This book … full accour
of 'mat … n approach
to pr … hich has
… tur

A theory of programming language semantics

part b

standard semantics
store semantics
stack semantics

A theory of programming language semantics

ROBERT MILNE

AND

CHRISTOPHER STRACHEY

Oxford University Computing Laboratory
Programming Research Group

LONDON
CHAPMAN AND HALL

A Halsted Press Book
John Wiley & Sons, Inc., New York

A theory of programming language semantics
a single work in two parts

First published 1976
by Chapman and Hall Ltd.,
11 New Fetter Lane, London EC4P 4EE

Printed in Great Britain by
Whitstable Litho Ltd., Whitstable, Kent

ISBN 0 412 14260 0

*Distributed in the U.S.A. by Halsted Press,
a Division of John Wiley & Sons, Inc., New York*

Library of Congress Cataloging in Publishing Data

Milne, Robert
A theory of programming language semantics.

Bibliography: p.
Includes index.
1. Programming languages (Electronic computers) - Semantics. I. Strachey, Christopher, joint author.
II. Title.
QA76.7.M54 001.6′424′0142 76-25025
ISBN 0-470-98906-8 (Wiley)

CHAPTER THREE

STANDARD SEMANTICS

3.1. The general form of the semantic equations.

3.1.1. Variations in the presentation.

In appendix 1 and appendix 9 we give the idealized syntax and the standard semantics for a large programming language called Sal. We shall discuss its characteristics and the detailed equations from 3.2.1 onwards; in this section we are concerned with more general matters which would apply to any programming language. We shall start by outlining our notation, which has quite early origins [40,85].

For reasons which we shall discuss in 4.1.1 we need to provide several sorts of semantics for one language; theorems which we shall prove ensure that these different semantics do in fact correctly represent the same language. It is therefore convenient to separate those parts of the language description which remain the same for all the sorts of semantics from those which vary. The unchanging parts are collected in appendix 9; each appendix concerned with Sal lists the syntactic domains, which are uniformly known by the first three letters of their natural name and typed in bold face. With each syntactic domain is associated a certain upper case Greek letter, which will invariably denote a member of that domain, so that when writing Γ, for instance, we shall often omit to mention that Γ is a command belonging to the domain Com. This should cause no confusion, and even the fact that some of these letters are hard to distinguish from upper case Roman letters should not wreak havoc with comprehensibility, as in the semantic equations we never use Roman letters with serifs.

We supply the idealized syntax of Sal in a form similar to BNF [2]; the syntactic rules are ambiguous, but a sufficient number of brackets can be introduced to allow us to write any program in an unambiguous way. Naturally any concrète syntax would have to introduce extra lexical and syntactic rules to resolve the ambiguities and to allow programs to be written in an acceptable manner. In the examples which we shall give we shall insert sufficient brackets to ensure that the parsing is not in doubt.

The syntactic domains and the idealized syntax remain the same for all the sorts of semantics given for Sal. The same is true of the valuations $\mathcal{I}$, $\mathcal{H}$, $\mathcal{J}$ and $\mathcal{K}$ (to be described in 3.4.5 and 3.4.8), the purpose of which is the essentially syntactic one of collecting lists of identifiers; consequently we have relegated their definitions to appendix 9, which should be read in conjunction with the appendices containing the truly semantic parts of the language descriptions.

The rest of the standard semantics for Sal is given in appendix 1. We start by setting out the structure of the semantic domains. These are built up, often in a rather complex manner, from a much smaller number of basic domains. We use upper case bold face Roman letters to name semantic domains and lower case Greek letters for members of these semantic domains. As many domains are actually sums of other domains there is a certain amount of duplication in the use of the corresponding Greek letters. Thus, for example, we use β for a member of B and also for a member of V; the context generally makes clear which is intended.

Each syntactic domain needs one or more 'valuations', mappings which, except for $\mathcal{I}$, $\mathcal{H}$, $\mathcal{J}$ and $\mathcal{K}$, yield results in the semantic domains. The valuations (for which we use upper case script letters) are listed near the beginning of appendix 1; the definitions of them that are appropriate to standard semantics occupy the remainder of appendix 1.

For a language as extensive as Sal these definitions have to be rather long and the reader will frequently need to examine parts of them. In order to make it easier to locate and understand the required formulas we have consistently adopted certain conventions both of arrangement and of notation.

Firstly, to eliminate the need to turn pages continually, we have incorporated the appendices in a separate volume which includes most of the material to which frequent reference may be made while reading the main text of this book. Secondly, we have adopted a strictly uniform method of arranging the component parts of the definitions. The list of the valuations is in the same order as the list of syntactic domains. The definitions follow the same sequence (except, of course, those of $\mathcal{J}$, $\mathcal{H}$, $\mathcal{J}$ and $\mathcal{K}$, which appear in appendix 9). In the definition of a valuation for any particular syntactic domain there is an equation corresponding to each clause in the idealized syntax for that syntactic domain. These equations are arranged in the same sequence as the clauses in the idealized syntax. The equation is also identified by repeating the syntactic clause in the left hand side.

Thus, for instance, the final syntactic domain is Com (for commands) having Γ as a typical member. The syntax for commands is

$\Gamma ::= \Gamma_0 ; \Gamma_1 \mid \mathbf{if}\ E\ \mathbf{do}\ \Gamma \mid \mathbf{while}\ E\ \mathbf{do}\ \Gamma \mid \Theta \mid I : \Gamma \mid I :: \Gamma \mid (\Gamma)$

and the valuations applicable to commands are $\mathcal{C}$, $\mathcal{P}$, $\mathcal{Q}$, $\mathcal{J}$ and $\mathcal{K}$. The definition of each of these five valuations will have seven equations corresponding to the seven clauses in the syntax. For instance, in the definition of $\mathcal{C}$ there are the following equations:

$\mathcal{C}[\![\Gamma_0;\Gamma_1]\!] = \lambda\rho\theta.\mathcal{C}[\![\Gamma_0]\!]\rho(\mathcal{C}[\![\Gamma_1]\!]\rho\theta);$

$\mathcal{C}[\![\mathbf{if}\ E\ \mathbf{do}\ \Gamma]\!] = \lambda\rho\theta.\mathcal{R}[\![E]\!]\rho(\mathit{test}\langle\mathcal{C}[\![\Gamma]\!]\rho\theta,\theta\rangle).$

These are to be interpreted as meaning that if Γ_2 is of the form $\Gamma_0;\Gamma_1$ then $\mathcal{C}[\![\Gamma_2]\!]$ is given by the first equation, whilst if Γ_2 is of the form $\mathbf{if}\ E\ \mathbf{do}\ \Gamma$ then $\mathcal{C}[\![\Gamma_2]\!]$ is given by the second equation. As is usual with BNF, the syntax is not intended to indicate the equality of Γ_0 and Γ_1, so that to form a correct equation we must decorate them differently. In any one equation for a valuation, on the other hand, two occurrences of Γ_0, say, do, of course, mean the same thing; unlike BNF clauses, which are sometimes thought of as production rules, the equations for a valuation are interpreted conventionally, so we have introduced suffices on their left hand sides when necessary to identify the component parts. The "abstract syntax" introduced by McCarthy [46] can be used to express the same result, but, as it requires explicit predicates to test the form of the command and further selector functions to extract the components, it is a great deal more verbose. If we were to provide suitable definitions for the predicates and selectors needed, in abstract syntax our equations for $\mathfrak{C}$ might be combined in the formula

$\mathfrak{C}[\![\Gamma]\!] =$

$issequence[\![\Gamma]\!] \rightarrow \lambda\rho\theta.\mathfrak{C}[\![firstcommand[\![\Gamma]\!]]\!]\rho(\mathfrak{C}[\![secondcommand[\![\Gamma]\!]]\!]\rho\theta),$

$isconditional[\![\Gamma]\!] \rightarrow \lambda\rho\theta.\mathfrak{R}[\![boolean[\![\Gamma]\!]]\!]\rho(test\langle\mathfrak{C}[\![command[\![\Gamma]\!]]\!]\rho\theta,\theta\rangle),$

... .

The notation adopted in the appendices avoids the necessity of burdening the reader with remembering the names of thirty-seven predicates and fifty-three selectors (in the case of Sal).

In the equation for $\mathfrak{C}[\![$if E do $\Gamma]\!]$ we mentioned *test*, which is like several basic functions in being intended to shorten the equations; together with various others it will be defined in 3.3.4. There is another class of basic function, of which *update* is a member, which embodies identifiable fundamental concepts. Many of these functions have been mentioned already. As their exact definition depends on the language under discussion, we shall collect the versions of them appropriate to Sal in 3.3.2 and 3.3.3. As far as possible we shall give the functions evocative names which should help to reduce the need to refer to their definitions frequently. We provide a separate list of all the basic functions which gives references to the sections containing their definitions.

The remaining matters of notation do not need much discussion, as they have been raised in 1.1.2 already. The bound variables ρ and θ used with the λ-notation signify members of U and C respectively, as is indicated by the list of semantic domains given in appendix 1; a similar convention applies to other bound variables. The barred brackets $[\![$ and $]\!]$ are intended to be an aid to the eye in separating the syntactic expressions from the semantic ones; the angular brackets $\langle$ and $\rangle$ indicate lists.

We have decided to leave our notation informal at some points in an attempt to make formulas less lengthy and more comprehensible than they would otherwise be. As we shall hint in 3.1.3, this decision is reflected in our use of lists of semantic equations rather than MSL [60] or some other variant of the symbolism adopted in the fragmentary formula given for $\mathcal{C}[\![\Gamma]\!]$ above. It is also reflected in our omission (from the semantic equations) of functions converting elements of one value domain (V, E, D or W) into elements of another value domain; some of these functions will nevertheless be described in 3.3.5 in terms familiar to us from 2.4.4. In appendix 1 we retain functions that project members of the domains E and D into such summands as E*, J, F and G; however, even this concession to accuracy will be discarded in certain other appendices. To make our language "definitions" suitable for use in an automatic compiler generator or program verifier we would need to remove all this informality and to specify a set of programs which could be parsed unambiguously; indeed, more formality than we shall frequently provide may well be desirable for humans using mathematical semantics as well as for computers, even if it is often undesired.

3.1.2. The structure of syntactic domains.

The idealized syntax of Sal given in appendix 1 defines a collection of sets when we regard symbols such as fn, (), . and .. merely as combinations of punctuation and decoration which indicate to which summand of a domain an entity belongs. Thus the syntactic rules for abstractions give rise to a set, Abs, which is related to sets Ide and Exp by the equation

Abs=Exp+(Ide×Exp)+(Ide×Exp),

where the three summands correspond with the three clauses in the idealized syntax. The rules governing commands, however, demand the introduction of a set Com such that

Com=(Com×Com)+(Exp×Com)+(Exp×Com)+Blo+(Ide×Com)+(Ide×Com)+Com;

moreover the equation for Exp involves Blo, as an expression may be of the form Θ before E, and the equation for Blo in turn involves Com, as a block may be of the form block Γ. In short, the sets Exp, Abs, Seq, Dec, Blo and Com satisfy mutually recursive equations in which the domains Bas, Mon, Dya and Ide are presumed to be known.

These sets can be seen in two lights. In the first of these we take refuge in the fact that when discussing programming languages we are only concerned with programs having finite lengths, and any such program may be formed by connecting shorter programs in a certain manner. For the purposes of syntactic analysis, any two finite programs which differ only because different bases, operators and identifiers appear in them may ultimately be reduced to members of the same finite combination of the domains Bas, Mon, Dya and Ide. Thus equations like those above may be interpreted simply as statements about how to extract the appropriate combination of these four domains from any given program.

The second way of looking at these sets is to introduce a universal domain, on which can be defined retractions *Bas*, *Mon*, *Dya* and *Ide* such that Bas, Mon, Dya and Ide are the retracts associated with

these retractions. Now we are interested in solving such equations as
Abs=Exp+(Ide×Exp)+(Ide×Exp),
together with more complicated ones, like
Com=(Com×Com)+(Exp×Com)+(Exp×Com)+Blo+(Ide×Com)+(Ide×Com)+Com,
where we interpret the operators × and + in the sense provided by 2.4.2. Because these operators are continuous we may use the argument of 2.4.3 to show that there is a list of retractions, ⟨*Exp*,*Abs*,*Seq*,*Dec*,*Blo*,*Com*⟩, which satisfies an obvious set of equations including those above. We may therefore take Exp, Abs, Seq, Dec, Blo and Com to be the retracts associated with *Exp*, *Abs*, *Seq*, *Dec*, *Blo* and *Com* respectively.

The first view of the syntax evades the problem of showing that syntactic domains exist, but, as we shall see in 3.1.4, it cannot readily be extended to certain semantic domains. In order to unify the theory we shall follow Scott [78] in adopting the second view, which can be so extended. Because we are using "separated" products and sums this view allows us to find non-trivial solutions to such fixed point equations as Γ=Γ;Γ, in which one member of Com is a sequence of two commands that are identical with one another and with the original command. Such a command as this is of no significance in practice, and the valuation 𝔈 is defined by the means to be suggested in 3.1.3 we can show that its image under 𝔈 is ⊥.

In order to formalize the first view of the syntax we would, in fact, set up the least fixed point of a function in much the same way as we do when taking the second view. We would let ⟨Exp,Abs,Seq,Dec,Blo,Co be a list of six sets which could be formed as the least fixed point of a certain continuous function mapping a complete lattice into itself. Each element of this complete lattice would be a list of six subsets of the set of all finite strings of symbols appropriate to Sal; the partial ordering would be that induced by the relation ⊇ between subsets.

3.1.3. The nature of semantic valuations.

The example given near the end of 3.1.1 reveals a characteristic property of many of the equations for the valuations. At first glance they might appear to be circular in a very involved manner, as the expressions on the right contain instances of the application of valuations. This "circularity" is more apparent than real, however, as in most cases the syntactic argument of any valuation appearing on the right is a component part of the argument of the valuation on the left. Languages sometimes provide exceptions to this rule, but they should not lead to circularity; in the case of Sal there are eight such expressions (given by the equations for $\mathfrak{E}[\![B]\!]$, $\mathfrak{E}[\![I]\!]$, $\mathfrak{E}[\![\Phi]\!]$, $\mathfrak{E}[\![\Sigma]\!]$, $\mathfrak{L}[\![E]\!]$, $\mathfrak{R}[\![E]\!]$, $\mathfrak{G}[\![\Sigma]\!]$ and $\mathfrak{C}[\![\Theta]\!]$), but inspecting appendix 1 will confirm that no circularity arises through them.

Corresponding with the two interpretations of the syntax which were mentioned in 3.1.2 there are two ways in which we can regard these equations as defining the valuations. In the first we take advantage of the fact that we are dealing only with programs which are finite in length. In principle, therefore, we can take any valuation applied to a specific program and systematically use the equations to reduce the complexity of the syntactic arguments appearing in the valuations on the right. As the definitions are not circular and the initial program is finite, this process must come to an end after a finite number of steps with an expression which contains no valuations other than $\mathfrak{B}$, $\mathfrak{D}$ and $\mathfrak{W}$. With any reasonably sized program, of course, the result would be wholly unmanageable, but the fact that it can be done in principle ensures the existence of the valuations. A somewhat similar argument allows us to prove results by using 'structural induction' in the manner to be displayed in 3.5.1.

The second way of interpreting the valuations involves treating them as the least fixed point of a function which takes as its argument a list of eleven functions mapping syntactic domains into semantic ones. Formalizing this function properly would be lengthy since we should need to introduce the predicates and selectors discussed in 3.1.1. Though we shall use the less cumbersome notation suggested by the first view of the valuations our decision to allow the syntactic domains to contain infinite programs obliges us to adopt the second view of the valuations. However, our appeals to structural induction refer only to finite programs, since we still justify structural induction by applying arithmetic induction.

In equations such as $\mathcal{E}[\![\Phi]\!]=\lambda\rho\kappa.\kappa(\mathcal{F}[\![\Phi]\!]\rho)$ the two occurrences of the syntactic variable (in this case Φ) do not really represent members of the same domain. On the left hand side of the equation we are dealing with a member of the domain Exp which happens to lie in the summand called Abs, whereas on the right hand side we are concerned with the result obtained by mapping this member of Exp into Abs. Implicit mappings like this underly all our semantic equations except those for $\mathcal{L}[\![E]\!]$ and $\mathcal{R}[\![E]\!]$; thus the equation $\mathcal{C}[\![\Gamma_0;\Gamma_1]\!]=\lambda\rho\theta.\mathcal{C}[\![\Gamma_0]\!]\rho(\mathcal{C}[\![\Gamma_1]\!]\rho\theta)$ entails first testing a member of Com to ensure that it lies in the summand Com×Com, then obtaining the appropriate pair in Com×Com and finally applying a valuation to both halves of the pair. We shall usually omit all mention of the mappings between the syntactic domains and their summands (as we did when mentioning the "equation" $\Gamma=\Gamma;\Gamma$ in 3.1.2); in 3.5.2, however, clarity will demand that we act otherwise, so we shall naturally use the notation explained in 2.2.3. Our neglect of these mappings constitutes one of the points of informality alluded to in 3.1.1.

3.1.4. The need for recursive domain equations.

The standard semantics of Sal exhibited in appendix 1 demands the introduction of domains subject to equations which refer to one another; one domain may satisfy an equation that mentions another domain, the "definition" of which in turn requires the original domain. In particular, E is "equal to" L+B+E*+J+F and F is "equal to" E→K→C; these equalities differ somewhat from one another, so we shall discuss them separately.

The occurrence of E* in the equation for E is fairly innocuous. We know that the set of finite lists of integers is recursively isomorphic with the set of integers, so by encoding the members of E in a suitable manner we might hope to set up a similar isomorphism between E and a union of various sets, one of which would be E*. This hope could be fulfilled (after a fashion) if we were prepared to ignore the partial ordering on E; we would then be unable to use the function *fix* to form circular data structures satisfying such equations as *loop*=⟨*loop*,*loop*⟩. In Sal *fix* cannot be used for this purpose anyhow, but languages without such complicated declarations would permit structures to be set up in this way. Even in Sal the technique suggested above for embedding something like E* in E would be an unpleasant expedient; just as in 3.1.2, here the natural approach is to provide a function having a list of retractions as its least fixed point.

The fact that F is a summand of E leads to further difficulties, which we first alluded to in 1.1.3. If we were to try to take F to be the set of all functions mapping E into K→C cardinal arithmetic would demonstrate that E→K→C could not be embedded satisfactorily in E unless K→C were rather uninteresting. As Scott [80] has shown, however, if we confine our attention to continuous functions we can embed E→K→C in E using the method summarized in 2.4.3. Thus we define a function mapping lists of retractions of a universal domain into other lists; this function and the domains described in appendix 1 are related in the same way as the functor W and the domain W mentioned in 2.4.3. The domains we require can be taken to be the retracts associated with the retractions which together form the least fixed point of this function. This construction will be analysed at greater length in 3.3.5.

It might be argued that the need to solve recursive domain equations when defining Sal indicates not that such equations are central to the theory of computing but that Sal is far too elaborate. For several reasons, which we shall now discuss, we believe this view to be false.

In the first place, recursive domain equations arise naturally in the description of the syntax of languages and in the semantics of data structures (in which E*, or something resembling it, has to be embedded in E). Nowadays every attempt to provide a sound understanding of a programming language begins with a complete statement of the syntax of the language in a style which is not unlike that involving the domain equations mentioned in 3.1.2. Moreover the programming language concerned is very likely to provide facilities for setting up general data structures. In our opinion the least contrived way of obtaining mathematical insight into these matters is to provide domains which satisfy recursive equations.

Even if the syntax and the data structures available in Sal were to be treated by techniques other than those we have advocated, there would remain the question of how to make F into a summand of E. One obvious possibility is to ignore the problem by claiming that Sal uses a silly mechanism for passing parameters. According to this view only certain members of E should be permitted to be the parameters of procedures, so that F might be reduced to, say, L→K→C, which does not involve E to quite the same extent as E→K→C. Unfortunately adopting this expedient would entail rejecting the mechanism for passing parameters inherent in many existing languages, including ones which allow the types of variables to be checked statically. Thus Algol 60 [61] and Algol 68 [94] would need to be altered although Fortran [1] and Pal [24] would be left unchanged (in this respect at least).

This mention of Pal brings to light a further aspect of Sal which requires recursive domain equations. In designing Sal we have deliberately followed the practice adopted in Pal, whereby label and procedure values can be stored. In appendix 1 V, J, C and S coincide with B+E*+J+F, C, S→A and (L→(V×T))×V*×V* respectively, so it is plain that linking V and J causes the same difficulties as connecting E and F. Thus to avoid introducing recursive domain equations we would need not only to devise an entirely different method of passing parameters but also to eliminate stored label values (and, for that matter, stored procedure values too). It is tempting to suggest that this fact is an argument against stored label values, not one in favour of recursive domain equations, for such values merely magnify the problems involved in proving programs correct. However, this temptation must be resisted because of the likeness between labels and coroutines. Though explicit labels are often despised, coroutines are thought to be useful for certain special purposes; yet in 1.5.8 it became fairly apparent that a satisfactory semantics for coroutines must make use of things that are almost identical with stored label values.

The final reason why recursive domain equations seem to be important in a detailed study of programming languages is rather more technical. One of our intentions in this book is to demonstrate how implementations may in principle be proved correct. We shall put this intention into effect by setting up a series of sets of semantic equations in which the abstract entities found in standard semantics will gradually give way to bit patterns. In developing this series there will come a point where the "return link" available during a call of a procedure will need to be kept in a machine state that will be present during the mathematical modelling of the call. The semantic equations in which this happens will have to be proved equivalent, in some sense, with the original ones. As we shall see in 5.6.9, this cannot be done conveniently in one step if the "return link" is a part of a program or a pointer to a program; it can be done, however, if the "return link" is a continuation. In this situation a portion of the procedure value also becomes a continuation and the procedure call is modelled by supplying the machine state as an argument to that continuation. Thus the continuation must be a function that can take as an argument a member of a domain in which a domain of continuations is immersed. This reason for introducing recursive domain equations would be relevant even if the programming language concerned did not demand that J or F be a summand of V or E (provided that the language still made some procedures available).

By using the technique to be mentioned briefly in 5.6.9 we can, in fact, ascribe meanings to programs without resorting to the introduction of recursive domain equations so long as we manipulate pointers and bit patterns instead of fixed points and functions. This approach lacks aesthetic appeal, because to put it into effect we have to make an arbitrary choice of a particular machine, which must then be regarded as canonical. Doing this obscures the intentions underlying programming language designs and complicates proving the correctness of many programs and implementations.

The partial ordering imposed on the domains that we use are crucial under only two circumstances; these arise when we wish to form the least fixed point of a function and when we wish to solve recursive domain equations. Thus we could afford to treat some of our domains not as complete lattices but as sets without any mention of $\perp$ and $\top$. We have chosen not to do this in order to unify the theory by making all the entities in semantic equations be definable in terms of the language Lambda [81].

3.2. An informal description of Sal.

3.2.1. General design considerations.

In order to demonstrate the utility of the description techniques outlined from 1.3.3 onwards we shall analyse the mathematical semantics of a language in a way which is applicable to languages with very different features. Though the results to be verified later in this book depend to some extent on the details of the language adopted as a paradigm, we are convinced (and we hope to convince the reader also) that analogous results can be proved for other languages by using similar methods.

We have chosen for our main paradigm a language which, for no very good reason, we call Sal. This exhibits many of the programming language features discussed after 1.2.1. In order to forestall the criticism that our methods can only be used for small or simple languages we have made Sal large and complex. The penalties to be paid for doing this are that the semantic equations become intricate and that some, at any rate, of the proofs become longer than they might otherwise have been. Yet, in fact, without reducing the power of the language in some way (by, for example, abolishing the store), it does not seem easy to devise a language in which the more important results are significantly easier to prove. In particular, the alternative form of semantics to be discussed in 4.1.2 cannot be avoided.

When designing any language it is necessary to make many decisions about the semantics. Our decisions have been governed in varying degrees by four factors: Sal should bear a recognizable resemblance to "real" programming languages, be large enough to establish that our description techniques can be applied widely, illustrate several facets of the semantic theory clearly and have semantic equations with few silly or boring complications. These factors are not, of course, all equally relevant to programming languages intended for practical use.

Although we have devised a language specially, instead of adopting an existing language as our paradigm, we can readily formulate the semantics of existing languages using the methods of this book; indeed, the semantic valuations describing Pal [50], Algol 68 [51], Lisp [25], Algol 60 [59], Snobol [90], Gedanken [92] and other languages have already been constructed, and work is under way on a description of PL/I [9]. However, the languages popular at present tend to have curious semantic irregularities (which can lengthen the semantic equations by a quite disproportionate amount) and to confuse distinct concepts, thereby making the task of explication much harder; in fact one role of mathematical semantics is to help in the design of better languages through a clarification of what underlies programming constructs.

Languages in which the types of expressions of identifiers can always be determined statically (before executing the expressions) can be described formally along the lines mentioned in 1.7.2, but they require the introduction of uninteresting valuations which check and calculate the types of expressions as well as valuations like those in appendix 1. Consequently we have made Sal a language in which types are only known dynamically (during the execution of programs) in order to keep the semantic description short. We have also omitted from Sal all features which can give rise to parallel programs so that we can ignore the sequels and rosters described in 1.5.9. However, in designing Sal we have made no other significant concessions to simplicity; for instance, executing a Sal program may involve constructing and manipulating very elaborate data structures.

If the "ideal" programming language exists it is not Sal, which has several features of dubious merit. Thus locations can be adjoined to the area of store in use without executing an explicit generating expression such as grab (which was discussed in 1.4.4) and values are read from an input stream by executing a block, not the expression read; in both these cases the explicit expressions might well be preferable.

The execution of a recursive declaration may influence, or be influenced by, the store, so we require the complicated treatment of recursive declarations suggested in 1.9.6 rather than the simple analysis to be given in 3.9.6. Furthermore, calls and declarations by reference and by incidence are made available instead of calls and declarations by denotation (from which our chosen constructs could be obtained with the aid of grab and explicit coercions); there are also two forms of label setting, one of which creates label values that are stored and that can facilitate the execution of bizarre jumps back into blocks. All of this is deliberate, for we wish to illustrate the way in which mathematical semantics can handle both wise design decisions and foolish ones.

In the rest of this section we shall give a brief description of the constructs available in Sal; this description should aid understanding of the various sorts of semantics that we shall discuss for Sal. One major sort of semantics, standard semantics, has essentially been introduced already; after 3.4.1 we shall outline the semantic equations for Sal provided by standard semantics (although the details of many of the equations will be found only in appendix 1). Other sorts of semantics, such as store semantics and stack semantics (which will not become important until 4.1.2 and 5.1.2 respectively), will be explained in a less expansive manner, because they will only arise once the reader is fully conversant with Sal and with the way in which semantic equations are to be understood.

From 3.6.1 onwards we shall be concerned with applying the principles of mathematical semantics to proofs about programs and implementations. In particular, we shall develop techniques which can be used to verify the equivalence or correctness of programs and we shall demonstrate that two implementations of Sal are correct (in 4.6.8 and 5.6.8). The term 'standard semantics' in fact refers to the normative role played by this sort of semantics in proofs like the ones that we shall outline.

3.2.2. Constants.

The bases used in Sal are true, false, the integral numerals, the real numerals, the characters, the strings and the empty list, which are recognized by lexical analysis. We shall adopt the conventional notation for numerals and have very little need to use the others in our examples except for true, false and the empty list (which we shall write as ()). The meaning of a base resembles the meaning of any other constant in being independent of the environment.

Most of the primitive operations in Sal are performed by monadic or dyadic operators. We have chosen to include as many as possible of the "working" parts of the language in these categories rather than introduce special syntactic constructions for them. This allows us to simplify the syntax of the main part of the language at the expense of having a rather large number of monadic and dyadic operators, some of which are unfamiliar.

The ordinary monadic operators like +, - and ~ (logical negation) have their usual meanings. In order to manipulate data structures, which are in general members of the domain E*, we need predicates to discover the type of an element of E (in other words, of which summand it is a member); there is one such predicate for each domain which is a summand of E or B. These are written in a uniform manner as isL, isB, isE*, isJ, isF, isT, isN, isR, isH and isH*. Not all of these are equally useful, but they all have a similar form. Thus for any expression E the expression isLE would produce a value in T which would be *true* if executing E yielded a member of the L summand of E (including its separated ⊥ and ⊤ elements) and *false* if it yielded a member (including ⊥ or ⊤) of any other summand of E. The tests for membership of T, N, R, H and H*, which are summands of B (which is itself a summand of E), take their argument from E, not B, and only yield a value *true* if it is a member both of B and of the relevant summand. Thus isNE has the same effect as isBE?isNE!false when E is idempotent (as will become clear in 3.8.7).

We need the operator # in order to find the "lengths" of structures lying in the summand E* of E. If the R-value of an expression E happens to be a structure, executing #E gives the length of that structure, so #() is 0.

The last two monadic operators are the most interesting. The operator $ provides an explicit coercion such that when E is any expression the E-value of $E is the R-value of E. The operator £ can be applied with impunity only to a procedure. It is intended to ensure that during an application of the procedure the actual parameter introduces a location which is not already in use. Thus if executing the actual parameter yields a location the content is copied into a new location, but if executing the actual parameter yields a stored value, this is put into a new location; in both cases the new location is then passed to the procedure as an argument. The chief significance of £ arises from the fact that it operates on procedures themselves and does not have to be attached to any actual parameters. It will be used in 3.5.8 to construct a transformation which replaces incidence (in abstractions, declarations and label settings) by reference in a way that preserves the effects of programs.

The ordinary mathematical dyadic operators (which include the arithmetic relations) present no interesting problems. Various matters having practical importance have to be decided in a somewhat arbitrary manner; for example, coercions between integers and real numbers could be permitted in both directions, one direction or not at all. In 3.4.1 we shall simply give semantic equations for certain operators which we shall allow to act only on integers; equations which incorporated coercions or which allowed the operators to act usefully on real numbers would be longer (but no more profound) than the ones that we shall present.

In Sal characters in H and strings in H* can be yielded as results by the execution of expressions. Hence we could provide operators for comparing and changing strings related to the operators available in Snobol [28]. We have omitted to do this just because such operators can be simply described within our present conceptual framework.

Though there are several dyadic operators for manipulating structures in useful ways, they are not independent of one another. In Sal we have introduced three of these operators: ↓, which allows elements to be selected from structures, †, which allows elements to be removed from the fronts of structures, and &, which allows elements to be appended to the fronts of structures in the manner described in 1.6.4. The operators ↓ and † have meanings which correspond closely with the meanings of the analogous operators that were defined on the semantic domains in 2.2.3. We have not provided the syntactic notation $E_0,\ldots,E_{n-1}$ corresponding with the one occasionally used for the semantic domains; were we to wish to write a list of expressions in the idealized syntax we could introduce the notation E_0,Ξ_0, where Ξ_0 would be a member of a new syntactic domain and would typically take either the form E_1 or the form E_1,Ξ_1. We have not needed to provide an explicit concatenation operator in Sal, because if we use the Sal declaration rec *c*==fn*u*..fn*v*..(#*u*=0)?*v*!((*u*↓1)&*c*(*u*†1)*v*) then whenever the R-values of *u* and *v* are structures the E-value of *c*(*u*)(*v*) is a structure obtained by contenating them. Also of interest are the Sal declarations *l*==fn*x*.fn*v*..*x*&*v* and *r*==fn*x*..fn*v*..*x*&*v*; as should become clear in 1.2.5, the application *l*(*x*)(*v*) attaches the L-value of *x* to the front of the E-value of *v* and the application *r*(*x*)(*v*) attaches the R-value of *x* to the front of the E-value of *v* (so long as the E-value of *v* is a structure). These operators and functions provide counterparts to some of those available in a language akin to APL [33].

3.2.3. Names.

The names available in a programming languages are those individual pieces of syntax which a programmer can endow with meaning. The Sal operators are constants, not names, for no operator can be given a meaning by a declaration. Moreover, as Sal provides dynamic types only it has no need of declarations of indications like those found in Algol 68 [94].

Languages can provide both explicit labels and implicit labels (as was discussed in 1.5.5); indeed names other than labels could in principle be given meanings implicitly instead of explicitly. However, in Sal there is just one implicit name, which is the label res. In fact the only names used in Sal are the identifiers needed to denote members of D (the domain of denoted values) and res; this fact has repercussions on the structure of the environment, as we shall see in 3.3.3. The identifiers will as usual be taken to be members of a domain Ide which is a flat lattice (in the sense explained in 2.2.1).

3.2.4. Expressions.

The characteristic property of an expression is that usually it returns a value, although it may also have a side effect which changes the store. In extreme cases it may produce a jump so that the computation continues from a different point in the program. A feature of Sal which is absent from most programming languages is that in some circumstances control is able to jump back into the execution of an expression (if it has been started once). Any explicit labels set inside a Sal expression must be within blocks to which their scopes are limited.

Bases, identifiers and abstractions are all simple forms of expressions. The clauses OE and $E_0 \Omega E_1$ represent the use of prefixed monadic operators and infixed dyadic operators respectively. One feature of note is that many operations defined on data structures, which in other languages are expressed by special syntactic constructions, are provided in Sal by special monadic or dyadic operators. This device shortens and simplifies the language description.

The construct $E_0 ? E_1 ! E_2$ is the conditional expression which in Algol 60 [61] would be **if** E_0 **then** E_1 **else** E_2. We use this unfamiliar notation partly for its brevity but also because we want to avoid confusion with the conditional command (which uses **if**) or with a metalanguage conditional term which might be written as $\varepsilon_0 \rightarrow \varepsilon_1, \varepsilon_2$.

The purpose of allowing Σ as an expression is to make it possible to jump out of an expression altogether (in order to terminate the program as the result of an error condition), thereby allowing the abrupt termination of the execution of a complicated expression by using **res** E or **goto** E.

We provide a juxtaposition of the form $E_0 E_1$ to represent a procedure application. The expression E_0, which yields the procedure, may be any expression, not just an identifier.

The expression val E_1 unceremoniously returns the E-value of E_0 if during its execution the expression res E_0 is encountered. If no expression of the form res E_0 is encountered the value of val E_1 is the same as that of E_1; val and res clauses may be nested, although other clauses may intervene. A res clause is always associated with its smallest surrounding val clause.

The construct Δ inside E corresponds rather closely to an Algol 60 block: the declaration Δ has a range which extends throughout E but not beyond, and in the terminology of 1.3.2 we say that the declaration Δ "governs" the expression E. If several declarations are required to govern E this can be achieved by using one of the more complex forms of declaration. According to appendix 1, Sal declarations cannot govern blocks or commands directly; as we shall show in 3.7.3, they can do this indirectly, so the language loses no expressive power on this account.

The construct Θ before E indicates that the block Θ is to be executed, presumably altering the store in some way, and then the expression E is to be executed with the store produced. The body of a procedure is often in this form.

The final construct, (E), is included to allow ambiguities of parsing to be resolved; the brackets have no effect on the execution of E.

3.2.5. Abstractions.

Abstractions in Sal are procedures rather than routines, because, when executed, they return values as well as, possibly, altering the store. The form fn()E has a parameter list of length zero. To distinguish between the procedure itself and an instance of its application, the idealized syntax of Sal insists on the presence of an empty list (which can be written as ()) when an application is intended.

The other two forms of abstraction require parameter lists of length one. Applying the abstraction fnI.E to an actual parameter involves executing E, the body of fnI.E, in an environment in which I denotes a location; this location is the L-value of E if the E-value of E equals the L-value of E and is a fresh location containing the R-value of E if the E-value of E equals the R-value of E. Applying fnI..E necessitates executing E in an environment in which I denotes the R-value of E.

We have restricted attention to procedures with at most one parameter each; allowing several parameters (by introducing constructs like fn$I_0, I_1, \ldots, I_{n-1}$.E) complicates the language without introducing anything significantly new. As a list of expressions could be viewed as an expression we could achieve the same effect by passing a list as an actual parameter and using $I{\downarrow}m$ in the body in place of I_m. Another way of producing the effect of procedures with several parameters permissible in Sal entails applying "higher-order" procedures which return procedures as results; for example, instead of using an abstraction that might be written as fnI_0, I_1.E we could use fnI_0.(fnI_1.E). If Φ_0 stands for the first of these abstractions and Φ_1 stands for the second, we could get the effect of an application of Φ_0 such as $\Phi_0(E_0, E_1)$ by using the repeated application $(\Phi_1 E_0)E_1$.

One way of providing routines in Sal will be discussed in 3.7.1.

3.2.6. Sequencers.

Sequencers differ from commands and blocks in that they make no use at all of their continuations. The form res E_0 is only useful inside an expression of the form val E_1 (although it may well be buried deeply inside). Its effect is to terminate immediately the execution of E_1 giving it the value obtained by executing E_0. This construction, or something akin to it, is required for escapes from the middles of bodies of procedures.

The form goto E is the familiar unconditional jump, but in Sal E can be a perfectly general expression, not just an identifier.

Sequencers can be used either as expressions or as blocks, though not as Sal declarations.

In place of the syntax supplied in appendix 1 we could adopt one in which Θ before Σ would be a sequencer belonging to the domain Seq whenever Σ and Θ were respectively a sequencer and a block; enlarging Seq in this way would be consistent with our view of what constitutes a sequencer, but would entail defining the valuation for sequencers on the construction Θ before Σ. However, because every sequencer can be viewed as an expression in Sal and because the construct Θ before E is available in Sal we can avoid introducing Θ before Σ explicitly in the syntax. Likewise in a language having a "double-armed" conditional command of the form if E do Γ_0 or Γ_1 and allowing every sequencer to be a block (and hence a command) there would be no need to include if E do Σ_0 or Σ_1 among the members of Seq. As we shall hint in 3.2.8, a similar phenomenon occurs with combinations of blocks; for instance, $\Theta_0;\Theta_1$ need not appear in the syntax for blocks because when the blocks Θ_0 and Θ_1 are regarded as commands they can be compounded to produce the command $\Theta_0;\Theta_1$, which can be taken to be equivalent with block $(\Theta_0;\Theta_1)$. Analogous remarks apply to if E do Θ and to while E do Θ.

3.2.7. Declarations.

The only declarations available in Sal are declarations by worth, just as the only abstractions are abstractions by worth. Executing I=E (a non-recursive declaration by worth and reference) in an environment ρ involves executing E in ρ to obtain an L-value which I is then made to denote. Similarly, executing I==E (a non-recursive declaration by worth and incidence) in ρ involves executing E in ρ to obtain an R-value which I is then made to denote.

Of greater interest are **rec** I=E and **rec** I==E, the recursive declarations analysed in 1.9.4 and 1.9.5 respectively. Executing either of these entails finding the R-value of E in an environment which provides an informed guess about the value that I ought to denote. In the case of **rec** I=E the R-value of E is used to update a location that I is made to denote, whereas in the case of **rec** I==E the R-value of E is taken to be what I must ultimately denote.

In Sal declarations can be combined in all the ways discussed in 1.9.3; thus Δ_0 **and** Δ_1, Δ_0 **within** Δ_1 and Δ_0 **around** Δ_1 are legitimate declarations when Δ_0 and Δ_1 are declarations, and to make matters less ambiguous than they would otherwise be we let (Δ) be a declaration whenever Δ is a declaration. In addition, any declaration, Δ, can be used to create a recursive declaration, **rec** Δ.

3.2.8. Blocks.

The distinction between blocks and commands is entirely concerned with the scope of labels. In common with many other languages Sal allows labels to be set without being previously declared. Thus the scope of a label can extend beyond the command in which it is set. A block, however, prevents the outward spread of label scopes, and thus prevents any direct attempt to jump into it. Nonetheless a block can still be entered at a point other than its beginning if a label I set in it is assigned to an identifier having a wider scope; this can only happen if the block has already been executed once before, since outside it I does not denote the appropriate label value.

Executing the assignment $E_0 := E_1$ entails coercing the result of executing E_0 to produce its L-value, α, and coercing the result of executing E_1 to produce its R-value, β. No attention is paid to the type of the previous content of α or the type of β, so an assignment can alter the type of the content of a location quite freely.

The store is also changed by the execution of get E and of put E, which provide rudimentary input and output facilities. Thus get E allows a location yielded by executing E to be updated with a value taken from an input stream, whereas put E allows a value yielded by executing E to be sent to an (otherwise inaccessible) output stream. However, fit E merely provides a means of obtaining the side effect of executing E while discarding the result.

The introduction of Σ both provides goto sequencers and allows a result to be returned from, for example, the body of a procedure. Use is made of block Γ to turn a command Γ into a block which limits the scopes of the labels set in it.

Among the blocks need not be mentioned those combinations of blocks which can be obtained by viewing blocks as commands.

3.2.9. Commands.

Commands are similar in many respects to blocks but do not confine the scopes of labels set in them.

Naturally $\Gamma_0;\Gamma_1$ allows for the normal sequencing of commands. By using the notions to be discussed in 3.6.1 we can easily show that the sequencing of commands is associative. Thus $\Gamma_0;(\Gamma_1;\Gamma_2)$ and $(\Gamma_0;\Gamma_1);\Gamma_2$ are equivalent in every way. In future, therefore, we shall generally omit parsing brackets in sequences of commands and write $\Gamma_0;\Gamma_1;\Gamma_2$ for both these commands. Since Γ, rather than Θ, occurs in the "single-armed" conditional construct if E do Γ, jumps can be made from outside into if E do Γ without requiring assignments to labels. We have not introduced a "double-armed" conditional command into the basic part of Sal, as it enlarges the language without introducing any new ideas. It is possible to construct a Sal command which has the same effect, although the most obvious candidate, which is probably fit (E ?(block Γ_0 before 0) !(block Γ_1 before 0)) (where the purpose of fit is merely to throw away the unwanted result of the chosen arm having the form Θ before E), is not satisfactory because its arms are blocks, not commands. An appropriate equivalent of a "double-armed" conditional command will be presented in 3.7.3.

The execution of while E do Γ involves first executing E; if the result obtained is *true*, the command Γ is obeyed and the process is repeated but if the result is *false* the execution of the loop is ended. Even in the latter case the loop cannot usually be said to have no effect, as E may already have produced a side effect which is not reversed at the finish of the process. Because Γ, the body of while E do Γ, is a command it can be entered directly by a jump without testing E; however, the normal process of testing E will still follow the termination of Γ. It is, of course, possible to jump out of the body of a while loop.

A block Θ is evidently also a command but requires no special syntactic marker to indicate the fact.

The constructs I:Γ and I::Γ are label setting commands. As with abstractions and declarations I:Γ sets its label by reference while I::Γ sets it by incidence. Each of these commands in effect gives a fresh meaning to I, since the labels explicitly set in a block produce an environment for the block. Any label setting command forms a label value in this environment; I:Γ makes I denote a new location which it updates with the label value, whereas I::Γ makes I denote the label value directly. A programmer who makes assignments to labels declared by reference can produce outrageously obscure programs.

In appendix 1 (Γ) is included among the commands to enable parsing ambiguities to be avoided.

3.3. The operations on the domains.

3.3.1. The value domains and continuation domains.

Choosing the semantic domains is a crucial part of the design of any programming language which was discussed in general terms in 1.6.5. In this section we shall describe the choices made when designing Sal.

As can be seen from appendix 1, we have deliberately made the domains and syntax of Sal very large and regular. Doing this creates difficulties (in, for example, the semantics of recursive declarations, which will be analysed in 3.4.5) but also reduces the need for tests and special cases. It might be thought that by restricting the generality of the language a simpler set of semantic equations could be used and that the proofs of results analogous to 5.3.9 and our other theorems would be shorter. We have not yielded to the temptation to prune Sal partly because we want to demonstrate the power of mathematical semantics and partly because the introduction of restrictions often complicates and lengthens the equations instead of making them more succinct.

The domains appropriate to any programming language can be built from certain simple domains by forming sums, products, function spaces and limit spaces in the manner outlined in 2.4.3. Thus the domains described in 2.2.2 can be used to form a domain of 'basic values', B, such that $B=T+N+R+H+H^*$; every proper member of B is a truth value, an integer, a "real" number, a character or a string of characters. In appendix 1 this version of B will be taken to be the domain of basic values for Sal, but another version could be used if more bases and operators were made available.

The domain of 'stored values', V, has perhaps a greater effect on the language than any other. In Sal V is rather large, since it includes both label values, which belong to J, and procedure values, which belong to F; more precisely, V=B+E*+J+F, so when β is a typical member of V it can be a basic value, a list of expressed values, a label value or a procedure value. The ability to store members of E*, J and F has consequences which were considered in 3.1.4.

The summand E* is needed because Sal allows programmers to set up general data structures. The domain E is such that any component of a structure can be either a location or a member of any summand of V. Together with the possibility of using recursive declarations (as discussed in 1.9.4) this fact enables us to construct an extremely large class of data structures including some which are re-entrant. We shall not have space to examine these structures in this book, but one example was given in 1.6.4.

In Sal the domain of 'expressed values', E, includes the domain of locations, L, and all the summands of V, and therefore satisfies the equation E=L+B+E*+J+F. When ε is a typical member of E it is said to be an 'L-value' if $\varepsilon \in L$ and to be an 'R-value' if $\varepsilon \in B$, $\varepsilon \in E^*$, $\varepsilon \in J$ or $\varepsilon \in F$. The fact that all the summands of E except L yield R-values (being also summands of V) is not a necessary feature. Many languages have elements of E which cannot be stored; an example of this phenomenon is provided by label values in Algol 60 [61].

The designer of a language can also determine the domain of 'denoted values', D; a typical member of D must be designated by δ. In Sal we have decided to make D rather large, with the consequence that any expressed value can also be denoted; doing so allows us to declare by incidence "everything that can be declared by reference". Again this is not a necessary choice, for integers in Algol 60 cannot be denoted. In Sal the only summand of D that does not appear in E as well is G, which is intended to assist with the formulation of the semantics of recursive declarations in a way which will be made clear in 3.4.5. Consequently in the standard semantics of Sal D=L+B+E*+J+F+G, as can be seen from appendix 1.

Those entities which arise in the course of computations form the domain of 'witnessed values', W, which has ω as a typical member. Plainly every stored, expressed or denoted value must be witnessed, but in Sal there are other witnessed values which can be associated with the syntactic object res by an expression of the form val E ; as we shall explain in 3.3.3, these values are expression continuations which belong to a domain K and which are kept in the environment. Hence W=L+B+E*+J+F+G+K in the standard semantics of Sal; later sorts of semantics will require emendations to this equation, because they will bring to the fore more of the entities handled by implementations.

We shall describe the domain of 'stores', S, and the domain of 'environments', U, in 3.3.2 and 3.3.3 respectively; suffice it to say at this stage that the members of S give a ready supply of members of V whereas the members of U yield members of D and of K in the standard semantics of Sal. The domain of 'answers', A, will not be analysed at all, although in standard semantics it can most aptly be taken to comprise either stores or output components of stores (which in our treatment can be taken to be members of V*); essentially all that we have to assume about A is that it can be constructed from the other domains by using the operators described in 2.4.2, but for convenience we shall occasionally impose more specific restrictions on the functor which produces it.

A 'command continuation' is signified by θ and is drawn from the domain C which is S→A when only serial programs are considered. In standard semantics a 'label value', which lies in the domain J, has the same structure as a command continuation, so J=C. An 'expression continuation', κ, and a 'declaration continuation', χ, belong to K, which is E→C, and X, which is U→C, respectively; this version of X should not be confused with the universal domain of 2.4.2.

A typical 'procedure value' is denoted by ϕ and belongs to F, which in the standard semantics of Sal is $E \to K \to C$. The structure of this domain reflects the design decision to restrict abstractions in Sal to ones having only a single parameter. If we had allowed abstractions having lists of parameters (which form a feature of many programming languages), we would have taken F to be $E^* \to K \to C$ unless we had treated the lists of parameters in the way adopted for fn()E in Sal, when F would have remained $E \to K \to C$.

Allied to F in standard semantics is the domain G, which is $K \to C$.

3.3.2. Some basic functions acting on stores.

In 1.4.2 we mentioned possible models for the store; here we shall content ourselves with giving the structure of the stores that we have chosen for Sal and with defining the basic functions which operate on them.

In Sal a typical store, σ, is a member of the domain S which has the structure $(L\to(V\times T))\times V^*\times V^*$ where L is the domain of locations, V is the domain of stored values and T is the domain of truth values. Intuitively the first component of σ, in $L\to(V\times T)$, gives for every location, α, a value in V (its content) and a value in T indicating whether α is "in use". The second and third components of σ are rudimentary input and output streams respectively; they can only be altered by executing the blocks get E and put E.

Though the basic features of this model for storage are needed by any domain of stores which could be used in the semantics of Sal many of its details are arbitrary. We could, for example, equally well regard S as $(L\to V)\times(L\to T)\times V^*\times V^*$ or even $(L\to(V+\{error\}))\times V^*\times V^*$; a member of the second of these domains associates with any location in L either a content in V or an indication that the location is not in use. In a language in which coroutines are permitted we might take S to be $(L\to(V\times T))\times(I\to(C\times T))\times V^*\times V^*$ for the reasons put forward in 1.5.8; here I would be a domain of coroutine tags and C would be the domain of command continuations. Some languages, among them being Algol 68 [94], need stores with more elaborate input and output components, but they do not involve more profound concepts on that score alone.

Just as we have chosen to define the domain S completely, not to specify it by rules, so we give the equations defining the basic functions acting on S instead of axioms governing the functions. An adequate set of axioms would be lengthy and uninteresting, and in practice it would specify the results of applying the functions to all arguments other than $\bot$ and $\top$ (that is, to all proper arguments). Thus no significant degree of generality is lost by defining the functions fully; moreover, though axioms might be preferable in a mechanical system for proving theorems about semantic equations, definitions have a greater attraction to the intuition of humans.

There is only one constant store of interest; it is $\mathit{empty}\in S$, which is defined in our model by

$\mathit{empty}=\langle\lambda\alpha.\langle \mathit{false},\mathit{false}\rangle,\langle\rangle,\langle\rangle\rangle$.

The content of every location in *empty* has been arbitrarily chosen to be *false*; another possible choice would be a special value $\mathit{unused}\in B$.

For examining locations in the store we use $\mathit{hold}\in L\to S\to V$ and $\mathit{area}\in L\to S\to T$, which are defined thus;

$\mathit{hold}=\lambda\alpha\sigma.(\sigma\downarrow 1)\alpha\downarrow 1$;

$\mathit{area}=\lambda\alpha\sigma.(\sigma\downarrow 1)\alpha\downarrow 2$.

These give the content and accessibility of every location in the store.

To perform the basic operation of updating a location we use $\mathit{update}\in L\to V\to S\to S$, for which

$\mathit{update}=\lambda\alpha\beta\sigma.\langle(\lambda\alpha'.(\alpha'=\alpha)\to\langle\beta,\mathit{true}\rangle,(\sigma\downarrow 1)\alpha'),\sigma\downarrow 2,\sigma\downarrow 3\rangle$.

Thus if $\sigma_1=\mathit{update}\,\alpha\beta\sigma_0$, σ_1 coincides with σ_0 at every point except for the pair in $V\times T$ associated with α. In σ_1 this is $\langle\beta,\mathit{true}\rangle$ irrespective of its value in σ_0. Thus *update* not only changes the content of a location but also marks it as being in use. Here it is the only basic function which can mark a location as being in use; we shall provide no function to reverse this operation until 5.1.4.

The semantic equations arrange that improper expressed values and stores need never be passed on as arguments to continuations. This fact is intuitively obvious, but a proper account of it involves an appeal to inclusive predicates formed using operators different from those underlying the predicates to be discussed in 4.2.3. Nevertheless some justification for our definition of *update*, and hence for our model of storage, can be gleaned from the following properties:

(i) if α_0 and α_1 are distinct proper locations then $update\,\alpha_0\beta_0 \circ update\,\alpha_1\beta_1 = update\,\alpha_1\beta_1 \circ update\,\alpha_0\beta_0$, so that assignments to distinct locations commute;

(ii) if α is a proper location then $update\,\alpha\beta_0 \circ update\,\alpha\beta_1 = update\,\alpha\beta_0$, so that repeated assignments to a single location can be replaced by the last one only.

The semantic equations often require the introduction of a location which "has not yet been used" (that is to say, for which $area\,\alpha\sigma = false$). If no such location exists (because a finite store is "full") the result *error* is obtained. We therefore introduce $new \in S \to (L + \{error\})$, which is unlike the other basic functions in that we do not define it but merely provide axioms which influence it. More precisely, we demand that *new* be any continuous function such that:

(i) if σ is a store having $\bigwedge\{area\,\alpha\sigma \mid \top \sqsupseteq \alpha \sqsupseteq \bot\} = false$ then $new\,\sigma|L$ is a proper location and $area(new\,\sigma|L)\sigma = false$;

(ii) if σ is a store having $\bigwedge\{area\,\alpha\sigma \mid \top \sqsupseteq \alpha \sqsupseteq \bot\} = true$ then $new\,\sigma$ is *error*.

For every σ $new\,\sigma$ merely gives a location; it does not mark the location as being in use.

These axioms for *new* have rather untoward consequences which will be described in 4.2.6 and which suggest that the axioms should be amended. The amendments required involve either adopting coalesced products and sums, as we did elsewhere [52:1.2.2], or specifying the effect of *new* only on stores belonging to a certain set. We shall discuss the latter possibility briefly in 4.2.6.

We also need iterated versions of *update* and *new*. As the intention of these functions is simple we shall define them recursively; normal definitions can be obtained by introducing *fix* in the way outlined in 2.3.2. Thus $updates \in L^* \to V^* \to S \to S$ is such that $updates = \lambda\alpha^*\beta^*\sigma.(\#\alpha^* = 0) \to \sigma, updates(\alpha^* \dagger 1)(\beta^* \dagger 1)(update(\alpha^* \downarrow 1)(\beta^* \downarrow 1)\sigma)$.

We assume for simplicity that the assignments are performed from left to right, so that $\alpha^*\downarrow 1$ is updated first. If the list α^* contains no repeated elements the properties of *update* ensure that the order in which the assignments are done is irrelevant.

In addition we let $news \in N \to S \to (L^* + \{error\})$ satisfy the equation

$$news = \lambda\nu\sigma.(\nu=0)\to\langle\rangle,$$
$$new\sigma E L \to news(\nu-1)(update(new\sigma|L)(false)\sigma)\S\langle new\sigma|L\rangle,$$
$$error.$$

The occurrence of *update* is intended to mark the location selected by *new* as being in use, in order that the list of locations returned by *news* may not contain repeated elements. If the store is "full" the function *news* provides not a list of locations but *error*.

3.3.3. Some basic functions acting on environments.

In the standard semantics of Sal, a typical environment, ρ, is a member of the domain U, which we take to be $(\text{Ide}\to D^*)\times K^*$. This is a more complex domain than that discussed in 1.3.3, in that it is constructed using D^* instead of D. Because of this, during the execution of a program the environment now associates with any identifier not just the value which the identifier has been declared to denote most recently but also those denoted values appropriate to the identifier in unfinished activations of other pieces of program. The most recently declared values associated with identifiers form the 'local environment'; the 'entire environment' consists of all the denoted values set up in as yet unfinished activations. As we shall see in 3.5.6, in standard semantics we could quite safely use only local environments, which were therefore the only ones considered in 1.3.3. However, in 4.1.2 we shall introduce semantic equations in which entire environments are needed; to avoid defining new operations on such environments we have decided to allow all our environments to make identifiers correspond with members of D^*, not just members of D.

As was indicated in 3.3.1, in Sal the expression val E is executed by executing E in an environment which associates with the name res the continuation for the complete expression; escape mechanisms of this nature were discussed in 1.5.4. Since expressions of the form val E can nest within one another in the same way as expressions preceded by declarations of identifiers any environment in U provides res with a list in K^* instead of one member of K.

Analogous to the store *empty* is $arid\in U$, which is subject to the equation

$arid=\langle(\lambda I.\langle\rangle),\langle\rangle\rangle$.

Strictly speaking, when ρ is an environment and I is an identifier we should write $(\rho\downarrow 1)[\![I]\!]$ for the list of denoted values associated with I by ρ. However, for the sake of convenience we shall invariably shorten $(\rho\downarrow 1)[\![I]\!]$ to $\rho[\![I]\!]$; as a useful aid to the memory we shall also write $\rho[\![res]\!]$ rather than $\rho\downarrow 2$. The values most recently declared for I and res will be $\rho[\![I]\!]\downarrow 1$ and $\rho[\![res]\!]\downarrow 1$ respectively.

Whenever I is an identifier, ρ is an environment, δ is a denoted value and κ is an expression continuation we alter ρ thus:

$\rho[\delta/I]=\langle(\lambda I'.(I'=I)\rightarrow\langle\delta\rangle\S\rho[\![I]\!],\rho[\![I']\!]),\rho[\![res]\!]\rangle$;

$\rho[\kappa/res]=\langle(\lambda I.\rho[\![I]\!]),\langle\kappa\rangle\S\rho[\![res]\!]\rangle$.

Likewise when I^* is in Ide^* and δ^* is in D^* we let

$\rho[\delta^*/I^*]=((\#I^*=0)\rightarrow\rho,(\rho[\delta^*\dagger 1/I^*\dagger 1])[\delta^*\downarrow 1/I^*\downarrow 1])$

in order that we may declare several identifiers simultaneously.

We need a function for combining environments; to extend ρ_0 by ρ_1 we use $divert\rho_0\rho_1$ where in standard semantics $divert\in U\rightarrow U\rightarrow U$ is given by the equation

$divert=\lambda\rho_0\rho_1.\langle\lambda I.\rho_1[\![I]\!]\S\rho_0[\![I]\!],\rho_1[\![res]\!]\S\rho_0[\![res]\!]\rangle$.

Note that the entries in ρ_1 come above those in ρ_0. The definitions are such that $\rho[\delta/I]=divert\rho(arid[\delta/I])$ and $\rho[\kappa/res]=divert\rho(arid[\kappa/res])$ while $divert(divert\rho_0\rho_1)\rho_2=divert\rho_0(divert\rho_1\rho_2)$ for all environments.

Although we do not need entire environments in standard semantics *divert* appears in the equations of appendix 1. The reason for this is that because declarations will return only little environments (in a manner to be explained in 3.4.4) there must be some means of masking one entry in an environment by another. Were we to wish not to view U as being $(Ide\rightarrow D^*)\times K^*$ but instead to permit environments to associate at most one denoted value with each identifier, we would be unable to define a continuous analogue of *divert* by taking U to be $(Ide\rightarrow D)\times K$; every little environment would need to indicate which identifiers had been declared, so U would have to be something like $(Ide\rightarrow(D\times T))\times K$ or $(Ide\rightarrow(D+\{error\}))\times K$. We would not, however, need to turn K into $K\times T$ or $K+\{error\}$, since *divert* is only required by declarations which set up denoted values for identifiers (not by ones which provide meanings for res).

3.3.4. Functions involving continuations.

In order to terminate a program when an error condition is discovered we use the basic command continuation $\mathit{wrong} \in C$; we could give *wrong* other parameters besides a store, but no new insights would be gained by doing so. We shall not discuss the properties of *wrong* beyond remarking that it forms part of the interface between a program and the operating system under which it is run.

The two functions to be discussed next test the domains of their arguments to ensure the failure of attempts to supply something other than a truth value to a conditional expression or to update a location with something which is not a stored value. In both cases the discovery of an error leads to the application of a version of *wrong*. Thus $\mathit{test} \in (C \times C) \to W \to C$ and $\mathit{assign} \in C \to W \to W \to C$ satisfy the following equations:

$$\mathit{test} = \lambda\langle\theta_0, \theta_1\rangle\omega.\, \omega E B \to (\omega | B E T \to (\omega | B | T \to \theta_0, \theta_1), \mathit{wrong}), \mathit{wrong};$$

$$\mathit{assign} = \lambda\theta\omega_0\omega_1\sigma.\, \omega_0 E L \wedge (\omega_1 E B \vee \omega_1 E E^* \vee \omega_1 E J \vee \omega_1 E F) \to \theta(\mathit{update}(\omega_0 | L)\omega_1\sigma), \mathit{wrong}\sigma.$$

We have chosen to make *test* and *assign* draw their arguments from the domain of witnessed values, W, instead of from the domain of expressed values, E, because this course of action will enable us to avoid defining *test* and *assign* anew in 5.1.4. Thus those equations in appendix 1 which involve these functions must also make implicit use of mappings which transform members of E into members of W. In addition *assign* itself involves a mapping which we have not mentioned explicitly, because members of the summands B, E*, J and F of W must be shifted into V before being put into locations; functions which achieve this effect have been defined in 2.4.4, but only in formal contexts, such as those of 3.3.5 and 4.1.5, will we make use of them in anything other than a covert manner.

The functions *lv* and *rv* perform the coercions necessary to change E-values into L-values or R-values. The definition of these functions is partly a matter of taste; for instance, lv need not entail making occasional assignments to unused locations and rv could check that locations were in the available area of storage before taking their contents. In Sal, however, $lv \in K \to K$ and $rv \in K \to K$ are defined thus:

$lv = \lambda \kappa \varepsilon \sigma . \varepsilon E L \to \kappa \varepsilon \sigma , new \sigma E L \to assign(\kappa(new \sigma | L))(new \sigma | L) \varepsilon \sigma , wrong \sigma ;$

$rv = \lambda \kappa \varepsilon \sigma . \varepsilon E L \to \kappa(hold(\varepsilon | L) \sigma) \sigma , \kappa \varepsilon \sigma .$

Here again we are using implicit mappings between summands of different domains; some of these mappings could be eliminated by taking lv to be in $K \to L \to C$ and rv to be in $K \to V \to C$ and by making the valuations $\mathcal{L}$ and $\mathcal{R}$ (to be explained in 3.4.2) be members of $Exp \to U \to (L \to C) \to C$ and $Exp \to U \to (V \to C) \to C$ respectively.

In order to adjoin some new locations to the area of available storage we let ψ range over members of $L^* \to C$ and define $tie \in (L^* \to C) \to N \to C$ by the equation

$tie = \lambda \psi \nu \sigma . (\nu = 0) \to \psi \langle \rangle \sigma ,$

$\quad new \sigma E L \to tie(\lambda \alpha^* . \psi(\alpha^* \S \langle new \sigma | L \rangle))(\nu - 1)(update(new \sigma | L)(false) \sigma) ,$

$\quad wrong \sigma .$

In 1.5.7 we mentioned the function run, which is intended to allow the order of evaluation of two expressions to be left unspecified. To define $run \in ((K \to C) \times (K \to C)) \to (E \to E \to C) \to C$ we introduce $veer$, which is either permutation of 0 and 1, and we write

$run = \lambda \langle \gamma_0 , \gamma_1 \rangle \psi . \gamma_{veer 0}(\lambda \varepsilon_{veer 0} . \gamma_{veer 1}(\lambda \varepsilon_{veer 1} . \psi \varepsilon_0 \varepsilon_1))$

when ε_0 and ε_1 range over members of E, γ_0 and γ_1 range over members of $K \to C$ and ψ ranges over members of $E \to E \to C$. Because the order in which declarations are evaluated can be varied in Sal we also need $run \in ((X \to C) \times (X \to C)) \to (U \to U \to C) \to C$, which differs from the function defined above only in the domains to which its arguments belong; thus E, $K \to C$ and $E \to E \to C$ have to give way to U, $X \to C$ and $U \to U \to C$ respectively. Different occurrences of run in appendix 1 may be viewed as being induced by different versions of $veer$.

3.3.5. Functors yielding the domains.

The domains V, E, D, W and so on mentioned in this section are the sets of fixed points of certain retractions, which here we designate by the corresponding Italic letters (*V*, *E*, *D*, *W* and so on). Because some of the equations for the domains refer to one another, the equations for the retractions do likewise; for instance, the equation V=B+E*+J+F gives rise to the equation $V=B+E^*+J+F$ where the retractions defined in 2.4.2 are such that if B=T+N+R+H+H* then $B=T+N+R+H+H^*$. Consequently we assume that the list $\langle V,E,D,W,\ldots\rangle$ is the least fixed point of a continuous function which maps the complete lattice of lists of retractions of a universal domain into itself.

From 4.2.3 onwards we shall need this assumption (in connection with applications of 2.5.3). Obviously a function X having the full list $\langle V,E,D,W,\ldots\rangle$ as its least fixed point would be too cumbersome to manipulate, for its parameter would be a list of thirteen retractions (on the assumption that the retractions *T*, *L*, *B* and *Ide* are given). Fortunately, we do not have to use such a function, since the length of the argument list required can be greatly reduced for a reason that we shall now outline. Most of the components of the fixed point do not appear on the right hand sides of the equations which they obey; the only exception in the case of Sal is provided by the equation $E=L+B+E^*+J+F$. Consequently for most values of m $X\langle X_0,\ldots,X_n\rangle{\downarrow}m$ is independent of X_m, so by picking such a value of m and applying 2.3.9 (or at any rate the version of 2.3.9 appropriate to functions taking argument lists of length thirteen) we may eliminate X_m from the argument list while retaining the right least fixed point. This process may be repeated until finally we obtain a function X and a corresponding value of n for which $X\langle X_0,\ldots,X_n\rangle{\downarrow}m$ depends on X_m for every m with $n{\ge}m{\ge}0$. If the equation governing the retraction A (for the domain of answers) can be expressed in terms of V and E, the standard semantics of Sal allows the final form of X to take an argument list of length two and to have $\langle V,E\rangle$ as its least fixed point; however, the store semantics and stack semantics to be discussed in 4.1.3 and 5.1.4 involve functions with $\langle V,E,S,U\rangle$ and $\langle V,E,W\rangle$ as their least fixed points. Functions like these may not be unique, for suitable versions of A would permit the adoption of a function having not $\langle V,E\rangle$ but $\langle E,S\rangle$ as its least fixed point.

What we have just been describing is a perfectly normal technique for simplifying functions which owe their interest only to their fixed points. It makes no use of the knowledge that the functions we are considering have argument lists composed of retractions generating domains for programming languages. The domains needed by a particular programming language can be formed from the four value domains, V, E, D and W. Moreover, as we remarked in 3.3.1, the stored, expressed and denoted values must be among the witnessed values, so V, E and D are sums of certain of the summands of W. When dealing with the standard semantics of Sal we can express this fact in terms of the mappings *push* and *mask* introduced in 2.4.4 by noting that $V=push\langle 4,-1\rangle \circ W \circ push\langle 3,1\rangle$, $E=W\circ mask4$ and $D=W\circ mask5$ because $V=B+E^*+J+F$, $E=L+B+E^*+J+F$, $D=L+B+E^*+J+F+G$ and $W=L+B+E^*+J+F+G+K$ according to appendix 1.

As all the retractions required by the standard semantics of Sal can be obtained from V and E they can also be obtained from W. This suggests that rather than employing a function having $\langle V,E\rangle$ as its least fixed point we use a function W with W as its least fixed point. When X is a variable representing a retraction of a universal domain we let

$$W=\lambda X.L+B+(EX)^*+JX+FX+GX+KX,$$

where the functions appearing in the definition of W are built up in the manner prescribed by 2.4.2. More specifically, we provide equations relating the value domains by writing:

$V=\lambda X.push\langle 4,-1\rangle \circ X \circ push\langle 3,1\rangle$;

$E=\lambda X.X \circ mask4$;

$D=\lambda X.X \circ mask5$.

To reflect the fact that $S=(L\rightarrow(V\times T))\times V^*\times V^*$ and that $U=(Ide\rightarrow D^*)\times K^*$ we define functions S and U thus:

$S=\lambda X.(L\rightarrow(VX\times T))\times(VX)^*\times(VX)^*$;

$U=\lambda X.(Ide\rightarrow(DX)^*)\times(DX)^*$.

On the assumption that A is a continuous functor for which $A=AW$ the functions providing retractions for the continuation domains are as follows:

$C=\lambda X.SX\rightarrow AX$;

$K=\lambda X.EX\rightarrow CX$;

$X=\lambda X.UX\rightarrow CX$.

Because $J=C$, $F=E\rightarrow K\rightarrow C$ and $G=K\rightarrow C$ the remaining functions are set up in the following manner:

$J=\lambda X.CX$;

$F=\lambda X.EX\rightarrow KX\rightarrow CX$;

$G=\lambda X.KX\rightarrow CX$.

In the standard semantics of Sal D, U and X play no part in the determination of W, so they will usually be ignored.

Because the operators defined on retractions in 4.2.2 can actually handle any continuous function mapping a universal domain into itself, when X is a retraction WX is at least continuous. Unfortunately WX need not be a retraction, for VX and EX need not coincide with $VX\circ VX$ and $EX\circ EX$ respectively. If, however, X is a retraction such that $mask4\circ X=X\circ mask4$ then WX is also a retraction and $mask4\circ WX=WX\circ mask4$. Moreover, it is obvious that $mask4\circ\bot=\bot\circ mask4$, and we know from 2.4.1 that the least upper bound of a directed set of continuous functions is a retraction if each of the functions is a retraction; hence by applying the induction rule of 2.3.2 we may infer that $fix(W)$ is a retraction. Further applications of the induction rule serve to confirm that $\langle V(\mathit{fix}(W)),E(\mathit{fix}(W))\rangle$ is the least fixed point of the final version of the function X mentioned above.

The construction underlying the domains we are using can therefore be summarized in the assertion that $\mathit{fix}(W)$ is a retraction for which W is the set of fixed points; the other retractions we require take forms such as $S(\mathit{fix}(W))$ and $U(\mathit{fix}(W))$. According to the usage of 2.4.3 a retraction mapping a universal domain on to **W** may be written as $\lambda\omega.\omega$, since ω is a typical member of **W**, so we can write this assertion as $\lambda\omega.\omega=\mathit{fix}(W)$. In the more advanced uses of the semantics of a programming language an equation like this is crucial and must be regarded as part of the language definition along with the semantic equations.

Though all our applications of the knowledge that $\lambda\omega.\omega=\mathit{fix}(W)$ can be expressed as applications of the claim that $\langle\lambda\beta.\beta,\lambda\varepsilon.\varepsilon\rangle$ is the least fixed point of X, in practice we prefer to use W, because it has a definition that is not intolerably prolix. Although W and the other functions described above are not functors in the sense given in 2.4.1, we shall nevertheless refer to them as functors. All that we need to suppose about A, for instance, is that if X is a retraction for which $\mathit{mask}4\circ X=X\circ\mathit{mask}4$ (or even just for which $\mathit{mask}4\circ X=\mathit{mask}4\circ X\circ\mathit{mask}4$) then AX is also a retraction and that if v is a directed set of such retractions then $A(\bigsqcup v)=\bigsqcup\{AX \mid X\in v\}$; as was intimated in 3.3.1, usually A can be taken to be S or V* (which comprises the output components of stores), so A can be S or $\lambda X.(VX)^*$.

3.4. The semantic equations for Sal.

3.4.1. The valuations $\mathcal{B}$, $\mathcal{V}$ and $\mathcal{W}$.

The valuations of standard semantics are intended to give an abstract mathematical meaning to a program. This should be independent of any machine implementation and so cannot contain details of the representation of any of the objects concerned. Hence in standard semantics we are not concerned with the details of number representations, word lengths and similar questions, though we could reasonably discuss such matters when dealing with a particular computer, such as that to be described in 5.4.1. Nevertheless even at this stage we should not ignore the fact that implementations take account of these things; because our aim is to be able to show that implementations correctly reflect the standard semantic equations, we must make some allowance for the introduction of finite representations and other machine characteristics. These manifest themselves in two rather different ways.

The first of these ways requires the replacement of the standard mathematical operations by approximations to them; thus the addition of integers is implemented on a machine by an operation which is accurate only when the integers are confined within bounds determined by the word length of the machine. This in itself would not require any major alteration in the equations for standard semantics; all that would be necessary would be a reinterpretation of the standard mathematical operators. We should, of course, have to check any proofs about programs which made use of the properties of the operators, as, for example, we could no longer assert that $n+1$ was always greater than n; in this book, however, we do not provide any such proofs.

The second way in which the implementations of mathematical operators can influence the semantic equations arises from their handling of exceptional conditions and errors. In some implementations such events as the mismatching of types and the overflow of registers are treated as errors and cause 'traps' (which are forcible transfers of control) when they occur. This means that there can be an error exit from the application of a monadic or dyadic operator or even from the evaluation of a base (although this last possibility could be detected by a compiler). In order to deal with this contingency we supply the valuations concerned with a continuation as an extra argument. If the result is "normal", as almost always happens, the continuation is applied to it, but if the operator induces a jump (or a trap) the continuation may be ignored. The situation is thus typical of those which, according to 1.5.1, require a more sophisticated treatment of sequencing than is available in the absence of continuations.

The only valuation applicable to bases is $\mathfrak{B}$ which is a member of Bas→K→C. We shall leave most of the details of $\mathfrak{B}$ unspecified, but from time to time in example programs we shall make tacit use of equations such as:

$\mathfrak{B}[\![\text{true}]\!]=\lambda\kappa.\kappa(\mathit{true});$

$\mathfrak{B}[\![\text{false}]\!]=\lambda\kappa.\kappa(\mathit{false});$

$\mathfrak{B}[\![()]\!]=\lambda\kappa.\kappa\langle\rangle.$

In the last of these equations ⟨⟩ is the empty list in E*.

The valuation for monadic operators, $\mathfrak{O}$, is also given a continuation as an argument and so is a member of Mon→K→E→C (or Mon→K→K). An error exit may be invoked if an attempt is made to apply an operator to an object of unsuitable type. Thus, for instance,

$\mathfrak{O}[\![-]\!]=\lambda\kappa.\mathit{rv}(\lambda\varepsilon.\varepsilon\text{E}\text{B}\rightarrow(\varepsilon|\text{B}\text{E}\text{N}\rightarrow\kappa(-(\varepsilon|\text{B}|\text{N})),\mathit{wrong}),\mathit{wrong}).$

The minus sign, -, on the right hand side of this equation is the normal mathematical prefixed operator. The tests ensure that it is only applied to an integer (not to a real number) and *rv* arranges that the R-value of an expression is taken.

The tests for membership of summands need equations such as:

$\mathcal{O}[\![\mathrm{isL}]\!]=\lambda\kappa\varepsilon.\kappa(\varepsilon\mathrm{E}\mathrm{L});$

$\mathcal{O}[\![\mathrm{isN}]\!]=\lambda\kappa\varepsilon.\kappa(\varepsilon\mathrm{E}\mathrm{B}\rightarrow\varepsilon|\mathrm{B}\mathrm{E}\mathrm{N},\mathit{false}).$

The equation for # takes the form

$\mathcal{O}[\![\#]\!]=\lambda\kappa.\mathit{rv}(\varepsilon\mathrm{E}\mathrm{E}^{*}\rightarrow\kappa(\#(\varepsilon|\mathrm{E}^{*})),\mathit{wrong}),$

which allows us to test R-values in E* but not those members of the summand B which lie in H*.

Following the account given in 3.2.2 we write:

$\mathcal{O}[\![\$]\!]=\lambda\kappa.\mathit{rv}\kappa;$

$\mathcal{O}[\![\pounds]\!]=\lambda\kappa.\mathit{rv}(\lambda\varepsilon.\varepsilon\mathrm{E}\mathrm{F}\rightarrow\kappa(\lambda\varepsilon'\kappa'.\mathit{rv}(\mathit{lv}(\lambda\varepsilon''.(\varepsilon|\mathrm{F})\varepsilon''\kappa'))\varepsilon'),\mathit{wrong}).$

As will be seen in 5.6.1 the second of these is awkward to implement.

We shall not stop to give all the equations for the ordinary arithmetic prefixed and infixed operators. To allow for possible error exits we take $\mathcal{W}$ to belong to Dya→K→E→E→C. As an example, if no implicit coercions between integers and real numbers were allowed and if addition could be performed only on integers we might set

$$\mathcal{W}[\![+]\!]=\lambda\kappa\varepsilon'\varepsilon''.(\lambda\psi.\mathit{rv}(\lambda\varepsilon.\mathit{rv}(\lambda\varepsilon'''.(\varepsilon'''\mathrm{E}\mathrm{B}\rightarrow\varepsilon'''|\mathrm{B}\mathrm{E}\mathrm{N},\mathit{false})\rightarrow\psi\varepsilon(\varepsilon'''|\mathrm{B}|\mathrm{N}),\mathit{wrong})\varepsilon'')\varepsilon')$$
$$(\lambda\varepsilon\nu.(\varepsilon\mathrm{E}\mathrm{B}\rightarrow\varepsilon|\mathrm{B}\mathrm{E}\mathrm{N},\mathit{false})\rightarrow\kappa((\varepsilon|\mathrm{B}|\mathrm{N})+\nu),\mathit{wrong}).$$

In a formula as complicated as this one has to be a local subsidiary function ψ (which here is a member of E→N→C) is needed in order to improve legibility. The value of ψ is given by the second line of the formula, in which care has been taken to avoid clashes of variables; consequently the body of this λ-expression can be substituted for the term $\psi\varepsilon(\varepsilon'''|\mathrm{B}|\mathrm{N})$ in the first line with little change.

To provide a test for equality between integers we let

$$\mathcal{W}[\![=]\!]=\lambda\kappa\varepsilon'\varepsilon''.(\lambda\psi.\mathit{rv}(\lambda\varepsilon.\mathit{rv}(\lambda\varepsilon'''.(\varepsilon'''\mathrm{E}\mathrm{B}\rightarrow\varepsilon'''|\mathrm{B}\mathrm{E}\mathrm{N},\mathit{false})\rightarrow\psi\varepsilon(\varepsilon'''|\mathrm{B}|\mathrm{N}),\mathit{wrong})\varepsilon'')\varepsilon')$$
$$(\lambda\varepsilon\nu.(\varepsilon\mathrm{E}\mathrm{B}\rightarrow\varepsilon|\mathrm{B}\mathrm{E}\mathrm{N},\mathit{false})\rightarrow\kappa((\varepsilon|\mathrm{B}|\mathrm{N})=\nu),\mathit{wrong}).$$

Here we have used the continuous predicate $(\varepsilon|\mathrm{B}|\mathrm{N})=\nu$ (which must be defined in the manner indicated in 2.2.2) in order to ensure that the continuations we use are continuous.

When E_0 has an R-value which is a string and when E_1 has an R-value which is an integer we may select a component of the structure by writing $E_0 \downarrow E_1$, where

$$\mathfrak{W}[\![\downarrow]\!] = \lambda\kappa\varepsilon'\varepsilon''.(\lambda\psi.\mathit{rv}(\lambda\varepsilon.\mathit{rv}(\lambda\varepsilon'''.(\varepsilon'''\mathsf{E}\mathrm{B}\rightarrow\varepsilon'''|\mathrm{B}\mathsf{E}\mathrm{N},\mathit{false})\rightarrow\psi\varepsilon(\varepsilon'''|\mathrm{B}|\mathrm{N}),\mathit{wrong})\varepsilon'')\varepsilon')$$
$$(\lambda\varepsilon\nu.\varepsilon\mathsf{E}\mathrm{E}^{*}\rightarrow(\#(\varepsilon|\mathrm{E}^{*})\geq\nu\geq 1\rightarrow\kappa((\varepsilon|\mathrm{E}^{*})\downarrow\nu),\mathit{wrong}),\mathit{wrong}).$$

To chop off a chunk of a structure we write $E_0 \dagger E_1$ and assume that

$$\mathfrak{W}[\![\dagger]\!] = \lambda\kappa\varepsilon'\varepsilon''.(\lambda\psi.\mathit{rv}(\lambda\varepsilon.\mathit{rv}(\lambda\varepsilon'''.(\varepsilon'''\mathsf{E}\mathrm{B}\rightarrow\varepsilon'''|\mathrm{B}\mathsf{E}\mathrm{N},\mathit{false})\rightarrow\psi\varepsilon(\varepsilon'''|\mathrm{B}|\mathrm{N}),\mathit{wrong})\varepsilon'')\varepsilon')$$
$$(\lambda\varepsilon\nu.\varepsilon\mathsf{E}\mathrm{E}^{*}\rightarrow(\#(\varepsilon|\mathrm{E}^{*})\geq\nu\geq 1\rightarrow\kappa((\varepsilon|\mathrm{E}^{*})\dagger\nu),\mathit{wrong}),\mathit{wrong}).$$

In a similar way we act in accordance with 1.6.4 by setting

$$\mathfrak{W}[\![\&]\!] = \lambda\kappa\varepsilon'\varepsilon''.\mathit{rv}(\lambda\varepsilon.\varepsilon\mathsf{E}\mathrm{E}^{*}\rightarrow\kappa(\langle\varepsilon'\rangle\,\S\,(\varepsilon|\mathrm{E}^{*})),\mathit{wrong})\varepsilon''.$$

It is this operator, &, that is responsible for our decision to take $\mathfrak{W}$ to be a member of Dya→K→E→E→C instead of a member of Dya→K→V→V→C. Were $\mathfrak{W}$ to belong to the latter domain applying & would only allow us to attach stored values, not locations, to the fronts of lists in E*; to obtain general lists it would be necessary to view & not as an operator but rather as a distinct syntactic entity such that $\mathcal{E}[\![E_0\&E_1]\!]$ was $\lambda\rho\kappa.\mathit{run}\langle\mathcal{E}[\![E_0]\!]\rho,\mathcal{R}[\![E_1]\!]\rho\rangle(\lambda\varepsilon'\varepsilon''.\varepsilon''\mathsf{E}\mathrm{E}^{*}\rightarrow\kappa(\langle\varepsilon'\rangle\S(\varepsilon''|\mathrm{E}^{*})),\mathit{wrong})$. Under these circumstances $\mathcal{E}[\![E_0\Omega E_1]\!]$ could safely be taken to be $\lambda\rho\kappa.\mathit{run}\langle\mathcal{R}[\![E_0]\!]\rho,\mathcal{R}[\![E_1]\!]\rho\rangle(\mathfrak{W}[\![\Omega]\!]\kappa)$. In addition, if we were to dispense with isL and to introduce coercions into operators like isN we could make $\mathcal{O}$ into a member of Mon→K→V→C and let $\mathcal{E}[\![\mathrm{O}E]\!]$ be $\lambda\rho\kappa.\mathcal{R}[\![E]\!]\rho(\mathcal{O}[\![\mathrm{O}]\!]\kappa)$. We could even take $\mathcal{B}$, $\mathcal{O}$ and $\mathfrak{W}$ to be in Bas→(E+{*error*}), Mon→E→(E+{*error*}) and Dya→E→E→(E+{*error*}) respectively and let $\mathcal{E}[\![\mathrm{B}]\!]=\lambda\rho\kappa.\mathit{ev}\kappa(\mathcal{B}[\![\mathrm{B}]\!])$, $\mathcal{E}[\![\mathrm{O}E]\!]=\lambda\rho\kappa.\mathcal{R}[\![E]\!]\rho(\lambda\varepsilon.\mathit{ev}\kappa(\mathcal{O}[\![\mathrm{O}]\!]\varepsilon))$ and $\mathcal{E}[\![E_0\Omega E_1]\!]=\lambda\rho\kappa.\mathit{run}\langle\mathcal{R}[\![E_0]\!]\rho,\mathcal{R}[\![E_1]\!]\rho\rangle(\lambda\varepsilon'\varepsilon''.\mathit{ev}\kappa(\mathfrak{W}[\![\Omega]\!]\varepsilon'\varepsilon''))$; here $\mathit{ev}\in\mathrm{K}\rightarrow(\mathrm{E}+\{\mathit{error}\})\rightarrow\mathrm{C}$ is given by an equation such as

$$\mathit{ev}=\lambda\kappa\varepsilon.\varepsilon\mathsf{E}\mathrm{E}\rightarrow\kappa(\varepsilon|\mathrm{E}),\mathit{wrong}$$

when ε is allowed to range over members of E+{*error*}. A treatment of constants which is reminiscent of this will be adopted in 1.9.2.

3.4.2. The valuations $\mathcal{E}$, $\mathcal{L}$ and $\mathcal{R}$.

In a language such as Sal in which types are determined dynamically the valuation for calculating the E-values of expressions is a member of Exp→U→K→C; the valuations that obtain L-values and R-values can also be taken to belong to Exp→U→K→C, as we explained in 1.5.7. Here we shall discuss the versions of these valuations that are defined in appendix 1.

A typical base in the domain Bas is signified by B. In 3.4.1 we introduced a version of $\mathcal{B}$ in the domain Bas→K→C in order to handle errors, so for every B in Bas we demand that

$\mathcal{E}[\![B]\!]=\lambda\rho\kappa.\mathcal{B}[\![B]\!]\kappa$;

in particular, $\mathcal{E}[\![\mathrm{true}]\!]=\lambda\rho\kappa.\kappa(\mathit{true})$ and $\mathcal{E}[\![\mathrm{false}]\!]=\lambda\rho\kappa.\kappa(\mathit{false})$.

Executing the expression OE involves supplying the E-value of the expression E to the function represented by the monadic operator O. The differences between distinct operators reside in the valuation $\mathcal{O}$ described in 3.4.1 so one semantic equation governs OE, irrespective of the nature of O. Thus since $\mathcal{O}$ belongs to Mon→K→E→C

$\mathcal{E}[\![\mathrm{OE}]\!]=\lambda\rho\kappa.\mathcal{E}[\![\mathrm{E}]\!]\rho(\mathcal{O}[\![\mathrm{O}]\!]\kappa)$.

One equation is also enough to model the execution of the expression $E_0\Omega E_1$, in which Ω is a dyadic operator, because $\mathcal{W}$ explains how operators differ. As we wish to allow either E_0 or E_1 to be executed first we make use of *run*, which we discussed in 3.3.4. Evidence akin to that put forward in the discussion of $E_0:=E_1$ in 1.5.7 suggests that as $\mathcal{W}$ is in Dya→K→E→E→C

$\mathcal{E}[\![E_0\Omega E_1]\!]=\lambda\rho\kappa.\mathit{run}\langle\mathcal{E}[\![E_0]\!]\rho,\mathcal{E}[\![E_1]\!]\rho\rangle(\mathcal{W}[\![\Omega]\!]\kappa)$.

The execution of the conditional expression $E_0?E_1!E_2$ starts by finding the R-value of E_0. If this is a truth value, the E-value of E_1 or E_2 is formed in the same environment; however, if it is not a truth value the computation leads to an error by invoking the command continuation *wrong*. The simple but rather lengthy expression required to perform these tests is summarized in the basic function *test*, which was defined in 3.3.4. Any side effects arising from the execution of E_0 come into play before E_1 or E_2 is executed; in particular if the execution of E_0 ends because of an error (or any other jump out of E_0) then the choice between E_1 and E_2 is never made. An explanation of an equation which resembles

$$\mathfrak{E}[\![E_0?E_1!E_2]\!]=\lambda\rho\kappa.\mathfrak{R}[\![E_0]\!]\rho(test\langle\mathfrak{E}[\![E_1]\!]\rho\kappa,\mathfrak{E}[\![E_2]\!]\rho\kappa\rangle)$$

was given in 1.5.3.

The four forms of expression described above could exist in a language which was purely arithmetic in nature. Identifiers, however, are more interesting. The equation for I in an environment ρ and with a continuation κ uses $\rho[\![I]\!]\downarrow 1$, which is what I currently denotes in ρ. If $\rho[\![I]\!]\downarrow 1$ lies in one of the summands of D which is also a summand of E (that is, if $\rho[\![I]\!]\downarrow 1$ lies in L, B, E*, J or F) it can be supplied to the expression continuation κ as an argument. If, however, $\rho[\![I]\!]\downarrow 1$ lies in G, which is K→C, κ is provided to it as an argument. As K is E→C in both situations a member of C is eventually obtained. Consequently we can safely let

$$\mathfrak{E}[\![I]\!]=\lambda\rho\kappa.\rho[\![I]\!]\downarrow 1\mathrm{E}G\rightarrow(\rho[\![I]\!]\downarrow 1|G)\kappa,\kappa(\rho[\![I]\!]\downarrow 1).$$

Executing an abstraction (but not, of course, a procedure application) produces no side effect, so when F is the domain of procedure values we can expect there to be a valuation $\mathfrak{F}$ in Abs→U→F such that if Φ is any abstraction

$$\mathfrak{E}[\![\Phi]\!]=\lambda\rho\kappa.\kappa(\mathfrak{F}[\![\Phi]\!]\rho);$$

the definition of $\mathfrak{F}$ to be given in 3.4.3 will make it plain that in $\mathfrak{F}[\![\Phi]\!]\rho$ the environment ρ at the time of abstraction is indeed embedded in the procedure value.

The equation governing a procedure application of the form E_0E_1 follows the pattern laid down in 1.8.5. The R-value of E_0 and the E-value of E_1 are found in either possible order with the aid of *run*; if the R-value of E_0 is a procedure value in F it is applied to the

E-value of E_1, but otherwise there is an immediate error exit. Thus we use the equation

$\mathcal{E}[\![E_0E_1]\!]=\lambda\rho\kappa.run\langle\mathcal{R}[\![E_0]\!]\rho,\mathcal{E}[\![E_1]\!]\rho\rangle(\lambda\varepsilon'\varepsilon''.\varepsilon'\in F\rightarrow(\varepsilon'|F)\varepsilon''\kappa,wrong)$.

A sequencer provides its own continuation in the manner described in 1.5.4. Hence when $\mathcal{S}$ is a suitable member of Seq→U→C (to be discussed in 3.4.3) and when Σ is any sequencer as in 1.5.3 we can let

$\mathcal{E}[\![\Sigma]\!]=\lambda\rho\kappa.\mathcal{S}[\![\Sigma]\!]\rho$.

Executing val E in an environment ρ and with a continuation κ is the same as executing E in ρ[κ/res] and with κ; here ρ[κ/res] differs from ρ only because it makes res denote κ. Hence when we write

$\mathcal{E}[\![\texttt{val}\ E]\!]=\lambda\rho\kappa.\mathcal{E}[\![E]\!]\rho[\kappa/\texttt{res}]$

we are continuing to use a version of the equation for val E introduced in 1.5.4.

After a little practice a "narrative" account of most of the equations in appendix 1 can readily be prepared. This is partly because the valuations express the underlying fundamental concepts clearly and partly because the notation helps us to gain an overall grasp of each equation: the positioning of the continuations in the semantic equations is such that when we read an equation from left to right we are tracing the execution sequence. According to the equation

$\mathcal{E}[\![\Delta\ \texttt{inside}\ E]\!]=\lambda\rho\kappa.\mathcal{D}[\![\Delta]\!]\rho(\lambda\rho'.\mathcal{E}[\![E]\!](divert\,\rho\rho')\kappa)$,

for example, executing Δ inside E in an environment ρ involves executing Δ in ρ to produce a little environment which can be appended to ρ with the aid of *divert* and then executing E in the resulting extended environment; E is followed by the expression continuation that originally followed Δ inside E.

To arrange that the equation governing Θ before E captures the effect of executing first the block Θ and then the expression E (presumably in an altered store), we set

$\mathcal{E}[\![\Theta\ \texttt{before}\ E]\!]=\lambda\rho\kappa.\mathcal{G}[\![\Theta]\!]\rho(\mathcal{E}[\![E]\!]\rho\kappa)$;

thus Θ before E provides the chief Sal expression the execution of which can modify the store. We use a block here, rather than any command, as we want to prevent the scope of labels set inside it from spreading outside the whole expression.

As the sole purpose of brackets in Sal is to allow us to be confident that there are many programs which can be parsed unambiguously, whenever ρ is an environment and κ is an expression continuation we let $\mathcal{E}[\![(E)]\!]\rho\kappa=\mathcal{E}[\![E]\!]\rho\kappa$.

We take $\mathcal{L}$ and $\mathcal{R}$ to be members of $\text{Exp}\to\text{U}\to\text{K}\to\text{C}$ which coerce the E-value of an expression to provide the L-value and the R-value respectively. Thus when E is any expression $\mathcal{L}[\![E]\!]\rho\kappa=\mathcal{E}[\![E]\!]\rho(lv\kappa)$ and $\mathcal{R}[\![E]\!]\rho\kappa=\mathcal{E}[\![E]\!]\rho(rv\kappa)$ provided that lv and rv are defined as in 3.3.4.

3.4.3. The valuations $\mathfrak{F}$ and $\mathfrak{S}$.

In standard semantics an abstraction needs only an environment to give it a value in F, the domain of 'procedure values'; hence it requires a valuation $\mathfrak{F}\in\mathsf{Abs}\to\mathsf{U}\to\mathsf{F}$. The language Sal has been designed so that F is a summand of V, E and D, but this is not the case for all programming languages; in Algol 60 [61], for example, procedures can be denoted but not stored, so F is not a summand of V.

Programming languages often use procedures without parameters - sometimes explicitly and sometimes, as in the Algol 60 call by name, in a less obvious manner. Care is needed to distinguish between a call of a procedure without parameters and any other mention of the procedure identifier. Although some languages permit an empty parameter list to be omitted and distinguish between an application of the procedure and another use of the procedure by different syntactic means, in Sal an empty list must be retained for an application. The semantic equation for a parameterless procedure is therefore

$$\mathfrak{F}[\![\mathsf{fn}(\,)\mathsf{E}]\!]=\lambda\rho.\lambda\epsilon\kappa.rv(\lambda\epsilon'.\epsilon'\mathsf{E}\mathsf{E}^*\to((\#(\epsilon'|\mathsf{E}^*)=0)\to\mathfrak{E}[\![\mathsf{E}]\!]\rho\kappa,wrong),wrong)\epsilon.$$

The first test, $\epsilon'\mathsf{E}\mathsf{E}^*$, is required because $\#(\epsilon'|\mathsf{E}^*)$ is useless unless $\epsilon'\mathsf{E}\mathsf{E}^*$; the second test, $\#(\epsilon'|\mathsf{E}^*)=0$, is needed for the purpose of checking that an empty list of expressed values having length zero is supplied as the argument. The function rv is used so that the argument allegedly giving an empty list is taken by R-value.

Procedures needing non-empty parameter lists can be created in several ways which differ in the manner in which the formal parameters are made to correspond with the expressions forming the actual parameters of an application. In Sal we have included no procedure needing more than one parameter in order to reduce the number of equations for the language. Since it is possible to pass a long list of expressions as one parameter, we have not lost any significant generality by not providing procedures having several parameters each.

The two main methods of passing parameters to procedures which are available in Sal have close parallels to the two forms of simple non-recursive declaration. An 'abstraction by reference' is written as fnI.E and needs the semantic equation

$\mathcal{F}[\![\text{fnI.E}]\!]=\lambda\rho.\lambda\varepsilon\kappa.lv(\lambda\varepsilon'.\mathcal{E}[\![E]\!]\rho[\varepsilon'/I]\kappa)\varepsilon.$

This ensures that the actual parameter provided at an application is coerced by lv to yield a location ε'. The body, E, of the procedure is then executed in the environment $\rho[\varepsilon'/I]$ (which is the original environment in which the abstraction was executed extended by making the formal parameter I denote the value ε'). The corresponding declaration is the 'declaration by reference' written as I=E; as will be proved in 3.6.4, the expressions $(\text{fnI.E}_0)\text{E}_1$ and I=E_1 inside E_0 are equivalent in the rather strong sense that replacing one by the other does not alter the outcome of any program.

The other method of passing parameters provided in Sal is closely related to the familiar call by value found in Algol 60. It entails executing the actual parameter so as to obtain an R-value at the moment of application. The formal parameter is then made to denote the resulting R-value while the body of the procedure is executed. This differs from the Algol 60 rule, where the formal parameter is made to denote a location which initially contains the R-value of the actual parameter. In order to avoid confusion with existing familiar terms, we use the term 'abstraction by incidence' for the method of passing parameters available in Sal, in accordance with the terminology adhered to in 1.8.5 and 1.9.2. Because the pertinent formal parameter denotes an R-value, assignments to it in Sal are pointless - a situation in sharp contrast to that pertaining in Algol 60, where a parameter "called by value" is effectively an initialized local variable denoting a location. We use the notation fnI..E for a typical abstraction by incidence and we let

$\mathcal{F}[\![\text{fn}I..E]\!]=\lambda\rho.\lambda\varepsilon\kappa.rv(\lambda\varepsilon'.\mathcal{E}[\![E]\!]\rho[\varepsilon'/I]\kappa)\varepsilon.$

Thus assignments to I in the body of fnI..E have nugatory effects when an application of fnI..E is executed. There is a corresponding 'declaration by incidence', for which the notation is I==E, and a connection between the expressions $(\text{fn}I..E_0)E_1$ and $(I==E_1)$ inside E_0.

It is worth noting that every procedure value in Sal incorporates the entire environment in which it is created, although we shall indicate in 3.5.6 that a truncated environment, known as a 'free variable list', will suffice; this gives only the values denoted by the names occurring free in the procedure.

The only discrepancy between the equation for res E below and that in 1.5.4 arises from the fact that now we are using $(\text{Ide}\to\text{D}^*)\times\text{K}^*$, not $(\text{Ide}\to\text{D})\times\text{K}$, as the domain of environments. Thus instead of taking $\rho[\![\text{res}]\!]$ to be a continuation we check that the name res has at least one entry in the environment ρ and (under these circumstances), use $\rho[\![\text{res}]\!]\downarrow 1$; accordingly we set up $\mathcal{S}\in\text{Seq}\to\text{U}\to\text{C}$ by letting

$\mathcal{S}[\![\text{res } E]\!]=\lambda\rho.\mathcal{E}[\![E]\!](\lambda\varepsilon.\#\rho[\![\text{res}]\!]>0\to(\rho[\![\text{res}]\!]\downarrow 1)\varepsilon,wrong).$

The sequencer goto E retains the meaning given in 1.5.4: if the value of E is a label value in J (which is C in standard semantics) it is applied to the store, whilst if it is not a label value an error results, so

$\mathcal{S}[\![\text{goto } E]\!]=\lambda\rho.\mathcal{R}[\![E]\!]\rho(\lambda\varepsilon.\varepsilon\,\text{E}\,\text{J}\to\varepsilon|\text{J},wrong).$

Above we have introduced a usage which henceforth we shall adhere to quite consistently: we have shortened the terms "abstraction by worth and reference" and "abstraction by worth and incidence" to "abstraction by reference" and "abstraction by incidence" respectively. This is in keeping with the tendency among language designers to ignore abstractions by name and abstractions by text. Similarly the "declarations by reference" and "declarations by incidence" which we shall now discuss should strictly be called "declarations by worth and reference" and "declarations by worth and incidence".

3.4.4. The valuation $\mathfrak{D}$.

The principal valuation applicable to declarations is $\mathfrak{D}$. In the case of recursive declarations only there are subsidiary valuations $\mathfrak{T}$, $\mathfrak{I}$ and $\mathfrak{H}$ used by the equation for $\mathfrak{D}[\![\text{rec } \Delta]\!]$; we shall defer the discussion of these valuations and this equation until 3.4.5.

The execution of a declaration is in some ways rather similar to that of an expression: each requires an environment in U and a continuation and produces a result (in either U or E). In standard semantics a declaration continuation belongs to U→C whereas an expression continuation belongs to E→C. When the execution of a declaration is successful and actually needs the continuation, the argument passed to the continuation is a so-called 'little environment' having an entry for every identifier which is associated with a denoted value by the declaration. This environment can be used to extend the environment in which an expression or a declaration is to be executed or simply to increase the size of the environment created by another declaration. Here we shall consider only the interaction of different declarations, because the connection between declarations and expressions (which is the only way in which declarations influence the rest of Sal) was discussed above, in 3.4.2, when we dealt with Δ inside E. Label settings, which alter the environment in much the same manner as declarations, will be described in 3.4.8.

The equations for $\mathfrak{D}[\![\text{I=E}]\!]$ and $\mathfrak{D}[\![\text{I==E}]\!]$ have similar structures. If the declarations are executed in an environment ρ and with a continuation χ, the outcome of I=E is calculated by first finding the L-value of E in the same environment, ρ, and then supplying the continuation χ with an environment containing only one entry; this environment is obtained by extending the empty environment *arid* by making I denote the L-value obtained from E. Thus we write

$\mathcal{D}[\![I=E]\!]=\lambda\rho\chi.\mathcal{L}[\![E]\!]\rho(\lambda\varepsilon.\chi(arid[\varepsilon/I]))$.

The execution of I==E has a analogous effect except that I is made to denote the R-value of E; as an R-value in Sal cannot be a location, subsequent assignments to I can serve only to fill the store with rubbish. Accordingly we let

$\mathcal{D}[\![I==E]\!]=\lambda\rho\chi.\mathcal{R}[\![E]\!]\rho(\lambda\varepsilon.\chi(arid[\varepsilon/I]))$.

The multiple declarations available in Sal were discussed in 1.9.3. The purpose of Δ_0 and Δ_1 is to allow a declaration in which Δ_0 and Δ_1 are executed in a common environment to provide two little environments; these environments are united by using *divert* (which we defined in 3.3.3) and are passed on to the declaration continuation. We introduce *run* to avoid determining the order in which Δ_0 and Δ_1 should be executed (just in case Δ_0 and Δ_1 produce side effects which influence the result).

Executing Δ_0 within Δ_1 involves executing Δ_1 in the environment produced by Δ_0 and returning, as a result, only the little environment produced by Δ_1.

The declaration Δ_0 around Δ_1 permits us to execute Δ_1 in the environment produced by Δ_0 and to unite the environment produced by Δ_0 and the environment produced by Δ_1.

When we want to we shall assume that every declaration taking either the form Δ_0 and Δ_1 or the form Δ_0 around Δ_1 is such that the list $\mathcal{I}[\![\Delta_0]\!]\S\mathcal{H}[\![\Delta_0]\!]$ (which comprises the identifiers declared in Δ_0 and having ranges extending beyond Δ_0) has no elements in common with $\mathcal{I}[\![\Delta_1]\!]\S\mathcal{H}[\![\Delta_1]\!]$ (which comprises the identifiers declared in Δ_1 and having ranges extending beyond Δ_1); we could obviously ensure the validity of this assumption by introducing suitable syntactic constraints into the semantics of Sal. The valuations $\mathcal{I}$ and $\mathcal{H}$ will be mentioned again in 3.4.4, when we shall discuss recursive declarations in Sal.

We choose to make (Δ) mean the same thing as Δ, just as we choose to make (E) mean the same thing as E.

3.4.5. The valuations $\mathcal{T}$, $\mathcal{I}$ and $\mathcal{H}$.

The equation for $\mathcal{D}[\![\mathrm{rec}\ \Delta]\!]$ is the most complex in the whole set of semantic equations for Sal. The reasons for this were discussed between 1.9.4 and 1.9.6, where various possibilities were examined. We confine ourselves here to noting that the difficulty springs from a combination of general declarations by reference and a desire to confine the occurrence of the side effects of a declaration to the time when it is executed.

Some of the complexity of the equation given in appendix 1 is hidden by our choice of basic functions operating on the store. In particular the fact that *news* does not alter the area of the store is responsible for the mention of *update* in the definition of *tie*. The need to deal with the possibility that executing the declaration may exhaust the storage available is responsible for the test that *new* returns a location rather than *error*. However, when σ is a store and ν is an integer such that $news\nu\sigma$ is a list of proper locations we can verify that whenever ψ is any member of the domain $\mathrm{L}^*\to\mathrm{C}$ $tie\psi\nu\sigma=\psi(news\nu\sigma|\mathrm{L}^*)(updates(news\nu\sigma|\mathrm{L}^*)(use\nu)\sigma)$; here $use\nu$ is a list of ν occurrences of *false* which is set up in the manner described in 2.3.2. This fact will be significant in 3.4.8 also.

In order that we may simplify the equation for $\mathcal{D}[\![\mathrm{rec}\ \Delta]\!]$ we shall introduce a valuation $\mathcal{A}\in\mathrm{Dec}\to\mathrm{U}\to\mathrm{G}^*$ to replace the $\lambda\psi$ abstraction in the formula given in appendix 1. If we do this the formula for $\mathcal{D}[\![\mathrm{rec}\ \Delta]\!]$ becomes merely

$$\lambda\rho\chi.tie(\lambda\alpha^*\sigma.\mathcal{T}[\![\Delta]\!](fix(\lambda\rho'.\rho[\alpha^*/\mathcal{I}[\![\Delta]\!]][\mathcal{A}[\![\Delta]\!]\rho'\sigma/\mathcal{H}[\![\Delta]\!]]))\chi\sigma)(\#\mathcal{I}[\![\Delta]\!]),$$

where $\mathcal{A}[\![\Delta]\!]$ is

$$\lambda\rho'\sigma.map(\lambda\mathrm{I}\kappa\sigma'.\mathcal{T}[\![\Delta]\!]\rho'(\lambda\rho''\sigma''.\rho''[\![\mathrm{I}]\!]\downarrow 1\mathrm{E}\mathrm{G}\to wrong\sigma'',\kappa(\rho''[\![\mathrm{I}]\!]\downarrow 1)\sigma')\sigma)(\mathcal{H}[\![\Delta]\!]).$$

The valuations $\mathcal{I}$ and $\mathcal{H}$, which both belong to $\mathrm{Dec}\to\mathrm{Ide}^*$, collect up the lists of identifiers declared by reference and by incidence respectively. These valuations, together with $\mathcal{J}$ and $\mathcal{K}$ (which will be discussed in 3.4.8), are really syntactic functions and so have the same definitions for all the sets of semantic equations we give for Sal. They are therefore collected together in appendix 9 and not repeated for each sort of semantics.

The valuation $\mathfrak{T}$ can be regarded as providing a first guess at $\mathfrak{D}$ before the recursion has been set up. It only differs from $\mathfrak{D}$ in the clauses for I=E and rec Δ. The reason for the first difference is that in order to set up the fixed point for the environment of a recursive definition we need to know all the locations denoted by the identifiers declared by reference. Thus we cannot use *lv* for any individual mention of I=E; the formula for $\mathfrak{T}$⟦I=E⟧ must utilize an environment in which the location denoted by I has been settled using the formula for $\mathfrak{D}$⟦rec Δ⟧. Its purpose, then, is to update this location using the R-value of E produced in the fixed point environment. The partial environment produced (and passed as an argument to the continuation) could have been found more easily, for it is merely the empty environment, *arid*, extended by the value which I is already assumed to denote.

The value of $\mathfrak{T}$⟦rec Δ⟧ is merely that of $\mathfrak{T}$⟦Δ⟧, for the fixed point in the environment is constructed by $\mathfrak{D}$, not by $\mathfrak{T}$.

We can now approach the evaluation of rec Δ using $\mathfrak{D}$. Looking at the simplified equation above it can be seen that the first step is to claim the locations for the identifiers declared by reference. This is done by using *tie* with two arguments (which are a rather complicated continuation belonging to L*→C and an integer in the domain N). We need to fill these locations immediately with some dummy value in order to prevent them being claimed (by *lv*, for instance) during the evaluation of other parts of the declaration before they have finally been updated with their correct values by declarations of the form I=E. The dummy value used is immaterial in this context; the definition of *tie* given in 3.3.4 makes this value be *false*, but another value could reasonably be used. The locations claimed by *tie* are turned into the values denoted by the corresponding elements of $\mathcal{I}[\![\Delta]\!]$ by using $\rho[\alpha^*/\mathcal{I}[\![\Delta]\!]]$ in the argument for *fix*.

The identifiers declared by incidence are collected by $\mathcal{H}[\![\Delta]\!]$ and set up to denote the list of recursion values produced by $\mathcal{A}[\![\Delta]\!]\rho'\sigma$. Here ρ' is the fixed point environment and σ is the store in which the locations claimed by *tie* contain suitable values. The definition of $\mathcal{A}$ has been chosen to have the same bound variables as its only occurrence so that although $\mathcal{A}$ is correctly defined as a valuation, the expression $\mathcal{A}[\![\Delta]\!]\rho'\sigma$ occurring on the right of the equation for $\mathcal{D}[\![\text{rec }\Delta]\!]$ can be replaced by the body of the λ-expression defining $\mathcal{A}[\![\Delta]\!]$ without producing any clashes of variables.

The definition of *map* ensures that the function

$\lambda I\kappa\sigma'.\mathcal{T}[\![\Delta]\!]\rho'(\lambda\rho''\sigma''.\rho''[\![I]\!]\downarrow 1 \mathsf{E} G \to wrong\sigma'',\kappa(\rho''[\![I]\!]\downarrow 1)\sigma')\sigma$

is applied in turn to each of the identifiers in the list $\mathcal{H}[\![\Delta]\!]$, which are those declared by incidence. If we write ϕ for

$\lambda I\kappa\sigma'.\lambda\rho''\sigma''.(\rho''[\![I]\!]\downarrow 1 \mathsf{E} G \to wrong\sigma'',\kappa(\rho''[\![I]\!]\downarrow 1)\sigma')$, the function applied by *map* to each identifier becomes

$\lambda I\kappa\sigma'.\mathcal{T}[\![\Delta]\!]\rho'(\phi[\![I]\!]\kappa\sigma')\sigma$,

where ρ' will ultimately become the fixed point environment.

In fact $\mathcal{T}[\![\Delta]\!]\rho'$ may have side effects on σ and may even ignore $\phi[\![I]\!]\kappa\sigma'$ altogether because of a jump (in which case the whole declaration rec Δ is abortive). If however it is successful even with a side effect, it will produce a partial environment ρ'' which is independent of $\phi[\![I]\!]\kappa\sigma'$ although, of course, it depends on ρ' and σ. We are going to identify ρ' with the fixed point environment which mentions what the members of $\mathcal{I}[\![\Delta]\!]$ and $\mathcal{H}[\![\Delta]\!]$ denote.

As we shall assume that in every declaration Δ the combined list of identifiers $\mathcal{I}[\![\Delta]\!]\S\mathcal{H}[\![\Delta]\!]$ contains no repetitions, $\rho''[\![I]\!]$ will be a unit list; moreover in practice the equations will ensure that its single member $\rho''[\![I]\!]\downarrow 1$ is not in G so we can temporarily write ε for $\rho''[\![I]\!]\downarrow 1$ and ignore the conditional in ϕ. We shall let σ be the store in which the whole recursive declaration rec Δ is executed when all the locations needed for declarations by reference have been claimed. Actually ε is the R-value of the expression used in the declaration for I (which, as I is declared by incidence, will be I==E) executed in the presence of the final fixed point environment (or in some extension of it formed by within and around declarations) and in the presence of a certain store; after the execution of E this store will become σ''.

The result of passing ρ'' to $\phi[\![I]\!]\kappa\sigma'$ is $\lambda\sigma''.\kappa\varepsilon\sigma'$ (which is a member of C), so the final denoted value associated with I by application of $\lambda I\kappa\sigma'.\mathcal{T}[\![\Delta]\!]\rho'(\phi[\![I]\!]\kappa\sigma')\sigma$ is, we may hope, something like

$\lambda\kappa\sigma'.(\lambda\sigma''.\kappa\varepsilon\sigma')\sigma''=\lambda\kappa\sigma'.\kappa\varepsilon\sigma'=\lambda\kappa.\kappa\varepsilon$,

provided that Δ is not left by a jump. Thus the final value denoted by I is a member of G whose dependence on the original store is now incorporated in the value of ε.

Any future use of the value $\lambda\kappa.\kappa\varepsilon$ must come from a reference to I in the environment ρ' (or some extension of it which does not mask the denotation of I). If this is evaluated with a continuation κ' we shall need to find the value of $\mathcal{E}[\![I]\!]\rho'\kappa'$. The equation for $\mathcal{E}[\![I]\!]$ shows that as $\rho'[\![I]\!]\downarrow 1\in G$ this value will be $\kappa'\varepsilon$ which introduces no further side effects.

At the end of 1.9.6 we mentioned that the general equations governing recursive declarations can be simplified in the usual practical situations. In particular, as we shall remark again in 3.9.6, we can easily prove that

$\mathcal{D}[\![\text{rec } I==\Phi]\!]=\lambda\rho\chi.\chi(arid[fix(\lambda\phi.\mathcal{F}[\![\Phi]\!]\rho[\phi/I])/I])$

and that mutually recursive procedures can be handled conveniently.

3.4.6. The valuation $\mathfrak{G}$.

Most of the equations governing $\mathfrak{G}$, which in standard semantics belongs to Blo→U→C→C, reflect the fact that the scopes of labels are not allowed to spread outside any expressions in which they appear. This is so because the only expression which incorporates either a block or a command is Θ before E. It follows that the constructs discussed below are naturally blocks, in that they confine the scopes of labels occurring in them; in Sal they do not yield results in E. The equation for block Γ, which is the only one concerned with setting labels, is more complex and will not be discussed until 3.4.8.

Executing fit E merely causes the result of executing E to be ignored; doing this obviously has a justification if E has a side effect or if there is a need for a command with no effect. The block get E allows the L-value of E to be updated with the first element of the input region of the store, provided that this region is not empty; the input region of the store produced consists of the original region truncated by one element. By contrast, whenever put E is executed, the R-value of E is added to the end of the output region of the store leaving the other components of the store unchanged.

The execution of an assignment of the form $E_0:=E_1$ entails finding the L-value of E_0 and the R-value of E_1 in either order; for this reason *run* must be used. The location thus obtained is then updated with the stored value without any regard being paid to the type of the previous content of E_0; this entails allowing the types of expressions to be dynamic. The use of $\mathcal{L}$ and $\mathcal{R}$ ensures that arguments of the correct type are supplied to *assign*. The definition of *li* we have adopted ensures that even an attempt to update a member of V such as an integer will not cause an error stop (unless the store is full); instead a new location, which may never again be accessible, will be given this member of V as its content.

A sequencer, Σ say, is also a block in Sal; naturally it merely ignores the continuation in C which it is given when treated as a block.

Because Sal provides no means of constructing one block from two others which does not involve regarding blocks as commands there is no need for a bracketed block, (Θ), to be featured in the idealized syntax of blocks.

3.4.7. The valuation $\mathfrak{C}$.

The equation for $\mathfrak{C}[\![\Gamma_0;\Gamma_1]\!]$ provides the simplest example of the use of continuations to explain the normal sequencing of commands while still allowing jumps. The value is obtained by executing Γ_0 in an environment ρ but with a continuation of the form $\mathfrak{C}[\![\Gamma_1]\!]\rho\theta$ in which the command Γ_1 is "followed by" θ. If there is a jump out of Γ_0 or if Γ_0 fails to terminate normally, the continuation $\mathfrak{C}[\![\Gamma_1]\!]\rho\theta$ is never invoked.

The intention of **if** E **do** Γ is to provide a "single-armed" conditional command. The R-value of E is found and if this is the truth value *true* then Γ is performed followed by the continuation of **if** E **do** Γ; if E yields the value *false* this continuation is used immediately. If E does not yield a truth value the function *test* causes an immediate error exit. Any side effects which E may have take place in any case, and the single arm is a command (not a block).

The equation for **while** E **do** Γ reflects the idea that this command has approximately the same effect as **if** E **do** (Γ; **while** E **do** Γ). The equivalence is only approximate, however, because we cannot allow label settings in Γ to be repeated; an exact version of the equivalence will be proved in 3.6.6. Thus when θ'' is taken to be $\mathfrak{C}[\![$**while** E **do** $\Gamma]\!]\rho\theta$ as in 1.5.3 it should also be $\mathfrak{C}[\![$**if** E **do** (Γ; **while** E **do** Γ)$]\!]\rho\theta$. Using the previous equations this value can be seen to be $\mathfrak{R}[\![E]\!]\rho(test\langle\mathfrak{C}[\![\Gamma]\!]\rho\theta'',\theta\rangle)$. We thus get an equation for θ'' which can be solved by taking a fixed point: if we let θ'' be $fix(\lambda\theta'.\mathfrak{R}[\![E]\!]\rho(test\langle\mathfrak{C}[\![\Gamma]\!]\rho\theta',\theta\rangle))$ then
$\theta''=(\lambda\theta'.\mathfrak{R}[\![E]\!]\rho(test\langle\mathfrak{C}[\![\Gamma]\!]\rho\theta',\theta\rangle))\theta''=\mathfrak{R}[\![E]\!]\rho(test\langle\mathfrak{C}[\![\Gamma]\!]\rho\theta'',\theta\rangle)$.

A block is the only kind of command to which $\mathfrak{G}$ may be applied. It limits the scopes of labels appearing in it but in all other respects is a normal command; owing to this $\mathfrak{C}$ can be defined on it.

The commands I:Γ and I::Γ serve only to set the label I; the command Γ has its usual value as far as $\mathfrak{C}$ is concerned. The subsidiary valuations governing the ways in which $I:\Gamma$ and $I::\Gamma$ permit us to set labels will be explained in 3.4.8.

The command (Γ) is introduced to allow ambiguities of parsing to be resolved as usual.

3.4.8. The valuations $\mathfrak{P}$, $\mathfrak{Q}$, $\mathfrak{J}$ and $\mathfrak{K}$.

The equation for $\mathfrak{G}[\![\text{block } \Gamma]\!]$ is intended to restrict the scopes of the labels set in Γ, so it necessitates forming the environment which contains the denoted values appropriate to these labels. As this is also the environment which must be used with the valuations applied to Γ, it must be formed by taking a fixed point. In fact block Γ has a close analogy with rec Δ, for both require environments which are constructed with the aid of *fix* and which are used when evaluating parts of the constructs; moreover both depend on a number of subsidiary valuations which handle identifiers set or declared by reference in a different manner from identifiers set or declared by incidence.

The valuations $\mathfrak{J}$ and $\mathfrak{K}$, which are defined in appendix 9, serve to collect into lists the label identifiers set by reference and incidence respectively; they are thus analogous to $\mathfrak{I}$ and $\mathfrak{H}$ and are syntactic rather than semantic in nature. The valuation $\mathfrak{C}$ plays a part which corresponds with that of $\mathfrak{T}$ in recursive declarations. The chief difference is that while the body of rec Δ is itself a declaration, so that $\mathfrak{T}$ takes a declaration as an argument, the body of block Γ is a command (and not a block) so that $\mathfrak{C}$ operates on commands rather than blocks. The purpose of $\mathfrak{C}$ is to provide a value for the command Γ once the appropriate fixed point environment has been found.

As blocks and commands are largely disjoint, the definition of $\mathfrak{C}$, unlike that of $\mathfrak{T}$, is the chief valuation for a number of important constructs. For this reason in 3.4.7 we discussed its clauses individually without alluding to the role of labels.

As was indicated in 3.4.7, in Sal labels are set by making use of the commands I:Γ and I::Γ. However, unlike the corresponding elementary declarations I=E and I==E, the value corresponding with the label I incorporates its continuation in an essential way. This is so because the value of a label represents the effect of the program from the label point onwards and is therefore a member of J (which in standard semantics is the same as C); in fact it has the value $\mathcal{C}[\![\Gamma]\!]\rho\theta$ when θ is the continuation actually supplied to Γ. In the case of a label I set by reference, I:Γ, this value has to be stored in the location which is denoted by I. As $\mathcal{C}[\![\Gamma]\!]\rho\theta$ is in $S\to A$ and S has a factor which is $L\to(V\times T)$, the inclusion of J in V makes the domains V, S and C subject to mutually recursive equations.

We need to associate the individual label values with the appropriate members of the lists of identifiers produced by $\mathcal{J}[\![\Gamma]\!]$ and $\mathcal{K}[\![\Gamma]\!]$. We do this by using two further subsidiary valuations, $\mathcal{P}$ and $\mathcal{Q}$, which collect the values of the labels set by reference and by incidence into lists which correspond term by term with the lists produced by $\mathcal{J}$ and $\mathcal{K}$. The equations for these two valuations differ from one another only in how they treat the relevant label setting commands. We shall only comment on $\mathcal{P}$, which collects the list of values of labels set by reference; the corresponding list of identifiers is formed by $\mathcal{J}$.

In the case of the command $\Gamma_0;\Gamma_1$, $\mathcal{J}$ merely concatenates the two sublists for Γ_0 and Γ_1; $\mathcal{P}[\![\Gamma_0;\Gamma_1]\!]\rho\theta$ does much the same but uses $\mathcal{C}[\![\Gamma_1]\!]\rho\theta$ as the continuation for Γ_0 because after the execution of a jump to a label in Γ_0 both the remainder of Γ_0 and the command Γ_1 must be executed.

The equation for $\mathcal{P}[\![$if E do $\Gamma]\!]$ reflects the fact that if there is a label inside Γ then the continuation supplied to it must include the continuation for the whole command. As the expression E effectively blocks the scopes of labels set anywhere inside it, it makes no contribution to $\mathcal{J}$ or $\mathcal{P}$.

The equation for $\mathcal{P}[\![$while E do $\Gamma]\!]$ can be explained by the same sort of reasoning as that used in the description of $\mathcal{C}[\![$while E do $\Gamma]\!]$; the repeated mention of Γ on the right hand side of the equation causes no difficulties as the value of $\mathfrak{C}[\![\Gamma]\!]$ is independent of any labels that may be set in Γ.

A block contains no labels which have scopes spreading beyond its edges, so for every Θ both $\mathfrak{P}[\![\Theta]\!]$ and $\mathfrak{Q}[\![\Theta]\!]$ are $\lambda\rho\theta.\langle\rangle$ while both $\mathfrak{J}[\![\Theta]\!]$ and $\mathfrak{K}[\![\Theta]\!]$ are $\langle\rangle$. The effect of $\mathfrak{P}[\![I{:}\Gamma]\!]$ is very different as this is required to add the label value for I to the front of the list it produces. If ρ is the environment and θ the continuation provided for I:E, the appropriate label value is $\mathfrak{C}[\![I{:}\Gamma]\!]\rho\theta$. By contrast, as $I{::}\Gamma$ provides a label set by incidence, not one set by reference, applying $\mathfrak{P}$ to it does not cause a new element to be appended at the front of the list $\mathfrak{P}[\![\Gamma]\!]\rho\theta$.

We can at last approach the equation for $\mathfrak{G}[\![\text{block } \Gamma]\!]$ itself. The first step is to claim the new locations required for the labels set by reference. This is done by the mention of the function *tie* in the equation. This function provides a list, α^*, which consists of members of L, unless the store has been exhausted in the course of claiming the new locations; if the store has been exhausted an error exit occurs through an application of *wrong*. It also arranges to update the elements of the list α^* with dummy values (just as it did at the corresponding stage in 3.4.5), although they are later updated directly with their final values. The next step is to form the appropriate fixed point environment, ρ'. This is obtained by extending ρ so as to denote elements of $\mathfrak{J}[\![\Gamma]\!]$ and $\mathfrak{K}[\![\Gamma]\!]$ by elements of α^* and $\mathfrak{Q}[\![\Gamma]\!]\rho'\theta$ respectively. Then the original store σ is changed by assigning to the elements of α^* the values in the list $\mathfrak{P}[\![\Gamma]\!]\rho'\theta$, thereby producing an altered store, say σ'. The final value of $\mathfrak{G}[\![\text{block } \Gamma]\!]\rho\theta\sigma$ is then $\mathfrak{C}[\![\Gamma]\!]\rho'\theta\sigma'$. When applying the equation for block Γ we shall always assume that $\mathfrak{J}[\![\Gamma]\!]\S\mathfrak{K}[\![\Gamma]\!]$ is devoid of repetitions; likewise, as we mentioned in 3.4.5, when applying the equation for rec Δ we shall suppose that the list $\mathfrak{I}[\![\Delta]\!]\S\mathfrak{H}[\![\Delta]\!]$ has no repeated elements.

3.5. Some elementary properties of the semantic equations.

3.5.1. Structural induction.

In the rest of this book we shall frequently wish to prove propositions about the semantic properties of classes of members of syntactic domains. Typically such a proposition may assert that if an expression, E say, satisfies a premise which we write as $e⟦E⟧=true$ (for some predicate e) then it satisfies a consequence which we write as $E⟦E⟧=true$ (for some predicate E). In order to establish such a result we carry out a 'structural induction' over all or some of the equations for the valuations. Here we shall describe this notion and give a trivial example.

In a structural induction, associated with each or certain of the valuations for the language there are predicates; we generally distinguish these predicates by using upper and lower case italic letters corresponding with the script letters for the valuations. For any expression E we usually expect the equation $e⟦E⟧=true$ to say something about the syntactic structure of E and the equation $E⟦E⟧=true$ to say something about the nature of $\mathcal{E}⟦E⟧$. Because expressions can be built up from other sorts of syntactic entities, such as declarations and blocks (owing to the existence of the expressions Δ **inside** E and Θ **before** E), we often need other predicates which are naturally named D and d or G and g; declarations and blocks in turn give rise to members of other syntactic domains so yet more predicates may be needed. In fact the semantics of Sal requires fourteen semantic valuations (including $\mathcal{B}$, $\mathcal{O}$ and $\mathcal{W}$ but excluding $\mathcal{I}$, $\mathcal{H}$, $\mathcal{J}$ and $\mathcal{K}$), so a structural induction over the whole of the language may in principle involve twenty-eight predicates.

The inductive step in a structural induction generally proceeds as follows. For an expression, E say, we stipulate that $e⟦E⟧=true$ and examine the semantic equations governing the forms that E can take;

if E is E_0E_1 for instance, we assume that if $r[\![E_0]\!]=true$ then $R[\![E_0]\!]=true$ and that if $e[\![E_1]\!]=true$ then $E[\![E_1]\!]=true$ (since $\mathcal{E}[\![E_0E_1]\!]$ is constructed from $\mathcal{R}[\![E_0]\!]$ and $\mathcal{E}[\![E_1]\!]$) and endeavour to prove that $E[\![E_0E_1]\!]=true$. When each of these possible forms for E is such that $E[\![E]\!]=true$ we can safely assert that $E[\![E]\!]=true$. Likewise for a declaration Δ and a block Θ we may posit that $d[\![\Delta]\!]=true$ and that $g[\![\Theta]\!]=true$ and try to show that $D[\![\Delta]\!]=true$ and that $G[\![\Theta]\!]=true$ by making suitable assumptions about the constituents of Δ and Θ.

In the course of verifying the inductive step we need to examine semantic equations the right hand sides of which are formed using syntactic entities for which there is no suitable inductive hypothesis; one such is the equation for $\mathcal{E}[\![I]\!]$, since if we wish to show that $E[\![E]\!]=true$ when E is I we cannot assume that $E[\![I]\!]=true$. These equations form the basis of the structural induction, just as taking ν to be 0 provides the basis in an arithmetic induction on the integer ν.

If we adopt the first view of the syntactic domains mentioned in 3.1.2 we can vindicate our use of structural induction by applying arithmetic induction to the lengths of programs. If, however, we adopt the second view of the syntactic domains we can apply arithmetic induction to justify using structural induction only when attention is restricted to finite programs and when no circularity arises in the definition of the valuations; when circularity does occur (as it will do in 4.6.1) we shall be obliged to appeal to the induction principle given in 2.3.2.

As an illustrative structural induction we shall consider something that is usually taken for granted - the proof that whenever Γ is a command $\#\mathcal{P}[\![\Gamma]\!]\rho\theta=\#\mathcal{J}[\![\Gamma]\!]$ for all ρ and θ. We set $P=\lambda\Gamma.\bigwedge\{\bigwedge\{\#\mathcal{P}[\![\Gamma]\!]\rho\theta=\#\mathcal{J}[\![\Gamma]\!]\mid\theta\}\mid\rho\}$ (so that $P[\![\Gamma]\!]=true$ if and only if $\#\mathcal{P}[\![\Gamma]\!]\rho\theta=\#\mathcal{J}[\![\Gamma]\!]$ for all ρ and θ) and $p=\lambda\Gamma.true$, since we want to show that $P[\![\Gamma]\!]=true$ without placing any restrictions on Γ.

Thus we conclude that whenever Γ is a command $P[\![\Gamma]\!]$ is *true*. By analogous reasoning we can deduce that whenever Γ is a command $\#\mathcal{Q}[\![\Gamma]\!]\rho\theta=\#\mathcal{K}[\![\Gamma]\!]$ for all ρ and θ; in the proof of this we naturally make $Q=\lambda\Gamma.\bigwedge\{\bigwedge\{\#\mathcal{Q}[\![\Gamma]\!]\rho\theta=\#\mathcal{K}[\![\Gamma]\!]\mid\theta\}\mid\rho\}$ and $q=\lambda\Gamma.\mathit{true}$.

The proof that we have just given is abnormal, in that it involves only one semantic valuation so only seven cases need to be considered, all of which are trivial. In most of the structural inductions we use it is impossible to confine the argument to a single semantic valuation and we have to consider each of the equations in all the valuations. There are sixty of these equations in appendix 1. Hence a detailed structural induction on the whole language would be a formidable task. Fortunately in many cases the result is trivially obvious, while other cases fall into a small number of groups, the members of which can be treated similarly. We shall rarely give more than a single example from each group. Finally, some propositions depend on structural inductions which are so like those required for other propositions that we omit the details of the proofs altogether.

Even after this drastic pruning the proofs in this book are often long, complicated and rather tedious. The difficulty springs, we think, from the fact that the programming language under consideration is itself a very complex mathematical construct. Unfortunately, attempts to simplify matters by cutting down the language do little to improve the situation unless they are so severe as to reduce the power of the language greatly.

A somewhat more elaborate, but still essentially elementary, example of structural induction will be discussed in 3.9.4; others will be mentioned in 3.5.5 and 3.5.6. The role of structural induction in proofs that implementations are correct will be examined in 4.6.1. Straightforward inductions on the lengths of programs will underlie 4.6.7 and 5.6.7.

In order to show that $P\llbracket\Gamma_0;\Gamma_1\rrbracket=true$ when $P\llbracket\Gamma_0\rrbracket=true$ and $P\llbracket\Gamma_1\rrbracket=true$, we note that, because $P\llbracket\Gamma_0\rrbracket=true$, $\#\mathcal{P}\llbracket\Gamma_0\rrbracket\rho\theta=\#\mathcal{J}\llbracket\Gamma_0\rrbracket$ for all ρ and θ; in particular $\#\mathcal{P}\llbracket\Gamma_0\rrbracket\rho(\mathcal{C}\llbracket\Gamma_1\rrbracket\rho\theta)=\#\mathcal{J}\llbracket\Gamma_0\rrbracket$ for all ρ and θ. Moreover, as $P\llbracket\Gamma_1\rrbracket=true$, $\#\mathcal{P}\llbracket\Gamma_1\rrbracket\rho\theta=\#\mathcal{J}\llbracket\Gamma_1\rrbracket$ for all ρ and θ, so in fact $\#\mathcal{P}\llbracket\Gamma_0\rrbracket\rho(\mathcal{C}\llbracket\Gamma_1\rrbracket\rho\theta)+\#\mathcal{P}\llbracket\Gamma_1\rrbracket\rho\theta=\#\mathcal{J}\llbracket\Gamma_0\rrbracket+\#\mathcal{J}\llbracket\Gamma_1\rrbracket$ for all ρ and θ. However, according to appendix 1 $\mathcal{P}\llbracket\Gamma_0;\Gamma_1\rrbracket=\lambda\rho\theta.\mathcal{P}\llbracket\Gamma_0\rrbracket\rho(\mathcal{C}\llbracket\Gamma_1\rrbracket\rho\theta)\S\mathcal{P}\llbracket\Gamma_1\rrbracket\rho\theta$, and according to appendix 9 $\mathcal{J}\llbracket\Gamma_0;\Gamma_1\rrbracket=\mathcal{J}\llbracket\Gamma_0\rrbracket\S\mathcal{J}\llbracket\Gamma_1\rrbracket$. By combining these pieces of information we deduce that $\#\mathcal{P}\llbracket\Gamma_0;\Gamma_1\rrbracket\rho\theta=\#\mathcal{J}\llbracket\Gamma_0;\Gamma_1\rrbracket$ for all ρ and θ; in other words $P\llbracket\Gamma_0;\Gamma_1\rrbracket=true$.

The arguments for if E do Γ and while E do Γ are even simpler, as in both cases the lists concerned are the same length as those for Γ. More fully, if $P\llbracket\Gamma\rrbracket=true$ then $\#\mathcal{P}\llbracket\Gamma\rrbracket\rho\theta=\#\mathcal{J}\llbracket\Gamma\rrbracket$ and $\#\mathcal{P}\llbracket\Gamma\rrbracket\rho(fix(\lambda\theta'.\mathcal{R}\llbracket E\rrbracket\rho(test\langle\mathcal{C}\llbracket\Gamma\rrbracket\rho\theta',\theta\rangle)))=\#\mathcal{J}\llbracket\Gamma\rrbracket$ for all ρ and θ, so

$$\begin{aligned}\#\mathcal{P}\llbracket\text{if E do }\Gamma\rrbracket\rho\theta&=\#\mathcal{P}\llbracket\Gamma\rrbracket\rho\theta\\&=\#\mathcal{J}\llbracket\Gamma\rrbracket\\&=\#\mathcal{J}\llbracket\text{if E do }\Gamma\rrbracket\end{aligned}$$

and

$$\begin{aligned}\#\mathcal{P}\llbracket\text{while E do }\Gamma\rrbracket\rho\theta&=\#\mathcal{P}\llbracket\Gamma\rrbracket\rho(fix(\lambda\theta'.\mathcal{R}\llbracket E\rrbracket\rho(test\langle\mathcal{C}\llbracket\Gamma\rrbracket\rho\theta',\theta\rangle)))\\&=\#\mathcal{J}\llbracket\Gamma\rrbracket\\&=\#\mathcal{J}\llbracket\text{while E do }\Gamma\rrbracket\end{aligned}$$

for all ρ and θ; consequently $P\llbracket\text{if E do }\Gamma\rrbracket=true$ and $P\llbracket\text{while E do }\Gamma\rrbracket=true$.

The case of Θ provides the basis for the induction: we know automatically that $P\llbracket\Theta\rrbracket=true$, since by virtue of appendix 1 $\mathcal{P}\llbracket\Theta\rrbracket=\lambda\rho\theta.\langle\rangle$ and by virtue of appendix 9 $\mathcal{J}\llbracket\Theta\rrbracket=\langle\rangle$.

When proving that $P\llbracket I:\Gamma\rrbracket=true$ when $P\llbracket\Gamma\rrbracket=true$ we observe that $\#\mathcal{P}\llbracket\Gamma\rrbracket\rho\theta=\#\mathcal{J}\llbracket\Gamma\rrbracket$ for all ρ and θ; hence $1+\#\mathcal{P}\llbracket\Gamma\rrbracket\rho\theta=1+\#\mathcal{J}\llbracket\Gamma\rrbracket$ for all ρ and θ and indeed $\#\mathcal{P}\llbracket I:\Gamma\rrbracket\rho\theta=\#\mathcal{J}\llbracket I:\Gamma\rrbracket$ for all ρ and θ, so $P\llbracket I:\Gamma\rrbracket=true$.

The arguments for $I::\Gamma$ and (Γ) are very similar to those for if E do Γ and while E do Γ, because again the lists concerned are the same length as those for Γ.

3.5.2. Occurrences of names.

We have often used the phrase "free occurrence of a name" without giving it more than an informal definition. Now that we have a full set of the standard semantic equations for Sal we can give a rigorous definition of the term. We can do this by defining a predicate $\mathit{free}\in(\mathsf{Exp}+\mathsf{Abs}+\mathsf{Seq}+\mathsf{Dec}+\mathsf{Blo}+\mathsf{Com})\to(\mathsf{Ide}+\{\mathsf{res}\})\to\mathsf{T}$ by an induction on the constructs of Sal. The intention is that $\mathit{free}\llbracket \mathrm{E}\rrbracket\llbracket \mathrm{K}\rrbracket$, for example, should have the value *true* if there is a free occurrence of the name K in E and the value *false* otherwise. Here we are using K as a variable ranging over members of the domain $\mathsf{Ide}+\{\mathsf{res}\}$, which contains all the names available in Sal.

A full definition of *free* requires an equation for each clause of the idealized syntax; as there are thirty-seven such clauses the full definition is rather long. Fortunately the equations for most of the clauses are trivial and can be omitted. We give below the more interesting equations in the order in which the clauses they refer to appear in the idealized syntax. For expressions we write:

$\mathit{free}\llbracket \mathrm{B}\rrbracket=\lambda \mathrm{K}.\mathit{false}$;

$\mathit{free}\llbracket \mathrm{I}\rrbracket=\lambda \mathrm{K}.\mathrm{K}\in\mathsf{Ide}\to(\mathrm{K}|\mathsf{Ide}=\mathrm{I}),\mathit{false}$;

$\mathit{free}\llbracket \Phi\rrbracket=\lambda \mathrm{K}.\mathit{free}\llbracket \Phi|\mathsf{Abs}\rrbracket\llbracket \mathrm{K}\rrbracket$;

$\mathit{free}\llbracket \Sigma\rrbracket=\lambda \mathrm{K}.\mathit{free}\llbracket \Sigma|\mathsf{Seq}\rrbracket\llbracket \mathrm{K}\rrbracket$;

$\mathit{free}\llbracket \mathbf{val}\ \mathrm{E}\rrbracket=\lambda \mathrm{K}.\mathit{free}\llbracket \mathrm{E}\rrbracket\llbracket \mathrm{K}\rrbracket\wedge(\mathrm{K}\in\mathsf{Ide})$;

$\mathit{free}\llbracket \Delta\ \mathbf{inside}\ \mathrm{E}\rrbracket=\lambda \mathrm{K}.\mathit{free}\llbracket \Delta\rrbracket\llbracket \mathrm{K}\rrbracket$

$\qquad\vee(\mathit{free}\llbracket \mathrm{E}\rrbracket\llbracket \mathrm{K}\rrbracket\wedge(\mathrm{K}\in\mathsf{Ide}\to\sim(\mathrm{K}|\mathsf{Ide}\in\mathfrak{I}\llbracket \Delta\rrbracket\S\mathcal{H}\llbracket \Delta\rrbracket),\mathit{true}))$.

For abstractions we write:

$\mathit{free}\llbracket \mathbf{fn}()\mathrm{E}\rrbracket=\lambda \mathrm{K}.\mathit{free}\llbracket \mathrm{E}\rrbracket\llbracket \mathrm{K}\rrbracket$;

$\mathit{free}\llbracket \mathbf{fn}\mathrm{I}.\mathrm{E}\rrbracket=\lambda \mathrm{K}.\mathit{free}\llbracket \mathrm{E}\rrbracket\llbracket \mathrm{K}\rrbracket\wedge(\mathrm{K}\in\mathsf{Ide}\to\sim(\mathrm{K}|\mathsf{Ide}=\mathrm{I}),\mathit{true})$;

$\mathit{free}\llbracket \mathbf{fn}\mathrm{I}..\mathrm{E}\rrbracket=\lambda \mathrm{K}.\mathit{free}\llbracket \mathrm{E}\rrbracket\llbracket \mathrm{K}\rrbracket\wedge(\mathrm{K}\in\mathsf{Ide}\to\sim(\mathrm{K}|\mathsf{Ide}=\mathrm{I}),\mathit{true})$.

For sequencers we write:

$\mathit{free}\llbracket \mathbf{res}\ \mathrm{E}\rrbracket=\lambda \mathrm{K}.\mathit{free}\llbracket \mathrm{E}\rrbracket\llbracket \mathrm{K}\rrbracket\vee\sim(\mathrm{K}\in\mathsf{Ide})$;

$\mathit{free}\llbracket \mathbf{goto}\ \mathrm{E}\rrbracket=\lambda \mathrm{K}.\mathit{free}\llbracket \mathrm{E}\rrbracket\llbracket \mathrm{K}\rrbracket$.

For declarations we write:

$\mathit{free}[\![\mathrm{I=E}]\!]=\lambda\mathrm{K}.\mathit{free}[\![\mathrm{E}]\!][\![\mathrm{K}]\!]$;

$\mathit{free}[\![\mathrm{I==E}]\!]=\lambda\mathrm{K}.\mathit{free}[\![\mathrm{E}]\!][\![\mathrm{K}]\!]$;

$\mathit{free}[\![\Delta_0 \;\mathbf{and}\; \Delta_1]\!]=\lambda\mathrm{K}.\mathit{free}[\![\Delta_0]\!][\![\mathrm{K}]\!]\vee\mathit{free}[\![\Delta_1]\!][\![\mathrm{K}]\!]$;

$\mathit{free}[\![\Delta_0 \;\mathbf{within}\; \Delta_1]\!]=\lambda\mathrm{K}.\mathit{free}[\![\Delta_0]\!][\![\mathrm{K}]\!]$

$\qquad\qquad\vee(\mathit{free}[\![\Delta_1]\!][\![\mathrm{K}]\!]\wedge(\mathrm{K}\sqsubseteq\mathrm{Ide}\rightarrow\sim(\mathrm{K}|\mathrm{Ide}\in\mathfrak{I}[\![\Delta_0]\!]\,\S\,\mathfrak{H}[\![\Delta_0]\!]),\mathit{true}))$;

$\mathit{free}[\![\Delta_0 \;\mathbf{around}\; \Delta_1]\!]=\lambda\mathrm{K}.\mathit{free}[\![\Delta_0]\!][\![\mathrm{K}]\!]$

$\qquad\qquad\vee(\mathit{free}[\![\Delta_1]\!][\![\mathrm{K}]\!]\wedge(\mathrm{K}\sqsubseteq\mathrm{Ide}\rightarrow\sim(\mathrm{K}|\mathrm{Ide}\in\mathfrak{I}[\![\Delta_0]\!]\,\S\,\mathfrak{H}[\![\Delta_0]\!]),\mathit{true}))$;

$\mathit{free}[\![\mathbf{rec}\;\Delta]\!]=\lambda\mathrm{K}.\mathit{free}[\![\Delta]\!][\![\mathrm{K}]\!]\wedge(\mathrm{K}\sqsubseteq\mathrm{Ide}\rightarrow\sim(\mathrm{K}|\mathrm{Ide}\in\mathfrak{I}[\![\Delta]\!]\,\S\,\mathfrak{H}[\![\Delta]\!]),\mathit{true})$.

For blocks we write:

$\mathit{free}[\![\Sigma]\!]=\lambda\mathrm{K}.\mathit{free}[\![\Sigma|\mathrm{Seq}]\!][\![\mathrm{K}]\!]$;

$\mathit{free}[\![\mathbf{block}\;\Gamma]\!]=\lambda\mathrm{K}.\mathit{free}[\![\Gamma]\!][\![\mathrm{K}]\!]\wedge(\mathrm{K}\sqsubseteq\mathrm{Ide}\rightarrow\sim(\mathrm{K}|\mathrm{Ide}\in\mathfrak{J}[\![\Gamma]\!]\,\S\,\mathfrak{K}[\![\Gamma]\!]),\mathit{true})$.

For commands we write:

$\mathit{free}[\![\Theta]\!]=\lambda\mathrm{K}.\mathit{free}[\![\Theta|\mathrm{Blo}]\!][\![\mathrm{K}]\!]$;

$\mathit{free}[\![\mathrm{I}:\Gamma]\!]=\lambda\mathrm{K}.\mathit{free}[\![\Gamma]\!][\![\mathrm{K}]\!]\vee(\mathrm{K}\sqsubseteq\mathrm{Ide}\rightarrow(\mathrm{K}|\mathrm{Ide}=\mathrm{I}),\mathit{false})$;

$\mathit{free}[\![\mathrm{I}::\Gamma]\!]=\lambda\mathrm{K}.\mathit{free}[\![\Gamma]\!][\![\mathrm{K}]\!]\vee(\mathrm{K}\sqsubseteq\mathrm{Ide}\rightarrow(\mathrm{K}|\mathrm{Ide}=\mathrm{I}),\mathit{false})$.

In these equations we have used the set membership sign, $\in$, to indicate membership of a list.

The equation for $\mathit{free}[\![\Phi]\!]$ when Φ is considered as an expression indicates that the value is to be found from the equation for the appropriate clause with Φ considered as an abstraction; a similar remark applies to sequencers considered as expressions or blocks and to blocks considered as commands. This usage is in keeping with the convention of 2.2.3 whereby | indicates a mapping into a summand of a domain; the domain concerned here may be Exp, Blo or Com.

Conventionally, the names having free occurrences in a construct are said to be the 'free variables' of the construct; the 'bound variables' of the construct are those names appearing in it which are not free variables. This usage accords with that adopted in λ-calculus [17].

3.5.3. The pruning of environments.

As many environments contain more entries than are needed, we shall introduce some "pruning" functions which cut out unwanted entries. The usual situation is that the environment is supplied to the equation for a syntactic element and the form of pruning required depends on the syntactic element. Thus, for example, we can cut down an environment ρ to the latest entry for each of the free variables of a piece of program by means of

$rend \in (\mathrm{Exp}+\mathrm{Abs}+\mathrm{Seq}+\mathrm{Dec}+\mathrm{Blo}+\mathrm{Com}) \to U \to U$, which satisfies the equation

$$rend = \lambda X\rho.\langle(\lambda I.\, free[\![X]\!][\![I]\!] \wedge (\#\rho[\![I]\!]>0) \to \langle \rho[\![I]\!]\downarrow 1\rangle, \langle\rangle),$$
$$(free[\![X]\!][\![\mathrm{res}]\!] \wedge (\#\rho[\![\mathrm{res}]\!]>0) \to \langle \rho[\![\mathrm{res}]\!]\downarrow 1\rangle, \langle\rangle)\rangle,$$

when we allow X to range over members of Exp+Abs+Seq+Dec+Blo+Com, a domain which contains all the syntactic entities available in Sal.

This function prunes an environment of unnecessary entries; however the original environment may not have had entries for all the free variables, in which case the corresponding entries produced by *rend* will be empty lists. We therefore nee d a function to assure us that there are indeed suitable entries for each of the free variables. To do this we use $rent \in (\mathrm{Exp}+\mathrm{Abs}+\mathrm{Seq}+\mathrm{Dec}+\mathrm{Blo}+\mathrm{Com}) \to U \to T$, for which

$$rent = \lambda X\rho. \bigwedge\{\sim free[\![X]\!][\![I]\!] \vee (\#\rho[\![I]\!]>0) \mid I\} \wedge (\sim free[\![X]\!][\![\mathrm{res}]\!] \vee (\#\rho[\![\mathrm{res}]\!]>0)),$$

when X is again allowed to range over members of the domain Exp+Abs+Seq+Dec+Blo+Com.

In the same way as *rend* cuts down an environment to the entries for free variables, a certain function can be used to cut down the little environment produced by a declaration to the latest entry for each of its declared variables. We do this with the aid of a function $slim \in \mathrm{Dec} \to U \to U$ such that

$$slim = \lambda\Delta\rho.\langle(\lambda I.\, I \in \mathfrak{I}[\![\Delta]\!]\,\S\,\mathcal{H}[\![\Delta]\!] \wedge (\#\rho[\![I]\!]>0) \to \langle\rho[\![I]\!]\downarrow 1\rangle, \langle\rangle), \langle\rangle\rangle.$$

Evidently as declarations only affect identifiers $(slim[\![\Delta]\!]\rho)[\![\mathrm{res}]\!]$ is always an empty list.

Not unlike *rent* is the function $full \in \mathrm{Dec} \to U \to T$, which reveals whether an environment has an entry for each of the identifiers declared in a declaration; it satisfies the equation

$$full = \lambda\Delta\rho . \bigwedge\{I \in \mathcal{J}[\![\Delta]\!] \S \mathcal{H}[\![\Delta]\!] \rightarrow (\#\rho[\![I]\!] > 0), (\#\rho[\![I]\!] = 0) \mid I\} \wedge (\#\rho[\![\mathbf{res}]\!] = 0).$$

The way we have constructed our standard semantic equations leads us to have intuitive views about some properties of these functions. Thus we expect to be able to cut down an environment by using *rend* without altering most of the valuations. Similarly we should be able to cut down the little environments produced by declarations with the aid of *slim* without altering their effect, and, moreover, we expect the result of applying *full* to such a little environment to be *true*. We shall now formalize these intuitive feelings.

3.5.4. Free variable lists.

We can express the view that a pruned environment is adequate for a valuation by saying, for example, that $\mathcal{E}[\![E]\!]\rho$ and $\mathcal{E}[\![E]\!](rend[\![E]\!]\rho)$ should have the same value for all ρ. When we attempt to prove this, we have to use a structural induction, so constructs like Θ before E and Δ inside E bring in other valuations. The syntactic valuations $\mathcal{I}$, $\mathcal{H}$, $\mathcal{J}$ and $\mathcal{K}$ given in appendix 9 do not use an environment and so are not really involved. For all the others, with the exception of $\mathcal{T}$ (which we shall discuss below), the required equations are typified by

$\mathcal{E}[\![E]\!]=\mathcal{E}[\![E]\!]\circ rend[\![E]\!]$.

There are ten of these equations (dealing with $\mathcal{E}$, $\mathcal{L}$, $\mathcal{R}$, $\mathcal{F}$, $\mathcal{S}$, $\mathcal{D}$, $\mathcal{G}$, $\mathcal{C}$, $\mathcal{P}$ and $\mathcal{Q}$); for example when Δ is any declaration we ought to know that

$\mathcal{D}[\![\Delta]\!]=\mathcal{D}[\![\Delta]\!]\circ rend[\![\Delta]\!]$.

The valuation $\mathcal{T}$ is intended to be applied to a declaration in an environment in which the identifiers to be declared have already been given an entry. Thus we cannot use *rend* to prune its environment as this only leaves entries for the free variables. We consequently need a further pruning function, $tear\in\mathrm{Dec}\to\mathrm{U}\to\mathrm{U}$; when applied to a declaration and an environment *tear* should produce an environment in which there are entries for the declared identifiers (as well as for the free variables), so we let

$tear=\lambda\Delta\rho.\langle(\lambda I.(free[\![\Delta]\!][\![I]\!]\vee I\in\mathcal{I}[\![\Delta]\!]\S\mathcal{H}[\![\Delta]\!])\wedge(\#\rho[\![I]\!]>0)\to\langle\rho[\![I]\!]\downarrow 1\rangle,\langle\rangle),$

$\qquad(free[\![\Delta]\!][\![\mathrm{res}]\!]\wedge(\#\rho[\![\mathrm{res}]\!]>0)\to\langle\rho[\![\mathrm{res}]\!]\downarrow 1\rangle,\langle\rangle)\rangle.$

The appropriate equation for $\mathcal{T}$ is therefore

$\mathcal{T}[\![\Delta]\!]=\mathcal{T}[\![\Delta]\!]\circ tear[\![\Delta]\!]$.

The function $torn\in\mathrm{Dec}\to\mathrm{U}\to\mathrm{T}$ tells us whether an environment is adequate for use with $\mathcal{T}$; it tests that there is an entry for all the free variables of Δ and all the declared identifiers. It bears the same relationship to *tear* as *rent* does to *rend* and is defined by the equation

$torn=\lambda\Delta\rho.rent[\![\Delta]\!]\rho\wedge full[\![\Delta]\!](slim[\![\Delta]\!]\rho)$.

We can express the knowledge that the little environments produced by declarations can be pruned with impunity by using *slim* as follows :

$\mathscr{D}[\![\Delta]\!]=\lambda\rho\chi.\mathscr{D}[\![\Delta]\!]\rho(\chi\circ slim[\![\Delta]\!])$;

$\mathscr{T}[\![\Delta]\!]=\lambda\rho\chi.\mathscr{T}[\![\Delta]\!]\rho(\chi\circ slim[\![\Delta]\!])$.

Finally, the fact that declarations produce entries for all their declared identifiers can be expressed thus:

$\mathscr{D}[\![\Delta]\!]=\lambda\rho\chi.\mathscr{D}[\![\Delta]\!]\rho(\lambda\rho'.full[\![\Delta]\!]\rho'\rightarrow\chi\rho',wrong)$;

$\mathscr{T}[\![\Delta]\!]=\lambda\rho\chi.\mathscr{T}[\![\Delta]\!]\rho(\lambda\rho'.full[\![\Delta]\!]\rho'\rightarrow\chi\rho',wrong)$.

The proofs that these equations hold involve structural inductions, but although they are long and tedious to write out at all fully, they are also elementary in character. We shall content ourselves with stating them (in 3.5.5 and 3.5.6), leaving an examination of the proofs to those who wish to make quite sure that they know what constitutes a structural induction.

It is worth noting that if $\mathscr{T}$ were defined not on Dec but on some other domain, such as Def or Dep (which will be described in 3.9.6), we would eliminate *tear* and *torn* in favour of *rend* and *rent* by extending the definitions of *rend* and *rent* to handle members of this new domain.

This is a convenient point at which to mention certain functions which will be used in passing in 3.8.2 but which will not really be needed until 4.1.3. We set up $chop\in\mathrm{Exp}\rightarrow\mathrm{U}\rightarrow\mathrm{U}$ by writing

$chop=\lambda\mathrm{E}\rho.\langle\lambda\mathrm{I}.\rho[\![\mathrm{I}]\!]\dagger(free[\![\mathrm{E}]\!][\![\mathrm{I}]\!]\rightarrow1,0),\rho[\![\mathbf{res}]\!]\dagger(free[\![\mathrm{E}]\!][\![\mathbf{res}]\!]\rightarrow1,0)\rangle$,

so that if E and ρ are such that $rent[\![\mathrm{E}]\!]\rho=true$ then $\rho=divert(chop[\![\mathrm{E}]\!]\rho)(rend[\![\mathrm{E}]\!]\rho)$. In addition we describe $clip\in\mathrm{Dec}\rightarrow\mathrm{U}\rightarrow\mathrm{U}$ and $snip\in\mathrm{Com}\rightarrow\mathrm{U}\rightarrow\mathrm{U}$ as follows:

$clip=\lambda\Delta\rho.\langle\lambda\mathrm{I}.\rho[\![\mathrm{I}]\!]\dagger(\mathrm{I}\in\mathscr{I}[\![\Delta]\!]\S\mathscr{H}[\![\Delta]\!]\rightarrow1,0),\rho[\![\mathbf{res}]\!]\rangle$;

$snip=\lambda\Gamma\rho.\langle\lambda\mathrm{I}.\rho[\![\mathrm{I}]\!]\dagger(\mathrm{I}\in\mathscr{I}[\![\Gamma]\!]\S\mathscr{H}[\![\Gamma]\!]\rightarrow1,0),\rho[\![\mathbf{res}]\!]\rangle$.

Slightly different definitions will be given in 4.1.4.

3.5.5. Proposition.

In Sal any Δ is such that, for the valuations outlined in 3.4.4 and 3.4.5, $\mathcal{D}[\![\Delta]\!]=\lambda\rho\chi.\mathcal{D}[\![\Delta]\!]\rho(\lambda\rho'.\mathit{full}[\![\Delta]\!]\rho'\to\chi\rho',\mathit{wrong})$ and $\mathcal{T}[\![\Delta]\!]=\lambda\rho\chi.\mathcal{T}[\![\Delta]\!]\rho(\lambda\rho'.\mathit{full}[\![\Delta]\!]\rho'\to\chi\rho',\mathit{wrong})$, provided that the list $\mathcal{I}[\![\Delta]\!]\S\mathcal{H}[\![\Delta]\!]$ contains no repeated elements.

◁This proposition suggests that the little environments yielded by declarations contain entries only for the identifiers declared. It can be proved by induction on the structure of Sal declarations without any investigation of the properties of other Sal constructs.▷

Because $\rho'=\mathit{slim}[\![\Delta]\!]\rho'$ whenever Δ and ρ' are such that $\mathit{full}[\![\Delta]\!]\rho'=\mathit{true}$ we may deduce from this result that $\mathcal{D}[\![\Delta]\!]=\lambda\rho\chi.\mathcal{D}[\![\Delta]\!]\rho(\lambda\rho'.\chi(\mathit{slim}[\![\Delta]\!]\rho'))$ and $\mathcal{T}[\![\Delta]\!]=\lambda\rho\chi.\mathcal{T}[\![\Delta]\!]\rho(\lambda\rho'.\chi(\mathit{slim}[\![\Delta]\!]\rho'))$.

This is the first result in which we have to insist that for any declaration taking either the form Δ_0 and Δ_1 or the form Δ_0 around Δ_1 the list $\mathcal{I}[\![\Delta_0]\!]\S\mathcal{H}[\![\Delta_0]\!]$ has no elements in common with $\mathcal{I}[\![\Delta_1]\!]\S\mathcal{H}[\![\Delta_1]\!]$.

3.5.6. Proposition.

In Sal all E, Φ, Σ, Δ, Θ and Γ are such that, for the valuations described from 3.4.1 onwards, $\mathcal{E}[\![E]\!]=\mathcal{E}[\![E]\!]\circ rend[\![E]\!]$, $\mathcal{L}[\![E]\!]=\mathcal{L}[\![E]\!]\circ rend[\![E]\!]$, $\mathcal{R}[\![E]\!]=\mathcal{R}[\![E]\!]\circ rend[\![E]\!]$, $\mathcal{H}[\![\Phi]\!]=\mathcal{H}[\![\Phi]\!]\circ rend[\![\Phi]\!]$, $\mathcal{S}[\![\Sigma]\!]=\mathcal{S}[\![\Sigma]\!]\circ rend[\![\Sigma]\!]$, $\mathcal{D}[\![\Delta]\!]=\mathcal{D}[\![\Delta]\!]\circ rend[\![\Delta]\!]$, $\mathcal{T}[\![\Delta]\!]=\mathcal{T}[\![\Delta]\!]\circ tear[\![\Delta]\!]$, $\mathcal{G}[\![\Theta]\!]=\mathcal{G}[\![\Theta]\!]\circ rend[\![\Theta]\!]$, $\mathcal{C}[\![\Gamma]\!]=\mathcal{C}[\![\Gamma]\!]\circ rend[\![\Gamma]\!]$, $\mathcal{P}[\![\Gamma]\!]=\mathcal{P}[\![\Gamma]\!]\circ rend[\![\Gamma]\!]$ and $\mathcal{Q}[\![\Gamma]\!]=\mathcal{Q}[\![\Gamma]\!]\circ rend[\![\Gamma]\!]$.

◁This proposition expresses the fact that when applying the valuations for standard semantics we really only need free variable lists. Its proof involves a structural induction over the whole language, but the necessary notions are no more interesting than those underlying 3.5.5. Although the proposition has been stated in terms appropriate to Sal, suitable analogues of it hold in very many conventional programming languages.▷

3.5.7. Exits from expressions.

In 5.1.8 we shall require a valuation $\mathfrak{X}\in\text{Exp}\rightarrow\text{Exp}^*$; when E is any expression the list $\mathfrak{X}[\![E]\!]$ is intended to comprise those portions of E concerned with what expressed values may result from executing E rather than with how the store may be changed by executing E. Accordingly we let:

$\mathfrak{X}[\![E_0?E_1!E_2]\!]=\mathfrak{X}[\![E_1]\!]\S\mathfrak{X}[\![E_2]\!]$;

$\mathfrak{X}[\![\Theta \text{ before } E]\!]=\mathfrak{X}[\![E]\!]$.

Since $\mathfrak{X}$ is purely syntactic in nature it cannot handle many constructs in a very satisfactory manner. For instance, we are obliged to write:

$\mathfrak{X}[\![E_0E_1]\!]=\langle E_0E_1\rangle$;

$\mathfrak{X}[\![\Delta \text{ inside } E]\!]=\langle\Delta \text{ inside } E\rangle$.

A full account of $\mathfrak{X}$ appears in appendix 9.

If E is an expression any member of $\mathfrak{X}[\![E]\!]$ can be termed an 'exit' of E; should the execution of E terminate without any jumps being made one exit of E must have been executed.

3.5.8. Syntactic transformations preserving meaning.

In a practical implementation each declaration by incidence must in fact be carried out by placing the denoted value in a storage cell and treating the declaration as if it were one by reference. The implementation must ensure that no further assignments are made to this storage cell so that the outcome of any program is useful. As Sal allows explicit declarations by reference as well as by incidence, it is reasonable to think that it should be possible to transform a program containing declarations by incidence into one containing only declarations by reference; moreover, it should be possible to carry out this transformation in a systematic manner.

This transformation, which is a syntactic one, can be specified by mutually recursive functions which are defined fully in appendix 7; we shall denote such syntactic transformations as these by lower case script letters. For reasons to be discussed below, the transformations that we require at the moment cannot belong to Dec→Dec but must be given more complex natures, which nevertheless still only use information which can be made available before programs are executed.

Syntactic transformations like these are intended to preserve the meanings of programs as far as possible. In the present case the meanings remain largely unchanged because the syntactic transformation sets up a correspondence between denoted values and locations containing comparable stored values. Thus typically we substitute I=E for certain occurrences of I==E and apply analogous translations to certain declarations and abstractions. Unfortunately we cannot simply change I==E into I=E as the latter declaration may introduce sharing which could cause unwanted side effects. For example, there is no equivalence between

```
        u=0              and              u=0
inside v==u                      inside v=u
inside u:=1                      inside u:=1
before v                         before v
```

as one yields 0 whilst the other yields a location containing 1 because the identifiers *u* and *v* denote the same location. When dealing with this what we need is a new unshared location for I set up in much the same manner as that required in an Algol 60 [61] call by value; this location provides a declaration by unshared reference of the form discussed in 1.9.2. We can write this in Sal by using the operator $, described in 3.2.2 and defined in 3.4.1, to replace I==E by I=$E.

The consequence of our choice for the function *lv* in Sal is that assignments to identifiers declared by incidence are legal though generally futile. If we replace I==E by I=$E, however, a subsequent assignment to I is no longer so harmless, for it makes the content of the location denoted by I in the transformed program differ from the value denoted by I according to the original program. Thus it is plain that

```
        w==0             and              w=$0
inside w:=1                      inside w:=1
before w                         before w
```

are not connected, since one of these programs produces 0 as its result and the other produces a location containing 1. To deal with this situation we arrange that all occurrences of I inside the scope of a declaration changed from incidence to reference are replaced by $I. In a right hand context this merely takes the content of the location denoted by I; in a left hand context it introduces a fresh location.

When recursive declarations by incidence are transformed into recursive declarations by reference there is no need to make sure that the identifiers declared do not denote locations which are already in use, since the semantic equations of appendix 1 ensure that this happens automatically. Hence in the context of a recursive declaration I==E may be changed into I=E instead of into I=$E.

Similar remarks are pertinent when a label set by incidence is replaced by one set by reference. Though we can change I::Γ into I:Γ without much ado, we must also arrange that every time I occurs in a left hand context within the scope of the label setting it is preceded by $.

When converting an abstraction by incidence into one by reference, however, it is not enough to replace all occurrences of the parameter I in the body of the abstraction by occurrences of $I, since abstractions by reference, like declarations by reference, introduce the possibility of sharing. Here the sharing that concerns us is that between the actual parameter of a procedure and a free variable of the procedure. Thus the programs

x=0	and	*x*=0
inside *f*=fn*y*..*x*:=1 before *y*		inside *f*=fn*y*.*x*:=1 before $*y*
inside *f*(*x*)		inside *f*(*x*)

are not equivalent because one yields 0 whereas the other yields 1, even though both bring about assignments. Although in this case we could save the situation by writing *f*($*x*) in place of *f*(*x*) this trick is not available to us in the general case, as the expression E_0E_1 does not allow us to tell whether E_0 is a procedure which has been altered or not: in general the value of E_0 cannot be found until the program is run. Thus we cannot perform a suitable syntactic transformation by such a simple means. Instead we make use of the operation £, which, as indicated in 3.4.1, operates directly on the value of the procedure; this enables us to replace fnI..E_2 by £(fnI.E_3) where E_2 differs from E_3 in that every occurrence of I in the former must become $I in the latter.

In order to change I into \$I in such cases as this we introduce an analogue of the environment which indicates nothing more than the fact that an identifier has had its declaration switched from incidence to reference. We shall use the letter ψ to stand for this entity which resembles an environment and which is a member of the domain $Ide \to T^*$. We need $\psi[\![I]\!]$ to be a list of truth values as declarations can nest. The most recent value, which is $\psi[\![I]\!]\downarrow 1$, is *true* if the declaration of I has been altered by the syntactic transformation and *false* if it has not. As ψ behaves similarly to ρ we shall use the notations $\psi[\varepsilon/I]$ and $\psi[\varepsilon^*/I^*]$ to extend ψ in the way in which we extend ρ according to 3.3.3.

In the transformations that we shall need to examine we shall not want to replace all the occurrences of incidence by reference. We therefore introduce an extra function *opt* which we shall use to select those instances which are to be transformed. The nature of *opt* is arbitrary and we could use differing definitions for it on different occasions. Even the domain to which these versions of *opt* belong is to a large extent arbitrary though it is obviously convenient to supply *opt* both with an identifier and with a member of $Ide \to T^*$. We therefore take *opt* to be a member of $Ide \to (Ide \to T^*) \to T$. Corresponding to each version of *opt* we need an iterated function, *opts*, which belongs to $Ide^* \to (Ide \to T^*) \to T^*$ and is given by the equation

$opts = \lambda I^* \psi . map(\lambda I . opt[\![I]\!]\psi) I^*$.

Here we have not endeavoured to prove that the transformations in appendix 7 do preserve the meanings of programs; indeed, as we shall see in 4.1.1, doing so is not feasible within the framework of standard semantics. Nevertheless this task has been performed before [52:2.5.9] using store semantics. Moreover, in the result leading up to 5.3.9 we shall effectively carry out part of it, albeit in a special situation; how to adapt our methods to the general situation should become clear.

3.6. Elementary equivalences.

3.6.1. Replaceable commands.

One role of the theory of programming languages is to provide mathematical justifications for claims about programs. In this section we shall consider claims about when two programs, or parts of programs, "have the same meaning". Standard semantics will be our yardstick for comparing the meanings of programs, so we shall not consider such questions as whether two programs run for distinct lengths of time. Although we shall be able to show that several pairs of Sal constructions are equivalent in meaning there are some matters beyond the power of standard semantics. Thus certain problems involving two programs which use the store differently cannot be handled adequately here for reasons which will be discussed more fully in 4.1.1; such problems can, however, be tackled in terms of the store semantics to be described in 4.1.2. The equivalences to be considered below will be termed 'elementary' because they require the use of standard semantics but not the use of other sorts of semantics.

For every syntactic domain in Sal there is a notion of equivalence: one member of the domain will be said to be 'equivalent' with another in an appropriate semantics if each valuation defined on the domain produces the same value when applied to one of these two members as it does when applied to the other. The most interesting Sal equivalences are those in standard semantics which concern Exp and Blo, since a Sal program may be an expression or a block; two expressions, E_0 and E_1, are equivalent if $\mathcal{E}[\![E_0]\!]=\mathcal{E}[\![E_1]\!]$, $\mathcal{L}[\![E_0]\!]=\mathcal{L}[\![E_1]\!]$ and $\mathcal{R}[\![E_0]\!]=\mathcal{R}[\![E_1]\!]$ whereas two blocks, Θ_0 and Θ_1, are equivalent if $\mathcal{G}[\![\Theta_0]\!]=\mathcal{G}[\![\Theta_1]\!]$. From the definitions of $\mathcal{L}$ and $\mathcal{R}$ it is apparent that E_0 and E_1 are inevitably equivalent when $\mathcal{E}[\![E_0]\!]=\mathcal{E}[\![E_1]\!]$; similarly Θ_0 and Θ_1 are equivalent when viewed as commands if they are equivalent when viewed as blocks.

A simple structural induction involving the syntax of Sal

shows that any member of the syntactic domains is equivalent with any other member which differs from it only in that certain components are replaced by equivalent ones. For instance, if Δ_0 is equivalent with Δ_1 and E_0 is equivalent with E_1 then certainly $\mathfrak{D}[\![\Delta_0]\!]=\mathfrak{D}[\![\Delta_1]\!]$ and $\mathfrak{E}[\![E_0]\!]=\mathfrak{E}[\![E_1]\!]$ so

$$\begin{aligned}\mathfrak{E}[\![\Delta_0 \texttt{ inside } E_0]\!] &= \lambda\rho\kappa.\mathfrak{D}[\![\Delta_0]\!]\rho(\lambda\rho'.\mathfrak{E}[\![E_0]\!](divert\rho\rho')\kappa)\\ &= \lambda\rho\kappa.\mathfrak{D}[\![\Delta_1]\!]\rho(\lambda\rho'.\mathfrak{E}[\![E_0]\!](divert\rho\rho')\kappa)\\ &= \lambda\rho\kappa.\mathfrak{D}[\![\Delta_1]\!]\rho(\lambda\rho'.\mathfrak{E}[\![E_1]\!](divert\rho\rho')\kappa)\\ &= \mathfrak{E}[\![\Delta_1 \texttt{ inside } E_1]\!];\end{aligned}$$

hence Δ_0 inside E_0 is equivalent with Δ_1 inside E_1.

Were it impossible to replace components by equivalent ones in this way our notion of equivalence would be quite unsatisfactory. Yet in arranging that it is satisfactory we have made it very restrictive, and this becomes a nuisance when we try to substitute one command for another. Though those expressions which we wish to exchange are generally equivalent in the sense described above, this is not so for labelled commands. Thus, for example, one assertion familiar from programming manuals is that while E do Γ "has the same effect as" I::if E do (Γ;goto I) when I is chosen suitably. Obviously these two commands are not equivalent, because distinct values are obtained when $\mathfrak{C}$ is applied to them; indeed not even I::while E do Γ and I::if E do (Γ;goto I) are equivalent, although these commands do at least have the same image under $\mathfrak{K}$. There is nevertheless a sense in which these commands do have the same effect, for in a complete program they will form parts of blocks, and these blocks will arrange that I denotes the right label value. However we cannot be content to prove merely that block while E do Γ is equivalent with block I::if E do (Γ;goto I), because jumps leading into while E do Γ from a surrounding block will be ruled out if block while E do Γ is used instead of while E do Γ. Hence we shall actually endeavour to compare any two suitable commands, Γ_0 and Γ_1 say, by developing

Γ_0 and Γ_1, that is implied by the equivalence of Γ_0 and Γ_1 and that implies the equivalence of block Γ_0 and block Γ_1. In seeking this we must be guided by the principle that in any context Γ_0 should be an adequate substitute for Γ_1 when they are related.

To avoid the complexities that arise when one command replaces another in an arbitrary block we shall examine constraints on Γ_0 and Γ_1 which establish that block Γ_0 and block Γ_1 are equivalent. For convenience we define $form \in \mathsf{Com} \to \mathsf{U} \to \mathsf{C} \to \mathsf{S} \to \mathsf{U} \to \mathsf{U}$ by setting

$form = \lambda\Gamma\rho_0\theta\sigma\rho_1 . \rho_0[(\lambda\nu.news\nu\sigma \in \mathsf{L}^* \to news\nu\sigma|\mathsf{L}^*, use\nu)(\#\mathcal{J}[\![\Gamma]\!])/\mathcal{J}[\![\Gamma]\!]][\mathcal{Q}[\![\Gamma]\!]\rho_1\theta/\mathcal{K}[\![\Gamma]\!]]$;

according to appendix 1, when $1 \geq n \geq 0$ for any ρ, θ and σ either

$news(\#\mathcal{J}[\![\Gamma_n]\!])\sigma$ is not a proper list of locations or

$\mathcal{G}[\![\text{block } \Gamma_n]\!]\rho\theta\sigma = \mathcal{C}[\![\Gamma_n]\!]\rho_n\theta\sigma_n$,

where $\rho_n = fix(form[\![\Gamma_n]\!]\rho\theta\sigma)$ and $\sigma_n = updates(news(\#\mathcal{H}[\![\Gamma_n]\!])\sigma|\mathsf{L}^*)(\mathcal{P}[\![\Gamma_n]\!]\rho_n\theta)\sigma$.

Consequently to ensure that $\mathcal{G}[\![\text{block } \Gamma_0]\!]\rho\theta\sigma = \mathcal{G}[\![\text{block } \Gamma_1]\!]\rho\theta\sigma$ we insist that so long as $news(\#\mathcal{H}[\![\Gamma_0]\!])\sigma$ or $news(\#\mathcal{H}[\![\Gamma_1]\!])\sigma$ is a proper list of locations they are both proper lists such that $\mathcal{C}[\![\Gamma_0]\!]\rho_0\theta = \mathcal{C}[\![\Gamma_1]\!]\rho_1\theta$ and $\sigma_0 = \sigma_1$. When σ is allowed to vary there is no guarantee that $\sigma_0 = \sigma_1$ unless $news(\#\mathcal{H}[\![\Gamma_0]\!])\sigma = news(\#\mathcal{H}[\![\Gamma_1]\!])\sigma$ and $\mathcal{P}[\![\Gamma_0]\!]\rho_0\theta = \mathcal{P}[\![\Gamma_1]\!]\rho_1\theta$. Our chances of verifying that $\mathcal{C}[\![\Gamma_0]\!]\rho_0\theta = \mathcal{C}[\![\Gamma_1]\!]\rho_1\theta$ and that $\mathcal{P}[\![\Gamma_0]\!]\rho_0\theta = \mathcal{P}[\![\Gamma_1]\!]\rho_1\theta$ are improved greatly if we stipulate that $\rho_0 = \rho_1$; moreover when ρ varies this condition is enough to assure us that $news(\#\mathcal{J}[\![\Gamma_0]\!])\sigma = news(\#\mathcal{J}[\![\Gamma_1]\!])\sigma$ even when $news(\#\mathcal{J}[\![\Gamma_0]\!])\sigma$ or $news(\#\mathcal{J}[\![\Gamma_1]\!])\sigma$ is not a proper list of locations.

The reasoning of the previous paragraph motivates the following definition. A command Γ_0 is 'replaceable' by a command Γ_1 if and only if it satisfies three conditions, to wit:

(i) $\lambda\rho\theta\sigma.fix(form[\![\Gamma_0]\!]\rho\theta\sigma) = \lambda\rho\theta\sigma.fix(form[\![\Gamma_1]\!]\rho\theta\sigma)$;

(ii) $\lambda\rho\theta\sigma.\mathcal{C}[\![\Gamma_0]\!](fix(form[\![\Gamma_0]\!]\rho\theta\sigma))\theta = \lambda\rho\theta\sigma.\mathcal{C}[\![\Gamma_1]\!](fix(form[\![\Gamma_1]\!]\rho\theta\sigma))\theta$;

(iii) $\lambda\rho\theta\sigma.\mathcal{P}[\![\Gamma_0]\!](fix(form[\![\Gamma_0]\!]\rho\theta\sigma))\theta = \lambda\rho\theta\sigma.\mathcal{P}[\![\Gamma_1]\!](fix(form[\![\Gamma_1]\!]\rho\theta\sigma))\theta$.

Plainly if Γ_0 is equivalent with Γ_1 then Γ_0 is replaceable by Γ_1; in addition, appendix 1 indicates that if Γ_1 is replaceable by Γ_1 then block Γ_0 is equivalent with block Γ_1. Yet even more than this is true, for any block is equivalent with a block which differs from it only because some commands are substituted for others by which they are replaceable. This is an immediate consequence of the fact that block Γ_0 is equivalent with block Γ_1 when Γ_0 is replaceable by Γ_1, since we can also confirm that:

(i) if Γ_0 is replaceable by Γ_2 and if Γ_1 is replaceable by Γ_3 then $\Gamma_0;\Gamma_1$ is replaceable by $\Gamma_2;\Gamma_3$ provided that $\mathfrak{H}[\![\Gamma_0]\!]\S\mathfrak{K}[\![\Gamma_0]\!]$ and $\mathfrak{H}[\![\Gamma_1]\!]\S\mathfrak{K}[\![\Gamma_1]\!]$ have no elements in common;

(ii) if E_0 is equivalent with E_1 and if Γ_0 is replaceable by Γ_1 then if E_0 do Γ_0 is replaceable by if E_1 do Γ_1;

(iii) if E_0 is equivalent with E_1 and if Γ_0 is replaceable by Γ_1 then while E_0 do Γ_0 is replaceable by while E_1 do Γ_1;

(iv) if Θ_0 is equivalent with Θ_1 then Θ_0 is replaceable by Θ_1;

(v) if Γ_0 is replaceable by Γ_1 then $I:\Gamma_0$ is replaceable by $I:\Gamma_1$ provided that I does not belong to the list $\mathfrak{H}[\![\Gamma_0]\!]\S\mathfrak{K}[\![\Gamma_0]\!]$;

(vi) if Γ_0 is replaceable by Γ_1 then $I::\Gamma_0$ is replaceable by $I::\Gamma_1$ provided that I does not belong to the list $\mathfrak{H}[\![\Gamma_0]\!]\S\mathfrak{K}[\![\Gamma_0]\!]$;

(vii) if Γ_0 is replaceable by Γ_1 then (Γ_0) is replaceable by (Γ_1).

The techniques required by the proofs of these properties are all embodied in the proof of (i), which we shall discuss shortly. The need for such a discussion might be viewed as one instance of the malign effect of allowing the scopes of labels to spread throughout sequences of commands; the proof involves a certain amount of tedious manipulation and should perhaps be examined only after reading less complex calculations, such as that in 3.6.4.

3.6.2. Proposition.

If Γ_0 is replaceable by Γ_2 and Γ_1 is replaceable by Γ_3 then $\Gamma_0;\Gamma_1$ is replaceable by $\Gamma_2;\Gamma_3$ provided that $\mathfrak{J}[\![\Gamma_0]\!]\S\mathfrak{K}[\![\Gamma_0]\!]$ has no members in common with $\mathfrak{J}[\![\Gamma_1]\!]\S\mathfrak{K}[\![\Gamma_1]\!]$.

◂The proof of this proposition unfortunately requires some rather laborious manipulation of semantic expressions. Although this is not an uncommon feature of propositions it is an unwelcome one, and the reader may well feel justified in omitting the verification of some of the details of this proof or in taking the entire result on trust for the moment. In setting out the proof we have attempted to distinguish those steps which depend only on the formal elaboration of the formulas concerned from those which make some appeal to less shallow mathematical properties.

The main part of the argument is concerned with the first of the three conditions for replaceability given in 3.6.1, so we shall need to examine the effect on $\lambda\rho\theta\sigma.\mathit{fix}(\mathit{form}[\![\Gamma_0;\Gamma_1]\!]\rho\theta\sigma)$ of replacing one or both of Γ_0 and Γ_1 by Γ_2 and Γ_3 respectively.

We start by establishing some trivial results concerning the lists of locations required for the labels set by reference. Thus we select any ρ_0, θ_0 and σ_0 for which $\mathit{news}(\#\mathfrak{J}[\![\Gamma_0;\Gamma_1]\!])\sigma_0$ is a proper list of locations; for all other ρ_0, θ_0 and σ_0 the result is obviously true, as the supply of new locations is insufficient. Now we let $\alpha^*_0=\mathit{news}(\#\mathfrak{J}[\![\Gamma_0]\!])\sigma_0$, $\sigma_1=\mathit{updates}\,\alpha^*_0(\mathit{use}(\#\mathfrak{J}[\![\Gamma_0]\!]))\sigma_0$ and $\alpha^*_1=\mathit{news}(\#\mathfrak{J}[\![\Gamma_1]\!])\sigma_1$. Here α^*_0 and α^*_1 are the lists of locations needed for the labels set by reference in Γ_0 and Γ_1 respectively; σ_1 has been introduced because, as was discussed in 3.3.2, *new* does not mark the locations it claims as being used, so that α^*_0 must be updated (thereby marking them as being used) before claiming α^*_1 in order to ensure that α^*_0 and α^*_1 are disjoint. The conditions on Γ_0 and Γ_2 and on Γ_1 and Γ_3 ensure that $\#\mathfrak{J}[\![\Gamma_0]\!]=\#\mathfrak{J}[\![\Gamma_2]\!]$ and that $\#\mathfrak{J}[\![\Gamma_1]\!]=\#\mathfrak{J}[\![\Gamma_3]\!]$; hence $\alpha^*_0=\mathit{news}(\#\mathfrak{J}[\![\Gamma_2]\!])\sigma_0$ and

$\alpha^*_1 = news(\#\mathfrak{J}[\![\Gamma_3]\!])\sigma_1$.

We now introduce a convenient abbreviation which is connected with *form* (defined as in 3.6.1) but which is more general. When m is 0 or 2 and n is 1 or 3 we define $\psi_{mn} \in U \to U \to U \to U$ by

$$\psi_{mn} = \lambda\rho'\rho''\rho'''.(\lambda\delta^*.\rho_0[\alpha^*_0 \S \alpha^*_1/\mathfrak{J}[\![\Gamma_m]\!] \S \mathfrak{J}[\![\Gamma_n]\!]][\delta^*/\mathfrak{K}[\![\Gamma_m]\!] \S \mathfrak{K}[\![\Gamma_n]\!]])$$
$$(\mathfrak{Q}[\![\Gamma_m]\!]\rho'(\mathfrak{C}[\![\Gamma_n]\!]\rho''\theta_0) \S \mathfrak{Q}[\![\Gamma_n]\!]\rho'''\theta_0).$$

By using the definition of *form*, the equations in appendix 1, and the fact that α^*_0 and α^*_1 are proper lists of locations unaffected by the values of m and n we can verify that for all ρ', ρ'' and ρ''' $\lambda\rho.\psi_{mn}\rho\rho\rho = form[\![\Gamma_m;\Gamma_n]\!]\rho_0\theta_0\sigma_0$, that

$\lambda\rho.\psi_{mn}\rho'\rho''\rho = form[\![\Gamma_n]\!](\rho_0[\alpha^*_0/\mathfrak{J}[\![\Gamma_m]\!]][\mathfrak{Q}[\![\Gamma_m]\!]\rho'(\mathfrak{C}[\![\Gamma_n]\!]\rho''\theta_0)/\mathfrak{K}[\![\Gamma_m]\!]])\theta_0\sigma_1$ and that

$\lambda\rho.\psi_{mn}\rho\rho''\rho''' = form[\![\Gamma_m]\!](\rho_0[\alpha^*_1/\mathfrak{J}[\![\Gamma_n]\!]][\mathfrak{Q}[\![\Gamma_n]\!]\rho'''\theta_0/\mathfrak{K}[\![\Gamma_n]\!]])(\mathfrak{C}[\![\Gamma_n]\!]\rho''\theta_0)\sigma_0$.

Applying the last two of these together with the first conditions for the replaceability of Γ_0 by Γ_2 and Γ_1 by Γ_3 establishes that $fix(\lambda\rho.\psi_{m1}\rho'\rho''\rho) = fix(\lambda\rho.\psi_{m3}\rho'\rho''\rho)$ for all ρ' and for all ρ'' such that $\mathfrak{C}[\![\Gamma_1]\!]\rho''\theta_0 = \mathfrak{C}[\![\Gamma_3]\!]\rho''\theta_0$, whilst $fix(\lambda\rho.\psi_{0n}\rho\rho''\rho''') = fix(\lambda\rho.\psi_{2n}\rho\rho''\rho''')$ for all ρ'' and for all ρ'''. These results are essentially obtained by manipulation alone.

We next make use of the nature of *fix* to provide us with further preliminary results; to this end we set $\rho_1 = fix(\lambda\rho'.fix(\lambda\rho''.fix(\lambda\rho.\psi_{01}\rho'\rho''\rho)))$. One application of 2.3.5 shows that $\rho_1 = fix(\lambda\rho'.fix(\lambda\rho.\psi_{01}\rho'\rho'\rho))$ and a second application of the same proposition reveals that $\rho_1 = fix(\lambda\rho.\psi_{01}\rho\rho\rho)$. Furthermore the properties of *fix* given in 2.3.2 show that

$$\begin{aligned}\rho_1 &= (\lambda\rho'.fix(\lambda\rho''.fix(\lambda\rho.\psi_{01}\rho'\rho''\rho)))\rho_1\\ &= fix(\lambda\rho''.fix(\lambda\rho.\psi_{01}\rho_1\rho''\rho))\\ &= (\lambda\rho''.fix(\lambda\rho.\psi_{01}\rho_1\rho''\rho))\rho_1\\ &= fix(\lambda\rho.\psi_{01}\rho_1\rho_1\rho).\end{aligned}$$

Because Γ_1 is replaceable by Γ_3 and

$\rho_1 = fix(form[\![\Gamma_1]\!](\rho_0[\alpha^*_0/\mathfrak{J}[\![\Gamma_0]\!]][\mathfrak{Q}[\![\Gamma_0]\!]\rho_1(\mathfrak{C}[\![\Gamma_1]\!]\rho_1\theta_0)/\mathfrak{K}[\![\Gamma_0]\!]])\theta_0\sigma_1)$

we know that $\mathfrak{C}[\![\Gamma_1]\!]\rho_1\theta_0 = \mathfrak{C}[\![\Gamma_3]\!]\rho_1\theta_0$. Hence $fix(\lambda\rho.\psi_{01}\rho_1\rho_1\rho) = fix(\lambda\rho.\psi_{03}\rho_1\rho_1\rho)$

and $\rho_1 = \mathit{fix}(\lambda\rho.\psi_{03}\rho_1\rho_1\rho)$; in particular, as

$$\begin{aligned}\rho_1 &= (\lambda\rho.\psi_{03}\rho_1\rho_1\rho)\rho_1\\ &= \psi_{03}\rho_1\rho_1\rho_1\\ &= (\lambda\rho.\psi_{03}\rho\rho_1\rho_1)\rho_1,\end{aligned}$$

ρ_1 is a fixed point of $\lambda\rho.\psi_{03}\rho\rho_1\rho_1$ and $\rho_1 \sqsupseteq \mathit{fix}(\lambda\rho.\psi_{03}\rho\rho_1\rho_1)$. However we have already noted that $\mathit{fix}(\lambda\rho.\psi_{03}\rho\rho_1\rho_1) = \mathit{fix}(\lambda\rho.\psi_{23}\rho\rho_1\rho_1)$, so $\rho_1 \sqsupseteq \mathit{fix}(\lambda\rho.\psi_{23}\rho\rho_1\rho_1)$. This inequality in turn shows that $\rho_1 \sqsupseteq (\lambda\rho''.\mathit{fix}(\lambda\rho.\psi_{23}\rho\rho''\rho_1))\rho_1$ and that $\rho_1 \sqsupseteq \mathit{fix}(\lambda\rho''.\mathit{fix}(\lambda\rho.\psi_{23}\rho\rho''\rho_1))$; from this it follows by a similar argument that $\rho_1 \sqsupseteq (\lambda\rho'''.\mathit{fix}(\lambda\rho''.\mathit{fix}(\lambda\rho.\psi_{23}\rho\rho''\rho''')))\rho_1$ and that $\rho_1 \sqsupseteq \mathit{fix}(\lambda\rho'''.\mathit{fix}(\lambda\rho''.\mathit{fix}(\lambda\rho.\psi_{23}\rho\rho''\rho''')))$. Applying 2.3.5 again, $\mathit{fix}(\lambda\rho'''.\mathit{fix}(\lambda\rho''.\mathit{fix}(\lambda\rho.\psi_{23}\rho\rho''\rho'''))) = \mathit{fix}(\lambda\rho.\psi_{23}\rho\rho\rho)$ and $\rho_1 \sqsupseteq \mathit{fix}(\lambda\rho.\psi_{23}\rho\rho\rho)$.

Since $\rho_1 = \mathit{fix}(\lambda\rho.\psi_{01}\rho\rho\rho)$, $\mathit{fix}(\lambda\rho.\psi_{01}\rho\rho\rho) \sqsupseteq \mathit{fix}(\lambda\rho.\psi_{23}\rho\rho\rho)$. The symmetry of the situation dictates that in fact $\mathit{fix}(\lambda\rho.\psi_{01}\rho\rho\rho) = \mathit{fix}(\lambda\rho.\psi_{23}\rho\rho\rho)$; thus, recalling that $\lambda\rho.\psi_{mn}\rho\rho\rho = \mathit{form}[\![\Gamma_m;\Gamma_n]\!]\rho_0\theta_0\sigma_0$ when m is 0 or 2 and n is 1 or 3, we infer that $\mathit{fix}(\mathit{form}[\![\Gamma_0;\Gamma_1]\!]\rho_0\theta_0\sigma_0) = \mathit{fix}(\mathit{form}[\![\Gamma_2;\Gamma_3]\!]\rho_0\theta_0\sigma_0)$.

Because $\rho_1 = \mathit{fix}(\lambda\rho.\psi_{23}\rho\rho\rho)$ and because (in accordance with 2.3.5) $\mathit{fix}(\lambda\rho'''.\mathit{fix}(\lambda\rho''.\mathit{fix}(\lambda\rho.\psi_{23}\rho\rho''\rho'''))) = \mathit{fix}(\lambda\rho.\psi_{23}\rho\rho\rho)$,

$$\begin{aligned}\rho_1 &= (\lambda\rho'''.\mathit{fix}(\lambda\rho''.\mathit{fix}(\lambda\rho.\psi_{23}\rho\rho''\rho''')))\rho_1\\ &= \mathit{fix}(\lambda\rho''.\mathit{fix}(\lambda\rho.\psi_{23}\rho\rho''\rho_1))\\ &= (\lambda\rho''.\mathit{fix}(\lambda\rho.\psi_{23}\rho\rho''\rho_1))\rho_1\\ &= \mathit{fix}(\lambda\rho.\psi_{23}\rho\rho_1\rho_1).\end{aligned}$$

In view of the definition of ψ_{mn} this establishes that $\rho_1 = \mathit{fix}(\mathit{form}[\![\Gamma_2]\!](\rho_0[\alpha*_1/\mathfrak{J}[\![\Gamma_3]\!]][\mathfrak{A}[\![\Gamma_3]\!]\rho_1\theta_0/\mathfrak{K}[\![\Gamma_3]\!]])(\mathfrak{C}[\![\Gamma_3]\!]\rho_1\theta_0)\sigma_0)$; consequently $\mathfrak{C}[\![\Gamma_0]\!]\rho_1(\mathfrak{C}[\![\Gamma_3]\!]\rho_1\theta_0) = \mathfrak{C}[\![\Gamma_2]\!]\rho_1(\mathfrak{C}[\![\Gamma_3]\!]\rho_1\theta_0)$ and $\mathfrak{P}[\![\Gamma_0]\!]\rho_1(\mathfrak{C}[\![\Gamma_3]\!]\rho_1\theta_0) = \mathfrak{P}[\![\Gamma_2]\!]\rho_1(\mathfrak{C}[\![\Gamma_3]\!]\rho_1\theta_0)$ as Γ_0 is replaceable by Γ_2. The reasoning which has already been used to show that $\mathfrak{C}[\![\Gamma_1]\!]\rho_1\theta_0 = \mathfrak{C}[\![\Gamma_3]\!]\rho_1\theta_0$ reveals also that $\mathfrak{P}[\![\Gamma_1]\!]\rho_1\theta_0 = \mathfrak{P}[\![\Gamma_3]\!]\rho_1\theta_0$. Hence $\mathfrak{C}[\![\Gamma_0;\Gamma_1]\!]\rho_1\theta_0 = \mathfrak{C}[\![\Gamma_2;\Gamma_3]\!]\rho_1\theta_0$ and $\mathfrak{P}[\![\Gamma_0;\Gamma_1]\!]\rho_1\theta_0 = \mathfrak{P}[\![\Gamma_2;\Gamma_3]\!]\rho_1\theta_0$. ▸

3.6.3. Equivalent blocks.

For block Γ_0 to be equivalent with block Γ_1 it is sufficient that Γ_0 be replaceable by Γ_1 but it is not necessary: if, for instance, Γ_0 is l:l:=false and Γ_1 is l:l:=false;m::l:=false then in Sal all three equalities given in the definition of 'replaceable' are invalid but nonetheless $\mathfrak{G}[\![\text{block } \Gamma_0]\!]=\mathfrak{G}[\![\text{block } \Gamma_1]\!]$. A more significant limitation on the usefulness of these equalities is the fact that $\lambda\rho\theta\sigma.fix(form[\![\Gamma_0]\!]\rho\theta\sigma)$ will not coincide with $\lambda\rho\theta\sigma.fix(form[\![\Gamma_1]\!]\rho\theta\sigma)$ unless $\mathcal{K}[\![\Gamma_0]\!]$ is a permutation of $\mathcal{K}[\![\Gamma_1]\!]$. This is rather irksome because we may wish to give fresh names to labels or to insert extra ones, as we do when changing while E do Γ into I::if E do (Γ;goto I). Luckily two rather trivial results about standard semantics come to our aid. The first of these asserts that if the identifiers in a program are altered in such a way that the distinct free variables of every component remain distinct then the meaning of the program is preserved throughout the change; the formal statement and inductive proof of this result will be left to the interested reader. The second result is similar in every respect to 3.5.6, which justifies the use of free variable lists, and affirms that any block is equivalent with a block which differs from it by omitting those labels that are set by incidence but are not referred to except at their points of setting.

The latter of these two results is the more important, for it clarifies the connection between while loops and conditional commands. In 3.6.7 we shall verify that I::while E do Γ is replaceable by I::if E do (Γ;goto I). If the smallest block surrounding while E do Γ has no mention of I except within the range of a declaration of I then it is equivalent with the block which contains I::while E do Γ in place of one occurrence of while E do Γ. Consequently it is also equivalent with the block which contains I:;if E do (Γ;goto I) instead.

Thus when it is applied in conjunction with results such as those mentioned above the concept of the "replaceable" command can produce proofs about useful properties of programs. Nevertheless it is not entirely adequate, as it cannot handle any transformations of labels set by reference which may change the allocation of storage. These will be mentioned in 5.3.8, so here we shall simply assert that:

(i) (fn()E)() is equivalent with E;

(ii) (fnI.E_0)E_1 is equivalent with I=E_1 **inside** E_0;

(iii) (fnI..E_0)E_1 is equivalent with I==E_1 **inside** E_0;

(iv) (Δ_0 **within** Δ_1) **inside** E is equivalent with Δ_0 **inside** (Δ_1 **inside** E) provided that no member of $\mathfrak{I}[\![\Delta_0]\!]\S\mathfrak{K}[\![\Delta_0]\!]$ which is not a member of $\mathfrak{I}[\![\Delta_1]\!]\S\mathfrak{K}[\![\Delta_1]\!]$ occurs free in E;

(v) (Δ_0 **around** Δ_1) **inside** E is equivalent with Δ_0 **inside** (Δ_1 **inside** E);

(vi) Δ **within** I=E is equivalent with I=(Δ **inside** E) provided that I is not a member of $\mathfrak{I}[\![\Delta]\!]\S\mathfrak{K}[\![\Delta]\!]$;

(vii) Δ **within** I==E is equivalent with I==(Δ **inside** E);

(viii) (Δ_0 **within** Δ_1) **within** Δ_2 is equivalent with Δ_0 **within** (Δ_1 **within** Δ_2) provided that no member of $\mathfrak{I}[\![\Delta_0]\!]\S\mathfrak{K}[\![\Delta_0]\!]$ which is not a member of $\mathfrak{I}[\![\Delta_1]\!]\S\mathfrak{K}[\![\Delta_1]\!]$ occurs free in Δ_2;

(ix) (Δ_0 **around** Δ_1) **within** Δ_2 is equivalent with Δ_0 **within** (Δ_1 **within** Δ_2);

(x) (Δ_0 **around** Δ_1) **around** Δ_2 is equivalent with Δ_0 **around** (Δ_1 **around** Δ_2);

(xi) (Γ_0;Γ_1);Γ_2 is equivalent with Γ_0;(Γ_1;Γ_2);

(xii) **block** Γ is equivalent with Γ provided that $\mathfrak{J}[\![\Gamma]\!]=\langle\rangle$ and $\mathfrak{K}[\![\Gamma]\!]=\langle\rangle$;

(xiii) **block** (Γ_0;Γ_1) is equivalent with (**block** Γ_0);(**block** Γ_1) provided that no member of $\mathfrak{J}[\![\Gamma_0]\!]\S\mathfrak{K}[\![\Gamma_0]\!]$ occurs free in Γ_1, $\mathfrak{J}[\![\Gamma_0]\!]=\langle\rangle$ and no member of $\mathfrak{K}[\![\Gamma_1]\!]$ occurs free in Γ_0;

(xiv) while E do Γ_0 is equivalent with if E do (Γ_0;while E do Γ_1) when Γ_1 is Γ_0 without its outermost level of label settings;

(xv) I::while E do Γ is replaceable by I::if E do (Γ;goto I).

Though many of these properties may seem intuitively obvious, intuition is not always a good guide and it is reassuring to be able to prove them; several will be verified shortly to illustrate the techniques needed. The syntactic constructs having these properties are perfectly general; the process of executing them may produce side effects, jumps and computations which do not terminate. After 3.8.1 we shall consider some equivalences which only hold if this generality is restricted.

By the phrase "Γ_1 is Γ_0 without its outermost level of label settings" we mean that Γ_1 is identical with Γ_0 except that the binding occurrence of each label occurring free in Γ_0 is absent from Γ_1; thus outside any block embedded in Γ_0 each label setting of the form I:Γ_2 or I::Γ_2 appearing in Γ_0 is replaced by Γ_3 in Γ_1 where Γ_3 is Γ_2 without its outermost level of label settings. After proving (xiv) in 3.6.6 we shall mention a more formal explanation of this notion.

3.6.4. Proposition.

If I is a Sal identifier and E_0 and E_1 are Sal expressions then $(\text{fn} I.E_0)E_1$ is equivalent with $I=E_1$ inside E_0.

⊲Notice first that if Φ is any abstraction then

$$\mathcal{R}[\![(\Phi)]\!]=\lambda\rho\kappa.\mathcal{E}[\![(\Phi)]\!]\rho(rv\kappa)=\lambda\rho\kappa.\mathcal{E}[\![\Phi]\!]\rho(rv\kappa)=\lambda\rho\kappa.rv\kappa(\mathcal{F}[\![\Phi]\!]\rho)=\lambda\rho\kappa.\kappa(\mathcal{F}[\![\Phi]\!]\rho).$$

Hence the definition of *run* given in 3.3.4 ensures that

$$\lambda\rho.\,run\langle\mathcal{R}[\![(\Phi)]\!]\rho,\mathcal{E}[\![E_1]\!]\rho\rangle=\lambda\rho\psi.\mathcal{E}[\![E_1]\!]\rho(\psi(\mathcal{F}[\![\Phi]\!]\rho)),$$

where we momentarily use ψ to represent an element of $E\to E\to C$. In particular,

$$\begin{aligned}\mathcal{E}[\![(\Phi)E_1]\!]&=\lambda\rho\kappa.\,run\langle\mathcal{R}[\![(\Phi)]\!]\rho,\mathcal{E}[\![E_1]\!]\rho\rangle(\lambda\varepsilon'\varepsilon''.\varepsilon'\mathsf{E}F\to(\varepsilon'|F)\varepsilon''\kappa,wrong)\\&=\lambda\rho\kappa.\mathcal{E}[\![E_1]\!]\rho((\lambda\varepsilon'\varepsilon''.\varepsilon'\mathsf{E}F\to(\varepsilon'|F)\varepsilon''\kappa,wrong)(\mathcal{F}[\![\Phi]\!]\rho))\\&=\lambda\rho\kappa.\mathcal{E}[\![E_1]\!]\rho(\lambda\varepsilon.\mathcal{F}[\![\Phi]\!]\rho\varepsilon\kappa).\end{aligned}$$

According to the equations of appendix 1, however,

$$\mathcal{F}[\![\text{fn}I.E_0]\!]=\lambda\rho.\lambda\varepsilon\kappa.lv(\lambda\varepsilon'.\mathcal{E}[\![E_0]\!]\rho[\varepsilon'/I]\kappa)\varepsilon.$$

In consequence,

$$\begin{aligned}\mathcal{E}[\![(\text{fn}I.E_0)E_1]\!]&=\lambda\rho\kappa.\mathcal{E}[\![E_1]\!]\rho(\lambda\varepsilon.lv(\lambda\varepsilon'.\mathcal{E}[\![E_0]\!]\rho[\varepsilon'/I]\kappa)\varepsilon)\\&=\lambda\rho\kappa.\mathcal{E}[\![E_1]\!]\rho(lv(\lambda\varepsilon.\mathcal{E}[\![E_0]\!]\rho[\varepsilon/I]\kappa))\\&=\lambda\rho\kappa.\mathcal{L}[\![E_1]\!]\rho(\lambda\varepsilon.\mathcal{E}[\![E_0]\!]\rho[\varepsilon/I]\kappa)\\&=\lambda\rho\kappa.\mathcal{L}[\![E_1]\!]\rho(\lambda\varepsilon.(\lambda\rho'.\mathcal{E}[\![E_0]\!](divert\rho\rho')\kappa)(arid[\varepsilon/I]))\\&=\lambda\rho\kappa.\mathcal{D}[\![I=E_1]\!]\rho(\lambda\rho'.\mathcal{E}[\![E_0]\!](divert\rho\rho')\kappa)\\&=\mathcal{E}[\![I=E_1\text{ inside }E_0]\!].\triangleright\end{aligned}$$

We have given a full proof of this proposition in order to illustrate the trivial sort of complexity which arises very easily. We introduced *run* into the semantic equations in order to avoid prescribing an order of execution; hence above we had to remove it by observing that the relevant expressions were commutative.

The expression $(\text{fn}I.E_0)E_1$ leads to a considerably more complicated scheme of evaluation than does $I=E_1$ inside E_0. This is so because an abstraction can be applied other than at the point where it is set up.

3.6.5. Proposition.

If I is a Sal identifier, E is a Sal expression and Δ is a Sal declaration then Δ within I=E is equivalent with I=(Δ inside E) provided that I does not belong to $\mathscr{I}\llbracket\Delta\rrbracket\S\mathscr{H}\llbracket\Delta\rrbracket$.

◁The equations of appendix 1 reveal that

$$
\begin{aligned}
\mathscr{D}\llbracket\Delta\ \mathtt{within}\ \mathrm{I{=}E}\rrbracket &= \lambda\rho\chi.\mathscr{D}\llbracket\Delta\rrbracket\rho(\lambda\rho'.\mathscr{D}\llbracket\mathrm{I{=}E}\rrbracket(\mathit{divert}\rho\rho')\chi)\\
&= \lambda\rho\chi.\mathscr{D}\llbracket\Delta\rrbracket\rho(\lambda\rho'.\mathscr{L}\llbracket\mathrm{E}\rrbracket(\mathit{divert}\rho\rho')(\lambda\varepsilon.\chi(\mathit{arid}[\varepsilon/\mathrm{I}])))\\
&= \lambda\rho\chi.\mathscr{D}\llbracket\Delta\rrbracket\rho(\lambda\rho'.\mathfrak{E}\llbracket\mathrm{E}\rrbracket(\mathit{divert}\rho\rho')(\mathit{lv}(\lambda\varepsilon.\chi(\mathit{arid}[\varepsilon/\mathrm{I}]))))\\
&= \lambda\rho\chi.\mathfrak{E}\llbracket\Delta\ \mathtt{inside}\ \mathrm{E}\rrbracket\rho(\mathit{lv}(\lambda\varepsilon.\chi(\mathit{arid}[\varepsilon/\mathrm{I}])))\\
&= \lambda\rho\chi.\mathscr{L}\llbracket\Delta\ \mathtt{inside}\ \mathrm{E}\rrbracket\rho(\lambda\varepsilon.\chi(\mathit{arid}[\varepsilon/\mathrm{I}]))\\
&= \mathscr{D}\llbracket\mathrm{I}=(\Delta\ \mathtt{inside}\ \mathrm{E})\rrbracket
\end{aligned}
$$

whether or not I belongs to $\mathscr{I}\llbracket\Delta\rrbracket\S\mathscr{H}\llbracket\Delta\rrbracket$.

The proof involving $\mathscr{T}$ instead of $\mathscr{D}$ is somewhat more complicated. We introduce the entity $\psi\in\mathrm{X}\to\mathrm{U}\to\mathrm{W}\to\mathrm{C}$, which is given by

$\psi=\lambda\chi\rho\omega.(\#\rho\llbracket\mathrm{I}\rrbracket>0)\to\mathit{assign}(\chi(\mathit{arid}[\rho\llbracket\mathrm{I}\rrbracket\downarrow 1/\mathrm{I}]))(\rho\llbracket\mathrm{I}\rrbracket\downarrow 1)\omega,\mathit{wrong}$;

as we know that I is not a member of the list $\mathscr{I}\llbracket\Delta\rrbracket\S\mathscr{H}\llbracket\Delta\rrbracket$,

$\lambda\rho'.\lambda\rho.\rho\llbracket\mathrm{I}\rrbracket\downarrow 1=\lambda\rho'.\lambda\rho.(\mathit{divert}\rho(\mathit{slim}\llbracket\Delta\rrbracket\rho'))\llbracket\mathrm{I}\rrbracket\downarrow 1$ and

$\lambda\rho'.\lambda\chi\rho\omega.\psi\chi\rho\omega=\lambda\rho'.\lambda\chi\rho\omega.\psi\chi(\mathit{divert}\rho(\mathit{slim}\llbracket\Delta\rrbracket\rho'))\omega$. Of course,

$\mathscr{T}\llbracket\mathrm{I{=}E}\rrbracket=\lambda\rho\chi.\mathscr{R}\llbracket\mathrm{E}\rrbracket\rho(\psi\chi\rho)$, so by applying 3.5.5 we see that

$$
\begin{aligned}
\mathscr{T}\llbracket\Delta\ \mathtt{within}\ \mathrm{I{=}E}\rrbracket &= \lambda\rho\chi.\mathscr{D}\llbracket\Delta\rrbracket\rho(\lambda\rho'.\mathscr{T}\llbracket\mathrm{I{=}E}\rrbracket(\mathit{divert}\rho\rho')\chi)\\
&= \lambda\rho\chi.\mathscr{D}\llbracket\Delta\rrbracket\rho(\lambda\rho'.\mathscr{T}\llbracket\mathrm{I{=}E}\rrbracket(\mathit{divert}\rho(\mathit{slim}\llbracket\Delta\rrbracket\rho'))\chi)\\
&= \lambda\rho\chi.\mathscr{D}\llbracket\Delta\rrbracket\rho(\lambda\rho'.(\lambda\rho''.\mathscr{R}\llbracket\mathrm{E}\rrbracket\rho''(\psi\chi\rho''))(\mathit{divert}\rho(\mathit{slim}\llbracket\Delta\rrbracket\rho')))\\
&= \lambda\rho\chi.\mathscr{D}\llbracket\Delta\rrbracket\rho(\lambda\rho'.\mathscr{R}\llbracket\mathrm{E}\rrbracket(\mathit{divert}\rho(\mathit{slim}\llbracket\Delta\rrbracket\rho'))(\psi\chi\rho))\\
&= \lambda\rho\chi.\mathscr{D}\llbracket\Delta\rrbracket\rho(\lambda\rho'.\mathscr{R}\llbracket\mathrm{E}\rrbracket(\mathit{divert}\rho\rho')(\psi\chi\rho))\\
&= \lambda\rho\chi.\mathscr{D}\llbracket\Delta\rrbracket\rho(\lambda\rho'.\mathfrak{E}\llbracket\mathrm{E}\rrbracket(\mathit{divert}\rho\rho')(\mathit{rv}(\psi\chi\rho)))\\
&= \lambda\rho\chi.\mathfrak{E}\llbracket\Delta\ \mathtt{inside}\ \mathrm{E}\rrbracket\rho(\mathit{rv}(\psi\chi\rho))\\
&= \lambda\rho\chi.\mathscr{R}\llbracket\Delta\ \mathtt{inside}\ \mathrm{E}\rrbracket\rho(\psi\chi\rho)\\
&= \mathscr{T}\llbracket\mathrm{I}=(\Delta\ \mathtt{inside}\ \mathrm{E})\rrbracket.
\end{aligned}
$$

Obviously $\mathscr{I}\llbracket\Delta\ \mathtt{within}\ \mathrm{I{=}E}\rrbracket=\mathscr{I}\llbracket\mathrm{I}=(\Delta\ \mathtt{inside}\ \mathrm{E})\rrbracket$ and $\mathscr{H}\llbracket\Delta\ \mathtt{within}\ \mathrm{I{=}E}\rrbracket=\mathscr{H}\llbracket\mathrm{I}=(\Delta\ \mathtt{inside}\ \mathrm{E})\rrbracket$, so Δ within I=E and I=(Δ inside E) are indeed equivalent.▷

The hypothesis that I does not belong to $\mathfrak{I}[\![\Delta]\!]\S\mathfrak{H}[\![\Delta]\!]$ highlights one quirk of recursive **within** declarations in Sal: the influence of Δ_0 in **rec** (Δ_0 **within** Δ_1) may spread beyond Δ_1 if Δ_1 contains declarations by reference. For example, the execution of **rec** (x==0 **within** x=0) gives rise to an error and does not yield a little environment in which x denotes a location containing 0.

Because we may wish to substitute one declaration, Δ_0, for another, Δ_1, when $\mathfrak{D}[\![\Delta_0]\!]$ coincides with $\mathfrak{D}[\![\Delta_1]\!]$ while $\mathfrak{T}[\![\Delta_0]\!]$ does not equal $\mathfrak{T}[\![\Delta_1]\!]$ we could choose to regard $\mathfrak{T}$, $\mathfrak{I}$ and $\mathfrak{H}$ as valuations defined not on Dec but on a domain isomorphic with Dec. In this situation the definition of "equivalent" given in 3.6.1 would imply that Δ_0 and Δ_1 were equivalent if $\mathfrak{D}[\![\Delta_0]\!]=\mathfrak{D}[\![\Delta_1]\!]$, so that Δ **within** I=E and I=(Δ **inside** E) would be equivalent even if I were in the list $\mathfrak{I}[\![\Delta]\!]\S\mathfrak{H}[\![\Delta]\!]$ (while **rec** I=E and I=(I=**false** **inside** I:=E **before** I) would also be equivalent).

3.6.6. Proposition.

If E is a Sal expression and Γ_0 is a Sal command then **while** E **do** Γ_0 is equivalent with **if** E **do** (Γ_0; **while** E **do** Γ_1) when Γ_1 is Γ_0 with the outermost level of label settings omitted.

◁The label settings removed from Γ_0 when Γ_1 is formed are precisely those which engender $\mathcal{J}[\![\Gamma_0]\!]$ and $\mathcal{K}[\![\Gamma_0]\!]$. By induction on the structure of Γ_0 we can therefore show that $\mathcal{C}[\![\Gamma_0]\!]=\mathcal{C}[\![\Gamma_1]\!]$, whilst $\mathcal{J}[\![\Gamma_1]\!]=\langle\rangle$ and $\mathcal{K}[\![\Gamma_1]\!]=\langle\rangle$.

Writing Γ_{n+2} for **while** E **do** Γ_n when $1\geq n\geq 0$ we infer from appendix 1 that

$$\begin{aligned}\mathcal{C}[\![\Gamma_2]\!]&=\lambda\rho\theta.\mathit{fix}(\lambda\theta'.\mathcal{R}[\![E]\!]\rho(\mathit{test}\langle\mathcal{C}[\![\Gamma_0]\!]\rho\theta',\theta\rangle))\\&=\lambda\rho\theta.\mathit{fix}(\lambda\theta'.\mathcal{R}[\![E]\!]\rho(\mathit{test}\langle\mathcal{C}[\![\Gamma_1]\!]\rho\theta',\theta\rangle))\\&=\mathcal{C}[\![\Gamma_3]\!].\end{aligned}$$

By applying the rules involving *fix* we see that

$$\begin{aligned}\mathcal{C}[\![\Gamma_2]\!]&=\lambda\rho\theta.\mathit{fix}(\lambda\theta'.\mathcal{R}[\![E]\!]\rho(\mathit{test}\langle\mathcal{C}[\![\Gamma_0]\!]\rho\theta',\theta\rangle))\\&=\lambda\rho\theta.\mathcal{R}[\![E]\!]\rho(\mathit{test}\langle\mathcal{C}[\![\Gamma_0]\!]\rho(\mathit{fix}(\lambda\theta'.\mathcal{R}[\![E]\!]\rho(\mathit{test}\langle\mathcal{C}[\![\Gamma_0]\!]\rho\theta',\theta\rangle))),\theta\rangle)\\&=\lambda\rho\theta.\mathcal{R}[\![E]\!]\rho(\mathit{test}\langle\mathcal{C}[\![\Gamma_0]\!]\rho(\mathcal{C}[\![\Gamma_2]\!]\rho\theta),\theta\rangle)\\&=\lambda\rho\theta.\mathcal{R}[\![E]\!]\rho(\mathit{test}\langle\mathcal{C}[\![\Gamma_0]\!]\rho(\mathcal{C}[\![\Gamma_3]\!]\rho\theta),\theta\rangle)\\&=\lambda\rho\theta.\mathcal{R}[\![E]\!]\rho(\mathit{test}\langle\mathcal{C}[\![\Gamma_0;\Gamma_3]\!]\rho\theta,\theta\rangle)\\&=\lambda\rho\theta.\mathcal{R}[\![E]\!]\rho(\mathit{test}\langle\mathcal{C}[\![(\Gamma_0;\Gamma_3)]\!]\rho\theta,\theta\rangle)\\&=\mathcal{C}[\![\mathbf{if}\ E\ \mathbf{do}\ (\Gamma_0;\Gamma_3)]\!].\end{aligned}$$

Because $\mathcal{P}[\![\Gamma_1]\!]=\lambda\rho\theta.\langle\rangle$ we know that $\mathcal{P}[\![\Gamma_3]\!]=\lambda\rho\theta.\langle\rangle$ and therefore that

$$\begin{aligned}\mathcal{P}[\![\Gamma_2]\!]&=\lambda\rho\theta.\mathcal{P}[\![\Gamma_0]\!]\rho(\mathit{fix}(\lambda\theta'.\mathcal{R}[\![E]\!]\rho(\mathit{test}\langle\mathcal{C}[\![\Gamma_0]\!]\rho\theta',\theta\rangle)))\\&=\lambda\rho\theta.\mathcal{P}[\![\Gamma_0]\!]\rho(\mathcal{C}[\![\Gamma_2]\!]\rho\theta)\\&=\lambda\rho\theta.\mathcal{P}[\![\Gamma_0]\!]\rho(\mathcal{C}[\![\Gamma_3]\!]\rho\theta)\\&=\lambda\rho\theta.\mathcal{P}[\![\Gamma_0]\!]\rho(\mathcal{C}[\![\Gamma_3]\!]\rho\theta)\S\mathcal{P}[\![\Gamma_3]\!]\rho\theta\\&=\mathcal{P}[\![\Gamma_0;\Gamma_3]\!]\\&=\mathcal{P}[\![(\Gamma_0;\Gamma_3)]\!]\\&=\mathcal{P}[\![\mathbf{if}\ E\ \mathbf{do}\ (\Gamma_0;\Gamma_3)]\!].\end{aligned}$$

Similarly $\mathcal{Q}[\![\Gamma_2]\!]=\mathcal{Q}[\![$if E do $(\Gamma_0;\Gamma_3)]\!]$, $\mathcal{J}[\![\Gamma_2]\!]=\mathcal{J}[\![$if E do $(\Gamma_0;\Gamma_3)]\!]$ and $\mathcal{K}[\![\Gamma_2]\!]=\mathcal{K}[\![$if E do $(\Gamma_0;\Gamma_3)]\!]$.⊁

Note that although $\mathcal{C}[\![\Gamma_2]\!]=\mathcal{C}[\![$if E do $(\Gamma_0;\Gamma_2)]\!]$ the analogous equations involving $\mathcal{P}$, $\mathcal{Q}$, $\mathcal{J}$ and $\mathcal{K}$ need not be valid. Furthermore we can only show that Γ_2 is equivalent with (if E do Γ_0);Γ_3 when E is idempotent (in a sense to be described in 3.8.7).

Strictly speaking, when verifying the proposition above we should have introduced a function *make*, say, which removed the outermost label settings from commands. This function would be defined by such recursive equations as $make[\![I:\Gamma]\!]=make[\![\Gamma]\!]$ and $make[\![I::\Gamma]\!]=make[\![\Gamma]\!]$, so we could easily show that $\mathcal{C}[\![\Gamma]\!]=\mathcal{C}[\![make[\![\Gamma]\!]]\!]$ for all Γ; moreover Γ_1 would be $make[\![\Gamma_0]\!]$ by definition.

3.6.7. Proposition.

If I is a Sal identifier, E is a Sal expression and Γ is a Sal command then I::while E do Γ is replaceable by I::if E do (Γ;goto I).

$\triangleleft$Select any continuation θ_0 and let $\chi=\mathcal{J}[\![\text{goto I}]\!]$ and $\gamma=\lambda\rho\theta.\mathcal{R}[\![E]\!]\rho(test\langle\mathcal{C}[\![\Gamma]\!]\rho\theta,\theta_0\rangle)$. When Γ_0 is I::while E do Γ and Γ_1 is I::if E do (Γ;goto I) appendix 1 makes it plain that $\lambda\rho.\mathcal{C}[\![(\Gamma;\text{goto I})]\!]\rho\theta_0=\lambda\rho.\mathcal{C}[\![\Gamma]\!]\rho(\chi\rho)$, $\lambda\rho.\mathcal{C}[\![\Gamma_0]\!]\rho\theta_0=\lambda\rho.fix(\gamma\rho)$ and $\lambda\rho.\mathcal{C}[\![\Gamma_1]\!]\rho\theta_0=\lambda\rho.\gamma\rho(\chi\rho)$, owing to our definitions of Γ_0 and Γ_1. Moreover $\lambda\rho.\mathcal{Q}[\![(\Gamma;\text{goto I})]\!]\rho\theta_0=\lambda\rho.\mathcal{Q}[\![\Gamma]\!]\rho(\chi\rho)$, so in fact $\lambda\rho.\mathcal{Q}[\![\Gamma_0]\!]\rho\theta_0=\lambda\rho.\langle\mathcal{C}[\![\Gamma_0]\!]\rho\theta_0\rangle\,\S\,\mathcal{Q}[\![\Gamma]\!]\rho(\mathcal{C}[\![\Gamma_0]\!]\rho\theta_0)=\lambda\rho.\langle fix(\gamma\rho)\rangle\,\S\,\mathcal{Q}[\![\Gamma]\!]\rho(fix(\gamma\rho))$ and $\lambda\rho.\mathcal{Q}[\![\Gamma_1]\!]\rho\theta_0=\lambda\rho.\langle\mathcal{C}[\![\Gamma_1]\!]\rho\theta_0\rangle\,\S\,\mathcal{Q}[\![(\Gamma;\text{goto I})]\!]\rho\theta_0=\lambda\rho.\langle\gamma\rho(\chi\rho)\rangle\,\S\,\mathcal{Q}[\![\Gamma]\!]\rho(\chi\rho)$.

Choose an environment ρ_2 and define ψ_0 and ψ_1 by setting $\psi_n=\lambda\rho.\rho_2[\mathcal{Q}[\![\Gamma_n]\!]\rho\theta_0/\mathcal{K}[\![\Gamma_n]\!]]$ if $1\geq n\geq 0$. From the definition of χ, if $\rho_1=fix\psi_1$ then $\chi\rho_1=\rho_1[\![I]\!]\downarrow 1=\gamma\rho_1(\chi\rho_1)$; consequently $\chi\rho_1$ is a fixed point of $\gamma\rho_1$ and $\chi\rho_1\sqsupseteq fix(\gamma\rho_1)$. Now

$$\begin{aligned}\rho_1&=\psi_1\rho_1\\ &=\rho_2[\gamma\rho_1(\chi\rho_1)/I][\mathcal{Q}[\![\Gamma]\!]\rho_1(\chi\rho_1)/\mathcal{K}[\![\Gamma]\!]]\\ &\sqsupseteq\rho_2[\gamma\rho_1(fix(\gamma\rho_1))/I][\mathcal{Q}[\![\Gamma]\!]\rho_1(fix(\gamma\rho_1))/\mathcal{K}[\![\Gamma]\!]]\\ &=\psi_0\rho_1.\end{aligned}$$

As $\rho_1\sqsupseteq\psi_0\rho_1$ the properties of fix ensure that $\rho_1\sqsupseteq\rho_0$ where $\rho_0=fix\psi_0$. However, $\chi\rho_0=\rho_0[\![I]\!]\downarrow 1=fix(\gamma\rho_0)$, so

$$\begin{aligned}\rho_0&=\psi_0\rho_0\\ &=\rho_2[fix(\gamma\rho_0)/I][\mathcal{Q}[\![\Gamma]\!]\rho_0(fix(\gamma\rho_0))/\mathcal{K}[\![\Gamma]\!]]\\ &=\rho_2[\gamma\rho_0(\chi\rho_0)/I][\mathcal{Q}[\![\Gamma]\!]\rho_0(\chi\rho_0)/\mathcal{K}[\![\Gamma]\!]]\\ &=\psi_1\rho_0.\end{aligned}$$

Hence $\rho_0\sqsupseteq fix\psi_1$ and in fact $\rho_0=\rho_1$; in particular $\mathcal{C}[\![\Gamma_0]\!]\rho_0\theta_0=fix(\gamma\rho_0)=\chi\rho_0=\chi\rho_1=\gamma\rho_1(\chi\rho_1)=\mathcal{C}[\![\Gamma_1]\!]\rho_1\theta_0$, whilst as $\lambda\rho.\mathcal{P}[\![\Gamma_0]\!]\rho\theta_0=\lambda\rho.\mathcal{P}[\![\Gamma]\!]\rho(\mathcal{C}[\![\Gamma_0]\!]\rho\theta_0)=\lambda\rho.\mathcal{P}[\![\Gamma]\!]\rho(fix(\gamma\rho))$ and $\lambda\rho.\mathcal{P}[\![\Gamma_1]\!]\rho\theta_0=\lambda\rho.\mathcal{P}[\![(\Gamma;\text{goto I})]\!]\rho\theta_0=\lambda\rho.\mathcal{P}[\![\Gamma]\!]\rho(\chi\rho)$ necessarily $\mathcal{P}[\![\Gamma_0]\!]\rho_0\theta_0=\mathcal{P}[\![\Gamma_1]\!]\rho_1\theta_0$.

Because $\mathcal{H}[\![\Gamma_0]\!]=\mathcal{H}[\![\Gamma_1]\!]$ the proof above is valid when there are ρ_3 and σ_0 for which $\psi_n=form[\![\Gamma_n]\!]\rho_3\theta_0\sigma_0$ if $1\geq n\geq 0$. This means that Γ_0 is replaceable by Γ_1.▸

The label I may, of course, be omitted under the circumstances discussed in 3.6.3.

3.7. Further standard uses of the semantic equations.

3.7.1. Routines.

Large though Sal is, it still does not contain all the features commonly found in programming languages. There are, for instance, no routines (abstractions having bodies that are blocks instead of expressions), no declarations governing blocks rather than expressions or other declarations, and no "double-armed" conditional commands. It would have been simple to incorporate such constructions in Sal and to provide them with natural semantic equations, but doing so would have involved lengthening those proofs in later sections which depend on structural inductions. If these extra constructions were to add any great depth to the language there would be a strong case for including them and enduring the longer proofs, but in fact they introduce nothing new, being largely notational conveniences for users. We shall therefore regard them as 'auxiliary constructions', and for each we shall give both a semantic equation in the ordinary way and an equivalent Sal construction. We shall also verify that some of these auxiliary constructions are indeed equivalent with ones in Sal. Once we have extended the language in this manner we shall be able to make use of these extra constructions in proofs about programs; at the same time we shall not need to discuss the appropriate semantic equations when dealing with structural inductions.

The auxiliary constructions fn()Θ, fnI.Θ and fnI..Θ correspond with the three forms of procedure abstraction available in Sal; they will be termed 'routines'. The semantic distinction between procedures and routines is that on application the former yield results which are expressed values whereas the latter do not. Thus a procedure application requires a continuation drawn from the domain K and a routine application requires one drawn from C. One way of bringing this about would be to add a block E_0E_1 to Blo and to extend E to include routine values belonging to E→C→C; the equation for a routine application would check that the R-value of E_0 was a routine value before trying to apply it. This approach to the semantics of routines is perfectly satisfactory and straightforward but it involves altering the domain structure. We can avoid this unwelcome operation by using the existing Sal block fit E, the role of which is to evaluate E for its side effect and then throw away the expressed value yielded. By arranging that a routine value returns a dummy result of some sort we can view it in the same manner as a procedure value and keep it in the domain E→K→C. The penalty for taking this easy way out appears at first sight to be that all routine applications have to be written as fit (E_0E_1); however, this can be evaded by providing a block E_0E_1 with the same meaning as fit (E_0E_1). We shall do this and ignore the parsing problems presented by fn()E_0E_1, for example, as being completely out of keeping with our concentration on the abstract syntax of the language. A routine application will be taken to be a block rather than a command because any labels appearing in E_0E_1 have scopes which are confined by the expressions E_0 and E_1.

An interesting situation arises if we try to introduce a sequencer, return say, which is intended to terminate immediately the current activation of the smallest surrounding routine by providing a jump to the end of this routine. If we want to avoid altering the domain U, we can try to make use of the res component of the environment. This yields an expression continuation and is set by a val expression. We therefore make return equivalent to res 0, so that we now have to ensure that the res component of the environment is properly set up when the routine is applied. This can be done by making fn()Θ equivalent with fn()(val (Θ before 0)) and by giving analogous equivalences for fnI.Θ and fnI..Θ.

These considerations lead to the following semantic equations for routines:

$\mathfrak{F}[\![\mathbf{fn}()\Theta]\!]=\lambda\rho.\lambda\varepsilon\kappa.\mathit{rv}(\lambda\varepsilon'.\varepsilon'\mathsf{E}\mathsf{E}^{*}\to((\#(\varepsilon'|\mathsf{E}^{*})=0)\to\mathfrak{G}[\![\Theta]\!]\rho[\kappa/\mathbf{res}](\kappa 0),\mathit{wrong}),\mathit{wrong})\varepsilon;$

$\mathfrak{F}[\![\mathbf{fn}\mathrm{I}.\Theta]\!]=\lambda\rho.\lambda\varepsilon\kappa.\mathit{lv}(\lambda\varepsilon'.\mathfrak{G}[\![\Theta]\!]\rho[\varepsilon'/\mathrm{I}][\kappa/\mathbf{res}](\kappa 0))\varepsilon;$

$\mathfrak{F}[\![\mathbf{fn}\mathrm{I}..\Theta]\!]=\lambda\rho.\lambda\varepsilon\kappa.\mathit{rv}(\lambda\varepsilon'.\mathfrak{G}[\![\Theta]\!]\rho[\varepsilon'/\mathrm{I}][\kappa/\mathbf{res}](\kappa 0))\varepsilon.$

We also introduce the **return** sequencer having the equation

$\mathfrak{J}[\![\mathbf{return}]\!]=\lambda\rho.((\#\rho[\![\mathbf{res}]\!]>0)\to(\rho[\![\mathbf{res}]\!]\downarrow 1)0,\mathit{wrong}),$

and the block E_0E_1, which has a meaning given by

$\mathfrak{G}[\![E_0E_1]\!]=\lambda\rho\theta.\mathit{run}\langle\mathfrak{L}[\![E_0]\!]\rho,\mathfrak{R}[\![E_1]\!]\rho\rangle(\lambda\varepsilon'\varepsilon''.\varepsilon'\mathsf{E}\mathsf{F}\to(\varepsilon'|\mathsf{F})\varepsilon''(\lambda\varepsilon.\theta),\mathit{wrong}).$

By using appendix 1 we can readily deduce that

(i) fn()Θ is equivalent with fn()(val (Θ before 0));

(ii) fnI.Θ is equivalent with fnI.(val (Θ before 0));

(iii) fnI..Θ is equivalent with fnI..(val (Θ before 0));

(iv) return is equivalent with res 0;

(v) E_0E_1 is equivalent with fit (E_0E_1) as a block.

In 3.7.2 we shall establish (ii); the other equivalences are equally easy to prove.

3.7.2. Proposition.

If I is an identifier and Θ is a block then fnI.Θ is equivalent with fnI.val (Θ before 0).

⊲According to appendix 1,

$$\mathcal{F}[\![\text{fnI.}\Theta]\!]=\lambda\rho.\lambda\varepsilon\kappa.\mathcal{l}v(\lambda\varepsilon'.\mathcal{G}[\![\Theta]\!]\rho[\varepsilon'/\mathrm{I}][\kappa/\text{res}](\kappa 0))\varepsilon$$

$$=\lambda\rho.\lambda\varepsilon\kappa.\mathcal{l}v(\lambda\varepsilon'.\mathcal{G}[\![\Theta]\!]\rho[\varepsilon'/\mathrm{I}][\kappa/\text{res}](\mathcal{E}[\![0]\!]\rho[\alpha/\mathrm{I}][\kappa/\text{res}]\kappa))\varepsilon$$

$$=\lambda\rho.\lambda\varepsilon\kappa.\mathcal{l}v(\lambda\varepsilon'.\mathcal{E}[\![\Theta\text{ before }0]\!]\rho[\varepsilon'/\mathrm{I}][\kappa/\text{res}]\kappa)\varepsilon$$

$$=\lambda\rho.\lambda\varepsilon\kappa.\mathcal{l}v(\lambda\varepsilon'.\mathcal{E}[\![\text{val }(\Theta\text{ before }0)]\!]\rho[\varepsilon'/\mathrm{I}]\kappa)\varepsilon$$

$$=\mathcal{F}[\![\text{fnI.val }(\Theta\text{ before }0)]\!].$$

As $\mathcal{E}[\![\Phi]\!]=\lambda\rho\kappa.\kappa(\mathcal{F}[\![\Phi]\!]\rho)$ for every abstraction Φ, fnI.Θ and fnI.val (Θ before 0) are equivalent.⊳

Before moving on to a new topic we must mention some more auxiliary constructions.

3.7.3. Other auxiliary constructions.

The Sal construction Θ before E allows an expression to be produced as the result of a block. It is often convenient, however, to be able to return a value before reaching the end of the block. This can be done by using val (Θ before E) and using res E inside Θ if an immediate return is wanted. On many occasions the end of the block is never reached, so the expression E becomes rather pointless. We therefore provide the auxiliary expression val Θ, which is equivalent to val (Θ before goto 0) and has the semantic equation

$\mathcal{E}[\![\text{val } \Theta]\!]=\lambda\rho\kappa.\mathcal{G}[\![\Theta]\!]\rho[\kappa/\text{res}](\mathit{wrong})$.

This equation ensures that erroneously running off the end of the block Θ gives a dynamic failure report. We could, of course, have made val Θ into a block by introducing the equation

$\mathcal{G}[\![\text{val } \Theta]\!]=\lambda\rho\theta.\mathcal{G}[\![\Theta]\!]\rho[\lambda\varepsilon.\theta/\text{res}]\theta$.

Another block is Δ inside Θ, in which the declaration Δ is intended to govern the block Θ in the same sort of way as it does E in the expression Δ inside E. This construction corresponds with the Algol 60 [61] species of block; it is worth noting that any labels set in Θ are inside the scope of the declaration Δ, so if there is a clash of names the label settings prevail. The block Δ inside Θ is equivalent with fit (Δ inside (Θ before 0)) because it has the semantic equation

$\mathcal{G}[\![\Delta \text{ inside } \Theta]\!]=\lambda\rho\theta.\mathcal{D}[\![\Delta]\!]\rho(\lambda\rho'.\mathcal{G}[\![\Theta]\!](\mathit{divert}\rho\rho')\theta)$.

In fact it is sometimes convenient to write an explicit statement which enables the execution of a program to be terminated abruptly. To this end we define

$\mathcal{X}[\![\text{error}]\!]=\lambda\rho\theta.\mathit{wrong}$.

Another valuable facility is the dummy block which is needed when the end of a group of commands has to be labelled. Executing dummy has no discernible effect on machine states and provides no labels,

so dummy can be given the semantics of a block by writing
$\mathfrak{G}[\![\text{dummy}]\!]=\lambda\rho\theta.\theta.$

Because blocks are inevitably commands, the constructs $\Theta_0;\Theta_1$, if E do Θ and while E do Θ yield commands. However no labels set in these particular commands have scopes which propagate outside, so we could actually view these commands as blocks and introduce such equations as
$\mathfrak{G}[\![\Theta_0;\Theta_1]\!]=\lambda\rho\theta.\mathfrak{G}[\![\Theta_0]\!]\rho(\mathfrak{G}[\![\Theta_1]\!]\rho\theta).$
Indeed whenever the outermost commands embedded in a command Γ are actually blocks Γ can itself be treated as a block.

Many programming languages also have a conditional command which provides two possible courses of action corresponding with the two truth values that may result from evaluating the premise of the conditional command. To model this facility we write:

$\mathfrak{C}[\![\text{if E do }\Gamma_0\text{ or }\Gamma_1]\!]=\lambda\rho\theta.\mathfrak{R}[\![E]\!]\rho(test\langle\mathfrak{C}[\![\Gamma_0]\!]\rho\theta,\mathfrak{C}[\![\Gamma_1]\!]\rho\theta\rangle);$

$\mathfrak{P}[\![\text{if E do }\Gamma_0\text{ or }\Gamma_1]\!]=\lambda\rho\theta.\mathfrak{P}[\![\Gamma_0]\!]\rho\theta\S\mathfrak{P}[\![\Gamma_1]\!]\rho\theta;$

$\mathfrak{Q}[\![\text{if E do }\Gamma_0\text{ or }\Gamma_1]\!]=\lambda\rho\theta.\mathfrak{Q}[\![\Gamma_0]\!]\rho\theta\S\mathfrak{Q}[\![\Gamma_1]\!]\rho\theta;$

$\mathfrak{H}[\![\text{if E do }\Gamma_0\text{ or }\Gamma_1]\!]=\mathfrak{H}[\![\Gamma_0]\!]\S\mathfrak{H}[\![\Gamma_1]\!];$

$\mathfrak{K}[\![\text{if E do }\Gamma_0\text{ or }\Gamma_1]\!]=\mathfrak{K}[\![\Gamma_0]\!]\S\mathfrak{K}[\![\Gamma_1]\!].$

Further cosmetic effects can be obtained by setting:

$\mathfrak{C}[\![\Gamma\text{ repeatwhile E}]\!]=\lambda\rho\theta.fix(\lambda\theta'.\mathfrak{C}[\![\Gamma]\!]\rho(\mathfrak{R}[\![E]\!]\rho(test\langle\theta',\theta\rangle)));$

$\mathfrak{P}[\![\Gamma\text{ repeatwhile E}]\!]=\lambda\rho\theta.\mathfrak{P}[\![\Gamma]\!]\rho(fix(\lambda\theta'.\mathfrak{R}[\![E]\!]\rho(test\langle\mathfrak{C}[\![\Gamma]\!]\rho\theta',\theta\rangle)));$

$\mathfrak{Q}[\![\Gamma\text{ repeatwhile E}]\!]=\lambda\rho\theta.\mathfrak{Q}[\![\Gamma]\!]\rho(fix(\lambda\theta'.\mathfrak{R}[\![E]\!]\rho(test\langle\mathfrak{C}[\![\Gamma]\!]\rho\theta',\theta\rangle)));$

$\mathfrak{H}[\![\Gamma\text{ repeatwhile E}]\!]=\mathfrak{H}[\![\Gamma]\!];$

$\mathfrak{K}[\![\Gamma\text{ repeatwhile E}]\!]=\mathfrak{K}[\![\Gamma]\!].$

Manipulations very similar to those required by 3.7.2 permit us to establish that when we presume that the syntactic domains for Sal include these auxiliary constructions (as well as the usual features of the language) and when we define the valuations on these constructions in the manner stipulated above then:

(i) val Θ is equivalent with val (Θ before goto 0);

(ii) Δ inside Θ is equivalent with fit (Δ inside (Θ before 0));

(iii) error is equivalent with goto 0;

(iv) dummy is equivalent with fit 0;

(v) $\Theta_0;\Theta_1$ is equivalent with block ($\Theta_0;\Theta_1$);

(vi) if E do Γ or dummy is equivalent with if E do Γ;

(vii) Γ_0 repeatwhile E is equivalent with Γ_0; while E do Γ_1 when Γ_1 is Γ_0 without its outermost level of label settings;

(viii) (if E do Γ_0 or Γ_1);I::dummy is replaceable by if E do (Γ_0;goto I);Γ_1;I::fit 0.

Only (vii) and (viii) have proofs which are not quite trivial.

The introduction of auxiliary constructions provides several elementary properties similar to those discussed in 3.6.3. Hence:

(i) (fn()Θ)() is equivalent with val Θ;

(ii) (fnI.Θ before error)E is equivalent with I=E inside val Θ;

(iii) (fnI..Θ before error)E is equivalent with I==E inside val Θ;

(iv) (Δ_0 within Δ_1) inside Θ is equivalent with Δ_0 inside (Δ_1 inside Θ) provided that no member of $\mathfrak{I}[\![\Delta_0]\!]\S\mathfrak{K}[\![\Delta_0]\!]$ which is not a member of $\mathfrak{I}[\![\Delta_1]\!]\S\mathfrak{K}[\![\Delta_1]\!]$ occurs free in Θ;

(v) (Δ_0 around Δ_1) inside Θ is equivalent with Δ_0 inside (Δ_1 inside Θ);

(vi) (if E do Γ_0 or Γ_1);Γ_2 is equivalent with if E do ($\Gamma_0;\Gamma_2$) or ($\Gamma_1;\Gamma_3$) and with if E do ($\Gamma_0;\Gamma_3$) or ($\Gamma_1;\Gamma_2$) when Γ_3 is Γ_2 without its outermost level of label settings;

(vii) if E do (Γ repeatwhile E) is equivalent with while E do Γ;

(viii) I::Γ repeatwhile E is replaceable by I::Γ;if E do goto I.

The proofs of these results will be omitted, as they follow the lines of the earlier ones. They can in turn be combined with these others to provide such equivalences as that between Γ_0 repeatwhile E and Γ_0;if E do (Γ_1 repeatwhile E) when Γ_1 is Γ_0 without its outermost level of label settings.

3.7.4. Proposition.

If E is a Sal expression and Γ_0 is a Sal command then Γ_0 repeatwhile E is equivalent with Γ_0;while E do Γ_1 when Γ_1 is Γ_0 with the outermost level of label settings omitted.

⊲The labels set at the outermost level are just those which are not set in a component block, so $\mathcal{C}[\![\Gamma_0]\!]=\mathcal{C}[\![\Gamma_1]\!]$, $\lambda\rho\theta.\mathcal{P}[\![\Gamma_1]\!]\rho\theta\S\mathcal{Q}[\![\Gamma_1]\!]\rho\theta=\lambda\rho\theta.\langle\rangle$ and $\mathcal{J}[\![\Gamma_1]\!]\S\mathcal{K}[\![\Gamma_1]\!]=\langle\rangle$. This means that if Γ_2 is Γ_0 repeatwhile E and Γ_3 is Γ_0;while E do Γ_1 then

$$\begin{aligned}\mathcal{P}[\![\Gamma_2]\!]&=\lambda\rho\theta.\mathcal{P}[\![\Gamma_0]\!]\rho\theta(\mathit{fix}(\lambda\theta'.\mathcal{R}[\![E]\!]\rho(\mathit{test}\langle\mathcal{C}[\![\Gamma_0]\!]\rho\theta',\theta\rangle)))\\&=\lambda\rho\theta.\mathcal{P}[\![\Gamma_0]\!]\rho\theta(\mathit{fix}(\lambda\theta'.\mathcal{R}[\![E]\!]\rho(\mathit{test}\langle\mathcal{C}[\![\Gamma_1]\!]\rho\theta',\theta\rangle)))\\&=\lambda\rho\theta.\mathcal{P}[\![\Gamma_0]\!]\rho\theta(\mathcal{C}[\![\text{while E do }\Gamma_1]\!]\rho\theta)\\&=\mathcal{P}[\![\Gamma_3]\!];\end{aligned}$$

similarly $\mathcal{Q}[\![\Gamma_2]\!]=\mathcal{Q}[\![\Gamma_3]\!]$, $\mathcal{J}[\![\Gamma_2]\!]=\mathcal{J}[\![\Gamma_3]\!]$ and $\mathcal{K}[\![\Gamma_2]\!]=\mathcal{K}[\![\Gamma_3]\!]$. Thus to show that Γ_2 and Γ_3 are equivalent we have now only to verify that $\mathcal{C}[\![\Gamma_2]\!]=\mathcal{C}[\![\Gamma_3]\!]$.

By 2.3.6 we know that if ψ_0 and ψ_1 are continuous members of C→C then $\mathit{fix}(\lambda\theta.\psi_0(\psi_1\theta))=\psi_0(\mathit{fix}(\lambda\theta.\psi_1(\psi_0\theta)))$. In particular, if we choose any ρ_0 and θ_0 and let $\psi_0=\lambda\theta.\mathcal{C}[\![\Gamma_0]\!]\rho_0\theta$ and $\psi_1=\lambda\theta.\mathcal{R}[\![E]\!]\rho_0(\mathit{test}\langle\theta,\theta_0\rangle)$ we can assert that

$$\begin{aligned}\mathcal{C}[\![\Gamma_2]\!]\rho_0\theta_0&=\mathit{fix}(\lambda\theta.\mathcal{C}[\![\Gamma_0]\!]\rho_0(\mathcal{R}[\![E]\!]\rho_0(\mathit{test}\langle\theta,\theta_0\rangle)))\\&=\mathcal{C}[\![\Gamma_0]\!]\rho_0(\mathit{fix}(\lambda\theta.\mathcal{R}[\![E]\!]\rho_0(\mathit{test}\langle\mathcal{C}[\![\Gamma_0]\!]\rho_0\theta,\theta_0\rangle)))\\&=\mathcal{C}[\![\Gamma_0]\!]\rho_0(\mathit{fix}(\lambda\theta.\mathcal{R}[\![E]\!]\rho_0(\mathit{test}\langle\mathcal{C}[\![\Gamma_1]\!]\rho_0\theta,\theta_0\rangle)))\\&=\mathcal{C}[\![\Gamma_0]\!]\rho_0(\mathcal{C}[\![\text{while E do }\Gamma_1]\!]\rho_0\theta_0)\\&=\mathcal{C}[\![\Gamma_3]\!]\rho_0\theta_0.\end{aligned}$$

As this is so for all ρ_0 and θ_0, Γ_2 is equivalent with Γ_3.⊳

<u>3.7.5. Proposition.</u>

If I is an identifier, E is an expression and Γ_0 and Γ_1 are commands then (if E do Γ_0 or Γ_1);I::dummy is replaceable by if E do (Γ_0;goto I);Γ_1;I::fit 0.

⊲Let Γ_2 be (if E do Γ_0 or Γ_1);I::dummy and let Γ_3 be if E do (Γ_0;goto I);Γ_1;I::fit 0. The semantic equations indicate that $\mathfrak{Q}[\![\Gamma_2]\!]=\lambda\rho\theta.\mathfrak{Q}[\![\Gamma_0]\!]\rho\theta\S\mathfrak{Q}[\![\Gamma_1]\!]\rho\theta\S\langle\theta\rangle$ and that $\mathfrak{Q}[\![\Gamma_3]\!]=\lambda\rho\theta.\mathfrak{Q}[\![\Gamma_0]\!]\rho(\chi\rho)\S\mathfrak{Q}[\![\Gamma_1]\!]\rho\theta\S\langle\theta\rangle$ where $\chi=\mathfrak{J}[\![\text{goto I}]\!]$.

Select any environment ρ_2 and any continuation θ_0, and set $\psi_n=\lambda\rho.\rho_2[\mathfrak{Q}[\![\Gamma_{n+2}]\!]\rho\theta_0/\mathfrak{R}[\![\Gamma_{n+2}]\!]]$ for $1\geq n\geq 0$. If $\rho_0=fix\psi_0$ and $\rho_1=fix\psi_1$ then $\chi\rho_0=\rho_0[\![I]\!]\downarrow 1=\theta_0$ whilst $\chi\rho_1=\rho_1[\![I]\!]\downarrow 1=\theta_0$. Hence

$$
\begin{aligned}
\rho_0&=\psi_0\rho_0\\
&=\rho_2[\mathfrak{Q}[\![\Gamma_0]\!]\rho_0\theta_0/\mathfrak{R}[\![\Gamma_0]\!]][\mathfrak{Q}[\![\Gamma_1]\!]\rho_0\theta_0/\mathfrak{R}[\![\Gamma_1]\!]][\theta_0/I]\\
&=\rho_2[\mathfrak{Q}[\![\Gamma_0]\!]\rho_0(\chi\rho_0)/\mathfrak{R}[\![\Gamma_0]\!]][\mathfrak{Q}[\![\Gamma_1]\!]\rho_0\theta_0/\mathfrak{R}[\![\Gamma_1]\!]][\theta_0/I]\\
&=\psi_1\rho_0
\end{aligned}
$$

and similarly $\rho_1=\psi_0\rho_1$. Since ρ_0 is a fixed point of ψ_1 and ρ_1 is a fixed point of ψ_0 the properties of *fix* ensure that $\rho_0\sqsupseteq\rho_1$ and that $\rho_1\sqsupseteq\rho_0$, so $\rho_0=\rho_1$. Now

$$
\begin{aligned}
\mathfrak{C}[\![\Gamma_2]\!]\rho_0\theta_0&=\mathfrak{R}[\![E]\!]\rho_0(test\langle\mathfrak{C}[\![\Gamma_0]\!]\rho_0\theta_0,\mathfrak{C}[\![\Gamma_1]\!]\rho_1\theta_0\rangle)\\
&=\mathfrak{R}[\![E]\!]\rho_1(test\langle\mathfrak{C}[\![\Gamma_0]\!]\rho_1(\chi\rho_1),\mathfrak{C}[\![\Gamma_1]\!]\rho_1\theta_0\rangle)\\
&=\mathfrak{C}[\![\Gamma_3]\!]\rho_1\theta_0\,;
\end{aligned}
$$

in addition,

$$
\begin{aligned}
\mathfrak{P}[\![\Gamma_2]\!]\rho_0\theta_0&=\mathfrak{P}[\![\Gamma_0]\!]\rho_0\theta_0\S\mathfrak{P}[\![\Gamma_1]\!]\rho_0\theta_0\\
&=\mathfrak{P}[\![\Gamma_0]\!]\rho_1(\chi\rho_1)\S\mathfrak{P}[\![\Gamma_1]\!]\rho_1\theta_0\\
&=\mathfrak{P}[\![\Gamma_3]\!]\rho_1\theta_0.
\end{aligned}
$$

As $fix\psi_0=fix\psi_1$ even when there are ρ_3 and σ_0 such that $\psi_n=form[\![\Gamma_{n+2}]\!]\rho_3\theta_0\sigma_0$ for $1\geq n\geq 0$, the command Γ_2 must be replaceable by Γ_3.⊳

By arguing as in 3.6.3 we could now demonstrate that if the smallest block surrounding if E do Γ_0 or Γ_1 has no mention of I then it is equivalent with a block obtained from it by replacing one occurrence of if E do Γ_0 or Γ_1 by if E do (Γ_0;goto I);Γ_1;I::fit 0.

3.7.6. An induction rule for loops.

According to the equations in appendix 1, if E is any Sal expression and if Γ is any Sal command then for every environment ρ and for every continuation θ $\mathcal{C}$⟦while E do Γ⟧ρθ=*fix*ψ where ψ=λθ′.$\mathcal{R}$⟦E⟧ρ(*test*⟨$\mathcal{C}$⟦Γ⟧ρθ′,θ⟩). The properties of *fix* described in 2.3.2 therefore ensure that $\mathcal{C}$⟦while E do Γ⟧ρθ⊒ψ($\mathcal{C}$⟦while E do Γ⟧ρθ) and that if *c* is an inclusive function mapping C into some domain then, for any θ, *c*($\mathcal{C}$⟦while E do Γ⟧ρθ)=⊥ provided that *c*⊥=⊥ and that *c*(ψθ′)=⊥ whenever *c*θ′=⊥. All the proofs about while loops which we have given hitherto are based on these assertions, but they could equally well rely on a formulation of the characteristics of loops which we shall now outline.

We proceed by defining ≥, a relation between commands, by stipulating that whenever Γ_0 and Γ_1 are commands $\Gamma_0 \geq \Gamma_1$ if and only if $\mathcal{C}$⟦Γ_0⟧⊒$\mathcal{C}$⟦Γ_1⟧. Though the relation ≥ is reflexive and transitive it is not antisymmetric (as is shown by while true do fit 0 and while true do fit 1). Nonetheless we may speak of a set of commands as being directed by ≥ simply by taking ≥ to be the relation mentioned in the definition of "directed set" given in 2.2.1; we may even refer to least upper bounds under ≥. As such bounds need not exist we consider a function ξ mapping Com into some domain to be "monotonic", "inclusive" or "continuous" with respect to ≥ if and only if whenever x is a directed subset of Com having a least upper bound Γ_∞ under ≥ then every least upper bound of {ξ⟦Γ⟧|Γ∈x} is related to Γ_∞ by inequalities analogous to those appearing in the definitions in 2.3.1.

The inequality in $\mathcal{C}$⟦while E do Γ⟧ρθ mentioned above shows that while E do Γ≥if E do Γ;(while E do Γ).

Moreover we can establish the following induction rule: if φ is a mapping of Com into some domain then φ⟦while E do Γ⟧=⊥ provided that φ⟦while true do fit 0⟧=⊥, that φ⟦if E dc (Γ;Γ′)⟧=⊥ whenever φ⟦Γ′⟧=⊥, and that ϕ is "inclusive" with respect to $\geq$. This rule can be validated by demonstrating from the semantic equations and the properties of *fix* that if Γ_0 is taken to be while true do fit 0 and if Γ_{n+1} is taken to be if E do $(\Gamma;\Gamma_n)$ when $n\geq 0$ then $\{\Gamma_n | n\geq 0\}$ is a set directed by $\geq$ and having while E do Γ as a least upper bound. We can characterize the semantics of while E do Γ completely by postulating not only the inequality and the induction rule described in the sentences above but also the equations $\mathcal{P}[\![\text{while E do }\Gamma]\!]=\lambda\rho\theta.\mathcal{P}[\![\Gamma]\!]\rho(\mathcal{C}[\![\text{while E do }\Gamma]\!]\rho\theta)$, $\mathcal{Q}[\![\text{while E do }\Gamma]\!]=\lambda\rho\theta.\mathcal{Q}[\![\Gamma]\!]\rho(\mathcal{C}[\![\text{while E do }\Gamma]\!]\rho\theta)$, $\mathcal{J}[\![\text{while E do }\Gamma]\!]=\mathcal{J}[\![\Gamma]\!]$ and $\mathcal{K}[\![\text{while E do }\Gamma]\!]=\mathcal{K}[\![\Gamma]\!]$.

In applications of the induction rule mentioned in the preceding paragraph the function ϕ often maps Com into the domain T′ described in 2.2.2 in such a way that for certain functions ξ_0 and ξ_1 which take Com into Com $\phi=\lambda\Gamma'.(\xi_0[\![\text{while E do }\Gamma]\!]\geq\xi_1[\![\Gamma']\!])$ when $\geq$ is regarded as a mapping of Com×Com into T′ in an obvious manner; evidently when ξ_1 is "continuous" with respect to $\geq$ then ϕ is "inclusive". Should we wish to prove not an equivalence result but a result which holds only for some environment ρ and for some continuation θ we can arrange that $\phi=\lambda\Gamma.c(\mathcal{C}[\![\Gamma]\!]\rho\theta)$ where c is an inclusive function taking C into T′, when ϕ is again "inclusive". In order to illustrate the use of the rule in 3.7.7 we shall prove an equivalence involving the auxiliary constructions discussed in 3.7.3; to help us we shall postulate that for all Γ_0 and Γ_1

$\Gamma_0\geq(\text{while true do fit }0);\Gamma_1\geq\text{while true do fit }0$,

from which it follows that

while true do fit $0\geq(\text{while true do fit }0);\Gamma_1$,

but doing this can evidently be justified by an appeal to appendix 1.

In 3.9.6 we shall provide induction rules which will express the properties of a certain class of recursive declarations in terms of within declarations and in terms of syntactic substitutions.

3.7.7. Proposition.

Let E_0 and E_1 be Sal expressions and let Γ_0, Γ_1, Γ_2 and Γ_3 be Sal commands; for any command Γ define $\xi_0[\![\Gamma]\!]$ and $\xi_1[\![\Gamma]\!]$ to be if E_0 do $(\Gamma_0;\Gamma)$ or Γ_1 and if E_1 do $(\Gamma_2;\Gamma)$ or Γ_3 respectively. If $\xi_0[\![$while true do fit 0$]\!]$ is equivalent with $\xi_1[\![$while true do fit 0$]\!]$ whereas $\xi_0[\![\xi_1[\![\Gamma]\!]]\!]$ is equivalent with $\xi_1[\![\xi_0[\![\Gamma]\!]]\!]$ for every command Γ then (while E_0 do Γ_0);Γ_1 is equivalent with (while E_1 do Γ_2);Γ_3 provided that $\mathcal{P}[\![\Gamma_0]\!]=\mathcal{P}[\![\Gamma_2]\!]$, $\mathcal{Q}[\![\Gamma_0]\!]=\mathcal{Q}[\![\Gamma_2]\!]$, $\mathcal{J}[\![\Gamma_0]\!]=\mathcal{J}[\![\Gamma_2]\!]$, $\mathcal{K}[\![\Gamma_0]\!]=\mathcal{K}[\![\Gamma_2]\!]$, $\mathcal{P}[\![\Gamma_1]\!]=\mathcal{P}[\![\Gamma_3]\!]$, $\mathcal{Q}[\![\Gamma_1]\!]=\mathcal{Q}[\![\Gamma_3]\!]$, $\mathcal{J}[\![\Gamma_1]\!]=\mathcal{J}[\![\Gamma_3]\!]$ and $\mathcal{K}[\![\Gamma_1]\!]=\mathcal{K}[\![\Gamma_3]\!]$.

$\triangleleft$For every command Γ we let $\xi_2[\![\Gamma]\!]$ be if E_0 do $(\Gamma_0;\Gamma)$ and $\xi_3[\![\Gamma]\!]$ be if E_1 do $(\Gamma_2;\Gamma)$; when we adopt the relation $\geq$ defined in 3.7.6 the semantic equations given in 3.7.3 reveal that $\xi_0[\![\Gamma;\Gamma_1]\!]\geq\xi_2[\![\Gamma]\!];\Gamma_1\geq\xi_0[\![\Gamma;\Gamma_1]\!]$ and $\xi_1[\![\Gamma;\Gamma_3]\!]\geq\xi_3[\![\Gamma]\!];\Gamma_3\geq\xi_1[\![\Gamma;\Gamma_3]\!]$ for each Γ. We wish to demonstrate that (while E_0 do Γ_0);$\Gamma_1\geq$(while E_1 do Γ_2);Γ_3 (among other things).

We know from 3.7.6 that

while E_0 do $\Gamma_0\geq\xi_2[\![$while E_0 do $\Gamma_0]\!]$

so, since actually $\xi_2[\![\Gamma]\!];\Gamma_1\geq\xi_0[\![\Gamma;\Gamma_1]\!]$ for any command Γ,

(while E_0 do Γ_0);$\Gamma_1\geq\xi_0[\![$(while E_0 do Γ_0);$\Gamma_1]\!]$.

Because all the operations available for forming commands out of other commands are "monotonic" with respect to $\geq$, ξ_0 and ξ_1 are "monotonic"; hence the stipulation that

(while E_0 do Γ_0);$\Gamma_1\geq$while true do fit 0

and the assumption that

$\xi_0[\![$while true do fit 0$]\!]\geq\xi_1[\![$while true do fit 0$]\!]$

conspire with the fact that

while true do fit 0$\geq$(while true do fit 0);Γ_1

to ensure that

(while E_0 do Γ_0);$\Gamma_1\geq\xi_1[\![$(while true do fit 0);$\Gamma_1]\!]$.

Moreover, if a command Γ is such that (while E_0 do Γ_0);$\Gamma_1\geq\xi_1[\![\Gamma_0;\Gamma_1]\!]$

the "monotonic" nature of ξ_0 allows us to assert that

$$\begin{aligned}(\text{while } E_0 \text{ do } \Gamma_0);\Gamma_1 &\geq \xi_0[\![(\text{while } E_0 \text{ do } \Gamma_0);\Gamma_1]\!]\\ &\geq \xi_0[\![\xi_1[\![\Gamma;\Gamma_1]\!]]\!]\\ &\geq \xi_1[\![\xi_0[\![\Gamma;\Gamma_1]\!]]\!]\\ &\geq \xi_1[\![\xi_2[\![\Gamma]\!];\Gamma_1]\!]\end{aligned}$$

in accordance with the hypothesis that $\xi_0[\![\xi_1[\![\Gamma]\!]]\!]$ is equivalent with $\xi_1[\![\xi_0[\![\Gamma]\!]]\!]$ for all Γ. Consequently when we regard $\geq$ as a mapping of Com×Com into T′ the mapping ϕ_0 which is defined by the equation $\phi_0=\lambda\Gamma.((\text{while } E_0 \text{ do } \Gamma_0);\Gamma_1\geq\xi_1[\![\Gamma;\Gamma_1]\!])$ is such that $\phi_0[\![\text{while true do fit } 0]\!]=\mathit{true}$ and $\phi_0[\![\xi_2[\![\Gamma]\!]]\!]=\mathit{true}$ whenever Γ satisfies the equation $\phi_0[\![\Gamma]\!]=\mathit{true}$. Clearly $\lambda\Gamma.\xi_1[\![\Gamma;\Gamma_1]\!]$ is "continuous" so ϕ_0 is "inclusive" and we may invoke the induction rule given in 3.7.6, thereby inferring that $\phi_0[\![\text{while } E_0 \text{ do } \Gamma_0]\!]=\mathit{true}$ or that $(\text{while } E_0 \text{ do } \Gamma_0);\Gamma_1\geq\xi_1[\![(\text{while } E_0 \text{ do } \Gamma_0);\Gamma_1]\!]$.

We shall now show that from the inequality $(\text{while } E_0 \text{ do } \Gamma_0);\Gamma_1\geq\xi_1[\![(\text{while } E_0 \text{ do } \Gamma_0);\Gamma_1]\!]$ we can deduce that $(\text{while } E_0 \text{ do } \Gamma_0);\Gamma_1\geq(\text{while } E_1 \text{ do } \Gamma_1);\Gamma_2$. To this end we suppose that Γ_4 is any command having $\Gamma_4\geq\xi_1[\![\Gamma_4]\!]$, and we note that

$\Gamma_4\geq(\text{while true do fit } 0);\Gamma_3$

by virtue of the postulates in 3.7.3. If $\Gamma_4\geq\Gamma;\Gamma_3$ for some command Γ the "monotonic" properties of ξ_1 ensure that

$$\begin{aligned}\Gamma_4 &\geq \xi_1[\![\Gamma_4]\!]\\ &\geq \xi_1[\![\Gamma;\Gamma_3]\!]\\ &\geq \xi_3[\![\Gamma]\!];\Gamma_3,\end{aligned}$$

because $\xi_1[\![\Gamma;\Gamma_3]\!]\geq\xi_3[\![\Gamma]\!];\Gamma_3$ as usual. Thus by setting $\phi_2=\lambda\Gamma.(\Gamma_4\geq\Gamma;\Gamma_3)$ we produce a function ϕ_2 mapping Com into T′ for which $\phi_2[\![\text{while true do fit } 0]\!]=\mathit{true}$ and $\phi_2[\![\xi_3[\![\Gamma]\!]]\!]=\mathit{true}$ whenever Γ is such that $\phi_2[\![\Gamma]\!]=\mathit{true}$. As $\lambda\Gamma.\Gamma;\Gamma_3$ is "continuous", ϕ_2 is "inclusive"; hence translating $\xi_3[\![\Gamma]\!]$ into if E_1 do $(\Gamma_2;\Gamma)$ reveals that we may apply the induction rule of 3.7.6 and conclude that $\phi_2[\![\text{while } E_1 \text{ do } \Gamma_2]\!]=\mathit{true}$.

When Γ_4 is taken to be (while E_0 do Γ_0);Γ_1 this indicates that (while E_0 do Γ_0);$\Gamma_1 \geq$(while E_1 do Γ_2);Γ_3.

The introduction of ϕ_1, ϕ_3 and Γ_5 (which reverse the roles of (while E_0 do Γ_0);Γ_1 and (while E_1 do Γ_2);Γ_3 in ϕ_0, ϕ_2 and Γ_4) allows us to establish in the same manner that

(while E_1 do Γ_2);$\Gamma_3 \geq$(while E_0 do Γ_0);Γ_1;

indeed, this inequality follows simply from the symmetry of the situation. Together with the earlier inequality it guarantees that

$\mathfrak{C}[\![$(while E_0 do Γ_0);$\Gamma_1]\!] = \mathfrak{C}[\![$(while E_1 do Γ_2);$\Gamma_3]\!]$.

The equations governing the auxiliary valuations and the conditions imposed in the statement of the result therefore imply that

$$\begin{aligned}\mathfrak{P}[\![(\text{while } E_0 \text{ do } \Gamma_0);\Gamma_1]\!] &= \lambda\rho\theta.\mathfrak{P}[\![\Gamma_0]\!]\rho(\mathfrak{C}[\![(\text{while } E_0 \text{ do } \Gamma_0);\Gamma_1]\!]\rho\theta)\S\mathfrak{P}[\![\Gamma_1]\!]\rho\theta\\ &= \lambda\rho\theta.\mathfrak{P}[\![\Gamma_2]\!]\rho(\mathfrak{C}[\![(\text{while } E_0 \text{ do } \Gamma_0);\Gamma_1]\!]\rho\theta)\S\mathfrak{P}[\![\Gamma_3]\!]\rho\theta\\ &= \lambda\rho\theta.\mathfrak{P}[\![\Gamma_2]\!]\rho(\mathfrak{C}[\![(\text{while } E_1 \text{ do } \Gamma_2);\Gamma_3]\!]\rho\theta)\S\mathfrak{P}[\![\Gamma_3]\!]\rho\theta\\ &= \mathfrak{P}[\![(\text{while } E_1 \text{ do } \Gamma_2);\Gamma_3]\!]\end{aligned}$$

whereas

$$\begin{aligned}\mathfrak{J}[\![(\text{while } E_0 \text{ do } \Gamma_0);\Gamma_1]\!] &= \mathfrak{J}[\![\Gamma_0]\!]\S\mathfrak{J}[\![\Gamma_1]\!]\\ &= \mathfrak{J}[\![\Gamma_2]\!]\S\mathfrak{J}[\![\Gamma_3]\!]\\ &= \mathfrak{J}[\![(\text{while } E_1 \text{ do } \Gamma_2);\Gamma_3]\!];\end{aligned}$$

remarks similar to those concerning $\mathfrak{P}$ and $\mathfrak{J}$ apply to $\mathfrak{Q}$ and $\mathfrak{K}$, so (while E_0 do Γ_0);Γ_1 is equivalent with (while E_1 do Γ_2);Γ_3.⊳

This result will be seen from a different angle in 3.8.4.

3.7.8. Assertions about commands.

We shall continue this account of certain uses of standard semantics by showing how rules which govern the correctness of commands can be formulated in terms of the appropriate semantic equations. To this end we introduce a predicate a which maps the domain of answers, A, into T′; as it is intended to check whether or not the answer produced by a program is correct according to some criterion, a is generally concerned with the output components of stores. When s is a predicate mapping the domain of stores, S, into T′ we temporarily take $s \rightarrow a$ to be the predicate defined on S→A by the equation

$$s \rightarrow a = \lambda\theta.\bigwedge\{a(\theta\sigma) \mid s\sigma\};$$

likewise when s_0 and s_1 are two predicates defined on S we set up $(s_0 \rightarrow a) \rightarrow (s_1 \rightarrow a)$ on (S→A)→(S→A) by writing

$$(s_0 \rightarrow a) \rightarrow (s_1 \rightarrow a) = \lambda\psi.\bigwedge\{(s_1 \rightarrow a)(\psi\theta) \mid (s_0 \rightarrow a)\theta\}.$$

These conventions of notation should not be confused with those of 2.5.5, which will not be needed until 3.8.2.

For any continuation θ the assertion that $(s \rightarrow a)\theta = true$ is tantamount to the claim that if σ is any store for which $s\sigma = true$ then, because $a(\theta\sigma) = true$, θ produces a correct answer when applied to σ. Thus for any command Γ and for any environment ρ the statement that $((s_0 \rightarrow a) \rightarrow (s_1 \rightarrow a))(\mathcal{C}[\![\Gamma]\!]\rho) = true$ for some s_0 and s_1 can be interpreted as indicating that if a given continuation produces a correct answer when applied to a store subject to s_0 then Γ itself yields a correct answer when supplied with that continuation and a store subject to s_1.

When Γ_0 and Γ_1 are any commands for which there are predicates s_0, s_1 and s_2 such that $((s_2 \rightarrow a) \rightarrow (s_0 \rightarrow a))(\mathcal{C}[\![\Gamma_0]\!]\rho) = true$ and $((s_1 \rightarrow a) \rightarrow (s_2 \rightarrow a))(\mathcal{C}[\![\Gamma_1]\!]\rho) = true$ in some environment ρ, we can confirm that $((s_1 \rightarrow a) \rightarrow (s_0 \rightarrow a))(\mathcal{C}[\![\Gamma_0;\Gamma_1]\!]\rho) = true$ by noting that if θ satisfies $(s_1 \rightarrow a)\theta = true$ then $(s_2 \rightarrow a)(\mathcal{C}[\![\Gamma_1]\!]\rho\theta) = true$ and $(s_0 \rightarrow a)(\mathcal{C}[\![\Gamma_0]\!]\rho(\mathcal{C}[\![\Gamma_1]\!]\rho\theta)) = true$.

When given predicates u and s (defined on U and S respectively) we shall suppose that E is an expression such that, for some $\phi\in U\to S\to E$, $\lambda\kappa.\mathfrak{E}[\![E]\!]\rho\kappa\sigma=\lambda\kappa.\kappa(\phi\rho\sigma)\sigma$ whenever $u\rho=\mathit{true}$ and $s\sigma=\mathit{true}$. After choosing one ρ having $u\rho=\mathit{true}$, we obtain a predicate s_2 mapping S into T$'$ by writing $s_2=\lambda\sigma.((\phi\rho\sigma\,\mathsf{E}\,L\to \mathit{hold}(\phi\rho\sigma|L)\sigma,\phi\rho\sigma)\equiv \mathit{true})$. If there are predicates s_0 and s_1 for which $s\sigma=\mathit{true}$ whenever $s_0\sigma\vee s_1\sigma=\mathit{true}$, and if there is a command Γ for which $((s_0\to a)\to((\lambda\sigma.s_1\sigma\wedge s_2\sigma)\to a))(\mathfrak{C}[\![\Gamma]\!]\rho)=\mathit{true}$, we can prove that $((s_0\to a)\to((\lambda\sigma.(s_0\sigma\wedge{\sim}s_2\sigma)\vee(s_1\sigma\wedge s_2\sigma))\to a))(\mathfrak{C}[\![\texttt{if}\ E\ \texttt{do}\ \Gamma]\!]\rho)=\mathit{true}$ provided that $a\bot=\mathit{true}$, $a\top=\mathit{true}$ and $a(\mathit{wrong}\sigma)=\mathit{true}$ for every σ; the proof merely involves observing that if θ satisfies $(s_0\to a)\theta=\mathit{true}$ then $((\lambda\sigma.s_1\sigma\wedge s_2\sigma)\to a)(\mathfrak{C}[\![\Gamma]\!]\rho\theta)=\mathit{true}$ and $((\lambda\sigma.(s_0\sigma\wedge{\sim}s_2\sigma)\vee(s_1\sigma\wedge s_2\sigma))\to a)(\lambda\sigma.\mathit{rv}(\mathit{test}\langle\mathfrak{C}[\![\Gamma]\!]\rho\theta,\theta\rangle)(\phi\rho\sigma)\sigma)=\mathit{true}$ (since $\mathit{rv}(\mathit{test}\langle\mathfrak{C}[\![\Gamma]\!]\rho\theta,\theta\rangle)(\phi\rho\sigma)\sigma$ is $\mathfrak{C}[\![\Gamma]\!]\rho\theta\sigma$ whenever $s_2\sigma$ is true and $\bot$, $\top$, $\mathit{wrong}\sigma$ or $\theta\sigma$ whenever $s_2\sigma$ is false).

Thus in order to handle errors we demand that $a(\mathit{wrong}\sigma)=\mathit{true}$ for all σ; intuitively this means that answers satisfy a if they are produced by erroneous computations as well as if they are correct. We also insist that $a\bot=\mathit{true}$ (and that $a\top=\mathit{true}$), but the full significance of doing so becomes apparent only when we consider commands which may explicitly give rise to unending computations. Once such command is, of course, the while loop, for which we may state the following rule: if Γ is such that

$(((\lambda\sigma.(s_0\sigma\wedge{\sim}s_2\sigma)\vee(s_1\sigma\wedge s_2\sigma))\to a)\to((\lambda\sigma.s_1\sigma\wedge s_2\sigma)\to a))(\mathfrak{C}[\![\Gamma]\!]\rho)=\mathit{true}$ then

$(((\lambda\sigma.s_0\sigma\wedge{\sim}s_2\sigma)\to a)\to((\lambda\sigma.(s_0\sigma\wedge{\sim}s_2\sigma)\vee(s_1\sigma\wedge s_2\sigma))\to a))(\mathfrak{C}[\![\texttt{while}\ E\ \texttt{do}\ \Gamma]\!]\rho)=\mathit{true}$

provided that E, ρ and s_2 are related as in the preceding paragraph. To verify this rule we either manipulate the semantic equations or apply the induction rule introduced in 3.7.6; here we shall adopt the latter method, though it naturally provides no real reduction in the effort required. Accordingly we let $c=(\lambda\sigma.(s_0\sigma\wedge{\sim}s_2\sigma)\vee(s_1\sigma\wedge s_2\sigma))\to a$ and $\eta=\lambda\Gamma'.(((\lambda\sigma.s_0\sigma\wedge{\sim}s_2\sigma)\to a)\to c)(\mathfrak{C}[\![\Gamma']\!]\rho)$, and we endeavour to establish that $\eta[\![\texttt{while}\ E\ \texttt{do}\ \Gamma]\!]=\mathit{true}$. Because $a\bot=\mathit{true}$, we can show in turn that $c\bot=\mathit{true}$, that $(((\lambda\sigma.s_0\sigma\wedge\sim s_2\sigma)\rightarrow a)\rightarrow c)\bot = true$ and that $\eta[\![\text{while true do fit 0}]\!] = true$. When Γ' is any command for which $\eta[\![\Gamma']\!] = true$ the fact that $(c\rightarrow((\lambda\sigma.s_1\sigma\wedge s_2\sigma)\rightarrow a))(\mathcal{C}[\![\Gamma]\!]\rho) = true$ combines with the hypothesis that $(((\lambda\sigma.s_0\sigma\wedge\sim s_2\sigma)\rightarrow a)\rightarrow c)(\mathcal{C}[\![\Gamma']\!]\rho) = true$ to ensure that $(((\lambda\sigma.s_0\sigma\wedge\sim s_2\sigma)\rightarrow a)\rightarrow((\lambda\sigma.s_1\sigma\wedge s_2\sigma)\rightarrow a))(\mathcal{C}[\![\Gamma;\Gamma']\!]\rho) = true$; consequently the rule for conditional commands discussed above allows us to assert that $(((\lambda\sigma.s_0\sigma\wedge\sim s_2\sigma)\rightarrow a)\rightarrow c)(\mathcal{C}[\![\text{if E do }(\Gamma;\Gamma')]\!]\rho) = true$ and that $\eta[\![\text{if E do }(\Gamma;\Gamma')]\!] = true$. Hence provided that η is "inclusive" in the sense explained in 3.7.6 we can infer that $\eta[\![\text{while E do }\Gamma]\!] = true$. If a is inclusive we can prove that c and $((\lambda\sigma.s_0\sigma\wedge\sim s_2\sigma)\rightarrow a)\rightarrow c$ are inclusive (and that η is "inclusive"). We therefore add the assumption that a is inclusive to the constraints imposed on a in order to declare with a clear conscience that

$$(((\lambda\sigma.s_0\sigma\wedge\sim s_2\sigma)\rightarrow a)\rightarrow((\lambda\sigma.(s_0\sigma\wedge\sim s_2\sigma)\vee(s_1\sigma\wedge s_2\sigma))\rightarrow a))(\mathcal{C}[\![\text{while E do }\Gamma]\!]\rho) = true$$

when $(((\lambda\sigma.(s_0\sigma\wedge\sim s_2\sigma)\vee(s_1\sigma\wedge s_2\sigma))\rightarrow a)\rightarrow((\lambda\sigma.s_1\sigma\wedge s_2\sigma)\rightarrow a))(\mathcal{C}[\![\Gamma]\!]\rho) = true$.

In order to handle the formalism of Hoare [31] we introduce a domain of 'formulas', For; we shall write a typical formula as the Greek letter P and we shall let a rule appear as $P_0\{\Gamma\}P_1$, where Γ is a command and P_0 and P_1 are formulas. A formula may take one of the forms E (where E is a programming language expression without side effects), ~E (where E is a programming language expression without side effects), $P_0\wedge P_1$ (where P_0 and P_1 are arbitrary formulas) and $P_0\vee P_1$ (where P_0 and P_1 are arbitrary formulas). We can define a valuation $\mathcal{U}$ on For in such a way that for any formula P, for any environment ρ and for any store σ $\mathcal{U}[\![P]\!]\rho\sigma$ belongs to T'. Strictly speaking, the definition of $\mathcal{U}$ demands the use of the conjugate valuation $\P\mathcal{R}$ to be described in 3.9.1, because (when $\sqsupseteq$ is regarded as an operator mapping its arguments into elements of T') we let:

$\mathcal{U}[\![E]\!] = \lambda\rho\sigma.(((\P\mathcal{R}[\![E]\!]\rho\sigma|(E\times S))\downarrow 1)\sqsupseteq true)$;

$\mathcal{U}[\![\sim E]\!] = \lambda\rho\sigma.(((\P\mathcal{R}[\![E]\!]\rho\sigma|(E\times S))\downarrow 1)\sqsupseteq false)$.

However, here it is enough to note that if ρ and σ are such that

$\lambda\kappa.\mathcal{R}[\![E]\!]\rho\kappa\sigma=\lambda\kappa.\kappa\varepsilon\sigma$ for some $\varepsilon\in E$ then $\mathcal{U}[\![E]\!]\rho\sigma=(\varepsilon\sqsupseteq true)$ and $\mathcal{U}[\![\sim E]\!]\rho\sigma=(\varepsilon\sqsupseteq false)$. We extend $\mathcal{U}$ to conjunctions and disjunctions of formulas as follows:

$\mathcal{U}[\![P_0\wedge P_1]\!]=\lambda\rho\sigma.\mathcal{U}[\![P_0]\!]\rho\sigma\wedge\mathcal{U}[\![P_1]\!]\rho\sigma$;

$\mathcal{U}[\![P_0\vee P_1]\!]=\lambda\rho\sigma.\mathcal{U}[\![P_0]\!]\rho\sigma\vee\mathcal{U}[\![P_1]\!]\rho\sigma$.

If we wanted to, we could easily make the domain For have members other than the ones that we have just mentioned; these might, for instance, make assertions about the output from programs.

Henceforth we shall take u and s to be predicates defined on U and S respectively and we shall abbreviate $(\lambda\sigma.\mathcal{U}[\![P]\!]\rho\sigma\wedge s\sigma)$ to $\mathcal{U}[\![P]\!]\rho\wedge s$ (for any formula P and for any environment ρ). If Γ is a command while P_0 and P_1 are formulas we shall view the rule $P_0\{\Gamma\}P_1$ as being 'valid' with respect to u and s if and only if

$((\mathcal{U}[\![P_1]\!]\rho\wedge s\rightarrow a)\rightarrow(\mathcal{U}[\![P_0]\!]\rho\wedge s\rightarrow a))(\mathcal{C}[\![\Gamma]\!]\rho)=true$

whenever ρ is an environment for which $u\rho=true$ and whenever a is an inclusive predicate mapping S into T′ in such a way that $a\bot=true$, $a\top=true$ and $(s\rightarrow a)(wrong)=true$. Thus the rule $P_0\{\Gamma\}P_1$ is valid with respect to u and s if and only if (for each inclusive predicate a having $a\bot=true$, $a\top=true$ and $(s\rightarrow a)(wrong)=true$) $a(\mathcal{C}[\![\Gamma]\!]\rho\theta\sigma)=true$ whenever ρ, θ and σ are chosen in such a manner that $u\rho=true$, $(\mathcal{U}[\![P_1]\!]\rho\wedge s\rightarrow a)\theta=true$ and $\mathcal{U}[\![P_0]\!]\rho\sigma\wedge s\sigma=true$. We could eliminate the requirement that $a\top$ be *true* were u and s to be designed suitably, but we shall not bother to do so.

The remarks in our earlier paragraphs can now be seen to vindicate particular rules of the form $P_0\{\Gamma\}P_1$. To demonstrate that this is so we make u and s be predicates such that, for some expression E without side effects, if $u\rho=true$ and $s\sigma=true$ then $\lambda\kappa.\mathcal{E}[\![E]\!]\rho\kappa\sigma=\lambda\kappa.\kappa(\phi\rho\sigma)\sigma$ where $(\phi\rho\sigma EL\rightarrow hold(\phi\rho\sigma|L)\sigma,\phi\rho\sigma)$ is either *true* or *false*. We can safely assert that:

(i) if Γ_0 and Γ_1 are any commands for which there are formulas P_0, P_1 and P_2 such that the rules $P_0\{\Gamma_0\}P_2$ and $P_2\{\Gamma_1\}P_1$ are valid with respect to u and s then the rule $P_0\{\Gamma_0;\Gamma_1\}P_1$ is valid with respect to u and s;

(ii) if Γ is any command for which there are formulas P_0 and P_1 such that the rule $(P_1\wedge E)\{\Gamma\}P_0$ is valid with respect to u and s then the rule $((P_0\wedge\sim E)\vee(P_1\wedge E))\{\texttt{if}\ E\ \texttt{do}\ \Gamma\}P_0$ is valid with respect to u and s;

(iii) if Γ is any command for which there are formulas P_0 and P_1 such that the rule $(P_1\wedge E)\{\Gamma\}((P_0\wedge\sim E)\vee(P_1\wedge E))$ is valid with respect to u and s then the rule $((P_0\wedge\sim E)\vee(P_1\wedge E))\{\texttt{while}\ E\ \texttt{do}\ \Gamma\}(P_0\wedge\sim E)$ is valid with respect to u and s.

To verify (i), for example, we select some environment ρ, take s_n to be $\mathcal{LL}[\![P_n]\!]\rho\wedge s$ when $2\geq n\geq 0$, and consider our paragraph about $\Gamma_0;\Gamma_1$. The second and third assertions, (ii) and (iii), take more familiar forms when P_0 is identified with P_1, in that if $(P_0\wedge E)\{\Gamma\}P_0$ is valid with respect to u and s then $P_0\{\texttt{if}\ E\ \texttt{do}\ \Gamma\}P_0$ and $P_0\{\texttt{while}\ E\ \texttt{do}\ \Gamma\}(P_0\wedge\sim E)$ are valid with respect to u and s.

Having provided a syntax for formulas we can analyse the validity of $(P[E/I])\{I{:=}E\}P$, a rule governing certain assignments which involves the substitution of the expression E for every free occurrence of the identifier I in the formula P (together, of course, with the changing of names to avoid clashes of bound variables). In order to prove that, for some u, s and a, $((\mathcal{LL}[\![P]\!]\rho\wedge s\rightarrow a)\rightarrow(\mathcal{LL}[\![P[E/I]]\!]\rho\wedge s\rightarrow a))(\mathcal{C}[\![I{:=}E]\!]\rho)=true$ for every environment ρ such that $u\rho=true$, we assume that there is some $\phi\in U\rightarrow S\rightarrow E$ for which $\lambda\kappa.\mathcal{E}[\![E]\!]\rho\kappa\sigma=\lambda\kappa.\kappa(\phi\rho\sigma)\sigma$ whenever $u\rho=true$ and $s\sigma=true$ and that $\rho[\![I]\!]\downarrow 1$ is a proper location whenever $u\rho=true$; under these assumptions we have to show that $(\mathcal{LL}[\![P[E/I]]\!]\rho\wedge s\rightarrow a)(\lambda\sigma.rv(assign\,\theta(\rho[\![I]\!]\downarrow 1))(\phi\rho\sigma)\sigma)=true$ whenever $u\rho=true$ and $(\mathcal{LL}[\![P]\!]\rho\wedge s\rightarrow a)\theta=true$. This equation in turn reduces to the assertion that if ρ and σ_0 are such that $u\rho=true$ and $\mathcal{LL}[\![P[E/I]]\!]\rho\sigma_0\wedge s\sigma_0=true$ then setting

$\sigma_1 = update(\rho[\![I]\!]\downarrow 1|L)(\phi\rho\sigma_0 \mathrm{E} L \rightarrow hold(\phi\rho\sigma_0|L)\sigma_0, \phi\rho\sigma_0)\sigma_0$ provides a store σ_1 such that $\mathcal{U}[\![P]\!]\rho\sigma_1 \wedge s\sigma_1 = true$. So long as $\mathcal{U}[\![P[\$I/I]]\!] = \mathcal{U}[\![P]\!]$ it might seem that the statement that $\mathcal{U}[\![P]\!]\rho\sigma_1 = true$ could be justified (in the absence of sharing) by induction on the structure of P, since, in terms that will be explained in 3.9.1, $\P\mathcal{R}[\![I'[E/I]]\!]\rho\sigma_0 = \P\mathcal{R}[\![I']\!]\rho\sigma_1$ for every identifier I′; in reality, however, the situation is more complex that this would suggest, as P may contain an application of a procedure the body of which has I as one of its free variables. Thus when validating the rule (P[E/I]){I:=E}P for languages that are not extremely simple we would use sets of semantic equations in which procedure values would mention explicit free variable lists; these sets of semantic equations would actually yield variants of store semantics, which will be discussed after 4.1.1.

Several rules taking the form $P_0\{\Gamma\}P_1$ (including the ones outlined above) have been given detailed justifications in terms of mathematical semantics, using notions of validity related to that adopted above [23,42]. Recent work on rules governing the properties of program schemes has also been discussed extensively [4]. This work, like much else that follows a similar approach [11,49], depends on special cases of the induction principle described in 2.3.2. In this connection we should also mention some intriguing results [30] which use the fixed points of functions that are not continuous in proofs that programs terminate.

3.7.9. Predicate transformers.

Here we shall analyse the treatment of correctness problems propounded by Dijkstra [22], using techniques like those introduced in 3.7.8; to this end we shall devise a correspondence between command continuations and certain entities like the formulas of 3.7.8 by viewing continuations as predicates that map stores into truth values. For each command continuation θ and for each store σ we expect $\theta\sigma$ to be *true* if and only if the computation represented by θ produces the "correct" outcome when started in the presence of a store signified by σ; accordingly we want a computation that never ends to be represented by the continuation $\lambda\sigma.false$. When the least element of A, the domain of answers, is written as $\perp$, conventionally the continuation $\lambda\sigma.\perp$ represents an unending computation; hence if A is to consist of elements written as *true* and *false* we must demand that *false* be the least element of A. Thus, as was noted by Mayoh [47], we must make A be the domain T″ described in 2.2.2, so that $true \sqsupseteq false$ in A, and we shall let C be $S\to T''$ throughout the course of this discussion.

We now set up a domain of 'claims', Cla. A typical claim, written as Ψ, may take one of the forms E (where E is a programming language expression without side effects), ~E (where E is a programming language expression without side effects), $\Psi_0\wedge\Psi_1$ (where Ψ_0 and Ψ_1 are arbitrary claims) and $\Psi_0\vee\Psi_1$ (where Ψ_0 and Ψ_1 are arbitrary claims), but it may alternatively be constructed from an infinite sequence of claims; when $\{\Psi_n|n\geq 0\}$ is such a sequence the claim constructed from it is signified by $\bigvee\{\Psi_n|n\geq 0\}$. For any claim Ψ, for any environment ρ and for any store σ we can create a member of T″, $\mathcal{V}[\![\Psi]\!]\rho\sigma$, by regarding $\sqsupseteq$ as an operator mapping its arguments into elements of T″; as we want $\mathcal{V}[\![\Psi]\!]\rho$ to be a command continuation in C (which is $S\to T''$ for the present) we formulate the valuation $\mathcal{V}$ in such a way that $\mathcal{V}[\![\Psi]\!]\rho$ is continuous. Because *true* and *false* are isolated in E (in the sense that we gave to this term in 2.4.6) we know that

$\mathcal{V}[\![E]\!]\rho$ and $\mathcal{V}[\![\sim E]\!]\rho$ are continuous if in accordance with 3.7.8 we set:

$\mathcal{V}[\![E]\!]=\lambda\rho\sigma.(((\P\mathcal{R}[\![E]\!]\rho\sigma|(E\times S))\downarrow 1)\sqsupseteq \mathit{true});$

$\mathcal{V}[\![\sim E]\!]=\lambda\rho\sigma.(((\P\mathcal{R}[\![E]\!]\rho\sigma|(E\times S))\downarrow 1)\sqsupseteq \mathit{false}).$

Likewise if $\mathcal{V}[\![\Psi_0]\!]\rho$ and $\mathcal{V}[\![\Psi_1]\!]\rho$ are continuous the fact that $\wedge$ and $\vee$ are continuous operations defined on T″ ensures that $\mathcal{V}[\![\Psi_0\wedge\Psi_1]\!]\rho$ and $\mathcal{V}[\![\Psi_0\vee\Psi_1]\!]\rho$ are continuous when:

$\mathcal{V}[\![\Psi_0\wedge\Psi_1]\!]=\lambda\rho\sigma.\mathcal{V}[\![\Psi_0]\!]\rho\sigma\wedge\mathcal{V}[\![\Psi_1]\!]\rho\sigma;$

$\mathcal{V}[\![\Psi_0\wedge\Psi_1]\!]=\lambda\rho\sigma.\mathcal{V}[\![\Psi_0]\!]\rho\sigma\vee\mathcal{V}[\![\Psi_1]\!]\rho\sigma.$

Finally, we handle the infinite sequence $\{\Psi_n|n\geq 0\}$ by letting

$\mathcal{V}[\![\bigvee\{\Psi_n|n\geq 0\}]\!]=\lambda\rho\sigma.\bigsqcup\{\mathcal{V}[\![\Psi_n]\!]\rho\sigma|n\geq 0\}.$

Induction on the structure of Ψ makes it plain that when ρ is any environment $\mathcal{V}[\![\Psi]\!]\rho$ is continuous; indeed, $\mathcal{V}$ is in Cla→U→S→T″.

Formulas deal with the "partial correctness" of a program, in that they are intended to indicate whether the execution of the program produces the correct outcome on the assumption that it terminates. Claims, however, concern the "total correctness" of a program, as they indicate whether the execution the program terminates with the correct outcome. It is for this reason that the semantics of a formula, as defined by $\mathcal{U}$, does not need any mention of the least upper bound of a set directed by $\sqsupseteq$ whereas the semantics of a claim, as defined by $\mathcal{V}$, may demand the introduction of a least upper bound. In fact our use of least upper bounds in this connection is precisely analogous to the use of existential quantifiers in discussions of termination, for $\mathcal{V}[\![\bigvee\{\Psi_n|n\geq 0\}]\!]\rho\sigma$ is *true* (for some ρ and σ) if and only if there exists an integer $n\geq 0$ such that $\mathcal{V}[\![\Psi_n]\!]\rho\sigma$ is *true*.

From the description of T″ in 2.2.2 it is clear that for all ρ and σ $\bigsqcup\{\mathcal{V}[\![\Psi_n]\!]\rho\sigma|n\geq 0\}$ is the least upper bound of the sequence $\{\mathcal{V}[\![\Psi_n]\!]\rho c|n\geq 0\}$ under $\sqsupseteq$. Hence, when we order Cla by demanding that whenever Ψ_0 and Ψ_1 are commands $\Psi_0\geq\Psi_1$ if and only if $\mathcal{V}[\![\Psi_0]\!]\sqsupseteq\mathcal{V}[\![\Psi_1]\!]$, $\bigvee\{\Psi_n|n\geq 0\}$ becomes a least upper bound of the sequence $\{\Psi_n|n\geq 0\}$ under $\geq$. We could amend the syntax of claims so that, when the sequence

$\{\Psi_n|n\geq 0\}$ was defined inductively (as, in practice, would always be the case), we could replace the claim $\bigvee\{\Psi_n|n\geq 0\}$, which formally requires an infinite piece of paper for its full expression, by a finite claim which would be a least upper bound for $\{\Psi_n|n\geq 0\}$; in 3.7.6 the same technique allowed us to replace the sequence $\{\Gamma_n|n\geq 0\}$ (where Γ_0 is while true do fit 0 and Γ_{n+1} is if E do $(\Gamma;\Gamma_n)$ when $n\geq 0$) by while E do Γ. We have chosen not to eliminate the syntactic form $\bigvee\{\Psi_n|n\geq 0\}$ because of the convenient way in which the notion of syntactic substitution may be extended to it: for any expression E and any identifier I we let $(\bigvee\{\Psi_n|n\geq 0\})[E/I]$ be $\bigvee\{\Psi_n[E/I]|n\geq 0\}$. Of course, when the expressions that appear in claims are constrained so that in them \$I may be substituted for I without changing their meanings, we may prove by structural induction that for any claim Ψ $\mathcal{V}[\![\Psi[E/I]]\!]\rho\sigma=\mathcal{V}[\![\Psi]\!]\rho[\varepsilon/I]\sigma$ if ρ, σ and ε are such that $\lambda\kappa.\mathcal{R}[\![E]\!]\rho\kappa\sigma=\lambda\kappa.\kappa\varepsilon\sigma$.

Next we introduce predicates u and s (defined on U and S respectively); these predicates are intended to ensure among other things that the values which we manipulate are proper. Having demonstrated how claims correspond with continuations, we can speak of a pair of claims, $\langle\Psi_0,\Psi_1\rangle$ say, as comprising a 'pre-condition' Ψ_0 and a 'post-condition' Ψ_1 for a command Γ with respect to u and s if and only if

$$\mathcal{V}[\![\Psi_0]\!]\rho\sigma\sqsubseteq\mathcal{C}[\![\Gamma]\!]\rho(\mathcal{V}[\![\Psi_1]\!]\rho)\sigma$$

whenever ρ and σ are such that $u\rho=true$ and $s\sigma=true$; thus $\langle\Psi_0,\Psi_1\rangle$ comprises a pre-condition and a post-condition for Γ with respect to u and s if and only if $\mathcal{C}[\![\Gamma]\!]\rho(\mathcal{V}[\![\Psi_1]\!]\rho)\sigma=true$ whenever ρ and σ are such that $u\rho=true$, $s\sigma=true$ and $\mathcal{V}[\![\Psi_0]\!]\rho\sigma=true$. Intuitively this means that if the claim Ψ_0 "holds" before the execution of Γ then executing Γ produces a state in which Ψ_1 "holds"; hence $\langle\Psi_0,\Psi_1\rangle$ is being used as a measure of the correctness of Γ.

For the benefit of those who are already familiar with the conjugate valuations to be discussed in 3.9.1 we shall now devote a (parenthetical) paragraph to the relation between the definitions just given and the concept of validity that was discussed in 3.7.8. Provided that $\P\mathcal{C}$ is conjugate to $\mathcal{C}$ for Γ under

$$(\lambda\langle \rho_0,\rho_1\rangle .(\rho_0\equiv\rho_1)\wedge u\rho_0)\rightarrow(\lambda\langle \theta_0,\theta_1\rangle .(\theta_0\equiv\theta_1))\rightarrow(\lambda\langle \theta_0,\theta_1\rangle .(\theta_0\equiv\theta_1))$$

(and that $(\P\mathcal{C}\llbracket\Gamma\rrbracket\rho\sigma|S)=true$ if $u\rho=true$, $s\sigma=true$ and $\P\mathcal{C}\llbracket\Gamma\rrbracket\rho\sigma\sqsubseteq S$), we can exploit the connection between $\mathcal{U}$ and $\mathcal{V}$ which holds when formulas are regarded as claims in order to establish the following little result: if $\langle P_0,P_1\rangle$ comprises a pre-condition P_0 and a post-condition P_1 for Γ with respect to u and s then $P_0\{\Gamma\}P_1$ is valid with respect to u and s (where the answer domain adopted for the version of $\mathcal{U}$ underlying the notion of validity need not be T″ when s is "chosen sensibly"). We shall not provide the rather messy proof of this result, but will content ourselves with pointing out that its converse does not hold, essentially because the system under discussion here handles failures to terminate and errors differently from that considered in 3.7.8; for instance, the rule true{while true do dummy}true is valid with respect to $\lambda\rho.true$ and $\lambda\sigma.true$ although

$$\mathcal{V}\llbracket\text{true}\rrbracket\sqsupseteq\lambda\rho.\mathcal{C}\llbracket\text{while true do dummy}\rrbracket\rho(\mathcal{V}\llbracket\text{true}\rrbracket\rho),$$

and the rule true{error}true is valid with respect to $\lambda\rho.true$ and $\lambda\sigma.true$ although

$$\mathcal{V}\llbracket\text{true}\rrbracket\sqsupseteq\lambda\rho.\mathcal{C}\llbracket\text{error}\rrbracket\rho(\mathcal{V}\llbracket\text{true}\rrbracket\rho),$$

so long as *wrong* is $\lambda\sigma.false$.

A pair of claims, $\langle\Psi_0,\Psi_1\rangle$ say, is of particular interest if, for a certain Γ and for predicates u and s like those mentioned above,

$$\mathcal{V}\llbracket\Psi_0\rrbracket\rho\sigma=\mathcal{C}\llbracket\Gamma\rrbracket\rho(\mathcal{V}\llbracket\Psi_1\rrbracket\rho)\sigma$$

whenever $u\rho=true$ and $s\sigma=true$; in this situation Ψ_0 is "weakest" among the pre-conditions for which Ψ_1 can be the post-condition, since the claim Ψ_0 "holds" (in that $\mathcal{V}\llbracket\Psi_0\rrbracket\rho\sigma=true$ for some ρ and σ having $u\rho=true$ and $s\sigma=true$) only if Ψ_2 "holds" when Ψ_2 is any claim such that $\langle\Psi_2,\Psi_1\rangle$ comprises a pre-condition and a post-condition for Γ with respect to u and s. In order to create a uniform method for obtaining "weakest" pre-conditions from given commands and post-conditions we consider an arbitrary mapping, $\mathfrak{t}$, belonging to Com→Cla→Cla; the intention is that for any Γ and Ψ $\langle \mathfrak{t}\llbracket\Gamma\rrbracket\llbracket\Psi\rrbracket,\Psi\rangle$ should comprise a pre-condition and a post-condition for Γ such that $\mathfrak{t}\llbracket\Gamma\rrbracket\llbracket\Psi\rrbracket$ is "weakest" among the pre-conditions for which Ψ can be the post-condition. Thus we shall regard a mapping $\mathfrak{t}$ as 'satisfactory' for a command Γ with respect to predicates u and s if and only if for every claim Ψ

$$\mathfrak{V}\llbracket\mathfrak{t}\llbracket\Gamma\rrbracket\llbracket\Psi\rrbracket\rrbracket\rho\sigma=\mathfrak{C}\llbracket\Gamma\rrbracket\rho(\mathfrak{V}\llbracket\Psi\rrbracket\rho)\sigma$$

whenever ρ and σ are such that $u\rho=true$ and $s\sigma=true$; under these circumstances $\mathfrak{t}\llbracket\Gamma\rrbracket$ is the 'predicate transformer' for Γ.

In order to illustrate the utility of the definition in the previous paragraph we shall show how to form predicate transformers for various commands. The simplest of these is **dummy**, for which, in accordance with 3.7.3, we provide the semantic equation

$$\mathfrak{C}\llbracket\textbf{dummy}\rrbracket=\lambda\rho\theta.\theta.$$

Consequently if, for some Ψ, ρ and σ, $\mathfrak{V}\llbracket\mathfrak{t}\llbracket\textbf{dummy}\rrbracket\llbracket\Psi\rrbracket\rrbracket\rho\sigma$ is to be $\mathfrak{C}\llbracket\textbf{dummy}\rrbracket\rho(\mathfrak{V}\llbracket\Psi\rrbracket\rho)\sigma$, $\mathfrak{V}\llbracket\mathfrak{t}\llbracket\textbf{dummy}\rrbracket\llbracket\Psi\rrbracket\rrbracket\rho\sigma$ must be $\mathfrak{V}\llbracket\Psi\rrbracket\rho\sigma$. It is therefore plain that, if we set

$$\mathfrak{t}\llbracket\textbf{dummy}\rrbracket=\lambda\Psi.\Psi,$$

$\mathfrak{t}$ will be satisfactory for **dummy** with respect to u and s, no matter what the nature of u and s may be.

Another elementary argument is provided by **error**, which by virtue of 3.7.3 gives the equation

$$\mathfrak{C}\llbracket\textbf{error}\rrbracket=\lambda\rho\theta.wrong.$$

As we are currently concerned with the correctness of commands, we are content to view *false* as the answer appropriate to any computation that is incorrect; we therefore let *wrong* be $\lambda\sigma.false$. We make certain that, for some Ψ, ρ and σ, $\mathfrak{V}\llbracket\mathfrak{t}\llbracket\textbf{error}\rrbracket\llbracket\Psi\rrbracket\rrbracket\rho\sigma$ coincides with $\mathfrak{C}\llbracket\textbf{error}\rrbracket\rho(\mathfrak{V}\llbracket\Psi\rrbracket\rho)\sigma$ by setting

$$\mathfrak{t}\llbracket\textbf{error}\rrbracket=\lambda\Psi.\textbf{false};$$

indeed this equation makes $\mathfrak{T}$ satisfactory for error with respect to u and s whatever we take u and s to be. If we wanted to distinguish erroneous computations from unending computations we would replace T″ by a domain containing elements in addition to *true* and *false*; though the definition of $\surd$ would need to be changed, the essentials of our reasoning would remain unaltered.

The discussion in 3.7.8 of the rule (P[E/I]){I:=E}P can easily be adapted to confirming that if for some suitable E

$\mathfrak{T}[\![I{:=}E]\!]=\lambda\Psi.\Psi[E/I]$

then $\mathfrak{T}$ is satisfactory for I:=E with respect to certain predicates, u and s. These predicates are such that if, whenever $u\rho=true$ and $s\sigma=true$, $\lambda\kappa.\mathfrak{R}[\![E]\!]\rho\kappa\sigma$ is $\lambda\kappa.\kappa\varepsilon\sigma$ (for some proper ε) and $\rho[\![I]\!]\downarrow 1$ is a proper location that is accessible through ρ and σ "only because I denotes it". How to formalize this vague phrase should become apparent after 4.1.2, for the predicate transformer for I:=E is best analysed in terms of a variant of store semantics; only in rather simple languages is standard semantics adequate for the purpose.

A further example is provided by the predicate transformer appropriate to $\Gamma_0;\Gamma_1$ when Γ_0 and Γ_1 are any suitable commands; we require a condition under which setting

$\mathfrak{T}[\![\Gamma_0;\Gamma_1]\!]=\lambda\Psi.\mathfrak{T}[\![\Gamma_0]\!][\![\mathfrak{T}[\![\Gamma_1]\!][\![\Psi]\!]]\!]$

makes $\mathfrak{T}$ satisfactory for $\Gamma_0;\Gamma_1$ with respect to some predicates, u and s, on the assumption that $\mathfrak{T}$ is satisfactory for Γ_0 with respect to u and s and $\mathfrak{T}$ is satisfactory for Γ_1 with respect to u and s. Accordingly we set up a relation ~ between continuations by stipulating that when θ_0 and θ_1 are members of C $\theta_0\sim\theta_1$ if and only if $\theta_0\sigma=\theta_1\sigma$ whenever σ is a store for which $s\sigma=true$; the required condition can now be expressed as the supposition that $\mathcal{C}[\![\Gamma_0]\!]\rho\theta_0\sim\mathcal{C}[\![\Gamma_0]\!]\rho\theta_0$ and $\mathcal{C}[\![\Gamma_1]\!]\rho\theta_0\sim\mathcal{C}[\![\Gamma_1]\!]\rho\theta_1$ whenever ρ, θ_0 and θ_1 are chosen in such a manner that $u\rho=true$ and $\theta_0\sim\theta_1$. When showing that this supposition is what we need, we take Ψ to be any claim and ρ to be any environment for which $u\rho=true$. Evidently

$\mathcal{V}[\![\mathfrak{t}[\![\Gamma_1]\!][\![\Psi]\!]]\!]\rho\sim\mathcal{C}[\![\Gamma_1]\!]\rho(\mathcal{V}[\![\Psi]\!]\rho)$

(since $\mathfrak{t}$ is satisfactory for Γ_1 with respect to u and s), so

$\mathcal{C}[\![\Gamma_0]\!]\rho(\mathcal{V}[\![\mathfrak{t}[\![\Gamma_1]\!][\![\Psi]\!]]\!]\rho)\sim\mathcal{C}[\![\Gamma_0]\!]\rho(\mathcal{C}[\![\Gamma_1]\!]\rho(\mathcal{V}[\![\Psi]\!]\rho))$;

however, as $\mathfrak{t}$ is satisfactory for Γ_1 with respect to u and s we also know that

$\mathcal{V}[\![\mathfrak{t}[\![\Gamma_0]\!][\![\mathfrak{t}[\![\Gamma_1]\!][\![\Psi]\!]]\!]]\!]\rho\sim\mathcal{C}[\![\Gamma_0]\!]\rho(\mathcal{V}[\![\mathfrak{t}[\![\Gamma_1]\!][\![\Psi]\!]]\!]\rho)$,

whilst

$\mathcal{V}[\![\mathfrak{t}[\![\Gamma_0;\Gamma_1]\!][\![\Psi]\!]]\!]\rho=\mathcal{V}[\![\mathfrak{t}[\![\Gamma_0]\!][\![\mathfrak{t}[\![\Gamma_1]\!][\![\Psi]\!]]\!]]\!]\rho$

and

$\mathcal{C}[\![\Gamma_0]\!]\rho(\mathcal{C}[\![\Gamma_1]\!]\rho(\mathcal{V}[\![\Psi]\!]\rho))=\mathcal{C}[\![\Gamma_0;\Gamma_1]\!]\rho(\mathcal{V}[\![\Psi]\!]\rho)$

according to the definitions. Hence the transitive nature of $\sim$ ensures that for any Ψ

$\mathcal{V}[\![\mathfrak{t}[\![\Gamma_0;\Gamma_1]\!][\![\Psi]\!]]\!]\rho\sim\mathcal{C}[\![\Gamma_0;\Gamma_1]\!]\rho(\mathcal{V}[\![\Psi]\!]\rho)$

whenever $u\rho=true$, and we may conclude that $\mathfrak{t}$ is satisfactory for $\Gamma_0;\Gamma_1$ with respect to u and s.

Naturally for **if** E **do** Γ we let

$\mathfrak{t}[\![\textbf{if}\ \mathrm{E}\ \textbf{do}\ \Gamma]\!]=\lambda\Psi.(\Psi\wedge\sim\mathrm{E})\vee(\mathfrak{t}[\![\Gamma]\!][\![\Psi]\!]\wedge\mathrm{E})$.

If $\mathfrak{t}$ is satisfactory for Γ with respect to u and s then elementary manipulations show that $\mathfrak{t}$ is satisfactory for **if** E **do** Γ with respect to u and s so long as $\lambda\kappa.\mathcal{R}[\![\mathrm{E}]\!]\rho\kappa\sigma$ is $\lambda\kappa.\kappa\varepsilon\sigma$ (for some ε such that $\varepsilon|\mathrm{B}|\mathrm{T}$ is either *true* or *false*) whenever $u\rho=true$ and $s\sigma=true$.

When providing a predicate transformer for the loop **while** E **do** Γ we define a sequence of mappings, $\{\phi_n|n\geq0\}$, having $\phi_n\epsilon\mathrm{Cla}\to\mathrm{Cla}$ for each $n\geq0$; more specifically, we let $\phi_n=\lambda\Psi.\mathrm{false}$ and, when $n\geq0$, $\phi_{n+1}=\lambda\Psi.(\Psi\wedge\sim\mathrm{E})\vee(\mathfrak{t}[\![\Gamma]\!][\![\phi_n[\![\Psi]\!]]\!]\wedge\mathrm{E})$. In addition we at last introduce an infinite disjunction by letting

$\mathfrak{t}[\![\textbf{while}\ \mathrm{E}\ \textbf{do}\ \Gamma]\!]=\lambda\Psi.\bigvee\{\phi_n[\![\Psi]\!]\,|\,n\geq0\}$.

Of course we assume that $\mathfrak{t}$ is satisfactory for Γ with respect to u and s and that $\lambda\kappa.\mathcal{R}[\![\mathrm{E}]\!]\rho\kappa\sigma$ is $\lambda\kappa.\kappa\varepsilon\sigma$ (for some ε such that $\varepsilon|\mathrm{B}|\mathrm{T}$ is either *true* or *false*) whenever $u\rho$=*true* and $s\sigma$=*true*. In addition we introduce a relation ~ such that, for any θ_0 and θ_1, $\theta_0 \sim \theta_1$ if and only if $\theta_0\sigma=\theta_1\sigma$ whenever σ is a store for which $s\sigma$=*true*; in terms of this relation we stipulate that $\mathfrak{C}[\![\Gamma]\!]\rho\theta_0 \sim \mathfrak{C}[\![\Gamma]\!]\rho\theta_1$ whenever ρ, θ_0 and θ_1 are selected so that $u\rho$=*true* and $\theta_0 \sim \theta_1$. Under these circumstances we may prove that $\mathfrak{t}$ is satisfactory for **while** E **do** Γ with respect to *u* and *s* as follows. We choose any claim Ψ and any environment ρ for which $u\rho$=*true* and we set $\psi=\lambda\theta.\mathfrak{R}[\![E]\!]\rho(test\langle\mathfrak{C}[\![\Gamma]\!]\rho\theta,\mathcal{V}[\![\Psi]\!]\rho\rangle)$. By induction on *n* we can demonstrate that for all $n \geq 0$

$\mathcal{V}[\![\phi_n[\![\Psi]\!]]\!]\rho \sim \psi^n(\lambda\sigma.false)$,

so, whenever $s\sigma$=*true*,

$\bigvee\{\mathcal{V}[\![\phi_n[\![\Psi]\!]]\!]\rho\sigma \mid n \geq 0\} = \bigvee\{\psi^n(\lambda\sigma.false)\sigma \mid n \geq 0\}$;

moreover, according to the definition given above,

$\mathcal{V}[\![\bigvee\{\phi_n[\![\Psi]\!] \mid n \geq 0\}]\!]\rho\sigma = \bigvee\{\mathcal{V}[\![\phi_n[\![\Psi]\!]]\!]\rho\sigma \mid n \geq 0\}$,

whilst, as $\lambda\sigma.false$ is the least element of C,

$\bigvee\{\psi^n(\lambda\sigma.false)\sigma \mid n \geq 0\} = \mathfrak{C}[\![\textbf{while } E \textbf{ do } \Gamma]\!]\rho(\mathcal{V}[\![\Psi]\!]\rho)\sigma$.

Hence for every ρ and σ such that $u\rho$=*true* and $s\sigma$=*true*

$\mathcal{V}[\![\bigvee\{\phi_n[\![\Psi]\!] \mid n \geq 0\}]\!]\rho\sigma = \mathfrak{C}[\![\textbf{while } E \textbf{ do } \Gamma]\!]\rho(\mathcal{V}[\![\Psi]\!]\rho)\sigma$,

and we may assert that $\mathfrak{t}$ is satisfactory for **while** E **do** Γ with respect to *u* and *s*.

We could perform similar verifications for "guarded commands", but instead we shall move on to another topic - how to associate a predicate transformer with the sequencer **goto** I. In order to do this we take $\mathfrak{t}$ to be a member not of **Com→Cla→Cla** but of **Com→Cla→(Ide→Cla*)→Cla**, where the members of **Ide→Cla*** provide correspondences between identifiers and claims. The use of **Ide→Cla*** instead of **Ide→Cla** is designed merely to allow us to adapt our notation for environments (proposed in 3.3.3) to the present situation: when ψ is a typical member of **Ide→Cla***, when I* is in **Ide*** and when Ψ* is in **Cla***, we take ψ[Ψ*/I*] to be the member of **Ide→Cla*** obtained by extending ψ so that I*↓ν corresponds with $\Psi^*\downarrow\nu$ when $\#\mathrm{I}^*\geq\nu\geq 0$. We now view $\mathfrak{t}$ as being satisfactory for Γ with respect to u and s if and only if for every claim Ψ

$\mathfrak{V}\llbracket\mathfrak{t}\llbracket\Gamma\rrbracket\llbracket\Psi\rrbracket\psi\rrbracket\rho\sigma_0=\mathfrak{C}\llbracket\Gamma\rrbracket\rho(\mathfrak{V}\llbracket\Psi\rrbracket\rho)\sigma_0$

whenever ρ, σ_0 and ψ are such that $u\rho=true$, $s\sigma_0=true$ and (for each I with $\rho\llbracket\mathrm{I}\rrbracket\downarrow 1\in\mathrm{J}$ and for each σ_1 with $s\sigma_1=true$) $\mathfrak{V}\llbracket\psi\llbracket\mathrm{I}\rrbracket\downarrow 1\rrbracket\rho\sigma_1=(\rho\llbracket\mathrm{I}\rrbracket\downarrow 1|\mathrm{J})\sigma_1$. The equations given for $\mathfrak{t}$ in earlier paragraphs carry across unchanged, except for the insertion of an extra argument, ψ, at suitable points, so that, for instance:

$\mathfrak{t}\llbracket\mathrm{I}:=\mathrm{E}\rrbracket=\lambda\Psi\psi.\Psi[\mathrm{E}/\mathrm{I}]$;

$\mathfrak{t}\llbracket\Gamma_0;\Gamma_1\rrbracket=\lambda\Psi\psi.\mathfrak{t}\llbracket\Gamma_0\rrbracket\llbracket\mathfrak{t}\llbracket\Gamma_1\rrbracket\llbracket\Psi\rrbracket\psi\rrbracket\psi$.

In addition we are now permitted to write

$\mathfrak{t}\llbracket\textbf{goto}\ \mathrm{I}\rrbracket=\lambda\Psi\psi.\psi\llbracket\mathrm{I}\rrbracket\downarrow 1$,

thereby illustrating how the predicate transformer for **goto** I simply disregards the claim supplied to it as an argument. To deal with **block** Γ we suppose that there exist mappings $\mathfrak{p}$ and $\mathfrak{q}$ in $\mathrm{Com}\to\mathrm{Cla}\to(\mathrm{Ide}\to\mathrm{Cla}^*)\to\mathrm{Cla}$ that enable us to list the claims appropriate to the labels set in commands, and we define a sequence of functions, $\{\phi_n|n\geq 0\}$, with $\phi_n\in\mathrm{Cla}\to(\mathrm{Ide}\to\mathrm{Cla}^*)\to(\mathrm{Ide}\to\mathrm{Cla}^*)$ by setting

$\phi_0=\lambda\Psi\psi.\psi[map(\lambda\mathrm{I}.\mathrm{false})(\mathfrak{J}\llbracket\Gamma\rrbracket\S\mathfrak{K}\llbracket\Gamma\rrbracket)/\mathfrak{J}\llbracket\Gamma\rrbracket\S\mathfrak{K}\llbracket\Gamma\rrbracket]$ and, when $n\geq 0$,

$\phi_{n+1}=\lambda\Psi\psi.\psi[\mathfrak{p}\llbracket\Gamma\rrbracket\llbracket\Psi\rrbracket(\phi_n\llbracket\Psi\rrbracket\psi)/\mathfrak{J}\llbracket\Gamma\rrbracket][\mathfrak{q}\llbracket\Gamma\rrbracket\llbracket\Psi\rrbracket(\phi_n\llbracket\Psi\rrbracket\psi)/\mathfrak{K}\llbracket\Gamma\rrbracket]$;

after introducing ϕ_∞, a member of $\mathrm{Cla}\to(\mathrm{Ide}\to\mathrm{Cla}^*)\to(\mathrm{Ide}\to\mathrm{Cla}^*)$ for which

$\phi_\infty=\lambda\Psi\psi.\psi[map(\lambda\mathrm{I}.\bigvee\{(\phi_n\llbracket\Psi\rrbracket\psi)\llbracket\mathrm{I}\rrbracket\downarrow 1|n\geq 0\})(\mathfrak{J}\llbracket\Gamma\rrbracket\S\mathfrak{K}\llbracket\Gamma\rrbracket)/\mathfrak{J}\llbracket\Gamma\rrbracket\S\mathfrak{K}\llbracket\Gamma\rrbracket]$, we can finally let

$\mathfrak{t}\llbracket\textbf{block}\ \Gamma\rrbracket=\lambda\Psi\psi.\mathfrak{t}\llbracket\Gamma\rrbracket\llbracket\Psi\rrbracket(\phi_\infty\llbracket\Psi\rrbracket\psi)$.

The mappings $\mathfrak{p}$ and $\mathfrak{q}$ resemble the valuations $\mathfrak{P}$ and $\mathfrak{Q}$ defined in appendix 1 (for in them Cla and Ide→Cla* play the roles allocated to C and U in appendix 1), so here we shall not define them but will simply remark that:

$\mathfrak{p}\llbracket\mathrm{I}:\Gamma\rrbracket=\lambda\Psi\psi.\langle\mathfrak{t}\llbracket\Gamma\rrbracket\llbracket\Psi\rrbracket\psi\rangle\S\mathfrak{p}\llbracket\Gamma\rrbracket\llbracket\Psi\rrbracket\psi$;

$\mathfrak{q}\llbracket\mathrm{I}::\Gamma\rrbracket=\lambda\Psi\psi.\langle\mathfrak{t}\llbracket\Gamma\rrbracket\llbracket\Psi\rrbracket\psi\rangle\S\mathfrak{q}\llbracket\Gamma\rrbracket\llbracket\Psi\rrbracket\psi$.

We shall leave for the reader the proof that $\mathfrak{t}$ is satisfactory for the commands goto I and block Γ with respect to suitable predicates defined on U and S.

The analogy between claims and continuations extends from commands to expressions and declarations: there are 'expression claims' and 'declaration claims', which provide post-conditions for expressions and declarations in the manner in which our present 'command claims' provide post-conditions for commands. As claims other than command claims are governed by rather untidy syntactic rules we shall not consider them here.

The verifications above could be modified somewhat if E and S were not complete lattices but partially ordered sets without any mention of $\top$, so that there would be no $\varepsilon \in E$ for which ε could be $\top$ or $\varepsilon|B|T$ could be $\top$. Under these circumstances, the definitions of $\mathcal{V}[\![E]\!]$ and $\mathcal{V}[\![\sim E]\!]$ could be simplified and the predicate s could be taken to be continuous when regarded as a mapping of S into T″; hence for any continuation θ in S→T″ the mapping $\lambda\sigma.\theta\sigma\wedge s\sigma$ could be taken to be a continuation in S→T″. Accordingly we would be able to view $\mathcal{c}$ as being satisfactory for Γ with respect to u and s if and only if

$\lambda\sigma.\mathcal{V}[\![\mathcal{c}[\![\Gamma]\!][\![\Psi]\!]\psi]\!]\rho\sigma\wedge s\sigma=\lambda\sigma.\mathcal{C}[\![\Gamma]\!]\rho(\lambda\sigma.\mathcal{V}[\![\Psi]\!]\rho\sigma\wedge s\sigma)\sigma\wedge s\sigma$

whenever ρ and ψ were such that $u\rho=true$ and, for every identifier I with $\rho[\![I]\!]\downarrow 1 \mathrm{E} J$, $\lambda\sigma.\mathcal{V}[\![\psi[\![I]\!]\downarrow 1]\!]\rho\sigma\wedge s\sigma=\lambda\sigma.(\rho[\![I]\!]\downarrow 1|J)\sigma\wedge s\sigma$. The modified verifications would be more elegant than those outlined above, because they would not require the use of the relation ~ between command continuations. This fact provides some support for replacing complete lattices by partially ordered sets in which every countable directed set has a least upper bound.

The answer domain, A, can now revert to being something other than T″. Never again in this book will we specify precisely what A must be, although occasionally we shall consider examples of what A could be and in 4.6.1 we shall even place constraints on the structure of A.

3.8. Restricted equivalences.

3.8.1. Possible forms of constraint.

Great generality has deliberately been provided in Sal; in particular, expressions may have side effects or even bring about jumps in the flow of control. Many practical programs, however, do not make use of this generality and therefore have interesting properties which are not shared by all Sal programs; for instance, of particular concern to people who wish to ban the use of labels are those expressions and blocks which give rise to no jumps.

Those equivalences which can be proved for certain special parts of programs in particular situations will be called 'restricted'. Their validity depends on constraining the semantics of programs in ways which will be our chief concern in this section. There are also syntactic constraints, which imply certain semantic ones, and it is these that a programmer will generally want to consider; they are, however, more elaborate in form than the semantic constraints for three reasons. Firstly, they often depend on the context and may be influenced by peculiar features of programs. Secondly, they are critically dependent on the details of the programming language; Sal has been devised principally to exhibit a wide range of semantic features, so a detailed examination of its syntactic constraints would not be in the spirit of this essay and might well be a waste of time. Finally, the correctness of syntactic constraints has to be established by a structural induction over the language. Accordingly we shall work in terms of semantic constraints.

To illustrate the need to restrict the stores supplied as arguments to valuations we shall consider the relation between the Sal commands (while $l \geq k$ do $(m:=m\times k;k:=k+1)$);$(k:=0;l:=0)$ and (while $l \geq k$ do $(m:=m\times l;l:=l-1)$);$(k:=0;l:=0)$, which we shall designate by Γ_4 and Γ_5 respectively. These commands can be embedded in expressions E_2 and E_3, which are k=1 and l=n inside block Γ_4 before m and k=1 and l=n inside block Γ_5 before m respectively; they thereby provide two methods of multiplying the value initially stored in the location denoted by m by the factorial of the value which is actually denoted by n (if that value is an integer), but the stores produced during the execution of Γ_4 differ from those produced during the execution of Γ_5 except at the beginning and end of the computation.

In order to establish the equivalence of E_2 and E_3 we try to apply 3.7.7 to Γ_4 and Γ_5 by substituting E_0 for $l \geq k$, Γ_0 for $(m{:=}m\times k;k{:=}k+1)$, Γ_1 for $(k{:=}0;l{:=}0)$, E_1 for $l \geq k$, Γ_2 for $(m{:=}m\times l;l{:=}l-1)$ and Γ_3 for $(k{:=}0;l{:=}0)$. When the operators $\geq$, $\times$ and $+$ are interpreted in the obvious ways we can show that if E_0 do (Γ_0;while true do fit 0) or Γ_1 is equivalent with if E_1 do (Γ_2;while true do fit 0) or Γ_3, since we have carefully made E_0 coincide with E_1 and Γ_1 coincide with Γ_3. However, as we shall now see, we are unable to verify that for an environment ρ $\mathfrak{C}[\![$if E_0 do (Γ_0;((if E_1 do Γ_2 or Γ_3);Γ)) or $\Gamma_1]\!]\rho$ equals $\mathfrak{C}[\![$if E_1 do (Γ_2;((if E_0 do Γ_1 or Γ_2);Γ)) or $\Gamma_3]\!]\rho$ for every command Γ even if k, l and m denote distinct locations in this environment. Under these circumstances we set $\alpha_0=\rho[\![k]\!]\downarrow 1|L$, $\alpha_1=\rho[\![l]\!]\downarrow 1|L$, $\alpha_2=\rho[\![m]\!]\downarrow 1|L$, $\beta_0=hold\alpha_0\sigma$, $\beta_1=hold\alpha_1\sigma$ and $\beta_2=hold\alpha_2\sigma$ for some store σ. We then observe that $\lambda\theta.\mathfrak{C}[\![$if E_0 do (Γ_0;((if E_1 do Γ_2 or Γ_3);Γ)) or $\Gamma_1]\!]\rho\theta\sigma$ is $\lambda\theta.\theta(update\alpha_0 0(update\alpha_1 0\sigma))$ if $\beta_0>\beta_1$, $\lambda\theta.\mathfrak{C}[\![\Gamma]\!]\rho\theta(update\alpha_0 0(update\alpha_1 0(update\alpha_2(\beta_2\times\beta_0)\sigma)))$ if $\beta_0+1>\beta_1\geq\beta_0$ and $\lambda\theta.\mathfrak{C}[\![\Gamma]\!]\rho\theta(update\alpha_0(\beta_0+1)(update\alpha_1(\beta_1-1)(update\alpha_2((\beta_2\times\beta_0)\times\beta_1)\sigma)))$ if $\beta_1\geq\beta_0+1$; however $\lambda\theta.\mathfrak{C}[\![$if E_1 do (Γ_2;((if E_0 do Γ_0 or Γ_1);Γ)) or $\Gamma_3]\!]\rho\theta\sigma$ is $\lambda\theta.\theta(update\alpha_0 0(update\alpha_1 0\sigma))$ if $\beta_0>\beta_1$, $\lambda\theta.\mathfrak{C}[\![\Gamma]\!]\rho\theta(update\alpha_0 0(update\alpha_1 0(update\alpha_2(\beta_2\times\beta_1)\sigma)))$ if $\beta_1\geq\beta_0>\beta_1-1$ and $\lambda\theta.\mathfrak{C}[\![\Gamma]\!]\rho\theta(update\alpha_0(\beta_0+1)(update\alpha_1(\beta_1-1)(update\alpha_2((\beta_2\times\beta_1)\times\beta_0)\sigma)))$

if $\beta_1-1\geq\beta_0$. These quantities are equal provided that $(\beta_2\times\beta_0)\times\beta_1=(\beta_2\times\beta_1)\times\beta_0$ and that if $\beta_0+1>\beta_1\geq\beta_0$ (or, in other words, if $\beta_1\geq\beta_0>\beta_1-1$) then $\beta_2\times\beta_0=\beta_2\times\beta_1$. The first of these conditions is satisfied, as multiplication is associative and commutative, but the second presents a difficulty: although the test $l\geq k$ eliminates the danger of trying to multiply entities which cannot be multiplied, it does nothing to ensure that β_0 and β_1 are integers rather than real numbers (for which $\beta_2\times\beta_0$ need not equal $\beta_2\times\beta_1$ if $\beta_0+1>\beta_1\geq\beta_0$).

To avoid this difficulty we could adopt one of three courses of action: we could replace $l\geq k$ by $(l\geq k)\wedge$isN$k\wedge$isNl, we could insist on the use of a language having static types (so the environment would indicate that α_0 and α_1 had to contain integers) or we could somehow constrain the stores involved in a version of 3.7.7. The first of these would make Γ_4 and Γ_5 even more artificial than at present, when they are already written implausibly in order to guarantee the equivalence of if E_0 do (Γ_0;while true do fit 0) or Γ_1 and if E_1 do (Γ_2;while true do fit 0) or Γ_3. The second would be satisfactory here but would be inadequate if we wished to relate two commands which computed the same results only when certain locations held not merely integers but positive integers. Hence we shall actually resort to the third course of action despite its reliance on the complicated symbolism which we shall discuss next. An account of how we handle Γ_4 and Γ_5 in terms of this symbolism will be presented in 3.8.4.

The treatment of restricted equivalences to be given hereafter may be fully comprehensible only to those who have a thorough grasp of the kinds of manipulations needed when proving elementary equivalences. However, it provides a useful (but inessential) preparation for 4.2.1, where we shall start to discuss congruences between different sorts of semantics.

3.8.2. Similarity.

Currently we are more interested in the equivalence of programs than we are in correctness, so we wish to analyse the effects of supplying stores σ_0 and σ_1 as arguments to two expressions which we hope to relate. The connection between these stores will be expressed by the equation $s\langle\sigma_0,\sigma_1\rangle=true$, where s is some predicate mapping S×S into the domain T′ described in 2.2.2; in the simplest cases, such as the equivalences mentioned in 3.6.3, $s\langle\sigma_0,\sigma_1\rangle$ will be *true* if and only if $\sigma_0=\sigma_1$, but we could demand, for example, that $s\langle\sigma_0,\sigma_1\rangle$ be *false* unless $hold\alpha_0\sigma_0$ and $hold\alpha_1\sigma_1$ are integers when α_0 and α_1 are certain locations. If θ_0 and θ_1 are command continuations belonging to S→A and if $s\langle\sigma_0,\sigma_1\rangle=true$ we might well want to establish that $\theta_0\sigma_0=\theta_1\sigma_1$ or even that $a\langle\theta_0\sigma_0,\theta_1\sigma_1\rangle=true$, where the predicate a (which maps A×A into T′) may conceivably not be the identity relation. For convenience we let

$s\to a=\lambda\langle\theta_0,\theta_1\rangle.\bigwedge\{a\langle\theta_0\sigma_0,\theta_1\sigma_1\rangle\mid s\langle\sigma_0,\sigma_1\rangle\}$,

so that $s\to a$ is a predicate such that $(s\to a)\langle\theta_0,\theta_1\rangle=true$ if and only if $a\langle\theta_0\sigma_0,\theta_1\sigma_1\rangle=true$ whenever $s\langle\sigma_0,\sigma_1\rangle=true$.

In general when x_0 and x_1 are any predicates which map a universal domain X into T′ we write

$x_0\to x_1=\lambda\chi.\bigwedge\{x_1\langle arrow(cross\chi\downarrow 1)(cross\chi'\downarrow 1),arrow(cross\chi\downarrow 2)(cross\chi'\downarrow 2)\rangle\mid x_0\chi'\}$;

this definition is simply a special case of that given in 2.5.5, but the properties discussed in 2.5.6 will not be required until 4.2.3. Just as $W_0\to W_1\to W_2$ is taken to be $W_0\to(W_1\to W_2)$ when W_0, W_1 and W_2 are domains so $x_0\to x_1\to x_2$ is taken to mean $x_0\to(x_1\to x_2)$; thus if, say, $(x_0\to x_1\to x_2)\langle\chi_0,\chi_1\rangle=true$ and $x_1\langle\chi_2,\chi_3\rangle=true$ then $(x_0\to x_2)\langle\lambda\chi.arrow(arrow\chi_0\chi)\chi_2,\lambda\chi.arrow(arrow\chi_1\chi)\chi_3\rangle=true$. In practice we shall of course deal not with explicit retractions of a universal domain but will adopt the usage mentioned in 2.4.3, so that *arrow* will not appear; consequently if, say, w_n is a predicate defined on $W_n \times W_n$ for $2 \geq n \geq 0$ then $w_0 \to w_1 \to w_2$ will be a predicate defined on $(W_0 \to W_1 \to W_2) \times (W_0 \to W_1 \to W_2)$ having $(w_0 \to w_2)\langle \lambda\omega.\omega_0\omega\omega_2, \lambda\omega.\omega_1\omega\omega_3\rangle = true$ whenever $(w_0 \to w_1 \to w_2)\langle \omega_0, \omega_1\rangle = true$ and $w_1\langle \omega_2, \omega_3\rangle = true$.

Any predicate defined on pairs of elements drawn from one domain will be denoted by a lower case Italic letter (possibly together with a subscript) which corresponds with the name given to the domain in appendix 1. In particular, e will map $E \times E$ into T', u will map $U \times U$ into T' and c will map $C \times C$ into T', so that $e \to c$ and $u \to c$ will be defined on $K \times K$ and $X \times X$ respectively; however, as we indicated in 2.3.1, we could express everything we wish to say about predicates in terms of certain subsets of domains.

We can now generalize the notion of equivalence which was introduced in 3.6.1. For any predicate q mapping $(U \to K \to C) \times (U \to K \to C)$ into T' we shall regard an expression E_0 as being 'LR-similar' to an expression E_1 under q if and only if $q\langle \mathcal{L}[\![E_0]\!], \mathcal{R}[\![E_1]\!]\rangle = true$. Evidently there are nine properties like that of being LR-similar (EE, EL, ER, LE, LL, LR, RE, RL and RR) but they are often connected with one another; if, for instance, q takes the form $u \to k \to c$ for some u, k and c such that $(k \to k)\langle lv, lv\rangle = true$ and $(k \to k)\langle rv, rv\rangle = true$ then whenever E_0 is EE-similar to E_1 under q it is also LL-similar and RR-similar to E_1 under q. Furthermore, if q is $(\lambda\langle \rho_0, \rho_1\rangle.(\rho_0 \equiv \rho_1)) \to (\lambda\langle \kappa_0, \kappa_1\rangle.(\kappa_0 \equiv \kappa_1)) \to (\lambda\langle \theta_0, \theta_1\rangle.(\theta_0 \equiv \theta_1))$, E_0 is EE-similar to E_1 under q precisely when it is equivalent with E_1.

Naturally we may speak of the similarity of other features of languages besides expressions. Thus when q maps $(U \to F) \times (U \to F)$ into T' an abstraction Φ_0 will be taken to be 'FF-similar' to an abstraction Φ_1 under q if and only if $q\langle \mathcal{H}[\![\Phi_0]\!], \mathcal{H}[\![\Phi_1]\!]\rangle = true$. Likewise when q maps $(U \to C) \times (U \to C)$ into T' a sequencer Σ_0 will be taken to be 'SS-similar' to a sequencer Σ_1 under q if and only if $q\langle \mathcal{S}[\![\Sigma_0]\!], \mathcal{S}[\![\Sigma_1]\!]\rangle = true$. There is an obvious parallel between these definitions and those in 3.6.1.

The notion of similarity appropriate to declarations closely resembles that appropriate to expressions: if q takes $(U\to X\to C)\times(U\to X\to C)$ into T' a declaration Δ_0 will be taken to be 'DT-similar' to a declaration Δ_1 under q if and only if $q\langle\mathfrak{D}[\![\Delta_0]\!],\mathfrak{T}[\![\Delta_1]\!]\rangle=true$. Two declarations may be similar in four main ways (DD, DT, TD and TT) but only two of these have practical significance. Also, when q maps Ide*×Ide* into T' Δ_0 will be 'II-similar' or 'HH-similar' to Δ_1 under q provided that $q\langle\mathfrak{I}[\![\Delta_0]\!],\mathfrak{I}[\![\Delta_1]\!]\rangle=true$ or $q\langle\mathfrak{H}[\![\Delta_0]\!],\mathfrak{H}[\![\Delta_1]\!]\rangle=true$.

When q is a predicate defined on $(U\to C\to C)\times(U\to C\to C)$ a block Θ_0 will be 'GG-similar' to a block Θ_1 under q if and only if $q\langle\mathfrak{G}[\![\Theta_0]\!],\mathfrak{G}[\![\Theta_1]\!]\rangle=true$, whereas a command Γ_0 will be 'CC-similar' to a command Γ_1 under q if and only if $q\langle\mathfrak{C}[\![\Gamma_0]\!],\mathfrak{C}[\![\Gamma_1]\!]\rangle=true$. Analogous definitions permit us to speak of Γ_0 as being 'PP-similar' or 'QQ-similar' to Γ_1 under q when q maps $(U\to C\to J^*)\times(U\to C\to J^*)$ into T' and to speak of Γ_0 as being 'JJ-similar' or 'KK-similar' to Γ_1 under q when q maps Ide*×Ide* into T'. We shall not deal with the mixed forms of similarity between declarations (IH and HI) and between commands (PQ, QP, IJ and JI) because analysing them in general involves store semantics, which will not be described until 4.1.2.

Suitable predicates would allow us to set up relations of similarity between expressions belonging to different languages, but we shall not discuss them as we are concerned with principles rather than details; instead we shall enumerate some results which refer to the standard semantics of Sal. When the predicates and parts of programs mentioned may be chosen arbitrarily we may assert that:

(i) if $(k\to c)\langle\mathfrak{B}[\![B_0]\!],\mathfrak{B}[\![B_1]\!]\rangle=true$ then B_0 is EE-similar to B_1 under $u\to k\to c$;

(ii) if E_0 is EE-similar to E_1 under $u\to k_1\to c$ and if $(k_0\to k_1)\langle\mathfrak{O}[\![O_0]\!],\mathfrak{O}[\![O_1]\!]\rangle=true$ then O_0E_0 is EE-similar to O_1E_1 under $u\to k_0\to c$;

(iii) if E_0 is EE-similar to E_2 under $u\to(e_0\to c)\to c$, if E_1 is

EE-similar to E_3 under $u\to(e_1\to c)\to c$ and if
$(k\to e_0\to e_1\to c)\langle\mathcal{W}[\![\Omega_0]\!],\mathcal{W}[\![\Omega_1]\!]\rangle=\mathit{true}$ then $E_0\Omega_0E_1$ is EE-similar
to $E_2\Omega_1E_3$ under $u\to k\to c$;

(iv) if E_0 is RR-similar to E_3 under $u\to(e\to c_1)\to c_0$, if E_1 is
EE-similar to E_4 under $u\to k\to c_1$, if E_2 is EE-similar to E_5
under $u\to k\to c_1$ and if
$(c_1\to c_1\to e\to c_1)\langle\lambda\theta'\theta''.\mathit{test}\langle\theta',\theta''\rangle,\lambda\theta'\theta''.\mathit{test}\langle\theta',\theta''\rangle\rangle=\mathit{true}$ then
$E_0?E_1!E_2$ is EE-similar with $E_3?E_4!E_5$ under $u\to k\to c_0$;

(v) if $(u\to e)\langle\lambda\rho.\rho[\![I_0]\!]\downarrow 1,\lambda\rho.\rho[\![I_1]\!]\downarrow 1\rangle=\mathit{true}$ or if
$(u\to(e\to c)\to c)\langle\lambda\rho.\rho[\![I_0]\!]\downarrow 1,\lambda\rho.\rho[\![I_1]\!]\downarrow 1\rangle=\mathit{true}$ then I_0 is EE-similar
to I_1 under $u\to(e\to c)\to c$;

(vi) if Φ_0 is FF-similar to Φ_1 under $u\to f$ and if $e\langle\phi_0,\phi_1\rangle=\mathit{true}$
whenever $f\langle\phi_0,\phi_1\rangle=\mathit{true}$ then Φ_0 is EE-similar to Φ_1 under
$u\to(e\to c)\to c$;

(vii) if E_0 is RR-similar to E_2 under $u\to(e_0\to c)\to c$, if E_1 is
EE-similar to E_3 under $u\to(e_1\to c\to c)$ and if
$(e_0\to e_1\to k\to c)\langle\xi,\xi\rangle=\mathit{true}$ (where $\xi=\lambda\varepsilon'\varepsilon''\kappa.(\varepsilon'\mathrm{E}\mathsf{F}\to(\varepsilon'|\mathsf{F})\varepsilon''\kappa,\mathit{wrong})$)
then E_0E_1 is EE-similar to E_2E_3 under $u\to k\to c$;

(viii) if Σ_0 is SS-similar to Σ_1 under $u\to c$ then Σ_0 is EE-similar to
Σ_1 under $u\to k\to c$;

(ix) if E_0 is EE-similar to E_1 under $u_1\to k\to c$ and if
$u_1=\lambda\langle\rho_0,\rho_1\rangle.u_0\langle\mathit{chop}[\![\mathsf{res}\ 0]\!]\rho_0,\mathit{chop}[\![\mathsf{res}\ 0]\!]\rho_1\rangle\wedge k\langle\rho_0[\![\mathsf{res}]\!]\downarrow 1,\rho_1[\![\mathsf{res}]\!]\downarrow 1\rangle$
then val E_0 is EE-similar to val E_1 under $u_0\to k\to c$;

(x) if E_0 is EE-similar to E_1 under $u_2\to k\to c_1$, if Δ_0 is DD-similar
to Δ_1 under $u_0\to((\lambda\langle\rho_0,\rho_1\rangle.u_1\langle\rho_0,\rho_1\rangle\wedge u_3\langle\rho_0,\rho_1\rangle)\to c_1)\to c_0$, if
$u_2=\lambda\langle\rho_0,\rho_1\rangle.u_0\langle\mathit{clip}[\![\Delta_0]\!]\rho_0,\mathit{clip}[\![\Delta_1]\!]\rho_1\rangle\wedge u_1\langle\mathit{slim}[\![\Delta_0]\!]\rho_0,\mathit{slim}[\![\Delta_1]\!]\rho_1\rangle$
and if $u_3=\lambda\langle\rho_0,\rho_1\rangle.\mathit{full}[\![\Delta_0]\!]\rho_0\wedge\mathit{full}[\![\Delta_1]\!]\rho_1$ then
Δ_0 inside E_0 is EE-similar to Δ_1 inside E_1 under
$u_0\to k\to c_0$;

(xi) if E_0 is EE-similar to E_1 under $u\to k\to c_1$ and if Θ is GG-similar to Θ_1 under $c_1 \to c_0$ then Θ_0 before E_0 is EE-similar to Θ_1 before E_1 under $u \to k \to c_0$;

(xii) if E_0 is EE-similar to E_1 under $u \to k \to c$ then (E_0) is EE-similar to (E_1) under $u \to k \to c$.

Equally banal assertions may be made about similar declarations blocks and commands, but we shall not bother to give them. Results somewhat akin to these are required for 4.3.9, so hints about how to verify (vii), for example, can be gleaned from 4.3.1. We shall pass over the pertinent proofs, observing only that the fact that every declaration is DD-similar to itself under $(\lambda\langle \rho_0, \rho_1\rangle . (\rho_0 \equiv \rho_1)) \to (u_3 \to (\lambda\langle \theta_0, \theta_1\rangle . (\theta_0 \equiv \theta_1))) \to (\lambda\langle \theta_0, \theta_1\rangle . (\theta_0 \equiv \theta_1))$ (where u_3 is defined as in (x)) may be used instead of 3.5.5 when proving 3.5.6.

Fortunately these results about similarity are not the only ones we can provide; others can be obtained by recalling the equivalence properties listed in 3.6.3 and by appealing to the relations to be discussed in 3.8.5 and 3.8.7. There are certain other simple constraints which sometimes ensure that parts of two programs are similar. For instance, when E is an expression and q is a predicate taking $(U \to K \to C) \times (U \to K \to C)$ into T′, E will be said to be 'without side effects' under q if $q\langle \mathcal{E}[\![E]\!], \lambda\rho\kappa\sigma.\kappa(\phi\rho\sigma)\sigma\rangle = true$ for some $\phi \in U \to S \to E$ and to be 'without store dependence' under q if $q\langle \mathcal{E}[\![E]\!], \lambda\rho\kappa\sigma.\mathcal{E}[\![E]\!]\rho(\lambda\varepsilon'\sigma'.\kappa\varepsilon'\sigma)(empty)\rangle = true$ (where $empty$ is defined as in 3.3.2); plainly an abstraction is without side effects and without store dependence under $(\lambda\langle \rho_0, \rho_1\rangle . (\rho_0 \equiv \rho_1)) \to ((\lambda\langle \varepsilon_0, \varepsilon_1\rangle . (\varepsilon_0 \equiv \varepsilon_1)) \to c) \to c$ whenever c is a predicate mapping $C \times C$ into T′. We shall discuss expressions which do not give rise to jumps in 3.9.1; among them will be the expressions without side effects. After 3.9.4 we shall be especially concerned with declarations without side effects and without store dependence.

3.8.3. Some useful properties of least fixed points.

It should be evident that often the commands which we wish to relate contain while loops and the appropriate proofs depend on the properties of *fix*. However, whereas the results mentioned in 3.6.3 and 3.7.3 concern equivalent commands (and therefore the equality of fixed points) those of interest to us here deal with similar commands, which generate distinct fixed points that nonetheless resemble one another. Consequently some obvious propositions about *fix* have to be cast in an unconventional mould before they can be of use to us.

In order to modify these propositions we introduce complete lattices W_0 and W_1 on both of which are defined relations written as $\sim$, and we suppose that these relations become inclusive when viewed in the natural way as mappings of $W_0 \times W_0$ and $W_1 \times W_1$ into T'. When $\psi_0 \in W_0 \to W_0$, $\psi_1 \in W_0 \to W_0$, $\psi_2 \in W_1 \to W_1$ and $\psi_3 \in W_1 \to W_0$ are four continuous functions we recall the adjective "transitive" from 2.2.1 and claim that:

(i) if $\bot \sim \bot$ in W_0 and if $\psi_0 \omega_0 \sim \psi_1 \omega_1$ for every $\omega_0 \in W_0$ and every $\omega_1 \in W_0$ having $\omega_0 \sim \omega_1$, then $fix\psi_0 \sim fix\psi_1$;

(ii) if $\bot \sim \bot$ in both W_0 and W_1, if $\psi_1 \bot \sim \psi_3 \bot$, if $\psi_0 \omega_0 \sim \psi_0 \omega_1$ and $\psi_1(\psi_0 \omega_0) \sim \psi_0(\psi_1 \omega_1)$ for every $\omega_0 \in W_0$ and every $\omega_1 \in W_0$ having $\omega_0 \sim \omega_1$, and if $\psi_2 \omega_2 \sim \psi_2 \omega_2$ and $\psi_0(\psi_3 \omega_2) \sim \psi_3(\psi_2 \omega_2)$ for every $\omega_2 \in W_1$ having $\omega_2 \sim \omega_2$, then $\psi_1(fix\psi_0) \sim \psi_3(fix\psi_2)$ provided that $\sim$ is transitive on W_0;

(iii) if $\bot \sim \bot$ in W_0, if $\psi_0 \bot \sim \psi_1 \bot$, and if $\psi_0 \omega_0 \sim \psi_0 \omega_1$, $\psi_1 \omega_0 \sim \psi_1 \omega_1$ and $\psi_0(\psi_1 \omega_1) \sim \psi_1(\psi_0 \omega_0)$ for every $\omega_0 \in W_0$ and every $\omega_1 \in W_0$ having $\omega_0 \sim \omega_1$, then $fix\psi_0 \sim fix\psi_1$ provided that $\sim$ is transitive on W_0.

Each of these three claims can be established by forming a continuous function ψ and an inclusive predicate ϕ to which the induction principle of 2.3.2 may be applied. In the case of (i) ψ and ϕ are defined on $W_0 \times W_0$ as $\lambda\langle \omega_0, \omega_1 \rangle . \langle \psi_0 \omega_0, \psi_1 \omega_1 \rangle$ and $\lambda\langle \omega_0, \omega_1 \rangle . (\omega_0 \sim \omega_1)$

respectively, whilst in the case of (ii) ψ and ϕ are defined on $W_0 \times W_1$ as $\lambda\langle\omega_0,\omega_1\rangle.\langle\psi_0\omega_0,\psi_2\omega_1\rangle$ and $\lambda\langle\omega_0,\omega_1\rangle.(\omega_0\sim\omega_0)\wedge(\omega_1\sim\omega_1)\wedge(\psi_1\omega_0\sim\psi_3\omega_1)$ respectively. The most striking claim is the third, which we shall investigate in detail by setting $\psi=\lambda\langle\omega_0,\omega_1\rangle.\langle\psi_0\omega_0,\psi_1\omega_1\rangle$ and $\phi=\lambda\langle\omega_0,\omega_1\rangle.(\omega_0\sim\omega_1)\wedge(\psi_0\omega_0\sim\psi_1\omega_1)$. For this choice of ψ and ϕ it is plain that $\phi\langle\perp,\perp\rangle=true$; moreover if $\langle\omega_0,\omega_1\rangle$ is any pair for which $\phi\langle\omega_0,\omega_1\rangle=true$ then $\psi_0(\psi_0\omega_0)\sim\psi_0(\psi_1\omega_1)$ and $\psi_1(\psi_0\omega_0)\sim\psi_1(\psi_1\omega_1)$ since $\psi_0\omega_0\sim\psi_1\omega_1$, whereas $\psi_0(\psi_1\omega_1)\sim\psi_1(\psi_0\omega_0)$ (by virtue of our assumptions about ψ_0 and ψ_1), so $\psi_0(\psi_0\omega_0)\sim\psi_1(\psi_1\omega_1)$ and, since $\psi_0\omega_0\sim\psi_1\omega_1$, $\phi(\psi\langle\omega_0,\omega_1\rangle)=true$. Hence by induction $\phi(fix\psi)=true$; however, implicit in 2.3.9 is the knowledge that $fix\psi=\langle fix\psi_0,fix\psi_1\rangle$, so in fact $\phi\langle fix\psi_0,fix\psi_1\rangle=true$ and $fix\psi_0\sim fix\psi_1$.

When (iii) is used we often know that the relation $\sim$ defined on W_0 is 'symmetric', in that if $\omega_0\in W_0$ and $\omega_1\in W_0$ are any elements for which $\omega_0\sim\omega_1$ then $\omega_1\sim\omega_0$. If $\sim$ is symmetric as well as transitive, $\omega_0\sim\omega_0$ whenever $\omega_0\in W_0$ is such that $\omega_0\sim\omega_1$ for some $\omega_1\in W_0$; if, in addition, $\psi_4\in W_0\to W_0$, $\psi_5\in W_0\to W_0$, $\psi_6\in W_0\to W_0$ and $\psi_7\in W_0\to W_0$ are continuous functions, $\psi_6(fix\psi_4)\sim\psi_7(fix\psi_5)$ provided that $\perp\sim\perp$, that $\psi_6\perp\sim\psi_7\perp$, that $\psi_6(\psi_4\perp)\sim\psi_7(\psi_5\perp)$ and that $\psi_4\omega_0\sim\psi_4\omega_1$, $\psi_5\omega_0\sim\psi_5\omega_1$, $\psi_4(\psi_5\omega_0)\sim\psi_5(\psi_4\omega_1)$, $\psi_4(\psi_6\omega_0)\sim\psi_6(\psi_4\omega_1)$ and $\psi_5(\psi_7\omega_0)\sim\psi_7(\psi_5\omega_1)$ whenever $\omega_0\sim\omega_1$.

If the relation $\sim$ given for W_0 is both symmetric and transitive it may be said to be 'restrictive', as in part it serves to sieve out certain elements of W_0 by comparing them with themselves. When $1\geq n\geq 0$, any predicate w_n mapping $W_n\times W_n$ into T' induces a relation $\sim$ such that for every $\omega_0\in W_n$ and every $\omega_1\in W_n$ $\omega_0\sim\omega_1$ if and only if $w_n\langle\omega_0,\omega_1\rangle=true$; we shall view w_n as being restrictive, symmetric, or transitive when the relation $\sim$ induced by w_n in this way is restrictive, symmetric, or transitive. Because we shall use several predicates having these attributes, here we shall not adopt the diacritical convention which was introduced in 2.5.4 in readiness for asymmetric situations, such as that of 4.2.1. The value of restrictive predicates is greatly increased by the fact that if w_0 and w_1 are restrictive then so is $w_0 \rightarrow w_1$; moreover, if w_1 is inclusive then so is $w_0 \rightarrow w_1$ and if $w_1\langle \bot,\bot\rangle = true$ then $(w_0 \rightarrow w_1)\langle \bot,\bot\rangle = true$.

In arguments involving **while** loops W_0 and W_1 are frequently taken to be C and K respectively and the two versions of ~ are induced by predicates c and k mapping C×C and K×K into T′. Thus (i) is required, for example, in the proof that **while** E_0 **do** Γ_0 is CC-similar to **while** E_1 **do** Γ_1 under $u \rightarrow c \rightarrow c$ provided that E_0 is RR-similar to E_1 under $u \rightarrow (e \rightarrow c) \rightarrow c$, Γ_0 is CC-similar to Γ_1 under $u \rightarrow c \rightarrow c$, $(c \rightarrow c \rightarrow e \rightarrow c)\langle \lambda\theta'\theta''.test\langle\theta',\theta''\rangle, \lambda\theta'\theta''.test\langle\theta',\theta''\rangle\rangle = true$, c is inclusive and $c\langle \bot,\bot\rangle = true$; only a special case of this will be established in the course of 3.8.8, but the general case can be analysed as easily. The second result above, (ii), will be applied twice in the course of 3.8.6, which will present the details of a complicated proof; for the benefit of those who are impatient, in the next paragraph we shall outline a rather unorthodox use of (ii). In 3.8.4 we shall return to the original motivation for this work and demonstrate how 3.7.7 can be generalized by applying (iii).

The proof which we shall now sketch indicates that **while** E **do** Γ can be regarded as a series of assignments when E and Γ are themselves composed of assignments. We suppose that there are functions $\psi_0 \in V^* \rightarrow T$, $\psi_1 \in V^* \rightarrow V^*$ and $\psi_2 \in V^* \rightarrow V^*$ and that there is a list of proper locations, α^*, for which

$(u \rightarrow (e \rightarrow s \rightarrow a) \rightarrow s \rightarrow a)\langle \mathcal{R}[\![E]\!], \lambda\rho\kappa\sigma.alter(\kappa(\psi_0(map(\lambda\alpha.hold\alpha\sigma)\alpha^*)))\alpha^*\psi_1\sigma\rangle = true$ and $(u \rightarrow (s \rightarrow a) \rightarrow s \rightarrow a)\langle \mathcal{C}[\![\Gamma]\!], \lambda\rho\theta.alter\theta\alpha^*\psi_2\rangle = true$ for predicates e, u, s and a, where $alter \in C \rightarrow L^* \rightarrow (V^* \rightarrow V^*) \rightarrow C$ is defined by the equation

$alter = \lambda\theta\alpha^*\psi\sigma.(\lambda\beta^*.\beta^* E V^* \rightarrow \theta(updates\alpha^*\beta^*\sigma), \bot)(\psi(map(\lambda\alpha.hold\alpha\sigma)\alpha^*))$.

Moreover we insist that if σ_1 is part of a pair $\langle\sigma_0,\sigma_1\rangle$ having $s\langle\sigma_0,\sigma_1\rangle = true$ then $\psi_1(map(\lambda\alpha.hold\alpha\sigma_1)\alpha^*)$ and $\psi_2(\psi_1(map(\lambda\alpha.hold\alpha\sigma_1)\alpha^*))$ are proper members of V*, with the consequence that

$\lambda\theta\psi.alter(alter\theta\alpha^*\psi)\alpha^*\psi_1\sigma_1=\lambda\theta\psi.alter\theta\alpha^*(\psi\circ\psi_1)\sigma_1$ and $\lambda\theta\psi.alter(alter\theta\alpha^*\psi)\alpha^*(\psi_2\circ\psi_1)\sigma_1=\lambda\theta\psi.alter\theta\alpha^*(\psi\circ\psi_2\circ\psi_1)\sigma_1$; we also require that if $s\langle\sigma_0,\sigma_1\rangle=true$ then there is some σ_2 for which $s\langle\sigma_2,updates\alpha^*(\psi_2(\psi_1(map(\lambda\alpha.hold\alpha\sigma_1)\alpha^*)))\sigma_1\rangle=true$. We now let $\phi_0=\lambda\rho\theta'\theta''.\mathcal{R}[\![E]\!]\rho(test\langle\mathcal{C}[\![\Gamma]\!]\rho\theta'',\theta'\rangle)$ and $\phi_1=\lambda\rho\theta'\theta''\sigma.(\psi_0(map(\lambda\alpha.hold\alpha\sigma)\alpha^*)\rightarrow alter\theta''\alpha^*(\psi_2\circ\psi_1)\sigma,alter\theta'\alpha^*\psi_1\sigma)$; clearly if $\langle\rho_0,\rho_1\rangle$ and $\langle\theta_0,\theta_1\rangle$ are chosen in such a manner that $u\langle\rho_0,\rho_1\rangle=true$ and $(s\rightarrow a)\langle\theta_0,\theta_1\rangle=true$ then $((s\rightarrow a)\rightarrow(s\rightarrow a))\langle\phi_0\rho_0\theta_0,\phi_1\rho_1\theta_1\rangle=true$ provided that $e\langle\varepsilon_0,\varepsilon_1\rangle=true$ only when either $\varepsilon_0=\varepsilon_1$ and $\varepsilon_0=true$ or $\varepsilon_0=\varepsilon_1$ and $\varepsilon_0=false$. Hence by assuming that a is inclusive and that $a\langle\bot,\bot\rangle=true$ (so that $s\rightarrow a$ is inclusive and $(s\rightarrow a)\langle\bot,\bot\rangle=true$) we may demonstrate with the aid of (i) that $(s\rightarrow a)\langle fix(\phi_0\rho_0\theta_0),fix(\phi_1\rho_1\theta_1)\rangle=true$; indeed $(u\rightarrow(s\rightarrow a)\rightarrow(s\rightarrow a))\langle\mathcal{C}[\![\texttt{while E do }\Gamma]\!],\lambda\rho\theta.fix(\phi_1\rho\theta)\rangle=true$. More than this is true, however, for if we define $\phi_2\in(V^*\rightarrow V^*)\rightarrow(V^*\rightarrow V^*)$ by setting $\phi_2=\lambda\psi\beta^*.(\psi_0\beta^*\rightarrow\psi(\psi_2(\psi_1\beta^*)),\psi_1\beta^*)$ then $(s\rightarrow a)\langle fix(\phi_0\rho_0\theta_0),alter\theta_1\alpha^*(fix\phi_2)\rangle=true$. To verify this we define a relation $\sim$ on C by demanding that $\theta_2\sim\theta_3$ if and only if $\theta_2\sigma_1=\theta_3\sigma_1$ whenever σ_1 is drawn from a pair $\langle\sigma_0,\sigma_1\rangle$ having $s\langle\sigma_0,\sigma_1\rangle=true$, and we note that we have merely to show that $fix(\phi_1\rho_1\theta_1)\sim alter\theta_1\alpha^*(fix\phi_2)$. Thus, recalling (ii), we take W_0 to be C and W_1 to be $V^*\rightarrow V^*$, on which the relation $\sim$ becomes the test for equality, and we make the functions ψ_0, ψ_1, ψ_2 and ψ_3 referred to in (ii) correspond with our present $\phi_1\rho_1\theta_1$, $\lambda\theta.\theta$, ϕ_2 and $alter\theta_1\alpha^*$. It is plain that we can be confident that $fix(\phi_1\rho_1\theta_1)\sim alter\theta_1\alpha^*(fix\phi_2)$ once we have verified that $\phi_1\rho_1\theta_1\theta_2\sim\phi_1\rho_1\theta_1\theta_3$ and $\phi_1\rho_1\theta_1(alter\theta_1\alpha^*\psi)\sim alter\theta_1\alpha^*(\phi_2\psi)$ for all θ_2 and θ_3 having $\theta_2\sim\theta_3$ and for all $\psi\in V^*\rightarrow V^*$; doing this is a mundane task which we shall leave to the reader along with much else. Consequently whenever $\langle\rho_0,\rho_1\rangle$, $\langle\theta_0,\theta_1\rangle$ and $\langle\sigma_0,\sigma_1\rangle$ satisfy the equations $u\langle\rho_0,\rho_1\rangle=true$, $(s\rightarrow a)\langle\theta_0,\theta_1\rangle=true$ and $s\langle\sigma_0,\sigma_1\rangle=true$ then

$a\langle fix(\phi_0\rho_0\theta_0)\sigma_0, alter\theta_1\alpha^*(fix\phi_2)\sigma_1\rangle = true$; in other words, $(u\rightarrow(s\rightarrow a)\rightarrow(s\rightarrow a))\langle\mathcal{C}[\![$while E do $\Gamma]\!], \lambda\rho\theta.alter\theta\alpha^*(fix\phi_2)\rangle = true$.

It is comforting to be able to establish this last equation, for it demonstrates that the semantics which we have adopted for **while** loops is intuitively satisfactory, in that the outcomes predicted by the semantic equations for loops formed from assignments coincide with what happens in practice unless the program fails to terminate; among the programs to which these remarks are relevant are all those to be discussed in 3.8.4 (and indeed most of the results to be mentioned there can be verified with the aid of the equations above). Further evidence for the satisfactory nature of our modelling of **while** loops will emerge later.

In 3.8.4 we shall give some further applications of the definitions provided in 3.8.2; they will include a generalization of 3.7.7 and yet another rule about the similarity of **while** loops, both of which will be illustrated by proofs about particular programs. Those who wish to avoid the confusing and intricate details of these proofs should try turning to 3.8.5. In fact the proofs are intended merely to demonstrate that standard semantics can be used to justify not only equivalences between members of classes of program (such as that between (fnI.E_1)E_0 and I=E_0 **inside** E_1) but also equivalences between individual programs. However, though equivalences of the former kind can easily be analysed in terms of semantic equations alone, equivalences of the latter kind are perhaps best established by first transforming the programs concerned with the aid of results like those listed in 3.6.3 and 3.7.3 and then applying correctness techniques; for instance, when establishing equivalences between the programs to be discussed in 3.8.4 we could make frequent appeals to the correctness result proved two paragraphs above. Likewise propositions about pieces of program that commute are best established by instantiating general results about representatives of classes of program; some such results will be mentioned in 3.8.5.

3.8.4. Illustrative examples.

As was hinted in 3.8.3, here we shall extend 3.7.7 in the manner required by 3.8.1. Accordingly we take E_0, Γ_0, Γ_1, E_1, Γ_2 and Γ_3 to be expressions and commands such that $c\langle\psi_0\bot,\psi_1\bot\rangle=true$, $(c\to c)\langle\psi_0,\psi_0\rangle=true$, $(c\to c)\langle\psi_1,\psi_1\rangle=true$ and $(c\to c)\langle\psi_0\circ\psi_1,\psi_1\circ\psi_0\rangle=true$ where $\psi_0=\lambda\theta'.\mathcal{R}[\![E_0]\!]\rho(test\langle\mathcal{C}[\![\Gamma_0]\!]\rho\theta',\mathcal{C}[\![\Gamma_1]\!]\rho\theta\rangle)$ and $\psi_1=\lambda\theta'.\mathcal{R}[\![E_1]\!]\rho(test\langle\mathcal{C}[\![\Gamma_2]\!]\rho\theta',\mathcal{C}[\![\Gamma_3]\!]\rho\theta\rangle)$ for some ρ and θ and for a certain predicate c; we also assume that c is restrictive and inclusive and that $c\langle\bot,\bot\rangle=true$. When $\langle\theta_0,\theta_1\rangle$ is any pair of continuations having $c\langle\theta_0,\theta_1\rangle=true$ we may safely claim that $c\langle\psi_0\theta_0,\psi_0\theta_1\rangle=true$, that $c\langle\psi_1\theta_0,\psi_1\theta_1\rangle=true$ and that $c\langle\psi_0(\psi_1\theta_1),\psi_1(\psi_0\theta_0)\rangle=true$ since c is symmetric. Moreover c is transitive, so when $\sim$ is the relation induced by c we may apply the third result listed in 3.8.3 and conclude that $fix\psi_0\sim fix\psi_1$ (or, in other words, that $c\langle fix\psi_0,fix\psi_1\rangle=true$); by translating this result into the terminology introduced in 3.8.2 we see that (while E_0 do Γ_0);Γ_1 is CC-similar to (while E_1 do Γ_2);Γ_3 under $u\to c_0\to c_1$ where the predicates u, c_0 and c_1 are given by the equations $u=\lambda\langle\rho_0,\rho_1\rangle.(\rho_0\equiv\rho)\wedge(\rho_1\equiv\rho)$, $c_0=\lambda\langle\theta_0,\theta_1\rangle.(\theta_0\equiv\theta)\wedge(\theta_1\equiv\theta)$ and $c_1=c$. We can express the equations $c\langle\bot,\bot\rangle=true$ and $c\langle\psi_0\bot,\psi_1\bot\rangle=true$ as the assertions that while true do fit 0 is CC-similar to while true do fit 0 under $u\to c_0\to c_1$ and that $\xi_0[\![$while true do fit 0$]\!]$ is CC-similar to $\xi_1[\![$while true do fit 0$]\!]$ under $u\to c_0\to c_1$ when ξ_0 and ξ_1 are defined as in 3.7.7; however, the other assumptions made above cannot readily be turned into relations of similarity. Nevertheless, were we to replace the induction rule given in 3.7.6 by one in which the inclusive predicate referred to pairs of commands rather than to individual commands, we could prove the following analogue of 3.7.7: if while true do fit 0, $\xi_0[\![$while true do fit 0$]\!]$, $\xi_0[\![\Gamma_8]\!]$, $\xi_1[\![\Gamma_8]\!]$ and $\xi_0[\![\xi_1[\![\Gamma_8]\!]]\!]$ are CC-similar to while true do fit 0, $\xi_1[\![$while true do fit 0$]\!]$, $\xi_0[\![\Gamma_9]\!]$, $\xi_1[\![\Gamma_9]\!]$ and $\xi_1[\![\xi_0[\![\Gamma_9]\!]]\!]$ (respectively) under $u\to c_0\to c_1$ whenever

Γ_8 is CC-similar to Γ_9 under $u \to c_0 \to c_1$ then (while E_0 do Γ_0);Γ_1 is CC-similar to (while E_1 do Γ_2);Γ_3 under $u \to c_0 \to c_1$. The premises of this result are, of course, slightly weaker than those of the one which we have just established, but, as we shall demonstrate in the next paragraph, in practice this is unimportant.

When Γ_4 is (while $l \geq k$ do $(m{:=}m \times k; k{:=}k+1)$);$(k{:=}0; l{:=}0)$ and Γ_5 is (while $l \geq k$ do $(m{:=}m \times l; l{:=}l-1)$);$(k{:=}0; l{:=}0)$ we can relate
$k=1$ and $l=n$ inside block Γ_4 before m to
$k=1$ and $l=n$ inside block Γ_5 before m as follows. We begin by viewing $\equiv$, $\geq$ and $>$ as mappings into T′ in the way outlined in 2.2.2 and by setting

$$\begin{aligned} u_0 = \lambda\langle\alpha_0,\alpha_1\rangle\langle\rho_0,\rho_1\rangle.(\rho_0 \equiv \rho_1) \\ \wedge(\#\rho_0[\![m]\!] > 0 \to (\rho_0[\![m]\!] \downarrow 1 \mathsf{E} \mathsf{L}), \mathit{true}) \\ \wedge(\#\rho_0[\![m]\!] > 0 \to \sim(\alpha_0 \equiv \rho_0[\![m]\!] \downarrow 1 | \mathsf{L}) \wedge \sim(\alpha_1 \equiv \rho_0[\![m]\!] \downarrow 1 | \mathsf{L}), \mathit{true}) \\ \wedge(\alpha_0 \equiv \rho_0[\![k]\!] \downarrow 1 | \mathsf{L}) \wedge (\alpha_1 \equiv \rho_0[\![l]\!] \downarrow 1 | \mathsf{L}) \wedge \sim(\alpha_0 \equiv \alpha_1), \end{aligned}$$

$$\begin{aligned} s_0 = \lambda\langle\alpha_0,\alpha_1\rangle\langle\sigma_0,\sigma_1\rangle.(\sigma_0 \equiv \sigma_1) \\ \wedge(\mathit{hold}\alpha_0\sigma_0 \mathsf{E} \mathsf{B} \to (\mathit{hold}\alpha_0\sigma_0 | \mathsf{B}) \mathsf{E} \mathsf{N}, \mathit{false}) \\ \wedge(\mathit{hold}\alpha_1\sigma_0 \mathsf{E} \mathsf{B} \to (\mathit{hold}\alpha_1\sigma_0 | \mathsf{B}) \mathsf{E} \mathsf{N}, \mathit{false}) \end{aligned}$$

and $c_0 = \lambda\langle\alpha_0,\alpha_1\rangle.s_0\langle\alpha_0,\alpha_1\rangle \to (\lambda\langle o_0,o_1\rangle.(o_0 \equiv o_1))$. When we fix the locations α_0 and α_1 we obtain predicates $u_0\langle\alpha_0,\alpha_1\rangle$, $s_0\langle\alpha_0,\alpha_1\rangle$ and $c_0\langle\alpha_0,\alpha_1\rangle$ defined on U×U, S×S and C×C respectively; we may therefore set $c_1 = c_0\langle\alpha_0,\alpha_1\rangle$ and observe that for any pair $\langle\theta_0,\theta_1\rangle$ $c_1\langle\theta_0,\theta_1\rangle = \mathit{true}$ if and only if $\theta_0\sigma_0 = \theta_1\sigma_1$ whenever $s_0\langle\alpha_0,\alpha_1\rangle\langle\sigma_0,\sigma_1\rangle = \mathit{true}$. Plainly c_1 is restrictive and inclusive, while $c_1\langle\bot,\bot\rangle = \mathit{true}$, $c_1\langle\top,\top\rangle = \mathit{true}$ and $c_1\langle \mathit{wrong},\mathit{wrong}\rangle = \mathit{true}$. If E_0 is $l \geq k$, Γ_0 is $(m{:=}m \times k, k{:=}k+1)$, Γ_1 is $(k{:=}0; l{:=}0)$, E_1 is $l \geq k$, Γ_2 is $(m{:=}m \times l; l{:=}l-1)$ and Γ_3 is $(k{:=}0; l{:=}0)$ it is clear that $c_1\langle\psi_0\bot,\psi_1\bot\rangle = \mathit{true}$, that $(c_1 \to c_1)\langle\psi_0,\psi_0\rangle = \mathit{true}$ and that $(c_1 \to c_1)\langle\psi_1,\psi_1\rangle = \mathit{true}$ when $\psi_0 = \lambda\theta'.\mathcal{R}[\![E_0]\!]\rho(\mathit{test}\langle\mathcal{C}[\![\Gamma_0]\!]\rho\theta',\mathcal{C}[\![\Gamma_1]\!]\rho\theta\rangle)$ and $\psi_1 = \lambda\theta'.\mathcal{R}[\![E_1]\!]\rho(\mathit{test}\langle\mathcal{C}[\![\Gamma_2]\!]\rho\theta',\mathcal{C}[\![\Gamma_3]\!]\rho\theta\rangle)$ for any ρ and θ having $u_0\langle\alpha_0,\alpha_1\rangle\langle\rho,\rho\rangle = \mathit{true}$. Moreover if $\langle\sigma_0,\sigma_1\rangle$ and $\langle\theta_0,\theta_1\rangle$ are such that $s_0\langle\alpha_0,\alpha_1\rangle\langle\sigma_0,\sigma_1\rangle = \mathit{true}$ and $c_1\langle\theta_0,\theta_1\rangle = \mathit{true}$ there is some pair $\langle\sigma_2,\sigma_3\rangle$ for which $s_0\langle\alpha_0,\alpha_1\rangle\langle\sigma_2,\sigma_3\rangle=true$ and for which $\langle\psi_0(\psi_1\theta_0)\sigma_0,\psi_1(\psi_0\theta_1)\sigma_1\rangle$ is $\langle\bot,\bot\rangle$, $\langle\top,\top\rangle$, $\langle wrong\sigma_2,wrong\sigma_3\rangle$, $\langle\theta\sigma_2,\theta\sigma_3\rangle$ or $\langle\theta_0\sigma_2,\theta_1\sigma_3\rangle$; consequently $(c_1\to c_1)\langle\psi_0\circ\psi_1,\psi_1\circ\psi_0\rangle=true$ and we may apply the result established above. This ensures that $c_1\langle fix\psi_0,fix\psi_1\rangle=true$ and therefore that $c_1\langle\mathcal{C}[\![\Gamma_4]\!]\rho\theta,\mathcal{C}[\![\Gamma_5]\!]\rho\theta\rangle=true$ for every ρ and θ such that $u_0\langle\alpha_0,\alpha_1\rangle\langle\rho,\rho\rangle=true$; in particular, if E_4 is block Γ_4 before m and E_5 is block Γ_5 before m then $c_1\langle\mathcal{E}[\![E_4]\!]\rho\kappa,\mathcal{E}[\![E_5]\!]\rho\kappa\rangle=true$ for every ρ and κ having $u_0\langle\alpha_0,\alpha_1\rangle\langle\rho,\rho\rangle=true$. Indeed because $u_0\langle\alpha_0,\alpha_1\rangle$ is symmetric and antisymmetric we may assert that E_4 is EE-similar to E_5 under $u_0\langle\alpha_0,\alpha_1\rangle\to(\lambda\langle\kappa_0,\kappa_1\rangle.(\kappa_0\equiv\kappa_1))\to c_0\langle\alpha_0,\alpha_1\rangle$. If we set up u_1 and x_0 by writing

$$u_1=\lambda\langle\rho_0,\rho_1\rangle.(\rho_0\equiv\rho_1)\wedge(\rho_0[\![m]\!]\downarrow 1\,E\,L)\wedge(\rho_0[\![n]\!]\downarrow 1\,E\,B\to(\rho_0[\![n]\!]\downarrow 1|B)\,E\,N,false)\text{ and}$$

$$\begin{aligned}x_0=\lambda\langle\chi_0,\chi_1\rangle.\bigwedge\{&c_0\langle\rho_0[\![k]\!]\downarrow 1|L,\rho_0[\![l]\!]\downarrow 1|L\rangle\langle\chi_0\rho_0,\chi_1\rho_1\rangle\\&|u_0\langle\rho_0[\![k]\!]\downarrow 1|L,\rho_0[\![l]\!]\downarrow 1|L\rangle\langle\rho_0,\rho_1\rangle\\&\wedge(\#\rho_0[\![m]\!]\equiv 0)\wedge(\#\rho_0[\![n]\!]\equiv 0)\wedge(\rho_0[\![k]\!]\downarrow 1\,E\,L)\wedge(\rho_0[\![l]\!]\downarrow 1\,E\,L)\}\end{aligned}$$

it becomes clear that because α_0 and α_1 may be varied at will we have actually demonstrated that $x_0\langle\lambda\rho'.\mathcal{E}[\![E_4]\!](divert\rho\rho')\kappa,\lambda\rho'.\mathcal{E}[\![E_5]\!](divert\rho\rho')\kappa\rangle=true$ for every ρ and κ for which $u_1\langle\rho,\rho\rangle=true$. Furthermore, the declaration k=1 and l=n is DD-similar to k=1 and l=n under $u_1\to x_0\to(\lambda\langle\theta_0,\theta_1\rangle.(\theta_0\equiv\theta_1))$, so in fact when $u_1\langle\rho,\rho\rangle=true$

$(x_0\to(\lambda\langle\theta_0,\theta_1\rangle.(\theta_0\equiv\theta_1)))\langle\mathcal{D}[\![k=1\text{ and }l=n]\!]\rho,\mathcal{D}[\![k=1\text{ and }l=n]\!]\rho\rangle=true$

and $(\lambda\langle\theta_0,\theta_1\rangle.(\theta_0\equiv\theta_1))\langle\mathcal{E}[\![E_2]\!]\rho\kappa,\mathcal{E}[\![E_3]\!]\rho\kappa\rangle=true$ where E_2 is k=1 and l=n inside E_4 and E_3 is k=1 and l=n inside E_5. Hence E_2 is EE-similar to E_3 under $u_1\to(\lambda\langle\kappa_0,\kappa_1\rangle.(\kappa_0\equiv\kappa_1))\to(\lambda\langle\theta_0,\theta_1\rangle.(\theta_0\equiv\theta_1))$, and we could even proceed to show that fn$n$..isNn?(m=1 inside E_2)!n is equivalent with fn$n$..isNn?(m=1 inside E_3)!n. Much the same analysis is suitable when n is not known to denote a location and the declaration k=1 and l=n is replaced by k=1 and l=\$$n$.

The example which we have just discussed can also be handled using another rule governing similarities between certain while loops.

In order to express this we introduce a predicate u (defined on $U \times U$), predicates s_0 and s_1 (defined on $S \times S$) and a predicate a (defined on $A \times A$), and we suppose that E_0 and E_1 are expressions for which there are functions $\phi_0 \in U \to S \to T$ and $\phi_1 \in U \to S \to T$ such that $\phi_0 \rho_0 \sigma_0$ and $\phi_1 \rho_1 \sigma_1$ are proper and equal while $\langle \mathcal{R}[\![E_0]\!] \rho_0 \kappa_0 \sigma_0, \mathcal{R}[\![E_1]\!] \rho_1 \kappa_1 \sigma_1 \rangle = \langle \kappa_0 (\phi_0 \rho_0 \sigma_0) \sigma_0, \kappa_1 (\phi_1 \rho_1 \sigma_1) \sigma_1 \rangle$ whenever $u \langle \rho_0, \rho_1 \rangle = true$, $(\lambda \langle \kappa_0, \kappa_1 \rangle . (\kappa_0 \equiv \kappa_1)) \langle \kappa_0, \kappa_1 \rangle = true$ and $s_0 \langle \sigma_0, \sigma_1 \rangle \vee s_1 \langle \sigma_0, \sigma_1 \rangle = true$. We now fix on one particular pair $\langle \rho_0, \rho_1 \rangle$ for which $u \langle \rho_0, \rho_1 \rangle = true$ and let $s_2 = \lambda \langle \sigma_0, \sigma_1 \rangle . (\phi_0 \rho_0 \sigma_0 \equiv true) \wedge (\phi_1 \rho_1 \sigma_1 \equiv true)$,
$c_0 = (\lambda \langle \sigma_0, \sigma_1 \rangle . s_0 \langle \sigma_0, \sigma_1 \rangle \wedge \sim s_2 \langle \sigma_0, \sigma_1 \rangle) \to a$,
$c_1 = (\lambda \langle \sigma_0, \sigma_1 \rangle . (s_0 \langle \sigma_0, \sigma_1 \rangle \wedge \sim s_2 \langle \sigma_0, \sigma_1 \rangle) \vee (s_1 \langle \sigma_0, \sigma_1 \rangle \wedge s_2 \langle \sigma_0, \sigma_1 \rangle)) \to a$ and
$c_2 = (\lambda \langle \sigma_0, \sigma_1 \rangle . s_1 \langle \sigma_0, \sigma_1 \rangle \wedge s_2 \langle \sigma_0, \sigma_1 \rangle) \to a$. When we assume that Γ_0 and Γ_1 are commands for which $(c_1 \to c_2) \langle \mathcal{C}[\![\Gamma_0]\!] \rho_0, \mathcal{C}[\![\Gamma_1]\!] \rho_1 \rangle = true$ we can prove that $(c_0 \to c_1) \langle \mathcal{C}[\![\texttt{while } E_0 \texttt{ do } \Gamma_0]\!] \rho_0, \mathcal{C}[\![\texttt{while } E_1 \texttt{ do } \Gamma_1]\!] \rho_1 \rangle = true$ provided that a is inclusive and $a \langle \bot, \bot \rangle = true$; in 3.7.8 we established a certain rule due to Hoare [31] which resembles this one, so we shall not describe the proof needed here beyond remarking that it involves one application of the first result listed in 3.8.3. A similar rule connecting `if` E_0 `do` Γ_0 to `if` E_1 `do` Γ_1 can also be established by following the approach outlined in 3.7.8.

We shall use our latest rule for `while` loops to relate k=1 `inside block ((while` $n \geq k$ `do` $(m:=m \times k; k:=k+1)$`);`k`:=0) before` m and $l=n$ `inside block while` $l \geq 1$ `do` $(m:=m \times l; l:=l-1)$ `before` m, which compute the factorial function less quaintly than the expressions considered before and which cannot be compared using a variant of 3.7.7. Evidently in this case we may presume that

$\phi_0 = \lambda \rho \sigma . ((\rho[\![n]\!] \downarrow 1 | B | N) \geq (hold(\rho[\![k]\!] \downarrow 1 | L) \sigma | B | N))$ and that

$\phi_1 = \lambda \rho \sigma . ((hold(\rho[\![l]\!] \downarrow 1 | L) \sigma | B | N) \geq 1)$. For convenience we let

$$\begin{aligned} u_3 = \lambda \langle \alpha_0, \alpha_1 \rangle \langle \nu_0, \nu_1 \rangle \langle \rho_0, \rho_1 \rangle . &(\alpha_0 \equiv \rho_0[\![k]\!] \downarrow 1 | L) \wedge (\alpha_1 \equiv \rho_0[\![m]\!] \downarrow 1 | L) \\ &\wedge (\alpha_0 \equiv \rho_1[\![l]\!] \downarrow 1 | L) \wedge (\alpha_1 \equiv \rho_1[\![m]\!] \downarrow 1 | L) \\ &\wedge (\nu_0 \equiv \rho_0[\![n]\!] \downarrow 1 | B | N) \wedge \sim(\alpha_0 \equiv \alpha_1), \end{aligned}$$

and, when $\psi\in N\to N$ is the factorial function defined by the equation

$\psi=\lambda\nu.((\nu=0)\to 1,\nu\times\psi(\nu-1))$,

rather informally we write

$$s_3=\lambda\langle\alpha_0,\alpha_1\rangle\langle\nu_0,\nu_1\rangle\langle\sigma_0,\sigma_1\rangle.(\sigma_0\equiv update\,\alpha_0(hold\,\alpha_0\sigma_0)(update\,\alpha_1(hold\,\alpha_1\sigma_0)\sigma_1))$$
$$\wedge((hold\,\alpha_0\sigma_0|B|N)+(hold\,\alpha_0\sigma_1|B|N)\equiv\nu_0+1)$$
$$\wedge((hold\,\alpha_1\sigma_0|B|N)\div\psi((hold\,\alpha_0\sigma_0|B|N)-1)\equiv\nu_1)$$
$$\wedge((hold\,\alpha_1\sigma_0|B|N)\times\psi(hold\,\alpha_0\sigma_1|B|N)\equiv\nu_1\times\psi\nu_0)$$
$$\wedge((hold\,\alpha_0\sigma_0|B|N)\geq 1).$$

Given two locations, α_0 and α_1, and two integers, ν_0 and ν_1, we can suppose that $\langle\rho_0,\rho_1\rangle$ is any pair for which $u_3\langle\alpha_0,\alpha_1\rangle\langle\nu_0,\nu_1\rangle\langle\rho_0,\rho_1\rangle=true$ and we can set $s_0=s_3\langle\alpha_0,\alpha_1\rangle\langle\nu_0,\nu_1\rangle$, $s_1=s_3\langle\alpha_0,\alpha_1\rangle\langle\nu_0,\nu_1\rangle$ and $s_2=\lambda\langle\sigma_0,\sigma_1\rangle.(\phi_0\rho_0\sigma_0\equiv true)\wedge(\phi_1\rho_1\sigma_1\equiv true)$. As $s_0=\lambda\langle\sigma_0,\sigma_1\rangle.(s_0\langle\sigma_0,\sigma_1\rangle\wedge\sim s_2\langle\sigma_0,\sigma_1\rangle)\vee(s_1\langle\sigma_0,\sigma_1\rangle\wedge s_2\langle\sigma_0,\sigma_1\rangle)$, when we provide a predicate a and define c_0, c_1 and c_2 in the manner proposed in the previous paragraph we know that $c_1=s_0\to a$; moreover, a simple calculation shows that

$(c_1\to c_2)\langle\mathfrak{C}[\![m:=m\times k;k:=k+1]\!]\rho_0,\mathfrak{C}[\![m:=m\times l;l:=l-1]\!]\rho_1\rangle=true$.

Consequently $(c_0\to c_1)\langle\mathfrak{C}[\![\Gamma_6]\!]\rho_0,\mathfrak{C}[\![\Gamma_7]\!]\rho_1\rangle=true$ where Γ_6 is while $n\geq k$ do $(m:=m\times k;k:=k+1)$ and Γ_7 is while $l\geq 1$ do $(m:=m\times l;l:=l-1)$, whilst it is plain that

$(((\lambda\langle\sigma_0,\sigma_1\rangle.(\sigma_0\equiv\sigma_1))\to a)\to c_0)\langle\mathfrak{C}[\![k:=0]\!]\rho_0,\mathfrak{C}[\![\text{fit }0]\!]\rho_1\rangle=true$; on combining these equations we see that

$(((\lambda\langle\varepsilon_0,\varepsilon_1\rangle.(\varepsilon_0\equiv\varepsilon_1))\to(\lambda\langle\sigma_0,\sigma_1\rangle.(\sigma_0\equiv\sigma_1))\to a)\to(s_0\to a))\langle\mathfrak{E}[\![E_6]\!]\rho_0,\mathfrak{E}[\![E_7]\!]\rho_1\rangle=true$

when E_6 is block $((\Gamma_6);k:=0)$ before m and E_7 is block Γ_7 before m. Because s_0 is independent of $\langle\rho_0,\rho_1\rangle$ we may therefore assert that E_6 is EE-similar to E_7 under

$u_3\langle\alpha_0,\alpha_1\rangle\langle\nu_0,\nu_1\rangle\to(\lambda\langle\kappa_0,\kappa_1\rangle.(\kappa_0\equiv\kappa_1))\to(s_3\langle\alpha_0,\alpha_1\rangle\langle\nu_0,\nu_1\rangle\to(\lambda\langle o_0,o_1\rangle.(o_0\equiv o_1)))$

(where we have chosen to make $a=\lambda\langle o_0,o_1\rangle.(o_0\equiv o_1)$ for brevity). We now let

$u_1=\lambda\langle\rho_0,\rho_1\rangle.(\rho_0\equiv\rho_1)\wedge(\rho_0[\![m]\!]\downarrow 1\in L)\wedge(\rho_0[\![n]\!]\downarrow 1\in B\to(\rho_0[\![n]\!]\downarrow 1|B)\in N,false)$

as before; in addition we write

$$x_1=\lambda\langle\alpha_1\rangle\langle\nu_0\rangle\langle\chi_0,\chi_1\rangle.\bigwedge\{\chi_0\rho_0\sigma_0\equiv\chi_1\rho_1\sigma_1$$
$$|u_3\langle\rho_0[\![k]\!]\downarrow 1|\mathsf{L},\alpha_1\rangle\langle\nu_0,hold\alpha_1\sigma_0|\mathsf{B}|\mathsf{N}\rangle\langle\rho_0,\rho_1\rangle$$
$$\wedge(\#\rho_0[\![m]\!]\equiv 0)\wedge(\#\rho_0[\![n]\!]\equiv 0)\wedge(\rho_0[\![k]\!]\downarrow 1\mathsf{E}\mathsf{L})$$
$$\wedge s_3\langle\rho_0[\![k]\!]\downarrow 1|\mathsf{L},\alpha_1\rangle\langle\nu_0,hold\alpha_1\sigma_0|\mathsf{B}|\mathsf{N}\rangle\langle\sigma_0,\sigma_1\rangle$$
$$\wedge(hold\alpha_1\sigma_0\equiv hold\alpha_1\sigma_1)\}.$$

and

$$c_4=\lambda\langle\alpha_1\rangle\langle\theta_0,\theta_1\rangle.\bigwedge\{\theta_0\sigma_0\equiv\theta_1\sigma_1|(\sigma_0\equiv\sigma_1)\wedge(hold\alpha_1\sigma_0\mathsf{E}\mathsf{B}\rightarrow(hold\alpha_1\sigma_0|\mathsf{B})\mathsf{E}\mathsf{N},false)\}.$$

Because we have shown that

$$x_1\langle\rho[\![m]\!]\downarrow 1|\mathsf{L}\rangle\langle\rho[\![n]\!]\downarrow 1|\mathsf{B}|\mathsf{N}\rangle\langle\lambda\rho'.\mathcal{E}[\![\mathrm{E}_6]\!](divert\rho\rho')\kappa,\lambda\rho'.\mathcal{E}[\![\mathrm{E}_7]\!](divert\rho\rho')\kappa\rangle=true$$

for every ρ and κ such that $u_1\langle\rho,\rho\rangle=true$, we may use the fact that

$$(x_1\langle\rho[\![m]\!]\downarrow 1|\mathsf{L}\rangle\langle\rho[\![n]\!]\downarrow 1|\mathsf{B}|\mathsf{N}\rangle\rightarrow c_4\langle\rho[\![m]\!]\downarrow 1|\mathsf{L}\rangle)\langle\mathcal{D}[\![k=1]\!]\rho,\mathcal{D}[\![l=n]\!]\rho\rangle=true$$

when $u_1\langle\rho,\rho\rangle=true$ to demonstrate that

$$c_4\langle\rho[\![m]\!]\downarrow 1|\mathsf{L}\rangle\langle\mathcal{E}[\![k=1\ \texttt{inside}\ \mathrm{E}_6]\!]\rho\kappa,\mathcal{E}[\![l=n\ \texttt{inside}\ \mathrm{E}_7]\!]\rho\kappa\rangle=true$$

for all ρ and κ having $u_1\langle\rho,\rho\rangle=true$. As in the case of our earlier example we could even verify that fn*n*..isN*n*?(*m*=1 inside *k*=1 inside E_6)!*n* is equivalent with fn*n*..isN*n*?(*m*=1 inside *l*=*n* inside E_7)!*n*.

The reader may enjoy designing a language in which the arrangements for discarding storage that is no longer needed make it possible to delete the assignment *k*:=1 from E_6 when establishing this equivalence. However, we shall now return to more abstract considerations which will, for instance, provide conditions under which (if E_0 do (while E_1 do Γ_1));(while E_0 do Γ_0) is equivalent with if E_0 do (if E_1 do ((while E_1 do Γ_1);Γ_0);(while E_0 do Γ_0)) for suitable expressions (E_0 and E_1) and for suitable commands (Γ_0 and Γ_1).

3.8.5. Commutativity.

Expressions E_0 and E_1 should be deemed to commute if evaluating E_0 before E_1 produces the same answer as evaluating E_1 before E_0. Plainly the implications of this intuitive notion of commutativity depend upon whether $\mathcal{E}$, $\mathcal{L}$ or $\mathcal{R}$ is used to evaluate E_0 and E_1. When q is a predicate mapping $(U\to(E\to E\to C)\to C)\times(U\to(E\to E\to C)\to C)$ into T' we shall therefore say that E_0 is 'LR-commutative' with E_1 under q if and only if $q\langle\lambda\rho\psi.\mathcal{L}[\![E_0]\!]\rho(\lambda\varepsilon'.\mathcal{R}[\![E_1]\!]\rho(\lambda\varepsilon''.\psi\varepsilon'\varepsilon'')),\lambda\rho\psi.\mathcal{R}[\![E_1]\!]\rho(\lambda\varepsilon''.\mathcal{L}[\![E_0]\!]\rho(\lambda\varepsilon'.\psi\varepsilon'\varepsilon''))\rangle=true$ when ψ represents a member of $E\to E\to C$. There are altogether nine properties akin to that of being LR-commutative (EE, EL, ER, LE, LL, LR, RE, RL and RR); harmless amusement may be obtained by trying to demonstrate that in Sal they are independent of one another provided that q is of the form $u\to(\lambda\langle\psi_0,\psi_1\rangle.(\psi_0\equiv\psi_1))\to(\lambda\langle\theta_0,\theta_1\rangle.(\theta_0\equiv\theta_1))$ for a suitable restrictive predicate u. The demands imposed by this sort of version of q are fairly severe, for if x is allowed by u to denote a location which initially contains 1 then x:=-x before \$$x$ is not XY-commutative with x:=-x before \$$x$ under this version of q when X and Y are any of E, L and R; moreover even 0 is not LL-commutative with 0 under this version of q, for if E_0 is a suitable store writing $\alpha_0=new\sigma_0$, $\sigma_1=update\alpha_0 0\sigma_0$, $\alpha_1=new\sigma_1$ and $\sigma_2=update\alpha_1 0\sigma_1$ shows that in Sal $\lambda\rho\psi.run\langle\mathcal{L}[\![0]\!]\rho,\mathcal{L}[\![0]\!]\rho\rangle\psi\sigma_0$ may be either $\lambda\rho\psi.\psi\alpha_0\alpha_1\sigma_2$ or $\lambda\rho\psi.\psi\alpha_1\alpha_0\sigma_2$. Were lv to be $\lambda\kappa\varepsilon.(\varepsilon\mathsf{E}L\to\kappa\varepsilon,wrong)$ such oddities as this would disappear, since $\lambda\rho\psi.run\langle\mathcal{L}[\![0]\!]\rho,\mathcal{L}[\![0]\!]\rho\rangle\psi\sigma_0$ would be $\lambda\rho\psi.wrong\sigma_0$ whatever the order in which run (defined as in 3.3.4) applied its arguments; however in practice it is often enough to know that 0 is LL-commutative with 0 under $u\to(\lambda\langle\psi_0,\psi_1\rangle.(\psi_0\equiv(\lambda\varepsilon'\varepsilon''.\psi_1\varepsilon''\varepsilon')))\to(\lambda\langle\theta_0,\theta_1\rangle.(\theta_0\equiv\theta_1))$.

There are conditions in which one abstraction could be taken to be 'FF-commutative' with another or in which one sequencer could be taken to be 'SS-commutative' with another, but they have no interest and will not be described. When q maps

$(U\to(U\to U\to C)\to C)\times(U\to(U\to U\to C)\to C)$ into T′ we shall view a declaration Δ_0 as being 'DT-commutative' with a declaration Δ_1 under q if and only if $q\langle\lambda\rho\psi.\mathfrak{D}[\![\Delta_0]\!]\rho(\lambda\rho'.\mathfrak{T}[\![\Delta_1]\!]\rho(\lambda\rho''.\psi\rho'\rho'')),\lambda\rho\psi.\mathfrak{T}[\![\Delta_1]\!]\rho(\lambda\rho''.\mathfrak{D}[\![\Delta_0]\!]\rho(\lambda\rho'.\psi\rho'\rho''))\rangle=\mathit{true}$ when ψ ranges over members of $U\to U\to C$. Of the four chief manners in which declarations may commute in Sal (DD, DT, TD and TT) only two are important in allowing us to interchange portions of and declarations.

When q takes $(U\to C\to C)\times(U\to C\to C)$ into T′ we shall speak of a block Θ_0 as being 'GG-commutative' with a block Θ_1 under q if and only if $q\langle\lambda\rho\theta.\mathfrak{G}[\![\Theta_0]\!]\rho(\mathfrak{G}[\![\Theta_1]\!]\rho\theta),\lambda\rho\theta.\mathfrak{G}[\![\Theta_1]\!]\rho(\mathfrak{G}[\![\Theta_0]\!]\rho\theta)\rangle=\mathit{true}$; likewise we shall speak of a command Γ_0 as being 'CC-commutative' with a command Γ_1 under q if and only if $q\langle\lambda\rho\theta.\mathfrak{C}[\![\Gamma_0]\!]\rho(\mathfrak{C}[\![\Gamma_1]\!]\rho\theta),\lambda\rho\theta.\mathfrak{C}[\![\Gamma_1]\!]\rho(\mathfrak{C}[\![\Gamma_0]\!]\rho\theta)\rangle=\mathit{true}$. An alternative to this form of commutativity would entail stipulating that $\Gamma_0;\Gamma_1$ be replaceable by $\Gamma_1;\Gamma_0$ in the sense discussed in 3.6.1.

We may wish to make an expression E commute with a declaration Δ, so when q is a predicate defined on $(U\to(E\to U\to C)\to C)\times(U\to(E\to U\to C)\to C)$ we shall take E to be 'ED-commutative' with Δ under q if and only if $q\langle\lambda\rho\psi.\mathfrak{E}[\![E]\!]\rho(\lambda\varepsilon.\mathfrak{D}[\![\Delta]\!]\rho(\lambda\rho'.\psi\varepsilon\rho')),\lambda\rho\psi.\mathfrak{D}[\![\Delta]\!]\rho(\lambda\rho'.\mathfrak{E}[\![E]\!]\rho(\lambda\varepsilon.\psi\varepsilon\rho'))\rangle=\mathit{true}$ where ψ is taken to be a typical member of $E\to U\to C$; evidently we can provide six definitions like this (ED, ET, LD, LT, RD and RT). Furthermore, when q maps $(U\to(E\to C)\to C)\times(U\to(E\to C)\to C)$ into T′ we shall say that E is 'EG-commutative' with a block Θ if and only if $q\langle\lambda\rho\kappa.\mathfrak{E}[\![E]\!]\rho(\lambda\varepsilon.\mathfrak{G}[\![\Theta]\!]\rho(\kappa\varepsilon)),\lambda\rho\kappa.\mathfrak{G}[\![\Theta]\!]\rho(\mathfrak{E}[\![E]\!]\rho\kappa)\rangle=\mathit{true}$ and that E is 'EC-commutative' with a command Γ if and only if $q\langle\lambda\rho\kappa.\mathfrak{E}[\![E]\!]\rho(\lambda\varepsilon.\mathfrak{C}[\![\Gamma]\!]\rho(\kappa\varepsilon)),\lambda\rho\kappa.\mathfrak{C}[\![\Gamma]\!]\rho(\mathfrak{E}[\![E]\!]\rho\kappa)\rangle=\mathit{true}$; naturally we can describe six terms in this fashion (EG, EC, LG, LC, RG and RC), and indeed we can even introduce four notions of commutativity for declarations and blocks or commands (DG, DC, TG and TC).

Several results about commutativity concern the ability to move a conditional expression or a while loop past other portions of programs. If, for example, E_0 is ER-commutative with E_1 under

$u \rightarrow (e_0 \rightarrow e_1 \rightarrow c_2) \rightarrow c_1$ whereas E_0 is EE-commutative with E_2 and E_3 under $u \rightarrow (e_0 \rightarrow e_2 \rightarrow c_0) \rightarrow c_2$ we might expect E_0 to be EE-commutative with $E_1 ? E_2 ! E_3$ under $u \rightarrow (e_0 \rightarrow e_2 \rightarrow c_0) \rightarrow c_1$; however our expectations would be fulfilled only if E_1 returned a truth value, as can be seen by taking E_0 to be res 0 and E_1 to be 0. To formalize what is meant by "returning a truth value" we shall say that a predicate e defined on E×E 'filters out truth values' when for any $\varepsilon_0 \in E$ and any $\varepsilon_1 \in E$ $e\langle \varepsilon_0, \varepsilon_1 \rangle = true$ only if either $\varepsilon_0 = \varepsilon_1$ and $\varepsilon_0 = true$ or $\varepsilon_0 = \varepsilon_1$ and $\varepsilon_0 = false$.

It is clear that if e filters out truth values then $(c \rightarrow c \rightarrow e \rightarrow c)\langle \lambda\theta'\theta''.test\langle \theta', \theta'' \rangle, \lambda\theta'\theta''.test\langle \theta', \theta'' \rangle \rangle = true$ for any predicate c mapping C×C into T'. Furthermore when γ_0 and γ_1 are members of K→C for which $((e_0 \rightarrow c_0) \rightarrow c_1)\langle \gamma_0, \gamma_1 \rangle = true$, when $(e_0 \rightarrow c_0)\langle \kappa_0, \kappa_1 \rangle = true$, when $(e_0 \rightarrow c_0)\langle \kappa_2, \kappa_3 \rangle = true$ and when $e_1\langle \varepsilon_0, \varepsilon_1 \rangle = true$ where e_1 filters out truth values, we know that $\langle \gamma_0(\lambda\varepsilon.test\langle \kappa_0\varepsilon, \kappa_2\varepsilon \rangle \varepsilon_0), test\langle \gamma_1\kappa_1, \gamma_1\kappa_3 \rangle \varepsilon_1 \rangle$ is either $\langle \gamma_0(\lambda\varepsilon.\kappa_0\varepsilon), \gamma_1\kappa_1 \rangle$ or $\langle \gamma_0(\lambda\varepsilon.\kappa_2\varepsilon), \gamma_1\kappa_3 \rangle$, so that $c_1\langle \gamma_0(\lambda\varepsilon.test\langle \kappa_0\varepsilon, \kappa_2\varepsilon \rangle \varepsilon_0), test\langle \gamma_1\kappa_1, \gamma_1\kappa_3 \rangle \varepsilon_1 \rangle = true$ and $(e_1 \rightarrow c_1)\langle \lambda\varepsilon'.\gamma_0(\lambda\varepsilon''.test\langle \kappa_0\varepsilon'', \kappa_2\varepsilon'' \rangle \varepsilon'), test\langle \gamma_1\kappa_1, \gamma_1\kappa_3 \rangle \rangle = true$; indeed $q\langle \lambda\gamma\kappa'\kappa''\varepsilon'.\gamma(\lambda\varepsilon''.test\langle \kappa\varepsilon'', \kappa\varepsilon'' \rangle \varepsilon'), \lambda\gamma\kappa'\kappa''.test\langle \gamma\kappa', \gamma\kappa'' \rangle \rangle = true$ where q is $((e_0 \rightarrow c_0) \rightarrow c_1) \rightarrow (e_0 \rightarrow c_0) \rightarrow (e_0 \rightarrow c_0) \rightarrow e_1 \rightarrow c_1$, provided that e_1 filters out truth values. This final equation is central to the proofs of results involving expressions which return truth values; naturally there are many such expressions, because several of the constants and operators available in Sal only pass truth values on to their continuations.

Some results about commutativity will be gathered below. They can all be established by simple means the more intricate of which are typified by the proof to be given in 3.8.6. Throughout any result X and Y are to be interpreted as E, L or R whilst U and V are to be interpreted as D or T; the predicates referred to will be any defined on the appropriate domains, so that u, for instance, will be an arbitrary mapping of U×U into T′. Accordingly (i), for example, indicates among other things that E_2 is LR-commutative with E_3 under $u\to(e_0\to e_1\to c)\to c$ when E_0 is LR-commutative with E_1 under $u\to(e_0\to e_1\to c)\to c$, E_0 is LL-similar to E_2 under $u\to(e_0\to c)\to c$, E_1 is RR-similar to E_3 under $u\to(e_1\to c)\to c$ and e_0, e_1, u and c are restrictive; results analogous to this particular one hold if E_0, E_1, E_2 and E_3 are replaced by four declarations, blocks or commands. More fully, we know that:

(i) if E_0 is XY-commutative with E_1 under $u\to(e_0\to e_1\to c)\to c$, if E_0 is XX-similar to E_2 under $u\to(e_0\to c)\to c$, if E_1 is YY-similar to E_3 under $u\to(e_1\to c)\to c$ and if e_0, e_1, u and c are restrictive then E_2 is XY-commutative with E_3 under $u\to(e_0\to e_1\to c)\to c$;

(ii) if E_0 is without side effects under $u\to(e_0\to c)\to c$, if E_1 is without side effects under $u\to(e_1\to c)\to c$ and if e_0, e_1, u and c are restrictive then E_0 is EE-commutative with E_1 under $u\to(e_0\to e_1\to c)\to c$;

(iii) if E_1 is without side effects under $u\to(e_0\to c)\to c$, if E_1 is without store dependence under $u\to(e_0\to c)\to c$ and if e_0, e_1, u and c are restrictive then E_0 is EX-commutative with E_1 under $u\to(e_0\to e_1\to c)\to c$;

(iv) if E_0 is XR-commutative with E_1 under $u\to(e_0\to e_1\to c_2)\to c_1$, if E_0 is XY-commutative with E_2 and E_3 under $u\to(e_0\to e_2\to c_0)\to c_2$, if E_0 is XX-similar to E_0 under $u\to(e_0\to c_2)\to c_2$, if E_1 is RR-similar to E_1 under $u\to(e_1\to c_2)\to c_1$, if E_2 and E_3 are XX-similar to E_2 and E_3 (respectively) under $u\to(e_2\to c_0)\to c_2$, if e_1 filters out truth values and if e_0, e_2, c_0, c_1 and c_2 are restrictive then E_0 is XY-commutative with $E_1?E_2!E_3$ under $u\to(e_0\to e_2\to c_0)\to c_1$;

(v) if E_0 is XY-commutative with E_1 under $u_2\to(e_0\to e_1\to c_0)\to c_2$, if E_0 is XD-commutative with Δ under $u_0\to(e_0\to u_1\to c_2)\to c_1$, if E_0 is XX-similar to E_0 under $u_0\to(e_0\to c_2)\to c_1$, if E_1 is YY-similar to E_1 under $u_2 \to (e_1 \to c_0) \to c_2$, if Δ is DD-similar to Δ under $u_0 \to (u_1 \to c_2) \to c_1$, if e_0, e_1, u_1, c_0, c_1 and c_2 are restrictive, if $u_2 = \lambda \langle \rho_0, \rho_1 \rangle . (u_0 \langle clip[\![\Delta]\!]\rho_0, clip[\![\Delta]\!]\rho_1 \rangle \wedge u_1 \langle slim[\![\Delta]\!]\rho_0, slim[\![\Delta]\!]\rho_1 \rangle)$ and if no member of $\mathfrak{I}[\![\Delta]\!] \S \mathfrak{H}[\![\Delta]\!]$ occurs free in E_0 then E_0 is XY-commutative with Δ inside E_1 under $u_0 \to (e_0 \to e_1 \to c_0) \to c_1$;

(vi) if E_0 is XY-commutative with E_1 under $u \to (e_0 \to e_1 \to c_0) \to c_2$, if E_0 is XG-commutative with Θ under $u \to (e_0 \to c_2) \to c_1$, if E_0 is XX-similar to E_0 under $u \to (e_0 \to c_2) \to c_2$, if E_1 is YY-similar to E_1 under $u \to (e_1 \to c_0) \to c_2$, if Θ is GG-similar to Θ under $u \to c_2 \to c_1$ and if e_0, e_1, c_0, c_1 and c_2 are restrictive then E_0 is XY-commutative with Θ before E_1 under $u \to (e_0 \to e_1 \to c_0) \to c_1$;

(vii) if E_0 is XL-commutative with E_1 under $u_0 \to (e_0 \to e_1 \to c_0) \to c_1$ and if $(e_1 \to u_1)\langle \lambda\varepsilon.arid[\varepsilon/I], \lambda\varepsilon.arid[\varepsilon/I] \rangle = true$ then E_0 is XD-commutative with I=E_1 under $u_0 \to (e_0 \to u_1 \to c_0) \to c_1$;

(viii) if E_0 is XR-commutative with E_1 under $u_0 \to (e_0 \to u_1 \to c_0) \to c_1$ and if $(e_1 \to u_1)\langle \lambda\varepsilon.arid[\varepsilon/I], \lambda\varepsilon.arid[\varepsilon/I] \rangle = true$ then E_0 is XU-commutative with I==E_1 under $u_0 \to (e_0 \to u_1 \to c_0) \to c_1$;

(ix) if E is XU-commutative with Δ_0 under $u_0 \to (e \to u_1 \to c) \to c$, if E is XU-commutative with Δ_1 under $u_0 \to (e \to u_2 \to c) \to c$, if E is XX-similar to E under $u_0 \to (e \to c) \to c$, if Δ_0 is UU-similar to Δ_0 under $u_0 \to (u_1 \to c) \to c$, if Δ_1 is UU-similar to Δ_1 under $u_0 \to (u_2 \to c) \to c$, if e, u_1, u_2 and c are restrictive, if $u_3 = \lambda \langle \rho_0, \rho_1 \rangle . (u_1 \langle slim[\![\Delta_0]\!]\rho_0, slim[\![\Delta_0]\!]\rho_1 \rangle \wedge u_2 \langle slim[\![\Delta_1]\!]\rho_0, slim[\![\Delta_1]\!]\rho_1 \rangle)$ and if $\mathfrak{I}[\![\Delta_0]\!] \S \mathfrak{H}[\![\Delta_0]\!]$ and $\mathfrak{I}[\![\Delta_1]\!] \S \mathfrak{H}[\![\Delta_1]\!]$ are disjoint, then E is XU-commutative with Δ_0 and Δ_1 under $u_0 \to (e \to u_3 \to c) \to c$;

(x) if E_0 is XE-commutative with E_1 under $u \to (e_0 \to e_1 \to c_0) \to c_1$ then E_0 is XG-commutative with fit E_1 under $u \to (e_0 \to c_0) \to c_1$;

(xi) if E_0 is EL-commutative with E_1 under $u \to (e_0 \to e_1 \to c_1) \to c_1$, if E_0 is ER-commutative with E_2 under $u \to (e_0 \to e_2 \to c_1) \to c_1$, if E_0 is EE-similar to E_0 under $u \to (e_0 \to c_1) \to c_1$, if E_1 is LL-similar to

E_1 under $u \to (e_1 \to c_1) \to c_1$, if E_2 is RR-similar to E_2 under $u \to (e_2 \to c_1) \to c_1$, if $(u \to (e_0 \to c_0) \to (e_1 \to e_2 \to c_1))\langle \xi_0, \xi_1 \rangle = \mathit{true}$ (where $\langle \xi_0, \xi_1 \rangle = \langle \lambda\rho\kappa\varepsilon'\varepsilon''.\mathscr{E}[\![E]\!]\rho(\lambda\varepsilon.\mathit{assign}(\kappa\varepsilon)\varepsilon'\varepsilon''), \lambda\rho\kappa.\mathit{assign}(\mathscr{E}[\![E]\!]\rho\kappa)\rangle$), if $(c_0 \to e_1 \to e_2 \to c_0)\langle \mathit{assign}, \mathit{assign}\rangle = \mathit{true}$, and if e_0, e_1, e_2, c_0 and c_1 are restrictive then E_0 is EG-commutative with $E_1 := E_2$ under $u \to (e_0 \to c_0) \to c_1$;

(xii) if E is XC-commutative with Γ_0 under $u \to (e \to c_2) \to c_1$, if E is XC-commutative with Γ_1 under $u \to (e \to c_0) \to c_2$, if E is XX-similar to E under $u \to (e \to c_2) \to c_2$, if Γ_0 is CC-similar to Γ_0 under $u \to c_2 \to c_1$, if Γ_1 is CC-similar to Γ_1 under $u \to c_0 \to c_2$ and if e, c_0, c_1 and c_2 are restrictive then E is XC-commutative with $\Gamma_0;\Gamma_1$ under $u \to (e \to c_0) \to c_1$;

(xiii) if E_0 is XR-commutative with E_1 under $u \to (e_0 \to e_1 \to c_0) \to c_1$, if E_0 is XC-commutative with Γ under $u \to (e_0 \to c_0) \to c_0$, if E_0 is XX-similar to E_0 under $u \to (e_0 \to c_0) \to c_0$, if E_1 is RR-similar to E_1 under $u \to (e_1 \to c_0) \to c_1$, if Γ is CC-similar to Γ under $u \to c_0 \to c_0$, if e_1 filters out truth values and if e_0, c_0 and c_1 are restrictive then E_0 is XC-commutative with **if** E_1 **do** Γ under $u \to (e_0 \to c_0) \to c_1$;

(xiv) if E_0 is XR-commutative with E_1 under $u \to (e_0 \to e_1 \to c) \to c$, if E_0 is XC-commutative with Γ under $u \to (e_0 \to c) \to c$, if E_0 is XC-commutative with **while true do fit 0** under $u \to (e_0 \to c) \to c$, if E_0 is XX-similar to E_0 under $u \to (e_0 \to c) \to c$, if E_1 is RR-similar to E_1 under $u \to (e_1 \to c) \to c$, if Γ is CC-similar to Γ under $u \to c \to c$, if e_0, e_1 and c are restrictive, if c is inclusive and if $c\langle \bot, \bot \rangle = \mathit{true}$ then E_0 is XC-commutative with **while** E_1 **do** Γ under $u \to (e_0 \to c) \to c$;

(xv) if E is XG-commutative with Θ under $u \to (e \to c) \to c$ then E is XC-commutative with Θ under $u \to (e \to c) \to c$.

With the exceptions of (i) and (ii) all these results have valid counterparts in which E_0 (or, in certain cases, E) is replaced by a declaration, a block or a command; moreover there are many other properties of commutativity which we have not bothered to list, such as those which govern when an expression commutes with function applications and with assorted kinds of declarations and blocks.

From these results we may obtain others; for instance, (vi) ensures that if E_0 and E_1 are LL-commutative under $u_0 \to (e_0 \to e_1 \to c_0) \to c_1$, if $(e_0 \to u_1)\langle \lambda\varepsilon.arid[\varepsilon/I_0], \lambda\varepsilon.arid[\varepsilon/I_0]\rangle = true$ and if $(e_1 \to u_2)\langle \lambda\varepsilon.arid[\varepsilon/I_1], \lambda\varepsilon.arid[\varepsilon/I_1]\rangle = true$ then $I=E_0$ and $I=E_1$ are DD-commutative under $u_0 \to (u_1 \to u_2 \to c_0) \to c_1$. In this connection the most interesting result is (xi), which the reader may use to provide general conditions under which two assignments commute.

Commutativity properties produce various results about similarity which will not be mentioned until 3.8.7 because they also involve the notion of idempotence. Here we shall merely remark that:

(i) if E is RR-similar to E under $u \to (e \to c_0) \to c_1$ and if e filters out truth values then fit $E is CC-similar to if E do fit 0 under $u \to (e \to c_0) \to c_1$;

(ii) if Γ is CC-commutative with while true do fit 0 under $u \to c \to c$, if Γ is CC-similar to Γ under $u \to c \to c$, if c is restrictive and inclusive and if $c\langle \bot, \bot\rangle = true$ then while true do Γ is CC-similar to while true do fit 0;

(iii) if Δ_0 is UU-commutative with Δ_1 under $u_0 \to (u_1 \to u_2 \to c_0) \to c_1$, if u_0, u_1, u_2, c_0 and c_1 are restrictive, if $u_3 = \lambda\langle \rho_0, \rho_1\rangle.(u_1\langle slim[\![\Delta_0]\!]\rho_0, slim[\![\Delta_0]\!]\rho_1\rangle \wedge u_2\langle slim[\![\Delta_1]\!]\rho_0, slim[\![\Delta_1]\!]\rho_1\rangle)$ and if $\mathfrak{I}[\![\Delta_0]\!]\S\mathfrak{K}[\![\Delta_0]\!]$ and $\mathfrak{I}[\![\Delta_1]\!]\S\mathfrak{K}[\![\Delta_1]\!]$ are disjoint then Δ_0 and Δ_1 is UU-similar to Δ_1 and Δ_0 under $u_0 \to (u_3 \to c_0) \to c_1$;

(iv) if Γ_0 is CC-commutative with Γ_1 under $u \to c_0 \to c_1$ then $\Gamma_0;\Gamma_1$ is CC-similar to $\Gamma_1;\Gamma_0$ under $u \to c_0 \to c_1$.

The interested reader will be able to find other results like these four before proceeding to the example proof to be given in 3.8.6.

3.8.6. Proposition.

Let E_0 and E_1 be Sal expressions and let Γ be a Sal command; suppose that for certain predicates e_0, e_1, u and c E_0 is ER-commutative with E_1 under $u\to(e_0\to e_1\to c)\to c$, E_0 is EC-commutative with Γ under $u\to(e_0\to c)\to c$, E_0 is EC-commutative with while true do fit 0 under $u\to(e_0\to c)\to c$, E_0 is EE-similar to E_0 under $u\to(e_0\to c)\to c$, E_1 is RR-similar to E_1 under $u\to(e_1\to c)\to c$, and Γ is CC-similar to Γ under $u\to c\to c$. Then E_0 is EC-commutative with while E_1 do Γ provided that e_0 is restrictive, e_1 filters out truth values, c is restrictive and inclusive and $c\langle\bot,\bot\rangle=true$.

◁In order to confirm that E_0 is EC-commutative with while E_1 do Γ under $u\to(e_0\to c)\to c$ we shall show that if $\langle\rho_0,\rho_1\rangle$ is chosen in such a way that $u\langle\rho_0,\rho_1\rangle=true$ then $((e_0\to c)\to c)\langle\lambda\kappa.\gamma_0(\lambda\varepsilon.fix(\phi_0(\kappa\varepsilon))),\lambda\kappa.fix(\phi_1(\gamma_1\kappa))\rangle=true$ where $\gamma_n=\mathcal{E}[\![E_0]\!]\rho_n$, $\xi_n=\lambda\theta'\theta''.test\langle\mathcal{C}[\![\Gamma]\!]\rho_n\theta'',\theta'\rangle$, $\gamma_{n+2}=\mathcal{R}[\![E_1]\!]\rho_n$ and $\phi_n=\lambda\theta'\theta''.\gamma_{n+2}(\xi_n\theta'\theta'')$ when $1\geq n\geq 0$. In the course of doing this we shall make two appeals to the second result about fixed points listed in 3.8.3 (and on both occasions W_0 will be C, W_1 will be K and ψ_1 will be $\lambda\theta.\theta$). One of these appeals will be complicated by the generality of our notions of similarity and commutativity; to clarify some of its details the reader may wish to consider the simple special case in which e_0, u and c are $\lambda\langle\varepsilon_0,\varepsilon_1\rangle.(\varepsilon_0\equiv\varepsilon_1)$, $\lambda\langle\rho_0,\rho_1\rangle.(\rho_0\equiv\rho_1)$ and $\lambda\langle\theta_0,\theta_1\rangle.(\theta_0\equiv\theta_1)$ respectively.

We begin by noting that for any κ_0, κ_1 and ε_0

$$\begin{aligned}\phi_0(\kappa_0\varepsilon_0)((\lambda\kappa.\kappa\varepsilon_0)\kappa_1)&=\phi_0(\kappa_0\varepsilon_0)(\kappa_1\varepsilon_0)\\&=(\lambda\kappa.\kappa\varepsilon_0)(\lambda\varepsilon.\phi_0(\kappa_0\varepsilon)(\kappa_1\varepsilon))\\&=(\lambda\kappa.\kappa\varepsilon_0)((\lambda\kappa\varepsilon.\phi_0(\kappa_0\varepsilon)(\kappa\varepsilon))\kappa_1).\end{aligned}$$

However, the second result in 3.8.3 assures us that, among other things, if $\psi_0\in C\to C$, $\psi_1\in C\to C$, $\psi_2\in K\to K$ and $\psi_3\in K\to C$ are such that $\psi_1\bot=\psi_3\bot$, $\psi_1(\psi_0\theta_0)=\psi_0(\psi_1\theta_0)$ and $\psi_0(\psi_3\kappa_1)=\psi_3(\psi_2\kappa_1)$ for all θ_0 and κ_1 then $\psi_1(fix\psi_0)=\psi_3(fix\psi_2)$. Hence by setting $\psi_0=\phi_0(\kappa_0\varepsilon_0)$, $\psi_1=\lambda\theta.\theta$,

$\psi_2=\lambda\kappa\varepsilon.\phi_0(\kappa_0\varepsilon)(\kappa\varepsilon)$ and $\psi_3=\lambda\kappa.\kappa\varepsilon_0$ we are able to infer that $fix(\phi_0(\kappa_0\varepsilon_0))=fix(\lambda\kappa\varepsilon.\phi_0(\kappa_0\varepsilon)(\kappa\varepsilon))\varepsilon_0$. This equation is valid for all κ_0 and ε_0, so $\lambda\varepsilon.fix(\phi_0(\kappa_0\varepsilon))=fix(\lambda\kappa\varepsilon.\phi_0(\kappa_0\varepsilon)(\kappa\varepsilon))$ and $\gamma_0(\lambda\varepsilon.fix(\phi_0(\kappa_0\varepsilon)))=\gamma_0(fix(\lambda\kappa\varepsilon.\phi_0(\kappa_0\varepsilon)(\kappa\varepsilon)))$ for all κ_0.

We can therefore establish that $((e_0\to c)\to c)\langle\lambda\kappa.\gamma_0(fix(\phi_0(\kappa\varepsilon))),\lambda\kappa.fix(\phi_1(\gamma_1\kappa))\rangle=true$ simply by proving that $c\langle\gamma_0(fix(\lambda\kappa\varepsilon.\phi_0(\kappa_0\varepsilon)(\kappa\varepsilon))),fix(\phi_1(\gamma_1\kappa_1))\rangle=true$ for every pair $\langle\kappa_0,\kappa_1\rangle$ subject to the equation $(e_0\to c)\langle\kappa_0,\kappa_1\rangle=true$. We shall do this by selecting such a pair and verifying that, if $\psi_0=\phi_1(\gamma_1\kappa_1)$, $\psi_1=\lambda\theta.\theta$, $\psi_2=\lambda\kappa\varepsilon.\phi_0(\kappa_0\varepsilon)(\kappa\varepsilon)$ and $\psi_3=\gamma_0$, the functions ψ_0, ψ_1, ψ_2 and ψ_3 satisfy the conditions required by the second result mentioned in 3.8.3 when ~ is induced by $\lambda\langle\theta',\theta''\rangle.c\langle\theta'',\theta'\rangle$ on C and by $\lambda\langle\kappa',\kappa''\rangle.(e_0\to c)\langle\kappa'',\kappa'\rangle$ on K. We know that c is transitive and inclusive and that $c\langle\bot,\bot\rangle=true$; in consequence we need only examine the validity of the conditions to the effect that $e_0\to c$ is inclusive, that $(e_0\to c)\langle\bot,\bot\rangle=true$, that $c\langle\bot,\gamma_0\bot\rangle=true$, that $c\langle\phi_1(\gamma_1\kappa_1)\theta_2,\phi_1(\gamma_1\kappa_1)\theta_3\rangle=true$ whenever $c\langle\theta_2,\theta_3\rangle=true$, and that $(e_0\to c)\langle\lambda\varepsilon.\phi_0(\kappa_0\varepsilon)(\kappa_2\varepsilon),\lambda\varepsilon.\phi_0(\kappa_0\varepsilon)(\kappa_3\varepsilon)\rangle=true$ and $c\langle\gamma_0(\lambda\varepsilon.\phi_0(\kappa_0\varepsilon)(\kappa_2\varepsilon)),\phi_1(\gamma_1\kappa_1)(\gamma_0\kappa_3)\rangle=true$ whenever $k\langle\kappa_2,\kappa_3\rangle=true$.

The definition of $x_0\to x_1$ given in 3.8.2 obviously makes $x_0\to x_1$ inclusive whenever x_1 is inclusive; hence as c is inclusive $e_0\to c$ must be inclusive. Similarly, because $c\langle\bot,\bot\rangle=true$ it is plain that $(e_0\to c)\langle\kappa_2,\kappa_3\rangle=true$ for any pair $\langle\kappa_2,\kappa_3\rangle$ such that $\langle\kappa_2\varepsilon_0,\kappa_3\varepsilon_1\rangle=\langle\bot,\bot\rangle$ whenever $e_0\langle\varepsilon_0,\varepsilon_1\rangle=true$; in particular, $(e_0\to c)\langle\bot,\bot\rangle=true$. An elementary calculation is enough to confirm that $\mathcal{C}[\![$**while true do fit** 0$]\!]=\bot$, so, as E_0 is EC-commutative with **while true do fit** 0 under $u\to(e_0\to c)\to c$, we know that when $(e_0\to c)\langle\kappa_2,\kappa_3\rangle=true$ $c\langle\gamma_0(\lambda\varepsilon.\bot\rho_0(\kappa_2\varepsilon)),\bot\rho_1(\gamma_1\kappa_3)\rangle=true$ or, in other words, that $c\langle\gamma_0\bot,\bot\rangle=true$.

Because Γ is CC-similar to Γ under $u\to c\to c$, we know that

$c\langle \mathfrak{C}\llbracket\Gamma\rrbracket\rho_0\theta_2, \mathfrak{C}\llbracket\Gamma\rrbracket\rho_1\theta_3\rangle = \mathit{true}$ if $\langle\theta_2,\theta_3\rangle$ is any pair for which $c\langle\theta_2,\theta_3\rangle = \mathit{true}$; hence if $\langle\theta_0,\theta_1\rangle$ satisfies $c\langle\theta_0,\theta_1\rangle = \mathit{true}$ we may safely assert that $(e_1\to c)\langle\xi_0\theta_0\theta_2,\xi_1\theta_1\theta_3\rangle = \mathit{true}$. Indeed, as E_1 is RR-similar to E_1 under $u\to(e_1\to c)\to c$, $((e_1\to c)\to c)\langle\gamma_2,\gamma_3\rangle = \mathit{true}$, $c\langle\gamma_2(\xi_0\theta_0\theta_2),\gamma_3(\xi_1\theta_1\theta_3)\rangle = \mathit{true}$ and $c\langle\phi_0\theta_0\theta_2,\phi_1\theta_1\theta_3\rangle = \mathit{true}$. Moreover, E_0 is EE-similar to E_0 under $u\to(e_0\to c)\to c$ so the stipulations that $u\langle\rho_0,\rho_1\rangle = \mathit{true}$ and that $(e_0\to c)\langle\kappa_0,\kappa_1\rangle = \mathit{true}$ ensure that $c\langle\gamma_0\kappa_0,\gamma_1\kappa_1\rangle = \mathit{true}$; thus setting $\langle\theta_0,\theta_1\rangle = \langle\gamma_0\kappa_0,\gamma_1\kappa_1\rangle$ reveals that $c\langle\phi_0(\gamma_0\kappa_0)\theta_2,\phi_1(\gamma_1\kappa_1)\theta_3\rangle = \mathit{true}$ whenever $c\langle\theta_2,\theta_3\rangle = \mathit{true}$.

For any $\langle\kappa_2,\kappa_3\rangle$ and $\langle\varepsilon_0,\varepsilon_1\rangle$ such that $(e_0\to c)\langle\kappa_2,\kappa_3\rangle = \mathit{true}$ and $e_0\langle\varepsilon_0,\varepsilon_1\rangle = \mathit{true}$ we may presume that $c\langle\kappa_0\varepsilon_0,\kappa_1\varepsilon_1\rangle = \mathit{true}$ and that $c\langle\kappa_2\varepsilon_0,\kappa_3\varepsilon_1\rangle = \mathit{true}$. Accordingly writing $\langle\theta_0,\theta_1\rangle = \langle\kappa_0\varepsilon_0,\kappa_1\varepsilon_1\rangle$ and $\langle\theta_2,\theta_3\rangle = \langle\kappa_2\varepsilon_0,\kappa_3\varepsilon_1\rangle$ establishes that $(e_1\to c)\langle\xi_0(\kappa_0\varepsilon_0)(\kappa_2\varepsilon_0),\xi_1(\kappa_1\varepsilon_1)(\kappa_3\varepsilon_1)\rangle = \mathit{true}$ and that $c\langle\phi_0(\kappa_0\varepsilon_0)(\kappa_2\varepsilon_0),\phi_1(\kappa_1\varepsilon_1)(\kappa_3\varepsilon_1)\rangle = \mathit{true}$. Since $\langle\varepsilon_0,\varepsilon_1\rangle$ can be any pair for which $e_0\langle\varepsilon_0,\varepsilon_1\rangle = \mathit{true}$, we deduce that $(e_0\to e_1\to c)\langle\lambda\varepsilon.\xi_0(\kappa_0\varepsilon)(\kappa_2\varepsilon),\lambda\varepsilon.\xi_1(\kappa_1\varepsilon)(\kappa_3\varepsilon)\rangle = \mathit{true}$ and that $(e_0\to c)\langle\lambda\varepsilon.\phi_0(\kappa_0\varepsilon)(\kappa_2\varepsilon),\lambda\varepsilon.\phi_1(\kappa_1\varepsilon)(\kappa_3\varepsilon)\rangle = \mathit{true}$. The assumption that E_0 is ER-commutative with E_1 under $u\to(e_0\to e_1\to c)\to c$ now implies that $c\langle\gamma_0(\lambda\varepsilon.\gamma_2(\xi_0(\kappa_0\varepsilon)(\kappa_2\varepsilon))),\gamma_3(\lambda\varepsilon''.\gamma_1(\lambda\varepsilon'.\xi_1(\kappa_1\varepsilon')(\kappa_3\varepsilon')\varepsilon''))\rangle = \mathit{true}$ or, in other words, that $c\langle\gamma_0(\lambda\varepsilon.\phi_0(\kappa_0\varepsilon)(\kappa_2\varepsilon)),\gamma_3(\lambda\varepsilon''.\gamma_1(\lambda\varepsilon'.\xi_1(\kappa_1\varepsilon')(\kappa_3\varepsilon')\varepsilon''))\rangle = \mathit{true}$.

If $\langle\varepsilon_2,\varepsilon_3\rangle$ is any pair for which $e_1\langle\varepsilon_2,\varepsilon_3\rangle = \mathit{true}$, $\langle\gamma_0(\lambda\varepsilon.\xi_0(\kappa_0\varepsilon)(\kappa_2\varepsilon)\varepsilon_2),\xi_1(\gamma_1\kappa_1)(\gamma_1\kappa_3)\varepsilon_3\rangle$ is either $\langle\gamma_0(\lambda\varepsilon.\mathfrak{C}\llbracket\Gamma\rrbracket\rho_0(\kappa_2\varepsilon)),\mathfrak{C}\llbracket\Gamma\rrbracket\rho_1(\gamma_1\kappa_3)\rangle$ or $\langle\gamma_0\kappa_0,\gamma_1\kappa_1\rangle$, because e_1 filters out truth values. As E_0 is EC-commutative with Γ under $u\to(e_0\to c)\to c$, $c\langle\gamma_0(\lambda\varepsilon.\mathfrak{C}\llbracket\Gamma\rrbracket\rho_0(\kappa_2\varepsilon)),\mathfrak{C}\llbracket\Gamma\rrbracket\rho_1(\gamma_1\kappa_3)\rangle = \mathit{true}$; furthermore $c\langle\gamma_0\kappa_0,\gamma_1\kappa_1\rangle = \mathit{true}$, because E_0 is EE-similar to E_0 under $u\to(e_0\to c)\to c$, so $c\langle\gamma_0(\lambda\varepsilon.\xi_0(\kappa_0\varepsilon)(\kappa_2\varepsilon)\varepsilon_2),\xi_1(\gamma_1\kappa_1)(\gamma_1\kappa_3)\varepsilon_3\rangle = \mathit{true}$ when $e_1\langle\varepsilon_2,\varepsilon_3\rangle = \mathit{true}$. Consequently $(e_1\to c)\langle\lambda\varepsilon''.\gamma_0(\lambda\varepsilon'.\xi_0(\kappa_0\varepsilon')(\kappa_2\varepsilon')\varepsilon''),\xi_1(\gamma_1\kappa_1)(\gamma_1\kappa_3)\rangle = \mathit{true}$ and, since E_1 is RR-similar to E_1 under $u\to(e_1\to c)\to c$,

$c\langle\gamma_2(\lambda\varepsilon''.\gamma_0(\lambda\varepsilon'.\xi_0(\kappa_0\varepsilon')(\kappa_2\varepsilon')\varepsilon'')),\gamma_1(\xi_1(\gamma_1\kappa_1)(\gamma_1\kappa_3))\rangle=true$;

this equation can of course be written as

$c\langle\gamma_2(\lambda\varepsilon''.\gamma_0(\lambda\varepsilon'.\xi_0(\kappa_0\varepsilon')(\kappa_2\varepsilon')\varepsilon'')),\phi_1(\gamma_1\kappa_1)(\gamma_1\kappa_3)\rangle=true$.

We must next relate $\gamma_2(\lambda\varepsilon''.\gamma_0(\lambda\varepsilon'.\xi_0(\kappa_0\varepsilon')(\kappa_2\varepsilon')\varepsilon''))$ and $\gamma_3(\lambda\varepsilon''.\gamma_1(\lambda\varepsilon'.\xi_1(\kappa_1\varepsilon')(\kappa_3\varepsilon')\varepsilon''))$. This we do by observing that when $e_1\langle\varepsilon_2,\varepsilon_3\rangle=true$ $(e_0\to c)\langle\lambda\varepsilon.\xi_0(\kappa_1\varepsilon)(\kappa_2\varepsilon)\varepsilon_2),\lambda\varepsilon.\xi_1(\kappa_1\varepsilon)(\kappa_3\varepsilon)\varepsilon_3\rangle=true$, so that $c\langle\gamma_0(\lambda\varepsilon.\xi_0(\kappa_1\varepsilon)(\kappa_2\varepsilon)\varepsilon_2),\gamma_1(\lambda\varepsilon.\xi_1(\kappa_1\varepsilon)(\kappa_3\varepsilon)\varepsilon_3)\rangle=true$ because E_0 is EE-similar to E_0 under $u\to(e_0\to c)\to c$. Hence $(e_1\to c)\langle\lambda\varepsilon''.\gamma_0(\xi_0(\kappa_0\varepsilon')(\kappa_2\varepsilon')\varepsilon''),\lambda\varepsilon''.\gamma_1(\xi_1(\kappa_1\varepsilon')(\kappa_3\varepsilon')\varepsilon'')\rangle=true$ and by applying the fact that E_1 is RR-similar to E_1 under $u\to(e_1\to c)\to c$ for the final time we infer that

$c\langle\gamma_2(\lambda\varepsilon''.\gamma_0(\lambda\varepsilon'.\xi_0(\kappa_0\varepsilon')(\kappa_2\varepsilon')\varepsilon'')),\gamma_3(\lambda\varepsilon''.\gamma_1(\lambda\varepsilon'.\xi_1(\kappa_1\varepsilon')(\kappa_3\varepsilon')\varepsilon''))\rangle=true$

At this point we recall the knowledge that e_0 and c are restrictive. The fact that $c\langle\phi_0(\gamma_0\kappa_0)\theta_2,\phi_1(\gamma_1\kappa_1)\theta_3\rangle=true$ whenever $c\langle\theta_2,\theta_3\rangle=true$ allows us to assert that $c\langle\phi_1(\gamma_1\kappa_1)\theta_2,\phi_1(\gamma_1\kappa_1)\theta_3\rangle=true$ whenever $c\langle\theta_2,\theta_3\rangle=true$; likewise, because $e_0\to c$ is restrictive (in view of the remarks in 3.8.3), the knowledge that $(e_0\to c)\langle\lambda\varepsilon.\phi_0(\kappa_0\varepsilon)(\kappa_2\varepsilon),\lambda\varepsilon.\phi_1(\kappa_1\varepsilon)(\kappa_3\varepsilon)\rangle=true$ whenever $(e_0\to c)\langle\kappa_2,\kappa_3\rangle=true$ reveals that $(e_0\to c)\langle\lambda\varepsilon.\phi_0(\kappa_0\varepsilon)(\kappa_2\varepsilon),\lambda\varepsilon.\phi_0(\kappa_0\varepsilon)(\kappa_3\varepsilon)\rangle=true$ whenever $(e_0\to c)\langle\kappa_2,\kappa_3\rangle=true$. Moreover if $(e_0\to c)\langle\kappa_2,\kappa_3\rangle=true$ we can combine the equations $(c\to c)\langle\phi_1(\gamma_1\kappa_1),\phi_1(\gamma_1\kappa_1)\rangle=true$, $c\langle\gamma_0\kappa_3,\gamma_1\kappa_3\rangle=true$, $c\langle\gamma_0(\lambda\varepsilon.\phi_0(\kappa_0\varepsilon)(\kappa_2\varepsilon)),\gamma_3(\lambda\varepsilon''.\gamma_1(\lambda\varepsilon'.\xi_1(\kappa_1\varepsilon')(\kappa_3\varepsilon')\varepsilon''))\rangle=true$, $c\langle\gamma_2(\lambda\varepsilon''.\gamma_0(\lambda\varepsilon'.\xi_0(\kappa_0\varepsilon')(\kappa_2\varepsilon')\varepsilon'')),\phi_1(\gamma_1\kappa_1)(\gamma_1\kappa_3)\rangle=true$ and $c\langle\gamma_2(\lambda\varepsilon''.\gamma_0(\lambda\varepsilon'.\xi_0(\kappa_0\varepsilon')(\kappa_2\varepsilon')\varepsilon'')),\gamma_3(\lambda\varepsilon''.\gamma_1(\lambda\varepsilon'.\xi_1(\kappa_1\varepsilon')(\kappa_3\varepsilon')\varepsilon''))\rangle=true$ in order to show that $c\langle\gamma_0(\lambda\varepsilon.\phi_0(\kappa_0\varepsilon)(\kappa_2\varepsilon)),\phi_1(\gamma_1\kappa_1)(\gamma_0\kappa_3)\rangle=true$.

Now that all the conditions needed by the second result listed in 3.8.3 are known to be satisfied we may assert that $c\langle\gamma_0(fix(\lambda\varepsilon\kappa.\phi_0(\kappa_0\varepsilon)(\kappa\varepsilon))),fix(\phi_1(\gamma_1\kappa_1))\rangle=true$ if $\langle\kappa_0,\kappa_1\rangle$ is such that $(e_0\to c)\langle\kappa_0,\kappa_1\rangle=true$. Hence $((e_0\to c)\to c)\langle\lambda\kappa.\gamma_0(\lambda\varepsilon.fix(\phi_0(\kappa\varepsilon))),\lambda\kappa.fix(\phi_1(\gamma_1\kappa))\rangle=true$ where if $1\geq n\geq 0$

γ_n and ϕ_n are determined by an arbitrarily chosen pair $\langle\rho_0,\rho_1\rangle$ having $u\langle\rho_0,\rho_1\rangle=true$. By inspecting the semantic equation we can confirm that this indicates that E_0 is EC-commutative with while E_1 do Γ under $u\to(e_0\to c)\to c$.$\triangleright$

This proof could have been shortened by using rules of inference such as that to the effect that if $(w_0\to w_1)\langle\omega_0,\omega_1\rangle=true$ and $(w_1\to w_2)\langle\omega_2,\omega_3\rangle=true$ for some $\langle\omega_0,\omega_1\rangle$ and $\langle\omega_2,\omega_3\rangle$ then $(w_0\to w_2)\langle\lambda\omega.\omega_2(\omega_0\omega),\lambda\omega.\omega_3(\omega_1\omega)\rangle=true$. We have avoided doing this merely to make the argument less abstract; naturally rules of inference would be preferred by those who had carried out other such proofs (or for a programming system intended to check proofs).

The assumption that E_0 is EC-commutative with while true do fit 0 under $u\to(e_0\to c)\to c$ is intended to ensure that adjoining E_0 to the front of an unending program produces an unending program. The need for some such assumption is demonstrated by taking E_0, E_1 and Γ to be res 0, true and fit 0 respectively, when all the other hypotheses in the statement of the result are satisfied but the conclusion is invalid if e_0, u and c are tests for equality. However, there are other assumptions which will serve our purposes equally well. For instance, when we take Γ_0 to be if E_1 do Γ and Γ_{n+1} to be if E_1 do $(\Gamma;\Gamma_n)$ for $n\geq 0$ then no matter how E_0 is related to while true do fit 0 we can easily confirm that E_0 is EC-commutative with while E_1 do Γ under $u\to(e_0\to c)\to c$ provided that for some $m\geq 0$ while E_1 do Γ is CC-similar to Γ_m under $u\to(e_0\to c)\to c$; indeed even without making this provision we can prove that, in the notation adopted above, $((e_0\to c)\to c)\langle\lambda\kappa.\gamma_0(\lambda\varepsilon.fix(\phi_0(\kappa\varepsilon))),\lambda\kappa.\phi_1(\gamma_1\kappa)(\gamma_1(\lambda\varepsilon.fix(\phi_1(\kappa\varepsilon))))\rangle=true$.

3.8.7. Idempotence.

When q maps $(U\to(E\to E\to C)\to C)\times(U\to(E\to E\to C)\to C)$ into T', we shall say that an expression E is 'E-idempotent' under q if and only if $q\langle\lambda\rho\psi.\mathcal{E}[\![E]\!]\rho(\lambda\varepsilon.\psi\varepsilon\varepsilon),\lambda\rho.run\langle\mathcal{E}[\![E]\!]\rho,\mathcal{E}[\![E]\!]\rho\rangle\rangle=true$ when ψ ranges over members of $E\to E\to C$; L-idempotence and, more significantly, R-idempotence can be defined similarly. If q is of the form $u\to(e\to e\to c_0)\to c_1$ for some e, u, c_0 and c_1 these definitions are not influenced by the order in which run applies its arguments, because when γ_0 and γ_1 are members of $K\to C$ for which $((e\to e\to c_0)\to c_1)\langle\lambda\psi.\gamma_0(\lambda\varepsilon.\psi\varepsilon\varepsilon),\lambda\psi.\gamma_1(\lambda\varepsilon'.\gamma_1(\lambda\varepsilon''.\psi\varepsilon'\varepsilon''))\rangle=true$, say, the knowledge that $(e\to e\to c_0)\langle\psi_0,\psi_1\rangle=true$ if and only if $(e\to e\to c_0)\langle\lambda\varepsilon'\varepsilon''.\psi_0\varepsilon''\varepsilon',\lambda\varepsilon'\varepsilon''.\psi_1\varepsilon''\varepsilon'\rangle=true$ ensures that $((e\to e\to c_0)\to c_1)\langle\lambda\psi.\gamma_0(\lambda\varepsilon.\psi\varepsilon\varepsilon),\lambda\psi.\gamma_1(\lambda\varepsilon''.\gamma_1(\lambda\varepsilon'.\psi\varepsilon'\varepsilon''))\rangle=true$.

We could introduce analogous concepts of D-idempotence and T-idempotence for declarations but there is little point in doing so. When q is a predicate defined on $(U\to C\to C)\times(U\to C\to C)$, a block Θ will be said to be 'G-idempotent' under q if and only if $q\langle\mathcal{G}[\![\Theta]\!],\lambda\rho\theta.\mathcal{G}[\![\Theta]\!]\rho(\mathcal{G}[\![\Theta]\!]\rho\theta)\rangle=true$, whilst a command Γ will be said to be 'C-idempotent' under q if and only if $q\langle\mathcal{C}[\![\Gamma]\!],\lambda\rho\theta.\mathcal{C}[\![\Gamma]\!]\rho(\mathcal{C}[\![\Gamma]\!]\rho\theta)\rangle=true$.

In our lists of results about idempotence we shall adopt the usages introduced in 3.8.5; thus the letter X will stand for E, L or R and we shall implicitly regard u, for example, as being any predicate mapping $U\times U$ into T'. To obtain a supply of idempotent portions of programs we apply such obvious properties as the following:

(i) if E_0 is X-idempotent under $u\to(e\to e\to c)\to c$, if E_0 is XX-similar to E_1 and if e, u and c are restrictive then E_1 is X-idempotent under $u\to(e\to e\to c)\to c$;

(ii) if E is without side effects under $u\to(e\to c)\to c$ and if e, u and c are restrictive then E is E-idempotent under $u\to(e\to e\to c)\to c$;

(iii) if E_0 is R-idempotent under $u\to(e_0\to e_0\to c)\to c$, if E_1 and E_2 are

X-idempotent under $u \to (e_1 \to e_1 \to c) \to c$, if E_0 is RX-commutative with E_1 and E_2 under $u \to (e_0 \to e_1 \to c) \to c$, if E_0 is RR-similar to E_0 under $u \to (e_0 \to c) \to c$, if E_1 and E_2 are XX-similar to E_1 and E_2 (respectively) under $u \to (e_1 \to c) \to c$, if e_0 filters out truth values and if e_1 and c are restrictive then $E_0 ? E_1 ! E_2$ is X-idempotent under $u \to (e_1 \to e_1 \to c) \to c$;

(iv) if Σ is SS-similar to Σ under $u \to c_1$ then Σ is XX-idempotent under $u \to (e_0 \to e_1 \to c_0) \to c_1$;

(v) if E is E-idempotent under $u \to (e \to c_0) \to c_1$ then fit E is G-idempotent under $u \to c_0 \to c_1$;

(vi) if Σ is SS-similar to Σ under $u \to c_1$ then Σ is G-idempotent under $u \to c_0 \to c_1$.

Clearly there are results akin to (i) which discuss the idempotence of declarations, blocks and commands rather than expressions.

Of more interest are certain connections between similarity, commutativity and idempotence, to wit:

(i) if E is X-idempotent under $u \to (e \to e \to c) \to c$ and if e, u and c are restrictive then E is XX-similar to E under $u \to (e \to c) \to c$;

(ii) if E is E-idempotent under $u \to (e \to c) \to c$ then E is EE-similar to fit E before E under $u \to (e \to c) \to c$,

(iii) if Γ is C-idempotent under $u \to c \to c$ then Γ is CC-similar to $\Gamma;\Gamma$ under $u \to c \to c$;

(iv) if Γ is C-idempotent under $u \to c \to c$, if Γ is CC-similar to Γ under $u \to c \to c$, if c is restrictive and inclusive and if $c\langle \bot, \bot \rangle = true$ then while true do Γ is CC-similar to Γ;while true do fit 0;

(v) if E_0 is R-idempotent under $u \to (e_0 \to e_0 \to c) \to c$, if E_0 is RR-similar to E_0 under $u \to (e_0 \to c) \to c$, if E_1, E_2, E_3 and E_4 are XX-similar to E_1, E_2, E_3 and E_4 (respectively) under $u \to (e_1 \to c) \to c$, if e_0 filters out truth values and if e_1 and c are restrictive then $E_0 ? E_1 ! E_2$ is XX-similar to $E_0 ? E_1 ! (E_0 ? E_3 ! E_2)$,

$E_0?(E_0?E_1!E_4)!E_2$ and $E_0?(E_0?E_1!E_4)!(E_0?E_3!E_2)$ under $u \to (e_1 \to c) \to c$;

(vi) if E is R-idempotent under $u \to (e \to e \to c) \to c$, if E is RR-similar to E under $u \to (e \to c) \to c$, if Γ is CC-similar to Γ under $u \to c \to c$, if e filters out truth values and if c is restrictive then if E do Γ is CC-similar to if E do (if E do Γ) under $u \to c \to c$;

(vii) if E is R-idempotent under $u \to (e \to e \to c) \to c$, if E is RR-similar to E under $u \to (e \to c) \to c$, if Γ is CC-similar to Γ under $u \to c \to c$, if e filters out truth values, if c is restrictive and inclusive and if $c\langle \bot, \bot \rangle = true$ then while E do Γ is CC-similar to if E do (while E do Γ), while E do (if E do Γ), while E do (while E do Γ) and (if E do Γ);(while E do Γ) under $u \to c \to c$;

(viii) if E is R-idempotent under $u \to (e \to e \to c) \to c$, if E is RR-similar to E under $u \to (e \to c) \to c$, if Γ_0 is CC-similar to Γ_0 under $u \to c \to c$, if Γ_1 is CC-similar to Γ_1 under $u \to c \to c$, if e filters out truth values, if c is restrictive and inclusive and if $c\langle \bot, \bot \rangle = true$ then while E do Γ_0 is CC-similar to (while E do Γ_0);(if E do Γ_1) and (while E do Γ_0);(while E do Γ_1) under $u \to c \to c$;

(ix) if E is R-idempotent under $u \to (e \to e \to c) \to c$, if E is RC-commutative with Γ_0 under $u \to (e \to c) \to c$, if E is RR-similar to E under $u \to (e \to c) \to c$, if Γ_0 is CC-similar to Γ_0 under $u \to c \to c$, if Γ_1 is CC-similar to Γ_1 under $u \to c \to c$, if e filters out truth values and if c is restrictive then (if E do Γ_0);(if E do Γ_1) is CC-similar to if E do (Γ_0;Γ_1) and if E do (Γ_0;if E do Γ_1) under $u \to c \to c$;

(x) if E is R-idempotent under $u \to (e \to e \to c) \to c$, if E is RC-commutative with Γ_0 under $u \to (e \to c) \to c$, if E is RR-similar to E under $u \to (e \to c) \to c$, if Γ_0 is CC-similar to Γ_0 under $u \to c \to c$, if Γ_1 is CC-similar to Γ_1 under $u \to c \to c$, if e filters out truth values, if

c is restrictive and inclusive and if $c\langle\perp,\perp\rangle = true$ then
(if E do Γ_0);(while E do Γ_1) is CC-similar to
if E do (Γ_0;while E do Γ_1), if E do (Γ_0;Γ_1;while E do Γ_1) and
(if E do (Γ_0;Γ_1));(while E do Γ_1) under $u \to c \to c$;

(xi) if E is R-idempotent under $u \to (e \to e \to c) \to c$, if E is RC-commutative with Γ under $u \to (e \to c) \to c$, if E is RR-similar to E under $u \to (e \to c) \to c$, if Γ is CC-similar to Γ under $u \to c \to c$, if *e* filters out truth values, if *c* is restrictive and inclusive, and if $c\langle\perp,\perp\rangle = true$ then while E do Γ is CC-similar to if E do (while true do Γ) under $u \to c \to c$.

Again there are analogues of (i) which analyse declarations, blocks and commands instead of expressions. Moreover we can obtain other results by combining these with equivalence and similarity properties. For instance, if E is R-idempotent under $u \to (e \to e \to c) \to c$, if E is RR-similar to E under $u \to (e \to c) \to c$ and if Γ is CC-similar to Γ under $u \to c \to c$ for suitable *e*, *u* and *c*, then it follows from (viii) that while E do Γ is C-idempotent under $u \to c \to c$; when, in addition, Γ is C-idempotent under $u \to c \to c$ and E is RC-commutative with Γ under $u \to (e \to c) \to c$, (ix) assures us that if E do Γ is C-idempotent under $u \to c \to c$ whereas (iv) and (xi) together indicate that while E do Γ is actually CC-similar to if E do (Γ;while true do fit 0) under $u \to c \to c$. Under the circumstances pertaining in (xi) we even know that while E do Γ is CC-similar to if E do (while true do fit 0) under $u \to c \to c$ provided that Γ is CC-commutative with while true do fit 0 under $u \to c \to c$ (whether or not Γ is C-idempotent under $u \to c \to c$).

Results such as these can be established easily; those in which we insist that an expression returns a truth value are the only ones having interesting proofs, and even they rely simply on certain equations which we shall justify in the first four paragraphs of the proof of 3.8.8. Accordingly we shall discuss just part of one of them, namely (vii).

3.8.8. Proposition.

Let E be a Sal expression and let Γ be a Sal command; suppose that for certain predicates e, u and c E is R-idempotent under $u\to(e\to e\to c)\to c$, E is RR-similar to E under $u\to(e\to c)\to c$ and Γ is CC-similar to Γ under $u\to c\to c$. Then while E do Γ is CC-similar to (if E do Γ);(while E do Γ) under $u\to c\to c$ provided that e filters out truth values, c is restrictive and inclusive and $c\langle\bot,\bot\rangle = true$.

◂We begin by considering any pair $\langle\gamma_0,\gamma_1\rangle$ such that γ_0 and γ_1 are members of K→C for which $((e\to e\to c)\to c)\langle\lambda\psi.\gamma_0(\lambda\varepsilon.\psi\varepsilon\varepsilon), run\langle\gamma_1,\gamma_1\rangle\rangle = true$ and $((e\to c)\to c)\langle\gamma_0,\gamma_1\rangle = true$. Because e and c are restrictive, in accordance with the remarks in 3.8.3 we know that $e\to c$ and $(e\to c)\to c$ are restrictive. Hence if $\langle\psi_0,\psi_1\rangle$ is subject to the equation $(e\to e\to c)\langle\psi_0,\psi_1\rangle = true$ we know not only that $(e\to c)\langle\lambda\varepsilon.\psi_0\varepsilon\varepsilon,\lambda\varepsilon.\psi_1\varepsilon\varepsilon\rangle = true$ but also that $(e\to c)\langle\lambda\varepsilon.\psi_0\varepsilon\varepsilon,\lambda\varepsilon.\psi_0\varepsilon\varepsilon\rangle = true$; this ensures that $c\langle\gamma_0(\lambda\varepsilon.\psi_0\varepsilon\varepsilon),\gamma_1(\lambda\varepsilon.\psi_0\varepsilon\varepsilon)\rangle = true$, so in fact $c\langle\gamma_1(\lambda\varepsilon.\psi_0\varepsilon\varepsilon), run\langle\gamma_1,\gamma_1\rangle\psi_1\rangle = true$ since $c\langle\gamma_0(\lambda\varepsilon.\psi_0\varepsilon\varepsilon), run\langle\gamma_1,\gamma_1\rangle\psi_1\rangle = true$ and c is restrictive. Consequently $((e\to e\to c)\to c)\langle\lambda\psi.\gamma_1(\lambda\varepsilon.\psi\varepsilon\varepsilon), run\langle\gamma_1,\gamma_1\rangle\rangle = true$, whilst $((e\to c)\to c)\langle\gamma_1,\gamma_1\rangle = true$ as $(e\to c)\to c$ is restrictive; for convenience we shall therefore disregard γ_0 and concentrate on the properties of γ_1.

When $\langle\kappa_0,\kappa_1\rangle$ and $\langle\kappa_2,\kappa_3\rangle$ are any pairs for which $(e\to c)\langle\kappa_0,\kappa_1\rangle = true$ and $(e\to c)\langle\kappa_2,\kappa_3\rangle = true$ it is plain that $(e\to e\to c)\langle\lambda\varepsilon'\varepsilon''.test\langle\kappa_0\varepsilon'',\kappa_2\varepsilon''\rangle\varepsilon',\lambda\varepsilon'\varepsilon''.test\langle\kappa_1\varepsilon'',\kappa_3\varepsilon''\rangle\varepsilon'\rangle = true$, so by applying the fact that $((e\to e\to c)\to c)\langle\lambda\psi.\gamma_1(\lambda\varepsilon.\psi\varepsilon\varepsilon), run\langle\gamma_1,\gamma_1\rangle\rangle = true$ we learn that

$c\langle\gamma_1(\lambda\varepsilon.test\langle\kappa_0\varepsilon,\kappa_2\varepsilon\rangle\varepsilon),\gamma_1(\lambda\varepsilon'.\gamma_1(\lambda\varepsilon''.test\langle\kappa_1\varepsilon'',\kappa_3\varepsilon''\rangle\varepsilon'))\rangle = true$

and even that

$c\langle\gamma_1(test\langle\kappa_0(true),\kappa_2(false)\rangle),\gamma_1(\lambda\varepsilon'.\gamma_1(\lambda\varepsilon''.test\langle\kappa_1\varepsilon'',\kappa_3\varepsilon''\rangle\varepsilon'))\rangle = true$

since $test\langle\kappa_0(true),\kappa_2(false)\rangle = \lambda\varepsilon.test\langle\kappa_0\varepsilon,\kappa_2\varepsilon\rangle\varepsilon$. Furthermore, $(e\to c)\langle\kappa_1,\kappa_1\rangle = true$ and $(e\to c)\langle\kappa_3,\kappa_3\rangle = true$ because $e\to c$ is restrictive, so the reasoning of 3.8.5 and the knowledge that e filters out truth values while $((e\to c)\to c)\langle\gamma_1,\gamma_1\rangle=\mathit{true}$ ensure that

$(e\to c)\langle\lambda\varepsilon'.\gamma_1(\lambda\varepsilon''.\mathit{test}\langle\kappa_1\varepsilon'',\kappa_3\varepsilon''\rangle\varepsilon'),\mathit{test}\langle\gamma_1\kappa_1,\gamma_1\kappa_3\rangle\rangle=\mathit{true}$

and therefore that, as $((e\to c)\to c)\langle\gamma_1,\gamma_1\rangle=\mathit{true}$,

$c\langle\gamma_1(\lambda\varepsilon'.\gamma_1(\lambda\varepsilon''.\mathit{test}\langle\kappa_1\varepsilon'',\kappa_3\varepsilon''\rangle\varepsilon')),\gamma_1(\mathit{test}\langle\gamma_1\kappa_1,\gamma_1\kappa_3\rangle)\rangle=\mathit{true}$.

Another use of the transitive nature of c now shows that

$c\langle\gamma_1(\mathit{test}\langle\kappa_0(\mathit{true}),\kappa_2(\mathit{false})\rangle),\gamma_1(\mathit{test}\langle\gamma_1\kappa_1,\gamma_1\kappa_3\rangle)\rangle=\mathit{true}$

whenever $(e\to c)\langle\kappa_0,\kappa_1\rangle=\mathit{true}$ and $(e\to c)\langle\kappa_2,\kappa_3\rangle=\mathit{true}$.

Provided that $(e\to c)\langle\kappa_2,\kappa_3\rangle=\mathit{true}$ the final result of the previous paragraph can be specialized by setting $\langle\kappa_0,\kappa_1\rangle=\langle\lambda\varepsilon.\theta_0,\lambda\varepsilon.\theta_1\rangle$ for some $\langle\theta_0,\theta_1\rangle$ having $c\langle\theta_0,\theta_1\rangle=\mathit{true}$; under these circumstances

$c\langle\gamma_1(\mathit{test}\langle\theta_0,\kappa_2(\mathit{false})\rangle),\gamma_1(\mathit{test}\langle\gamma_1(\lambda\varepsilon.\theta_1),\gamma_1\kappa_3\rangle)\rangle=\mathit{true}$.

As c is restrictive we may assert that $c\langle\theta_1,\theta_1\rangle=\mathit{true}$,

$(e\to c)\langle\lambda\varepsilon.\theta_1,\lambda\varepsilon.\theta_1\rangle=\mathit{true}$, and $(e\to c)\langle\kappa_3,\kappa_3\rangle=\mathit{true}$; hence because $c\langle\gamma_1,\gamma_1\rangle=\mathit{true}$ we can deduce that $c\langle\gamma_1(\lambda\varepsilon.\theta_1),\gamma_1(\lambda\varepsilon.\theta_1)\rangle=\mathit{true}$, $c\langle\gamma_1\kappa_3,\gamma_1\kappa_3\rangle=\mathit{true}$ and $(e\to c)\langle\lambda\varepsilon.\gamma_1\kappa_3,\lambda\varepsilon.\gamma_1\kappa_3\rangle=\mathit{true}$, with the effect that

$c\langle\gamma_1(\mathit{test}\langle\theta_1,\gamma_1\kappa_3\rangle),\gamma_1(\mathit{test}\langle\gamma_1(\lambda\varepsilon.\theta_1),\gamma_1(\lambda\varepsilon.\gamma_1\kappa_3)\rangle)\rangle=\mathit{true}$.

The fact that $(e\to c)\langle\kappa_3,\kappa_3\rangle=\mathit{true}$ also indicates that

$(e\to e\to c)\langle\lambda\varepsilon.\kappa_3,\lambda\varepsilon.\kappa_3\rangle=\mathit{true}$, so $c\langle\gamma_1\kappa_3,\gamma_1(\lambda\varepsilon.\gamma_1\kappa_3)\rangle=\mathit{true}$ owing to the equation $((e\to e\to c)\to c)\langle\lambda\psi.\gamma_1(\lambda\varepsilon.\psi\varepsilon\varepsilon),\mathit{run}\langle\gamma_1,\gamma_1\rangle\rangle=\mathit{true}$; since $c\langle\gamma_1(\lambda\varepsilon.\theta_1),\gamma_1(\lambda\varepsilon.\theta_1)\rangle=\mathit{true}$ we observe that

$(e\to c)\langle\mathit{test}\langle\gamma_1(\lambda\varepsilon.\theta_1)\ \gamma_1\kappa_3\rangle\ \ \mathit{test}\langle\gamma_1(\lambda\varepsilon.\theta_1)\ \gamma_1(\lambda\varepsilon.\gamma_1\kappa_3)\rangle\rangle=\mathit{true}$

and indeed that, as $((e\to c)\to c)\langle\gamma_1,\gamma_1\rangle=\mathit{true}$,

$c\langle\gamma_1(\mathit{test}\langle\gamma_1(\lambda\varepsilon.\theta_1),\gamma_1\kappa_3\rangle),\gamma_1(\mathit{test}\langle\gamma_1(\lambda\varepsilon.\theta_1),\gamma_1(\lambda\varepsilon.\gamma_1\kappa_3)\rangle)\rangle=\mathit{true}$.

The restrictive properties of c therefore imply that

$c\langle\gamma_1(\mathit{test}\langle\theta_0,\kappa_2(\mathit{false})\rangle),\gamma_1(\mathit{test}\langle\theta_1,\gamma_1\kappa_3\rangle)\rangle=\mathit{true}$

whenever $c\langle\theta_0,\theta_1\rangle=\mathit{true}$ and $(e\to c)\langle\kappa_2,\kappa_3\rangle=\mathit{true}$.

We have thus established that, when $c\langle\theta_0,\theta_1\rangle=\mathit{true}$,

$(e\to c)\langle\kappa_0,\kappa_1\rangle=\mathit{true}$ and $(e\to c)\langle\kappa_2,\kappa_3\rangle=\mathit{true}$,

$c\langle\gamma_1(\mathit{test}\langle\kappa_0(\mathit{true}),\kappa_2(\mathit{false})\rangle),\gamma_1(\mathit{test}\langle\gamma_1\kappa_1,\gamma_1\kappa_3\rangle)\rangle=\mathit{true}$

and

$c\langle \gamma_1(test\langle \theta_0, \kappa_2(false)\rangle), \gamma_1(test\langle \theta_1, \gamma_1\kappa_3\rangle)\rangle = true$;

similarly

$c\langle \gamma_1(test\langle \kappa_0(true), \theta_0\rangle), \gamma_1(test\langle \gamma_1\kappa_1, \theta_1\rangle)\rangle = true$.

These results are crucial when proving those properties of idempotent expressions which depend on the fact that e filters out truth values; generally they are applied in situations where

$\langle \kappa_0, \kappa_1\rangle = \langle test\langle \theta_2, \theta_4\rangle, test\langle \theta_3, \theta_5\rangle\rangle$ and $\langle \kappa_2, \kappa_3\rangle = \langle test\langle \theta_6, \theta_8\rangle, test\langle \theta_7, \theta_9\rangle\rangle$

(when the continuations satisfy the equations $c\langle \theta_2, \theta_3\rangle = true$, $c\langle \theta_4, \theta_5\rangle = true$, $c\langle \theta_6, \theta_7\rangle = true$ and $c\langle \theta_8, \theta_9\rangle = true$).

At last we can turn to the particular assertions which are of most interest at the moment. Thus we choose any $\langle \rho_0, \rho_1\rangle$ and $\langle \theta_0, \theta_1\rangle$ having $u\langle \rho_0, \rho_1\rangle = true$ and $c\langle \theta_0, \theta_1\rangle = true$ and we set $\gamma_n = \mathcal{R}[\![\mathrm{E}]\!]\rho_n$, $\theta_{n+2} = \mathcal{C}[\![\texttt{while E do }\Gamma]\!]\rho_n\theta_n$ and $\theta_{n+4} = \mathcal{C}[\![\Gamma]\!]\rho_n\theta_{n+2}$ if $1 \geq n \geq 0$; we wish to prove that

$c\langle \mathcal{C}[\![\texttt{while E do }\Gamma]\!]\rho_0\theta_0, \mathcal{C}[\![(\texttt{if E do }\Gamma);(\texttt{while E do }\Gamma)]\!]\rho_1\theta_1\rangle = true$.

According to the semantic equations in appendix 1,

$\theta_3 = fix(\lambda\theta.\mathcal{R}[\![\mathrm{E}]\!]\rho_1(test\langle \mathcal{C}[\![\Gamma]\!]\rho_1\theta, \theta_1\rangle))$, so

$$\begin{aligned}\theta_3 &= (\lambda\theta.\mathcal{R}[\![\mathrm{E}]\!]\rho_1(test\langle \mathcal{C}[\![\Gamma]\!]\rho_1\theta, \theta_1\rangle))\theta_3\\ &= \mathcal{R}[\![\mathrm{E}]\!]\rho_1(test\langle \mathcal{C}[\![\Gamma]\!]\rho_1\theta_3, \theta_1\rangle)\\ &= \mathcal{R}[\![\mathrm{E}]\!]\rho_1(test\langle \theta_5, \theta_1\rangle)\\ &= \gamma_1(test\langle \theta_5, \theta_1\rangle).\end{aligned}$$

The semantic equations also show that

$$\begin{aligned}\mathcal{C}[\![(\texttt{if E do }\Gamma);(\texttt{while E do }\Gamma)]\!]\rho_1\theta_1 &= \mathcal{C}[\![\texttt{if E do }\Gamma]\!]\rho_1(\mathcal{C}[\![\texttt{while E do }\Gamma]\!]\rho_1\theta_1)\\ &= \mathcal{C}[\![\texttt{if E do }\Gamma]\!]\rho_1\theta_3\\ &= \mathcal{R}[\![\mathrm{E}]\!]\rho_1(test\langle \mathcal{C}[\![\Gamma]\!]\rho_1\theta_3, \theta_3\rangle)\\ &= \mathcal{R}[\![\mathrm{E}]\!]\rho_1(test\langle \theta_5, \theta_3\rangle)\\ &= \gamma_1(test\langle \theta_5, \theta_3\rangle).\end{aligned}$$

When $\langle \theta_6, \theta_7\rangle$ is any pair of continuations for which $c\langle \theta_6, \theta_7\rangle = true$ we know that $c\langle \mathcal{C}[\![\Gamma]\!]\rho_0\theta_6, \mathcal{C}[\![\Gamma]\!]\rho_1\theta_7\rangle = true$ since Γ is CC-similar to Γ under $u \rightarrow c \rightarrow c$; hence

$(e \to c)\langle test\langle \mathcal{C}[\![\Gamma]\!]\rho_0\theta_6, \theta_0\rangle, test\langle \mathcal{C}[\![\Gamma]\!]\rho_1\theta_7, \theta_1\rangle\rangle = true$, and
$c\langle \mathcal{R}[\![E]\!]\rho_0(test\langle \mathcal{C}[\![\Gamma]\!]\rho_0\theta_6, \theta_0\rangle), \mathcal{R}[\![E]\!]\rho_1(test\langle \mathcal{C}[\![\Gamma]\!]\rho_1\theta_7, \theta_1\rangle)\rangle = true$
because E is RR-similar to E under $u \to (e \to c) \to c$. As c is inclusive and $c\langle \bot, \bot\rangle = true$, if we form a relation ~ from c and apply the first result listed in 3.8.3 we may infer that
$c\langle fix(\lambda\theta.\mathcal{R}[\![E]\!]\rho(test\langle \mathcal{C}[\![\Gamma]\!]\rho_0\theta, \theta_0\rangle)), fix(\lambda\theta.\mathcal{R}[\![E]\!]\rho_1(test\langle \mathcal{C}[\![\Gamma]\!]\rho_1\theta, \theta_1\rangle))\rangle = true$
and that $c\langle \theta_2, \theta_3\rangle = true$; indeed, owing to the arbitrary way in which we have chosen $\langle \rho_0, \rho_1\rangle$ and $\langle \theta_0, \theta_1\rangle$, we may even claim that while E do Γ is CC-similar to while E do Γ under $u \to c \to c$. In order to achieve our aim of proving that $c\langle \theta_2, \gamma_1(test\langle \theta_5, \theta_3\rangle)\rangle = true$ we have therefore only to confirm that $c\langle \theta_3, \gamma_1(test\langle \theta_5, \theta_3\rangle)\rangle = true$ and to apply the fact that c is transitive; in fact by eliminating θ_3 by means of the equation above we reduce this problem to that of showing that $c\langle \gamma_1(test\langle \theta_5, \theta_1\rangle), \gamma_1(test\langle \theta_5, \gamma_1(test\langle \theta_5, \theta_1\rangle)\rangle)\rangle = true$.

Since Γ is CC-similar to Γ under $u \to c \to c$ while $u\langle \rho_0, \rho_1\rangle = true$ and $c\langle \theta_2, \theta_3\rangle = true$, we may assert that $c\langle \theta_4, \theta_5\rangle = true$. The restrictive nature of E therefore ensures that $c\langle \theta_5, \theta_5\rangle = true$ and also that $c\langle \theta_1, \theta_1\rangle = true$, from which it follows that
$(e \to c)\langle test\langle \theta_5, \theta_1\rangle, test\langle \theta_5, \theta_1\rangle\rangle = true$. However, because E is R-idempotent under $u \to (e \to e \to c) \to c$ and E is RR-similar to E under $u \to (e \to c) \to c$ we know that $(e \to e \to c)\langle \lambda\psi.\gamma_0(\lambda\varepsilon.\psi\varepsilon\varepsilon), run\langle \gamma_1, \gamma_1\rangle\rangle = true$ and that $((e \to c) \to c)\langle \gamma_0, \gamma_1\rangle = true$; consequently we can be sure that
$(c \to (e \to c) \to c)\langle \lambda\theta\kappa.\gamma_1(test\langle \theta, \kappa(false)\rangle), \lambda\theta\kappa.\gamma_1(test\langle \theta, \gamma_1\kappa\rangle)\rangle = true$.
In particular, since $((e \to c) \to c)\langle \gamma_1, \gamma_1\rangle = true$,
$c\langle \gamma_1(test\langle \theta_5, test\langle \theta_5, \theta_1\rangle(false)\rangle), \gamma_1(test\langle \theta_5, \gamma_1(test\langle \theta_5, \theta_1\rangle)\rangle)\rangle = true$,
and by writing this more briefly we see that
$c\langle \gamma_1(test\langle \theta_5, \theta_1\rangle), \gamma_1(test\langle \theta_5, \gamma_1(test\langle \theta_5, \theta_1\rangle)\rangle)\rangle = true$.

As we explained above, the fact that c is transitive ensures that $c\langle \theta_2, \gamma_1(test\langle \theta_5, \theta_3\rangle)\rangle = true$ whenever θ_2, θ_3, θ_5 and γ_1 are properly constructed from pairs $\langle \rho_0, \rho_1\rangle$ and $\langle \theta_0, \theta_1\rangle$ for which

$u\langle\rho_0,\rho_1\rangle = true$ and $c\langle\theta_0,\theta_1\rangle = true$. Accordingly $(u\to(e\to c)\to c)\langle\mathcal{C}[\![\text{while E do }\Gamma]\!],\mathcal{C}[\![(\text{if E do }\Gamma);(\text{while E do }\Gamma)]\!]\rangle = true$ and while E do Γ is CC-similar to (if E do Γ);(while E do Γ) under $u\to(e\to c)\to c$.➤

Though this proof may appear long it is not really so, for its first four paragraphs are applicable in many other proofs and its seventh paragraph really provides simply a special case of a result mentioned in 3.8.2. Thus only four paragraphs are concerned with the details of the present result.

Instead of demanding that e filter out truth values in such propositions as that above we could insist that e and u be restrictive, that $(u\to(e\to c)\to c)\langle\mathcal{R}[\![\text{E}]\!],\lambda\rho\kappa.\mathcal{R}[\![\text{E}]\!]\rho(truth\,\kappa)\rangle = true$ and that $((e\to c)\to(e\to c))\langle truth, truth\rangle = true$ where $truth$ is given by the equation $truth = \lambda\kappa\varepsilon.\varepsilon E B\to(\varepsilon|B E T\to((\varepsilon|B|T = true)\vee(\varepsilon|B|T = false)\to\kappa\varepsilon,\bot), wrong), wrong$; the changes to our arguments necessitated by adopting this approach are rather dull and will therefore be omitted.

When Γ_0 and Γ_1 are commands which differ only in that Γ_1 lacks the outermost level of label settings found in Γ_0 we know that $\mathcal{C}[\![\text{while E do }\Gamma_0]\!] = \mathcal{C}[\![\text{while E do }\Gamma_1]\!]$. Consequently the proposition above allows us to assert that while E do Γ_0 is CC-similar to (if E do Γ_0);(while E do Γ_1) under $u\to c\to c$; in particular if E is R-idempotent under $(\lambda\langle\rho_0,\rho_1\rangle.(\rho_0\equiv\rho_1))\to(e\to(\lambda\langle\theta_0,\theta_1\rangle.(\theta_0\equiv\theta_1)))\to(\lambda\langle\theta_0,\theta_1\rangle.(\theta_0\equiv\theta_1))$ then while E do Γ_0 is equivalent with (if E do Γ_0);(while E do Γ_1) since Γ_0 is PP-similar and QQ-similar to Γ_0 under $(\lambda\langle\rho_0,\rho_1\rangle.(\rho_0\equiv\rho_1))\to(\lambda\langle\theta_0,\theta_1\rangle.(\theta_0\equiv\theta_1))\to(\lambda\langle\theta^*_0,\theta^*_1\rangle.(\theta^*_0\equiv\theta^*_1))$ and Γ_0 is JJ-similar and KK-similar to Γ_0 under $\lambda\langle I^*_0,I^*_1\rangle.(I^*_0\equiv I^*_1)$. This result can be established directly, without appealing to the proposition above; the proof required can be obtained by simplifying that needed above through taking u to be $\lambda\langle\rho_0,\rho_1\rangle.(\rho_0\equiv\rho_1)$ and c to be $\lambda\langle\theta_0,\theta_1\rangle.(\theta_0\equiv\theta_1)$.

3.9. Recursive procedures.

3.9.1. Conjugate valuations.

The equations of appendix 1 require continuations merely to provide an understanding of jumps and of certain aspects of unending computations [70]. A program containing no features that produce jumps might therefore be expected to have a semantics from which continuations would be absent. That this is actually the case has been known for some time; indeed early work on mathematical semantics [82] used a formalism making no mention of continuations. We shall now demonstrate how certain Sal programs can be given meanings in terms of a variant of that formalism; these meanings will be used later to vindicate the semantic equations for recursive declarations.

The execution of an expression generally serves just to pass an expressed value and a store on to the continuation, which remains unperturbed; in fact when the expression is without side effects the store may also be unchanged. Similarly, executing a Sal declaration entails passing on an environment and a store, whilst executing a block or a command involves altering the store. This suggests that we interpret parts of programs not as entities which map one continuation into another but as entities which transform stores into stores (perhaps together with some other things). Thus instead of the domains $K \to C$, $X \to C$ and $C \to C$ (or $(E \to S \to A) \to (S \to A)$, $(U \to S \to A) \to (S \to A)$ and $(S \to A) \to (S \to A)$) required in appendix 1 we need $S \to (E \times S)$, $S \to (U \times S)$ and $S \to S$.

Exceptions to this principle occur when an explicit jump is brought about by a sequencer, when a procedure is applied, when an improper expressed value is supplied as an argument to a function such as *test*, when the program fails to terminate or when an error produces an invocation of *wrong*. We shall prohibit the first of these situations from arising by suitable syntactic constraints, and in 4.2.7 we shall hint at how inclusive predicates enable us to cope with the second.

In order to cater for the third, fourth and fifth we shall use not $S\rightarrow(E\times S)$, $S\rightarrow(U\times S)$ and $S\rightarrow S$ but $S\rightarrow(A+(E\times S))$, $S\rightarrow(A+(U\times S))$ and $S\rightarrow(A+S)$ where A is the answer domain appropriate to appendix 1; A will be of importance because it includes the range of the error function, *wrong*. Corresponding with the valuations $\mathfrak{E}$, $\mathfrak{L}$ and $\mathfrak{R}$, which are defined on $Exp\rightarrow U\rightarrow K\rightarrow C$, will therefore be valuations $\P\mathfrak{E}$, $\P\mathfrak{L}$ and $\P\mathfrak{R}$ belonging to $Exp\rightarrow U\rightarrow S\rightarrow(A+(E\times S))$. In addition $\mathfrak{D}$ and $\mathfrak{T}$, which are elements of $Dec\rightarrow U\rightarrow X\rightarrow C$, will tally with valuations $\P\mathfrak{D}$ and $\P\mathfrak{T}$ in $Dec\rightarrow U\rightarrow S\rightarrow(A+(U\times S))$, whereas $\mathfrak{G}$ and $\mathfrak{C}$ will produce $\P\mathfrak{G}$ and $\P\mathfrak{C}$, both of which will be in $U\rightarrow S\rightarrow(A+S)$.

To formalize the connections between these various valuations we proceed as follows. We suppose that $\{W_i \mid n+n\geq i>0\}$ is a family of domains for which there is a family of predicates $\{w_j \mid n\geq j\geq 1\}$ such that when $n\geq j\geq 1$ w_j maps $W_j\times W_{n+j}$ into the domain T' of 2.2.2; we also introduce integers $k\geq 1$, $l\geq 1$ and $m\geq 0$ having $k+l+m+1=n$, and we allow ω_i to signify a typical member of W_i when $n+n\geq i\geq 0$. If ϕ ranges over members of $W_{n+k+l+1}\rightarrow\ldots\rightarrow W_{n+k+l+m}\rightarrow(W_{n+n}+W_0)$, ψ ranges over members of $W_{n+k+l+1}\rightarrow\ldots\rightarrow W_{n+k+l+m}\rightarrow W_{n+n}$ and o ranges over members of $W_{n+n}+(W_{n+k+l+1}\times\ldots\times W_{n+k+l+m})$ we write

$$fit=\lambda\phi o.\, o\,E\,W_{n+n}\rightarrow o,$$
$$\phi((o|(W_{n+k+l+1}\times\ldots\times W_{n+k+l+m}))\downarrow 1)\ldots((o|(W_{n+k+l+1}\times\ldots\times W_{n+k+l+m}))\downarrow m),$$

so that $fit\phi o$ is invariably a member of $W_{n+n}+W_0$, and

$$set=\lambda\psi o.\, o\,E\,W_{n+n}\rightarrow o|W_{n+n},$$
$$\psi((o|(W_{n+k+l+1}\times\ldots\times W_{n+k+l+m}))\downarrow 1)\ldots((o|(W_{n+k+l+1}\times\ldots\times W_{n+k+l+m}))\downarrow m),$$

so that $set\psi o$ is in W_{n+n}. Given a syntactic domain named Dom, an element X of Dom and a valuation $\mathfrak{X}$ belonging to

$$Dom\rightarrow W_1\rightarrow\ldots\rightarrow W_k\rightarrow(W_{k+l+1}\rightarrow\ldots\rightarrow W_{k+l+m}\rightarrow W_n)\rightarrow(W_{k+1}\rightarrow\ldots\rightarrow W_{k+l}\rightarrow W_n)$$

we shall say that a valuation $\P\mathfrak{X}$ defined on

$$Dom\rightarrow W_{n+1}\rightarrow\ldots\rightarrow W_{n+k}\rightarrow W_{n+k+1}\rightarrow\ldots\rightarrow W_{n+k+l}\rightarrow(W_{n+n}+(W_{n+k+l+1}\times\ldots\times W_{n+k+l+m}))$$

is 'conjugate' to $\mathfrak{X}$ for X under q if and only if $q\langle\mathfrak{X}[\![X]\!],\xi\rangle=true$ where

$\xi=\lambda\omega_{n+1}\ldots\omega_{n+k}\psi\omega_{n+k+1}\ldots\omega_{n+k+l}.set\psi(¶\mathfrak{X}[\![X]\!]\omega_{n+1}\ldots\omega_{n+k}\omega_{n+k+1}\ldots\omega_{n+k+l})$ and where, in terms of the notation introduced in 3.8.2, $q=w_1\to\ldots\to w_k\to(w_{k+l+1}\to\ldots\to w_{k+l+m}\to w_n)\to(w_{k+1}\to\ldots\to w_{k+l}\to w_n)$. Naturally these definitions carry across almost unchanged to situations in which m is 1, when we presume that *fit*, *set* and ¶$\mathfrak{X}$ are set up using $W_{n+k+l+1}$ instead of $W_{n+k+l+1}\times\ldots\times W_{n+k+l+m}$.

As we are considering only serial programs the family $\{W_j|n\geq j\geq 1\}$ will be composed from E, U, S and A and we shall assume, for the present, that $\{W_{n+j}|n\geq j\geq 1\}$ is formed in the same way. We shall also fix our attention on four predicates, e, u, s and a, which are defined on E×E, U×U, S×S and A×A respectively and which together produce the family $\{w_j|n\geq j\geq 1\}$.

When finding conjugates for the main valuations of appendix 1 we identify W_l and W_{n+l} with S, W_{k+l} and W_{n+k+l} with S, W_{k+l+m} and $W_{n+k+l+m}$ with S and W_n and W_{n+n} with A; moreover we let k be 1, l be 1 and m be 1 or 2 and we take W_1 and W_{n+1} to be E or U unless m is 1. Thus of particular importance in 3.9.2 will be the versions of *set* defined on $(E\to S\to A)\to(A+(E\times S))\to A$, $(U\to S\to A)\to(A+(U\times S))\to A$ and $(S\to A)\to(A+S)\to A$; these are given by the equations
$set=\lambda\kappa o.o\,E\,A\to o|A,\kappa((o|(E\times S))\downarrow 1)((o|(E\times S))\downarrow 2)$,
$set=\lambda\chi o.o\,E\,A\to o|A,\chi((o|(U\times S))\downarrow 1)((o|(U\times S))\downarrow 2)$ and
$set=\lambda\theta o.o\,E\,A\to o|A,\theta(o|S)$ when o is allowed to represent successively a member of A+(E×S), a member of A+(U×S), and a member of A+S.

3.9.2. Programs without jumps.

We naturally wish to define $\P\mathcal{E}$, $\P\mathcal{L}$ and $\P\mathcal{R}$ in such a way that when $\P\mathcal{E}$ is conjugate to $\mathcal{E}$ for an expression E under $u\to(e\to s\to a)\to(s\to a)$ then $\P\mathcal{L}$ and $\P\mathcal{R}$ are conjugate to $\mathcal{L}$ and $\mathcal{R}$ (respectively) for E under $u\to(e\to s\to a)\to(s\to a)$. This means that when $(u\to(e\to s\to a)\to(s\to a))\langle\mathcal{E}[\![E]\!],\lambda\rho\kappa.set\kappa\circ(\P\mathcal{E}[\![E]\!]\rho)\rangle=true$ we want to be sure that $(u\to(e\to s\to a)\to(s\to a))\langle\mathcal{L}[\![E]\!],\lambda\rho\kappa.set\kappa\circ(\P\mathcal{L}[\![E]\!]\rho)\rangle=true$ and that $(u\to(e\to s\to a)\to(s\to a))\langle\mathcal{R}[\![E]\!],\lambda\rho\kappa.set\kappa\circ(\P\mathcal{R}[\![E]\!]\rho)\rangle=true$. We therefore insist that, for every pair $\langle\varepsilon_0,\varepsilon_1\rangle$ belonging to E such that at least one of ε_0 or ε_1 is either improper or a location in L, $e\langle\varepsilon_0,\varepsilon_1\rangle=true$ if and only if $\varepsilon_0=\varepsilon_1$. Implicitly transforming members of L and V into members of E enables us to set

$$s=\lambda\langle\sigma_0,\sigma_1\rangle.\bigwedge\{e\langle hold\alpha_0\sigma_0,hold\alpha_1\sigma_1\rangle\wedge(area\alpha_0\sigma_0\equiv area\alpha_1\sigma_1)\mid e\langle\alpha_0,\alpha_1\rangle\}$$
$$\wedge((\#\sigma_0\downarrow2\equiv\#\sigma_1\downarrow2)\to\bigwedge\{e\langle\sigma_0\downarrow2\downarrow\nu,\sigma_1\downarrow2\downarrow\nu\rangle\mid\#\sigma_0\downarrow2\geq\nu\geq1\},false)$$
$$\wedge((\#\sigma_1\downarrow3\equiv\#\sigma_1\downarrow3)\to\bigwedge\{e\langle\sigma_0\downarrow3\downarrow\nu,\sigma_1\downarrow3\downarrow\nu\rangle\mid\#\sigma_0\downarrow3\geq\nu\geq1\},false);$$

in addition we assume that $a\langle\bot,\bot\rangle=true$, that $a\langle\top,\top\rangle=true$, and that $a\langle wrong\sigma_0,wrong\sigma_1\rangle=true$ and $new\sigma_0=new\sigma_1$ whenever $s\langle\sigma_0,\sigma_1\rangle=true$. Under these circumstances it is easy to demonstrate that $((e\to s\to a)\to(e\to s\to a))\langle lv,\lambda\kappa.set\kappa\circ\phi_0\rangle=true$ and that $((e\to s\to a)\to(e\to s\to a))\langle rv,\lambda\kappa.set\kappa\circ\phi_1\rangle=true$ where ϕ_0 and ϕ_1 are the members of $E\to S\to(A+(E\times S))$ given by the equations $\phi_0=\lambda\varepsilon\sigma.(\varepsilon E L\to\langle\varepsilon,\sigma\rangle,new\sigma E L\to\langle new\sigma|L,update(new\sigma|L)\varepsilon\sigma\rangle,wrong\sigma)$ and $\phi_1=\lambda\varepsilon\sigma.(\varepsilon E L\to\langle hold(\varepsilon|L)\sigma,\sigma\rangle,\langle\varepsilon,\sigma\rangle)$; plainly here *set* must be deemed to be a member of $(E\to S\to A)\to(A+(E\times S))\to A$. When *fit* is a member of $(E\to S\to(A+(E\times S)))\to(A+(E\times S))\to(A+(E\times S))$, for every expression E we set $\P\mathcal{L}[\![E]\!]=\lambda\rho.fit\phi_0\circ\P\mathcal{E}[\![E]\!]\rho$ and $\P\mathcal{R}[\![E]\!]=\lambda\rho.fit\phi_1\circ\P\mathcal{E}[\![E]\!]\rho$. As $\lambda\kappa\phi.set(set\kappa\circ\phi)=\lambda\kappa\phi.set\kappa\circ fit\phi$, we know that $\lambda\rho\kappa.set\kappa\circ(\P\mathcal{L}[\![E]\!]\rho)=\lambda\rho\kappa.set(set\kappa\circ\phi_0)\circ(\P\mathcal{E}[\![E]\!]\rho)$ and that $\lambda\rho\kappa.set\kappa\circ(\P\mathcal{R}[\![E]\!]\rho)=\lambda\rho\kappa.set(set\kappa\circ\phi_1)\circ(\P\mathcal{E}[\![E]\!]\rho)$; hence when $(u\to(e\to s\to a)\to(s\to a))\langle\mathcal{E}[\![E]\!],\lambda\rho\kappa.set\kappa\circ(\P\mathcal{E}[\![E]\!]\rho\kappa)\rangle=true$, we may safely assume that $\mathcal{L}$ and $\mathcal{R}$ satisfy the equations

$(u\to(e\to s\to a)\to(s\to a))\langle \mathcal{L}[\![E]\!], \lambda\rho\kappa.set\kappa\circ(\P\mathcal{L}[\![E]\!]\rho\kappa)\rangle = true$ and

$(u\to(e\to s\to a)\to(s\to a))\langle \mathcal{R}[\![E]\!], \lambda\rho\kappa.set\kappa\circ(\P\mathcal{R}[\![E]\!]\rho\kappa)\rangle = true$.

If we are to have any confidence that the valuation $\P\mathcal{E}$ exists we must be able to remove the continuations which are among the arguments of $\mathcal{B}$, $\mathcal{O}$ and $\mathcal{W}$. Accordingly we presume that there are valuations $\P\mathcal{B}$, $\P\mathcal{O}$ and $\P\mathcal{W}$ which belong to

$Bas\to S\to(A+(E\times S))$, $Mon\to E\to S\to(A+(E\times S))$ and $Dya\to E\to E\to S\to(A+(E\times S))$

and are conjugate to $\mathcal{B}$, $\mathcal{O}$ and $\mathcal{W}$ for all B, O and Ω under $(e\to s\to a)\to(s\to a)$, $(e\to s\to a)\to(e\to s\to a)$ and $(e\to s\to a)\to(e\to e\to s\to a)$ respectively. Less ambiguously, we demand that for all B, O and Ω

$((e\to s\to a)\to(s\to a))\langle \mathcal{B}[\![B]\!], \lambda\kappa.set\kappa\circ(\P\mathcal{B}[\![B]\!])\rangle = true$,

$((e\to s\to a)\to(e\to s\to a))\langle \mathcal{O}[\![O]\!], \lambda\kappa\varepsilon.set\kappa\circ(\P\mathcal{O}[\![O]\!]\varepsilon)\rangle = true$ and

$((e\to s\to a)\to(e\to e\to s\to a))\langle \mathcal{W}[\![\Omega]\!], \lambda\kappa\varepsilon'\varepsilon''.set\kappa\circ(\P\mathcal{W}[\![\Omega]\!]\varepsilon'\varepsilon'')\rangle = true$ where

the version of *set* required is that provided for $(E\to S\to A)\to(A+(E\times S))\to A$. This demand is not unreasonable, for bases are without side effects and without store dependence, while operators are intended mainly to convert elements of E into one another; as was hinted in 3.4.1, were we to supply members of V (instead of members of E) as arguments to operators, almost every operator would also be without store dependence.

To construct $\P\mathcal{B}$, $\P\mathcal{O}$ and $\P\mathcal{W}$ we strengthen the constraints on E by requiring that any pair $\langle \varepsilon_0, \varepsilon_1\rangle$ drawn from E is such that when either ε_0 or ε_1 is a basic value in B $e\langle \varepsilon_0, \varepsilon_1\rangle = true$ if and only if $\varepsilon_0 = \varepsilon_1$ whilst when either ε_0 or ε_1 is in E* $e\langle \varepsilon_0, \varepsilon_1\rangle = true$ if and only if both ε_0 and ε_1 are in E*, $\#(\varepsilon_0|E^*) = \#(\varepsilon_1|E^*)$ and $\bigwedge\{e\langle (\varepsilon_0|E^*)\downarrow\nu, (\varepsilon_1|E^*)\downarrow\nu\rangle \mid \#(\varepsilon_0|E^*)\geq\nu\geq 1\} = true$. We may now blithely define $\P\mathcal{B}$ by means of such equations as $\P\mathcal{B}[\![\mathbf{true}]\!] = \lambda\sigma.\langle true, \sigma\rangle$ and $\P\mathcal{B}[\![\mathbf{false}]\!] = \lambda\sigma.\langle false, \sigma\rangle$. Likewise we may set up $\P\mathcal{O}$ and $\P\mathcal{W}$ for those operators which do not act on label or procedure values; for example, $\mathcal{O}[\![\$]\!] = \phi_1$ and $\P\mathcal{W}[\![\&]\!] = \lambda\varepsilon'\varepsilon''.fit(\lambda\varepsilon\sigma.\varepsilon E E^*\to\langle\langle \varepsilon'\rangle \S (\varepsilon|E^*), \sigma\rangle, wrong\sigma)\circ\phi_1\varepsilon''$ when

ϕ_1 is defined as above. In practice $\phi_1\varepsilon\sigma$ cannot belong to the summand A of A+(E×S), so we could dispense with part of the equation for $\P\mathfrak{W}[\![\&]\!]$; however a slight change in the definition of *rv* given in 3.3.4 would entail setting $\phi_1=\lambda\varepsilon\sigma.(\varepsilon\in L\to(area(\varepsilon|L)\sigma\to\langle hold(\varepsilon|L)\sigma,\sigma\rangle,wrong\,\sigma),\langle\varepsilon,\sigma\rangle)$, when this equation would be needed. If we choose expressions E, E_0 and E_1 in such a way that $\P\mathcal{E}[\![E]\!]$, $\P\mathcal{E}[\![E_0]\!]$ and $\P\mathcal{E}[\![E_1]\!]$ exist we may define $\P\mathcal{E}[\![B]\!]$, $\P\mathcal{E}[\![OE]\!]$ and $\P\mathcal{E}[\![E_0\Omega E_1]\!]$ by setting $\P\mathcal{E}[\![B]\!]=\lambda\rho.\P\mathfrak{B}[\![B]\!]$, $\P\mathcal{E}[\![OE]\!]=\lambda\rho.fit(\P\mathcal{O}[\![O]\!])\circ\P\mathcal{E}[\![E]\!]\rho$ and either $\P\mathcal{E}[\![E_0\Omega E_1]\!]=\lambda\rho.fit(\lambda\varepsilon'.fit(\lambda\varepsilon''.\P\mathfrak{W}[\![\Omega]\!]\varepsilon'\varepsilon'')\circ\P\mathcal{E}[\![E_1]\!]\rho)\circ\P\mathcal{E}[\![E_0]\!]\rho$ or $\P\mathcal{E}[\![E_0\Omega E_1]\!]=\lambda\rho.fit(\lambda\varepsilon''.fit(\lambda\varepsilon'.\P\mathfrak{W}[\![\Omega]\!]\varepsilon'\varepsilon'')\circ\P\mathcal{E}[\![E_0]\!]\rho)\circ\P\mathcal{E}[\![E_1]\!]\rho$, depending on the order in which *run* applies its arguments. Furthermore if $\P\mathcal{E}$ is conjugate to $\mathcal{E}$ for E, E_0 and E_1 under $u\to(e\to s\to a)\to(s\to a)$ we can readily confirm that $\P\mathcal{E}$ is conjugate to $\mathcal{E}$ for B, OE and $E_0\Omega E_1$ under $u\to(e\to s\to a)\to(s\to a)$.

In the standard semantics of Sal which appears in appendix 1 the valuation $\mathfrak{F}$ is defined on Abs→U→F where F is E→K→C; thus $\mathfrak{F}$ is actually a member of Abs→U→E→(E→S→A)→(S→A). This suggests that we seek a valuation $\P\mathfrak{F}$ belonging to Abs→U→E→S→(A+(E×S)) which is conjugate to $\mathfrak{F}$ for certain abstractions under $u\to e\to(e\to s\to a)\to(s\to a)$. Such a valuation can indeed be formed; for instance we can let $\P\mathcal{E}[\![\mathrm{fn}I..E]\!]=\lambda\rho\varepsilon.fit(\lambda\varepsilon'.\mathcal{E}[\![E]\!]\rho[\varepsilon'/I])\circ\phi_1\varepsilon$.
However, we cannot now set $\P\mathfrak{F}[\![\Phi]\!]=\lambda\rho\sigma.\langle\P\mathfrak{H}[\![\Phi]\!]\rho,\sigma\rangle$ for any abstraction Φ, since if we wish to prove that $(u\to(e\to s\to a)\to(s\to a))\langle\mathfrak{F}[\![\Phi]\!],\lambda\rho\kappa.set\kappa\circ(\P\mathfrak{H}[\![\Phi]\!]\rho)\rangle=true$ we must ascribe a meaning to $\lambda\rho\kappa.\kappa(\P\mathfrak{H}[\![\Phi]\!]\rho)$ and thus view E→S→(A+(E×S)) as a summand of E. We shall disregard this strategem until 4.2.7, preferring instead to write $\P\mathfrak{F}[\![\Phi]\!]=\lambda\rho\sigma.\langle\mathfrak{F}[\![\Phi]\!]\rho,\sigma\rangle$ where $\mathfrak{F}$ is the valuation provided by appendix 1.

Having decided how to treat procedures we can complete our account of *e* by stipulating that, for every pair $\langle\varepsilon_0,\varepsilon_1\rangle$ belonging to **E** and having at least one of ε_0 and ε_1 in the summand J or the summand F, $e\langle \varepsilon_0,\varepsilon_1\rangle = true$ if and only if $\varepsilon_0=\varepsilon_1$. After collecting all our information about e together we may write

$$e=\lambda\langle \varepsilon_0,\varepsilon_1\rangle.(\varepsilon_0\equiv\bot)\vee(\varepsilon_1\equiv\bot)\rightarrow(\varepsilon_0\equiv\bot)\wedge(\varepsilon_1\equiv\bot),$$
$$(\varepsilon_0\equiv\top)\vee(\varepsilon_1\equiv\top)\rightarrow(\varepsilon_0\equiv\top)\wedge(\varepsilon_1\equiv\top),$$
$$\varepsilon_0 E \mathrm{L}\wedge\varepsilon_1 E \mathrm{L}\rightarrow(\varepsilon_0|\mathrm{L}\equiv\varepsilon_1|\mathrm{L}),$$
$$\varepsilon_0 E \mathrm{B}\wedge\varepsilon_1 E \mathrm{B}\rightarrow(\varepsilon_0|\mathrm{B}\equiv\varepsilon_1|\mathrm{B}),$$
$$\varepsilon_0 E \mathrm{E}^*\wedge\varepsilon_1 E \mathrm{E}^*\rightarrow(\lambda\langle \varepsilon^*_0,\varepsilon^*_1\rangle.(\#\varepsilon^*_0\equiv\#\varepsilon^*_1)\rightarrow\bigwedge\{e\langle \varepsilon^*_0\downarrow\nu,\varepsilon^*_1\downarrow\nu\rangle\mid\#\varepsilon^*_0\geq\nu\geq1\},$$
$$false)$$
$$(\langle \varepsilon_0|\mathrm{E}^*,\varepsilon_1|\mathrm{E}^*\rangle),$$
$$\varepsilon_0 E \mathrm{J}\wedge\varepsilon_1 E \mathrm{J}\rightarrow(\varepsilon_0|\mathrm{J}\equiv\varepsilon_1|\mathrm{J}),$$
$$\varepsilon_0 E \mathrm{F}\wedge\varepsilon_1 E \mathrm{F}\rightarrow(\varepsilon_0|\mathrm{F}\equiv\varepsilon_1|\mathrm{F}),$$
$$false.$$

This version of e permits us to define $\P\mathcal{O}$ and $\P\mathcal{W}$ on those operators which act on label and procedure values simply by converting $\mathcal{O}$ and $\mathcal{W}$ appropriately; thus

$$\mathcal{O}[\![\mathcal{E}]\!]=\lambda\varepsilon.fit(\lambda\varepsilon'\sigma.\varepsilon' E \mathrm{F}\rightarrow\langle\lambda\varepsilon''\kappa.rv(lv(\lambda\varepsilon'''.(\varepsilon'|\mathrm{F})\varepsilon'''\kappa))\varepsilon'',\sigma\rangle,wrong\sigma)\circ\phi_1\varepsilon.$$

Anyone who has followed us this far may have formed a shrewd suspicion that $e=\lambda\langle \varepsilon_0,\varepsilon_1\rangle.(\varepsilon_0\equiv\varepsilon_1)$. This is indeed the case when e is the least fixed point of the obvious equation (as can be proved by applying the technique to be developed in 3.9.8); we shall not prove this fact but will assume it, with the effect that $e=\lambda\langle \varepsilon_0,\varepsilon_1\rangle.(\varepsilon_0\equiv\varepsilon_1)$ and $s=\lambda\langle \sigma_0,\sigma_1\rangle.(\sigma_0\equiv\sigma_1)$. Here is perhaps also the place to admit that we shall take a to be the test for equality between members of A by writing $a=\lambda\langle o_0,o_1\rangle.(o_0\equiv o_1)$. Nevertheless, although $e\rightarrow s\rightarrow a$, for instance, becomes $\lambda\langle \kappa_0,\kappa_1\rangle.(\kappa_0\equiv\kappa_1)$ we shall continue to use the notation $e\rightarrow s\rightarrow a$, because much of our argument will pass across unchanged to the situation in 4.2.7, where e will not be $\lambda\langle \varepsilon_0,\varepsilon_1\rangle.(\varepsilon_0\equiv\varepsilon_1)$. The sole reason for taking e, s and a to be tests for equality is to prove 3.9.3, which is intended to ensure that $(u\rightarrow e)\langle \mathcal{H}[\![\Phi]\!],\mathcal{H}[\![\Phi]\!]\rangle = true$ (and therefore that $(u\rightarrow(e\rightarrow s\rightarrow a)\rightarrow(s\rightarrow a))\langle \mathcal{E}[\![\Phi]\!],\lambda\rho\kappa.set\kappa\circ(\P\mathcal{E}[\![\Phi]\!]\rho)\rangle = true$); when this reason becomes redundant, as it will do in 4.2.7, we shall be free to set up e, s and a differently.

The nature of u is governed by the semantic equation for identifiers, which evidently dictates that if $u\langle\rho_0,\rho_1\rangle=true$ and if $\rho_0[\![I]\!]\downarrow 1$ and $\rho_1[\![I]\!]\downarrow 1$ are in those summands of D which are also summands of E then $e\langle\rho_0[\![I]\!]\downarrow 1,\rho_1[\![I]\!]\downarrow 1\rangle$ should be $true$; when $\rho_0[\![I]\!]\downarrow 1$ is in G we allow $\rho_1[\![I]\!]\downarrow 1$ either to be in G (in which case $((e\to s\to a)\to(s\to a))\langle\rho_0[\![I]\!]\downarrow 1,\rho_1[\![I]\!]\downarrow 1\rangle$ must be $true$) or to be in a summand of E (in which case $((e\to s\to a)\to(s\to a))\langle\rho_0[\![I]\!]\downarrow 1,\lambda\kappa.\kappa(\rho_1[\![I]\!]\downarrow 1)\rangle$ must be $true$). In symbolic terms, when

$$\begin{aligned}d=\lambda\langle\delta_0,\delta_1\rangle.\ &(\delta_0\equiv\bot)\wedge(\delta_1\equiv\bot)\to(\delta_0\equiv\bot)\wedge(\delta_1\equiv\bot),\\ &(\delta_0\equiv\top)\wedge(\delta_1\equiv\top)\to(\delta_0\equiv\top)\wedge(\delta_1\equiv\top),\\ &\delta_0\mathsf{E}\mathrm{G}\to((e\to s\to a)\to(s\to a))\langle\delta_0,\lambda\kappa.(\delta_1\mathsf{E}\mathrm{G}\to\delta_1\kappa,\kappa\delta_1)\rangle,\\ &\delta_1\mathsf{E}\mathrm{G}\to false,\\ &e\langle\delta_0,\delta_1\rangle,\end{aligned}$$

(so that if δ_0 and δ_1 are any denoted values subject to the restriction $d\langle\delta_0,\delta_1\rangle=true$ then either $\delta_0=\delta_1$ or $\delta_0=\lambda\kappa.\kappa\delta_1$) we agree to let

$$\begin{aligned}u=\lambda\langle\rho_0,\rho_1\rangle.\ &\bigwedge\{(\#\rho_0[\![I]\!]\equiv\#\rho_1[\![I]\!])\to\bigwedge\{d\langle\rho_0[\![I]\!]\downarrow\nu,\rho_1[\![I]\!]\downarrow\nu\rangle\mid\#\rho_0[\![I]\!]\geq\nu\geq 1\},false\mid I\}\\ &\wedge(\rho_0[\![\mathsf{res}]\!]\equiv\rho_1[\![\mathsf{res}]\!]).\end{aligned}$$

Thus when $\P\mathcal{E}[\![I]\!]=\lambda\rho\sigma.(\rho[\![I]\!]\downarrow 1\mathsf{E}\mathrm{G}\to wrong\sigma,\langle\rho[\![I]\!]\downarrow 1,\sigma\rangle)$ and $u\langle\rho_0,\rho_1\rangle=true$ we know that $((e\to s\to a)\to(s\to a))\langle\mathcal{E}[\![I]\!]\rho_0,\lambda\kappa.set\kappa\circ(\P\mathcal{E}[\![I]\!]\rho_1)\rangle=true$ provided that $\rho_1[\![I]\!]\downarrow 1$ is not a member of G.

For any element X of Exp+Abs+Seq+Dec+Blo+Com and for any list I* in Ide* we shall say that X is 'orderly' in I* if and only if outside the bodies of abstractions X contains:

(i) no mention of the syntactic structures E_0E_1, Σ, val E, I:Γ and I::Γ;

(ii) no declaration of the form rec Δ such that an element of the list $\mathcal{H}[\![\Delta]\!]$ occurs free in Δ outside the body of an abstraction;

(iii) no free occurrence of any member of the list I*.

In addition we shall set:

$u_0 = \lambda I^* \langle \rho_0, \rho_1 \rangle . u\langle \rho_0, \rho_1 \rangle \wedge \bigwedge\{ I \in I^* \mid \rho_1[\![I]\!] \downarrow 1 \in G \}$;

$u_1 = \lambda I^* \langle \rho_0, \rho_1 \rangle . u\langle \rho_0, \rho_1 \rangle \wedge \bigwedge\{ (\rho_0[\![I]\!] \downarrow 1 \equiv \bot) \vee (\rho_0[\![I]\!] \downarrow 1 \equiv \top) \to \mathit{false}, \sim(\rho_0[\![I]\!] \downarrow 1 \in G) \mid I \in I^* \}$;

$u_2 = \lambda I^* \langle \rho_0, \rho_1 \rangle . (\lambda \phi . u\langle \phi\rho_0, \phi\rho_1 \rangle)(\lambda \rho . \langle \lambda I . ((I \in I^*) \to \langle\rangle, \rho[\![I]\!]), \rho[\![\mathrm{res}]\!] \rangle)$.

The first of these definitions could be given more formally by introducing a suitable assemblage of recursive functions, but there is little point in doing so since the intuitive content of the notion is what is important. Essentially we are trying to restrict programs in such a way that they do not require continuations either to set up labels (as in val E, I:Γ and I::Γ) or to bring about jumps (as in Σ). The elimination of terms of the form E_0E_1 allows us to stop abstractions from being applied and thus to stop continuations from being supplied to abstractions, so any syntactic structure may occur inside the body of an abstraction. Together with the use of u_0 and the constraints on the identifiers declared recursively or appearing as free variables outside abstractions the omission of E_0E_1 can also serve to prevent a continuation from being passed to a member of G which fails to terminate or causes a jump.

Although the connection between the valuations of standard semantics and certain conjugate valuations is of interest in its own right, here we are investigating it mainly because of the justification that it provides for the semantics of recursive declarations which we have adopted. Accordingly in the definitions above we have not tried to reduce the restrictions on X to a minimum but merely to provide a class of constructs which includes every reasonable recursive declaration. A different class of constructs will be suggested in 4.2.7; now, however, we must make use of our present one. For convenience in doing so we introduce one final predicate, j, such that

$j = \lambda \langle \theta^*_0, \theta^*_1 \rangle . (\#\theta^*_0 \equiv \#\theta^*_1) \to \bigwedge\{ (s \to a)\langle \theta^*_0 \downarrow \nu, \theta^*_1 \downarrow \nu \rangle \mid \#\theta^*_0 \geq \nu \geq 1 \}, \mathit{false}$.

Those who wish to do so may skip the proofs (though not the statements) of the next two results.

3.9.3. Proposition.

In Sal all E, Φ, Σ, Δ, Θ and Γ are such that, in terms of the predicates of 3.9.2, E is EE-similar, LL-similar and RR-similar to E under $u\to(e\to s\to a)\to(s\to a)$, Φ is FF-similar to Φ under $u\to e\to(e\to s\to a)\to(s\to a)$, Σ is SS-similar to Σ under $u\to(s\to a)$, Δ is DD-similar and TT-similar to Δ under $u\to(u\to s\to a)\to(s\to a)$, Θ is GG-similar to Θ under $u\to(s\to a)\to(s\to a)$, Γ is CC-similar to Γ under $u\to(s\to a)\to(s\to a)$, and Γ is PP-similar and QQ-similar to Γ under $u\to(s\to a)\to j$.

◁ We begin by noting that when $u\langle\rho_0,\rho_1\rangle=true$ then for any identifier I if $\rho_0[\![I]\!]\downarrow1=\bot$ then $\rho_1[\![I]\!]\downarrow1=\bot$, if $\rho_0[\![I]\!]\downarrow1=\top$ then $\rho_1[\![I]\!]\downarrow1=\top$, if $\rho_0[\![I]\!]\downarrow1$ is a summand of E then $\rho_1[\![I]\!]\downarrow1$ is in a summand of E and $e\langle\rho_0[\![I]\!]\downarrow1,\rho_1[\![I]\!]\downarrow1\rangle=true$, and if $\rho_0[\![I]\!]\downarrow1$ is in G then either $\rho_1[\![I]\!]\downarrow1$ is in G and $((e\to s\to a)\to(s\to a))\langle\rho_0[\![I]\!]\downarrow1,\rho_1[\![I]\!]\downarrow1\rangle=true$ or $\rho_1[\![I]\!]\downarrow1$ is in a summand of E and $(e\to s\to a)\langle\rho_0[\![I]\!]\downarrow1,\lambda\kappa.\kappa(\rho_0[\![I]\!]\downarrow1)\rangle=true$. Since $a\langle\bot,\bot\rangle=true$ and $a\langle\top,\top\rangle=true$, under all these circumstances $((e\to s\to a)\to(s\to a))\langle\mathcal{E}[\![I]\!]\rho_0,\mathcal{E}[\![I]\!]\rho_1\rangle=true$ and, as $\langle\rho_0,\rho_1\rangle$ can be any pair for which $u\langle\rho_0,\rho_1\rangle=true$, I is EE-similar to I under $u\to(e\to s\to a)\to(s\to a)$.

We can now proceed by using a trivial structural induction (or just by quoting the results in 3.8.2). Thus, for example, if $u\langle\rho_0,\rho_1\rangle=true$ and $u\langle\rho_2,\rho_3\rangle=true$ then $u\langle divert\rho_0\rho_2,divert\rho_1\rho_3\rangle=true$, so when E is EE-similar to E under $u\to(e\to s\to a)\to(s\to a)$ and Δ is DD-similar to Δ under $u\to(u\to s\to a)\to(s\to a)$ Δ **inside** E must be EE-similar to Δ **inside** E under $u\to(e\to s\to a)\to a$. The other cases requiring examination are equally simple; the only interest is provided by **rec** Δ and **block** Γ (which apply the facts that $a\langle\bot,\bot\rangle=true$ and that d is inclusive) and by **while** E **do** Γ (which involves the assumptions that $a\langle\bot,\bot\rangle=true$ and that a is inclusive).▷

In fact we only need to know that every abstraction Φ satisfies $(u\to e)\langle\mathcal{F}[\![\Phi]\!],\mathcal{F}[\![\Phi]\!]\rangle=true$, but proving this obviously entails establishing the more general result given above.

3.9.4. Proposition.

Suppose that E, Δ, Θ and Γ are orderly in some list I*. There are valuations $\P\mathfrak{E}$, $\P\mathfrak{L}$, $\P\mathfrak{R}$, $\P\mathfrak{D}$, $\P\mathfrak{T}$, $\P\mathfrak{G}$ and $\P\mathfrak{C}$ such that, in terms of the predicates of 3.9.2, $\P\mathfrak{E}$ is conjugate to $\mathfrak{E}$ for E under $u_0 I^* \to (e\to s\to a)\to(s\to a)$, $\P\mathfrak{L}$ is conjugate to $\mathfrak{L}$ for E under $u_0 I^* \to (e\to s\to a)\to(s\to a)$, $\P\mathfrak{R}$ is conjugate to $\mathfrak{R}$ for E under $u_0 I^* \to (e\to s\to a)\to(s\to a)$, $\P\mathfrak{D}$ is conjugate to $\mathfrak{D}$ for Δ under $u_0 I^* \to (u_1(\mathfrak{I}[\![\Delta]\!]\S\mathfrak{H}[\![\Delta]\!])\to s\to a)\to(s\to a)$, $\P\mathfrak{T}$ is conjugate to $\mathfrak{T}$ for Δ under $u_0 I^* \to (u_1(\mathfrak{I}[\![\Delta]\!]\S\mathfrak{H}[\![\Delta]\!])\to s\to a)\to(s\to a)$, $\P\mathfrak{G}$ is conjugate to $\mathfrak{G}$ for Θ under $u_0 I^* \to (s\to a)\to(s\to a)$ and $\P\mathfrak{C}$ is conjugate to $\mathfrak{C}$ for Γ under $u_0 I^* \to (s\to a)\to(s\to a)$. In addition when $\langle\rho_0,\rho_1\rangle$ and $\langle\sigma_0,\sigma_1\rangle$ are chosen in such a way that $u_2 I^*\langle\rho_0,\rho_1\rangle = true$ and $s\langle\sigma_0,\sigma_1\rangle = true$ then unless $\P\mathfrak{E}[\![E]\!]\rho_2\sigma_1$ is drawn from the summand E×S of A+(E×S) for every ρ_2 having $u_2 I^*\langle\rho_0,\rho_2\rangle = true$ $\P\mathfrak{E}[\![E]\!]\rho_1\sigma_1$ is not in E×S and $((e\to s\to a)\to a)\langle\lambda\kappa.\mathfrak{E}[\![E]\!]\rho_0\kappa\sigma_0, \lambda\kappa.set\kappa(\P\mathfrak{E}[\![E]\!]\rho_1\sigma_1)\rangle = true$; analogous remarks apply to $\mathfrak{L}$, $\mathfrak{R}$, $\mathfrak{D}$, $\mathfrak{T}$, $\mathfrak{G}$ and $\mathfrak{C}$.

∢Predictably the proof of this result involves an induction on the structure of those programs which are orderly for some list of identifiers. In the course of this induction we need to define the valuations such as $\P\mathfrak{E}$ by means of mutually recursive equations. Some of these equations were given in 3.9.2, where we indicated, for instance, how to demonstrate that if $\P\mathfrak{E}$ is conjugate to $\mathfrak{E}$ for E, E_0 and E_1 under $u_0 I^* \to (e\to s\to a)\to(s\to a)$ then $\P\mathfrak{E}$ can be set up on B, OE and $E_0 \Omega E_1$ in such a way that $\P\mathfrak{E}$ is conjugate to $\mathfrak{E}$ for B, OE and $E_0 \Omega E_1$ under $u_0 I^* \to (e\to s\to a)\to(s\to a)$. Here we shall simply provide a few more portions of the definitions of the valuations and explain how to carry out the appropriate parts of the structural induction for two of them.

We already know the descriptions of $\P\mathfrak{L}$ and $\P\mathfrak{R}$ in terms of $\P\mathfrak{E}$, so without a qualm we may let $\P\mathfrak{E}[\![E_0?E_1!E_2]\!]$ be
$\lambda\rho.fit(\lambda\varepsilon.\varepsilon\mathrm{E}\mathrm{B}\to(\varepsilon|\mathrm{B}\mathrm{E}\mathrm{T}\to(\varepsilon|\mathrm{B}|\mathrm{T}\to\P\mathfrak{E}[\![E_1]\!]\rho, \P\mathfrak{E}[\![E_2]\!]\rho), wrong), wrong)\circ(\P\mathfrak{R}[\![E_0]\!]\rho)$.
As was hinted in 3.9.2 we take $\P\mathfrak{E}[\![I]\!]$ to be

$\lambda\rho\sigma.(\rho[\![I]\!]\downarrow 1 \in G \to wrong\sigma, \langle \rho[\![I]\!]\downarrow 1, \sigma\rangle)$ and $\P\mathcal{E}[\![\Phi]\!]$ to be $\lambda\rho\sigma.\langle \mathcal{F}[\![\Phi]\!]\rho,\sigma\rangle$ (where $\mathcal{F}$ is, of course, the valuation defined in appendix 1). It is plain that if I is orderly in I* then I is not an element of I* so $(u_2 I^* \to (e\to s\to a)\to(s\to a))\langle \mathcal{E}[\![I]\!], \lambda\rho\kappa.set\kappa\circ(\P\mathcal{E}[\![I]\!]\rho)\rangle = true$ and unless $\#\rho_1[\![I]\!]=0$ $\P\mathcal{E}[\![I]\!]\rho_1\sigma_1$ is in E×S if $u_2 I^*\langle \rho_0,\rho_1\rangle = true$ and $s\langle\sigma_0,\sigma_1\rangle = true$; moreover $(u_0 I^* \to (e\to s\to a)\to(s\to a))\langle \mathcal{E}[\![\Phi]\!], \lambda\rho\kappa.set\kappa\circ(\P\mathcal{E}[\![\Phi]\!]\rho)\rangle = true$, in accordance with 3.9.3, and $\P\mathcal{E}[\![\Phi]\!]\rho_1\sigma_1$ is always in E×S when $u_2 I^*\langle\rho_0,\rho_1\rangle = true$ and $s\langle\sigma_0,\sigma_1\rangle = true$. Likewise $\P\mathcal{E}[\![\Delta \text{ inside } E]\!]$, $\P\mathcal{E}[\![\Theta \text{ before } E]\!]$ and $\P\mathcal{E}[\![(E)]\!]$ can be safely written as $\lambda\rho.fit(\lambda\rho'.\P\mathcal{E}[\![E]\!](divert\rho\rho'))\circ(\P\mathcal{D}[\![\Delta]\!]\rho)$, $\lambda\rho.fit(\P\mathcal{E}[\![E]\!]\rho)\circ(\P\mathcal{G}[\![\Theta]\!]\rho)$ and $\lambda\rho.\P\mathcal{E}[\![E]\!]\rho$ respectively when fit is taken to be a member of $(U\to S\to(A+(E\times S)))\to(A+(U\times S))\to(A+(E\times S))$ (in the case of Δ inside E) or a member of $(S\to(A+(E\times S)))\to(A+S)\to(A+(E\times S))$ (in the case of Θ before E).

These remarks should suffice to clarify the construction of ¶𝓔 and its counterparts; the details can be filled in by any interested reader while we proceed to examine the lengthier parts of the induction, which concern rec Δ and while E do Γ. One of these will require the distinction between u and u_1 and will introduce the second half of the statement of the present result as an aid in establishing the first; the other will show why even in a program known to be free from errors we cannot hope to replace $\lambda\rho\theta.set\theta\circ(\P\mathcal{C}[\![\text{while } E \text{ do } \Gamma]\!]\rho)$ by $\lambda\rho\theta.\theta\circ(\P\mathcal{C}[\![\text{while } E \text{ do } \Gamma]\!]\rho)$ unless we consider no continuation θ for which $\theta\bot$ is not ⊥.

Accordingly we first suppose that rec Δ is orderly in I* for some list I*, so that Δ is orderly in I^*_0 when I^*_0 is composed by concatenating $\mathcal{K}[\![\Delta]\!]$ with the result of deleting from I* those elements which belong to $\mathcal{I}[\![\Delta]\!]$; that is,

$$I^*_0 = (fix(\lambda\psi I^*_1.(\#I^*_1=0)\to\langle\rangle, I^*_1\downarrow 1\in\mathcal{I}[\![\Delta]\!]\to\psi(I^*_1\dagger 1), \langle I^*_1\downarrow 1\rangle \S \psi(I^*_1\dagger 1))I^*)\S\mathcal{K}[\![\Delta]\!].$$

It is therefore natural to assume an inductive hypothesis to the effect that, when $x=u_1(\mathfrak{I}[\![\Delta]\!]\S\mathfrak{H}[\![\Delta]\!])\to s\to a$, $\P\mathcal{T}$ is conjugate to $\mathcal{T}$ for Δ under $u_0 I^*{}_0\to x\to(s\to a)$ and that when $u_2 I^*{}_0\langle\rho_0,\rho_1\rangle=true$ and $s\langle\sigma_0,\sigma_1\rangle=true$ then $\P\mathcal{T}[\![\Delta]\!]\rho_1\sigma_1$ is not in U×S and $(x\to a)\langle\lambda\chi.\mathcal{T}[\![\Delta]\!]\rho_0\chi\sigma_0,\lambda\chi.set\chi(\P\mathcal{T}[\![\Delta]\!]\rho_1\sigma_1)\rangle=true$ provided that for every ρ_2 with $u_2 I^*{}_0\langle\rho_0,\rho_2\rangle=true$ $\P\mathcal{T}[\![\Delta]\!]\rho_2\sigma_1$ is not in U×S. With the aid of these assumptions we can demonstrate that $\P\mathfrak{D}$ is conjugate to $\mathfrak{D}$ for rec Δ under $u_0 I^*\to(x\to s\to a)\to(s\to a)$ and that if $u_2 I^*\langle\rho_0,\rho_1\rangle=true$ and $s\langle\sigma_0,\sigma_1\rangle=true$ then $\P\mathfrak{D}[\![\text{rec }\Delta]\!]\rho_1\sigma_1$ is not drawn from U×S and $(x\to a)\langle\lambda\chi.\mathfrak{D}[\![\text{rec }\Delta]\!]\rho_0\chi\sigma_0,\lambda\chi.set\chi(\P\mathfrak{D}[\![\text{rec }\Delta]\!]\rho_1\sigma_1)\rangle=true$ unless $\P\mathfrak{D}[\![\text{rec }\Delta]\!]\rho_2\sigma_1$ is in U×S for every ρ_2 with $u_2 I^*\langle\rho_0,\rho_2\rangle=true$; here $\mathfrak{D}[\![\text{rec }\Delta]\!]$ is

$$\lambda\rho\sigma.(\lambda\sigma'.(\lambda\alpha^*.(\lambda\psi.(\lambda\rho'.\alpha^*\in L^*\to\P\mathcal{T}[\![\Delta]\!]\rho'\sigma',wrong\sigma')$$

$$(fix(\lambda\rho''.\rho[\alpha^*/\mathfrak{I}[\![\Delta]\!]][map(\psi\rho'')(\mathfrak{H}[\![\Delta]\!])/\mathfrak{H}[\![\Delta]\!]])))$$

$$(\lambda\rho''I.\P\mathcal{T}[\![\Delta]\!]\rho''\sigma'\in A\to\bot,(\lambda\delta.\delta\in G\to\bot,\delta)(((\P\mathcal{T}[\![\Delta]\!]\rho''\sigma'|(U\times S))\downarrow 1)[\![I]\!]\downarrow 1)))$$

$$(news(\#\mathfrak{I}[\![\Delta]\!])\sigma))$$

$$(fix(\lambda\xi\nu\sigma''.(\nu=0)\to\sigma'',new\sigma''\in L\to\xi(\nu-1)(update(new\sigma''|L)(false)\sigma''),\sigma'')(\#\mathfrak{I}[\![\Delta]\!])\sigma).$$

We first select arbitrary pairs $\langle\rho_0,\rho_1\rangle$ and $\langle\sigma_0,\sigma_1\rangle$ for which $u_0 I^*\langle\rho_0,\rho_1\rangle=true$ and $s\langle\sigma_0,\sigma_1\rangle=true$ and we let $\alpha^*=news(\#\mathfrak{I}[\![\Delta]\!])\sigma_0$, so that $\alpha^*=news(\#\mathfrak{I}[\![\Delta]\!])\sigma_1$. Unless $\alpha^*\in L^*$ it is immediately clear that now $(x\to a)\langle\lambda\chi.\mathfrak{D}[\![\text{rec }\Delta]\!]\rho_0\chi\sigma_0,\lambda\chi.set\chi(\P\mathfrak{D}[\![\text{rec }\Delta]\!]\rho_1\sigma_1)\rangle=true$; hence we assume that $\alpha^*\in L^*$ and we set $\rho_2=\rho_0[\alpha^*/\mathfrak{I}[\![\Delta]\!]]$, $\rho_3=\rho_1[\alpha^*/\mathfrak{I}[\![\Delta]\!]]$, $\sigma_2=updates\,\alpha^*(use(\#\mathfrak{I}[\![\Delta]\!]))\sigma_0$ and $\sigma_3=updates\,\alpha^*(use(\#\mathfrak{I}[\![\Delta]\!]))\sigma_1$, with the effect that $u_0 I^*\langle\rho_2,\rho_3\rangle=true$ and $s\langle\sigma_2,\sigma_3\rangle=true$. By making two appeals to 2.3.6 we can demonstrate that $\lambda\chi.\mathfrak{D}[\![\text{rec }\Delta]\!]\rho_0\chi\sigma_0=\lambda\chi.\mathcal{T}[\![\Delta]\!]\rho_2[fix\phi_0/\mathfrak{H}[\![\Delta]\!]]\chi\sigma_2$ and that $\P\mathfrak{D}[\![\text{rec }\Delta]\!]\rho_1\sigma_1=\P\mathcal{T}[\![\Delta]\!]\rho_3[fix\phi_1/\mathfrak{H}[\![\Delta]\!]]\sigma_3$ where (now)

$$\phi_0=\lambda\delta^*.(\lambda\psi.map(\psi(\rho_2[\delta^*/\mathfrak{H}[\![\Delta]\!]]))(\mathfrak{H}[\![\Delta]\!]))$$

$$(\lambda\rho''I.\lambda\kappa''\sigma''.\mathcal{T}[\![\Delta]\!]\rho''(\lambda\rho'\sigma'.\rho'[\![I]\!]\downarrow 1\in G\to wrong\sigma',\kappa''(\rho'[\![I]\!]\downarrow 1)\sigma'')\sigma_2)$$

and

$$\phi_1=\lambda\delta^*.(\lambda\psi.map(\psi(\rho_3[\delta^*/\mathfrak{H}[\![\Delta]\!]]))(\mathfrak{H}[\![\Delta]\!]))$$

$$(\lambda\rho''I.\P\mathcal{T}[\![\Delta]\!]\rho''\sigma_3\in A\to\bot,(\lambda\delta.\delta\in G\to\bot,\delta)(((\P\mathcal{T}[\![\Delta]\!]\rho''\sigma_3|(U\times S))\downarrow 1)[\![I]\!]\downarrow 1).$$

Hence to show that $(x\to a)\langle\lambda\chi.\mathfrak{D}[\![\text{rec }\Delta]\!]\rho_0\chi\sigma_0,\lambda\chi.set\chi(\P\mathfrak{D}[\![\text{rec }\Delta]\!]\rho_1\sigma_1)\rangle=true$

we have only to verify inductively that
$(x\to a)\langle \lambda\chi.\mathcal{T}[\![\Delta]\!]\rho_1[fix\phi_0/\mathcal{H}[\![\Delta]\!]]\chi\sigma_2,\lambda\chi.set\chi(\P\mathcal{T}[\![\Delta]\!]\rho_3[fix\phi_1/\mathcal{H}[\![\Delta]\!]]\sigma_2)\rangle = true$.

We let δ^*_0 and δ^*_1 be lists of length $\#\mathcal{H}[\![\Delta]\!]$ for which $(x\to a)\langle \lambda\chi.\mathcal{T}[\![\Delta]\!]\rho_2[\delta^*_0/\mathcal{H}[\![\Delta]\!]]\chi\sigma_2,\lambda\chi.set\chi(\P\mathcal{T}[\![\Delta]\!]\rho_3[\delta^*_1/\mathcal{H}[\![\Delta]\!]]\sigma_2)\rangle = true$; for brevity we set $\rho_4=\rho_2[\delta^*_0/\mathcal{H}[\![\Delta]\!]]$, $\rho_5=\rho_3[\delta^*_1/\mathcal{H}[\![\Delta]\!]]$, $\rho_6=\rho_2[\phi_0\delta^*_0/\mathcal{H}[\![\Delta]\!]]$ and $\rho_7=\rho_3[\phi_1\delta^*_1/\mathcal{H}[\![\Delta]\!]]$. For any pairs $\langle\kappa_0,\kappa_1\rangle$ and $\langle\sigma_4,\sigma_5\rangle$ such that $(e\to s\to a)\langle\kappa_0,\kappa_1\rangle = true$ and $s\langle\sigma_4,\sigma_5\rangle = true$ (and for any integer ν having $\#\mathcal{H}[\![\Delta]\!]\geq\nu\geq 1$) the continuations χ_0 and χ_1 obtained by setting $\chi_0=\lambda\rho\sigma.(\rho[\![\mathcal{H}[\![\Delta]\!]\downarrow\nu]\!]\downarrow 1 \mathsf{E} \mathsf{G}\to wrong\sigma,\kappa_0(\rho[\![\mathcal{H}[\![\Delta]\!]\downarrow\nu]\!]\downarrow 1)\sigma_4)$ and $\chi_1=\lambda\rho\sigma.\kappa_1(\rho[\![\mathcal{H}[\![\Delta]\!]\downarrow\nu]\!]\downarrow 1 \mathsf{E} \mathsf{G}\to\bot,\rho[\![\mathcal{H}[\![\Delta]\!]\downarrow\nu]\!]\downarrow 1)\sigma_5$ satisfy the equation $x\langle\chi_0,\chi_1\rangle = true$, so $a\langle\mathcal{T}[\![\Delta]\!]\rho_4\chi_0\sigma_2,set\chi_1(\P\mathcal{T}[\![\Delta]\!]\rho_5\sigma_3)\rangle = true$; consequently if $\P\mathcal{T}[\![\Delta]\!]\rho_5\sigma_3$ is in $\mathsf{U}\times\mathsf{S}$ $a\langle\mathcal{T}[\![\Delta]\!]\rho_4\chi_0\sigma_2,(\lambda\langle\rho,\sigma\rangle.\chi_1\rho\sigma)(\P\mathcal{T}[\![\Delta]\!]\rho_5\sigma_3|(\mathsf{U}\times\mathsf{S}))\rangle = true$ or, in other words, $\phi_0\delta^*_0$ and $\phi_1\delta^*_1$ are such that $a\langle(\phi_0\delta^*_0\downarrow\nu)\kappa_0\sigma_4,\kappa_1(\phi_1\delta^*_1\downarrow\nu)\sigma_5\rangle = true$. In view of the arbitrary nature of $\langle\kappa_0,\kappa_1\rangle$ and $\langle\sigma_4,\sigma_5\rangle$ this means that if $\mathcal{T}[\![\Delta]\!]\rho_5\sigma_3$ is in $\mathsf{U}\times\mathsf{S}$ then $d\langle\phi_0\delta^*_0\downarrow\nu,\phi_1\delta_1{}^*\downarrow\nu\rangle = true$ whenever $\#\mathcal{H}[\![\Delta]\!]\geq\nu\geq 1$, so $u_0\mathrm{I}^*_0\langle\rho_6,\rho_7\rangle = true$ and $(x\to a)\langle\lambda\chi.\mathcal{T}[\![\Delta]\!]\rho_6\chi\sigma_2,\lambda\chi.set\chi(\P\mathcal{T}[\![\Delta]\!]\rho_7\sigma_3)\rangle = true$ in accordance with the inductive hypothesis concerning Δ. This hypothesis also indicates that $(x\to a)\langle\lambda\chi.\mathcal{T}[\![\Delta]\!]\rho_6\chi\sigma_2,\lambda\chi.set\chi(\P\mathcal{T}[\![\Delta]\!]\rho_7\sigma_3)\rangle = true$ when $\P\mathcal{T}[\![\Delta]\!]\rho_5\sigma_3$ is not in the summand $\mathsf{U}\times\mathsf{S}$ of $\mathsf{A}+(\mathsf{U}\times\mathsf{S})$, because $u_2\mathrm{I}^*_0\langle\rho_6,\rho_5\rangle = true$. Thus in every case
$(x\to a)\langle\lambda\chi.\mathcal{T}[\![\Delta]\!]\rho_2[\phi_0\delta^*_0/\mathcal{H}[\![\Delta]\!]]\chi\sigma_2,\lambda\chi.set\chi(\P\mathcal{T}[\![\Delta]\!]\rho_3[\phi_1\delta^*_1/\mathcal{H}[\![\Delta]\!]]\sigma_3)\rangle = true$.

As $d\langle\bot,\bot\rangle = true$ writing $\rho_8=\rho_2[map(\lambda\mathrm{I}.\bot)(\#\mathcal{H}[\![\Delta]\!])/\mathcal{H}[\![\Delta]\!]]$ and $\rho_9=\rho_3[map(\lambda\mathrm{I}.\bot)(\mathcal{H}[\![\Delta]\!])/\mathcal{H}[\![\Delta]\!]]$ provides us with environments ρ_8 and ρ_9 having $u_0\mathrm{I}^*_0\langle\rho_8,\rho_9\rangle = true$; another application of the hypothesis about Δ therefore assures us that $(x\to a)\langle\lambda\chi.\mathcal{T}[\![\Delta]\!]\rho_8\chi\sigma_2,\lambda\chi.set\chi(\P\mathcal{T}[\![\Delta]\!]\rho_9\sigma_3)\rangle = true$. Since a is inclusive $x\to a$ is inclusive; furthermore all the necessary functions are continuous, so the predicate
$\lambda\langle\delta^*_0,\delta^*_1\rangle.(x\to a)\langle\lambda\chi.\mathcal{T}[\![\Delta]\!]\rho_2[\delta^*_0/\mathcal{H}[\![\Delta]\!]]\chi\sigma_2,\lambda\chi.set\chi(\P\mathcal{T}[\![\Delta]\!]\rho_3[\delta^*_1/\mathcal{H}[\![\Delta]\!]]\sigma_3)\rangle$ is inclusive. When taken in conjunction with the preceding paragraph

the induction rule of 2.3.2 therefore establishes that

$(x\to a)\langle\lambda\chi.\mathfrak{T}[\![\Delta]\!]\rho_2[fix\phi_0/\mathfrak{H}[\![\Delta]\!]]\chi\sigma_2,\lambda\chi.set\chi(\P\mathfrak{T}[\![\Delta]\!]\rho_3[fix\phi_1/\mathfrak{H}[\![\Delta]\!]]\sigma_3)\rangle=true$

and also that if $\P\mathfrak{T}[\![\Delta]\!]\rho_3[fix\phi_1/\mathfrak{H}[\![\Delta]\!]]\sigma_3$ is U×S then

$u_0 I^*{}_0\langle\rho_2[fix\phi_0/\mathfrak{H}[\![\Delta]\!]],\rho_3[fix\phi_1/\mathfrak{H}[\![\Delta]\!]]\rangle=true$.

We have now demonstrated that when $\langle\rho_0,\rho_1\rangle$ and $\langle\sigma_0,\sigma_1\rangle$ are chosen in such a way that $u_0 I^*\langle\rho_0,\rho_1\rangle=true$ and $s\langle\sigma_0,\sigma_1\rangle=true$ then $(x\to a)\langle\lambda\chi.\mathfrak{D}[\![\text{rec }\Delta]\!]\rho_0\chi\sigma_0,\lambda\chi.set\chi(\P\mathfrak{D}[\![\text{rec }\Delta]\!]\rho_1\sigma_1)\rangle=true$. Accordingly $\P\mathfrak{D}$ is conjugate to $\mathfrak{D}$ for rec Δ under $u_0 I^*\to x\to(s\to a)$, and thus we have proved part of what we originally set out to demonstrate.

Similar, but simpler, arguments show that when $u_2 I^*\langle\rho_0,\rho_1\rangle=true$ and $s\langle\sigma_0,\sigma_1\rangle=true$ then $\P\mathfrak{D}[\![\text{rec }\Delta]\!]\rho_1\sigma_1$ is not drawn from U×S and as a result $(x\to a)\langle\lambda\chi.\mathfrak{D}[\![\text{rec }\Delta]\!]\rho_0\chi\sigma_0,\lambda\chi.set\chi(\P\mathfrak{D}[\![\text{rec }\Delta]\!]\rho_1\sigma_1)\rangle=true$ provided that $\P\mathfrak{D}[\![\text{rec }\Delta]\!]\rho_2\sigma_1$ is not in U×S for any ρ_2 such that $u_2 I^*\langle\rho_0,\rho_2\rangle=true$.

Next we shall turn to the study of while E do Γ. Thus we suppose that while E do Γ is orderly in I* for some list I*, so that E and Γ are orderly in I*; moreover we demand that $\P\mathfrak{R}$ be conjugate to $\mathfrak{R}$ for E under $u_0 I^*\to(e\to s\to a)\to(s\to a)$, that $\P\mathfrak{C}$ be conjugate to $\mathfrak{C}$ for Γ under $u_0 I^*\to(s\to a)\to(s\to a)$, that when $u_2 I^*\langle\rho_0,\rho_1\rangle=true$ and $s\langle\sigma_0,\sigma_1\rangle=true$ $\P\mathfrak{R}[\![E]\!]\rho_1\sigma_1$ cannot be in E×S and $((e\to s\to a)\to a)\langle\lambda\kappa.\mathfrak{R}[\![E]\!]\rho_0\kappa\sigma_0,\lambda\kappa.set\kappa(\P\mathfrak{R}[\![E]\!]\rho_1\sigma_1)\rangle=true$ unless $\P\mathfrak{R}[\![E]\!]\rho_2\sigma_1$ is in E×S for every ρ_2 having $u_2 I^*\langle\rho_0,\rho_2\rangle=true$, and that when $u_2 I^*\langle\rho_0,\rho_1\rangle=true$ and $s\langle\sigma_0,\sigma_1\rangle=true$ $\P\mathfrak{C}[\![\Gamma]\!]\rho_1\sigma_1$ cannot be in S and $((s\to a)\to a)\langle\lambda\theta.\mathfrak{C}[\![\Gamma]\!]\rho_0\theta\sigma_0,\lambda\theta.set\theta(\P\mathfrak{C}[\![\Gamma]\!]\rho_1\sigma_1)\rangle=true$ unless $\P\mathfrak{C}[\![\Gamma]\!]\rho_2\sigma_1$ is in S for every ρ_2 having $u_2 I^*\langle\rho_0,\rho_2\rangle=true$. We shall demonstrate that $\P\mathfrak{C}$ is conjugate to $\mathfrak{C}$ for while E do Γ under $u_0 I^*\to(s\to a)\to(s\to a)$; the other part of the result concerning while E do Γ can be established with no difficulty whatever. Naturally we take $\P\mathfrak{C}[\![\text{while E do }\Gamma]\!]$ to be $\lambda\rho.fix(\lambda\phi.fit(\psi_2\langle fit\phi\circ(\P\mathfrak{C}[\![\Gamma]\!]\rho),\phi_2\rangle)\circ(\P\mathfrak{R}[\![E]\!]\rho))$ where ψ_2 is $\lambda\langle\phi',\phi''\rangle\epsilon.\epsilon E B\to(\epsilon|BET\to(\epsilon|B|T\to\phi',\phi''),wrong),wrong)$ and where ϕ_2 is that member of S→(A+S) such that $\lambda\sigma.\sigma=\lambda\sigma.\phi_2\sigma|S$.

When given arbitrary pairs $\langle\rho_0,\rho_1\rangle$ and $\langle\theta_0,\theta_1\rangle$ such that

$u_0 I^*\langle \rho_0,\rho_1\rangle = true$ and $(s\to a)\langle \theta_0,\theta_1\rangle = true$ we wish to demonstrate that $(s\to a)\langle \mathcal{C}[\![\text{while E do }\Gamma]\!]\rho_0\theta_0, set\theta_1\circ(\P\mathcal{C}[\![\text{while E do }\Gamma]\!]\rho_1)\rangle = true$. This merely entails verifying inductively that $(s\to a)\langle fix\psi_0, set\theta_1\circ fix\psi_1\rangle = true$ where $\psi_0=\lambda\theta.\mathcal{R}[\![E]\!]\rho_0(test\langle \mathcal{C}[\![\Gamma]\!]\rho_0\theta,\theta_0\rangle)$ as usual and where $\psi_1=\lambda\theta.fit(\psi_2\langle fit\phi\circ(\P\mathcal{C}[\![\Gamma]\!]\rho_1),\phi_2\rangle)\circ(\P\mathcal{R}[\![E]\!]\rho_1)$. We shall do this with assistance from the equations $\lambda\theta\phi.set(set\theta\circ\phi)=\lambda\theta\phi.set\theta\circ fit\phi$ and $\lambda\theta\langle\phi',\phi''\rangle\varepsilon.test\langle set\theta\circ\phi', set\theta\circ\phi''\rangle\varepsilon=\lambda\theta\langle\phi',\phi''\rangle\varepsilon.set\theta\circ\psi_2\langle\phi',\phi''\rangle\varepsilon$, which are valid when ϕ ranges over members of $S\to(A+S)$.

We take $\langle\theta,\phi\rangle$ to be any pair drawn from $(S\to A)\times(S\to(A+S))$ for which $(s\to a)\langle\theta, set\theta_1\circ\phi\rangle = true$. Because $\P\mathcal{C}$ is conjugate to $\mathcal{C}$ for Γ under $u_0 I^*\to(s\to a)\to(s\to a)$, $(s\to a)\langle \mathcal{C}[\![\Gamma]\!]\rho_0\theta, set(set\theta_1\circ\phi)\circ(\P\mathcal{C}[\![\Gamma]\!]\rho_1)\rangle = true$; since, in addition, $(s\to a)\langle\theta_0, set\theta_1\circ\phi_2\rangle = true$, the fact that $((s\to a)\to(s\to a)\to(e\to s\to a))\langle\lambda\theta'\theta''.test\langle\theta',\theta''\rangle,\lambda\theta'\theta''.test\langle\theta',\theta''\rangle\rangle = true$ ensures that $(e\to s\to a)\langle test\langle\mathcal{C}[\![\Gamma]\!]\rho_0\theta,\theta_0\rangle, test\langle set(set\theta_1\circ\phi)\circ(\P\mathcal{C}[\![\Gamma]\!]\rho_1), set\theta_1\circ\phi_2\rangle\rangle = true$. However, we know that $set(set\theta_1\circ\phi)=set\theta_1\circ fit\phi$ and that $test\langle set\theta_1\circ fit\phi\circ(\P\mathcal{C}[\![\Gamma]\!]\rho_1), set\theta_1\circ\phi_2\rangle = \lambda\varepsilon.set\theta_1\circ\psi_2\langle fit\phi\circ(\P\mathcal{C}[\![\Gamma]\!]\rho_1),\phi_2\rangle\varepsilon$, so $(e\to s\to a)\langle test\langle\mathcal{C}[\![\Gamma]\!]\rho_0\theta,\theta_0\rangle,\lambda\varepsilon.set\theta_1\circ\psi_2\langle fit\phi\circ(\P\mathcal{C}[\![\Gamma]\!]\rho_1),\phi_2\rangle\varepsilon\rangle = true$. As $\P\mathcal{R}$ is conjugate to $\mathcal{R}$ for E under $u_0 I^*\to(e\to s\to a)\to(s\to a)$, and as $\mathcal{R}[\![E]\!]\rho_0(test\langle\mathcal{C}[\![\Gamma]\!]\rho_0\theta,\theta_0\rangle)=\psi_0\theta$, $(s\to a)\langle\psi_0\theta, set(\lambda\varepsilon.set\theta_1\circ\psi_2\langle fit\phi\circ(\P\mathcal{C}[\![\Gamma]\!]\rho_1),\phi_2\rangle\varepsilon)\circ(\P\mathcal{R}[\![E]\!]\rho_1)\rangle = true$. It is clear that $set(\lambda\varepsilon.set\theta_1\circ\psi_2\langle fit\phi\circ(\P\mathcal{C}[\![\Gamma]\!]\rho_1),\phi_2\rangle\varepsilon)=set\theta_1\circ fit(\psi_2\langle fit\phi\circ(\P\mathcal{C}[\![\Gamma]\!]\rho_1),\phi_2\rangle)$ and that $fit(\psi_2\langle fit\phi\circ(\P\mathcal{C}[\![\Gamma]\!]\rho_1),\phi_2\rangle)\circ(\P\mathcal{R}[\![E]\!]\rho_1)=\psi_1\phi$, so actually $(s\to a)\langle\psi_0\theta, set\theta_1\circ\psi_1\phi\rangle = true$.

From the definition of *set* given in 3.9.1 it follows that $set\theta_1\circ\bot=\bot$ even when $\theta_1\bot$ is not $\bot$; consequently the assumption that $a\langle\bot,\bot\rangle = true$ implies that $(s\to a)\langle\bot, set\theta_1\circ\bot\rangle = true$. The inclusive nature of a ensures that $\lambda\langle\theta,\phi\rangle.(s\to a)\langle\theta, set\theta_1\circ\phi\rangle$ is an predicate mapping $(S\to A)\times(S\to(A+S))$ into T'; hence in accordance with the induction principle of 2.3.2 $(s\to a)\langle fix\psi_0, set\theta_1\circ fix\psi_1\rangle = true$.

Now that we have shown that $(s\to a)\langle fix\psi_0, set\theta_1 \circ fix\psi_1\rangle = true$ we may assert that

$(s\to a)\langle \mathcal{C}[\![\text{while E do }\Gamma]\!]\rho_0\theta_0, set\theta_1\circ(\P\mathcal{C}[\![\text{while E do }\Gamma]\!]\rho_1)\rangle = true$. However, our reasoning has made no use of properties of $\langle \rho_0,\rho_1\rangle$ and $\langle \theta_0,\theta_1\rangle$ beyond those contained in the equations $u_0\mathrm{I}^*\langle \rho_0,\rho_1\rangle = true$ and $(s\to a)\langle \theta_0,\theta_1\rangle = true$. Consequently $\P\mathcal{C}$ is conjugate to $\mathcal{C}$ for while E do Γ under $u_0\mathrm{I}^*\to(s\to a)\to(s\to a)$.

An argument which parallels that above justifies the claim that when $u_2\mathrm{I}^*\langle \rho_0,\rho_1\rangle = true$ and $s\langle \sigma_0,\sigma_1\rangle = true$ then $\P\mathcal{C}[\![\text{while E do }\Gamma]\!]\rho_1\sigma_1$ is not drawn from S and $((s\to a)\to a)\langle \lambda\theta.\mathcal{C}[\![\text{while E do }\Gamma]\!]\rho_0\theta\sigma_0, \lambda\theta.set\theta(\P\mathcal{C}[\![\text{while E do }\Gamma]\!]\rho_1\sigma_1)\rangle = true$ unless $\P\mathcal{C}[\![\text{while E do }\Gamma]\!]\rho_2\sigma_1$ is in S for every ρ_2 such that $u_2\mathrm{I}^*\langle \rho_0,\rho_2\rangle = true$.

This completes as much of the proof of the result as we intend to provide. The other parts of the structural induction are far less intricate than those that we have discussed.▷

One final gloss on this result should be noted. When rec Δ is the recursive declaration discussed in the proof we know that if $\langle \rho_0,\rho_1\rangle$ and $\langle \sigma_0,\sigma_1\rangle$ are chosen in such a way that $u_0\mathrm{I}^*\langle \rho_0,\rho_1\rangle$ and $s\langle \sigma_0,\sigma_1\rangle$ are *true* and $news(\#\mathcal{J}[\![\Delta]\!])\sigma_0$ is proper then, in the notation adopted above, $\lambda\chi.\mathcal{D}[\![\text{rec }\Delta]\!]\rho_0\chi\sigma_0 = \lambda\chi.\mathcal{T}[\![\Delta]\!]\rho_2[fix\phi_0/\mathcal{H}[\![\Delta]\!]]\chi\sigma_2$ where when $\P\mathcal{T}[\![\Delta]\!]\rho_3[fix\phi_1/\mathcal{H}[\![\Delta]\!]]\sigma_3$ is in U×S $u\langle \rho_2[fix\phi_0/\mathcal{H}[\![\Delta]\!]], \rho_3[fix\phi_1/\mathcal{H}[\![\Delta]\!]]\rangle = true$. Hence from 3.9.3 we may deduce that when $\P\mathcal{D}[\![\text{rec }\Delta]\!]\rho_1\chi\sigma_1$ is in U×S $\lambda\chi.\mathcal{D}[\![\text{rec }\Delta]\!]\rho_0\chi\sigma_0 = \lambda\chi.\mathcal{T}[\![\Delta]\!]\rho_3[fix\phi_1/\mathcal{H}[\![\Delta]\!]]\chi\sigma_3$; thus because no element of the list $fix\phi_1$ is in G we can eliminate members of G from the environment while retaining the use of $\mathcal{T}$ when considering recursive declarations. Indeed, if we were to amend the syntax of Sal so that declarations would be allowed to be recursive only when they were orderly in ⟨⟩, we would be able to dispense with the summand G of D while retaining an accurate set of semantic equations.

3.9.5. Simple applications.

Those who have endured reading the entire proof of 3.9.4 may be comforted to learn that in the remainder of this book they will not encounter another single proposition having such a lengthy proof. Though more complex results will be established later they will always be split up into manageable portions. We have chosen to treat 3.9.4 as one proposition rather than as a sequence of lemmas because we wish to emphasize not the result itself but its applications to recursive declarations.

Thus we are especially interested in the fact that if rec Δ is orderly in I* then $\P\mathfrak{D}$ is conjugate to $\mathfrak{D}$ for rec Δ under $u_0 I^* \to (u_1(\mathfrak{I}[\![\Delta]\!] \S \mathfrak{K}[\![\Delta]\!]) \to s \to a) \to (s \to a)$ when $\P\mathfrak{D}[\![\text{rec } \Delta]\!]$ is defined as in 3.9.4. Indeed, when $u_0 I^* \langle \rho_0, \rho_1 \rangle$ and $s\langle \sigma_0, \sigma_1 \rangle$ are *true* and $\P\mathfrak{D}[\![\text{rec } \Delta]\!] \rho_1 \sigma_1$ is in U×S there exist an environment ρ_2 and a store σ_2 such that $\rho_2[\![\mathfrak{K}[\![\Delta]\!] \downarrow \nu]\!] \downarrow 1$ is not in G when $\#\mathfrak{K}[\![\Delta]\!] \geq \nu \geq 1$,

$$\langle \rho_2, \sigma_2 \rangle = (\lambda \rho . \P\mathfrak{T}[\![\Delta]\!] \rho (updates(news(\#\mathfrak{I}[\![\Delta]\!])\sigma_1)(use(\#\mathfrak{I}[\![\Delta]\!]))\sigma_1) \mid (U \times S))$$
$$(\rho_1[news(\#\mathfrak{I}[\![\Delta]\!])\sigma_1 / \mathfrak{I}[\![\Delta]\!]][map(\lambda I . \rho_2[\![I]\!] \downarrow 1)(\mathfrak{K}[\![\Delta]\!]) / \mathfrak{K}[\![\Delta]\!]]),$$

and $\lambda\chi . \mathfrak{D}[\![\text{rec } \Delta]\!] \rho_0 \chi \sigma_0 = \lambda\chi . \chi \rho_2 \sigma_2$. By introducing a variant of the function *knit* to be described in 4.2.5 we could even show that $\rho_2[\![\mathfrak{I}[\![\Delta]\!] \downarrow \nu]\!] \downarrow 1 = news(\#\mathfrak{I}[\![\Delta]\!])\sigma_1 \downarrow \nu$ when $\#\mathfrak{I}[\![\Delta]\!] \geq \nu \geq 1$ and that $\rho_2 = slim[\![\Delta]\!] \rho_2$, so in fact

$$\langle \rho_2, \sigma_2 \rangle = \P\mathfrak{T}[\![\Delta]\!](divert \rho_1 \rho_2)(updates(news(\#\mathfrak{I}[\![\Delta]\!])\sigma_1)(use(\#\mathfrak{I}[\![\Delta]\!]))\sigma_1) \mid (U \times S).$$

Consequently the meaning ascribed to rec Δ satisfies the criterion governing recursive declarations which was laid down at the beginning of 1.9.4, and when $\#\mathfrak{K}[\![\Delta]\!] \geq \nu \geq 1$ $\rho_2[\![\mathfrak{K}[\![\Delta]\!] \downarrow \nu]\!] \downarrow 1$ is one of the expressed values obtained by executing Δ in the store provided at the time of declaration and by discarding the side effect (as can be seen most clearly by setting $\#\mathfrak{I}[\![\Delta]\!] = 0$). Because $\lambda\chi . \mathfrak{D}[\![\text{rec } \Delta]\!] \rho_0 \chi \sigma_0 = \lambda\chi . \chi \rho_2 \sigma_2$ we have at last confirmed the correctness of the intuitions used in 1.9.5 to justify our semantic equations for recursive declarations which do not give rise to jumps.

Only one point remains in doubt - the relation between recursive declarations by reference and recursive declarations by incidence. This has been discussed fully elsewhere [52:2.7.7] and will be touched upon in the present work in 4.1.1 and 5.3.9. Here we shall merely remark that when rec Δ is orderly in I* for some list I* the transformations of 3.5.8 can be used to convert rec Δ into a declaration which has almost the same properties and which contains no recursive declarations by incidence.

The concept of orderliness explained in 3.9.2 excludes from consideration such recursive declarations as rec *r*==*r*&(). This declaration might be expected to produce a looping structure which merely points at itself, as does the declaration rec *r*=*r*&(); however, according to the semantic equations of appendix 1, 𝔇⟦rec *r*==*r*&()⟧=⊥. In order to cater for such declarations we would take E to be L+B+E*+J+F+G while continuing to take D to be L+B+E*+J+F+G and V to be B+E*+J+F. Then we would set:

lv=λκεσ.εEL→κεσ,εEG→(ε|G)(*lv*κ)σ,*new*σEL→*assign*(κ(*new*σ|L))(*new*σ|L)εσ,*wrong*σ;

rv=λκεσ.εEL→κ(*hold*(ε|L)σ)σ,εEG→(ε|G)(*rv*κ)σ,κεσ.

We would also turn 𝔈⟦I⟧ into λρκ.κ(ρ⟦I⟧↓1) and 𝔇⟦rec Δ⟧ into

λρχ.(λψ.*tie*(λα*σ.𝔗⟦Δ⟧(*fix*(λρ'.ρ[α*/𝔍⟦Δ⟧][*map*(ψρ'σ)(ℌ⟦Δ⟧)/ℌ⟦Δ⟧]))χσ)(#𝔍⟦Δ⟧))

(λρ'σ.λI.λκσ'.𝔗⟦Δ⟧ρ'(λρ"σ".κ(ρ"⟦I⟧↓1)σ')σ).

Such equations for *lv* and *rv* differ from those given in 3.3.4 by being recursive, but this growth in complexity is perhaps offset by the simplicity of the proposed versions of 𝔈⟦I⟧ and 𝔇⟦rec Δ⟧. Altering the semantic equations in this manner would make 𝔇⟦rec *r*==*r*&()⟧=λρχ.χ(*arid*[*fix*(λγ.λκ.κ(⟨γ⟩))/*r*]), so *r* would denote a perfectly respectable loop. Unfortunately ¶𝔇⟦rec *r*==*r*&()⟧ would be λρσ.⟨*arid*[*fix*(λε.⟨ε⟩)/*r*],σ⟩, so verifying a proposition analogous to 3.9.4 would entail making *e* compare members of G with members of (other summands of) E just as *d* does at present; that is, were γ in G but ε not in G $e\langle \gamma,\varepsilon\rangle$ would be *true* only if $((e\rightarrow s\rightarrow a)\rightarrow(s\rightarrow a))\langle \gamma,\lambda\kappa.\kappa\varepsilon\rangle$ were *true*. Because E* is a summand of V, under these circumstances e and s would be connected recursively in a way which would render their existence suspect (as we shall see in a different situation in 4.2.1); how to lay such suspicions at rest will be discussed in 4.2.7. Analogous considerations here deter us from pursuing what happens when $\P\mathfrak{E}\llbracket\Phi\rrbracket=\lambda\rho\sigma.\langle\P\mathfrak{F}\llbracket\Phi\rrbracket\rho,\sigma\rangle$ (where $\P\mathfrak{F}$ is in $\mathrm{Abs}\rightarrow\mathrm{U}\rightarrow\mathrm{E}\rightarrow\mathrm{S}\rightarrow(\mathrm{A}+(\mathrm{E}\times\mathrm{S})))$ and from dwelling on the role of recursive predicates in some proofs about the similarity of programs containing function applications.

An interesting use of 3.9.4 concerns the relation between recursive and and around declarations. If $\mathfrak{T}\llbracket\Delta_0$ and $\Delta_1\rrbracket$ is $\lambda\rho\chi.run\langle\mathfrak{T}\llbracket\Delta_0\rrbracket\rho,\mathfrak{T}\llbracket\Delta_1\rrbracket\rho\rangle(\lambda\rho'\rho''.\chi(divert\rho'\rho''))$ and $\mathfrak{T}\llbracket\Delta_0$ around $\Delta_1\rrbracket$ $\lambda\rho\chi.\mathfrak{T}\llbracket\Delta_0\rrbracket\rho(\lambda\rho'.\mathfrak{T}\llbracket\Delta_1\rrbracket(divert\rho\rho')(\lambda\rho''.\chi(divert\rho'\rho'')))$ it is natural to take $\P\mathfrak{T}\llbracket\Delta_0$ and $\Delta_1\rrbracket$ to be $\lambda\rho.fit(\lambda\rho'.fit(\lambda\rho''\sigma.\langle divert\rho'\rho'',\sigma\rangle)\circ\P\mathfrak{T}\llbracket\Delta_1\rrbracket\rho)\circ\P\mathfrak{T}\llbracket\Delta_0\rrbracket\rho$ (provided that *run* applies its arguments from left to right) and to take $\P\mathfrak{T}\llbracket\Delta_0$ around $\Delta_1\rrbracket$ to be $\lambda\rho.fit(\lambda\rho'.fit(\lambda\rho''\sigma.\langle divert\rho'\rho'',\sigma\rangle)\circ\P\mathfrak{T}\llbracket\Delta_1\rrbracket(divert\rho\rho'))\circ\P\mathfrak{T}\llbracket\Delta_0\rrbracket\rho$. When we adopt these interpretations of the declarations we can prove that when rec (Δ_0 and Δ_1) is orderly in I* then it is DD-similar to rec (Δ_0 around Δ_1) under $u_0\mathrm{I}^*\rightarrow(u\rightarrow s\rightarrow a)\rightarrow(s\rightarrow a)$ provided that $\mathfrak{I}\llbracket\Delta_0\rrbracket\S\mathfrak{H}\llbracket\Delta_0\rrbracket$ and $\mathfrak{I}\llbracket\Delta_1\rrbracket\S\mathfrak{R}\llbracket\Delta_1\rrbracket$ are disjoint. There is even a more general result about the substitution of Δ_0 and Δ_1 for Δ_0 around Δ_1 in arbitrary recursive declarations which are orderly in I*; to establish this we would formulate a notion of 'replaceable' declarations which would resemble that provided for commands in 3.6.1 but which would depend on $\P\mathfrak{T}$ rather than $\mathfrak{Q}$. In the absence of orderliness this result does not hold, as can be seen by comparing rec (u==0 and v==u) with rec (u==0 around v==u).

3.9.6. Some induction rules for recursion.

The relation between $\mathcal{D}[\![\text{rec }\Delta]\!]$ and $\P\mathcal{T}[\![\Delta]\!]$ which we have described cannot be simplified significantly unless we suppose that Δ is both without side effects and without store dependence. In order to provide declarations subject to these restrictions we introduce a domain of 'definitions', Def, the members of which are built up by combining declarations by incidence that make identifiers denote abstractions. Thus if A represents a typical Sal definition its syntax is governed by the BNF [2] rule

$A::=I==\Phi|A_0 \text{ and } A_1|A_0 \text{ within } A_1|A_0 \text{ around } A_1|\text{rec } A|(A).$

Evidently there is a continuous mapping of Def into Dec which converts every definition into a Sal declaration "having the same form". In our usual cavalier fashion we can ignore this mapping by pretending that the valuation $\mathcal{H}$ provided for Dec in appendix 9 is defined on Def; hence when A is a member of Def $\mathcal{H}[\![A]\!]$ can be taken to be a list of the identifiers which are declared in A but which can have scopes extending beyond A. If in addition we tacitly map members of F (the domain of procedure values) into members of D (the domain of denoted values) we can set up $\mathcal{M}$, a valuation belonging to Def→U→D*, thus:

$\mathcal{M}[\![I==\Phi]\!]=\lambda\rho.\langle\mathcal{F}[\![\Phi]\!]\rho\rangle$;

$\mathcal{M}[\![A_0 \text{ and } A_1]\!]=\lambda\rho.\mathcal{M}[\![A_0]\!]\rho\S\mathcal{M}[\![A_1]\!]\rho$;

$\mathcal{M}[\![A_0 \text{ within } A_1]\!]=\lambda\rho.\mathcal{M}[\![A_0]\!]\rho[\mathcal{M}[\![A_0]\!]\rho/\mathcal{H}[\![A_0]\!]]$;

$\mathcal{M}[\![A_0 \text{ around } A_1]\!]=\lambda\rho.\mathcal{M}[\![A_0]\!]\rho\S\mathcal{M}[\![A_1]\!]\rho[\mathcal{M}[\![A_0]\!]\rho/\mathcal{H}[\![A_0]\!]]$;

$\mathcal{M}[\![\text{rec } A]\!]=\lambda\rho.fix(\lambda\delta^*.\mathcal{N}[\![A]\!]\rho[\delta^*/\mathcal{N}[\![A]\!]])$;

$\mathcal{M}[\![(A)]\!]=\lambda\rho.\mathcal{M}[\![A]\!]\rho$.

These equations for $\mathcal{M}$ mention $\mathcal{N}$, a valuation belonging to Def→U→D*, just as the equations for $\mathcal{D}$ given in appendix 1 mention $\mathcal{T}$. The equations for $\mathcal{N}$ enable us to ignore occurrences of rec outside the first halves of within declarations, since they are as follows:

$\mathcal{N}[\![I==\Phi]\!] = \lambda\rho.\langle \mathcal{F}[\![\Phi]\!]\rho\rangle$;

$\mathcal{N}[\![A_0 \text{ and } A_1]\!] = \lambda\rho.\mathcal{N}[\![A_0]\!]\rho \S \mathcal{N}[\![A_1]\!]\rho$;

$\mathcal{N}[\![A_0 \text{ within } A_1]\!] = \lambda\rho.\mathcal{N}[\![A_1]\!]\rho[\mathcal{M}[\![A_0]\!]\rho/\mathcal{H}[\![A_0]\!]]$;

$\mathcal{N}[\![A_0 \text{ around } A_1]\!] = \lambda\rho.\mathcal{N}[\![A_0]\!]\rho \S \mathcal{N}[\![A_1]\!]\rho[\mathcal{N}[\![A_0]\!]\rho/\mathcal{H}[\![A_0]\!]]$;

$\mathcal{M}[\![\text{rec } A]\!] = \lambda\rho.\mathcal{N}[\![A]\!]\rho$;

$\mathcal{N}[\![(A)]\!] = \lambda\rho.\mathcal{N}[\![A]\!]\rho$.

Induction on the structure of definitions allows us to demonstrate that for each A in Def

$\P\mathcal{D}[\![A]\!] = \lambda\rho\sigma.\langle arid[\mathcal{M}[\![A]\!]\rho/\mathcal{H}[\![A]\!]],\sigma\rangle$

and

$\P\mathcal{T}[\![A]\!] = \lambda\rho\sigma.\langle arid[\mathcal{N}[\![A]\!]\rho/\mathcal{H}[\![A]\!]],\sigma\rangle$,

whereas

$\mathcal{D}[\![A]\!] = \lambda\rho\chi.\chi(arid[\mathcal{M}[\![A]\!]\rho/\mathcal{H}[\![A]\!]])$

and

$\mathcal{T}[\![A]\!] = \lambda\rho\chi.\chi(arid[\mathcal{N}[\![A]\!]\rho/\mathcal{H}[\![A]\!]])$;

the occurrences of A on the left hand sides of these equations really signify the member of Dec that corresponds with A (as does the occurrence of A in the term $\mathcal{H}[\![A]\!]$). The equations themselves can be established without appealing to 3.9.4, though naturally they depend on the validity of 3.9.3.

Other declarations may sometimes be regarded as members of the domain Def; for instance, if the execution of each base can never have side effects or be influenced by the store, so that $\mathcal{B}[\![B]\!] = \lambda\kappa.\kappa((\P\mathcal{B}[\![B]\!](empty)\,|\,(E\times S))\downarrow 1)$ for every B in Bas, we can allow I==B to be a member of Def. In addition any expression of the form \$E which is without side effects and without store dependence under $u\to(e\to s\to a)\to(s\to a)$ may be permitted to appear on the right hand side of a declaration by incidence belonging to Def; thus $\mathcal{M}$ and $\mathcal{N}$ may be defined on I==£Φ, which is equivalent with I==\$(£Φ).

In conjunction with the equations governing $\mathcal{M}$ and $\mathcal{N}$ the properties

$\mathcal{D}[\![A]\!]=\lambda\rho\chi.\chi(arid[\mathcal{M}[\![A]\!]\rho/\mathcal{H}[\![A]\!]])$

and

$\mathcal{T}[\![A]\!]=\lambda\rho\chi.\chi(arid[\mathcal{N}[\![A]\!]\rho/\mathcal{H}[\![A]\!]])$

express many of our expectations about recursive procedures, since they show that, for example, when I is any identifier and Φ is any abstraction

$\mathcal{D}[\![\text{rec } I==\Phi]\!]=\lambda\rho\chi.\chi(arid[fix(\lambda\phi.\mathcal{H}[\![\Phi]\!]\rho[\phi/I])/I])$.

Another intuitive account of recursive procedures is provided by certain induction rules which will be described below. In order to formulate these rules we isolate some definitions, the 'depositions', which form a domain Dep; when Λ represents a typical deposition its syntax is subject to the rule

$\Lambda::=I==\Phi|\Lambda_0 \text{ and } \Lambda_1|A \text{ within } \Lambda|\Lambda_0 \text{ around } \Lambda_1|(\Lambda)$,

so a deposition is really a definition which has no occurrences of rec outside the first halves of within declarations. For our present purpose the importance of depositions arises from the fact that for every Λ in Dep

$\mathcal{M}[\![\Lambda]\!]=\mathcal{N}[\![\Lambda]\!]$

when we embed Dep in Def in the way adopted for embedding Def in Dec. This equation can be justified by performing an induction on the structure of depositions.

Much as in 3.7.6 we set up a relation $\geq$ by demanding that whenever Δ_0 and Δ_1 are declarations $\Delta_0\geq\Delta_1$ if and only if $\mathcal{D}[\![\Delta_0]\!]\sqsupseteq\mathcal{D}[\![\Delta_1]\!]$. Again $\geq$ is reflexive and transitive but not antisymmetric; however we may speak of a 'directed set' of elements of Dec which we may hope to have a least upper bound under $\geq$. Naturally we view a function ξ taking Dec into Dec as "monotonic", "inclusive" or "continuous" with respect to $\geq$ if and only if when x is a subset of Dec which is directed by $\geq$ and which has a least upper bound Δ_∞ under $\geq$ then each least upper bound of $\{\xi[\![\Delta]\!]|\Delta\epsilon x\}$ is connected to Δ_∞ by inequalities comparable with those given in 2.3.1.

When Λ is any deposition the equation

$\mathcal{M}[\![\text{rec } \Lambda]\!]=\lambda\rho.fix(\lambda\delta^*.\mathcal{N}[\![\Lambda]\!]\rho[\delta^*/\mathcal{H}[\![\Lambda]\!]]$

shows that

$\mathcal{M}[\![\text{rec } \Lambda]\!]=\lambda\rho.\mathcal{N}[\![\Lambda]\!]\rho[\mathcal{M}[\![\text{rec } \Lambda]\!]\rho/\mathcal{H}[\![\Lambda]\!]]$

by virtue of the properties of *fix* mentioned in 2.3.2; however,

$\mathcal{M}[\![(\text{rec } \Lambda) \text{ within } \Lambda]\!]=\lambda\rho.\mathcal{M}[\![\Lambda]\!]\rho[\mathcal{M}[\![\text{rec } \Lambda]\!]\rho/\mathcal{H}[\![\Lambda]\!]]$

and

$\mathcal{M}[\![\Lambda]\!]=\mathcal{N}[\![\Lambda]\!]$,

so

$\mathcal{M}[\![\text{rec } \Lambda]\!]=\mathcal{M}[\![(\text{rec } \Lambda) \text{ within } \Lambda]\!]$.

In particular,

rec Λ≥(rec Λ) within Λ;

indeed, we also know that

(rec Λ) within Λ≥rec Λ,

but we prefer to regard this second inequality as being derived from an induction rule which resembles the rule given in 3.7.6 in the way that the inequality

rec Λ≥(rec Λ) within Λ

resembles the inequality

while E do Γ≥if E do (Γ;while E do Γ).

To set up the induction rule for recursive depositions we imagine that folly is an abstraction in Abs for which $\mathcal{F}[\![\text{folly}]\!]=\lambda\rho.\lambda\varepsilon\kappa.\bot$; owing to the nature of *lv* and *rv* such an abstraction cannot be obtained from the forms fn()E, fnI.E and fnI..E, which are the only ones available in Sal, so we are obliged to posit its existence for the sake of argument. Now we set up a function *lessen*:Ide*→Dep such that

$lessen=\lambda I^*.(\#I^*=1)\rightarrow(I^*\downarrow 1==\text{folly}),(I^*\downarrow 1==\text{folly and } lessen(I^*\dagger 1))$,

so that when Λ is any deposition $lessen(\mathcal{H}[\![\Lambda]\!])$ is a deposition having $\mathcal{M}[\![lessen(\mathcal{H}[\![\Lambda]\!])]\!]=\lambda\rho.map(\lambda I.\lambda\varepsilon\kappa.\bot)(\mathcal{H}[\![\Lambda]\!])$. The induction rule that interests us is as follows: if φ is a mapping of Dec into some domain and if Λ is any deposition then $\phi[\![\text{rec } \Lambda]\!]=\bot$ provided that $\phi[\![lessen(\mathcal{H}[\![\Lambda]\!])]\!]=$

that $\phi[\![\Lambda' \text{ within } \Lambda]\!]=\bot$ whenever $\phi[\![\Lambda']\!]=\bot$ and $\mathcal{H}[\![\Lambda']\!]=\mathcal{H}[\![\Lambda]\!]$, and that ϕ is "inclusive" with respect to $\geq$. Obviously this rule can be justified by noting that when Λ_0 is $lessen(\mathcal{H}[\![\Lambda]\!])$ and when Λ_{n+1} is Λ_n within Λ for each $n\geq 0$ then $\{\Lambda_n | n\geq 0\}$ is a directed set under $\geq$ having rec Λ as a least upper bound. Together with the inequality

rec $\Lambda \geq$(rec Λ) within Λ

and the equation

$\mathcal{M}[\![\text{rec } \Lambda]\!]=\mathcal{M}[\![\Lambda]\!]$

the rule suffices to characterize the behaviour of rec Λ when Λ is any member of Dep. However, this characterization is not valid for an arbitrary definition (unless no member of $\mathcal{H}[\![A]\!]$ occurs free in A); this can be demonstrated by applying the valuations to

x==fn()0 within rec x==fn()x and to rec (x==fn()0 within rec x==fn()x).

The properties of rec Λ can also be formulated in terms of syntactic substitution in the following manner. When I* is a list of identifiers and E* is a list of expressions having #I*=#E* for any expression E we take E[E*/I*] to be the expression obtained by substituting $E^*\downarrow\nu$ for every free occurrence of $I^*\downarrow\nu$ in E whenever $\#I^*\geq\nu\geq 1$ so long as care is taken to avoid the "capture of bound variables" [17]; the inductive definition of E[E*/I*] and of the corresponding notions for declarations, blocks and commands can safely be omitted. When the identifiers in I* are distinct and when, for $\#I^*\geq\nu\geq 1$, $E^*\downarrow\nu$ is without side effects and without store dependence under $(\lambda\langle\rho_0,\rho_1\rangle.(\rho_0\equiv\rho_1))\rightarrow(\lambda\langle\kappa_0,\kappa_1\rangle.(\kappa_0\equiv\kappa_1))\rightarrow(\lambda\langle\theta_0,\theta_1\rangle.(\theta_0\equiv\theta_1))$ structural induction (or an application of the results about similarity which were listed in 3.8.3) shows that for every expression E

$\mathcal{E}[\![E[E^*/I^*]]\!]=\lambda\rho.\mathcal{E}[\![E]\!]\rho[map(\lambda E'.(\P\mathcal{E}[\![E']\!]\rho(empty)|(E\times S))\downarrow 1)(E^*)/I^*]$,

and equations analogous to this one hold for all the other valuations except $\mathcal{T}$; in particular

$\mathcal{M}[\![\Lambda[E^*/I^*]]\!]=\lambda\rho.\mathcal{M}[\![\Lambda]\!]\rho[map(\lambda E'.(\P\mathcal{E}[\![E']\!]\rho(empty)|(E\times S))\downarrow 1)(E^*)/I^*]$.

For any deposition Λ' and for any ν having $\#\mathcal{H}[\![\Lambda']\!]\geq\nu\geq 1$ Λ' inside $\mathcal{H}[\![\Lambda']\!]\downarrow\nu$

is without side effects and without store dependence under $(\lambda\langle\rho_0,\rho_1\rangle.(\rho_0\equiv\rho_1))\rightarrow(\lambda\langle\kappa_0,\kappa_1\rangle.(\kappa_0\equiv\kappa_1))\rightarrow(\lambda\langle\theta_0,\theta_1\rangle.(\theta_0\equiv\theta_1))$; moreover
$\P\mathcal{E}[\![\Lambda'$ inside $\mathcal{H}[\![\Lambda']\!]\downarrow\nu]\!]=\lambda\rho\sigma.\langle\mathcal{M}[\![\Lambda']\!]\rho\downarrow\nu,\sigma\rangle$.
Hence if Λ is a deposition such that $\mathcal{H}[\![\Lambda]\!]$ contains no repeated elements and such that $\mathcal{H}[\![\Lambda']\!]=\mathcal{H}[\![\Lambda]\!]$ the fact that
$\mathcal{M}[\![\Lambda'$ within $\Lambda]\!]=\lambda\rho.\mathcal{M}[\![\Lambda]\!]\rho[\mathcal{M}[\![\Lambda']\!]\rho/\mathcal{H}[\![\Lambda']\!]]$
ensures that if we let E* be *map*(λI.Λ′ inside I)($\mathcal{H}[\![\Lambda]\!]$) and I* be $\mathcal{H}[\![\Lambda]\!]$ then
$\mathcal{M}[\![\Lambda'$ within $\Lambda]\!]=\mathcal{M}[\![\Lambda[map(\lambda I.\Lambda'$ inside $I)(\mathcal{H}[\![\Lambda]\!])/\mathcal{H}[\![\Lambda]\!]]]\!]$.
Consequently
rec $\Lambda\geq\Lambda[map(\lambda I.($rec $\Lambda)$ inside $I)(\mathcal{H}[\![\Lambda]\!])/\mathcal{H}[\![\Lambda]\!]]$;
furthermore if ϕ maps Dec into some domain then $\phi[\![$rec $\Lambda]\!]=\perp$ provided that $\phi[\![lessen(\mathcal{H}[\![\Delta]\!])]\!]=\perp$, that $\phi[\![\Lambda[map(\lambda I.\Lambda'$ inside $I)(\mathcal{H}[\![\Lambda]\!])/\mathcal{H}[\![\Lambda]\!]]]\!]=\perp$ whenever $\phi[\![\Lambda']\!]=\perp$ and $\mathcal{H}[\![\Lambda']\!]=\mathcal{H}[\![\Lambda]\!]$, and that ϕ is "inclusive" with respect to $\geq$.

There are other versions of this induction rule, but they have little importance. Here we shall merely remark that the rule above vindicates a "copy rule" of Algol 60 [61]: if I is an identifier and Φ is an abstraction then, when Φ_0 is folly and Φ_{n+1} is $\Phi_n[\Phi/I]$ for $n\geq 0$, $\mathcal{D}[\![$rec $I==\Phi]\!]=\bigsqcup\{\mathcal{D}[\![I==\Phi_n]\!]\mid n\geq 0\}$. Needless to say, a similar equation governs declarations of mutually recursive procedures; detailed proofs of the analogous result for program schemes have already been given [3,73].

When we allow other declarations, such as I==B, to appear in definitions we are obliged to take folly not to be an abstraction such that $\mathcal{F}[\![$folly$]\!]=\lambda\rho.\lambda\epsilon\kappa.\perp$ but to be a base such that $(\P\mathcal{B}[\![$folly$]\!](empty)\mid(E\times S))\downarrow 1=\perp$ (where $\perp$ is the least element of E); thus instead of using the element $\perp$ in the domain Abs we could use the element $\perp$ in the syntactic domain Bas.

While on this subject we should perhaps point out that if Λ is any deposition and if Δ is any declaration then Λ around Δ is equivalent with Λ and $(\Lambda$ within $\Delta)$ (so long as $\mathcal{I}[\![\Lambda]\!]\S\mathcal{H}[\![\Lambda]\!]$ is disjoint from $\mathcal{I}[\![\Delta]\!]\S\mathcal{H}[\![\Delta]\!]$).

3.9.7. Alterations to programs.

Now that we have confirmed that recursive declarations of procedures behave satisfactorily we can discuss how to simplify programs containing them. Thus, for instance, when I is any identifier and A is any definition such that I is not a member of $\mathfrak{R}[\![A]\!]$ we can show that $\mathfrak{D}[\![$rec (A and I==Φ)$]\!]=\mathfrak{D}[\![$rec (A[Φ/I] and I==Φ)$]\!]$ by carrying out manipulations like those mentioned in 3.9.6. If, in addition, the abstraction Φ contains no free occurrence of I then neither does A[Φ/I] so $\mathfrak{D}[\![$rec (A[Φ/I] and I==Φ)$]\!]=\mathfrak{D}[\![$(rec A[Φ/I]) around I==Φ$]\!]$ when the semantics of around declarations is that provided in 3.9.6; consequently $\mathfrak{D}[\![$rec (A and I==Φ)$]\!]=\mathfrak{D}[\![$(rec A[Φ/I]) around I==Φ$]\!]$ and we can reduce the "amount of recursion" in declarations of suitable mutually recursive procedures. Indeed when no member of $\mathfrak{R}[\![A]\!]$ appears free in A[Φ/I] we may eliminate the recursive nature of the declaration, because under these circumstances $\mathfrak{D}[\![$rec A[Φ/I]$]\!]=\mathfrak{D}[\![$A[Φ/I]$]\!]$.

Another result with some interest is the equivalence (in the sense of 3.6.1) between the expressions
rec I_0==fnI_1..(E_0?(Θ before (I_0E_1))!E_2) inside ($I_0$0) and
block (while E_0 do (Θ;fit \$$E_1$)) before E_2, which holds whenever I_0 and I_1 are distinct identifiers that do not appear free in E_0, E_1, E_2 and Θ. This can be established by an elementary induction which makes use of the fact that $\mathfrak{D}[\![$rec I==Φ$]\!]=\lambda\rho\chi.\chi(arid[fix(\lambda\phi.\mathfrak{F}[\![\Phi]\!]\rho[\phi/I])/I])$ for any identifier I and for any abstraction Φ.

The most familiar while loops are typified by
while (I_3:=I_0I_3 before I_1I_3) do (Θ_0;I_3:=I_2I_3;Θ_1), where the blocks Θ_0 and Θ_1 may be fit 0. When Φ is
fnI_5..(I_5==I_0I_5 inside (I_1I_5?(Θ_0 before (I_5==I_2I_5 inside Θ_1 before I_4I_5))!I_5))
we can often relate this loop to the assignment
I_3:=(rec I_4==Φ inside I_4I_3) in the following manner. We suppose that I_3, I_4 and I_5 are distinct identifiers which are not identical with

I_0, I_1 or I_2 and which do not appear free in Θ_0 or Θ_1, and we introduce predicates e_0, e_1, s, u and a. For these we demand that $e_0\langle\varepsilon_0,\varepsilon_1\rangle = true$ only if $\varepsilon_0=\varepsilon_1$, that e_1 filter out truth values, that s be restrictive, that $u\langle\rho_0,\rho_1\rangle = true$ only if $\rho_0=\rho_1$ and $\rho_0[\![I_3]\!]\downarrow 1$ is a proper location, that a be restrictive and inclusive and that $a\langle\bot,\bot\rangle = true$. In addition we stipulate that when $2\geq n\geq 0$ I_n is RR-similar to fnI_5..I_nI_5 under $u\to(e_0\to s\to a)\to(s\to a)$, that when $2\geq n\geq 0$ fnI_5..(I_3:=I_5 before I_nI_5) is FF-similar to fnI_5..(I_n==I_nI_5 inside (I_3:=I_5 before I_n)) under $u\to e_0\to(e_0\to s\to a)\to(s\to a)$, that fn$I_5$..$I_1I_5$ is FF-similar to fnI_5..I_1I_5 under $u\to e_0\to(e_1\to s\to a)\to(s\to a)$ and that when $1\geq n\geq 0$ fnI_5..(I_3:=I_5 before (Θ_n before 0) is FF-similar to fnI_5..(Θ_n before (I_3:=I_5 before 0)); thus in effect we insist that assignments to I_3 commute with the procedures represented by I_0, I_1 and I_2 and with the blocks Θ_0 and Θ_1. Under these circumstances an application of the second result listed in 3.8.3 serves to establish that while (I_3:=I_0I_3 before I_1I_3) do (Θ_0;I_3:=I_2I_3;Θ_1) is CC-similar to I_3:=(rec I_4==Φ inside I_4I_3) under $u\to(s\to a)\to(s\to a)$ when Φ is the abstraction given above. We shall leave verifying this result to the reader along with providing the corresponding connection between while loops composed of multiple assignments (instead of assignments to I_4) and certain recursive procedures; this connection has an obvious relevance to examples such as those in 3.8.4.

3.9.8. Termination.

When $\bot$ is the answer returned by a program according to the semantic equations we expect intuitively that the program will not terminate. We are therefore interested in finding methods which indicate whether particular programs return the answer $\bot$. Often the only reason why the answer $\bot$ may be returned is that *fix* appears in the semantic equations. In this situation the method of investigation is generally straightforward: for any domains, W_0 and W_1 say, and for any continuous function $\psi\in(W_0\to W_1)\to(W_0\to W_1)$, the induction principle of 2.3.2 allows us to show that $fix\psi\omega=\bot$ whenever ω belongs to a certain subset of W_0 simply by proving that, for every $\phi\in W_0\to W_1$, if $\phi\omega=\bot$ whenever ω belongs to the subset concerned then $\psi\phi\omega=\bot$ whenever ω belongs to the subset concerned. By this means we can verify that, for instance, $\mathcal{C}[\![\texttt{while}\ b\ \texttt{do}\ n{:=}{-n}]\!]\rho\theta\sigma=\bot$ whenever $((hold(\rho[\![b]\!]\downarrow 1|\mathsf{L})\sigma)|\mathsf{B}|\mathsf{T})=true$ and $(hold(\rho[\![n]\!]\downarrow 1|\mathsf{L})\sigma|\mathsf{B})\in\mathsf{N}$; here it is appropriate to choose one particular environment, ρ, and one particular continuation, θ, to let $\psi=\lambda\theta'.\mathcal{R}[\![b]\!]\rho(test\langle\mathcal{C}[\![n{:=}{-n}]\!]\rho\theta',\theta\rangle)$ and to take the "subset concerned" to comprise those stores in which the content of $\rho[\![b]\!]\downarrow 1|\mathsf{L}$ is *true* and in which the content of $\rho[\![n]\!]\downarrow 1|\mathsf{L}$ is an integer.

Needless to say, the properties of *fix* are relevant to recursive declarations by incidence as well as to `while` loops. Thus in order to show that $\mathcal{E}[\![\texttt{rec}\ f{==}\texttt{fn}n.f(0)\ \texttt{inside}\ f(1)]\!]\rho\kappa\sigma=\bot$ for any suitable ρ, κ and σ we proceed as follows. We select any environment, ρ, any expression continuation, κ, and any store, σ, and we let $\chi=\lambda\rho'.\mathcal{E}[\![f(1)]\!](divert\rho\rho')\kappa$ and $\psi=\lambda\phi.\mathcal{H}[\![\texttt{fn}n.f(0)]\!]\rho[\phi/f]$ (where ϕ is deemed to range over the procedure values); evidently

$$\begin{aligned}\mathcal{E}[\![\texttt{rec}\ f{==}\texttt{fn}n.f(0)\ \texttt{inside}\ f(1)]\!]\rho\kappa\sigma &= \chi(arid[fix\psi/f])\sigma\\ &= \mathcal{E}[\![f(1)]\!]\rho[fix\psi/f]\kappa\sigma\\ &= fix\psi 1\kappa\sigma.\end{aligned}$$

Now we assume that ϕ is a procedure value such that when ε is any expressed value belonging to a certain set, e, and when σ is any store belonging to a certain set, s, then $\phi\varepsilon\kappa\sigma=\bot$; e and s will be delineated below. We wish to show that $\psi\phi\varepsilon\kappa\sigma=\bot$ whenever $\varepsilon\in$e and $\sigma\in$s so we calculate by writing

$$\psi\phi\varepsilon\kappa\sigma=\mathcal{H}[\![\text{fn}\,n.f(0)]\!]\rho[\phi/f]\varepsilon\kappa\sigma$$

$$=lv(\lambda\varepsilon.\mathcal{E}[\![f(0)]\!]\rho[\phi/f][\varepsilon/n]\kappa)\varepsilon\sigma.$$

As we want 1 to belong to e, $\psi\phi\varepsilon\kappa\sigma$ can only be guaranteed to be $\bot$ if $new\sigma$EL; hence we demand that for every $\sigma\in$S $new\sigma$EL and we observe that, when ε is in e, when σ is in s and when the value of the check εEL is *false*, then

$$\psi\phi\varepsilon\kappa\sigma=\mathcal{E}[\![f(0)]\!]\rho[\phi/f][new\sigma|\text{L}/n]\kappa(update(new\sigma|\text{L})\varepsilon\sigma)$$

$$=\phi 0\kappa(update(new\sigma|\text{L})\varepsilon\sigma).$$

In order to apply our assumption about ϕ we now insist that 0 belong to e and that, whenever ε is in e, whenever σ is in s and whenever the value of the check εEL is *false*, then $update(new\sigma|\text{L})\varepsilon\sigma$ is in s; if this is so, $\psi\phi\varepsilon\kappa\sigma$ must be $\bot$. Hence an obvious extension of the remarks in the previous paragraph shows that we can prove that $fix\psi 1\kappa\sigma=\bot$ whenever $\sigma\in$S by taking e to be the set containing only 0 and 1 and by taking s to be the set such that $\sigma\in$s if and only if $new\sigma$ is a proper location and $update(new\sigma|\text{L})\varepsilon\sigma\in$s whenever $\varepsilon\in$e.

In fact in the example that we have just been considering we could have let e be any set of expressed values to which 0 and 1 belonged but from which $\top$ was excluded; the need for excluding $\top$ becomes apparent when $lv(\lambda\varepsilon.\mathcal{E}[\![f(0)]\!]\rho[\phi/f][\varepsilon/n])\top\sigma$ is analysed. The set s, however, is rather special; indeed, we ensure that it exists by letting the domain of locations, L, be infinite and by taking s to be a set of stores such that $\sigma\in$s only when the set $\{\alpha|area\alpha\sigma=true\}$ is finite.

The technique used above to analyse recursive declarations by incidence is not appropriate for recursive declarations by reference.

To verify that $\mathcal{E}[\![\text{rec } f\text{=fn}n.f(0) \text{ inside } f(1)]\!]\rho\kappa\sigma=\bot$ we adapt a method developed by Park [63] for relating the "paradoxical combinator" [18] to the function *fix* in the original λ-calculus models of Scott [80]. We shall outline the adapted form of this method in the next paragraph.

When ρ is any environment, κ is any expression continuation and σ is any store such that *new*σ is a proper location, on setting $\chi=\lambda\rho'.\mathcal{E}[\![f(1)]\!](divert\rho\rho')\kappa$, $\alpha=new\sigma|\text{L}$ and $\phi=\mathcal{H}[\![\text{fn}n.f(0)]\!]\rho[\alpha/f]$ we see from appendix 1 that

$$\mathcal{E}[\![\text{rec } f\text{=fn}n.f(0) \text{ inside } f(1)]\!]\rho\kappa\sigma=\chi(arid[\alpha/f])(update\alpha\phi\sigma)$$
$$=\mathcal{E}[\![f(1)]\!]\rho[\alpha/f]\kappa(update\alpha\phi\sigma)$$
$$=\phi 1\kappa(update\alpha\phi\sigma).$$

Here the recursive nature of φ arises from the fact that α contains φ, rather than from the use of a least fixed point, so we must confirm that $\phi 1\kappa(update\alpha\phi\sigma)=\bot$ by studying the store. We therefore let e be the set containing just 0 and 1, as before, and we let s be the set $\{\sigma'|(area\alpha\sigma'=true)\wedge(\phi\sqsupseteq hold\alpha\sigma')\}$; in addition we recall from 3.3.5 that all the domains we need are produced from the retraction *fix*(W) when W is a certain functor that creates the domain of witnessed values. We therefore suppose that *X* is some retraction such that $\lambda\omega.\omega\sqsupseteq X$, $mask^4\circ X=X\circ mask^4$ and $(\text{F}X\phi)\varepsilon\kappa\sigma'=\bot$ for all $\varepsilon\in$e and for all $\sigma'\in$s and we endeavour to show that $(\text{F}(\text{W}X)\phi)\varepsilon\kappa\sigma'=\bot$ for all $\varepsilon\in$e and for all $\sigma'\in$s; here the functors we require are defined as in 3.3.5. For all ε and σ'

$$((\text{F}(\text{W}X))\phi)\varepsilon\kappa\sigma = \text{F}(\text{W}X)(\mathcal{H}[\![\text{fn}n.f(0)]\!]\rho[\alpha/f])\varepsilon\kappa\sigma'$$
$$=\text{C}(\text{W}X)((\mathcal{H}[\![\text{fn}n.f(0)]\!]\rho[\alpha/f])(\text{E}(\text{W}X)\varepsilon)(\text{K}(\text{W}X)\kappa))\sigma'$$
$$=\text{A}(\text{W}X)((\mathcal{H}[\![\text{fn}n.f(0)]\!]\rho[\alpha/f])(\text{E}(\text{W}X)\varepsilon)(\text{K}(\text{W}X)\kappa)(\text{S}(\text{W}X)\sigma'))$$
$$\sqsubseteq\text{A}(\text{W}X)((\mathcal{H}[\![\text{fn}n.f(0)]\!]\rho[\alpha/f])\varepsilon\kappa(\text{S}(\text{W}X)\sigma'))$$
$$\sqsubseteq\mathcal{H}[\![\text{fn}n.f(0)]\!]\rho[\alpha/f]\varepsilon\kappa(\text{S}(\text{W}X)\sigma')$$
$$=lv(\lambda\varepsilon.\mathcal{E}[\![f(0)]\!]\rho[\alpha/f][\varepsilon/n])\varepsilon\kappa(\text{S}(\text{W}X)\sigma').$$

If ε is in e and σ' is in s then *new*σ' is a proper location and we may define a store σ" in s by setting $\sigma''=update(new\sigma'|\text{L})\varepsilon(\text{S}(\text{W}X)\sigma')$;

plainly $new(S(WX)\sigma')\sqsubseteq\sigma''$ so

$$((F(WX))\phi)\varepsilon\kappa\sigma'\sqsubseteq\mathcal{E}[\![f(0)]\!]\rho[\alpha/f][\varepsilon/n]\varepsilon\kappa\sigma''$$
$$=\mathcal{R}[\![f]\!]\rho[\alpha/f][\varepsilon/n](\lambda\varepsilon'.\varepsilon'\mathsf{E}F\to(\varepsilon'|F)0\kappa,wrong)\sigma''$$
$$=\mathcal{E}[\![f]\!]\rho[\alpha/f][\varepsilon/n](rv(\lambda\varepsilon'.\varepsilon'\mathsf{E}F\to(\varepsilon'|F)0\kappa,wrong))\sigma''$$
$$=rv(\lambda\varepsilon'.\varepsilon'\mathsf{E}F\to(\varepsilon'|F)0\kappa,wrong)\alpha\sigma''$$
$$=(\lambda\varepsilon'.\varepsilon'\mathsf{E}F\to(\varepsilon'|F)0\kappa,wrong)(hold\alpha\sigma'')\sigma''$$
$$=(\lambda\varepsilon'.\varepsilon'\mathsf{E}F\to(\varepsilon'|F)0\kappa,wrong)(VX(hold\alpha\sigma'))\sigma''$$
$$\sqsubseteq(\lambda\varepsilon'.\varepsilon'\mathsf{E}F\to(\varepsilon'|F)0\kappa,wrong)(VX\phi)\sigma''$$
$$=(FX\phi)0\kappa\sigma''.$$

In the final links of this chain of equations we have tacitly converted first $VX(hold\alpha\sigma')$ and then $VX\phi$ into members of E, but inserting explicit mappings from V into E makes no crucial difference to the argument. Because 0 is in e and σ'' is in s we can safely assert that $(FX\phi)0\kappa\sigma''=\bot$; consequently $(F(WX)\phi)\varepsilon\kappa\sigma'=\bot$ whenever ε is in e and σ' is in s; moreover $\lambda\omega.\omega\sqsupseteq WX$ and $mask4\circ WX=WX\circ mask4$. A short chain of equations like that above is enough to demonstrate that $(F\bot\phi)\varepsilon\kappa\sigma'=\bot$ whenever ε is in e and σ' is in s (since $hold\alpha(S\bot\sigma')=\bot$ no matter what the nature of σ' may be), so by applying the induction principle of 2.3.2 we can conclude that $(F(fix(W))\phi)\varepsilon\kappa\sigma'=\bot$ whenever ε is in e and σ' is in s; as $fix(W)=\lambda\omega.\omega$, in fact $F(fix(W))\phi=\phi$ and $\phi\varepsilon\kappa\sigma'=\bot$ whenever ε is in e and σ' is in s. In particular,

$\mathcal{E}[\![$rec f=fn$n.f(0)$ inside $f(1)]\!]\rho\kappa\sigma=\bot$.

We can place our latest argument in a more general context in the following manner. When W, W_0 and W_1 are functors defined on the retractions of a universal domain X we can produce domains W_0 and W_1 by setting $W_0=\{\chi|\chi=W_0(fix(W))\chi\}$ and $W_1=\{\chi|\chi=W_1(fix(W))\chi\}$ in the way put forward in 2.4.3. If $\phi\in W_0\to W_1$ is a continuous function we can show that $\phi\omega=\bot$ for all ω in a certain subset of W_0 by verifying that $((W_0\bot\to W_1\bot)\phi)\omega=\bot$ for each ω in the subset and by proving that if, for some retraction X having $\lambda\omega.\omega\sqsupseteq X$, $((W_0X\to W_1X)\phi)\omega=\bot$ for each ω in the subset then $((W_0(WX)\to W_1(WX))\phi)\omega=\bot$ for each ω in the subset; under these circumstances $(W_0(\mathit{fix}(W)) \to W_1(\mathit{fix}(W)))\omega = \bot$ for each ω in the subset.

Another method for analysing recursive declarations by reference involves first applying a known result [52:2.7.7] to change the declarations into equivalent recursive declarations by incidence and then using the properties of *fix* in the way sketched above. As we shall soon explain, in the proof of this "known result" we need a sort of semantics besides that developed in this chapter so that we can relate the equations

$\mathcal{D}[\![\texttt{rec } I=\Phi]\!] = \lambda\rho\chi.\mathit{lv}(\lambda\varepsilon.\mathit{assign}(\chi(\mathit{arid}[\varepsilon/I]))\varepsilon(\mathcal{F}[\![\Phi]\!]\rho[\varepsilon/I]))(\mathit{false})$

and

$\mathcal{D}[\![\texttt{rec } I==\Phi]\!] = \lambda\rho\chi.\chi(\mathit{arid}[\mathit{fix}(\lambda\phi.\mathcal{H}[\![\Phi]\!]\rho[\phi/I])/I])$

which can be derived from the equations in appendix 1.

CHAPTER FOUR

STORE SEMANTICS

4.1. State vectors.

4.1.1. Some nasty equivalence problems.

Implicit in appendix 1 are simple equations which give the values of rec I=Φ and rec I==Φ when I is an identifier and Φ is an abstraction. These values cannot possibly coincide, as only one involves using *new* to add a location to the available storage. However unless this location is subsequently updated it should not affect the outcome of applying Φ except by providing a means whereby the value of Φ can refer to itself. To dispel the haze surrounding the link between rec I=Φ and rec I==Φ this location and its content must therefore be related to a procedure value $\phi \epsilon F$ kept in an environment which itself is incorporated in ϕ. In 3.4.2 F was E→K→C, so the environments in procedure values did not appear in the semantic equation for E_0E_1; here we shall split up these and other values in order to reveal which locations are accessed during computations. Before doing this we shall mention two further equivalence problems which require that domains like F be modified.

Usually while E do Γ is believed to mean the same as I::if E do (Γ;goto I) when I is an identifier which does not occur free in the expression E or the command Γ. Provided that the label I is set by incidence we can readily confirm this belief within standard semantics; according to 3.6.7, for example, if Θ_0 is chosen to be an arbitrary block in which I does not occur, and if Θ_1 coincides with Θ_0 except for the replacement of one instance of while E do Γ by I::if E do (Γ;goto I), then $\mathcal{G}[\![\Theta_0]\!]$ equals $\mathcal{G}[\![\Theta_1]\!]$. In a language like Pal [24] this result cannot be established, since every label is set by reference and the semantic equations for such a label require an increase in the area of store whereas the equations for while loops do not. Nevertheless there remains a nagging feeling that a satisfactory theory of programming languages should tell us more than this, for we would like to find an equivalence between the block Θ_0 which we mentioned above and the block Θ_2 that differs from it only because one occurrence of while E do Γ is transmuted into I:if E do (Γ;goto I). We cannot demand that $\mathcal{G}[\![\Theta_0]\!]$ be equal to $\mathcal{G}[\![\Theta_2]\!]$, since the location denoted by I will send the storage allocated by Θ_0 "out of step" with that allocated by Θ_2: an identifier declared in Θ_0 may well be associated with two distinct locations by Θ_0 and Θ_2. Moreover we cannot give I the semantics of a label set by incidence, since a particular environment may permit a library procedure in Θ_2 to access the location which I should properly denote; in any case such an artifice would run counter to a basic principle of Pal, which allows only locations to be denoted. Consequently we seem compelled to study the equivalence of Θ_0 and Θ_2 by comparing the locations referred to by Θ_0 with those needed by Θ_2.

A third matter which cannot be handled well in standard semantics is the problem of demonstrating that two commands commute. If Γ_0 and Γ_1 are any commands which do not require access to common locations then under certain circumstances $\Gamma_0;\Gamma_1$ and $\Gamma_1;\Gamma_0$ must "have the same effect". Again this last phrase has to be given an elaborate interpretation before this assertion can be understood, for certainly $\mathcal{C}[\![\Gamma_0;\Gamma_1]\!]$ need not coincide with $\mathcal{C}[\![\Gamma_1;\Gamma_0]\!]$: when Γ_0 and Γ_1 both contain declarations by reference then the contents of some locations after executing $\Gamma_0;\Gamma_1$ may differ from the contents after executing $\Gamma_1;\Gamma_0$. Furthermore in standard semantics we cannot provide an adequate account of which locations are actually accessed by Γ_0 and Γ_1, because if an identifier appearing in Γ_0 or Γ_1 denotes a procedure value the equations of appendix 1 will not indicate which locations appear in the appropriate free variable list.

Equivalence problems which, like these three, deal with classes of program instead of individual programs cannot be dismissed as unimportant. Before such rules as those discussed in 3.7.8 are used for program verification their validity should be established relative to the semantics of the programming language. Rules about recursive procedures, for instance, can be justified easily unless the procedures are declared by reference, as they may be in Algol 68 [94], when we have to resort to the technique which we need in any case to prove the equivalence of **rec** I=Φ and **rec** I==Φ. Thus correctness proofs for programs often tacitly assume that such equivalences have already been confirmed. To assist with the process of confirmation we shall now introduce store semantics, which corresponds with standard semantics in many ways but which allows these equivalences to be expressed clearly. As we shall explain in 5.2.1 and 5.6.9, store semantics also seems to be needed as an intermediary in proofs of the correctness of implementations in which Sal programs are compiled before being run; indeed, this will be a major role of store semantics in this book. Applications of store semantics that cannot be carried out in terms of standard semantics depend on one essential feature of store semantics: the fact that it allows us to list the locations which are accessible at any point in a computation. What this means should become clear in 5.2.2.

We shall shortly outline the salient features of store semantics before moving on to a proof that the description of Sal yielded by it corresponds closely with the description provided by standard semantics; the outcome of this proof will be stated in 4.3.7. Thereafter we shall relate the store semantics of Sal to an implementation in which Sal programs are interpreted on a particular machine; setting up mathematical accounts of the implementation will occupy us from 4.4.1 onwards, and the connection between store semantics and the implementation will not be made completely secure until 4.6.9.

4.1.2. Stacks.

If we wish to know which locations are accessible from a program by passing through a particular environment $\rho\in U$ we cannot just enumerate those identifiers which denote members of L. The application of a procedure within the program will mask ρ with the environment which was present when the procedure was originally given its value. Consequently to trace the accessible locations we must inspect not merely ρ but the environments associated with procedure values in ρ.

The valuation $\mathfrak{F}$ for standard semantics seals all the information about a procedure into a member of $E\to K\to C$. To extract the environment we could regard the value of a procedure as a member of $(E\to K\to C)\times U$ instead, so that $\mathfrak{F}[\![\mathrm{fnI.E}]\!]\rho$, for instance, would be $\langle\lambda\varepsilon\kappa.\mathcal{l}v(\lambda\varepsilon'.\mathfrak{E}[\![E]\!]\rho[\varepsilon'/I]\kappa)\varepsilon,\rho\rangle$. This would not be satisfactory, however, since were the procedure to be applied we would have no formal way of saying that the second component of the relevant member of $(E\to K\to C)\times U$ was actually incorporated in the first. Hence we are obliged to make use of this second component by passing it as a parameter when we apply the procedure, and so we take $\mathfrak{F}[\![\mathrm{fnI.E}]\!]\rho$ to be something rather like $\langle\lambda\rho'\varepsilon\kappa.\mathcal{l}v(\lambda\varepsilon'.\mathfrak{E}[\![E]\!]\rho'[\varepsilon'/I]\kappa)\varepsilon,\rho\rangle$, which does not seal an environment into its first component. More accurately, in appendix 2 we continue to define $\mathfrak{F}$ as an element of $Abs\to U\to F$ but we make F into $O\times U$, where O is a domain containing the "pure code" generated by parts of programs without any reference to specific environments. Dealing with a language not unlike Lisp [44] in which procedures were given environments at the time of application instead of at the time of abstraction would entail turning F into O.

Just as environments occur in the values of procedures and routines so environments and continuations are needed when labels are set up; moreover the locations accessible by passing through an environment include those obtainable from the label values in the environment. In standard semantics the label settings I:Γ and I::Γ both produce the label value $\mathcal{C}[\![\Gamma]\!]\rho\theta$ when provided with a suitable environment and a continuation. By analogy with abstractions we might be tempted to extract the environment from this value simply by forming the pair $\langle \lambda\rho'.\mathcal{C}[\![\Gamma]\!]\rho'\theta,\rho\rangle$. Unfortunately, sealed into the continuation θ is another environment which should contribute to the list of locations required by the label value; this is manifested by I:fit true and I::fit true, which yield the pair $\langle \lambda\rho'.\theta,\rho\rangle$. When we split up a label value we must therefore take care that the "state transformation" component no longer has an environment embedded in it. Thus rather than viewing θ as a member of C (which is S→A unless parallel processes are considered) we tentatively regard it as a member of U→C. Every continuation now requires an environment as an argument; the changes to the semantic equations necessitated by this fact are typified by $\mathcal{C}[\![\Gamma_0;\Gamma_1]\!]$, which ceases to be $\lambda\rho\theta.\mathcal{C}[\![\Gamma_0]\!]\rho(\mathcal{C}[\![\Gamma_1]\!]\rho\theta)$ and becomes $\lambda\rho\theta.\mathcal{C}[\![\Gamma_0]\!]\rho(\lambda\rho'.\mathcal{C}[\![\Gamma_1]\!]\rho'\theta)$. Here ρ has to be the entire environment, which has entries for all the declarations encountered "up to the present program point", because if we preserved only a local environment having entries for the free variables of the block we would be unable to trace all the locations accessible from outer blocks.

This does not exhaust the complications caused by splitting label values into their constituents. In common with Gedanken [69], Sal permits identifiers to have label values assigned to them, so control may return to an expression which has already been executed once. Thus after the execution of 0+((block *l*:*m*:=*l*) before 1) executing goto *m* will involve jumping back to the point labelled *l*, performing the assignment of *l* to *m* once more and adding 0 to 1. If the execution of this expression takes place from left to right the numeral 0 is not evaluated after the jump is made; instead 0 is embedded in the label value when *l* is set for the first time. In standard semantics the continuation for l takes care of the embedding, but we cannot let this happen in store semantics for the following reason. For the block **0**:=((block l:m:=l) before 1) the analogue of the integer 0 needed above is a new location $\alpha \in L$ which is given 0 as its content. One effect of goto m is to change the content of α to 1, so α must be listed among the locations which are required by the label value. To bring this about all the anonymous quantities which might be needed after a jump are retained as the third component of a label value (along with the continuation and the environment). These quantities result from the execution of expressions, so they are all expressed values in E; the third component of a label value is therefore a 'stack' belonging to E^*. Hence we actually demand that the domain of label values, J, be $Z \times U \times Y$ where Z is $U \to Y \to C$, Y is E^* and C is $S \to A$.

To keep the anonymous quantities separate from the continuation for a program we are obliged to formulate the valuations which normally take continuations as arguments in such a way that they depend on stacks as well. Accordingly the valuations retain their earlier significance but acquire new arguments, so that $\mathcal{E}$, for instance, belongs to $Exp \to Z \to U \to Y \to C$. We also ensure that the members of Z are continuations which do not provide any information about the environment or the stack. Consequently we can identify the domain 0 of "pure code" with $Z \to Z$ and regard $\mathfrak{E}$ as an element of $Exp \to 0$. In fact it will be shown in 5.5.7 that valuations like $\mathfrak{E}$ can be obtained by translating high level languages into machine codes; indeed, if it did not rely so heavily on fix, in store semantics $\mathfrak{E}[\![E]\!]$ would provide all the information known by a certain implementation after the expression E had been compiled but before it had been executed. In this situation there are no differences between continuations appropriate to expressions, declarations and commands: all of the continuations belong to Z, a typical member of which is signified by ζ, and many of the valuations have range 0, a typical member of which is signified by ξ. Usually expressions adjoin an element to the top of the stack, declarations append a layer of denoted values to the environment and commands alter the store; this threefold distinction is reflected in the members of O which the relevant valuations produce, not in the continuations supplied as arguments.

Many implementations require a stack which differs from that appropriate to store semantics by containing linkage information for procedure calls as well as local quantities. We could modify appendix 2 so that our equations would model this kind of stack; indeed this is one of the changes carried out in appendix 3. However our present version of the stack is quite adequate for devising notions of program equivalence. These notions involve introducing the concept of a 'state' of a machine which belongs to a domain P. For parallel programs P becomes $U \times Y \times S \times Q \times H$, just as C becomes $S \to Q \to H \to A$, but since we deal mainly with serial programs we shall take P to be $U \times Y \times S$. We shall use π to denote a typical member of P and υ to denote a typical member of Y.

Because the equations of appendix 2 simulate an implementation in which complex parts of states can be stored by assignment the resulting description of Sal is termed its 'store semantics'. Analysing these equations in the way to be outlined in 5.6.9 shows that they capture the essence of a very general, but inefficient, implementation technique: well-nigh every high-level language can be given an implementation which could be couched in terms of a variant of store semantics. This claim can also be made about the interpreters of Landin [37], which can be related to store semantics by applying the methods to be described in 4.6.2. General remarks about proofs that implementations are correct will be found in 5.6.9; they could be read at this stage in an attempt to motivate some of what we shall now discuss. We shall formalize the intuitive connection between standard semantics and store semantics from 4.2.1 onwards.

4.1.3. The recurrence of states.

Arguments similar to those concerning label values lead us to view $\rho[\![\text{res}]\!]$ as a member of J* where J is $Z\times U\times Y$. Thus executing either res E or goto E entails discarding not just continuations but environments and stacks as well. Indeed it does not matter what stack is supplied to a sequencer Σ when it is executed, for, as will be confirmed in 4.3.3, appendix 2 would remain a reasonable description of Sal if we took $\mathcal{E}[\![\Sigma]\!]$ and $\mathcal{G}[\![\Sigma]\!]$ to be $\lambda\zeta\rho\upsilon\sigma.\mathcal{S}[\![\Sigma]\!](\mathit{rend}[\![\Sigma]\!]\rho)\langle\rangle\sigma$. We have chosen not to do this because the formulas actually adopted are more generally applicable: modified forms of them are valid in the stack semantics of Sal, in which a label value does not contain an explicit stack but merely a pointer that indicates the height of the stack at the time of the setting of the label. Indeed these particular formulas even remain valid in languages akin to BCPL [72] in which J is just $Z\times U$ (with the effect that jumps back into expressions can cause trouble); however, in 4.3.3 we shall show also that the continuations for standard semantics correspond with label values belonging to $Z\times U\times Y$.

In order to record all the locations which may be referred to while computing we must subject G to the same scrutiny as F and S. At first sight it might seem that we should take G to be $O\times U\times Y\times S$; then the execution of rec Δ would entail giving each identifier I in the list $\mathcal{H}[\![\Delta]\!]$ an initial value like $\langle\mathcal{T}[\![\Delta]\!],\rho,\upsilon,\sigma\rangle$ where υ would be the stack before the declaration was executed. This version of G implies that the value of I is more heavily dependent on the state $\langle\rho,\upsilon,\sigma\rangle$ than is actually the case. Stacks are obtained when the continuations of standard semantics are split up, so they have to be included in label values. However members of G do not contain continuations; instead they contain mappings of continuations into continuations and affect the stacks supplied to them only by adding extra elements. Hence the component Y is as redundant in G as it would be in F and we can allow G to be $O\times U\times S$.

A comparison with appendix 1 suggests that if for some I, Δ and ρ′ we know that ρ′⟦I⟧↓1 equals ⟨𝒯⟦Δ⟧,ρ,σ⟩ then, for any ζ′, υ′ and σ′, ℰ⟦I⟧ζ′ρ′υ′σ′ should be 𝒯⟦Δ⟧ζ″ρ⟨⟩σ where ζ″ is essentially λρ″υ″σ″.ζ′ρ′(⟨ρ″⟦I⟧↓1⟩§υ″)σ′. Unfortunately, adopting this approach to recursive declarations violates the principle that no continuation should conceal information about locations which may be required during a computation. We must therefore alter the equations so that the analogue of ζ″ extracts ρ′, υ′ and σ′ from part of the state supplied as an argument to it. To this end we change the domain of environments, U, into (Ide→D*)×J*×P* where P is U×Y×S; for convenience we let ρ⟦rec⟧ be the third component of any ρ∈U, and we extend the conventions and functions of 3.3.3 to ρ⟦rec⟧ by dealing with it in the same way as we dealt with ρ⟦res⟧. Now we introduce *recur*=λIζρυσ.(λ⟨ρ′,υ′,σ′⟩.ρ⟦I⟧↓1∈G→*wrong*σ,ζρ′(⟨ρ⟦I⟧↓1⟩§υ′)σ′)(ρ⟦rec⟧↓1) and demand that an identifier I be given an initial value of the form ⟨λζ.𝒯⟦Δ⟧(*recur*⟦I⟧ζ),ρ,σ⟩ when it is recursively declared by incidence; moreover if ρ′⟦I⟧↓1 coincides with this particular initial value we take ℰ⟦I⟧ζ′ρ′υ′σ′ to be 𝒯⟦Δ⟧(*recur*⟦I⟧ζ′)ρ[⟨ρ′,υ′,σ′⟩/rec]⟨⟩σ for all ζ′, υ′ and σ′. Though in appendix 2 members of P are kept in the environment in precisely the manner indicated here, we could arrange to keep them in the stack or the store instead; for the purpose of tracing the accessible locations all that matters is that somewhere in each state there be a place for preserving one other state when elaborate recursive declarations by incidence are allowed.

Splitting up continuations in the manner outlined above provides us with the entire environment, although as we pointed out in 3.5.6 parts of programs are influenced only by what their free variables denote. Consequently the members of F and G with which we deal need include only little environments to give meaning to the variables encoded in the appropriate members of O. For this reason the definitions of $\mathcal{E}$ and $\mathcal{D}$ in appendix 2 make use of the function *rend* introduced in 3.5.3. We could go further than this by restricting the store in a member of $O\times U\times S$ so that only the accessible locations would have to be copied when executing a recursive declaration, but in practice tracing these locations might be time-consuming.

Any continuation for store semantics is intended to describe a sequence of machine instructions but not the entities on which these instructions act, so the state supplied to this continuation must include the entire environment and the stack. In particular, when we apply a procedure which has $\varepsilon\in O\times U$ as its value we cannot be content to provide $\varepsilon\downarrow 1$ with the environment $\varepsilon\downarrow 2$; instead we must pile $\varepsilon\downarrow 2$ on top of the environment ρ pertaining at the time of application. Thus in terms of the functions defined in 3.3.3 we provide $\varepsilon\downarrow 1$ with $\mathit{divert}\rho(\varepsilon\downarrow 2)$. To restore the original environment after executing the procedure we do not introduce a continuation of the form $\lambda\rho'.\zeta\rho$; reasoning analogous to that motivating the use of *recur* obliges us to remove the top layer from $\mathit{divert}\rho(\varepsilon\downarrow 2)$ when it becomes superfluous. This we shall do by incorporating a function $\mathit{chop}\in \mathrm{Exp}\to U\to U$ in the equation giving the value of an abstraction Φ so that after Φ has been applied the environment loses the layer set up by the free variables and parameters of Φ. Accordingly

$\mathit{chop}=\lambda E\rho.\langle \lambda I.\rho[\![I]\!]\dagger(\mathit{free}[\![E]\!][\![I]\!]\to 1,0),\rho[\![\mathrm{res}]\!]\dagger(\mathit{free}[\![E]\!][\![\mathrm{res}]\!]\to 1,0),\rho[\![\mathrm{rec}]\!]\rangle$.

Because the formal parameter of an abstraction may not occur free in the body the equations for fnI.E and fnI..E require the use of $\mathit{chop}[\![IE]\!]$ rather than $\mathit{chop}[\![E]\!]$.

Another means of reducing the size of the environment is provided by the function $\mathit{revert}\in U\to U\to U$, which satisfies

$$\mathit{revert}=\lambda\rho_1\rho_0.\langle \lambda I.\rho_1[\![I]\!]\dagger(\#\rho_1[\![I]\!]-\#\rho_0[\![I]\!])\rangle \S\langle \rho_1[\![\mathrm{res}]\!]\dagger(\#\rho_1[\![\mathrm{res}]\!]-\#\rho_0[\![\mathrm{res}]\!])\rangle \S\langle \rho_1[\![\mathrm{rec}]\!]\dagger(\#\rho_1[\![\mathrm{rec}]\!]-\#\rho_0[\![\mathrm{rec}]\!])\rangle .$$

The reason for introducing *revert* in such a laconically dismissive way should become apparent in 4.1.4.

Though we are now able to select a third component from ρ by writing ρ⟦rec⟧ (whereas the standard semantics of Sal provides only ρ⟦I⟧ and ρ⟦res⟧), we are not suggesting that rec is an implicit name (in the sense in which we used this term in 3.2.3). Instead of taking U to be $(Ide \to D^*) \times J^* \times P^*$ in appendix 2 we should really make U be $(Ide \to D^*) \times J^*$ and make S be $(L \to (V \times T)) \times V^* \times V^* \times P$. However, as the need for preserving members of P is forced upon us only by recursive declarations with side effects, which ought really to be banned, we have allowed ourselves to be lax about U. Because environments now have three components we are obliged to adopt a definition of *arid* different from that given in 3.3.3; in fact
$arid = \langle (\lambda I.\langle\rangle), \langle\rangle, \langle\rangle\rangle$.

4.1.4. The conservation of environments.

Though standard semantics distinguishes sharply between the environment created by a declaration and the environment in which the succeeding expression is executed, here our wish to model an implementation which always has the entire state at its behest militates against doing this. When Δ inside E is executed in an environment ρ, a new layer is added to ρ, E is executed in the resulting environment, and finally the extra layer is removed. To mimic the removal we could use a continuation of the form $\zeta\circ revert\rho$; however, in contrast to the situation discussed in our earlier work [52:2.1.1], here a compiler can predict the size of the layer, so we actually use $\zeta\circ clip[\![\Delta]\!]$, which models a more efficient implementation. It should nevertheless be noted that as $\zeta\circ revert\rho$ requires a knowledge only of the size of ρ, not of specific denoted values, like $\zeta\circ clip[\![\Delta]\!]$ it is faithful to the intention that continuations should not have parts of the machine state deeply embedded in them. Since the environment must be pruned in the execution of block Γ, as well as that of Δ inside E, we define $clip\in \mathrm{Dec}\to \mathrm{U}\to \mathrm{U}$ and $snip\in \mathrm{Com}\to \mathrm{U}\to \mathrm{U}$ thus:

$$clip=\lambda\Delta\rho.\langle\lambda I.\rho[\![I]\!]\dagger(I\in\mathcal{I}[\![\Delta]\!]\S\mathcal{H}[\![\Delta]\!]\to 1,0),\rho[\![\mathrm{res}]\!],\rho[\![\mathrm{rec}]\!]\rangle\ ;$$

$$snip=\lambda\Gamma\rho.\langle\lambda I.\rho[\![I]\!]\dagger(I\in\mathcal{J}[\![\Gamma]\!]\S\mathcal{K}[\![\Gamma]\!]\to 1,0),\rho[\![\mathrm{res}]\!],\rho[\![\mathrm{rec}]\!]\rangle\ .$$

According to appendix 1, when Δ_0 and Δ_1 is executed in an environment ρ both Δ_0 and Δ_1 must be executed in an environments having the same top layer as ρ. This layer is masked when Δ_0 is executed and must therefore be retrieved before the execution of Δ_1. To do this we introduce $swap\in \mathrm{Dec}\to \mathrm{U}\to \mathrm{U}$, which satisfies

$$swap=\lambda\Delta\rho.\langle\lambda I.((I\in\mathcal{I}[\![\Delta]\!]\S\mathcal{H}[\![\Delta]\!])\to((\#\rho[\![I]\!]\geq 2)\to\langle\rho[\![I]\!]\downarrow 2\rangle,\langle\rho[\![I]\!]\downarrow 1\rangle),\langle\rangle)\S\rho[\![I]\!]\rangle$$
$$\S\langle\rho[\![\mathrm{res}]\!]\rangle\S\langle\rho[\![\mathrm{rec}]\!]\rangle\ .$$

If the execution of Δ_0 precedes that of Δ_1 we can adjust the environment suitably by applying $swap[\![\Delta_0]\!]$ before executing Δ_1 and $clip[\![\Delta_0]\!]$ afterwards; moreover, in a properly composed program, $clip[\![\Delta_0]\!]$ equals $clip[\![\Delta_0$ and $\Delta_1]\!]\circ swap[\![\Delta_1]\!]$, as $\mathcal{I}[\![\Delta_0]\!]\S\mathcal{H}[\![\Delta_0]\!]$ and $\mathcal{I}[\![\Delta_1]\!]\S\mathcal{H}[\![\Delta_1]\!]$ are disjoint.

The declaration Δ_0 within Δ_1 receives a treatment similar to that given to Δ inside E, since after the execution of Δ_1 the values attached to identifiers by Δ_0 will still be lurking around in the environment and may obscure the original values. To eliminate these superfluous values we first formulate the function *slim* of 3.5.3 in a manner appropriate to our present version of U; thus

$slim = \lambda\Delta\rho.\langle(\lambda I.I \in \mathcal{I}[\![\Delta]\!] \S \mathcal{H}[\![\Delta]\!] \wedge (\#\rho[\![I]\!]>0) \to \langle\rho[\![I]\!]\downarrow 1\rangle, \langle\rangle), \langle\rangle, \langle\rangle\rangle$.

Using this form of *slim* we now define $trim \in \mathrm{Dec} \to \mathrm{Dec} \to \mathrm{U} \to \mathrm{U}$ by

$trim = \lambda\Delta_0\Delta_1\rho.divert(clip[\![\Delta_0]\!](clip[\![\Delta_1]\!]\rho))(slim[\![\Delta_1]\!]\rho)$.

The effect of $trim[\![\Delta_0]\!][\![\Delta_1]\!]$ on ρ is to discard $\rho[\![I]\!]\downarrow 1$ when I is in $\mathcal{I}[\![\Delta_0]\!] \S \mathcal{H}[\![\Delta_0]\!]$ but not in $\mathcal{I}[\![\Delta_1]\!] \S \mathcal{H}[\![\Delta_1]\!]$ and to discard $\rho[\![I]\!]\downarrow 2$ when I is in both $\mathcal{I}[\![\Delta_0]\!] \S \mathcal{H}[\![\Delta_0]\!]$ and $\mathcal{I}[\![\Delta_1]\!] \S \mathcal{H}[\![\Delta_1]\!]$.

We also adopt *trim* in the equation governing recursive declarations. The identifiers declared in **rec** Δ are given one set of values before the execution of Δ and another set in the course of the execution. To ensure that only the latter of these sets affects the size of the ultimate environment we apply $trim[\![\Delta]\!][\![\Delta]\!]$.

There is a difference between the function *tear* required by **rec** Δ and that given in 3.5.4 which corresponds with the difference between the two forms of *slim*; thus we let

$tear = \lambda\Delta\rho.\langle(\lambda I.(free[\![\Delta]\!][\![I]\!] \vee I \in \mathcal{I}[\![\Delta]\!] \S \mathcal{H}[\![\Delta]\!]) \wedge (\#\rho[\![I]\!]>0) \to \langle\rho[\![I]\!]\downarrow 1\rangle, \langle\rangle),$

$\quad (free[\![\Delta]\!][\![\mathbf{res}]\!] \wedge (\#\rho[\![\mathbf{res}]\!]>0) \to \langle\rho[\![\mathbf{res}]\!]\downarrow 1\rangle, \langle\rangle), \rho[\![\mathbf{rec}]\!]\rangle$.

Because the conversion from standard semantics to store semantics does not alter the way in which the domain S is constructed from L, V and T, the definitions of *hold*, *area*, *update*, *updates*, *new* and *news* can be carried across unchanged to the present situation. We can even adopt a function *wrong* which belongs to the domain C for store semantics; we shall also suppose $test \in (\mathrm{C} \times \mathrm{C}) \to \mathrm{W} \to \mathrm{C}$, $assign \in \mathrm{C} \to \mathrm{W} \to \mathrm{W} \to \mathrm{C}$ and $tie \in (\mathrm{L}^* \to \mathrm{C}) \to \mathrm{N} \to \mathrm{C}$ to be defined precisely as in 3.3.4. However, we shall replace *lv* and *rv* by *mv* and *sv*, members of O which are constructed as follows:

$mv = \lambda\zeta\rho\upsilon\sigma.\upsilon{\downarrow}1\in L\to\zeta\rho\upsilon\sigma, new\sigma\in L\to assign(\zeta\rho(\langle new\sigma|L\rangle\S\upsilon{\dagger}1))(new\sigma|L)(\upsilon{\downarrow}1)\sigma, wrong\sigma;$

$sv = \lambda\zeta\rho\upsilon\sigma.\upsilon{\downarrow}1\in L\to\zeta\rho(\langle hold(\upsilon{\downarrow}1|L)\sigma\rangle\S\upsilon{\dagger}1)\sigma, \zeta\rho\upsilon\sigma.$

The function *run*, which was introduced to allow orders of evaluation to remain unspecified, is also ill-suited for store semantics. We therefore provide $earn\in(O\times O)\to O$, which handles the evaluation of expressions, and $deal\in(O\times O)\to O$, which handles the evaluation of declarations. In terms of the permutation *veer* of 3.3.4,

$earn = \lambda\langle\xi_0,\xi_1\rangle\zeta.\xi_{veer0}(\xi_{veer1}(\lambda\rho\upsilon\sigma.\zeta\rho((veer0=0)\to\upsilon,\langle\upsilon{\downarrow}2\rangle\S\langle\upsilon{\downarrow}1\rangle\S\upsilon{\dagger}2)\sigma))$

$deal = \lambda\langle\xi_0,\xi_1\rangle\zeta.\xi_{veer0}(\xi_{veer1}\zeta).$

Similar considerations oblige us to let the valuations $\mathcal{B}$, $\mathcal{O}$ and $\mathcal{W}$ used in appendix 2 be members of $\mathrm{Bas}\to O$, $\mathrm{Mon}\to O$ and $\mathrm{Dya}\to O$ respectively.

At any point in the execution of a program we can list all the locations that are accessible by delving into the environment, the stack and the store; one function which does this for us will be defined in 5.1.2. Consequently we might reasonable expect there to be a function *novel* such that, for any ρ, υ and σ, if there are any locations which are not accessible through ρ, υ and σ then $novel\rho\upsilon\sigma$ must be one of them and if there are no such locations then $novel\rho\upsilon\sigma$ must be *error*; we could even use *novel* instead of *new* in the definition of *mv*. Such a function does exist, but using it in the definition of *mv* obliges us either to introduce some continuations that are not continuous functions or to handle recursion without using least fixed points; elsewhere [52:2.4.4] we have discussed why this is so and how to include suitable discontinuous functions in domains satisfying recursive equations.

Several projection functions are omitted from appendix 2; thus $(\lambda\rho\upsilon\sigma.\upsilon{\downarrow}2\in F\to(\upsilon{\downarrow}2{\downarrow}1)\zeta(divert\rho(\upsilon{\downarrow}2{\downarrow}2))(\langle\upsilon{\downarrow}1\rangle\S\upsilon{\dagger}2)\sigma, wrong\sigma)$, which appears in the equation governing E_0E_1, should really be written as the formula $(\lambda\rho\upsilon\sigma.\upsilon{\downarrow}2\in F\to((\upsilon{\downarrow}2|F){\downarrow}1)\zeta(divert\rho((\upsilon{\downarrow}2|F){\downarrow}2))(\langle\upsilon{\downarrow}1\rangle\S\upsilon{\dagger}2)\sigma, wrong\sigma)$. This kind of laxity (which is indulged in for the sake of brevity) should not be confusing at this stage, but sometimes (in 4.3.1, for example) we shall mention the projection functions just to try to be helpful.

4.1.5. The formation of the domains.

Three of the value domains given in appendix 2 have the same surface structure as their counterparts in appendix 1; thus V=B+E*+J+F, E=L+B+E*+J+F and D=L+B+E*+J+F+G. The domain W, however, differs from the domain of witnessed values for standard semantics, since it has to take into account the fact that the third components of environments contain states which can be obtained during computations by applying *recur*. Consequently we let W=L+B+E*+J+F+G+J+P in store semantics; when only serial programs are considered, P=U×Y×S. The two summands of W called J refer to label values and to the entities set up by val expressions; these summands have to be distinct because in predicates such as those of 5.2.4 a continuation is subjected to tests which depend on whether it arises from a label value or is connected with res. In both situations J=Z×U×Y and J is the retract associated with the retraction $(\lambda\zeta.\zeta)\times(\lambda\rho.\rho)\times(\lambda\upsilon.\upsilon)$, which can be written as $\lambda\langle\zeta,\rho,\upsilon\rangle.\langle\zeta,\rho,\upsilon\rangle$; moreover F=O×S and G=O×U×S, so F and G are associated with the retractions $\lambda\langle\xi,\rho\rangle.\langle\xi,\rho\rangle$ and $\lambda\langle\xi,\rho,\sigma\rangle.\langle\xi,\rho,\sigma\rangle$.

In 4.2.3 we shall need to be sure that the domains suited to appendix 2 are the retracts associated with the fixed point of a continuous function defined on lists of retractions of a universal domain. Here we shall therefore provide a functor, W, such that W can be assumed to be the retract associated with *fix*(W); the other domains will be the retracts associated with retractions obtained from *fix*(W) by the means mentioned in 3.3.5. When X represents a retraction of a universal domain we let

$$W=\lambda X.L+B+(EX)^{*}+(ZX\times UX\times YX)+(OX\times UX)+(OX\times UX\times SX)+(ZX\times UX\times YX)+PX,$$

where the functor U differs from that defined in 3.3.5. We use the mappings *push* and *mask* introduced in 2.4.4 in order to form functors governing stored, expressed and denoted values thus:

$V=\lambda X.push\langle 4,-1\rangle \circ X \circ push\langle 3,1\rangle$;

$E=\lambda X.X\circ mask4$;

$D=\lambda X.X\circ mask5$.

Though the functor for the domain of stores retains the form given to it in 3.3.5, we now have to introduce an extra functor (for the domain of stacks) and we have to modify the functor for the domain of environments. Because $S=(L\to(V\times T))\times V^*\times V^*$, $Y=E^*$ and $U=(Ide\to D^*)\times J^*\times P^*$ these functors are as follows:

$S=\lambda X.(L\to(VX\times T))\times(VX)^*\times(VX)^*$;

$Y=\lambda X.(EX)^*$;

$U=\lambda X.(Ide\to(DX)^*)\times(reject\circ X\circ flag6)^*\times(reject\circ X\circ flag7)^*$.

The simple retractions T, L, B and Ide are familiar to us from 3.3.5, but the bizarre forms needed by the second and third factors of UX perhaps require some explanation. The argument supplied to a retraction X will be regarded as a member of W, so in order to make X act on members of the domains J and P (which occur the equation for U) we first convert them into members of the relevant summands of W, then apply X and finally extract the significant portion of the result; we perform these operations using the functions *flag* and *reject* defined in 2.4.4. We can now provide a suitable equation for P, the functor for the domain of states, by writing

$P=\lambda X.UX\times YX\times SX$.

These funçtors, together with A (a functor for the domain of answers) are required by the definition of Z, which governs pure continuations. As $Z=U\to Y\to S\to A$, we set

$Z=\lambda X.UX\to YX\to SX\to AX$.

Similarly the fact that $O=Z\to Z$ suggests the equation

$O=\lambda X.ZX\to ZX$.

We now make the assumption that if X is any retraction of the universal domain having $X\circ mask4=mask4\circ X$, $X\circ mask5=mask5\circ X$,

$X \circ \mathit{flag}6 = X \circ \mathit{flag}6 \circ \mathit{reject} \circ X \circ \mathit{flag}6$ and $X \circ \mathit{flag}7 = X \circ \mathit{flag}7 \circ \mathit{reject} \circ X \circ \mathit{flag}7$ then AX is a retraction (so that WX is a retraction satisfying these conditions). Moreover we suppose that whenever ν is a directed set of retractions each of which is subject to the conditions imposed on X above then $A(\bigsqcup \nu) = \bigsqcup\{AX \mid X \in \nu\}$. Under these circumstances we may form the retraction *fix*(W) and we can demand, for example, that the retractions V(*fix*(W)), E(*fix*(W)) and D(*fix*(W)) give rise to the retracts V, E and D. Hence we shall stipulate that W must be the retract associated with *fix*(W), and we shall regard the other retractions required as being obtained from *fix*(W) by applying the functors introduced above. Thus besides asserting that $\lambda\omega.\omega = \mathit{fix}(W)$ we shall tacitly use such equations as $\lambda\sigma.\sigma = S(\lambda\omega.\omega)$, $\lambda\upsilon.\upsilon = Y(\lambda\omega.\omega)$ and $\lambda\rho.\rho = U(\lambda\omega.\omega)$ (together with more complicated ones like $\lambda\langle\zeta,\rho,\upsilon\rangle.\langle\zeta,\rho,\upsilon\rangle = Z(\lambda\omega.\omega)\times U(\lambda\omega.\omega)\times Y(\lambda\omega.\omega)$).

The suppositions made about A can, of course, be changed to reflect any sort of dependence of A on W. The domains engendered by the changes are of little interest to us, because in store semantics A is often taken to be P, with the effect that A becomes P (which certainly satisfies the hypotheses above).

4.1.6. The vectorial convention.

Of particular importance in store semantics is the domain of states, P, which for serial programs can be identified with U×Y×S. As a typical member of P is denoted by π whereas typical members of U, Y and S are denoted by ρ, υ and σ respectively, from 5.2.1 onwards we shall find it convenient to identify π with $\langle \rho,\upsilon,\sigma\rangle$, thereby giving the equations $\pi{\downarrow}1=\rho$, $\pi{\downarrow}2=\upsilon$ and $\pi{\downarrow}3=\sigma$. This convention will extend also to subscripted and accented variables, so that underlying the use of π as a variable will be such unstated equalities as $\langle \acute{\pi}_1,\grave{\pi}_1\rangle=\langle\langle \acute{\rho}_1,\acute{\upsilon}_1,\acute{\sigma}_1\rangle,\langle \grave{\rho}_1,\grave{\upsilon}_1,\grave{\sigma}_1\rangle\rangle$. Unpleasant though this usage is, it does have the virtue of abbreviating formulae such as those to be given in 5.2.2.

4.2. Recursive relations.

4.2.1. Congruent equations.

Our analysis of programming languages involves two kinds of relation between semantic equations, which we shall term 'equivalence' and 'congruence'. Equivalence problems are those concerned with proofs that two programs written in the same language have identical or similar meanings according to one set of semantic equations, whereas congruence problems are those which deal with the connections between two different sets of semantic equations. The distinction between these kinds of problem is not entirely rigid, and in cases more complex than those of 4.3.7 the appropriate methods of proof often coincide; moreover in investigations such as that to be described in 5.2.1 it is sometimes convenient to establish that two sets of equations are congruent by verifying that one set ascribes to each program a meaning which corresponds with the meaning given to an equivalent program by the other set. Nonetheless the main matter to be discussed in this section is purely a congruence problem: in order to be sure that Sal programs which are equivalent in store semantics are also equivalent in standard semantics we wish to verify that the two sorts of semantics are closely related. We shall begin by clarifying what is to be understood by this rather loose phrasing.

Continuations are functions which map arguments embodying aspects of the machine state into final answers of programs. In both standard semantics and store semantics A signifies the domain of answers, but we need not assume that the two versions of A are the same; similar remarks apply to the other domains and valuations used in the appendices, since we can interpret S, for instance, as the domain of stores for either standard semantics or store semantics without fear of confusion. This economical nomenclature allows the diacritical convention of 2.5.4 to be adopted; thus here β will be taken to be a pair of environments, $\langle\acute{\rho},\grave{\rho}\rangle$, such that $\acute{\rho}$ belongs to the domain U needed by standard semantics and $\grave{\rho}$ belongs to the domain U required by store semantics. Needless to say, the primitive lattices (such as L, B, T and N) remain unchanged when we move from one set of semantic equations to the other.

Because the answer domains may not coincide we cannot relate these two sorts of semantics by demanding that $\mathfrak{G}[\![\Theta]\!]\acute{\rho}\theta\acute{\sigma}$ be equal to $\mathfrak{G}[\![\Theta]\!]\zeta\grave{\rho}\upsilon\grave{\sigma}$ for any Sal block Θ and for all "suitable" θ, ζ, υ, $\hat{\rho}$ and $\hat{\sigma}$. We can, however, insist that the pair $\langle\mathfrak{G}[\![\Theta]\!]\acute{\rho}\theta\acute{\sigma},\mathfrak{G}[\![\Theta]\!]\zeta\grave{\rho}\upsilon\grave{\sigma}\rangle$ be subject to some predicate a defined on A×A; when the two versions of A are identical this predicate can be equality, but generally it will be a more elaborate function for which $a\langle\bot,\bot\rangle$ must be *true* if $\bot$ is the answer given by a non-terminating program.

Just as we require a predicate a which reveals when two answers match so we need a predicate s to determine which pairs in S×S are "suitable". Not all pairs are "suitable", for when m denotes a location α the value of **goto** m depends heavily on what the store contains: only if we are sure that $a\langle(hold\,\alpha\acute{\sigma})\acute{\sigma},(hold\,\alpha\grave{\sigma})(hold\,\alpha\acute{\sigma}\downarrow 2)(hold\,\alpha\grave{\sigma}\downarrow 3)\grave{\sigma}\rangle$ is *true* do we know that $a\langle\mathfrak{G}[\![\mathbf{goto}\ m]\!](arid[\alpha/m])\theta\acute{\sigma},\mathfrak{G}[\![\mathbf{goto}\ m]\!]\zeta(arid[\alpha/m])\upsilon\grave{\sigma}\rangle$ is *true*. Accordingly we stipulate that stores $\acute{\sigma}$ and $\grave{\sigma}$ cannot satisfy $s\hat{\sigma}=true$ unless locations $\acute{\alpha}$ and $\grave{\alpha}$ which correspond are such that the pair $\langle hold\,\acute{\alpha}\acute{\sigma},hold\,\grave{\alpha}\grave{\sigma}\rangle$ is "suitable" and $area\,\acute{\alpha}\acute{\sigma}=area\,\grave{\alpha}\grave{\sigma}$. Provided that the storage allocation for standard semantics is kept in step with that for store semantics (in a sense to be made plain in 4.2.6) we can let l, the correspondence between locations, be such that $l\hat{\alpha}$ is *true* if and only if $\acute{\alpha}\in$L is equal to $\grave{\alpha}\in$L. Under these particular circumstances $s\hat{\sigma}$ cannot be *true* unless $\bigwedge\{(area\,\acute{\alpha}\acute{\sigma}\equiv area\,\grave{\alpha}\grave{\sigma})\wedge v\langle hold\,\acute{\alpha}\acute{\sigma},hold\,\grave{\alpha}\grave{\sigma}\rangle \mid l\hat{\alpha}\}$ is *true* for some predicate v which maps V×V into the domain T′ described in 2.2.2.

This predicate v is intended to indicate whether stored values $\acute{\beta}$ and $\grave{\beta}$ are "suitable" in that the role of $\acute{\beta}$ in standard semantics is the same as the role of $\grave{\beta}$ in store semantics. As the program goto *m* demonstrates, when $\acute{\beta}$ and $\grave{\beta}$ are label values it is reasonable to allow $v\hat{\beta}$ to be *true* only if whenever $s\hat{\sigma}=$*true* the effect of applying $\acute{\beta}$ to $\acute{\sigma}$ is properly related to the effect on $\grave{\sigma}$ of the jump represented by $\grave{\beta}$. Thus when $\hat{\beta}$ is a pair of label values having $v\hat{\beta}=$*true* $\hat{\beta}$ must satisfy $c\hat{\beta}=$*true* where c is a predicate such that no $\theta\epsilon C$ and $\langle\zeta,\rho,\upsilon\rangle\epsilon Z\times U\times Y$ can have $c\langle\theta,\langle\zeta,\rho,\upsilon\rangle\rangle$ equal to *true* unless $a\langle\theta\acute{\sigma},\zeta\rho\upsilon\grave{\sigma}\rangle$ is *true* for all $\hat{\sigma}$ with $s\hat{\sigma}=$*true*.

The equations governing v, s and c must therefore refer to one another recursively. However, we cannot establish the existence of these predicates by an appeal to the Tarski fixed point theorem [89] because the role of s in our account of c prevents them from being the fixed points of monotonic functions. Instead we shall exploit the assumption that the domains which we use are induced by the least fixed points of functors like those defined in 3.3.5 and 4.1.5; the relevance of this knowledge will emerge in 4.2.3, but first we shall describe the predicates more fully. Not until 4.2.5 will we explain how they are employed in the proof that the standard semantics of Sal is congruent with the store semantics of Sal.

4.2.2. The links required by the domains.

The store set up by evaluating a program using standard semantics must yield input and output which correspond with those provided by store semantics. It is therefore unreasonable to expect stores $\acute{\sigma}$ and $\grave{\sigma}$ to have $s\hat{\sigma}$ equal to *true* unless the entries in the input and output components of $\acute{\sigma}$ satisfy v when paired with the appropriate portions of $\grave{\sigma}$. As the domains named S are both of the form $(L\rightarrow(V\times T))\times V^{*}\times V^{*}$, we exhaust the constraints which can be imposed on $\hat{\sigma}$ by adopting the equation

$$\begin{aligned} s=\lambda\hat{\sigma}.\bigwedge\{(\mathit{area}\acute{\alpha}\acute{\sigma}\equiv\mathit{area}\grave{\alpha}\grave{\sigma})\wedge v\langle\mathit{hold}\acute{\alpha}\acute{\sigma},\mathit{hold}\grave{\alpha}\grave{\sigma}\rangle \mid l\hat{\alpha}\} \\ \wedge((\#\acute{\sigma}\downarrow 2\equiv\#\grave{\sigma}\downarrow 2)\rightarrow\bigwedge\{v\langle\acute{\sigma}\downarrow 2\downarrow\nu,\grave{\sigma}\downarrow 2\downarrow\nu\rangle \mid \#(\grave{\sigma}\downarrow 2)\geq\nu\geq 1\},\mathit{false}) \\ \wedge((\#\acute{\sigma}\downarrow 3\equiv\#\grave{\sigma}\downarrow 3)\rightarrow\bigwedge\{v\langle\acute{\sigma}\downarrow 3\downarrow\nu,\grave{\sigma}\downarrow 3\downarrow\nu\rangle \mid \#(\acute{\sigma}\downarrow 3)\geq\nu\geq 1\},\mathit{false}). \end{aligned}$$

Because the semantic equations ensure that the store $\perp$ need never be supplied as an argument to a continuation the effect (on this store) of standard semantics need not coincide with that of store semantics. Indeed, the "coalesced" products and sums used in other work [52:1.2.2] are such that these two sorts of semantics do produce different effects when the store $\perp$ is discussed; here, however, the effects coincide, so we can take $s\langle\perp,\perp\rangle$ to be *true*.

We must let $v\langle\perp,\perp\rangle$ be *true* when $s\langle\perp,\perp\rangle$ is *true*, since otherwise from stores that were equivalent could be extracted values that were not. The equation satisfied by v makes use of four further predicates, each of which handles one summand of V. The most trivial of these predicates, b, maps pairs in B×B into truth values in such a way that whenever $\acute{\beta}$ and $\grave{\beta}$ are proper members of B $v\hat{\beta}$ is $b\hat{\beta}$. For all our purposes we tacitly assume that $b\hat{\beta}$ is *true* if and only if $\acute{\beta}\in B$ is equal to $\grave{\beta}\in B$, but we could choose to do otherwise; thus, for example, we might wish to prove that one program was equivalent with another obtained from it by interchanging **true** with **false** and ∧ with ∨ and by setting ~ before the premise of every loop or conditional clause, in which case $b\langle true, false\rangle$ would need to be *true* and $b\langle true, true\rangle$ would be *false*. When $\acute{\beta}$ and $\grave{\beta}$ are both in E* their components are paired and tested by a predicate e, which maps E×E into T′; only if $e\langle(\acute{\beta}|E^*)\downarrow\nu,(\grave{\beta}|E^*)\downarrow\nu\rangle$ is *true* whenever $\#(\acute{\beta}|E^*)\geq\nu\geq1$ can $v\hat{\beta}$ be *true*. Analogous to the test c applied to label values is the predicate f which provides $v\hat{\beta}$ when $\acute{\beta}$ and $\grave{\beta}$ are procedure values. More formally,

$$
\begin{aligned}
v=\lambda\hat{\beta}.\,&(\acute{\beta}\equiv\bot)\vee(\grave{\beta}\equiv\bot)\rightarrow(\acute{\beta}\equiv\bot)\wedge(\grave{\beta}\equiv\bot),\\
&(\acute{\beta}\equiv\top)\vee(\grave{\beta}\equiv\top)\rightarrow(\acute{\beta}\equiv\top)\wedge(\grave{\beta}\equiv\top),\\
&\acute{\beta}\in B\wedge\grave{\beta}\in B\rightarrow l\langle\acute{\beta}|L,\grave{\beta}|L\rangle,\\
&\acute{\beta}\in E^*\wedge\grave{\beta}\in E^*\rightarrow(\lambda\langle\varepsilon^*_0,\varepsilon^*_1\rangle.(\#\varepsilon^*_0\equiv\#\varepsilon^*_1)\rightarrow\bigwedge\{e\langle\varepsilon^*_0\downarrow\nu,\varepsilon^*_1\downarrow\nu\rangle\,|\,\#\varepsilon^*_0\geq\nu\geq1\},\\
&\qquad\qquad\qquad\qquad\qquad false)\\
&\qquad\qquad(\langle\acute{\beta}|E^*,\grave{\beta}|E^*\rangle),\\
&\acute{\beta}\in J\wedge\grave{\beta}\in J\rightarrow c\langle\acute{\beta}|J,\grave{\beta}|J\rangle,\\
&\acute{\beta}\in F\wedge\grave{\beta}\in F\rightarrow f\langle\acute{\beta}|F,\grave{\beta}|F\rangle,\\
&false.
\end{aligned}
$$

Expression continuations in Sal may be called upon to handle the expressed value $\bot$ when they are obliged to handle the store $\bot$. Consequently $e\langle\bot,\bot\rangle$, like $s\langle\bot,\bot\rangle$, must be *true* and we can build up e in the same way as v. Since an expressed value may be in L we write

$$
\begin{aligned}
e=\lambda\hat{\varepsilon}.\,&(\acute{\varepsilon}\equiv\bot)\vee(\grave{\varepsilon}\equiv\bot)\rightarrow(\acute{\varepsilon}\equiv\bot)\wedge(\grave{\varepsilon}\equiv\bot),\\
&(\acute{\varepsilon}\equiv\top)\vee(\grave{\varepsilon}\equiv\top)\rightarrow(\grave{\varepsilon}\equiv\top)\wedge(\grave{\varepsilon}\equiv\top),\\
&\acute{\varepsilon}\in L\vee\grave{\varepsilon}\in L\rightarrow(\acute{\varepsilon}\in L\wedge\grave{\varepsilon}\in L\rightarrow l\langle\acute{\varepsilon}|L,\grave{\varepsilon}|L\rangle, false),\\
&v\hat{\varepsilon}.
\end{aligned}
$$

The predicate for command continuations, c, is given by

$$c=\lambda\langle\theta,\langle\zeta,\rho,\upsilon\rangle\rangle.\bigwedge\{a\langle\theta\acute{\sigma},\zeta\rho\upsilon\grave{\sigma}\rangle\,|\,s\hat{\sigma}\}.$$

Expression continuations can be handled similarly by introducing a predicate k such that for no $\kappa\in K$ and $\langle\zeta,\rho,\upsilon\rangle\in Z\times U\times Y$ can $k\langle\kappa,\langle\zeta,\rho,\upsilon\rangle\rangle$ be *true* unless $a\langle\kappa\acute{\varepsilon}\acute{\sigma},\zeta\rho(\langle\grave{\varepsilon}\rangle\S\upsilon)\grave{\sigma}\rangle$ is *true* whenever $e\hat{\varepsilon}$ and $s\hat{\sigma}$ are *true*; thus

$$k=\lambda\langle\kappa,\langle\zeta,\rho,\upsilon\rangle\rangle.\bigwedge\{c\langle\kappa\acute{\varepsilon},\langle\zeta,\rho,\langle\grave{\varepsilon}\rangle\S\upsilon\rangle\rangle\,|\,e\hat{\varepsilon}\}.$$

In standard semantics the representation of a procedure is a mapping which produces a member of A when supplied with a parameter in E, a continuation in K and a store in S; hence if ϕ is such a representation whilst $\varepsilon \in E$ and $\kappa \in K$ then $\phi\varepsilon\kappa$ is actually in C. In store semantics, however, a procedure is applied by superimposing its free variable list on the entire environment and by regarding the top element of the stack as the parameter; thus, if $\langle \xi,\rho \rangle$ is taken to be a procedure, at the time of application $\langle \zeta,\rho',\langle \varepsilon \rangle \S \upsilon,\sigma \rangle$ is replaced by $\langle \xi\zeta,\mathit{divert}\rho'\rho,\langle \varepsilon \rangle \S \upsilon,\sigma \rangle$. Such versions of procedures may be related by writing

$$f=\lambda\langle \phi,\langle \xi,\rho \rangle\rangle . \bigwedge\{c\langle \phi\acute{\varepsilon}\kappa,\langle \xi\zeta,\mathit{divert}\rho'\rho,\langle \grave{\varepsilon} \rangle \S \upsilon \rangle\rangle \mid e\hat{\varepsilon} \wedge k\langle \kappa,\langle \zeta,\rho',\upsilon \rangle\rangle \}.$$

Now v has been explicated insofar as is possible without showing that it exists. Our proof of the congruence requires other predicates; because they do not depend on v recursively we shall delay our discussion of them until 4.2.4.

4.2.3. The forging of these links.

In 2.2.2 we remarked that T′ is a complete lattice having ∨ as its join operation and *true* as its least element. Consequently there is a close connection between the equations governing the predicates of 4.2.2 and the operators defined on inclusive functions in 2.5.5 provided that we take the range of these functions to be T′ and identify the element *check* needed by the operators with *false*. This connection is not, of course, fortuitous, for just as we can establish the relation between S, V and C by using the fixed points of functors on universal domains so we can set up *s*, *v* and *c* by introducing suitable predictors. In fact 2.5.3 seems to be as crucial to demonstrating the congruence of different semantic equations as 2.3.3 is to proving the existence of the entities that appear in the equations.

In the argument that follows we shall take X to be a universal domain; a typical inclusive predicate mapping X into T′ will be denoted by *x* and a typical retraction of X will be denoted by *X*. We indicated in 3.3.5 that the domains suited to the standard semantics of Sal are determined by the assumption that W is the set of fixed points of a certain retraction, *fix*(W), which is itself the least fixed point of W, a continuous functor on X. In a similar manner the domains for the store semantics of Sal depend upon the relevant version of the domain of witnessed values, which is the set of fixed points of another retraction that again takes the form *fix*(W) for a suitable functor called W. Hence here we shall provide a mapping w which is actually a predictor for W∘W and which nevertheless provides the predicates we require when 2.5.3. is invoked.

The form taken by w cannot be as simple as 2.5.5 might suggest, because we have to set up a correspondence between two domains having different structures; that for standard semantics takes the form

L+B+E*+J+F+G+K, whereas that for store semantics takes the form L+B+E*+J+F+G+J+P. However, we do not wish to compare any witnessed value for standard semantics with a member of the domain P for store semantics. Moreover, since the predicates of 4.2.2 do not demand a knowledge of what values may be denoted but merely a knowledge of what values may be expressed, we can ignore those summands of the two versions of W which are not also summands of the two versions of E. Hence in the present instance we may assume that

$w=\lambda x.(l+b+(ex)^*+cx+fx)\circ(\lambda\hat{\omega}.\hat{\omega})$.

As in 4.2.2, we take l and b to be the identity predicates defined on L×L and B×B; thus $l=\lambda\hat{\alpha}.(\acute{\alpha}\equiv\grave{\alpha})$ and $b=\lambda\hat{\beta}.(\acute{\beta}\equiv\grave{\beta})$, where momentarily $\hat{\beta}$ is taken to be a typical member of B×B, not a typical member of V×V. Because *check* is being interpreted as *false*, and because B=T+N+R+H+H* in the case of Sal, we may write $b=t+n+r+h+h^*$, where t, n, r and h are the identity predicates for T×T, N×N, R×R and H×H respectively; more explicitly, we let $t=\lambda\hat{\varepsilon}.(\acute{\varepsilon}\equiv\grave{\varepsilon})$ (when $\hat{\varepsilon}$ is only allowed to be a member of T×T rather than a member of E×E) and we could define n, r and h in a similar fashion.

The equation for w bears a resemblance to the equation for W given in 3.3.5, so we expect the equation for v, which generates v, to be similar to that for V. Recalling the function *mask* defined in 2.4.4 and the fact that $\lambda\hat{\beta}.\hat{\beta}$ is the retraction of X on to V×V, we write

$v=\lambda x.x\circ(push\langle 3,1\rangle\times push\langle 3,1\rangle)\circ(\lambda\hat{\beta}.\hat{\beta})$;

taking v to be $\lambda x.x\circ push\langle 3,1\rangle$ would not reflect the fact that v tests members of V×V, not members of V.

Likewise to generate e we introduce e; as it is given by the equation

$e=\lambda x.x\circ(mask4\times mask4)\circ(\lambda\hat{\varepsilon}.\hat{\varepsilon})$,

it is connected with E in the way in which v is connected with V.

These equations provide more than enough to enable us to

define a mapping s which generates functions acting on pairs of stores. Because the functor called S in 3.3.5 satisfies

$S=\lambda X.(L\to(VX\times T))\times(VX)^*\times(VX)^*$,

we set

$s=\lambda x.((l\to(vx\times t))\times(vx)^*\times(vx)^*)\circ(\lambda\hat{\theta}.\hat{\theta})$.

The mapping c diverges more strongly from the pattern laid down in 2.5.5, since label values belong to C in standard semantics and to Z×U×Y in store semantics. However, we already know what equation we want the predicate *c* to satisfy, so if we introduce a mapping a to generate the predicate *a* we may write

$c=\lambda x.\lambda\langle\theta,\langle\zeta,\rho,\upsilon\rangle\rangle.\bigwedge\{ax\langle\theta\acute{\theta},\zeta\rho\upsilon\grave{\theta}\rangle\mid sx\hat{\theta}\}$.

Because $sx\hat{\theta}=true$ if and only if $(sx\hat{\theta}\equiv true)=true$ this equation can be turned into

$c=\lambda x.\lambda\langle\theta,\langle\zeta,\rho,\upsilon\rangle\rangle.\bigwedge\{ax\langle\theta\acute{\theta},\zeta\rho\upsilon\grave{\theta}\rangle\mid sx\hat{\theta}\equiv true\}$,

We have defined s in such a way that when $\lambda\hat{\theta}.\hat{\theta}$ is the retraction of X on to S×S then $s=\lambda x.sx\circ(\lambda\hat{\theta}.\hat{\theta})$ and

$c=\lambda x.\lambda\langle\theta,\langle\zeta,\rho,\upsilon\rangle\rangle.\bigwedge\{ax\langle\theta(cross\,\chi\downarrow 1),\zeta\rho\upsilon(cross\,\chi\downarrow 2)\rangle\mid sx\chi\equiv true\}$.

Since $\lambda\langle\theta,\langle\zeta,\rho,\upsilon\rangle\rangle.\langle\theta,\zeta\rho\upsilon\rangle$ is a function which first maps X into C×(Z×U×Y) and then maps C×(Z×U×Y) into C×C, we may factor it out in the same way as we factored out $\lambda\hat{\theta}.\hat{\theta}$, thereby obtaining the equation

$$c=\lambda x.(\lambda\chi.\bigwedge\{ax\langle arrow(cross\,\chi\downarrow 1)(cross\,\chi'\downarrow 1),arrow(cross\,\chi\downarrow 2)(cross\,\chi'\downarrow 2)\rangle \mid sx\chi'\equiv true\})\circ(\lambda\langle\theta,\langle\zeta,\rho,\upsilon\rangle\rangle.\langle\theta,\zeta\rho\upsilon\rangle).$$

As *true* is the least element of T′, we may translate this into the more formal style of 2.5.5 by writing

$c=\lambda x.(sx\to ax)\circ(\lambda\langle\theta,\langle\zeta,\rho,\upsilon\rangle\rangle.\langle\theta,\zeta\rho\upsilon\rangle)$.

To emphasize the unity of purpose underlying the predicates of 4.2.2 we shall adopt the same technique when defining the other mappings; for instance, the mapping k which generates *k* is given by

$k=\lambda x.(ex\to cx)\circ(\lambda\langle\kappa,\langle\zeta,\rho,\upsilon\rangle\rangle.\langle\kappa,(\lambda\varepsilon.\langle\zeta,\rho,\langle\varepsilon\rangle\S\upsilon\rangle)\rangle)$.

More interesting is f, which provides the predicate f governing procedure values. Varying the order in which arguments are supplied to members of F produces an assortment of definitions of f; the one appropriate to the equations in 4.2.3 is

$f=\lambda x.(ex\rightarrow kx\rightarrow cx)\circ(\lambda\langle\phi,\langle\xi,\rho\rangle\rangle.\langle\phi,(\lambda\varepsilon.\lambda\langle\zeta,\rho',\upsilon\rangle.\langle\xi\zeta,divert\rho'\rho,\langle\varepsilon\rangle\S\upsilon\rangle)\rangle)$.

These last three equations illustrate why we have chosen to incorporate retractions such as $\lambda\hat{\beta}.\hat{\beta}$ in the definitions of the mappings rather than taking v, for instance, to be simply $\lambda x.x\circ(push\langle 3,1\rangle\times push\langle 3,1\rangle)$: were we not to do so we would need analogues of $\lambda\langle\theta,\langle\zeta,\rho,\upsilon\rangle\rangle.\langle\theta,\zeta\rho\upsilon\rangle$, $\lambda\langle\kappa,\langle\zeta,\rho,\upsilon\rangle\rangle.\langle\kappa,(\lambda\varepsilon.\langle\zeta,\rho,\langle\varepsilon\rangle\S\upsilon\rangle)\rangle$ and $\lambda\langle\phi,\langle\xi,\rho\rangle\rangle.\langle\phi,(\lambda\varepsilon.\lambda\langle\zeta,\rho',\upsilon\rangle.\langle\xi\zeta,divert\rho'\rho,\langle\varepsilon\rangle\S\upsilon\rangle)\rangle$ which would use *arrow* and *cross* and would be too long to be comprehensible. As a penalty for introducing these retractions, when proving that w is a predictor for W⊛W we are not allowed to consider a retraction X unless $X\circ(\lambda\hat{\omega}.\hat{\omega})=(\lambda\hat{\omega}.\hat{\omega})\circ X$.

Thus we now wish to find two functions called W which are functors (in the loose sense discussed in 3.3.5) and which are such that w is a predictor for W⊛W based on a pair $\langle x_0,X_0\rangle$ and bounded by a set y. Naturally we let $\langle x_0,X_0\rangle=\langle(\lambda\chi.true),(\lambda\chi.\bot)\times(\lambda\chi.\bot)\rangle$; in addition we follow the leads suggested by 3.3.5 and 4.1.5 by taking a retraction X to belong to y if and only if $X=acute(X)\times grave(X)$, $acute(X)\circ(\lambda\acute{\omega}.\acute{\omega})=(\lambda\acute{\omega}.\acute{\omega})\circ acute(X)$, $acute(X)\circ mask4=mask4\circ acute(X)$, $grave(X)\circ(\lambda\grave{\omega}.\grave{\omega})=(\lambda\grave{\omega}.\grave{\omega})\circ grave(X)$, $grave(X)\circ mask4=mask4\circ grave(X)$, $grave(X)\circ mask5=mask5\circ grave(X)$, $grave(X)\circ flag6=grave(X)\circ flag6\circ reject\circ grave(X)\circ flag6$ and $grave(X)\circ flag7=grave(X)\circ flat7\circ reject\circ grave(X)\circ flat7$. Obviously $X_0\epsilon$y, so we must endeavour to ensure that if $\langle x_1,X_1\rangle$ and $\langle x_2,X_2\rangle$ are pairs for which $\langle x_2,X_2\rangle\geq\langle x_1,X_1\rangle\geq\langle x_0,X_0\rangle$ and $X_n\epsilon$y when $2\geq n\geq 0$ then $\langle wx_2,(W⊛W)X_2\rangle\geq\langle wx_1,(W⊛W)X_1\rangle\geq\langle wx_0,(W⊛W)X_0\rangle$ and $(W⊛W)X_n\epsilon$y when $2\geq n\geq 0$.

For standard semantics we make W and the other functors take precisely the same forms as in 3.3.5; for instance

$W=\lambda X.L+B+(EX)^{\star}+CX+FX+GX+KX.$

Plainly the version of W appropriate to store semantics must be similar to that above if we are to have any hope of proving that w is a predictor for W⊛W. Hence we assume that

$W=\lambda X.L+B+(EX)^{\star}+CX+FX+GX+KX+PX,$

when the functors appearing in this equation are suitably selected. The functors V, E, S and A, which are among those needed when explaining this equation, retain the meanings ascribed to them in 4.1.5; thus E, for example, is still given by the equation

$E=\lambda X.X\circ mask4.$

We shall discuss the remaining functors later.

For the pairs $\langle x_1,X_1\rangle$ and $\langle x_2,X_2\rangle$ which were introduced above we can readily verify that $\langle vx_2,(V\circledast V)X_2\rangle \geq\langle vx_1,(V\circledast V)X_1\rangle \geq\langle vx_0,(V\circledast V)X_0\rangle$, that $\langle ex_2(E\circledast E)X_2\rangle \geq\langle ex_1,(E\circledast E)X_1\rangle \geq\langle ex_0,(E\circledast E)X_0\rangle$, and that, in accordance with 2.5.6, $\langle sx_2,(S\circledast S)X_2\rangle \geq\langle sx_1,(S\circledast S)X_1\rangle \geq\langle sx_0,(S\circledast S)X_0\rangle$; here, we are, of course, using both versions of each of the functors V, E and S. For instance, to show that $vx_2\sqsupseteq vx_1\circ(V\circledast V)X_1$ we note that

$$\begin{aligned}
push\langle 3,1\rangle\circ(\lambda\acute{\beta}.\acute{\beta}) &= push\langle 3,1\rangle\circ V(\lambda\acute{\omega}.\acute{\omega})\\
&= push\langle 3,1\rangle\circ push\langle 4,-1\rangle\circ(\lambda\acute{\omega}.\acute{\omega})\circ push\langle 3,1\rangle\\
&= push\langle 4,0\rangle\circ(\lambda\acute{\omega}.\acute{\omega})\circ push\langle 3,1\rangle\\
&= (\lambda\acute{\omega}.\acute{\omega})\circ push\langle 4,0\rangle\circ push\langle 3,1\rangle\\
&= (\lambda\acute{\omega}.\acute{\omega})\circ push\langle 3,1\rangle
\end{aligned}$$

and that, as $X_1=acute(X_1)\times grave(X_1)$,

$$\begin{aligned}
acute(X_1)\circ push\langle 3,1\rangle &= acute(X_1)\circ push\langle 4,0\rangle\circ push\langle 3,1\rangle\\
&= push\langle 4,0\rangle\circ acute(X_1)\circ push\langle 3,1\rangle\\
&= push\langle 3,1\rangle\circ push\langle 4,-1\rangle\circ acute(X_1)\circ push\langle 3,1\rangle\\
&= push\langle 3,1\rangle\circ V(acute(X_1)),
\end{aligned}$$

so that

$$V(acute(X_1))\circ(\lambda\acute{\beta}.\acute{\beta})=push\langle 4,-1\rangle\circ acute(X_1)\circ push\langle 3,1\rangle\circ(\lambda\acute{\beta}.\acute{\beta})$$
$$=push\langle 4,-1\rangle\circ acute(X_1)\circ(\lambda\acute{\omega}.\acute{\omega})\circ push\langle 3,1\rangle$$
$$=push\langle 4,-1\rangle\circ(\lambda\acute{\omega}.\acute{\omega})\circ acute(X_1)\circ push\langle 3,1\rangle$$
$$=push\langle 4,-1\rangle\circ(\lambda\acute{\omega}.\acute{\omega})\circ push\langle 3,1\rangle\circ V(acute(X_1))$$
$$=V(\lambda\acute{\omega}.\acute{\omega})\circ V(acute(X_1))$$
$$=(\lambda\acute{\beta}.\acute{\beta})\circ V(acute(X_1));$$

we can confirm that

$$grave(X_1)\circ push\langle 3,1\rangle\circ(\lambda\acute{\beta}.\acute{\beta})=push\langle 3,1\rangle\circ(\lambda\acute{\beta}.\acute{\beta})\circ V(grave(X_1))$$

in the same manner, so in fact

$$vx_2=x_2\circ(push\langle 3,1\rangle\times push\langle 3,1\rangle)\circ(\lambda\hat{\beta}.\hat{\beta})$$
$$\sqsupseteq x_1\circ X_1\circ(push\langle 3,1\rangle\times push\langle 3,1\rangle)\circ(\lambda\hat{\beta}.\hat{\beta})$$
$$=x_1\circ(push\langle 3,1\rangle\times push\langle 3,1\rangle)\circ(\lambda\hat{\beta}.\hat{\beta})\circ(V\circledast V)X_1$$
$$=vx_1\circ(V\circledast V)X_1.$$

Less obvious are the functors required by c, k and f. When a is a predictor for $A\circledast A$ based on the pair $\langle x_0,X_0\rangle$ and bounded by the set y then, because s is a predictor for $S\circledast S$, 2.5.6 plainly assures us that $\lambda x.ax\to sx$ is a predictor for $(\lambda X.SX\to AX)\circledast(\lambda X.SX\to AX)$. Hence to show that the pairs $\langle x_1,X_1\rangle$ and $\langle x_2,X_2\rangle$ introduced above are such that $\langle cx_2,(C\circledast C)X_2\rangle\geq\langle cx_1,(C\circledast C)X_1\rangle\geq\langle cx_0,(C\circledast C)X_0\rangle$ we have only to insist that $\lambda X.(\lambda\theta.\theta)\circ CX=\lambda X.(SX\to AX)\circ(\lambda\theta.\theta)$ in standard semantics and that $\lambda X.(\lambda\langle\zeta,\rho,\upsilon\rangle.\zeta\rho\upsilon)\circ CX=\lambda X.(SX\to AX)\circ(\lambda\langle\zeta,\rho,\upsilon\rangle.\zeta\rho\upsilon)$ in store semantics. For brevity we therefore define the version of C appropriate to store semantics by setting

$$C=\lambda X.\lambda\langle\zeta,\rho,\upsilon\rangle.\langle\lambda\rho'\upsilon'.(SX\to AX)(\zeta\rho'\upsilon'),\rho,\upsilon\rangle$$

instead of by following the elaborate conventions of 2.4.2; were we to introduce analogous retractions into the definitions of V, E, and S (so that $V(acute(X_1))$ for example, would become $push\langle 4,-1\rangle\circ acute(X_1)\circ push\langle 3,1\rangle\circ(\lambda\acute{\beta}.\acute{\beta})$) we could replace the requirement that $(\lambda\hat{\omega}.\hat{\omega})\circ X_1=X_1\circ(\lambda\hat{\omega}.\hat{\omega})$ by the requirement that $(\lambda\hat{\omega}.\hat{\omega})\circ X_1\circ(\lambda\hat{\omega}.\hat{\omega})=X_1\circ(\lambda\hat{\omega}.\hat{\omega})$.

Similar arguments concerning expression continuations reveal that for the purposes of demonstrating that

$\langle kx_2,(K\circledast K)X_2\rangle \geq \langle kx_1,(K\circledast K)X_1\rangle \geq \langle kx_0,(K\circledast K)X_0\rangle$ an adequate version of K appropriate to store semantics can be provided by the equation

$K=\lambda X.\lambda\langle\zeta,\rho,\upsilon\rangle.\langle\lambda\rho'\upsilon'.(SX\to AX)(\zeta\rho'((\#\upsilon'=0)\to\langle\rangle,\langle EX(\upsilon'\downarrow 1)\rangle\S\upsilon'\dagger 1)),\rho,\upsilon\rangle.$

The functor F for standard semantics resembles the corresponding functors C and K in being defined as in 3.3.5; it thus takes the form $\lambda X.EX\to KX\to CX$. The form of the mapping f suggests that for store semantics F satisfies the equation

$$F=\lambda X.\lambda\langle\xi,\rho\rangle.(\lambda\xi'.\langle\xi'\circ\xi\circ\xi',\rho\rangle)$$
$$(\lambda\zeta'\rho'\upsilon'.(SX\to AX)(\zeta'\rho'((\#\upsilon'=0)\to\langle\rangle,\langle EX(\upsilon'\downarrow 1)\rangle\S\upsilon'\dagger 1))).$$

On grounds of uniformity with the foregoing we assume that the functor G for store semantics is such that

$$G=\lambda X.\lambda\langle\xi,\rho,\sigma\rangle.(\lambda\xi'.\langle\lambda\zeta'\rho'\upsilon'.(SX\to AX)(\xi(\xi'\zeta')\rho'\upsilon'),\rho,\sigma\rangle)$$
$$(\lambda\zeta'\rho'\upsilon'.(SX\to AX)(\zeta'\rho'((\#\upsilon'=0)\to\langle\rangle,\langle EX(\upsilon'\downarrow 1)\rangle\S\upsilon'\dagger 1))),$$

and that the functor P in the present instance is such that

$P=\lambda X.\lambda\langle\rho,\upsilon,\sigma\rangle.\langle\rho,\upsilon,\sigma\rangle.$

However the versions of G and P given in 4.1.5 would be equally suitable for Sal, since the fact that G does not occur among the summands of V and E allows us to ignore it when defining w; if G did appear as part of V or E, we would require the version of G given above (together with that given in 3.3.5).

If temporarily we provide a functor, X, appropriate to store semantics by writing

$X=\lambda X.L+B+(EX)^*+(ZX\times UX\times YX)+(OX\times UX)+(OX\times UX\times SX)+(ZX\times UX\times YX)+(UX\times YX\times SX)$

(so that X is the version of W defined in 4.1.5) then we may make use of the remarks in 4.1.5 which postulate that $\lambda\hat{\omega}.\hat{\omega}=fix(X)$. Bearing in mind such equations as

$\lambda\langle\zeta,\rho,\upsilon\rangle.\langle\zeta,\rho,\upsilon\rangle=Z(\lambda\hat{\omega}.\hat{\omega})\times U(\lambda\hat{\omega}.\hat{\omega})\times Y(\lambda\hat{\omega}.\hat{\omega})$ we can observe that $W(\lambda\hat{\omega}.\hat{\omega})=\lambda\hat{\omega}.\hat{\omega}$ and therefore that $\lambda\hat{\omega}.\hat{\omega}\sqsupseteq fix(W)$ when

$W=\lambda X.L+B+(EX)^*+CX+FX+GX+KX+PX.$

Moreover if X is a retraction of the universal domain for which $fix(\mathrm{W})\sqsupseteq X$ and $(\lambda\chi.\bot)\times X\in\mathrm{y}$ (where y is the set of retractions which we introduced above) then $fix(\mathrm{W})\sqsupseteq \mathrm{X}X$ and $(\lambda\chi.\bot)\times\mathrm{X}X\in\mathrm{y}$ because of the assumptions made about the functor A in 4.1.5; consequently the induction rule of 2.3.2 allows us to assert that $fix(\mathrm{W})\sqsupseteq fix(\mathrm{X})$. The inequalities established in this paragraph thus ensure that $\lambda\acute{\omega}.\acute{\omega}=fix(\mathrm{W})$ no matter which of the versions of G and P suggested above are actually inserted in the equation for W.

In 3.3.5 we stipulated that $\lambda\acute{\omega}.\acute{\omega}=fix(\mathrm{W})$ where the version of W appropriate to standard semantics is subject to the equation
$\mathrm{W}=\lambda X.L+B+(\mathrm{E}X)^{*}+\mathrm{C}X+\mathrm{F}X+\mathrm{K}X.$
As was intimated in 2.5.4, $\bigsqcup\{(\mathrm{W}\circledast\mathrm{W})^{n}|n\geq 0\}=fix(\mathrm{W})\times fix(\mathrm{W})$ when both versions of W appear in $\mathrm{W}\circledast\mathrm{W}$, so $\bigsqcup\{(\mathrm{W}\circledast\mathrm{W})^{n}|n\geq 0\}=\lambda\hat{\omega}.\hat{\omega}$. Examining the definition of w reveals that w is a predictor for $\mathrm{W}\circledast\mathrm{W}$ based on the pair $\langle x_0,X_0\rangle$ and bounded by the set y; furthermore $X_0\in\mathrm{y}$ and $(\mathrm{W}\circledast\mathrm{W})X_0\in\mathrm{y}$. In accordance with 2.5.3 there is therefore a unique inclusive predicate w for which $w=\mathrm{w}w\circ(\lambda\hat{\omega}.\hat{\omega})$ and $w\langle\bot,\bot\rangle=true$; the definition of w shows that $w=\mathrm{w}w$, and we may obtain the predicates v, e, s, c, k, f and a of 4.2.2 by writing $v=\mathrm{v}w$, $e=\mathrm{e}w$, $s=\mathrm{s}w$, $c=\mathrm{c}w$, $k=\mathrm{k}w$, $f=\mathrm{f}w$ and $a=\mathrm{a}w$.

The functors and predictors introduced above can be modified in several minor ways, all of which produce the same version of w. By defining analogues of functors and predictors intended to act on lists of retractions and predicates, not on individual retractions and predicates, we could even prove the existence of v and e without the use of w; in the proof we would employ a function having $\langle\mathrm{V}(\lambda\acute{\omega}.\acute{\omega}),\mathrm{E}(\lambda\acute{\omega}.\acute{\omega})\rangle$ as its least fixed point, and we would be able to take the set corresponding with y to be the complete lattice of all retractions if the functions acting on lists of retractions and predicates were chosen well. Such proofs are valid whatever the value of *check*, but when *check* is *true* v and e become $\lambda\hat{\beta}.true$ and $\lambda\hat{\varepsilon}.true$ respectively.

4.2.4. Subsidiary predicates.

The predicates of 4.2.2 could have been made to restrict attention to those stores in which proper locations have proper contents. Such restrictions as this can be incorporated in the structure of the domains [52:1.2.2] without modifying the construction of the predicates greatly. Any decision about whether to adopt domains which do not have so many redundant improper elements can therefore be made irrespective of what predicates are required. There is, however, one situation in which the improper elements cannot be deleted from domains: the application of the Knaster fixed point theorem [36] to facilitate recursion involved "seeding" the environment with $\bot$, so if $\rho[\bot/\mathrm{I}]$ and $\langle\zeta,\bot,\upsilon\rangle$ were identified with $\bot$ in U and $\bot$ in D respectively the equation for block Γ in appendix 2 would cause the entire environment to collapse to $\bot$. This cannot happen in standard semantics, where a label entry point having $\bot$ as its environment produces a store transformation belonging to C.

For convenience, in keeping with the remarks above we test D in a way which accepts that the denoted value $\bot$ is legitimate (even if the stored value $\bot$ is shunned). Any denoted value which cannot be returned as the result of an expression evaluation is a recursion value which must belong to G; such entities are tested by a predicate g which by analogy with f is subject to

$$g=\lambda\langle\gamma,\langle\xi,\rho,\sigma\rangle\rangle.\bigwedge\{\dot{c}\langle\gamma\kappa,\langle\lambda\rho''\upsilon''\sigma''.\xi\zeta\rho[\langle\rho'',\upsilon'',\sigma''\rangle/\mathbf{rec}]\langle\rangle\sigma,\rho',\upsilon\rangle\rangle\mid k\langle\kappa,\langle\zeta,\rho',\upsilon\rangle\rangle\}.$$

From e and g we form the predicate for denoted values, d, thus:

$$\begin{aligned}d=\lambda\hat{\delta}.\ &(\acute{\delta}\equiv\bot)\vee(\grave{\delta}\equiv\bot)\to(\acute{\delta}\equiv\bot)\wedge(\grave{\delta}\equiv\bot),\\ &(\acute{\delta}\equiv\top)\vee(\grave{\delta}\equiv\top)\to(\acute{\delta}\equiv\top)\wedge(\grave{\delta}\equiv\top),\\ &\acute{\delta}\,E\,\mathrm{G}\vee\grave{\delta}\,E\,\mathrm{G}\to(\acute{\delta}\,E\,\mathrm{G}\wedge\grave{\delta}\,E\,\mathrm{G}\to g\langle\acute{\delta}|\mathrm{G},\grave{\delta}|\mathrm{G}\rangle,\mathit{false}),\\ &e\hat{\delta}.\end{aligned}$$

To complete this chain of definitions we give that for u, which is

$$\begin{aligned}u=\lambda\hat{\rho}.\bigwedge\{&((\#\acute{\rho}[\![\mathrm{I}]\!]=0)\to\mathit{true},d\langle\acute{\rho}[\![\mathrm{I}]\!]\downarrow1,\grave{\rho}[\![\mathrm{I}]\!]\downarrow1\rangle)\wedge(\#\acute{\rho}[\![\mathrm{I}]\!]\leq\#\grave{\rho}[\![\mathrm{I}]\!])\mid\mathrm{I}\}\\ &\wedge((\#\acute{\rho}[\![\mathbf{res}]\!]=0)\to\mathit{true},k\langle\acute{\rho}[\![\mathbf{res}]\!]\downarrow1,\grave{\rho}[\![\mathbf{res}]\!]\downarrow1\rangle)\wedge(\#\acute{\rho}[\![\mathbf{res}]\!]\leq\#\grave{\rho}[\![\mathbf{res}]\!]).\end{aligned}$$

4.2.5. Syntactic predicates.

We can now clarify what is meant by the assertion that the standard semantics for an expression E is congruent with its store semantics: when supplied with arguments related by the predicates above the two versions of $\mathcal{E}[\![E]\!]$ must produce answers related by these predicates. As declarations in standard semantics are treated differently from those in store semantics we restrict attention to those environments which contain an entry for every free variable of E; thus we regard E as having equivalent standard and store semantics if

$c\langle \mathcal{E}[\![E]\!]\acute{\rho}\kappa, \langle \mathcal{E}[\![E]\!]\zeta, \grave{\rho}, \upsilon\rangle\rangle = true$ whenever $k\langle \kappa, \langle \zeta, \grave{\rho}, \upsilon\rangle\rangle \wedge u\hat{\rho} \wedge rent[\![E]\!]\acute{\rho} = true$

where *rent* is defined as in 3.5.3. More formally, we introduce predicates E, L and R such that:

$E = \lambda E.\bigwedge\{c\langle \mathcal{E}[\![E]\!]\acute{\rho}\kappa, \langle \mathcal{E}[\![E]\!]\zeta, \grave{\rho}, \upsilon\rangle\rangle \mid k\langle \kappa, \langle \zeta, \grave{\rho}, \upsilon\rangle\rangle \wedge u\hat{\rho} \wedge rent[\![E]\!]\acute{\rho}\}$;

$L = \lambda E.\bigwedge\{c\langle \mathcal{L}[\![E]\!]\acute{\rho}\kappa, \langle \mathcal{L}[\![E]\!]\zeta, \grave{\rho}, \upsilon\rangle\rangle \mid k\langle \kappa, \langle \zeta, \grave{\rho}, \upsilon\rangle\rangle \wedge u\hat{\rho} \wedge rent[\![E]\!]\acute{\rho}\}$;

$R = \lambda E.\bigwedge\{c\langle \mathcal{R}[\![E]\!]\acute{\rho}\kappa, \langle \mathcal{R}[\![E]\!]\zeta, \grave{\rho}, \upsilon\rangle\rangle \mid k\langle \kappa, \langle \zeta, \grave{\rho}, \upsilon\rangle\rangle \wedge u\hat{\rho} \wedge rent[\![E]\!]\acute{\rho}\}$.

In practice we know that the expressed value supplied to the continuation κ is a location when $\mathcal{L}[\![E]\!]\rho\kappa$ is being considered and a stored value when $\mathcal{R}[\![E]\!]\rho\kappa$ is being considered. We could have incorporated this useful information in the definitions of L and R in the way in which we shall include similar information in the definitions of predicates called D and T. Our decision not to do this makes L and R uniform with E, but it sometimes creates trifling complications in proofs; these complications could be eliminated equally well by taking the valuations $\mathcal{L}$ and $\mathcal{R}$ pertinent to standard semantics to be members of $\mathrm{Exp}\to\mathrm{U}\to(\mathrm{L}\to\mathrm{C})\to\mathrm{C}$ and $\mathrm{Exp}\to\mathrm{U}\to(\mathrm{V}\to\mathrm{C})\to\mathrm{C}$ respectively.

For abstractions we set

$F = \lambda\Phi.\bigwedge\{f\langle \mathcal{F}[\![\Phi]\!]\acute{\rho}, \mathcal{F}[\![\Phi]\!](rend[\![\Phi]\!]\grave{\rho})\rangle \mid u\hat{\rho} \wedge rent[\![\Phi]\!]\acute{\rho}\}$.

Similarly sequencers are handled using

$S = \lambda\Sigma.\bigwedge\{c\langle \mathcal{S}[\![\Sigma]\!]\acute{\rho}, \langle \mathcal{S}[\![\Sigma]\!], \grave{\rho}, \upsilon\rangle\rangle \mid u\hat{\rho} \wedge rent[\![\Sigma]\!]\acute{\rho}\}$.

In this equation υ is a bound variable which is allowed to range over all the members of Y.

Whereas the standard continuation κ supplied to any expression takes exactly one expressed value as an argument, the size of the environment handed on by a declaration to a continuation χ depends on the declaration. We can capture this dependence by recalling the function *slim* introduced in 3.5.3 and by writing

$$knit=\lambda\Delta\hat{\rho}_0\hat{\rho}_1.(\acute{\rho}_0 \equiv slim\llbracket\Delta\rrbracket\acute{\rho}_0)\wedge(\grave{\rho}_0 \equiv divert\grave{\rho}_1(slim\llbracket\Delta\rrbracket\grave{\rho}_0))$$
$$\wedge\bigwedge\{\acute{\rho}_0\llbracket I\rrbracket\downarrow 1 \in \mathrm{G} \mid I\in\mathfrak{J}\llbracket\Delta\rrbracket\S\mathfrak{K}\llbracket\Delta\rrbracket\}.$$

The predicates for declarations, *D* and *T*, which correspond with *E* are therefore given by the following equations:

$$D=\lambda\Delta.\bigwedge\{c\langle\mathfrak{D}\llbracket\Delta\rrbracket\acute{\rho}_0\chi,\langle\mathfrak{D}\llbracket\Delta\rrbracket\zeta,\grave{\rho}_0,\upsilon\rangle\rangle$$
$$\mid u\hat{\rho}_0\wedge rent\llbracket\Delta\rrbracket\acute{\rho}_0\wedge\bigwedge\{c\langle\chi\acute{\rho}_1,\langle\zeta,\grave{\rho}_1,\upsilon\rangle\rangle\mid u\hat{\rho}_1\wedge knit\llbracket\Delta\rrbracket\hat{\rho}_1\hat{\rho}_0\}\};$$
$$T=\lambda\Delta.\bigwedge\{c\langle\mathfrak{T}\llbracket\Delta\rrbracket\acute{\rho}_0\chi,\langle\mathfrak{T}\llbracket\Delta\rrbracket\zeta,\grave{\rho}_0,\upsilon\rangle\rangle$$
$$\mid u\hat{\rho}_0\wedge torn\llbracket\Delta\rrbracket\acute{\rho}_0\wedge\bigwedge\{c\langle\chi\acute{\rho}_1,\langle\zeta,\grave{\rho}_1,\upsilon\rangle\rangle\mid u\hat{\rho}_1\wedge knit\llbracket\Delta\rrbracket\hat{\rho}_1\hat{\rho}_0\}\}.$$

Likewise to deal with blocks we write

$$G=\lambda\Theta.\bigwedge\{c\langle\mathfrak{G}\llbracket\Theta\rrbracket\acute{\rho}\theta,\langle\mathfrak{G}\llbracket\Theta\rrbracket\zeta,\grave{\rho},\upsilon\rangle\rangle\mid c\langle\theta,\langle\zeta,\grave{\rho},\upsilon\rangle\rangle\wedge u\hat{\rho}\wedge rent\llbracket\Gamma\rrbracket\grave{\rho}\}.$$

The analogous predicates for handling commands are defined thus:

$$C=\lambda\Gamma.\bigwedge\{c\langle\mathfrak{C}\llbracket\Gamma\rrbracket\acute{\rho}\theta,\langle\mathfrak{C}\llbracket\Gamma\rrbracket\zeta,\grave{\rho},\upsilon\rangle\rangle\mid c\langle\theta,\langle\zeta,\grave{\rho},\upsilon\rangle\rangle\wedge u\hat{\rho}\wedge rent\llbracket\Gamma\rrbracket\grave{\rho}\};$$
$$P=\lambda\Gamma.\bigwedge\{c\langle\mathfrak{P}\llbracket\Gamma\rrbracket\acute{\rho}\theta\downarrow\nu,\mathfrak{P}\llbracket\Gamma\rrbracket\zeta\grave{\rho}\upsilon\downarrow\nu\rangle\mid c\langle\theta,\langle\zeta,\grave{\rho},\upsilon\rangle\rangle\wedge u\hat{\rho}\wedge rent\llbracket\Gamma\rrbracket\grave{\rho}\wedge(\#\mathfrak{J}\llbracket\Gamma\rrbracket\geq\nu\geq 1)\};$$
$$Q=\lambda\Gamma.\bigwedge\{c\langle\mathfrak{Q}\llbracket\Gamma\rrbracket\acute{\rho}\theta\downarrow\nu,\mathfrak{Q}\llbracket\Gamma\rrbracket\zeta\grave{\rho}\upsilon\downarrow\nu\rangle\mid c\langle\theta,\langle\zeta,\grave{\rho},\upsilon\rangle\rangle\wedge u\hat{\rho}\wedge rent\llbracket\Gamma\rrbracket\grave{\rho}\wedge(\#\mathfrak{K}\llbracket\Gamma\rrbracket\geq\nu\geq 1)\}.$$

Applications of predicates like *P* and *Q* often tacitly involve the assumptions that for every ρ and every θ $\#\mathfrak{P}\llbracket\Gamma\rrbracket\rho\theta=\#\mathfrak{J}\llbracket\Gamma\rrbracket$ and $\#\mathfrak{Q}\llbracket\Gamma\rrbracket\rho\theta=\#\mathfrak{K}\llbracket\Gamma\rrbracket$; we could include these assumptions in the definitions of *P* and *Q* without any difficulty, but we do not need to, owing to the remarks made in 3.5.1.

To demonstrate that the standard semantics of Sal is congruent with the store semantics we have to show that store semantics reflects the outcome of any program (on the assumption that standard semantics does so). Thus suppose, for instance, that the outcome of a program which consists of an expression E without free variables is held to be given by $\mathcal{E}[\![E]\!](arid)(\lambda\varepsilon\sigma.\sigma)(empty)$; then we would want to show that it could also be given by $\mathcal{E}[\![E]\!](\lambda\rho\upsilon\sigma.\sigma)(arid)\langle\rangle(empty)$, in which store semantics is used. When A is taken to be S, a can taken to be s, so that certainly $k\langle(\lambda\varepsilon\sigma.\sigma),\langle(\lambda\rho\upsilon\sigma.\sigma),arid,\langle\rangle\rangle\rangle$ can be regarded as $true$. Because $u\langle arid,arid\rangle$ and $s\langle empty,empty\rangle$ are both $true$ $a\langle\mathcal{E}[\![E]\!](arid)(\lambda\varepsilon\sigma.\sigma)(empty),\mathcal{E}[\![E]\!](\lambda\rho\upsilon\sigma.\sigma)(arid)\langle\rangle(empty)\rangle$ will be $true$ provided that $E[\![E]\!]=true$. Analogous remarks apply to any program which is simply a block, Θ say, having no free variables.

Consequently we can view standard semantics and store semantics as congruent if we can show that every Sal program is constrained by equations typified by $E[\![E]\!]=true$ (which must hold when E is any expression) and $G[\![\Theta]\!]=true$ (which must hold when Θ is any block). These equalities can in fact be established under certain circumstances by means of an induction on the structure of programs. This induction (which will be started in 4.3.1) takes the form of many lemmas, one for each Sal construct. As these lemmas follow an obvious pattern we shall not scruple to prove only the more interesting ones and to leave the remainder to the reader; a summary of their implications will be given in 4.3.7.

The circumstances governing the equations are very simple. Since fix will be applied in 4.3.5 and 4.3.6, we demand that a be inclusive in the sense of 2.3.1; in this situation u and c are also inclusive. Since ⊥ and ⊤ can be the outcomes of programs while error exits are provided by two functions named $wrong$ we insist that $a\langle\bot,\bot\rangle=true$, that $a\langle\top,\top\rangle=true$ and that $(s\rightarrow a)\langle wrong,wrong\rangle=true$. Since we want $E[\![B]\!]$, $E[\![OE]\!]$ and $E[\![E_0\Omega E_1]\!]$ to be $true$ if $E[\![E]\!]$, $E[\![E_0]\!]$ and $E[\![E_1]\!]$ are $true$ we suppose that for all B, O and Ω

$(k\rightarrow c)\langle\mathcal{B}[\![B]\!],(\lambda\langle\zeta,\rho,\upsilon\rangle.\langle\mathcal{B}[\![B]\!]\zeta,\rho,\upsilon\rangle)\rangle=true$,

$(k\rightarrow e\rightarrow c)\langle\mathcal{O}[\![O]\!],(\lambda\langle\zeta,\rho,\upsilon\rangle.\lambda\varepsilon.\langle\mathcal{O}[\![O]\!]\zeta,\rho,\langle\varepsilon\rangle\S\upsilon\rangle)\rangle=true$ and

$(k\rightarrow e\rightarrow e\rightarrow c)\langle\mathcal{W}[\![\Omega]\!],(\lambda\langle\rho,\upsilon,\sigma\rangle.\lambda\varepsilon'.\lambda\varepsilon''.\langle\mathcal{W}[\![\Omega]\!]\zeta,\rho,\langle\varepsilon''\rangle\S\langle\varepsilon'\rangle\S\upsilon\rangle)\rangle=true$;

this is a perfectly reasonable assumption which essentially states that the operators which act on members of J and F make no use of the ways in which labels and procedures are represented in the semantic equations. Finally, since $s\hat{\sigma}$ can be *true* only if $v\langle hold\,\alpha\acute{\sigma}, hold\,\alpha\grave{\sigma}\rangle$ is *true* for all $\alpha\in L$ we require that the two *new* functions correspond, in that $new\acute{\sigma}=new\grave{\sigma}$ when $s\hat{\sigma}=true$; if this is so a brief argument demonstrates that $(k\to k)\langle lv,(\lambda\langle\zeta,\rho,\upsilon\rangle.\langle mv\zeta,\rho,\upsilon\rangle)\rangle$ and $(k\to k)\langle rv,(\lambda\langle\zeta,\rho,\upsilon\rangle.\langle sv\zeta,\rho,\upsilon\rangle)\rangle$ are *true* (and therefore that $L[\![E]\!]$ and $R[\![E]\!]$ are *true* whenever E is an expression for which $E[\![E]\!]$ is *true*). The conditions under which this requirement may be imposed on the *new* functions will be discussed in 4.2.6. They depend crucially on the fact that $\lambda\alpha.area\,\alpha\acute{\sigma}=\lambda\alpha.area\,\alpha\grave{\sigma}$ when $s\hat{\sigma}=true$; in 5.2.1 this will not be the case, so we shall be obliged to introduce a method of pairing off locations which is more complex than that provided by l.

4.2.6. Storage allocation.

In order to relate the *new* function for standard semantics to that for store semantics in the manner required in 4.2.5 we define a retraction X_0 by the equation $X_0=L+B+(\mathrm{E}X_0)^{*}+(\lambda\chi.\mathrm{C}(\lambda\acute{\omega}.\acute{\omega})\bot)+(\lambda\chi.\mathrm{F}(\lambda\acute{\omega}.\acute{\omega})\bot)$ where C and F are the functors used in 4.2.3 when discussing standard semantics. When we introduce any *new* function for standard semantics, setting $\psi=new\circ\mathrm{S}X_0\circ(\lambda\breve{\sigma}.\breve{\sigma})$ provides a function, ψ, which maps the domain S for store semantics into the domain $\mathrm{L}+\{error\}$. For any store $\breve{\sigma}$ $\lambda\alpha.area\alpha\breve{\sigma}=\lambda\alpha.area\alpha(\mathrm{S}X_0\breve{\sigma})$, so $\psi\breve{\sigma}=error$ if $\bigwedge\{area\alpha\breve{\sigma}\mid\top\sqsupseteq\alpha\sqsupseteq\bot\}=true$ and $area(\psi\breve{\sigma}\mid\mathrm{L})\breve{\sigma}=false$ if $\bigwedge\{area\alpha\breve{\sigma}\mid\top\sqsupseteq\alpha\sqsupseteq\bot\}=false$. In addition, it is reasonable to assume that $new=new\circ\mathrm{S}X_0\circ(\lambda\acute{\sigma}.\acute{\sigma})$, because doing so expresses the view that *new* should not be influenced by the members of J and F which are stored; thus whenever $s\hat{\sigma}=true$ we may claim fairly that $new\acute{\sigma}=\psi\breve{\sigma}$, since $new\acute{\sigma}=new(\mathrm{S}X_0\acute{\sigma})$ and $\mathrm{S}X_0\acute{\sigma}=\mathrm{S}X_0\breve{\sigma}$. Hence *new* and $new\circ\mathrm{S}X_0\circ(\lambda\breve{\sigma}.\breve{\sigma})$ (which is ψ) are, respectively, a *new* function for standard semantics and a *new* function for store semantics; together they satisfy the requirements of 4.2.5.

Not every *new* function for store semantics can be obtained from one for standard semantics in this way; any *new* function for which $new\langle(\lambda\alpha.\langle false,\langle\bot,arid,\langle 0\rangle\rangle\rangle),\langle\rangle,\langle\rangle\rangle$ differs from $new\langle(\lambda\alpha.\langle false,\langle\bot,arid,\langle 1\rangle\rangle\rangle),\langle\rangle,\langle\rangle\rangle$ supplies evidence for this. If, however, $new=new\circ\mathrm{S}X_1\circ(\lambda\breve{\sigma}.\breve{\sigma})$ where

$$X_1=L+B+(\mathrm{E}X_1)^{*}+(\lambda\chi.(\mathrm{Z}(\lambda\grave{\omega}.\grave{\omega})\times\mathrm{U}(\lambda\grave{\omega}.\grave{\omega})\times\mathrm{Y}(\lambda\grave{\omega}.\grave{\omega}))\bot)+(\lambda\chi.(\mathrm{O}(\lambda\grave{\omega}.\grave{\omega})\times\mathrm{U}(\lambda\grave{\omega}.\grave{\omega}))\bot)$$

then *new* corresponds with a *new* function for standard semantics which is actually $new\circ\mathrm{S}X_0\circ(\lambda\acute{\sigma}.\acute{\sigma})$.

In 3.3.2 we hinted that the axioms governing *new* left something to be desired; here we shall explain what this is. We take σ_0 and σ_1 to be any stores such that setting $\sigma_2=\langle(\lambda\alpha.\langle\bot,area\alpha\sigma_0\rangle),\bot,\bot\rangle$ provides a store σ_2 for which $\sigma_2=\langle(\lambda\alpha.\langle\bot,area\alpha\sigma_1\rangle),\bot,\bot\rangle$ and we suppose that $new\sigma_0$, $new\sigma_1$ and $new\sigma_2$ are all proper locations; according to 3.3.2 this supposition is reasonable if $\bigwedge\{area\alpha\sigma_2 | \top \sqsupseteq \alpha \sqsupseteq \bot\}$ is *false*. Because $\sigma_0 \sqsupseteq \sigma_2$ and $\sigma_1 \sqsupseteq \sigma_2$, the continuous nature of *new* ensures that $new\sigma_0 \sqsupseteq new\sigma_2$ and $new\sigma_1 \sqsupseteq new\sigma_2$; hence as L is a flat lattice $new\sigma_0 = new\sigma_2$ and $new\sigma_1 = new\sigma_2$. In other words, whenever σ_0 and σ_1 are two stores having identical areas $new\sigma_0$ and $new\sigma_1$ coincide. Thus some storage allocation functions are debarred from being *new* functions simply on the ground that they depend on the content of the store; in particular, if *new'* and *new"* are two *new* functions and α_0 is any location $\lambda\sigma.(hold\alpha_0\sigma E B \rightarrow new'\sigma, new''\sigma)$ cannot be a *new* function. This unsatisfactory state of affairs can best be remedied by modifying the axioms governing *new* so that $new\sigma_2$ no longer has to be proper. To this end we let e be the set of proper expressed values for standard semantics, l be the set of proper locations and t be the set of proper truth values; thus e is included in E, l is included in L and t is included in T. We now take s to be the set of stores such that $hold\alpha\sigma\epsilon e$ and $area\alpha\sigma\epsilon t$ whenever $\alpha\epsilon l$, such that $\#\sigma{\downarrow}2$ is proper and $\sigma{\downarrow}2{\downarrow}\nu\epsilon e$ whenever $\#\sigma{\downarrow}2 \geq \nu \geq 1$, and such that $\#\sigma{\downarrow}3$ is proper and $\sigma{\downarrow}3{\downarrow}\nu\epsilon e$ whenever $\#\sigma{\downarrow}3 \geq \nu \geq 1$. Doing this enables us to take *new* to be any continuous function for which:

(i) if $\sigma\epsilon s$ satisfies the equation $\bigwedge\{area\alpha\sigma | \alpha\epsilon l\} = false$ then $new\sigma | L\epsilon l$ and $area(new\sigma | L)\sigma = false$;

(ii) if $\sigma\epsilon s$ satisfies the equation $\bigwedge\{area\alpha\sigma | \alpha\epsilon l\} = true$ then $new\sigma$ is *error*.

When *new'* and *new"* satisfy these axioms certainly $\lambda\sigma.(hold\alpha_0\sigma E B \rightarrow new'\sigma, new''\sigma)$ satisfies them as well, but $\lambda\sigma.(hold\alpha_0\sigma E B \rightarrow (hold\alpha_0\sigma E T \rightarrow new'\sigma, new''\sigma), new''\sigma)$ does not do so. If we wished to regard both these functions (and others like them) as *new* functions we would retain the axioms above while adopting a more restrictive version of e; in fact, we would define e recursively by letting $\epsilon\epsilon e$ precisely when $\epsilon | L\epsilon l$, when $\epsilon | B$ is a proper member of a summand of B, when $\#(\varepsilon|E^*)$ is proper and $(\varepsilon|E^*)\downarrow\nu\in\varepsilon$ for $\#(\varepsilon|E^*)\geq\nu\geq 1$, when $\varepsilon\mathsf{E}J$ or when $\varepsilon\mathsf{E}F$.

In the definition of s given above we have for convenience identified members of V with the corresponding members of E. If we wanted to investigate such sets as s in detail we would be more rigorous in this respect. In fact, we would set up operations ×, +, * and → which would act on sets (rather than the predicates of 2.5.5) and would allow us to discard the improper elements of a sum. Thus if x_m were a set of elements of X_m when $n\geq m\geq 0$ then $x_0+\ldots+x_n$ would be, in effect, the union of $x_0,\ldots,x_n$ regarded as a set of elements of $X_0+\ldots+X_n$; the elements $\bot$ and $\top$ in $X_0+\ldots+X_n$ would not belong to this set. The equations $e=l+b+e^*+J+F$ and $b=t+n+r+h+h^*$ implicit in the preceding paragraph could be solved by appealing to 2.3.2 without the use of an analogue of 2.5.3 because the function having e as its fixed point would be continuous, owing to the absence of →; indeed, equations somewhat similar to this will be solved in 4.2.7 (along with ones that do need appeals to 2.5.3).

It should perhaps be mentioned that adopting the axioms for *new* suggested above (rather than those in 3.3.2) does not invalidate the argument in our opening paragraph: if *new* is a function which satisfies these axioms and which equals $new\circ SX_0\circ(\lambda\sigma.\sigma)$ then $new\circ SX_0\circ(\lambda\hat{\sigma}.\hat{\sigma})$ also satisfies these axioms (and $new\sigma=(new\circ SX_0\circ(\lambda\hat{\sigma}.\hat{\sigma}))\hat{\sigma}$ whenever $s\hat{\sigma}=true$).

At this point those who wish to avoid the forthcoming digression (which harks back to 3.9.1) may move on to 4.3.1 in order to start the inductive proof that the equations given in appendix 1 are congruent with those given in appendix 2.

4.2.7. The removal of continuations.

Before turning to the structural induction we shall indicate how the methods explained in 4.2.3 can be used to establish propositions like 3.9.4 when the domains on which the valuations $\mathcal{E}$ and $¶\mathcal{E}$ are defined do not coincide. We shall assume that for every abstraction Φ $¶\mathcal{E}[\![\Phi]\!]=\lambda\rho\sigma.\langle ¶\mathcal{F}[\![\Phi]\!]\rho,\sigma\rangle$ where $¶\mathcal{F}$ is the member of $\mathrm{Abs}\to\mathrm{U}\to\mathrm{E}\to\mathrm{S}\to(\mathrm{A}+(\mathrm{E}\times\mathrm{S}))$ mentioned in 3.9.2; thus the domains E, S and U will differ from their counterparts in appendix 1, but A will remain the domain of answers for standard semantics (although it will be intended solely to receive error messages). Because sequencers will not be permitted in programs and because $¶\mathcal{D}[\![\mathrm{rec}\ \Delta]\!]$ will be treated as in 3.9.4, we must form the value domains for the conjugate valuations from L, B, E* and F, where F is $\mathrm{E}\to\mathrm{S}\to(\mathrm{A}+(\mathrm{E}\times\mathrm{S}))$; in fact V has to be B+E*+F, E has to be L+B+E*+F and D has to be L+B+E*+F. These value domains may be embedded in a domain of witnessed values, W, which is L+B+E*+F and which must be compared with the domain L+B+E*+J+F+G+K given in appendix 1. In the new situation F is $\mathrm{E}\to(\mathrm{E}\to\mathrm{S}\to\mathrm{A})\to(\mathrm{S}\to\mathrm{A})$ and G is $(\mathrm{E}\to\mathrm{S}\to\mathrm{A})\to(\mathrm{S}\to\mathrm{A})$.

Naturally $\acute{\omega}$ will be a typical member of the domain of witnessed values needed in appendix 1, whilst $\grave{\omega}$ will be a typical member of the domain W introduced in the preceding paragraph; accents will be used similarly with members of the other domains, so that the diacritical convention can be freely invoked. Thus occurrences of $\lambda\grave{\varepsilon}\grave{\kappa}.set\grave{\kappa}\circ((\grave{\omega}|\mathrm{F})\grave{\varepsilon})$ will refer to that version of *set* which is defined on $\mathrm{E}\to\mathrm{S}\to\mathrm{A}$ (where E and S are domains needed by the conjugate valuations). When x represents an inclusive predicate mapping a universal domain into T′ we can define inclusive predicates vx and sx on V×V and S×S respectively by means of the equations

$$\mathrm{v}=\lambda x.x\circ(push\langle 3,1\rangle\times push\langle 2,1\rangle)\times(\lambda\hat{\beta}.\hat{\beta})$$

and

$$\mathrm{s}=\lambda x.((l\to(\mathrm{v}x\times t))\times(\mathrm{v}x)^{*}\times(\mathrm{v}x)^{*})\circ(\lambda\hat{\sigma}.\hat{\sigma})$$

where l and t are explained in 4.2.3. In appendix 1 E is L+B+E*+J+F, but, as was mentioned in 3.9.5, by making E be L+B+E*+J+F+G we could give rec r==r&() a sensible meaning; when E is L+B+E*+J+F we let

$$\mathrm{e}=\lambda x.x\circ(mask4\times mask3)\circ(\lambda\hat{\varepsilon}.\hat{\varepsilon}),$$

whereas when E is L+B+E*+J+F+G we let

$$\mathrm{e}=\lambda x.x\circ(mask5\times mask3)\circ(\lambda\hat{\varepsilon}.\hat{\varepsilon}).$$

We can now provide a function ϕ such that if x is a mapping of inclusive predicates into inclusive predicates then so is ϕx; this function is given in terms of the notation of 2.5.5 by the equation

$$\begin{aligned}\phi=\lambda\mathrm{x}x\hat{\omega}.\ &(\acute{\omega}\equiv\bot)\vee(\grave{\omega}\equiv\bot)\rightarrow(\acute{\omega}\equiv\bot)\wedge(\grave{\omega}\equiv\bot),\\ &(\acute{\omega}\equiv\top)\vee(\grave{\omega}\equiv\top)\rightarrow(\acute{\omega}\equiv\top)\wedge(\grave{\omega}\equiv\top),\\ &\acute{\omega}\mathrm{E}\mathrm{L}\wedge\grave{\omega}\mathrm{E}\mathrm{L}\rightarrow l\langle\acute{\omega}|\mathrm{L},\grave{\omega}|\mathrm{L}\rangle,\\ &\acute{\omega}\mathrm{E}\mathrm{B}\wedge\grave{\omega}\mathrm{E}\mathrm{B}\rightarrow b\langle\acute{\omega}|\mathrm{B},\grave{\omega}|\mathrm{B}\rangle,\\ &\acute{\omega}\mathrm{E}\mathrm{E}^*\wedge\grave{\omega}\mathrm{E}\mathrm{E}^*\rightarrow(\mathrm{e}x)^*\langle\acute{\omega}|\mathrm{E}^*,\grave{\omega}|\mathrm{E}^*\rangle,\\ &\acute{\omega}\mathrm{E}\mathrm{F}\wedge\grave{\omega}\mathrm{E}\mathrm{F}\rightarrow(\mathrm{e}x\rightarrow(\mathrm{e}x\rightarrow\mathrm{s}x\rightarrow a)\rightarrow(\mathrm{s}x\rightarrow a))\langle\acute{\omega}|\mathrm{F},(\lambda\grave{\varepsilon}\grave{\kappa}.set\grave{\kappa}\circ((\grave{\omega}|\mathrm{F})\grave{\varepsilon}))\rangle,\\ &\acute{\omega}\mathrm{E}\mathrm{G}\rightarrow\bigvee\{\mathrm{e}(\mathrm{x}x)\langle\acute{\varepsilon},\grave{\omega}\rangle\wedge(\acute{\omega}|\mathrm{G}\equiv(\lambda\acute{\kappa}.\acute{\kappa}\acute{\varepsilon}))|\acute{\varepsilon}\},\\ &false.\end{aligned}$$

Here l, b and a are the tests for equality defined on L×L, B×B and A×A respectively, while $\acute{\varepsilon}$ is a bound variable subject to existential quantification. Because of the presence of existential quantifiers it is not immediately obvious that if x maps inclusive predicates into inclusive predicates then so does ϕx; to show that this actually happens we have to appeal to the nature of A in the manner described in the next paragraph.

Here we briefly take ε_0 and ε_1 to be members of E having $\lambda\kappa.\kappa\varepsilon_0\sqsupseteq\lambda\kappa.\kappa\varepsilon_1$. There can be no isolated element ε_2 for which $\varepsilon_1\sqsupseteq\varepsilon_2$ and for which it is not the case that $\varepsilon_0\sqsupseteq\varepsilon_2$, since under these circumstances defining κ_2 to be $\lambda\varepsilon.(\varepsilon\sqsupseteq\varepsilon_2\rightarrow\top,\bot)$ yields a continuous mapping such that $\kappa_2\varepsilon_1\sqsupseteq\kappa_2\varepsilon_0$ (provided that A contains at least two elements). Hence when z is a set containing only every isolated ε_2 having $\varepsilon_1\sqsupseteq\varepsilon_2$ we know that $\varepsilon_0\sqsupseteq\bigsqcup z$; however, we shall assume that the functor A is constructed simply by combining the operators defined in 2.4.2. so that, by virtue of 2.4.6, $\varepsilon_1 = \bigsqcup z$ and $\varepsilon_0 \sqsupseteq \varepsilon_1$. Consequently whenever ε_0 and ε_1 are members of E such that $\lambda\kappa.\kappa\varepsilon_0 \sqsupseteq \lambda\kappa.\kappa\varepsilon_1$ we may conclude that $\varepsilon_0 \sqsupseteq \varepsilon_1$.

Now we are in a position to confirm that ϕ has the properties which it is intended to have, in that if x maps inclusive predicates into inclusive predicates, if x is an inclusive predicate and if w is a directed set in W×W then $\bigsqcup\{\phi x x\hat{\omega} \mid \hat{\omega} \in w\} \sqsupseteq \phi x x(\bigsqcup w)$. As $\phi x x(\bigsqcup w)$ must be either *true* or *false*, and as *false*$\sqsupseteq$*true* in T′, this inequality can be established merely by verifying that $\phi x x(\bigsqcup w) = true$ whenever $\bigsqcup\{\phi x x\hat{\omega} \mid \hat{\omega} \in w\} = true$. Because l, b, $(ex)^*$ and $ex \rightarrow (ex \rightarrow sx \rightarrow a) \rightarrow (sx \rightarrow a)$ are evidently inclusive and because *set* is continuous this verification is simple unless w is a pair such that $(\bigsqcup w){\downarrow}1 \mathrm{E} G$. In this situation we can assume that for every $\hat{\omega} \in w$ either $\hat{\omega} = \langle \bot, \bot \rangle$ or $\acute{\omega} \mathrm{E} G$, in which case there is some $\acute{\varepsilon}_{\hat{\omega}}$ in E for which $e(xx)\langle \acute{\varepsilon}_{\hat{\omega}}, \grave{\omega} \rangle = true$ and $(\acute{\omega} \mid G \equiv (\lambda\acute{\kappa}.\acute{\kappa}\acute{\varepsilon}_{\hat{\omega}})) = true$. Since **w** is a directed set, $\{\lambda\acute{\kappa}.\acute{\kappa}\acute{\varepsilon}_{\hat{\omega}} \mid \hat{\omega} \in w\}$ is also a directed set, and, in accordance with the previous paragraph, $\{\acute{\varepsilon}_{\hat{\omega}} \mid \hat{\omega} \in w\}$ must be a directed set. As xx is inclusive $e(xx)$ is inclusive so $e(xx)\langle \bigsqcup\{\acute{\varepsilon}_{\hat{\omega}} \mid \hat{\omega} \in w\}, \bigsqcup\{\grave{\omega} \mid \hat{\omega} \in w\} \rangle = true$ and $(\bigsqcup\{\acute{\omega} \mid \hat{\omega} \in w\} \mid G \equiv \bigsqcup\{\lambda\acute{\kappa}.\acute{\kappa}\acute{\varepsilon}_{\hat{\omega}} \mid \hat{\omega} \in w\}) = true$. The fact that $\bigsqcup\{\lambda\acute{\kappa}.\acute{\kappa}\acute{\varepsilon}_{\hat{\omega}} \mid \hat{\omega} \in w\} = \lambda\acute{\kappa}.\acute{\kappa}(\bigsqcup\{\acute{\varepsilon}_{\hat{\omega}} \mid \hat{\omega} \in w\})$ therefore ensures that $\phi x x(\bigsqcup w) = true$ when $(\bigsqcup w){\downarrow}1 \mathrm{E} G$. Thus in all the possible situations $\bigsqcup\{\phi x x\hat{\omega} \mid \hat{\omega} \in w\} \sqsupseteq \phi x x(\bigsqcup w)$ and ϕx maps inclusive predicates into inclusive predicates. A full account of this proof (and of a proof that certain recursive predicates exist) has been given independently by Reynolds [71].

Actually ϕ is a continuous function, as will be demonstrated in the next paragraph. In consequence, we can form its least fixed point, which is an element of the complete lattice of mappings of inclusive predicates into inclusive predicates; because *true* is the least element of T′, $\lambda x\chi.true$ is the least element of this complete lattice and $fix\phi = \bigsqcup\{\phi^n(\lambda x\hat{\omega}.true) \mid n \geq 0\}$. On setting $w = fix\phi$ we see that

$$
\begin{aligned}
w=\lambda x\hat{\omega}.\ & (\acute{\omega}\equiv\bot)\vee(\grave{\omega}\equiv\bot)\rightarrow(\acute{\omega}\equiv\bot)\wedge(\grave{\omega}\equiv\bot),\\
& (\acute{\omega}\equiv\top)\vee(\grave{\omega}\equiv\top)\rightarrow(\acute{\omega}\equiv\top)\wedge(\grave{\omega}\equiv\top),\\
& \acute{\omega}\mathrm{E}\mathrm{L}\wedge\grave{\omega}\mathrm{E}\mathrm{L}\rightarrow l\langle\acute{\omega}|\mathrm{L},\grave{\omega}|\mathrm{L}\rangle,\\
& \acute{\omega}\mathrm{E}\mathrm{B}\wedge\grave{\omega}\mathrm{E}\mathrm{B}\rightarrow b\langle\acute{\omega}|\mathrm{B},\grave{\omega}|\mathrm{B}\rangle,\\
& \acute{\omega}\mathrm{E}\mathrm{E}^*\wedge\grave{\omega}\mathrm{E}\mathrm{E}^*\rightarrow(ex)^*\langle\acute{\omega}|\mathrm{E}^*,\grave{\omega}|\mathrm{E}^*\rangle,\\
& \acute{\omega}\mathrm{E}\mathrm{F}\wedge\grave{\omega}\mathrm{E}\mathrm{F}\rightarrow(ex\rightarrow(ex\rightarrow sx\rightarrow a)\rightarrow(sx\rightarrow a))\langle\acute{\omega}|\mathrm{F},(\lambda\grave{\epsilon}\grave{\kappa}.set\grave{\kappa}\circ((\grave{\omega}|\mathrm{F})\grave{\epsilon}))\rangle,\\
& \acute{\omega}\mathrm{E}\mathrm{G}\rightarrow\bigvee\{e(wx)\langle\acute{\epsilon},\grave{\omega}\rangle\wedge(\acute{\omega}|\mathrm{G}\equiv(\lambda\acute{\kappa}.\acute{\kappa}\acute{\epsilon}))\,|\,\acute{\epsilon}\},\\
& false.
\end{aligned}
$$

In order to show that ϕ is continuous we introduce X (an arbitrary directed set comprising mappings of inclusive predicates into inclusive predicates), together with an inclusive predicate x and a pair $\hat{\omega}$. Unless $\acute{\omega}\mathrm{E}\mathrm{G}$ it is plain that $\phi(\bigsqcup\mathrm{X})x\hat{\omega}=\bigsqcup\{\phi\mathrm{x}x\hat{\omega}\,|\,\mathrm{x}\in\mathrm{X}\}$; if, however, $\acute{\omega}\mathrm{E}\mathrm{G}$ we have to investigate the situation more fully by using the knowledge that for all $\acute{\epsilon}$, because e is continuous,

$$
\begin{aligned}
e((\bigsqcup\mathrm{X})x)\langle\acute{\epsilon},\grave{\omega}\rangle &= e(\bigsqcup\{\mathrm{x}x\,|\,\mathrm{x}\in\mathrm{X}\})\langle\acute{\epsilon},\grave{\omega}\rangle\\
&=\bigsqcup\{e(\mathrm{x}x)\,|\,\mathrm{x}\in\mathrm{X}\}\langle\acute{\epsilon},\grave{\omega}\rangle\\
&=\bigsqcup\{e(\mathrm{x}x)\langle\acute{\epsilon},\grave{\omega}\rangle\,|\,\mathrm{x}\in\mathrm{X}\}
\end{aligned}
$$

(so that, as *true* is the least element of T', $e((\bigsqcup\mathrm{X})x)\langle\acute{\epsilon},\grave{\omega}\rangle=true$ if and only if $e(\mathrm{x}x)\langle\acute{\epsilon},\grave{\omega}\rangle=true$ for every $\mathrm{x}\in\mathrm{X}$). When $\acute{\omega}\mathrm{E}\mathrm{G}$ and $\phi(\bigsqcup\mathrm{X})x\hat{\omega}=true$ we observe that there is some $\acute{\epsilon}$ for which $e((\bigsqcup\mathrm{X})x)\langle\acute{\epsilon},\grave{\omega}\rangle=true$ and $(\acute{\omega}|\mathrm{G}\equiv(\lambda\acute{\kappa}.\acute{\kappa}\acute{\epsilon}))=true$, so for each $\mathrm{x}\in\mathrm{X}$ $e(\mathrm{x}x)\langle\acute{\epsilon},\grave{\omega}\rangle=true$ and $(\acute{\omega}|\mathrm{G}\equiv(\lambda\acute{\kappa}.\acute{\kappa}\acute{\epsilon}))=true$ (or, in other words, $\phi(\mathrm{x}x)\hat{\omega}=true$); hence $\bigsqcup\{\phi(\mathrm{x}x)\hat{\omega}\,|\,\mathrm{x}\in\mathrm{X}\}=true$. When $\acute{\omega}\mathrm{E}\mathrm{G}$ and $\bigsqcup\{\phi(\mathrm{x}x)\hat{\omega}\,|\,\mathrm{x}\in\mathrm{X}\}=true$ we know that whenever $\mathrm{x}\in\mathrm{X}$ there is some $\acute{\epsilon}_{\mathrm{x}}$ in E such that $e(\mathrm{x}x)\langle\acute{\epsilon}_{\mathrm{x}},\grave{\omega}\rangle=true$ and $(\acute{\omega}|\mathrm{G}\equiv(\lambda\acute{\kappa}.\acute{\kappa}(\acute{\epsilon}_{\mathrm{x}})))=true$, with the effect that if $\mathrm{x}_0\in\mathrm{X}$ and $\mathrm{x}_1\in\mathrm{X}$ then $\lambda\kappa.\kappa(\acute{\epsilon}_{\mathrm{x}_0})=\lambda\kappa.\kappa(\acute{\epsilon}_{\mathrm{x}_1})$ and indeed $\acute{\epsilon}_{\mathrm{x}_0}=\acute{\epsilon}_{\mathrm{x}_1}$; consequently if $\acute{\epsilon}=\bigsqcup\{\acute{\epsilon}_{\mathrm{x}}\,|\,\mathrm{x}\in\mathrm{X}\}$ we may infer successively that for every $\mathrm{x}\in\mathrm{X}$ $e(\mathrm{x}x)\langle\acute{\epsilon},\grave{\omega}\rangle=true$ and $(\acute{\omega}|\mathrm{G}\equiv(\lambda\acute{\kappa}.\acute{\kappa}\acute{\epsilon}))=true$, that for every $\mathrm{x}\in\mathrm{X}$ $\phi\mathrm{x}x\hat{\omega}=true$, and that $\phi(\bigsqcup\mathrm{X})x\hat{\omega}=true$. Thus, when $\acute{\omega}\mathrm{E}\mathrm{G}$, $\phi(\bigsqcup\mathrm{X})x\hat{\omega}=true$ if and only if $\bigsqcup\{\phi\mathrm{x}x\hat{\omega}\,|\,\mathrm{x}\in\mathrm{X}\}=true$, and since $\phi(\bigsqcup\mathrm{X})x\hat{\omega}$ and $\bigsqcup\{\phi\mathrm{x}x\hat{\omega}\,|\,\mathrm{x}\in\mathrm{X}\}$ can take solely the values *true* and *false* we may deduce that $\phi(\bigsqcup\mathrm{X})\mathrm{x}\hat{\omega}=\bigsqcup\{\phi\mathrm{x}x\hat{\omega}\,|\,\mathrm{x}\in\mathrm{X}\}$.

This equation completes the proof that $\phi(\bigsqcup x)x\hat{\omega}=\bigsqcup\{\phi x x\hat{\omega} \mid x\in x\}$ for all suitable x, x and $\hat{\omega}$, so ϕ must be continuous and w can be $fix\phi$.

The next objective in our pursuit of the relation between the two domains called W is to find an inclusive predicate ω having ω=wω. To this end we assemble a collection of functors rather like that provided in 4.2.3. Thus when X signifies a retraction of the universal domain we set up VX and SX, which are appropriate to the domains V and S defined in appendix 1, with the aid of the equations

$V=\lambda X.X\circ push\langle 3,1\rangle$

and

$S=\lambda X.(L\to(VX\times T))\times(VX)^*\times(VX)^*$

when L and T are as in 2.4.2. In addition if E is L+B+E*+J+F we set

$E=\lambda X.X\circ mask4$,

whilst if E is L+B+E*+J+F+G we set

$E=\lambda X.X\circ mask5$.

Naturally W complements w by being recursive; in fact when

$C=\lambda X.SX\to AX$

we introduce ψ, which is given by the equation

$$\psi=\lambda XX.L+B+(EX)^*+C(\lambda\hat{\omega}.\hat{\omega})+(EX\to(EX\to SX\to A(\lambda\hat{\omega}.\hat{\omega}))\to(SX\to A(\lambda\hat{\omega}.\hat{\omega})))$$
$$+((E(XX)\to C(\lambda\hat{\omega}.\hat{\omega}))\to C(\lambda\hat{\omega}.\hat{\omega}))+(E(\lambda\hat{\omega}.\hat{\omega})\to C(\lambda\hat{\omega}.\hat{\omega}))$$

and we let $W=fix\psi$, so that

$$W=\lambda X.L+B+(EX)^*+C(\lambda\hat{\omega}.\hat{\omega})+(EX\to(EX\to SX\to A(\lambda\hat{\omega}.\hat{\omega}))\to(SX\to A(\lambda\hat{\omega}.\hat{\omega})))$$
$$+((E(WX)\to C(\lambda\hat{\omega}.\hat{\omega}))\to C(\lambda\hat{\omega}.\hat{\omega}))+(E(\lambda\hat{\omega}.\hat{\omega})\to C(\lambda\hat{\omega}.\hat{\omega})).$$

In the case of the domains needed by the conjugate valuations,

$V=\lambda X.X\circ push\langle 2,1\rangle$

and

$S=\lambda X.(L\to(VX\times T))\times(VX)^*\times(VX)^*$;

in addition, because E and W are both L+B+E*+F,

$E=\lambda X.X\circ mask3$

and

$W=\lambda X.L+B+(EX)^*+(EX\to SX\to(A(\lambda\hat{\omega}.\hat{\omega})+(EX\times SX)))$.

When $x_0=\lambda\chi.true$ and $X_0=(\lambda\chi.\bot)\times(\lambda\chi.\bot)$ it is clear that $\langle \mathrm{w}x_0,(\mathrm{W}\circledast\mathrm{W})X_0\rangle \geq \langle x_0,X_0\rangle$; moreover we can confirm inductively that $\bigsqcup\{(\mathrm{W}\circledast\mathrm{W})^n X_0 \mid n\geq 0\}=\lambda\hat{\omega}.\hat{\omega}$ and that w is a predictor for $\mathrm{W}\circledast\mathrm{W}$ based on $\langle x_0,X_0\rangle$ and bounded by a set y (the delineation of which will be left to the reader). We shall indicate how to carry out one of the necessary inductions in the next paragraph; here we merely remark that according to 2.5.3 they imply that there is a unique inclusive predicate w having $w=\mathrm{w}w$ (and having $\langle w,\lambda\hat{\omega}.\hat{\omega}\rangle \geq \langle x_0,X_0\rangle$, for what it is worth). If $v=\mathrm{v}w$, $e=\mathrm{e}w$ and $s=\mathrm{s}w$ the knowledge that $\mathrm{e}w=\mathrm{e}(\mathrm{w}w)$ assures us that

$w=\lambda\hat{\omega}.(\acute{\omega}\equiv\bot)\vee(\grave{\omega}\equiv\bot)\to(\acute{\omega}\equiv\bot)\wedge(\grave{\omega}\equiv\bot),$

$(\acute{\omega}\equiv\top)\vee(\grave{\omega}\equiv\top)\to(\acute{\omega}\equiv\top)\wedge(\grave{\omega}\equiv\top),$

$\acute{\omega}\mathrm{E}\mathrm{L}\wedge\grave{\omega}\mathrm{E}\mathrm{L}\to l\langle \acute{\omega}|\mathrm{L},\grave{\omega}|\mathrm{L}\rangle,$

$\acute{\omega}\mathrm{E}\mathrm{B}\wedge\grave{\omega}\mathrm{E}\mathrm{B}\to b\langle \acute{\omega}|\mathrm{B},\grave{\omega}|\mathrm{B}\rangle,$

$\acute{\omega}\mathrm{E}\mathrm{E}^*\wedge\grave{\omega}\mathrm{E}\mathrm{E}^*\to e^*\langle \acute{\omega}|\mathrm{E}^*,\grave{\omega}|\mathrm{E}^*\rangle,$

$\acute{\omega}\mathrm{E}\mathrm{F}\wedge\grave{\omega}\mathrm{E}\mathrm{F}\to(e\to(e\to s\to a)\to(s\to a))\langle \acute{\omega}|\mathrm{F},(\lambda\varepsilon\kappa.set\kappa\circ((\grave{\omega}|\mathrm{F})\varepsilon))\rangle,$

$\acute{\omega}\mathrm{E}\mathrm{G}\to\bigvee\{e\langle \acute{\varepsilon},\grave{\omega}\rangle\wedge(\acute{\omega}|\mathrm{G}\equiv(\lambda\kappa.\kappa\acute{\varepsilon}))|\acute{\varepsilon}\},$

$false.$

Now we resume the proof that w is a predictor for $\mathrm{W}\circledast\mathrm{W}$ based on $\langle x_0,X_0\rangle$ and bounded by y. Thus we suppose that $\langle x_1,X_1\rangle$ and $\langle x_2,X_2\rangle$ are pairs of inclusive predicates and retractions having $\langle x_2,X_2\rangle \geq\langle x_1,X_1\rangle \geq\langle x_0,X_0\rangle$ and $X_n\epsilon\mathrm{y}$ when $2\geq n\geq 0$, and we try to show that $\langle \mathrm{w}x_2,(\mathrm{W}\circledast\mathrm{W})X_2\rangle \geq\langle \mathrm{w}x_1,(\mathrm{W}\circledast\mathrm{W})X_1\rangle \geq\langle \mathrm{w}x_0,(\mathrm{W}\circledast\mathrm{W})X_0\rangle$ and that $(\mathrm{W}\circledast\mathrm{W})X_n\epsilon\mathrm{y}$ when $2\geq n\geq 0$. Because $\mathrm{w}=fix\phi$ and one version of W satisfies the equation $\mathrm{W}=fix\psi$ we proceed inductively by introducing any x and X such that $\langle \mathrm{x}x_2,(\mathrm{X}\circledast\mathrm{W})X_2\rangle \geq\langle \mathrm{x}x_1,(\mathrm{X}\circledast\mathrm{W})X_1\rangle \geq\langle \mathrm{x}x_0,(\mathrm{X}\circledast\mathrm{W})X_0\rangle$ and $(\mathrm{X}\circledast\mathrm{W})X_n\epsilon\mathrm{y}$ when $2\geq n\geq 0$. For any pair $\hat{\omega}$ it is immediately plain from 2.5.6 that unless $\acute{\omega}\mathrm{E}\mathrm{G}$ $\phi\mathrm{x}x_2\hat{\omega}\supseteq\phi\mathrm{x}x_1(((\psi\mathrm{X}\circledast\mathrm{W})X_1)\hat{\omega})$ and $\phi\mathrm{x}x_1\hat{\omega}\supseteq\phi\mathrm{x}x_2(((\psi\mathrm{X}\circledast\mathrm{W})X_1)\hat{\omega})$, since v, e, s and $\lambda x.a$ are predictors for $\mathrm{V}\circledast\mathrm{V}$, $\mathrm{E}\circledast\mathrm{E}$, $\mathrm{S}\circledast\mathrm{S}$ and $\lambda X.\mathrm{A}(\lambda\hat{\omega}.\acute{\omega})\times\mathrm{A}(\lambda\hat{\omega}.\grave{\omega})$ (respectively) based on $\langle x_0,X_0\rangle$ and bounded by y. If $\acute{\omega}\mathrm{E}\mathrm{G}$ and $\phi\mathrm{x}x_2\hat{\omega}=true$

there is some $\acute{\epsilon}$ for which $\mathrm{e}(\mathrm{x}x_2)\langle\acute{\epsilon},\grave{\omega}\rangle=true$ and $(\acute{\omega}|\mathrm{G}\equiv(\lambda\acute{\kappa}.\acute{\kappa}\acute{\epsilon}))=true$, so, as $\langle\mathrm{x}x_2,(\mathrm{X}\circledast\mathrm{W})X_2\rangle\geq\langle\mathrm{x}x_1,(\mathrm{X}\circledast\mathrm{W})X_1\rangle$ and as e is a predictor for $\mathrm{E}\circledast\mathrm{E}$ based on $\langle x_0,X_0\rangle$ and bounded by y, $\mathrm{e}(\mathrm{x}x_1)(((\mathrm{E}\circledast\mathrm{E})(\mathrm{X}\circledast\mathrm{W})X_1)\langle\acute{\epsilon},\grave{\omega}\rangle)=true$ and $(((\mathrm{E}(\mathrm{X}(acute(X_1)))\rightarrow\mathrm{C}(\lambda\acute{\omega}.\acute{\omega}))\rightarrow\mathrm{C}(\lambda\acute{\omega}.\acute{\omega}))(\acute{\omega}|\mathrm{G})\equiv(\lambda\acute{\kappa}.\acute{\kappa}(\mathrm{E}(\mathrm{X}(acute(X_1)))\acute{\epsilon})))=true$; hence $\mathrm{e}(\mathrm{x}x_1)\langle\mathrm{E}(\mathrm{X}(acute(X_1))\acute{\epsilon},\mathrm{W}(grave(X_1))\grave{\omega}\rangle=true$ and $((\psi\mathrm{X}(acute(X_1))\acute{\omega})|\mathrm{G}\equiv(\lambda\acute{\kappa}.\acute{\kappa}(\mathrm{E}(\mathrm{X}(acute(X_1)))\acute{\epsilon})))=true$ or, in other words, $\phi\mathrm{x}x_1(((\psi\mathrm{X}\circledast\mathrm{W})X_1)\hat{\omega})=true$. This ensures that $\phi\mathrm{x}x_2\hat{\omega}\sqsupseteq\phi\mathrm{x}x_1(((\psi\mathrm{X}\circledast\mathrm{W})X_1)\hat{\omega})$ even when $\hat{\omega}\sqsubseteq\mathrm{G}$, since $\phi\mathrm{x}x_2\hat{\omega}$ can only be *true* or *false*; similarly $\phi\mathrm{x}x_1\hat{\omega}\sqsupseteq\phi\mathrm{x}x_2(((\psi\mathrm{X}\circledast\mathrm{W})X_2)\hat{\omega})$ under all circumstances. Simple calculations establish that $(\psi\mathrm{X}\circledast\mathrm{W})X_1=(\psi\mathrm{X}\circledast\mathrm{W})X_2\circ(\psi\mathrm{X}\circledast\mathrm{W})X_1$, that $(\psi\mathrm{X}\circledast\mathrm{W})X_1=(\psi\mathrm{X}\circledast\mathrm{W})X_1\circ(\psi\mathrm{X}\circledast\mathrm{W})X_2$ and that $(\psi\mathrm{X}\circledast\mathrm{W})X_1\sqsupseteq(\psi\mathrm{X}\circledast\mathrm{W})X_2$, so actually $\langle\phi\mathrm{x}x_2,(\psi\mathrm{X}\circledast\mathrm{W})X_2\rangle\geq\langle\phi\mathrm{x}x_1,(\psi\mathrm{X}\circledast\mathrm{W})X_1\rangle$; indeed, the same argument also demonstrates that $\langle\phi\mathrm{x}x_1,(\psi\mathrm{X}\circledast\mathrm{W})X_1\rangle\geq\langle\phi\mathrm{x}x_0,(\psi\mathrm{X}\circledast\mathrm{W})X_0\rangle$. Thus if $\langle\mathrm{x}x_2,(\mathrm{X}\circledast\mathrm{W})X_2\rangle\geq\langle\mathrm{x}x_1,(\mathrm{X}\circledast\mathrm{W})X_1\rangle\geq\langle\mathrm{x}x_0,(\mathrm{X}\circledast\mathrm{W})X_0\rangle$ and $(\mathrm{X}\circledast\mathrm{W})X_n\in\mathrm{y}$ when $2\geq n\geq 0$ we can verify that $\langle\phi\mathrm{x}x_2,(\psi\mathrm{X}\circledast\mathrm{W})X_2\rangle\geq\langle\phi\mathrm{x}x_1,(\psi\mathrm{X}\circledast\mathrm{W})X_1\rangle\geq\langle\phi\mathrm{x}x_0,(\psi\mathrm{X}\circledast\mathrm{W})X_0\rangle$ and $(\psi\mathrm{X}\circledast\mathrm{W})X_n\in\mathrm{y}$ when $2\geq n\geq 0$; because $\langle(\lambda x\chi.true)x_2,((\lambda X\chi.\bot)\circledast\mathrm{W})X_2\rangle\geq\langle(\lambda x\chi.true)x_1,((\lambda X\chi.\bot)\circledast\mathrm{W})X_1\rangle$ and $\langle(\lambda x\chi.true)x_1,((\lambda X\chi.\bot)\circledast\mathrm{W})X_1\rangle\geq\langle(\lambda x\chi.true)x_0,((\lambda X\chi.\bot)\circledast\mathrm{W})X_0\rangle$ we may therefore appeal to the induction principle of 2.3.2 to ensure that $\langle\mathrm{w}x_2,(\mathrm{W}\circledast\mathrm{W})X_2\rangle\geq\langle\mathrm{w}x_1,(\mathrm{W}\circledast\mathrm{W})X_1\rangle\geq\langle\mathrm{w}x_0,(\mathrm{W}\circledast\mathrm{W})X_0\rangle$ and that $(\mathrm{W}\circledast\mathrm{W})X_n\in\mathrm{y}$ when $2\geq n\geq 0$. The reader is invited to investigate where this argument breaks down when w and W satisfy equations that are not recursive.

As was remarked above, we may confidently assert that there is an inclusive predicate w such that $w=\mathrm{w}w$. With impunity we may therefore define inclusive predicates d and u by writing $d=\mathrm{d}w$ and $u=\mathrm{u}w$ where

$\mathrm{d}=\lambda x.x\circ(mask5\times mask3)\circ(\lambda\hat{\delta}.\hat{\delta})$

and

$\mathrm{u}=\lambda x\hat{\rho}.\bigwedge\{(\mathrm{d}x)^*\langle\acute{\rho}[\![\mathrm{I}]\!],\grave{\rho}[\![\mathrm{I}]\!]\rangle\,|\,\mathrm{I}\}$.

When using these definitions we view an entity X in

Exp+Abs+Seq+Dec+Blo+Com as being 'regular' if and only if X contains:

(i) no mention of the syntactic structures Σ, val E, I:Γ and I::Γ;

(ii) no declaration of the form rec Δ such that an element of the list $\mathcal{H}[\![\Delta]\!]$ occurs free in Δ outside the body of an abstraction which is not an exit (in the sense of 3.5.7) of an expression E_0 appearing in an application E_0E_1 in Δ.

Thus rec *f*=fn*x*.*f* is regular whereas rec *f*==(*y*?fn*x*.*f*!*y*)*y* is not regular. If we wish to regard rec *r*==*r*&() as a useful declaration in the way suggested in 3.9.5 we can allow X to be regular even when it is not subject to (ii) provided that every occurrence of a member of $\mathcal{H}[\![\Delta]\!]$ in rec Δ outside an abstraction that is not applied is such that only $\mathcal{E}$, not $\mathcal{L}$ or $\mathcal{R}$, is required for its evaluation; obviously there are syntactic constraints which suffice to make sure that this happens.

When we take $\P\mathcal{E}[\![E_0E_1]\!]$ to be equal to

$$\lambda\rho.fit(\lambda\varepsilon'.fit(\lambda\varepsilon''.\varepsilon'\mathsf{E}\mathsf{F}\rightarrow(\varepsilon'|\mathsf{F})\varepsilon'',wrong)\circ\P\mathcal{E}[\![E_1]\!]\rho)\circ(\P\mathcal{R}[\![E_0]\!]\rho)$$

and set up the remaining equations in the definition of $\P\mathcal{E}$ along the lines laid down in 3.9.2, we can establish by methods identical with those adopted in 3.9.4 that whenever E is regular $\P\mathcal{E}$ is conjugate to $\mathcal{E}$ for E under $u\rightarrow(e\rightarrow s\rightarrow a)\rightarrow(s\rightarrow a)$ (provided that $\P\mathcal{B}$, $\P\mathcal{O}$ and $\P\mathcal{W}$ are related suitably to $\mathcal{B}$, $\mathcal{O}$ and $\mathcal{W}$); naturally analogous remarks apply to the other valuations, such as $\P\mathcal{D}$ and $\P\mathcal{T}$.

If we ignore such declarations as rec *r*==*r*&() we are at liberty to take E to be L+B+E*+J+F (as is done in appendix 1) instead of L+B+E*+J+F+G. In this situation we can set up *e* (as well as *v* and *s*) without needing to compare members of G with elements of the domain E which is L+B+E*+F; consequently G can be given a trivial role in the equation for *w*. More precisely, we can let *w*=w*w*, where

$$
\begin{aligned}
\mathrm{w}=\lambda x\hat{\omega}.\,&(\acute{\omega}\equiv\bot)\vee(\grave{\omega}\equiv\bot)\rightarrow(\acute{\omega}\equiv\bot)\wedge(\grave{\omega}\equiv\bot),\\
&(\acute{\omega}\equiv\top)\vee(\grave{\omega}\equiv\top)\rightarrow(\acute{\omega}\equiv\top)\wedge(\grave{\omega}\equiv\top),\\
&\acute{\omega}\mathsf{E}\mathrm{L}\wedge\grave{\omega}\mathsf{E}\mathrm{L}\rightarrow l\langle\acute{\omega}|\mathrm{L},\grave{\omega}|\mathrm{L}\rangle,\\
&\acute{\omega}\mathsf{E}\mathrm{B}\wedge\grave{\omega}\mathsf{E}\mathrm{B}\rightarrow b\langle\acute{\omega}|\mathrm{B},\grave{\omega}|\mathrm{B}\rangle,\\
&\acute{\omega}\mathsf{E}\mathrm{E}^*\wedge\grave{\omega}\mathsf{E}\mathrm{E}^*\rightarrow(\mathrm{e}x)^*\langle\acute{\omega}|\mathrm{E}^*,\grave{\omega}|\mathrm{E}^*\rangle,\\
&\acute{\omega}\mathsf{E}\mathrm{F}\wedge\grave{\omega}\mathsf{E}\mathrm{F}\rightarrow(\mathrm{e}x\rightarrow(\mathrm{e}x\rightarrow\mathrm{s}x\rightarrow a)\rightarrow(\mathrm{s}x\rightarrow a))\langle\acute{\omega}|\mathrm{F},(\lambda\grave{\epsilon}\grave{\kappa}.\,set\grave{\kappa}\circ((\grave{\omega}|\mathrm{F})\grave{\epsilon}))\rangle,\\
&false.
\end{aligned}
$$

The mappings v, e, s and u take the forms provided above, but now

$$
\begin{aligned}
\mathrm{d}=\lambda x\hat{\delta}.\,&(\acute{\delta}\equiv\bot)\vee(\grave{\delta}\equiv\bot)\rightarrow(\acute{\delta}\equiv\bot)\wedge(\grave{\delta}\equiv\bot),\\
&(\acute{\delta}\equiv\top)\vee(\grave{\delta}\equiv\top)\rightarrow(\acute{\delta}\equiv\top)\wedge(\grave{\delta}\equiv\top),\\
&\acute{\delta}\mathsf{E}\mathrm{G}\rightarrow\bigvee\{\mathrm{e}x\langle\acute{\epsilon},\grave{\delta}\rangle\wedge(\acute{\delta}|\mathrm{G}\equiv(\lambda\acute{\kappa}.\acute{\kappa}\acute{\epsilon}))|\acute{\epsilon}\},\\
&\mathrm{e}x\hat{\delta}.
\end{aligned}
$$

The predicates vω, eω, dω, sω and uω coincide with the versions of v, e, d, s and u set up above (though our present version of w is not that used before), so we can still prove results about conjugate valuations. However, because the latest version of w satisfies an equation which is not recursive we do not need to show that it is the least fixed point of a continuous function and we can drastically simplify the proof that w is a predictor for W∘W based on $\langle x_0,X_0\rangle$ and bounded by y. Indeed, we can even let the version of W appropriate to the domain L+B+E*+J+F+G+K be given by the equation

$$
\begin{aligned}
\mathrm{W}=\lambda X.\,&L+B+(\mathrm{E}X)^*+\mathrm{C}(\lambda\acute{\omega}.\acute{\omega})+(\mathrm{E}X\rightarrow(\mathrm{E}X\rightarrow\mathrm{S}X\rightarrow\mathrm{A}(\lambda\acute{\omega}.\acute{\omega}))\rightarrow(\mathrm{S}X\rightarrow\mathrm{A}(\lambda\acute{\omega}.\acute{\omega})))\\
&+((\mathrm{E}(\lambda\acute{\omega}.\acute{\omega})\rightarrow\mathrm{C}(\lambda\acute{\omega}.\acute{\omega}))\rightarrow\mathrm{C}(\lambda\acute{\omega}.\acute{\omega}))+(\mathrm{E}(\lambda\acute{\omega}.\acute{\omega})\rightarrow\mathrm{C}(\lambda\acute{\omega}.\acute{\omega})).
\end{aligned}
$$

Those who still have the energy to examine the structural induction mentioned in 4.2.5 may now do so.

4.3. The congruence between standard semantics and store semantics.

4.3.1. Lemma.

If E_0 and E_1 are Sal expressions such that $R[\![E_0]\!] \wedge E[\![E_1]\!] = true$ then $E[\![E_0E_1]\!] = true$.

◁It is enough to show that $c\langle \mathcal{E}[\![E_0E_1]\!]\acute{\rho}\kappa, \langle \mathcal{E}[\![E_0E_1]\!]\zeta_0, \grave{\rho}, \upsilon\rangle\rangle = true$ whenever $k\langle\kappa, \langle\zeta_0, \grave{\rho}, \upsilon\rangle\rangle \wedge u\hat{\rho} \wedge rent[\![E_0E_1]\!]\hat{\rho} = true$. This will be established on the assumption that $run = \lambda\langle\gamma_0, \gamma_1\rangle\psi.\gamma_0(\lambda\varepsilon'.\gamma_1(\lambda\varepsilon''.\psi\varepsilon'\varepsilon''))$, so that expressions are evaluated from left to right; the proof needed when evaluations proceed from right to left is very similar. Thus it will be shown that if $\psi = \lambda\varepsilon'\varepsilon''.(\varepsilon' \mathsf{E} F \rightarrow (\varepsilon'|F)\varepsilon''\kappa, wrong)$ and $\zeta_1 = \lambda\rho\upsilon\sigma.(\upsilon\downarrow 2 \mathsf{E} F \rightarrow ((\upsilon\downarrow 2|F)\downarrow 1)\zeta_0(divert\rho((\upsilon\downarrow 2|F)\downarrow 2))(\langle\upsilon\downarrow 1\rangle \S \upsilon\dagger 2)\sigma, wrong\sigma)$ then $c\langle \mathcal{R}[\![E_0]\!]\acute{\rho}(\lambda\varepsilon'.\mathcal{E}[\![E_1]\!]\acute{\rho}(\lambda\varepsilon''.\psi\varepsilon'\varepsilon'')), \langle \mathcal{R}[\![E_0]\!](\mathcal{E}[\![E_1]\!]\zeta_1), \grave{\rho}, \upsilon\rangle\rangle = true$.

In fact it is quite sufficient to verify that $k\langle\lambda\varepsilon'.\mathcal{E}[\![E_1]\!]\acute{\rho}(\lambda\varepsilon''.\psi\varepsilon'\varepsilon''), \langle\mathcal{E}[\![E_1]\!]\zeta_1, \grave{\rho}, \upsilon\rangle\rangle = true$, because $R[\![E_0]\!] = true$ and $u\hat{\rho} \wedge rent[\![E_0]\!]\hat{\rho} = true$. Thus an attempt must be made to show that $c\langle\mathcal{E}[\![E_1]\!]\acute{\rho}(\psi\acute{\varepsilon}_0), \langle\mathcal{E}[\![E_1]\!]\zeta_1, \grave{\rho}, \langle\grave{\varepsilon}_0\rangle \S \upsilon\rangle\rangle = true$ for each $\hat{\varepsilon}_0$ having $e\hat{\varepsilon}_0 = true$; as $E[\![E_1]\!] = true$ and $u\hat{\rho} \wedge rent[\![E_1]\!]\hat{\rho} = true$ this can be done by demonstrating that $k\langle\psi\acute{\varepsilon}_0, \langle\zeta_1, \grave{\rho}, \langle\grave{\varepsilon}_0\rangle \S \upsilon\rangle\rangle = true$ or that $c\langle\psi\acute{\varepsilon}_0\acute{\varepsilon}_1, \langle\zeta_1, \grave{\rho}, \langle\grave{\varepsilon}_1\rangle \S \langle\grave{\varepsilon}_0\rangle \S \upsilon\rangle\rangle = true$ if $\hat{\varepsilon}_1$ is chosen to be an arbitrary pair such that $e\hat{\varepsilon}_1 = true$.

When $e\hat{\varepsilon}_0 = true$ it is plain that, unless $\hat{\varepsilon}_0$ is $\langle\bot,\bot\rangle$ or $\langle\top,\top\rangle$, either $\acute{\varepsilon}_0$ and $\grave{\varepsilon}_0$ are both outside their respective versions of F or $\acute{\varepsilon}_0 \mathsf{E} F$ and $\grave{\varepsilon}_0 \mathsf{E} F$. If $\hat{\varepsilon}_0$ is $\langle\bot,\bot\rangle$ or $\langle\top,\top\rangle$, $\langle\psi\acute{\varepsilon}_0\acute{\varepsilon}_1, \zeta_1\grave{\rho}(\langle\grave{\varepsilon}_1\rangle \S \langle\grave{\varepsilon}_0\rangle \S \upsilon)\rangle$ is $\langle\bot,\bot\rangle$ or $\langle\top,\top\rangle$; otherwise $\langle\psi\acute{\varepsilon}_0\acute{\varepsilon}_1, \zeta_1\grave{\rho}(\langle\grave{\varepsilon}_1\rangle \S \langle\grave{\varepsilon}_0\rangle \S \upsilon)\rangle$ is $\langle wrong, wrong\rangle$ or $\langle(\acute{\varepsilon}_0|F)\acute{\varepsilon}_1\kappa, ((\grave{\varepsilon}_0|F)\downarrow 1)\zeta_0(divert\grave{\rho}((\grave{\varepsilon}_0|F)\downarrow 2))(\langle\grave{\varepsilon}_1\rangle \S \upsilon)\rangle$ (depending on whether or not $\acute{\varepsilon}_0 \mathsf{E} F$ and $\grave{\varepsilon}_0 \mathsf{E} F$). The assumptions made about a in 4.2.5 ensure that $(s\rightarrow a)\langle\bot,\bot\rangle = true$, $(s\rightarrow a)\langle\top,\top\rangle = true$ and $(s\rightarrow a)\langle wrong, wrong\rangle = true$; furthermore, when $\acute{\varepsilon}_0 \mathsf{E} F$ and $\grave{\varepsilon}_0 \mathsf{E} F$ $f\langle\acute{\varepsilon}_0|F, \grave{\varepsilon}_0|F\rangle = true$ so $c\langle(\acute{\varepsilon}_0|F)\acute{\varepsilon}_1\kappa, \langle((\grave{\varepsilon}_0|F)\downarrow 1)\zeta_0, divert\grave{\rho}((\grave{\varepsilon}_0|F)\downarrow 2), \upsilon\rangle\rangle = true$ (or, in other words, $(s\rightarrow a)\langle(\acute{\varepsilon}_0|F)\acute{\varepsilon}_1\kappa, ((\grave{\varepsilon}_0|F)\downarrow 1)\zeta_0(divert\grave{\rho}((\grave{\varepsilon}_0|F)\downarrow 2))\upsilon\rangle = true$) and $k\langle\kappa, \langle\zeta_0, \grave{\rho}, \upsilon\rangle\rangle \wedge e\hat{\varepsilon}_1 = true$. Hence under all circumstances

$(s \to a)\langle \psi\acute{\epsilon}_0\acute{\epsilon}_1, \zeta_1\grave{\rho}(\langle \grave{\epsilon}_1\rangle \S \langle \grave{\epsilon}_0\rangle \S \upsilon)\rangle = true$, and, because $c = \lambda\langle \theta, \langle \zeta, \rho, \upsilon\rangle\rangle . (s \to a)\langle \theta, \zeta\rho\upsilon\rangle$, $c\langle \psi\acute{\epsilon}_0\acute{\epsilon}_1, \langle \zeta_1, \grave{\rho}, \langle \grave{\epsilon}_1\rangle \S \langle \grave{\epsilon}_0\rangle \S \upsilon\rangle\rangle = true$.

This equation holds for any $\hat{\epsilon}_1$ selected in such a way that $e\hat{\epsilon}_1 = true$, so $k\langle \psi\acute{\epsilon}_0, \langle \zeta_1, \grave{\rho}, \langle \grave{\epsilon}_0\rangle \S \upsilon\rangle\rangle = true$. In turn this shows that $c\langle \mathcal{E}[\![E_1]\!] \acute{\rho}(\psi\acute{\epsilon}_0), \langle \mathcal{E}[\![E_1]\!] \zeta_1, \grave{\rho}, \langle \grave{\epsilon}_0\rangle \S \upsilon\rangle\rangle = true$ for every $\hat{\epsilon}_0$ subject to the constraint that $e\hat{\epsilon}_0 = true$; consequently $k\langle \lambda\epsilon'.\mathcal{E}[\![E_1]\!] \acute{\rho}(\lambda\epsilon''.\psi\epsilon'\epsilon''), \langle \mathcal{E}[\![E_1]\!] \zeta_1, \grave{\rho}, \upsilon\rangle\rangle = true$. It is even the case that $c\langle \mathcal{R}[\![E_0]\!] \acute{\rho}(\lambda\epsilon'.\mathcal{E}[\![E_1]\!] \acute{\rho}(\lambda\epsilon''.\psi\epsilon'\epsilon'')), \langle \mathcal{R}[\![E_0]\!] (\mathcal{E}[\![E_1]\!] \zeta_1), \grave{\rho}, \upsilon\rangle\rangle = true$, which is tantamount to asserting that E_0E_1 satisfies the equation $c\langle \mathcal{E}[\![E_0E_1]\!] \acute{\rho}\kappa, \langle \mathcal{E}[\![E_0E_1]\!] \zeta_0, \grave{\rho}, \upsilon\rangle\rangle = true$. Because this equation is valid whenever $k\langle \kappa, \langle \zeta_0, \grave{\rho}, \upsilon\rangle\rangle \wedge u\hat{\rho} \wedge rent[\![E_0E_1]\!] \acute{\rho} = true$, in fact $E[\![E_0E_1]\!] = true$.⊳

We shall treat the remaining parts of the structural induction in a more cursory manner than the foregoing. Indeed we shall omit many of them entirely, since making only minor changes to the proof of 4.3.2, for instance, would allow us to verify that $F[\![\mathsf{fn}()E]\!] = true$ and $F[\![\mathsf{fn}I.E]\!] = true$ when $E[\![E]\!] = true$.

4.3.2. Lemma.

If E is a Sal expression such that $E[\![E]\!]=true$ then $F[\![\mathrm{fnI..E}]\!]=true$.

◂When Φ is an abstraction we wish to know that $F[\![\Phi]\!]=true$ in order that we may verify that $E[\![\Phi]\!]=true$. To prove that Φ satisfies the equation $F[\![\Phi]\!]=true$ it is sufficient to demonstrate that if $\hat{\rho}$ is any pair of environments having $u\hat{\rho}\wedge rent[\![\Phi]\!]\acute{\rho}=true$ then $f\langle\mathfrak{F}[\![\Phi]\!]\acute{\rho},\mathfrak{F}[\![\Phi]\!](rend[\![\Phi]\!]\grave{\rho})\rangle=true$. The equations for the predicates given in 4.2.3 indicate that this can be done by confirming that whenever $\hat{\varepsilon}$, $\hat{\sigma}$ and $\langle\kappa_0,\langle\zeta_0,\grave{\rho},\upsilon\rangle\rangle$ are chosen in such a manner that $k\langle\kappa_0,\langle\zeta_0,\grave{\rho}_0,\upsilon\rangle\rangle\wedge e\hat{\varepsilon}\wedge s\hat{\sigma}=true$ then

$a\langle\mathfrak{F}[\![\Phi]\!]\acute{\rho}\acute{\varepsilon}\kappa_0\acute{\sigma},(\mathfrak{F}[\![\Phi]\!](rend[\![\Phi]\!]\grave{\rho})\downarrow1)\zeta_0(divert\grave{\rho}_0(\mathfrak{F}[\![\Phi]\!](rend[\![\Phi]\!]\grave{\rho})\downarrow2))(\langle\grave{\varepsilon}\rangle\S\upsilon)\grave{\sigma}\rangle=true$.

If Φ is fnI..E this involves showing that $a\langle rv\kappa_1\acute{\varepsilon}\acute{\sigma},sv\zeta_1\grave{\rho}_1(\langle\grave{\varepsilon}\rangle\S\upsilon)\grave{\sigma}\rangle=true$ where $\kappa_1=\lambda\varepsilon.\mathcal{E}[\![E]\!]\acute{\rho}[\varepsilon/I]\kappa_0$, $\zeta_1=\lambda\rho\upsilon\sigma.\mathcal{E}[\![E]\!](\zeta_0\circ chop[\![IE]\!])\rho[\upsilon\downarrow1/I](\upsilon\dagger1)\sigma$ and $\grave{\rho}_1=divert\grave{\rho}_0(rend[\![\mathrm{fnI..E}]\!]\grave{\rho})$.

Setting $\hat{\beta}=\langle(\acute{\varepsilon}\,E\,L\to hold(\acute{\varepsilon}|L)\acute{\sigma},\acute{\varepsilon}),(\grave{\varepsilon}\,E\,L\to hold(\grave{\varepsilon}|L)\grave{\sigma},\grave{\varepsilon})\rangle$ provides $\hat{\beta}$, for which $v\hat{\beta}=true$ (because $e\hat{\varepsilon}\wedge s\hat{\sigma}=true$) and for which $\langle rv\kappa_1\acute{\varepsilon}\acute{\sigma},sv\zeta_1\grave{\rho}_1(\langle\grave{\varepsilon}\rangle\S\upsilon)\grave{\sigma}\rangle$ is $\langle\kappa_1\acute{\beta}\acute{\sigma},\zeta_1\grave{\rho}_1(\langle\grave{\beta}\rangle\S\upsilon)\grave{\sigma}\rangle$, $\langle\bot,\bot\rangle$ or $\langle\top,\top\rangle$. In view of the assumption that $a\langle\bot,\bot\rangle=true$ and $a\langle\top,\top\rangle=true$ and the knowledge that, according to 3.5.6, $\mathcal{E}[\![E]\!]=\mathcal{E}[\![E]\!]\circ rend[\![E]\!]$ in standard semantics, it is now necessary only to establish that

$a\langle\mathcal{E}[\![E]\!](rend[\![E]\!](\acute{\rho}[\acute{\beta}/I]))\kappa_0\acute{\sigma},\mathcal{E}[\![E]\!](\zeta_0\circ chop[\![IE]\!])\grave{\rho}_1[\grave{\beta}/I]\upsilon\grave{\sigma}\rangle=true$. However, $u\langle rend[\![E]\!](\acute{\rho}[\acute{\beta}/I]),\grave{\rho}_1[\grave{\beta}/I]\rangle\wedge rent(rend[\![E]\!](\acute{\rho}[\acute{\beta}/I]))=true$ since $u\hat{\rho}\wedge rent[\![\mathrm{fnI..E}]\!]\acute{\rho}=true$ and $v\hat{\beta}=true$; moreover as $rent[\![\mathrm{fnI..E}]\!]\grave{\rho}=true$

$$
\begin{aligned}
k\langle\kappa_0,\langle\zeta_0\circ chop[\![IE]\!],\grave{\rho}_1[\grave{\beta}/I],\upsilon\rangle\rangle &=(e\to s\to a)\langle\kappa_0,(\lambda\varepsilon.(\zeta_0\circ chop[\![IE]\!])(\grave{\rho}_1[\grave{\beta}/I])(\langle\varepsilon\rangle\S\upsilon))\rangle\\
&=(e\to s\to a)\langle\kappa_0,(\lambda\varepsilon.\zeta_0\grave{\rho}_0(\langle\varepsilon\rangle\S\upsilon))\rangle\\
&=k\langle\kappa_0,\langle\zeta_0,\grave{\rho}_0,\upsilon\rangle\rangle .
\end{aligned}
$$

As $k\langle\kappa_0,\langle\zeta_0,\grave{\rho}_0,\upsilon\rangle\rangle=true$, from the fact that $E[\![E]\!]=true$ it follows that $a\langle\mathcal{E}[\![E]\!](rend[\![E]\!](\acute{\rho}[\acute{\beta}/I]))\kappa_0\acute{\sigma},\mathcal{E}[\![E]\!](\zeta_0\circ chop[\![IE]\!])\grave{\rho}_1[\grave{\beta}/I]\upsilon\grave{\sigma}\rangle=true$ and therefore that $a\langle rv\kappa_1\acute{\varepsilon}\acute{\sigma},sv\zeta_1\grave{\rho}_1(\langle\grave{\varepsilon}\rangle\S\upsilon)\grave{\sigma}\rangle=true$.

The generality of this last equation ensures that $F[\![\mathrm{fnI..E}]\!]=true$.▸

4.3.3. Lemma.

If E is a Sal expression such that $\mathcal{E}[\![\mathrm{E}]\!]=true$ then $\mathcal{S}[\![\mathbf{res}\ \mathrm{E}]\!]=true$.

⊲The argument follows a pattern which should by now be becoming familiar. If Σ is any sequencer the definitions in 4.2.5 indicate that to confirm that $\mathcal{S}[\![\Sigma]\!]=true$ it is enough to prove that if $\hat{\rho}$ is any pair of environments for which $u\hat{\rho}\wedge rent[\![\Sigma]\!]\acute{\rho}=true$ and if υ is any stack then $c\langle\mathfrak{S}[\![\Sigma]\!]\acute{\rho},\langle\mathfrak{S}[\![\Sigma]\!],\grave{\rho},\upsilon\rangle\rangle=true$. When Σ is **res** E and $\mathcal{E}[\![\mathrm{E}]\!]=true$ the appendices show that this equation can be established by proving that $k\langle\kappa,\langle\zeta,\grave{\rho},\upsilon\rangle\rangle=true$ where $\kappa=\acute{\rho}[\![\mathbf{res}]\!]\downarrow 1$ and

$\zeta=\lambda\rho\upsilon\sigma.((\#\rho[\![\mathbf{res}]\!]>0)\rightarrow(\rho[\![\mathbf{res}]\!]\downarrow 1\downarrow 1)(\rho[\![\mathbf{res}]\!]\downarrow 1\downarrow 2)(\langle\upsilon\downarrow 1\rangle\,\S\,\rho[\![\mathbf{res}]\!]\downarrow 1\downarrow 3)\sigma,wrong\sigma)$.

The knowledge that $u\hat{\rho}\wedge rent[\![\mathbf{res}\ \mathrm{E}]\!]\acute{\rho}=true$ ensures not only that $\#\acute{\rho}[\![\mathbf{res}]\!]>0$ and that $\#\grave{\rho}[\![\mathbf{res}]\!]>0$ but that $k\langle\acute{\rho}[\![\mathbf{res}]\!]\downarrow 1,\grave{\rho}[\![\mathbf{res}]\!]\downarrow 1\rangle=true$. Moreover $\lambda\varepsilon.\zeta\grave{\rho}(\langle\varepsilon\rangle\,\S\,\upsilon)=\lambda\varepsilon.(\grave{\rho}[\![\mathbf{res}]\!]\downarrow 1\downarrow 1)(\grave{\rho}[\![\mathbf{res}]\!]\downarrow 1\downarrow 2)(\langle\varepsilon\rangle\,\S\,\grave{\rho}[\![\mathbf{res}]\!]\downarrow 1\downarrow 3)$, so actually

$$\begin{aligned}k\langle\kappa,\langle\zeta,\grave{\rho},\upsilon\rangle\rangle &=(e\rightarrow s\rightarrow a)\langle\kappa,(\lambda\varepsilon.\zeta\grave{\rho}(\langle\varepsilon\rangle\,\S\,\upsilon))\rangle\\ &=(e\rightarrow s\rightarrow a)\langle\kappa,(\lambda\varepsilon.(\grave{\rho}[\![\mathbf{res}]\!]\downarrow 1\downarrow 1)(\grave{\rho}[\![\mathbf{res}]\!]\downarrow 1\downarrow 2)(\langle\varepsilon\rangle\,\S\,\grave{\rho}[\![\mathbf{res}]\!]\downarrow 1\downarrow 3))\rangle\\ &=k\langle\kappa,\grave{\rho}[\![\mathbf{res}]\!]\downarrow 1\rangle,\end{aligned}$$

and $k\langle\kappa,\langle\zeta,\grave{\rho},\upsilon\rangle\rangle=true$. Consequently $c\langle\mathfrak{S}[\![\mathbf{res}\ \mathrm{E}]\!]\rho,\langle\mathfrak{S}[\![\mathbf{res}\ \mathrm{E}]\!],\grave{\rho},\upsilon\rangle\rangle=true$ for every $\hat{\rho}$ having $u\hat{\rho}\wedge rent[\![\mathbf{res}\ \mathrm{E}]\!]\acute{\rho}=true$ and for every υ; more briefly, $\mathcal{S}[\![\mathbf{res}\ \mathrm{E}]\!]=true$.⊳

This result and the corresponding result for **goto** E (which can be established in a very similar manner) justify the assertion in 4.1.3 that instead of taking $\mathfrak{E}[\![\Sigma]\!]$ and $\mathfrak{G}[\![\Sigma]\!]$ to be $\lambda\zeta.\mathfrak{S}[\![\Sigma]\!]$ in store semantics we could let them be $\lambda\zeta\rho\upsilon\sigma.\mathfrak{S}[\![\Sigma]\!](rend[\![\Sigma]\!]\rho)\langle\rangle\sigma$. Furthermore these results demonstrate that the continuations used in standard semantics are abstract versions of label entry points which preserve the stacks present at the times that the labels are set.

4.3.4. Lemma.

If Δ_0 and Δ_1 are Sal declarations such that $D[\![\Delta_0]\!] \wedge T[\![\Delta_1]\!] = true$ then $T[\![\Delta_0 \text{ within } \Delta_1]\!] = true$.

◁Let Δ be Δ_0 within Δ_1 and choose any $\hat{\rho}_0$ for which $u\hat{\rho}_0 \wedge torn[\![\Delta]\!]\acute{\rho}_0 = true$. Suppose that χ, ζ_0 and υ are selected in such a way that $c\langle \chi\acute{\rho}_1, \langle \zeta_0, \grave{\rho}_1, \upsilon\rangle\rangle = true$ for each $\hat{\rho}_1$ having $u\hat{\rho}_1 \wedge knit[\![\Delta]\!]\hat{\rho}_1\hat{\rho}_0 = true$; it is enough to show that $c\langle \mathfrak{T}[\![\Delta]\!]\acute{\rho}_0\chi, \langle \mathfrak{T}[\![\Delta]\!]\zeta_0, \grave{\rho}_0, \upsilon\rangle\rangle = true$.

When $\zeta_1 = \zeta_0 \circ trim[\![\Delta_0]\!][\![\Delta_1]\!]$, $\mathfrak{T}[\![\Delta]\!]\zeta_0 = \mathfrak{D}[\![\Delta_0]\!](\mathfrak{T}[\![\Delta_1]\!]\zeta_1)$; hence because $D[\![\Delta_0]\!] = true$ and $u\hat{\rho}_0 \wedge rent[\![\Delta_0]\!]\acute{\rho}_0 = true$ the desired result can be established by proving that

$c\langle (\lambda\rho.\mathfrak{T}[\![\Delta_1]\!](divert\acute{\rho}_0\rho)\chi)\acute{\rho}_2, \langle \mathfrak{T}[\![\Delta_1]\!]\zeta_1, \grave{\rho}_2, \upsilon\rangle\rangle = true$ for each $\hat{\rho}_2$ subject to the equation $u\hat{\rho}_2 \wedge knit[\![\Delta_0]\!]\hat{\rho}_2\hat{\rho}_0 = true$. For any such $\hat{\rho}_2$, setting $\hat{\rho}_3 = \langle divert\acute{\rho}_0\acute{\rho}_2, \grave{\rho}_2\rangle$ yields a pair, $\hat{\rho}_3$, for which $u\hat{\rho}_3 \wedge torn[\![\Delta_1]\!]\acute{\rho}_3 = true$. Consequently the assumption that $T[\![\Delta_1]\!] = true$ ensures that $c\langle \mathfrak{T}[\![\Delta_1]\!]\acute{\rho}_3\chi, \langle \mathfrak{T}[\![\Delta_1]\!]\zeta_1, \grave{\rho}_3, \upsilon\rangle\rangle = true$ provided that $c\langle \chi\acute{\rho}_4, \langle \zeta_1, \grave{\rho}_4, \upsilon\rangle\rangle = true$ whenever $\hat{\rho}_4$ is formed in such a way that $u\hat{\rho}_4 \wedge knit[\![\Delta_1]\!]\hat{\rho}_4\hat{\rho}_3 = true$.

Given any pair $\hat{\rho}_4$ for which $u\hat{\rho}_4 \wedge knit[\![\Delta_1]\!]\hat{\rho}_4\hat{\rho}_3 = true$, writing $\hat{\rho}_5 = \langle \acute{\rho}_4, trim[\![\Delta_0]\!][\![\Delta_1]\!]\grave{\rho}_4\rangle$ provides a pair, $\hat{\rho}_5$, having $\zeta_1\grave{\rho}_4 = \zeta_0\grave{\rho}_5$ (and therefore having $c\langle \chi\acute{\rho}_4, \langle \zeta_1, \grave{\rho}_4, \upsilon\rangle\rangle = c\langle \chi\acute{\rho}_5, \langle \zeta_0, \grave{\rho}_5, \upsilon\rangle\rangle$). Moreover, in accordance with the definitions in 4.1.4,

$$\begin{aligned}
\grave{\rho}_5 &= trim[\![\Delta_0]\!][\![\Delta_1]\!]\grave{\rho}_4 \\
&= divert(clip[\![\Delta_0]\!](clip[\![\Delta_1]\!]\grave{\rho}_4))(slim[\![\Delta_1]\!]\grave{\rho}_4) \\
&= divert(clip[\![\Delta_0]\!](clip[\![\Delta_1]\!](divert\grave{\rho}_3(slim[\![\Delta_1]\!]\grave{\rho}_4))))(slim[\![\Delta_1]\!]\grave{\rho}_4) \\
&= divert(clip[\![\Delta_0]\!]\grave{\rho}_3)(slim[\![\Delta_1]\!]\grave{\rho}_4) \\
&= divert(clip[\![\Delta_0]\!]\grave{\rho}_2)(slim[\![\Delta_1]\!]\grave{\rho}_4) \\
&= divert(clip[\![\Delta_0]\!](divert\grave{\rho}_0(slim[\![\Delta_0]\!]\grave{\rho}_2)))(slim[\![\Delta_1]\!]\grave{\rho}_4) \\
&= divert\grave{\rho}_0(slim[\![\Delta_1]\!]\grave{\rho}_4),
\end{aligned}$$

because $\#\grave{\rho}_4[\![I]\!] \geq \#\acute{\rho}_4[\![I]\!]$ and $\#\acute{\rho}_4[\![I]\!] > 0$ when $I \in \mathfrak{I}[\![\Delta_1]\!] \S \mathfrak{H}[\![\Delta_1]\!]$ while $\#\grave{\rho}_2[\![I]\!] \geq \#\acute{\rho}_2[\![I]\!]$ and $\#\acute{\rho}_2[\![I]\!] > 0$ when $I \in \mathfrak{I}[\![\Delta_0]\!] \S \mathfrak{H}[\![\Delta_0]\!]$. Since $\mathfrak{I}[\![\Delta]\!] = \mathfrak{I}[\![\Delta_1]\!]$ and $\mathfrak{H}[\![\Delta]\!] = \mathfrak{H}[\![\Delta_1]\!]$, $\acute{\rho}_5 = slim[\![\Delta]\!]\acute{\rho}_5$ and $\grave{\rho}_5 = divert\grave{\rho}_0(slim[\![\Delta]\!]\grave{\rho}_5)$. The knowledge that

$u\hat{\rho}_4 \wedge knit[\![\Delta_1]\!]\hat{\rho}_4\hat{\rho}_3 = true$ now reveals that $u\hat{\rho}_5 \wedge knit[\![\Delta]\!]\hat{\rho}_5\hat{\rho}_0 = true$, and this fact in turn implies that $c\langle\chi\acute{\rho}_5,\langle\zeta_0,\grave{\rho}_5,\upsilon\rangle\rangle = true$.

Tracing back through the argument shows successively that $c\langle\chi\acute{\rho}_4,\langle\zeta_1,\grave{\rho}_4,\upsilon\rangle\rangle = true$, that $c\langle\mathcal{T}[\![\Delta_1]\!]\acute{\rho}_3\chi,\langle\mathcal{T}[\![\Delta_1]\!]\zeta_1,\grave{\rho}_3,\upsilon\rangle\rangle = true$, that $c\langle\mathcal{D}[\![\Delta_0]\!]\acute{\rho}_0(\lambda\rho.\mathcal{T}[\![\Delta_1]\!](divert\acute{\rho}_0\rho)\chi),\langle\mathcal{D}[\![\Delta_0]\!](\mathcal{T}[\![\Delta_1]\!]\zeta_1),\grave{\rho}_0,\upsilon\rangle\rangle = true$ and that $c\langle\mathcal{T}[\![\Delta]\!]\acute{\rho}_0\chi,\langle\mathcal{T}[\![\Delta]\!]\zeta_0,\grave{\rho}_0,\upsilon\rangle\rangle = true$. As $\hat{\rho}_0$, χ, ζ_0 and υ may be any entities satisfying the conditions imposed above, it follows from the definitions in 4.2.5 that $T[\![\Delta]\!] = true$.$\triangleright$

4.3.5. Lemma.

If Γ is a Sal command such that $C[\![\Gamma]\!]\wedge P[\![\Gamma]\!]\wedge Q[\![\Gamma]\!]=true$ then $G[\![\text{block }\Gamma]\!]=true$.

⊲If Θ is any block, to prove that $G[\![\Theta]\!]=true$ it is enough to verify that, whenever $c\langle\theta,\langle\zeta_0,\grave{\rho}_0,\upsilon\rangle\rangle\wedge u\hat{\rho}_0\wedge rent[\![\Theta]\!]\acute{\rho}_0=true$, $c\langle\mathfrak{G}[\![\Theta]\!]\acute{\rho}_0\theta,\langle\mathfrak{G}[\![\Theta]\!]\zeta_0,\grave{\rho}_0,\upsilon\rangle\rangle=true$ (or $(s\rightarrow a)\langle\mathfrak{G}[\![\Theta]\!]\acute{\rho}_0\theta,\mathfrak{G}[\![\Theta]\!]\zeta_0\grave{\rho}_0\upsilon\rangle=true$). In the situation of immediate concern Θ is block Γ where $C[\![\Gamma]\!]=true$; however, according to the semantic equations given in appendix 1 and appendix 2, there are entities $\acute{\psi}_0$ and $\grave{\psi}_0$ (belonging to the versions of $L^*\rightarrow C$ appropriate to standard semantics and store semantics respectively) such that $\langle\mathfrak{G}[\![\text{block }\Gamma]\!]\acute{\rho}_0\theta,\mathfrak{G}[\![\text{block }\Gamma]\!]\zeta_1\grave{\rho}_0\upsilon\rangle$ is really $\langle tie\acute{\psi}_0(\#\mathcal{J}[\![\Gamma]\!]),tie\grave{\psi}_0(\#\mathcal{J}[\![\Gamma]\!])\rangle$, where the functions called *tie* are those suggested in 3.3.4 and 4.1.4. To show that $c\langle\mathfrak{G}[\![\text{block }\Gamma]\!]\acute{\rho}_0\theta,\langle\mathfrak{G}[\![\text{block }\Gamma]\!]\zeta_0,\grave{\rho}_0,\upsilon\rangle\rangle=true$ it is therefore enough to prove that $(s\rightarrow a)\langle tie\acute{\psi}_0(\#\mathcal{J}[\![\Gamma]\!]),tie\grave{\psi}_0(\#\mathcal{J}[\![\Gamma]\!])\rangle=true$. How to do this will now be sketched.

With the aid of induction it can be shown that the two versions of *tie* are such that if $\hat{\sigma}_0$ is any pair of stores for which $s\hat{\sigma}_0=true$ and if ν is any integer for which $\nu\geq 0$ then $\langle(\lambda\acute{\psi}.tie\acute{\psi}\nu\acute{\sigma}_0),(\lambda\grave{\psi}.tie\grave{\psi}\nu\grave{\sigma}_0)\rangle$ takes one of four forms – $\langle(\lambda\acute{\psi}.\bot),(\lambda\grave{\psi}.\bot)\rangle$, $\langle(\lambda\acute{\psi}.\top),(\lambda\grave{\psi}.\top)\rangle$, $\langle(\lambda\acute{\psi}.wrong\acute{\sigma}_1),(\lambda\grave{\psi}.wrong\grave{\sigma}_1)\rangle$ (for some $\hat{\sigma}_1$ having $s\hat{\sigma}_1=true$) and $\langle(\lambda\acute{\psi}.\acute{\psi}\acute{\alpha}^*\acute{\sigma}_1),(\lambda\grave{\psi}.\grave{\psi}\grave{\alpha}^*\grave{\sigma}_1)\rangle$ (for some $\hat{\sigma}_1$, $\acute{\alpha}^*$ and $\grave{\alpha}^*$ having $s\hat{\sigma}_1=true$, $l^*\langle\acute{\alpha}^*,\grave{\alpha}^*\rangle=true$ and $\#\acute{\alpha}^*=\nu$). The induction can rely either on the fact that each version of *tie* is the least fixed point of a function in a suitable domain (structured as $((L^*\rightarrow C)\rightarrow N\rightarrow C)\rightarrow((L^*\rightarrow C)\rightarrow N\rightarrow C))$ or on arithmetic induction; in both cases it depends on the knowledge that $new\acute{\sigma}_0=new\grave{\sigma}_0$ and (if $new\acute{\sigma}_0\in L$) $l\langle new\acute{\sigma}_0|L,new\grave{\sigma}_0|L\rangle=true$ whenever $s\hat{\sigma}_0=true$. The appropriate inductive arguments will be left to the reader.

The remark at the beginning of the previous paragraph indicates that, if $\hat{\sigma}_0$ is such that $s\hat{\sigma}_0=true$ then $a\langle\acute{\psi}_0(\#\mathcal{J}[\![\Gamma]\!])\acute{\sigma}_0,\grave{\psi}_0(\#\mathcal{J}[\![\Gamma]\!])\grave{\sigma}_0\rangle$ is

$a\langle\bot,\bot\rangle$, $a\langle\top,\top\rangle$, $a\langle wrong\acute{\sigma}_1, wrong\grave{\sigma}_1\rangle$ (for some $\hat{\sigma}_1$ having $s\hat{\sigma}_1=true$) or $a\langle\psi_0\acute{\alpha}^*\acute{\sigma}_1,\grave{\psi}_0\grave{\alpha}^*\grave{\sigma}_1\rangle$ (for some $\hat{\sigma}_1$, $\acute{\alpha}^*$ and $\grave{\alpha}^*$ having $s\hat{\sigma}_1=true$, $l^*\langle\acute{\alpha}^*,\grave{\alpha}^*\rangle=true$ and $\#\acute{\alpha}^*=\#\mathcal{J}[\![\Gamma]\!]$). The assumptions made in 4.2.5 will therefore ensure that $a\langle tie\acute{\psi}_0(\#\mathcal{J}[\![\Gamma]\!])\acute{\sigma}_0, tie\grave{\psi}_0(\#\mathcal{J}[\![\Gamma]\!])\grave{\sigma}_0\rangle=true$ provided that $a\langle\acute{\psi}_0\acute{\alpha}^*\acute{\sigma}_1,\grave{\psi}_0\grave{\alpha}^*\grave{\sigma}_1\rangle=true$ for any $\hat{\sigma}_1$, $\acute{\alpha}^*$ and $\grave{\alpha}^*$ having $s\hat{\sigma}_1=true$, $l^*\langle\acute{\alpha}^*,\grave{\alpha}^*\rangle=true$ and $\#\acute{\alpha}^*=\#\mathcal{J}[\![\Gamma]\!]$; the validity of this proviso will be established below for an arbitrary choice of $\hat{\sigma}_1$, $\acute{\alpha}^*$ and $\grave{\alpha}^*$.

When $\hat{\rho}_1=\langle\acute{\rho}_0[\acute{\alpha}^*/\mathcal{J}[\![\Gamma]\!]],\grave{\rho}_0[\grave{\alpha}^*/\mathcal{J}[\![\Gamma]\!]]\rangle$ it is plain that $u\hat{\rho}_1=true$, since $u\hat{\rho}_0\wedge l^*\langle\acute{\alpha}^*,\grave{\alpha}^*\rangle=true$. Appeals to the properties of fix given in 2.3.2 reveal that if

$\hat{\rho}_2=\langle fix(\lambda\acute{\rho}.\acute{\rho}_1[\mathcal{Q}[\![\Gamma]\!]\acute{\rho}\theta/\mathcal{K}[\![\Gamma]\!]]), fix(\lambda\grave{\rho}.\grave{\rho}_1[\mathcal{Q}[\![\Gamma]\!]\zeta_1\grave{\rho}\upsilon/\mathcal{K}[\![\Gamma]\!]])\rangle$ and $\zeta_1=\zeta_0\circ clip[\![\Gamma]\!]$ then $\hat{\rho}_1=\langle\acute{\rho}_2[fix\acute{\phi}/\mathcal{K}[\![\Gamma]\!]],\grave{\rho}_2[fix\grave{\phi}/\mathcal{K}[\![\Gamma]\!]]\rangle$, where $\hat{\phi}=\langle(\lambda\acute{\delta}^*.\mathcal{Q}[\![\Gamma]\!]\acute{\rho}_1[\acute{\delta}^*/\mathcal{K}[\![\Gamma]\!]]\theta),(\lambda\grave{\delta}^*.\mathcal{Q}[\![\Gamma]\!]\zeta_1\grave{\rho}_1[\grave{\delta}^*/\mathcal{K}[\![\Gamma]\!]])\rangle$. Hence to show that $u\hat{\rho}_2=true$ it is sufficient to prove that $d^*\langle fix\acute{\phi},fix\grave{\phi}\rangle=true$. To this end suppose that $\acute{\delta}^*$ and $\grave{\delta}^*$ are lists of denoted values having $d^*\langle\acute{\delta}^*,\grave{\delta}^*\rangle=true$ and $\#\acute{\delta}^*=\#\mathcal{K}[\![\Gamma]\!]$; evidently $u\langle\acute{\rho}_1[\acute{\delta}^*/\mathcal{K}[\![\Gamma]\!]],\grave{\rho}_1[\grave{\delta}^*/\mathcal{K}[\![\Gamma]\!]]\rangle=true$ and $rent[\![\Gamma]\!]\acute{\rho}_1[\acute{\delta}^*/\mathcal{K}[\![\Gamma]\!]]=true$ whilst

$$\begin{aligned}c\langle\theta,\langle\zeta_1,\grave{\rho}_1[\grave{\delta}^*/\mathcal{K}[\![\Gamma]\!]],\upsilon\rangle\rangle &=(s\to a)\langle\theta,\zeta_1\grave{\rho}_1[\grave{\delta}^*/\mathcal{K}[\![\Gamma]\!]]\upsilon\rangle\\ &=(s\to a)\langle\theta,\zeta_0\grave{\rho}_0\upsilon\rangle\\ &=c\langle\theta,\langle\zeta_0,\grave{\rho}_0,\upsilon\rangle\rangle,\end{aligned}$$

so, because $Q[\![\Gamma]\!]=true$,

$c^*\langle\mathcal{Q}[\![\Gamma]\!]\acute{\rho}_1[\acute{\delta}^*/\mathcal{K}[\![\Gamma]\!]]\theta,\mathcal{Q}[\![\Gamma]\!]\grave{\zeta}_1\grave{\rho}_1[\grave{\delta}^*/\mathcal{K}[\![\Gamma]\!]]\upsilon\rangle=true$ (and indeed $d^*\langle\acute{\phi}\acute{\delta}^*,\grave{\phi}\grave{\delta}^*\rangle=true$ and $\#\acute{\phi}\acute{\delta}^*=\#\mathcal{K}[\![\Gamma]\!]$). As $d\langle\bot,\bot\rangle=true$ and as d^* is inclusive (in the sense described in 2.3.1) $d^*\langle fix\acute{\phi},fix\grave{\phi}\rangle=true$. Consequently $u\hat{\rho}_2=true$; moreover $rent[\![\Gamma]\!]\acute{\rho}_2=true$.

Since $P[\![\Gamma]\!]=true$, reasoning like that above ensures that $c^*\langle\mathcal{P}[\![\Gamma]\!]\acute{\rho}_2\theta,\mathcal{P}[\![\Gamma]\!]\zeta_1\grave{\rho}_2\upsilon\rangle=true$, so $v^*\langle\mathcal{P}[\![\Gamma]\!]\acute{\rho}_2\theta,\mathcal{P}[\![\Gamma]\!]\zeta_1\grave{\rho}_2\upsilon\rangle=true$. In conjunction with the equations $s\hat{\sigma}_1=true$ and $l^*\langle\acute{\alpha}^*,\grave{\alpha}^*\rangle=true$ this establishes that $s\hat{\sigma}_2=true$ where

$\hat{\sigma}_2=\langle updates\acute{\alpha}^*(\mathcal{P}[\![\Gamma]\!]\acute{\rho}_2\theta)\acute{\sigma}_1, updates\grave{\alpha}^*(\mathcal{P}[\![\Gamma]\!]\zeta_1\grave{\rho}_2\upsilon)\grave{\sigma}_1\rangle$. Indeed because $C[\![\Gamma]\!]=true$ it is even the case that $c\langle\mathcal{C}[\![\Gamma]\!]\acute{\rho}_2\theta,\langle\mathcal{C}[\![\Gamma]\!]\zeta_1,\grave{\rho}_2,\upsilon\rangle\rangle=true$ and

$a\langle \mathcal{C}[\![\Gamma]\!]\acute{\rho}_2\theta\acute{\sigma}_2, \mathcal{C}[\![\Gamma]\!]\zeta_1\grave{\rho}_2\upsilon\grave{\sigma}_2\rangle = true$. However, according to the semantic equations $\langle \mathcal{C}[\![\Gamma]\!]\acute{\rho}_2\theta\acute{\sigma}_2, \mathcal{C}[\![\Gamma]\!]\zeta_1\grave{\rho}_2\upsilon\grave{\sigma}_2\rangle$ is actually $\langle \phi_0\acute{\alpha}*\acute{\sigma}_1, \phi_0\grave{\alpha}*\grave{\sigma}_1\rangle$, so, tracing back through the argument,
$a\langle tie\acute{\psi}_0(\#\mathcal{J}[\![\Gamma]\!])\acute{\sigma}_0, tie\grave{\psi}_0(\#\mathcal{J}[\![\Gamma]\!])\grave{\sigma}_0\rangle = true$ whenever $s\hat{\sigma}_0 = true$.▷

Now that $(s \to a)\langle tie\acute{\psi}_0(\#\mathcal{J}[\![\Gamma]\!]), tie\grave{\psi}_0(\#\mathcal{J}[\![\Gamma]\!])\rangle = true$ it is clear that $c\langle \mathcal{G}[\![\text{block } \Gamma]\!]\acute{\rho}_0\theta, \langle \mathcal{G}[\![\text{block } \Gamma]\!]\zeta_0, \grave{\rho}_0, \upsilon\rangle\rangle = true$. This equation is valid whenever $c\langle \theta, \langle \zeta_0, \grave{\rho}_0, \upsilon\rangle\rangle \wedge u\hat{\rho}_0 \wedge rent[\![\text{block } \Gamma]\!]\acute{\rho}_0 = true$, so $G[\![\text{block } \Gamma]\!] = true$.

The proof above resembles the one which establishes that, for any declaration Δ, $D[\![\text{rec } \Delta]\!] = true$ when $T[\![\Delta]\!] = true$. The result about the two versions of *tie* which is used in it is a generalization of the equation $((l^* \to s \to a) \to n \to (s \to a))\langle tie, tie\rangle = true$ where n is $\lambda\hat{\nu}.(\acute{\nu} \equiv \grave{\nu})$ (the test for equality between integers); this equation can naturally be justified by induction.

4.3.6. Lemma.

If E is a Sal expression and Γ is a Sal command such that $R[\![E]\!] \wedge C[\![\Gamma]\!] = true$ then $C[\![\text{while E do }\Gamma]\!] = true$.

⋖Select any pair $\hat{\rho}$ for which $u\hat{\rho} \wedge rent[\![\text{while E do }\Gamma]\!]\acute{\rho} = true$, together with any θ_0, ζ_0 and υ for which $c\langle \theta_0, \langle \zeta_0, \grave{\rho}, \upsilon\rangle\rangle = true$. Let $\psi = \lambda\theta.\mathfrak{R}[\![E]\!]\acute{\rho}(test\langle \mathfrak{C}[\![\Gamma]\!]\acute{\rho}\theta, \theta_0\rangle)$ and $\xi = \lambda\zeta.\mathfrak{R}[\![E]\!](\lambda\rho\upsilon\sigma.test\langle \mathfrak{C}[\![\Gamma]\!]\zeta\rho(\upsilon\dagger 1), \zeta_0\rho(\upsilon\dagger 1)\rangle(\upsilon\downarrow 1)\sigma)$, so that it is enough to confirm that $c\langle fix\psi, \langle fix\xi, \grave{\rho}, \upsilon\rangle\rangle = true$ by applying the induction rule provided in 2.3.2.

Introduce any θ_1 and ζ_1 for which $c\langle \theta_1, \langle \zeta_1, \grave{\rho}, \upsilon\rangle\rangle = true$ and set $\zeta_2 = \lambda\rho\upsilon\sigma.test\langle \mathfrak{C}[\![\Gamma]\!]\zeta_1\rho(\upsilon\dagger 1), \zeta_0\rho(\upsilon\dagger 1)\rangle(\upsilon\downarrow 1)\sigma$; because $R[\![E]\!] = true$ and $u\hat{\rho} \wedge rent[\![E]\!]\acute{\rho} = true$, in order to show that $c\langle \psi\theta_1, \langle \xi\zeta_1, \grave{\rho}, \upsilon\rangle\rangle = true$ it suffices to verify that $k\langle test\langle \mathfrak{C}[\![\Gamma]\!]\acute{\rho}\theta_1, \theta_0\rangle, \langle \zeta_2, \grave{\rho}, \upsilon\rangle\rangle = true$. Accordingly, take $\hat{\varepsilon}$ to be any pair of expressed values such that $e\hat{\varepsilon} = true$. Examining the definition of $test$ given in 3.1.4 reveals that $\langle test\langle \mathfrak{C}[\![\Gamma]\!]\acute{\rho}\theta_1, \theta_0\rangle\acute{\varepsilon}, \zeta_2\grave{\rho}(\langle\grave{\varepsilon}\rangle \S \upsilon)\rangle$ can only be $\langle \mathfrak{C}[\![\Gamma]\!]\acute{\rho}\theta_1, \mathfrak{C}[\![\Gamma]\!]\zeta_1\grave{\rho}\upsilon\rangle$, $\langle \theta_0, \zeta_0\grave{\rho}\upsilon\rangle$, $\langle \bot, \bot\rangle$, $\langle \top, \top\rangle$ or $\langle wrong, wrong\rangle$, because $e = l+b+e^*+c+f$ and $b = t+n+r+h+h^*$. The assumption made in 4.2.5 (to the effect that $a\langle \bot, \bot\rangle = true$, $a\langle \top, \top\rangle = true$ and $(s\rightarrow a)\langle wrong, wrong\rangle = true$) and the fact that $C[\![\Gamma]\!] = true$ thus indicate that $a\langle test\langle \mathfrak{C}[\![\Gamma]\!]\acute{\rho}\theta_1, \theta_0\rangle\acute{\varepsilon}\acute{\sigma}, \zeta_2\grave{\rho}(\langle\grave{\varepsilon}\rangle \S \upsilon)\grave{\sigma}\rangle = true$ for every $\hat{\sigma}$ having $s\hat{\sigma} = true$. Hence $k\langle test\langle \mathfrak{C}[\![\Gamma]\!]\acute{\rho}\theta_1, \theta_0\rangle, \langle \zeta_2, \grave{\rho}, \upsilon\rangle\rangle = true$ and $c\langle \psi\theta_1, \langle \xi\zeta_1, \grave{\rho}, \upsilon\rangle\rangle = true$ provided that $c\langle \theta_1, \langle \zeta_1, \grave{\rho}, \upsilon\rangle\rangle = true$.

The insistence that $a\langle \bot, \bot\rangle = true$ implies that $c\langle \bot, \langle \bot, \grave{\rho}, \upsilon\rangle\rangle = true$, so as c is inclusive $c\langle fix\psi, \langle fix\xi, \grave{\rho}, \upsilon\rangle\rangle = true$ by virtue of the induction rule given in 2.3.2. In consequence, $c\langle \mathfrak{C}[\![\text{while E do }\Gamma]\!]\acute{\rho}\theta_0, \langle \mathfrak{C}[\![\text{while E do }\Gamma]\!]\zeta_0, \grave{\rho}, \upsilon\rangle\rangle = true$, and the arbitrary nature of the choice of $\hat{\rho}$, θ_0, ζ_0 and υ ensures that $C[\![\text{while E do }\Gamma]\!] = true$.⋗

This result clearly remains valid whatever forms are taken by the two versions of E and B so long as T is a summand of B and B is a summand of E. Were we to adopt definitions of *e* and *b* which debarred the improper values along the lines mentioned in 4.2.2 we could dispense with the requirement that $a\langle \top,\top\rangle = true$ (though not with the requirement that $a\langle \bot,\bot\rangle = true$).

4.3.7. Theorem.

Suppose that $a\langle \bot,\bot\rangle = true$, $a\langle \top,\top\rangle = true$ and $(s\to a)\langle wrong, wrong\rangle = true$ and that $new\acute{\sigma} = new\grave{\sigma}$ whenever $\hat{\sigma}$ is such that $s\hat{\sigma} = true$. Assume also that for all B, O and Ω $(k\to c)\langle \mathcal{B}[\![B]\!], (\lambda\langle\zeta,\rho,\upsilon\rangle.\langle\mathcal{B}[\![B]\!]\zeta,\rho,\upsilon\rangle)\rangle = true$, $(k\to e\to c)\langle \mathcal{O}[\![O]\!], (\lambda\langle\zeta,\rho,\upsilon\rangle.\lambda\varepsilon.\langle\mathcal{O}[\![O]\!]\zeta,\rho,\langle\varepsilon\rangle\S\upsilon\rangle)\rangle = true$ and $(k\to e\to e\to c)\langle \mathcal{W}[\![\Omega]\!], (\lambda\langle\zeta,\rho,\upsilon\rangle.\lambda\varepsilon'.\lambda\varepsilon''.\langle\mathcal{W}[\![\Omega]\!]\zeta,\rho,\langle\varepsilon''\rangle\S\langle\varepsilon'\rangle\S\upsilon\rangle)\rangle = true$. All E, Φ, Σ, Δ, Θ and Γ are such that, in terms of the predicates of 4.2.5, $E[\![E]\!]\wedge L[\![E]\!]\wedge R[\![E]\!] = true$, $F[\![\Phi]\!] = true$, $S[\![\Sigma]\!] = true$, $D[\![\Delta]\!]\wedge T[\![\Delta]\!] = true$, $G[\![\Theta]\!] = true$ and $C[\![\Gamma]\!]\wedge P[\![\Gamma]\!]\wedge Q[\![\Gamma]\!] = true$; thus the standard semantics of any Sal program is congruent with the store semantics of the same program.

◁This theorem is simply a summary of the foregoing lemmas and their unstated companions. Because no special features of Sal have been needed in the course of the argument a similar theorem holds for every other language which can be given a standard semantics.▷

4.4. Interpreters.

4.4.1. Controls.

As we have already hinted, there is a superficial resemblance between the semantic equations of appendix 2 and an evaluating mechanism which differs from that due to Landin [37] only in having no "dump". There is, however, also a profound distinction: the sorts of semantics which we have described up till now form label and procedure values from members of abstract function spaces, whereas interpreters akin to that for VDL [43] operate by manipulating texts. Thus, in an interpreter, executing an expression which happens to be an abstraction, Φ say, simply entails placing on the stack Φ (or something like it) and an environment; the body of a procedure is evaluated only when the procedure is applied, not when the corresponding abstraction is set up.

Although we can view a typical procedure value as being a pair of the form $\langle \Phi,\rho \rangle$ we cannot regard label values in quite such an attractive light. Not only must a label value include information about anonymous expressed values (as was explained in 4.1.2); it must also indicate to what point in the program the label is attached, and this point cannot be represented purely by part of the text of the block in which the label appears. The inadequacy of such a representation is shown most clearly in the case of the values associated with **res** by **val** expressions, in which the "block" does not exist since **res** labels the end of a piece of text; however, it is equally unsatisfactory to represent the destination of the label I in I:Γ by means of Γ alone, because doing so does not describe what happens when the execution of Γ comes to a conclusion. Thus we are obliged to associate with a label not a piece of a Sal block but an entity rather more like a continuation. In an interpreter this entity cannot be a continuation in a function domain such as the version of Z described in 4.1.2, but it can be a text of some sort which when executed has the effect of a continuation. The continuations used in appendix 2 are built out of functions some of which (*mv* and *sv*, for instance) have no counterparts in Sal, so we cannot hope to put together the corresponding text simply from Sal constructs, though it may well have such constructs embedded in it. We therefore require an additional language, Sap, containing not only versions of the features of Sam but also orders such as mv and sv; when they are executed these orders alter the environment, the stack and the store in simple ways that are not available explicitly in Sal.

An interpretive implementation of a language intermingles the activities of code generation and code execution which a conventional compiler separates. In our case, interpreting a Sal expression involves first decomposing the expression into a list of Sap 'orders' and then executing this list; however, the list may itself contain further Sal expressions which in turn must be decomposed before execution can proceed. The valuation $\mathscr{e}$ that converts Sal expressions into lists of Sap orders is not recursive, by contrast with the valuation to be described in 5.4.1 (where we shall discuss compilers); $\mathscr{e}[\![E_0 E_1]\!]$, for example, is $\langle \mathrm{r}\ E_0\rangle \S \langle \mathrm{e}\ E_1\rangle \S \langle \mathrm{apply}\rangle$, in which $\mathrm{r}\ E_0$ and $\mathrm{e}\ E_1$ are orders that will expand in the course of execution to yield entities resembling $\mathscr{r}[\![E_0]\!]$ and $\mathscr{e}[\![E_1]\!]$ respectively. The execution of the orders l E and r E entails expanding the expression E into short strings of orders which must then be executed; more precisely if Con is the domain of Sap 'controls' (which are simply lists of Sap orders) we expand E by defining $\mathscr{e}$, $\mathscr{l}$ and $\mathscr{r}$ on Exp→Con in such a way that $\mathscr{l}[\![E]\!]$ is $\langle \mathrm{e}\ E\rangle \S \langle \mathrm{mv}\rangle$ and $\mathscr{r}[\![E]\!]$ is $\langle \mathrm{e}\ E\rangle \S \langle \mathrm{sv}\rangle$.

Alongside $\mathscr{e}$, $\mathscr{l}$ and $\mathscr{r}$ we require valuations which are also not recursive and which convert abstractions, sequencers, declarations, blocks and commands into controls; thus we take $\mathscr{f}$ to be in Abs→Con, $\mathscr{s}$ to be in Seq→Con, $\mathscr{d}$ and $\mathscr{t}$ to be in Dec→Con, $\mathscr{g}$ to be in Blo→Con and $\mathscr{c}$ to be in Com→Con. A full account of all these functions is presented in appendix

5 together with definitions of $\mathfrak{p}$ and $\mathfrak{q}$, members of Com→Con* which collect up the controls appropriate to the labels set up in a command. Later we shall also require valuations $\mathfrak{b}$, $\mathfrak{o}$ and $\mathfrak{w}$ which we shall not describe beyond remarking that $\mathfrak{b}$ is in Bas→Con, $\mathfrak{o}$ is in Mon→Con and $\mathfrak{w}$ is in Dya→Con; more exacting restrictions will be placed on these valuations in 4.6.2 and 4.6.5.

Those Sap orders which represent Sal constructs (such as **e** E, **l** E and **r** E) can themselves be converted into Sap controls (such as $\mathfrak{e}[\![E]\!]$, $\mathfrak{l}[\![E]\!]$ and $\mathfrak{r}[\![E]\!]$) with the aid of a valuation which we shall describe in 4.4.2. These controls are crucial to our interpretive implementation of Sal and deserve to be singled out for special mention. Accordingly, when H_0 and H_1 are any Sap controls we shall say that 'H_1 is concealed in H_0' if and only if there is some integer ν such that $\#H_0 \geq \nu \geq 1$ and such that one of the following fifteen conditions holds:

(i) $H_0{\downarrow}\nu=\mathbf{b}\ B$ and $H_1=\mathfrak{b}[\![B]\!]$ for some B;

(ii) $H_0{\downarrow}\nu=\mathbf{o}\ O$ and $H_1=\mathfrak{o}[\![O]\!]$ for some O;

(iii) $H_0{\downarrow}\nu=\mathbf{w}\ \Omega$ and $H_1=\mathfrak{w}[\![\Omega]\!]$ for some Ω;

(iv) $H_0{\downarrow}\nu=\mathbf{e}\ E$ and $H_1=\mathfrak{e}[\![E]\!]$ for some E;

(v) $H_0{\downarrow}\nu=\mathbf{r}\ E$ and $H_1=\mathfrak{l}[\![E]\!]$ for some E;

(vi) $H_0{\downarrow}\nu=\mathbf{l}\ E$ and $H_1=\mathfrak{r}[\![E]\!]$ for some E;

(vii) $H_0{\downarrow}\nu=\mathbf{f}\ \Phi$ and $H_1=\mathfrak{f}[\![\Phi]\!]$ for some Φ;

(viii) $H_0{\downarrow}\nu=\mathbf{s}\ \Sigma$ and $H_1=\mathfrak{s}[\![\Sigma]\!]$ for some Σ;

(ix) $H_0{\downarrow}\nu=\mathbf{d}\ \Delta$ and $H_1=\mathfrak{d}[\![\Delta]\!]$ for some Δ;

(x) $H_0{\downarrow}\nu=\mathbf{t}\ \Delta$ and $H_1=\mathfrak{t}[\![\Delta]\!]$ for some Δ;

(xi) $H_0{\downarrow}\nu=\mathbf{g}\ \Theta$ and $H_1=\mathfrak{g}[\![\Theta]\!]$ for some Θ;

(xii) $H_0{\downarrow}\nu=\mathbf{c}\ \Gamma$ and $H_1=\mathfrak{c}[\![\Gamma]\!]$ for some Γ;

(xiii) $H_0{\downarrow}\nu=\mathbf{t}\ \langle \nu',\Delta\rangle$ and $H_1=\langle \mathbf{t}\ \Delta\rangle \S \langle \mathbf{occur}\ \mathfrak{h}[\![\Delta]\!]{\downarrow}\nu'\rangle$ for some ν' and for some Δ;

(xiv) $H_0{\downarrow}\nu=\mathbf{p}\ \langle \nu',\Gamma\rangle$ and $H_1=\mathfrak{p}[\![\Gamma]\!]{\downarrow}\nu'$ for some ν' and for some Γ;

(xv) $H_0{\downarrow}\nu=\mathbf{q}\ \langle \nu',\Gamma\rangle$ and $H_1=\mathfrak{q}[\![\Gamma]\!]{\downarrow}\nu'$ for some ν' and for some Γ.

The valuations referred to in this definition are of course those provided by appendix 5. Though the concept underlying this definition is of great importance, the definition itself will not be used much until 4.6.5.

It can be seen from appendix 5 that some members of Ord, the domain of Sap orders, take "parameters" which are numerical in nature; for instance, move 1 and pick 2, which appear in the equation for $\mathcal{e}[\![E_0?E_1!E_2]\!]$, can be viewed as the results of supplying move and pick with the parameters 1 and 2 respectively. Strictly speaking we should take these parameters to be numerals, not numbers, and we should turn these numerals into numbers only when we apply the valuations which model the execution of orders; thus move 1 and pick 2 should be replaced by move 1 and pick 2 in such equations as that for $\mathcal{e}[\![E_0?E_1!E_2]\!]$. In order to simplify our notation we shall not be scrupulously formalistic in this respect.

Before embarking on an explanation of how orders are executed we should perhaps make one point clear. We could have devised an "interpreter" which resembled not the equations of appendix 2 but those of appendix 1 in its mode of operation. However, because the continuations used in standard semantics incorporate environments and expressed values, some of the orders which would take the place of Sap orders would need to be given environments and expressed values as parameters. Those who doubt that the net effect would be considerably less elegant than the one provided by our present interpreter should examine what would become of $\mathcal{e}[\![E_0E_1]\!]$. Our methods for proving the correctness of interpreters (which will be illustrated in the results leading up to 4.6.8) have been used by Stoy [84] to verify the correctness of an "interpreter" for a language based on semantic equations akin to those in appendix 1; they have also been used [52:3.6.6] to analyse valuations which depend on neither continuations nor controls.

4.4.2. Orders.

The valuations defined in appendix 5 merely serve to expand Sal programs into Sap controls. They provide no indication of how these controls can be executed, and indeed they are almost incomprehensible in the absence of such an indication. Our next task must therefore be to introduce a valuation, $\mathcal{Z}$, which describes the execution of controls; when composed with the valuations of appendix 5 this valuation will then demonstrate how Sal can be implemented through the mediation of an interpreter.

Every control consists of a list of orders each member of which can be given a meaning more or less on its own. Consequently we can expect to define $\mathcal{Z}$ on Con in terms of a valuation $\mathcal{A}$ which takes a member of Ord as an argument. When T is in Ord $\mathcal{A}[\![T]\!]$ must show how executing T should affect the state vector; thus the set of equations for $\mathcal{A}$, which in our case is provided in appendix 11, corresponds with what is often called the 'transition function' [56] for an interpreter, whereas $\mathcal{Z}$ (which is effectively an iterated version of $\mathcal{A}$) is sometimes termed the 'evaluation function'.

When U, Y and S signify suitable domains of environments, stacks and stores, at first sight it might seem that we could take $\mathcal{A}$ to belong to $\text{Ord}\to U\to Y\to S\to(U\times Y\times S)$; then $\mathcal{A}$ would ascribe to **drop** and **turn** the values $\lambda\rho\upsilon\sigma.\langle\rho,\upsilon\dagger 1,\sigma\rangle$ and $\lambda\rho\upsilon\sigma.\langle\rho,\langle\upsilon\downarrow 2\rangle\S\langle\upsilon\downarrow 1\rangle\S\upsilon\dagger 2,\sigma\rangle$ respectively. However, such orders as **move** ν and **pick** ν are intended to bring about the skipping of some steps in the natural control path, and this is best achieved by passing a control as an argument to $\mathcal{A}[\![T]\!]$ for every T in Ord. This control, H say, indicates what will happen next during the interpretation if the execution of T does not entail making a jump. Since H is a list of orders, for every integer ν having $\#H\geq\nu\geq 0$ $H\dagger\nu$ is also a control; it shows what will happen later if the set $\{T\}\cup\{H\downarrow\nu'\,|\,\nu\geq\nu'\geq 1\}$ contains no orders giving rise to jumps. Thus to capture the effect of jumping forward along the control path we must take $\mathcal{A}$ to be in

$Ord \to Con \to U \to Y \to S \to (Con \times U \times Y \times S)$ at least, so that if $\mathcal{A}[\![T]\!][\![H]\!]\rho\upsilon\sigma$ has $H \dagger \nu$ as one component the first ν steps of the control H will be omitted. Yet even this domain is unsuitable for $\mathcal{A}$, because it offers no means of handling errors such as those that may arise in the execution of read. The simplest way to provide a treatment of errors is to let $\mathcal{A}$ be a member of $Ord \to Con \to U \to Y \to S \to (\{error\} + (Con \times U \times Y \times S))$; however, as we wish to impose a degree of uniformity on all the sorts of semantics that we consider, we shall actually regard $\mathcal{A}$ as being in $Ord \to Con \to U \to Y \to S \to (A + (Con \times U \times Y \times S))$ by using a function $wrong \in S \to A$ and a domain A. This version of A and the answer domain called A in appendix 2 can have a common overall structure (in terms of W) but may nonetheless not be identical, since the corresponding versions of W differ in ways to be described in 4.4.3.

It will be noted that as Con is a syntactic domain a typical member of it is denoted by the upper case Greek letter H in keeping with the principles enunciated in 1.1.1; to use a lower case Greek letter, such as ζ, for this purpose would be rather misleading even if it would give the equations of appendix 11 a slightly more familiar appearance. In any case, the semantic analogue of a control is not always a continuation signified by ζ but an entity which will be called a 'consecution' (and which, not unnaturally, will be denoted by η); the reason for this is to be sought in the fact that from the control H can be derived the set $\{H \dagger \nu \mid \#H \geq \nu \geq 0\}$, which comprises $1 + \#H$ controls, whilst the only continuation "derivable" from a continuation is itself. We shall discuss this point at greater length in 4.5.1.

Now that it is clear to which domain $\mathcal{A}$ belongs it can be seen that many of the equations of appendix 11 mimic simple operations on states which combine to form equations like those of appendix 2; naturally here we regard such functions as *update* as being defined on our present versions of the domains, not on those described in 4.1.5. For example, find is intended merely to arrange that *false* be put on top of the stack whilst insert has a close connection with *assign* (as is made plain by the definition of *assign* provided in 3.3.4). More interesting than these are the orders which when executed may discard part, or all, of the control supplied to them; they include not only move ν and pick ν but also jump and leap. Several orders are concerned with manipulating the environment in ways like those found in appendix 2. Because the overall structure of the environment domain remains similar to that considered in 4.1.4 we may safely continue to use such functions as *clip*, *swap* and *trim*. Thus even occur I has an obvious connection with the function *recur* introduced in 4.1.3; however an understanding of amend I (and also of t $\langle \nu,\Delta\rangle$, p $\langle \nu,\Gamma\rangle$ and q $\langle \nu,\Gamma\rangle$) must await our definition of *fold*, which will be given in 4.4.4.

Any one of the remaining Sap orders (b B, o O, w Ω, e E, l E, r E, f Φ, s Σ, d Δ, t Δ, g Θ, c Γ, t $\langle \nu,\Delta\rangle$, p $\langle \nu,\Gamma\rangle$ and q $\langle \nu,\Gamma\rangle$) will form a new Sap control when subjected to the version of $\mathcal{A}$ provided in appendix 11; according to the definition in 4.4.1, this new control may be said to be concealed in any control in which the order appears. Applying $\mathcal{A}$ to b B, o O or w Ω serves to attach this new control (which is $\mathfrak{b}[\![B]\!]$, $\mathfrak{o}[\![O]\!]$ or $\mathfrak{w}[\![\Omega]\!]$) to the front of the control supplied as an argument to $\mathcal{A}$. The orders e E, l E, r E, d Δ, t Δ, g Θ and c Γ also permit the control supplied as an argument to be extended by the appropriate controls set up by the valuations of appendix 5. The meanings accorded by $\mathcal{A}$ to f Φ and s Σ diverge from the pattern set by b B, o O and w Ω, in that executing f Φ results in the lengthening of the stack by the addition of a procedure value and executing s Σ entails replacing the control by $\mathfrak{s}[\![\Sigma]\!]$. The definition of $\mathfrak{f}[\![\Phi]\!]$ shows that we have chosen not to treat the value of a procedure Φ as a pair of the form $\langle \Phi,\rho\rangle$, despite what was proposed in 4.4.1; instead we are regarding it as a pair of the form $\langle H,\rho\rangle$ in which H is a short list of orders.

In order to execute a list of Sap orders we first execute

the initial order using the rest of the list as the control and we then proceed to execute the list of orders formed as a result of the initial execution; if the list is empty or if an error happens the process of execution must come to an immediate end. When the process finally does end we are left with either an element of $U \times Y \times S$ or a member of A; however, in practice only part of any member of $U \times Y \times S$ may be available as an answer for the programmer. To model all this we introduce $\mathit{process} \in U \to Y \to S \to A$, which is intended to extract an answer in A from a state in $U \times Y \times S$, and $\mathit{proceed} \in (Con \to U \to Y \to S \to A) \to (Con \to U \to Y \to S \to A)$. We shall say nothing about *process* for the moment, but we shall define *proceed* provisionally by writing

$$\begin{aligned}\mathit{proceed} = \lambda\psi H\rho\upsilon\sigma.\,&(\#H=0) \to \mathit{process}\,\rho\upsilon\sigma,\\ &\mathcal{A}[\![H{\downarrow}1]\!][\![H{\dagger}1]\!]\rho\upsilon\sigma \mathsf{E} A \to \mathcal{A}[\![H{\downarrow}1]\!][\![H{\dagger}1]\!]\rho\upsilon\sigma \,|\, A,\\ &(\lambda\langle H',\rho',\upsilon',\sigma'\rangle.\,\psi[\![H']\!]\rho'\upsilon'\sigma')(\mathcal{A}[\![H{\downarrow}1]\!][\![H{\dagger}1]\!]\rho\upsilon\sigma \,|\, (Con \times U \times Y \times S));\end{aligned}$$

now we take the valuation $\mathcal{Z}$ to be the least fixed point of *proceed*, so $\mathcal{Z} = \mathit{fix}(\mathit{proceed})$. We shall present another equation for *proceed* in 4.6.2; however, the value of $\mathcal{Z}$ will remain unchanged until well beyond 4.6.9. We have lost no generality by providing *process* and letting A be an answer domain (rather than a mere repository of error messages), for we can always take A to be $\{\mathit{error}\} + (U \times Y \times S)$ if we wish.

From the orders mentioned in appendix 11 we can construct all the controls taking the forms $\mathfrak{e}[\![E]\!]$, $\mathfrak{l}[\![E]\!]$, $\mathfrak{r}[\![E]\!]$, $\mathfrak{f}[\![\Phi]\!]$, $\mathfrak{s}[\![\Sigma]\!]$, $\mathfrak{d}[\![\Delta]\!]$, $\mathfrak{t}[\![\Delta]\!]$, $\mathfrak{g}[\![\Theta]\!]$, $\mathfrak{r}[\![\Gamma]\!]$, $\mathfrak{p}[\![\Gamma]\!]{\downarrow}\nu'$ and $\mathfrak{q}[\![\Gamma]\!]{\downarrow}\nu''$ (when $\#\mathfrak{p}[\![\Gamma]\!] \geq \nu' \geq 1$ and $\#\mathfrak{q}[\![\Gamma]\!] \geq \nu'' \geq 1$). Applying the valuations $\mathfrak{b}$, $\mathfrak{o}$ and $\mathfrak{w}$, however, may well produce controls containing orders which never occur in appendix 11. Such orders will be termed 'secret', for they will never appear explicitly and we shall say nothing about them beyond hoping that they satisfy certain assumptions which we shall lay down from time to time. Since secret orders are generally needed merely for performing elementary operations on stacks their meanings are as simple to grasp as those of the most elementary orders mentioned in appendix 11.

4.4.3. An assortment of state valuations.

At last we can form an interpreter for Sal by tying together the definitions in appendix 5 and appendix 11. To illustrate this we introduce valuations $\mathcal{E}$, $\mathcal{L}$ and $\mathcal{R}$ which we take to be those members of Exp→Con→U→Y→S→A such that:

$\mathcal{E}=\lambda EH.\mathcal{Z}[\![\mathfrak{e}[\![E]\!]\S H]\!]$;

$\mathcal{L}=\lambda EH.\mathcal{Z}[\![\mathfrak{r}[\![E]\!]\S H]\!]$;

$\mathcal{R}=\lambda EH.\mathcal{Z}[\![\mathfrak{l}[\![E]\!]\S H]\!]$.

For a reason which will emerge shortly we make $\mathcal{F}$ be an element of Abs→U→(Con×U) by writing

$\mathcal{F}=\lambda\Phi\rho.\langle\mathfrak{f}[\![\Phi]\!],\rho\rangle$.

Similarly $\mathcal{S}$ belongs to Seq→U→Y→S→A, being given by the definition

$\mathcal{S}=\lambda\Sigma\rho\upsilon\sigma.\mathcal{Z}[\![\mathfrak{s}[\![\Sigma]\!]]\!]\rho\upsilon\sigma$.

By analogy with $\mathcal{E}$, $\mathcal{L}$ and $\mathcal{R}$ we let $\mathcal{D}$ and $\mathcal{T}$ be the mappings in Dec→Con→U→Y→S→A for which:

$\mathcal{D}=\lambda\Delta H.\mathcal{Z}[\![\mathfrak{d}[\![\Delta]\!]\S H]\!]$;

$\mathcal{T}=\lambda\Delta H.\mathcal{Z}[\![\mathfrak{t}[\![\Delta]\!]\S H]\!]$.

For handling blocks we require $\mathcal{G}$, a member of the domain Blo→Con→U→Y→S→A which satisfies the equation

$\mathcal{G}=\lambda\Theta H.\mathcal{Z}[\![\mathfrak{g}[\![\Theta]\!]\S H]\!]$.

Finally, commands demand the introduction not merely of $\mathcal{C}$, which is in Com→Con→U→Y→S→A, but also of $\mathcal{P}$ and $\mathcal{Q}$, which lie in Com→Con→U→Y→Ide*→(Con×U×Y×Ide*). Hence we set:

$\mathcal{C}=\lambda\Gamma H.\mathcal{Z}[\![\mathfrak{c}[\![\Gamma]\!]\S H]\!]$;

$\mathcal{P}=\lambda\Gamma H\rho\upsilon I^*.map(\lambda H'.\langle(map(\lambda I.\text{amend } I)I^*)\S H'\S H,\rho,\upsilon,I^*\rangle)(\mathfrak{p}[\![\Gamma]\!])$;

$\mathcal{Q}=\lambda\Gamma H\rho\upsilon I^*.map(\lambda H'.\langle(map(\lambda I.\text{amend } I)I^*)\S H'\S H,\rho,\upsilon,I^*\rangle)(\mathfrak{q}[\![\Gamma]\!])$.

By inspecting appendix 11 and applying the knowledge that $\mathcal{Z}=proceed(\mathcal{Z})$ we can confirm immediately that $\mathcal{E}=\lambda EH.\mathcal{Z}[\![\langle\text{ e } E\rangle\S H]\!]$, $\mathcal{L}=\lambda EH.\mathcal{Z}[\![\langle\text{ l } E\rangle\S H]\!]$ and $\mathcal{R}=\lambda EH.\mathcal{Z}[\![\langle\text{ r } E\rangle\S H]\!]$; similarly $\mathcal{D}=\lambda\Delta H.\mathcal{Z}[\![\langle\text{ d }\Delta\rangle\S H]\!]$ and $\mathcal{T}=\lambda\Delta H.\mathcal{Z}[\![\langle\text{ t }\Delta\rangle\S H]\!]$, whilst $\mathcal{G}=\lambda\Theta H.\mathcal{Z}[\![\langle\text{ g }\Theta\rangle\S H]\!]$ and $\mathcal{C}=\lambda\Gamma H.\mathcal{Z}[\![\langle\text{ c }\Gamma\rangle\S H]\!]$.

Naturally $\mathfrak{F}$ is not $\lambda\Phi H.\mathfrak{Z}\llbracket\langle f\ \Phi\rangle\S H\rrbracket$ and $\mathfrak{S}$ is not $\lambda\Sigma H.\mathfrak{Z}\llbracket\langle s\ \Sigma\rangle\S H\rrbracket$, but $\lambda\Phi H.\mathfrak{Z}\llbracket\langle f\ \Phi\rangle\S H\rrbracket$ is $\lambda\Phi H\rho\upsilon\sigma.\mathfrak{Z}\llbracket H\rrbracket\rho(\langle\mathfrak{F}\llbracket\Phi\rrbracket(rend\llbracket\Phi\rrbracket\rho)\rangle\S\upsilon)\sigma$ and $\lambda\Sigma H.\mathfrak{Z}\llbracket\langle s\ \Sigma\rangle\S H\rrbracket$ is $\lambda\Sigma H.\mathfrak{S}\llbracket\Sigma\rrbracket$. We can also demonstrate that when $map(\lambda I.\rho\llbracket I\rrbracket\downarrow 1)(\mathfrak{J}\llbracket\Gamma\rrbracket)$ is a list of $\#\mathfrak{J}\llbracket\Gamma\rrbracket$ distinct proper locations then $\lambda H\upsilon\sigma.\mathfrak{Z}\llbracket fix(\lambda\psi\nu.(\nu=0)\to\langle\rangle,\langle \text{view}\ \mathfrak{J}\llbracket\Gamma\rrbracket\downarrow\nu\rangle\S\langle p\ \langle\nu,\Gamma\rangle\rangle\S\langle\text{insert}\rangle\S\psi(\nu-1))(\#\mathfrak{J}\llbracket\Gamma\rrbracket)\S H\rrbracket\rho\upsilon\sigma$ is $\lambda H\upsilon\sigma.\mathfrak{Z}\llbracket H\rrbracket\rho\upsilon(updates(map(\lambda I.\rho\llbracket I\rrbracket\downarrow 1)(\mathfrak{J}\llbracket\Gamma\rrbracket))(\mathfrak{P}\llbracket\Gamma\rrbracket\llbracket H\dagger 1\rrbracket\rho\upsilon\langle\rangle)\sigma)$. In addition if we let $grip\in \text{Ide}^*\to\text{U}\to\text{U}$ be such that $grip=\lambda I^*\rho.\langle\lambda I.\rho\llbracket I\rrbracket\dagger(I\in I^*\to 1,0),\rho\llbracket\text{res}\rrbracket,\rho\llbracket\text{rec}\rrbracket\rangle$ then $\lambda\Gamma H.\mathfrak{Z}\llbracket fix(\lambda\psi\nu.(\nu=0)\to\langle\rangle,\langle q\ \langle\nu,\Gamma\rangle\rangle\S\psi(\nu-1))(\#\mathfrak{K}\llbracket\Gamma\rrbracket)\S H\rrbracket$ is $\lambda\Gamma H\rho\upsilon\sigma.\mathfrak{Z}\llbracket H\rrbracket\rho[\mathfrak{Q}\llbracket\Gamma\rrbracket\llbracket H\dagger(1+3\times\#\mathfrak{J}\llbracket\Gamma\rrbracket+\#\mathfrak{K}\llbracket\Gamma\rrbracket)\rrbracket\rho\upsilon(\mathfrak{K}\llbracket\Gamma\rrbracket)/\mathfrak{K}\llbracket\Gamma\rrbracket]$; a similar connection exists between $\lambda\Delta H.\mathfrak{Z}\llbracket fix(\lambda\psi\nu.(\nu=0)\to\langle\rangle,\langle t\ \langle\nu,\Delta\rangle\rangle\S\psi(\nu-1))(\#\mathfrak{K}\llbracket\Delta\rrbracket)\S H\rrbracket$ and a certain function involving t Δ.

Even more than this is true, however, since by making repeated use of the fact that $\mathfrak{Z}=proceed(\mathfrak{Z})$ and by taking over *tie* to our present situation we can verify that $\mathfrak{E}$, $\mathfrak{L}$, $\mathfrak{R}$, $\mathfrak{F}$, $\mathfrak{S}$, $\mathfrak{D}$, $\mathfrak{T}$, $\mathfrak{G}$ and $\mathfrak{C}$ satisfy a set of equations which is presented in appendix 4. Furthermore obvious inductions on the structure of commands reveal that $\mathfrak{P}$ and $\mathfrak{Q}$ are governed by recursive equations which are also provided in appendix 4.

The equations of appendix 4 differ from those in appendix 2 in four main respects. Firstly, rather than taking continuations as arguments the new valuations take controls, which are unevaluated pieces of Sap text (so that $\mathfrak{E}\llbracket E_0 E_1\rrbracket$, for instance, is $\lambda H.\mathfrak{R}\llbracket E_0\rrbracket(\langle e\ E_1\rangle\S\langle\text{apply}\rangle\S H)$); likewise label and procedure values contain controls instead of semantic entities such as continuations. Secondly, although the equations for the valuations remain recursive, none of them involves more than one occurrence of a valuation other than $\mathfrak{F}$, $\mathfrak{P}$ or $\mathfrak{Q}$; these three valuations are devices for abbreviation which may appear as often as is convenient, since they are independent of $\mathfrak{Z}$ and evoke no notion of execution. Thirdly, while loops cannot be handled by means of *fix* owing to the absence of explicit backward jumps from the order code of the interpreter, which according to the definition of $\mathcal{A}$ "throws away" the text in the course of executing it; thus $\mathcal{Z}$[[while E do Γ]] is λH.$\mathcal{R}$[[E]][[⟨pick 2⟩§⟨c Γ⟩§⟨c while E do Γ⟩§H]], not something like λH.$\mathcal{Z}$[[⟨r E⟩§⟨pick 2⟩§⟨c Γ⟩§⟨move -4⟩§H]]. Fourthly, *fix* does not occur in the equations for $\mathfrak{D}$[[rec Δ]] and $\mathfrak{T}$[[block Γ]], whilst *fold* does occur there. The first three of these features are specific to interpreters, but the fourth could arise in a suitably modified version of appendix 2; however, unless *fix* can be removed from semantic equations we have no assurance that they can be implemented. The role of *fold* in facilitating recursion will become clear in 4.4.4.

The domains appropriate to the semantic equations provided in appendix 4 are slightly different from those for the store semantics for Sal. As in appendix 2, we let V=B+E*+J+F, E=L+B+E*+J+F and D=L+B+E*+J+F+G, but now we change the detailed structure of J, F and G by setting J=Con×U×Y×Ide*, F=Con×U and G=Con×U×S×Ide*. Furthermore we write U=(Ide→D*)×K*×P*, where K=Con×U×Y and P=U×Y×S, so, although it is still the case that Y=E* and that S=(L→(V×T))×V*×V*, W=L+B+E*+J+F+G+K+P. The particular treatment of recursion which we have adopted entails keeping lists of identifiers as components of members of G and J but not as components of members of F and K; the reason for this is that members of G and J are set up by semantic equations which might be expected to mention fixed points, whereas in Sal members of F and K are not set up by such equations. Providing recursive procedures by the means hinted at in 1.9.7 would entail turning F into Con×U×Ide*.

The valuations defined for Sal in appendix 4 are 'operational', because they give labels and procedures values that have as constituents not functions but controls (which are pieces of program). As we have just explained, these valuations can be obtained by composing the translating functions given in appendix 5 with the operational valuations provided for Sap in appendix 11. However, more than this is true, for the 'denotational' valuations supplied for Sal in appendix 2, in which functions are present instead of controls, can themselves be obtained by composing the translating functions with certain denotational valuations for Sap described in appendix 10; these valuations govern the 'consecution semantics' of Sap, which we shall discuss in 4.5.1. After 4.6.1 we shall relate our two sorts of semantics for Sap to one another, thereby connecting appendix 4 with appendix 2 in a precise manner. At the end of 4.6.9 we shall even indicate how we can link appendix 4 with appendix 1 in a way which demonstrates that our interpreter for Sal is correct relative to standard semantics; by this we mean that for every Sal program the answer arrived at by executing the program using the interpreter is "like" (and, in some cases, is identical with) the answer predicted for the program by standard semantics.

The relations between the valuations of interest to us in this chapter can conveniently be illustrated on a diagram in which arrows indicate functions defined in the appendices mentioned alongside the arrows; two complete paths between one point and another reveal functions that coincide, and bracketed references point to the proofs of the main congruences. These congruences themselves depend on other important results; thus, as we shall observe later, in order to prove 4.6.8 we must establish 4.5.2 and 4.5.3.

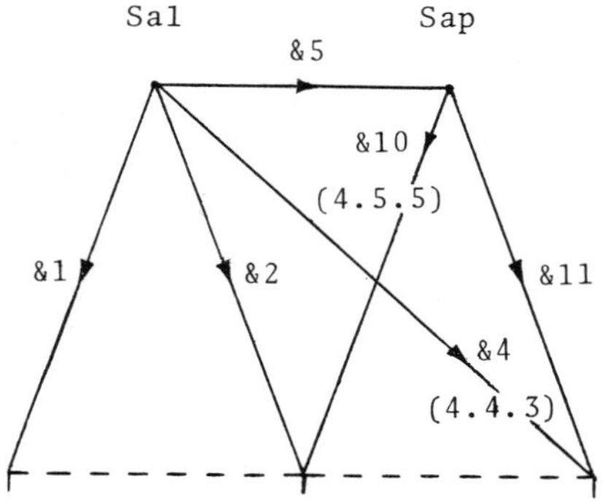

4.4.4. The folding of environments.

In order to account for *fold* we first define $wrap \in U \to D \to D$ by means of the equation

$$wrap = \lambda\rho\delta.(\lambda\phi.\delta E J \to \langle(\delta|J)\downarrow 1,((\delta|J)\downarrow 2)[\phi((\delta|J)\downarrow 4)/(\delta|J)\downarrow 4],(\delta|J)\downarrow 3,\langle\rangle\rangle,$$
$$\delta E G \to \langle(\delta|G)\downarrow 1,((\delta|G)\downarrow 2)[\phi((\delta|G)\downarrow 2)/(\delta|G)\downarrow 4],(\delta|G)\downarrow 3,\langle\rangle\rangle,$$
$$\delta)$$
$$(\lambda I^*.map(\lambda I.\rho[\![I]\!]\downarrow 1)I^*).$$

We can now let $fold \in Ide^* \to U \to U$ be described recursively by

$$fold = \lambda I^*\rho.(\#I^*=0) \to \rho,$$
$$(\#\rho[\![I^*\downarrow 1]\!]=0) \to fold(I^*\dagger 1)\rho,$$
$$fold(I^*\dagger 1)((grip\langle I^*\downarrow 1\rangle\rho)[wrap\rho(\rho[\![I^*\downarrow 1]\!]\downarrow 1)/I^*\downarrow 1]).$$

It should be noted in passing that $\lambda\rho.wrap = \lambda\rho'\rho''\delta.wrap\rho'(wrap\rho''\delta)$, so induction on $\#I^*$ can be used to demonstrate that $foldI^* = \lambda\rho.fold[\![I^*\downarrow\nu]\!](foldI^*\rho)$ for any list I^* and for any integer ν having $\#I^* \geq \nu \geq 1$. At this point, we shall also define for convenience a function $coil \in Con \to U \to U$ such that

$$coil = \lambda H\rho.(\#H=0) \to \rho,$$
$$\bigvee\{H\downarrow 1 \equiv \text{amend } I|I\} \to \bigsqcup\{(H\downarrow 1 \equiv \text{amend } I) \to coil[\![H\dagger 1]\!](fold\langle I\rangle\rho),\perp|I\},$$
$$\rho.$$

Thus if H and I^* are related by the equation $H=(map(\lambda I.\text{amend } I)I^*)\S(H\dagger\#I^*)$ then $coil[\![H]\!]=foldI^*$. The utility of *coil* will become apparent in 4.6.1; here we shall merely point out that for every control H $\mathcal{Z}[\![H]\!]=\mathcal{Z}[\![H]\!]\circ coil[\![H]\!]$, as may be demonstrated by induction on the least integer ν such that either $H\dagger\nu$ is $\langle\rangle$ or $(H\dagger\nu)\downarrow 1$ is not of the form amend I for any identifier I.

Were we to set up a more "realistic" domain of environments, such as $(Ide\times D)^*\times K^*\times P^*$, we could make it quite evident that *fold* and its associates could be implemented; however, this refinement can safely be left to the reader.

To understand the value of *wrap* in facilitating recursion it is best to consider what happens in some detail. Thus we assume that block Γ is supplied with a control H_0, an environment ρ_0, a stack σ_0 and a store σ_0 having $\#\mathfrak{J}\llbracket\Gamma\rrbracket$ unused locations. Under these circumstances, a succession of environments may be formed by setting $\rho_1=\rho_0[\mathit{news}(\#\mathfrak{J}\llbracket\Gamma\rrbracket)\sigma_0/\mathfrak{J}\llbracket\Gamma\rrbracket]$, $\rho_2=\rho_1[\mathfrak{Q}\llbracket\Gamma\rrbracket\llbracket H_1\rrbracket\rho_1\upsilon_0(\mathfrak{K}\llbracket\Gamma\rrbracket)/\mathfrak{K}\llbracket\Gamma\rrbracket]$ and $\rho_3=\mathit{fold}(\mathfrak{K}\llbracket\Gamma\rrbracket)\rho_2$, where $H_1=\langle \text{snip } \Gamma\rangle\S H_0$. Indeed if $\sigma_1=\mathit{updates}(\mathit{news}(\#\mathfrak{J}\llbracket\Gamma\rrbracket)\sigma_0)(\mathfrak{P}\llbracket\Gamma\rrbracket\llbracket H_1\rrbracket\rho_3\upsilon_1\langle\rangle)\sigma_0$ we know that $\mathfrak{G}\llbracket \text{block } \Gamma\rrbracket\llbracket H_0\rrbracket\rho_0\upsilon_0\sigma_0=\mathfrak{C}\llbracket\Gamma\rrbracket\llbracket H_1\rrbracket\rho_3\upsilon_1\sigma_1$. Inside Γ the execution of goto $\mathfrak{H}\llbracket\Gamma\rrbracket\downarrow\nu$ proceeds normally but that of goto $\mathfrak{K}\llbracket\Gamma\rrbracket\downarrow\nu$ requires further investigation. Certainly appendix 4 shows that for any environment ρ_4 with $\rho_4\llbracket\mathfrak{K}\llbracket\Gamma\rrbracket\downarrow\nu\rrbracket\downarrow 1=\rho_3\llbracket\mathfrak{K}\llbracket\Gamma\rrbracket\downarrow\nu\rrbracket\downarrow 1$ and for any stack υ_1 and any store σ_2 we may assert that

$$
\begin{aligned}
\mathfrak{J}\llbracket \text{goto } \mathfrak{K}\llbracket\Gamma\rrbracket\downarrow\nu\rrbracket\rho_4\upsilon_1\sigma_2 &= \mathfrak{R}\llbracket\mathfrak{K}\llbracket\Gamma\rrbracket\downarrow\nu\rrbracket\llbracket\langle \text{jump}\rangle\rrbracket\rho_4\upsilon_1\sigma_2\\
&= \mathfrak{E}\llbracket\mathfrak{K}\llbracket\Gamma\rrbracket\downarrow\nu\rrbracket\llbracket\langle \text{sv}\rangle\S\langle \text{jump}\rangle\rrbracket\rho_4\upsilon_1\sigma_2\\
&= \mathfrak{Z}\llbracket\langle \text{sv}\rangle\S\langle \text{jump}\rangle\rrbracket\rho_4(\langle\rho_4\llbracket\mathfrak{K}\llbracket\Gamma\rrbracket\downarrow\nu\rrbracket\downarrow 1\rangle\S\upsilon_1)\sigma_2\\
&= \mathfrak{Z}\llbracket\langle \text{jump}\rangle\rrbracket\rho_4(\langle\rho_4\llbracket\mathfrak{K}\llbracket\Gamma\rrbracket\downarrow\nu\rrbracket\downarrow 1\rangle\S\upsilon_1)\sigma_2\\
&= \mathfrak{Z}\llbracket\rho_4\llbracket\mathfrak{K}\llbracket\Gamma\rrbracket\downarrow\nu\rrbracket\downarrow 1\downarrow 1\rrbracket(\rho_4\llbracket\mathfrak{K}\llbracket\Gamma\rrbracket\downarrow\nu\rrbracket\downarrow 1\downarrow 2)(\rho_4\llbracket\mathfrak{K}\llbracket\Gamma\rrbracket\downarrow\nu\rrbracket\downarrow 1\downarrow 3)\sigma_2.
\end{aligned}
$$

Moreover, writing $I^*=\mathit{fix}(\lambda\psi\nu'.(\nu'=0)\rightarrow\langle\rangle,\psi(\nu'-1)\S\mathfrak{K}\llbracket\Gamma\rrbracket\downarrow\nu')(\nu-1))$, $\rho_5=\mathit{fold}I^*\rho_2$ and $\rho_6=\rho_1[\mathit{map}(\lambda I.\rho_5\llbracket I\rrbracket)(\mathfrak{K}\llbracket\Gamma\rrbracket)/\mathfrak{K}\llbracket\Gamma\rrbracket]$ provides environments for which

$$
\begin{aligned}
\rho_3\llbracket\mathfrak{K}\llbracket\Gamma\rrbracket\downarrow\nu\rrbracket\downarrow 1 &= (\mathit{fold}(\mathfrak{K}\llbracket\Gamma\rrbracket)\rho_2)\llbracket\mathfrak{K}\llbracket\Gamma\rrbracket\downarrow\nu\rrbracket\downarrow 1\\
&= \mathit{wrap}(\rho_2\llbracket\mathfrak{K}\llbracket\Gamma\rrbracket\downarrow\nu\rrbracket\downarrow 1)\rho_5\\
&= \mathit{wrap}(\mathfrak{Q}\llbracket\Gamma\rrbracket\llbracket H_1\rrbracket\rho_1\upsilon_0(\mathfrak{K}\llbracket\Gamma\rrbracket)\downarrow\nu)\rho_5\\
&= \mathit{wrap}\langle(\mathit{map}(\lambda I.\text{amend } I)(\mathfrak{K}\llbracket\Gamma\rrbracket))\S\mathfrak{q}\llbracket\Gamma\rrbracket\downarrow\nu\S H_1,\rho_1,\upsilon_0,\mathfrak{K}\llbracket\Gamma\rrbracket\rangle\rho_5\\
&= \langle(\mathit{map}(\lambda I.\text{amend } I)(\mathfrak{K}\llbracket\Gamma\rrbracket))\S\mathfrak{q}\llbracket\Gamma\rrbracket\downarrow\nu\S H_1,\rho_6,\upsilon_0,\langle\rangle\rangle.
\end{aligned}
$$

However, by induction on ν we can verify that $\rho_6=\mathit{fold}I^*\rho_2$, so $\rho_6=\mathit{fold}I^*\rho_6$ and

$\rho_3 = \mathit{fold}(\mathcal{K}[\![\Gamma]\!])\rho_2$

$\quad = \mathit{fold}(\mathrm{I}^*\S\mathcal{K}[\![\Gamma]\!]\dagger(\nu-1))\rho_2$

$\quad = \mathit{fold}(\mathcal{K}[\![\Gamma]\!]\dagger(\nu-1))(\mathit{fold}\mathrm{I}^*\rho_2)$

$\quad = \mathit{fold}(\mathcal{K}[\![\Gamma]\!]\dagger(\nu-1))\rho_6$

$\quad = \mathit{fold}(\mathcal{K}[\![\Gamma]\!]\dagger(\nu-1))(\mathit{fold}\mathrm{I}^*\rho_6)$

$\quad = \mathit{fold}(\mathrm{I}^*\S\mathcal{K}[\![\Gamma]\!]\dagger(\nu-1))\rho_6$

$\quad = \mathit{fold}(\mathcal{K}[\![\Gamma]\!])\rho_6.$

As $\lambda\mathrm{H}.\mathcal{Z}[\![(\mathit{map}(\lambda\mathrm{I}.\mathrm{amend\ I})(\mathcal{K}[\![\Gamma]\!]))\S\mathrm{H}]\!] = \lambda\mathrm{H}\rho\upsilon\sigma.\mathcal{Z}[\![\mathrm{H}]\!](\mathit{fold}(\mathcal{K}[\![\Gamma]\!])\rho)\upsilon\sigma$,

$\mathcal{S}[\![\mathrm{goto}\ \mathcal{K}[\![\Gamma]\!]\downarrow\nu]\!]\rho_4\upsilon_1\sigma_2 = \mathcal{Z}[\![(\mathit{map}(\lambda\mathrm{I}.\mathrm{amend\ I})(\mathcal{K}[\![\Gamma]\!]))\S\mathcal{Q}[\![\Gamma]\!]\downarrow\nu\S\mathrm{H}_1]\!]\rho_6\upsilon_0\sigma_3$

$\qquad = \mathcal{Z}[\![\mathcal{Q}[\![\Gamma]\!]\downarrow\nu\S\mathrm{H}_1]\!](\mathit{fold}(\mathcal{K}[\![\Gamma]\!])\rho_6)\upsilon_0\sigma_3$

$\qquad = \mathcal{Z}[\![\mathcal{Q}[\![\Gamma]\!]\downarrow\nu\S\mathrm{H}_1]\!]\rho_3\upsilon_0\sigma_3.$

Consequently when a jump is made to the point labelled by $\mathcal{K}[\![\Gamma]\!]\downarrow\nu$ the corresponding control is evaluated in an environment identical with the environment in which Γ is executed.

In a similar fashion the meaning ascribed to rec Δ in appendix 4 makes each member of $\mathcal{H}[\![\Delta]\!]$ denote a element of G having an environment component in which each member of $\mathcal{H}[\![\Delta]\!]$ denotes an element of G having an environment component lacking the appropriate entries for the members of $\mathcal{H}[\![\Delta]\!]$; only when a member of $\mathcal{H}[\![\Delta]\!]$ is looked up in the environment are these entries provided by the control, which takes the form $(\mathit{map}(\lambda\mathrm{I}.\mathrm{amend\ I}))\S\langle \mathrm{t}\ \Delta\rangle\S\langle \mathrm{occur}\ \mathcal{H}[\![\Delta]\!]\downarrow\nu\rangle$. Further insight into this mechanism may be obtained by examining a simple program such as rec $(f{=}{=}\mathrm{fn}x..gx$ and $g{=}{=}\mathrm{fn}x..fx)$ inside $f0$; this particular program naturally gives the value $\perp$ when $\mathcal{E}$ is applied to it (as can be established by recalling that $\mathcal{Z}=\mathit{fix}(\mathit{proceed})$).

We could modify this treatment of $\mathcal{D}[\![\mathrm{rec}\ \Delta]\!]$ and $\mathcal{G}[\![\mathrm{block}\ \Gamma]\!]$ by altering the meanings of $\mathrm{t}\langle\nu,\Delta\rangle$ and $\mathrm{q}\langle\nu,\Gamma\rangle$ so that, for example, in the notation used above $\rho_3[\![\mathcal{K}[\![\Gamma]\!]\downarrow\nu]\!]\downarrow1$ would be

$\langle \mathit{map}(\lambda\mathrm{I}.\mathrm{amend\ I})(\mathcal{K}[\![\Gamma]\!]\dagger(\nu-1))\S\mathcal{Q}[\![\Gamma]\!]\downarrow\nu\S\mathrm{H}_1,\rho_1,\upsilon_0,\mathcal{K}[\![\Gamma]\!]\rangle$,

$\langle \mathit{map}(\lambda\mathrm{I}.\mathrm{amend\ I})(\mathcal{K}[\![\Gamma]\!])\S\mathcal{Q}[\![\Gamma]\!]\downarrow\nu\S\mathrm{H}_1,\mathit{grip}\mathrm{I}^*\rho_2,\upsilon_0,\mathrm{I}^*\rangle$ or even

$\langle map(\lambda I.\mathrm{amend}\ I)(\mathfrak{K}[\![\Gamma]\!]\dagger(\nu-1))\S\mathfrak{Q}[\![\Gamma]\!]\downarrow\nu\S H_1, grip\, I^*\rho_2, \upsilon_0, I^*\rangle$. Furthermore unnecessary copying could be eliminated by allowing label and procedure values to include not environments and stacks but pointers into the current environment and stack (or into another environment and stack in the case of label and procedure values which had been passed out of their scopes). We cannot, however, remove $fold(\mathfrak{H}[\![\Delta]\!])$ and $fold(\mathfrak{K}[\![\Gamma]\!])$ from the equations for $\mathfrak{D}[\![\mathrm{rec}\ \Delta]\!]$ and $\mathfrak{G}[\![\mathrm{block}\ \Gamma]\!]$ without introducing *wrap* elsewhere; this is demonstrated by the simple program rec (f==fn$x$..gx and g==fn$x$..fx) inside (g==fn$x$..0 inside f0). Other variations on appendix 4 can easily be formalized, but they serve largely to complicate the semantic equations without yielding much new insight.

4.5. The identity between store semantics and consecution semantics.

4.5.1. Consecutions.

Since Sal can be given a semantics based on continuations as well as one based on controls we may reasonably hope that the same will be true of Sap. Accordingly we could attempt to construct a valuation $\mathcal{A}$ belonging to Ord→Z→Z where the domain Z would actually be that described in 4.1.2. At first such an attempt would appear to succeed, for evidently we would take $\mathcal{A}[\![\mathrm{mv}]\!]$ and $\mathcal{A}[\![\mathrm{sv}]\!]$, for instance, to be $\lambda\zeta\rho\upsilon\sigma.mv\zeta\rho\upsilon\sigma$ and $\lambda\zeta\rho\upsilon\sigma.sv\zeta\rho\upsilon\sigma$ respectively when we remembered the definitions of *mv* and *sv* which were given in 4.1.4. However, the attempt would founder on the difficulties involved in ascribing meanings to move ν, pick ν and link ν. These orders require the introduction of not just one continuation but two: that formed from the control following the order and that obtained by missing out orders from the control. Corresponding to a control H is a set of continuations generated by $\{H\dagger\nu \mid \#H\geq\nu\geq 0\}$, and it is this set that is of concern to us here. To formalize what we need we shall use a domain H, which we shall define to be N→Z (although Z* would be equally suitable); we shall call a member of H a 'consecution' and we shall designate it by η.

When $\mathcal{A}$ is presumed to be a member of Ord→H→Z instead of Ord→Z→Z we can fulfil the expectation that Sap orders may be given meanings in terms of continuations. Simple orders may be handled in roughly the way proposed above; in particular $\mathcal{A}[\![\mathrm{mv}]\!]$ and $\mathcal{A}[\![\mathrm{sv}]\!]$ can be $\lambda\eta\rho\upsilon\sigma.mv(\eta 0)\rho\upsilon\sigma$ and $\lambda\eta\rho\upsilon\sigma.sv(\eta 0)\rho\upsilon\sigma$ respectively. Here η0 is regarded as the continuation corresponding to the control H which in appendix 11 would follow the order, so naturally ην is viewed as the continuation corresponding to H†ν. Thus whereas in appendix 11 $\mathcal{A}[\![\mathrm{move}\ \nu]\!]$ is equal to $\lambda H\rho\upsilon\sigma.\langle H\dagger\nu,\rho,\upsilon,\sigma\rangle$ here it is equal to $\lambda\eta\rho\upsilon\sigma.\eta\nu\rho\upsilon\sigma$, and analogous remarks apply to $\mathcal{A}[\![\mathrm{pick}\ \nu]\!]$ and $\mathcal{A}[\![\mathrm{link}\ \nu]\!]$. Even the controls $H\dagger(-1+3\times\nu)$ and $H\dagger(\nu+3\times\#\mathcal{J}[\![\Gamma]\!]+\#\mathcal{K}[\![\Gamma]\!])$ (which appear in the equations governing $p\langle\nu,\Gamma\rangle$ and $q\langle\nu,\Gamma\rangle$ respectively) make way for $\eta(-1+3\times\nu)$ and $\eta(\nu+3\times\#\mathcal{J}[\![\Gamma]\!]+\#\mathcal{K}[\![\Gamma]\!])$. An account of our latest version of $\mathcal{A}$ is contained in appendix 10. This resembles appendix 11 in ignoring those Sap orders which are secret and which may therefore arise in controls such as $\mathfrak{b}[\![B]\!]$, $\mathfrak{o}[\![O]\!]$ and $\mathfrak{w}[\![\Omega]\!]$.

Our mention of $p\langle\nu,\Gamma\rangle$ and $q\langle\nu,\Gamma\rangle$ brings to the fore the sole difference between appendix 10 and appendix 11 which is not related to the distinctions between consecutions and controls. The valuation $\mathcal{A}$ which we are discussing here is supposed to act upon precisely the same domains as the valuations of appendix 2. Because these domains make no provision for the use of *fold* we are obliged to handle recursion with the aid of *fix*. Consequently in appendix 10 $t\langle\nu,\Delta\rangle$ and $q\langle\nu,\Gamma\rangle$ (and indeed amend I) are treated in ways which seem rather odd from the standpoint of appendix 11; it would seem much more natural to endow them with meanings which would reflect their earlier meanings much more directly, so that $\mathcal{A}[\![\text{amend I}]\!]$, for instance, would be not $\lambda\eta\rho\upsilon\sigma.\eta 0\rho\upsilon\sigma$ but $\lambda\eta\rho\upsilon\sigma.\eta 0(\mathit{fold}\langle I\rangle\rho)\upsilon\sigma$. Obviously this course of action would entail adopting domains for our present version of $\mathcal{A}$ which would not coincide with those needed by appendix 2.

The orders $t\langle\nu,\Delta\rangle$, $p\langle\nu,\Gamma\rangle$ and $q\langle\nu,\Gamma\rangle$ depend for their meanings on the valuations defined in appendix 2, but they are independent of appendix 5 in this particular formulation of the 'consecution semantics' of Sap. This is true of any order T such that there is a control concealed in $\langle T\rangle$ (in the sense explained in 4.4.1); $\mathcal{A}[\![b\ B]\!]$, $\mathcal{A}[\![o\ O]\!]$ and $\mathcal{A}[\![w\ \Omega]\!]$, for instance, are $\lambda\eta\rho\upsilon\sigma.\mathfrak{B}[\![B]\!](\eta 0)\rho\upsilon\sigma$, $\lambda\eta\rho\upsilon\sigma.\mathfrak{O}[\![O]\!](\eta 0)\rho\upsilon\sigma$ and $\lambda\eta\rho\upsilon\sigma.\mathfrak{W}[\![\Omega]\!](\eta 0)\rho\upsilon\sigma$, whilst $\mathcal{A}[\![f\ \Phi]\!]$ is $\lambda\eta\rho\upsilon\sigma.\eta 0\rho(\langle\mathfrak{F}[\![\Phi]\!](\mathit{rend}[\![\Phi]\!]\rho)\rangle\S\upsilon)\sigma$ and $\mathcal{A}[\![s\ \Sigma]\!]$ is $\lambda\eta\rho\upsilon\sigma.\mathfrak{S}[\![\Sigma]\!]\rho\upsilon\sigma$.

To express the effect of applying $\mathcal{A}$ to the orders in a control H "until there is nothing left to do" we introduce a valuation $\mathcal{Y}$

in Con→Z→Z which involves supplying $\mathscr{A}$ with the order H↓1 and the consecution corresponding to the control H†1. More concisely, we arrange that $\mathscr{Y}=\lambda H\zeta.((\#H=0)\rightarrow\zeta,\mathscr{A}[\![H{\downarrow}1]\!](\lambda\nu.\mathscr{Y}[\![(H{\dagger}1){\dagger}\nu]\!]\zeta))$ by setting $\mathscr{Y}=fix(\lambda\psi H\zeta.(\#H=0)\rightarrow\zeta,\mathscr{A}[\![H{\downarrow}1]\!](\lambda\nu.\psi[\![(H{\dagger}1){\dagger}\nu]\!]\zeta))$.

The Sap orders which are generated from Sal programs by applying the valuations given in appendix 5 always satisfy certain constraints. In particular move ν, pick ν and link ν (and also p ⟨ν,Γ⟩ and q ⟨ν,Γ⟩) are not allowed to produce jumps forwards, while t ⟨ν,Δ⟩ and q ⟨ν,Δ⟩ appear only in certain predictable sequences. Accordingly we shall say that a Sap control H is 'cohesive' if and only if whenever $\#H\geq\nu\geq 1$ the following conditions hold:

(i) if H↓ν is move ν′, pick ν′ or link ν′ for any ν′ then $\#(H{\dagger}\nu)\geq\nu'\geq 0$;

(ii) if H↓ν is p ⟨ν′,Γ⟩ for any ν′ and Γ then $\#(H{\dagger}\nu)\geq -1+3\times\nu'\geq 0$;

(iii) if H↓ν is q ⟨ν′,Γ⟩ for any ν′ and Γ then $\#(H{\dagger}\nu)\geq\nu'+3\times\#\mathscr{J}[\![\Gamma]\!]+\#\mathscr{K}[\![\Gamma]\!]\geq 0$.

Here we are supposing for simplicity that any secret order T is such that $\mathscr{A}[\![T]\!]=\lambda\eta.\xi(\eta 0)$ for some $\xi\in 0$; if this is not the case the notion of a cohesive control must be altered in a manner which will be implicit in the proof of 4.5.2.

Though cohesive controls will be the ones of most concern to us in the immediate future any Sap control generated by expanding a Sal program has other useful properties besides that of being cohesive. To summarize them we shall call a Sap control H 'adhesive' if and only if when $\#H\geq\nu\geq 1$ the order H↓ν is such that:

(i) if H↓ν is t ⟨ν′,Δ⟩ for any ν′ and Δ then $\#\mathscr{K}[\![\Delta]\!]\geq\nu'\geq 1$ and whenever $\#\mathscr{K}[\![\Delta]\!]\geq\nu''\geq 1$ H↓(ν+ν′−ν″) is t ⟨ν″,Δ⟩ and H↓(ν+ν′−ν″+#𝒦⟦Δ⟧) is amend $\mathscr{K}[\![\Delta]\!]{\downarrow}(\#\mathscr{K}[\![\Delta]\!]-\nu'')$;

(ii) if H↓ν is q ⟨ν′,Γ⟩ for any ν′ and Γ then $\#\mathscr{K}[\![\Gamma]\!]\geq\nu'\geq 1$ and whenever $\#\mathscr{K}[\![\Gamma]\!]\geq\nu''\geq 1$ H↓(ν+ν′−ν″) is q ⟨ν″,Γ⟩ and H↓(ν+ν′−ν″+#𝒦⟦Γ⟧) is amend $\mathscr{K}[\![\Gamma]\!]{\downarrow}(\#\mathscr{K}[\![\Gamma]\!]-\nu'')$;

(iii) if $H\downarrow\nu$ is move ν', pick ν' or link ν' for any ν' and if $((H\dagger\nu)\dagger\nu')\downarrow 1$ is t $\langle\nu'',\Delta\rangle$ for any ν'' and Δ then $\nu''=\#\mathcal{K}[\![\Delta]\!]$;

(iv) if $H\downarrow\nu$ is p $\langle\nu',\Gamma\rangle$ for any ν' and Γ and if $((H\dagger\nu)\dagger(-1+3\times\nu'))\downarrow 1$ is t $\langle\nu'',\Delta\rangle$ for any ν'' and Δ then $\nu''=\#\mathcal{K}[\![\Delta]\!]$;

(v) if $H\downarrow\nu$ is q $\langle\nu',\Gamma\rangle$ for any ν' and Γ and if $((H\dagger\nu)\dagger(\nu'+3\times\#\mathcal{J}[\![\Gamma]\!]+\#\mathcal{K}[\![\Gamma]\!]))\downarrow 1$ is t $\langle\nu'',\Delta\rangle$ for any ν'' and Δ then $\nu''=\#\mathcal{K}[\![\Delta]\!]$;

(vi) if $H\downarrow\nu$ is move ν', pick ν' or link ν' for any ν' and if $((H\dagger\nu)\dagger\nu')\downarrow 1$ is q $\langle\nu'',\Gamma\rangle$ for any ν'' and Γ then $\nu''=\#\mathcal{K}[\![\Gamma]\!]$;

(vii) if $H\downarrow\nu$ is p $\langle\nu',\Gamma'\rangle$ for any ν' and Γ' and if $((H\dagger\nu)\dagger(-1+3\times\nu'))\downarrow 1$ is q $\langle\nu'',\Gamma''\rangle$ for any ν'' and Γ'' then $\nu''=\#\mathcal{K}[\![\Gamma'']\!]$;

(viii) if $H\downarrow\nu$ is q $\langle\nu',\Gamma'\rangle$ for any ν' and Γ' and if $((H\dagger\nu)\dagger(\nu'+3\times\#\mathcal{J}[\![\Gamma']\!]+\#\mathcal{K}[\![\Gamma'']\!]))\downarrow 1$ is q $\langle\nu'',\Gamma''\rangle$ for any ν'' and Γ'' then $\nu''=\#\mathcal{K}[\![\Gamma'']\!]$.

Thus when H is adhesive and $H\downarrow\nu$ is move ν', pick ν' or link ν' $(H\dagger\nu)\dagger\nu'$ is also adhesive; similar remarks apply when H is adhesive and $H\downarrow\nu$ is p $\langle\nu',\Gamma\rangle$ or q $\langle\nu',\Gamma\rangle$. Evidently if H_0 is cohesive and adhesive and if H_1 is adhesive then $H_0\S H_1$ is adhesive.

From time to time we shall write $\mathit{cohere}[\![H]\!]=\mathit{true}$ if and only if the control H is cohesive and $\mathit{adhere}[\![H]\!]=\mathit{true}$ if and only if the control H is adhesive.

On examining the version of $\mathcal{A}$ provided in appendix 10 we see that when T is any order that is not secret we can find a list $\nu^*\in N^*$ and a function $\psi\in Z^*\to O$ such that $\mathcal{A}[\![T]\!]=\lambda\eta.\psi(\mathit{map}\,\eta\nu^*)(\eta 0)$; moreover we can arrange that ψ does not depend on those integer "parameters" appearing in T which form part of arguments of η in the equation for $\mathcal{A}[\![T]\!]$. If T is link ν, for instance, we can take ν^* to be $\langle\nu\rangle$ and ψ to be $\lambda\zeta^*\zeta\rho\upsilon\sigma.\zeta\rho[\langle\zeta^*\downarrow 1,\rho,\upsilon\rangle/\mathrm{res}]$, since $\mathcal{A}[\![\text{link }\nu]\!]$ is $\lambda\eta\rho\upsilon\sigma.\eta 0\rho[\langle\eta\nu,\rho,\upsilon\rangle/\mathrm{res}]$. Usually ν^* can be $\langle\rangle$, for only move ν, pick ν, link ν, p $\langle\nu,\Gamma\rangle$ and q $\langle\nu,\Gamma\rangle$ mention "parameters" for pointing into controls; these five exceptional orders demand that ν^* be $\langle\nu\rangle$, $\langle\nu\rangle$, $\langle\nu\rangle$, $\langle -1+3\times\nu\rangle$ and

$\langle \nu+3\times\#\mathcal{J}[\![\Gamma]\!]+\#\mathcal{K}[\![\Gamma]\!]\rangle$ respectively. Thus we are really suggesting that a control is cohesive if and only if whenever $\#H\geq\nu\geq1$ the list ν^* appropriate to $H\dagger\nu$ is such that $\#H\geq\nu+\nu^*\downarrow\nu'\geq\nu$ for each ν' having $\#\nu^*\geq\nu'\geq1$; it is satisfactory to phrase the definition above in this way even when all we assume about each secret instruction, T say, is that $\mathcal{A}[\![T]\!]=\lambda\eta.\psi(map\eta\nu^*)(\eta 0)$ for some $\nu^*\in N^*$ and for some $\psi\in Z^*\to O$ which is not influenced by the code pointers present in T. We could formalize the derivation of ν^* and ψ from T by introducing additional valuations, but there is little to be gained by doing so.

In 4.5.5 we shall relate the semantics of Sap discussed above (and presented in appendix 10) to the semantics of Sal given in appendix 2; essentially we shall show that the equations in appendix 2 can be obtained by applying the valuation $\mathcal{Y}$ to Sap controls generated from Sal programs with the aid of the equations in appendix 5. Before then, however, we shall verify some properties of cohesive controls that are intuitively obvious and we shall indicate why we are interested only in those controls that are cohesive and adhesive. Not until 4.6.1 will we again require the semantics for Sap provided in appendix 11; at that point we shall begin to analyse the connection between our two sorts of semantics for Sap. This connection is complicated, because of a need to consider solely adhesive controls. Nonetheless, the theorem which we shall prove in 4.6.8 will allow us to establish the correctness of our interpreter for Sal, for, as we shall hint in 4.6.9, standard semantics provides every Sal program with an answer which can, in effect, also be obtained by executing the program using the interpreter underlying appendix 5 and appendix 11. A similar result (concerning the correctness of a compiler) will be explained in detail in 5.6.9.

The diagram provided in 4.4.3 may be helpful to those who are confused by the intricate relations between the different sorts of semantics that we have introduced in the course of developing our interpreter for Sal.

4.5.2. Proposition.

If H is a cohesive Sap control then

$\lambda\eta.\mathcal{Y}[\![H]\!]=\lambda\eta\zeta.((\#H=0)\to\zeta,\mathcal{A}[\![H\downarrow 1]\!](\lambda\nu.(\#H-1\geq\nu\geq 0)\to\mathcal{Y}[\![(H\dagger 1)\dagger\nu]\!]\zeta,\eta\nu))$.

◁Patently the valuation $\mathcal{A}$ referred to is that provided by appendix 10. This indicates that unless #H=0 or H↓1 is move ν′, pick ν′, link ν′, p ⟨ν′,Γ⟩ or q ⟨ν′,Γ⟩ for some ν′ and some Γ there is some $\xi\in 0$ with $\mathcal{A}[\![H\downarrow 1]\!]=\lambda\eta.\xi(\eta 0)$; under these circumstances, for any $\zeta\in Z$ and for any $\eta\in H$

$$\begin{aligned}\mathcal{A}[\![H\downarrow 1]\!](\lambda\nu.\mathcal{Y}[\![(H\dagger 1)\dagger\nu]\!]\zeta)&=\xi((\lambda\nu.\mathcal{Y}[\![(H\dagger 1)\dagger\nu]\!]\zeta)0)\\&=\xi(\mathcal{Y}[\![H\dagger 1]\!]\zeta)\\&=\xi((\lambda\nu.(\#H-1\geq\nu\geq 0)\to\mathcal{Y}[\![(H\dagger 1)\dagger\nu]\!]\zeta,\eta\nu)0)\\&=\mathcal{A}[\![H\downarrow 1]\!](\lambda\nu.(\#H-1\geq\nu\geq 0)\to\mathcal{Y}[\![(H\dagger 1)\dagger\nu]\!]\zeta,\eta\nu).\end{aligned}$$

Of greater interest is what happens when H↓1 is move ν′, pick ν′, link ν′, p ⟨ν′,Γ⟩ or q ⟨ν′,Γ⟩, for then we have to appeal to the knowledge that H is cohesive. If H↓1 is move ν′, for instance, then we know that $\#(H\dagger 1)\geq\nu'\geq 0$, so for any $\zeta\in 0$ and any $\eta\in H$

$$\begin{aligned}\mathcal{A}[\![H\downarrow 1]\!](\lambda\nu.\mathcal{Y}[\![(H\dagger 1)\dagger\nu]\!]\zeta)&=(\lambda\nu.\mathcal{Y}[\![(H\dagger 1)\dagger\nu]\!]\zeta)\nu'\\&=\mathcal{Y}[\![(H\dagger 1)\dagger\nu']\!]\zeta\\&=(\lambda\nu.((\#H-1\geq\nu\geq 0)\to\mathcal{Y}[\![(H\dagger 1)\dagger\nu]\!]\zeta,\eta\nu)\nu'\\&=\mathcal{A}[\![H\downarrow 1]\!](\lambda\nu.(\#H-1\geq\nu\geq 0)\to\mathcal{Y}[\![(H\dagger 1)\dagger\nu]\!]\zeta,\eta\nu).\end{aligned}$$

The other cases require very similar arguments which together with the equation $\mathcal{Y}=\lambda H\zeta.((\#H=0)\to\zeta,\mathcal{A}[\![H\downarrow 1]\!](\lambda\nu.\mathcal{Y}[\![(H\dagger 1)\dagger\nu]\!]\zeta))$ allow us to assert that in fact

$\lambda\eta.\mathcal{Y}[\![H]\!]=\lambda\eta\zeta.((\#H=0)\to\zeta,\mathcal{A}[\![H\downarrow 1]\!](\lambda\nu.(\#H-1\geq\nu\geq 0)\to\mathcal{Y}[\![(H\dagger 1)\dagger\nu]\!]\zeta,\eta\nu))$

when H is a cohesive control.▷

4.5.3. Proposition.

If H_0 and H_1 are Sap controls such that H_0 is cohesive then $\mathscr{Y}\llbracket H_0 \S H_1 \rrbracket = \lambda\zeta.\mathscr{Y}\llbracket H_0 \rrbracket(\mathscr{Y}\llbracket H_1 \rrbracket\zeta)$.

◁Because the valuation $\mathscr{Y}$ satisfies the recursive equation $\mathscr{Y} = \lambda H\zeta.((\# H=0)\to\zeta, \mathscr{A}\llbracket H{\downarrow}1\rrbracket(\lambda\nu.\mathscr{Y}\llbracket (H{\dagger}1){\dagger}\nu\rrbracket\zeta)$ it is natural to try to verify this result by induction on the length of the Sap control; proofs by induction on this length are the counterparts for Sap of the structural inductions needed by Sal.

Accordingly we assume that H_0 is a cohesive control for which $\# H_0>0$ and that if H_2 is a cohesive control having $\# H_0>\# H_2$ then $\mathscr{Y}\llbracket H_2 \S H_1\rrbracket=\lambda\zeta.\mathscr{Y}\llbracket H_2\rrbracket(\mathscr{Y}\llbracket H_1\rrbracket\zeta)$ for every control H_1. Since H_0 is cohesive, whenever $\# H_0-1\geq\nu\geq 0$ $(H_0{\dagger}1){\dagger}\nu$ is cohesive and $\# H_0>\#((H_0{\dagger}1){\dagger}\nu)$; consequently whenever $\# H_0-1\geq\nu\geq 0$ $\mathscr{Y}\llbracket((H_0{\dagger}1){\dagger}\nu)\S H_1\rrbracket=\lambda\zeta.\mathscr{Y}\llbracket(H_0{\dagger}1){\dagger}\nu\rrbracket(\mathscr{Y}\llbracket H_1\rrbracket\zeta)$, in accordance with the inductive hypothesis. However,

$$\mathscr{Y}\llbracket H_0\S H_1\rrbracket=\lambda\zeta.\mathscr{A}\llbracket(H_0\S H_1){\downarrow}1\rrbracket(\lambda\nu.\mathscr{Y}\llbracket((H_0\S H_1){\dagger}1){\dagger}\nu\rrbracket\zeta)$$
$$=\lambda\zeta.\mathscr{A}\llbracket H_0{\downarrow}1\rrbracket(\lambda\nu.\mathscr{Y}\llbracket((H_0\S H_1){\dagger}1){\dagger}\nu\rrbracket\zeta)$$
$$=\lambda\zeta.\mathscr{A}\llbracket H_0{\downarrow}1\rrbracket(\lambda\nu.(\# H_1-1\geq\nu\geq 0)\to\mathscr{Y}\llbracket((H_0{\dagger}1){\dagger}\nu)\S H_1\rrbracket\zeta,\mathscr{Y}\llbracket((H_0\S H_1){\dagger}1){\dagger}\nu\rrbracket\zeta),$$

so actually

$$\mathscr{Y}\llbracket H_0\S H_1\rrbracket=\lambda\zeta.\mathscr{A}\llbracket H_0{\downarrow}1\rrbracket(\lambda\nu.(\# H_1-1\geq\nu\geq 0)\to\mathscr{Y}\llbracket(H_0{\dagger}1){\dagger}\nu\rrbracket(\mathscr{Y}\llbracket H_1\rrbracket\zeta),\mathscr{Y}\llbracket((H_0\S H_1){\dagger}1){\dagger}\nu\rrbracket\zeta)$$

On recalling that H_0 is cohesive we may apply 4.5.2 to H_0, thereby obtaining the equation

$$\mathscr{Y}\llbracket H_0\S H_1\rrbracket=\lambda\zeta.\mathscr{A}\llbracket H_0{\downarrow}1\rrbracket(\lambda\nu.\mathscr{Y}\llbracket(H_0{\dagger}1){\dagger}\nu\rrbracket(\mathscr{Y}\llbracket H_1\rrbracket\zeta)).$$

In addition the definition of $\mathscr{Y}$ ensures that

$$\lambda\zeta.\mathscr{Y}\llbracket H_0\rrbracket(\mathscr{Y}\llbracket H_1\rrbracket\zeta)=\lambda\zeta.\mathscr{A}\llbracket H_0{\downarrow}1\rrbracket(\lambda\nu.\mathscr{Y}\llbracket(H_0{\dagger}1){\dagger}\nu\rrbracket(\mathscr{Y}\llbracket H_1\rrbracket\zeta));$$

hence $\mathscr{Y}\llbracket H_0\S H_1\rrbracket=\lambda\zeta.\mathscr{Y}\llbracket H_0\rrbracket(\mathscr{Y}\llbracket H_1\rrbracket\zeta)$.

When H_0 is a control with $\# H_0=0$ it is plain that $\mathscr{Y}\llbracket H_0\rrbracket=\lambda\zeta.\zeta$ and that $\mathscr{Y}\llbracket H_0\S H_1\rrbracket=\mathscr{Y}\llbracket H_1\rrbracket$, so $\mathscr{Y}\llbracket H_0\S H_1\rrbracket=\lambda\zeta.\mathscr{Y}\llbracket H_0\rrbracket(\mathscr{Y}\llbracket H_1\rrbracket\zeta)$ trivially. Hence the basis of the induction on the length of H_0 is valid; indeed, we can conclude that $\mathscr{Y}\llbracket H_0\S H_1\rrbracket=\lambda\zeta.\mathscr{Y}\llbracket H_0\rrbracket(\mathscr{Y}\llbracket H_1\rrbracket\zeta)$ whenever H_0 is cohesive.▷

4.5.4. Proposition.

In Sal all E, Φ, Σ, Δ, Θ and Γ are such that $\mathfrak{e}[\![E]\!]$, $\mathfrak{l}[\![E]\!]$, $\mathfrak{r}[\![E]\!]$, $\mathfrak{f}[\![\Phi]\!]$, $\mathfrak{s}[\![\Sigma]\!]$, $\mathfrak{d}[\![\Delta]\!]$, $\mathfrak{t}[\![\Delta]\!]$, $\mathfrak{g}[\![\Theta]\!]$, $\mathfrak{c}[\![\Gamma]\!]$, $\mathfrak{p}[\![\Gamma]\!]\downarrow\nu'$ and $\mathfrak{q}[\![\Gamma]\!]\downarrow\nu''$ are cohesive and adhesive Sap controls whenever $\#\mathfrak{p}[\![\Gamma]\!]\geq\nu'\geq1$ and $\#\mathfrak{q}[\![\Gamma]\!]\geq\nu''\geq1$.

◁The proof of this emerges immediately from an inspection of the definitions of $\mathfrak{e}$ and the other valuations which appear in appendix 5. As these valuations are not recursive (with the exceptions of $\mathfrak{p}$ and $\mathfrak{q}$) structural inductions are needed only to show that $\mathfrak{p}[\![\Gamma]\!]\downarrow\nu'$ and $\mathfrak{q}[\![\Gamma]\!]\downarrow\nu''$ are cohesive and adhesive whenever $\#\mathfrak{p}[\![\Gamma]\!]\geq\nu'\geq1$ and $\#\mathfrak{q}[\![\Gamma]\!]\geq\nu''\geq1$.▷

This result has been stated largely for the sake of completeness. However, based on it is 4.5.5, which concerns the relation between appendix 2 and appendix 5.

4.5.5. Proposition.

In Sal all E, Φ, Σ, Θ and Γ are such that $\mathcal{E}[\![E]\!]=\mathcal{Y}[\![\mathfrak{e}[\![E]\!]]\!]$, $\mathcal{L}[\![E]\!]=\mathcal{Y}[\![\mathfrak{l}[\![E]\!]]\!]$, $\mathcal{R}[\![E]\!]=\mathcal{Y}[\![\mathfrak{r}[\![E]\!]]\!]$, $\mathcal{H}[\![\Phi]\!]=\lambda\rho.\langle\mathcal{Y}[\![\mathfrak{f}[\![\Phi]\!]]\!],\rho\rangle$, $\lambda\zeta.\mathcal{S}[\![\Sigma]\!]=\mathcal{Y}[\![\mathfrak{s}[\![\Sigma]\!]]\!]$, $\mathcal{D}[\![\Delta]\!]=\lambda\zeta.\mathcal{Y}[\![\mathfrak{d}[\![\Delta]\!]]\!]\zeta$, $\mathcal{T}[\![\Delta]\!]=\mathcal{Y}[\![\mathfrak{t}[\![\Delta]\!]]\!]$, $\mathcal{G}[\![\Theta]\!]=\mathcal{Y}[\![\mathfrak{g}[\![\Theta]\!]]\!]$, $\mathcal{C}[\![\Gamma]\!]=\mathcal{Y}[\![\mathfrak{c}[\![\Gamma]\!]]\!]$, $\mathcal{P}[\![\Gamma]\!]=\lambda\zeta\rho\upsilon.map(\lambda H.\langle\mathcal{Y}[\![H]\!]\zeta,\rho,\upsilon\rangle)(\mathfrak{p}[\![\Gamma]\!])$ and $\mathcal{Q}[\![\Gamma]\!]=\lambda\zeta\rho\upsilon.map(\lambda H.\langle\mathcal{Y}[\![H]\!]\zeta,\rho,\upsilon\rangle)(\mathfrak{q}[\![\Gamma]\!])$.

◁Much of this result can be proved without recourse to inductions on the structure of Sal programs, for it relies upon the way in which $\mathcal{Y}$ is defined in appendix 10 on such orders as e E, l E and r E. We shall demonstrate the technique required simply by examining one case, that involving while E do Γ.

We fix attention on one particular continuation ζ and take η to be the consecution $\lambda\nu.\mathcal{Y}[\![\mathfrak{c}[\![\mathtt{while}\ E\ \mathtt{do}\ \Gamma]\!]\dagger\nu]\!]\zeta$. Thus we wish to demonstrate that η0 coincides with $\mathcal{Y}[\![\mathtt{while}\ E\ \mathtt{do}\ \Gamma]\!]\zeta$, which is $fix\xi$ where $\xi=\lambda\zeta'.\mathcal{R}[\![E]\!](\lambda\rho\upsilon\sigma.test\langle\mathcal{C}[\![\Gamma]\!]\zeta'\rho(\upsilon\dagger1),\zeta\rho(\upsilon\dagger1)\rangle(\upsilon\downarrow1)\sigma)$. Evidently appendix 5 assures us that

$$\eta0=\mathcal{Y}[\![(\langle\mathtt{r}\ E\rangle\S\langle\mathtt{pick}\ 2\rangle\S\langle\mathtt{c}\ \Gamma\rangle\S\langle\mathtt{c}\ \mathtt{while}\ E\ \mathtt{do}\ \Gamma\rangle)\dagger0]\!]\zeta$$
$$=\mathcal{Y}[\![\langle\mathtt{r}\ E\rangle\S\langle\mathtt{pick}\ 2\rangle\S\langle\mathtt{c}\ \Gamma\rangle\S\langle\mathtt{c}\ \mathtt{while}\ E\ \mathtt{do}\ \Gamma\rangle]\!]\zeta$$
$$=\mathcal{A}[\![\mathtt{r}\ E]\!](\lambda\nu.\mathcal{Y}[\![((\langle\mathtt{r}\ E\rangle\S\langle\mathtt{pick}\ 2\rangle\S\langle\mathtt{c}\ \Gamma\rangle\S\langle\mathtt{c}\ \mathtt{while}\ E\ \mathtt{do}\ \Gamma\rangle)\dagger1)\dagger\nu]\!]\zeta)$$
$$=\mathcal{R}[\![E]\!]((\lambda\nu.\mathcal{Y}[\![((\langle\mathtt{r}\ E\rangle\S\langle\mathtt{pick}\ 2\rangle\S\langle\mathtt{c}\ \Gamma\rangle\S\langle\mathtt{c}\ \mathtt{while}\ E\ \mathtt{do}\ \Gamma\rangle)\dagger1)\dagger\nu]\!]\zeta)0)$$
$$=\mathcal{R}[\![E]\!](\mathcal{Y}[\![\langle\mathtt{pick}\ 2\rangle\S\langle\mathtt{c}\ \Gamma\rangle\S\langle\mathtt{c}\ \mathtt{while}\ E\ \mathtt{do}\ \Gamma\rangle]\!]\zeta)$$

whilst

$$\eta1=\mathcal{Y}[\![(\langle\mathtt{r}\ E\rangle\S\langle\mathtt{pick}\ 2\rangle\S\langle\mathtt{c}\ \Gamma\rangle\S\langle\mathtt{c}\ \mathtt{while}\ E\ \mathtt{do}\ \Gamma\rangle)\dagger1]\!]\zeta$$
$$=\mathcal{Y}[\![\langle\mathtt{pick}\ 2\rangle\S\langle\mathtt{c}\ \Gamma\rangle\S\langle\mathtt{c}\ \mathtt{while}\ E\ \mathtt{do}\ \Gamma\rangle]\!]\zeta$$
$$=\mathcal{A}[\![\mathtt{pick}\ 2]\!](\lambda\nu.\mathcal{Y}[\![((\langle\mathtt{pick}\ 2\rangle\S\langle\mathtt{c}\ \Gamma\rangle\S\langle\mathtt{c}\ \mathtt{while}\ E\ \mathtt{do}\ \Gamma\rangle)\dagger1)\dagger\nu]\!]\zeta).$$

By continuing our examination of η we see that

$$\eta2=\mathcal{Y}[\![(\langle\mathtt{r}\ E\rangle\S\langle\mathtt{pick}\ 2\rangle\S\langle\mathtt{c}\ \Gamma\rangle\S\langle\mathtt{c}\ \mathtt{while}\ E\ \mathtt{do}\ \Gamma\rangle)\dagger2]\!]\zeta$$
$$=\mathcal{Y}[\![\langle\mathtt{c}\ \Gamma\rangle\S\langle\mathtt{c}\ \mathtt{while}\ E\ \mathtt{do}\ \Gamma\rangle]\!]\zeta$$
$$=\mathcal{A}[\![\mathtt{c}\ \Gamma]\!](\lambda\nu.\mathcal{Y}[\![((\langle\mathtt{c}\ \Gamma\rangle\S\langle\mathtt{c}\ \mathtt{while}\ E\ \mathtt{do}\ \Gamma\rangle)\dagger1)\dagger\nu]\!]\zeta)$$
$$=\mathcal{C}[\![\Gamma]\!]((\lambda\nu.\mathcal{Y}[\![((\langle\mathtt{c}\ \Gamma\rangle\S\langle\mathtt{c}\ \mathtt{while}\ E\ \mathtt{do}\ \Gamma\rangle)\dagger1)\dagger\nu]\!]\zeta)0)$$
$$=\mathcal{C}[\![\Gamma]\!](\mathcal{Y}[\![\langle\mathtt{c}\ \mathtt{while}\ E\ \mathtt{do}\ \Gamma\rangle]\!]\zeta)$$

and also that

$$\eta 3=\mathcal{Y}\llbracket(\langle \mathrm{r\ E}\rangle \S \langle \mathrm{pick\ 2}\rangle \S \langle \mathrm{c}\ \Gamma\rangle \S \langle \mathrm{c\ while\ E\ do}\ \Gamma\rangle)\dagger 3\rrbracket\zeta$$
$$=\mathcal{Y}\llbracket\langle \mathrm{c\ while\ E\ do}\ \Gamma\rangle\rrbracket\zeta$$
$$=\mathcal{A}\llbracket \mathrm{c\ while\ E\ do}\ \Gamma\rrbracket(\lambda\nu.\mathcal{Y}\llbracket((\langle \mathrm{c\ while\ E\ do}\ \Gamma\rangle)\dagger 1)\dagger\nu\rrbracket\zeta)$$
$$=\mathcal{C}\llbracket \mathrm{while\ E\ do}\ \Gamma\rrbracket((\lambda\nu.\mathcal{Y}\llbracket((\langle \mathrm{c\ while\ E\ do}\ \Gamma\rangle)\dagger 1)\dagger\nu\rrbracket\zeta)0)$$
$$=\mathcal{C}\llbracket \mathrm{while\ E\ do}\ \Gamma\rrbracket(\mathcal{Y}\llbracket\langle\rangle\rrbracket\zeta)$$

whilst

$$\eta 4=\mathcal{Y}\llbracket(\langle \mathrm{r\ E}\rangle \S \langle \mathrm{pick\ 2}\rangle \S \langle \mathrm{c}\ \Gamma\rangle \S \langle \mathrm{c\ while\ E\ do}\ \Gamma\rangle)\dagger 4\rrbracket\zeta$$
$$=\mathcal{Y}\llbracket\langle\rangle\rrbracket\zeta$$
$$=\zeta.$$

As $(\lambda\nu.\mathcal{Y}\llbracket((\langle \mathrm{pick\ 2}\rangle \S \langle \mathrm{c}\ \Gamma\rangle \S \langle \mathrm{c\ while\ E\ do}\ \Gamma\rangle)\dagger 1)\dagger\nu\rrbracket\zeta)0=\eta 2$ and $(\lambda\nu.\mathcal{Y}\llbracket((\langle \mathrm{pick\ 2}\rangle \S \langle \mathrm{c}\ \Gamma\rangle \S \langle \mathrm{c\ while\ E\ do}\ \Gamma\rangle)\dagger 1)\dagger\nu\rrbracket\zeta)2=\eta 4$ the semantics provided for pick ν' in appendix 10 reveals that

$$\eta 1=\lambda\rho\upsilon\sigma.\mathit{test}\langle\eta 2\rho(\upsilon\dagger 1),\eta 4\rho(\upsilon\dagger 1)\rangle(\upsilon\downarrow 1)\sigma$$
$$=\lambda\rho\upsilon\sigma.\mathit{test}\langle\mathcal{C}\llbracket\Gamma\rrbracket(\mathcal{Y}\llbracket\langle \mathrm{c\ while\ E\ do}\ \Gamma\rangle\rrbracket\zeta)\rho(\upsilon\dagger 1),\eta 4\rho(\upsilon\dagger 1)\rangle(\upsilon\downarrow 1)\sigma$$
$$=\lambda\rho\upsilon\sigma.\mathit{test}\langle\mathcal{C}\llbracket\Gamma\rrbracket(\eta 3)\rho(\upsilon\dagger 1),\eta 4\rho(\upsilon\dagger 1)\rangle(\upsilon\downarrow 1)\sigma$$
$$=\lambda\rho\upsilon\sigma.\mathit{test}\langle\mathcal{C}\llbracket\Gamma\rrbracket(\mathcal{C}\llbracket \mathrm{while\ E\ do}\ \Gamma\rrbracket(\mathcal{Y}\llbracket\langle\rangle\rrbracket\zeta)\rho(\upsilon\dagger 1),\eta 4\rho(\upsilon\dagger 1)\rangle(\upsilon\downarrow 1)\sigma$$
$$=\lambda\rho\upsilon\sigma.\mathit{test}\langle\mathcal{C}\llbracket\Gamma\rrbracket(\mathcal{C}\llbracket \mathrm{while\ E\ do}\ \Gamma\rrbracket\zeta)\rho(\upsilon\dagger 1),\zeta\rho(\upsilon\dagger 1)\rangle(\upsilon\downarrow 1)\sigma.$$

When we combine the implications of these equations we may therefore establish that

$$\eta 0=\mathcal{R}\llbracket \mathrm{E}\rrbracket(\mathcal{Y}\llbracket\langle \mathrm{pick2}\rangle \S \langle \mathrm{c}\ \Gamma\rangle \S \langle \mathrm{c\ while\ E\ do}\ \Gamma\rangle\rrbracket\zeta)$$
$$=\mathcal{R}\llbracket \mathrm{E}\rrbracket(\eta 1)$$
$$=\mathcal{R}\llbracket \mathrm{E}\rrbracket(\lambda\rho\upsilon\sigma.\mathit{test}\langle\mathcal{C}\llbracket\Gamma\rrbracket(\mathcal{C}\llbracket \mathrm{while\ E\ do}\ \Gamma\rrbracket\zeta)\rho(\upsilon\dagger 1),\zeta\rho(\upsilon\dagger 1)\rangle(\upsilon\downarrow 1)\sigma$$
$$=\xi(\mathcal{C}\llbracket \mathrm{while\ E\ do}\ \Gamma\rrbracket\zeta).$$

However, since $\mathcal{C}\llbracket \mathrm{while\ E\ do}\ \Gamma\rrbracket\zeta=\mathit{fix}\xi$ (according to appendix 2), the account of *fix* given in 2.3.2 ensures that

$$\mathcal{C}\llbracket \mathrm{while\ E\ do}\ \Gamma\rrbracket\zeta=\xi(\mathcal{C}\llbracket \mathrm{while\ E\ do}\ \Gamma\rrbracket\zeta).$$

Consequently $\mathcal{C}\llbracket \mathrm{while\ E\ do}\ \Gamma\rrbracket\zeta=\eta 0$ no matter how ζ is chosen (provided that η is $\lambda\nu.\mathcal{Y}\llbracket c\llbracket \mathrm{while\ E\ do}\ \Gamma\rrbracket\dagger\nu\rrbracket\zeta$), and we may confidently claim that $\mathcal{C}\llbracket \mathrm{while\ E\ do}\ \Gamma\rrbracket=\mathcal{Y}\llbracket c\llbracket \mathrm{while\ E\ do}\ \Gamma\rrbracket\rrbracket$.

Because $\mathfrak{p}$ and $\mathfrak{q}$ are defined recursively, in order to prove that $\mathscr{P}\llbracket \mathtt{while}\ E\ \mathtt{do}\ \Gamma\rrbracket = \lambda\zeta\rho\upsilon.map(\lambda H.\langle\mathscr{Y}\llbracket H\rrbracket\zeta,\rho,\upsilon\rangle)(\mathfrak{p}\llbracket \mathtt{while}\ E\ \mathtt{do}\ \Gamma\rrbracket)$ and that $\mathscr{Q}\llbracket \mathtt{while}\ E\ \mathtt{do}\ \Gamma\rrbracket = \lambda\zeta\rho\upsilon.map(\lambda H.\langle\mathscr{Y}\llbracket H\rrbracket\zeta,\rho,\upsilon\rangle)(\mathfrak{q}\llbracket \mathtt{while}\ E\ \mathtt{do}\ \Gamma\rrbracket)$ we are obliged to introduce suitable inductive hypotheses implying that $\mathscr{P}\llbracket\Gamma\rrbracket = \lambda\zeta\rho\upsilon.map(\lambda H.\langle\mathscr{Y}\llbracket H\rrbracket\zeta,\rho,\upsilon\rangle)(\mathfrak{p}\llbracket\Gamma\rrbracket)$ and that $\mathscr{Q}\llbracket\Gamma\rrbracket = \lambda\zeta\rho\upsilon.map(\lambda H.\langle\mathscr{Y}\llbracket H\rrbracket\zeta,\rho,\upsilon\rangle)(\mathfrak{q}\llbracket\Gamma\rrbracket)$. When $\#\mathfrak{p}\llbracket\Gamma\rrbracket\geq\nu'\geq 1$ and $\#\mathfrak{q}\llbracket\Gamma\rrbracket\geq\nu''\geq 1$, we know that $\mathfrak{p}\llbracket\Gamma\rrbracket\downarrow\nu'$ and $\mathfrak{q}\llbracket\Gamma\rrbracket\downarrow\nu''$ are cohesive in view of 4.5.4, so according to 4.5.3 we may assert that

$$\mathscr{Y}\llbracket\mathfrak{p}\llbracket\Gamma\rrbracket\downarrow\nu'\S\langle \mathtt{c\ while}\ E\ \mathtt{do}\ \Gamma\rangle\rrbracket = \mathscr{Y}\llbracket\mathfrak{p}\llbracket\Gamma\rrbracket\downarrow\nu'\rrbracket(\mathscr{Y}\llbracket\langle \mathtt{c\ while}\ E\ \mathtt{do}\ \Gamma\rangle\rrbracket\zeta)$$

$$\mathscr{Y}\llbracket\mathfrak{q}\llbracket\Gamma\rrbracket\downarrow\nu''\S\langle \mathtt{c\ while}\ E\ \mathtt{do}\ \Gamma\rangle\rrbracket = \mathscr{Y}\llbracket\mathfrak{q}\llbracket\Gamma\rrbracket\downarrow\nu''\rrbracket(\mathscr{Y}\llbracket\langle \mathtt{c\ while}\ E\ \mathtt{do}\ \Gamma\rangle\rrbracket\zeta).$$

In addition appendix 10 shows that

$$\begin{aligned}\mathscr{Y}\llbracket\langle \mathtt{c\ while}\ E\ \mathtt{do}\ \Gamma\rangle\rrbracket &= \lambda\zeta.\mathscr{A}\llbracket \mathtt{c\ while}\ E\ \mathtt{do}\ \Gamma\rrbracket(\lambda\nu.\mathscr{Y}\llbracket((\langle \mathtt{c\ while}\ E\ \mathtt{do}\ \Gamma\rangle)\dagger 1)\dagger\nu\rrbracket\zeta)\\ &= \lambda\zeta.\mathscr{C}\llbracket \mathtt{while}\ E\ \mathtt{do}\ \Gamma\rrbracket((\lambda\nu.\mathscr{Y}\llbracket((\langle \mathtt{c\ while}\ E\ \mathtt{do}\ \Gamma\rangle)\dagger 1)\dagger\nu\rrbracket\zeta)0)\\ &= \lambda\zeta.\mathscr{C}\llbracket \mathtt{while}\ E\ \mathtt{do}\ \Gamma\rrbracket(\mathscr{Y}\llbracket\langle\rangle\rrbracket\zeta)\\ &= \mathscr{C}\llbracket \mathtt{while}\ E\ \mathtt{do}\ \Gamma\rrbracket.\end{aligned}$$

Consequently by virtue of appendix 2

$$\begin{aligned}\mathscr{P}\llbracket \mathtt{while}\ E\ \mathtt{do}\ \Gamma\rrbracket &= \lambda\zeta.\mathscr{P}\llbracket\Gamma\rrbracket(\mathscr{C}\llbracket \mathtt{while}\ E\ \mathtt{do}\ \Gamma\rrbracket\zeta)\\ &= \lambda\zeta\rho\upsilon.map(\lambda H.\langle\mathscr{Y}\llbracket H\rrbracket(\mathscr{C}\llbracket \mathtt{while}\ E\ \mathtt{do}\ \Gamma\rrbracket\zeta),\rho,\upsilon\rangle)(\mathfrak{p}\llbracket\Gamma\rrbracket)\\ &= \lambda\zeta\rho\upsilon.map(\lambda H.\langle\mathscr{Y}\llbracket H\rrbracket(\mathscr{Y}\llbracket\langle \mathtt{c\ while}\ E\ \mathtt{do}\ \Gamma\rangle\rrbracket\zeta),\rho,\upsilon\rangle)(\mathfrak{p}\llbracket\Gamma\rrbracket)\\ &= \lambda\zeta\rho\upsilon.map(\lambda H.\langle\mathscr{Y}\llbracket H\S\langle \mathtt{c\ while}\ E\ \mathtt{do}\ \Gamma\rangle\rrbracket\zeta,\rho,\upsilon\rangle)(\mathfrak{p}\llbracket\Gamma\rrbracket)\\ &= \lambda\zeta\rho\upsilon.map(\lambda H.\langle\mathscr{Y}\llbracket H\rrbracket\zeta,\rho,\upsilon\rangle)(\mathfrak{p}\llbracket \mathtt{while}\ E\ \mathtt{do}\ \Gamma\rrbracket)\end{aligned}$$

and similarly $\mathscr{Q}\llbracket \mathtt{while}\ E\ \mathtt{do}\ \Gamma\rrbracket$ is identical with $\lambda\zeta\rho\upsilon.map(\lambda H.\langle\mathscr{Y}\llbracket H\rrbracket\zeta,\rho,\upsilon\rangle)(\mathfrak{q}\llbracket \mathtt{while}\ E\ \mathtt{do}\ \Gamma\rrbracket)$.⊁

Throughout the proof of this result we require the knowledge that *fix* produces a fixed point but not a guarantee that this fixed point is the least possible. Moreover we have to appeal to the cohesive nature of certain Sap controls and to perform structural inductions only when verifying that $\mathfrak{p} = \lambda\Gamma\zeta\rho\upsilon.map(\lambda H.\langle\mathscr{Y}\llbracket H\rrbracket\zeta,\rho,\upsilon\rangle)(\mathfrak{p}\llbracket\Gamma\rrbracket)$ and that $\mathscr{Q} = \lambda\Gamma\zeta\rho\upsilon.map(\lambda H.\langle\mathscr{Y}\llbracket H\rrbracket\zeta,\rho,\upsilon\rangle)(\mathfrak{q}\llbracket\Gamma\rrbracket)$. This situation contrasts with the one which will be present in the lemmas to be discussed before 5.5.7.

The definition of $\mathscr{A}$ given in appendix 10 allows us to infer from this result that $\lambda E.\mathscr{A}[\![\mathrm{e}\ E]\!]=\lambda E\eta.\mathscr{Y}[\![\boldsymbol{e}[\![E]\!]]\!](\eta 0)$, $\lambda E.\mathscr{A}[\![\mathrm{l}\ E]\!]=\lambda E\eta.\mathscr{Y}[\![\boldsymbol{l}[\![E]\!]]\!](\eta 0)$, $\lambda E.\mathscr{A}[\![\mathrm{r}\ E]\!]=\lambda E\eta.\mathscr{Y}[\![\boldsymbol{r}[\![E]\!]]\!](\eta 0)$, $\lambda\Phi.\mathscr{A}[\![\mathrm{f}\ \Phi]\!]=\lambda\Phi\eta\rho\upsilon\sigma.\eta 0\rho(\langle\langle\mathscr{Y}[\![\boldsymbol{f}[\![\Phi]\!]]\!],\mathit{rend}[\![\Phi]\!]\rho\rangle\rangle\S\upsilon)\sigma$, $\lambda\Sigma\eta\nu.\mathscr{A}[\![\mathrm{s}\ \Sigma]\!]\eta=\lambda\Sigma\eta\nu.\mathscr{Y}[\![\boldsymbol{s}[\![\Sigma]\!]]\!](\eta\nu)$, $\lambda\Delta.\mathscr{A}[\![\mathrm{d}\ \Delta]\!]=\lambda\Delta\eta.\mathscr{Y}[\![\boldsymbol{d}[\![\Delta]\!]]\!](\eta 0)$, $\lambda\Delta.\mathscr{A}[\![\mathrm{t}\ \Delta]\!]=\lambda\Delta\eta.\mathscr{Y}[\![\boldsymbol{t}[\![\Delta]\!]]\!](\eta 0)$, $\lambda\Theta.\mathscr{A}[\![\mathrm{g}\ \Theta]\!]=\lambda\Theta\eta.\mathscr{Y}[\![\boldsymbol{g}[\![\Theta]\!]]\!](\eta 0)$ and $\lambda\Gamma.\mathscr{A}[\![\mathrm{c}\ \Gamma]\!]=\lambda\Gamma\eta.\mathscr{Y}[\![\boldsymbol{c}[\![\Gamma]\!]]\!](\eta 0)$. We can even provide meanings for $\mathrm{t}\ \langle\nu,\Delta\rangle$, $\mathrm{p}\ \langle\nu,\Gamma\rangle$ and $\mathrm{q}\ \langle\nu,\Gamma\rangle$ in terms of $\mathscr{Y}[\![\boldsymbol{t}[\![\Delta]\!]]\!]$, $\mathit{map}(\lambda H.\mathscr{Y}[\![H]\!])(\boldsymbol{p}[\![\Gamma]\!])$ and $\mathit{map}(\lambda H.\mathscr{Y}[\![H]\!])(\boldsymbol{q}[\![\Gamma]\!])$. Thus we could have started off by defining $\mathscr{A}$ and $\mathscr{Y}$ in a mutually recursive manner without reference to the valuations given in appendix 2. The equations which we actually use to describe e E, l E and r E would then need to be justified by appealing to the fact that $\mathscr{A}$ and $\mathscr{Y}$ would together be the least fixed point of a particular equation.

By 4.5.2 $\lambda\eta.\mathscr{Y}[\![\langle T\rangle]\!]=\lambda\eta\zeta.\mathscr{A}[\![T]\!](\lambda\nu.(\nu=0)\rightarrow\zeta,\eta\nu)$ whenever T is an order such that $\langle T\rangle$ is cohesive. Hence in fact $\lambda E.\mathscr{Y}[\![\langle\mathrm{e}\ E\rangle]\!]=\lambda E.\mathscr{Y}[\![\boldsymbol{e}[\![E]\!]]\!]$, $\lambda E.\mathscr{Y}[\![\langle\mathrm{l}\ E\rangle]\!]=\lambda E.\mathscr{Y}[\![\boldsymbol{l}[\![E]\!]]\!]$ and $\lambda E.\mathscr{Y}[\![\langle\mathrm{r}\ E\rangle]\!]=\lambda E.\mathscr{Y}[\![\boldsymbol{r}[\![E]\!]]\!]$; analogous equations apply to the other Sap orders which involve features of Sal.

In this result we have tacitly assumed that $\mathit{veer}0=0$; were this not to be the case we would simply have to alter the equations of appendix 4 and appendix 5 in obvious ways. Accordingly we shall not mention the requirement that $\mathit{veer}0=0$ even in such major results as 4.6.8.

4.6. The conformity between consecution semantics and control semantics.

4.6.1. Computational induction.

We have now provided two sorts of semantics for Sap, one involving consecutions and the other involving controls. From these two sorts of semantics we have even derived two sets of equations for Sal which are presented in appendix 2 and appendix 4. Only the first of these sets of equations for Sal is adequate by itself to supply a meaning to any Sal program; the other relies on the translation of Sal into Sap described in appendix 5 and on the semantics of Sap provided in appendix 11. Thus according to appendix 2 $\mathcal{E}[\![E_0E_1]\!]$, for instance, depends on E_0 and E_1 only through $\mathcal{R}[\![E_0]\!]$ and $\mathcal{E}[\![E_1]\!]$, but according to appendix 4 $\mathcal{E}[\![E_0E_1]\!]$ is a function of $\mathcal{R}[\![E_0]\!]$ and the Sap orders **e** E_1 and apply. This distinction between these two sets of equations for Sal is of great practical importance, for it implies that, though induction on the structure of Sal programs may be used to prove results about appendix 2, 'computational induction' on the lengths of computations is needed when verifying useful results about the interpreter represented by appendix 4. Indeed a major virtue of denotational semantics is that it allows us to establish the properties of certain sets of semantic equations simply by means of structural inductions; in these sets the meaning of a program emerges directly from the meanings of the components of that program (so that $\mathcal{E}[\![E_0E_1]\!]$ depends on E_0 and E_1 only through $\mathcal{R}[\![E_0]\!]$ and $\mathcal{E}[\![E_1]\!]$). We shall return to this point in a different context in 5.6.9; in the mean time we shall merely mention that it influences how we handle our next task, which is to establish a formal connection between appendix 2 and appendix 4 by relating the two sorts of semantics that we have given for Sap.

In order to explain what this connection must be we observe that we can turn any control into a member of O (which is Z→Z) simply by applying $\mathcal{Y}$; thus if H is the control given by a label appearing in a program which is followed by the continuation ζ then $\mathcal{Y}[\![H]\!]\zeta$ is the member of Z provided by the label, whilst if H is the control generated from a procedure then $\mathcal{Y}[\![H]\!]$ is the member of O provided by the procedure. In fact we can even convert any witnessed value belonging to the domain W appropriate to appendix 11 into a satisfactory member of the domain W for appendix 10. For this purpose we let ζ be a continuation, ψ be a function taking Z into a continuous mapping between the two domains called W and $\acute{\omega}$ be a witnessed value suited to control semantics; doing this enables us to provide $furling\psi\zeta\acute{\omega}$ (a witnessed value suited to consecution semantics) by recalling the function $coil$ defined in 4.4.4 and by setting

$$
\begin{aligned}
furling=\lambda\psi\zeta\acute{\omega}.\,&\acute{\omega}\,\mathsf{E}\,\mathsf{L}\rightarrow\acute{\omega},\\
&\acute{\omega}\,\mathsf{E}\,\mathsf{B}\rightarrow\acute{\omega},\\
&\acute{\omega}\,\mathsf{E}\,\mathsf{E}^{*}\rightarrow(\mathrm{E}(\psi\zeta))^{*}(\acute{\omega}|\mathsf{E}^{*}),\\
&\acute{\omega}\,\mathsf{E}\,\mathsf{J}\rightarrow\langle\mathcal{Y}[\![(\acute{\omega}|\mathsf{J})\downarrow 1]\!]\zeta,\mathrm{U}(\psi\zeta)(coil[\![(\acute{\omega}|\mathsf{J})\downarrow 1]\!]((\acute{\omega}|\mathsf{J})\downarrow 2)),\mathrm{Y}(\psi\zeta)((\acute{\omega}|\mathsf{J})\downarrow 3)\\
&\acute{\omega}\,\mathsf{E}\,\mathsf{F}\rightarrow\langle\mathcal{Y}[\![(\acute{\omega}|\mathsf{F})\downarrow 1]\!],\mathrm{U}(\psi\zeta)((\acute{\omega}|\mathsf{F})\downarrow 2)\rangle,\\
&\acute{\omega}\,\mathsf{E}\,\mathsf{G}\rightarrow\langle\mathcal{Y}[\![(\acute{\omega}|\mathsf{G})\downarrow 1]\!],\mathrm{U}(\psi\zeta)(coil[\![(\acute{\omega}|\mathsf{G})\downarrow 1]\!]((\acute{\omega}|\mathsf{G})\downarrow 2)),\mathrm{S}(\psi\zeta)((\acute{\omega}|\mathsf{G})\downarrow 3)\rangle\\
&\acute{\omega}\,\mathsf{E}\,\mathsf{K}\rightarrow\langle\mathcal{Y}[\![(\acute{\omega}|\mathsf{K})\downarrow 1]\!]\zeta,\mathrm{U}(\psi\zeta)((\acute{\omega}|\mathsf{K})\downarrow 2),\mathrm{Y}(\psi\zeta)((\acute{\omega}|\mathsf{K})\downarrow 3)\rangle,\\
&\mathrm{P}(\psi\zeta)(\acute{\omega}|\mathsf{P}).
\end{aligned}
$$

Here $\psi\zeta$ is not a retraction, but this need not deter us from referring to $\mathrm{E}(\psi\zeta)$, $\mathrm{U}(\psi\zeta)$, $\mathrm{Y}(\psi\zeta)$, $\mathrm{S}(\psi\zeta)$ and $\mathrm{P}(\psi\zeta)$, because E, U, Y, S and P can be defined on continuous functions (regarded as mappings of the underlying universal domain into itself) as well as on retractions. Moreover because E, U, Y, S and P do not depend on the detailed structure of the summands of W we may actually identify the versions of these functors appropriate to appendix 11 with the versions needed in 4.1.5. Thus we still set:

$\mathrm{V}=\lambda X.push\langle 4,-1\rangle\circ X\circ push\langle 3,1\rangle$;

$\mathrm{E}=\lambda X.X\circ mask4$;

$\mathrm{D}=\lambda X.X\circ mask5$.

Under these circumstances we have:

$S=\lambda X.(L\to(VX\times T))\times(VX)^*\times(VX)^*$;

$Y=\lambda X.(EX)^*$;

$U=\lambda X.(Ide\to(DX)^*)\times(reject\circ X\circ flag6)^*\times(reject\circ X\circ flag7)^*$.

Consequently it is reasonable to write

$P=\lambda X.UX\times YX\times SX$.

For any ζ and $\hat{\omega}$ we are interested in the element $fix(furling)\zeta\hat{\omega}$ belonging to the domain W for appendix 10. Accordingly we let

$furl=fix(furling)$

and we note that if, say, $\hat{\omega}\in E^*$ then $furl\zeta\hat{\omega}$ is actually $map(furl\zeta\circ mask4)(\hat{\omega}|E^*)$. We have taken $\psi\zeta$ instead of ψ to be the mapping between the two versions of W in order to make the definition of $furl$ (as $fix(furling)$ instead of $\psi\zeta.fix(\lambda\psi.furling\psi\zeta)$) uniform with the definition of $curl$ to be given in 4.6.2.

When ζ is a continuation and $\hat{\epsilon}$ is an expressed value appropriate to appendix 11 we are only able to view $E(furl\zeta)\hat{\epsilon}$ as an element of the domain E for appendix 10 because the two versions of E have a common structure in terms of W; analogous remarks apply to U, Y, S and P. However, more than a common structure is required, for though we can regard $Ide\to(D(furl\zeta))^*$, for instance, as a mapping taking a domain suited to appendix 11 into a domain suited to appendix 10 we cannot satisfactorily do the same with $D(furl\zeta)\to Ide^*$. The domains on which we can induce satisfactory mappings using $furl\zeta$ are those built from W by combining $\times$, $+$, $*$ and $\to$ in such a way that "W never appears to the left of the symbol $\to$"; we could give a more formal description of this class of combinations, but there is little point in doing so. Henceforth we shall assume that the domains called A in appendix 11 and appendix 10 have a common structure in terms of W which belongs to this class of combinations; this will ensure that if $\hat{\sigma}$ is in the domain of answers introduced in 4.4.2 then $A(furl\zeta)\hat{\sigma}$ is in the domain of answers mentioned in 4.1.2. Naturally this assumption is entirely reasonable, since A is most likely to be S, V* or P (perhaps with another summand intended to hold error messages) and so $A(\mathit{furl}\,\zeta)$ can probably be taken to be $S(\mathit{furl}\,\zeta)$, $(V(\mathit{furl}\,\zeta))^*$ or $P(\mathit{furl}\,\zeta)$.

If H is a control and ζ is a continuation then from any state, $\langle \acute{\rho},\acute{\upsilon},\acute{\sigma}\rangle$, suitable for control semantics we can obtain $A(\mathit{furl}\,\zeta)(\mathcal{Z}[\![H]\!]\acute{\rho}\acute{\upsilon}\acute{\sigma})$ and $\mathcal{Y}[\![H]\!]\zeta(U(\mathit{furl}\,\zeta)\acute{\rho})(Y(\mathit{furl}\,\zeta)\acute{\upsilon})(S(\mathit{furl}\,\zeta)\acute{\sigma})$. The first of these members of the domain of answers for appendix 10 represents the effect of executing H in the presence of the state $\langle \acute{\rho},\acute{\upsilon},\acute{\sigma}\rangle$ and converting the answer yielded into a more abstract form; the second results from applying $\mathcal{Y}[\![H]\!]\zeta$ to an environment, a stack and a store which are the counterparts of $\acute{\rho}$, $\acute{\upsilon}$ and $\acute{\sigma}$ in consecution semantics. The equation governing $\mathcal{Z}$ incorporates *process*, a function which is intended to finish everything off at the end of the execution of the control, whereas the continuation ζ appearing in $\mathcal{Y}[\![H]\!]\zeta$ could in principle be any member of Z, not just one expressing what happens on completing the executing of H. Thus, if we wish to compare $A(\mathit{furl}\,\zeta)(\mathcal{Z}[\![H]\!]\acute{\rho}\acute{\upsilon}\acute{\sigma})$ with $\mathcal{Y}[\![H]\!]\zeta(U(\mathit{furl}\,\zeta)\acute{\rho})(Y(\mathit{furl}\,\zeta)\acute{\upsilon})(S(\mathit{furl}\,\zeta)\acute{\sigma})$ even when H is $\langle\rangle$, we must make sure that applying *process* to $\acute{\rho}$, $\acute{\upsilon}$ and $\acute{\sigma}$ is very like applying ζ to an environment, a stack and a store akin to $\acute{\rho}$, $\acute{\upsilon}$, and $\acute{\sigma}$; in fact we must demand that ζ be subject to the equation

$$A(\mathit{furl}\,\zeta)(\mathit{process}\,\acute{\rho}\acute{\upsilon}\acute{\sigma})=\zeta(U(\mathit{furl}\,\zeta)\acute{\rho})(Y(\mathit{furl}\,\zeta)\acute{\upsilon})(S(\mathit{furl}\,\zeta)\acute{\sigma})$$

whenever $\langle \acute{\rho},\acute{\upsilon},\acute{\sigma}\rangle$ is a suitable state. We should therefore be satisfied that control semantics was congruent with consecution semantics if we could confirm that

$$A(\mathit{furl}\,\zeta)(\mathcal{Z}[\![H]\!]\acute{\rho}\acute{\upsilon}\acute{\sigma})=\mathcal{Y}[\![H]\!]\zeta(U(\mathit{furl}\,\zeta)\acute{\rho})(Y(\mathit{furl}\,\zeta)\acute{\upsilon})(S(\mathit{furl}\,\zeta)\acute{\sigma})$$

for every H, every $\langle \acute{\rho},\acute{\upsilon},\acute{\sigma}\rangle$ and every ζ constrained in the manner suggested.

Unfortunately the final equation in the preceding paragraph is not always valid, as may be seen by taking H to be $\langle\,\mathbf{t}\,\langle\nu,\Delta\rangle\rangle$ or $\langle\,\mathbf{amend}\ I\rangle$ for some identifier I such that $U(\mathit{furl}\,\zeta)\acute{\rho}$ differs from $U(\mathit{furl}\,\zeta)(\mathit{fold}\langle I\rangle\acute{\rho})$. Even so, we might expect it to be true when $\acute{\rho}$ coincides with $\mathit{fold}\langle I\rangle\acute{\rho}$ for any I; yet the expectation is mistaken, as is shown by letting H be ⟨jump⟩ and by supposing that $((\acute{\upsilon}\downarrow 1)|J)\downarrow 1$ is ⟨t ⟨ν,Δ⟩⟩ or ⟨amend I⟩ where $U(\mathit{furl}\,\zeta)(\mathit{coil}[\![(\acute{\upsilon}\downarrow 1|J)\downarrow 1]\!]((\acute{\upsilon}\downarrow 1|J)\downarrow 2))$ differs from $U(\mathit{furl}\,\zeta)(\mathit{fold}\langle I\rangle((\acute{\upsilon}\downarrow 1)|J)\downarrow 2))$. The assertion also fails when H is ⟨apply⟩§⟨write⟩ and $((\acute{\upsilon}\downarrow 2)|F)\downarrow 1$ is ⟨move 1⟩. We can, however, take heart from the belief that none of these cases can ever arise during the execution of Sal programs, for 4.5.4 allows us to concern ourselves with a control only when it is adhesive (and with a label value, $\langle H,\acute{\rho},\acute{\upsilon},I^*\rangle$ say, only when $\lambda I.\mathit{coil}[\![H]\!]\acute{\rho}=\lambda I.\mathit{fold}\langle I\rangle(\mathit{coil}[\![H]\!]\acute{\rho})$ and $I^*=\langle\rangle$). Accordingly we shall confine our attention to adhesive controls and to states which are "reliable" in a sense to be explained in 4.6.2; the only controls obtained by delving into such states will themselves be adhesive. Our discussion of these controls and states will culminate in the proof in 4.6.8 that

$$A(\mathit{furl}\,\zeta)(\mathcal{Z}[\![H]\!]\acute{\rho}\acute{\upsilon}\acute{\sigma})=\mathcal{Y}[\![H]\!]\zeta(U(\mathit{furl}\,\zeta)\acute{\rho})(Y(\mathit{furl}\,\zeta)\acute{\upsilon})(S(\mathit{furl}\,\zeta)\acute{\sigma})$$

under reasonable conditions.

4.6.2. The explicit connection between functions and program texts.

We must now confess that we require the diacritical convention of 2.5.4 again. However, here $\acute{\omega}$ will be a witnessed value in the version of W appropriate to appendix 11 whilst $\grave{\omega}$ will belong to the version of W needed by appendix 10 (as it did also in 4.2.1). Using this notation we can readily set up a continuous function, *curling*; when supplied with any inclusive predicate, ϕ, mapping the version of W appropriate to appendix 11 into T′ this provides another inclusive predicate, *curling*ϕ. If *cohere* and *adhere* have the properties given to them in 4.5.1,

$$
\begin{aligned}
\mathit{curling}=\lambda\phi\acute{\omega}.\,&(\acute{\omega}\equiv\bot)\rightarrow \mathit{true},\\
&(\acute{\omega}\equiv\top)\rightarrow \mathit{true},\\
&\acute{\omega}\in\mathsf{L}\rightarrow \mathit{true},\\
&\acute{\omega}\in\mathsf{B}\rightarrow \mathit{true},\\
&\acute{\omega}\in\mathsf{E}^*\rightarrow(\mathrm{e}(\lambda\hat{\omega}.\phi\acute{\omega}))^*\langle\acute{\omega}|\mathsf{E}^*,\mathit{furl}\bot\acute{\omega}|\mathsf{E}^*\rangle,\\
&\acute{\omega}\in\mathsf{J}\rightarrow \mathit{adhere}\llbracket(\acute{\omega}|\mathsf{J})\downarrow 1\rrbracket\\
&\qquad\wedge\mathrm{u}(\lambda\hat{\omega}.\phi\acute{\omega})\langle \mathit{coil}\llbracket(\acute{\omega}|\mathsf{J})\downarrow 1\rrbracket((\acute{\omega}|\mathsf{J})\downarrow 2),(\mathit{furl}\bot\acute{\omega}|\mathsf{J})\downarrow 2\rangle\\
&\qquad\wedge\mathrm{y}(\lambda\hat{\omega}.\phi\acute{\omega})\langle(\acute{\omega}|\mathsf{J})\downarrow 3,(\mathit{furl}\bot\acute{\omega}|\mathsf{J})\downarrow 3\rangle\\
&\qquad\wedge((\acute{\omega}|\mathsf{J})\downarrow 4\equiv\langle\,\rangle),\\
&\acute{\omega}\in\mathsf{F}\rightarrow \mathit{cohere}\llbracket(\acute{\omega}|\mathsf{F})\downarrow 1\rrbracket\wedge \mathit{adhere}\llbracket(\acute{\omega}|\mathsf{F})\downarrow 1\rrbracket\\
&\qquad\wedge\mathrm{u}(\lambda\hat{\omega}.\phi\acute{\omega})\langle(\acute{\omega}|\mathsf{F})\downarrow 2,(\mathit{furl}\bot\acute{\omega}|\mathsf{F})\downarrow 2\rangle,\\
&\acute{\omega}\in\mathsf{G}\rightarrow \mathit{cohere}\llbracket(\acute{\omega}|\mathsf{G})\downarrow 1\rrbracket\wedge \mathit{adhere}\llbracket(\acute{\omega}|\mathsf{G})\downarrow 1\rrbracket\\
&\qquad\wedge\mathrm{u}(\lambda\hat{\omega}.\phi\acute{\omega})\langle \mathit{coil}\llbracket(\acute{\omega}|\mathsf{G})\downarrow 1\rrbracket((\acute{\omega}|\mathsf{G})\downarrow 2),(\mathit{furl}\bot\acute{\omega}|\mathsf{G})\downarrow 2\rangle\\
&\qquad\wedge\mathrm{s}(\lambda\hat{\omega}.\phi\acute{\omega})\langle(\acute{\omega}|\mathsf{G})\downarrow 3,(\mathit{furl}\bot\acute{\omega}|\mathsf{G})\downarrow 3\rangle\\
&\qquad\wedge((\acute{\omega}|\mathsf{G})\downarrow 4\equiv\langle\,\rangle),\\
&\acute{\omega}\in\mathsf{K}\rightarrow \mathit{adhere}\llbracket(\acute{\omega}|\mathsf{K})\downarrow 1\rrbracket\\
&\qquad\wedge\mathrm{u}(\lambda\hat{\omega}.\phi\acute{\omega})\langle(\acute{\omega}|\mathsf{K})\downarrow 2,(\mathit{furl}\bot\acute{\omega}|\mathsf{J})\downarrow 2\rangle\\
&\qquad\wedge\mathrm{y}(\lambda\hat{\omega}.\phi\acute{\omega})\langle(\acute{\omega}|\mathsf{K})\downarrow 3,(\mathit{furl}\bot\acute{\omega}|\mathsf{J})\downarrow 3\rangle,\\
&\mathrm{p}(\lambda\hat{\omega}.\phi\acute{\omega})\langle\acute{\omega}|\mathsf{P},\mathit{furl}\bot\acute{\omega}|\mathsf{P}\rangle.
\end{aligned}
$$

Once again we have freely adapted old notation to a new situation by mentioning $\mathrm{e}(\lambda\hat{\omega}.\phi\acute{\omega})$, $\mathrm{u}(\lambda\hat{\omega}.\phi\acute{\omega})$, $\mathrm{y}(\lambda\hat{\omega}.\phi\acute{\omega})$, $\mathrm{s}(\lambda\hat{\omega}.\phi\acute{\omega})$ and $\mathrm{p}(\lambda\hat{\omega}.\phi\acute{\omega})$, which are predicates defined on E×E, U×U, Y×Y, S×S and P×P respectively. When we apply the diacritical convention to these (and other) products of domains and when we make use of the functions defined in 2.4.4 we may set

$v=\lambda x.x\circ(push\langle 3,1\rangle\times push\langle 3,1\rangle)\circ(\lambda\hat{\beta}.\hat{\beta});$

$e=\lambda x.x\circ(mask4\times mask4)\circ(\lambda\hat{\epsilon}.\hat{\epsilon});$

$d=\lambda x.x\circ(mask5\times mask5)\circ(\lambda\hat{\delta}.\hat{\delta}).$

We also provide l and t, the tests for equality between members of L and between members of T, so that after identifying *check* with *false* in the equations of 2.5.5 we may define:

$s=\lambda x.((l\rightarrow(vx\times t))\times(vx)^*\times(vx)^*)\circ(\lambda\hat{\sigma}.\hat{\sigma})$

$y=\lambda x.(ex)^*\circ(\lambda\hat{\upsilon}.\hat{\upsilon});$

$u=\lambda x\hat{\rho}.\bigwedge\{(dx)^*\langle\acute{\rho}[\![I]\!],\grave{\rho}[\![I]\!]\rangle\mid I\}$

$\qquad\wedge(x\circ flag6)^*\langle\acute{\rho}[\![\mathrm{res}]\!],\grave{\rho}[\![\mathrm{res}]\!]\rangle\wedge(x\circ flag7)^*\langle\acute{\rho}[\![\mathrm{rec}]\!],\grave{\rho}[\![\mathrm{rec}]\!]\rangle.$

With the aid of u, y and s we define p by writing

$p=\lambda x.(ux\times yx\times sx)\circ(\lambda\hat{\pi}.\hat{\pi}).$

Because *curling* is a continuous function mapping a domain of inclusive predicates into itself we may form its least fixed point, *curl*, by writing

$curl=fix(curling);$

though *curl* is an inclusive predicate subject to a recursive equation its existence can be established without any resort to 2.5.3, since it is a fixed point of a continuous function. The terms involving $furl\,\iota\acute{\omega}$ in the equation for *curling* simply ensure that e, u, y, s and p are supplied with the right types of arguments; they could have been omitted, but we would then have needed to use lengthy forms of predicates instead of a group of familiar predictors. Thus in such formulas as $u(\lambda\hat{\omega}.curl\,\acute{\omega})\hat{\rho}$, $y(\lambda\hat{\omega}.curl\,\acute{\omega})\hat{\upsilon}$ and $s(\lambda\hat{\omega}.curl\,\acute{\omega})\hat{\sigma}$, for example, only $\acute{\rho}$, $\acute{\upsilon}$ and $\acute{\sigma}$ are really important; $\grave{\rho}$, $\grave{\upsilon}$ and $\grave{\sigma}$ could be eliminated in favour of $U(furl\,\zeta)\acute{\rho}$, $Y(furl\,\zeta)\acute{\upsilon}$ and $S(furl\,\zeta)\acute{\sigma}$ for any ζ so long as they "have the right shapes".

When $\langle \acute{\rho},\acute{\upsilon},\acute{\sigma}\rangle$ is a state belonging to the domain P appropriate to appendix 11 for brevity we shall call $\langle \acute{\rho},\acute{\upsilon},\acute{\sigma}\rangle$ 'reliable' if and only if $p(\lambda\hat{\omega}.curl\acute{\omega})\langle\langle \acute{\rho},\acute{\upsilon},\acute{\sigma}\rangle, P(furl\bot)\langle \acute{\rho},\acute{\upsilon},\acute{\sigma}\rangle\rangle = true$. If $\langle \acute{\rho},\acute{\upsilon},\acute{\sigma}\rangle$ is reliable we know that $\lambda I.\acute{\rho} = \lambda I.fold\langle I\rangle\acute{\rho}$, for the equation $u(\lambda\hat{\omega}.curl\acute{\omega})\langle \acute{\rho}, U(furl\bot)\acute{\rho}\rangle = true$ ensures that when I is any identifier for which $\#\acute{\rho}[\![I]\!]>0$ then $d(\lambda\hat{\omega}.curl\acute{\omega})\langle \acute{\rho}[\![I]\!]\downarrow 1, D(furl\bot)(\acute{\rho}[\![I]\!]\downarrow 1)\rangle = true$ and $wrap\acute{\rho}(\acute{\rho}[\![I]\!]\downarrow 1) = \acute{\rho}[\![I]\!]\downarrow 1$.

Having at last restricted the controls and states of interest to us we can begin to relate $A(furl\zeta)(\mathcal{Z}[\![H]\!]\acute{\rho}\acute{\upsilon}\acute{\sigma})$ and $\mathcal{Y}[\![H]\!]\zeta(U(furl\zeta)\acute{\rho})(Y(furl\zeta)\acute{\upsilon})(S(furl\zeta)\acute{\sigma})$. An obvious approach to this task involves induction on the length of H; thus we might try to prove that $A(furl\zeta)(\mathcal{Z}[\![H_0]\!]\acute{\rho}_0\acute{\upsilon}_0\acute{\sigma}_0) = \mathcal{Y}[\![H_0]\!]\zeta(U(furl\zeta)\acute{\rho}_0)(Y(furl\zeta)\acute{\sigma}_0)(S(furl\zeta)\acute{\sigma}_0)$ by examining $\mathcal{A}[\![H_0\downarrow 1]\!]$ on the assumption that $A(furl\zeta)(\mathcal{Z}[\![H_1]\!]\acute{\rho}_1\acute{\upsilon}_1\acute{\sigma}_1) = \mathcal{Y}[\![H_1]\!]\zeta(U(furl\zeta)\acute{\rho}_1)(Y(furl\zeta)\acute{\sigma}_1)(S(furl\zeta)\acute{\sigma}_1)$ for every adhesive control H_1 having $\#H_0 - 1 \geq \#H_1 \geq 0$ and for every reliable state $\langle \acute{\rho}_1,\acute{\upsilon}_1,\acute{\sigma}_1\rangle$. Unfortunately an attempt to validate this equation will break down if $H_0\downarrow 1$ is jump, apply or view I, since the control created by applying $\mathcal{A}[\![H_0\downarrow 1]\!]$ may have length greater than $\#H_0 - 1$.

In fact though equations involving the valuation $\mathcal{Y}$ alone can be justified by structural induction alone those involving $\mathcal{Z}$ as well cannot be established by this means. Essentially the reason for this is that the recursion implicit in the definition of $\mathcal{Y}$ is of a different nature from that underlying $\mathcal{Z}$: $\mathcal{Y}$ is defined simply by recursion on the length of the control supplied to it as an argument, whilst $\mathcal{Z}$ is defined by computing a control using $\mathcal{A}$ and then passing that control to $\mathcal{Z}$. For us to rely solely on structural induction when proving things about $\mathcal{Z}$ would be no more reasonable than to appeal just to induction on the area of the store, say, when verifying propositions about $\mathcal{E}$; in both cases we would be endeavouring to establish a property of programs by imposing static limits on quantities which can vary dynamically during computations in unpredictable ways.

When formalizing the connection between appendix 11 and appendix 10 we are therefore obliged to use our knowledge that $\mathbf{Z}=\mathit{fix}(\mathit{proceed})$. We could try to do this by showing that for any ψ and some ζ

$A(\mathit{furl}\zeta)(\mathit{proceed}\psi[\![H_0]\!]\acute{\rho}_0\acute{\upsilon}_0\acute{\sigma}_0)=\mathcal{Y}[\![H_0]\!]\zeta(U(\mathit{furl}\zeta)\acute{\rho}_0)(Y(\mathit{furl}\zeta)\acute{\upsilon}_0)(S(\mathit{furl}\zeta)\acute{\sigma}_0)$

on the assumption that

$A(\mathit{furl}\zeta)(\psi[\![H_1]\!]\acute{\rho}_1\acute{\upsilon}_1\acute{\sigma}_1)=\mathcal{Y}[\![H_1]\!]\zeta(U(\mathit{furl}\zeta)\acute{\rho}_1)(Y(\mathit{furl}\zeta)\acute{\upsilon}_1)(S(\mathit{furl}\zeta)\acute{\sigma}_1)$

whenever H_1 is adhesive and $\langle\acute{\rho}_1,\acute{\upsilon}_1,\acute{\sigma}_1\rangle$ is reliable; however, such an argument would not allow us to conclude that

$A(\mathit{furl}\zeta)(\mathbf{Z}[\![H_0]\!]\acute{\rho}_0\acute{\upsilon}_0\acute{\sigma}_0)=\mathcal{Y}[\![H_0]\!]\zeta(U(\mathit{furl}\zeta)\acute{\rho}_0)(Y(\mathit{furl}\zeta)\acute{\upsilon}_0)(S(\mathit{furl}\zeta)\acute{\sigma}_0)$

by appealing to the induction principle of 2.3.2, because we would not believe that in general

$A(\mathit{furl}\zeta)(\bot[\![H_0]\!]\acute{\rho}_0\acute{\upsilon}_0\acute{\sigma}_0)=\mathcal{Y}[\![H_1]\!]\zeta(U(\mathit{furl}\zeta)\acute{\rho}_1)(Y(\mathit{furl}\zeta)\acute{\upsilon}_1)(S(\mathit{furl}\zeta)\acute{\sigma}_1)$.

Nevertheless since

$A(\mathit{furl}\zeta)(\bot[\![H_1]\!]\acute{\rho}_1\acute{\upsilon}_1\acute{\sigma}_1)\sqsubseteq\mathcal{Y}[\![H_1]\!]\zeta(U(\mathit{furl}\zeta)\acute{\rho}_1)(Y(\mathit{furl}\zeta)\acute{\upsilon}_1)(S(\mathit{furl}\zeta)\acute{\sigma}_1)$

we can still establish inductively that

$A(\mathit{furl}\zeta)(\mathbf{Z}[\![H_0]\!]\acute{\rho}_0\acute{\upsilon}_0\acute{\sigma}_0)\sqsubseteq\mathcal{Y}[\![H_0]\!]\zeta(U(\mathit{furl}\zeta)\acute{\rho}_0)(Y(\mathit{furl}\zeta)\acute{\upsilon}_0)(S(\mathit{furl}\zeta)\acute{\sigma}_0)$;

this job will be undertaken in 4.6.4.

When we attempt to confirm that

$A(\mathit{furl}\zeta)(\mathit{proceed}\psi[\![H_0]\!]\acute{\rho}_0\acute{\upsilon}_0\acute{\sigma}_0)\sqsubseteq\mathcal{Y}[\![H_0]\!]\zeta(U(\mathit{furl}\zeta)\acute{\rho}_0)(Y(\mathit{furl}\zeta)\acute{\upsilon}_0)(S(\mathit{furl}\zeta)\acute{\sigma}_0)$

by assuming that

$\mathit{halt}\zeta(\psi[\![H_1]\!]\acute{\rho}_1\acute{\upsilon}_1\acute{\sigma}_1)\sqsubseteq\mathcal{Y}[\![H_1]\!]\zeta(U(\mathit{furl}\zeta)\acute{\rho}_1)(Y(\mathit{furl}\zeta)\acute{\upsilon}_1)(S(\mathit{furl}\zeta)\acute{\sigma}_1)$

whenever H_1 is adhesive and $\langle\acute{\rho}_1,\acute{\upsilon}_1,\acute{\sigma}_1\rangle$ is reliable, we run into trouble if $H_0{\downarrow}1$ is t $\langle\nu,\Delta\rangle$ or q $\langle\nu,\Gamma\rangle$, as then $\mathit{proceed}\psi[\![H_0]\!]\acute{\rho}_0\acute{\upsilon}_0\acute{\sigma}_0=\psi[\![H_0{\dagger}1]\!]\acute{\rho}_1\acute{\upsilon}_0\acute{\sigma}_0$ where $\langle\acute{\rho}_1,\acute{\upsilon}_0,\acute{\sigma}_0\rangle$ is not reliable (because H_1 differs from $\mathit{fold}(\mathcal{H}[\![\Delta]\!])\acute{\rho}_1$ or $\mathit{fold}(\mathcal{K}[\![\Gamma]\!])\acute{\rho}_1$). To circumvent this trouble we amend our definition of $\mathit{proceed}\in(\mathsf{Con}\to\mathsf{U}\to\mathsf{Y}\to\mathsf{S}\to\mathsf{A})\to(\mathsf{Con}\to\mathsf{U}\to\mathsf{Y}\to\mathsf{S}\to\mathsf{A})$ so that

$proceed = \lambda\psi H\acute{\rho}\acute{\upsilon}\acute{\sigma}.(\#H=0) \to process\,\acute{\rho}\acute{\upsilon}\acute{\sigma},$

$\mathcal{A}[\![H{\downarrow}1]\!][\![H{\dagger}1]\!]\acute{\rho}\acute{\upsilon}\acute{\sigma}\,E\,A \to \mathcal{A}[\![H{\downarrow}1]\!][\![H{\dagger}1]\!]\acute{\rho}\acute{\upsilon}\acute{\sigma}|A,$

$(\lambda\langle H',\acute{\rho}',\acute{\upsilon}',\acute{\sigma}'\rangle.\bigvee\{H'{\downarrow}1 \equiv \text{amend } I|I\} \to proceed\,\psi[\![H']\!]\acute{\rho}'\acute{\upsilon}'\acute{\sigma}',$

$\bigvee\{\bigvee\{H{\downarrow}1 \equiv \text{t } \langle\nu,\Delta\rangle\,|\nu\}|\Delta\} \to proceed\,\psi[\![H']\!]\acute{\rho}'\acute{\upsilon}'\acute{\sigma}',$

$\bigvee\{\bigvee\{H{\downarrow}1 \equiv \text{q } \langle\nu,\Gamma\rangle\,|\nu\}|\Gamma\} \to proceed\,\psi[\![H']\!]\acute{\rho}'\acute{\upsilon}'\acute{\sigma}',$

$\psi[\![H']\!]\acute{\rho}'\acute{\upsilon}'\acute{\sigma}'$

$(\mathcal{A}[\![H{\downarrow}1]\!][\![H{\dagger}1]\!]\rho\upsilon\sigma|(Con\times U\times Y\times S)).$

We shall leave it to the reader to verify with the aid of 2.3.2 that when *proceed* is set up in this manner $\mathcal{Z}=fix(proceed)$ provided that $\mathcal{Z}$ is defined as in appendix 11.

The argument about *proceed* in 4.6.3 is tiresomely tortuous, so the reader may well choose to skip it for the present. Indeed, although the set of proofs which we are about to provide follows a simple pattern (to be laid down in 4.6.5) it does so in a way which is far from perspicuous, owing to the differences between our two treatments of amend I, t $\langle\nu,\Delta\rangle$ and q $\langle\nu,\Gamma\rangle$. A less obscure set of proofs conforming to the same pattern will be discussed from 5.6.3 onwards and should perhaps be studied first.

The proof of 4.6.3 requires us to impose various constraints on the functions that we are considering. Thus we demand that $\lambda\zeta.A(furl\,\zeta)\bot=\lambda\zeta.\bot$, $\lambda\zeta.A(furl\,\zeta)\top=\lambda\zeta.\top$, $\lambda\zeta.A(furl\,\zeta)(wrong\,\acute{\sigma})=\lambda\zeta.wrong(S(furl\,\zeta)\acute{\sigma})$ and $\lambda\zeta.new\,\acute{\sigma}=\lambda\zeta.new(S(furl\,\zeta)\acute{\sigma})$ whenever $\acute{\sigma}$ is such that $s(\lambda\hat{\omega}.curl\,\acute{\omega})\langle\acute{\sigma},S(furl\bot)\acute{\sigma}\rangle=true$ (though actually slightly weaker restrictions on *wrong* and *new* suffice for the proof of 4.6.8); naturally the versions of *wrong* and *new* appropriate to appendix 11 are used on the left hand sides of these equations, whereas the versions appropriate to appendix 10 appear on the right hand sides. If H_0 is an adhesive control such that $H_0{\downarrow}1$ is a secret order and if $\langle\acute{\rho}_0,\acute{\upsilon}_0,\acute{\sigma}_0\rangle$ is a reliable state, we shall suppose that, when $\mathcal{A}[\![H_0{\downarrow}1]\!][\![H_0{\dagger}1]\!]\acute{\rho}_0\acute{\upsilon}_0\acute{\sigma}_0$ is not in $Con\times U\times Y\times S$,

$\lambda\zeta.A(furl\zeta)(\mathcal{A}[\![H_0\downarrow 1]\!][\![H_0\dagger 1]\!]\rho_0\upsilon_0\sigma_0|A)=\lambda\zeta.\mathcal{Y}[\![H_0]\!]\zeta(U(furl\zeta)\rho_0)(Y(furl\zeta)\upsilon_0)(S(furl\zeta)\sigma_0)$ and that, when $\mathcal{A}[\![H_0\downarrow 1]\!][\![H_0\dagger 1]\!]\rho_0\upsilon_0\sigma_0$ is in $Con\times U\times Y\times S$, $\lambda\psi.proceed\psi[\![H_0]\!]\rho_0\upsilon_0\sigma_0=\lambda\psi.\psi[\![H_1]\!]\rho_1\upsilon_1\sigma_1$ (for some adhesive control H_1 and for some reliable state $\langle\rho_1,\upsilon_1,\sigma_1\rangle$ such that $\lambda\zeta.\mathcal{Y}[\![H_0]\!]\zeta(U(furl\zeta)\rho_0)(Y(furl\zeta)\upsilon_0)(S(furl\zeta)\sigma_0)$ coincides with $\lambda\zeta.\mathcal{Y}[\![H_1]\!]\zeta(U(furl\zeta)\rho_1)(Y(furl\zeta)\upsilon_1)(S(furl\zeta)\sigma_1)$); why this is a reasonable supposition will become apparent in 4.6.3, when we shall show that the claim it makes about $H_0\downarrow 1$ is certainly valid when $H_0\downarrow 1$ is not secret. On top of all this we shall extend 4.5.4 and 4.5.5 by assuming that for all B, O and Ω $\mathcal{B}[\![B]\!]$, $\mathcal{O}[\![O]\!]$ and $\mathcal{W}[\![\Omega]\!]$ are cohesive and adhesive controls such that $\mathcal{B}[\![B]\!]=\mathcal{Y}[\![\mathfrak{b}[\![B]\!]]\!]$, $\mathcal{O}[\![O]\!]=\mathcal{Y}[\![\mathfrak{o}[\![O]\!]]\!]$ and $\mathcal{W}[\![\Omega]\!]=\mathcal{Y}[\![\mathfrak{w}[\![\Omega]\!]]\!]$ when we apply the valuations $\mathcal{B}$, $\mathcal{O}$ and $\mathcal{W}$ implicit in appendix 2.

4.6.3. Lemma.

Let H_0 be an adhesive Sap control having $\#H_0>0$ and let $\langle\acute{\rho}_0,\acute{\upsilon}_0,\acute{\sigma}_0\rangle$ be a reliable state; take ζ to be any continuation and set $\langle\grave{\rho}_0,\grave{\upsilon}_0,\grave{\sigma}_0\rangle=P(\mathit{furl}\zeta)\langle\acute{\rho}_0,\acute{\upsilon}_0,\acute{\sigma}_0\rangle$. Unless $\mathcal{A}[\![H_0{\downarrow}1]\!][\![H_0{\dagger}1]\!]\acute{\rho}_0\acute{\upsilon}_0\acute{\sigma}_0\in\mathrm{Con}\times\mathrm{U}\times\mathrm{Y}\times\mathrm{S}$, $A(\mathit{furl}\zeta)(\mathcal{A}[\![H_0{\downarrow}1]\!][\![H_0{\dagger}1]\!]\acute{\rho}_0\acute{\upsilon}_0\acute{\sigma}_0|A)=\mathcal{Y}[\![H_0]\!]\zeta\grave{\rho}_0\grave{\upsilon}_0\grave{\sigma}_0$. If $\mathcal{A}[\![H_0{\downarrow}1]\!][\![H_0{\dagger}1]\!]\acute{\rho}_0\acute{\upsilon}_0\acute{\sigma}_0\in\mathrm{Con}\times\mathrm{U}\times\mathrm{Y}\times\mathrm{S}$, there exists an adhesive Sap control H_1, together with a reliable state $\langle\acute{\rho}_1,\acute{\upsilon}_1,\acute{\sigma}_1\rangle$, such that $\lambda\psi.\mathit{proceed}\psi[\![H_0]\!]\acute{\rho}_0\acute{\upsilon}_0\acute{\sigma}_0=\lambda\psi.\psi[\![H_1]\!]\acute{\rho}_1\acute{\upsilon}_1\acute{\sigma}_1$ and $\mathcal{Y}[\![H_0]\!]\zeta\grave{\rho}_0\grave{\upsilon}_0\grave{\sigma}_0=\mathcal{Y}[\![H_1]\!]\zeta\grave{\rho}_1\grave{\upsilon}_1\grave{\sigma}_1$ where $\langle\grave{\rho}_1,\grave{\upsilon}_1,\grave{\sigma}_1\rangle=P(\mathit{furl}\zeta)\langle\acute{\rho}_1,\acute{\upsilon}_1,\acute{\sigma}_1\rangle$.

⊲The proof of this result proceeds simply by comparing the meaning ascribed to $H_0{\downarrow}1$ by appendix 11 with the meaning ascribed to $H_0{\downarrow}1$ by appendix 10; when $H_0{\downarrow}1$ is secret the suppositions made in 4.6.2 ensure that the result holds. Here we shall simply examine what happens when $H_0{\downarrow}1$ is one of five orders (move ν, jump, apply, p $\langle\nu,\Gamma\rangle$ and q $\langle\nu,\Gamma\rangle$), leaving the remaining possibilities to the reader.

Before examining these orders we shall discuss one feature of the version of *proceed* provided in 4.6.2. We take H_0 to be a control, I* to be a list of identifiers and $\langle\acute{\rho}_0,\acute{\upsilon}_0,\acute{\sigma}_0\rangle$ to be a state such that writing $\langle H_2,\acute{\rho}_2,\acute{\upsilon}_2,\acute{\sigma}_2\rangle=\mathcal{A}[\![H_0{\downarrow}1]\!][\![H_0{\dagger}1]\!]\acute{\rho}_0\acute{\upsilon}_0\acute{\sigma}_0|(\mathrm{Con}\times\mathrm{U}\times\mathrm{Y}\times\mathrm{S})$ produces an adhesive control H_2 and a state $\langle\acute{\rho}_2,\acute{\upsilon}_2,\acute{\sigma}_2\rangle$ for which $\langle\mathit{coil}[\![H_2]\!]\acute{\rho}_2,\acute{\upsilon}_2,\acute{\sigma}_2\rangle$ is reliable. When ν is the least integer for which either $H_2{\downarrow}\nu$ is $\langle\rangle$ or $(H_2{\dagger}\nu){\downarrow}1$ is not of the form amend I for any I we may show by induction on ν that $\lambda\psi.\mathit{proceed}\psi[\![H_0]\!]\acute{\rho}_0\acute{\upsilon}_0\acute{\sigma}_0=\lambda\psi.\psi[\![H_2{\dagger}\nu]\!](\mathit{coil}[\![H]\!]\acute{\rho}_2)\acute{\upsilon}_2\acute{\sigma}_2$ and, of course, that $\mathcal{Y}[\![H_2]\!]=\mathcal{Y}[\![H_2{\dagger}\nu]\!]$. Hence if, in addition, there is some ζ and a state $\langle\grave{\rho}_0,\grave{\upsilon}_0,\grave{\sigma}_0\rangle$ such that $\mathcal{Y}[\![H_0]\!]\zeta\grave{\rho}_0\grave{\upsilon}_0\grave{\sigma}_0=\mathcal{Y}[\![H_2]\!]\zeta(U(\mathit{furl}\zeta)(\mathit{coil}[\![H]\!]\acute{\rho}_1))(Y(\mathit{furl}\zeta)\acute{\upsilon}_1)(S(\mathit{furl}\zeta)\acute{\sigma}_1)$, we may conclude that there exists an adhesive control H_1 (which is $H_2{\dagger}\nu$), together with a reliable state $\langle\acute{\rho}_1,\acute{\upsilon}_1,\acute{\sigma}_1\rangle$ (which is $\langle\mathit{coil}[\![H]\!]\acute{\rho}_2,\acute{\upsilon}_2,\acute{\sigma}_2\rangle$), for which $\lambda\psi.\mathit{proceed}\psi[\![H_0]\!]\acute{\rho}_0\acute{\upsilon}_0\acute{\sigma}_0=\lambda\psi.\psi[\![H_1]\!]\acute{\rho}_1\acute{\upsilon}_1\acute{\sigma}_1$ and

$\mathcal{Y}[\![H_0]\!]\zeta\grave{\rho}_0\grave{\upsilon}_0\grave{\sigma}_0=\mathcal{Y}[\![H_1]\!]\zeta\grave{\rho}_1\grave{\upsilon}_1\grave{\sigma}_1$ where $\langle\grave{\rho}_1,\grave{\upsilon}_1,\grave{\sigma}_1\rangle=P(\mathit{furl}\zeta)\langle\acute{\rho}_1,\acute{\upsilon}_1,\acute{\sigma}_1\rangle$.

We now select any adhesive control H_0 and any reliable state $\langle\acute{\rho}_0,\acute{\upsilon}_0,\acute{\sigma}_0\rangle$, and for some continuation ζ we let $\langle\grave{\rho}_0,\grave{\upsilon}_0,\grave{\sigma}_0\rangle=P(\mathit{furl}\zeta)\langle\acute{\rho}_0,\acute{\upsilon}_0,\acute{\sigma}_0\rangle$ in readiness for our examination of $H_0\downarrow 1$.

When $H_0\downarrow 1$ is move ν appendix 11 indicates that $\mathcal{A}[\![H_0\downarrow 1]\!][\![H_0\dagger 1]\!]\acute{\rho}_0\acute{\upsilon}_0\acute{\sigma}_0|(\mathrm{Con}\times U\times Y\times S)=\langle(H_0\dagger 1)\dagger\nu,\acute{\rho}_0,\acute{\upsilon}_0,\acute{\sigma}_0\rangle$ and that $\mathcal{Y}[\![H_0]\!]\zeta\grave{\rho}_0\grave{\upsilon}_0\grave{\sigma}_0=\mathcal{Y}[\![(H_0\dagger 1)\dagger\nu]\!]\zeta\grave{\rho}_0\grave{\upsilon}_0\grave{\sigma}_0$ where $(H_0\dagger 1)\dagger\nu$ is adhesive and where $\langle\mathit{coil}[\![(H_0\dagger 1)\dagger\nu]\!]\acute{\rho}_0,\acute{\upsilon}_0,\acute{\sigma}_0\rangle$ is reliable. Consequently the remarks above allow us to assert the existence of an adhesive control H_1 and a reliable state $\langle\acute{\rho}_1,\acute{\upsilon}_1,\acute{\sigma}_1\rangle$ (which here is actually $\langle\grave{\rho}_0,\grave{\upsilon}_0,\grave{\sigma}_0\rangle$) having $\lambda\psi.\mathit{proceed}\psi[\![H_0]\!]\acute{\rho}_0\acute{\upsilon}_0\acute{\sigma}_0=\lambda\psi.\psi[\![H_1]\!]\acute{\rho}_1\acute{\upsilon}_1\acute{\sigma}_1$ and $\mathcal{Y}[\![H_0]\!]\zeta\grave{\rho}_0\grave{\upsilon}_0\grave{\sigma}_0=\mathcal{Y}[\![H_1]\!]\zeta\grave{\rho}_1\grave{\upsilon}_1\grave{\sigma}_1$ where $\langle\grave{\rho}_1,\grave{\upsilon}_1,\grave{\sigma}_1\rangle=P(\mathit{furl}\zeta)\langle\acute{\rho}_1,\acute{\upsilon}_1,\acute{\sigma}_1\rangle$.

When $H_0\downarrow 1$ is jump the situation is materially more complicated, for $\mathcal{A}[\![H_0\downarrow 1]\!][\![H_0\dagger 1]\!]\acute{\rho}_0\acute{\upsilon}_0\acute{\sigma}_0$ is $\perp$, $\top$, $\mathit{wrong}\acute{\sigma}_0$ or $\langle\acute{\upsilon}_0\downarrow 1\downarrow 1,\acute{\upsilon}_0\downarrow 1\downarrow 2,\acute{\upsilon}_0\downarrow 1\downarrow 3,\acute{\sigma}_0\rangle$ (and $\mathcal{Y}[\![H_0]\!]\zeta\grave{\rho}_0\grave{\upsilon}_0\grave{\sigma}_0$ is $\perp$, $\top$, $\mathit{wrong}\grave{\sigma}_0$ or $(\grave{\upsilon}_0\downarrow 1\downarrow 1)(\grave{\upsilon}_0\downarrow 1\downarrow 2)(\grave{\upsilon}_0\downarrow 1\downarrow 3)\grave{\sigma}_0)$, depending on whether $\acute{\upsilon}_0\downarrow 1$ is $\perp$, $\top$, a member of a summand of E other than J or a member of the summand J. Owing to the assumptions made about *wrong* in 4.6.1 we may conclude that $A(\mathit{furl}\zeta)(\mathcal{A}[\![H_0\downarrow 1]\!][\![H_0\dagger 1]\!]\acute{\rho}_0\acute{\upsilon}_0\acute{\sigma}_0|A)=\mathcal{Y}[\![H_0]\!]\zeta\grave{\rho}_0\grave{\upsilon}_0\grave{\sigma}_0$ unless $\mathcal{A}[\![H_0\downarrow 1]\!][\![H_0\dagger 1]\!]\acute{\rho}_0\acute{\upsilon}_0\acute{\sigma}_0\in\mathrm{Con}\times U\times Y\times S$; thus we concentrate on considering what happens when $\acute{\upsilon}_0\downarrow 1$ is a member of the summand J. Under these circumstances we note that $\acute{\upsilon}_0\downarrow 1|J$ is $\langle H_2,\acute{\rho}_2,\acute{\upsilon}_2,I^*\rangle$ for some H_2, $\acute{\rho}_2$, $\acute{\upsilon}_2$ and I^* such that $\mathcal{A}[\![H_0\downarrow 1]\!][\![H_0\dagger 1]\!]\acute{\rho}_0\acute{\upsilon}_0\acute{\sigma}_0|(\mathrm{Con}\times U\times Y\times S)=\langle H_2,\acute{\rho}_2,\acute{\upsilon}_2,\acute{\sigma}_0\rangle$, H_2 is adhesive, $u(\lambda\hat{\omega}.\mathit{curl}\hat{\omega})\langle\mathit{coil}[\![H_2]\!]\acute{\rho}_2,U(\mathit{furl}\perp)(\mathit{coil}[\![H_2]\!]\acute{\rho}_2)\rangle=\mathit{true}$ and $y(\lambda\hat{\omega}.\mathit{curl}\hat{\omega})\langle\acute{\upsilon}_2,Y(\mathit{furl}\perp)\acute{\upsilon}_2\rangle=\mathit{true}$ (because $e(\lambda\hat{\omega}.\mathit{curl}\hat{\omega})\langle\acute{\upsilon}_0\downarrow 1,E(\mathit{furl}\perp)(\upsilon_0\downarrow 1)\rangle=\mathit{true}$). However, according to appendix 10,

$\mathcal{Y}[\![H_0]\!]\zeta\grave\rho_0\grave\upsilon_0\grave\sigma_0=\mathcal{A}[\![H_0\downarrow 1]\!](\lambda\nu.\mathcal{Y}[\![(H_0\dagger 1)\dagger\nu]\!]\zeta)\grave\rho_0\grave\upsilon_0\grave\sigma_0$

$=(\grave\upsilon_0\downarrow 1\downarrow 1)(\grave\upsilon_0\downarrow 1\downarrow 2)(\grave\upsilon_0\downarrow 1\downarrow 3)\grave\sigma_0$

$=\mathcal{Y}[\![H_2]\!]\zeta(U(\mathit{furl}\zeta)(\mathit{fold}I{*}\acute\rho_2))(Y(\mathit{furl}\zeta)\acute\upsilon_2)(S(\mathit{furl}\zeta)\acute\sigma_0)$,

since $\grave\upsilon_0\downarrow 1$, being $E(\mathit{furl}\zeta)(\acute\upsilon_0\downarrow 1)$, is $\langle\mathcal{Y}[\![H_2]\!]\zeta,U(\mathit{furl}\zeta)(\mathit{coil}[\![H_2]\!]\acute\rho_2),Y(\mathit{furl}\zeta)\acute\upsilon_2\rangle$. The remarks above now give us an adhesive control H_1 and a reliable state $\langle\acute\rho_1,\acute\upsilon_1,\acute\sigma_1\rangle$ having $\lambda\psi.\mathit{proceed}\psi[\![H_0]\!]\acute\rho_0\acute\upsilon_0\acute\sigma_0=\lambda\psi.\psi[\![H_1]\!]\acute\rho_1\acute\upsilon_1\acute\sigma_1$ and $\mathcal{Y}[\![H_0]\!]\zeta\grave\rho_0\grave\upsilon_0\grave\sigma_0=\mathcal{Y}[\![H_1]\!]\zeta\grave\rho_1\grave\upsilon_1\grave\sigma_1$ where $\langle\grave\rho_1,\grave\upsilon_1,\grave\sigma_1\rangle=P(\mathit{furl}\zeta)\langle\acute\rho_1,\acute\upsilon_1,\acute\sigma_1\rangle$.

When $H_0\downarrow 1$ is apply $\mathcal{A}[\![H_0\downarrow 1]\!][\![H_0\dagger 1]\!]\acute\rho_0\acute\upsilon_0\acute\sigma_0$ is $\bot$, $\top$ $\mathit{wrong}\acute\sigma_0$ or $\langle\acute\upsilon_0\downarrow 2\downarrow 1\S(H_0\dagger 1),\mathit{divert}\acute\rho_0(\acute\upsilon_0\downarrow 2\downarrow 2),\langle\acute\upsilon_0\downarrow 1\rangle\S\acute\upsilon_0\dagger 2,\acute\sigma_0\rangle$ whereas $\mathcal{Y}[\![H_0]\!]\zeta\grave\rho_0\grave\upsilon_0\grave\sigma_0$ is $\bot$, $\top$, $\mathit{wrong}\grave\sigma_0$ or $(\grave\upsilon_0\downarrow 2\downarrow 1)(\mathcal{Y}[\![H_0\dagger 1]\!]\zeta)(\mathit{divert}\grave\rho_0(\grave\upsilon_0\downarrow 2\downarrow 2))(\langle\grave\upsilon_0\downarrow 1\rangle\S\grave\upsilon_0\dagger 2)\grave\sigma_0$. Since $\grave\upsilon_0\downarrow 2=E(\mathit{furl}\zeta)(\acute\upsilon_0\downarrow 2)$ and $\grave\sigma_0=S(\mathit{furl}\zeta)\acute\sigma_0$, unless $\mathcal{A}[\![H_0\downarrow 1]\!][\![H_0\dagger 1]\!]\acute\rho_0\acute\upsilon_0\acute\sigma_0\in Con\times U\times Y\times S$ the required result follows immediately from our assumptions about *wrong*. If $\mathcal{A}[\![H_0\downarrow 1]\!][\![H_0\dagger 1]\!]\acute\rho_0\acute\upsilon_0\acute\sigma_0\in Con\times U\times Y\times S$ we take $\acute\upsilon_2\downarrow 2|F$ to be $\langle H_3,\acute\rho_3\rangle$ for some H_3 and $\acute\rho_3$; plainly we may assert that H_3 is cohesive and adhesive and that $u(\lambda\hat\omega.\mathit{curl}\hat\omega)\langle\acute\rho_3,U(\mathit{furl}\bot)\acute\rho_3\rangle=\mathit{true}$, as $e(\lambda\hat\omega.\mathit{curl}\hat\omega)\langle\acute\upsilon_0\downarrow 2,E(\mathit{furl}\bot)(\acute\upsilon_0\downarrow 2)\rangle=\mathit{true}$. Hence by supposing that H_0 is adhesive and that $\langle\acute\rho_0,\acute\upsilon_0,\acute\sigma_0\rangle$ is reliable we actually ensure that $H_3\S(H_0\dagger 1)$ is adhesive and that $\langle\mathit{divert}\acute\rho_0\acute\rho_3,\langle\acute\upsilon_0\downarrow 1\rangle\S\acute\upsilon_0\dagger 2,\acute\sigma_0\rangle$ is reliable; moreover the cohesive nature of H_3 allows us to assert that $\mathcal{Y}[\![H_3\S(H_0\dagger 1)]\!]\zeta=\mathcal{Y}[\![H_3]\!](\mathcal{Y}[\![H_0\dagger 1]\!]\zeta)$ by virtue of 4.5.3. By setting $H_2=H_3\S(H_0\dagger 1)$ and $\langle\acute\rho_2,\acute\upsilon_2,\acute\sigma_2\rangle=\langle\mathit{divert}\acute\rho_0\acute\rho_3,\langle\acute\upsilon_0\downarrow 1\rangle\S\upsilon_0\dagger 2,\acute\sigma_0\rangle$ we therefore obtain an adhesive control H_2 and a reliable state $\langle\acute\rho_2,\acute\upsilon_2,\acute\sigma_2\rangle$ governed by the equation $\mathcal{A}[\![H_0\downarrow 1]\!][\![H_0\dagger 1]\!]\acute\rho_0\acute\upsilon_0\acute\sigma_0|(Con\times U\times Y\times S)=\langle H_2,\acute\rho_2,\acute\upsilon_2,\acute\sigma_2\rangle$; because $\grave\upsilon_0\downarrow 2=\langle\mathcal{Y}[\![H_3]\!],U(\mathit{furl}\zeta)\grave\rho_3\rangle$, we also know that

$$\mathcal{Y}[\![H_0]\!]\zeta\grave\rho_0\grave\upsilon_0\grave\sigma_0=\mathcal{A}[\![H_0\downarrow 1]\!](\lambda\nu.\mathcal{Y}[\![(H_0\dagger 1)\dagger\nu]\!]\zeta)\grave\rho_0\grave\upsilon_0\grave\sigma_0$$
$$=(\grave\upsilon_0\downarrow 2\downarrow 1)((\lambda\nu.\mathcal{Y}[\![(H_0\dagger 1)\dagger\nu]\!]\zeta)0)(\mathit{divert}\grave\rho_0(\grave\upsilon_0\downarrow 2\downarrow 2))(\langle\grave\upsilon_0\downarrow 1\rangle\S\grave\upsilon_0\dagger 2)\grave\sigma_0$$
$$=\mathcal{Y}[\![H_3]\!](\mathcal{Y}[\![H_0\dagger 1]\!]\zeta)(\mathit{divert}\grave\rho_0(\mathrm{U}(\mathit{furl}\zeta)\acute\rho_3))(\langle\grave\upsilon_0\downarrow 1\rangle\S\grave\upsilon_0\dagger 2)\grave\sigma_0$$
$$=\mathcal{Y}[\![H_2]\!]\zeta(\mathrm{U}(\mathit{furl}\zeta)(\mathit{divert}\acute\rho_0\acute\rho_3))(\mathrm{Y}(\mathit{furl}\zeta)(\langle\acute\upsilon_0\downarrow 1\rangle\S\acute\upsilon_0\dagger 2))(\mathrm{S}(\mathit{furl}\zeta)\acute\sigma_0)$$
$$=\mathcal{Y}[\![H_2]\!]\zeta(\mathrm{U}(\mathit{furl}\zeta)\acute\rho_2)(\mathrm{Y}(\mathit{furl}\zeta)\acute\upsilon_2)(\mathrm{S}(\mathit{furl}\zeta)\acute\sigma_2).$$

Consequently we may infer that there exists an adhesive control H_1, together with a reliable state $\langle\acute\rho_1,\acute\upsilon_1,\acute\sigma_1\rangle$, for which $\lambda\psi.\mathit{proceed}\psi[\![H_0]\!]\acute\rho_0\acute\upsilon_0\acute\sigma_0=\lambda\psi.\psi[\![H_1]\!]\acute\rho_1\acute\upsilon_1\acute\sigma_1$ and $\mathcal{Y}[\![H_0]\!]\zeta\grave\rho_0\grave\upsilon_0\grave\sigma_0=\mathcal{Y}[\![H_1]\!]\zeta\grave\rho_1\grave\upsilon_1\grave\sigma_1$ where $\langle\grave\rho_1,\grave\upsilon_1,\grave\sigma_1\rangle=\mathrm{P}(\mathit{furl}\zeta)\langle\acute\rho_1,\acute\upsilon_1,\acute\sigma_1\rangle$.

When $H_0\downarrow 1$ is p $\langle\nu,\Gamma\rangle$ for some ν and Γ we know that $\mathcal{A}[\![H_0\downarrow 1]\!][\![H_0\dagger 1]\!]\acute\rho_0\acute\upsilon_0\acute\sigma_0$ is $\langle H_0\dagger 1,\acute\rho_0,\langle\acute\varepsilon_0\rangle\S\acute\upsilon_0,\acute\sigma_0\rangle$ where $\acute\varepsilon_0=\langle\wp[\![\Gamma]\!]\downarrow\nu\S((H_0\dagger 1)\dagger(-1+3\times\nu)),\acute\rho_0,\acute\upsilon_0\dagger 1,\langle\rangle\rangle$. Here $\wp[\![\Gamma]\!]\downarrow\nu$ is cohesive and adhesive by virtue of 4.5.4 whereas $(H_0\dagger 1)\dagger(-1+3\times\nu)$ is adhesive (in accordance with the definitions in 4.5.1), so, when $H_2=\wp[\![\Gamma]\!]\downarrow\nu\S((H_0\dagger 1)\dagger(-1+3\times\nu))$, H_2 is adhesive, just as is $H_0\dagger 1$; moreover $\mathrm{u}(\lambda\hat\omega.\mathit{curl}\hat\omega)\langle\mathit{coil}[\![H_2]\!]\acute\rho_2,\mathrm{U}(\mathit{furl}\bot)(\mathit{coil}[\![H_2]\!]\acute\rho_2)\rangle=\mathit{true}$ and $y(\lambda\hat\omega.\mathit{curl}\hat\omega)\langle\acute\upsilon_0\dagger 1,\mathrm{Y}(\mathit{furl}\bot)(\acute\upsilon_0\dagger 1)\rangle=\mathit{true}$ since $\langle\acute\rho_0,\acute\upsilon_0,\acute\sigma_0\rangle$ is reliable. Hence not only is $H_0\dagger 1$ adhesive but $\langle\acute\rho_0,\langle\acute\varepsilon_0\rangle\S\acute\upsilon_0,\acute\sigma_0\rangle$ is reliable (as an inspection of the definition of *curl* in 4.6.1 will readily confirm). However, as $\wp[\![\Gamma]\!]\downarrow\nu$ is cohesive, when $\grave\varepsilon_0=\mathcal{P}[\![\Gamma]\!](\mathcal{Y}[\![(H_0\dagger 1)\dagger(-1+3\times\nu)]\!]\zeta)\grave\rho_0(\grave\upsilon_0\dagger 1)\downarrow\nu$ we may apply first 4.5.3 and then 4.5.5 in order to demonstrate that

$$\mathrm{E}(\mathit{furl}\zeta)\acute\varepsilon_0=\langle\mathcal{Y}[\![\wp[\![\Gamma]\!]\downarrow\nu\S((H_0\dagger 1)\dagger(-1+3\times\nu))]\!]\zeta,\mathrm{U}(\mathit{furl}\zeta)(\mathit{fold}\langle\rangle\acute\rho_0),\mathrm{Y}(\mathit{furl}\zeta)(\acute\upsilon_0\dagger 1)\rangle$$
$$=\langle\mathcal{Y}[\![\wp[\![\Gamma]\!]\downarrow\nu]\!](\mathcal{Y}[\![(H_0\dagger 1)\dagger(-1+3\times\nu)]\!]\zeta),\mathrm{U}(\mathit{furl}\zeta)\acute\rho_0,(\mathrm{Y}(\mathit{furl}\zeta)\acute\upsilon_0)\dagger 1\rangle$$
$$=\langle\mathcal{Y}[\![\wp[\![\Gamma]\!]\downarrow\nu]\!](\mathcal{Y}[\![(H_0\dagger 1)\dagger(-1+3\times\nu)]\!]\zeta),\grave\rho_0,\grave\upsilon_0\dagger 1\rangle$$
$$=\mathcal{P}[\![\Gamma]\!](\mathcal{Y}[\![(H_0\dagger 1)\dagger(-1+3\times\nu)]\!]\zeta)\grave\rho_0(\grave\upsilon_0\dagger 1)\downarrow\nu$$
$$=\grave\varepsilon_0;$$

in addition appendix 10 indicates that, because $H_0\downarrow 1$ is p $\langle\nu,\Gamma\rangle$, $\mathcal{Y}[\![H_0]\!]\zeta\grave\rho_0\grave\upsilon_0\grave\sigma_0=\mathcal{Y}[\![H_0\dagger 1]\!]\zeta\grave\rho_0(\langle\grave\varepsilon_0\rangle\S\grave\upsilon_0)\grave\sigma_0$. Consequently there must be an adhesive control H_1 and a reliable state $\langle\acute\rho_1,\acute\upsilon_1,\acute\sigma_1\rangle$ (which here is actually $\langle \acute{\rho}_0, \langle \acute{\epsilon}_0 \rangle \S \acute{\upsilon}_0, \acute{\sigma}_0 \rangle$) for which $\lambda\psi.\mathit{proceed}\psi[\![H_0]\!]\acute{\rho}_0\acute{\upsilon}_0\acute{\sigma}_0 = \lambda\psi.\psi[\![H_1]\!]\acute{\rho}_1\acute{\upsilon}_1\acute{\sigma}_1$ and $\mathcal{Y}[\![H_0]\!]\zeta\grave{\rho}_0\grave{\upsilon}_0\grave{\sigma}_0 = \mathcal{Y}[\![H_1]\!]\zeta\grave{\rho}_1\grave{\upsilon}_1\grave{\sigma}_1$ where $\langle \grave{\rho}_1, \grave{\upsilon}_1, \grave{\sigma}_1 \rangle = P(\mathit{furl}\zeta)\langle \acute{\rho}_1, \acute{\upsilon}_1, \acute{\sigma}_1 \rangle$.

When $H_0 \downarrow 1$ is $\mathtt{q}\ \langle \nu, \Gamma \rangle$ for some ν and Γ the adhesive nature of H_0 ensures that $\nu = \#\mathcal{K}[\![\Gamma]\!]$ and that whenever $\#\mathcal{K}[\![\Gamma]\!] \geq \nu' \geq 1$ $H_0 \downarrow \nu'$ is $\mathtt{q}\ \langle 1-\nu'+\#\mathcal{K}[\![\Gamma]\!], \Gamma \rangle$ and $H_0 \downarrow (\nu'+\#\mathcal{K}[\![\Gamma]\!])$ is amend $\mathcal{K}[\![\Gamma]\!] \downarrow \nu$. Consequently, when $H_2 = H_0 \dagger (\#\mathcal{K}[\![\Gamma]\!])$ and $H_3 = H_0 \dagger (1+3\times\#\mathcal{J}[\![\Gamma]\!]+2\times\#\mathcal{K}[\![\Gamma]\!])$, appendix 11 shows that $\lambda\psi.\mathit{proceed}\psi[\![H_0]\!]\acute{\rho}_0\acute{\upsilon}_0\acute{\sigma}_0 = \lambda\psi.\mathit{proceed}\psi[\![H_2]\!]\acute{\rho}_2\acute{\upsilon}_0\acute{\sigma}_0$, where $\acute{\rho}_2 = \acute{\rho}_0[\mathit{map}(\lambda H.\langle (\mathit{map}(\lambda I.\text{amend } I)(\mathcal{K}[\![\Gamma]\!]))\S H \S H_3, \acute{\rho}_0, \acute{\upsilon}_0, \mathcal{K}[\![\Gamma]\!] \rangle)(\mathcal{Q}[\![\Gamma]\!])/\mathcal{K}[\![\Gamma]\!]]$, whilst appendix 10 shows that $\mathcal{Y}[\![H_0]\!]\zeta\grave{\rho}_0\grave{\upsilon}_0\grave{\sigma}_0 = \mathcal{Y}[\![H_2]\!]\zeta\grave{\rho}_2\grave{\upsilon}_0\grave{\sigma}_0$, where $\grave{\rho}_2 = \mathit{fix}(\lambda\grave{\rho}.\grave{\rho}_0[\mathcal{Q}[\![\Gamma]\!](\mathcal{Y}[\![H_3]\!]\zeta)\grave{\rho}\grave{\upsilon}_0/\mathcal{K}[\![\Gamma]\!]])$. As $\#\mathcal{K}[\![\Gamma]\!] \geq 1$, there is a control H_4, to wit $H_0 \dagger (-1+\#\mathcal{K}[\![\Gamma]\!])$, such that $\langle H_2, \acute{\rho}_2, \acute{\upsilon}_0, \acute{\sigma}_0 \rangle = \mathcal{A}[\![H_4 \downarrow 1]\!][\![H_4 \dagger 1]\!]\acute{\rho}_4\acute{\upsilon}_0\acute{\sigma}_0 | (\text{Con}\times\text{U}\times\text{Y}\times\text{S})$, $\lambda\psi.\mathit{proceed}\psi[\![H_0]\!]\acute{\rho}_0\acute{\upsilon}_0\acute{\sigma}_0 = \lambda\psi.\mathit{proceed}\psi[\![H_0]\!]\acute{\rho}_4\acute{\upsilon}_0\acute{\sigma}_0$ and $\mathcal{Y}[\![H_0]\!]\zeta\grave{\rho}_0\grave{\upsilon}_0\grave{\sigma}_0 = \mathcal{Y}[\![H_4]\!]\zeta\grave{\rho}_4\grave{\upsilon}_0\grave{\sigma}_0$ for a certain pair ρ_4 (the precise definition of which will be omitted); furthermore H_2 is adhesive, in accordance with the definitions in 4.5.1. Thus the remarks at the beginning of the proof of the present result will allow us to infer the existence of an adhesive control H_1 and a reliable state $\langle \acute{\rho}_1, \acute{\upsilon}_1, \acute{\sigma}_1 \rangle$ for which $\lambda\psi.\mathit{proceed}\psi[\![H_0]\!]\acute{\rho}_0\acute{\upsilon}_0\acute{\sigma}_0 = \lambda\psi.\psi[\![H_1]\!]\acute{\rho}_1\acute{\upsilon}_1\acute{\sigma}_1$ and $\mathcal{Y}[\![H_0]\!]\zeta\grave{\rho}_0\grave{\upsilon}_0\grave{\sigma}_0 = \mathcal{Y}[\![H_1]\!]\zeta\grave{\rho}_1\grave{\upsilon}_1\grave{\sigma}_1$ (where $\langle \grave{\rho}_1, \grave{\upsilon}_1, \grave{\sigma}_1 \rangle = P(\mathit{furl}\zeta)\langle \acute{\rho}_1, \acute{\upsilon}_1, \acute{\sigma}_1 \rangle$) immediately we have demonstrated that $\langle \mathit{coil}[\![H_2]\!]\acute{\rho}_2, \acute{\upsilon}_0, \acute{\sigma}_0 \rangle$ is reliable and that $\langle \grave{\rho}_2, \grave{\upsilon}_0, \grave{\sigma}_0 \rangle = P(\mathit{furl}\zeta)\langle \mathit{coil}[\![H_2]\!]\acute{\rho}_2, \acute{\upsilon}_0, \acute{\sigma}_0 \rangle$. Even this task reduces to that of showing that when $\acute{\rho}_3 = \mathit{coil}[\![H_2]\!]\acute{\rho}_2$ and $\grave{\rho}_3 = \grave{\rho}_2$ then $u(\lambda\hat{\omega}.\mathit{curl}\hat{\omega})\langle \acute{\rho}_3, U(\mathit{furl}\bot)\acute{\rho}_3 \rangle = \mathit{true}$ and $\grave{\rho}_3 = U(\mathit{furl}\zeta)\acute{\rho}_3$, since we already know a great deal about $\hat{\upsilon}_0$ and $\hat{\sigma}_0$. To demonstrate that $u(\lambda\hat{\omega}.\mathit{curl}\hat{\omega})\langle \acute{\rho}_3, U(\mathit{furl}\bot)\acute{\rho}_3 \rangle = \mathit{true}$ and that $\grave{\rho}_3 = U(\mathit{furl}\zeta)\acute{\rho}_3$ we appeal to the induction principle of 2.3.2 after analysing the definitions of *curl*, *furl* and $\grave{\rho}_3$ in terms of least fixed points. Thus we assume that ϕ, ψ and $\grave{\rho}$ are entities such that $\mathit{curl} \sqsupseteq \phi$ (so that ϕ is an inclusive

predicate mapping W into T′), $furl \sqsupseteq \psi$ (so that ψ is a continuous function defined on Z), $u(\lambda\hat{\omega}.\phi\acute{\omega})\langle\acute{\rho}_3,U(furl\bot)\acute{\rho}_3\rangle = true$, $U(\psi\zeta)\acute{\rho}_3 \sqsubseteq \grave{\rho}_3$ and $U(furl\zeta)\acute{\rho}_3 \sqsupseteq \grave{\rho}$. Induction on ν' and arguments like those needed for $p\langle\nu,\Gamma\rangle$ allow us to verify that, when $\#\mathfrak{K}[\![\Gamma]\!] \geq \nu' \geq 1$ and $I^* = fix(\lambda\xi\nu''.(\nu''>\nu')\rightarrow\langle\rangle,\langle\mathfrak{K}[\![\Gamma]\!]\downarrow\nu''\rangle\S\xi(\nu''+1))1$, every ν'' with $\nu' \geq \nu'' \geq 1$ is such that
$d(\lambda\hat{\omega}.curling\phi\acute{\omega})\langle foldI^*\acute{\rho}_2[\![I^*\downarrow\nu'']\!]\downarrow 1,D(furl\bot)(foldI^*\acute{\rho}_2[\![I^*\downarrow\nu'']\!]\downarrow 1)\rangle = true$,
$D(furling\psi\zeta)(foldI^*\acute{\rho}_2[\![I^*\downarrow\nu'']\!]\downarrow 1) \sqsubseteq \grave{\rho}_3[\![I^*\downarrow\nu'']\!]\downarrow 1$ and
$D(furl\zeta)(foldI^*\acute{\rho}_2[\![I^*\downarrow\nu'']\!]\downarrow 1) \sqsupseteq \mathfrak{Q}[\![\Gamma]\!](\mathfrak{Y}[\![H_3]\!]\zeta)\grave{\rho}\grave{\upsilon}_0\downarrow\nu''$. Taking ν' to be $\#\mathfrak{K}[\![\Gamma]\!]$ shows that $u(\lambda\hat{\omega}.curling\phi\acute{\omega})\langle\acute{\rho}_3,U(furl\bot)\acute{\rho}_3\rangle = true$, $U(furling\psi\zeta)\acute{\rho}_3 \sqsubseteq \grave{\rho}_3$ and $U(furl\zeta)\acute{\rho}_3 \sqsupseteq \grave{\rho}_0[\mathfrak{Q}[\![\Gamma]\!](\mathfrak{Y}[\![H_3]\!]\zeta)\grave{\rho}\grave{\upsilon}_0/\mathfrak{K}[\![\Gamma]\!]]$, as in fact $curl \sqsupseteq curling\phi$ and $furl \sqsupseteq furling\psi$. We know, however, that $curl \sqsupseteq \lambda\acute{\omega}.true$, $furl \sqsupseteq \lambda\zeta\acute{\omega}.\bot$, $u(\lambda\hat{\omega}.true)\langle\acute{\rho}_3,U(furl\bot)\acute{\rho}_3\rangle = true$, $U(\lambda\acute{\omega}.\bot)\acute{\rho}_3 \sqsubseteq \grave{\rho}_3$ and $U(furl\zeta)\acute{\rho}_3 \sqsupseteq \bot$, so the continuous natures of u and U allow us to infer from the induction rule of 2.3.2 that $u(\lambda\hat{\omega}.fix(curling)\acute{\omega})\langle\acute{\rho}_3,U(furl\bot)\acute{\rho}_3\rangle = true$
$U(fix(furling)\zeta)\acute{\rho}_3 \sqsubseteq \grave{\rho}_3$ and $U(furl\zeta)\acute{\rho}_3 \sqsupseteq fix(\lambda\grave{\rho}.\grave{\rho}_0[\mathfrak{Q}[\![\Gamma]\!](\mathfrak{Y}[\![H_3]\!]\zeta)\grave{\rho}\grave{\upsilon}_0/\mathfrak{K}[\![\Gamma]\!]])$.
Hence $u(\lambda\hat{\omega}.curl\acute{\omega})\langle\acute{\rho}_3,U(furl\bot)\acute{\rho}_3\rangle = true$ and $\grave{\rho}_3 = U(furl\zeta)\acute{\rho}_3$, and this implies that there exists an adhesive control H_1, together with a reliable state $\langle\acute{\rho}_1,\acute{\upsilon}_1,\acute{\sigma}_1\rangle$, for which
$\lambda\psi.proceed\psi[\![H_0]\!]\acute{\rho}_0\acute{\upsilon}_0\acute{\sigma}_0 = \lambda\psi.\psi[\![H_1]\!]\acute{\rho}_1\acute{\upsilon}_1\acute{\sigma}_1$ and $\mathfrak{Y}[\![H_0]\!]\zeta\grave{\rho}_0\grave{\upsilon}_0\grave{\sigma}_0 = \mathfrak{Y}[\![H_1]\!]\zeta\grave{\rho}_1\grave{\upsilon}_1\grave{\sigma}_1$
where $\langle\grave{\rho}_1,\grave{\upsilon}_1,\grave{\sigma}_1\rangle = P(furl\zeta)\langle\acute{\rho}_1,\acute{\upsilon}_1,\acute{\sigma}_1\rangle$.

This concludes our discussion of the proof that we can find an adhesive control H_1 and a reliable state $\langle\acute{\rho}_1,\acute{\upsilon}_1,\acute{\sigma}_1\rangle$ having $\lambda\psi.proceed\psi[\![H_0]\!]\acute{\rho}_0\acute{\upsilon}_0\acute{\sigma}_0 = \lambda\psi.\psi[\![H_1]\!]\acute{\rho}_1\acute{\upsilon}_1\acute{\sigma}_1$ and $\mathfrak{Y}[\![H_0]\!]\zeta\grave{\rho}_0\grave{\upsilon}_0\grave{\sigma}_0 = \mathfrak{Y}[\![H_1]\!]\sigma\grave{\rho}_1\grave{\upsilon}_1\grave{\sigma}_1$ (where $\langle\grave{\rho}_1,\grave{\upsilon}_1,\grave{\sigma}_1\rangle = P(furl\zeta)\langle\acute{\rho}_1,\acute{\upsilon}_1,\acute{\sigma}_1\rangle$). The other possible versions of $H_0\downarrow 1$ require analyses no more intricate than the five given above; the main complications arise in the case of $t\langle\nu,\Delta\rangle$, and even these can be handled by the means adopted for $q\langle\nu,\Gamma\rangle$.⊁

Were the equations for amend I, $t\langle\nu,\Delta\rangle$ and $q\langle\nu,\Gamma\rangle$ in appendix 10 to resemble the corresponding equations in appendix 11 we would be able to prove the following result, which is more elegant than that above: if

$p(\lambda\hat{\omega}.\mathit{curl}\,\acute{\omega})\langle\langle\acute{\rho}_0,\acute{\upsilon}_0,\acute{\sigma}_0\rangle,P(\mathit{furl}\,\bot)\langle\acute{\rho}_0,\acute{\upsilon}_0,\acute{\sigma}_0\rangle\rangle=\mathit{true}$ and

$\langle\acute{\rho}_0,\acute{\upsilon}_0,\acute{\sigma}_0\rangle=P(\mathit{furl}\,\zeta)\langle\grave{\rho}_0,\grave{\upsilon}_0,\grave{\sigma}_0\rangle$ (for suitable versions of *curl* and *furl*) then for any control H_0 with $\#H_0>0$ either

$A(\mathit{furl}\,\zeta)(\mathcal{A}[\![H_0\downarrow 1]\!][\![H_0\dagger 1]\!]\acute{\rho}_0\acute{\upsilon}_0\acute{\sigma}_0|A)=\mathcal{Y}[\![H_0]\!]\zeta\acute{\rho}_0\acute{\upsilon}_0\acute{\sigma}_0$ or

$\mathcal{A}[\![H_0\downarrow 1]\!][\![H_0\dagger 1]\!]\acute{\rho}_0\acute{\upsilon}_0\acute{\sigma}_0|(\mathrm{Con}\times\mathrm{U}\times\mathrm{Y}\times\mathrm{S})=\langle H_1,\acute{\rho}_1,\acute{\upsilon}_1,\acute{\sigma}_1\rangle$ for some control H_1 and some state $\langle\acute{\rho}_1,\acute{\upsilon}_1,\acute{\sigma}_1\rangle$ having

$p(\lambda\hat{\omega}.\mathit{curl}\,\acute{\omega})\langle\langle\acute{\rho}_0,\acute{\upsilon}_0,\acute{\sigma}_0\rangle,P(\mathit{furl}\,\bot)\langle\acute{\rho}_0,\acute{\upsilon}_0,\acute{\sigma}_0\rangle\rangle=\mathit{true}$ and

$\mathcal{Y}[\![H_0]\!]\zeta\grave{\rho}_0\grave{\upsilon}_0\grave{\sigma}_0=\mathcal{Y}[\![H_1]\!]\zeta\grave{\rho}_1\grave{\upsilon}_1\grave{\sigma}_1$ where $\langle\grave{\rho}_1,\grave{\upsilon}_1,\grave{\sigma}_1\rangle=P(\mathit{furl}\,\zeta)\langle\acute{\rho}_1,\acute{\upsilon}_1,\acute{\sigma}_1\rangle$.

An even more attractive result than this will be provided in 5.6.3, where the analogue of *curl* will be $\lambda\grave{\omega}.\mathit{true}$.

4.6.4. Proposition.

If H is an adhesive Sap control, ⟨ρ́,ύ,σ́⟩ is a reliable state and ζ is a continuation such that

$A(furl\zeta)(process\acute{\rho}\acute{\upsilon}\acute{\sigma})=\zeta(U(furl\zeta)\acute{\rho})(Y(furl\zeta)\acute{\upsilon})(S(furl\zeta)\acute{\sigma})$ whenever ⟨ρ́,ύ,σ́⟩ is a reliable state then

$A(furl\zeta)(\mathcal{Z}[\![H]\!]\acute{\rho}\acute{\upsilon}\acute{\sigma})\sqsubseteq\mathcal{Y}[\![H]\!]\zeta(U(furl\zeta)\acute{\rho})(Y(furl\zeta)\acute{\upsilon})(S(furl\zeta)\acute{\sigma})$.

⊲As was intimated in 4.6.2, in order to verify this result we are obliged to use the equation $\mathcal{Z}=fix(proceed)$ and to apply the induction principle described in 2.3.2. Throughout the proof we shall take ζ to be a continuation such that

$A(furl\zeta)(process\acute{\rho}\acute{\upsilon}\acute{\sigma})=\zeta(U(furl\zeta)\acute{\rho})(Y(furl\zeta)\acute{\upsilon})(S(furl\zeta)\acute{\sigma})$

if ⟨ρ́,ύ,σ́⟩ is any reliable state.

Naturally we assume that $\psi\in Con\to U\to Y\to S\to A$ is such that

$A(furl\zeta)(\psi[\![H]\!]\acute{\rho}\acute{\upsilon}\acute{\sigma})\sqsubseteq\mathcal{Y}[\![H]\!]\zeta(U(furl\zeta)\acute{\rho})(Y(furl\zeta)\acute{\upsilon})(S(furl\zeta)\acute{\sigma})$

whenever H is adhesive and ⟨ρ́,ύ,σ́⟩ is reliable, and we attempt to prove that in addition

$A(furl\zeta)(proceed\psi[\![H]\!]\acute{\rho}\acute{\upsilon}\acute{\sigma})\sqsubseteq\mathcal{Y}[\![H]\!]\zeta(U(furl\zeta)\acute{\rho})(Y(furl\zeta)\acute{\upsilon})(S(furl\zeta)\acute{\sigma})$

whenever H is adhesive and ⟨ρ́,ύ,σ́⟩ is reliable. After selecting any adhesive control H_0 and any reliable state $\langle\acute{\rho}_0,\acute{\upsilon}_0,\acute{\sigma}_0\rangle$ we let $\langle\grave{\rho}_0,\grave{\upsilon}_0,\grave{\sigma}_0\rangle=P(furl\zeta)\langle\acute{\rho}_0,\acute{\upsilon}_0,\acute{\sigma}_0\rangle$. When $\#H_0=0$,

$$\begin{aligned}A(furl\zeta)(proceed\psi[\![H_0]\!]\acute{\rho}_0\acute{\upsilon}_0\acute{\sigma}_0)&=A(furl\zeta)(process\acute{\rho}_0\acute{\upsilon}_0\acute{\sigma}_0)\\&=\zeta\grave{\rho}_0\grave{\upsilon}_0\grave{\sigma}_0\\&=\mathcal{Y}[\![H_0]\!]\zeta\grave{\rho}_0\grave{\upsilon}_0\grave{\sigma}_0\end{aligned}$$

in accordance with what we have stipulated about ζ. When $\#H_0>0$ but $\mathcal{A}[\![H_0\downarrow1]\!][\![H_0\dagger1]\!]\acute{\rho}_0\acute{\upsilon}_0\acute{\sigma}_0$ is not a member of $Con\times U\times Y\times S$,

$$\begin{aligned}A(furl\zeta)(proceed\psi[\![H_0]\!]\acute{\rho}_0\acute{\upsilon}_0\acute{\sigma}_0)&=A(furl\zeta)(\mathcal{A}[\![H_0\downarrow1]\!][\![H_0\dagger1]\!]\acute{\rho}_0\acute{\upsilon}_0\acute{\sigma}_0|A)\\&=\mathcal{Y}[\![H_0]\!]\zeta\grave{\rho}_0\grave{\upsilon}_0\grave{\sigma}_0\end{aligned}$$

by virtue of 4.6.3. When $\#H_0>0$ and $\mathcal{A}[\![H_0\downarrow1]\!][\![H_0\dagger1]\!]\acute{\rho}_0\acute{\upsilon}_0\acute{\sigma}_0$ is a member of $Con\times U\times Y\times S$, 4.6.3 assures us that there exists an adhesive control H_1, together with a reliable state $\langle\acute{\rho}_1,\acute{\upsilon}_1,\acute{\sigma}_1\rangle$, for which

$proceed\,\psi[\![H_0]\!]\acute{\rho}_0\acute{\upsilon}_0\acute{\sigma}_0=\psi[\![H_1]\!]\acute{\rho}_1\acute{\upsilon}_1\acute{\sigma}_1$ and $\mathcal{Y}[\![H_0]\!]\zeta\grave{\rho}_0\grave{\upsilon}_0\grave{\sigma}_0=\mathcal{Y}[\![H_1]\!]\zeta\grave{\rho}_1\grave{\upsilon}_1\grave{\sigma}_1$ (where $\langle\grave{\rho}_1,\grave{\upsilon}_1,\grave{\sigma}_1\rangle=P(furl\,\zeta)\langle\acute{\rho}_1,\acute{\upsilon}_1,\acute{\sigma}_1\rangle$), so the inductive hypothesis indicates that in fact

$$
\begin{aligned}
A(furl\,\zeta)(proceed\,\psi[\![H_0]\!]\acute{\rho}_0\acute{\upsilon}_0\acute{\sigma}_0) &= A(furl\,\zeta)(\psi[\![H_1]\!]\acute{\rho}_1\acute{\upsilon}_1\acute{\sigma}_1)\\
&\sqsubseteq \mathcal{Y}[\![H_1]\!]\zeta\grave{\rho}_1\grave{\upsilon}_1\grave{\sigma}_1\\
&= \mathcal{Y}[\![H_0]\!]\zeta\grave{\rho}_0\grave{\upsilon}_0\grave{\sigma}_0 .
\end{aligned}
$$

The only other possible situations (which arise when $\#H_0=\bot$ or $\#H_0=\top$) are uninteresting. Hence we may actually assert that

$A(furl\,\zeta)(proceed\,\psi[\![H]\!]\acute{\rho}\acute{\upsilon}\acute{\sigma})\sqsubseteq\mathcal{Y}[\![H]\!]\zeta(U(furl\,\zeta)\acute{\rho})(Y(furl\,\zeta)\acute{\upsilon})(S(furl\,\zeta)\acute{\sigma})$

whenever H is an adhesive control and $\langle\acute{\rho},\acute{\upsilon},\acute{\sigma}\rangle$ is a reliable state.

Plainly $A(furl\,\zeta)(\bot[\![H]\!]\acute{\rho}\acute{\upsilon}\acute{\sigma})\sqsubseteq\mathcal{Y}[\![H]\!]\zeta\grave{\rho}\grave{\upsilon}\grave{\sigma}$ for all H, $\langle\acute{\rho},\acute{\upsilon},\acute{\sigma}\rangle$ and $\langle\grave{\rho},\grave{\upsilon},\grave{\sigma}\rangle$, and we have just proved that if

$A(furl\,\zeta)(\psi[\![H]\!]\acute{\rho}\acute{\upsilon}\acute{\sigma})\sqsubseteq\mathcal{Y}[\![H]\!]\zeta(U(furl\,\zeta)\acute{\rho})(Y(furl\,\zeta)\acute{\upsilon})(S(furl\,\zeta)\acute{\sigma})$

whenever H is adhesive and $\langle\acute{\rho},\acute{\upsilon},\acute{\sigma}\rangle$ is reliable then

$A(furl\,\zeta)(proceed\,\psi[\![H]\!]\acute{\rho}\acute{\upsilon}\acute{\sigma})\sqsubseteq\mathcal{Y}[\![H]\!]\zeta(U(furl\,\zeta)\acute{\rho})(Y(furl\,\zeta)\acute{\upsilon})(S(furl\,\zeta)\acute{\sigma})$

whenever H is adhesive and $\langle\acute{\rho},\acute{\upsilon},\acute{\sigma}\rangle$ is reliable. Hence as $\mathcal{Z}=fix(proceed)$ (and as the inequality relation defines an inclusive predicate) we may conclude by applying the induction principle that

$A(furl\,\zeta)(\mathcal{Z}[\![H]\!]\acute{\rho}\acute{\upsilon}\acute{\sigma})\sqsubseteq\mathcal{Y}[\![H]\!]\zeta(U(furl\,\zeta)\acute{\rho})(Y(furl\,\zeta)\acute{\upsilon})(S(furl\,\zeta)\acute{\sigma})$

when H is an adhesive Sap control and $\langle\acute{\rho},\acute{\upsilon},\acute{\sigma}\rangle$ is a reliable state.$\triangleright$

A result closely allied to this one will be established in 5.6.4 for a language which is even more primitive than Sap.

4.6.5. The implicit connection between functions and program texts.

We have now proved that if H is any adhesive control, $\langle\acute\rho,\acute\upsilon,\acute\sigma\rangle$ is any reliable control and H is any continuation for which

$A(furl\zeta)(process\,\acute\rho\acute\upsilon\acute\sigma)=\zeta(U(furl\zeta)\acute\rho)(Y(furl\zeta)\acute\upsilon)(S(furl\zeta)\acute\sigma)$

whenever $\langle\acute\rho,\acute\upsilon,\acute\sigma\rangle$ is reliable then

$A(furl\zeta)(\mathcal{Z}[\![H]\!]\acute\rho\acute\upsilon\acute\sigma)\sqsubseteq\mathcal{Y}[\![H]\!]\zeta(U(furl\zeta)\acute\rho)(Y(furl\zeta)\acute\upsilon)(S(furl\zeta)\acute\sigma)$.

Encouraging though this inequality may be, it is not the relation that we set out to establish in 4.6.1; in addition to it we need to be sure that

$A(furl\zeta)(\mathcal{Z}[\![H]\!]\acute\rho\acute\upsilon\acute\sigma)\sqsupseteq\mathcal{Y}[\![H]\!]\zeta(U(furl\zeta)\acute\rho)(Y(furl\zeta)\acute\upsilon)(S(furl\zeta)\acute\sigma)$.

We justified the first of these two inequalities using an inductive argument which depended on the definition of $\mathcal{Z}$ as a least fixed point; we therefore naturally try to justify the second of them using an induction based on the fact that $\mathcal{Y}$, too, is a least fixed point. Though this induction is essentially an induction on the structure of H it is not entirely straightforward, because when $H{\downarrow}1$ is jump, apply or view I the equations of appendix 11 provide us not with a control to which $\mathcal{Y}$ can be applied but with a continuation in which $\mathcal{Y}$ is hidden away. Reasoning like that in 4.2.1 therefore compels us to seek for predicates defined on products of homonymous domains, such as W×W, which do not allow us to claim that a control H matches a continuation $\mathcal{Y}[\![H]\!]\zeta$ unless $A(furl\zeta)(\mathcal{Z}[\![H]\!]\acute\rho\acute\upsilon\acute\sigma)$ resembles $\mathcal{Y}[\![H]\!]\zeta\grave\rho\grave\upsilon\grave\sigma$ whenever $\langle\acute\rho,\acute\upsilon,\acute\sigma\rangle$ and $\langle\grave\rho,\grave\upsilon,\grave\sigma\rangle$ are states that correspond. In turn $\langle\acute\rho,\acute\upsilon,\acute\sigma\rangle$ and $\langle\grave\rho,\grave\upsilon,\grave\sigma\rangle$ are not allowed to correspond unless every control which can be obtained by delving into $\langle\acute\rho,\acute\upsilon,\acute\sigma\rangle$ (and which is therefore a component of a witnessed value such as $\acute\rho[\![I]\!]{\downarrow}\nu$, $\acute\upsilon{\downarrow}\nu$ or $hold\,\alpha\acute\sigma$ for some I, ν and α) matches the appropriate continuation extracted from $\langle\grave\rho,\grave\upsilon,\grave\sigma\rangle$.

We might attempt to insist that $\langle\acute\rho,\acute\upsilon,\acute\sigma\rangle$ correspond with $\langle\acute\rho,\acute\upsilon,\acute\sigma\rangle$ only if $p(\lambda\hat\omega.curl\hat\omega)\langle\langle\acute\rho,\acute\upsilon,\acute\sigma\rangle,\langle\grave\rho,\grave\upsilon,\grave\sigma\rangle\rangle=true$ and $\langle\grave\rho,\grave\upsilon,\grave\sigma\rangle=P(furl\zeta)\langle\acute\rho,\acute\upsilon,\acute\sigma\rangle$; this was, after all, how we set about proving that

$A(furl\zeta)(\mathcal{Z}[\![H]\!]\acute{\rho}\acute{\upsilon}\acute{\sigma})\sqsubseteq\mathcal{Y}[\![H]\!]\zeta(U(furl\zeta)\acute{\rho})(Y(furl\zeta)\acute{\upsilon})(S(furl\zeta)\acute{\sigma})$.

However, this kind of correspondence is not satisfactory when we want to use induction on the structure of H in order to establish that

$A(furl\zeta)(\mathcal{Z}[\![H]\!]\acute{\rho}\acute{\upsilon}\acute{\sigma})\sqsupseteq\mathcal{Y}[\![H]\!]\zeta(U(furl\zeta)\acute{\rho})(Y(furl\zeta)\acute{\upsilon})(S(furl\zeta)\acute{\sigma})$.

The difficulty is that the controls obtained by delving into $\langle\acute{\rho},\acute{\upsilon},\acute{\sigma}\rangle$ may have structures much more complex than that of H and may be "brought to the surface" when $H\downarrow 1$ is jump, apply or view I; we have already mentioned this point in 4.6.2, but it is worth repeating. Only by treating the continuations obtained by delving into $\langle\grave{\rho},\grave{\upsilon},\grave{\sigma}\rangle$ as abstract entities in their own right (rather than as objects produced by applying *furl*ζ) can we hope to prove results by induction on the structure of H alone. Consequently we require predicates which reflect not the nature of the domains for control semantics but the nature of the domains for consecution semantics; moreover because these domains satisfy recursive equations the predicates must do likewise. These predicates do not provide an explicit mapping of controls into continuations; in fact with any adhesive control H they implicitly associate several controls, many of which may not be of the form $\mathcal{Y}[\![H]\!]\zeta$ for any ζ.

The situation that we are considering is in fact typical of problems involving the congruence of two sets of semantic equations, one of which requires recursive domains to do what the other does without recursive domains. Generally these problems concern proofs that operational valuations, such as those given in appendix 11, have the same effect as denotational valuations, such as those given in appendix 10; the essential distinction between these kinds of valuation is that the operational valuations treat the values of labels and procedures as pieces of program (or as pointers to pieces of program) rather than as members of abstract function spaces. One such problem has been analysed by Gordon [25] using techniques quite unlike those being discussed here. Congruence problems of this type can be solved by means of two inductions which establish two contrasting inequalities. The first of these relies heavily on the tacit assumption that the operational valuations in fact form the least fixed point of a set of mutually recursive equations; in our present case this induction was given in 4.6.4. The second involves inspecting the sizes of the programs supplied to the denotational valuations and demands the introduction of predicates constructed with the aid of 2.5.3; in our present case the predicates will be set up shortly and the induction will result from combining 4.6.6 and 4.6.7. Another congruence problem which adheres to this pattern will be examined in 5.6.2. For the benefit of those interested in a situation in which the second of the two inductions reduces to a very conventional structural induction, elsewhere [52:3.6.6] we have related two sets of semantic equations for expressions of indications in Algol 68 [94].

Following our usual practice we shall build up the predicates that we need by introducing an inclusive predicate w. This maps pairs of witnessed values into elements of T′ in such a way that $w\hat{\omega}=\mathit{true}$ if and only if $\acute{\omega}$ and $\grave{\omega}$ correspond suitably; hence from it we can obtain some of the other predicates that we require simply by recalling the functions v, e, d, s, y, u and p provided in 5.6.2 and by setting up vw, ew, dw, sw, yw, uw and pw. When $\hat{\omega}$ is a pair of label or procedure values, the equation satisfied by $w\hat{\omega}$ must mention a predicate zw which compares controls with continuations; evidently we would like $\mathrm{z}w\langle H,\zeta\rangle$ to be *true* if and only if $\mathbf{Z}[\![H]\!]\acute{\rho}\acute{\upsilon}\acute{\sigma}$ and $\zeta\grave{\rho}\grave{\upsilon}\grave{\sigma}$ correspond whenever $\hat{\rho}$, $\hat{\upsilon}$ and $\hat{\sigma}$ satisfy the equations $\mathrm{u}w\hat{\rho}=\mathit{true}$, $\mathrm{y}w\hat{\upsilon}=\mathit{true}$ and $\mathrm{s}w\hat{\sigma}=\mathit{true}$. Accordingly we supply a function a, which maps inclusive predicates into inclusive predicates in a manner subject to the equation $\mathrm{a}=\lambda x.\mathrm{a}x\circ(\lambda\hat{\sigma}.\hat{\sigma})$; here $\acute{\sigma}$ ranges over members of the domain appropriate to appendix 11 whereas $\grave{\sigma}$ ranges over members of the domain A needed by appendix 10. No attempt will be made to define a before 5.6.9; however, for the purposes of 5.6.6, we shall assume that

$a\omega\langle\bot,\bot\rangle=true$ and $a\omega\langle\top,\top\rangle=true$. In addition we shall let $z=\lambda x.(ux\rightarrow yx\rightarrow sx\rightarrow ax)\circ(\lambda\langle H,\zeta\rangle.\langle \mathcal{Z}[\![H]\!],\zeta\rangle)$.

When $\acute{\omega}$ and $\grave{\omega}$ are drawn from their respective versions of J we want $w\hat{\omega}$ to be *true* only if $z\omega\langle(\acute{\omega}|J)\downarrow 1,(\grave{\omega}|J)\downarrow 1\rangle=true$, $u\omega\langle coil[\![(\acute{\omega}|J)\downarrow 1]\!](\acute{\omega}|J)\downarrow 2,(\grave{\omega}|J)\downarrow 2\rangle=true$, $y\omega\langle(\acute{\omega}|J)\downarrow 3,(\grave{\omega}|J)\downarrow 3\rangle=true$ and $(\acute{\omega}|J)\downarrow 4=\langle\rangle$; for our later convenience we shall also demand that $adhere[\![(\acute{\omega}|J)\downarrow 1]\!]=true$. Similarly, when $\acute{\omega}$ and $\grave{\omega}$ are drawn from their respective versions of F we wish $w\hat{\omega}$ to be *true* only if $z\omega\langle((\acute{\omega}|F)\downarrow 1)\S H,((\grave{\omega}|F)\downarrow 1)\zeta\rangle=true$ and $u\omega\langle(\acute{\omega}|F)\downarrow 2,(\grave{\omega}|F)\downarrow 2\rangle=true$ whenever H and ζ are such that $z\omega\langle H,\zeta\rangle=true$; in this case our later discussions (in 4.6.9) make it desirable to insist also that $cohere[\![(\acute{\omega}|F)\downarrow 1]\!]=true$ and $adhere[\![(\acute{\omega}|F)\downarrow 1]\!]=true$. Consequently ω must be a fixed point of a function, w, which is not continuous, and the existence of ω must be demonstrated by an appeal to 2.5.3. By extending our remarks about $w\hat{\omega}$ to the summands of W other than J and F we see that it is reasonable to define w by setting

$$
\begin{aligned}
\mathrm{w}=\lambda x\hat{\omega}.\ & (\acute{\omega}\equiv\bot)\vee(\grave{\omega}\equiv\bot)\rightarrow(\grave{\omega}\equiv\bot),\\
& (\acute{\omega}\equiv\top)\vee(\grave{\omega}\equiv\top)\rightarrow(\acute{\omega}\equiv\top)\wedge(\grave{\omega}\equiv\top),\\
& \acute{\omega}\mathrm{E}\mathrm{L}\wedge\grave{\omega}\mathrm{E}\mathrm{L}\rightarrow l\langle\acute{\omega}|\mathrm{L},\grave{\omega}|\mathrm{L}\rangle,\\
& \acute{\omega}\mathrm{E}\mathrm{B}\wedge\grave{\omega}\mathrm{E}\mathrm{B}\rightarrow b\langle\acute{\omega}|\mathrm{B},\grave{\omega}|\mathrm{B}\rangle,\\
& \acute{\omega}\mathrm{E}\mathrm{E}^*\wedge\grave{\omega}\mathrm{E}\mathrm{E}^*\rightarrow(\mathrm{e}x)^*\langle\acute{\omega}|\mathrm{E}^*,\grave{\omega}|\mathrm{E}^*\rangle,\\
& \acute{\omega}\mathrm{E}\mathrm{J}\wedge\grave{\omega}\mathrm{E}\mathrm{J}\rightarrow \mathrm{z}x\langle(\acute{\omega}|\mathrm{J})\downarrow1,(\grave{\omega}|\mathrm{J})\downarrow1\rangle\\
& \qquad\wedge \mathit{adhere}[\![(\acute{\omega}|\mathrm{J})\downarrow1]\!]\\
& \qquad\wedge \mathrm{u}x\langle \mathit{coil}[\![(\acute{\omega}|\mathrm{J})\downarrow1]\!]((\acute{\omega}|\mathrm{J})\downarrow2),(\grave{\omega}|\mathrm{J})\downarrow2\rangle\\
& \qquad\wedge \mathrm{y}x\langle(\acute{\omega}|\mathrm{J})\downarrow3,(\grave{\omega}|\mathrm{J})\downarrow3\rangle\\
& \qquad\wedge((\acute{\omega}|\mathrm{J})\downarrow4\equiv\langle\rangle),\\
& \acute{\omega}\mathrm{E}\mathrm{F}\wedge\grave{\omega}\mathrm{E}\mathrm{F}\rightarrow(\mathrm{z}x\rightarrow\mathrm{z}x)\langle\lambda\mathrm{H}.((\acute{\omega}|\mathrm{F})\downarrow1)\S\mathrm{H},(\grave{\omega}|\mathrm{F})\downarrow1\rangle\\
& \qquad\wedge \mathit{cohere}[\![(\acute{\omega}|\mathrm{F})\downarrow1]\!]\wedge \mathit{adhere}[\![(\acute{\omega}|\mathrm{F})\downarrow1]\!]\\
& \qquad\wedge \mathrm{u}x\langle(\acute{\omega}|\mathrm{F})\downarrow2,(\grave{\omega}|\mathrm{F})\downarrow2\rangle,\\
& \acute{\omega}\mathrm{E}\mathrm{G}\wedge\grave{\omega}\mathrm{E}\mathrm{G}\rightarrow(\mathrm{z}x\rightarrow\mathrm{z}x)\langle\lambda\mathrm{H}.((\acute{\omega}|\mathrm{G})\downarrow1)\S\mathrm{H},(\grave{\omega}|\mathrm{G})\downarrow1\rangle\\
& \qquad\wedge \mathit{cohere}[\![(\acute{\omega}|\mathrm{G})\downarrow1]\!]\wedge \mathit{adhere}[\![(\acute{\omega}|\mathrm{G})\downarrow1]\!]\\
& \qquad\wedge \mathrm{u}x\langle \mathit{coil}[\![(\acute{\omega}|\mathrm{G})\downarrow1]\!]((\acute{\omega}|\mathrm{G})\downarrow2),(\grave{\omega}|\mathrm{G})\downarrow2\rangle\\
& \qquad\wedge \mathrm{y}x\langle(\acute{\omega}|\mathrm{G})\downarrow3,(\grave{\omega}|\mathrm{G})\downarrow3\rangle\\
& \qquad\wedge((\acute{\omega}|\mathrm{G})\downarrow4\equiv\langle\rangle),\\
& \acute{\omega}\mathrm{E}\mathrm{K}\wedge\grave{\omega}\mathrm{E}\mathrm{J}\rightarrow \mathrm{z}x\langle(\acute{\omega}|\mathrm{K})\downarrow1,(\grave{\omega}|\mathrm{J})\downarrow1\rangle\\
& \qquad\wedge \mathit{adhere}[\![(\acute{\omega}|\mathrm{K})\downarrow1]\!]\\
& \qquad\wedge \mathrm{u}x\langle(\acute{\omega}|\mathrm{K})\downarrow2,(\acute{\omega}|\mathrm{J})\downarrow2\rangle\\
& \qquad\wedge \mathrm{y}x\langle(\acute{\omega}|\mathrm{K})\downarrow3,(\grave{\omega}|\mathrm{J})\downarrow3\rangle\\
& \qquad\wedge((\acute{\omega}|\mathrm{K})\downarrow4\equiv\langle\rangle),\\
& \acute{\omega}\mathrm{E}\mathrm{P}\wedge\grave{\omega}\mathrm{E}\mathrm{P}\rightarrow \mathrm{p}x\langle\acute{\omega}|\mathrm{P},\grave{\omega}|\mathrm{P}\rangle,\\
& \mathit{false}.
\end{aligned}
$$

Here l and b are the tests for equality between members of L and between members of T; the reasons for making $\mathrm{w}x\langle\acute{\omega},\bot\rangle$ be *true* for all $\acute{\omega}$ and x will become apparent in 4.6.7 and 4.6.8.

The functor W which governs the version of W appropriate to appendix 11 is given by the equation

$W=\lambda X.L+B+(EX)^*+(Con\times UX\times YX\times Ide^*)+(Con\times UX)+(Con\times UX\times SX\times Ide^*)+(Con\times UX\times YX)+PX$,

where we let *Con* and *Ide* be retractions of the universal domain having Con and Ide as their respective sets of fixed points; naturally we stipulate that $\lambda\acute{\omega}.\acute{\omega}=fix(W)$. In addition the assumptions made in 4.1.5 allow us to insist that $\lambda\grave{\omega}.\grave{\omega}=fix(W)$, where

$W=\lambda X.L+B+(EX)^*+(ZX\times UX\times YX)+(OX\times UX)+(OX\times UX\times SX)+(ZX\times UX\times YX)+PX$,

provided that

$Z=\lambda X.UX\to YX\to SX\to AX$

and that

$O=\lambda X.ZX\to ZX$.

We shall not say much about either of the functors named A until 4.6.9 although we shall presume that they satisfy the conditions laid down in 4.1.5.

Next we introduce a set of retractions, y, such that X is in y if and only if $X=acute(X)\times grave(X)$, $X\circ(\lambda\hat{\omega}.\hat{\omega})=(\lambda\hat{\omega}.\hat{\omega})\circ X$, $X\circ(mask4\times mask4)=(mask4\times mask4)\circ X$, $X\circ(mask5\times mask5)=(mask5\times mask5)\circ X$, $X\circ(flag6\times flag6)=X\circ(flag6\times flag6)\circ(reject\times reject)\circ X\circ(flag6\times flag6)$ and $X\circ(flag7\times flag7)=X\circ(flag7\times flag7)\circ(reject\times reject)\circ X\circ(flag7\times flag7)$. We now assume that a is a predictor for $A\circledast A$ based on $\langle(\lambda\chi.true),(\lambda\chi.\bot)\times(\lambda\chi.\bot)\rangle$ and bounded by y (as is certainly the case if A is S, V* or P); under these circumstances, 2.5.6 enables us to verify that z is a predictor for $(\lambda X.Con)\circledast Z$ based on $\langle(\lambda\chi.true),(\lambda\chi.\bot)\times(\lambda\chi.\bot)\rangle$ and bounded by y. From this it follows that w is a predictor for $W\circledast W$ based on $\langle(\lambda\chi.true),(\lambda\chi.\bot)\times(\lambda\chi.\bot)\rangle$ and bounded by y. In addition, $\langle w(\lambda\chi.true),(W\circledast W)((\lambda\chi.\bot)\times(\lambda\chi.\bot))\rangle\geq\langle(\lambda\chi.true),(\lambda\chi.\bot)\times(\lambda\chi.\bot)\rangle$, whilst since $\lambda\acute{\omega}.\acute{\omega}=fix(W)$ and $\lambda\grave{\omega}.\grave{\omega}=fix(W)$ (provided that the correct version of W is used in each case), $\lambda\hat{\omega}.\hat{\omega}=\bigsqcup\{(W\circledast W)^n((\lambda\chi.\bot)\times(\lambda\chi.\bot))\mid n\geq 0\}$; accordingly 2.5.3 assures us that there is a unique inclusive predicate ω having $\omega=\mathrm{w}\omega$ and $\omega\langle\bot,\bot\rangle=true$. When given this predicate we set $v=\mathrm{v}\omega$, $e=\mathrm{e}\omega$, $d=\mathrm{d}\omega$, $s=\mathrm{s}\omega$, $y=\mathrm{y}\omega$, $u=\mathrm{u}\omega$, $p=\mathrm{p}\omega$, $z=\mathrm{z}\omega$ and $a=\mathrm{a}\omega$ in the usual way; by doing so we obtain such equations as

$z=(u\to y\to s\to a)\circ(\lambda\langle H,\zeta\rangle.\langle \mathcal{Z}\llbracket H\rrbracket,\zeta\rangle)$,

so that for any H and any ζ $z\langle H,\zeta\rangle=true$ if and only if

$a\langle \mathcal{Z}\llbracket H\rrbracket\acute{\rho}\acute{\upsilon}\acute{\sigma},\zeta\grave{\rho}\grave{\upsilon}\grave{\sigma}\rangle=true$ whenever $\hat{\rho}$, $\hat{\upsilon}$ and $\hat{\sigma}$ are governed by the equations $u\hat{\rho}=true$, $y\hat{\upsilon}=true$ and $s\hat{\sigma}=true$.

One variant of our chosen equation for w should be noted. When $\acute{\omega}$ and $\grave{\omega}$ are drawn from their respective versions of J we could take $wx\hat{\omega}$ to be *true* if and only if

$(sx\to ax)\langle \mathcal{Z}\llbracket(\acute{\omega}|J)\downarrow 1\rrbracket((\acute{\omega}|J)\downarrow 2)((\acute{\omega}|J)\downarrow 3),((\grave{\omega}|J)\downarrow 1)((\grave{\omega}|J)\downarrow 2)((\grave{\omega}|J)\downarrow 3)\rangle=true$

and $(\acute{\omega}|J)\downarrow 4=\langle\rangle$; when $\acute{\omega}$ and $\grave{\omega}$ are other kinds of witnessed value we could modify $wx\hat{\omega}$ in a similar fashion. We have rejected this revised equation for w because it requires us to introduce functors like those of 4.2.3 instead of the simple versions of W used when confirming that w exists.

We have constructed w in order that we may demonstrate that if H is any adhesive control then $z\langle H,\mathcal{Y}\llbracket H\rrbracket\zeta\rangle=true$ (so long as $z\langle\langle\rangle,\zeta\rangle=true$); combining the claims made in 4.6.4 with this equality will enable us to deduce in 4.6.8 that if $A(furl\,\zeta)\acute{\sigma}\sqsupseteq\grave{\sigma}$ for every $\hat{\sigma}$ having $a\hat{\sigma}=true$ then

$A(furl\,\zeta)(\mathcal{Z}\llbracket H\rrbracket\acute{\rho}\acute{\upsilon}\acute{\sigma})=\mathcal{Y}\llbracket H\rrbracket\zeta(U(furl\,\zeta)\acute{\rho})(Y(furl\,\zeta)\acute{\upsilon})(S(furl\,\zeta)\acute{\sigma})$

whenever $\langle\acute{\rho},\acute{\upsilon},\acute{\sigma}\rangle$ is reliable. It is tempting to try to prove that $z\langle H,\mathcal{Y}\llbracket H\rrbracket\zeta\rangle=true$ by a straightforward induction on the length of H. However, if we try to prove that $z\langle H_0,\mathcal{Y}\llbracket H_0\rrbracket\zeta\rangle=true$ by assuming only that $z\langle H_1,\mathcal{Y}\llbracket H_1\rrbracket\zeta\rangle=true$ for every adhesive control H_1 having $\#H_0-1\geq\#H_1\geq 0$, we encounter difficulties when $H_0\downarrow 1$ is e E, say, as we then have to show that $z\langle \mathscr{e}\llbracket E\rrbracket\S(H_0\dagger 1),\mathcal{Y}\llbracket\mathscr{e}\llbracket E\rrbracket\S(H_0\dagger 1)\rrbracket\zeta\rangle=true$ although $\mathscr{e}\llbracket E\rrbracket\S(H_0\dagger 1)$ is sure to have length greater than $\#H_0-1$. In Sap the length of a control is not an accurate measure of complexity of structure, since any control may have other controls concealed in it by the means described in the definition in 4.4.1; moreover these other controls may have yet more controls concealed in them, and if one of them is

$\mathfrak{c}[\![\text{while } E \text{ do } \Gamma]\!]$ this process of producing new controls may be iterated indefinitely. Hence in any induction on the lengths of a control H we are obliged to assume that the controls concealed in H (in the sense explained in 4.4.1) are subject to certain constraints. Because the controls which can be concealed in H are precisely those which can be formed by applying the valuations of appendix 5 to Sal programs, we can hope to confirm that they do indeed satisfy the constraints by performing an induction on the structure of Sal programs. If we were interested in the properties of Sal rather than the properties of Sap we would carry out only this second induction; however, since we are concerned with Sap itself and since the result established by the first induction shortens the second induction, we shall actually discuss them both (in 4.6.6 and 4.6.7). The approach adopted by Gordon [26] entails dealing with the high-level language without mentioning the order code of the underlying interpreter.

Naturally we are obliged to make some more assumptions about those parts of the semantics of Sap which we have left unspecified. Thus we insist that if $\hat{\sigma}$ is any pair of stores for which $s\hat{\sigma}=true$ and if $\acute{\sigma}$ is any answer then $a\langle\acute{\sigma},\perp\rangle=true$, $a\langle\top,\top\rangle=true$, $a\langle wrong\acute{\sigma}, wrong\grave{\sigma}\rangle=true$ and $new\acute{\sigma}\sqsupseteq new\grave{\sigma}$; doing so will be justified in 4.6.9. If H_0 is an adhesive control such that $H_0{\downarrow}1$ is a secret operator and such that $(z\rightarrow z)\langle H_1,\mathfrak{y}[\![H_1]\!]\rangle=true$ whenever H_1 is a control concealed in H_0, we shall suppose that, when H_0 is cohesive and $(z\rightarrow z)\langle\lambda H.(H_0{\dagger}\nu)\S H,\mathfrak{y}[\![H_0{\dagger}\nu]\!]\rangle=true$ for every cohesive and adhesive control of the form $H_0{\dagger}\nu$ having $\#H_0\geq\nu\geq 1$, $(z\rightarrow z)\langle\lambda H.H_0\S H,\mathfrak{y}[\![H_0]\!]\rangle=true$ and that, when $z\langle\langle\rangle,\zeta\rangle=true$ and $z\langle H_0{\dagger}\nu,\mathfrak{y}[\![H_0{\dagger}\nu]\!]\zeta\rangle=true$ for every adhesive control of the form $H_0{\dagger}\nu$ having $\#H_0\geq\nu\geq 1$, $z\langle H_0,\mathfrak{y}[\![H_0]\!]\zeta\rangle=true$; this supposition may appear bizarre, but it is precisely what we shall establish in 4.6.6 for orders that are not secret. We shall also assume that for all B, O and Ω $\mathfrak{b}[\![B]\!]$, $\mathfrak{o}[\![O]\!]$ and $\mathfrak{w}[\![\Omega]\!]$ are truly primitive, in that there are no controls concealed in $\mathfrak{b}[\![B]\!]$, $\mathfrak{o}[\![O]\!]$ or $\mathfrak{w}[\![\Omega]\!]$.

4.6.6. Lemma.

Let H_0 be an adhesive Sap control such that $(z\rightarrow z)\langle \lambda H.H_1 \S H, \mathcal{Y}[\![H_1]\!]\rangle = true$ whenever H_1 is a control concealed in H_0. If H_0 is cohesive then $(z\rightarrow z)\langle \lambda H.H_0 \S H, \mathcal{Y}[\![H_0]\!]\rangle = true$ whilst if ζ is a continuation for which $z\langle\langle\rangle,\zeta\rangle = true$ then $z\langle H_0, \mathcal{Y}[\![H_0]\!]\zeta\rangle = true$.

⊲The proof of this result requires an induction on the length of H_0. Thus we suppose that H_0 is an adhesive control having $(z\rightarrow z)\langle \lambda H.H_1 \S H, \mathcal{Y}[\![H_1]\!]\rangle = true$ whenever H_1 is concealed in H_0; as our inductive hypothesis we use the assumption that, whenever ν is an integer such that $\#H_0 \geq \nu \geq 1$ and $H_0 \dagger \nu$ is adhesive, if $H_0 \dagger \nu$ is cohesive then $(z\rightarrow z)\langle \lambda H.(H_0 \dagger \nu)\S H, \mathcal{Y}[\![H_0 \dagger \nu]\!]\rangle = true$ whilst if ζ is a continuation for which $z\langle\langle\rangle,\zeta\rangle = true$ then $z\langle H_0 \dagger \nu, \mathcal{Y}[\![H_0 \dagger \nu]\!]\zeta\rangle = true$. Our task is to demonstrate that if H_0 is cohesive then $z\langle H_0 \S H_1, \mathcal{Y}[\![H_0]\!]\zeta\rangle = true$ when $z\langle H_1,\zeta\rangle = true$ and that under all circumstances $z\langle H_0, \mathcal{Y}[\![H_0]\!]\zeta\rangle = true$ when $z\langle\langle\rangle,\zeta\rangle = true$. To unify these two possibilities we introduce a control H_1 and a continuation ζ such that $z\langle H_1,\zeta\rangle = true$, we insist that $H_1 = \langle\rangle$ unless H_0 is known to be cohesive, and we let $H_2 = H_0 \S H_1$. Either H_0 is cohesive, in which case when $\#H_0 \geq \nu \geq 0$ $H_0 \dagger \nu$ is cohesive and $\mathcal{Y}[\![H_2 \dagger \nu]\!]\zeta = \mathcal{Y}[\![H_0 \dagger \nu]\!](\mathcal{Y}[\![H_1]\!]\zeta)$ (in accordance with 4.5.3), or $H_1 = \langle\rangle$, in which case $\mathcal{Y}[\![H_2 \dagger \nu]\!]\zeta = \mathcal{Y}[\![H_0 \dagger \nu]\!](\mathcal{Y}[\![H_1]\!]\zeta)$ for each ν. Consequently our task reduces to showing that $z\langle H_2, \mathcal{Y}[\![H_2]\!]\zeta\rangle = true$ on the assumption that $z\langle H_2 \dagger \nu, \mathcal{Y}[\![H_2 \dagger \nu]\!]\zeta\rangle = true$ for all ν such that $\#H_0 \geq \nu \geq 1$ and $H_0 \dagger \nu$ is adhesive.

We now select arbitrary pairs $\hat{\rho}_0$, $\hat{\upsilon}_0$ and $\hat{\sigma}_0$ for which $u\hat{\rho}_0 = true$, $y\hat{\upsilon}_0 = true$ and $s\hat{\sigma}_0 = true$; demonstrating that $z\langle H_2, \mathcal{Y}[\![H_2]\!]\zeta\rangle = true$ really only involves proving that $a\langle \mathcal{Z}[\![H_2]\!]\acute{\rho}_0\acute{\upsilon}_0\acute{\sigma}_0, \mathcal{Y}[\![H_2]\!]\zeta\grave{\rho}_0\grave{\upsilon}_0\grave{\sigma}_0\rangle = true$. The validity of this equation is obvious when $\#H_0 = 0$, as then $H_2 = H_1$ and $\mathcal{Y}[\![H_2]\!]\zeta = \mathcal{Y}[\![H_1]\!]\zeta$, so we demand that $\#H_0 > 0$; as in 4.6.3 our discussion of this situation will be limited to examining what happens if $H_2 \downarrow 1$ is one of five orders (move ν, jump, apply, p $\langle\nu,\Gamma\rangle$ and q $\langle\nu,\Gamma\rangle$).

When $H_2{\downarrow}1$ is move ν for some ν the equations of appendix 11 show that $\mathcal{Z}[\![H_2]\!]\acute\rho_0\acute\upsilon_0\acute\sigma_0=\mathcal{Z}[\![(H_2{\dagger}1){\dagger}\nu]\!]\acute\rho_0\acute\upsilon_0\acute\sigma_0$ whereas the equations of appendix 10 indicate that $\mathcal{Y}[\![H_2]\!]\zeta\grave\rho_0\grave\upsilon_0\grave\sigma_0=\mathcal{Y}[\![(H_2{\dagger}1){\dagger}\nu]\!]\zeta\grave\rho_0\grave\upsilon_0\grave\sigma_0$. Either $\#(H_0{\dagger}1)\geq\nu\geq0$ or $H_1=\langle\rangle$, so $(H_2{\dagger}1){\dagger}\nu=((H_0{\dagger}1){\dagger}\nu)\S H_1$ where $(H_0{\dagger}1){\dagger}\nu$ is adhesive (as is made plain by the definitions in 4.5.1); hence, in accordance with our inductive hypothesis, $z\zeta\langle(H_2{\dagger}1){\dagger}\nu,\mathcal{Y}[\![(H_2{\dagger}1){\dagger}\nu]\!]\zeta\rangle=true$. In view of the assumption that $u\hat\rho_0=true$, $y\hat\upsilon_0=true$ and $s\hat\sigma_0=true$ we may now assert that $a\langle\mathcal{Z}[\![(H_2{\dagger}1){\dagger}\nu]\!]\acute\rho_0\acute\upsilon_0\acute\sigma_0,\mathcal{Y}[\![(H_2{\dagger}1){\dagger}\nu]\!]\zeta\grave\rho_0\grave\upsilon_0\grave\sigma_0\rangle=true$. From this it follows that $a\langle\mathcal{Z}[\![H_2]\!]\acute\rho_0\acute\upsilon_0\acute\sigma_0,\mathcal{Y}[\![H_2]\!]\sigma\grave\rho_0\grave\upsilon_0\grave\sigma_0\rangle=true$.

When $H_2{\downarrow}1$ is jump $\mathcal{A}[\![H_2{\downarrow}1]\!][\![H_2{\dagger}1]\!]\acute\rho_0\acute\upsilon_0\acute\sigma_0$ may be $\bot$, $\top$, $wrong\acute\sigma_0$ or $\langle\acute\upsilon_0{\downarrow}1{\downarrow}1,\acute\upsilon_0{\downarrow}1{\downarrow}2,\acute\upsilon_0{\downarrow}1{\downarrow}3,\acute\sigma_0\rangle$, depending on whether $\acute\upsilon_0{\downarrow}1$ is $\bot$, $\top$, a member of a summand of E other than J or a member of the summand J. Since $e\langle\acute\upsilon_0{\downarrow}1,\grave\upsilon_0{\downarrow}1\rangle=true$ we know that, unless $\grave\upsilon_0{\downarrow}1$ is $\bot$ (in which case $\mathcal{Y}[\![H_2]\!]\sigma\grave\rho_0\grave\upsilon_0\grave\sigma_0$ is $\bot$ and therefore $d\langle\mathcal{Z}[\![H_2]\!]\acute\rho_0\acute\upsilon_0\acute\sigma_0,\mathcal{Y}[\![H_2]\!]\zeta\grave\rho_0\grave\upsilon_0\grave\sigma_0\rangle=true$ automatically), $\mathcal{A}[\![H_2{\downarrow}1]\!][\![H_2{\dagger}1]\!]\acute\rho_0\acute\upsilon_0\acute\sigma_0$ is $\bot$, $\top$, $wrong\acute\sigma_0$ or $\langle\acute\upsilon_0{\downarrow}1{\downarrow}1,\grave\upsilon_0{\downarrow}1{\downarrow}2,\acute\upsilon_0{\downarrow}1{\downarrow}3,\acute\sigma_0\rangle$ exactly when $\mathcal{Y}[\![H_2]\!]\zeta\grave\rho_0\grave\upsilon_0\grave\sigma_0$ is $\bot$, $\top$, $wrong\grave\sigma_0$ or $(\grave\upsilon_0{\downarrow}1{\downarrow}1)(\grave\upsilon_0{\downarrow}1{\downarrow}2)(\grave\upsilon_0{\downarrow}1{\downarrow}3)\grave\sigma_0$. As we are given that $a\langle\bot,\bot\rangle=true$, $a\langle\top,\top\rangle=true$ and $(s\to a)\langle wrong,wrong\rangle=true$ we have only to discuss the situation arising when $\grave\upsilon_0{\downarrow}1$ is in J. Under these circumstances the knowledge that $e\langle\acute\upsilon_0{\downarrow}1,\grave\upsilon_0{\downarrow}1\rangle=true$ ensures that writing $\langle H_3,\acute\rho_1,\acute\upsilon_1,I^*\rangle$ for $\acute\upsilon_0{\downarrow}1|J$ produces a control H_3, an environment $\acute\rho_1$ and a stack $\acute\upsilon_1$ such that $z\langle H_3,\grave\upsilon_0{\downarrow}1{\downarrow}1\rangle=true$, $u\langle coil[\![H_3]\!]\acute\rho_1,\grave\upsilon_0{\downarrow}1{\downarrow}2\rangle=true$ and $y\langle\acute\upsilon_1,\grave\upsilon_0{\downarrow}1{\downarrow}3\rangle=true$. Consequently the definitions of the predicates given in 4.6.5 reveal that $a\langle\mathcal{Z}[\![H_3]\!](coil[\![H_3]\!]\acute\rho_1)\acute\upsilon_1\acute\sigma_0,(\grave\upsilon_0{\downarrow}1{\downarrow}1)(\grave\upsilon_0{\downarrow}1{\downarrow}2)(\grave\upsilon_0{\downarrow}1{\downarrow}3)\grave\sigma_0\rangle=true$, and since $\mathcal{Z}[\![H_2]\!]\acute\rho_0\acute\upsilon_0\acute\sigma_0=\mathcal{Z}[\![H_3]\!]\acute\rho_1\acute\upsilon_1\acute\sigma_0$ and $\mathcal{Z}[\![H_3]\!]\acute\rho_1\acute\upsilon_1\acute\sigma_0=\mathcal{Z}[\![H_3]\!](coil[\![H_3]\!]\acute\rho_1)\acute\upsilon_1\acute\sigma_0$ (in accordance with the remarks in 4.4.4) we may conclude that $a\langle\mathcal{Z}[\![H_2]\!]\acute\rho_0\acute\upsilon_0\acute\sigma_0,\mathcal{Y}[\![H_2]\!]\zeta\grave\rho_0\grave\upsilon_0\grave\sigma_0\rangle=true$.

When $H_2{\downarrow}1$ is apply we may fairly claim that

$\mathcal{A}[\![H_2\downarrow 1]\!][\![H_2\dagger 1]\!]\acute{\rho}_0\acute{\upsilon}_0\acute{\sigma}_0$ is $\bot$, $\top$, $wrong\acute{\sigma}_0$ or $\langle\acute{\upsilon}_0\downarrow 1\downarrow 2\S(H_2\dagger 1), divert\acute{\rho}_0(\acute{\upsilon}_0\downarrow 2\downarrow 2), \langle\acute{\upsilon}_0\downarrow 1\rangle\S\acute{\upsilon}_0\dagger 2, \acute{\sigma}_0\rangle$; moreover, unless $\grave{\upsilon}_0\downarrow 2$ is $\bot$, the fact that $e\langle\acute{\upsilon}_0\downarrow 2,\grave{\upsilon}_0\downarrow 2\rangle = true$ ensures that $\mathcal{Y}[\![H_2]\!]\zeta\grave{\rho}_0\grave{\upsilon}_0\grave{\sigma}_0$ is $\bot$, $\top$ $wrong\grave{\sigma}_0$ or $(\grave{\upsilon}_0\downarrow 2\downarrow 1)(\mathcal{Y}[\![H_2\dagger 1]\!]\zeta)(divert\grave{\rho}_0(\grave{\upsilon}_0\downarrow 2\downarrow 2))(\langle\grave{\upsilon}_0\downarrow 1\rangle\S\grave{\upsilon}_0\dagger 2)\grave{\sigma}_0$ depending on whether $\acute{\upsilon}_0\downarrow 2$ is $\bot$, $\top$, a member of a summand of E other than F, or a member of the summand F. Reasons similar to those considered above therefore permit us to be satisfied with analysing only what happens if $\grave{\upsilon}_0\downarrow 1$ is in F. Because $\#H_0>\#(H_0\dagger 1)$ and $H_2\dagger 1$ is adhesive, $z\langle H_2\dagger 1, \mathcal{Y}[\![H_2\dagger 1]\!]\zeta\rangle = true$, and we actually know that if $\grave{\upsilon}_0\downarrow 1$ is in F
$z\langle\acute{\upsilon}_0\downarrow 2\downarrow 1\S(H_2\dagger 1),(\grave{\upsilon}_0\downarrow 2\downarrow 1)(\mathcal{Y}[\![H_2\dagger 1]\!]\zeta)\rangle = true$,
$u\langle divert\acute{\rho}_0(\acute{\upsilon}_0\downarrow 2\downarrow 1), divert\grave{\rho}_0(\grave{\upsilon}_0\downarrow 2\downarrow 2)\rangle = true$ and
$y\langle\langle\acute{\upsilon}_0\downarrow 1\rangle\S\acute{\upsilon}_0\dagger 2, \langle\grave{\upsilon}_0\downarrow 1\rangle\S(\grave{\upsilon}_0\dagger 2)\rangle = true$ since $u\hat{\rho}_0 = true$ and $y\hat{\upsilon}_0 = true$. In consequence, after setting $H_3 = \acute{\upsilon}_0\downarrow 2\downarrow 1\S(H_2\dagger 1)$, $\acute{\rho}_1 = divert\acute{\rho}_0(\acute{\upsilon}_0\downarrow 2\downarrow 1)$ and $\acute{\upsilon}_1 = \langle\acute{\upsilon}_0\downarrow 1\rangle\S\acute{\upsilon}_0\dagger 2$, we may infer that
$a\langle\mathcal{Z}[\![H_3]\!]\acute{\rho}_1\acute{\upsilon}_1\acute{\sigma}_0, (\grave{\upsilon}_0\downarrow 2\downarrow 1)(divert\grave{\rho}_0(\grave{\upsilon}_0\downarrow 2\downarrow 2))(\langle\grave{\upsilon}_0\downarrow 1\rangle\S\grave{\upsilon}_0\dagger 2)\grave{\sigma}_0\rangle = true$ where $\mathcal{Z}[\![H_2]\!]\acute{\rho}_0\acute{\upsilon}_0\acute{\sigma}_0 = \mathcal{Z}[\![H_3]\!]\acute{\rho}_1\acute{\upsilon}_1\acute{\sigma}_0$; indeed we even know that
$a\langle\mathcal{Z}[\![H_2]\!]\acute{\rho}_0\acute{\upsilon}_0\acute{\sigma}_0, \mathcal{Y}[\![H_2]\!]\zeta\grave{\rho}_0\grave{\upsilon}_0\grave{\sigma}_0\rangle = true$.

When $H_2\downarrow 1$ is p $\langle\nu,\Gamma\rangle$ for some ν and Γ letting
$\acute{\varepsilon}_0 = \langle\mathfrak{p}[\![\Gamma]\!]\downarrow\nu\S((H_2\dagger 1)\dagger(-1+3\times\nu)), \acute{\rho}_0, \acute{\upsilon}_0\dagger 1, \langle\rangle\rangle$ and
$\grave{\varepsilon}_0 = \mathcal{P}[\![\Gamma]\!](\mathcal{Y}[\![(H_2\dagger 1)\dagger(-1+3\times\nu)]\!]\zeta)\grave{\rho}_0(\grave{\upsilon}_0\dagger 1)\downarrow\nu$ yields a pair $\hat{\varepsilon}_0$ for which
$\mathcal{Z}[\![H_2]\!]\acute{\rho}_0\acute{\upsilon}_0\acute{\sigma}_0 = \mathcal{Z}[\![H_2\dagger 1]\!]\acute{\rho}_0(\langle\acute{\varepsilon}_0\rangle\S\acute{\upsilon}_0)\acute{\sigma}_0$ and $\mathcal{Y}[\![H_2]\!]\zeta\grave{\rho}_0\grave{\upsilon}_0\grave{\sigma}_0 = \mathcal{Y}[\![H_2\dagger 1]\!]\zeta\grave{\rho}_0(\langle\grave{\varepsilon}_0\rangle\S\grave{\upsilon}_0)\grave{\sigma}_0$.
As $\#H_0\geq 1\geq 1$ and $H_0\dagger 1$ is adhesive, we are assuming that $z\langle H_2\dagger 1, \mathcal{Y}[\![H_2\dagger 1]\!]\zeta\rangle = true$; hence as $u\hat{\rho}_0 = true$, $y\hat{\upsilon}_0 = true$ and $s\hat{\sigma}_0 = true$ we may justifiably assert that $a\langle\mathcal{Z}[\![H_2]\!]\acute{\rho}_0\acute{\upsilon}_0\acute{\sigma}_0, \mathcal{Y}[\![H_2]\!]\zeta\grave{\rho}_0\grave{\upsilon}_0\grave{\sigma}_0\rangle = true$ once we have shown that $e\hat{\varepsilon}_0 = true$. Since $u\hat{\rho}_0 = true$ we certainly know that $u\langle coil[\![\acute{\varepsilon}_0\downarrow 1]\!](\acute{\varepsilon}_0\downarrow 2), \grave{\varepsilon}_0\downarrow 2\rangle = true$; likewise since $y\hat{\upsilon}_0 = true$ we are sure that $y\langle\acute{\varepsilon}_0\downarrow 3, \grave{\varepsilon}_0\downarrow 3\rangle = true$. Either $\#(H_0\dagger 1)\geq -1+3\times\nu\geq 0$ or $H_1 = \langle\rangle$, so $(H_2\dagger 1)\dagger(-1+3\times\nu) = ((H_0\dagger 1)\dagger(-1+3\times\nu))\S H_1$ where $(H_0\dagger 1)\dagger(-1+3\times\nu)$ is adhesive; consequently our inductive assumption ensures that
$z\langle(H_2\dagger 1)\dagger(-1+3\times\nu), \mathcal{Y}[\![(H_2\dagger 1)\dagger(-1+3\times\nu)]\!]\zeta\rangle = true$. The fact that $H_0\downarrow 1$ is

p $\langle \nu,\Gamma\rangle$ indicates that $\mathfrak{p}[\![\Gamma]\!]\downarrow\nu$ is concealed in H_0, so

$(z\rightarrow z)\langle \mathfrak{p}[\![\Gamma]\!]\downarrow\nu,\mathfrak{Y}[\![\mathfrak{p}[\![\Gamma]\!]\downarrow\nu]\!]\rangle = true$; from this it follows that

$z\langle \mathfrak{p}[\![\Gamma]\!]\downarrow\nu\S((H_2\dagger 1)\dagger(-1+3\times\nu)),\mathfrak{Y}[\![\mathfrak{p}[\![\Gamma]\!]\downarrow\nu]\!](\mathfrak{Y}[\![(H_2\dagger 1)\dagger(-1+3\times\nu)]\!]\zeta)\rangle = true$

and indeed that $z\langle \acute{\varepsilon}_0\downarrow 1,\grave{\varepsilon}_0\downarrow 1\rangle = true$ owing to the equation

$\lambda\grave{\rho}\grave{\upsilon}.\mathfrak{P}[\![\Gamma]\!](\mathfrak{Y}[\![(H_2\dagger 1)\dagger(-1+3\times\nu)]\!]\zeta)\grave{\rho}\grave{\upsilon}\downarrow\nu = \lambda\grave{\rho}\grave{\upsilon}.\langle \mathfrak{Y}[\![\mathfrak{p}[\![\Gamma]\!]\downarrow\nu]\!](\mathfrak{Y}[\![(H_2\dagger 1)\dagger(-1+3\times\nu)]\!]\zeta,\grave{\rho},\grave{\upsilon}\rangle$

implicit in 4.5.5. To summarize all this, $e\hat{\varepsilon}_0 = true$ and, as was intimated above, $a\langle \mathfrak{X}[\![H_2]\!]\acute{\rho}_0\acute{\upsilon}_0\acute{\sigma}_0,\mathfrak{Y}[\![H_2]\!]\zeta\grave{\rho}_0\grave{\upsilon}_0\grave{\sigma}_0\rangle = true$.

When $H_2\downarrow 1$ is q $\langle \nu,\Gamma\rangle$ for some ν and Γ the adhesive properties of H_0 assures us that if $H_3 = H_2\dagger(1+3\times\#\mathfrak{J}[\![\Gamma]\!]+2\times\#\mathfrak{K}[\![\Gamma]\!])$ and $H_4 = H_2\dagger(2\times\#\mathfrak{K}[\![\Gamma]\!])$ then $\mathfrak{X}[\![H_2]\!]\acute{\rho}_0\acute{\upsilon}_0\acute{\sigma}_0 = \mathfrak{X}[\![H_4]\!](fold(\mathfrak{K}[\![\Gamma]\!])\acute{\rho}_1)\acute{\upsilon}_0\acute{\sigma}_0$ and $\mathfrak{Y}[\![H_2]\!]\zeta\grave{\rho}_0\grave{\upsilon}_0\grave{\sigma}_0 = \mathfrak{Y}[\![H_4]\!]\zeta\grave{\rho}_1\grave{\upsilon}_0\grave{\sigma}_0$ when we define $\hat{\rho}_1$ by setting

$\acute{\rho}_1 = \acute{\rho}_0[map(\lambda H.\langle(map(\lambda I.\text{amend } I)(\mathfrak{K}[\![\Gamma]\!]))\S H\S H_3,\acute{\rho}_0,\acute{\upsilon}_0,\mathfrak{K}[\![\Gamma]\!]\rangle)(\mathfrak{q}[\![\Gamma]\!])/\mathfrak{K}[\![\Gamma]\!]]$

and $\grave{\rho}_1 = fix(\lambda\grave{\rho}.\grave{\rho}_0[\mathfrak{Q}[\![\Gamma]\!](\mathfrak{Y}[\![H_3]\!]\zeta)\grave{\rho}\grave{\upsilon}_0/\mathfrak{K}[\![\Gamma]\!]])$ (so that

$\grave{\rho}_1 = \grave{\rho}_0[fix(\lambda\grave{\delta}^*.\mathfrak{Q}[\![\Gamma]\!](\mathfrak{Y}[\![H_3]\!]\zeta)\grave{\rho}_0[\grave{\delta}^*/\mathfrak{K}[\![\Gamma]\!]]\grave{\upsilon}_0)/\mathfrak{K}[\![\Gamma]\!]])$. Arguments akin to those used above indicate that $H_0\dagger(1+3\times\#\mathfrak{J}[\![\Gamma]\!]+2\times\#\mathfrak{K}[\![\Gamma]\!])$ and $H_0\dagger(2\times\#\mathfrak{K}[\![\Gamma]\!])$ are adhesive controls having $H_3 = H_0\dagger(1+3\times\#\mathfrak{J}[\![\Gamma]\!]+2\times\#\mathfrak{K}[\![\Gamma]\!])\S H_1$ and $H_4 = (H_0\dagger(2\times\#\mathfrak{K}[\![\Gamma]\!]))\S H_1$; consequently $z\langle H_3,\mathfrak{Y}[\![H_3]\!]\zeta\rangle = true$ and $z\langle H_4,\mathfrak{Y}[\![H_4]\!]\zeta\rangle = true$ by virtue of our inductive hypothesis. Hence in order to prove that $a\langle \mathfrak{X}[\![H_2]\!]\acute{\rho}_0\acute{\upsilon}_0\acute{\sigma}_0,\mathfrak{Y}[\![H_2]\!]\zeta\grave{\rho}_0\grave{\upsilon}_0\grave{\sigma}_0\rangle = true$ we need only verify that $u\langle fold(\mathfrak{K}[\![\Gamma]\!])\acute{\rho}_1,\grave{\rho}_1\rangle = true$. For this purpose it helps to notice that when $\#\mathfrak{K}[\![\Gamma]\!]\geq\nu'\geq 1$ $\mathfrak{q}[\![\Gamma]\!]\downarrow\nu'$ is a cohesive and adhesive control concealed in H_0, so

$(z\rightarrow z)\langle(map(\lambda I.\text{amend } I)(\mathfrak{K}[\![\Gamma]\!]))\S\mathfrak{q}[\![\Gamma]\!]\downarrow\nu'\S H_3,\mathfrak{Y}[\![\mathfrak{q}[\![\Gamma]\!]\downarrow\nu'\S H_3]\!]\rangle = true$ where

$\lambda\grave{\rho}\grave{\upsilon}.\mathfrak{Q}[\![\Gamma]\!](\mathfrak{Y}[\![H_3]\!]\zeta)\grave{\rho}\grave{\upsilon}\downarrow\nu' = \lambda\grave{\rho}\grave{\upsilon}.\langle\mathfrak{Y}[\![\mathfrak{q}[\![\Gamma]\!]\downarrow\nu'\S H_3]\!]\zeta,\grave{\rho},\grave{\upsilon}\rangle$. If $\grave{\delta}^*$ is a list of $\#\mathfrak{K}[\![\Gamma]\!]$ values having $d\langle fold(\mathfrak{K}[\![\Gamma]\!])\acute{\rho}_1[\![\mathfrak{K}[\![\Gamma]\!]\downarrow\nu']\!]\downarrow 1,\grave{\delta}^*\downarrow\nu'\rangle = true$ whenever $\#\mathfrak{K}[\![\Gamma]\!]\geq\nu'\geq 1$ then induction on ν' indicates that, when $\#\mathfrak{K}[\![\Gamma]\!]\geq\nu'\geq 1$ and

$I^* = fix(\lambda\xi\nu''.(\nu''>\nu')\rightarrow\langle\rangle,\langle\mathfrak{K}[\![\Gamma]\!]\downarrow\nu''\rangle\S\xi(\nu''+1))1$,

$d\langle fold I^*\acute{\rho}_1[\![I^*\downarrow\nu'']\!]\downarrow 1,\mathfrak{Q}[\![\Gamma]\!](\mathfrak{Y}[\![H_3]\!]\zeta)\grave{\rho}_0[\grave{\delta}^*/\mathfrak{K}[\![\Gamma]\!]]\grave{\upsilon}_0\downarrow\nu''\rangle = true$

for every ν'' with $\nu'\geq\nu''\geq 1$; in particular

$d\langle fold(\mathfrak{K}[\![\Gamma]\!])\acute{\rho}_1[\![\mathfrak{K}[\![\Gamma]\!]\downarrow\nu'']\!]\downarrow 1,\mathfrak{Q}[\![\Gamma]\!](\mathfrak{Y}[\![H_3]\!]\zeta)\grave{\rho}_0[\grave{\delta}^*/\mathfrak{K}[\![\Gamma]\!]]\grave{\upsilon}_0\downarrow\nu''\rangle = true$

for every ν'' with $\#\mathfrak{K}[\![\Gamma]\!]\geq\nu''\geq 1$. The definition of w in 4.6.5 shows that $d\langle \mathit{fold}(\mathfrak{K}[\![\Gamma]\!])\acute{\rho}_1[\![\mathfrak{K}[\![\Gamma]\!]\dagger\nu'']\!]\dagger 1,\bot\rangle = \mathit{true}$ whenever $\#\mathfrak{K}[\![\Gamma]\!]\geq\nu''\geq 1$, so as $u\hat{\rho}_0 = \mathit{true}$ we may conclude that $u\langle \mathit{fold}(\mathfrak{K}[\![\Gamma]\!])\acute{\rho}_1,\grave{\rho}_1\rangle = \mathit{true}$ and therefore that $a\langle \mathfrak{Z}[\![H_2]\!]\acute{\rho}_0\acute{\upsilon}_0\acute{\sigma}_0,\mathfrak{Y}[\![H_2]\!]\zeta\grave{\rho}_0\grave{\upsilon}_0\grave{\sigma}_0\rangle = \mathit{true}$.

In view of the arbitrary natures of $\hat{\rho}_0$, $\hat{\upsilon}_0$ and $\hat{\sigma}_0$ these paragraphs, and others like them, confirm that $z\langle H_0\S H_1,\mathfrak{Y}[\![H_0]\!](\mathfrak{Y}[\![H_1]\!]\zeta)\rangle = \mathit{true}$ for these particular versions of H_0 and H_1. By induction on the length of H_0 it follows that if H_0 is cohesive then $(z\to z)\langle \lambda H.H_0\S H,\mathfrak{Y}[\![H_0]\!]\rangle = \mathit{true}$ and that if $z\langle\langle\rangle,\zeta\rangle = \mathit{true}$ then $z\langle H_0,\mathfrak{Y}[\![H_0]\!]\zeta\rangle = \mathit{true}$.▸

The equations in appendix 11 and appendix 10 actually indicate rather more than what we have established here, for it can be verified that, if T is any order which is not secret and which is not move ν, pick ν, link ν, t $\langle\nu,\Delta\rangle$, p $\langle\nu,\Gamma\rangle$ or q $\langle\nu,\Gamma\rangle$ (for any ν, Δ or Γ), then $\mathfrak{A}[\![T]\!]=\lambda\eta.\xi(\eta 0)$ for some $\xi\in O$ having $(z\to z)\langle\lambda H.\langle\Gamma\rangle\S H,\xi\rangle = \mathit{true}$.

4.6.7. Proposition.

If H_0 and H_1 are Sap controls such that H_1 is concealed in H_0 then $(z\to z)\langle \lambda H.H_1\S H,\mathfrak{y}[\![H_1]\!]\rangle = \mathit{true}$.

⊲This property of controls really concerns Sal rather than Sap so its proof proceeds by induction on the structure of Sal programs. The basis of the induction, which concerns what happens when H_1 is $\mathfrak{b}[\![B]\!]$, $\mathfrak{o}[\![O]\!]$ or $\mathfrak{w}[\![\Omega]\!]$ for some B, O or Ω, is handled as follows. We note that the suppositions mentioned in 4.6.2 ensure that H_1 is cohesive and adhesive and that the assumptions made in 4.6.5 indicate that there are no controls concealed in H_1. Hence we may use 4.6.6 (which depends on other claims made about secret orders) to show that $(z\to z)\langle \lambda H.H_1\S H,\mathfrak{y}[\![H_1]\!]\rangle = \mathit{true}$.

As an example of how the induction continues we consider the situation when H_1 is $\mathfrak{e}[\![E_0E_1]\!]$ for some E_0 and E_1. Under these circumstances, we have to show that $(z\to z)\langle \lambda H.\mathfrak{e}[\![E_0E_1]\!]\S H,\mathfrak{y}[\![\mathfrak{e}[\![E_0E_1]\!]]\!]\rangle = \mathit{true}$ on the premises that $(z\to z)\langle \lambda H.\mathfrak{r}[\![E_1]\!]\S H,\mathfrak{y}[\![\mathfrak{r}[\![E_0]\!]]\!]\rangle = \mathit{true}$ and that $(z\to z)\langle \lambda H.\mathfrak{e}[\![E_1]\!]\S H,\mathfrak{y}[\![\mathfrak{e}[\![E_1]\!]]\!]\rangle = \mathit{true}$. According to appendix 4, $\mathfrak{e}[\![E_0E_1]\!] = \langle r\ E_0\rangle\S\langle e\ E_1\rangle\S\langle \mathrm{apply}\rangle$ so $\mathfrak{r}[\![E_0]\!]$ and $\mathfrak{e}[\![E_1]\!]$ are the only controls concealed in $\mathfrak{e}[\![E_0E_1]\!]$ in the way made plain in appendix 11. As 4.5.4 indicates that $\mathfrak{e}[\![E_0E_1]\!]$ is cohesive and adhesive we may apply 4.6.6, thereby establishing that $(z\to z)\langle \lambda H.\mathfrak{e}[\![E_0E_1]\!]\S H,\mathfrak{y}[\![\mathfrak{e}[\![E_0E_1]\!]]\!]\rangle = \mathit{true}$.

All except one of the other cases in the induction have precisely the same pattern as E_0E_1, in that they involve appealing first to 4.5.4 and then to 4.6.6. The exception is the proof that $(z\to z)\langle \lambda H.\mathfrak{c}[\![\text{while } E \text{ do } \Gamma]\!]\S H,\mathfrak{y}[\![\mathfrak{c}[\![\text{while } E \text{ do } \Gamma]\!]]\!]\rangle = \mathit{true}$, in which it is assumed that $(z\to z)\langle \lambda H.\mathfrak{r}[\![E]\!]\S H,\mathfrak{y}[\![\mathfrak{r}[\![E]\!]]\!]\rangle = \mathit{true}$ and that $(z\to z)\langle \lambda H.\mathfrak{c}[\![\Gamma]\!]\S H,\mathfrak{y}[\![\mathfrak{c}[\![\Gamma]\!]]\!]\rangle = \mathit{true}$. The valuation $\mathfrak{c}$ provided by appendix 4 is such that $\mathfrak{c}[\![\text{while } E \text{ do } \Gamma]\!] = \langle r\ E\rangle\S\langle \text{pick } 2\rangle\S\langle c\ \Gamma\rangle\S\langle c \text{ while } E \text{ do } \Gamma\rangle$, so in accordance with appendix 11 the controls concealed in $\mathfrak{c}[\![\text{while } E \text{ do } \Gamma]\!]$ are $\mathfrak{r}[\![E]\!]$, $\mathfrak{c}[\![\Gamma]\!]$ and $\mathfrak{c}[\![\text{while } E \text{ do } \Gamma]\!]$. Thus in order to infer that $(z{\to}z)\langle \lambda H.\mathfrak{c}[\![\text{while E do }\Gamma]\!]\S H,\mathfrak{Y}[\![\mathfrak{c}[\![\text{while E do }\Gamma]\!]]\!]\rangle = \mathit{true}$ by applying 4.6.6 it appears that we have to demand not only that $(z{\to}z)\langle \lambda H.\mathfrak{r}[\![E]\!]\S H,\mathfrak{Y}[\![\mathfrak{r}[\![E]\!]]\!]\rangle = \mathit{true}$ and that $(z{\to}z)\langle \lambda H.\mathfrak{c}[\![\Gamma]\!]\S H,\mathfrak{Y}[\![\mathfrak{c}[\![\Gamma]\!]]\!]\rangle = \mathit{true}$ but also that $(z{\to}z)\langle \lambda H.\mathfrak{c}[\![\text{while E do }\Gamma]\!]\S H,\mathfrak{Y}[\![\mathfrak{c}[\![\text{while E do }\Gamma]\!]]\!]\rangle = \mathit{true}$. This circularity can be removed by an appeal to the induction principle of 2.3.2; the need for this appeal stems from the fact that the proof that $\mathfrak{C}[\![\text{while E do }\Gamma]\!] = \mathfrak{Y}[\![\mathfrak{c}[\![\text{while E do }\Gamma]\!]]\!]$ (given in 4.5.5) does not depend on the minimal nature of the fixed point generated by *fix*.

To clarify what we mean we shall now give the inductive proof that $(z{\to}z)\langle \lambda H.\mathfrak{c}[\![\text{while E do }\Gamma]\!]\S H,\mathfrak{Y}[\![\mathfrak{c}[\![\text{while E do }\Gamma]\!]]\!]\rangle = \mathit{true}$ when $(z{\to}z)\langle \lambda H.\mathfrak{r}[\![E]\!]\S H,\mathfrak{Y}[\![\mathfrak{r}[\![E]\!]]\!]\rangle = \mathit{true}$ and $(z{\to}z)\langle \lambda H.\mathfrak{c}[\![\Gamma]\!]\S H,\mathfrak{Y}[\![\mathfrak{c}[\![\Gamma]\!]]\!]\rangle = \mathit{true}$. For this purpose we shall take $\langle H,\zeta\rangle$ to be a pair comprising a control and a continuation for which $z\langle H,\zeta\rangle = \mathit{true}$ and we shall demonstrate that $z\langle \mathfrak{c}[\![\text{while E do }\Gamma]\!]\S H,\mathfrak{Y}[\![\mathfrak{c}[\![\text{while E do }\Gamma]\!]]\!]\zeta\rangle = \mathit{true}$; if there is no such pair $\langle H,\zeta\rangle$ the required result is trivial.

We suppose that ζ' is any continuation having $z\langle \mathfrak{c}[\![\text{while E do }\Gamma]\!]\S H,\zeta'\rangle = \mathit{true}$; as we can tell from appendix 11 that $\mathfrak{X}[\![\langle \text{c while E do }\Gamma\rangle\S H]\!] = \mathfrak{X}[\![\mathfrak{c}[\![\text{while E do }\Gamma]\!]\S H]\!]$, $z\langle\langle \text{c while E do }\Gamma\rangle\S H,\zeta'\rangle = \mathit{true}$. Because $(z{\to}z)\langle \lambda H.\mathfrak{c}[\![\Gamma]\!]\S H,\mathfrak{Y}[\![\mathfrak{c}[\![\Gamma]\!]]\!]\rangle = \mathit{true}$ and $\lambda H.\mathfrak{X}[\![\langle \text{c }\Gamma\rangle\S H]\!] = \lambda H.\mathfrak{X}[\![\mathfrak{c}[\![\Gamma]\!]\S H]\!]$ we also know that $(z{\to}z)\langle \lambda H.\langle \text{c }\Gamma\rangle\S H,\mathfrak{Y}[\![\mathfrak{c}[\![\Gamma]\!]]\!]\rangle = \mathit{true}$ and therefore that $z\langle\langle \text{c }\Gamma\rangle\S\langle \text{c while E do }\Gamma\rangle\S H,\mathfrak{Y}[\![\mathfrak{c}[\![\Gamma]\!]]\!]\zeta'\rangle = \mathit{true}$. In addition $z\langle H,\zeta\rangle = \mathit{true}$, so by comparing the meaning ascribed to pick ν in appendix 11 with the meaning supplied by appendix 10 we see that $z\langle\langle \text{pick }2\rangle\S\langle \text{c }\Gamma\rangle\S\langle \text{c while E do }\Gamma\rangle\S H,\zeta''\rangle = \mathit{true}$ where $\zeta'' = \lambda\rho\upsilon\sigma.\mathit{test}\langle \mathfrak{Y}[\![\mathfrak{c}[\![\Gamma]\!]]\!]\zeta'\rho(\upsilon{\dagger}1),\zeta\rho(\upsilon{\dagger}1)\rangle(\upsilon{\downarrow}1)\sigma$. Since $(z{\to}z)\langle \lambda H.\mathfrak{r}[\![E]\!]\S H,\mathfrak{Y}[\![\mathfrak{r}[\![E]\!]]\!]\rangle = \mathit{true}$ and $\lambda H.\mathfrak{X}[\![\langle \text{r E}\rangle\S H]\!] = \lambda H.\mathfrak{X}[\![\mathfrak{r}[\![E]\!]\S H]\!]$ we may assert that $(z{\to}z)\langle \lambda H.\langle \text{r E}\rangle\S H,\mathfrak{Y}[\![\mathfrak{r}[\![E]\!]]\!]\rangle = \mathit{true}$; consequently $z\langle\langle \text{r E}\rangle\S\langle \text{pick }2\rangle\S\langle \text{c }\Gamma\rangle\S\langle \text{c while E do }\Gamma\rangle\S H,\mathfrak{Y}[\![\mathfrak{r}[\![E]\!]]\!]\zeta''\rangle = \mathit{true}$. However, from 4.5.5 we know that $\mathfrak{R}[\![E]\!] = \mathfrak{Y}[\![\mathfrak{r}[\![E]\!]]\!]$ and that $\mathfrak{C}[\![\Gamma]\!] = \mathfrak{Y}[\![\mathfrak{c}[\![\Gamma]\!]]\!]$, so we can state this equation in the form

$z\langle \mathfrak{C}[\![\text{while E do }\Gamma]\!]\S H, \mathfrak{R}[\![E]\!](\lambda\rho\upsilon\sigma.\mathit{test}\langle \mathfrak{C}[\![\Gamma]\!]\zeta'\rho(\upsilon\dagger 1), \zeta\rho(\upsilon\dagger 1)\rangle(\upsilon\downarrow 1)\sigma)\rangle = \mathit{true}$.

The definitions of the predicates given in 4.6.5 make it plain that $z\langle \mathfrak{C}[\![\text{while E do }\Gamma]\!]\S H, \bot\rangle = \mathit{true}$ since $a\langle \delta, \bot\rangle = \mathit{true}$ for every δ in A. Hence as z is an inclusive predicate and as $\mathfrak{C}[\![\text{while E do }\Gamma]\!]\zeta = \mathit{fix}(\lambda\zeta'.\mathfrak{R}[\![E]\!](\lambda\rho\upsilon\sigma.\mathit{test}\langle \mathfrak{C}[\![\Gamma]\!]\zeta'\rho(\upsilon\dagger 1), \zeta\rho(\upsilon\dagger 1)\rangle(\upsilon\downarrow 1)\sigma))$, $z\langle \mathfrak{C}[\![\text{while E do }\Gamma]\!]\S H, \mathfrak{C}[\![\text{while E do }\Gamma]\!]\zeta\rangle = \mathit{true}$. Another appeal to 4.5.5 indicates that $\mathfrak{C}[\![\text{while E do }\Gamma]\!] = \mathfrak{Y}[\![\mathfrak{C}[\![\text{while E do }\Gamma]\!]]\!]$, so $z\langle \mathfrak{C}[\![\text{while E do }\Gamma]\!]\S H, \mathfrak{Y}[\![\mathfrak{C}[\![\text{while E do }\Gamma]\!]]\!]\rangle = \mathit{true}$; because $\langle H, \zeta\rangle$ may be any pair having $z\langle H, \zeta\rangle = \mathit{true}$ we may safely conclude that $(z\to z)\langle \lambda H.\mathfrak{C}[\![\text{while E do }\Gamma]\!]\S H, \mathfrak{Y}[\![\mathfrak{C}[\![\text{while E do }\Gamma]\!]]\!]\rangle = \mathit{true}$.

We shall not consider any other cases in the structural induction, for, as we have already remarked, the remainder are closely similar to the proof about $E_0 E_1$.‣

By using the consequences of this result in the statement of 4.6.6 we now obtain the result that we really want: whenever H_0 is an adhesive control and ζ is a continuation, if H_0 is cohesive then $(z\to z)\langle \lambda H.H_0\S H, \mathfrak{Y}[\![H_0]\!]\rangle = \mathit{true}$ whilst if $z\langle\langle\rangle, \zeta\rangle = \mathit{true}$ then $z\langle H_0, \mathfrak{Y}[\![H_0]\!]\zeta\rangle = \mathit{true}$. The reason for this is that any control H_1 concealed in H_0 must be subject to the equation $(z\to z)\langle \lambda H.H_1\S H, \mathfrak{Y}[\![H_1]\!]\rangle = \mathit{true}$.

4.6.8. Theorem.

Suppose that $\lambda\zeta.\mathrm{A}(\mathit{furl}\zeta)\bot=\lambda\zeta.\bot$, $\lambda\zeta.\mathrm{A}(\mathit{furl}\zeta)\top=\lambda\zeta.\top$, $a\langle\acute{\sigma},\bot\rangle=\mathit{true}$ and $a\langle\top,\top\rangle=\mathit{true}$ for every $\acute{\sigma}$. Assume that $\mathrm{A}(\mathit{furl}\zeta)(\mathit{wrong}\acute{\sigma})=\mathit{wrong}\grave{\sigma}$ and $\mathit{new}\acute{\sigma}=\mathit{new}\grave{\sigma}$ for all $\hat{\sigma}$ and ζ having $s(\lambda\hat{\omega}.\mathit{curl}\acute{\omega})\hat{\sigma}=\mathit{true}$ and $\mathrm{S}(\mathit{furl}\zeta)\acute{\sigma}=\grave{\sigma}$ that $a\langle\mathit{wrong}\acute{\sigma},\mathit{wrong}\grave{\sigma}\rangle=\mathit{true}$ and $\mathit{new}\acute{\sigma}\sqsupseteq\mathit{new}\grave{\sigma}$ for every $\hat{\sigma}$ having $s\hat{\sigma}=\mathit{true}$. Insist also that for all B, O and Ω the controls $\mathfrak{b}[\![\mathrm{B}]\!]$, $\mathfrak{o}[\![\mathrm{O}]\!]$ and $\mathfrak{w}[\![\Omega]\!]$ are cohesive and adhesive, have no controls concealed in them and satisfy the equations $\mathfrak{B}[\![\mathrm{B}]\!]=\mathfrak{Y}[\![\mathfrak{b}[\![\mathrm{B}]\!]]\!]$, $\mathfrak{O}[\![\mathrm{O}]\!]=\mathfrak{Y}[\![\mathfrak{o}[\![\mathrm{O}]\!]]\!]$ and $\mathfrak{W}[\![\Omega]\!]=\mathfrak{Y}[\![\mathfrak{w}[\![\Omega]\!]]\!]$. Take the secret orders to be restricted in the ways mentioned in 4.6.2 and 4.6.5. Let ζ be any continuation such that $\mathrm{A}(\mathit{furl}\zeta)(\mathit{process}\acute{\rho}\acute{\upsilon}\acute{\sigma})=\zeta(\mathrm{U}(\mathit{furl}\zeta)\acute{\rho})(\mathrm{Y}(\mathit{furl}\zeta)\acute{\upsilon})(\mathrm{S}(\mathit{furl}\zeta)\acute{\sigma})$ whenever $\langle\acute{\rho},\acute{\upsilon},\acute{\sigma}\rangle$ is reliable and such that $z\langle\langle\rangle,\zeta\rangle=\mathit{true}$. If H is an adhesive Sap control and $\langle\acute{\rho},\acute{\upsilon},\acute{\sigma}\rangle$ is a reliable state then
$\mathrm{A}(\mathit{furl}\zeta)(\mathfrak{Z}[\![\mathrm{H}]\!]\acute{\rho}\acute{\upsilon}\acute{\sigma})=\mathfrak{Y}[\![\mathrm{H}]\!]\zeta(\mathrm{U}(\mathit{furl}\zeta)\acute{\rho})(\mathrm{Y}(\mathit{furl}\zeta)\acute{\upsilon})(\mathrm{S}(\mathit{furl}\zeta)\acute{\sigma})$
provided that $\mathrm{A}(\mathit{furl}\zeta)\acute{\sigma}\sqsupseteq\grave{\sigma}$ whenever $a\hat{\sigma}=\mathit{true}$.

⊲We shall simply consider one typical continuation, ζ, such that $\mathrm{A}(\mathit{furl}\zeta)(\mathit{process}\acute{\rho}\acute{\upsilon}\acute{\sigma})=\zeta(\mathrm{U}(\mathit{furl}\zeta)\acute{\rho})(\mathrm{Y}(\mathit{furl}\zeta)\acute{\upsilon})(\mathrm{S}(\mathit{furl}\zeta)\acute{\sigma})$ whenever $\langle\acute{\rho},\acute{\upsilon},\acute{\sigma}\rangle$ is reliable and such that $z\langle\langle\rangle,\zeta\rangle=\mathit{true}$. When we introduce any Sap control, H say, 4.6.6 and 4.6.7 together imply that $(z\rightarrow z)\langle\lambda\mathrm{H}'.\mathrm{H}\S\mathrm{H}',\mathfrak{Y}[\![\mathrm{H}]\!]\rangle=\mathit{true}$ if H is cohesive and adhesive and that $z\langle\mathrm{H},\mathfrak{Y}[\![\mathrm{H}]\!]\zeta\rangle=\mathit{true}$ if H is adhesive. In the next two paragraphs we shall sketch how to use this knowledge to prove inductively that $w\langle\acute{\omega},\mathit{furl}\zeta\acute{\omega}\rangle=\mathit{true}$ when $\acute{\omega}$ is any witnessed value for which $\mathit{curl}\acute{\omega}=\mathit{true}$.

We let ψ be any mapping such that $\psi\zeta$ is a continuous function taking the version of W appropriate to appendix 11 into the version of W appropriate to appendix 10 and such that $w\langle\acute{\omega},\psi\zeta\acute{\omega}\rangle=\mathit{true}$ for every $\acute{\omega}$ with $\mathit{curl}\acute{\omega}=\mathit{true}$. The functions provided in 4.6.1 and 4.6.2 are evidently contrived so that $e\langle\acute{\epsilon},\mathrm{E}(\psi\zeta)\acute{\epsilon}\rangle=\mathit{true}$ for every $\acute{\epsilon}$ having $e(\lambda\hat{\omega}.\mathit{curl}\acute{\omega})\langle\acute{\epsilon},\mathrm{E}(\mathit{furl}\bot)\acute{\epsilon}\rangle=\mathit{true}$, $u\langle\acute{\rho},\mathrm{U}(\psi\zeta)\acute{\rho}\rangle=\mathit{true}$ for every $\acute{\rho}$ having $u(\lambda\hat{\omega}.\mathit{curl}\acute{\omega})\langle\acute{\rho},\mathrm{U}(\mathit{furl}\bot)\acute{\rho}\rangle=\mathit{true}$, $y\langle\acute{\upsilon},\mathrm{Y}(\psi\zeta)\acute{\upsilon}\rangle=\mathit{true}$ for every $\acute{\upsilon}$ having

$y(\lambda\hat{\omega}.\mathit{curl}\acute{\omega})\langle\acute{\upsilon},Y(\mathit{furl}\bot)\acute{\upsilon}\rangle=\mathit{true}$, $s\langle\acute{\sigma},S(\psi\zeta)\acute{\sigma}\rangle=\mathit{true}$ for every $\acute{\sigma}$ having $s(\lambda\hat{\omega}.\mathit{curl}\acute{\omega})\langle\acute{\sigma},S(\mathit{furl}\bot)\acute{\sigma}\rangle=\mathit{true}$ and $p\langle\acute{\pi},P(\psi\zeta)\acute{\pi}\rangle=\mathit{true}$ for every $\acute{\pi}$ having $p(\lambda\hat{\omega}.\mathit{curl}\acute{\omega})\langle\acute{\pi},P(\mathit{furl}\bot)\acute{\pi}\rangle=\mathit{true}$. Hence we can now verify that if $\hat{\omega}$ is any witnessed value for which $\mathit{curl}\hat{\omega}=\mathit{true}$ then $w\langle\acute{\omega},\mathit{furling}\psi\zeta\hat{\omega}\rangle=\mathit{true}$; when $\hat{\omega}\in J$, for instance, we write $\langle H,\acute{\rho},\acute{\upsilon},I^*\rangle$ for $\hat{\omega}|J$ and note that $\langle\mathcal{Y}[\![H]\!]\zeta,U(\psi\zeta)(\mathit{coil}[\![H]\!]\acute{\rho}),Y(\psi\zeta)\acute{\upsilon}\rangle$ is $\mathit{furling}\psi\zeta\hat{\omega}|J$, where $z\langle H,\mathcal{Y}[\![H]\!]\zeta\rangle=\mathit{true}$, $u\langle\mathit{coil}[\![H]\!]\acute{\rho},U(\psi\zeta)(\mathit{coil}[\![H]\!]\acute{\rho})\rangle=\mathit{true}$, $y\langle\acute{\upsilon},Y(\psi\zeta)\acute{\upsilon}\rangle=\mathit{true}$ and $I^*=\langle\rangle$ because H is adhesive, $u(\lambda\hat{\omega}.\mathit{curl}\acute{\omega})\langle\mathit{coil}[\![H]\!]\acute{\rho},U(\mathit{furl}\bot)(\mathit{coil}[\![H]\!]\acute{\rho})\rangle=\mathit{true}$, $y(\lambda\hat{\omega}.\mathit{curl}\acute{\omega})\langle\acute{\upsilon},Y(\mathit{furl}\bot)\acute{\upsilon}\rangle=\mathit{true}$ and $I^*=\langle\rangle$.

The argument of the preceding paragraph demonstrates that if ψ is such that $w\langle\acute{\omega},\psi\zeta\hat{\omega}\rangle=\mathit{true}$ for every $\hat{\omega}$ with $\mathit{curl}\hat{\omega}=\mathit{true}$ then $\mathit{furling}\psi$ is such that $w\langle\acute{\omega},\mathit{furling}\psi\zeta\hat{\omega}\rangle=\mathit{true}$ for every $\hat{\omega}$ with $\mathit{curl}\hat{\omega}=\mathit{true}$. Furthermore, in 4.6.5 we carefully arranged that $w\langle\acute{\omega},\bot\rangle=\mathit{true}$ for each $\hat{\omega}$, so certainly $w\langle\acute{\omega},(\lambda\zeta\hat{\omega}.\bot)\zeta\hat{\omega}\rangle=\mathit{true}$ for every $\hat{\omega}$ with $\mathit{curl}\hat{\omega}=\mathit{true}$. As w is inclusive the induction principle of 2.3.2 allows us to assert that $w\langle\acute{\omega},\mathit{fix}(\mathit{furling})\zeta\hat{\omega}\rangle=\mathit{true}$ for every $\hat{\omega}$ with $\mathit{curl}\hat{\omega}=\mathit{true}$; in other words, $w\langle\acute{\omega},\mathit{furl}\zeta\hat{\omega}\rangle=\mathit{true}$ when $\hat{\omega}$ is any witnessed value for which $\mathit{curl}\hat{\omega}=\mathit{true}$.

From the fact that $w\langle\acute{\omega},\mathit{furl}\zeta\hat{\omega}\rangle=\mathit{true}$ whenever $\mathit{curl}\hat{\omega}=\mathit{true}$ we can infer that if $\langle\acute{\rho},\acute{\upsilon},\acute{\sigma}\rangle$ is any reliable state then $u\langle\acute{\rho},U(\mathit{furl}\zeta)\acute{\rho}\rangle=\mathit{true}$, $y\langle\acute{\upsilon},Y(\mathit{furl}\zeta)\acute{\upsilon}\rangle=\mathit{true}$ and $s\langle\acute{\sigma},S(\mathit{furl}\zeta)\acute{\sigma}\rangle=\mathit{true}$. If H is any adhesive control we know that $z\langle H,\mathcal{Y}[\![H]\!]\zeta\rangle=\mathit{true}$, so the definition of z given in 4.6.5 indicates that

$a\langle\mathcal{Z}[\![H]\!]\acute{\rho}\acute{\upsilon}\acute{\sigma},\mathcal{Y}[\![H]\!]\zeta(U(\mathit{furl}\zeta)\acute{\rho})(Y(\mathit{furl}\zeta)\acute{\upsilon})(S(\mathit{furl}\zeta)\acute{\sigma})\rangle=\mathit{true}$ for this particular state. Assuming that $A(\mathit{furl}\zeta)\acute{\alpha}\sqsupseteq\grave{\alpha}$ whenever $\hat{\alpha}$ is such that $a\hat{\alpha}=\mathit{true}$ in turn reveals that

$A(\mathit{furl}\zeta)(\mathcal{Z}[\![H]\!]\acute{\rho}\acute{\upsilon}\acute{\sigma})\sqsupseteq\mathcal{Y}[\![H]\!]\zeta(U(\mathit{furl}\zeta)\acute{\rho})(Y(\mathit{furl}\zeta)\acute{\upsilon})(S(\mathit{furl}\zeta)\acute{\sigma})$;

however, in 4.6.4 we proved that

$A(\mathit{furl}\zeta)(\mathcal{Z}[\![H]\!]\acute{\rho}\acute{\upsilon}\acute{\sigma})\sqsubseteq\mathcal{Y}[\![H]\!]\zeta(U(\mathit{furl}\zeta)\acute{\rho})(Y(\mathit{furl}\zeta)\acute{\upsilon})(S(\mathit{furl}\zeta)\acute{\sigma})$,

so combining these inequalities demonstrates that

$A(\mathit{furl}\zeta)(\mathcal{Z}[\![H]\!]\grave{\rho}\grave{\upsilon}\grave{\sigma})=\mathcal{Y}[\![H]\!]\zeta(U(\mathit{furl}\zeta)\acute{\rho})(Y(\mathit{furl}\zeta)\acute{\upsilon})(S(\mathit{furl}\zeta)\acute{\sigma})$, ⊁

4.6.9. The assumptions underlying the basic result.

Though we have succeeded in demonstrating that
$A(furl\,\zeta)(\mathcal{X}[\![H]\!]\acute{\rho}\acute{\upsilon}\acute{\sigma})=\mathcal{Y}[\![H]\!]\zeta(U(furl\,\zeta)\acute{\rho})(Y(furl\,\zeta)\acute{\upsilon})(S(furl\,\zeta)\acute{\sigma})$
when H is adhesive and $\langle\acute{\rho},\acute{\upsilon},\acute{\sigma}\rangle$ is reliable, the proof of 4.6.8 involves making many assumptions which have not as yet been justified. Here we shall discuss these assumptions, paying particular attention to the requirement that $A(furl\,\zeta)\acute{\sigma}\sqsupseteq\grave{\sigma}$ whenever $a\hat{\sigma}=true$. We shall find it useful to have at our behest a retraction, W_0, such that, if $Z_0=\lambda\chi.Z(\lambda\tilde{\omega}.\tilde{\omega})\bot$ and $O_0=\lambda\chi.O(\lambda\tilde{\omega}.\tilde{\omega})\bot$ then
$W_0=L+B+(EW_0)^*+(Z_0\times UW_0\times YW_0)+(O_0\times UW_0)+(O_0\times UW_0\times SW_0)+(Z_0\times UW_0\times YW_0)+PW_0$,
where the functors are those mentioned in 4.6.1 and 4.6.5. When $\tilde{\omega}_0$ and $\tilde{\omega}_1$ are witnessed values appropriate to consecution semantics, the equation $W_0\tilde{\omega}_0=W_0\tilde{\omega}_1$ implies that $\tilde{\omega}_0$ and $\tilde{\omega}_1$ can be distinguished only by looking at members of Z or O; moreover, an application of the induction rule of 2.3.2 to the obvious function having W_0 as its least fixed point indicates that $W_0\circ furl\bot=W_0\circ furl\,\zeta$, $furl\bot\acute{\omega}\sqsupseteq W_0\tilde{\omega}$ and $w\langle\acute{\omega},W_0\tilde{\omega}\rangle=true$ for any ζ and for any $\hat{\omega}$ having $w\hat{\omega}=true$.

The conditions imposed on *wrong* in 4.6.2 and 4.6.5 can only be justified when the domains named A are known. However, examining a few possible versions of A, such as S, V* and P (with or without extra summands for holding error messages), should be enough to convince anyone that these conditions are perfectly fair.

We can say rather more than this about the restrictions placed on *new*, since they reflect the intuitive view that *new* should not depend on the code associated with label and procedure values. It is natural to demand that form of *new* appropriate to appendix 2 should satisfy the equation $new=new\circ SW_0\circ S(\lambda\tilde{\omega}.\tilde{\omega})$ (which actually ensures that this *new* function corresponds with one for standard semantics in the way discussed in 4.2.6). Under these circumstances, our remarks about W_0 show that

$$\begin{aligned}
new\circ S(furl\bot) &= new\circ SW_0\circ S(\lambda\tilde{\omega}.\tilde{\omega})\circ S(furl\bot)\\
&= new\circ SW_0\circ S(furl\bot)\\
&= new\circ SW_0\circ S(furl\zeta)\\
&= new\circ SW_0\circ S(\lambda\tilde{\omega}.\tilde{\omega})\circ S(furl\zeta)\\
&= new\circ S(furl\zeta)
\end{aligned}$$

for every ζ (as $S(furl\zeta)=S(\lambda\tilde{\omega}.\tilde{\omega})\circ S(furl\zeta)$) and that

$$\begin{aligned}
new(S(furl\bot)\acute{\sigma}) &\sqsupseteq new(SW_0\grave{\sigma})\\
&= new(SW_0(S(\lambda\tilde{\omega}.\tilde{\omega})\grave{\sigma}))\\
&= new\grave{\sigma}
\end{aligned}$$

for every $\hat{\sigma}$ with $s\hat{\sigma}=true$. In addition, $new\circ S(furl\bot)$ satisfies the axioms which any *new* function must obey; consequently letting $\psi=new\circ S(furl\bot)$ provides a function, ψ, which is a *new* function for control semantics having $\lambda\zeta.\psi=\lambda\zeta.new\circ S(furl\zeta)$ and $\psi\acute{\sigma}\sqsupseteq new\grave{\sigma}$ whenever $s\hat{\sigma}=true$ (provided that *new* is appropriate to appendix 10 and is subject to the equation $new=new\circ SW_0\circ S(\lambda\tilde{\omega}.\tilde{\omega})$). Thus we can be sure that there are lots of functions restricted in the ways suggested for *new* in 4.6.2 and 4.6.5.

If we were to supply semantic equations for the secret Sap orders we would be able to justify many more of the suppositions made in 4.6.8. In particular, we could extend 4.5.4 and 4.5.5, thereby establishing the desired properties of ♭, ⊙ and ⊛, and we could become certain that 4.6.3 and 4.6.6 are valid even when the controls concerned contain secret orders. None of this is of much interest to us here, for we chiefly wish to discuss the less trivial constraints on A and a in 4.6.8; it is to these that we shall now devote our attention.

In 4.6.8 we insisted on using a continuation, ζ, such that $A(furl\zeta)(process\acute{\rho}\acute{\upsilon}\acute{\sigma})=\zeta(U(furl\zeta)\acute{\rho})(Y(furl\zeta)\acute{\upsilon})(S(furl\zeta)\acute{\sigma})$ whenever $\langle\acute{\rho},\acute{\upsilon},\acute{\sigma}\rangle$ is reliable and such that $z\langle\langle\rangle,\zeta\rangle=true$ (or, in other words, such that $(u\to y\to s\to a)\langle process,\zeta\rangle=true$). These equations to which *process* and ζ must be subject resemble those governing the two versions of *wrong*, in that they can only be justified once the form taken by A has been settled. When we want a concrete example of what *process* and ζ are like we shall therefore let A be P and let *process* be $\lambda\acute{\rho}\acute{\upsilon}\acute{\sigma}.\langle\acute{\rho},\acute{\upsilon},\acute{\sigma}\rangle$; other choices for A and *process* could be discussed in a similar vein. Even after A and *process* have been fixed ζ may still be varied in accordance with the properties of A and a. When A is P and *process* is $\lambda\acute{\rho}\acute{\upsilon}\acute{\sigma}.\langle\acute{\rho},\acute{\upsilon},\acute{\sigma}\rangle$ the obvious versions of ζ are $\lambda\grave{\rho}\grave{\upsilon}\grave{\sigma}.\mathrm{P}W_0\langle\grave{\rho},\grave{\upsilon},\grave{\sigma}\rangle$ and $\lambda\grave{\rho}\grave{\upsilon}\grave{\sigma}.\langle\grave{\rho},\grave{\upsilon},\grave{\sigma}\rangle$; the conditions to the effect that $\mathrm{A}(\mathit{furl}\,\zeta)(\mathit{process}\,\acute{\rho}\acute{\upsilon}\acute{\sigma})=\zeta(\mathrm{U}(\mathit{furl}\,\zeta)\acute{\rho})(\mathrm{Y}(\mathit{furl}\,\zeta)\acute{\upsilon})(\mathrm{S}(\mathit{furl}\,\zeta)\acute{\sigma})$ whenever $\langle\acute{\rho},\acute{\upsilon},\acute{\sigma}\rangle$ is reliable and to the effect that $z\langle\langle\rangle,\zeta\rangle=\mathit{true}$ are satisfied by the first of these versions of ζ so long as A is $\lambda X.\mathrm{P}W_0\circ\mathrm{P}X$ and a is $\lambda x\hat{\sigma}.((\grave{\sigma}\equiv\bot)\rightarrow\mathit{true},\mathrm{p}x\hat{\sigma}\wedge(\grave{\sigma}\equiv\mathrm{P}W_0\grave{\sigma}))$ and by the second of these versions of ζ so long as A is P and a is $\lambda x\hat{\sigma}.((\grave{\sigma}\equiv\bot)\rightarrow\mathit{true},\mathrm{p}x\hat{\sigma})$.

Though we can guarantee that the conditions involving ζ are satisfied, we have greater problems with the demand that $\mathrm{A}(\mathit{furl}\,\zeta)\acute{\sigma}\sqsupseteq\grave{\sigma}$ whenever $a\hat{\sigma}=\mathit{true}$. If ζ is $\lambda\acute{\rho}\acute{\upsilon}\acute{\sigma}.\mathrm{P}W_0\langle\acute{\rho},\acute{\upsilon},\acute{\sigma}\rangle$ then when A is $\lambda X.\mathrm{P}W_0\circ\mathrm{P}X$ and a is $\lambda x\hat{\sigma}.((\grave{\sigma}\equiv\bot)\rightarrow\mathit{true},\mathrm{p}x\hat{\sigma}\wedge(\grave{\sigma}\equiv\mathrm{P}W_0\grave{\sigma}))$ the facts that $a=\mathrm{a}w$ and that $\mathit{furl}\,\zeta\acute{\omega}\sqsupseteq W_0\grave{\omega}$ whenever $w\hat{\omega}=\mathit{true}$ ensure that $\mathrm{A}(\mathit{furl}\,\zeta)\acute{\sigma}\sqsupseteq\grave{\sigma}$ whenever $a\hat{\sigma}=\mathit{true}$; however, if ζ is $\lambda\acute{\rho}\acute{\upsilon}\acute{\sigma}.\langle\acute{\rho},\acute{\upsilon},\acute{\sigma}\rangle$ then when A is P and a is $\lambda x\hat{\sigma}.((\grave{\sigma}\equiv\bot)\rightarrow\mathit{true},\mathrm{p}x\hat{\sigma})$ we only know that $\mathrm{A}(\mathit{furl}\,\zeta)\acute{\sigma}\sqsupseteq\mathrm{A}W_0\grave{\sigma}$ whenever $\mathrm{a}\hat{\sigma}=\mathit{true}$, and we cannot do better than this by taking a to be $\lambda x\hat{\sigma}.(\mathrm{A}(\mathit{furl}\,\zeta)\acute{\sigma}\sqsupseteq\grave{\sigma})$ without sacrificing the assurance that $z\langle\langle\rangle,\zeta\rangle=\mathit{true}$. More generally, when A takes any of the forms permitted in 4.6.1, if we assume that a coincides with $\lambda x\hat{\sigma}.\mathrm{a}x\hat{\sigma}\wedge(\grave{\sigma}\equiv\mathrm{A}W_0\grave{\sigma})$ we may assert that $\mathrm{A}(\mathit{furl}\,\zeta)\acute{\sigma}\sqsupseteq\grave{\sigma}$ whenever $a\hat{\sigma}=\mathit{true}$ (and also that $\zeta=\lambda\grave{\rho}\grave{\upsilon}\grave{\sigma}.\mathrm{A}W_0(\zeta\grave{\rho}\grave{\upsilon}\grave{\sigma})$ and $\mathrm{A}=\lambda X.\mathrm{A}W_0\circ\mathrm{A}X$ if ζ obeys the conditions in 4.6.8 which involve it). In this situation we may apply 4.6.8 in conjunction with 4.5.4, thereby establishing, for instance, that when E is any Sal expression and when $\langle\acute{\rho},\acute{\upsilon},\acute{\sigma}\rangle$ is any reliable state

$A(\mathit{furl}\zeta)(\mathcal{E}[\![E]\!][\![\langle\rangle]\!]\acute{\rho}\acute{\upsilon}\acute{\sigma})=\mathcal{E}[\![E]\!]\zeta(U(\mathit{furl}\zeta)\acute{\rho})(Y(\mathit{furl}\zeta)\acute{\upsilon})(S(\mathit{furl}\zeta)\acute{\sigma})$,

where the valuation defined in appendix 4 appears on the left hand side of this equation and the valuation defined in appendix 2 appears on the right hand side; it is this result (and the corresponding results for the other Sal valuations) that we originally set out to verify in 4.6.1. If we do not assume that $\delta=AW_0\delta$ whenever $a\hat{\delta}=\mathit{true}$ we are unable to prove this result, because we do not know that $A(\mathit{furl}\zeta)\acute{\sigma}\sqsupseteq AW_0\delta$ whenever $a\hat{\delta}=\mathit{true}$; nevertheless, as we shall show below, we can still do somewhat more than baldly stating 4.6.4 and 4.6.7 in terms applicable to Sal.

In order to provide a substitute for the claim that $A(\mathit{furl}\zeta)\acute{\sigma}\sqsupseteq\delta$ whenever $a\hat{\delta}=\mathit{true}$ we use yet more predicates; these new predicates, however, will be defined upon pairs of values, both halves of which will be suited to consecution semantics. We shall let ϕ be a typical mapping such that for any ζ $\phi\zeta$ is an inclusive predicate taking pairs of witnessed values suited to appendix 10 into elements of T'. If we presume that a is defined on pairs of answers suited to appendix 10, so that $a=\lambda x.ax\circ(\lambda\langle\delta_0,\delta_1\rangle.\langle\delta_0,\delta_1\rangle)$ we may define a predicate, $\mathit{bond}\phi\zeta$, by writing

$$\mathit{bond}=\lambda\phi\zeta\langle\zeta_0,\zeta_1\rangle.\bigwedge\{a(\phi\zeta)\langle\zeta_0\grave{\rho}\grave{\upsilon}\grave{\sigma},\zeta_1\grave{\rho}\grave{\upsilon}\grave{\sigma}\rangle$$
$$|p(\lambda\hat{\omega}.\mathit{curl}\acute{\omega})\langle\langle\acute{\rho},\acute{\upsilon},\acute{\sigma}\rangle,\langle\grave{\rho},\grave{\upsilon},\grave{\sigma}\rangle\rangle\wedge(P(\mathit{furl}\zeta)\langle\acute{\rho},\acute{\upsilon},\acute{\sigma}\rangle\equiv\langle\grave{\rho},\grave{\upsilon},\grave{\sigma}\rangle)\}$$

Thus $\mathit{bond}\phi\zeta\langle\zeta_0,\zeta_1\rangle=\mathit{true}$ if and only if $a(\phi\zeta)\langle\zeta_0\grave{\rho}\grave{\upsilon}\grave{\sigma},\zeta_1\grave{\rho}\grave{\upsilon}\grave{\sigma}\rangle=\mathit{true}$ whenever $\langle\grave{\rho},\grave{\upsilon},\grave{\sigma}\rangle$ is of the form $P(\mathit{furl}\zeta)\langle\acute{\rho},\acute{\upsilon},\acute{\sigma}\rangle$ for some state $\langle\acute{\rho},\acute{\upsilon},\acute{\sigma}\rangle$ which is reliable.

Having set up *bond* we can create *burling*, which transforms any function, ϕ, mapping continuations into inclusive predicates, into another such function, $\mathit{burling}\phi$. Essentially we apply $\mathit{bond}\phi\zeta$ to pairs of components of witnessed values by letting

$$
\begin{aligned}
burling = \lambda\phi\zeta\langle\tilde{\omega}_0,\tilde{\omega}_1\rangle.\;&(\tilde{\omega}_0\equiv\bot)\vee(\tilde{\omega}_1\equiv\bot)\rightarrow(\tilde{\omega}_1\equiv\bot),\\
&(\tilde{\omega}_0\equiv\top)\vee(\tilde{\omega}_1\equiv\top)\rightarrow(\tilde{\omega}_0\equiv\top),\\
&\tilde{\omega}_0\mathsf{E}\mathsf{L}\wedge\tilde{\omega}_1\mathsf{E}\mathsf{L}\rightarrow(\tilde{\omega}_0|\mathsf{L}\sqsupseteq\tilde{\omega}_1|\mathsf{L}),\\
&\tilde{\omega}_0\mathsf{E}\mathsf{B}\wedge\tilde{\omega}_1\mathsf{E}\mathsf{B}\rightarrow(\tilde{\omega}_0|\mathsf{B}\sqsupseteq\tilde{\omega}_1|\mathsf{B}),\\
&\tilde{\omega}_0\mathsf{E}\mathsf{E}^*\wedge\omega_1\mathsf{E}\mathsf{E}^*\rightarrow(\mathrm{e}(\phi\zeta))^*\langle\tilde{\omega}_0|\mathsf{E}^*,\tilde{\omega}_1|\mathsf{E}^*\rangle,\\
&\tilde{\omega}_0\mathsf{E}\mathsf{J}\wedge\tilde{\omega}_1\mathsf{E}\mathsf{J}\rightarrow bond\phi\zeta\langle(\tilde{\omega}_0|\mathsf{J})\downarrow1,(\tilde{\omega}_1|\mathsf{J})\downarrow1\rangle\\
&\qquad\wedge\mathrm{u}(\phi\zeta)\langle(\tilde{\omega}_0|\mathsf{J})\downarrow2,(\tilde{\omega}_1|\mathsf{J})\downarrow2\rangle\\
&\qquad\wedge\mathrm{y}(\phi\zeta)\langle(\tilde{\omega}_0|\mathsf{J})\downarrow3,(\tilde{\omega}_1|\mathsf{J})\downarrow3\rangle,\\
&\tilde{\omega}_0\mathsf{E}\mathsf{F}\wedge\tilde{\omega}_1\mathsf{E}\mathsf{F}\rightarrow\bigwedge\{bond\phi\zeta\langle((\tilde{\omega}_0|\mathsf{F})\downarrow1)(\mathcal{Y}[\![\mathsf{H}]\!]\zeta),((\tilde{\omega}_1|\mathsf{F})\downarrow1)(\mathcal{Y}[\![\mathsf{H}]\!]\zeta)\rangle\\
&\qquad\qquad|\,adhere[\![\mathsf{H}]\!]\}\\
&\qquad\wedge\mathrm{u}(\phi\zeta)\langle(\tilde{\omega}_0|\mathsf{F})\downarrow2,(\tilde{\omega}_1|\mathsf{F})\downarrow2\rangle,\\
&\tilde{\omega}_0\mathsf{E}\mathsf{G}\wedge\tilde{\omega}_1\mathsf{E}\mathsf{G}\rightarrow\bigwedge\{bond\phi\zeta\langle((\tilde{\omega}_0|\mathsf{G})\downarrow1)(\mathcal{Y}[\![\mathsf{H}]\!]\zeta),((\tilde{\omega}_1|\mathsf{G})\downarrow1)(\mathcal{Y}[\![\mathsf{H}]\!]\zeta)\rangle\\
&\qquad\qquad|\,adhere[\![\mathsf{H}]\!]\}\\
&\qquad\wedge\mathrm{u}(\phi\zeta)\langle(\tilde{\omega}_0|\mathsf{G})\downarrow2,(\tilde{\omega}_1|\mathsf{G})\downarrow2\rangle\\
&\qquad\wedge\mathrm{s}(\phi\zeta)\langle(\tilde{\omega}_0|\mathsf{G})\downarrow3,(\tilde{\omega}_1|\mathsf{G})\downarrow3\rangle,\\
&\tilde{\omega}_0\mathsf{E}\mathsf{J}\wedge\tilde{\omega}_1\mathsf{E}\mathsf{J}\rightarrow bond\phi\zeta\langle(\tilde{\omega}_0|\mathsf{J})\downarrow1,(\tilde{\omega}_1|\mathsf{J})\downarrow1\rangle\\
&\qquad\wedge\mathrm{u}(\phi\zeta)\langle(\tilde{\omega}_0|\mathsf{J})\downarrow2,(\tilde{\omega}_1|\mathsf{J})\downarrow2\rangle\\
&\qquad\wedge\mathrm{y}(\phi\zeta)\langle(\tilde{\omega}_0|\mathsf{J})\downarrow3,(\tilde{\omega}_1|\mathsf{J})\downarrow3\rangle,\\
&\tilde{\omega}_0\mathsf{E}\mathsf{P}\wedge\tilde{\omega}_1\mathsf{E}\mathsf{P}\rightarrow\mathrm{p}(\phi\zeta)\langle\tilde{\omega}_0|\mathsf{P},\tilde{\omega}_1|\mathsf{P}\rangle,\\
&false.
\end{aligned}
$$

Here we take e, u, y, s and p to be constructed in the manner prescribed in 4.6.2 except that they map predicates into predicates defined on pairs of values suited to appendix 10; for instance, $\mathrm{p}=\lambda x.(\mathrm{u}x\times\mathrm{y}x\times\mathrm{s}x)\circ(\lambda\langle\tilde{\pi}_0,\tilde{\pi}_1\rangle.\langle\tilde{\pi}_0,\tilde{\pi}_1\rangle)$.

We now assume that a is continuous when regarded as a function which maps the domain of inclusive predicates into itself; this assumption is sure to be credible when A is formed as in 4.6.1, since in such a situation ax may be built up by associating x with the operators ×, +, * and → (defined in 2.5.5) in such a way that x "is not needed to the left of →". Both *bond* and *burl* become continuous functions, and the precedent of 4.6.2 dictates that we set

$burl = fix(burling)$,

with the effect that for any ζ $burl\zeta$ is inclusive. Just as in 3.8.3 here we regard a predicate x mapping some domain into T′ as being transitive if the relation induced by it is transitive (with the effect that $x\langle\chi_0,\chi_2\rangle = true$ whenever $x\langle\chi_0,\chi_1\rangle = true$ and $x\langle\chi_1,\chi_2\rangle = true$).

Next we take ζ to be any continuation for which $A(furl\zeta)(process\acute\rho\acute\upsilon\acute\sigma) = \zeta(U(furl\zeta)\acute\rho)(Y(furl\zeta)\acute\upsilon)(S(furl\zeta)\acute\sigma)$ whenever $\langle\acute\rho,\acute\upsilon,\acute\sigma\rangle$ is reliable and for which $z\langle\langle\rangle,\zeta\rangle = true$. We also make one further assumption about a: we demand that when x is a transitive inclusive predicate having $(\lambda\langle\grave\omega_0,\grave\omega_1\rangle.(\grave\omega_0 \sqsupseteq \grave\omega_1)) \sqsupseteq x$ and $w \sqsupseteq (\lambda\hat\omega.x\langle furl\zeta\acute\omega,\grave\omega\rangle)$ (so that $x\langle\grave\omega_0,\grave\omega_1\rangle = true$ and $x\langle furl\zeta\acute\omega,\grave\omega\rangle = true$ whenever $\grave\omega_0 \sqsupseteq \grave\omega_1$ and $w\hat\omega = true$) then $\mathrm{a}x$ is a transitive inclusive predicate having $(\lambda\langle\grave\delta_0,\grave\delta_1\rangle.(\grave\delta_0 \sqsupseteq \grave\delta_1)) \sqsupseteq \mathrm{a}x$ and $a \sqsupseteq (\lambda\hat\delta.\mathrm{a}x\langle A(furl\zeta)\acute\delta,\grave\delta\rangle)$. This demand is certainly reasonable if A is S, V* or P provided that a is chosen sensibly; for instance, if A is P we let a be $\lambda x\langle\grave\delta_0,\grave\delta_1\rangle.((\grave\delta_1 \equiv \bot) \rightarrow true, \mathrm{p}x\langle\grave\delta_0,\grave\delta_1\rangle \wedge (\grave\delta_1 \equiv PW_0\grave\delta_1))$ when ζ is $\lambda\grave\rho\grave\upsilon\grave\sigma.PW_0\langle\grave\rho,\grave\upsilon,\grave\sigma\rangle$ and we let a be $\lambda x\langle\grave\delta_0,\grave\delta_1\rangle.((\grave\delta_1 \equiv \bot) \rightarrow true, \mathrm{p}x\langle\grave\delta_0,\grave\delta_1\rangle)$ when ζ is $\lambda\grave\rho\grave\upsilon\grave\sigma.\langle\grave\rho,\grave\upsilon,\grave\sigma\rangle$.

As was demonstrated in 4.6.8, if $\langle\acute\rho,\acute\upsilon,\acute\sigma\rangle$ is reliable then $u\hat\rho = true$, $y\hat\upsilon = true$ and $s\hat\sigma = true$ when $\langle\grave\rho,\grave\upsilon,\grave\sigma\rangle = P(furl\zeta)\langle\acute\rho,\acute\upsilon,\acute\sigma\rangle$, so, if in addition H is an adhesive control and ζ' is any continuation for which $z\langle H,\zeta'\rangle = true$, then setting $\acute\delta = \mathcal{Z}[\![H]\!]\acute\rho\acute\upsilon\acute\sigma$, $\grave\delta_0 = \mathcal{Y}[\![H]\!]\zeta\grave\rho\grave\upsilon\grave\sigma$ and $\grave\delta_1 = \zeta'\grave\rho\grave\upsilon\grave\sigma$ provides elements such that $\grave\delta_0 \sqsupseteq A(furl\zeta)\acute\delta$ and $a\langle\acute\delta,\grave\delta_1\rangle = true$; consequently, when $\phi\zeta$ is a transitive inclusive predicate having $(\lambda\langle\grave\omega_0,\grave\omega_1\rangle.(\grave\omega_0 \sqsupseteq \grave\omega_1)) \sqsupseteq \phi\zeta$ and $w \sqsupseteq (\lambda\hat\omega.\phi\zeta\langle furl\zeta\acute\omega,\grave\omega\rangle)$, we know that $\mathrm{a}(\phi\zeta)\langle\grave\delta_0,A(furl\zeta)\acute\delta\rangle = true$ and $\mathrm{a}(\phi\zeta)\langle A(furl\zeta)\acute\delta,\grave\delta_1\rangle = true$ (and therefore that $\mathrm{a}(\phi\zeta)\langle\grave\delta_0,\grave\delta_1\rangle = true$). Indeed $\mathrm{a}(\phi\zeta)\langle\mathcal{Y}[\![H]\!]\zeta\grave\rho\grave\upsilon\grave\sigma,\zeta'\grave\rho\grave\upsilon\grave\sigma\rangle = true$ whenever H is adhesive, $z\langle H,\zeta'\rangle = true$ and $\langle\grave\rho,\grave\upsilon,\grave\sigma\rangle = P(furl\zeta)\langle\acute\rho,\acute\upsilon,\acute\sigma\rangle$ (for some reliable state $\langle\acute\rho,\acute\upsilon,\acute\sigma\rangle$). This means that $bond\phi\zeta\langle\mathcal{Y}[\![H]\!]\zeta,\zeta'\rangle = true$ so long as H is adhesive and $z\langle H,\zeta'\rangle = true$; in other words, $(\lambda\langle H,\zeta'\rangle.adhere[\![H]\!] \wedge z\langle H,\zeta'\rangle) \sqsupseteq (\lambda\langle H,\zeta'\rangle.bond\phi\zeta\langle\mathcal{Y}[\![H]\!]\zeta,\zeta'\rangle)$. We can extend these remarks to *burling* by examining the summands in which witnessed values may lie; on doing so we observe that $burling\phi\zeta$ is a transitive inclusive predicate having $(\lambda\langle\hat{\omega}_0,\hat{\omega}_1\rangle.(\hat{\omega}_0\sqsupseteq\hat{\omega}_1))\sqsupseteq burling\phi\zeta$ and $w\sqsupseteq(\lambda\hat{\omega}.burling\phi\zeta\langle furl\zeta\hat{\omega},\hat{\omega}\rangle)$.

Since $\lambda\langle\hat{\omega}_0,\hat{\omega}_1\rangle.true$ is a transitive inclusive predicate having $(\lambda\langle\hat{\omega}_0,\hat{\omega}_1\rangle.(\hat{\omega}_0\sqsupseteq\hat{\omega}_1))\sqsupseteq(\lambda\langle\hat{\omega}_0,\hat{\omega}_1\rangle.true)$ and $w\sqsupseteq(\lambda\hat{\omega}.(\lambda\langle\hat{\omega}_0,\hat{\omega}_1\rangle.true)\langle furl\zeta\hat{\omega},\hat{\omega}\rangle)$, applying the induction principle of 2.3.2 shows that $burl\zeta$ is transitive and that $(\lambda\langle\hat{\omega}_0,\hat{\omega}_1\rangle.(\hat{\omega}_0\sqsupseteq\hat{\omega}_1))\sqsupseteq burl\zeta$ and $w\sqsupseteq(\lambda\hat{\omega}.burl\zeta\langle furl\zeta\hat{\omega},\hat{\omega}\rangle)$; in other words, $burl\zeta\langle\hat{\omega}_0,\hat{\omega}_1\rangle=true$ and $burl\zeta\langle furl\zeta\hat{\omega},\hat{\omega}\rangle=true$ whenever $\hat{\omega}_0\sqsupseteq\hat{\omega}_1$ and $w\hat{\omega}=true$. If we now let $\geq$ be the ordering of the domain A such that $\delta_0\geq\delta_1$ if and only if $a(burl\zeta)\langle\delta_0,\delta_1\rangle=true$ we may deduce that $\geq$ is transitive, that $\delta_0\geq\delta_1$ whenever $\delta_0\sqsupseteq\delta_1$, and that $A(furl\zeta)\hat{\delta}\geq\hat{\delta}$ whenever $a\hat{\delta}=true$. The last of these deductions is our final substitute for the claim that $A(furl\zeta)\hat{\delta}\sqsupseteq\hat{\delta}$ whenever $a\hat{\delta}=true$; with its assistance we are able to claim that, according to 4.6.8, when H is adhesive and $\langle\hat{\rho},\hat{\upsilon},\hat{\sigma}\rangle$ is reliable

$A(furl\zeta)(\mathcal{Z}[\![H]\!]\hat{\rho}\hat{\upsilon}\hat{\sigma})\geq\mathcal{Y}[\![H]\!]\zeta(U(furl\zeta)\hat{\rho})(Y(furl\zeta)\hat{\upsilon})(S(furl\zeta)\hat{\sigma})$,

while we still know that

$\mathcal{Y}[\![H]\!]\zeta(U(furl\zeta)\hat{\rho})(Y(furl\zeta)\hat{\upsilon})(S(furl\zeta)\hat{\sigma})\sqsupseteq A(furl\zeta)(\mathcal{Z}[\![H]\!]\hat{\rho}\hat{\upsilon}\hat{\sigma})$.

These inequalities represent all that we can reasonably hope to establish, since they say that a label or procedure value obtained by delving into the answer $A(furl\zeta)(\mathcal{Z}[\![H]\!]\hat{\rho}\hat{\upsilon}\hat{\sigma})$ cannot be distinguished from its counterpart in $\mathcal{Y}[\![H]\!]\zeta(U(furl\zeta)\hat{\rho})(Y(furl\zeta)\hat{\upsilon})(S(furl\zeta)\hat{\sigma})$ by applying it to portions of state vectors that can arise during computations.

Thus unless $\hat{\delta}=AW_0\hat{\delta}$ whenever $a\hat{\delta}=true$ we must be content with the inequalities above. However, usually the answer domains do not discriminate between one label or procedure value and another, so we can insist that $\hat{\delta}=AW_0\hat{\delta}$ whenever $a\hat{\delta}=true$; in this situation we can appeal to 4.3.7 and adapt the argument to be given in 5.6.9 in order to deduce that, for instance, if E has no free variables

$\mathcal{E}[\![E]\!](arid)\kappa(empty)=A(furl\zeta)(\mathcal{Z}[\![\mathbf{e}[\![E]\!]]\!](arid)\langle\rangle(empty))$,

so long as κ and ζ are "suitable" continuations that model the ends of computations in standard semantics and store semantics respectively.

CHAPTER FIVE
STACK SEMANTICS

5.1. Idealized versions of realistic implementations.

5.1.1. Inefficiencies in general techniques.

The implementation technique underlying store semantics can be widely applied, but it is not very efficient. Every procedure value set up by it includes a little environment in order to cater for the possibility that an assignment may pass the free variables of the procedure out of the blocks in which they are declared. Even more complex are label values, which require not only private environments but surrogate stacks also; pointers into the environment and stack components of the machine state may be inadequate substitutes if label values are stored, because the components present when a label is set may have altered beyond recognition by the time it is activated. The worst inefficiences arise from the treatment of recursion in appendix 2, which demands that during the evaluation of a recursively declared identifier I there be three stores - the one forming part of $\rho[\![I]\!]\downarrow 1$, the one forming part of $\rho[\![\mathbf{rec}]\!]\downarrow 1$ and the one which can be modified by the evaluating mechanism. In this section we shall describe a formalism which embodies an efficient implementation; this avoids copying portions of the machine state by brandishing pointers at the stack, so the definition of Sal in appendix 3 (which uses the resulting equations) will be called a form of 'stack semantics'. Unfortunately this definition corresponds with that in appendix 1 only when programs satisfy certain syntactic constraints (to be explained in 5.1.8) that guarantee that locations are not referred to outside the pieces of program in which they are "really" needed.

Our aim is thus to model an implementation which reduces the storage and time needed for running Sal programs by moving information less often than the implementations suggested by store semantics. One fruitful source of reductions is provided by declarations, which in the equations of appendix 2 involve operations that merely shift elements from the stack into the environment. These operations can be avoided by making the environment map identifiers not into denoted values but into pointers which reveal where on the stack the appropriate denoted values can be found. This usage gives $\mathcal{D}[\![I=E]\!]$, for example, the value $\lambda\zeta.\mathcal{L}[\![E]\!](\lambda\rho\upsilon\sigma.\zeta\rho[\#\upsilon/I]\upsilon\sigma)$. At the end of executing Δ **inside** E the denoted values put on the stack by Δ are removed so that Δ **inside** E only increases the length of the stack by 1, like every other expression; as Δ may have within declarations embedded in it the number of denoted values to be removed may not be $\#\mathcal{I}[\![\Delta]\!]+\#\mathcal{H}[\![\Delta]\!]$ and must be computed with the aid of the valuation $\mathcal{Y}\in \mathrm{Dec}\to \mathrm{N}$ defined in appendix 9. While the expression part, E, of Δ **inside** E is being executed it may extend the stack far beyond the height reached by Δ either by activating more declarations or by introducing lots of anonymous quantities intended for later use. Thus at any point during the running of a program the stack will contain layers of denoted values (or of values drawn from the domain J required by res) interleaved with layers of anonymous quantities. A layer of denoted values and the layer of anonymous quantities above it will together be known as a 'working space'; every unfinished activation of Δ **inside** E will naturally produce its own working space.

An environment of the kind described in the preceding paragraph cannot be constructed when a program is being compiled, since a procedure call, declaration or label setting in the body of a recursive procedure may be executed in the presence of several different stack heights. Throughout the running of a program such an environment must therefore still be manipulated with the aid of functions like *chop*. Consequently we shall actually adopt the more sophisticated environments to be described in 5.1.2; these can be constructed by compilers, as they allow identifiers to be associated with denoted values kept on the stack by the means suggested by Dijkstra [21].

Before proceeding further the reader may wish to review our discussions of ranges and limitations (in 1.3.2) and of extents and lifetimes (in 1.4.3).

5.1.2. Displays.

For convenience we shall refer to any language feature which confines scopes to expressions or commands as a 'limitation'; in Sal the limitations therefore take the forms Φ, **val** E, Δ **inside** E and **block** Γ. When a limitation is being compiled every name introduced by it, whether an identifier or res, is tagged by a 'block number'. which, loosely speaking, we shall take to be one greater than the biggest among the block numbers of the names occurring free in the limitation. For reasons to be explained in 5.1.7 our sort of block number is unconventional, but this does not matter, for all we really need to do here is to associate every limitation appearing in the text of a program with an integer different from the integers provided for its free variables.

When an abstraction Φ is supplied with an actual parameter by a procedure call the implementation places on the stack the height of the stack at the start of the activation of that limitation which sets up the free variable of Φ having the biggest block number. Thus while a program is being run any call of Φ that has not yet been completely executed will have a working space containing a pointer to the working space utilized by an activation of a certain limitation which surrounds Φ in the program text. In fact analogous remarks apply to each activation of every limitation, not just to procedure calls, so unless it is at the bottom of the stack the working space for any activation of a limitation indicates the position on the stack of the working space for an activation of a second limitation. This second limitation gives a meaning to some name with a block number, ν say, one less than that of the names introduced by the first one. Because of the restrictions to be discussed in 5.1.8 the working space for the activation of the first limitation is nearer the top of the stack than that for the activation of the second. Just as the first working space usually points to a second so the second points to a third (unless ν is 1, when the bottom working space on the stack has been reached); hence there is a succession of working spaces, the positions of which form a chain consisting of $\nu+1$ integers, each pointing further down the stack than the one after. If the first working space is that at the top of the stack, this chain is termed the 'static chain' and is provided by a function $display \in Y \to N^*$ which will be described in 5.1.5. When $\#display\,\upsilon \geq \nu \geq 1$ the integer $display\,\upsilon \downarrow \nu$ gives the start of the working space which contains (among other things) the denoted value associated with any identifier which has ν as its block number and which appears in the text of the most recently activated limitation; in particular, $display\,\upsilon \downarrow (\#display\,\upsilon)$ is the length of the stack immediately after the activation of this limitation, as it is in the conventional description [68] of displays.

In order to find the denoted value associated with a name occurring in the most recently activated limitation it is not, of course, enough merely to know where the working space containing the value begins. However the 'offset', or position of the value relative to the start of the working space, can be calculated during the compilation of the program. This calculation presents no difficulty when the name is introduced by an abstraction or by val E, and it can be carried out for block Γ simply by ensuring that when $\#\mathfrak{J}[\![\Gamma]\!]+\#\mathfrak{K}[\![\Gamma]\!] \geq \nu \geq 1$ the identifier $(\mathfrak{J}[\![\Gamma]\!] \S \mathfrak{K}[\![\Gamma]\!]) \downarrow \nu$ requires the offset $\#\mathfrak{J}[\![\Gamma]\!]+\#\mathfrak{K}[\![\Gamma]\!]-\nu+1$. Greater complexity arises with Δ inside E, because the presence of within declarations may mean that if the component declarations of Δ increase the length of the stack in the order in which they are executed then when $\#\mathfrak{J}[\![\Delta]\!]+\#\mathfrak{H}[\![\Delta]\!] \geq \nu \geq 1$ the identifier $(\mathfrak{J}[\![\Delta]\!] \S \mathfrak{H}[\![\Delta]\!]) \downarrow \nu$ may need an offset which is not just a function of $\#\mathfrak{J}[\![\Delta]\!]$, $\#\mathfrak{H}[\![\Delta]\!]$ and ν. We could model an implementation which would allow the denoted value created by $\mathfrak{D}[\![I=E]\!]$, for instance, to be placed somewhere other than at the top of the stack; indeed the equation for $\mathcal{T}[\![I{=}{=}E]\!]$ in appendix 3 achieves precisely this. As we do not mind that $(\mathcal{I}[\![\Delta]\!]\S\mathcal{K}[\![\Delta]\!])\downarrow\nu$ does not tally with $\#\mathcal{I}[\![\Delta]\!]+\#\mathcal{K}[\![\Delta]\!]-\nu+1$ we shall not adopt this expedient; instead we shall use the valuation $\mathcal{Z}\in \mathrm{Dec}\to\mathrm{U}\to\mathrm{N}\to\mathrm{N}\to\mathrm{U}$ described in appendix 9 to make $(\mathcal{I}[\![\Delta]\!]\S\mathcal{K}[\![\Delta]\!])\downarrow\nu$ tally with an offset representing what happens when the components of Δ actually do lengthen the stack according to their order of execution.

The environments of appendix 3 therefore associate identifiers with pairs, each comprising a block number and the position of the appropriate denoted value relative to the start of the working space connected with that block number; res, however, is associated with block numbers only, since its offset is inevitably 1. To avoid introducing fresh descriptions of the functions of 3.3.3 we take U to be $(\mathrm{Ide}\to(\mathrm{N}\times\mathrm{N})^*)\times\mathrm{N}^*$ rather than $(\mathrm{Ide}\to(\mathrm{N}\times\mathrm{N}))\times\mathrm{N}$; we can easily verify by structural induction that suitable equations using $(\mathrm{Ide}\to(\mathrm{N}\times\mathrm{N}))\times\mathrm{N}$ are congruent with those in appendix 3. The discussion above indicates that, in the presence of an environment ρ and a stack υ, an identifier I corresponds with a denoted value occupying a position $(\mathit{display}\,\upsilon\downarrow(\rho[\![I]\!]\downarrow1\downarrow1)+\rho[\![I]\!]\downarrow1\downarrow2)$ from the bottom of υ; hence the denoted value itself is $\upsilon\downarrow(\#\upsilon-(\mathit{display}\,\upsilon\downarrow(\rho[\![I]\!]\downarrow1\downarrow1)+\rho[\![I]\!]\downarrow1\downarrow2)+1)$.

Now that the environment needed by a program can be determined by a compiler it has not to be manipulated during the running of the program. Unlike the equations of appendix 2 those of appendix 3 therefore do not need to supply environments as arguments to continuations. Accordingly Z is presumed to be $\mathrm{Y}\to\mathrm{C}$, where Y remains the domain of stacks and C is $\mathrm{S}\to\mathrm{A}$ for serial programs, so when O is $\mathrm{Z}\to\mathrm{Z}$ the valuations are typified by $\mathcal{E}$, which belongs to $\mathrm{Exp}\to\mathrm{U}\to\mathrm{O}$. As $\mathcal{C}[\![\Gamma_0;\Gamma_1]\!]$ becomes $\lambda\rho\zeta.\mathcal{C}[\![\Gamma_0]\!]\rho(\mathcal{C}[\![\Gamma_1]\!]\rho\zeta)$ the semantic equations can build environments into continuations; nevertheless we can still regard a member of Z as a "pure continuation" because the environment built into it will in practice refer neither to particular locations nor to absolute positions on the stack (by contrast with the environments incorporated in the continuations for standard semantics). Thus now $\mathcal{E}[\![E]\!]\rho$ represents all that is known after E has been compiled but before it has been executed, whereas in the version of store semantics explained in 4.1.2 the same role is played by $\mathcal{E}[\![E]\!]$.

The maximum among the block numbers of the names entered in an environment is given by a function $\mathit{lift}\in U\to N$ which is defined in terms of the notation of 2.2.2 by setting

$$\mathit{lift}=\lambda\rho.\bigvee\{(\#\rho[\![I]\!]>0)\to\rho[\![I]\!]\downarrow1\downarrow1,0 \mid \top\sqsupset I\sqsupset\bot\}\vee((\#\rho[\![res]\!]>0)\to\rho[\![res]\!]\downarrow1\downarrow1,0).$$

Consequently, when an environment ρ is supplied to Δ inside E, for example, every identifier declared by Δ is given $\mathit{lift}\rho+1$ as its block number. The structure we have chosen for U does not permit lift to be continuous unless Ide is finite; moreover if Ide is infinite there can be no continuous function which coincides with lift when applied to every environment ρ for which $\#\rho[\![I]\!]>0$ for only finitely many I. Were this important we could structure U as $(Ide\times(N\times N)^*)^*\times N^*$, thereby obtaining a continuous counterpart to lift; we shall not bother to do this because we do not really require $\mathcal{E}[\![E]\!]$ to be continuous for any E in stack semantics.

5.1.3. Label and procedure values.

Though we have eliminated operations which move elements from the stack into the environment we have yet to remove those portions of the machine state which store semantics includes in label and procedure values. Here we shall explain how such values are handled by stack semantics.

The treatment of labels implicit in appendix 3 is in part forced on us by our decision to build up environments during compilation. Now that the continuations we use incorporate environments we have no need to provide environment as components of label values. Hence when I is declared as a label we could represent it by $\langle \zeta,\upsilon\rangle$ where ζ is a certain continuation and υ is the stack just after I has been set. Under the restrictions to be imposed in 5.1.8, however, we can do even better than this. These restrictions prevent each label from being assigned to locations that are not local to the activation of the block in which it is set. When a **goto** sequencer is executed control therefore passes into a block the activation of which is unfinished; this means that the stack present when this block is first activated must be an initial segment of that present when the jump is made. Hence for the value of I we adopt $\langle \zeta,\#\upsilon-1\rangle$ instead of $\langle \zeta,\upsilon\rangle$, and we arrange that a jump to I reduces the stack height to $\#\upsilon$. The stack thereby obtained, which is υ, has to include the denoted values associated with the labels declared at the same time as I, since these labels remain in scope after the jump.

Reasons to be given in 5.1.5 dictate that the equations of appendix 3 provide every procedure value with a component which resembles an environment by being a member of $(\mathrm{Ide}\rightarrow(N\times N)^*)\times N^*$. For the moment this component will be disregarded, because when an abstraction, Φ, is compiled the appropriate environment is already known and can therefore be incorporated into the "pure code" component of the value given to Φ. This environment, ρ say, maps every free variable of Φ into a pair of integers which in conjunction with the static chain yields the denoted value associated with the free variable by υ_0, the stack present when Φ is set up. To ensure that this denoted value is also associated with the free variable by υ_1, the stack created by a call of Φ, we impose two conditions: firstly, the links in the static chain for υ_0 which are required by entries in ρ must equal the corresponding links in the static chain for υ_1 (so that $display\,\upsilon_0{\downarrow}\nu = display\,\upsilon_1{\downarrow}\nu$ when $lift\,\rho \geq \nu \geq 1$), and, secondly, the denoted values just above these links in υ_0 must be those found in the same positions in υ_1. This second condition is satisfied provided that Φ is called only inside the scopes of its free variables, since in this situation the portion of υ_0 containing the denoted values is an initial segment of υ_1. As part of the value of Φ we keep the integer $\nu_0 = ((lift\,\rho = 0) \rightarrow 0, display\,\upsilon_0{\downarrow}(lift\,\rho))$, which is also placed at the bottom of the working space for every call of Φ. There it acts as a static chain pointer, so if $\upsilon_0{\dagger}(\#\upsilon_0 - \nu_0) = \upsilon_1{\dagger}(\#\upsilon_1 - \nu_0)$ then, when $lift\,\rho \geq \nu \geq 1$,

$$display\,\upsilon_0{\downarrow}\nu = display(\upsilon_0{\dagger}(\#\upsilon_0 - \nu_0)){\downarrow}\nu = display(\upsilon_1{\dagger}(\#\upsilon_1 - \nu_0)){\downarrow}\nu = display\,\upsilon_1{\downarrow}\nu$$

and the first condition is satisfied. Hence within its scope Φ can be represented by "pure code" and a pointer; here and elsewhere by the 'scope' of a procedure we mean the intersection of the scopes of its free variables.

In accordance with the account above the valuation $\mathfrak{F}$ used in appendix 3 is a member of the domain Abs→U→Y→F. This means that the value of an abstraction, like that of a label, cannot usually be calculated before the execution of the program in which the abstraction appears. It is tempting to take the second component of a procedure to be a block number instead of a static chain pointer so that it could be produced by a compiler along with the first component; indeed some implementations do this. In the notation of the preceding paragraph, if υ_2 is the stack immediately before a call of Φ then this strategy involves letting $display\upsilon_1{\downarrow}\nu=display\upsilon_2{\downarrow}\nu$ whenever $lift\rho\geq\nu\geq1$. Unfortunately, it only ensures that $display\upsilon_0{\downarrow}\nu=display\upsilon_1{\downarrow}\nu$ when $lift\rho\geq\nu\geq1$ if the free variables of Φ have lower block numbers than the formal parameter of any procedure for which Φ is an argument. One program which does not meet this requirement is rec f=fn$g$.true?g0!f0 inside x=0 inside (f(fn$y$.x)); when executed using the strategy suggested here this yields a location containing the value of fn$y$.x although it should produce a location containing 0.

The treatment of procedures underlying appendix 3 differs in one other respect from that of appendix 2. The continuation for a procedure call is not supplied as an additional argument alongside the stack and the store; instead it is kept on the stack, from which it is retrieved at the end of the call by means of $jump\in$Z, which we define in terms of $wrong\in$C by setting $jump=\lambda\upsilon\sigma.\upsilon{\downarrow}2\,\mathsf{E}\,Z\to(\upsilon{\downarrow}2)(\langle\upsilon{\downarrow}1\rangle\,\S\,\upsilon{\dagger}2)\sigma,wrong\sigma$.
Thus now beside the anonymous quantities and denoted values on the stack there are return links (belonging to Z) and items from which the static chain can be formed.

Because a procedure is never applied outside the scope of any of its free variables, a res sequencer can be executed only when the corresponding activation of a val expression has not been completed. Consequently the stack present when control enters the val expression is part of that present when the statement is encountered. As is the case with labels the domain J appropriate to res is therefore taken to be Z×N where the second component provides stack heights. This component is really redundant here, for unlike a label res E cannot be passed as a parameter or assigned to a location without immediately causing a jump, so the stack height expected after the execution of res E can be determined from the static chain and the block number of res. More precisely, if υ is the stack before the execution of res E in an environment ρ and if ε is the expressed value yielded by E then $\langle\varepsilon\rangle \S \upsilon\dagger(\#\upsilon - \mathit{display}\,\upsilon\downarrow(\rho[\![\mathrm{res}]\!]\downarrow 1)+2)$ is the stack afterwards. Indeed we could even change the res component of the environment so that U would be $(\mathrm{Ide}\to(\mathrm{N}\times\mathrm{N})^*)\times(\mathrm{Z}\times\mathrm{N})^*$; under these circumstances res E would invoke the continuation $\rho[\![\mathrm{res}]\!]\downarrow 1\downarrow 1$ and produce the stack $\langle\varepsilon\rangle \S \upsilon\dagger(\#\upsilon - \mathit{display}\,\upsilon\downarrow(\rho[\![\mathrm{res}]\!]\downarrow 1\downarrow 2)+2)$. For the sake of uniformity between the two kinds of Sal sequencer we have chosen not to do this but rather to represent the effect of a val expression by placing a continuation and a stack height on the stack and by pointing into the stack through the environment; hence U is $(\mathrm{Ide}\to(\mathrm{N}\times\mathrm{N})^*)\times\mathrm{N}^*$.

5.1.4. The restoration of stores.

The constraints to be explained in 5.1.8 ensure not only that programs never refer to positions beyond the top of the stack but also that the locations adjoined to the store area during an activation of a limitation are never needed after the activation finishes. Hence space may be saved by removing these locations from the store at the same time as the working space for the activation is deleted from the stack. In contrast to the final size of the working space, which can be calculated using valuations such as $\mathcal{Y}$, the number of extra locations needed in the course of an activation cannot be known until the limitation is executed; the effect of while x do 0:=0, for instance, depends upon the value given to x. At the beginning of the activation the area of store already in use is therefore preserved with the static chain pointer; when the activation ends normally the area is reduced to this by an application of $restore \in (L \to T) \to S \to S$. On the assumption that S is $(L \to (V \times T)) \times V^* \times V^*$ we let ψ range temporarily over $L \to T$ and set

$restore = \lambda\psi\sigma.\langle \lambda\alpha.\langle (\sigma{\downarrow}1)\alpha{\downarrow}1, ((\sigma{\downarrow}1)\alpha{\downarrow}2) \wedge \psi\alpha\rangle, \sigma{\downarrow}2, \sigma{\downarrow}3\rangle$.

The area can be reduced whether the activation ends by control passing the last point in the text of the limitation or by a jump being made to a surrounding limitation. Accordingly, when a label is set up in a block we keep two members of $L \to T$; one of these is the area of store required when the activation of the block finishes normally, whilst the other is the area needed after the execution of a jump to the label and therefore mentions the locations introduced by the labels set by reference in the block.

Since the assignable part of the store is now handled in much the same way as the stack, we could amalgamate the two and discard locations in favour of positions on the stack. However we have followed the usual practice by distinguishing the stack from the store because otherwise the offsets for denoted values cannot necessarily be calculated when programs are being compiled. Thus if locations are regarded as positions on the stack the offset required by z in the declaration w=x?0!y within z==0 will depend on the content of x when y denotes a location, because w may denote either the same location as y or a fresh one. Even in languages which do not permit declarations like this the same difficulty may be caused by multiple declarations of arrays having bounds that are not known to the compiler.

The equations of appendix 3 therefore entail putting an area and a static chain pointer on the stack whenever a limitation is activated. These two pieces of information are enough for the purposes of an implementation, but in the semantics of limitations we actually provide not members of $(L\to T)\times N$, as would seem to be sensible, but members of $(L\to T)\times N\times N\times U$. The significance of the two final factors of $(L\to T)\times N\times N\times U$ will be explained in 5.1.5; here it is enough to note that they do not affect most of the primitive functions. For instance, when we introduce $wrong\in C$ to deal with errors we can describe $lose\in N\to Z\to Z$, which cuts back the stack and the store when an activation of a limitation ends, by writing

$$lose=\lambda\nu\zeta\upsilon\sigma.(\upsilon\downarrow\nu\,E\,(L\to T)\times N\times N\times U)\to\zeta(\langle\upsilon\downarrow 1\rangle\,\S\,\upsilon\dagger\nu)(restore(\upsilon\downarrow\nu\downarrow 1)\sigma),wrong\,\sigma.$$

As the stored values and expressed values required by stack semantics belong to the same kinds of domain as those required by store semantics, V is B+E*+J+F and E is L+B+E*+J+F. Our treatment of recursion (to be given in 5.1.6) enables recursive declarations by incidence to be comprehended without the use of a domain G resembling that of 4.1.3, so D reduces to L+B+E*+J+F. Any other intermediate values that arise in the course of a computation must be members of Z, $(L\to T)\times N\times N\times U$ or the version of J corresponding with res; furthermore all such values are kept on the stack. Consequently W is $L+B+E^*+J+F+J+Z+((L\to T)\times N\times N\times U)$ and Y is not E* but W*.

Since we are retaining the model for storage of 3.3.2 we shall continue to make liberal use of *hold*, *area*, *update*, *updates*, *new* and *news*; furthermore we can adopt functions $test \in (C \times C) \to W \to C$, $assign \in C \to W \to W \to C$ and $tie \in (L^* \to C) \to N \to C$ like those of 3.3.4. The continuations for stack semantics differ from the continuations for store semantics, so we provide functions for obtaining $\mathcal{L}$ and $\mathcal{R}$ from $\mathcal{E}$ thus:

$$nv = \lambda\zeta\upsilon\sigma.\upsilon{\downarrow}1 \in L \to \zeta\upsilon\sigma, new\sigma \in L \to assign(\zeta(\langle new\sigma | L\rangle \S \upsilon{\dagger}1))(new\sigma | L)(\upsilon{\downarrow}1)\sigma, wrong\sigma;$$

$$tv = \lambda\zeta\upsilon\sigma.\upsilon{\downarrow}1 \in L \to \zeta(\langle hold(\upsilon{\downarrow}1 | L)\sigma\rangle \S \upsilon{\dagger}1)\sigma, \zeta\upsilon\sigma.$$

Similar considerations lead us to supply a replacement for *earn*, namely $ease \in (O \times O) \to O$, which satisfies

$$ease = \lambda\langle \xi_0, \xi_1\rangle \zeta.\xi_{veer0}(\xi_{veer1}(\lambda\upsilon\sigma.\zeta((veer0=0) \to \upsilon, \langle \upsilon{\downarrow}2\rangle \S \langle \upsilon{\downarrow}1\rangle \S \upsilon{\dagger}2)\sigma)).$$

As in store semantics, the valuations $\mathfrak{B}$, $\mathfrak{M}$ and $\mathfrak{W}$ for stack semantics are members of Bas→O, Mon→O and Dya→O respectively, but the new form needed by O necessitates obvious changes in their definitions. Thus, for instance, $\mathfrak{M}[\![\$]\!]$ is now tv and $\mathfrak{M}[\![£]\!]$ is now

$$\lambda\zeta.tv(\lambda\upsilon\sigma.\upsilon{\downarrow}1 \in F \to \zeta(\langle\langle tv(nv(\upsilon{\downarrow}1{\downarrow}1)), \upsilon{\downarrow}1{\downarrow}2, \upsilon{\downarrow}1{\downarrow}3\rangle\rangle \S \upsilon{\dagger}1)\sigma, wrong\sigma).$$

5.1.5. Chains.

In most implementations every working space on a stack contains a pointer to the start of the working space immediately below it; the set of such pointers is known as the 'dynamic chain'. We do not have to provide an explicit dynamic chain because our use of the domain $(L\to T)\times N\times N\times U$ for the linkage information permits us to find where working spaces begin simply by examining the domains to which elements on the stack belong. To construct something akin to the dynamic chain we introduce $chain\in Y\to Y^*$, which satisfies

$chain=\lambda\upsilon.(\#\upsilon=0)\to\langle\rangle,(\upsilon\downarrow 1E(L\to T)\times N\times N\times U)\to\langle\upsilon\rangle\S chain(\upsilon\dagger 1),chain(\upsilon\dagger 1).$

As mentioned in 5.1.2, the static chain is formed with the help of a function $display\in Y\to N^*$; this is subject to

$display=\lambda\upsilon.(\#chain\upsilon=0)\to\langle\rangle,display(\upsilon\dagger(\#\upsilon-chain\upsilon\downarrow 1\downarrow 1\downarrow 2))\S\langle\#(chain\upsilon\downarrow 1)\rangle.$

Thus if $\#chain\upsilon>0$ then $chain\upsilon\downarrow 1=\upsilon\dagger(\#\upsilon-display\upsilon\downarrow(\#display\upsilon))$.

When $\upsilon\downarrow\nu\in(L\to T)\times N\times N\times U$ for some $\upsilon\in Y$ and $\nu\in N$, we intend $\upsilon\downarrow\nu\downarrow 3$ to be the distance from the bottom of υ to the top of the denoted values just above $\upsilon\downarrow\nu$, and we want $\upsilon\downarrow\nu\downarrow 4$ to reveal the absolute positions on the stack corresponding with every entry in the entire environment. To convert environments which give block numbers into those which give absolute positions on the stack we apply $twist\in U\to Y\to U$, which is given by

$twist=\lambda\rho\upsilon.\langle\lambda I.map(\lambda\langle\nu',\nu''\rangle.\langle display\upsilon\downarrow\nu',\nu''\rangle)(\rho[\![I]\!]),map(\lambda\nu.display\upsilon\downarrow\nu)(\rho[\![res]\!])\rangle.$

Any environment ρ and stack υ therefore associate

$\upsilon\downarrow(\#\upsilon-(twist\rho\upsilon[\![I]\!]\downarrow 1\downarrow 1+twist\rho\upsilon[\![I]\!]\downarrow 1\downarrow 2)+1)$ with an identifier I.

Of special importance is the fourth component of that member of $(L\to T)\times N\times N\times U$ which is nearest the top of the stack, since from it can be formed a member of $(Ide\to D^*)\times J^*$ which is analogous with the environment adopted in the equations of appendix 2. Consequently we provide a function $field\in Y\to U$, the purpose of which is to extract this environment; thus

$field = \lambda \upsilon.(\#display\upsilon=0)\rightarrow arid, \upsilon\downarrow(\#\upsilon - display\upsilon\downarrow(\#display\upsilon)+1)\downarrow 4.$

Thus at the start of an activation of every limitation a record is made of the area of the store, the last link in the static chain, the height of the stack and the "absolute" environment in which the execution of the limitation begins. We can create this record by using $size \in N\rightarrow N\rightarrow U\rightarrow Y\rightarrow S\rightarrow((L\rightarrow T)\times N\times N\times U)$, which is such that

$size = \lambda \nu_0 \nu_1 \rho\upsilon\sigma.\langle \lambda\alpha.area\alpha\sigma, ((\nu_0=0)\rightarrow 0, display\upsilon\downarrow\nu_0), \nu_1+\#\upsilon, divert(field\upsilon)(twist\rho\upsilon)\rangle.$

For example, in the presence of an environment ρ, a stack υ and a store σ the first step in the execution of **val** E is to put $size(lift\rho)2(arid[lift\rho+1/\mathbf{res}])\upsilon\sigma$ on the stack.

The link in the static chain needed by a call of a procedure is part of the value of the procedure and is not obtained from the block number of the variables set up in the limitation surrounding the call. Moreover, if the procedure value results from evaluating an abstraction with the aid of an environment ρ and a stack υ_1, the "absolute" environment appropriate to the procedure will be $twist\rho\upsilon_1$; however an application of *size* when the procedure is called in the presence of a stack υ_2 will give rise to $twist\rho\upsilon_2$. Because $display\upsilon_1$ may not coincide with $display\upsilon_2$ the environments $twist\rho\upsilon_1$ and $twist\rho\upsilon_2$ may differ. Hence the domain F is taken to be $Z\times N\times U$, $twist\rho\upsilon_1$ is kept as the third component of the procedure value and $bulk((lift\rho=0)\rightarrow 0, display\upsilon_1\downarrow(lift\rho))0(twist\rho\upsilon_1)\upsilon_2\sigma$ is added to the stack on calling the procedure; $bulk \in N\rightarrow N\rightarrow U\rightarrow Y\rightarrow S\rightarrow((L\rightarrow T)\times N\times N\times U)$ satisfies

$bulk = \lambda\nu_0\nu_1\rho\upsilon\sigma.\langle\lambda\alpha.area\alpha\sigma, \nu_0, \nu_1+\#\upsilon, divert(field\upsilon)\rho\rangle$,

so in general

$size = \lambda\nu_0\nu_1\rho\upsilon\sigma.bulk((\nu_0=0)\rightarrow 0, display\upsilon\downarrow\nu_0)\nu_1(twist\rho\upsilon)\upsilon\sigma.$

It should be stressed that the third and fourth factors of $(L\rightarrow T)\times N\times N\times U$ and the third factor of $Z\times N\times U$ are completely irrelevant to the implementation we are considering. We could easily provide semantic equations which did not include them at all by discarding the functions *act* and *aid* (to be defined in 5.1.6) and by defining *size* to be $\lambda\nu\upsilon\sigma.\langle\lambda\alpha.\mathit{area}\,\alpha\sigma,(\nu=0\rightarrow 0,\mathit{display}\,\upsilon\downarrow\nu)\rangle$ and *bulk* to be $\lambda\nu\upsilon\sigma.\langle\lambda\alpha.\mathit{area}\,\alpha\sigma,\nu\rangle$. Using a structural induction requiring very simple inclusive predicates (to relate the domains) we could then show that these equations were congruent with those of appendix 3. The roles of the additional factors of $(L\rightarrow T)\times N\times N\times U$ and $Z\times N\times U$ will be clarified in 5.2.2, when we shall consider the congruence between stack semantics and store semantics.

5.1.6. The creation of environments.

The valuations in appendix 3 can for the most part be formed quite easily. In particular they are usually members of natural analogues of Exp→U→O, the domain to which $\mathcal{E}$ belongs; thus, for instance, $\mathcal{S}$ is in Seq→U→Z, $\mathcal{G}$ is in Blo→U→O and $\mathcal{C}$ is in Com→U→O. However, $\mathcal{P}$ and $\mathcal{Q}$ produce label values only when both a continuation and a stack height are supplied, so they are in Com→U→Z→N→J*, just as $\mathcal{F}$ is a member of Abs→U→Y→F. Greater difficulties are presented by $\mathcal{D}$ and $\mathcal{T}$, which need two integer parameters (representing a block number and an offset); in contrast to the integer required by $\mathcal{P}$ and $\mathcal{Q}$ these parameters can be calculated by a compiler, so it is appropriate to view $\mathcal{D}$ and $\mathcal{T}$ as members of Dec→U→N→N→O rather than Dec→U→Z→N→N→Z. As $\mathcal{D}$ and $\mathcal{T}$ are complicated by within declarations they will be discussed at some length.

The equations of appendix 9 indicate that given a declaration Δ, an environment ρ and integers ν_0 and ν_1 the valuation $\mathcal{Z}\in$Dec→U→N→N→U superimposes the layer $\mathcal{Z}[\![\Delta]\!](\mathit{arid})\nu_0\nu_1$ on ρ; this layer maps every element of $\mathfrak{I}[\![\Delta]\!]\S\mathfrak{H}[\![\Delta]\!]$ to a pair, the first component of which is ν_0+1. Moreover the main effect of $\mathcal{D}[\![\Delta]\!]\rho\nu_0\nu_1$ is to extend the stack υ_0 supplied to it, giving a stack υ_1 such that if $\nu_1=\#\upsilon_0-\mathit{display}\,\upsilon_0\downarrow(\#\mathit{display}\,\upsilon_0)$ then when $\#\mathfrak{I}[\![\Delta]\!]+\#\mathfrak{H}[\![\Delta]\!]\geq\nu\geq1$ the denoted value associated with $(\mathfrak{I}[\![\Delta]\!]\S\mathfrak{H}[\![\Delta]\!])\downarrow\nu$ is $\upsilon_1\downarrow(\#\upsilon_1-(\mathit{display}\,\upsilon_1\downarrow(\#\mathit{display}\,\upsilon_1)+\mathcal{Z}[\![\Delta]\!](\mathit{arid})\nu_0\nu_1((\mathfrak{I}[\![\Delta]\!]\S\mathfrak{H}[\![\Delta]\!])\downarrow\nu)\downarrow1\downarrow2)+1)$ and $\nu_1+\mathcal{Y}[\![\Delta]\!]=\#\upsilon_1-\mathit{display}\,\upsilon_1\downarrow(\#\mathit{display}\,\upsilon_1)$. Consequently if Δ inside E is evaluated in an environment ρ the expression E is evaluated in the environment $\mathit{divert}\rho(\mathcal{Z}[\![\Delta]\!](\mathit{arid})(\mathit{lift}\rho)0)$ or $\mathcal{Z}[\![\Delta]\!]\rho(\mathit{lift}\rho)0$; likewise, if Δ_0 within Δ_1 is executed in an environment ρ at a time when the length of the static chain is ν_0+1 and the top of the stack is ν_1 positions above the highest member of (L→T)×N×N×U, then Δ_1 is executed in the environment $\mathcal{Z}[\![\Delta_0]\!]\rho\nu_0\nu_1$ at a time when the stack has grown by

$\mathcal{Y}[\![\Delta_0]\!]$ positions.

The declaration Δ_0 and Δ_1 is executed in a similar way to Δ_0 within Δ_1 except that both Δ_0 and Δ_1 are supplied with the environment ρ provided for the whole declaration. The equations governing $\mathcal{D}$ show that when Δ_0 is executed before Δ_1 the length of the stack increases first by $\mathcal{Y}[\![\Delta_0]\!]$ and then by $\mathcal{Y}[\![\Delta_1]\!]$ (giving a total increment of $\mathcal{Y}[\![\Delta_0$ and $\Delta_1]\!]$); furthermore $\mathcal{Z}[\![\Delta_0$ and $\Delta_1]\!]\rho\nu_0\nu_1$, the environment arising from $\mathcal{D}[\![\Delta_0$ and $\Delta_1]\!]\rho\nu_0\nu_1$, consists of ρ together with $\mathcal{Z}[\![\Delta_0]\!](arid)\nu_0\nu_1$ and $\mathcal{Z}[\![\Delta_1]\!](arid)\nu_0(\nu_1+\mathcal{Y}[\![\Delta_0]\!])$. Thus $\mathcal{Z}$ presumes that multiple declarations are evaluated from left to right, and would have to be modified were this not the case; for this reason we have not included a function resembling *deal* in the equations of appendix 3.

As intimated in 5.1.4, in stack semantics there is a parallel between a position on the stack and a location. We shall exploit this parallel to provide an approach to recursive declarations by incidence that avoids the use of *fix*; a similar approach can be incorporated in any sort of semantic equation which associates denoted values with identifiers through the indirect application of pointers. According to appendix 1, when rec I=E is executed a fresh location, α say, is updated with the result of executing E in an environment in which I denotes α; this result mimics a recursive one quite well, since if it is a procedure value, for example, embedded in it is usually an environment in which I denotes α (not what α once contained). Now that environments map identifiers into lists of pairs of pointers, recursive declarations by incidence will behave reasonably if treated in the same manner as recursive declarations by reference. Thus at a time when the lengths of the static chain and the topmost working space are ν_0+1 and ν_1 respectively executing either rec I=E or rec I==E in an environment ρ involves placing an expressed value ε at the top of the stack and executing E in the environment $\rho[\langle\nu_0+1,\nu_1+1\rangle/\text{I}]$.

In the case of rec I=E, ε is a location and can therefore be updated with β, the result given by E; in the case of rec I==E, ε is a stored value so the way to make I denote β is to substitute β for ε. The equivalent of *update* used to effect the substitution, $change \in \mathsf{N} \to \mathsf{W} \to \mathsf{Y} \to \mathsf{Y}$, satisfies

$$change = \lambda\nu\omega\upsilon.(\nu=1) \to \langle\omega\rangle \S \upsilon\dagger 1, \langle \upsilon\downarrow 1\rangle \S change(\nu-1)\omega(\upsilon\dagger 1).$$

The treatment of recursive declarations given in appendix 3 is basically a generalization of that described above. At the beginning of the execution of rec Δ a list comprising $\#\mathcal{I}[\![\Delta]\!]$ fresh locations and $\#\mathcal{R}[\![\Delta]\!]$ copies of *false* is concatenated with the stack. Then Δ is executed in an environment which makes every member of $\mathcal{I}[\![\Delta]\!]\S\mathcal{R}[\![\Delta]\!]$ correspond with a pair of pointers marking the position on the stack of the appropriate location or stored value. This environment can be obtained by applying $grow \in \mathsf{Ide}^* \to \mathsf{U} \to \mathsf{N} \to \mathsf{N} \to \mathsf{U}$, which is defined by

$$grow = \lambda I^*\rho\nu_0\nu_1.\rho[fix(\lambda\psi\nu.(\nu=0) \to \langle\rangle, \langle\langle \nu_0+1, \nu_1+\nu\rangle\rangle \S \psi(\nu-1))(\#I^*)/I^*].$$

Just as the calculation of $\mathcal{D}[\![\text{rec }\Delta]\!]\rho\nu_0\nu_1$ necessitates that of $\mathcal{T}[\![\Delta]\!](grow(\mathcal{I}[\![\Delta]\!]\S\mathcal{R}[\![\Delta]\!])\rho\nu_0\nu_1)\nu_0(\nu_1+\#\mathcal{I}[\![\Delta]\!]+\#\mathcal{R}[\![\Delta]\!])$ so the calculation of $\mathcal{G}[\![\text{block }\Gamma]\!]\rho$ necessitates that of $\mathcal{C}[\![\Gamma]\!](grow(\mathcal{H}[\![\Gamma]\!]\S\mathcal{K}[\![\Gamma]\!])\rho(lift\rho)0)$.

Because the stack is lengthened by $\#\mathcal{I}[\![\Delta]\!]+\#\mathcal{R}[\![\Delta]\!]$ immediately the execution of rec Δ starts, there is no need for further positions to be added when Δ is being executed, unless Δ contains within declarations; instead the denoted values occupying the positions provided are either given new contents or replaced by others, depending on whether they are locations or not. Thus, according to the description of $\mathcal{T}$, executing Δ_0 and Δ_1 from left to right entails extending the stack first by $\mathcal{Y}[\![\Delta_0]\!]-\#\mathcal{I}[\![\Delta_0]\!]-\#\mathcal{R}[\![\Delta_0]\!]$ positions and then by $\mathcal{Y}[\![\Delta_1]\!]-\#\mathcal{I}[\![\Delta_1]\!]-\#\mathcal{R}[\![\Delta_1]\!]$ positions, so that the ultimate extension is $\mathcal{Y}[\![\Delta_0 \text{ and } \Delta_1]\!]-\#\mathcal{I}[\![\Delta_0 \text{ and } \Delta_1]\!]-\#\mathcal{R}[\![\Delta_0 \text{ and } \Delta_1]\!]$; moreover, no application of $\mathcal{Z}$ is called for, as the environment handed on by Δ_0 and Δ_1 is simply that originally supplied.

In order to establish a connection between stack semantics

and store semantics the function *field* of 5.1.5 is used to provide an environment which slavishly follows the intricate metamorphoses of the entire environment for store semantics. Often these metamorphoses happen when an activation of a limitation is brought to an end; under these circumstances the changes in the dynamic chain will enable the environment yielded by *field* to keep in step. However, according to 4.1.4 some layers of the entire environment can be transformed during the execution of declarations, so similar transformations must be performed on the environment for stack semantics. Hence when ϕ is assumed temporarily to range over $U \to U$ the function $act \in (U \to U) \to Y \to Y$ is taken to be such that

$$act = \lambda\phi\upsilon.(\lambda\nu.change\,\nu\langle \upsilon{\downarrow}\nu{\downarrow}1, \upsilon{\downarrow}\nu{\downarrow}2, \upsilon{\downarrow}\nu{\downarrow}3, \phi(\upsilon{\downarrow}\nu{\downarrow}4)\rangle\upsilon)$$
$$(\#\upsilon - display\,\upsilon{\downarrow}(\#display\,\upsilon)+1),$$

and the functions *clip*, *swap* and *trim* of 4.1.4 are adapted to the present version of U by the omission of every mention of $\rho[\![rec]\!]$. Where $trim[\![\Delta_0]\!][\![\Delta_1]\!]$, for instance, occurs in appendix 2, $act(trim[\![\Delta_0]\!][\![\Delta_1]\!])$ must occur in appendix 3; the only exception to this principle is provided by the equations for Δ_0 and Δ_1, which in appendix 3 refer to $act(clip[\![\Delta_0]\!])$ rather than $act(clip[\![\Delta_0 \text{ and } \Delta_1]\!]) \circ act(swap[\![\Delta_1]\!])$, but this is unimportant because $\mathcal{J}[\![\Delta_0]\!]\S\mathcal{H}[\![\Delta_0]\!]$ and $\mathcal{J}[\![\Delta_1]\!]\S\mathcal{H}[\![\Delta_1]\!]$ are supposed to be disjoint.

The equations of appendix 2 manipulate the entire environment in other ways besides those implicit in *clip*, *swap* and *trim*. In particular they can adjoin new layers to the environment in a manner which is reflected in stack semantics by an increase in the amount of working space that is deemed to hold denoted values. We therefore have to introduce a function which can alter the third and fourth components of the topmost member of $(L \to T) \times N \times N \times U$ on the stack; this function, $aid \in N \to U \to Y \to Y$, satisfies

$$aid = \lambda\nu\rho\upsilon.(\lambda\nu'.change\,\nu'\langle \upsilon{\downarrow}\nu'{\downarrow}1, \upsilon{\downarrow}\nu'{\downarrow}2, \upsilon{\downarrow}\nu'{\downarrow}3+\nu, divert(\upsilon{\downarrow}\nu'{\downarrow}4)(twist\,\rho\upsilon)\rangle)$$
$$(\#\upsilon - display\,\upsilon{\downarrow}(\#display\,\upsilon)+1).$$

5.1.7. Alternative approaches.

The version of stack semantics put forward in 5.1.3 is not sacrosanct, and it has been adopted largely because it embodies a common method of implementation. Here we shall mention a few variations on this method which do not provide fresh insights into computing. Our intention is merely to demonstrate that semantic equations can be used to describe an implementation in as much detail as a given application may require and that such equations can be validated relative to standard semantics by the means we shall discuss in 5.2.6.

The domain Y could be taken to be $N \to W$ instead of W^*; this would permit every memory cell which may be included in the stack to contain something even if the stack had not expanded enough to fill it, so the relevant semantic equations would need an extra argument indicating how much of the stack was in use. They might also include a 'display', a member of N^* intended to mimic the static chain; in an implementation, a display allows identifiers to be associated with denoted values more rapidly than does the corresponding static chain, but it has to be modified at the beginning and end of every activation of a limitation. Were both a pointer to the top of the used stack and a display to be exhibited in the semantics, the main adjustments to the scheme underlying appendix 3 would arise from the fact that Z would become $N \to N^* \to Y \to C$; consequently it would be a trivial and uninteresting task to prove that the display could be kept in step with the static chain if the obvious means for updating it were adopted.

To eliminate *lift* from the equations of appendix 3 we could provide all the valuations other than $\mathfrak{D}$ and $\mathfrak{T}$ with an extra parameter, an integer which would be interpreted as a block number; $\mathfrak{H}[\![\text{fn}\,\text{I}.\text{E}]\!]\rho\nu\upsilon{\downarrow}1$, for instance, would turn into

$$nv(\lambda\upsilon'\sigma'.\mathfrak{E}[\![\text{E}]\!]\rho[\langle\nu+1,1\rangle/\text{I}](\nu+1)(lose3(jump))(aid1(arid[\langle\nu+1,1\rangle/\text{I}])\upsilon')\sigma').$$

Changing the valuations in this way would produce the conventional sort of block number, which for any definition is one greater than the block number of the definition surrounding it in a program text. These block numbers have a disadvantage which leads us to prefer the use of *lift*. Calling a procedure anywhere within its scope (in the sense of 5.1.3) should lead to a sensible result, but in fact if conventional block numbers are used trouble may ensue when a procedure is called outside the limitation in which it is set up, whether or not its scope is confined to that limitation. Even such a trivial program as x==0 inside ((y==0 inside fn$z$.x)0) will produce nonsense, although it might reasonably be expected to be equivalent with x==0 inside ((fn$z$.x)0). Naturally the equations of appendix 3 provide an abstraction Φ with a meaning that is satisfactory throughout its scope only because $\mathcal{E}[\![\Phi]\!]$ is $\lambda\rho\zeta\upsilon\sigma.\zeta(\langle\mathcal{F}[\![\Phi]\!](rend[\![\Phi]\!]\rho)\upsilon\rangle\,\S\,\upsilon)\sigma$; taking $\mathcal{E}[\![\Phi]\!]$ to be $\lambda\rho\zeta\upsilon\sigma.\zeta(\langle\mathcal{F}[\![\Phi]\!]\rho\upsilon\rangle\,\S\,\upsilon)\sigma$ would give rise to the same defect as introducing block numbers into the valuations.

By ensuring that an abstraction Φ was never passed as a parameter to a procedure having a wider scope we could arrange to discard the second component of the value of Φ in favour of the biggest among the block numbers of the free variables of Φ; when Φ was called the appropriate static chain would be constructed by the means outlined in 5.1.3. Indeed, by modifying the predicate *found* (which will be discussed in 5.1.9), we could prove that label values, as well as the first two components of procedure values, could be formed during compilation provided that every program obeyed the constraints to be described in 5.1.8 and that no procedure had a wider scope than its actual parameter. In this situation we might use environments belonging to $(\text{Ide}\to((\text{N}\times\text{N})+(\text{Z}\times\text{N}))^*)\times\text{N}^*$ or even to $(\text{Ide}\to((\text{N}\times\text{N})+(\text{Z}\times\text{N}))^*)\times(\text{Z}\times\text{N})^*$ (in view of the discussion of res in 5.1.3). A typical label value would have two components, the second of which would be the block number of the label; thus if a jump were made to a label having $\langle\zeta,\nu\rangle$ as its value then the stack would shrink from υ, say, to $\upsilon\dagger(\#\upsilon-\upsilon\downarrow(\#\upsilon-\mathit{display}\upsilon\downarrow\nu+1)\downarrow3-1)$.

Though we have couched our discussion of static chains in terms of programs subject to fairly severe restrictions there is no need to do so. Even the environments and the versions of procedure and label values explained in the preceding paragraph could be adopted for arbitrary programs so long as care was taken when the restrictions ceased to hold. When an identifier could be supplied as a parameter to a procedure with a wider scope, assigned to an identifier having a wider scope, or passed out of its limitation, some additional code would have to be inserted during compilation. This code would be intended to replace the block number in a procedure or label value by a pointer to the top of the static chain in a copy of an appropriate portion of the stack; if υ were the stack when the code was executed and if ν were the block number, the "appropriate portion" would be $\upsilon\dagger(\#\upsilon-((\nu=0)\rightarrow0,\upsilon\downarrow(\#\upsilon-\mathit{display}\upsilon\downarrow\nu+1)\downarrow3))$ for a procedure value and $\upsilon\dagger(\#\upsilon-\upsilon\downarrow(\#\upsilon-\mathit{display}\upsilon\downarrow\nu+1)\downarrow3-1)$ for a label value. The equations resulting from this strategy would be congruent with the store semantics of Sal under almost all conditions, but they would not yield a form of stack semantics. The absence of copying, not the presence of a display, is what characterizes stack semantics, which is therefore typified not merely by appendix 3 but also by the radically different approach in our earlier work [52:3.1.1].

5.1.8. Syntactic constraints ensuring validity.

To indicate which Sal programs are executed correctly by the implementation embodied in appendix 3 we introduce predicates which test members of the various syntactic domains. When a program satisfies these predicates none of the names in it will be needed outside their scopes, so, as 5.3.9 will confirm, its stack semantics will be congruent with the store semantics of the program obtained from it by applying the transformations of appendix 7 in order to eliminate recursive declarations by incidence. The existence of conditional clauses implies that there will be many programs which do not satisfy the predicates but which nevertheless run correctly. The class of programs to be considered here is, however, wide enough for many practical purposes; in particular it includes all the Sal programs corresponding with programs written in Algol 60 [61] and other languages which allow only members of B to be stored or passed out of limitations.

The value which a name is made to denote in an activation of a limitation is only used outside that activation if it is placed on the stack or assigned to a location in the store. Thus our predicates must ensure, firstly, that no expression yields a result referring to positions on the stack or locations that are no longer accessible, and, secondly, that no assignment of the form $E_0:=E_1$ is such that the result of E_1 refers to positions on the stack or locations which become inaccessible before the result of E_0. In essence we therefore require $e \in \mathrm{Exp} \to \mathrm{U} \to \mathrm{N} \to \mathrm{T}$, which when supplied with an expression, an environment and a block number reveals whether the identifiers found at the exits of the expression have block numbers higher than the given one. Naturally we wish to test not simply the exits of the expression but also the exits of its constituents, so in appendix 8 we define e recursively.

Just as $\mathfrak{E}$ depends on other valuations so e depends on other predicates, such as $d \in \mathsf{Dec} \to \mathsf{U} \to \mathsf{N} \to \mathsf{T}$ and $t \in \mathsf{Dec} \to \mathsf{U} \to \mathsf{N} \to \mathsf{T}$. Both these take declarations, environments and block numbers as arguments, but by contrast with e they use the block numbers to form further environments along the lines laid down for $\mathfrak{D}$ and $\mathfrak{T}$ in 5.1.6. We need not bother to provide either d or t with a parameter measuring the offset, because a simple structural induction shows that if ρ_0 and ρ_1 are two environments for which
$\lambda I.map(\lambda\langle\nu',\nu''\rangle.\nu')(\rho_0[\![I]\!])=\lambda I.map(\lambda\langle\nu',\nu''\rangle.\nu')(\rho_1[\![I]\!])$ and
$\rho_0[\![\mathsf{res}]\!]=\rho_1[\![\mathsf{res}]\!]$ then $d[\![\Delta]\!]\rho_0=d[\![\Delta]\!]\rho_1$ and $t[\![\Delta]\!]\rho_0=t[\![\Delta]\!]\rho_1$ for every Δ.

The main role of d and t is to verify that e is satisfied by every expression embedded in a declaration to which they are applied, but $t[\![\Delta_0\ \mathsf{within}\ \Delta_1]\!]$ also examines whether $\mathfrak{I}[\![\Delta_0]\!]\S\mathfrak{K}[\![\Delta_0]\!]$ and $\mathfrak{I}[\![\Delta_1]\!]\S\mathfrak{K}[\![\Delta_1]\!]$ are disjoint. The necessity for such an examination is manifested even by such programs as $\mathsf{rec}\ (x\mathsf{=0}\ \mathsf{within}\ x\mathsf{==1})\ \mathsf{inside}\ (x\mathsf{+1})$ and its variants involving $x\mathsf{==0}$ and $x\mathsf{=1}$, all of which except for $\mathsf{rec}\ (x\mathsf{==0}\ \mathsf{within}\ x\mathsf{=1})\ \mathsf{inside}\ (x\mathsf{+1})$ yield the result 2 according to appendix 1 and the result 1 according to appendix 3. We could allow $\mathfrak{I}[\![\Delta_0]\!]\S\mathfrak{K}[\![\Delta_0]\!]$ and $\mathfrak{I}[\![\Delta_1]\!]\S\mathfrak{K}[\![\Delta_1]\!]$ to have elements in common if we were to calculate $\mathfrak{Z}[\![\mathsf{rec}\ \Delta]\!]$ by introducing a new valuation instead of by applying *grow*; we shall not do this, since there are other grounds, such as those of 3.6.5, for demanding that $\mathfrak{I}[\![\Delta_0]\!]\S\mathfrak{K}[\![\Delta_0]\!]$ be disjoint from $\mathfrak{I}[\![\Delta_1]\!]\S\mathfrak{K}[\![\Delta_1]\!]$ when $\Delta_0\ \mathsf{within}\ \Delta_1$ is evaluated using $\mathfrak{T}$.

Neither $g \in \mathsf{Blo} \to \mathsf{U} \to \mathsf{T}$ nor $c \in \mathsf{Com} \to \mathsf{U} \to \mathsf{T}$ has to be supplied with a parameter because no new values are placed on the stack when an activation of a block or a command ends. Nevertheless $g[\![E_0\mathsf{:=}E_1]\!]$ is obviously of crucial importance, since it checks that the result of E_1 has a scope at least as wide as that of any exit of E_0. The restriction on what can be an exit of E_0 is not too drastic in practice; the only interesting assignments prohibited by it are those in which E_0 is intended to extract a component from a structure belonging to E*, and, as it happens, in Sal a location can only be adjoined to a member of E* if first it has been associated with an identifier by a declaration or a procedure call.

Certain operators inevitably return results in B and therefore run no risk of passing members of L, E*, J or F out of limitations; several other operators, however, do run this risk and must therefore be applied only to expressions that are suitably restricted. To cater for this diversity we provide $o\in\mathsf{Mon}\to\mathsf{N}\to\mathsf{N}\to\mathsf{N}$ and $w\in\mathsf{Dya}\to\mathsf{N}\to\mathsf{N}\to(\mathsf{N}\times\mathsf{N})$, which supply e with block numbers. For any O and Ω the integers $o[\![\mathrm{O}]\!]\nu_0\nu_1$, $w[\![\Omega]\!]\nu_0\nu_1{\downarrow}1$ and $w[\![\Omega]\!]\nu_0\nu_1{\downarrow}2$ may be either ν_0 or ν_1; for instance, $w[\![+]\!]\nu_0\nu_1$ is $\langle\nu_0,\nu_0\rangle$, $w[\![\downarrow]\!]\nu_0\nu_1$ is $\langle\nu_1,\nu_0\rangle$ and $w[\![\&]\!]\nu_0\nu_1$ is $\langle\nu_1,\nu_1\rangle$.

The most interesting among the equations governing e is that governing abstractions. As an abstraction can act as an exit from an expression, the biggest among the block numbers of its free variables must be compared with the integer supplied to e. In addition an abstraction may be required by a procedure call, so its stack semantics will be sensible only if its bound variables never appear in its exits. For this purpose the formal parameter is viewed as one of the bound variables of the procedure because such programs as $((\mathsf{fn}x..(\mathsf{fn}y..x))0)1$ (which produces the value 1 according to stack semantics) are not ruled out by taking $f[\![\mathrm{fnI..E}]\!]$ to be $\lambda\rho\nu.e[\![\mathrm{E}]\!]\rho[\langle lift\rho+1,1\rangle/\mathrm{I}](lift\rho+1)$. To prevent E_0 from having a wider scope than E_1 $e[\![E_0E_1]\!]$ could be defined to be $\lambda\rho\nu.r[\![E_0]\!]\rho\nu\wedge e[\![E_1]\!]\rho(\bigwedge\{\mathrm{I}\in\mathfrak{X}[\![E_1]\!]\to\rho[\![\mathrm{I}]\!]{\downarrow}1{\downarrow}1,lift\rho\mid\top\sqsupseteq\mathrm{I}\sqsupseteq\bot\})$ when $\bigwedge\{(\mathrm{E}\mathsf{E}\mathsf{Ide})\vee(\mathrm{E}\mathsf{E}\mathsf{Bas})\vee(\mathrm{E}\mathsf{E}\mathsf{Abs})\vee(\mathrm{E}\mathsf{E}\mathsf{Seq})\vee\sim(\mathrm{E}\in\mathfrak{X}[\![E_0]\!])\mid\top\sqsupseteq\mathrm{E}\sqsupseteq\bot\}=true$.

Programs in which two identifiers denote the same location may be executed erroneously even when the assignments to the identifiers satisfy the constraints given in appendix 8; one such program is

f=fn$x$.x inside ((y==0 inside g==fn$z$.y inside h=f inside h:=g before f)]).
The same situation arises with an abstraction by reference as with a declaration by reference that is not recursive; either feature of the language can lead to there being a location denoted by two identifiers having different scopes. We could prohibit only those abstractions and non-recursive declarations containing assignments to the identifiers that they define, but the appropriate version of e would be rather complex. Consequently we actually choose to ban every abstraction by reference and non-recursive declaration by reference. We do not lose much generality by doing this because every program which conceals no assignments to any identifier defined by an abstraction by reference or a non-recursive declaration by reference is equivalent with the program obtained from it by placing $ before every identifier which denotes a location, by applying £ to every abstraction by reference and by inserting $ into every non-recursive declaration by reference. By inverting the transformations of appendix 7 we can turn this second program into one in which there is no occurrence of an abstraction by reference or a non-recursive declaration by reference; finally, if the resulting program obeys the constraints of appendix 8 then, in accordance with the theorem to be stated in 5.3.9, the stack semantics of the second program is congruent with the store semantics of a program which differs from it only in that recursive declarations by incidence are transformed into recursive declarations by reference. Generally these recursive declarations by incidence are orderly in ⟨⟩ (in the sense explained in 3.9.2); under these circumstances, a modification to the proof of 5.3.9 which we have explained before [52:2.7.7] enables us to avoid transforming the declarations into recursive declarations by reference so the stack semantics of the second program is congruent with the standard semantics of the same program.

5.1.9. Some semantic implications of these constraints.

When we come to analyse the stacks and stores which can really result from applying the valuations in appendix 3, of particular importance will be the entity analogous to the environment supplied as an argument in the equations of appendix 2. This entity is obtained by applying the function *field* defined in 5.1.5 and therefore does not coincide with the environment taken as a parameter by the valuations. Nonetheless for any stack υ produced during a computation $\mathit{field}\,\upsilon$ will satisfy various conditions. We know, for instance, that if $\mathit{field}\,\upsilon[\![I]\!]\geq\nu\geq 1$ for some I and ν then $\upsilon\downarrow(\#\upsilon-\mathit{field}\,\upsilon[\![I]\!]\downarrow\nu\downarrow 1+1)$ must be a member of $(L\rightarrow T)\times N\times N\times U$. We can summarize these conditions by introducing a predicate *tidy* such that

$$\begin{aligned}
\mathit{tidy}=\lambda\rho\upsilon.&(\lambda\psi.\bigwedge\{\bigwedge\{\#\rho[\![I]\!]\geq\nu\geq 1\rightarrow\psi(\rho[\![I]\!]\downarrow\nu),\mathit{true}\,|\,I\}\,|\,\nu\geq 0\})\\
&(\lambda\langle\nu',\nu''\rangle.\upsilon\downarrow(\#\upsilon-\nu'+1)\,\mathrm{E}\,(L\rightarrow T)\times N\times N\times U\rightarrow\upsilon\downarrow(\#\upsilon-\nu'+1)\downarrow 3\geq\nu'+\nu''\geq\nu'+1,\mathit{false})\\
&\wedge(\lambda\psi.\bigwedge\{\#\rho[\![\mathrm{res}]\!]\geq\nu\geq 1\rightarrow\psi(\rho[\![\mathrm{res}]\!]\downarrow\nu),\mathit{true}\,|\,\nu\geq 0\})\\
&\quad(\lambda\nu.\sim((\upsilon\downarrow(\#\upsilon-\nu+1)\,\mathrm{E}\,(L\rightarrow T)\times N\times N\times U)\wedge(\upsilon\downarrow(\#\upsilon-\nu)\,\mathrm{E}\,J))\rightarrow\mathit{false},\\
&\qquad\upsilon\downarrow(\#\upsilon-\nu+1)\downarrow 3=\upsilon\downarrow(\#\upsilon-\nu)\downarrow 2+2=\nu+1).
\end{aligned}$$

The syntactic constraints outlined in 5.1.8 naturally have semantic counterparts; in particular, when an expression E satisfies $e[\![E]\!]\rho\nu=\mathit{true}$ for some ρ and ν the expressed value, ω, adjoined to the stack at the end of the execution of E is subject to certain restrictions. Broadly speaking, these restrictions embody the fact that ω may be used freely until the end of the activation of that limitation which currently associates denoted values with names having ν as their block number. The clearest way to explain these restrictions is simply to enumerate them in an equation governing a predicate. Consequently we write

$found=\lambda\omega\nu\upsilon\sigma.\omega\in L\rightarrow(\nu=\#display\upsilon\rightarrow area\omega\sigma,(\upsilon\downarrow(\#\upsilon-display\upsilon\downarrow(\nu+1)+1)\downarrow 1)\omega)$

$\quad\wedge found(hold\omega\sigma)\nu\upsilon\sigma,$

$\omega\in B\rightarrow true,$

$\omega\in E^{*}\rightarrow\bigwedge\{found(\omega\downarrow\nu')\nu\upsilon\sigma\mid\#\omega\geq\nu'\geq 1\},$

$\omega\in J\rightarrow\bigvee\{chain\upsilon\downarrow\nu'\downarrow 1\downarrow 3=\omega\downarrow 2\mid\#(chain\upsilon)\geq\nu'\geq 1\}$

$\quad\wedge(\upsilon\downarrow(\#\upsilon-display\upsilon\downarrow\nu+1)\downarrow 3\geq\omega\downarrow 2),$

$\omega\in F\rightarrow((\nu=0)\rightarrow(\omega\downarrow 2=0)\wedge(\omega\downarrow 3=arid),$

$\quad\sim\bigvee\{\#(chain\upsilon\downarrow\nu')=\omega\downarrow 2\mid\#(chain\upsilon)\geq\nu'\geq 1\}\rightarrow(\omega\downarrow 2=0),$

$\quad((displau\upsilon\downarrow\nu\geq\omega\downarrow 2)\wedge tidy(\omega\downarrow 3)(\upsilon\dagger(\#\upsilon-\omega\downarrow 2+1)\downarrow 3)))),$

$\omega\in J\rightarrow\bigvee\{chain\upsilon\downarrow\nu'\downarrow 1\downarrow 3=\omega\downarrow 2+2\mid\#(chain\upsilon)\geq\nu'\geq 1\}$

$\quad\wedge(\upsilon\downarrow(\#\upsilon-display\upsilon\downarrow\nu+1)\downarrow 3\geq\omega\downarrow 2+2),$

$\omega\in Z\rightarrow true,$

$\bigwedge\{(\omega\downarrow 1)\alpha\vee\sim area\alpha\sigma\mid\alpha\}\wedge(\#\upsilon\geq\omega\downarrow 3\geq display\upsilon\downarrow\nu\geq\omega\downarrow 2\geq 0)\wedge tidy(\omega\downarrow 4)(\upsilon\dagger(\#\upsilon-\omega\downarrow 3))$

$\wedge(\bigvee\{\#(chain\upsilon\downarrow\nu')=\omega\downarrow 2\mid\#(chain\upsilon)\geq\nu'\geq 1\}\vee(\omega\downarrow 2=0)).$

Because an expressed value on the stack is generally produced by evaluating an expression it must be subject to a derivative of *found* when it is not at the top of the stack. Members of Z and (L→T)×N×N×U on the stack must also be constrained in a manner which we have incorporated in *found* even though they are not expressed values. The derivative we use is given by

$known=\lambda\omega\nu\upsilon\sigma.(\nu>\#chain\upsilon+1)\rightarrow false,$

$\quad(\nu=1)\rightarrow found\omega(\#display\upsilon)\upsilon\sigma,$

$\quad known\omega(\nu-1)((chain\upsilon\downarrow 1)\dagger 1)(restore(chain\upsilon\downarrow 1\downarrow 1\downarrow 1)\sigma);$

if υ is a stack formed during a computation then $known(\upsilon\downarrow(\#\upsilon-\nu_1+1))\nu_0\upsilon\sigma$ should be *true* whenever $\#chain\upsilon+1\geq\nu_0\geq 1$ and $((\nu_0=1)\rightarrow\#\upsilon,\#(chain\upsilon\downarrow(\nu_0-1))-1)\geq\nu_1\geq((\nu_0=\#chain\upsilon+1)\rightarrow 1,\#(chain\upsilon\downarrow\nu_0))$.

When ω is a location the expression for *found*ωνυσ mentions *found*(*hold*ωσ)νωσ, so in fact *found* examines not merely the entries on the stack but also some values which can be reached from them by tracing through the store. At first sight it might seem that if *hold*$\alpha\sigma$ is $\langle\alpha\rangle$ for some location α then *found*$\alpha\nu\upsilon\sigma$ must be $\bot$, as the conventions governing recursive definitions dictate that *found* must be the least fixed point of a function ϕ such that for all suitable ψ the value of $\phi\psi$ can be obtained by substituting ψ for every occurrence of *found* in the right hand side of the definition above. If ϕ is regarded as a continuous function from $W \to N \to Y \to S \to T$ into itself then certainly *fix*$\phi\alpha\nu\upsilon\sigma$ is $\bot$ when *hold*$\alpha\sigma$ is $\langle\alpha\rangle$. However, we actually take ϕ to be a continuous function from $W \Rightarrow N \Rightarrow Y \Rightarrow S \Rightarrow T'$ into itself, where T' is the domain described in 2.2.2; consequently *true* plays the role usually given to $\bot$, and *fix*$\phi\alpha\nu\upsilon\sigma$ is *true*. When regarding *found* as a member of $W \Rightarrow N \Rightarrow Y \Rightarrow S \Rightarrow T'$ we are obliged to make use of the implicit mapping of T into T′ which was mentioned in 2.2.2, since for any store σ and for any location α *area*$\alpha\sigma$ is a member of T, not T′.

Although it may be interesting that the properties of a Sal implementation can be expressed in semantic equations, we want to know more than this; in particular, we wish to be sure that the resulting semantic equations are "correct" relative to the standard semantics of Sal. In 5.3.1 we shall begin to show that this is indeed the case; before then, however, we must examine the properties of functions like *found* and we must formalize our notion of correctness. Doing this will occupy the whole of the next section, which will frequently seem intricate and will occasionally be difficult (as it will in 5.2.5, for instance). The complexity of our notion of correctness is, we believe, essential to the problem that we are considering, for an implementation inevitably requires a lot of "house-keeping" information which is absent from standard semantics. However, some readers may wish to take the notion on trust by proceeding straight to 5.3.9, in which we shall sum up the lemmas about correctness; those who do not wish to do this may be helped by studying part of 5.6.9 now in order to obtain a global view before becoming absorbed in small-scale detail.

5.2. Preparations for an inductive proof.

5.2.1. Shortcomings of direct connections.

Now that we have formulated the functions mentioned in appendix 3 the next task confronting us is to show that the standard semantics of Sal is congruent with its stack semantics at least when programs satisfy the predicates of appendix 8. We might hope to approach this task by adapting the proof of 4.3.7 in a straightforward way, but in fact obstacles which we shall describe below oblige us to adopt a much more tortuous route.

To simplify our account of these obstacles we shall suppose for the moment that the definition of *lose* given in 5.1.4 contains no mention of *restore*, so that the equations of appendix 3 never suggest that the area of available storage can be reduced. Under these circumstances the allocation of storage induced by standard semantics keeps in step with that induced by stack semantics; as in 4.2.1 we can express something of this fact in terms of the diacritical convention of 2.5.4 by providing a predicate l such that $l\hat{\alpha}$ is *true* if and only if $\acute{\alpha}$ and $\grave{\alpha}$ are proper locations which coincide. This predicate allows us to introduce s, v and c, which satisfy equations resembling those in 4.2.2 except by requiring an extra argument representing a stack. For instance, when $\acute{\sigma}$ and $\grave{\sigma}$ are deemed to be stores appropriate to standard semantics and to stack semantics respectively, then no $\theta \in C$, $\langle \zeta, \nu \rangle \in Z \times N$ and $\upsilon \in Y$ can have $c\langle \theta, \langle \zeta, \upsilon \downarrow \nu \rangle \rangle$ (or $v\langle \theta, \langle \zeta, \nu \rangle \rangle \upsilon$) equal to *true* unless $a\langle \theta\acute{\sigma}, lose1\zeta(\upsilon' \dagger (\#\upsilon' - \nu - 1))\grave{\sigma} \rangle$ is *true* for all $\hat{\sigma}$ and υ' such that $s\hat{\sigma}\upsilon' = true$ and $\upsilon' \dagger (\#\upsilon' - \nu - 1) = \upsilon \dagger (\#\upsilon - \nu - 1)$. These predicates are linked to the semantic equations by u, which is naturally such that $u\hat{\rho}\upsilon$ cannot be *true* unless

$c\langle \acute{\rho}[\![I]\!] \downarrow 1, \upsilon \dagger (\#\upsilon - display\,\upsilon \downarrow (\grave{\rho}[\![I]\!] \downarrow 1 \downarrow 1) - \grave{\rho}[\![I]\!] \downarrow 1 \downarrow 2 + 1) \rangle \upsilon$ is *true* for all I with $\acute{\rho}[\![I]\!] \downarrow 1 \in C$. Regrettably u and its associates cannot be applied in a structural induction like that outlined in 4.2.5 for two reasons.

Firstly, the stack supplied at a particular point in a computation, υ, may be reduced at the end of a block to, say, $\upsilon\dagger\nu$ without the store undergoing any change, and even if $v\langle hold\acute{\alpha}\acute{\sigma}, hold\grave{\alpha}\grave{\sigma}\rangle\upsilon = true$ for all $\hat{\alpha}$ having $l\hat{\alpha} = true$ we have no guarantee that $v\langle hold\acute{\alpha}\acute{\sigma}, hold\grave{\alpha}\grave{\sigma}\rangle(\upsilon\dagger\nu) = true$ for all such $\hat{\alpha}$; however, we can reasonably believe that $v\langle hold\acute{\alpha}\acute{\sigma}, hold\grave{\alpha}\grave{\sigma}\rangle\upsilon = true$ for all $\acute{\alpha}$ and $\grave{\alpha}$ which can be reached through the environments. Secondly, when we try to prove the lemma analogous to 4.3.5 we need to show that if certain Γ, $\hat{\rho}_0$, υ_0, θ and ζ_0 satisfy $u\hat{\rho}_0\upsilon_0 \wedge c\langle\theta, \langle\zeta_0, \#\upsilon_0 - 1\rangle\rangle\upsilon_0 = true$ then $u\hat{\rho}_1\upsilon_1 \wedge c\langle\theta, \langle\zeta_1, \#\upsilon_1 - 1\rangle\rangle\upsilon_1 = true$ for some $\hat{\rho}_1$, υ_1 and ζ_1 such that, when $\#\mathcal{K}[\![\Gamma]\!] \geq \nu \geq 1$, $\acute{\rho}_1[\![\mathcal{K}[\![\Gamma]\!]\downarrow\nu]\!]\downarrow 1 = \mathfrak{Q}[\![\Gamma]\!]\acute{\rho}_1\theta\downarrow\nu$, $\grave{\rho}_1[\![\mathcal{K}[\![\Gamma]\!]\downarrow\nu]\!]\downarrow 1 = \langle lift\grave{\rho}_0 + 1, \#\mathcal{K}[\![\Gamma]\!] - \nu + 1\rangle$ and $\upsilon_1\downarrow(\#\upsilon_1 - display\upsilon_1\downarrow(lift\grave{\rho}_0 + 1) - (\#\mathcal{K}[\![\Gamma]\!] - \nu + 1) + 1) = \mathfrak{Q}[\![\Gamma]\!]\grave{\rho}_1\zeta_1(\#\upsilon_1 - 1)\downarrow\nu$; although in 4.3.5 we could use the inclusive nature of u and the rules governing *fix* to show that the pair analogous with $\hat{\rho}_1$ was subject to u, here the claims that $c\langle\bot, \mathfrak{Q}[\![\Gamma]\!]\grave{\rho}_1\zeta_1(\#\upsilon_1 - 1)\downarrow\nu\rangle$ is not *true* and that $\grave{\rho}_1$ is not constructed using *fix* preclude doing this directly.

Like the semantics of block Γ, the semantics of rec Δ provided by appendix 3 makes no appeal to *fix* but instead relies upon pointers to stack positions where there may be label and procedure values having code components which mention the pointers. The standard semantics of recursive declarations is entirely different, as it needs *fix* and the domain G. Whereas the environments $\acute{\rho}_1$ and $\grave{\rho}_1$ of the preceding paragraph do at any rate pair label values for standard semantics with those for stack semantics, the corresponding environments set up on entry to a recursive declaration pair members of G with the dummy value *false*; furthermore such declarations as rec $x{=}{=}x$ are obviously given meanings by appendix 1 that are quite unlike the meanings accorded to them by appendix 3. Since in store semantics recursive declarations by incidence are deliberately intended to resemble recursive declarations by reference, it seems wise to exploit this resemblance when trying to prove that the semantic equations are satisfactory. This can be done by applying the transformations of appendix 7 to programs in such a way that recursive declarations by incidence are replaced by recursive declarations by reference. However, these transformations change the amount of storage required when running a program, so a program can only be shown to be equivalent with one obtained by transforming it if the predicates deal not with all the locations (as does *l*) but just with those that can be reached through the environments.

Thus whether or not we ignore the presence of *restore* in the definition of *lose* we need a means of delving into the store to reveal which locations are accessible from particular parts of programs; by providing predicates that do this we should be able both to set up a correspondence between pairs of states and to examine the connection between applying *fix* and constructing circular chains of pointers. In 4.1.1 we pointed out that such predicates are not available in standard semantics. We shall therefore verify that the equations of appendix 3 are satisfactory by relating them to those of appendix 2 and by making use of the congruence between standard semantics and store semantics established in 4.3.7. More precisely, we shall show in the proof of 5.3.9 that if two programs are formed by applying the transformations of appendix 7 (and two versions of *opt*) to a program text subject to the constraints of appendix 8 then the stack semantics of one of them is equivalent with the store semantics of the other so long as this latter program contains no recursive declarations by incidence. For the purposes of this proof we shall adopt the diacritical convention of 2.5.4 with the intention that, for instance, $\hat{\zeta}$ will be a pair of continuations such that $\acute{\zeta}$ and $\grave{\zeta}$ are appropriate to stack semantics and to store semantics respectively; furthermore, we shall make full use of the vectorial convention explained in 4.1.6, applying it to stack semantics as well as to store semantics. Because we shall combine the effects of these two conventions we shall tacitly identify the pair $\hat{\pi}_1$, say, both with $\langle \acute{\pi}_1, \grave{\pi}_1 \rangle$ and with $\langle\langle \acute{\rho}_1, \acute{\upsilon}_1, \acute{\sigma}_1 \rangle, \langle \grave{\rho}_1, \grave{\upsilon}_1, \grave{\sigma}_1 \rangle\rangle$, despite the fact that $\langle \acute{\upsilon}_1, \acute{\sigma}_1 \rangle$ rather than $\langle \acute{\rho}_1, \acute{\upsilon}_1, \acute{\sigma}_1 \rangle$ models the machine state produced by the implementation suggested by appendix 3.

5.2.2. Tracing algorithms.

Some of the locations accessible from a program are obtained by investigating the main values associated with entries in the environment and positions on the stack. In stack semantics all these values are kept on the stack, $\acute{\sigma}$, but in store semantics each value is of one of the forms $\grave{\rho}[\![\mathrm{I}]\!]{\downarrow}\nu$, $\grave{\rho}[\![\mathrm{res}]\!]{\downarrow}\nu$, $\grave{\rho}[\![\mathrm{rec}]\!]{\downarrow}\nu$ and $\grave{\upsilon}{\downarrow}\nu$ when $\grave{\rho}$ is the environment and $\grave{\upsilon}$ is the stack. As we wish to set up a correspondence between the locations required in stack semantics and those required in store semantics we have to make every value preserved on $\acute{\sigma}$ tally with the value adjoined to $\grave{\rho}$ or $\grave{\upsilon}$ "at the same time". The third component of every member of $(\mathrm{L}\rightarrow\mathrm{T})\times\mathrm{N}\times\mathrm{N}\times\mathrm{U}$ found in $\acute{\sigma}$ indicates how much of the working space is occupied by denoted values, so a stack comprising only the expressed values, $stick\,\acute{\sigma}$, can be obtained if we define $stick\in\mathrm{Y}\rightarrow\mathrm{Y}$ by

$$\begin{aligned}
stick=\lambda\upsilon.(\#\upsilon=0)\rightarrow\langle\rangle,\\
&(\upsilon{\downarrow}1\,\mathrm{E}\,\mathrm{Z}\vee\upsilon{\downarrow}1\,\mathrm{E}\,(\mathrm{L}\rightarrow\mathrm{T})\times\mathrm{N}\times\mathrm{N}\times\mathrm{U})\rightarrow stick(\upsilon{\dagger}1),\\
&(\#display\,\upsilon=0)\rightarrow\langle\upsilon{\downarrow}1\rangle\,\S\,stick(\upsilon{\dagger}1),\\
&(\#\upsilon\geq(1+\upsilon{\downarrow}(\#\upsilon-display\,\upsilon{\downarrow}(\#display\,\upsilon)+1){\downarrow}3))\rightarrow\langle\upsilon{\downarrow}1\rangle\,\S\,stick(\upsilon{\dagger}1),\\
&stick(\upsilon{\dagger}(\#\upsilon-display\,\upsilon{\downarrow}(\#display\,\upsilon)+1)).
\end{aligned}$$

The resulting list of expressed values can be exhibited alongside $\grave{\upsilon}$ by means of $\lambda\hat{\omega}.gyven\,\hat{\omega}\langle stick\,\acute{\sigma},\grave{\upsilon}\rangle$, where

$$gyven=\lambda\hat{\omega}\hat{\sigma}.\bigvee\{\hat{\omega}\equiv\langle\acute{\sigma}{\downarrow}\nu,\grave{\upsilon}{\downarrow}\nu\rangle\mid(\#\acute{\sigma}\geq\nu\geq1)\wedge(\#\grave{\upsilon}\geq\nu\geq1)\}.$$

Greater difficulties are encountered when we try to compare the denoted values kept on $\acute{\sigma}$ with the entries in $\grave{\rho}$. Though the environment for stack semantics, $\acute{\rho}$, allows us to extract some of the denoted values in $\acute{\sigma}$ by forming $\acute{\sigma}{\downarrow}(\#\acute{\sigma}-(display\,\upsilon{\downarrow}(\acute{\rho}[\![\mathrm{I}]\!]{\downarrow}1{\downarrow}1)+\acute{\rho}[\![\mathrm{I}]\!]{\downarrow}1{\downarrow}2)+1)$ for every I, we cannot necessarily extract them all by this means because $\acute{\rho}$ is purely a local environment. However, we have devised the equations of appendix 3 so that embedded in $\acute{\sigma}$ is an environment $field\,\acute{\sigma}$ which connects identifiers with all the positions on the stack occupied by the associated denoted values. Whereas the stack positions provided by entries in $\acute{\rho}$ depend on $\mathit{display}\acute{\upsilon}$, those provided by $\mathit{field}\acute{\upsilon}$ are absolute; were this not so $\mathit{field}\acute{\upsilon}$ would associate the wrong values with identifiers declared in the presence of a static chain not given by $\mathit{display}\acute{\upsilon}$. To set up this association we provide $\mathit{ravel}\in\mathsf{U}\to\mathsf{Y}\to((\mathsf{Ide}\to\mathsf{W}^*)\times\mathsf{W}^*)$, which satisfies

$\mathit{ravel}=\lambda\acute{\rho}\acute{\upsilon}.\langle\lambda\mathrm{I}.\mathit{map}(\lambda\langle\nu',\nu''\rangle.\acute{\upsilon}\downarrow(\#\acute{\upsilon}-\nu'-\nu''+1))(\acute{\rho}[\![\mathrm{I}]\!]),\mathit{map}(\lambda\nu.\acute{\upsilon}\downarrow(\#\acute{\upsilon}-\nu))(\acute{\rho}[\![\mathrm{res}]\!])\rangle$;

thus $\mathit{ravel}(\mathit{twist}\acute{\rho}\acute{\upsilon})\acute{\upsilon}[\![\mathrm{I}]\!]\downarrow 1$ is the value denoted by I if $\acute{\rho}$ is constructed during a compilation. Because $\mathit{twist}\acute{\rho}\acute{\upsilon}$ should constitute the top layer of $\mathit{field}\acute{\upsilon}$ we are particularly interested in $\mathit{ravel}(\mathit{field}\acute{\upsilon})\acute{\upsilon}$, which we write as $\mathit{level}\acute{\upsilon}$; we therefore obtain $\mathit{level}\in\mathsf{Y}\to((\mathsf{Ide}\to\mathsf{W}^*)\times\mathsf{W}^*)$ from the equation

$\mathit{level}=\lambda\acute{\upsilon}.\mathit{ravel}(\mathit{field}\acute{\upsilon})\acute{\upsilon}$.

We put the denoted values generated according to stack semantics into correspondence with the entries in the environment for store semantics by using $\lambda\hat{\omega}.\mathit{hoten}\hat{\omega}\langle\mathit{level}\acute{\upsilon},\grave{\rho}\rangle$, where by momentarily taking $\acute{\rho}$ to be a member of $(\mathsf{Ide}\to\mathsf{W}^*)\times\mathsf{W}^*$ we can define hoten thus:

$$\mathit{hoten}=\lambda\hat{\omega}\hat{\rho}.\bigvee\{\bigvee\{\hat{\omega}\equiv\langle\acute{\rho}[\![\mathrm{I}]\!]\downarrow\nu,\grave{\rho}[\![\mathrm{I}]\!]\downarrow\nu\rangle\mid(\#\acute{\rho}[\![\mathrm{I}]\!]\geq\nu\geq 1)\wedge(\#\grave{\rho}[\![\mathrm{I}]\!]\geq\nu\geq 1)\}\mid\mathrm{I}\}$$
$$\vee\bigvee\{\hat{\omega}\equiv\langle\acute{\rho}[\![\mathrm{res}]\!]\downarrow\nu,\grave{\rho}[\![\mathrm{res}]\!]\downarrow\nu\rangle\mid(\#\acute{\rho}[\![\mathrm{res}]\!]\geq\nu\geq 1)\wedge(\#\grave{\rho}[\![\mathrm{res}]\!]\geq\nu\geq 1)\}.$$

From a pair of witnessed values, $\hat{\omega}$, and a pair of states, $\hat{\pi}$, may be obtained further witnessed values. When $\acute{\omega}$ or $\grave{\omega}$ is a location, for instance, $\hat{\omega}$ gives rise to $\langle(\acute{\omega}\mathsf{E}\mathsf{L}\to\mathit{hold}\acute{\omega}\acute{\sigma},\acute{\omega}),(\grave{\omega}\mathsf{E}\mathsf{L}\to\mathit{hold}\grave{\omega}\grave{\sigma},\grave{\omega})\rangle$. When $\acute{\omega}$ and $\grave{\omega}$ are label values they yield all the pairs found by examining what would be the environments and stacks formed by executing jumps to the pertinent labels; in stack semantics the stack formed is a segment of that present before the jump, and the values on it can be put into correspondence with those arising from the second and third components of $\grave{\omega}$ by applying level and stick. When $\acute{\omega}$ and $\grave{\omega}$ are procedure values they yield those pairs representing the values denoted by the free variables of the relevant abstraction; the role of the third component of $\acute{\omega}$ is simply to indicate where on the stack these denoted values are situated. Because the programs which we shall evaluate using stack semantics will not contain recursive declarations by incidence we have no need to investigate what happens if $\grave{\omega}\text{E}G$.

The complete correspondence between states $\acute{\pi}$ and $\grave{\pi}$ can be produced by iterating the process whereby one pair of values gives rise to others. The algorithm which we adopt for doing this resembles in principle that used during the marking phase of a garbage collector, except that we choose not to form a list of those locations which have already been encountered. Instead we introduce an integer parameter to eliminate the possibility that $\perp$ might result from trying to trace which locations could be reached from a pair $\hat{\alpha}$ such that $\langle \mathit{hold}\acute{\alpha}\acute{\sigma}, \mathit{hold}\grave{\alpha}\grave{\sigma}\rangle = \langle\langle\acute{\alpha}\rangle, \langle\grave{\alpha}\rangle\rangle$. Thus we provide a function *seen* such that if $\mathit{seen}\,\nu\hat{\omega}_0\hat{\omega}_1\hat{\pi}$ is *true* then $\hat{\omega}_0$ can be reached from $\hat{\omega}_1$ in at most ν steps; consequently

$$
\begin{aligned}
\mathit{seen} = \lambda\nu\hat{\omega}_0\hat{\omega}_1\hat{\pi}.\,&(1>\nu)\rightarrow(\hat{\omega}_0\equiv\hat{\omega}_1),\\
&\acute{\omega}_1\text{E}L\vee\grave{\omega}_1\text{E}L\rightarrow \mathit{seen}(\nu-1)\hat{\omega}_0\langle(\acute{\omega}_1\text{E}L\rightarrow\mathit{hold}\acute{\omega}_1\acute{\sigma},\acute{\omega}_1),(\grave{\omega}_1\text{E}L\rightarrow\mathit{hold}\grave{\omega}_1\grave{\sigma},\grave{\omega}_1)\rangle\hat{\pi},\\
&\acute{\omega}_1\text{E}B\wedge\grave{\omega}_1\text{E}B\rightarrow \mathit{false},\\
&\acute{\omega}_1\text{E}E^*\wedge\grave{\omega}_1\text{E}E^*\rightarrow\bigvee\{\mathit{seen}(\nu-1)\hat{\omega}_0\langle\acute{\omega}_1\downarrow\nu,\grave{\omega}_1\downarrow\nu\rangle\hat{\pi}\mid \#\acute{\omega}_1\geq\nu\geq 1\},\\
&\acute{\omega}_1\text{E}J\wedge\grave{\omega}_1\text{E}J\rightarrow\bigvee\{\mathit{seen}(\nu-1)\hat{\omega}_0\hat{\omega}_2\hat{\pi},\\
&\qquad\qquad \mid \mathit{hoten}\hat{\omega}_2\langle \mathit{level}(\acute{\sigma}\dagger(\#\acute{\sigma}-\acute{\omega}_1\downarrow 2-1)),\grave{\omega}_1\downarrow 2\rangle,\\
&\qquad\qquad \vee\mathit{gyven}\hat{\omega}_2\langle \mathit{stick}(\acute{\sigma}\dagger(\#\acute{\sigma}-\omega_1\downarrow 2-1)),\grave{\omega}_1\downarrow 3\rangle\},\\
&\acute{\omega}_1\text{E}F\wedge\grave{\omega}_1\text{E}F\rightarrow\bigvee\{\mathit{seen}(\nu-1)\hat{\omega}_0\hat{\omega}_2\hat{\pi}\mid \mathit{hoten}\hat{\omega}_2\langle \mathit{ravel}(\acute{\omega}_1\downarrow 3)\acute{\sigma},\grave{\omega}_1\downarrow 2\rangle\},\\
&\acute{\omega}_1\text{E}J\wedge\grave{\omega}_1\text{E}J\rightarrow\bigvee\{\mathit{seen}(\nu-1)\hat{\omega}_0\hat{\omega}_2\hat{\pi}\\
&\qquad\qquad \mid \mathit{hoten}\hat{\omega}_2\langle \mathit{level}(\acute{\sigma}\dagger(\#\acute{\sigma}-\acute{\omega}_1\downarrow 2)),\grave{\omega}_1\downarrow 2\rangle\\
&\qquad\qquad \vee\mathit{gyven}\hat{\omega}_2\langle \mathit{stick}(\acute{\sigma}\dagger(\#\acute{\sigma}-\omega_1\downarrow 2)),\grave{\omega}_1\downarrow 3\rangle\},\\
&\mathit{false}.
\end{aligned}
$$

Values $\acute{\omega}$ and $\grave{\omega}$ correspond in the states $\acute{\pi}$ and $\grave{\pi}$ if they can be reached from a pair of values that is immediately accessible through the environments, the stacks or the input components of the stores available to a pair of programs. Here we shall regard values as being immediately accessible if they are found in the environments, the stacks or the input components of the stores, so we can enumerate all the pairs that tally by setting

$$kent=\lambda\hat{\omega}\hat{\pi}.\bigvee\{\bigvee\{seen\,\nu\hat{\omega}\hat{\omega}_0\hat{\pi}$$
$$|hoten\,\hat{\omega}_0\langle level\,\acute{\upsilon},\grave{\rho}\rangle\vee gyven\,\hat{\omega}_0\langle stick\,\acute{\upsilon},\grave{\upsilon}\rangle\vee gyven\,\hat{\omega}_0\langle\acute{\sigma}\downarrow 2,\grave{\sigma}\downarrow 2\rangle\}|\nu\geq 0\}.$$

We could dispense with the integer parameter in the definition of *seen* by using a recursive equation resembling that given for *found* in 5.1.9; in contrast with *found*, however, *seen* would map entities into the domain T″ described in 2.2.2, not into the domain T′, so $\bigvee$ would be the surrogate for $\bigsqcup$. We have chosen not to do this because proofs that entities are subject to *seen* perhaps gain in intuitive appeal what they lose in elegance when they are couched in terms of arithmetic induction on the integer parameter supplied to *seen* rather than the properties of *fix*. Thus, for instance, by induction on ν_1 we can readily prove that if ν_0, ν_1, $\hat{\omega}_0$, $\hat{\omega}_1$, $\hat{\omega}_2$ and $\hat{\pi}$ satisfy $seen\,\nu_0\hat{\omega}_1\hat{\omega}_0\hat{\pi}\wedge seen\,\nu_1\hat{\omega}_2\hat{\omega}_1\hat{\pi}=true$ then $seen(\nu_0+\nu_1)\hat{\omega}_2\hat{\omega}_0\hat{\pi}=true$ provided that $seen\,\nu_2\hat{\omega}_3\hat{\omega}_0\hat{\pi}$ is proper for all ν_2 and $\hat{\omega}_3$; as a corollary to this, if $seen\,\nu_0\hat{\omega}_1\hat{\omega}_0\hat{\pi}\wedge kent\,\hat{\omega}_0\hat{\pi}=true$ for some ν_0, $\hat{\omega}_0$, $\hat{\omega}_1$ and $\hat{\pi}$ then $kent\,\hat{\omega}_1\hat{\pi}=true$ provided that $seen\,\nu_1\hat{\omega}_3\hat{\omega}_2\hat{\pi}$ is proper for all ν_1, $\hat{\omega}_2$ and $\hat{\omega}_3$ such that $hoten\,\hat{\omega}_2\langle level\,\acute{\upsilon},\grave{\rho}\rangle\vee gyven\,\hat{\omega}_2\langle stick\,\acute{\upsilon},\grave{\upsilon}\rangle\vee gyven\,\hat{\omega}_2\langle\acute{\sigma}\downarrow 2,\grave{\sigma}\downarrow 2\rangle=true$. These statements mean that if $\hat{\omega}_1$ can be reached from $\hat{\omega}_0$ in ν_0 steps and if $\hat{\omega}_2$ can be reached from $\hat{\omega}_1$ in ν_1 steps then $\hat{\omega}_2$ can be reached from $\hat{\omega}_0$ in $\nu_0+\nu_1$ steps, whilst if $\hat{\omega}_1$ can be reached from $\hat{\omega}_0$ in ν_0 steps and if $\hat{\omega}_0$ is accessible in $\hat{\pi}$ then $\hat{\omega}_1$ is accessible in $\hat{\pi}$; they will be used frequently when we come to prove the lemmas leading up to 5.3.9.

In 5.2.3 and 5.2.4 we shall develop some of the predicates that we shall need when analysing the congruence between the store semantics of Sal and the stack semantics of Sal. To establish the existence of some of these predicates we shall be obliged to apply 2.5.3 in a rather complicated manner which will be presented in 5.2.5.

5.2.3. Resemblances between states.

Having provided a suitable tracing algorithm, we can now turn to a more detailed examination of the states generated during the evaluation of programs. For any command Γ subject to the constraints of appendix 8 we wish to compare the meanings ascribed by different sorts of semantics to two commands obtained by transforming Γ by using the rules of appendix 7 in two ways. Thus we are interested in relating $\mathcal{C}[\![\mathcal{T}[\![\Gamma]\!]\acute{\psi}]\!]\acute{\rho}\acute{\zeta}\acute{\upsilon}\acute{\sigma}$ and $\mathcal{C}[\![\mathcal{T}[\![\Gamma]\!]\grave{\psi}]\!]\grave{\zeta}\grave{\rho}\grave{\upsilon}\grave{\sigma}$ for some $\hat{\psi}$, $\hat{\rho}$, $\hat{\upsilon}$, $\hat{\sigma}$ and $\hat{\zeta}$; following the practice of 4.2.1 we therefore introduce a predicate a which maps pairs of members of A into truth values. If $\langle\acute{\upsilon},\acute{\sigma}\rangle$ and $\langle\grave{\rho},\grave{\upsilon},\grave{\sigma}\rangle$ themselves result from evaluating two commands formed with the aid of $\acute{\psi}$ and $\grave{\psi}$, they have to resemble one another vaguely and must be connected with $\hat{\psi}$ in a manner which indicates that the values denoted by a particular identifier I in $\acute{\upsilon}$ and $\grave{\rho}$ are produced by declarations obtained by transforming one declaration in two ways. This means that if, for instance, I is in scope and $level\acute{\upsilon}[\![I]\!]{\downarrow}1$ is a location whereas $\grave{\rho}[\![I]\!]{\downarrow}1$ is not then $\acute{\psi}[\![I]\!]{\downarrow}1$ must be $true$ and $\grave{\psi}[\![I]\!]{\downarrow}1$ must be $false$; this and other such properties of $\hat{\psi}$ can be captured by writing

$$
\begin{aligned}
apt = \lambda\hat{\psi}\langle\acute{\upsilon},\grave{\rho}\rangle.\textstyle\bigwedge\{ & (\#\grave{\rho}[\![I]\!]=0)\rightarrow true,\\
& \sim(level\acute{\upsilon}[\![I]\!]{\downarrow}1\,\mathsf{E}\,\mathsf{L})\wedge\sim(\grave{\rho}[\![I]\!]{\downarrow}1\,\mathsf{E}\,\mathsf{L})\rightarrow\sim\acute{\psi}[\![I]\!]{\downarrow}1\wedge\sim\grave{\psi}[\![I]\!]{\downarrow}1,\\
& \sim(level\acute{\upsilon}[\![I]\!]{\downarrow}1\,\mathsf{E}\,\mathsf{L})\rightarrow\sim\acute{\psi}[\![I]\!]{\downarrow}1\wedge\grave{\psi}[\![I]\!]{\downarrow}1,\\
& \sim(\grave{\rho}[\![I]\!]{\downarrow}1\,\mathsf{E}\,\mathsf{L})\rightarrow\acute{\psi}[\![I]\!]{\downarrow}1\wedge\sim\grave{\psi}[\![I]\!]{\downarrow}1,\\
& (\acute{\psi}[\![I]\!]{\downarrow}1\wedge\grave{\psi}[\![I]\!]{\downarrow}1)\vee\sim(\acute{\psi}[\![I]\!]{\downarrow}1\vee\grave{\psi}[\![I]\!]{\downarrow}1)\\
& |I\}.
\end{aligned}
$$

Hence when comparing $\mathcal{C}[\![\mathcal{T}[\![\Gamma]\!]\acute{\psi}]\!]\acute{\rho}\acute{\zeta}\acute{\upsilon}\acute{\sigma}$ and $\mathcal{C}[\![\mathcal{T}[\![\Gamma]\!]\grave{\psi}]\!]\grave{\zeta}\grave{\rho}\grave{\upsilon}\grave{\sigma}$ we demand not only that $c[\![\Gamma]\!]\acute{\rho}=true$ but also that $apt\hat{\psi}\langle\acute{\upsilon},rend[\![\Gamma]\!]\grave{\rho}\rangle=true$; furthermore $\acute{\rho}$ and $\acute{\upsilon}$ have to be linked by the relations $rend[\![\Gamma]\!](twist\acute{\rho}\acute{\upsilon})=rend[\![\Gamma]\!](field\acute{\upsilon})$ and $\#display\acute{\upsilon}=lift\acute{\rho}$, because otherwise $field\acute{\upsilon}$ will rarely indicate accurately what the free variables of Γ denote.

The "vague resemblance" between $\langle\acute{\upsilon},\acute{\sigma}\rangle$ and $\langle\grave{\rho},\grave{\upsilon},\grave{\sigma}\rangle$ is embodied in the assertion that $p_0\hat{\pi}=true$ for a certain predicate p_0. Rather more than this is known, however, for those values $\acute{\omega}$ and $\grave{\omega}$ which are accessible at corresponding points in $\acute{\pi}$ and $\grave{\pi}$ must be comparable in some sense; more precisely, they must satisfy $w\hat{\omega}\hat{\pi}=true$ where w is a predicate which may in principle depend on $\hat{\pi}$. Hence we actually expect $\acute{\pi}$ and $\grave{\pi}$ to be subject to a predicate p, which is akin to our earlier s and is given by

$p=\lambda\hat{\pi}.\bigwedge\{kent\hat{\omega}\hat{\pi}\rightarrow w\hat{\omega}\hat{\pi},true\,|\,\hat{\omega}\}\wedge p_0\hat{\pi}$.

Loosely speaking, continuations $\acute{\zeta}$ and $\grave{\zeta}$ are equivalent if when applied to equivalent states they yield answers related by a. We might hope to be able to demand that $\bigwedge\{a\langle\acute{\zeta}\acute{\upsilon}\acute{\sigma},\grave{\zeta}\grave{\rho}\grave{\upsilon}\grave{\sigma}\rangle\,|\,p\hat{\pi}\}=true$, but this is not possible. Our intention is, very roughly, to confirm that if $c[\![\Gamma]\!]\hat{\rho}=true$ and $\acute{\zeta}$ and $\grave{\zeta}$ are equivalent then $\mathfrak{C}[\![\mathfrak{c}[\![\Gamma]\!]\acute{\phi}]\!]\acute{\rho}\acute{\zeta}$ and $\mathfrak{C}[\![\mathfrak{c}[\![\Gamma]\!]\grave{\phi}]\!]\grave{\zeta}$ are also equivalent. Yet when Γ is x:=0, for example, the effect of $\mathfrak{c}[\![\Gamma]\!]\acute{\phi}$ depends on whether or not x denotes a location and may therefore not inevitably coincide with the effect of $\mathfrak{c}[\![\Gamma]\!]\grave{\phi}$; only if $apt\acute{\phi}\langle\acute{\upsilon},rend[\![\Gamma]\!]\grave{\rho}\rangle=true$ can we establish that $a\langle\mathfrak{C}[\![\mathfrak{c}[\![\Gamma]\!]\acute{\phi}]\!]\acute{\rho}\acute{\zeta}\acute{\upsilon}\acute{\sigma},\mathfrak{C}[\![\mathfrak{c}[\![\Gamma]\!]\grave{\phi}]\!]\grave{\zeta}\grave{\rho}\grave{\upsilon}\grave{\sigma}\rangle$ is *true*. Accordingly we have to adopt a predicate, c, which allows $\acute{\zeta}$ and $\grave{\zeta}$ to be equivalent even if $a\langle\acute{\zeta}\acute{\upsilon}\acute{\sigma},\grave{\zeta}\grave{\rho}\grave{\upsilon}\grave{\sigma}\rangle$ is not *true* except for certain pairs $\hat{\pi}$ such that $p\hat{\pi}$ is *true*. This can best be done by providing both $\hat{\zeta}$ and a pair of states as arguments for c, so that $a\langle\acute{\zeta}\acute{\upsilon}\acute{\sigma},\grave{\zeta}\grave{\rho}\grave{\upsilon}\grave{\sigma}\rangle$ need only be *true* when matches this pair of states to some extent. Hence we set

$c=\lambda\hat{\zeta}\hat{\pi}.\bigwedge\{a\langle\acute{\zeta}\acute{\upsilon}_0\acute{\sigma}_0,\grave{\zeta}\grave{\rho}_0\grave{\upsilon}_0\grave{\sigma}_0\rangle\,|\,p\hat{\pi}\wedge match0\hat{\pi}_0\hat{\pi}\}$.

The test $match0\hat{\pi}_0\hat{\pi}_1$ is intended to ensure that $\langle\acute{\upsilon}_0,\acute{\sigma}_0\rangle$ and $\langle\grave{\rho}_0,\grave{\upsilon}_0,\grave{\sigma}_0\rangle$ could conceivably be formed by evaluating two commands in the presence of the states $\langle\acute{\upsilon}_1,\acute{\sigma}_1\rangle$ and $\langle\grave{\rho}_1,\grave{\upsilon}_1,\grave{\sigma}_1\rangle$; it is independent of $\acute{\rho}_0$ and $\acute{\rho}_1$. The parameter 0 indicates that $\acute{\upsilon}_0$ has the same height as $\acute{\upsilon}_1$, so when $\langle\acute{\upsilon}_0,\acute{\sigma}_0\rangle$ and $\langle\grave{\rho}_0,\grave{\upsilon}_0,\grave{\sigma}_0\rangle$ are produced by the evaluation of expressions in the presence of $\langle\acute{\upsilon}_1,\acute{\sigma}_1\rangle$ and $\langle\grave{\rho}_1,\grave{\upsilon}_1,\grave{\sigma}_1\rangle$ then $match1\hat{\pi}_0\hat{\pi}_1$ is needed instead of $match0\hat{\pi}_0\hat{\pi}_1$. Since $\langle\acute{\upsilon}_1,\acute{\sigma}_1\rangle$ and $\langle\grave{\rho}_1,\grave{\upsilon}_1,\grave{\sigma}_1\rangle$ may themselves be imagined to result from evaluating two portions of very similar programs, we can insist that $\acute{\upsilon}_1$ be at least as high as the ceiling imposed on the topmost set of denoted values, and that $\acute{\upsilon}_1\downarrow\nu$ must not be a location unless $stick\grave{\upsilon}_1\downarrow\nu$ is one also. Consequently we set

$$
\begin{aligned}
match=\lambda\nu\hat{\pi}_0\hat{\pi}_1.&(YW_0(\acute{\upsilon}_0\dagger\nu)=YW_0\acute{\upsilon}_1)\wedge(UW_0\grave{\rho}_0=UW_0\grave{\rho}_1)\wedge(YW_0\grave{\upsilon}_0\dagger\nu=YW_0\grave{\upsilon}_1)\\
&\wedge\bigwedge\{area\alpha\acute{\sigma}_0\vee\sim area\alpha\acute{\sigma}_1 \mid \top\sqsupset\alpha\sqsupset\bot\}\\
&\wedge(\#chain\acute{\upsilon}_0=0\rightarrow true,(\#\acute{\upsilon}_0\geq chain\acute{\upsilon}_0\downarrow1\downarrow1\downarrow3+\nu))\\
&\wedge\bigwedge\{\acute{\upsilon}_0\downarrow\nu_0 E L\vee\acute{\upsilon}_0\downarrow\nu_0 E B\vee\acute{\upsilon}_0\downarrow\nu_0 E E^*\vee\acute{\upsilon}_0\downarrow\nu_0 E J\vee\acute{\upsilon}_0\downarrow\nu_0 E F \mid \nu\geq\nu_0\geq1\}\\
&\wedge\bigwedge\{(stick\acute{\upsilon}_0\downarrow\nu_0 E L\wedge\grave{\upsilon}_0\downarrow\nu_0 E L)\vee\sim(stick\acute{\upsilon}_0\downarrow\nu_0 E L\vee\grave{\upsilon}_0\downarrow\nu_0 E L)\mid\#\acute{\upsilon}_0\geq\nu_0\geq1\}.
\end{aligned}
$$

Here, for each domain W, W_0 is a retraction of W into itself which is "sufficiently large" to discriminate between members of different summands of W, whilst U and Y turn retractions of W into retractions of U and Y respectively in a way to be explained in 5.2.5.

By analogy with 4.2.2 we could introduce a predicate k such that

$k=\lambda\hat{\zeta}\hat{\pi}.\bigwedge\{a\langle\acute{\zeta}\acute{\upsilon}_0\acute{\sigma}_0,\grave{\zeta}\grave{\rho}_0\grave{\upsilon}_0\grave{\sigma}_0\rangle \mid p\hat{\pi}_0\wedge match1\hat{\pi}_0\hat{\pi}\}$,

and we might try to prove that if $k\hat{\zeta}\hat{\pi}=true$ then $c\langle\mathfrak{E}[\![\mathfrak{e}[\![E]\!]\acute{\psi}]\!]\acute{\rho}\acute{\zeta},\mathfrak{E}[\![\mathfrak{e}[\![E]\!]\grave{\psi}]\!]\grave{\zeta}\rangle\hat{\pi}=true$ for all suitable E, $\hat{\pi}$ and $\hat{\zeta}$, just as we shall confirm that $c\langle\mathfrak{C}[\![\mathfrak{c}[\![\Gamma]\!]\acute{\psi}]\!]\acute{\rho}\acute{\zeta},\mathfrak{C}[\![\mathfrak{c}[\![\Gamma]\!]\grave{\psi}]\!]\grave{\zeta}\rangle\hat{\pi}=true$ under certain circumstances when $c\hat{\zeta}\hat{\pi}=true$. This treatment of expressions would fail because it takes no account of the requirement that no value be passed outside its scope. This requirement can be incorporated in a predicate like k by using not $match1\hat{\pi}_0\hat{\pi}_1$ but $match1\hat{\pi}_0\hat{\pi}_1\wedge found(\acute{\upsilon}_0\downarrow1)\nu\acute{\upsilon}_0\acute{\sigma}_0$, where *found* is defined as in 5.1.9. Accordingly we let

$j=\lambda\hat{\zeta}\nu\hat{\pi}.\bigwedge\{a\langle\acute{\zeta}\acute{\upsilon}_0\acute{\sigma}_0,\grave{\zeta}\grave{\rho}_0\grave{\upsilon}_0\grave{\sigma}_0\rangle \mid p\hat{\pi}_0\wedge match1\hat{\pi}_0\hat{\pi}_1\wedge found(\acute{\upsilon}_0\downarrow1)\nu\acute{\upsilon}_0\acute{\sigma}_0\}$,

and we attempt to prove that $c\langle\mathfrak{E}[\![\mathfrak{e}[\![E]\!]\acute{\psi}]\!]\acute{\rho}\acute{\zeta},\mathfrak{E}[\![\mathfrak{e}[\![E]\!]\grave{\psi}]\!]\grave{\zeta}\rangle\hat{\pi}=true$ only when $j\hat{\zeta}\nu\hat{\pi}=true$ and $e[\![E]\!]\acute{\rho}\nu=true$ for some ν.

5.2.4. Correspondences between values.

Much of what must be said about predicates such as p_0 is virtually independent of the programming language considered and would apply to any proof requiring the use of tracing algorithms like that of 5.2.2. For example, when $\acute{\pi}$ is to resemble $\grave{\pi}$ the entire environment and the stack of anonymous quantities incorporated in $\acute{\pi}$ must have the same heights as the corresponding portions of $\grave{\pi}$; thus if we define *neat* by setting

$$neat=\lambda\hat{\rho}.\bigwedge\{\#\acute{\rho}[\![I]\!]=\#\grave{\rho}[\![I]\!] \mid I\}\wedge(\#\acute{\rho}[\![\mathrm{res}]\!]=\#\grave{\rho}[\![\mathrm{res}]\!])$$

then $neat\langle level\acute{\sigma},\grave{\rho}\rangle=true$ and $\#stick\acute{\sigma}=\grave{\vartheta}$ provided that $\acute{\pi}$ is suited to stack semantics and $\grave{\pi}$ is suited to store semantics.

Some aspects of $p_0\hat{\pi}$ arise from the difference between the storage allocated to $\acute{\pi}$ and that allocated to $\grave{\pi}$. To allow the areas of $\acute{\sigma}$ and of $\grave{\sigma}$ to be extended simultaneously we assume that they are finite but that L is infinite. In addition if $\hat{\omega}_0$ and $\hat{\omega}_0$ are pairs such that $\acute{\omega}_0 \in L$, $\grave{\omega}_1 \in L$, $\acute{\omega}_0=\acute{\omega}_1$ and $kent\hat{\omega}_0\hat{\pi}\wedge kent\hat{\omega}_1\hat{\pi}=true$ then we must ensure that $\grave{\omega}_0=\grave{\omega}_1$, since otherwise updating $\acute{\omega}_0$ and $\grave{\omega}_0$ using equivalent stored values might give $\acute{\omega}_0$ and $\grave{\omega}_1$ contents which were not equivalent. Because the equations of appendix 3 mention *change* as well as *update*, we subject the stack positions to a limitation akin to that imposed on the locations; this asserts that if I_0, I_1, ν_0 and ν_1 are such that $\grave{\rho}[\![I_1]\!]\downarrow\nu_1 \in L$ and $field\acute{\sigma}[\![I_0]\!]\downarrow\nu_0=field\acute{\sigma}[\![I_1]\!]\downarrow\nu_1$ then $\grave{\rho}[\![I_0]\!]\downarrow\nu_0=\grave{\rho}[\![I_1]\!]\downarrow\nu_1$.

Further features of $p_0\hat{\pi}$ stem from the fact that $\acute{\pi}$ is presumed to be generated by evaluating a transformed version of a program obeying the constraints of appendix 8. Thus in accordance with the comments in 5.1.9 the elements of the stack $\acute{\sigma}$ should be restricted by appropriate forms of *known* while when $\#chain\acute{\sigma}\geq\nu_0\geq\nu_1\geq 1$ the environment $chain\acute{\sigma}\downarrow\nu_0\downarrow 1\downarrow 4$ should be an extension of $chain\acute{\sigma}\downarrow\nu_1\downarrow 1\downarrow 4$; moreover when a pair $\hat{\omega}$ satisfies $kent\hat{\omega}\hat{\pi}=true$ it should also satisfy

$w_0\hat{\omega}\hat{\pi}=\mathit{true}$ (where w_0 is a predicate to be explained below). Similar considerations apply to the input and output components of $\acute{\sigma}$ and $\grave{\sigma}$. However, for our present purposes the most interesting constraint in appendix 8 is that which prohibits an identifier from denoting a location which is already in use when the identifier is declared; for convenience we amalgamate this condition with a full statement of that at the end of the preceding paragraph by writing

$$\begin{aligned}
&\mathit{pure}=\lambda\hat{\rho}_0\hat{\rho}_1\acute{\upsilon}\acute{\sigma}.\bigwedge\{\bigwedge\{\bigwedge\{\bigwedge\{(\acute{\rho}_0[\![I_0]\!]\downarrow\nu_0=\acute{\rho}_1[\![I_1]\!]\downarrow\nu_1)\rightarrow(UW_0\grave{\rho}_0[\![I_0]\!]\downarrow\nu_0=UW_0\grave{\rho}_1[\![I_1]\!]\downarrow\nu_1),\\
&\qquad\qquad\qquad\qquad\sim(\grave{\rho}_0[\![I_0]\!]\downarrow\nu_0\mathrm{EL})\vee\sim(\grave{\rho}_0[\![I_0]\!]\downarrow\nu_0=\grave{\rho}_1[\![I_1]\!]\downarrow\nu_1)\\
&\qquad\qquad\qquad\qquad|\#\acute{\rho}_1[\![I_1]\!]\geq\nu_1\geq1\}\\
&\qquad\qquad\qquad\quad|I_1\}\\
&\qquad\qquad\qquad\wedge\bigwedge\{(\#(\mathit{chain}\acute{\upsilon}\downarrow\nu_2)\geq\acute{\rho}_0[\![I_0]\!]\downarrow\nu_0\downarrow1)\rightarrow\mathit{true},\\
&\qquad\qquad\qquad\quad\sim(\mathit{twist}\acute{\rho}_0\acute{\upsilon}[\![I_0]\!]\downarrow\nu_0\mathrm{EL})\vee\sim\mathit{known}(\mathit{twist}\acute{\rho}_0\acute{\upsilon}[\![I_0]\!]\downarrow\nu_0)(\nu_2+1)\acute{\upsilon}\acute{\sigma}\\
&\qquad\qquad\qquad\quad|\#\mathit{chain}\acute{\upsilon}\geq\nu_2\geq1\}\\
&\qquad\qquad\qquad|\#\acute{\rho}_0[\![I_0]\!]\geq\nu_0\geq1\}\\
&\qquad\qquad\quad|I_0\}.
\end{aligned}$$

At last we can let

$$\begin{aligned}
&p_0=\lambda\hat{\pi}.\mathit{neat}\langle\mathit{level}\acute{\upsilon},\grave{\rho}\rangle\wedge(\#\mathit{stick}\acute{\upsilon}=\#\grave{\upsilon})\wedge(\#\acute{\sigma}\downarrow2=\#\grave{\sigma}\downarrow2)\wedge(\#\acute{\sigma}\downarrow3=\#\grave{\sigma}\downarrow3)\\
&\qquad\wedge\mathit{pure}\langle\mathit{field}\acute{\upsilon},\grave{\rho}\rangle\langle\mathit{field}\acute{\upsilon},\grave{\rho}\rangle\acute{\upsilon}\acute{\sigma}\\
&\qquad\wedge\bigwedge\{\bigwedge\{\mathit{area}\acute{\alpha}_m\acute{\sigma}\wedge\mathit{area}\grave{\alpha}_m\grave{\sigma}\,|\,n\geq m\geq1\}\rightarrow\bigvee\{\hat{\alpha}_m=\hat{\alpha}_l\,|\,n\geq l>m\geq1\},\mathit{false}\,|\,n\geq2\}\\
&\qquad\wedge\bigwedge\{\bigwedge\{\mathit{kent}\hat{\omega}_0\hat{\pi}\wedge\mathit{kent}\hat{\omega}_1\hat{\pi}\wedge(\acute{\omega}_0\mathrm{EL})\wedge(\acute{\omega}_0=\acute{\omega}_1)\rightarrow W_0\grave{\omega}_0=W_0\grave{\omega}_1,\ \mathit{true}\,|\,\hat{\omega}_1\}\,|\,\hat{\omega}_0\}\\
&\qquad\wedge\bigwedge\{\bigwedge\{\mathit{kent}\hat{\omega}_0\hat{\pi}\wedge\mathit{kent}\hat{\omega}_1\hat{\pi}\wedge(\grave{\omega}_0\mathrm{EL})\wedge(\grave{\omega}_0=\grave{\omega}_1)\rightarrow W_0\acute{\omega}_0=W_0\acute{\omega}_1,\ \mathit{true}\,|\,\hat{\omega}_1\}\,|\,\hat{\omega}_0\}\\
&\qquad\wedge\bigwedge\{\mathit{found}(\acute{\sigma}\downarrow2\downarrow\nu)0\acute{\upsilon}\acute{\sigma}\,|\,\#\acute{\sigma}\downarrow2\geq\nu\geq1\}\\
&\qquad\wedge\bigwedge\{\mathit{found}(\acute{\sigma}\downarrow3\downarrow\nu)0\acute{\upsilon}\acute{\sigma}\wedge w_0\langle\acute{\sigma}\downarrow3\downarrow\nu,\grave{\sigma}\downarrow3\downarrow\nu\rangle\hat{\pi}\,|\,\#\acute{\sigma}\downarrow3\geq\nu\geq1\}\\
&\qquad\wedge\bigwedge\{\bigwedge\{(\lambda\rho.\rho=\mathit{revert}\rho(\mathit{field}\acute{\upsilon}))(\nu_0=\#\mathit{chain}\acute{\upsilon}+1\rightarrow\mathit{arid},\mathit{field}(\mathit{chain}\acute{\upsilon}\downarrow\nu_0))\\
&\qquad\qquad\wedge\mathit{known}(\acute{\upsilon}\downarrow(\#\acute{\upsilon}-\nu_1+1))\nu_0\acute{\upsilon}\acute{\sigma}\\
&\qquad\qquad|(\nu_0=1\rightarrow\#\acute{\upsilon},\#(\mathit{chain}\upsilon\downarrow(\nu_0-1))-1)\geq\nu_1\geq(\nu_0=\#\mathit{chain}\acute{\upsilon}+1\rightarrow1,\#(\mathit{chain}\acute{\upsilon}\downarrow\nu_0))\}\\
&\qquad\quad|\#\mathit{chain}\acute{\upsilon}+1\geq\nu_0\geq1\}.
\end{aligned}$$

In general $\mathit{field}\acute{\upsilon}$ does not mention all the stack positions containing denoted values which may be required, because the occurrence of *act*(*trim*⟦Δ_0⟧⟦Δ_1⟧) in the equations given for Δ_0 within Δ_1 obliterates from *field*ύ the entries recording those members of 𝔍⟦Δ_0⟧§ℋ⟦Δ_0⟧ which appear as free variables of abstractions set up in Δ_1. Thus even such a simple declaration as *x*==0 within *f*==fn*y*.*x* will embed in the value of *f* a reference to an identifier *x* which is unnoticed by *field*ύ. Consequently the condition *pure*⟨*field*ύ,ρ̀⟩⟨*field*ύ,ρ̀⟩ύσ́=*true* does not provide all the limitations on the stack positions containing denoted values; in addition it is essential that *pure*⟨ώ↓3,ὼ↓2⟩⟨*field*ύ,ρ̀⟩ύσ́=*true* whenever ώ∈F and ὼ∈F are such that *kent*ω̂π̂=*true*. This restriction is the least straightforward of those which constitute w_0, for when *b* checks on pairs of basic values in the manner described in 4.2.3,

w_0=λω̂π̂. ώ∈L∨ὼ∈L→(ώ∈L→*area*ώσ́,*true*)∧(ὼ∈L→*area*ὼσ̀,*false*),

ώ∈B∧ὼ∈B→*b*ω̂,

ώ∈E*∧ὼ∈E*→#ώ=#ὼ∧⋀{(ώ↓ν∈L∧ὼ↓ν∈L)∨~(ώ↓ν∈L∨ὼ↓ν∈L)|#ώ≥ν≥1},

ώ∈J∧ὼ∈J→*neat*⟨*level*(ύ†(#ύ-ώ↓2-1)),ὼ↓2⟩∧(#*stick*(ύ†(#ύ-ώ↓2-1))=#ὼ↓3)

∧(*revert*(ὼ↓2)(UW_0ρ̀)=UW_0(ὼ↓2))∧(YW_0ὺ†(#ὺ-ὼ↓3)=YW_0(ὼ↓3))

∧⋁{#(*chain*ύ↓ν)=ώ↓2+1|#*chain*ύ≥ν≥1},

ώ∈F∧ὼ∈F→*neat*⟨ώ↓3,ὼ↓2⟩∧*pure*⟨ώ↓3,ὼ↓2⟩⟨*field*ύ,ρ̀⟩ύσ́

∧⋁{#(*chain*ύ↓ν)=ώ↓2|#*chain*ύ≥ν≥1},

ώ∈J∧ὼ∈J→*neat*⟨*level*(ύ†(#ύ-ώ↓2)),ὼ↓2⟩∧(#*stick*(ύ†(#ύ-ώ↓2))=#ὼ↓3)

∧(*revert*(ὼ↓2)(UW_0ρ̀)=UW_0(ὼ↓2))∧(YW_0ὺ†(#ὺ-ὼ↓3)=YW_0(ὼ↓3))

∧⋁{#(*chain*ύ↓ν)=ώ↓2+1|#*chain*ύ≥ν≥1},

false.

When *m* is made to denote a label value in a program there is no point in trying to show that *a*⟨𝔊⟦𝔤⟦goto *m*⟧φ́⟧ρ́ζ́ύσ́,𝔊⟦𝔤⟦goto *m*⟧ψ̀⟧ζ̀ρ̀ὺσ̀⟩=*true* for suitable ρ̂, ῠ, σ̂, ζ̂ and φ̂ unless the knowledge that *p*π̂=*true* provides information about the label values in ύ and ρ̀ associated with *m*. Taking δ́ and δ̀ to be these values, w_0δ̂π̂ must be *true* so that ύ↓(#ύ-δ́↓2) can belong to

$(L \to T) \times N \times N \times U$ and so that $\mathfrak{G}\llbracket \mathfrak{g}\llbracket \mathbf{goto}\ m \rrbracket \acute{\psi} \rrbracket \acute{\rho}\acute{\zeta}\acute{\upsilon}\acute{\sigma}$ can be $(\acute{\delta}{\downarrow}1)(\acute{\upsilon}{\dagger}(\#\acute{\upsilon}-\acute{\delta}{\downarrow}2-1))(\mathit{restore}(\acute{\upsilon}{\downarrow}(\#\acute{\upsilon}-\acute{\delta}{\downarrow}2){\downarrow}1)\acute{\sigma})$; furthermore $\mathfrak{G}\llbracket \mathfrak{g}\llbracket \mathbf{goto}\ m \rrbracket \grave{\psi} \rrbracket \grave{\rho}\grave{\zeta}\grave{\upsilon}\grave{\sigma}$ is $(\grave{\delta}{\downarrow}1)(\grave{\delta}{\downarrow}2)(\grave{\delta}{\downarrow}3)\grave{\sigma}$. Demanding that $c\langle \acute{\delta}{\downarrow}1, \grave{\delta}{\downarrow}1 \rangle \hat{\pi} = \mathit{true}$ is therefore of no help in verifying that

$$a\langle \mathfrak{G}\llbracket \mathfrak{g}\llbracket \mathbf{goto}\ m \rrbracket \acute{\psi} \rrbracket \acute{\rho}\acute{\zeta}\acute{\upsilon}\acute{\sigma}, \mathfrak{G}\llbracket \mathfrak{g}\llbracket \mathbf{goto}\ m \rrbracket \grave{\psi} \rrbracket \grave{\zeta}\grave{\rho}\grave{\upsilon}\grave{\sigma} \rangle = \mathit{true};$$

instead it must be insisted that

$$c\langle \acute{\delta}{\downarrow}1, \grave{\delta}{\downarrow}1 \rangle \langle\langle \acute{\rho}, \acute{\upsilon}{\dagger}(\#\acute{\upsilon}-\acute{\delta}{\downarrow}2-1), \mathit{restore}(\acute{\upsilon}{\downarrow}(\#\acute{\upsilon}-\acute{\delta}{\downarrow}2){\downarrow}1)\acute{\sigma}\rangle, \langle \grave{\delta}{\downarrow}2, \grave{\delta}{\downarrow}3, \grave{\sigma}\rangle\rangle = \mathit{true}.$$

Because a **goto** sequencer can contain a general expression instead of m the condition imposed on $\acute{\delta}$ and $\grave{\delta}$ must actually be imposed on every pair of labels values reached by tracing through $\langle \acute{\upsilon}, \acute{\sigma} \rangle$ and $\langle \grave{\rho}, \grave{\upsilon}, \grave{\sigma} \rangle$, not just on those pairs which are connected with identifiers; this will be done with the aid of the predicate w mentioned in 5.2.3.

A similar situation arises with **res** sequencers which are, however, complicated further by the fact that they increase the height of the stack supplied. However, if $s\llbracket \mathbf{res}\ \mathrm{E} \rrbracket \acute{\rho}$ is *true* then $e\llbracket \mathrm{E} \rrbracket \acute{\rho}0$ is *true* and the expressed value E adjoined to the stack by evaluating E in the presence of $\langle \acute{\upsilon}, \acute{\sigma} \rangle$ must satisfy $\mathit{found}\acute{\varepsilon}0\acute{\upsilon}\acute{\sigma} = \mathit{true}$. Since our main concern is with programs subject to the constraints of appendix 8 we demand that if $\mathit{kent}\hat{\omega}\hat{\pi}$ and $p\hat{\pi}$ are *true* then

$$j\langle \acute{\omega}{\downarrow}1, \grave{\omega}{\downarrow}1 \rangle 0 \langle\langle \acute{\rho}, \acute{\upsilon}{\dagger}(\#\acute{\upsilon}-\acute{\omega}{\downarrow}2), \mathit{restore}(\acute{\upsilon}{\downarrow}(\#\acute{\upsilon}-\acute{\omega}{\downarrow}2){\downarrow}1)\acute{\sigma}\rangle, \langle \grave{\omega}{\downarrow}2, \grave{\omega}{\downarrow}3, \grave{\sigma}\rangle\rangle$$

must be *true* when $\acute{\omega}$ and $\grave{\omega}$ belong to the domains called J that are required by **res**. The remaining differences between the treatment of these domains and that of the domains for label values stem from the fact that, according to appendix 3, evaluating a **res** sequencer involves discarding from the stack the member of $(L \to T) \times N \times N \times U$ set up alongside the member of J.

Procedure values require a more intricate analysis than label values because they are supplied with return links (in the form of continuations) as well as expressed values when they arise in the semantic equations; moreover these return links have to be checked by the predicate j, not by c, because they await stacks holding the results of procedure applications. Thus if $\hat{\zeta}$ satisfies $j\hat{\zeta}\nu\Uparrow_0=true$ for some ν and $\Uparrow_0$ it is tempting to expect that for reasonable procedure values, $\acute{\omega}$ and $\grave{\omega}$, $j\langle\acute{\omega}\downarrow 1,(\grave{\omega}\downarrow 1)\grave{\zeta}\rangle(\#display\acute{\upsilon}_1)\Uparrow_1$ will be $true$ when $\acute{\rho}_1=\acute{\rho}_0$, $\acute{\upsilon}_1=\langle bulk(\acute{\omega}\downarrow 2)2(\acute{\omega}\downarrow 3)\acute{\upsilon}_0\acute{\sigma}_0\rangle\S\langle\acute{\zeta}\rangle\S\acute{\upsilon}_0$, $\acute{\sigma}_1=\acute{\sigma}_0$, $\grave{\rho}_1=divert\grave{\rho}_0(\grave{\omega}\downarrow 2)$, $\grave{\upsilon}_1=\grave{\upsilon}_0$ and $\grave{\delta}_1=\grave{\delta}_0$. This expectation will not be fulfilled, however, unless $((\nu=0)\rightarrow 0,display\acute{\upsilon}_0\downarrow\nu)\geq\acute{\omega}\downarrow 2$, since even the constraints of appendix 8 allow the result returned by a procedure application to be the value taken by a free variable of the procedure. In addition, if $\acute{\omega}$ is of the form $\mathcal{H}\llbracket\mathbf{f}\llbracket \mathrm{fn\,I..E}\rrbracket\acute{\psi}\rrbracket(rend\llbracket\mathbf{f}\llbracket \mathrm{fn\,I..E}\rrbracket\acute{\psi}\rrbracket\acute{\rho})\acute{\upsilon}$ for some I, E, $\acute{\psi}$, $\acute{\rho}$ and $\acute{\upsilon}$, then to turn an expressed value adjoined to $\acute{\upsilon}_1$ into the actual parameter of the procedure $\#display\acute{\upsilon}_1$ must be taken to be $lift(rend\llbracket\mathbf{f}\llbracket \mathrm{fn\,I..E}\rrbracket\acute{\psi}\rrbracket\acute{\rho})+1$; because $lift(rend\llbracket\mathbf{f}\llbracket \mathrm{fn\,I..E}\rrbracket\acute{\psi}\rrbracket\acute{\rho})$ does not occur explicitly in $\acute{\omega}$ we actually require that $\#display(\acute{\upsilon}_0\dagger(\#\acute{\upsilon}_0-\acute{\omega}\downarrow 2))$ coincide with $\#display(\acute{\upsilon}\dagger(\#\acute{\upsilon}-\acute{\omega}\downarrow 2))$ instead. If $\grave{\omega}$ is $\mathcal{F}\llbracket\mathbf{f}\llbracket \mathrm{fn\,I..E}\rrbracket\grave{\psi}\rrbracket(rend\llbracket\mathbf{f}\llbracket \mathrm{fn\,I..E}\rrbracket\grave{\psi}\rrbracket\grave{\rho})$ for some $\grave{\psi}$ and $\grave{\rho}$ then we must ensure that $apt\acute{\psi}\langle\acute{\upsilon}_1,\grave{\omega}\downarrow 2\rangle=true$, and this can best be done by recalling that $apt\acute{\psi}\langle\acute{\upsilon},\grave{\omega}\downarrow 2\rangle$ has to be $true$ and by restricting $\acute{\upsilon}_1$ so that no entry in $ravel(\acute{\omega}\downarrow 3)\acute{\upsilon}_1$ is a location unless it equals the corresponding entry in $ravel(\acute{\omega}\downarrow 3)\acute{\upsilon}$. For convenience these last two conditions on $\acute{\upsilon}_0$ are incorporated in $tally$, which is given by

$$
\begin{aligned}
tally=\lambda\acute{\upsilon}_0\acute{\upsilon}_1.(\lambda\acute{\upsilon}_2.\,&(\#chain\acute{\upsilon}_1=0)\rightarrow(YW_0\acute{\upsilon}_1=YW_0\acute{\upsilon}_2),\\
&(YW_0(chain\acute{\upsilon}_1\downarrow 1)\dagger 1=YW_0(chain\acute{\upsilon}_2\downarrow 1)\dagger 1)\\
&\wedge\bigwedge\{chain\acute{\upsilon}_1\downarrow 1\downarrow 1\downarrow\nu=chain\acute{\upsilon}_2\downarrow 1\downarrow 1\downarrow\nu\mid 2\geq\nu\geq 1\}\\
&\wedge\bigwedge\{(\acute{\upsilon}_1\downarrow\nu\mathrm{EL}\wedge\acute{\upsilon}_2\downarrow\nu\mathrm{EL})\vee\sim(\acute{\upsilon}_1\downarrow\nu\mathrm{EL}\vee\acute{\upsilon}_2\downarrow\nu\mathrm{EL})\mid\#\acute{\upsilon}_1-\#(chain\acute{\upsilon}_1\downarrow 1)\geq\nu\geq 1\}\\
&(\acute{\upsilon}_0\dagger(\#\acute{\upsilon}_0-\#\acute{\upsilon}_1)).
\end{aligned}
$$

Hence if $kent\hat{\omega}\Uparrow$ and $p\Uparrow$ are $true$ for certain $\acute{\omega}\mathrm{EF}$ and $\grave{\omega}\mathrm{EF}$ we can presume that when $\Uparrow_1$ is as above $j\langle\acute{\omega}\downarrow 1,(\grave{\omega}\downarrow 1)\grave{\zeta}\rangle(\#display\acute{\upsilon}_1)\Uparrow_1$ will be $true$ provided that $j\hat{\zeta}\nu\Uparrow_0=true$, $found\acute{\omega}\nu\acute{\upsilon}_0\acute{\sigma}_0=true$ and $tally\acute{\upsilon}_0(\acute{\upsilon}\dagger(\#\acute{\upsilon}-((\acute{\omega}\downarrow 2=0)\rightarrow 0,\acute{\upsilon}\downarrow(\#\acute{\upsilon}-\acute{\omega}\downarrow 2+1)\downarrow 3)))=true$ for some ν.

To sum up our remarks about label and procedure values we introduce a predicate w such that

$$
\begin{aligned}
&w=\lambda\hat{\omega}\hat{\pi}.\sim w_0\hat{\omega}\hat{\pi}\rightarrow \mathit{false},\\
&\qquad \acute{\omega}\,\mathsf{E}\,\mathsf{J}\wedge\grave{\omega}\,\mathsf{E}\,\mathsf{J}\rightarrow\bigwedge\{c\langle\acute{\omega}\downarrow 1,\grave{\omega}\downarrow 1\rangle\langle\langle\acute{\rho}_0,\acute{\upsilon}_0,\acute{\sigma}_0\rangle,\langle\grave{\omega}\downarrow 2,\grave{\omega}\downarrow 3,\grave{\sigma}\rangle\rangle\\
&\qquad\qquad\qquad |(\acute{\upsilon}_0\equiv\acute{\upsilon}\dagger(\#\acute{\upsilon}-\acute{\omega}\downarrow 2-1))\\
&\qquad\qquad\qquad \wedge(\acute{\sigma}_0\equiv \mathit{restore}(\acute{\upsilon}\downarrow(\#\acute{\upsilon}-\acute{\omega}\downarrow 2)\downarrow 1)\acute{\sigma})\},\\
&\qquad \acute{\omega}\,\mathsf{E}\,\mathsf{F}\wedge\grave{\omega}\,\mathsf{E}\,\mathsf{F}\rightarrow\bigwedge\{j\langle\acute{\omega}\downarrow 1,(\grave{\omega}\downarrow 1)\grave{\zeta}\rangle(\#\mathit{display}\acute{\upsilon}_1)\langle\langle\acute{\rho}_0,\acute{\upsilon}_1,\acute{\sigma}_0\rangle,\langle\grave{\rho}_1,\grave{\upsilon}_0,\grave{\sigma}_0\rangle\rangle\\
&\qquad\qquad\qquad |(\acute{\upsilon}_1\equiv\langle \mathit{bulk}(\acute{\omega}\downarrow 2)2(\acute{\omega}\downarrow 3)\acute{\upsilon}_0\acute{\sigma}_0\rangle\S\langle\acute{\zeta}\rangle\S\acute{\upsilon}_0)\\
&\qquad\qquad\qquad \wedge(\grave{\rho}_1\equiv \mathit{divert}\grave{\rho}_0(\grave{\omega}\downarrow 2))\wedge j\nu\hat{\zeta}\hat{\pi}_0\wedge \mathit{found}\acute{\omega}\nu\acute{\upsilon}_0\acute{\sigma}_0\\
&\qquad\qquad\qquad \wedge \mathit{tally}\acute{\upsilon}_0(\acute{\upsilon}\dagger(\#\acute{\upsilon}-((\acute{\omega}\downarrow 2=0)\rightarrow 0,\acute{\upsilon}\downarrow(\#\acute{\upsilon}-\acute{\omega}\downarrow 2+1)\downarrow 3)))\},\\
&\qquad \acute{\omega}\,\mathsf{E}\,\mathsf{J}\wedge\grave{\omega}\,\mathsf{E}\,\mathsf{J}\rightarrow\bigwedge\{j0\langle\acute{\omega}\downarrow 1,\grave{\omega}\downarrow 1\rangle\langle\langle\acute{\rho}_0,\acute{\upsilon}_0,\acute{\sigma}_0\rangle,\langle\grave{\omega}\downarrow 2,\grave{\omega}\downarrow 3,\grave{\sigma}\rangle\rangle\\
&\qquad\qquad\qquad |(\acute{\upsilon}_0\equiv\acute{\upsilon}\dagger(\#\acute{\upsilon}-\acute{\omega}\downarrow 2))\\
&\qquad\qquad\qquad \wedge(\acute{\sigma}_0\equiv \mathit{restore}(\acute{\upsilon}\downarrow(\#\acute{\upsilon}-\acute{\omega}\downarrow 2)\downarrow 1)\acute{\sigma})\},\\
&\qquad \mathit{true}.
\end{aligned}
$$

We now have to sketch the rather tortuous proof that w exists; a slightly different construction, which we have used elsewhere [52:2.4.6] for predicates resembling w, may well be preferred by some.

5.2.5. Predictors providing suitable properties.

The discussion of 5.2.4 indicates that, in order to deal properly with procedure and label values, the predicate w has to mention c, which refers to w through the definition of p. Consequently we are obliged to resort to the use of predictors to demonstrate that w exists. In fact the generality of expressions in Sal ensures that predictors would be needed even if no label or procedure value could be stored, because in stack semantics such a value includes a continuation but not the stack which is finally supplied as an argument and which acts as a repository for further label and procedure values.

For any pair $\hat{\pi}$ we shall regard x as a variable ranging over the predicates which map a universal domain into the domain T′ described in 2.2.2, and we shall define p by

$$p=\lambda x.\lambda\hat{\pi}.\bigwedge\{kent\hat{\omega}\hat{\pi}\rightarrow x\langle\langle\acute{\omega},\acute{\pi}\rangle,\langle\grave{\omega},\grave{\pi}\rangle\rangle,true\mid\hat{\omega}\}\wedge p_0\hat{\pi}$$

where p_0 is the predicate introduced in 5.2.4. On the premise that we have a suitable mapping a, we can also introduce c, which is given by

$$c=\lambda x.\lambda\langle\langle\acute{\zeta},\acute{\pi}\rangle,\langle\grave{\zeta},\grave{\pi}\rangle\rangle.\bigwedge\{ax\langle\acute{\zeta}\acute{\upsilon}_0\acute{\sigma}_0,\grave{\zeta}\grave{\rho}_0\grave{\upsilon}_0\grave{\sigma}_0\rangle\mid px\hat{\pi}_0\wedge match0\hat{\pi}_0\hat{\pi}\};$$

by the same token

$$j=\lambda\nu.\lambda x.\lambda\langle\langle\acute{\zeta},\acute{\pi}\rangle,\langle\grave{\zeta},\grave{\pi}\rangle\rangle.\bigwedge\{ax\langle\acute{\zeta}\acute{\upsilon}_0\acute{\sigma}_0,\grave{\zeta}\grave{\rho}_0\grave{\upsilon}_0\grave{\sigma}_0\rangle\mid px\hat{\pi}_0\wedge match1\hat{\pi}_0\hat{\pi}\wedge found(\acute{\upsilon}_0+1)\nu\acute{\upsilon}_0\acute{\sigma}_0\}.$$

The collection of mappings is completed by defining w thus:

$$
\begin{aligned}
\mathrm{w} = \lambda x.\lambda\langle\langle\acute{\omega},\acute{\pi}\rangle,\langle\grave{\omega},\grave{\pi}\rangle\rangle.{\sim}w_0\hat{\omega}\hat{\pi}\rightarrow & \mathit{false}, \\
& \acute{\omega}\mathrm{E}\mathrm{J}\wedge\grave{\omega}\mathrm{E}\mathrm{J}\rightarrow\bigwedge\{\mathrm{c}x\langle\langle\acute{\omega}\downarrow 1,\langle\acute{\rho}_0,\acute{\upsilon}_0,\acute{\sigma}_0\rangle\rangle,\langle\grave{\omega}\downarrow 1,\langle\grave{\omega}\downarrow 2,\grave{\omega}\downarrow 3,\grave{\sigma}\rangle\rangle\rangle \\
& \qquad |(\acute{\upsilon}_0\equiv\acute{\upsilon}\dagger(\#\acute{\upsilon}-\acute{\omega}\downarrow 2-1)) \\
& \qquad \wedge(\acute{\sigma}_0\equiv\mathit{restore}(\acute{\upsilon}\downarrow(\#\acute{\upsilon}-\acute{\omega}\downarrow 2)\downarrow 1)\acute{\sigma})\}, \\
& \acute{\omega}\mathrm{E}\mathrm{F}\wedge\grave{\omega}\mathrm{E}\mathrm{F}\rightarrow\bigwedge\{\mathrm{j}\nu_1 x\langle\langle\acute{\omega}\downarrow 1,\langle\acute{\rho}_0,\acute{\upsilon}_1,\acute{\sigma}_0\rangle\rangle,\langle(\grave{\omega}\downarrow 1)\grave{\zeta},\langle\grave{\rho}_1,\grave{\upsilon}_0,\grave{\sigma}_0\rangle\rangle\rangle \\
& \qquad |(\nu_1\equiv\#\mathit{display}\acute{\upsilon}_1) \\
& \qquad \wedge(\nu_2\equiv(\#\acute{\upsilon}-((\acute{\omega}\downarrow 2=0)\rightarrow 0,\acute{\upsilon}\downarrow(\#\acute{\upsilon}-\acute{\omega}\downarrow 2+1)\downarrow 3)) \\
& \qquad \wedge(\acute{\upsilon}_1\equiv\langle\mathit{bulk}(\acute{\omega}\downarrow 2)2(\acute{\omega}\downarrow 3)\acute{\upsilon}_0\acute{\sigma}_0\rangle\S\langle\acute{\zeta}\rangle\S\acute{\upsilon}_0) \\
& \qquad \wedge(\grave{\rho}_1\equiv\mathit{divert}\grave{\rho}_0(\grave{\omega}\downarrow 2))\wedge\mathrm{j}\nu x\langle\langle\acute{\zeta},\acute{\pi}_0\rangle,\langle\grave{\zeta},\grave{\pi}_0\rangle\rangle \\
& \qquad \wedge\mathit{found}\acute{\omega}\nu\acute{\upsilon}_0\acute{\sigma}_0\wedge\mathit{tally}\acute{\upsilon}_0(\acute{\upsilon}\dagger\nu_2)\}, \\
& \acute{\omega}\mathrm{E}\mathrm{J}\wedge\grave{\omega}\mathrm{E}\mathrm{J}\rightarrow\bigwedge\{j0x\langle\langle\acute{\omega}\downarrow 1,\langle\acute{\rho}_0,\acute{\upsilon}_0,\acute{\sigma}_0\rangle\rangle,\langle\grave{\omega}\downarrow 1,\langle\grave{\omega}\downarrow 2,\grave{\omega}\downarrow 3,\grave{\sigma}\rangle\rangle\rangle \\
& \qquad |(\acute{\upsilon}_0\equiv\acute{\upsilon}\dagger(\#\acute{\upsilon}-\acute{\omega}\downarrow 2)) \\
& \qquad \wedge(\acute{\sigma}_0\equiv\mathit{restore}(\acute{\upsilon}\downarrow(\#\acute{\upsilon}-\acute{\omega}\downarrow 2)\downarrow 1)\acute{\sigma})\}, \\
& \mathit{true}.
\end{aligned}
$$

In view of the use to which w will be put we should perhaps have written explicit mappings from W into J and F in the definition above, but doing so would have made it even less easy to read.

Now that our mapping takes two pairs of elements drawn from assorted domains, we need another operation for applying two functors at the same time in addition to that introduced in 2.5.4. Whenever X_0 and X_1 are functors we let
$X_0 \text{¤} X_1=\lambda X.X_0(\mathit{acute}(X))\times X_1(\mathit{acute}(X))$.

Once we have shown that there is an inclusive predicate x which equals $\mathrm{w}x$ we shall be able to define the predicates w, p, c, j and a referred to in 5.2.3 by setting $w=\lambda\hat{\omega}\hat{\pi}.x\langle\langle\acute{\omega},\acute{\pi}\rangle,\langle\grave{\omega},\grave{\pi}\rangle\rangle$, $p=\mathrm{p}x$, $c=\lambda\hat{\zeta}\hat{\pi}.\mathrm{c}x\langle\langle\acute{\zeta},\acute{\pi}\rangle,\langle\grave{\zeta},\grave{\pi}\rangle\rangle$, $j=\lambda\hat{\zeta}\nu\hat{\pi}.\mathrm{j}\nu x\langle\langle\acute{\zeta},\acute{\pi}\rangle,\langle\grave{\zeta},\grave{\pi}\rangle\rangle$ and $a=\mathrm{a}x$. We shall show how to prove that x exists by exhibiting two functors called W and two functors called P, together with a pair $\langle x_0,X_0\rangle$ and a set y, such that w is a predictor for $(\mathrm{W}\text{¤}\mathrm{P})\circledast(\mathrm{W}\text{¤}\mathrm{P})$ based on $\langle x_0,X_0\rangle$ and bounded by y; in the expression $(\mathrm{W}\text{¤}\mathrm{P})\circledast(\mathrm{W}\text{¤}\mathrm{P})$ each version of W is adjacent to the corresponding version of P. Naturally X_0 will be $(W_0\times\mathrm{P}W_0)\times(W_0\times\mathrm{P}W_0)$

where the two versions of W_0 are those which make their first appearance in 2.5.3 (and where each occurrence of $(W_0 \times PW_0)$ involves only one version of W_0); furthermore x_0 will be $\lambda\langle\langle\acute{\omega},\acute{\pi}\rangle,\langle\grave{\omega},\grave{\pi}\rangle\rangle.w_0\hat{\omega}\hat{\pi}$.

To construct a functor W suitable for use with the domains of appendix 3 we recall the definitions of V, E, D, S, Y, P and Z which were given in 4.1.5 and we try to provide similar functions appropriate to the present situation. In stack semantics $V=B+E^*+J+F$ and $E=L+B+E^*+J+F$ but $D=L+B+E^*+J+F$, so as $W=L+B+E^*+J+F+J+Z+((L\to T)\times N\times N\times U)$ we take X to be a typical retraction of the universal domain and define V, E and D thus:

$V=\lambda X.push\langle 4,-1\rangle \circ X \circ push\langle 3,1\rangle$;

$E=\lambda X.X\circ mask4$,

$D=\lambda X.X\circ mask5$.

Since $S=(L\to(V\times T))\times V^*\times V^*$ and $Y=W^*$ in stack semantics we introduce functors S and Y such that:

$S=\lambda X.(L\to(VX\times T))\times(VX)^*\times(VX)^*$;

$Y=\lambda X.X^*$.

The domain of environments defined in appendix 3 obviously consists of the set of fixed points of the retraction U which satisfies the equation $U=(Ide\to(N\times N)^*)\times N^*$. Consequently we can set

$P=\lambda X.U\times YX\times SX$.

The functor Z differs from its counterpart for store semantics, being given by the equation

$Z=\lambda X.YX\to SX\to AX$.

As we wish to define W in terms of these functors, in the case of stack semantics we shall demand that if $\acute{\omega}$ is a label value then $\lambda X.(WX\acute{\omega}|J)\downarrow 1=\lambda X.ZX((\acute{\omega}|J)\downarrow 1)$ and that if $\acute{\omega}$ is a procedure value then $\lambda X.(WX\acute{\omega}|F)\downarrow 1=\lambda X.ZX((\acute{\omega}|F)\downarrow 1)$. In addition we shall assume that $\lambda X.(WX\grave{\omega}|J)\downarrow 1=\lambda X.ZX((\grave{\omega}|J)\downarrow 1)$ when $\grave{\omega}$ is a label value appropriate to store semantics and that $\lambda X.(WX\grave{\omega}|F)\downarrow 1=\lambda X.OX((\grave{\omega}|F)\downarrow 1)$ when $\grave{\omega}$ is a procedure value appropriate to store semantics; the functors Z and O referred to here are those defined in 4.1.5, but the functor W has yet to be given fully.

We are already in a position to decide on the content of the set y mentioned above, since we now know how to extract all the domains for stack semantics and store semantics from the domains of witnessed values. Bearing in mind the nature of the retractions outlined in 4.1.5 we take y to consist of those X which are retractions such that $X=acute(X)\times grave(X)$, where $acute(X)=W\times \mathrm{P}W$ for some retraction W having $(\lambda\acute{\omega}.\acute{\omega})\circ W=W\circ(\lambda\acute{\omega}.\acute{\omega})$ and $mask4\circ W=W\circ mask4$ and where $grave(X)=W\times \mathrm{P}W$ for some retraction W having $(\lambda\grave{\omega}.\grave{\omega})\circ W=W\circ(\lambda\grave{\omega}.\grave{\omega})$, $mask4\circ W=W\circ mask4$, $mask5\circ W=W\circ mask5$, $W\circ flag6=W\circ flag6\circ reject\circ W\circ flag6$ and $W\circ flag7=W\circ flag7\circ reject\circ W\circ flag7$.

In order to establish that w is a predictor for $(\mathrm{W}\mathbin{¤}\mathrm{P})\circledast(\mathrm{W}\mathbin{¤}\mathrm{P})$ based on $\langle x_0,X_0\rangle$ and bounded by y we must confirm that $\langle \mathrm{w}x_2,((\mathrm{W}\mathbin{¤}\mathrm{P})\circledast(\mathrm{W}\mathbin{¤}\mathrm{P}))X_2\rangle \geq\langle \mathrm{w}x_1,((\mathrm{W}\mathbin{¤}\mathrm{P})\circledast(\mathrm{W}\mathbin{¤}\mathrm{P}))X_1\rangle$ whenever $\langle x_2,X_2\rangle\geq\langle x_1,X_1\rangle\geq\langle x_0,X_0\rangle$ and $X_n\in\mathrm{y}$ when $2\geq n\geq 0$. An examination of the definition of w reveals that confirming this involves verifying that $\langle \mathrm{c}x_2,((\mathrm{Z}\mathbin{¤}\mathrm{P})\circledast(\mathrm{Z}\mathbin{¤}\mathrm{P}))X_2\rangle\geq\langle \mathrm{c}x_1,((\mathrm{Z}\mathbin{¤}\mathrm{P})\circledast(\mathrm{Z}\mathbin{¤}\mathrm{P}))X_1\rangle$, where one version of Z is that introduced above and the other is that defined in 4.1.5. The proof of this in turn demands applications of the inequality $\langle \mathrm{p}x_2,((\lambda X.\mathrm{P}(acute(X)))\circledast(\lambda X.\mathrm{P}(acute(X))))X_2\rangle\geq\langle \mathrm{p}x_1,(\lambda X.\mathrm{P}(acute(X)))\circledast(\lambda X.\mathrm{P}(acute(X))))X_1\rangle$. Thus, writing W_1 for $acute(acute(\mathrm{X}_1))$ and for $acute(grave(X_1))$, when any pair $\hat{\pi}_2$ satisfies $\mathrm{p}x_2\hat{\pi}_2=true$ we must know that $\mathrm{p}x_1\hat{\pi}_1=true$ where $\hat{\pi}_1=(\mathrm{P}W_1\times\mathrm{P}W_1)\hat{\pi}_2$; in particular, for every $\hat{\omega}_1$, $kent\hat{\omega}_1\hat{\pi}_1$ must be proper and if $kent\hat{\omega}_1\hat{\pi}_1$ is $true$ then $x_1\langle\langle\acute{\omega}_1,\acute{\pi}_1\rangle,\langle\grave{\omega}_1,\grave{\pi}_1\rangle\rangle$ must be $true$. One way to ensure that this happens is to arrange that $kent\hat{\omega}_1\hat{\pi}_1$ is proper and that when $kent\hat{\omega}_1\hat{\pi}_1$ is $true$ there is some $\hat{\omega}_2$ for which $\hat{\omega}_1=(W_1\times W_1)\hat{\omega}_2$ and $kent\hat{\omega}_2\hat{\pi}_2$ is $true$; in this last situation $x_2\langle\langle\acute{\omega}_2,\acute{\pi}_2\rangle,\langle\grave{\omega}_2,\grave{\pi}_2\rangle\rangle=true$ so since $\langle x_2,X_2\rangle\geq\langle x_1,X_1\rangle$

$x_1\langle acute(X_1)\langle \acute{\omega}_2,\hat{\pi}_2\rangle, grave(X_1)\langle \grave{\omega}_2,\hat{\pi}_2\rangle\rangle = true$ and $x_1\langle\langle \acute{\omega}_1,\hat{\pi}_1\rangle,\langle \grave{\omega}_1,\hat{\pi}_1\rangle\rangle = true$.

From the definition of *kent* given in 5.2.2 it is clear that to put into effect the arrangements suggested in the preceding paragraph it helps to require that if $\hat{\omega}_3$ and $\hat{\pi}$ are such that $seen\nu_0\hat{\omega}_4\hat{\omega}_3\hat{\pi}$ is proper for all ν_0 and $\hat{\omega}_4$ then for every ν_1 and $\hat{\omega}_5$ there is some $\hat{\omega}_6$ for which $seen\nu_1\hat{\omega}_5((W_1\times W_1)\hat{\omega}_3)((PW_1\times PW_1)\hat{\pi}) = seen\nu_1\hat{\omega}_6\hat{\omega}_3\hat{\pi}$ where $\hat{\omega}_5=(W_1\times W_1)\hat{\omega}_6$ when $seen\nu_1\hat{\omega}_5((W_1\times W_1)\hat{\omega}_3)((PW_1\times PW_1)\hat{\pi}) = true$. We can verify by induction on ν_1 that this requirement is fulfilled so long as the version of W_1 appropriate to stack semantics satisfies the equation

$$W_1 = L+B+(\mathrm{E}W_1)^*+(((\lambda\chi.W_1\chi|\mathrm{J})\dagger 1)\times N)+(((\lambda\chi.W_1\chi|\mathrm{F})\dagger 1)\times N\times U)$$
$$+(((\lambda\chi.W_1\chi|\mathrm{J})\dagger 1)\times N)+(\lambda\chi.W_1\chi|\mathrm{Z})+(\lambda\chi.W_1\chi|((\mathrm{L}\to\mathrm{T})\times\mathrm{N}\times\mathrm{N}\times\mathrm{U}))$$

and the version of W_1 appropriate to store semantics satisfies the equation

$$W_1 = L+B+(\mathrm{E}W_1)^*+(((\lambda\chi.W_1\chi|\mathrm{J})\dagger 1)\times \mathrm{U}W_1\times \mathrm{Y}W_1)+(((\lambda\chi.W_1\chi|\mathrm{F})\dagger 1)\times \mathrm{U}W_1)$$
$$+(\lambda\chi.W_1\chi|\mathrm{G})+(((\lambda\chi.W_1\chi|\mathrm{J})\dagger 1)\times \mathrm{U}W_1\times \mathrm{Y}W_1)+(\lambda\chi.W_1\chi|\mathrm{P}).$$

We are, of course, particularly interested in what happens when $W_1\times W_1=(\mathrm{W}\circ\mathrm{W})(W_0\times W_0)$, since we wish to apply 2.5.3.

When read in conjunction with the definition of *match* given in 5.2.3, that part of the definition of w which concerns procedure values suggests that if $\acute{\omega}$ is a witnessed value for stack semantics chosen so that $\acute{\omega}\mathrm{EZ}$ then $W_0\acute{\omega}$ should not be anything other than $\acute{\omega}$; similarly if $\acute{\omega}\mathrm{E}((\mathrm{L}\to\mathrm{T})\times\mathrm{N}\times\mathrm{N}\times\mathrm{U})$ then $W_0\acute{\omega}$ should be $\acute{\omega}$. We have already made assumptions about the value of $\lambda X.\mathrm{W}X\acute{\omega}$ when $\acute{\omega}\mathrm{EJ}$ or $\acute{\omega}\mathrm{EF}$, so for stack semantics we let

$$\mathrm{W}=\lambda X.L+B+(\mathrm{E}(\mathrm{W}X))^*+(\mathrm{Z}X\times N)+(\mathrm{Z}X\times N\times U)+(\mathrm{Z}X\times N)+\mathrm{Z}(\lambda\acute{\omega}.\acute{\omega})+((L\to T)\times N\times N\times U),$$

and we set $Z_0=\lambda\chi.\mathrm{Z}(\lambda\acute{\omega}.\acute{\omega})\bot$ and

$$W_0=L+B+(\mathrm{E}W_0)^*+(Z_0\times N)+(Z_0\times N\times U)+(Z_0\times N)+\mathrm{Z}(\lambda\acute{\omega}.\acute{\omega})+((L\to T)\times N\times N\times U).$$

In the case of store semantics the only aspect of W which is not determined by the assumptions and arguments advanced so far is the value of $\lambda X.\mathrm{W}X\grave{\omega}$ when $\grave{\omega}\mathrm{EG}$ or $\grave{\omega}\mathrm{EP}$. As the function *seen* described in 5.2.2 does not concern itself with the summands G and P to any great extent we could take $\lambda X.\mathrm{W}X\grave{\omega}$ to be $\lambda X.\grave{\omega}$ when $\grave{\omega}\mathrm{EG}$ or $\grave{\omega}\mathrm{EP}$. However, there are tracing algorithms which are important in problems involving store semantics alone [52:2.4.6] and which do deal with G and P. For such algorithms $\lambda X.WX\tilde{\omega}|G$ has to be $\lambda X.(OX\times U(WX)\times S(WX))(\tilde{\omega}|G)$ and $\lambda X.WX\tilde{\omega}|P$ has to be $\lambda X.P(WX)(\tilde{\omega}|P)$, so in the present situation we shall use the same values. Hence we express the version of W appropriate to store semantics in terms of the functors defined in 4.1.5 by means of the equation

$$W=\lambda X.L+B+(E(WX))^*+(ZX\times U(WX)\times Y(WX))+(OX\times U(WX))$$
$$+(OX\times U(WX)\times S(WX))+(ZX\times U(WX)\times Y(WX))+P(WX);$$

in addition we write $Z_0=\lambda\chi.Z(\lambda\tilde{\omega}.\tilde{\omega})\bot$, $O_0=\lambda\chi.O(\lambda\tilde{\omega}.\tilde{\omega})\bot$ and
$W_0=L+B+(EW_0)^*+(Z_0\times UW_0\times YW_0)+(O_0\times UW_0)+(O_0\times UW_0\times SW_0)+(Z_0\times UW_0\times YW_0)+PW_0.$

It may not be immediately apparent that these functors called W exist, so here we shall indicate how to prove this in the case of the second of them; the proof required by the first follows the same pattern. Those X which are retractions such that $(W_0\times PW_0)\times(X\times PX)\in y$ are the elements of a set z which is closed under the formation of least upper bounds of directed subsets. If we write temporarily

$$fun=\lambda X.\lambda X.L+B+(E(XX))^*+(ZX\times U(XX)\times Y(XX))+(OX\times U(XX))$$
$$+(OX\times U(XX)\times S(XX))+(ZX\times U(XX)\times Y(XX))+P(XX),$$

then when X is a continuous function mapping z into z so is fun(X), provided that the functor for the answer domain, A, maps z into the complete lattice of retractions of the universal domain. Indeed, since we stipulated in 4.1.5 that A must be continuous, fun is continuous and we can take W to be $fix(fun)$. The mode of construction of W ensures that if X is a retraction in z then so is WX. Moreover two extremely straightforward applications of the properties of fix given in 2.3.2 demonstrate that $fix(W)=fix(fun(\lambda X.X))$, so, as we postulated in 4.1.5 that $\lambda\tilde{\omega}.\tilde{\omega}=fix(fun(\lambda X.X))$, we can assert that $\lambda\tilde{\omega}.\tilde{\omega}=fix(W)$.

Similarly in the case of stack semantics we suppose that A is such that if X is a retraction of the universal domain for which

$(X\times PX)\times(W_0\times PW_0)\in y$ then AX is also a retraction and that if ν is any directed set of such retractions then $A(\bigsqcup\nu)=\bigsqcup\{AX\mid X\in\nu\}$. Under these circumstances we can readily show not only that the version of W appropriate to stack semantics exists but also that $\lambda\acute{\omega}.\acute{\omega}=fix(W)$ provided that we postulate that $\lambda\acute{\omega}.\acute{\omega}=fix(X)$, where $X=\lambda X.L+B+(EX)^*+(ZX\times N)+(ZX\times N\times U)+(ZX\times N)+(ZX\times N\times U)+ZX+((L\to T)\times N\times N\times U)$.

We can now demonstrate that p is a predictor for $(\lambda X.P(acute(X)))\circledast(\lambda X.P(acute(X)))$ based on $\langle x_0,X_0\rangle$ and bounded by y. Consequently, if we assume that a is a predictor for $(\lambda X.A(acute(X)))\circledast(\lambda X.A(acute(X)))$ based on $\langle x_0,X_0\rangle$ and bounded by y, then the fact that $match=\lambda\nu\hat{\pi}_0\hat{\pi}_1.match\nu((PW_0\times PW_0)\hat{\pi}_0)((PW_0\times PW_0)\hat{\pi}_1)$ allows us to infer that for every ν c and $j\nu$ are both predictors for $(Z\boxtimes P)\circledast(Z\boxtimes P)$ which are based on $\langle x_0,X_0\rangle$ and bounded by y. From this we can even deduce that w is a predictor for $(W\boxtimes P)\circledast(W\boxtimes P)$ based on $\langle x_0,X_0\rangle$ and bounded by y.

If we suppose that $\lambda x.\lambda\chi.ax\langle A(\lambda\acute{\omega}.\acute{\omega})\bot,A(\lambda\grave{\omega}.\grave{\omega})\bot\rangle=\lambda x.\lambda\chi.true$ we can prove that for every ν $\lambda x.\lambda\chi.cx((Z_0\times Z_0)\chi)=\lambda x.\lambda\chi.true$ and $\lambda x.\lambda\chi.jx\nu((Z_0\times Z_0)\chi)=\lambda x.\lambda\chi.true$; thus if $A(\lambda\acute{\omega}.\acute{\omega})\bot=AW_0\bot$ and $A(\lambda\grave{\omega}.\grave{\omega})\bot=AW_0\bot$ $\langle wx_0,((W\boxtimes P)\circledast(W\boxtimes P))X_0\rangle\geq\langle x_0,X_0\rangle$, since $x_0=\lambda\langle\langle\acute{\omega},\acute{\pi}\rangle,\langle\grave{\omega},\grave{\pi}\rangle\rangle.w_0\hat{\omega}\hat{\pi}$ and $X_0=(W_0\times PW_0)\times(W_0\times PW_0)$. As $X_0\in y$ and $((W\circledast P)\boxtimes(W\circledast P))X_0\in y$, it follows from 2.5.3 that there is a unique inclusive predicate x such that $x=wx\circ X$ and $\langle x,X\rangle\geq\langle x_0,X_0\rangle$ where $X=\bigsqcup\{((W\circledast P)\boxtimes(W\circledast P))^nX_0\mid n\geq 0\}$. The remarks in 2.5.4 indicate that $X=\bigsqcup\{(W\circledast P)^n(W_0\times PW_0)\mid n\geq 0\}\times\bigsqcup\{(W\circledast P)^n(W_0\times PW_0)\mid n\geq 0\}$, so in fact $X=(\bigsqcup\{W^nW_0\mid n\geq 0\}\times P(\bigsqcup\{W^nW_0\mid n\geq 0\}))\times(\bigsqcup\{W^nW_0\mid n\geq 0\}\times P(\bigsqcup\{W^nW_0\mid n\geq 0\}))$. Because $\lambda\acute{\omega}.\acute{\omega}\sqsupseteq W_0$ and $\lambda\acute{\omega}.\acute{\omega}=fix(W)$ in stack semantics whereas $\lambda\grave{\omega}.\grave{\omega}\sqsupseteq W_0$ and $\lambda\grave{\omega}.\grave{\omega}=fix(W)$ in store semantics we may now assert that $X=((\lambda\acute{\omega}.\acute{\omega})\times P(\lambda\acute{\omega}.\acute{\omega}))\times((\lambda\grave{\omega}.\grave{\omega})\times P(\lambda\grave{\omega}.\grave{\omega}))$; hence $x=wx$ and we can define w, p, c, j and a in terms of x in the manner described above.

Next we shall use the predicates that we have just formed.

5.2.6. The syntactic counterparts of these properties.

As was intimated in 5.2.3, we are interested in proving that $c\langle \mathcal{E}[\![\mathbf{e}[\![\mathrm{E}]\!]\phi]\!]\acute{\rho}\acute{\zeta},\mathcal{E}[\![\mathbf{e}[\![\mathrm{E}]\!]\psi]\!]\grave{\zeta}\rangle\hat{\pi}$ is *true* only when E, ϕ, $\acute{\rho}$, $\acute{\sigma}$, $\hat{\sigma}$ and $\hat{\zeta}$ satisfy certain conditions. Thus we can assume that there is some ν such that $e[\![\mathrm{E}]\!]\acute{\rho}\nu=\mathit{true}$, $\mathit{rend}[\![\mathrm{E}]\!](\mathit{twist}\acute{\rho}\acute{\sigma})=\mathit{rend}[\![\mathrm{E}]\!](\mathit{field}\acute{\sigma})$, $\mathit{apt}\phi\langle\acute{\sigma},\mathit{rend}[\![\mathrm{E}]\!]\grave{\rho}\rangle=\mathit{true}$, $\#\mathit{display}\acute{\sigma}=\mathit{lift}\acute{\rho}$ and $j\hat{\zeta}\nu\hat{\pi}=\mathit{true}$; the knowledge that $\mathit{rent}[\![\mathrm{E}]\!]\acute{\rho}=\mathit{true}$, which was required in 4.2.5, is here provided by the assumption that $e[\![\mathrm{E}]\!]\acute{\rho}\nu=\mathit{true}$. However, according to the equation governing c, $c\langle \mathcal{E}[\![\mathbf{e}[\![\mathrm{E}]\!]\phi]\!]\acute{\rho}\acute{\zeta},\mathcal{E}[\![\mathbf{e}[\![\mathrm{E}]\!]\psi]\!]\grave{\zeta}\rangle\hat{\pi}$ is trivially equal to *true* when there is no $\hat{\pi}_0$ such that $p\hat{\pi}_0$ and $\mathit{match}0\hat{\pi}_0\hat{\pi}$ are *true*; to avoid considering this situation we therefore take $p\hat{\pi}$ to be *true*. Remarks similar to these apply to $\mathcal{L}$ and $\mathcal{R}$, so for convenience we define three predicates on expressions by setting:

$$E=\lambda\mathrm{E}.\bigwedge\{c\langle \mathcal{E}[\![\mathbf{e}[\![\mathrm{E}]\!]\phi]\!]\acute{\rho}\acute{\zeta},\mathcal{E}[\![\mathbf{e}[\![\mathrm{E}]\!]\psi]\!]\grave{\zeta}\rangle\hat{\pi}$$
$$\mid e[\![\mathrm{E}]\!]\acute{\rho}\nu\wedge(\mathit{rend}[\![\mathrm{E}]\!](\mathit{twist}\acute{\rho}\acute{\sigma})=\mathit{rend}[\![\mathrm{E}]\!](\mathit{field}\acute{\sigma}))\wedge\mathit{apt}\phi\langle\acute{\sigma},\mathit{rend}[\![\mathrm{E}]\!]\grave{\rho}\rangle$$
$$\wedge(\#\mathit{display}\acute{\sigma}\geq\mathit{lift}\acute{\rho})\wedge p\hat{\pi}\wedge j\hat{\zeta}\nu\hat{\pi}\};$$

$$L=\lambda\mathrm{E}.\bigwedge\{c\langle \mathcal{L}[\![\mathbf{l}[\![\mathrm{E}]\!]\phi]\!]\acute{\rho}\acute{\zeta},\mathcal{L}[\![\mathbf{l}[\![\mathrm{E}]\!]\psi]\!]\grave{\zeta}\rangle\hat{\pi}$$
$$\mid l[\![\mathrm{E}]\!]\acute{\rho}\nu\wedge(\mathit{rend}[\![\mathrm{E}]\!](\mathit{twist}\acute{\rho}\acute{\sigma})=\mathit{rend}[\![\mathrm{E}]\!](\mathit{field}\acute{\sigma}))\wedge\mathit{apt}\phi\langle\acute{\sigma},\mathit{rend}[\![\mathrm{E}]\!]\grave{\rho}\rangle$$
$$\wedge(\#\mathit{display}\acute{\sigma}\geq\mathit{lift}\acute{\rho})\wedge p\hat{\pi}\wedge j\hat{\zeta}\nu\hat{\pi}\};$$

$$R=\lambda\mathrm{E}.\bigwedge\{c\langle \mathcal{R}[\![\mathbf{r}[\![\mathrm{E}]\!]\phi]\!]\acute{\rho}\acute{\zeta},\mathcal{R}[\![\mathbf{r}[\![\mathrm{E}]\!]\psi]\!]\grave{\zeta}\rangle\hat{\pi}$$
$$\mid r[\![\mathrm{E}]\!]\acute{\rho}\nu\wedge(\mathit{rend}[\![\mathrm{E}]\!](\mathit{twist}\acute{\rho}\acute{\sigma})=\mathit{rend}[\![\mathrm{E}]\!](\mathit{field}\acute{\sigma}))\wedge\mathit{apt}\phi\langle\acute{\sigma},\mathit{rend}[\![\mathrm{E}]\!]\grave{\rho}\rangle$$
$$\wedge(\#\mathit{display}\acute{\sigma}\geq\mathit{lift}\acute{\rho})\wedge p\hat{\pi}\wedge j\hat{\zeta}\nu\hat{\pi}\}.$$

Following the practice of 4.2.5, we do not bother to use variants of j specially suited to $\mathcal{L}$ and $\mathcal{R}$ in order to indicate that applying $\mathcal{L}$ adjoins a location to the stack whereas applying $\mathcal{R}$ adjoins a stored value.

The other valuations appearing in the equations for $\mathcal{E}$ also correspond with predicates. To handle $\mathcal{F}$, for instance, we let

$F=\lambda\Phi.\bigwedge\{w\hat{\varepsilon}\hat{\pi}\wedge found\,\acute{\varepsilon}(lift(rend[\![\Phi]\!]\acute{\rho}))\acute{\upsilon}\acute{\sigma}$

$\quad|f[\![\Phi]\!]\acute{\rho}\wedge(rend[\![\Phi]\!](twist\,\acute{\rho}\acute{\upsilon})=rend[\![\Phi]\!](field\,\acute{\upsilon}))\wedge apt\,\acute{\psi}\langle\acute{\upsilon},rend[\![\Phi]\!]\grave{\rho}\rangle$

$\quad\wedge(\#display\,\acute{\upsilon}\geq lift\,\acute{\rho})\wedge p\hat{\pi}$

$\quad\wedge(\hat{\varepsilon}\equiv\langle\mathfrak{F}[\![\mathfrak{f}[\![\Phi]\!]\acute{\psi}]\!](rend[\![\mathfrak{f}[\![\Phi]\!]\acute{\psi}]\!]\acute{\rho})\acute{\upsilon},\mathfrak{F}[\![\mathfrak{f}[\![\Phi]\!]\grave{\psi}]\!](rend[\![\mathfrak{f}[\![\Phi]\!]\grave{\psi}]\!]\grave{\rho})\rangle\}.$

Generally $rend[\![\mathfrak{f}[\![\Phi]\!]\acute{\psi}]\!]$ and $rend[\![\mathfrak{f}[\![\Phi]\!]\grave{\psi}]\!]$ coincide with $rend[\![\Phi]\!]$.

To deal with $\mathfrak{S}$ we introduce

$S=\lambda\Sigma.\bigwedge\{c\langle\mathfrak{S}[\![\mathfrak{s}[\![\Sigma]\!]\acute{\psi}]\!]\acute{\rho},\mathfrak{S}[\![\mathfrak{s}[\![\Sigma]\!]\grave{\psi}]\!]\rangle\hat{\pi}$

$\quad|s[\![\Sigma]\!]\acute{\rho}\wedge(rend[\![\Sigma]\!](twist\,\acute{\rho}\acute{\upsilon})=rend[\![\Sigma]\!](field\,\acute{\upsilon}))\wedge apt\,\acute{\psi}\langle\acute{\upsilon},rend[\![\Sigma]\!]\grave{\rho}\rangle$

$\quad\wedge(\#display\,\acute{\upsilon}\geq lift\,\acute{\rho})\wedge p\hat{\pi}\}.$

For any Σ if $S[\![\Sigma]\!]=true$ then plainly $E[\![\Sigma]\!]=true$.

In order to verify that $c\langle\mathfrak{D}[\![\mathfrak{d}[\![\Delta]\!]\acute{\psi}]\!]\acute{\rho}\nu_0\nu_1\acute{\zeta},\mathfrak{D}[\![\mathfrak{d}[\![\Delta]\!]\grave{\psi}]\!]\grave{\zeta}\rangle\hat{\pi}$ is *true* we use conditions which are more complex than those provided in the definition of E; these conditions account for the parameters ν_0 and ν_1 and make allowances for the intricate way in which declarations affect the size of the stack. Thus besides insisting that $d[\![\Delta]\!]\acute{\rho}\nu_0=true$, $rend[\![\Delta]\!](twist\,\acute{\rho}\acute{\upsilon})=rend[\![\Delta]\!](field\,\acute{\upsilon})$, $apt\,\acute{\psi}\langle\acute{\upsilon},rend[\![\Delta]\!]\grave{\rho}\rangle=true$, $\#display\,\acute{\upsilon}\geq lift\,\acute{\rho}$ and $p\hat{\pi}=true$ we must recall that, according to the discussion in 5.1.6, in practice $lift\,\rho+1\geq\nu_0+1\geq lift\,\acute{\rho}$, $\#display\,\acute{\upsilon}=\nu_0+1$ and $\#\acute{\upsilon}=\nu_1+display\,\upsilon\downarrow(\nu_0+1)=\acute{\upsilon}\downarrow(\#\acute{\upsilon}-display\,\acute{\upsilon}\downarrow(\nu_0+1)+1)\downarrow 3$. When $c\langle\mathfrak{T}[\![\mathfrak{t}[\![\Delta]\!]\acute{\psi}]\!]\acute{\rho}\nu_0\nu_1\acute{\zeta},\mathfrak{T}[\![\mathfrak{t}[\![\Delta]\!]\grave{\psi}]\!]\grave{\zeta}\rangle\hat{\pi}$ is being considered similar conditions are valid, but we also know that if I is an element of $\mathfrak{I}[\![\Delta]\!]\S\mathfrak{K}[\![\Delta]\!]$ then $\acute{\rho}[\![I]\!]\downarrow1\downarrow1=\nu_0+1$; moreover because recursive declarations by incidence have a form in stack semantics which is not always equivalent with their form in store semantics, $\mathfrak{K}[\![\mathfrak{t}[\![\Delta]\!]\grave{\psi}]\!]$ must be $\langle\rangle$. We can summarize these conditions by introducing a function *fine* such that in $fine[\![\Delta]\!]\nu_0\nu_1\nu_2\acute{\psi}\hat{\pi}$ taking ν_2 to be 0 or 1 corresponds with supplying Δ as an argument to $\mathfrak{D}$ or $\mathfrak{T}$. Hence:

$$fine=\lambda\Delta\nu_0\nu_1\nu_2\hat{\psi}\hat{\pi}.(\lambda\phi.\phi(twist\hat{\rho}_0\acute{\upsilon}_0)=\phi(field\acute{\upsilon}_0))(\nu_2=0\rightarrow rend[\![\Delta]\!],tear[\![\Delta]\!])$$
$$\wedge apt\hat{\psi}\langle\acute{\upsilon},(\nu_2=0\rightarrow rend[\![\Delta]\!]\hat{\rho},tear[\![\Delta]\!]\hat{\rho})\rangle$$
$$\wedge(\nu_0+1\geq lift\hat{\rho}\geq\nu_0)$$
$$\wedge(\#display\acute{\upsilon}=\nu_0+1)$$
$$\wedge(\#\acute{\upsilon}=\nu_1+display\acute{\upsilon}\downarrow(\nu_0+1)=\acute{\upsilon}\downarrow(\#\acute{\upsilon}+display\acute{\upsilon}\downarrow(\nu_0+1)+1)\downarrow 3)$$
$$\wedge\bigwedge\{(\nu_2=0)\vee\sim(I\in\mathcal{I}[\![\Delta]\!]\S\mathcal{K}[\![\Delta]\!])\rightarrow true,$$
$$(\hat{\rho}[\![I]\!]\downarrow 1\downarrow 1=\nu_0+1)\wedge((I\in\mathcal{K}[\![\Delta]\!])\rightarrow\hat{\psi}[\![I]\!]\downarrow 1,\sim(\hat{\psi}[\![I]\!]\downarrow 1\vee\hat{\psi}[\![I]\!]\downarrow 1))$$
$$|\top\sqsupseteq I\sqsupseteq\bot\}.$$

Evaluating an expression in the presence of states $\hat{\pi}_1$ and $\tilde{\pi}_1$ produces states $\hat{\pi}_0$ and $\tilde{\pi}_0$ such that $match1\hat{\pi}_0\hat{\pi}_1$ and $found(\acute{\upsilon}_1\downarrow 1)\nu\acute{\upsilon}_1\acute{\sigma}_1$ are *true* for some ν. When $\hat{\pi}_0$ is obtained by evaluating a declaration Δ, however, the relation between it and $\hat{\pi}_1$ depends on Δ and on whether $\mathcal{D}$ or $\mathcal{T}$ is the valuation chosen. Thus applying $\mathcal{D}$ ensures that $\#\acute{\upsilon}_0=\#\acute{\upsilon}_1+\mathcal{Y}[\![\Delta]\!]$ and that $field\acute{\upsilon}_0=divert(field\acute{\upsilon}_1)(twist(\mathcal{Z}[\![\mathcal{d}[\![\Delta]\!]\hat{\psi}]\!](arid)\nu_0\nu_1)\acute{\upsilon}_0)$ for suitable ν_0, ν_1 and ψ, whereas applying $\mathcal{T}$ ensures that $\#\acute{\upsilon}_0=\#\acute{\upsilon}_1+\mathcal{Y}[\![\Delta]\!]-\#\mathcal{I}[\![\Delta]\!]-\#\mathcal{K}[\![\Delta]\!]$ and that $field\acute{\upsilon}_0=divert(field\acute{\upsilon}_1)(slim[\![\Delta]\!](field\acute{\upsilon}_1))$. Both valuations are such that for any ν having $\#\acute{\upsilon}_1\geq\nu\geq 1$ the entity $\acute{\upsilon}_0\downarrow(\#\acute{\upsilon}_0-\#\acute{\upsilon}_1+\nu)$ can be a location if and only if $\acute{\upsilon}_1\downarrow\nu$ is a location, although the occurrence of *change* in the equations of appendix 3 means that $\acute{\upsilon}_0\downarrow(\#\acute{\upsilon}_0-\#\acute{\upsilon}_1+\nu)$ may not be identical with $\acute{\upsilon}_1\downarrow\nu$ when $\#\acute{\upsilon}_0-\#(chain\acute{\upsilon}_0\downarrow 1)\geq\nu\geq 1$. Equally obvious connections exist between $\acute{\sigma}_0$ and $\acute{\sigma}_1$, between $\hat{\rho}_0$ and $\hat{\rho}_1$ and between $\hat{\upsilon}_0$ and $\hat{\upsilon}_1$; we can combine them in a function *spun* which satisfies

$$spun=\lambda\Delta\nu_0\nu_1\nu_2\hat{\Phi}\hat{\pi}_0\hat{\pi}_1.(\lambda\acute{\psi}_0.(\lambda\grave{\psi}_0.(\lambda\nu.fine[\![\Delta]\!]\nu_0\nu\nu_2\hat{\Phi}_0\hat{\pi}_0)$$
$$(\nu_2=0\to\nu_1+\mathfrak{Y}[\![\Delta]\!],\nu_1+\mathfrak{Y}[\![\Delta]\!]-\#\mathfrak{J}[\![\Delta]\!]-\#\mathfrak{H}[\![\Delta]\!]))$$
$$(\nu_2=0\to\grave{\psi}[use(\#\mathfrak{J}[\![\Delta]\!])/\mathfrak{J}[\![\Delta]\!]][opts(\mathfrak{H}[\![\Delta]\!])\grave{\psi}/\mathfrak{H}[\![\Delta]\!]],\grave{\psi}))$$
$$(\nu_2=0\to\acute{\psi}[use(\#\mathfrak{J}[\![\Delta]\!])/\mathfrak{J}[\![\Delta]\!]][opts(\mathfrak{H}[\![\Delta]\!])\acute{\psi}/\mathfrak{H}[\![\Delta]\!]],\acute{\psi}))$$
$$\wedge(\acute{\rho}_0=(\nu_2=0\to\mathcal{Z}[\![\mathfrak{d}[\![\Delta]\!]\acute{\psi}]\!]\acute{\rho}_1\nu_0\nu_1,\acute{\rho}_1))$$
$$\wedge(field\acute{\upsilon}_0=divert(field\acute{\upsilon}_1)(slim[\![\Delta]\!](twist\acute{\rho}_0\acute{\upsilon}_0)))$$
$$\wedge tally\acute{\upsilon}_0\acute{\upsilon}_1$$
$$\wedge\bigwedge\{area\alpha\acute{\sigma}_0\vee\sim area\alpha\acute{\sigma}_1\mid\top\sqsupseteq\alpha\sqsupseteq\bot\}$$
$$\wedge(UW_0\grave{\rho}_0=UW_0(divert\grave{\rho}_1(slim[\![\Delta]\!](\nu_2=0\to\grave{\rho}_0,\grave{\rho}_1))))$$
$$\wedge(YW_0\grave{\upsilon}_0=YW_0\grave{\upsilon}_1).$$

In contrast to all our other predicates *fine* and *spun* really do depend on the members of $(\mathrm{Ide}\to(\mathrm{N}\times\mathrm{N})^*)\times\mathrm{N}^*$ which form components of their arguments.

When $fine[\![\Delta]\!]\nu_0\nu_1\nu_2\hat{\Phi}\hat{\pi}_1$ and $p\hat{\pi}_0$ are *true* there is at least one $\hat{\pi}_0$ for which $spun[\![\Delta]\!]\nu_0\nu_1\nu_2\hat{\Phi}\hat{\pi}_0\hat{\pi}_1$ and $p\hat{\pi}_1$ are *true*, so the condition $\bigwedge\{c\hat{\zeta}\hat{\pi}_0\mid spun[\![\Delta]\!]\nu_0\nu_1\nu_2\hat{\Phi}\hat{\pi}_0\hat{\pi}_1\wedge p\hat{\pi}_0\}=true$ is not satisfied vacuously. Consequently in the predicates for $\mathfrak{D}$ and $\mathfrak{T}$ this condition can play the role played by $j\hat{\zeta}\nu\hat{\pi}=true$ in the predicate for $\mathfrak{E}$, and we can usefully define:

$$D=\lambda\Delta.\bigwedge\{c\langle\mathfrak{D}[\![\mathfrak{d}[\![\Delta]\!]\acute{\psi}]\!]\acute{\rho}\nu_0\nu_1\acute{\zeta},\mathfrak{D}[\![\mathfrak{d}[\![\Delta]\!]\grave{\psi}]\!]\grave{\zeta}\rangle\hat{\pi}$$
$$\mid d[\![\Delta]\!]\acute{\rho}\nu_0\wedge fine[\![\Delta]\!]\nu_0\nu_1 0\hat{\Phi}\hat{\pi}\wedge p\hat{\pi}\wedge\bigwedge\{c\hat{\zeta}\hat{\pi}_0\mid spun[\![\Delta]\!]\nu_0\nu_1 0\hat{\Phi}\hat{\pi}_0\hat{\pi}\wedge p\hat{\pi}_0\}\};$$
$$T=\lambda\Delta.\bigwedge\{c\langle\mathfrak{T}[\![\mathfrak{t}[\![\Delta]\!]\acute{\psi}]\!]\acute{\rho}\nu_0\nu_1\acute{\zeta},\mathfrak{T}[\![\mathfrak{t}[\![\Delta]\!]\grave{\psi}]\!]\grave{\zeta}\rangle\hat{\pi}$$
$$\mid t[\![\Delta]\!]\acute{\rho}\nu_0\wedge fine[\![\Delta]\!]\nu_0\nu_1 1\hat{\Phi}\hat{\pi}\wedge p\hat{\pi}\wedge\bigwedge\{c\hat{\zeta}\hat{\pi}_0\mid spun[\![\Delta]\!]\nu_0\nu_1 1\hat{\Phi}\hat{\pi}_0\hat{\pi}\wedge p\hat{\pi}_0\}\}.$$

The predicate appropriate to $\mathfrak{G}$ differs from that for $\mathfrak{E}$ only because, by contrast with an expression, a block does not increase the height of the stack. Thus for certain $\hat{\pi}$ and $\hat{\zeta}$ we substitute the requirement that $g[\![\Theta]\!]\acute{\rho}$ and $c\hat{\zeta}\hat{\pi}$ be *true* for the requirement that $e[\![\mathrm{E}]\!]\acute{\rho}\nu$ and $j\hat{\zeta}\nu\hat{\pi}$ be *true*, and we set

$$G=\lambda\Theta.\bigwedge\{c\langle\mathfrak{G}[\![\mathfrak{g}[\![\Theta]\!]\phi]\!]\acute{\rho}\acute{\zeta},\mathfrak{G}[\![\mathfrak{g}[\![\Theta]\!]\psi]\!]\grave{\zeta}\rangle\hat{\pi}$$

$$|g[\![\Theta]\!]\acute{\rho}\wedge(rend[\![\Theta]\!](twist\acute{\rho}\acute{\upsilon})=rend[\![\Theta]\!](field\acute{\upsilon}))\wedge apt\Phi\langle\acute{\upsilon},rend[\![\Theta]\!]\grave{\rho}\rangle$$

$$\wedge(\#display\acute{\upsilon}\geq lift\acute{\rho})\wedge p\hat{\pi}\wedge c\hat{\zeta}\hat{\pi}\}.$$

From the definition of G immediately above we could obtain a predicate appropriate to $\mathfrak{C}$ simply by replacing terms involving Θ by the corresponding terms involving Γ; $g[\![\Theta]\!]\acute{\rho}$, for instance, would become $c[\![\Gamma]\!]\acute{\rho}$. However, the labels set by incidence in $\mathfrak{c}[\![\Gamma]\!]\phi$ may not coincide with those set by incidence in $\mathfrak{c}[\![\Gamma]\!]\psi$ so we are unable to introduce predicates P and Q analogous to those of 4.2.5. Consequently we actually adopt a predicate for $\mathfrak{C}$ which checks $\mathfrak{P}$ and $\mathfrak{Q}$ as well by pairing the elements of $\mathfrak{J}[\![\mathfrak{c}[\![\Gamma]\!]\phi]\!]\S\mathfrak{K}[\![\mathfrak{c}[\![\Gamma]\!]\phi]\!]$ and $\mathfrak{J}[\![\mathfrak{c}[\![\Gamma]\!]\psi]\!]\S\mathfrak{K}[\![\mathfrak{c}[\![\Gamma]\!]\psi]\!]$; the pairing is carried out by subjecting two "environments" to *hoten*; one of these "environments" is a member of (Ide→W*)×W* but the other is a member of the domain U provided by appendix 2. Accordingly we write

$$C=\lambda\Gamma.\bigwedge\{c\langle\mathfrak{C}[\![\mathfrak{c}[\![\Gamma]\!]\phi]\!]\acute{\rho}\acute{\zeta},\mathfrak{C}[\![\mathfrak{c}[\![\Gamma]\!]\psi]\!]\grave{\zeta}\rangle\hat{\pi}$$

$$\wedge\bigwedge\{w\hat{\delta}\hat{\pi}\wedge found\hat{\delta}(lift\acute{\rho})\grave{\upsilon}\acute{\sigma}\,|\,hoten\hat{\delta}\hat{\rho}_0\}$$

$$|c[\![\Gamma]\!]\acute{\rho}\wedge(rend[\![\Gamma]\!](twist\acute{\rho}\acute{\upsilon})=rend[\![\Gamma]\!](field\acute{\upsilon}))\wedge apt\Phi\langle\acute{\upsilon},rend[\![\Gamma]\!]\grave{\rho}\rangle$$

$$\wedge(\#display\acute{\upsilon}=lift\acute{\rho}+1)\wedge p\hat{\pi}\wedge c\hat{\zeta}\hat{\pi}$$

$$\wedge(\acute{\rho}_0\equiv arid[\mathfrak{P}[\![\mathfrak{c}[\![\Gamma]\!]\phi]\!]\acute{\rho}\acute{\zeta}(\#\acute{\upsilon}-1)/\mathfrak{J}[\![\mathfrak{c}[\![\Gamma]\!]\phi]\!]][\mathfrak{Q}[\![\mathfrak{c}[\![\Gamma]\!]\phi]\!]\acute{\rho}\acute{\zeta}(\#\acute{\upsilon}-1)/\mathfrak{K}[\![\mathfrak{c}[\![\Gamma]\!]\phi]\!]])$$

$$\wedge(\grave{\rho}_0\equiv arid[\mathfrak{P}[\![\mathfrak{c}[\![\Gamma]\!]\psi]\!]\grave{\zeta}\grave{\rho}\grave{\upsilon}/\mathfrak{J}[\![\mathfrak{c}[\![\Gamma]\!]\psi]\!]][\mathfrak{Q}[\![\mathfrak{c}[\![\Gamma]\!]\psi]\!]\grave{\zeta}\grave{\rho}\grave{\upsilon}/\mathfrak{K}[\![\mathfrak{c}[\![\Gamma]\!]\psi]\!]])\}.$$

As in 4.2.5 we now have to use structural induction in order to show that $E[\![\mathrm{E}]\!]=true$ when E is any expression. The conditions under which this is so will be stated in 4.3.9; before giving the more interesting portions of the induction, however, we shall establish some other results which essentially assert that stack semantics terminates the activations of limitations in a proper manner.

5.2.7. Proposition.

Suppose that $\hat{\pi}_0$ and $\hat{\pi}_1$ are such that $p_0\hat{\pi}_1 = true$ and that there are ν_0 and ν_1 for which $\acute{\upsilon}_0\dagger(\#\acute{\upsilon}_0-\nu_1)=\acute{\upsilon}_1\dagger(\#\acute{\upsilon}_1-\nu_1)$ and either $\nu_0=\#(chain\acute{\upsilon}_1)+1$ or $\nu_1=chain\acute{\upsilon}_1\downarrow\nu_0\downarrow 1\downarrow 3$. If $\langle(\acute{\omega}\text{EL}\rightarrow hold\acute{\omega}\acute{\sigma}_0,\acute{\omega}),(\grave{\omega}\text{EL}\rightarrow hold\grave{\omega}\grave{\sigma}_0,\grave{\omega})\rangle$ coincides with the pair $\langle(\acute{\omega}\text{EL}\rightarrow hold\acute{\omega}\acute{\sigma}_1,\acute{\omega}),(\grave{\omega}\text{EL}\rightarrow hold\grave{\omega}\grave{\sigma}_1,\grave{\omega})\rangle$ for every $\hat{\omega}$ having $kent\hat{\omega}\hat{\pi}_1\wedge known\acute{\omega}\nu_0\acute{\upsilon}_1\acute{\sigma}_1=true$, then every $\hat{\omega}_0$, $\hat{\omega}_1$ and ν which satisfy $seen\nu\hat{\omega}_0\hat{\omega}_1\hat{\pi}_0\wedge kent\hat{\omega}_1\hat{\pi}_1\wedge known\acute{\omega}_1\nu_0\acute{\upsilon}_1\acute{\sigma}_1=true$ must be such that $kent\hat{\omega}_0\hat{\pi}_1\wedge known\acute{\omega}_0\nu_0\acute{\upsilon}_1\acute{\sigma}_1=true$. Furthermore, if $\bigwedge\{(area\alpha\acute{\sigma}_0\vee{\sim}area\alpha\acute{\sigma}_1)\wedge(area\alpha\grave{\sigma}_0\vee{\sim}area\alpha\grave{\sigma}_1)\mid\alpha\}=true$, and if $\hat{\omega}$ is any pair subject to $w\hat{\omega}\hat{\pi}_1\wedge known\acute{\omega}\nu_0\acute{\upsilon}_1\acute{\sigma}_1=true$, then $w\hat{\omega}\hat{\pi}_0=true$.

$\vartriangleleft$Assume that for some ν any $\hat{\omega}_0$ and $\hat{\omega}_1$ having $seen\nu\hat{\omega}_0\hat{\omega}_1\hat{\pi}_0\wedge kent\hat{\omega}_1\hat{\pi}_1\wedge known\acute{\omega}_1\nu_0\acute{\upsilon}_1\acute{\sigma}_1=true$ must satisfy $kent\hat{\omega}_0\hat{\pi}_1\wedge known\acute{\omega}_0\nu_0\acute{\upsilon}_1\acute{\sigma}_1=true$; this is manifestly so when $\nu<1$. Let $\hat{\omega}_0$ and $\hat{\omega}_1$ be such that $seen(\nu+1)\hat{\omega}_0\hat{\omega}_1\hat{\pi}_0\wedge kent\hat{\omega}_1\hat{\pi}_1\wedge found\acute{\omega}_1\nu_1\acute{\upsilon}_1\acute{\sigma}_1=true$; we shall verify that $kent\hat{\omega}_0\hat{\pi}_1\wedge known\acute{\omega}_0\nu_0\acute{\upsilon}_1\acute{\sigma}_1=true$ by showing that there is some $\hat{\omega}_2$ with $seen\nu\hat{\omega}_0\hat{\omega}_2\hat{\pi}_0\wedge kent\hat{\omega}_2\hat{\pi}_1\wedge known\acute{\omega}_2\nu_0\acute{\upsilon}_1\acute{\sigma}_1=true$.

If $\acute{\omega}_1\text{EL}$ or $\grave{\omega}_1\text{EL}$ then $seen\nu\hat{\omega}_0\hat{\omega}_2\hat{\pi}_0=true$ when $\hat{\omega}_2$ is $\langle(\acute{\omega}_1\text{EL}\rightarrow hold\acute{\omega}_1\acute{\sigma}_0,\acute{\omega}_1),(\grave{\omega}_1\text{EL}\rightarrow hold\grave{\omega}_1\grave{\sigma}_0,\grave{\omega}_1)\rangle$. We know, however, that under these circumstances $\hat{\omega}_2$ is also $\langle(\acute{\omega}_1\text{EL}\rightarrow hold\acute{\omega}_1\acute{\sigma}_1,\acute{\omega}_1),(\grave{\omega}_1\text{EL}\rightarrow hold\grave{\omega}_1\grave{\sigma}_1,\grave{\omega}_1)\rangle$, so $kent\hat{\omega}_2\hat{\pi}_1\wedge known\acute{\omega}_2\nu_0\acute{\upsilon}_1\acute{\sigma}_1=true$ by virtue of the comments in 5.2.2 appropriate to our present version of *seen*.

If $\acute{\omega}_1\text{EJ}$ and $\grave{\omega}_1\text{EJ}$ then $seen\nu\hat{\omega}_0\hat{\omega}_2\hat{\pi}_0=true$ for some $\hat{\omega}_2$ having $hoten\hat{\omega}_2\langle level\acute{\upsilon}_2,\grave{\omega}_1\downarrow 2\rangle\vee gyven\hat{\omega}_2\langle stick\acute{\upsilon}_2,\grave{\omega}_1\downarrow 3\rangle=true$ when $\acute{\upsilon}_2=\acute{\upsilon}_0\dagger(\#\acute{\upsilon}_0-\hat{\omega}_1\downarrow 2)$. Because $known\acute{\omega}_1\nu_0\acute{\upsilon}_1\acute{\sigma}_1=true$, we can assert that $\nu_1\geq\acute{\omega}_1\downarrow 2$ (and $\#chain\acute{\upsilon}_1\geq\nu_0$) and therefore that $\acute{\upsilon}_2=\acute{\upsilon}_1\dagger(\#\acute{\upsilon}_1-\acute{\omega}_1\downarrow 2)$. Hence $seen1\hat{\omega}_2\hat{\omega}_1\hat{\pi}_1=true$ and, applying the remarks in 5.2.2, $kent\hat{\omega}_2\hat{\pi}_1=true$. Moreover there are certain integers ν_2 and ν_3 for which $\acute{\omega}_2=\acute{\upsilon}_0\downarrow(\#\acute{\upsilon}_0-\nu_2+1)$, $\nu_3\geq\nu_0$ and $((\nu_3=1)\rightarrow\#\acute{\upsilon}_1,\#(chain\acute{\upsilon}_1\downarrow(\nu_3-1))-1)\geq\nu_2\geq((\nu_3=\#chain\acute{\upsilon}_1+1)\rightarrow 1,\#(chain\acute{\upsilon}_1\downarrow\nu_3))$; we know that $known\acute{\omega}_2\nu_3\acute{\upsilon}_1\acute{\sigma}_1=true$, so actually $known\acute{\omega}_2\nu_0\acute{\upsilon}_1\acute{\sigma}_1=true$.

If $\acute{\omega}_1 \in F$ and $\grave{\omega}_1 \in F$ then $seen\nu\hat{\omega}_0\hat{\omega}_2\hat{\pi}_0=true$ for some $\hat{\omega}_2$ having $hoten\hat{\omega}_2\langle ravel(\acute{\omega}_1\downarrow 3)\acute{\upsilon}_0,\grave{\omega}_1\downarrow 2\rangle=true$. As $known\acute{\omega}_1\nu_0\acute{\upsilon}_1\acute{\sigma}_1=true$, either $\acute{\omega}_1\downarrow 2=0$ or there is some ν_2 having $\acute{\omega}_1\downarrow 2=\#(chain\acute{\upsilon}_1\downarrow\nu_2)$ and $\nu_0\geq\nu_2$; indeed if $\acute{\upsilon}_2=\acute{\upsilon}_1\dagger(\#\acute{\upsilon}_1-(\acute{\omega}_1\downarrow 2=0\rightarrow 0,chain\acute{\upsilon}_1\downarrow\nu_2\downarrow 1\downarrow 3))$ then $tidy(\acute{\omega}_1\downarrow 3)\acute{\upsilon}_2=true$, $\#\acute{\upsilon}_0-\nu_1\geq\#\acute{\upsilon}_2$, $hoten\hat{\omega}_2\langle ravel(\acute{\omega}_1\downarrow 3)\acute{\upsilon}_1,\grave{\omega}_1\downarrow 2\rangle=true$ and $kent\hat{\omega}_2\hat{\pi}_1=true$.
The fact that $tidy(\acute{\omega}_1\downarrow 3)\acute{\upsilon}_2=true$ also ensures that there are ν_3 and ν_4 such that $\acute{\omega}_2=\acute{\upsilon}_0\downarrow(\#\acute{\upsilon}_0-\nu_3+1)$, $\nu_4\geq\nu_0$ and
$((\nu_4=1)\rightarrow\#\acute{\upsilon}_1,\#(chain\acute{\upsilon}_1\downarrow(\nu_4-1))-)\geq\nu_3\geq((\nu_3=\#chain\acute{\upsilon}_1+1)\rightarrow 1,\#(chain\acute{\upsilon}_1\downarrow\nu_3))$, so $known\acute{\omega}_2\nu_0\acute{\upsilon}_1\acute{\sigma}_1=true$ in this case also.

Equally simple arguments are needed by the other summands of W, so we may conclude that whatever the nature of $\hat{\omega}_1$ there is some $\hat{\omega}_2$ for which $seen\nu\hat{\omega}_0\hat{\omega}_2\hat{\pi}_0\wedge kent\hat{\omega}_2\hat{\pi}_1\wedge known\acute{\omega}_2\nu_0\acute{\upsilon}_1\acute{\sigma}_1=true$.
From the inductive assumption we can therefore deduce that $kent\hat{\omega}_0\hat{\pi}_1\wedge known\acute{\omega}_0\nu_0\acute{\upsilon}_1\acute{\sigma}_1=true$.

The proof that $w\hat{\omega}\hat{\pi}_0$ is *true* when $w\hat{\omega}\hat{\pi}_1$ and $known\acute{\omega}\nu_0\acute{\upsilon}_1\acute{\sigma}_1$ are *true* merely requires an examination of the definition of w.▸

In particular, if $p\hat{\pi}_1=true$ then $w\hat{\omega}\hat{\pi}_0=true$ for every $\hat{\omega}$ such that $kent\hat{\omega}\hat{\pi}_1=true$, since in this situation $known\acute{\omega}\nu_0\acute{\upsilon}_1\acute{\sigma}_1=true$ inevitably.

5.2.8. Proposition.

Suppose that $\hat{\pi}_0$ and $\hat{\pi}_1$ are constrained in such a way that $neat\langle level\acute{\upsilon}_0,\grave{\rho}_0\rangle=true$, $\#stick\acute{\upsilon}_0=\#\grave{\upsilon}_0$, $UW_0\grave{\rho}_0=UW_0(revert\grave{\rho}_0\grave{\rho}_1)$, $YW_0\grave{\upsilon}_0=YW_0\grave{\upsilon}_1\dagger(\#\grave{\upsilon}_1-\#\grave{\upsilon}_0)$, $YW_0\acute{\upsilon}_0=YW_0\acute{\upsilon}_1\dagger(\nu_2-1)$, $\#\acute{\upsilon}_1-\nu_2+2=\#(chain\acute{\upsilon}_1\downarrow(\nu_3-1))$ and $\bigwedge\{(\acute{\upsilon}_1\downarrow(\nu_2-1)\downarrow1)\alpha\vee\sim area\alpha\acute{\sigma}_0|\alpha\}=true$ for certain ν_2 and ν_3. Let ν_0 and ν_1 be subject either to $\nu_1=0$ or to $\acute{\upsilon}_0\downarrow(\#\acute{\upsilon}_0-display\acute{\upsilon}_0\downarrow\nu_0+1)\downarrow3\geq\acute{\upsilon}_1\downarrow(\#\acute{\upsilon}_1-display\acute{\upsilon}_1\downarrow\nu_1+1)\downarrow3$. Assume that $\hat{\zeta}_0$ and $\hat{\zeta}_1$ can be chosen so that $j\hat{\zeta}_0\nu_0\hat{\pi}_0=true$ and so that every $\hat{\pi}_2$ having $match1\hat{\pi}_2\hat{\pi}_1=true$ gives rise to some $\grave{\rho}_3$ and $\grave{\upsilon}_3$ such that $UW_0\grave{\rho}_3=UW_0\grave{\rho}_0$, $YW_0\grave{\upsilon}_3=YW_0\grave{\upsilon}_0$, $\acute{\zeta}_1\acute{\upsilon}_2\acute{\sigma}_2=lose\nu_2\acute{\zeta}_0\acute{\upsilon}_2\acute{\sigma}_2$, $\grave{\zeta}_1\grave{\rho}_2\grave{\upsilon}_2\grave{\sigma}_2=\grave{\zeta}_0\grave{\rho}_3(\langle\grave{\upsilon}_2\downarrow1\rangle\S\grave{\upsilon}_3)\grave{\sigma}_2$ and $kent\hat{\omega}\hat{\pi}_2\wedge known\acute{\omega}\nu_3\acute{\upsilon}_2\acute{\sigma}_2=true$ whenever $hoten\hat{\omega}\langle level(\acute{\upsilon}_2\dagger\nu_2),\grave{\rho}_3\rangle\vee gyven\hat{\omega}\langle stick(\acute{\upsilon}_2\dagger\nu_2),\grave{\upsilon}_3\rangle=true$. Then $\hat{\zeta}_1$ satisfies $j\hat{\zeta}_1\nu_1\hat{\pi}_1=true$.

$\triangleleft$If there is no pair $\hat{\pi}_2$ for which $p\hat{\pi}_2$, $match1\hat{\pi}_2\hat{\pi}_1$ and $found(\acute{\upsilon}_2\downarrow1)\nu_1\acute{\upsilon}_2\acute{\sigma}_2$ are all *true* the result is trivial. Accordingly we assume that there actually is such a $\hat{\pi}_2$ and we attempt to prove that $a\langle\acute{\zeta}_1\acute{\upsilon}_2\acute{\sigma}_2,\grave{\zeta}_1\grave{\rho}_2\grave{\upsilon}_2\grave{\sigma}_2\rangle=true$. For this purpose we introduce $\hat{\pi}_4$, which is defined by taking the $\grave{\rho}_3$ and $\grave{\upsilon}_3$ corresponding to $\hat{\pi}_2$ and setting $\acute{\pi}_4=\langle\acute{\rho}_2,\langle\acute{\upsilon}_2\downarrow1\rangle\S\acute{\upsilon}_2\dagger\nu_2,restore(\acute{\upsilon}_2\downarrow\nu_2)\acute{\sigma}_2\rangle$ and $\grave{\pi}_4=\langle\grave{\rho}_3,\langle\grave{\upsilon}_2\downarrow1\rangle\S\grave{\upsilon}_3,\grave{\sigma}_3\rangle$; as $j\hat{\zeta}_0\nu_0\hat{\pi}_0=true$ and $\langle\acute{\zeta}_1\acute{\upsilon}_2\acute{\sigma}_2,\grave{\zeta}_1\grave{\rho}_2\grave{\upsilon}_2\grave{\sigma}_2\rangle=\langle\acute{\zeta}_0\acute{\upsilon}_4\acute{\sigma}_4,\grave{\zeta}_0\grave{\rho}_4\grave{\upsilon}_4\grave{\sigma}_4\rangle$, to confirm that $a\langle\acute{\zeta}_1\acute{\upsilon}_2\acute{\sigma}_2,\grave{\zeta}_1\grave{\rho}_2\grave{\upsilon}_2\grave{\sigma}_2\rangle=true$ we need only verify that $p\hat{\pi}_4$, $match1\hat{\pi}_4\hat{\pi}_0$ and $found(\acute{\upsilon}_4\downarrow1)\nu_0\acute{\upsilon}_4\acute{\sigma}_4$ are *true*.

Since $match1\hat{\pi}_2\hat{\pi}_0=true$ and $p_0\hat{\pi}_2=true$, if α is any location such that $area\alpha\acute{\sigma}_0=true$ then $(\acute{\upsilon}_2\downarrow\nu_2\downarrow1)\alpha=true$ while if $(\acute{\upsilon}_2\downarrow\nu_2\downarrow1)\alpha=true$ then $area\alpha\acute{\sigma}_2=true$ also. Consequently $\bigwedge\{area\alpha\acute{\sigma}_4\vee\sim area\alpha\acute{\sigma}_0|\alpha\}=true$, and this fact together with the knowledge that $UW_0\grave{\rho}_4=UW_0\grave{\rho}_0$ and $YW_0\grave{\upsilon}_4\dagger1=YW_0\grave{\upsilon}_0$ indicates that $match1\hat{\pi}_4\hat{\pi}_0=true$.

The construction of $\acute{\upsilon}_4$ from $\acute{\upsilon}_2$ ensures that either $\nu_1=0$ or $\acute{\upsilon}_4\downarrow(\#\acute{\upsilon}_4-display\acute{\upsilon}_4\downarrow\nu_0+1)\downarrow3\geq\acute{\upsilon}_2\downarrow(\#\acute{\upsilon}_2-display\acute{\upsilon}_2\downarrow\nu_1+1)\downarrow3$; hence either $\nu_1=0$

or in fact $chain\acute{\upsilon}_2\downarrow\nu_3\downarrow 1\downarrow 3=chain\acute{\upsilon}_4\downarrow 1\downarrow 1\downarrow 3\geq\acute{\upsilon}_4\downarrow(\#\acute{\upsilon}_2-display\acute{\upsilon}_2\downarrow\nu_1+1)\downarrow 3$. By recursion induction on the defining equation of *found* we can therefore establish that if $\acute{\omega}$ is any witnessed value having $found\acute{\omega}\nu_1\acute{\upsilon}_2\acute{\sigma}_2=true$ then $known\acute{\omega}\nu_3\acute{\upsilon}_2\acute{\sigma}_2\wedge known\acute{\omega}1\acute{\upsilon}_4\acute{\sigma}_4\wedge found\acute{\omega}\nu_0\acute{\upsilon}_4\acute{\sigma}_4=true$. In particular, as $found(\acute{\upsilon}_2\downarrow 1)\nu_1\acute{\upsilon}_2\acute{\sigma}_2$ is *true*, we can assert that $known(\acute{\upsilon}_4\downarrow 1)\nu_3\acute{\upsilon}_2\acute{\sigma}_2$, $known(\acute{\upsilon}_4\downarrow 1)1\acute{\upsilon}_4\acute{\sigma}_4$ and $found(\acute{\upsilon}_4\downarrow 1)\nu_0\acute{\upsilon}_4\acute{\sigma}_4$ are *true*.

Because $stick\acute{\upsilon}_4=\langle\acute{\upsilon}_4\downarrow 1\rangle\S stick(\acute{\upsilon}_4\dagger 1)$, any pair $\hat{\omega}$ meeting the condition $hoten\hat{\omega}\langle level\acute{\upsilon}_4,\grave{\rho}_4\rangle\vee gyven\langle stick\acute{\upsilon}_4,\grave{\upsilon}_4\rangle=true$ also satisfies $kent\hat{\omega}\hat{\pi}_2\wedge known\acute{\omega}\nu_3\acute{\upsilon}_2\acute{\sigma}_2=true$. In consequence we can apply 5.2.7 to $\hat{\pi}_2$ and $\hat{\pi}_4$ to obtain the result that every $\hat{\omega}$ with $kent\hat{\omega}\hat{\pi}_4=true$ is subject to $kent\hat{\omega}\hat{\pi}_2\wedge known\acute{\omega}\nu_3\acute{\upsilon}_2\acute{\sigma}_2=true$ while every $\hat{\omega}$ with $w\hat{\omega}\hat{\pi}_2\wedge known\acute{\omega}\nu_3\acute{\upsilon}_2\acute{\sigma}_2=true$ is subject to $w\hat{\omega}\hat{\pi}_4=true$. Taken in conjunction with the facts that $p\hat{\pi}_2=true$ and that $\acute{\upsilon}_4\dagger 1=(chain\acute{\upsilon}_2\downarrow(\nu_3-1))\dagger 1$ this means that $p\hat{\pi}_4=true$.

We have now shown that $p\hat{\pi}_4$, $match1\hat{\pi}_4\hat{\pi}_0$ and $found(\acute{\upsilon}_4\downarrow 1)\nu_0\acute{\upsilon}_4\acute{\sigma}_4$ are *true*, so we may rightly claim that $\alpha\langle\acute{\zeta}_1\acute{\upsilon}_2\acute{\sigma}_2,\grave{\zeta}_1\grave{\rho}_2\grave{\upsilon}_2\grave{\sigma}_2\rangle=true$. Since $\hat{\pi}_2$ can be any pair such that $p\hat{\pi}_2$, $match1\hat{\pi}_2\hat{\pi}_1$ and $found(\acute{\upsilon}_2\downarrow 1)\nu_1\acute{\upsilon}_2\acute{\sigma}_2$ are *true* we can conclude that $j\hat{\zeta}_1\nu_1\hat{\pi}_1=true$.$\triangleright$

5.2.9. Proposition.

If ν_0, ζ_0 and $\hat{\pi}_0$ are such that $j\zeta_0\nu_0\hat{\pi}_0=true$ then $j\langle jump,\zeta_0\rangle\nu_0\hat{\pi}_1=true$ where $\hat{\pi}_1=\langle\langle\acute{\rho}_0,\langle\zeta_0\rangle\S\acute{\upsilon}_0,\acute{\sigma}_0\rangle,\check{\pi}_0\rangle$.

$\triangleleft$Suppose that $\hat{\pi}_2$ is a pair for which $p\hat{\pi}_2$, $match1\hat{\pi}_2\hat{\pi}_1$ and $found(\acute{\upsilon}_2\downarrow 1)\nu_0\acute{\upsilon}_2\acute{\sigma}_2$ are *true*, and let $\hat{\pi}_3=\langle\langle\acute{\rho}_2,\langle\acute{\upsilon}_2\downarrow 1\rangle\S\acute{\upsilon}_2\dagger 2,\acute{\sigma}_2\rangle,\check{\pi}_2\rangle$. Because $match1\hat{\pi}_2\hat{\pi}_1=true$, $\acute{\upsilon}_2\downarrow 2=\zeta_0$ and $jump\acute{\upsilon}_2\acute{\sigma}_2=\zeta_0\acute{\upsilon}_3\acute{\sigma}_3$; hence to show that $a\langle jump\acute{\upsilon}_2\acute{\sigma}_2,\zeta_0\grave{\rho}_2\grave{\upsilon}_2\grave{\sigma}_2\rangle=true$ we have simply to establish that $p\hat{\pi}_3$, $match1\hat{\pi}_3\hat{\pi}_0$ and $found(\acute{\upsilon}_3\downarrow 1)\nu_0\acute{\upsilon}_3\acute{\sigma}_3$ are *true*.

Plainly $stick\acute{\upsilon}_3=stick\acute{\upsilon}_2$ and $stick\acute{\upsilon}_0=stick\acute{\upsilon}_1$, so, as $match1\hat{\pi}_2\hat{\pi}_1$ is *true*, $match1\hat{\pi}_3\hat{\pi}_0$ must be *true* also. In particular if $\#chain\acute{\upsilon}_3\geq 1$ then $\#\acute{\upsilon}_3\geq chain\upsilon_3\downarrow 1\downarrow 1\downarrow 3+1$, so we may actually presume that $found(\acute{\upsilon}_3\downarrow 1)\nu_0\acute{\upsilon}_3\acute{\sigma}_3=found(\acute{\upsilon}_2\downarrow 1)\nu_0\acute{\upsilon}_2\acute{\sigma}_2$ and $level\acute{\upsilon}_3=level\acute{\upsilon}_2$. Consequently any $\hat{\omega}$ such that $hoten\hat{\omega}\langle level\acute{\upsilon}_3,\grave{\rho}_3\rangle\vee gyven\langle stick\acute{\upsilon}_3,\grave{\upsilon}_3\rangle=true$ also satisfies $kent\hat{\omega}\hat{\pi}_2\wedge known\acute{\omega}\nu\acute{\upsilon}_2\acute{\sigma}_2=true$ for some ν. Thus if we apply 5.2.7 to $\hat{\pi}_3$ and $\hat{\pi}_2$ we can infer that every $\hat{\omega}$ with $kent\hat{\omega}\hat{\pi}_3=true$ is subject to $kent\hat{\omega}\hat{\pi}_2\wedge known\acute{\omega}\nu\acute{\upsilon}_2\acute{\sigma}_2=true$ for some ν, while every $\hat{\omega}$ having $w\hat{\omega}\hat{\pi}_2\wedge known\acute{\omega}\nu\acute{\upsilon}_2\acute{\sigma}_2=true$ is such that $w\hat{\omega}\hat{\pi}_3=true$. Because $p\hat{\pi}_2=true$ this means that $p\hat{\pi}_3=true$ and that $a\langle jump\acute{\upsilon}_2\acute{\sigma}_2,\zeta_0\grave{\rho}_2\grave{\upsilon}_2\grave{\sigma}_2\rangle=true$.

As $\hat{\pi}_2$ may be any pair for which $p\hat{\pi}_2$, $match1\hat{\pi}_2\hat{\pi}_1$ and $found(\acute{\upsilon}_2\downarrow 1)\nu_0\acute{\upsilon}_2\acute{\sigma}_2$ are *true* we can conclude that $j\langle jump,\zeta_0\rangle\nu_0\hat{\pi}_1$ is *true*.$\triangleright$

5.3. The congruence between store semantics and stack semantics.

5.3.1. Lemma.

If I is a Sal identifier then $E[\![\mathrm{I}]\!]=true$.

$\lessdot$Let $\Uparrow_0$ be such that $rend[\![\mathrm{I}]\!](twist\acute{\rho}_0\acute{\upsilon}_0)=rend[\![\mathrm{I}]\!](field\acute{\upsilon}_0)$; take any ν_0 and $\hat{\psi}$ for which $e[\![\mathrm{I}]\!]\acute{\rho}_0\nu_0=true$, $p\Uparrow_0=true$, $apt\hat{\psi}\langle\acute{\upsilon}_0,rend[\![\mathrm{I}]\!]\grave{\rho}_0\rangle=true$ and $\#display\acute{\upsilon}_0\geq lift\acute{\rho}_0$, and assume that $\acute{\zeta}$ and $\grave{\zeta}$ are continuations such that $j\hat{\zeta}\nu_0\Uparrow_0=true$. In order to show that $c\langle\mathcal{E}[\![e[\![\mathrm{I}]\!]\acute{\psi}]\!]\acute{\rho}_0\acute{\zeta},\mathcal{E}[\![e[\![\mathrm{I}]\!]\grave{\psi}]\!]\grave{\zeta}\rangle\Uparrow_0=true$ pick any $\Uparrow_1$ having $p\Uparrow_1\wedge match0\Uparrow_1\Uparrow_0=true$; set $\langle\nu_1,\nu_2\rangle=\acute{\rho}_0[\![\mathrm{I}]\!]\downarrow 1$, $\acute{\delta}=\acute{\upsilon}_1\downarrow(\#\acute{\upsilon}_1-display\acute{\upsilon}_1\downarrow\nu_1-\nu_2+1)$, $\grave{\delta}=\grave{\rho}_1[\![\mathrm{I}]\!]\downarrow 1$, $\acute{\varepsilon}=(\acute{\psi}[\![\mathrm{I}]\!]\downarrow 1\rightarrow hold\acute{\delta}\acute{\sigma}_1,\acute{\delta})$, $\grave{\varepsilon}=(\grave{\psi}[\![\mathrm{I}]\!]\downarrow 1\rightarrow hold\grave{\delta}\grave{\sigma}_1,\grave{\delta})$, $\nu_3=\#display\acute{\upsilon}_1$ and $\Uparrow_2=\langle\langle\acute{\rho}_1,\langle\acute{\varepsilon}\rangle\S\acute{\upsilon}_1,\acute{\sigma}_1\rangle,\langle\grave{\rho}_1,\langle\grave{\varepsilon}\rangle\S\grave{\upsilon}_1,\grave{\sigma}_1\rangle\rangle$.

The appendices and the definition of j given in 5.2.3 indicate that to establish that $a\langle\mathcal{E}[\![e[\![\mathrm{I}]\!]\acute{\psi}]\!]\acute{\rho}_0\acute{\zeta}\acute{\upsilon}_1\acute{\sigma}_1,\mathcal{E}[\![e[\![\mathrm{I}]\!]\grave{\psi}]\!]\grave{\zeta}\grave{\rho}_1\grave{\upsilon}_1\grave{\sigma}_1\rangle$ is *true* we have only to demonstrate that $found\acute{\varepsilon}\nu_0\acute{\upsilon}_2\acute{\sigma}_2$ and $p\Uparrow_2$ are *true*. As $rend[\![\mathrm{I}]\!](twist\acute{\rho}_0\acute{\upsilon}_0)=rend[\![\mathrm{I}]\!](field\acute{\upsilon}_0)$ and $match0\Uparrow_1\Uparrow_0=true$ we know that $\langle display\acute{\upsilon}_1\downarrow\nu_1,\nu_2\rangle=field\acute{\upsilon}_1[\![\mathrm{I}]\!]\downarrow 1$; moreover, as $p_0\Uparrow_1=true$ we can assume that $\#\acute{\upsilon}_1\geq field\acute{\upsilon}_1[\![\mathrm{I}]\!]\downarrow 1\downarrow 1+field\acute{\upsilon}_1[\![\mathrm{I}]\!]\downarrow 1\downarrow 2\geq 1$. Hence $\acute{\delta}$ is proper and equal to $level\acute{\upsilon}_1[\![\mathrm{I}]\!]\downarrow 1$.

The fact that $p_0\Uparrow_1=true$ ensures that if ν_4 is the unique integer for which $display\acute{\upsilon}_1\downarrow\nu_1=\#(chain\acute{\upsilon}_1\downarrow\nu_4)$ then $(\nu_4=1\rightarrow\#\acute{\upsilon}_1,\#(chain\acute{\upsilon}_1\downarrow(\nu_4-1))-1)\geq display\acute{\upsilon}_1\downarrow\nu_1+\nu_2$ and $\nu_2\geq 1$. Consequently when $\acute{\upsilon}_3=chain\acute{\upsilon}_1\downarrow\nu_4$ and $\acute{\upsilon}_4=(\nu_4=1\rightarrow\acute{\upsilon}_1,chain(\acute{\upsilon}_1\downarrow(\nu_4-1))\dagger 1)$ we may assert that $\acute{\delta}=\acute{\upsilon}_4\downarrow\nu_5$ cor some ν_5 having $\#\acute{\upsilon}_4-\#\acute{\upsilon}_3\geq\nu_5$. Using the knowledge that $p_0\Uparrow_1=true$ once more, we see that $\nu_1=\#display\acute{\upsilon}_3$ and that $found\acute{\delta}(\#display\acute{\upsilon}_3)\acute{\upsilon}_4(restore(\acute{\upsilon}_4\downarrow 1\downarrow 1)\acute{\sigma}_1)=true$. However, recursion induction on the definition of *found* establishes that if $\acute{\omega}$ is a witnessed value such that $found\acute{\omega}\nu_1\acute{\upsilon}_4(restore(\acute{\upsilon}_4\downarrow 1\downarrow 1)\acute{\sigma}_1)=true$ then $found\acute{\omega}\nu_3\acute{\upsilon}_2\acute{\sigma}_2\wedge found\acute{\omega}\nu_0\acute{\upsilon}_2\acute{\sigma}_2=true$ (since $\nu_3\geq\nu_0\geq\nu_1$ owing to the equation $e[\![\mathrm{I}]\!]\acute{\rho}_0\nu_0=true$). In particular, $found(\acute{\upsilon}_2\downarrow 1)\nu_3\acute{\upsilon}_2\acute{\sigma}_2$ and $found\acute{\varepsilon}\nu_0\acute{\upsilon}_2\acute{\sigma}_2$ are *true*.

Because $apt\hat{\psi}\langle \acute{\upsilon}_1, rend[\![I]\!]\grave{\rho}_1\rangle$ is known to be *true*, $\acute{\epsilon}$ and $\grave{\epsilon}$ are either both in L or both outside L; whichever happens $kent\,\hat{\epsilon}\hat{\varpi}_1=true$ and, more generally, $kent\,\hat{\omega}\hat{\varpi}_1=true$ for all $\hat{\omega}$ having $gyven\hat{\omega}\langle stick\acute{\upsilon}_2, \grave{\upsilon}_2\rangle=true$. For every $\hat{\omega}$ having $kent\,\hat{\omega}\hat{\varpi}_2=true$ applications of 5.2.7 to $\hat{\varpi}_2$ and $\hat{\varpi}_1$ now allow us to deduce successively that $kent\,\hat{\omega}\hat{\varpi}_1=true$, that $w\hat{\omega}\hat{\varpi}_1=true$ and that $w\hat{\omega}\hat{\varpi}_2=true$. Recursion induction also reveals that any $\acute{\omega}$ subject to $found\acute{\omega}\nu_3\acute{\upsilon}_1\acute{\sigma}_1=true$ satisfies $found\acute{\omega}\nu_3\acute{\upsilon}_2\acute{\sigma}_2=true$, so $known(\acute{\upsilon}_2\dagger\nu)1\acute{\upsilon}_2\acute{\sigma}_2=true$ when ν is any integer having $\#\acute{\upsilon}_2-(\#chain\acute{\upsilon}_2=0\rightarrow 0,\#(chain\acute{\upsilon}_2\dagger 1))\geq\nu\geq 1$. It is clear that $\hat{\varpi}_2$ meets the remaining conditions in the definition of p_0 because $\hat{\varpi}_1$ does so and because $apt\hat{\psi}\langle \acute{\upsilon}_1, rend[\![I]\!]\grave{\rho}_1\rangle=true$; hence $p\hat{\varpi}_2=true$.

Since $p\hat{\varpi}_2$, $match\,0\hat{\varpi}_1\hat{\varpi}_0$ and $found\acute{\epsilon}\nu_0\acute{\upsilon}_2\acute{\sigma}_2$ are *true*, $a\langle \mathcal{E}[\![e[\![I]\!]\acute{\psi}]\!]\acute{\rho}_0\acute{\zeta}\acute{\upsilon}_1\acute{\sigma}_1, \mathcal{E}[\![e[\![I]\!]\grave{\psi}]\!]\grave{\zeta}\grave{\rho}_1\grave{\upsilon}_1\grave{\sigma}_1\rangle=true$ for a certain $\hat{\varpi}_1$ chosen only so that $p\hat{\varpi}_1\wedge match\,0\hat{\varpi}_1\hat{\varpi}_0=true$. Hence $c\langle \mathcal{E}[\![e[\![I]\!]\acute{\psi}]\!]\acute{\rho}_0\acute{\zeta}, \mathcal{E}[\![e[\![I]\!]\grave{\psi}]\!]\grave{\zeta}\rangle\hat{\pi}_0=true$. whenever $\hat{\zeta}$ satisfies $j\hat{\zeta}\nu_0\hat{\varpi}_0=true$ for some ν_0 having $e[\![I]\!]\acute{\rho}_0\nu_0=true$. In terms of the definitions in 5.2.6 this means that $E[\![I]\!]=true$. ▷

Notice that this result must still hold even when all we know about $\hat{\zeta}$ is that there is a certain ν_6 having $\nu_4\geq\nu_6$ such that if $\hat{\varpi}$ satisfies $p\hat{\varpi}=true$, $match\,1\hat{\varpi}\hat{\varpi}_0=true$, $found(\acute{\upsilon}\dagger 1)\nu_0\acute{\upsilon}\acute{\sigma}=true$ and $known(\upsilon\dagger 1)(\nu_6+1)\acute{\upsilon}\acute{\sigma}\wedge(\acute{\upsilon}\dagger 1\,\mathrm{E}\,\mathrm{L})=false$ then $a\langle \acute{\zeta}\acute{\upsilon}\acute{\sigma}, \grave{\zeta}\grave{\rho}\grave{\upsilon}\grave{\sigma}\rangle=true$; this is so because the fact that $p_0\hat{\varpi}_1=true$ ensures that if $\acute{\epsilon}\,\mathrm{E}\,\mathrm{L}$ then $known\acute{\epsilon}(\nu_4+1)\acute{\upsilon}_1\acute{\sigma}_1=false$.

5.3.2. Lemma.

If E_0 and E_1 are Sal expressions such that $R[\![E_0]\!] \wedge E[\![E_1]\!]=\mathit{true}$ then $E[\![E_0E_1]\!]=\mathit{true}$.

$\triangleleft$In order to show that $E[\![E_0E_1]\!]=\mathit{true}$ we select any ν_0, $\hat\zeta_0$, $\hat\pi_0$ and $\hat\psi$ such that $e[\![E_0E_1]\!]\acute\rho_0\nu_0=\mathit{true}$, $p\hat\pi_0=\mathit{true}$, $\mathit{rend}[\![E_0E_1]\!](\mathit{twist}\acute\rho_0\acute\upsilon_0)=\mathit{rend}[\![E_0E_1]\!](\mathit{field}\acute\upsilon_0)$, $\mathit{apt}\hat\psi\langle\acute\upsilon_0,\mathit{rend}[\![E_0E_1]\!]\grave\rho_0\rangle=\mathit{true}$, $\#\mathit{display}\acute\upsilon_0\geq\mathit{lift}\acute\rho_0$ and $j\hat\zeta_0\nu_0\hat\pi_0=\mathit{true}$. As usual, we consider only what happens when expressions are evaluated from left to right; thus when $\acute\zeta_1=\lambda\acute\upsilon\acute\sigma.\acute\upsilon\downarrow 2\mathsf{E}\mathsf{F}\rightarrow(\acute\upsilon\downarrow 2\downarrow 1)((\acute\upsilon\downarrow 1)\S\langle \mathit{bulk}(\acute\upsilon\downarrow 2\downarrow 2)0(\acute\upsilon\downarrow 2\downarrow 3)\acute\upsilon\acute\sigma\rangle\S\langle\acute\zeta_0\rangle\S\acute\upsilon\dagger 2)\acute\sigma,\mathit{wrong}\acute\sigma$ and $\grave\zeta_1=\lambda\grave\rho\grave\upsilon\grave\sigma.\grave\upsilon\downarrow 2\mathsf{E}\mathsf{F}\rightarrow(\grave\upsilon\downarrow 2\downarrow 1)\grave\zeta_0(\mathit{divert}\grave\rho(\grave\upsilon\downarrow 2\downarrow 2))((\grave\upsilon\downarrow 1)\S\grave\upsilon\dagger 2)\grave\sigma,\mathit{wrong}\grave\sigma$, and when $\acute\zeta_2=\mathcal{E}[\![e[\![E_1]\!]\acute\psi]\!]\acute\rho_0\acute\zeta_1$ and $\grave\zeta_2=\mathcal{E}[\![e[\![E_1]\!]\grave\psi]\!]\grave\zeta_1$, we have to demonstrate that $c\langle\mathcal{R}[\![r[\![E_0]\!]\acute\psi]\!]\acute\rho_0\acute\zeta_2,\mathcal{R}[\![r[\![E_0]\!]\grave\psi]\!]\grave\zeta_2\rangle\hat\pi_0=\mathit{true}$. Since $R[\![E_0]\!]$ and $r[\![E_0]\!]\acute\rho_0\nu_0$ are true even this task reduces to showing that $j\hat\zeta_2\nu_0\hat\pi_0=\mathit{true}$.

Accordingly we choose any $\hat\pi_1$ for which $p\hat\pi_1$, $\mathit{match1}\hat\pi_1\hat\pi_0$ and $\mathit{found}(\acute\upsilon_1\downarrow 1)\nu_0\acute\upsilon_1\acute\sigma_1$ are true, and we try to prove that $a\langle\acute\zeta_2\acute\upsilon_1\acute\sigma_1,\grave\zeta_2\grave\rho_1\grave\upsilon_1\grave\sigma_1\rangle$ is true. For this purpose we need only verify that $j\hat\zeta_1\nu_1\hat\pi_1$ is true when $\nu_1=\mathit{lift}\acute\rho_0$, since we have assumed that $E[\![E_1]\!]$ and $e[\![E_1]\!]\acute\rho_0\nu_1$ are true and that $\mathit{field}\acute\upsilon_0$ coincides with $\mathit{field}\acute\upsilon_1$. Consequently we next introduce any $\hat\pi_2$ such that $p\hat\pi_2$, $\mathit{match1}\hat\pi_2\hat\pi_1$ and $\mathit{found}(\acute\upsilon_2\downarrow 1)\nu_1\acute\upsilon_2\acute\sigma_2$ are true. As $\mathit{match2}\hat\pi_2\hat\pi_0=\mathit{true}$ we know that $\mathit{gyven}\langle\acute\upsilon_2\downarrow 2,\grave\upsilon_2\downarrow 2\rangle\langle\mathit{stick}\acute\upsilon_2,\grave\upsilon_2\rangle=\mathit{true}$ and therefore that $w\langle\acute\upsilon_2\downarrow 2,\grave\upsilon_2\downarrow 2\rangle\hat\pi_2=\mathit{true}$. Hence, unless $\acute\upsilon_2\downarrow 2\mathsf{E}\mathsf{F}$ and $\grave\upsilon_2\downarrow 2\mathsf{E}\mathsf{F}$, $a\langle\acute\zeta_1\acute\upsilon_2\acute\sigma_2,\grave\zeta_1\grave\rho_2\grave\upsilon_2\grave\sigma_2\rangle$ is $a\langle\mathit{wrong}\acute\sigma_2,\mathit{wrong}\grave\sigma_2\rangle$, and to show that $j\hat\zeta_1\nu_0\hat\pi_1$ is true we concentrate on the situation which arises if $\acute\upsilon_2\downarrow 2\mathsf{E}\mathsf{F}$ and $\grave\upsilon_2\downarrow 2\mathsf{E}\mathsf{F}$. Under these circumstances $a\langle\acute\zeta_1\acute\upsilon_2\acute\sigma_2,\grave\zeta_1\grave\rho_2\grave\upsilon_2\grave\sigma_2\rangle$ is $a\langle(\acute\upsilon_2\downarrow 2\downarrow 1)\acute\upsilon_3\acute\sigma_3,(\grave\upsilon_2\downarrow 2\downarrow 1)\grave\zeta_0\grave\rho_3\grave\upsilon_3\grave\sigma_3\rangle$ where $\acute\pi_3=\langle\acute\upsilon_2\downarrow 2\downarrow 3,\langle\acute\upsilon_2\downarrow 1\rangle\S\langle \mathit{bulk}(\acute\upsilon_2\downarrow 2\downarrow 2)0(\acute\upsilon_2\downarrow 2\downarrow 3)\acute\upsilon_2\acute\sigma_2\rangle\S\langle\acute\zeta_0\rangle\S\acute\upsilon_2\dagger 2,\acute\sigma_2\rangle$ and $\grave\pi_3=\langle\mathit{divert}\grave\rho_2(\grave\upsilon_2\downarrow 2\downarrow 2),\langle\grave\upsilon_2\downarrow 1\rangle\S\grave\upsilon_2\dagger 2,\grave\sigma_2\rangle$.

A glance at the definition of j confirms that our initial assumption that $j\hat\zeta_0\nu_0\hat\pi_0=\mathit{true}$, together with the knowledge that $\bigwedge\{\mathit{area}\alpha\acute\sigma_2\vee\sim\mathit{area}\alpha\acute\sigma_0\mid\alpha\}=\mathit{true}$, ensures that $j\hat\zeta_0\nu_0\langle\langle\acute\rho_2,\acute\upsilon_2\dagger 2,\acute\sigma_2\rangle,\langle\grave\rho_2,\grave\upsilon_2\dagger 2,\grave\sigma_2\rangle\rangle=\mathit{true}$. Because $\mathit{match1}\hat\pi_2\hat\pi_1=\mathit{true}$ and

$\mathit{found}(\acute{\upsilon}_1{\downarrow}1)\nu_0\acute{\upsilon}_1\acute{\sigma}_1=\mathit{true}$ we know that $\mathit{found}(\acute{\upsilon}_2{\downarrow}2)\nu_0\acute{\upsilon}_2\acute{\sigma}_2=\mathit{true}$; in consequence the fact that $w\langle\acute{\upsilon}_2{\downarrow}2,\grave{\upsilon}_2{\downarrow}2\rangle\hat{\pi}_2=\mathit{true}$ implies that $j\langle\acute{\upsilon}_2{\downarrow}2{\downarrow}1,(\grave{\upsilon}_2{\downarrow}2{\downarrow}1)\grave{\zeta}_0\rangle\nu_2\langle\langle\acute{\rho}_3,\acute{\upsilon}_3{\dagger}1,\acute{\sigma}_3\rangle,\langle\grave{\rho}_3,\grave{\upsilon}_3{\dagger}1,\grave{\sigma}_3\rangle\rangle=\mathit{true}$ where $\nu_2=\#\mathit{display}\acute{\upsilon}_2$. Thus once we have established that $p\hat{\pi}_3$ is *true* we shall be able to infer that $a\langle\acute{\zeta}_1\acute{\upsilon}_2\acute{\sigma}_2,\grave{\zeta}_1\grave{\rho}_2\grave{\upsilon}_2\grave{\sigma}_2\rangle$ is *true*.

As $\mathit{match2}\hat{\pi}_2\hat{\pi}_0=\mathit{true}$ and $\mathit{found}(\acute{\upsilon}_2{\downarrow}2)\nu_0\acute{\upsilon}_2\acute{\sigma}_2=\mathit{true}$ we certainly know that $\mathit{tidy}(\acute{\upsilon}_2{\downarrow}2{\downarrow}3)(\acute{\upsilon}_2{\dagger}2)=\mathit{true}$. Consequently any $\hat{\omega}$ such that $\mathit{hoten}\hat{\omega}\langle\mathit{level}\acute{\upsilon}_3,\grave{\rho}_3\rangle=\mathit{true}$ satisfies $\mathit{hoten}\hat{\omega}\langle\mathit{level}\acute{\upsilon}_2,\grave{\rho}_2\rangle\vee\mathit{hoten}\langle\mathit{ravel}(\acute{\upsilon}_2{\downarrow}2{\downarrow}3)\acute{\upsilon}_2,\grave{\upsilon}_2{\downarrow}2\rangle=\mathit{true}$, whilst any $\hat{\omega}$ such that $\mathit{gyven}\hat{\omega}\langle\mathit{stick}\acute{\upsilon}_3,\grave{\upsilon}_3\rangle=\mathit{true}$ satisfies $\mathit{gyven}\hat{\omega}\langle\mathit{stick}\acute{\upsilon}_2,\grave{\upsilon}_2\rangle=\mathit{true}$; moreover in both cases there is some $\nu\geq1$ such that $\mathit{known}\hat{\omega}\nu\acute{\upsilon}_2\acute{\sigma}_2=\mathit{true}$, by virtue of the fact that $p_0\hat{\pi}_2=\mathit{true}$. Hence we may apply the remark following 5.2.7 to $\hat{\pi}_3$ and $\hat{\pi}_2$, obtaining the result that any $\hat{\omega}$ having $\mathit{kent}\hat{\omega}\hat{\pi}_3=\mathit{true}$ is subject to $w\hat{\omega}\hat{\pi}_3\wedge\mathit{kent}\hat{\omega}\hat{\pi}_2=\mathit{true}$; this means that if $p_0\hat{\pi}_3$ is *true* then $p\hat{\pi}_3$ must be *true*.

When ν_3 and ν_4 are any integers such that $\#\mathit{chain}\acute{\upsilon}_3+1\geq\nu_3\geq2$, $\nu_4\geq4$ and $\#\acute{\upsilon}_3+((\nu_3=\#\mathit{chain}\acute{\upsilon}_3+1)\rightarrow0,1-\#(\mathit{chain}\acute{\upsilon}_3{\downarrow}\nu_3))\geq\nu_4\geq\#\acute{\upsilon}_3-\#(\mathit{chain}\acute{\upsilon}_3{\downarrow}(\nu_3-1))+2$ then $\mathit{known}(\acute{\upsilon}_3{\downarrow}\nu_4)\nu_3\acute{\upsilon}_3\acute{\sigma}_3=\mathit{known}(\acute{\upsilon}_2{\downarrow}(\nu_4-1))(\nu_3-1)\acute{\upsilon}_2\acute{\sigma}_2$ and $\#\acute{\upsilon}_2+((\nu_3-1=\#\mathit{chain}\acute{\upsilon}_2+1)\rightarrow0,1-\#(\mathit{chain}\acute{\upsilon}_2{\downarrow}(\nu_3-1)))\geq\nu_4-1\geq\#\acute{\upsilon}_2-\#(\mathit{chain}\acute{\upsilon}_2{\downarrow}(\nu_3-2))+2$ since $\mathit{chain}\acute{\upsilon}_3=\langle\acute{\upsilon}_3{\dagger}1\rangle\S\mathit{chain}\acute{\upsilon}_2$. However, $p_0\hat{\pi}_2=\mathit{true}$ and $\mathit{known}(\acute{\upsilon}_3{\downarrow}2)1\acute{\upsilon}_3\acute{\sigma}_3\wedge\mathit{known}(\acute{\upsilon}_3{\downarrow}3)2\acute{\upsilon}_3\acute{\sigma}_3=\mathit{true}$, while we can convince ourselves that $\mathit{found}(\acute{\upsilon}_3{\downarrow}1)\nu_2\acute{\upsilon}_3\acute{\sigma}_3=\mathit{true}$ just by examining the implications of the knowledge that $\mathit{found}(\acute{\upsilon}_3{\downarrow}1)\nu_0\acute{\upsilon}_2\acute{\sigma}_2=\mathit{true}$. We can now deduce successively that $p_0\hat{\pi}_3=\mathit{true}$, that $p\hat{\pi}_3=\mathit{true}$, and that $a\langle\acute{\zeta}_1\acute{\upsilon}_2\acute{\sigma}_2,\grave{\zeta}_1\grave{\rho}_2\grave{\upsilon}_2\grave{\sigma}_2\rangle=\mathit{true}$.

As $\hat{\pi}_2$ may be any pair for which $p\hat{\pi}_2$, $\mathit{match1}\hat{\pi}_2\hat{\pi}_1$ and $\mathit{found}(\acute{\upsilon}_2{\downarrow}1)\nu_1\acute{\upsilon}_2\acute{\sigma}_2$ are *true*, $j\hat{\zeta}_1\nu_1\hat{\pi}_1$ must be *true*. This in turn shows that $c\hat{\zeta}_2\hat{\pi}_1$ is *true*, that $j\hat{\zeta}_2\nu_0\hat{\pi}_0$ is *true* and finally that $c\langle\mathscr{E}[\![e[\![E_0E_1]\!]\acute{\psi}]\!]\acute{\rho}_0\acute{\zeta}_0,\mathscr{E}[\![e[\![E_0E_1]\!]\grave{\psi}]\!]\grave{\zeta}_0\rangle\hat{\pi}_0$ is *true*.▷

Evidently the proof above is structured rather like that in 4.3.1.

5.3.3. Lemma.

If E is a Sal expression such that $E[\![E]\!]=true$ then $F[\![\mathrm{fnI..E}]\!]=true$.

⋖We assume that ν_0, $\hat{\pi}_0$ and Φ are such that $f[\![\Phi]\!]\acute{\rho}_0=true$, $p\hat{\pi}_0=true$, $rend[\![\Phi]\!](twist\acute{\rho}_0\acute{\upsilon}_0)=rend[\![\Phi]\!](field\acute{\upsilon}_0)apt\Phi\langle\acute{\upsilon}_0,rend[\![\Phi]\!]\grave{\rho}_0\rangle=true$ and $\#display\acute{\upsilon}_0\geq lift\acute{\rho}_0$ where Φ is fnI..E. After setting $\hat{\varepsilon}=\langle\mathcal{H}[\![f[\![\Phi]\!]\acute{\psi}]\!](rend[\![\Phi]\!]\acute{\rho}_0)\acute{\upsilon}_0,\mathcal{H}[\![f[\![\Phi]\!]\grave{\psi}]\!](rend[\![\Phi]\!]\grave{\rho}_0)\rangle$ and $\nu_0=lift(rend[\![\Phi]\!]\acute{\rho}_0)$ we try to prove that $found\acute{\varepsilon}\nu_0\acute{\upsilon}_0\acute{\sigma}_0$ and $w\hat{\varepsilon}\hat{\pi}_0$ are $true$.

We know that if $\nu_0=0$ then $\acute{\varepsilon}\downarrow 2=0$ and $\acute{\varepsilon}\downarrow 3=arid$ and that if $\acute{\varepsilon}\downarrow 2$ is not $\#(chain\acute{\upsilon}_0\downarrow\nu_2)$for some $\nu_2\geq 1$ then $\acute{\varepsilon}\downarrow 2=0$, so to confirm that $found\acute{\varepsilon}\nu_0\acute{\upsilon}_0\acute{\sigma}_0=true$ we have only to demonstrate that $tidy(\acute{\varepsilon}\downarrow 3)\acute{\upsilon}_5=true$, where $\acute{\upsilon}_5=\acute{\upsilon}_0\dagger(\#\acute{\upsilon}_0-((\acute{\varepsilon}\downarrow 2=0)\rightarrow 0,\acute{\upsilon}_0\downarrow(\#\acute{\upsilon}_0-\acute{\varepsilon}\downarrow 2+1)\downarrow 3))$. Plainly $twist(rend[\![\Phi]\!]\acute{\rho}_0)\acute{\upsilon}_0=rend[\![\Phi]\!](field\acute{\upsilon}_0)$; however, $tidy(field\acute{\upsilon}_0)\acute{\upsilon}_0=true$, so in fact $tidy(rend[\![\Phi]\!](field\acute{\upsilon}_0))\acute{\upsilon}_5=true$ and $found\acute{\varepsilon}\nu_0\acute{\upsilon}_0\acute{\sigma}_0=true$.

Let ν_1, $\hat{\pi}_1$ and $\hat{\zeta}_0$ be entities having $found\acute{\varepsilon}\nu_1\acute{\upsilon}_1\acute{\sigma}_1=true$, $tally\acute{\upsilon}_1\acute{\upsilon}_5=true$ and $j\hat{\zeta}_0\nu_1\hat{\pi}_1=true$; when we define $\hat{\pi}_4$ by setting $\acute{\pi}_2=\langle\acute{\varepsilon}\downarrow 3,\langle\lambda\alpha.area\acute{\alpha}\acute{\sigma}_1,\acute{\varepsilon}\downarrow 2,2+\#\acute{\upsilon}_1,divert(field\acute{\upsilon}_1)(\acute{\varepsilon}\downarrow 3)\rangle\S\langle\acute{\zeta}_0\rangle\S\acute{\upsilon}_1,\acute{\sigma}_1\rangle$ and $\grave{\pi}_2=\langle divert\grave{\rho}_1(\grave{\varepsilon}\downarrow 2),\grave{\upsilon}_1,\grave{\sigma}_1\rangle$ we wish to establish that $j\langle\acute{\varepsilon}\downarrow 1,(\grave{\varepsilon}\downarrow 1)\grave{\zeta}_0\rangle(\#display\acute{\upsilon}_0)\hat{\pi}_0=true$. To this end we pick any $\hat{\pi}_3$ such that $p\hat{\pi}_3$, $match1\hat{\pi}_3\hat{\pi}_2$ and $found(\acute{\upsilon}_3\downarrow 1)(\#display\acute{\upsilon}_0)\acute{\upsilon}_2\acute{\sigma}_2$ are all $true$, and we take $\hat{\zeta}_1$ to be $\langle lose3(jump),\grave{\zeta}_0\circ clip[\![\mathrm{IE}]\!]\rangle$. Because the storage areas are finite new provides proper locations; thus if we let $\hat{\alpha}=\langle new\acute{\sigma}_3,new\grave{\sigma}_3\rangle$, $\hat{\beta}=\langle(\acute{\upsilon}_3\downarrow 1\mathrm{E}L\rightarrow hold(\acute{\upsilon}_3\downarrow 1)\acute{\sigma}_3,\acute{\upsilon}_3\downarrow 1),(\grave{\upsilon}_3\downarrow 1\mathrm{E}L\rightarrow hold(\grave{\upsilon}_3\downarrow 1)\grave{\sigma}_3,\grave{\upsilon}_3\downarrow 1)\rangle$ $\hat{\rho}_4=\langle(rend[\![\mathrm{fnI..E}]\!]\acute{\rho}_0)[\langle\nu_0+1,1\rangle/\mathrm{I}],(rend[\![\mathrm{fnI..E}]\!]\grave{\rho}_0)[(opt[\![\mathrm{I}]\!]\grave{\psi}\rightarrow\grave{\alpha},\grave{\beta})/\mathrm{I}]\rangle$, $\hat{\upsilon}_4=\langle\langle(opt[\![\mathrm{I}]\!]\acute{\psi}\rightarrow\acute{\alpha},\acute{\beta})\rangle\S aid1(arid[\langle\nu_0+1,1\rangle/\mathrm{I}])(\acute{\upsilon}_3\dagger 1)\acute{\sigma}_3,\grave{\upsilon}_3\dagger 1\rangle$ and $\hat{\sigma}_4=\langle(opt[\![\mathrm{I}]\!]\acute{\psi}\rightarrow update\acute{\alpha}\acute{\beta}\acute{\sigma}_2,\acute{\sigma}_2),(opt[\![\mathrm{I}]\!]\grave{\psi}\rightarrow update\grave{\alpha}\grave{\beta}\grave{\sigma}_2,\grave{\sigma}_2)\rangle$ then according to the appendices $(\acute{\varepsilon}\downarrow 1)\acute{\upsilon}_3\acute{\sigma}_3=\acute{\mathcal{E}}[\![\mathrm{e}[\![\mathrm{E}]\!]\acute{\psi}[opt[\![\mathrm{I}]\!]\acute{\psi}/\mathrm{I}]]\!]\acute{\rho}_4\acute{\zeta}_1\acute{\upsilon}_4\acute{\sigma}_4$ and $(\grave{\varepsilon}\downarrow 1)\grave{\zeta}_0\grave{\rho}_3\grave{\upsilon}_3\grave{\sigma}_3=\grave{\mathcal{E}}[\![\mathrm{e}[\![\mathrm{E}]\!]\grave{\psi}[opt[\![\mathrm{I}]\!]\grave{\psi}/\mathrm{I}]]\!]\grave{\zeta}_1\grave{\rho}_4\grave{\upsilon}_4\grave{\sigma}_4$. It therefore seems sensible to attempt to prove that $p\hat{\pi}_4$ and certain other values are $true$.

Obviously $\acute{\upsilon}_4$ is designed so that if a pair $\hat{\omega}$ satisfies $hoten\hat{\omega}\langle level\acute{\upsilon}_4,\grave{\rho}_4\rangle\vee gyven\hat{\omega}\langle stick\acute{\upsilon}_4,\grave{\upsilon}_4\rangle=true$ then $kent\hat{\omega}\hat{\pi}_3=true$ unless, perhaps, $\hat{\omega}=\langle\acute{\alpha},\hat{\beta}\rangle$ or $\hat{\omega}=\langle\acute{\beta},\grave{\alpha}\rangle$. By applying 5.2.7 to $\hat{\pi}_3$ and $\hat{\pi}_4$ we see that every $\hat{\omega}$ with $kent\hat{\omega}\hat{\pi}_4=true$ has $kent\hat{\omega}\hat{\pi}_3=true$ unless $\hat{\omega}=\langle\acute{\alpha},\hat{\beta}\rangle$ or $\hat{\omega}=\langle\acute{\beta},\grave{\alpha}\rangle$, whilst every $\hat{\omega}$ with $w\hat{\omega}\hat{\pi}_3=true$ is subject to $w\hat{\omega}\hat{\pi}_4=true$. Whatever the nature of $\hat{\alpha}$ may be we can tell immediately that $p_0\hat{\pi}_4$ is *true* (since $p_0\hat{\pi}_3$ is *true*), so $p\hat{\pi}_4$ is *true*. Notice that $p_0\hat{\pi}_4$ would not necessarily be *true* if $\hat{\pi}_4$ were constructed from $\hat{\pi}_3$ in the manner required by fnI.E instead of in the manner required by fnI..E, since the rules governing $field\acute{\upsilon}_4$ might be violated.

As $display\acute{\upsilon}_0=display(\acute{\upsilon}_0\dagger(\#\acute{\upsilon}_0-\acute{\epsilon}\downarrow 2))\S(display\acute{\upsilon}_0\dagger\nu_0)$ and $display(\acute{\upsilon}_4\dagger(\#\acute{\upsilon}_4-\acute{\epsilon}\downarrow 2))=display(\acute{\upsilon}_0\dagger(\#\acute{\upsilon}_0-\acute{\epsilon}\downarrow 2))$, we can apply the assumption that $found\acute{\epsilon}\nu_1\acute{\upsilon}_1\acute{\sigma}_1=true$ to obtain

$$\begin{aligned}(\nu_1=0\rightarrow 0,display\acute{\upsilon}_1\downarrow\nu_1)&\geq\acute{\epsilon}\downarrow 2\\ &\geq((\nu_0=0)\rightarrow 0,display\acute{\upsilon}_0\downarrow\nu_0)\\ &\geq((\nu_0=0)\rightarrow 0,display(\acute{\upsilon}_4\dagger(\#\acute{\upsilon}_4-\acute{\epsilon}\downarrow 2))\downarrow\nu_0)\\ &\geq((\nu_0=0)\rightarrow 0,display\acute{\upsilon}_4\downarrow\nu_0).\end{aligned}$$

In particular, either $\nu_0=0$ or, since $p_0\hat{\pi}_3=true$, $\acute{\upsilon}_1\downarrow(\#\acute{\upsilon}_1-display\acute{\upsilon}_1\downarrow\nu_1+1)\downarrow 3\geq\acute{\upsilon}_4\downarrow(\#\acute{\upsilon}_4-display\acute{\upsilon}_4\downarrow\nu_0+1)\downarrow 3$. By 5.2.9, however, $j\langle jump,\grave{\zeta}_0\rangle\nu_1\langle\langle\acute{\rho}_1,\langle\acute{\zeta}_0\rangle\S\acute{\upsilon}_1,\acute{\sigma}_1\rangle,\hat{\pi}_1\rangle=true$. Thus all the conditions in the statement of 5.2.8 are satisfied when we substitute our present ν_1, ν_0, 3, 2, $\langle\langle\acute{\rho}_1,\langle\acute{\zeta}_0\rangle\S\acute{\upsilon}_1,\acute{\sigma}_1\rangle,\hat{\pi}_1\rangle$, $\hat{\pi}_4$, $\langle jump,\grave{\zeta}_0\rangle$ and $\hat{\zeta}_1$ for the ν_0, ν_1, ν_2, ν_3, $\hat{\pi}_0$, $\hat{\pi}_1$, $\hat{\zeta}_0$ and $\hat{\zeta}_1$ of 5.2.8, so $j\hat{\zeta}_1\nu_0\hat{\pi}_4=true$. Clearly $apt\langle\acute{\psi}[opt[\![\mathrm{I}]\!]\acute{\psi}/\mathrm{I}],\grave{\psi}[opt[\![\mathrm{I}]\!]\grave{\psi}/\mathrm{I}]\rangle\langle\acute{\upsilon}_4,rend[\![\mathrm{E}]\!]\grave{\rho}_4\rangle=true$ and $rend[\![\mathrm{E}]\!](twist\acute{\rho}_4\acute{\upsilon}_4)=rend[\![\mathrm{E}]\!](field\acute{\upsilon}_4)$, while we already know that $E[\![\mathrm{E}]\!]$ and $e[\![\mathrm{E}]\!]\acute{\rho}_4\nu_0$ are *true*, so $a\langle\mathbf{E}[\![\mathbf{e}[\![\mathrm{E}]\!]\acute{\psi}[opt[\![\mathrm{I}]\!]\acute{\psi}/\mathrm{I}]\acute{\rho}_4]\!]\acute{\zeta}_1,\mathbf{E}[\![\mathbf{e}[\![\mathrm{E}]\!]\grave{\psi}[opt[\![\mathrm{I}]\!]\grave{\psi}/\mathrm{I}]]\!]\grave{\zeta}_1\rangle=true$. Together with the fact that $p\hat{\pi}_4=true$ this ensures that $a\langle(\acute{\epsilon}\downarrow 1)\acute{\upsilon}_3\acute{\sigma}_3,(\grave{\epsilon}\downarrow 1)\grave{\zeta}_0\grave{\rho}_3\grave{\upsilon}_3\grave{\sigma}_3\rangle=true$. In view of our choice of $\hat{\pi}_3$ we can therefore conclude that $j\langle\acute{\epsilon}\downarrow 1,(\grave{\epsilon}\downarrow 1)\grave{\zeta}_0\rangle(\#display\acute{\upsilon}_0)\hat{\pi}_2=true$ and, more generally, that $w\hat{\epsilon}\hat{\pi}_0=true$.

As this holds for all suitable ν_0, $\hat{\pi}_0$ and $\hat{\psi}$, $F[\![\Phi]\!]=true$.▷

This proof should be compared with that in 4.3.2, just as the next proof should be compared with that in 4.3.3.

5.3.4. Lemma.

If E is a Sal expression such that $\mathcal{E}[\![E]\!]=true$ then $\mathcal{S}[\![$res E$]\!]=true$.

$\triangleleft$We know that $\mathcal{S}[\![\Sigma]\!]=true$ if $c\langle\mathfrak{S}[\![\mathfrak{s}[\![\Sigma]\!]\acute{\Phi}]\!]\rho_0,\mathfrak{S}[\![\mathfrak{s}[\![\Sigma]\!]\grave{\Phi}]\!]\rangle\hat{\pi}_0=true$ whenever $\hat{\pi}_0$ and $\hat{\Phi}$ are chosen so that $s[\![\Sigma]\!]\acute{\rho}_0=true$, $apt\hat{\Phi}\langle\acute{\upsilon}_0,rend[\![\Sigma]\!]\grave{\rho}_0\rangle=true$, $rend[\![\Sigma]\!](twist\acute{\rho}_0\acute{\upsilon}_0)=rend[\![\Sigma]\!](field\acute{\upsilon}_0)$, $\#display\acute{\upsilon}_0\geq lift\acute{\rho}_0$ and $p\hat{\pi}=true$. Accordingly when Σ is res E we pick any such $\hat{\pi}_0$ and $\hat{\Phi}$ and try to prove that $c\langle\mathfrak{E}[\![\mathfrak{e}[\![E]\!]\acute{\Phi}]\!]\acute{\rho}_0\acute{\zeta}_0,\mathfrak{E}[\![\mathfrak{e}[\![E]\!]\grave{\Phi}]\!]\grave{\zeta}_0\rangle\hat{\pi}_0=true$, where we define $\acute{\zeta}_0$ and $\grave{\zeta}_0$ by setting $\nu_0=\acute{\rho}_0[\![$res$]\!]\downarrow 1$,
$\acute{\zeta}_0=\lambda\acute{\upsilon}\acute{\sigma}.(\lambda\nu.\acute{\upsilon}\downarrow\nu\mathsf{E}\mathsf{J}\rightarrow lose(\nu+1)(\acute{\upsilon}\downarrow\nu\downarrow 1)\acute{\upsilon}\acute{\sigma},wrong\acute{\sigma})(\#\acute{\upsilon}-display\acute{\upsilon}\downarrow\nu_0)$ and
$\grave{\zeta}_0=\lambda\grave{\rho}\grave{\upsilon}\grave{\sigma}.((\#\grave{\rho}[\![res]\!]>0)\rightarrow(\grave{\rho}[\![res]\!]\downarrow 1\downarrow 1)(\grave{\rho}[\![res]\!]\downarrow 1\downarrow 2)(\langle\grave{\upsilon}\downarrow 1\rangle\S\grave{\rho}[\![res]\!]\downarrow 1\downarrow 3)\grave{\sigma},wrong\grave{\sigma})$;
we can rest assured that ν_0 is proper because $s[\![$res E$]\!]\acute{\rho}_0=true$.

Since $\mathcal{E}[\![E]\!]$ and $e[\![E]\!]\acute{\rho}_0 0$ are *true*, we need only establish that $j\hat{\zeta}_0 0\hat{\pi}_0=true$. To achieve this goal we select any $\hat{\pi}_1$ such that $p\hat{\pi}_1$, $match1\hat{\pi}_1\hat{\pi}_0$ and $found(\acute{\upsilon}_1\downarrow 1)0\acute{\upsilon}_1\acute{\sigma}_1$ are all *true* and we write $\nu_1=\#\acute{\upsilon}_1-display\acute{\upsilon}_1\downarrow\nu_0+1$, $\acute{\pi}_2=\langle\acute{\rho}_1,\acute{\upsilon}_1\dagger 1,\acute{\sigma}_1\rangle$ and $\grave{\pi}_2=\langle\grave{\rho}_1,\grave{\upsilon}_1\dagger 1,\grave{\sigma}_1\rangle$. From the fact that $p\hat{\pi}_1=true$ we can immediately deduce that $\acute{\upsilon}_1\downarrow(\nu_1-1)\mathsf{E}\mathsf{J}$ and $\acute{\upsilon}_1\downarrow\nu_1\mathsf{E}(\mathsf{L}\rightarrow\mathsf{T})\times\mathsf{N}\times\mathsf{N}\times\mathsf{U}$, and we may therefore safely define $\acute{\zeta}_1=\acute{\upsilon}_1\downarrow(\nu_1-1)\downarrow 1$, $\grave{\zeta}_1=\grave{\rho}_1[\![res]\!]\downarrow 1\downarrow 1$, $\acute{\pi}_3=\langle\acute{\rho}_1,\acute{\upsilon}_1\dagger\nu_1,restore(\acute{\upsilon}_1\downarrow\nu_1\downarrow 1)\acute{\sigma}_1\rangle$ and $\grave{\pi}_3=\langle\grave{\rho}_1[\![res]\!]\downarrow 1\downarrow 2,\grave{\rho}_1[\![res]\!]\downarrow 1\downarrow 3,\grave{\sigma}_1\rangle$. Moreover $\nu_1=\#\acute{\upsilon}_1-field\acute{\upsilon}_1[\![res]\!]\downarrow 1+1$ because $rend[\![$res E$]\!](twist\acute{\rho}_0\acute{\upsilon}_0)=rend[\![$res E$]\!](field\acute{\upsilon}_0)$ and $match1\hat{\pi}_1\hat{\pi}_0=true$, so $kent\langle\acute{\upsilon}_1\downarrow(\nu_1-1),\grave{\rho}_1[\![res]\!]\downarrow 1\rangle\hat{\pi}_1=true$. As $p\hat{\pi}_1=true$ this means that $\nu_1=\#\acute{\upsilon}_1-\acute{\upsilon}_1\downarrow(\nu_1-1)\downarrow 2$, $neat\langle level\acute{\upsilon}_3,\grave{\rho}_3\rangle=true$, $\#stick\acute{\upsilon}_3=\#\grave{\upsilon}_3$, $UW_0\grave{\rho}_3=UW_0(revert\grave{\rho}_3\grave{\rho}_2)$, $YW_0\grave{\upsilon}_0=YW_0\grave{\upsilon}_2\dagger(\#\grave{\upsilon}_2-\#\grave{\upsilon}_3)$ and $j\hat{\zeta}_1 0\hat{\pi}_3=true$; as $tidy(field\acute{\upsilon}_3)\acute{\upsilon}_3=true$ it also implies that any $\hat{\omega}$ having $hoten\hat{\omega}\langle level\acute{\upsilon}_3,\grave{\rho}_3\rangle\vee gyven\hat{\omega}\langle stick\acute{\upsilon}_3,\grave{\upsilon}_3\rangle=true$ must satisfy $kent\hat{\omega}\hat{\pi}_1\wedge known\hat{\omega}\nu_2\acute{\upsilon}_1\acute{\sigma}_1=true$ when ν_2 is the unique integer such that $\#\acute{\upsilon}_2-\nu_1+2=\#(chain\acute{\upsilon}_2\downarrow(\nu_2-1))$.

On exchanging 0, 0, ν_1, ν_2, $\hat{\pi}_3$, $\hat{\pi}_2$ and $\hat{\zeta}_1$ for the ν_0, ν_1, ν_2, ν_3, $\hat{\pi}_0$, $\hat{\pi}_1$ and $\hat{\zeta}_0$ of 5.2.8 we see that they satisfy all the relevant conditions in the statement of 5.2.8. We cannot, however, infer from this that $j\hat{\zeta}_0 0\hat{\pi}_2=true$ because we do not know that our present $\hat{\zeta}_0$ obeys all the constraints placed on the pair $\hat{\zeta}_1$ in 5.2.8. Nevertheless, $\acute{\zeta}_0\acute{\upsilon}_1\acute{\sigma}_1 = \mathit{lose}\nu_1\acute{\zeta}_1\acute{\upsilon}_1\acute{\sigma}_1$ and $\grave{\zeta}_0\grave{\rho}_1\grave{\upsilon}_1\grave{\sigma}_1 = \grave{\zeta}_1\grave{\rho}_3(\langle\grave{\upsilon}_1{\downarrow}1\rangle\S\grave{\upsilon}_3)\grave{\sigma}_3$, so by phrasing the proof of 5.2.8 in terms of $\hat{\pi}_1$ and $\hat{\zeta}_0$ (rather than the $\hat{\pi}_2$ and $\hat{\zeta}_1$ of 5.2.8) we can show that $a\langle\acute{\zeta}_0\acute{\upsilon}_1\acute{\sigma}_1,\grave{\zeta}_0\grave{\rho}_1\grave{\upsilon}_1\grave{\sigma}_1\rangle = \mathit{true}$.

As $\hat{\pi}_1$ may be any pair such that $p\hat{\pi}_1$, $\mathit{match}1\hat{\pi}_1\hat{\pi}_0$ and $\mathit{found}(\acute{\upsilon}_1{\downarrow}1)0\acute{\upsilon}_1\acute{\sigma}_1$ are true, we can now assert that $j\hat{\zeta}_0 0\hat{\pi}_0 = \mathit{true}$. This in turn ensures that $c\langle\mathcal{E}[\![\mathbf{e}[\![\mathrm{E}]\!]\acute{\psi}]\!]\acute{\rho}_0\acute{\zeta}_0,\mathcal{E}[\![\mathbf{e}[\![\mathrm{E}]\!]\grave{\psi}]\!]\grave{\zeta}_0\rangle\hat{\pi}_0 = \mathit{true}$ and therefore that $c\langle\mathcal{S}[\![\mathbf{s}[\![\mathrm{res\ E}]\!]\acute{\psi}]\!]\acute{\rho}_0,\mathcal{S}[\![\mathbf{s}[\![\mathrm{res\ E}]\!]\grave{\psi}]\!]\rangle\hat{\pi}_0 = \mathit{true}$. ▷

5.3.5. Lemma.

If E is a Sal expression such that $R[\![\mathrm{E}]\!]=true$ then $T[\![\mathrm{I==E}]\!]=true$.

$\lessdot$It is convenient to abbreviate I==E to Δ and to introduce any ν_0, ν_1, $\hat{\pi}_0$ and $\hat{\phi}$ having $t[\![\Delta]\!]\acute{\rho}_0\nu_0=true$, $fine[\![\Delta]\!]\nu_0\nu_1 1\hat{\phi}_0\hat{\pi}_0=true$ and $p\hat{\pi}_0=true$. We also need to provide arbitrary appropriate continuations $\acute{\zeta}_0$ and $\grave{\zeta}_0$ for which $c\hat{\zeta}_0\hat{\pi}=true$ whenever $\hat{\pi}$ satisfies $spun[\![\Delta]\!]\nu_0\nu_1 1\hat{\phi}\hat{\pi}\hat{\pi}_0\wedge p\hat{\pi}=true$. Once we have shown that $c\langle\mathcal{T}[\![\mathbf{t}[\![\Delta]\!]\acute{\phi}]\!]\acute{\rho}_0\nu_0\nu_1\acute{\zeta}_0,\mathcal{T}[\![\mathbf{t}[\![\Delta]\!]\grave{\psi}]\!]\grave{\zeta}_0\rangle\hat{\pi}_0=true$ for this typical choice of parameters we shall be able to infer that $T[\![\Delta]\!]=true$. In fact we shall do this on the premise that $\acute{\phi}[\![\mathrm{I}]\!]\downarrow 1=false$, which demands a more detailed analysis than its opposite.

Let $\langle\nu_2,\nu_3\rangle=\acute{\rho}_0[\![\mathrm{I}]\!]\downarrow 1$ and observe that $\nu_2=\nu_0+1$, $\mathcal{T}[\![\mathbf{t}[\![\Delta]\!]\acute{\phi}]\!]\acute{\rho}_0\nu_0\nu_1\acute{\zeta}_0=\mathcal{R}[\![\mathbf{r}[\![\mathrm{E}]\!]\acute{\phi}]\!]\acute{\rho}_0\acute{\zeta}_1$ and $\mathcal{T}[\![\mathbf{t}[\![\Delta]\!]\grave{\psi}]\!]\grave{\zeta}_0=\mathcal{R}[\![\mathbf{r}[\![\mathrm{E}]\!]\grave{\psi}]\!]\grave{\zeta}_1$ where $\acute{\zeta}_1=tv(\lambda\acute{\upsilon}\acute{\sigma}.\acute{\zeta}_0(aid0(arid[\langle\nu_2,\nu_3\rangle/\mathrm{I}])(change(\#\acute{\upsilon}\text{-}display\acute{\upsilon}\downarrow\nu_2-\nu_3+1)(\acute{\upsilon}\downarrow 1)\acute{\upsilon}))\acute{\sigma})$ and $\grave{\zeta}_1=sv(\lambda\grave{\rho}\grave{\upsilon}\grave{\sigma}.assign(\grave{\zeta}_0\grave{\rho}[\grave{\rho}[\![\mathrm{I}]\!]\downarrow 1/\mathrm{I}](\grave{\upsilon}\dagger 1))(\grave{\rho}[\![\mathrm{I}]\!]\downarrow 1)(\grave{\upsilon}\downarrow 1)\grave{\sigma})$.
Thus because $R[\![\mathrm{E}]\!]$ and $r[\![\mathrm{E}]\!]\acute{\rho}_0\nu_2$ are *true* we can content ourselves with proving that $j\hat{\zeta}_1\nu_2\hat{\pi}_0=true$. We select any pair $\hat{\pi}_1$ such that $p\hat{\pi}_1$, $match1\hat{\pi}_1\hat{\pi}_0$ and $found(\acute{\upsilon}_1\downarrow 1)\nu_2\acute{\upsilon}_1\acute{\sigma}_1$ are all *true* and note that $\grave{\rho}_1[\![\mathrm{I}]\!]\downarrow 1\in\mathsf{L}$ since $\grave{\psi}[\![\mathrm{I}]\!]\downarrow 1=true$. Now when we set $\grave{\alpha}=\grave{\rho}_1[\![\mathrm{I}]\!]\downarrow 1$, $\hat{\beta}=\langle(\acute{\upsilon}_1\downarrow 1\in\mathsf{L}\rightarrow hold(\acute{\upsilon}_1\downarrow 1)\acute{\sigma}_1,\acute{\upsilon}_1\downarrow 1),(\grave{\upsilon}_1\downarrow 1\in\mathsf{L}\rightarrow hold(\grave{\upsilon}_1\downarrow 1)\grave{\sigma}_1,\grave{\upsilon}_1\downarrow 1)\rangle$, $\acute{\pi}_2=\langle\acute{\rho}_0,aid0(arid[\langle\nu_2,\nu_3\rangle/\mathrm{I}])(change(\#\acute{\upsilon}_1\text{-}display\acute{\upsilon}_1\downarrow\nu_2-\nu_3+1)\acute{\beta}\acute{\upsilon}_1),\sigma_1\rangle$ and $\grave{\pi}_2=\langle\grave{\rho}_1[\grave{\alpha}/\mathrm{I}],\grave{\upsilon}_1\dagger 1,update\grave{\alpha}\grave{\beta}\grave{\sigma}_1\rangle$ we know that $\acute{\zeta}_1\acute{\upsilon}_1\acute{\sigma}_1=\acute{\zeta}_0\acute{\upsilon}_2\acute{\sigma}_2$ and that $\grave{\zeta}_1\grave{\rho}_1\grave{\upsilon}_1\grave{\sigma}_1=\grave{\zeta}_0\grave{\rho}_2\grave{\upsilon}_2\grave{\sigma}_2$. Hence to show that $j\hat{\zeta}_1\nu_0\hat{\pi}_0$ is *true* we concentrate on confirming that $p\hat{\pi}_2$ and $spun[\![\Delta]\!]\nu_0\nu_1 1\hat{\phi}\hat{\pi}_2\hat{\pi}_0$ are *true* when $\hat{\pi}_2$ is constructed in this way.

In fact as $hoten\langle level\acute{\upsilon}_1[\![\mathrm{I}]\!]\downarrow 1,\grave{\alpha}\rangle=true$ and $p\hat{\pi}_1=true$ there can be no ν such that $level\acute{\upsilon}_1[\![\mathbf{res}]\!]\downarrow\nu=level\acute{\upsilon}_1[\![\mathrm{I}]\!]\downarrow 1$. Furthermore, if $\grave{\alpha}=\grave{\upsilon}_2\downarrow\nu$ for some ν then $stick\acute{\upsilon}_1\downarrow\nu\in\mathsf{L}$ (since $match1\hat{\pi}_1\hat{\pi}_0=true$), which would contradict the facts that $kent\langle level\acute{\upsilon}_1[\![\mathrm{I}]\!]\downarrow 1,\grave{\alpha}\rangle\hat{\pi}_1=true$, that $p_0\hat{\pi}_1=true$ and that $level\acute{\upsilon}_1[\![\mathrm{I}]\!]\downarrow 1$ is not a member of L. In conjunction with the assumption that $p_0\hat{\pi}_1 = true$ this implies that any pair $\hat{\omega}$ having $hoten\hat{\omega}\langle level\acute{\upsilon}_2, \grave{\rho}_2\rangle \vee gyven\hat{\omega}\langle stick\acute{\upsilon}_2, \grave{\upsilon}_2\rangle = true$ either must equal $\langle\acute{\beta}, \grave{\alpha}\rangle$ or must be constrained by $(hoten\hat{\omega}\langle level\acute{\upsilon}_1, \grave{\rho}_1\rangle \vee gyven\hat{\omega}\langle stick\acute{\upsilon}_1, \grave{\upsilon}_1\rangle) \wedge \sim(\grave{\omega} = \grave{\alpha}) = true$. By induction on ν we can demonstrate that whenever $\hat{\omega}_0$ and $\hat{\omega}_1$ satisfy $seen\nu\hat{\omega}_0\hat{\omega}_1\hat{\pi}_2 \wedge ((\grave{\omega}_1 = \grave{\alpha}) \rightarrow (\acute{\omega}_1 = \acute{\beta}), kent\hat{\omega}_1\hat{\pi}_1 \wedge known\acute{\omega}_1 1\acute{\upsilon}_1\acute{\sigma}_1) = true$ they are also subject to $((\grave{\omega}_0 = \grave{\alpha}) \rightarrow (\acute{\omega}_0 = \acute{\beta}), kent\hat{\omega}_0\hat{\pi}_1 \wedge known\acute{\omega}_0 1\acute{\upsilon}_1\acute{\sigma}_1) = true$. Hence as $p\hat{\pi}_1 = true$ we can deduce that every $\hat{\omega}$ with $kent\hat{\omega}\hat{\pi}_2 = true$ is such that $((\grave{\omega} = \grave{\alpha}) \rightarrow (\acute{\omega} = \acute{\beta}), kent\hat{\omega}\hat{\pi}_1) = true$, $w\hat{\omega}\hat{\pi}_1 = true$ and $w\hat{\omega}\hat{\pi}_2 = true$. We can also verify immediately that $p_0\hat{\pi}_2 = true$, so actually $p\hat{\pi}_2 = true$; in addition $spun[\![\Delta]\!]\nu_0\nu_1 1\phi\hat{\pi}_2\hat{\pi}_0 = true$ simply because $fine[\![\Delta]\!]\nu_0\nu_1 1\phi\hat{\pi}_0 \wedge match 1\hat{\pi}_1\hat{\pi}_0 = true$. Consequently $a\langle\acute{\zeta}_0\acute{\upsilon}_2\acute{\sigma}_2, \grave{\zeta}_0\grave{\rho}_2\grave{\upsilon}_2\grave{\sigma}_2\rangle = true$, $j\hat{\zeta}_1\nu_2\hat{\pi}_0 = true$, $c\langle\mathcal{R}[\![r[\![E]\!]\acute{\psi}]\!]\acute{\rho}_0\acute{\zeta}_1, \mathcal{R}[\![r[\![E]\!]\grave{\psi}]\!]\grave{\zeta}_1\rangle\hat{\pi}_0 = true$ and $T[\![\Delta]\!] = true$.▷

The proof given above is more intricate and interesting than the proofs that $D[\![I==E]\!]$ and $T[\![I=E]\!]$ are *true* when $R[\![E]\!]$ is *true*.

5.3.6. Lemma.

If Δ_0 and Δ_1 are Sal declarations such that $D[\![\Delta_0]\!] \wedge T[\![\Delta_1]\!]=true$ then $T[\![\Delta_0$ within $\Delta_1]\!]=true$.

⊲Select any ν_0, ν_1, $\hat{\pi}_0$ and $\hat{\psi}_0$ for which $t[\![\Delta]\!]\acute{\rho}_0\nu_0=true$, $fine[\![\Delta]\!]\nu_0\nu_1 1\hat{\psi}_0\hat{\pi}_0=true$ and $p\hat{\pi}_0=true$ when the declaration Δ is taken to be Δ_0 within Δ_1. Suppose that $\hat{\zeta}_0$ satisfies $c\hat{\zeta}_0\hat{\pi}=true$ whenever $spun[\![\Delta]\!]\nu_0\nu_1 1\hat{\psi}_0\hat{\pi}\hat{\pi}_0 \wedge p\hat{\pi}=true$. As $D[\![\Delta_0]\!]$ and $d[\![\Delta_0]\!]\acute{\rho}_0\nu_0$ are $true$, to show that $c\langle \mathcal{T}[\![t[\![\Delta]\!]\acute{\psi}_0]\!]\acute{\rho}_0\nu_0\nu_1\acute{\zeta}_0, \mathcal{T}[\![t[\![\Delta]\!]\grave{\psi}_0]\!]\grave{\zeta}_0\rangle\hat{\pi}_0=true$ we have merely to prove that if we initially write $\nu_2=\nu_1+\mathcal{Y}[\![\Delta_0]\!]$, $\acute{\zeta}_1=\acute{\zeta}_0\circ act(trim[\![\Delta_0]\!][\![\Delta_1]\!])$, $\grave{\zeta}_1=\grave{\zeta}_0\circ trim[\![\Delta_0]\!][\![\Delta_1]\!]$, $\acute{\psi}_1=\acute{\psi}_0[use(\#\mathcal{J}[\![\Delta_0]\!])/\mathcal{J}[\![\Delta_0]\!]][opts(\mathcal{H}[\![\Delta_0]\!])\acute{\psi}_0/\mathcal{H}[\![\Delta_0]\!]]$, $\grave{\psi}_1=\grave{\psi}_0[use(\#\mathcal{J}[\![\Delta_0]\!])/\mathcal{J}[\![\Delta_0]\!]][opts(\mathcal{H}[\![\Delta_0]\!])\grave{\psi}_0/\mathcal{H}[\![\Delta_0]\!]]$, $\acute{\zeta}_2=\mathcal{T}[\![t[\![\Delta_1]\!]\acute{\psi}_1]\!]\acute{\rho}_1\nu_0\nu_2\acute{\zeta}_1$ and $\grave{\zeta}_2=\mathcal{T}[\![t[\![\Delta_1]\!]\grave{\psi}_1]\!]\grave{\zeta}_1$ then $c\hat{\zeta}_2\hat{\pi}_1=true$ when we choose $\hat{\pi}_1$ in such a way that $spun[\![\Delta_0]\!]\nu_0\nu_1 0\hat{\psi}_0\hat{\pi}_1\hat{\pi}_0 \wedge p\hat{\pi}_1=true$. For such a $\hat{\pi}_1$, $tear[\![\Delta_1]\!](twist\acute{\rho}_1\acute{\upsilon}_1)=tear[\![\Delta_1]\!](field\acute{\upsilon}_1)$ and $fine[\![\Delta_1]\!]\nu_0\nu_2 1\hat{\psi}_1\hat{\pi}_1=true$, so because $T[\![\Delta_1]\!]$ and $t[\![\Delta_1]\!]\acute{\rho}_1\nu_0$ are $true$ we now try to demonstrate that $c\hat{\zeta}_1\hat{\pi}=true$ for every $\hat{\pi}$ having $spun[\![\Delta_1]\!]\nu_0\nu_2 1\hat{\psi}_1\hat{\pi}\hat{\pi}_1=true$. Thus we introduce any $\hat{\pi}_2$ and $\hat{\pi}_3$ such that $spun[\![\Delta_1]\!]\nu_0\nu_2 1\hat{\psi}_1\hat{\pi}_2\hat{\pi}_1=true$, $p\hat{\pi}_3=true$ and $match 0\hat{\pi}_3\hat{\pi}_2=true$ and we define $\hat{\pi}_4$ by setting $\acute{\pi}_4=\langle\acute{\rho}_0, act(trim[\![\Delta_0]\!][\![\Delta_1]\!])\acute{\upsilon}_3, \acute{\sigma}_3\rangle$ and $\grave{\pi}_4=\langle trim[\![\Delta_0]\!][\![\Delta_1]\!]\grave{\rho}_3, \grave{\upsilon}_3, \grave{\sigma}_3\rangle$. As $\acute{\zeta}_1\acute{\upsilon}_3\acute{\sigma}_3=\acute{\zeta}_0\acute{\upsilon}_4\acute{\sigma}_4$ and $\grave{\zeta}_1\grave{\rho}_3\grave{\upsilon}_3\grave{\sigma}_3=\grave{\zeta}_0\grave{\rho}_4\grave{\upsilon}_4\grave{\sigma}_4$, establishing that $p\hat{\pi}_4$ and $spun[\![\Delta]\!]\nu_0\nu_1 1\hat{\psi}\hat{\pi}_4\hat{\pi}_0$ are $true$ will enable us to assert that $a\langle\acute{\zeta}_1\acute{\upsilon}_3\acute{\sigma}_3, \grave{\zeta}_1\grave{\rho}_3\grave{\upsilon}_3\grave{\sigma}_3\rangle=true$.

Because $p\hat{\pi}_3=true$ and $hoten\hat{\omega}\langle level\acute{\upsilon}_3, \grave{\rho}_3\rangle \vee gyven\hat{\omega}\langle stick\acute{\upsilon}_3, \grave{\upsilon}_3\rangle=true$ for all $\hat{\omega}$ such that $hoten\hat{\omega}\langle level\acute{\upsilon}_4, \grave{\rho}_4\rangle \vee gyven\hat{\omega}\langle stick\acute{\upsilon}_4, \grave{\upsilon}_4\rangle=true$, we can immediately apply 5.2.7 to confirm that $p\hat{\pi}_4=true$. To prove that $spun[\![\Delta]\!]\nu_0\nu_1 1\hat{\psi}_0\hat{\pi}_4\hat{\pi}_0=true$ we note that $fine[\![\Delta_0]\!]\nu_0\nu_1 0\hat{\psi}_0\hat{\pi}_0$, $fine[\![\Delta_0]\!]\nu_0\nu_2 0\hat{\psi}_1\hat{\pi}_1$ and $fine[\![\Delta_1]\!]\nu_0\nu_3 1\hat{\psi}_1\hat{\pi}_2$ are $true$ when $\nu_3=\nu_2+\mathcal{Y}[\![\Delta_1]\!]-\#\mathcal{J}[\![\Delta_1]\!]-\#\mathcal{H}[\![\Delta_1]\!]$; also $trim[\![\Delta_0]\!][\![\Delta_1]\!]=clip[\![\Delta_0]\!]$ as $\mathcal{J}[\![\Delta_0]\!]\S\mathcal{H}[\![\Delta_0]\!]$ and $\mathcal{J}[\![\Delta_1]\!]\S\mathcal{H}[\![\Delta_1]\!]$ have no elements in common. Hence

$$\begin{aligned}
\mathrm{U}W_0\grave{\rho}_4 &= \mathrm{U}W_0(\mathit{clip}[\![\Delta_0]\!]\grave{\rho}_3)\\
&= \mathrm{U}W_0(\mathit{clip}[\![\Delta_0]\!]\grave{\rho}_2)\\
&= \mathrm{U}W_0(\mathit{clip}[\![\Delta_0]\!](\mathit{divert}\grave{\rho}_1(\mathit{slim}[\![\Delta_1]\!]\grave{\rho}_1)))\\
&= \mathrm{U}W_0(\mathit{clip}[\![\Delta_0]\!](\mathit{divert}(\mathit{divert}\grave{\rho}_0(\mathit{slim}[\![\Delta_0]\!]\grave{\rho}_1))(\mathit{slim}[\![\Delta_1]\!]\grave{\rho}_1)))\\
&= \mathrm{U}W_0(\mathit{divert}\grave{\rho}_0(\mathit{slim}[\![\Delta_1]\!]\grave{\rho}_1))\\
&= \mathrm{U}W_0(\mathit{divert}\grave{\rho}_0(\mathit{slim}[\![\Delta_1]\!](\mathit{divert}\grave{\rho}_0(\mathit{slim}[\![\Delta_0]\!]\grave{\rho}_1))))\\
&= \mathrm{U}W_0(\mathit{divert}\grave{\rho}_0(\mathit{slim}[\![\Delta_1]\!]\grave{\rho}_0)),
\end{aligned}$$

and likewise $\mathit{field}\acute{\upsilon}_4=\mathit{divert}(\mathit{field}\acute{\upsilon}_0)(\mathit{slim}[\![\Delta_1]\!](\mathit{twist}\acute{\rho}_4\acute{\upsilon}_4))$. From this we infer successively that $\mathit{apt}\hat{\psi}_0\langle\acute{\upsilon}_4,\grave{\rho}_4\rangle=\mathit{true}$, that $\mathit{fine}[\![\Delta]\!]\nu_0\nu_3 1\hat{\Phi}_0\hat{\pi}_4=\mathit{true}$ and that $\mathit{spun}[\![\Delta]\!]\nu_0\nu_1 1\hat{\Phi}_0\hat{\pi}_4\hat{\pi}_0=\mathit{true}$.

Consequently $a\langle\acute{\zeta}_0\acute{\upsilon}_4\acute{\sigma}_4,\grave{\zeta}_0\grave{\rho}_4\grave{\upsilon}_4\grave{\sigma}_4\rangle=\mathit{true}$ when $\hat{\pi}_4$ is derived from $\hat{\pi}_3$ in the appropriate manner. This is so for every suitable $\hat{\pi}_3$, so $c\hat{\zeta}_1\hat{\pi}_2=\mathit{true}$ whenever $\mathit{spun}[\![\Delta_1]\!]\nu_0\nu_2 1\hat{\Phi}_1\hat{\pi}_2\hat{\pi}_1\wedge p\hat{\pi}_2=\mathit{true}$. As hinted above, this ensures that $c\hat{\zeta}_2\hat{\pi}_1=\mathit{true}$ if $\mathit{spun}[\![\Delta_0]\!]\nu_0\nu_1 1\hat{\Phi}_0\hat{\pi}_1\hat{\pi}_0=\mathit{true}$, and this in turn implies that $c\langle\mathcal{T}[\![\mathbf{t}[\![\Delta]\!]\acute{\psi}_0]\!]\acute{\rho}_0\nu_0\nu_1\acute{\zeta}_0,\mathcal{T}[\![\mathbf{t}[\![\Delta]\!]\hat{\psi}_0]\!]\grave{\zeta}_0\rangle\hat{\pi}_0=\mathit{true}$. Because ν_0, ν_1, $\hat{\zeta}_0$, $\hat{\pi}_0$ and $\hat{\Phi}_0$ can be any entities satisfying the constraints given in the definition of T this means that $T[\![\Delta]\!]=\mathit{true}$.▷

5.3.7. Lemma.

If E_0 and E_1 are Sal expressions such that $\mathcal{L}[\![E_0]\!] \wedge \mathcal{R}[\![E_1]\!] = \mathit{true}$ then $\mathcal{G}[\![E_0 := E_1]\!] = \mathit{true}$.

$\lessdot$Choose any $\hat{\zeta}_0$, $\hat{\pi}_0$ and $\hat{\psi}$ having $g[\![E_0 := E_1]\!]\acute{\rho}_0 = \mathit{true}$, $p\hat{\pi}_0 = \mathit{true}$, $\mathit{rend}[\![E_0 := E_1]\!](\mathit{twist}\acute{\rho}_0\acute{\upsilon}_0) = \mathit{rend}[\![E_0 := E_1]\!](\mathit{field}\acute{\upsilon}_0)$, $\mathit{apt}\hat{\psi}\langle\acute{\upsilon}_0, \mathit{rend}[\![E_0 := E_1]\!]\grave{\rho}_0\rangle = \mathit{true}$, $\#\mathit{display}\acute{\upsilon}_0 \geq \mathit{lift}\acute{\rho}_0$ and $c\hat{\zeta}_0\hat{\pi}_0 = \mathit{true}$. Define pairs of continuations, $\hat{\zeta}_1$ and $\hat{\zeta}_2$, by setting $\acute{\zeta}_1 = \mathit{tv}(\lambda\acute{\upsilon}\acute{\sigma}.\mathit{assign}(\acute{\zeta}_0(\acute{\upsilon}\dagger 2))(\acute{\upsilon}\downarrow 2)(\acute{\upsilon}\downarrow 1)\acute{\sigma})$, $\grave{\zeta}_1 = \mathit{sv}(\lambda\grave{\rho}\grave{\upsilon}\grave{\sigma}.\mathit{assign}(\grave{\zeta}_0\grave{\rho}(\grave{\upsilon}\dagger 2))(\grave{\upsilon}\downarrow 2)(\grave{\upsilon}\downarrow 1)\grave{\sigma})$, $\acute{\zeta}_2 = \mathcal{R}[\![r[\![E_1]\!]\acute{\psi}]\!]\acute{\rho}_0\acute{\zeta}_0$ and $\grave{\zeta}_2 = \mathcal{R}[\![r[\![E_1]\!]\grave{\psi}]\!]\grave{\zeta}_1$, and suppose that E_0 is evaluated before E_1, so that $\mathfrak{G}[\![g[\![E_0 := E_1]\!]\acute{\psi}]\!]\acute{\rho}_0\acute{\zeta}_0 = \mathfrak{L}[\![\ell[\![E_0]\!]\acute{\psi}]\!]\acute{\rho}_2\acute{\zeta}_2$ and $\mathfrak{G}[\![g[\![E_0 := E_1]\!]\grave{\psi}]\!]\grave{\zeta}_0 = \mathfrak{L}[\![\ell[\![E_0]\!]\grave{\psi}]\!]\grave{\zeta}_2$ because tv and sv are idempotent. Let $\nu_0 = \mathit{lift}\acute{\rho}_0$ and $\nu_1 = \bigwedge\{I \in \mathcal{I}[\![E_0]\!] \to \acute{\rho}_0[\![I]\!]\downarrow 1\downarrow 1, \nu_0 \mid I\}$, and take ν_2 to be the unique integer such that $\mathit{display}\acute{\upsilon}_0\downarrow\nu_1 = \#(\mathit{chain}\acute{\upsilon}_0\downarrow\nu_2)$; as $g[\![E_0 := E_1]\!]\acute{\rho}_0 = \mathit{true}$ we know that $r[\![E_1]\!]\acute{\rho}_0\nu_1 = \mathit{true}$.

Owing to the constraints imposed on E_0 we can make the following claim: if $\hat{\zeta}$ is such that every E subject to $p\hat{\pi} \wedge \mathit{match}1\hat{\pi}\hat{\pi}_0 \wedge (\sim\mathit{known}(\acute{\upsilon}\downarrow 1)(\nu_2+1)\acute{\upsilon}\acute{\sigma}) \wedge (\acute{\upsilon}\downarrow 1 \mathsf{E} \mathsf{L}) = \mathit{true}$ satisfies $a\langle\acute{\zeta}\acute{\upsilon}\acute{\sigma}, \grave{\zeta}\grave{\rho}\grave{\upsilon}\grave{\sigma}\rangle = \mathit{true}$ then $c\langle\mathfrak{L}[\![\ell[\![E_0]\!]\acute{\psi}]\!]\acute{\rho}_0\acute{\zeta}, \mathfrak{L}[\![\ell[\![E_0]\!]\grave{\psi}]\!]\grave{\zeta}\rangle\hat{\pi}_0 = \mathit{true}$. This can be established by induction on the structure of E_0 with the aid of the remark after 5.3.1, so long as we assume that $\mathcal{E}[\![E]\!] \wedge \mathcal{G}[\![\Theta]\!] = \mathit{true}$ whenever E and Θ are constituents of E_0. Though this claim is not an immediate consequence of the fact that $\mathcal{E}[\![E_0]\!] = \mathit{true}$ when we define $\mathcal{E}$ as in 5.2.6, it would be so were we to modify $\mathcal{E}$ either by demanding that if $\mathcal{E}[\![E_0]\!] = \mathit{true}$ then $\mathcal{E}[\![E]\!] \wedge \mathcal{G}[\![\Theta]\!] = \mathit{true}$ when E and Θ form parts of E_0 or by replacing the one integer parameter of j by two (corresponding with our present ν_0 and ν_1). We have not adopted one of these alternatives because both involve the introduction of extra notation bearing little conceptual weight. Those who are sceptical about the claim made above can either verify it by introducing such notation or restrict their attention to what happens when E_0 is simply an identifier.

Select any pair $\hat{\pi}_1$ which is constrained by $p\hat{\pi}_1 \wedge match1\hat{\pi}_1\hat{\pi}_0 \wedge (\sim known(\acute{\upsilon}_1\downarrow 1)(\nu_2+1)\acute{\upsilon}_1\acute{\sigma}_1) \wedge (\acute{\upsilon}_1\downarrow 1 \in L) = true$; we shall prove that $a\langle \acute{\zeta}_2\acute{\upsilon}_1\acute{\sigma}_1, \grave{\zeta}_2\grave{\rho}_1\grave{\upsilon}_1\grave{\sigma}_1\rangle = true$ by demonstrating that $c\hat{\zeta}_2\hat{\pi}_1 = true$. Since $R[\![E_1]\!] = true$ and $r[\![E_1]\!]\acute{\rho}_0\nu_1 = true$, doing so reduces to showing that $j\hat{\zeta}_1\nu_1\hat{\pi}_1 = true$. To this end we take any $\hat{\pi}_2$ for which $p\hat{\pi}_2$, $match1\hat{\pi}_2\hat{\pi}_1$ and $found(\acute{\upsilon}_2\downarrow 1)\nu_1\acute{\upsilon}_2\acute{\sigma}_2$ are *true*, and we set $\hat{\beta} = \langle(\acute{\upsilon}_2\downarrow 1 \in L \rightarrow hold(\acute{\upsilon}_2\downarrow 1)\acute{\sigma}_2, \acute{\upsilon}_2\downarrow 1), (\grave{\upsilon}_2\downarrow 1 \in L \rightarrow hold(\grave{\upsilon}_2\downarrow 1)\grave{\sigma}_2, \grave{\upsilon}_2\downarrow 1)\rangle$, $\hat{\alpha} = \langle \acute{\upsilon}_2\downarrow 2, \grave{\upsilon}_2\downarrow 2\rangle$, $\acute{\pi}_3 = \langle \acute{\rho}_2, \acute{\upsilon}_2\dagger 2, update\acute{\alpha}\acute{\beta}\acute{\sigma}_2\rangle$ and $\grave{\pi}_3 = \langle \grave{\rho}_2, \grave{\upsilon}_2\dagger 2, update\grave{\alpha}\grave{\beta}\grave{\sigma}_2\rangle$. Plainly $match0\hat{\pi}_3\hat{\pi}_0 = true$, so once we have confirmed that $p\hat{\pi}_3 = true$ the fact that $c\hat{\zeta}_0\hat{\pi}_0 = true$ will ensure that $a\langle \acute{\zeta}_1\acute{\upsilon}_2\acute{\sigma}_2, \grave{\zeta}_1\grave{\rho}_2\grave{\upsilon}_2\grave{\sigma}_2\rangle = true$.

We are unable to list those $\hat{\omega}$ for which $kent\hat{\omega}\hat{\pi}_3 = true$ merely by appealing to 5.2.7, because the conditions in the statement of that proposition do not hold. We can, however, carry out an induction along similar lines by taking ν_3 to be any integer such that $\#chain\acute{\upsilon}_2+1 \geq \nu_3 \geq 1$ and by assuming that for some ν any $\hat{\omega}_0$ and $\hat{\omega}_1$ having $seen\nu\hat{\omega}_0\hat{\omega}_1\hat{\pi}_3 \wedge kent\hat{\omega}_1\hat{\pi}_2 \wedge known\acute{\omega}_1\nu_3\acute{\upsilon}_2\acute{\sigma}_2 = true$ also satisfy $kent\hat{\omega}_0\hat{\pi}_2 \wedge known\acute{\omega}_0\nu_3\acute{\upsilon}_3\acute{\sigma}_3 = true$. Under this assumption we pick any $\hat{\omega}_0$ and $\hat{\omega}_1$ for which $seen(\nu+1)\hat{\omega}_0\hat{\omega}_1\hat{\pi}_3 \wedge kent\hat{\omega}_1\hat{\pi}_2 \wedge known\acute{\omega}_1\nu_3\acute{\upsilon}_2\acute{\sigma}_2 = true$. Unless $\acute{\omega}_1 \in L$ or $\grave{\omega}_1 \in L$ the argument required is virtually identical with that of 5.2.7 (since the fact that $match2\hat{\pi}_2\hat{\pi}_0 = true$ ensures that either $\#chain\acute{\upsilon}_2 = 0$ or $\#\acute{\upsilon}_3 \geq chain\acute{\upsilon}_3\downarrow 1\downarrow 1\downarrow 3$), so we shall suppose that $\acute{\omega}_1 \in L$ or $\grave{\omega}_1 \in L$. In this case $seen\nu\hat{\omega}_0\hat{\omega}_2\hat{\pi}_3 = true$ where $\hat{\omega}_2 = \langle(\acute{\omega}_1 \in L \rightarrow hold\acute{\omega}_1\acute{\sigma}_3, \acute{\omega}_1), (\grave{\omega}_1 \in L \rightarrow hold\grave{\omega}_1\grave{\sigma}_3, \grave{\omega}_1)\rangle$; moreover $\acute{\omega}_1 = \acute{\alpha}$ if and only if $\grave{\omega}_1 = \grave{\alpha}$, as $kent\hat{\omega}_1\hat{\pi}_2 \wedge p_0\hat{\pi}_2 = true$. Consequently $seen\nu\hat{\omega}_0\hat{\omega}_2\hat{\pi}_3 \wedge kent\hat{\omega}_2\hat{\pi}_3 \wedge known\acute{\omega}_2\nu_3\acute{\upsilon}_2\acute{\sigma}_2 = true$ for some $\hat{\omega}_2$ unless, perhaps, $\hat{\omega}_1 = \hat{\alpha}$. However, when $seen(\nu+1)\hat{\omega}_0\hat{\alpha}\hat{\pi}_3 \wedge known\acute{\alpha}\nu_3\acute{\upsilon}_2\acute{\sigma}_2 = true$ we can infer that $\nu_2 \geq \nu_3$ and therefore that $known\acute{\beta}\nu_3\acute{\upsilon}_2\acute{\sigma}_2 = true$ (since $known\acute{\beta}\nu_2\acute{\upsilon}_2\acute{\sigma}_2 = true$); in addition $seen\nu\hat{\omega}_0\hat{\beta}\hat{\pi}_3 \wedge kent\hat{\beta}\hat{\pi}_2 = true$. This means that there is always a pair $\hat{\omega}_2$ for which $seen\nu\hat{\omega}_0\hat{\omega}_2\hat{\pi}_3 \wedge kent\hat{\omega}_2\hat{\pi}_2 \wedge known\acute{\omega}_2\nu_3\acute{\upsilon}_2\acute{\sigma}_2 = true$, and by the principle of induction $kent\hat{\omega}_0\hat{\pi}_2$ and $known\acute{\omega}_0\nu_3\acute{\upsilon}_3\acute{\sigma}_3$ must be *true*.

Plainly $kent\hat{\omega}\hat{\pi}_2=true$ for every $\hat{\omega}$ such that $hoten\hat{\omega}\langle level\acute{\upsilon}_3,\grave{\rho}_3\rangle \vee gyven\hat{\omega}\langle stick\acute{\upsilon}_3,\grave{\upsilon}_3\rangle=true$, so $kent\hat{\omega}\hat{\pi}_2=true$ whenever $kent\hat{\omega}\hat{\pi}_3=true$. By applying 5.2.7 we now see that $p\hat{\pi}_3=true$, and we can deduce in turn that $a\langle\acute{\zeta}_1\acute{\upsilon}_2\acute{\sigma}_2,\grave{\zeta}_1\grave{\rho}_2\grave{\upsilon}_2\grave{\sigma}_2\rangle=true$, that $j\hat{\zeta}_1\nu_1\hat{\pi}_1=true$, that $c\hat{\zeta}_2\hat{\pi}_1=true$ and that $a\langle\acute{\zeta}_2\acute{\upsilon}_1\acute{\sigma}_1,\grave{\zeta}_2\grave{\rho}_2\grave{\upsilon}_2\grave{\sigma}_2\rangle=true$. Thus $\hat{\zeta}_2$ meets the conditions laid upon $\hat{\zeta}$ above and we can assert that $c\langle\mathcal{L}[\![\mathcal{E}[\![E_0]\!]\acute{\psi}]\!]\acute{\rho}_0\acute{\zeta}_2,\mathcal{L}[\![\mathcal{E}[\![E_0]\!]\grave{\psi}]\!]\grave{\zeta}_2\rangle\hat{\pi}_0=true$, which ensures that $G[\![E_0:=E_1]\!]=true$.▹

5.3.8. Lemma.

If Γ is a Sal command such that $C[\![\Gamma]\!]=true$ then $G[\![\text{block } \Gamma]\!]=true$.

◁Write Θ for block Γ, and suppose that $\hat{\zeta}_0$, $\hat{\pi}_0$ and Φ_0 satisfy $g[\![\Theta]\!]\acute{\rho}_0=true$, $apt\Phi_0\langle\acute{\upsilon}_0,rend[\![\Theta]\!]\grave{\rho}_0\rangle=true$, $rend[\![\Theta]\!](twist\acute{\rho}_0\acute{\upsilon}_0)=rend[\![\Theta]\!](field\acute{\upsilon}_0)$, $\#display\acute{\upsilon}_0\geq lift\acute{\rho}_0$, $p\hat{\pi}_0=true$ and $c\hat{\zeta}_0\hat{\pi}_0=true$. To show that $c\langle\mathfrak{G}[\![\mathfrak{g}[\![\Theta]\!]\acute{\psi}_0]\!]\acute{\rho}_0\acute{\zeta}_0,\mathfrak{G}[\![\mathfrak{g}[\![\Theta]\!]\grave{\psi}_0]\!]\grave{\zeta}_0\rangle\hat{\pi}_0=true$, pick any pair $\hat{\pi}_1$ having $p\hat{\pi}_1\wedge match0\hat{\pi}_1\hat{\pi}_0=true$ and set $\nu_0=lift\acute{\rho}_0$, $\nu_1=1+\#\mathcal{J}[\![\Gamma]\!]+\#\mathcal{K}[\![\Gamma]\!]$,

$\acute{\psi}_1=\acute{\psi}_0[use(\#\mathcal{J}[\![\Gamma]\!])/\mathcal{J}[\![\Gamma]\!]][opts(\mathcal{K}[\![\Gamma]\!])\acute{\psi}_0/\mathcal{K}[\![\Gamma]\!]]$,

$\grave{\psi}_1=\grave{\psi}_0[use(\#\mathcal{J}[\![\Gamma]\!])/\mathcal{J}[\![\Gamma]\!]][opts(\mathcal{K}[\![\Gamma]\!])\grave{\psi}_0/\mathcal{K}[\![\Gamma]\!]]$,

$\langle\acute{\alpha}^*,\grave{\alpha}^*\rangle=\langle news(\#\mathcal{J}[\![\mathfrak{c}[\![\Gamma]\!]\acute{\psi}_1]\!])\acute{\sigma}_1,news(\#\mathcal{J}[\![\mathfrak{c}[\![\Gamma]\!]\grave{\psi}_1]\!])\grave{\sigma}_1\rangle$ and

$\hat{\zeta}_1=\langle lose(\nu_1+1)(\lambda\acute{\upsilon}\acute{\sigma}.\acute{\zeta}_0(\acute{\upsilon}\dagger 1)\acute{\sigma}),\grave{\zeta}_0\circ snip[\![\Gamma]\!]\rangle$. Because $\acute{\sigma}_1$ and $\grave{\sigma}_1$ are finite in area both $\acute{\alpha}^*$ and $\grave{\alpha}^*$ can be assumed not to be *error*.

We now let $\nu_4=\nu_1+\#\acute{\upsilon}_1$, $\acute{\rho}_2=grow(\mathcal{J}[\![\mathfrak{c}[\![\Gamma]\!]\acute{\psi}_1]\!]\S\mathcal{K}[\![\mathfrak{c}[\![\Gamma]\!]\acute{\psi}_1]\!])\acute{\rho}_0\nu_0 0$

$\acute{\upsilon}_3=\acute{\alpha}^*\S\mathfrak{Q}[\![\mathfrak{c}[\![\Gamma]\!]\acute{\psi}_1]\!]\acute{\rho}_2\acute{\zeta}_1\nu_4\S\langle size\nu_0\nu_1(grow(\mathcal{J}[\![\mathfrak{c}[\![\Gamma]\!]\acute{\psi}_1]\!]\S\mathcal{K}[\![\mathfrak{c}[\![\Gamma]\!]\acute{\psi}_1]\!])(arid)\nu_0 0)\acute{\upsilon}_1\acute{\sigma}_1\rangle\S\acute{\upsilon}_1$

$\acute{\sigma}_2=updates\acute{\alpha}^*(\mathfrak{P}[\![\mathfrak{c}[\![\Gamma]\!]\acute{\psi}_1]\!]\acute{\rho}_2\acute{\zeta}_1\nu_4)\acute{\sigma}_1$ and $\acute{\upsilon}_2=\langle size(\nu_0+1)1(arid)\acute{\upsilon}_3\acute{\sigma}_2\rangle\S\acute{\upsilon}_2$, for which $\mathfrak{G}[\![\mathfrak{g}[\![\Theta]\!]\acute{\psi}_0]\!]\acute{\rho}_0\acute{\zeta}_0\acute{\upsilon}_1\acute{\sigma}_1=\mathfrak{C}[\![\mathfrak{c}[\![\Gamma]\!]\acute{\psi}_1]\!]\acute{\rho}_2\acute{\zeta}_1\acute{\upsilon}_2\acute{\sigma}_2$. Moreover, we define

$\grave{\rho}_2=fix(\lambda\rho.\rho_1[\grave{\alpha}^*/\mathcal{J}[\![\mathfrak{c}[\![\Gamma]\!]\grave{\psi}_1]\!]][\mathfrak{Q}[\![\mathfrak{c}[\![\Gamma]\!]\grave{\psi}_1]\!]\grave{\zeta}_1\rho\grave{\upsilon}_1/\mathcal{K}[\![\mathfrak{c}[\![\Gamma]\!]\grave{\psi}_1]\!]])$, $\grave{\upsilon}_2=\grave{\upsilon}_1$ and

$\grave{\sigma}_2=updates\grave{\alpha}^*(\mathfrak{P}[\![\mathfrak{c}[\![\Gamma]\!]\grave{\psi}_1]\!]\grave{\zeta}_1\grave{\rho}_2\grave{\upsilon}_1)\grave{\sigma}_1$, so that

$\mathfrak{G}[\![\mathfrak{g}[\![\Theta]\!]\grave{\psi}_0]\!]\grave{\zeta}_0\grave{\rho}_1\grave{\upsilon}_1\grave{\sigma}_1=\mathfrak{C}[\![\mathfrak{c}[\![\Gamma]\!]\grave{\psi}_1]\!]\grave{\zeta}_1\grave{\rho}_2\grave{\upsilon}_2\grave{\sigma}_2$.

When we set $\nu_2=\nu_1+2$ and $\nu_3=3$ we see that $\hat{\pi}_0$ and $\hat{\pi}_2$ are related in the way laid down for the $\hat{\pi}_0$ and $\hat{\pi}_1$ of 5.2.8. Furthermore every $\hat{\pi}_4$ having $match0\hat{\pi}_4\hat{\pi}_2=true$ gives rise to some $\grave{\rho}_5$ and $\grave{\upsilon}_5$ such that $UW_0\grave{\rho}_5=UW_0\grave{\rho}_0$, $YW_0\grave{\upsilon}_5=YW_0\grave{\upsilon}_0$,

$\acute{\zeta}_1\acute{\upsilon}_4\acute{\sigma}_4=lose(\nu_2-1)(\lambda\acute{\upsilon}\acute{\sigma}.\acute{\zeta}_0(\acute{\upsilon}\dagger 1)\acute{\sigma})\acute{\upsilon}_4\acute{\sigma}_4$ and $\grave{\zeta}_1\grave{\rho}_4\grave{\upsilon}_4\grave{\sigma}_4=\grave{\zeta}_0\grave{\rho}_5\grave{\upsilon}_5\grave{\sigma}_4$. Because $c\hat{\zeta}_0\hat{\pi}_0=true$ we may therefore adopt reasoning precisely parallel with that of 5.2.8 in order to conclude that $c\hat{\zeta}_1\hat{\pi}_2=true$.

Quite obviously $apt\Phi_1\langle\acute{\upsilon}_2,rend[\![\Gamma]\!]\grave{\rho}_2\rangle=true$, $rend[\![\Gamma]\!](twist\acute{\rho}_2\acute{\upsilon}_2)=rend[\![\Gamma]\!](field\acute{\upsilon}_2)$ and $\#display\acute{\upsilon}_2\geq lift\acute{\rho}_2$; in addition, we know that $C[\![\Gamma]\!]$ and $c[\![\Gamma]\!]\acute{\rho}_2$ are *true*. Hence from the definition of C given in 5.2.6 we deduce that

$c\langle \mathcal{C}[\![\mathtt{c}[\![\Gamma]\!]\acute{\psi}_1]\!]\acute{\rho}_2\acute{\zeta}_1, \mathcal{C}[\![\mathtt{c}[\![\Gamma]\!]\grave{\psi}_1]\!]\grave{\zeta}_1\rangle \hat{\pi}_2 = true$ and that if $\hat{\upsilon}_4 = map(\lambda I.\langle level\acute{\upsilon}_2[\![I]\!]\downarrow 1, \grave{\rho}_2[\![I]\!]\downarrow 1\rangle)(\mathcal{I}[\![\Gamma]\!]\S\mathcal{K}[\![\Gamma]\!])$ and $\hat{\upsilon}_5 = map(\lambda\hat{\omega}.\langle(\acute{\omega}\in L\to hold\acute{\omega}\acute{\sigma}_2,\acute{\omega}),(\grave{\omega}\in L\to hold\grave{\omega}\grave{\sigma}_2,\grave{\omega})\rangle)(\hat{\upsilon}_4)$ then $c\langle\acute{\upsilon}_5\downarrow\nu\downarrow 1,\grave{\upsilon}_5\downarrow\nu\downarrow 1\rangle\hat{\pi}_2 = true$ whenever $\#\acute{\upsilon}_5\geq\nu\geq 1$. Indeed we may even justifiably assert that any $\hat{\omega}$ such that $gyven\hat{\omega}\hat{\upsilon}_4\vee gyven\hat{\omega}\hat{\upsilon}_5 = true$ satisfies $w\hat{\omega}\hat{\pi}_2\wedge known\acute{\omega}2\acute{\upsilon}_2\acute{\sigma}_2 = true$.

If $\hat{\omega}$ is any pair with $kent\hat{\omega}\hat{\pi}_1\wedge known\acute{\omega}1\acute{\upsilon}_1\acute{\sigma}_1 = true$ then $hold\acute{\omega}\acute{\sigma}_2 = hold\acute{\omega}\acute{\sigma}_1$ when $\acute{\omega}\in L$ and $hold\grave{\omega}\grave{\sigma}_2 = hold\grave{\omega}\grave{\sigma}_1$ when $\grave{\omega}\in L$. We can therefore apply 5.2.7 to $\hat{\pi}_2$ and $\hat{\pi}_1$ to establish that every $\hat{\omega}_0$, $\hat{\omega}_1$ and ν_1 which satisfy $seen\nu\hat{\omega}_0\hat{\omega}_1\hat{\pi}_2\wedge kent\hat{\omega}_1\hat{\pi}_1\wedge known\acute{\omega}_1 1\acute{\upsilon}_1\acute{\sigma}_1 = true$ must be such that $kent\hat{\omega}_0\hat{\pi}_1 = true$. In conjunction with the fact that any $\hat{\omega}$ subject to $hoten\hat{\omega}\langle level\acute{\upsilon}_2,\grave{\rho}_2\rangle = true$ satisfies $hoten\hat{\omega}\langle level\acute{\upsilon}_1,\grave{\rho}_1\rangle\vee gyven\hat{\omega}\hat{\upsilon}_4 = true$ this result allows us to confirm by a simple induction on ν that $kent\hat{\omega}_0\hat{\pi}_1\vee gyven\hat{\omega}_0\hat{\upsilon}_4\vee gyven\hat{\omega}_0\hat{\upsilon}_5 = true$ whenever $\hat{\omega}_0$, $\hat{\omega}_1$ and ν are constrained by $seen\nu\hat{\omega}_0\hat{\omega}_1\hat{\pi}_1\wedge hoten\hat{\omega}_1\langle level\acute{\upsilon}_2,\grave{\rho}_2\rangle = true$. Since $stick\acute{\upsilon}_2 = stick\acute{\upsilon}_1$ we can now conclude that if $kent\hat{\omega}\hat{\pi}_2 = true$ then $kent\hat{\omega}\hat{\pi}_1\vee gyven\hat{\omega}\hat{\upsilon}_4\vee gyven\hat{\omega}\hat{\upsilon}_5 = true$. Because $p\hat{\pi}_1 = true$ and $\bigwedge\{(area\alpha\acute{\sigma}_2\vee\sim area\alpha\acute{\sigma}_1)\wedge(area\alpha\grave{\sigma}_2\vee\sim area\alpha\grave{\sigma}_1)\mid\alpha\} = true$, a second application of 5.2.7 reveals that $w\hat{\omega}\hat{\pi}_2 = true$ whenever $kent\hat{\omega}\hat{\pi}_1 = true$. By inspection any $\acute{\omega}$ having $known\acute{\omega}\nu\acute{\upsilon}_1\acute{\sigma}_1 = true$ for some ν with $\#(chain\acute{\upsilon}_1)+1\geq\nu\geq 1$ also satisfies $known\acute{\omega}(\nu+2)\acute{\upsilon}_2\acute{\sigma}_2 = true$, so in fact $p\hat{\pi}_2 = true$.

As $c\langle \mathcal{C}[\![\mathtt{c}[\![\Gamma]\!]\acute{\psi}_1]\!]\acute{\rho}_1\acute{\zeta}_1, \mathcal{C}[\![\mathtt{c}[\![\Gamma]\!]\grave{\psi}_1]\!]\grave{\zeta}_1\rangle \hat{\pi}_2$ and $p\hat{\pi}_2$ are both *true*, $a\langle\mathcal{G}[\![\mathtt{g}[\![\Theta]\!]\psi_0]\!]\acute{\rho}_0\acute{\zeta}_0\acute{\upsilon}_1\acute{\sigma}_1,\mathcal{G}[\![\mathtt{g}[\![\Theta]\!]\grave{\psi}_0]\!]\grave{\zeta}_0\grave{\rho}_1\grave{\upsilon}_1\grave{\sigma}_1\rangle$ must also be *true* in view of the definition of c. The pair $\hat{\pi}_1$ is restricted only by having $p\hat{\pi}_1\wedge match0\hat{\pi}_1\hat{\pi}_0 = true$, so $c\langle\mathcal{G}[\![\mathtt{g}[\![\Theta]\!]\acute{\psi}_0]\!]\acute{\rho}_0\acute{\zeta}_0,\mathcal{G}[\![\mathtt{g}[\![\Theta]\!]\grave{\psi}_0]\!]\grave{\zeta}_0\rangle\hat{\pi}_0 = true$ for our typical choice of $\hat{\zeta}_0$, $\hat{\pi}_0$ and $\hat{\phi}_0$. In consequence $G[\![\text{block }\Gamma]\!]$ has to be *true*. ▸

In contrast with 4.3.5 this proof only requires *fix* to generate a fixed point (rather than the minimal fixed point).

If $T[\![\Delta]\!] = true$ and for all $\grave{\psi}$ $opts(\mathcal{K}[\![\Delta]\!]\grave{\psi})\downarrow\nu = true$ when

$\#\mathcal{H}[\![\Delta]\!]\geq\nu\geq1$ the method of proof used above can be adopted when showing that $\mathcal{D}[\![\text{rec }\Delta]\!]=true$. The assumption about *opts* is needed in this case in order to ensure that $\mathcal{d}[\![\text{rec }\Delta]\!]\tilde{\psi}$ does not contain recursive declarations by incidence, which have a store semantics that is not invariably congruent with their stack semantics; nonetheless, as we shall mention again in 5.3.9, we can extend the proof that $\mathcal{D}[\![\text{rec }\Delta]\!]=true$ to cover all the useful recursive declarations by incidence if we appeal to a counterpart of 3.9.4 that is appropriate to store semantics instead of standard semantics.

5.3.9. Theorem.

Suppose that $a\langle\bot,\bot\rangle=true$, $a\langle\top,\top\rangle=true$ and $a\langle wrong(\pi\downarrow 3),wrong(\pi\downarrow 3)\rangle=true$ for every π such that $p\pi=true$. Assume also that for all B, O and Ω $c\langle\mathcal{B}[\![B]\!]\acute{\zeta}_0,\mathcal{B}[\![B]\!]\grave{\zeta}_0\rangle\pi_0=true$, $c\langle\mathcal{O}[\![O]\!]\acute{\zeta}_1,\mathcal{O}[\![O]\!]\grave{\zeta}_1\rangle\pi_1=true$ and $c\langle\mathcal{W}[\![\Omega]\!]\acute{\zeta}_2,\mathcal{W}[\![\Omega]\!]\grave{\zeta}_2\rangle\pi_2=true$ whenever $p\pi_0=true$, $j\zeta_0 0\pi_0=true$, $p\pi_1=true$, $\#display(\pi_1\downarrow 2)\geq lift(\pi_1\downarrow 1)$, $found(\pi_1\downarrow 2\downarrow 1)(o[\![O]\!](lift(\pi_1\downarrow 1))\nu_1)((\pi_1\downarrow 2)\dagger 1)(\pi_1\downarrow 3)=true$, $j\zeta_1\nu_1\pi_1=true$, $p\pi_2=true$, $\#display(\pi_2\downarrow 2)\geq lift(\pi_2\downarrow 1)$, $found(\pi_2\downarrow 2\downarrow 1)(w[\![\Omega]\!](lift(\pi_2\downarrow 1))\nu_2\downarrow 2)((\pi_2\downarrow 2)\dagger 2)(\pi_2\downarrow 3)=true$, $found(\pi_2\downarrow 2\downarrow 2)(w[\![\Omega]\!](lift(\pi_2\downarrow 1))\nu_2\downarrow 1)((\pi_2\downarrow 2)\dagger 2)(\pi_2\downarrow 3)=true$ and $j\zeta_2\nu\pi_2=true$. Let $\lambda I\psi.true$ be the version of *opt* used when recursive declarations are evaluated in terms of store semantics and suppose that the domain of locations, L, is infinite. All E, Φ, Σ, Δ, Θ and Γ are such that, in terms of the predicates of 5.2.6, $E[\![E]\!]\wedge L[\![E]\!]\wedge R[\![E]\!]=true$, $F[\![\Phi]\!]=true$, $S[\![\Sigma]\!]=true$, $D[\![\Delta]\!]\wedge T[\![\Delta]\!]=true$, $G[\![\Theta]\!]=true$ and $C[\![\Gamma]\!]=true$; thus the stack semantics of any Sal program constrained in the manner suggested in 5.1.8 is congruent with the store semantics of any program obtained by subjecting the given program to the transformations laid down in 3.5.8 in a way which removes all the recursive declarations by incidence.

∢The rather complicated conditions in the statement of this result simply ensure that for every B, O and Ω $E[\![B]\!]=true$, $E[\![OE]\!]=true$ and $E[\![E_0\Omega E_1]\!]=true$ whenever $E[\![E]\!]=true$, $E[\![E_0]\!]=true$ and $E[\![E_1]\!]=true$; the proof that is so is of no more interest than the proof that $L[\![E]\!]=true$ and $R[\![E]\!]=true$ if $E[\![E]\!]=true$. Moreover the conditions may themselves be shown to be valid for any base or operator that might reasonably appear in a programming language. As the portions of the structural induction which we have omitted raise no difficulties not encountered in the portions we have given we may conclude that $E[\![E]\!]=true$ whenever E is an expression and that analogous remarks apply to the other predicates defined in 5.2.6.

The constraint on the version of *opt* used when recursive declarations are evaluated in terms of store semantics is intended merely to ensure that $\mathcal{H}[\![\mathcal{d}[\![$rec $\Delta]\!]\hat{\psi}]\!]$ need never be anything other than $\langle\rangle$; it is not intended to influence the transformations given in appendix 8 in any other way. Even this constraint can be removed for those recursive declarations which are subject to the conditions laid down in the statement of 3.9.4. Thus, if we consider any recursive declaration rec Δ obtained by combining such simple declarations as $I{=}{=}\Phi$ according to the syntax of Sal, then we may assert that $\mathcal{D}[\![$rec $\Delta]\!]=true$ whether or not $\mathcal{H}[\![\mathcal{d}[\![$rec $\Delta]\!]\hat{\psi}]\!]$ is $\langle\rangle$. The proof of this follows the simple pattern set by 5.3.8, but because it rests on a version of the result described in 3.9.4 we shall not discuss it in detail here.

We can dispense with the requirement that L be infinite provided that we demand instead that $a\langle wrong(\hat{\pi}{\downarrow}3),\hat{\delta}\rangle$ and $a\langle\hat{\delta},wrong(\hat{\pi}{\downarrow}3)\rangle$ be *true* for all $\hat{\delta}\in A\times A$ and for all $\hat{\pi}\in P\times P$ such that $p\hat{\pi}=true$.

We are at last in a position where we can see how to analyse the connection between while E do Γ and I:if E do (Γ;goto I) which was alluded to in 4.1.1. By 3.5.6 we may replace an occurrence of while E do Γ in an expression, E_0, by I::while E do Γ provided that doing so does not create a hole in the scope of a mention of I; by this means we obtain a new expression, E_1, such that $\mathcal{E}[\![E_0]\!]=\mathcal{E}[\![E_1]\!]$ in standard semantics. In accordance with 3.6.7 the resulting occurrence of I::while E do Γ in E_1 may be removed in favour of I::if E do (Γ;goto I) with the effect that we form an expression, E_2, for which $\mathcal{E}[\![E_1]\!]=\mathcal{E}[\![E_2]\!]$ in standard semantics. We may produce another expression, E_3, by substituting I:if E do (Γ;goto I) for I::if E do (Γ;goto I). An analogue of 5.3.8 which involves store semantics alone allows us to assert that the meaning ascribed to E_2 by store semantics is related to the meaning given to E_3 by store semantics in a way suggested by the predicates of 5.2.6; the proof of this result will not be provided in this essay because it is almost identical with the proof that we have just given, but elsewhere [52:2.5.9] we have established the same kind of result for a precursor of Sal. Hence if the domain A appropriate to standard semantics consists of the output components of stores we can establish that, when X_0 is the retraction introduced in 4.2.6, $(VX_0)^*(\mathcal{E}[\![E_0]\!](arid)(\lambda\epsilon\sigma.\sigma{\downarrow}3)(empty))=(VX_0)^*(\mathcal{E}[\![E_3]\!](arid)(\lambda\epsilon\sigma.\sigma{\downarrow}3)(empty))$; setting up this equation involves making appeals to 4.3.7 in a way that we shall explain in 5.6.9.▸

5.4. Compilers.

5.4.1. Code generation.

Though we have claimed that the stack semantics of appendix 3 "embodies an implementation" we have yet to explain what is to be understood by this phrase. Intuitively we mean, of course, that the relevant semantic equations prescribe how the state of a computer memory changes as the execution of a program proceeds. Here we shall make this notion precise by introducing a machine code, Sam, into which Sal programs can be compiled; in 5.5.7 the value given to any Sal program by appendix 3 will be shown to be that provided by appendix 12 for the corresponding Sam program. We shall not analyse the equations of appendix 2 in a similar manner but we could do so by first removing *fix* from the semantics of declarations and blocks and then introducing a sophisticated machine code akin to part of Sap.

Both the compiling algorithm needed and the semantic equations can be regarded as terms written in a version of the language Lambda [81] containing suitable idioms; we shall not prove that a particular compiler written in a conventional programming language is "correct" by virtue of having the same semantics as the Lambda term for the algorithm. Moreover, in keeping with our neglect of parsing problems, we shall ignore matters of lexical and syntactic analysis so that we can concentrate on the code generation phase of the algorithm. Thus for us the compiling algorithm will be simply a set of mutually recursive functions which transform members of the syntactic domains for Sal into members of the domains for Sam. These functions resemble the valuations of appendix 3 by taking as arguments not merely pieces of program but also those entities such as the environment which, in the terminology of 5.1.2, can be determined by a compiler

Whereas in appendix 3 we deal with valuations belonging to such domains as $\text{Exp}\to\text{U}\to\text{O}$ in appendix 6 we provide functions which take their arguments not into O, a domain of "pure code", but into Pro, the domain of abstract Sam programs; in 5.4.2 we shall provide a way of converting members of Pro into members of O. The analogy with $\mathcal{E}$, $\mathcal{L}$ and $\mathcal{R}$ therefore leads us to introduce $\mathfrak{e}$, $\mathfrak{l}$ and $\mathfrak{r}$, which belong to Exp→U→Pro; as is indicated in appendix 6, the dependence of $\mathcal{E}$, $\mathcal{L}$ and $\mathcal{R}$ on $\mathcal{B}$, $\mathcal{O}$ and $\mathcal{W}$ is reflected in the dependence of $\mathfrak{e}$, $\mathfrak{l}$ and $\mathfrak{r}$ on $\mathfrak{b}$, $\mathfrak{o}$ and $\mathfrak{w}$, which belong to Bas→Pro, Mon→Pro and Dya→Pro respectively. Likewise $\mathcal{D}$ and $\mathcal{T}$ correspond with $\mathfrak{d}$ and $\mathfrak{t}$, members of Dec→U→N→N→Pro, whereas $\mathcal{G}$ and $\mathcal{C}$ are associated with $\mathfrak{g}$, in Blo→U→Pro, and $\mathfrak{c}$, in Com→U→Pro. The valuations of appendix 9 are needed in the definitions of these functions for purposes like those discussed in 5.1.6.

The remaining valuations in appendix 3 cannot be connected with translation functions quite so readily because they are not specified in terms of O. However, for any Φ, Σ, ρ and υ both $\mathcal{F}[\![\Phi]\!]\rho\upsilon{\downarrow}1$ and $\mathcal{S}[\![\Sigma]\!]\rho$ can be manipulated into the form $\xi(jump)$ for some $\xi\epsilon O$ which can reasonably be regarded as being obtained from a Sam program. Consequently we can set up $\mathfrak{f}$, a member of Abs→U→Pro, and $\mathfrak{s}$, a member of Seq→U→Pro, by adjoining a jump instruction to the end of the code appropriate to abstractions and statements; this instruction is aptly denoted by jump and is intended to invoke *jump* when evaluated.

We could set up label values in a similar manner which would involve the use of mappings $\mathfrak{p}$ and $\mathfrak{q}$ belonging to Com→U→Pro*; $\mathfrak{p}[\![I:\Gamma]\!]\rho{\downarrow}1$ and $\mathfrak{q}[\![I::\Gamma]\!]\rho{\downarrow}1$, the code for the label I, would then be $\mathfrak{c}[\![\Gamma]\!]\rho$ for any I, Γ and ρ. Instead, however, we take advantage of a major characteristic of machine code programs, which is that they are purely linear and do not contain nested commands like if E_0 do (Γ_0;if E_1 do Γ_1) (by contrast with high-level languages); in particular, any Sam program is simply a list of instructions, each of which can be marked by its position in the list. Furthermore, the code for any label set in a Sal block is simply a segment of the list of Sam instructions generated by the whole block. Hence $\mathfrak{p}$ and $\mathfrak{q}$ can be taken to be members of Com→N* rather than Com→U→Pro*, and they provide for every label a pointer to a segment of the code for the surrounding block, not the code for the label itself. For instance, when the body of the block is I:Γ or I::Γ the label I must be made to point at the first element of the program $\mathfrak{c}[\![\Gamma]\!]\rho$, so $\mathfrak{p}[\![\mathrm{I}:\Gamma]\!]\downarrow 1$ and $\mathfrak{q}[\![\mathrm{I}::\Gamma]\!]\downarrow 1$ are 1.

Since a Sam program, Π say, is a list of instructions we may speak of its length, which we represent by #Π in the usual way; there is no need to assume, as we do tacitly, that individual instructions are all of the same length, but nothing with conceptual significance is lost by doing so. By structural induction we can show that $\#\mathfrak{c}[\![\Gamma]\!]\rho_0=\#\mathfrak{c}[\![\Gamma]\!]\rho_1$ for any command Γ and any ρ_0 and ρ_1. Consequently to supply the labels in $\Gamma_0;\Gamma_1$ with suitable pointers we have only to increase the pointers supplied to the labels in Γ_1 by the length of the code generated by Γ_0 in any environment. For this reason $\mathfrak{p}[\![\Gamma_0;\Gamma_1]\!]$ and $\mathfrak{q}[\![\Gamma_0;\Gamma_1]\!]$ are taken to be respectively $\mathfrak{p}[\![\Gamma_0]\!]\S map(\lambda\nu.\nu+\#(\mathfrak{c}[\![\Gamma_0]\!]\langle\lambda\mathrm{I}.\langle\langle 0,0\rangle\rangle,\langle 0\rangle\rangle))(\mathfrak{p}[\![\Gamma_1]\!])$ and $\mathfrak{q}[\![\Gamma_0]\!]\S map(\lambda\nu.\nu+\#(\mathfrak{c}[\![\Gamma_0]\!]\langle\lambda\mathrm{I}.\langle\langle 0,0\rangle\rangle,\langle 0\rangle\rangle))(\mathfrak{q}[\![\Gamma_1]\!])$ in appendix 6; the environment $\langle\lambda\mathrm{I}.\langle\langle 0,0\rangle\rangle,\langle 0\rangle\rangle$ is used instead of *arid* to allow attention to be confined to those environments having an entry for each free variable of Γ_0.

The instruction jump caters for situations in which a jump must be made to a destination which cannot be predicted during compilation. There are, however, several Sal expressions and commands which compile into programs containing instructions which authorize jumps having known destinations; for example, the code for if E do Γ is obtained by inserting between the code for E and the code for Γ an instruction which sanctions a jump to the end of the code Γ if *false* is yielded by the execution of E. Hence certain Sam instructions must be given parameters which, strictly speaking, should be viewed as numerals that denote the positions of various pieces of code. To avoid introducing transfer functions between numerals and integers we shall actually take these parameters to be the lengths themselves. Thus the conditional jump instruction mentioned in the description of the code for **if** E **do** Γ is designated by **pick** ν, not by **pick** N (where N is a variable ranging over numerals). More formally, we regard the domain of Sam instructions, Ins, as a product of many other domains, among which is a copy of N for the instructions of the form **pick** ν. Words like **pick** serve only to indicate to which summands of Ins their parameters belong, so we can legitimately interpret the program ⟨**leap** ν⟩§⟨**move** ν⟩§⟨**pick** ν⟩ say, as ⟨**leap** ν,**move** ν,**pick** ν⟩.

Integer parameters are required by many Sam instructions besides those which concern pointers to pieces of program. Five of the instructions found in appendix 6 (namely **take** ⟨ν,ρ⟩, **join** ⟨ν,ρ⟩, **clip** Δ, **swap** Δ and **trim** $\langle\Delta_0,\Delta_1\rangle$) are especially bizarre, because among their parameters may be not just integers but environments and Sal declarations. The intention underlying **take** ⟨ν,ρ⟩ is to place on the stack a pointer to the code beginning at a position labelled ν, together with the second and third components of an abstraction evaluated in the environment ρ; **join** ⟨ν,ρ⟩, **clip** Δ, **swap** Δ and **trim** $\langle\Delta_0,\Delta_1\rangle$ enable *aid*νρ, *act*(*clip*⟦Δ⟧), *act*(*swap*⟦Δ⟧) and *act*(*trim*$[\![\Delta_0]\!][\![\Delta_1]\!]$) to be applied to the stack. Hence if every mention of the third and fourth factors of (L→T)×N×N×U and the third factor of Z×N×U were excised from the stack semantics of Sal by the means outlined in 5.1.5, the instruction **take** ⟨ν,ρ⟩ could become simply **take** ⟨ν,*lift*ρ⟩, whilst **join** ⟨ν,ρ⟩, **swap** Δ, **clip** Δ and **trim** $\langle\Delta_0,\Delta_1\rangle$ could be eliminated from appendix 6. Thus the instructions in Sam which do not correspond with ones in realistic machine codes are precisely the ones needed solely for the proof of 5.3.9.

5.4.2. Instructions.

Most of the instructions available in Sam merely facilitate altering the stack and the store; among these instructions are nv, tv and lose ν, which are connected with the functions *nv*, *tv* and *lose*ν described in 5.1.4. The instruction jump, however, gives rise to a jump to a destination in the code which is indicated by something kept on the stack so the semantic equation for jump must mention this change of destination. Here we shall bring this about by introducing continuations into the semantics of Sam; because the stack and store pertinent to an implementation of Sam have the same structure as those needed in appendix 3, we can take these continuations to belong to the domain Z. Hence executing jump may be modelled mathematically by applying *jump*, as defined in 5.1.3, to a member of Y and a member of S; though jump is in Ins (the domain of instructions) *jump* is in Z.

This discussion might give the impression that in appendix 12 the valuation for instructions, $\mathcal{A}$, should be in Ins→Z→Z, so that $\mathcal{A}$⟦jump⟧ would be $\lambda\zeta\upsilon\sigma.jump\upsilon\sigma$. However, this impression is not correct, for as yet we have not considered the instructions which regard certain parameters as 'code pointers' (integers indicating where particular pieces of code begin); these instructions are represented by move ν', pick ν', seek ν', load $\langle\nu',\nu''\rangle$, link $\langle\nu',\nu''\rangle$ and take $\langle\nu',\rho\rangle$ (in which ν' is interpreted as a code pointer). Such instructions can be given a meaning only when placed in the context of an entire program, since otherwise nothing can be said about what their parameters really signify. Supplying a Sam program Π with a continuation ζ brings into being several other continuations (one for each segment of Π). As Π is a linear list of instructions, these continuations can be formed in such a way that, when $1+\#\Pi\geq\nu\geq1$, the segment $\Pi\dagger(\nu-1)$ sets up a continuation $\mathcal{Y}$⟦Π⟧$\zeta\nu$ which reveals the effect of first evaluating $\Pi\dagger(\nu-1)$ and then applying ζ. Thus the execution of Π from the code position ν onwards can be modelled by the continuation $\mathcal{V}[\![\Pi]\!]\zeta\nu$, and, more generally, $\mathcal{V}[\![\Pi]\!]\zeta$ provides continuations for the code pointers appearing as parameters of instructions embedded in Π. The valuation $\mathcal{A}$ therefore requires an argument drawn from a domain H which we shall take to be N→Z (although Z* could also serve out purposes); any such argument will be termed a 'consecution' and will typically be denoted by η, just as it was in 4.5.1.

The role of consecutions in the equations of appendix 12 bears some resemblance to the part played by environments in governing the meanings of labels set by incidence. In a Sam program Π the instruction $\Pi{\downarrow}\nu$ may be move ν' where $\nu\geq\nu'\geq1$, so when $\Pi{\downarrow}\nu$ is encountered in the execution of Π control may jump "backwards" to $\Pi{\downarrow}\nu$. Hence the consecution $\mathcal{V}[\![\Pi]\!]\zeta$ must be defined recursively; it must also be supplied in full as an argument when $\Pi{\downarrow}\nu$ is evaluated, for usually a variant of it, such as $\mathcal{V}[\![\Pi\dagger(\nu-1)]\!]\zeta$, is an inadequate substitute.

We could regard $\mathcal{A}$ as belonging to Ins→H→Z→Z, when link $\langle\nu',\nu''\rangle$ (the instruction for creating a member of the domain J for res) would be described by setting

$\mathcal{A}[\![\text{link}\ \langle\nu',\nu''\rangle]\!]=\lambda\eta\zeta\upsilon\sigma.\zeta(\langle\langle\eta\nu',\nu''+\#\upsilon\rangle\rangle\S\upsilon)\sigma.$

Here the pertinent version of $\mathcal{V}$ would satisfy the equation

$\mathcal{V}=\lambda\Pi\zeta\nu.(\#\Pi\geq\nu\geq1\rightarrow\mathcal{A}[\![\Pi{\downarrow}\nu]\!](\mathcal{V}[\![\Pi]\!]\zeta)(\mathcal{V}[\![\Pi]\!]\zeta(\nu+1)),\zeta).$

This suggestion for the value of $\mathcal{V}$ makes it plain that there is no need to supply a continuation when evaluating an instruction; the entry in the consecution for the "next instruction along" will do just as well. Hence in appendix 12 we actually take $\mathcal{A}$ to be a member of Ins→H→H, and we write

$\mathcal{A}[\![\text{link}\ \langle\nu',\nu''\rangle]\!]=\lambda\eta\nu\upsilon\sigma.\eta\nu(\langle\langle\eta\nu',\nu''+\#\upsilon\rangle\rangle\S\upsilon)\sigma.$

We also provide $\mathcal{U}$, a valuation in Pro→Z→H→H, and $\mathcal{V}$, a valuation in Pro→Z→H, which are subject to:

$\mathcal{U}=\lambda\Pi\zeta\eta.(\#\Pi\geq\nu\geq1\rightarrow\mathcal{A}[\![\Pi{\downarrow}\nu]\!]\eta(\nu+1),\zeta),$

$\mathcal{V}=\lambda\Pi\zeta.fix(\mathcal{U}[\![\Pi]\!]\zeta).$

The equations governing load $\langle \nu', \nu'' \rangle$ and link $\langle \nu', \nu'' \rangle$ in appendix 12 have a common form but different intentions. Thus load $\langle \nu', \nu'' \rangle$ places on the stack something in the domain J needed by label values, whereas link $\langle \nu', \nu'' \rangle$ places on the stack the value required by a **res** sequencer. We could, of course, distinguish between the resulting two occurrences of $\langle \eta\nu', \nu''+\#\upsilon^* \rangle$ by injecting them into different summands of **W** with the aid of the function *flag* mentioned in 2.4.4.

In appendix 12 we specify how $\mathcal{A}$ is defined only for those Sam instructions which appear explicitly in appendix 6, although other instructions are necessary for the formation of $\mathfrak{b}$, $\mathfrak{o}$ and $\mathfrak{w}$. Any member of Ins that is not mentioned in appendix 12 will be called a 'secret instruction'. If Ξ is a member of Ins which happens to be secret we shall assume henceforth that $\mathcal{A}[\![\Xi]\!] = \lambda\eta\nu.\psi(map\,\eta\nu^*)(\eta\nu)$ for some $\nu^* \epsilon N^*$ and for some $\psi \epsilon Z^* \to O$; here we do not allow ψ to depend on those parameters of Ξ which are used as code pointers. This assumption is eminently reasonable, since it holds for every instruction mentioned in appendix 12; if Ξ is pick ν', for instance, ν^* is $\langle \nu' \rangle$ and ψ is $\lambda\zeta^*\zeta\upsilon\sigma.test\langle \zeta(\upsilon\dagger 1), (\zeta^*\downarrow 1)(\upsilon\dagger 1) \rangle (\upsilon\downarrow 1)\sigma$. In fact only when a parameter of Ξ is treated as a code pointer is it necessary to take ν^* to be anything other than $\langle\rangle$.

5.4.3. Code relocation.

When a Sal program is compiled into a Sam program Π by applying the algorithm of appendix 6, occurrences of move ν', pick ν', seek ν', load $\langle\nu',\nu''\rangle$, link $\langle\nu',\nu''\rangle$ and take $\langle\nu',\rho\rangle$ in Π define only 'relative addresses' in Π; thus if $\Pi\downarrow\nu$ is move ν', for instance, it is intended that when the program is executed there will be an unconditional jump to $\Pi\downarrow(\nu+\nu'+1)$, not to $\Pi\downarrow\nu'$. However, in common with many real machines, the abstract machine which we use to describe the meanings of Sam programs requires 'absolute addresses', for it perversely interprets move ν' as demanding a jump to $\Pi\downarrow\nu'$, whatever may be the whereabouts of move ν' in Π.

There are three ways of obviating this difficulty. Firstly, we could make the Sal compiler produce absolute addresses by providing all the translating functions with an extra argument revealing how much code had already been produced; $\mathfrak{c}[\![$if E do $\Gamma]\!]$, for example, would become $\lambda\rho\nu.\mathfrak{r}[\![E]\!]\rho\nu\S\langle\text{pick }\nu+1+\#\mathfrak{r}[\![E]\!]\rho\nu+\#\mathfrak{c}[\![\Gamma]\!]\rho(\nu+1+\#\mathfrak{c}[\![\Gamma]\!]\rho\nu)\rangle\S\mathfrak{c}[\![\Gamma]\!]\rho(\nu+1+\#\mathfrak{r}[\![E]\!]\rho\nu)$. Secondly, we could abandon the equations of appendix 12 in favour of ones which view the parameters of instructions as addresses known relative to the position of the instruction itself; then we would end up with equations such as

$\mathfrak{A}[\![\text{link }\langle\nu',\nu''\rangle]\!]=\lambda\eta\nu\upsilon\sigma.\eta\nu(\langle\langle\eta(\nu+\nu'),\nu''+\#\upsilon\rangle\rangle\S\upsilon)\sigma.$

Thirdly, we could introduce an additional mapping which would transform any Sam program containing relative addresses into one containing absolute addresses.

Compiling programs into absolute code is undesirable, because when presented with an expression like E_0E_1 we may wish to compile E_0 and E_1 separately but to execute them together. It is more sensible to provide a machine which interprets parameters as relative addresses, but this is not done by all designers. We shall therefore actually adopt the third way out of the difficulty by introducing $\mathfrak{a}$, a member of

Ins→N→Ins. This function models a relocating loader by modifying the code pointers appearing in Sam instructions; accordingly we let

$\mathfrak{a}[\![\text{link } \langle\nu',\nu''\rangle]\!]=\lambda\nu.\text{link}\,\langle\nu+\nu',\nu''\rangle$.

When an instruction is placed in a particular program the absolute address corresponding with its parameter can be obtained by applying $\mathfrak{x}$, a member of Pro→N→Pro, to the program; here the integer parameter supplied to $\mathfrak{x}$ has to be "rolled along" between one instruction and the next, so we arrange that $\mathfrak{x}=\lambda\Pi\nu.((\#\Pi=0)\rightarrow\langle\rangle,\langle\mathfrak{a}[\![\Pi\downarrow 1]\!](\nu+1)\S\mathfrak{x}[\![\Pi\dagger 1]\!](\nu+1))$ by letting ψ range over members of Pro→N→Pro and by writing $\mathfrak{x}=fix(\lambda\psi\Pi\nu.(\#\Pi=0)\rightarrow\langle\rangle,\langle\mathfrak{a}[\![\Pi\downarrow 1]\!](\nu+1)\rangle\S\psi[\![\Pi\dagger 1]\!](\nu+1))$.

In appendix 14 $\mathfrak{a}$ is defined for all the Sam instructions which are not secret; when extending it to the remaining instructions we arrange that if $\mathcal{A}[\![\Xi]\!]=\lambda\eta\nu.\psi(map\,\eta\nu^*)(\eta\nu)$ for some $\nu^*\in N^*$ and for some $\psi\in Z^*\rightarrow O$ then $\lambda\nu'.\mathcal{A}[\![\mathfrak{a}[\![\Xi]\!]\nu']\!]=\lambda\nu'\eta\nu.\psi(map(\lambda\nu''.\eta(\nu'+\nu''))\nu^*)(\eta\nu)$.

When Π is any program and when ν' and ν'' are arbitrary integers simple inductions on $\#\Pi$ allow us to infer that $\#\mathfrak{x}[\![\Pi]\!]\nu'=\#\Pi$ and that $\mathfrak{x}[\![\Pi]\!]\nu'\downarrow\nu''=\mathfrak{a}[\![\Pi\downarrow\nu'']\!](\nu'+\nu'')$. Hence by appealing to the definition of $\mathcal{L}$ given in 5.4.2 we deduce that

$$\begin{aligned}\lambda\zeta\eta.\mathcal{L}[\![\mathfrak{x}[\![\Pi]\!]\nu']\!]\zeta\eta\nu''&=\lambda\zeta\eta.(\#\mathfrak{x}[\![\Pi]\!]\nu'\geq\nu''\geq 1)\rightarrow\mathcal{A}[\![\mathfrak{x}[\![\Pi]\!]\nu'\downarrow\nu'']\!]\eta(\nu''+1),\zeta\\&=\lambda\zeta\eta.(\#\Pi\geq\nu''\geq 1)\rightarrow\mathcal{A}[\![\mathfrak{x}[\![\Pi]\!]\nu'\downarrow\nu'']\!]\eta(\nu''+1),\zeta\\&=\lambda\zeta\eta.(\#\Pi\geq\nu''\geq 1)\rightarrow\mathcal{A}[\![\mathfrak{a}[\![\Pi\downarrow\nu'']\!](\nu'+\nu'')]\!]\eta(\nu''+1),\zeta.\end{aligned}$$

In particular

$\mathcal{L}[\![\mathfrak{x}[\![\Pi]\!]1]\!]=\lambda\zeta\eta\nu.(\#\Pi\geq\nu\geq 1)\rightarrow\mathcal{A}[\![\mathfrak{a}[\![\Pi\downarrow\nu]\!](\nu+1)]\!]\eta(\nu+1),\zeta$,

whilst, as $\mathcal{V}[\![\mathfrak{x}[\![\Pi]\!]1]\!]=\lambda\zeta.\mathcal{L}[\![\mathfrak{x}[\![\Pi]\!]1]\!]\zeta(\mathcal{V}[\![\mathfrak{x}[\![\Pi]\!]1]\!]\zeta)$ owing to the properties of *fix* discussed in 2.3.2,

$\mathcal{V}[\![\mathfrak{x}[\![\Pi]\!]1]\!]=\lambda\zeta\nu.(\#\Pi\geq\nu\geq 1)\rightarrow\mathcal{A}[\![\mathfrak{a}[\![\Pi\downarrow\nu]\!](\nu+1)]\!](\mathcal{V}[\![\mathfrak{x}[\![\Pi]\!]1]\!]\zeta)(\nu+1),\zeta$;

this equation will be very useful when we come to the proofs of the lemmas leading up to 5.5.7.

We could have regarded $\mathfrak{x}$ as a mapping from one language into a different one, but there is nothing to be gained from so doing except perhaps a little extra clarity. Hence, although $\mathfrak{e}[\![E]\!]\rho$ will be a valid

Sam program for every expression E and every environment ρ, of more interest to us will be $\mathfrak{z}[\![\mathfrak{e}[\![E]\!]\rho]\!]1$. Programs such as this should not mention code pointers corresponding with positions far outside them, for when E_0 and E_1 are executed together there should be no wild jumps from the code for E_0 into that for E_1. More generally, the code produced by a compiler for any segment of a source language program should not need to refer to the code for any other segment, because otherwise the segments cannot be compiled entirely independently. Consequently, if Π is any program obtained by compiling a Sal expression, Π must be 'coherent', in that whenever $\#\Pi\geq\nu\geq 1$ if $\mathfrak{A}[\![\Pi\downarrow\nu]\!]=\lambda\eta\nu'.\psi(map\eta\nu^*)(\eta\nu')$ for some $\nu^*\in N^*$ and for some $\psi\in Z^*\to O$ then $\#\Pi\geq\nu+\nu^*\downarrow\nu''\geq 0$ for every ν'' having $\#\nu^*\geq\nu''\geq 1$. Thus, on the assumption that no secret instruction treats its parameters as code pointers (so that ν^* can be $\langle\rangle$ unless $\Pi\downarrow\nu$ is move ν', pick ν', seek ν', link $\langle\nu',\nu''\rangle$, load $\langle\nu',\nu''\rangle$ or take $\langle\nu',\rho\rangle$), Π is coherent if and only if whenever $\#\Pi\geq\nu\geq 1$ the following conditions are satisfied:

(i) if $\Pi\downarrow\nu$ is move ν', pick ν' or seek ν' for any ν' then $\#\Pi\geq\nu+\nu'\geq 0$;

(ii) if $\Pi\downarrow\nu$ is link $\langle\nu',\nu''\rangle$ or load $\langle\nu',\nu''\rangle$ for any ν' and ν'' then $\#\Pi\geq\nu+\nu'\geq 0$;

(iii) if $\Pi\downarrow\nu$ is take $\langle\nu',\rho\rangle$ for any ν' and ρ then $\#\Pi\geq\nu+\nu'\geq 0$.

When Π is coherent and when $\#\Pi\geq\nu\geq 1$ there should be a list $\nu^*\in N^*$ and a function $\psi\in Z^*\to O$ such that $\mathfrak{U}[\![\mathfrak{z}[\![\Pi]\!]1\downarrow\nu]\!]=\lambda\zeta\eta\nu'.\psi(map\eta\nu^*)(\eta\nu')$ and $1+\#\Pi\geq\nu^*\downarrow\nu''\geq 1$ whenever $\#\nu^*\geq\nu''\geq 1$.

If Π is any program we may write $cleave[\![\Pi]\!]=true$ to signify that Π is coherent. By a simple induction on the structure of Sal programs we could show that if $\mathfrak{b}[\![B]\!]$, $\mathfrak{o}[\![O]\!]$ and $\mathfrak{w}[\![\Omega]\!]$ are coherent for all B, O and Ω then $\mathfrak{e}[\![E]\!]\rho$ is coherent for every expression E and every environment ρ, but instead we shall incorporate the proof of this assertion in the less trivial arguments leading to 5.5.7.

Given two Sam programs, Π_0 and Π_1, and an integer, ν, we shall say that 'Π_1 is embedded in Π_0 after ν' if $\#\Pi_0-\#\Pi_1\geq\nu\geq 0$ and if

$\Pi_0\downarrow(\nu+\nu')=\Pi_1\downarrow\nu'$ whenever $\#\Pi_1\geq\nu'\geq 1$. In 5.4.4 and 5.4.5 we shall prove that a coherent program embedded in any other program has an effect that depends only on the continuation following it. This fact is of considerable interest in its own right, since there are many coherent Sam programs which do not result from compiling Sal programs. We established a similar property of Sap controls in 4.5.2 and 4.5.3.

The techniques for analysing implementations which concern us in this book are, we believe, sufficiently general to cater for proofs about the correctness of any implementation (even if it involves optimization). However, before pursuing them further the reader may wish to examine early work on the correctness of compilers, which has been surveyed well already [54]. As an aid to this examination we can provide a diagram indicating some of the results required when proving that our compiler is correct for those Sal programs that are constrained in accordance with appendix 8; we shall assume that the manner in which Sam programs are executed is given by appendix 13 (which we shall discuss in 5.6.1). This diagram should be interpreted in the way adopted for the diagram in 4.4.3; in essence it summarizes informally much of what we shall say in 5.6.9, where we shall outline the steps needed in proofs of the correctness of implementations.

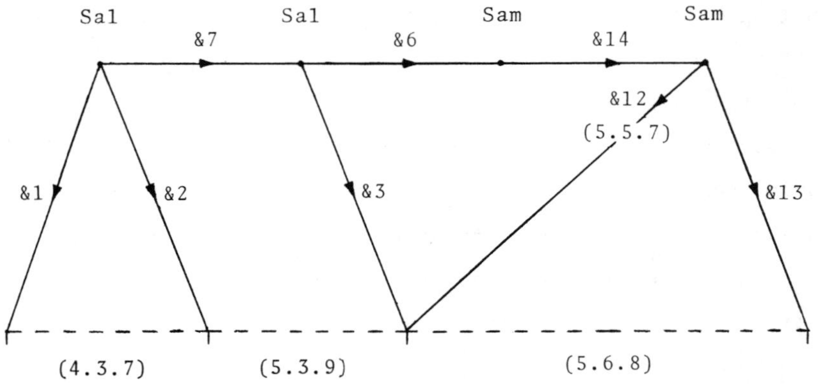

5.4.4. Proposition.

Let Π_0 and Π_1 be Sam programs and suppose that ν is an integer such that Π_1 is coherent and embedded in Π_0 after ν. If η_0 and η_1 are consecutions for which $\eta_0(\nu+\nu')=\eta_1\nu'$ whenever $1+\#\Pi_1\geq\nu'\geq 1$ and if ζ_0 and ζ_1 are arbitrary continuations then $\mathcal{U}[\![\mathcal{X}[\![\Pi_0]\!]1]\!]\zeta_0\eta_0(\nu+\nu')=\mathcal{U}[\![\mathcal{X}[\![\Pi_1]\!]1]\!]\zeta_1\eta_1\nu'$ whenever $\#\Pi_1\geq\nu'\geq 1$.

⊲We begin by letting Ξ be an arbitrary instruction such that $\mathcal{A}[\![\Xi]\!]=\lambda\eta\nu''.\psi(map\eta\nu^*)(\eta\nu'')$ for some $\nu^*\epsilon N^*$ and for some $\psi\epsilon Z^*\to 0$; here ψ is not influenced by the parameters of Ξ used as code pointers. As we mentioned in 5.4.3, the valuation $\mathcal{a}$ defined in appendix 14 is arranged in such a way that when ν' is any integer $\mathcal{A}[\![\mathcal{a}[\![\Xi]\!](\nu+\nu'+1)]\!]=\lambda\eta\nu''.\psi(map(\lambda\nu'''.\eta(\nu+\nu'+1+\nu'''))\nu^*)(\eta\nu'')$ and $\mathcal{A}[\![\mathcal{a}[\![\Xi]\!](\nu'+1)]\!]=\lambda\eta\nu''.\psi(map(\lambda\nu'''.\eta(\nu'+1+\nu'''))\nu^*)(\eta\nu'')$. In particular, if $1+\#\Pi_1\geq\nu'\geq 1$ and if $1+\#\Pi_1\geq\nu'+1+\nu^*\downarrow\nu'''\geq 1$ whenever $\#\nu^*\geq\nu'''\geq 1$ then

$$\begin{aligned}\mathcal{A}[\![\mathcal{a}[\![\Xi]\!](\nu+\nu'+1)]\!]\eta_0(\nu+\nu'+1)&=\psi(map(\lambda\nu'''.\eta_0(\nu+\nu'+1+\nu'''))\nu^*)(\eta_0(\nu+\nu'+1))\\&=\psi(map(\lambda\nu'''.\eta_0(\nu+\nu'+1+\nu'''))\nu^*)(\eta_1(\nu'+1))\\&=\psi(map(\lambda\nu'''.\eta_1(\nu'+1+\nu'''))\nu^*)(\eta_1(\nu'+1))\\&=\mathcal{A}[\![\mathcal{a}[\![\Xi]\!](\nu'+1)]\!]\eta_1(\nu'+1).\end{aligned}$$

Now we suppose that $\#\Pi_1\geq\nu'\geq 1$ and we identify $\Pi_1\downarrow\nu'$ with Ξ, the instruction discussed in the preceding paragraph; thus we may set $\mathcal{A}[\![\Pi_1\downarrow\nu']\!]=\lambda\eta\nu''.\psi(map\eta\nu^*)(\eta\nu'')$ when ν^* and ψ are as above. Plainly $1+\#\Pi_1\geq\nu'\geq 1$; moreover $1+\#\Pi_1\geq\nu'+1+\nu'''\downarrow\nu\ \geq 1$ whenever $\#\nu^*\geq\nu''\geq 1$, because Π_1 is coherent. Consequently $\mathcal{A}[\![\mathcal{a}[\![\Pi_1\downarrow\nu']\!](\nu+\nu'+1)]\!]\eta_0(\nu+\nu'+1)=\mathcal{A}[\![\mathcal{a}[\![\Pi_1\downarrow\nu']\!](\nu'+1)]\!]\eta_1(\nu'+1)$. The fact that Π_1 is embedded in Π_0 after ν ensures that $\#\Pi_0-\#\Pi_1\geq\nu\geq 1$ and that $\Pi_0\downarrow(\nu+\nu')=\Pi_1\downarrow\nu'$. Hence $\#\Pi_0\geq\nu+\nu'\geq 1$ and

$$
\begin{aligned}
\mathcal{U}[\![\mathcal{Z}[\![\Pi_0]\!]1]\!]\zeta_0\eta_0(\nu+\nu') &= \mathcal{A}[\![\mathcal{Z}[\![\Pi_0]\!]1\downarrow(\nu+\nu')]\!]\eta_0(\nu+\nu'+1)\\
&= \mathcal{A}[\![\mathcal{a}[\![\Pi_0\downarrow(\nu+\nu')]\!](\nu+\nu'+1)]\!]\eta_0(\nu+\nu'+1)\\
&= \mathcal{A}[\![\mathcal{a}[\![\Pi_1\downarrow\nu']\!](\nu+\nu'+1)]\!]\eta_0(\nu+\nu'+1)\\
&= \mathcal{A}[\![\mathcal{a}[\![\Pi_1\downarrow\nu']\!](\nu'+1)]\!]\eta_1(\nu'+1)\\
&= \mathcal{A}[\![\mathcal{Z}[\![\Pi_1]\!]1\downarrow\nu']\!]\eta_1(\nu'+1)\\
&= \mathcal{U}[\![\mathcal{Z}[\![\Pi_1]\!]1]\!]\zeta_1\eta_1\nu';
\end{aligned}
$$

moreover this chain of deductions is valid for each ν' such that $\#\Pi_1\geq\nu'\geq 1$.

To convince those those who mistrust the dependence of this argument on ν^* and ψ, which we have not bothered to define, we shall examine exactly what happens when $\Pi_1\downarrow\nu'$ is move ν'' for some ν'' (when ν^* is $\langle\nu''\rangle$ and ψ is $\lambda\zeta^*\zeta.\zeta^*\downarrow 1$). In this situation the coherent nature of Π_1 ensures that $1+\#\Pi_1\geq\nu'+1+\nu''\geq 1$ so $\eta_0(\nu+\nu'+1+\nu'')=\eta_1(\nu'+1+\nu'')$. Hence

$$
\begin{aligned}
\mathcal{A}[\![\mathcal{a}[\![\text{move }\nu'']\!](\nu+\nu'+1)]\!]\eta_0(\nu+\nu'+1) &= \mathcal{A}[\![\text{move }\nu+\nu'+1+\nu'']\!]\eta_0(\nu+\nu'+1)\\
&= \eta_0(\nu+\nu'+1+\nu'')\\
&= \eta_1(\nu'+1+\nu'')\\
&= \mathcal{A}[\![\text{move }\nu'+1+\nu'']\!]\eta_1(\nu'+1)\\
&= \mathcal{A}[\![\mathcal{a}[\![\text{move }\nu'']\!](\nu'+1)]\!]\eta_1(\nu'+1),
\end{aligned}
$$

while $\mathcal{U}[\![\mathcal{Z}[\![\Pi_0]\!]1]\!]\zeta_0\eta_0(\nu+\nu')=\mathcal{A}[\![\mathcal{a}[\![\Pi_0\downarrow(\nu+\nu')]\!](\nu+\nu'+1)]\!]\eta_0(\nu+\nu'+1)$ and $\mathcal{U}[\![\mathcal{Z}[\![\Pi_1]\!]1]\!]\zeta_1\eta_1\nu'=\mathcal{A}[\![\mathcal{a}[\![\Pi_1\downarrow\nu']\!](\nu'+1)]\!]\eta_1(\nu'+1)$ as usual. Because $\Pi_0\downarrow(\nu+\nu')$ is move ν'' it follows in this case at least that $\mathcal{U}[\![\mathcal{Z}[\![\Pi_0]\!]1]\!]\zeta_0\eta_0(\nu+\nu')=\mathcal{U}[\![\mathcal{Z}[\![\Pi_1]\!]1]\!]\zeta_1\eta_1\nu'.$ $\triangleright$

5.4.5. Proposition.

Let Π_0 and Π_1 be Sam programs and suppose that ν is an integer such that Π_1 is coherent and embedded in Π_0 after ν. If ζ_0 and ζ_1 are continuations for which $\zeta_1=\mathcal{V}\llbracket\Pi_0\rrbracket\zeta_0(\nu+1+\#\Pi_1)$ then $\mathcal{V}\llbracket\Pi_0\rrbracket\zeta_0(\nu+\nu')=\mathcal{V}\llbracket\Pi_1\rrbracket\zeta_1\nu'$ whenever $1+\#\Pi_1\geq\nu'\geq 1$.

◁For any ζ_0 and ζ_1 such that $\zeta_1=\mathcal{V}\llbracket\Pi_0\rrbracket\zeta_0(\nu+1+\#\Pi_1)$ we define ψ_0, ψ_1, η_0 and η_1 by setting $\psi_0=\mathcal{U}\llbracket\Pi_0\rrbracket\zeta_0$, $\psi_1=\mathcal{U}\llbracket\Pi_1\rrbracket\zeta_1$, $\eta_0=\lambda\nu'.((\nu+1+\#\Pi\geq\nu'\geq\nu+1)\rightarrow fix\psi_1(\nu'-\nu),fix\psi_0\nu')$ and $\eta_1=\lambda\nu'.((\#\Pi_1\geq\nu'\geq 1)\rightarrow fix\psi_0(\nu+\nu'),\zeta_1)$.

As $\eta_0(\nu+\nu')=fix\psi_1\nu'$ whenever $1+\#\Pi_1\geq\nu'\geq 1$, 4.5.4 assures us that $\psi_0\eta_0(\nu+\nu')=\psi_1(fix\psi_1)\nu'$ whenever $\#\Pi_1\geq\nu\geq 1$; moreover $\psi_0\eta_0(\nu+\nu')=fix\psi_0(\nu+\nu')$ whenever $1>\nu'$ or $\nu'>\#\Pi_1$. Because $fix\psi_1=\psi_1(fix\psi_1)$ and $fix\psi_0(\nu+1+\#\Pi_1)=fix\psi_1(1+\#\Pi_1)$ (and because $1+\#\Pi_1\geq\nu'\geq 1$ if and only if $\nu+1+\#\Pi_1\geq\nu+\nu'\geq\nu+1$) we may claim that $\psi_0\eta_0=\lambda\nu'.((\nu+1+\#\Pi_1\geq\nu'\geq\nu+1)\rightarrow fix\psi_1(\nu'-\nu),fix\psi_0\nu')$ or, in other words, that $\psi_0\eta_0=\eta_0$. Since $fix\psi_0$ is the least fixed point of ψ_0 this implies that $\eta_0\sqsupseteq fix\psi_0$.

Certainly $fix\psi_0(\nu+\nu')=\eta_1\nu'$ whenever $1+\#\Pi_1\geq\nu'\geq 1$, so by applying 4.5.4 again we infer that $\psi_0(fix\psi_0)(\nu+\nu')=\psi_1\eta_1\nu'$ whenever $1+\#\Pi_1\geq\nu'\geq 1$, while we know that $\zeta_1=\psi_1\eta_1\nu'$ whenever $1>\nu'$ or $\nu'>\#\Pi_1$. In view of the fact that $fix\psi_0=\psi_0(fix\psi_0)$ we may now assert that $\lambda\nu'.((1+\#\Pi_1\geq\nu'\geq 1)\rightarrow fix\psi_0(\nu+\nu'),\zeta_1)=\psi_1\eta_1$. Thus $\eta_1=\psi_1\eta_1$ and, as $fix\psi_1$ is the least fixed point of ψ_1, $\eta_1\sqsupseteq fix\psi_1$.

From the two inequalities established above we conclude that if ν' is any integer having $1+\#\Pi_1\geq\nu'\geq 1$ then $fix\psi_1(\nu+\nu'-\nu)\sqsupseteq fix\psi_0(\nu+\nu')$ and $fix\psi_0(\nu+\nu')\sqsupseteq fix\psi_1\nu'$. Consequently $fix\psi_0(\nu+\nu')=fix\psi_1\nu'$ whenever $1+\#\Pi_1\geq\nu'\geq 1$, and, because $fix\psi_0=\mathcal{V}\llbracket\Pi_0\rrbracket\zeta_0$ and $fix\psi_1=\mathcal{V}\llbracket\Pi_1\rrbracket\zeta_1$, $\mathcal{V}\llbracket\Pi_0\rrbracket\zeta_0(\nu+\nu')=\mathcal{V}\llbracket\Pi_1\rrbracket\zeta_1\nu'$ whenever $1+\#\Pi_1\geq\nu'\geq 1$.▷

It may be found illuminating to compare this result with 4.5.3, in which controls took the part of programs.

5.4.6. The decomposition of semantic equations.

From every Sam program Π and every continuation ζ can be obtained a consecution $\mathcal{V}\llbracket \Pi \rrbracket \zeta$ such that, when $1+\#\Pi \geq \nu \geq 1$, $\mathcal{V}\llbracket \Pi \rrbracket \zeta\nu$ transforms members of Y and S in a way consonant with starting the execution of Π at the beginning of the segment $\Pi\dagger(\nu-1)$. Of particular importance is $\mathcal{V}\llbracket \Pi \rrbracket \zeta 1$, because the execution of a program usually commences with the first instruction, even if later on jumps ensure that control does not always flow smoothly from each instruction to its successor in the program text. In the presence of an environment ρ, a Sal expression E can be converted into the Sam program $\mathfrak{z}\llbracket \mathfrak{e}\llbracket E \rrbracket \rho \rrbracket 1$, which in turn provides the continuation $\mathcal{V}\llbracket \mathfrak{z}\llbracket \mathfrak{e}\llbracket E \rrbracket \rho \rrbracket 1 \rrbracket \zeta 1$. This continuation is familiar to us already, however, since we can show that it coincides with $\mathcal{E}\llbracket E \rrbracket \rho\zeta$, provided that $\mathfrak{b}$, $\mathfrak{o}$ and $\mathfrak{w}$ generate "sensible" code and that *ease* evaluates pairs of expressions from left to right; if *ease* were to act in the opposite direction we would need a compiling algorithm slightly different from that displayed in appendix 6, since $\mathfrak{e}\llbracket E_0E_1 \rrbracket \rho$, for example, would have to be $\mathfrak{e}\llbracket E_1 \rrbracket \rho \S \mathfrak{r}\llbracket E_0 \rrbracket \rho \S\langle \text{turn}\rangle \S \langle \text{seek } 1\rangle \S\langle \text{jump}\rangle$.

When verifying that $\mathcal{E}\llbracket E \rrbracket = \lambda\rho\zeta.\mathcal{V}\llbracket \mathfrak{z}\llbracket \mathfrak{e}\llbracket E \rrbracket \rho \rrbracket 1 \rrbracket \zeta 1$ we resort, as usual, to induction on the structure of E. Thus, when E is E_0E_1, we assume that $\mathcal{R}\llbracket E_0 \rrbracket = \lambda\rho\zeta.\mathcal{V}\llbracket \mathfrak{z}\llbracket \mathfrak{r}\llbracket E_0 \rrbracket \rho \rrbracket 1 \rrbracket \zeta 1$ and that $\mathcal{E}\llbracket E_1 \rrbracket = \lambda\rho\zeta.\mathcal{V}\llbracket \mathfrak{z}\llbracket \mathfrak{e}\llbracket E_1 \rrbracket \rho \rrbracket 1 \rrbracket \zeta 1$ and then endeavour to show that $\lambda\rho\zeta.\mathcal{V}\llbracket \mathfrak{z}\llbracket \mathfrak{e}\llbracket E_0E_1 \rrbracket \rho \rrbracket 1 \rrbracket \zeta 1$ can be formed from $\lambda\rho\zeta.\mathcal{V}\llbracket \mathfrak{z}\llbracket \mathfrak{r}\llbracket E_0 \rrbracket \rho \rrbracket 1 \rrbracket \zeta 1$ and $\lambda\rho\zeta.\mathcal{V}\llbracket \mathfrak{z}\llbracket \mathfrak{e}\llbracket E_1 \rrbracket \rho \rrbracket 1 \rrbracket \zeta 1$ in the way in which $\mathcal{E}\llbracket E_0E_1 \rrbracket$ is formed from $\mathcal{R}\llbracket E_0 \rrbracket$ and $\mathcal{E}\llbracket E_1 \rrbracket$. To do this we must appeal to a result such as 5.4.5, which permits us to incorporate in $\mathcal{V}\llbracket \mathfrak{z}\llbracket \mathfrak{e}\llbracket E_0E_1 \rrbracket \rho \rrbracket 1 \rrbracket$ aspects of $\mathcal{V}\llbracket \mathfrak{z}\llbracket \mathfrak{r}\llbracket E_0 \rrbracket \rho \rrbracket 1 \rrbracket$ and $\mathcal{V}\llbracket \mathfrak{z}\llbracket \mathfrak{e}\llbracket E_1 \rrbracket \rho \rrbracket 1 \rrbracket$ so long as we know that $\mathfrak{r}\llbracket E_0 \rrbracket \rho$ and $\mathfrak{e}\llbracket E_1 \rrbracket \rho$ are coherent. As we remarked in 5.4.3, however, we can indeed show by structural induction that these two programs are coherent; moreover the fact that they are coherent ensures that $\mathfrak{e}\llbracket E_0E_1 \rrbracket \rho$ is also coherent. In consequence, it is convenient to adopt inductive hypotheses which not only relate the stack semantics of Sal to the consecution semantics of Sam but also handle the coherence of Sam programs.

To express these hypotheses succinctly we follow our habitual practice of introducing predicates which correspond with the valuations. Hence we set:

$E=\lambda E.(\mathcal{E}[\![E]\!]=\lambda\rho\zeta.\mathcal{N}[\![\mathfrak{z}[\![\mathfrak{e}[\![E]\!]\rho]\!]1]\!]\zeta 1)\wedge\bigwedge\{cleave(\mathfrak{e}[\![E]\!]\rho)\mid\rho\}$;

$L=\lambda E.(\mathcal{L}[\![E]\!]=\lambda\rho\zeta.\mathcal{N}[\![\mathfrak{z}[\![\mathfrak{l}[\![E]\!]\rho]\!]1]\!]\zeta 1)\wedge\bigwedge\{cleave(\mathfrak{l}[\![E]\!]\rho)\mid\rho\}$;

$R=\lambda E.(\mathcal{R}[\![E]\!]=\lambda\rho\zeta.\mathcal{N}[\![\mathfrak{z}[\![\mathfrak{r}[\![E]\!]\rho]\!]1]\!]\zeta 1)\wedge\bigwedge\{cleave(\mathfrak{r}[\![E]\!]\rho)\mid\rho\}$.

For abstractions we let

$F=\lambda\Phi.(\lambda\zeta.\mathcal{H}[\![\Phi]\!]=\lambda\zeta.\lambda\rho\upsilon.\langle\mathcal{N}[\![\mathfrak{z}[\![\mathfrak{f}[\![\Phi]\!]\rho]\!]1]\!]\zeta 1,((lift\rho=0)\rightarrow 0,display\upsilon\downarrow(lift\rho)),twist\rho\upsilon\rangle)$
$\quad\wedge\bigwedge\{cleave(\mathfrak{f}[\![\Phi]\!]\rho)\mid\rho\}$.

Similarly the predicate for sequencers satisfies

$S=\lambda\Sigma.(\lambda\zeta.\mathcal{S}[\![\Sigma]\!]=\lambda\zeta.\lambda\rho.\mathcal{N}[\![\mathfrak{z}[\![\mathfrak{s}[\![\Sigma]\!]\rho]\!]1]\!]\zeta 1)\wedge\bigwedge\{cleave(\mathfrak{s}[\![\Sigma]\!]\rho)\mid\rho\}$.

We could eliminate the final instruction, jump, from $\mathfrak{s}[\![$res E$]\!]\rho$ and $\mathfrak{s}[\![$goto E$]\!]\rho$ provided that we took both $\mathfrak{e}[\![\Sigma]\!]\rho$ and $\mathfrak{g}[\![\Sigma]\!]\rho$ to be $\mathfrak{s}[\![\Sigma]\!]\rho\S\langle$jump$\rangle$; under these circumstances we would wish to establish the equality of $\mathcal{S}[\![\Sigma]\!]$ and $\lambda\rho.\mathcal{N}[\![\mathfrak{z}[\![\mathfrak{s}[\![\Sigma]\!]\rho]\!]1]\!](jump)1$, not of $\lambda\zeta.\mathcal{S}[\![\Sigma]\!]$ and $\lambda\zeta.\lambda\rho.\mathcal{N}[\![\mathfrak{z}[\![\mathfrak{s}[\![\Sigma]\!]\rho]\!]1]\!]\zeta 1$. In a similar manner we could move the jump instruction occurring at the end of $\mathfrak{f}[\![$fn()E$]\!]\rho$, $\mathfrak{f}[\![$fnI.E$]\!]\rho$ and $\mathfrak{f}[\![$fnI..E$]\!]\rho$ into the equation for $\mathfrak{e}[\![\Phi]\!]\rho$. We have not done this, since the fact that jump occurs so frequently in appendix 6 is a feature of Sam rather than of a typical Sal compiler; many machine codes have distinct instructions for handling the two sorts of Sal sequencer.

The predicates for $\mathcal{D}$ and $\mathcal{T}$ are naturally closely analogous to those for $\mathcal{E}$, $\mathcal{L}$ and $\mathcal{R}$, being given by:

$D=\lambda\Delta.(\mathcal{D}[\![\Delta]\!]=\lambda\rho\nu'\nu''\zeta.\mathcal{N}[\![\mathfrak{z}[\![\mathfrak{d}[\![\Delta]\!]\rho\nu'\nu'']\!]1]\!]\zeta 1)$
$\quad\wedge\bigwedge\{\bigwedge\{\bigwedge\{cleave(\mathfrak{d}[\![\Delta]\!]\rho\nu'\nu'')\mid\rho\}\mid\nu'\}\mid\nu''\}$;

$T=\lambda\Delta.(\mathcal{T}[\![\Delta]\!]=\lambda\rho\nu'\nu''\zeta.\mathcal{N}[\![\mathfrak{z}[\![\mathfrak{t}[\![\Delta]\!]\rho\nu'\nu'']\!]1]\!]\zeta 1)$
$\quad\wedge\bigwedge\{\bigwedge\{\bigwedge\{cleave(\mathfrak{t}[\![\Delta]\!]\rho\nu'\nu'')\mid\rho\}\mid\nu'\}\mid\nu''\}$.

Equally simple is the predicate for blocks, which is subject to

$G=\lambda\Theta.(\mathfrak{G}[\![\Theta]\!]=\lambda\rho\zeta.\mathcal{V}[\![\mathfrak{x}[\![\mathfrak{g}[\![\Theta]\!]\rho]\!]1]\!]\zeta 1)\wedge\bigwedge\{cleave(\mathfrak{g}[\![\Theta]\!]\rho)\mid\rho\}.$

Any command Γ produces the continuation $\mathcal{V}[\![\mathfrak{x}[\![\mathfrak{c}[\![\Gamma]\!]\rho]\!]1]\!]\zeta 1$ when evaluated in the presence of an environment ρ and a continuation ζ. However, if $\#\mathfrak{J}[\![\Gamma]\!]+\#\mathfrak{K}[\![\Gamma]\!]\geq\nu\geq 1$ the label $(\mathfrak{J}[\![\Gamma]\!]\S\mathfrak{K}[\![\Gamma]\!])\downarrow\nu$ does not correspond with the continuation $\mathcal{V}[\![\mathfrak{x}[\![\mathfrak{c}[\![\Gamma]\!]\rho\dagger((\mathfrak{p}[\![\Gamma]\!]\S\mathfrak{q}[\![\Gamma]\!])\downarrow\nu\text{-}1)]\!]1]\!]\zeta 1$, as one might imagine, because $\mathfrak{c}[\![\Gamma]\!]\rho\dagger((\mathfrak{p}[\![\Gamma]\!]\S\mathfrak{q}[\![\Gamma]\!])\downarrow\nu\text{-}1)$ may not be coherent. Consequently to associate continuations with the labels in Γ we have to make use of $\mathcal{V}[\![\mathfrak{x}[\![\mathfrak{c}[\![\Gamma]\!]\rho]\!]1]\!]\zeta\nu$ when ν is not 1. More specifically, the predicates appropriate to $\mathfrak{C}$, $\mathfrak{P}$ and $\mathfrak{Q}$ are subject to:

$C=\lambda\Gamma.(\mathfrak{C}[\![\Gamma]\!]=\lambda\rho\zeta.\mathcal{V}[\![\mathfrak{x}[\![\mathfrak{c}[\![\Gamma]\!]\rho]\!]1]\!]\zeta)\wedge\bigwedge\{cleave(\mathfrak{c}[\![\Gamma]\!]\rho)\mid\rho\};$

$P=\lambda\Gamma.(\mathfrak{P}[\![\Gamma]\!]=\lambda\rho\zeta\nu.map(\lambda\nu'.\langle\mathcal{V}[\![\mathfrak{x}[\![\mathfrak{c}[\![\Gamma]\!]\rho]\!]1]\!]\zeta\nu',\nu\rangle)(\mathfrak{p}[\![\Gamma]\!]))$

$\wedge\bigwedge\{\bigwedge\{(\#\mathfrak{p}[\![\Gamma]\!]\geq\nu\geq 1)\rightarrow(1+\#\mathfrak{c}[\![\Gamma]\!]\rho\geq\mathfrak{p}[\![\Gamma]\!]\downarrow\nu\geq 1),true\mid\rho\}\mid\nu\};$

$Q=\lambda\Gamma.(\mathfrak{Q}[\![\Gamma]\!]=\lambda\rho\zeta\nu.map(\lambda\nu'.\langle\mathcal{V}[\![\mathfrak{x}[\![\mathfrak{c}[\![\Gamma]\!]\rho]\!]1]\!]\zeta\nu',\nu\rangle)(\mathfrak{q}[\![\Gamma]\!]))$

$\wedge\bigwedge\{\bigwedge\{(\#\mathfrak{q}[\![\Gamma]\!]\geq\nu\geq 1)\rightarrow(1+\#\mathfrak{c}[\![\Gamma]\!]\rho\geq\mathfrak{q}[\![\Gamma]\!]\downarrow\nu\geq 1),true\mid\rho\}\mid\nu\}.$

Some of the instructions in Sam have rather eccentric meanings, and several practical languages provide individual instructions for actions which in Sam must be simulated by groups of instructions. Indeed, we have deliberately devised Sam in such a way that it is not ideally suited to the construction of a Sal compiler. Thus many modifications can be made to $\mathfrak{a}$ and to the mappings of appendix 6 without invalidating the claim that $\mathfrak{E}[\![E]\!]=\lambda\rho\zeta.\mathcal{V}[\![\mathfrak{x}[\![\mathfrak{e}[\![E]\!]\rho]\!]1]\!]\zeta 1$ for every E; furthermore such modifications do not make the claim more difficult to justify. More major changes can be effected by allowing the parameters of Sam instructions to be pointers giving relative addresses in the code instead of absolute positions; under these circumstances, we know, for instance, that

$\mathfrak{A}[\![\text{link}\ \langle\nu',\nu''\rangle]\!]=\lambda\eta\nu\upsilon\sigma.\eta\nu(\langle\langle\eta(\nu+\nu'),\nu''+\#\upsilon\rangle\rangle\S\upsilon)\sigma,$

and instead of proving that $\mathfrak{E}[\![E]\!]$ coincides with $\lambda\rho\zeta.\mathcal{V}[\![\mathfrak{x}[\![\mathfrak{e}[\![E]\!]\rho]\!]1]\!]\zeta 1$ we have to prove that it equals $\lambda\rho\zeta.\mathcal{V}[\![\mathfrak{e}[\![E]\!]\rho]\!]\zeta 1$.

The next section will contain a few exemplary steps in the inductive proof that $E[\![E]\!]=true$ when E is any Sal expression.

5.5. The identity between stack semantics and consecution semantics.

5.5.1. Lemma.

If Φ is a Sal abstraction such that $F[\![\Phi]\!]=true$ then $E[\![\Phi]\!]=true$.

⊲When Φ is any abstraction having $F[\![\Phi]\!]=true$ we introduce any environment, ρ_0, and any continuation, ζ, appropriate to appendix 3. Doing so enables us to set $\rho_1=rend[\![\Phi]\!]\rho_0$ and $\eta=\mathcal{V}[\![\mathcal{Z}[\![\mathfrak{e}[\![\Phi]\!]\rho_0]\!]1]\!]\zeta$, where, according to appendix 6, $\mathfrak{e}[\![\Phi]\!]\rho_0$ is $\langle\text{take}\ \langle 1,\rho_1\rangle\rangle\ \S\langle\text{move}\ \#\mathfrak{f}[\![\Phi]\!]\rho_1\rangle\ \S\mathfrak{f}[\![\Phi]\!]\rho_1$.

The arguments in 5.4.3 indicate that

$\eta=\lambda\nu.(\#\mathfrak{e}[\![\Phi]\!]\rho_0\geq\nu\geq 1)\rightarrow\mathcal{A}[\![\mathfrak{a}[\![\mathfrak{e}[\![\Phi]\!]\rho_0\downarrow\nu]\!](\nu+1)]\!]\eta(\nu+1),\zeta,$

so by inspecting appendix 14 and appendix 12 we observe that

$\eta 1=\mathcal{A}[\![\mathfrak{a}[\![\mathfrak{e}[\![\Phi]\!]\rho_0\downarrow 1]\!]2]\!]\eta 2$

$\quad=\mathcal{A}[\![\mathfrak{a}[\![\text{take}\ \langle 1,\rho_1\rangle]\!]2]\!]\eta 2$

$\quad=\mathcal{A}[\![\text{take}\ \langle 3,\rho_1\rangle]\!]\eta 2$

$\quad=\lambda\upsilon\sigma.\eta 2(\langle\langle\eta 3,((lift\rho_1=0)\rightarrow 0,display\upsilon\downarrow(lift\rho_1)),twist\rho_1\upsilon\rangle\rangle\ \S\upsilon)\sigma,$

whereas

$\eta 2=\mathcal{A}[\![\mathfrak{a}[\![\mathfrak{e}[\![\Phi]\!]\rho\downarrow 2]\!]3]\!]\eta 3$

$\quad=\mathcal{A}[\![\mathfrak{a}[\![\text{move}\ \#\mathfrak{f}[\![\Phi]\!]\rho_1]\!]3]\!]\eta 3$

$\quad=\mathcal{A}[\![\text{move}\ 3+\#\mathfrak{f}[\![\Phi]\!]\rho_1]\!]\eta 3$

$\quad=\eta(3+\#\mathfrak{f}[\![\Phi]\!]\rho_1).$

Since $F[\![\Phi]\!]=true$ we know that $\mathfrak{f}[\![\Phi]\!]\rho_1$ is coherent; furthermore the structure of $\mathfrak{e}[\![\Phi]\!]\rho_0$ is such that $\mathfrak{f}[\![\Phi]\!]\rho_1$ is embedded in $\mathfrak{e}[\![\Phi]\!]\rho_0$ after 2. Consequently 5.4.5 assures us that

$\eta 3=\mathcal{V}[\![\mathcal{Z}[\![\mathfrak{f}[\![\Phi]\!]\rho_1]\!]1]\!](\eta(3+\#\mathfrak{f}[\![\Phi]\!]\rho_1))1.$

Furthermore $3+\#\mathfrak{f}[\![\Phi]\!]\rho_1=1+\#\mathfrak{e}[\![\Phi]\!]\rho_0$, so

$\eta(3+\#\mathfrak{f}[\![\Phi]\!]\rho_1)=\zeta.$

The definition of F provided in 5.4.6 makes it plain that

$\mathcal{H}[\![\Phi]\!]\rho_1=\lambda\upsilon.\langle\mathcal{V}[\![\mathcal{Z}[\![\mathfrak{f}[\![\Phi]\!]\rho_1]\!]1]\!]\zeta 1,((lift\rho_1=0)\rightarrow 0,display\upsilon\downarrow(lift\rho_1)),twist\rho_1\upsilon\rangle.$

By piecing these equations together we see that

$\eta 1=\lambda\upsilon\sigma.\zeta(\langle\mathcal{H}[\![\Phi]\!]\rho_1\upsilon\rangle\ \S\upsilon)\sigma.$

The fact that $\mathcal{E}[\![\Phi]\!]\rho_0\zeta=\lambda\upsilon\sigma.\zeta(\langle\mathcal{H}[\![\Phi]\!]\rho_1\upsilon\rangle\ \S\upsilon)\sigma$ now shows that

$\mathcal{E}[\![\Phi]\!]\rho_0\zeta = \mathcal{V}[\![z[\![e[\![\Phi]\!]\rho_0]\!]1]\!]\zeta$; in addition $e[\![\Phi]\!]\rho_0$ is coherent, since $f[\![\Phi]\!]\rho_1$ is coherent. As ρ_0 and ζ may be chosen at will, all the conditions required by the definition of E are satisfied and $E[\![\Phi]\!]=true$.▸

As will become clear in 5.5.2 and 5.5.3 many of the results to be summarized in 5.5.7 are no more difficult to prove than that described above.

5.5.2. Lemma.

If E is a Sal expression such that $E[\![\mathrm{E}]\!]=true$ then $E[\![\mathrm{val\ E}]\!]=true$.

$\vartriangleleft$When ρ_0 is any environment and ζ is any continuation we let $\rho_1=\rho_0[lift\rho_0+1/\mathrm{res}]$ and $\eta=\mathcal{V}[\![\mathfrak{z}[\![\mathfrak{e}[\![\mathrm{val\ E}]\!]\rho_0]\!]1]\!]\zeta$, and we presume that $E[\![\mathrm{val\ E}]\!]=true$.

From 5.4.3 we can glean the knowledge that

$\eta=\lambda\nu.(\#\mathfrak{e}[\![\mathrm{val\ E}]\!]\rho_0\geq\nu\geq1)\rightarrow\mathcal{A}[\![\mathfrak{a}[\![\mathfrak{e}[\![\mathrm{val\ E}]\!]\rho_0]\!](\nu+1)]\!]\eta(\nu+1),\zeta,$

which enables us to apply the equation for $\mathfrak{e}[\![\mathrm{val\ E}]\!]\rho_0$ given in appendix 6. Plainly appendix 14 and appendix 12 reveal that

$\eta1=\mathcal{A}[\![\mathfrak{a}[\![\mathfrak{e}[\![\mathrm{val\ E}]\!]\rho_0\downarrow1]\!]2]\!]\eta2$

$\quad=\mathcal{A}[\![\mathfrak{a}[\![\mathrm{save}\ lift\rho_0]\!]2]\!]\eta2$

$\quad=\mathcal{A}[\![\mathrm{save}\ lift\rho_0]\!]\eta2$

$\quad=\lambda\upsilon\sigma.\eta2(\langle size(lift\rho_0)1(arid)\upsilon\sigma\rangle\S\upsilon)\sigma;$

moreover

$\eta2=\mathcal{A}[\![\mathfrak{a}[\![\mathfrak{e}[\![\mathrm{val\ E}]\!]\rho_0\downarrow2]\!]3]\!]\eta3$

$\quad=\mathcal{A}[\![\mathfrak{a}[\![\mathrm{join}\ \langle1,arid[lift\rho_0+1/\mathrm{res}]\rangle]\!]3]\!]\eta3$

$\quad=\mathcal{A}[\![\mathrm{join}\ \langle1,arid[lift\rho_0+1/\mathrm{res}]\rangle]\!]\eta3$

$\quad=\lambda\upsilon\sigma.\eta3(aid1(arid[lift\rho_0+1/\mathrm{res}])\upsilon)\sigma$

and

$\eta3=\mathcal{A}[\![\mathfrak{a}[\![\mathfrak{e}[\![\mathrm{val\ E}]\!]\rho_0\downarrow3]\!]4]\!]\eta4$

$\quad=\mathcal{A}[\![\mathfrak{a}[\![\mathrm{link}\ \langle1+\#\mathfrak{e}[\![\mathrm{E}]\!]\rho_1,-1\rangle]\!]4]\!]\eta4$

$\quad=\mathcal{A}[\![\mathrm{link}\ \langle5+\#\mathfrak{e}[\![\mathrm{E}]\!]\rho_1,-1\rangle]\!]\eta4$

$\quad=\lambda\upsilon\sigma.\eta4(\langle\langle\eta(5+\#\mathfrak{e}[\![\mathrm{E}]\!]\rho_1),\#\upsilon-1\rangle\rangle\S\upsilon)\sigma.$

Since $\mathfrak{e}[\![\mathrm{E}]\!]\rho_1$ is coherent and embedded in $\mathfrak{e}[\![\mathrm{E}]\!]\rho_0$ after 3 we can infer from 5.4.5 that $\eta4=\mathcal{V}[\![\mathfrak{z}[\![\mathfrak{e}[\![\mathrm{E}]\!]\rho_1]\!]1]\!](\eta(4+\#\mathfrak{e}[\![\mathrm{E}]\!]\rho_1))1$. However, unravelling $\mathfrak{e}[\![\mathrm{val\ E}]\!]\rho_0$ also shows that

$\eta(4+\#\mathfrak{e}[\![\mathrm{E}]\!]\rho_1)=\mathcal{A}[\![\mathfrak{a}[\![\mathfrak{e}[\![\mathrm{val\ E}]\!]\rho_0\downarrow(4+\#\mathfrak{e}[\![\mathrm{E}]\!]\rho_1)]\!](5+\#\mathfrak{e}[\![\mathrm{E}]\!]\rho_1)]\!]\eta(5+\#\mathfrak{e}[\![\mathrm{E}]\!]\rho_1)$

$\qquad\qquad=\mathcal{A}[\![\mathfrak{a}[\![\mathrm{lose}\ 3]\!](5+\#\mathfrak{e}[\![\mathrm{E}]\!]\rho_1)]\!]\eta(5+\#\mathfrak{e}[\![\mathrm{E}]\!]\rho_1)$

$\qquad\qquad=lose3(\eta(5+\#\mathfrak{e}[\![\mathrm{E}]\!]\rho_1)),$

whilst, as $5+\#\mathfrak{e}[\![\mathrm{E}]\!]\rho_1=1+\#\mathfrak{e}[\![\mathrm{val\ E}]\!]\rho_0$,

$\eta(5+\#\mathcal{e}[\![E]\!]\rho_1)=\zeta$.

Because the definition of *aid* given in 5.1.6 shows that $\lambda\upsilon\sigma.aid1(arid[lift\rho_0+1/\text{res}])(\langle size(lift\rho_0)1(arid)\upsilon\sigma\rangle\S\upsilon)$ coincides with $\lambda\upsilon\sigma.\langle size(lift\rho_0)2(arid[lift\rho_0+1/\text{res}])\upsilon\sigma\rangle\S\upsilon$ and because the fact that $\mathcal{T}[\![\text{val } E]\!]=true$ ensures that

$\mathcal{E}[\![E]\!]\rho_1(lose3\zeta)=\mathcal{W}[\![\mathcal{z}[\![\mathcal{e}[\![E]\!]\rho_1]\!]1]\!](lose3\zeta)1$

we may safely conclude that

$\eta1=\lambda\upsilon\sigma.\mathcal{E}[\![E]\!]\rho_1(lose3\zeta)(\langle\langle\zeta,\#\upsilon\rangle\rangle\S\langle size(lift\rho_0)2(arid[lift\rho_0+1/\text{res}])\upsilon\sigma\rangle\S\upsilon)\sigma$.

A glance at appendix 3 now confirms that $\mathcal{E}[\![\text{val } E]\!]\rho_0\zeta=\mathcal{W}[\![\mathcal{z}[\![\mathcal{e}[\![\text{val } E]\!]\rho_0]\!]1]\!]\zeta1$, and it is clear that $\mathcal{e}[\![\text{val } E]\!]\rho_0$ is coherent. Since ρ_0 and ζ can be taken to be any environment and continuation, enough has been established for us to be able to assert that $E[\![\text{val } E]\!]=true$.▷

5.5.3. Lemma.

If E is a Sal expression such that $R\llbracket E\rrbracket = true$ then $S\llbracket \mathtt{goto}\ E\rrbracket = true$.

$\triangleleft$As usual we select any environment, ρ_0, and any continuation, ζ_0; having done so, we let $\eta = \mathfrak{V}\llbracket \mathfrak{z}\llbracket \mathfrak{s}\llbracket \mathtt{goto}\ E\rrbracket \rho_0\rrbracket 1\rrbracket \zeta$ and we try to show that $\mathfrak{S}\llbracket \mathtt{goto}\ E\rrbracket \rho_0 = \eta 1$ (and that $\mathfrak{s}\llbracket \mathtt{goto}\ E\rrbracket \rho_0$ is coherent) on the assumption that $R\llbracket E\rrbracket = true$. For this purpose we require the knowledge that $\mathfrak{s}\llbracket \mathtt{goto}\ E\rrbracket \rho_0$ is $\mathfrak{r}\llbracket E\rrbracket \rho_0 \S\langle \mathtt{adjust}\rangle \S\langle \mathtt{lose}\ 1\rangle \S\langle \mathtt{jump}\rangle$.

From the fact that $R\llbracket E\rrbracket = true$ it follows that $\mathfrak{r}\llbracket E\rrbracket \rho_0$ is coherent; hence, because in addition $\mathfrak{r}\llbracket E\rrbracket \rho_0$ is embedded in $\mathfrak{s}\llbracket \mathtt{goto}\ E\rrbracket \rho_0$ after 0, 5.4.5 tells us that

$\eta 1 = \mathfrak{V}\llbracket \mathfrak{z}\llbracket \mathfrak{r}\llbracket E\rrbracket \rho_0\rrbracket 1\rrbracket (\eta(1+\#\mathfrak{r}\llbracket E\rrbracket \rho_0))1.$

Another appeal to the assumption that $R\llbracket E\rrbracket = true$ shows that

$\mathfrak{R}\llbracket E\rrbracket \rho_0(\eta(1+\#\mathfrak{r}\llbracket E\rrbracket \rho_0)) = \mathfrak{V}\llbracket \mathfrak{z}\llbracket \mathfrak{r}\llbracket E\rrbracket \rho_0\rrbracket 1\rrbracket (\eta(1+\#\mathfrak{r}\llbracket E\rrbracket \rho_0)),$

so actually

$\eta 1 = \mathfrak{R}\llbracket E\rrbracket \rho_0(\eta(1+\#\mathfrak{r}\llbracket E\rrbracket \rho_0)).$

Next we apply the remarks in 5.4.3, which indicate that

$\eta = \lambda\nu.(\#\mathfrak{s}\llbracket \mathtt{goto}\ E\rrbracket \rho_0 \geq \nu \geq 1) \rightarrow \mathfrak{A}\llbracket \mathfrak{a}\llbracket \mathfrak{s}\llbracket \mathtt{goto}\ E\rrbracket \rho_0\rrbracket (\nu+1)\rrbracket \eta(\nu+1), \zeta,$

in order to verify that when $\nu = \#\mathfrak{r}\llbracket E\rrbracket \rho_0$

$$\begin{aligned}
\eta(1+\nu) &= \mathfrak{A}\llbracket \mathfrak{a}\llbracket \mathfrak{s}\llbracket \mathtt{goto}\ E\rrbracket \rho_0 \downarrow (1+\nu)\rrbracket (2+\nu)\rrbracket \eta(2+\nu)\\
&= \mathfrak{A}\llbracket \mathfrak{a}\llbracket \mathtt{adjust}\rrbracket (2+\nu)\rrbracket \eta(2+\nu)\\
&= \mathfrak{A}\llbracket \mathtt{adjust}\rrbracket \eta(2+\nu)\\
&= \lambda\upsilon\sigma.\, \upsilon\downarrow 1 \mathsf{E} \mathsf{J} \rightarrow (\lambda\nu'.\eta(2+\nu)((\langle \upsilon\downarrow\nu'\rangle \S\langle \upsilon\downarrow 1\downarrow 1\rangle \S \upsilon\dagger\nu')\sigma)(\#\upsilon - \upsilon\downarrow 1\downarrow 2), wrong\,\sigma,
\end{aligned}$$

whilst

$$\begin{aligned}
\eta(2+\nu) &= \mathfrak{A}\llbracket \mathfrak{a}\llbracket \mathfrak{s}\llbracket \mathtt{goto}\ E\rrbracket \rho_0 \downarrow (2+\nu)\rrbracket (3+\nu)\rrbracket \eta(3+\nu)\\
&= \mathfrak{A}\llbracket \mathfrak{a}\llbracket \mathtt{lose}\ 1\rrbracket (3+\nu)\rrbracket \eta(3+\nu)\\
&= \mathfrak{A}\llbracket \mathtt{lose}\ 1\rrbracket \eta(3+\nu)\\
&= lose 1(\eta(3+\nu))
\end{aligned}$$

and

$\eta(3+\nu)=\mathcal{A}[\![\mathfrak{a}[\![\mathfrak{s}[\![\text{goto E}]\!]\rho_0\downarrow(3+\nu)]\!](4+\nu)]\!]\eta(4+\nu)$

$\quad=\mathcal{A}[\![\mathfrak{a}[\![\text{jump}]\!](4+\nu)]\!]\eta(4+\nu)$

$\quad=\mathcal{A}[\![\text{jump}]\!]'\eta(4+\nu)$

$\quad=\mathit{jump}.$

In addition the definition of *jump* given in 5.1.3 permits us to point out that $\lambda\upsilon\sigma.\upsilon\downarrow 1\mathsf{E}J\rightarrow(\lambda\nu'.\mathit{lose}1(\mathit{jump})(\langle\upsilon\downarrow\nu'\rangle\S\langle\upsilon\downarrow 1\downarrow 1\rangle\S\upsilon\dagger\nu')(\#\upsilon-\upsilon\downarrow 1\downarrow 2),\mathit{wrong}\sigma$ is identical with $\lambda\upsilon\sigma.\upsilon\downarrow 1\mathsf{E}J\rightarrow\mathit{lose}1(\upsilon\downarrow 1\downarrow 1)(\upsilon\dagger(\#\upsilon-\upsilon\downarrow 1\downarrow 2-1))\sigma,\mathit{wrong}\sigma$; hence $\eta(1+\#\mathfrak{r}[\![E]\!]\rho_0)=\lambda\upsilon\sigma.\upsilon\downarrow 1\mathsf{E}J\rightarrow\mathit{lose}1(\upsilon\downarrow 1\downarrow 1)(\upsilon\dagger(\#\upsilon-\upsilon\downarrow 1\downarrow 2-1))\sigma,\mathit{wrong}\sigma.$

According to appendix 3, however, $\mathfrak{S}[\![\text{goto E}]\!]\rho_0=\mathfrak{R}[\![E]\!]\rho_0(\lambda\upsilon\sigma.\upsilon\downarrow 1\mathsf{E}J\rightarrow\mathit{lose}1(\upsilon\downarrow 1\downarrow 1)(\upsilon\dagger(\#\upsilon-\upsilon\downarrow 1\downarrow 2-1))\sigma,\mathit{wrong}\sigma)$; in consequence, as $\eta 1=\mathfrak{R}[\![E]\!]\rho_0(\eta(1+\#\mathfrak{r}[\![E]\!]\rho))$ we may conclude that $\mathfrak{S}[\![\text{goto E}]\!]\rho_0=\mathfrak{V}[\![\mathfrak{z}[\![\mathfrak{s}[\![\text{goto E}]\!]\rho_0]\!]1]\!]\zeta 1$. When taken together with the assurance that $\mathfrak{s}[\![\text{goto E}]\!]\rho_0$ is coherent this implies that $\mathcal{S}[\![\text{goto E}]\!]=\mathit{true}$.▷

The pace at which we treat results like this will now quicken. In particular, in 5.5.4 the features which are distinctive to the proofs that $\mathcal{D}[\![\text{rec }\Delta]\!]=\mathit{true}$ and that $\mathcal{G}[\![\text{block }\Gamma]\!]=\mathit{true}$ will be emphasized at the expense of the features which are common to all the results underlying 5.5.7.

5.5.4. Lemma.

If Γ is a Sal command such that $C[\![\Gamma]\!]\wedge P[\![\Gamma]\!]\wedge Q[\![\Gamma]\!]=true$ then $G[\![\text{block }\Gamma]\!]=true$.

◁We begin in the conventional manner by supposing that Γ is any command for which $C[\![\Gamma]\!]=true$, $P[\![\Gamma]\!]=true$ and $Q[\![\Gamma]\!]=true$ and by introducing any environment, ρ_0, any continuation, ζ_0, any stack, υ_0, and any store, σ_0, suited to appendix 3. In order to convince ourselves that $G[\![\text{block }\Gamma]\!]=true$ we want to be able to show that
$\mathfrak{C}[\![\text{block }\Gamma]\!]\rho_0\zeta_0\upsilon_0\sigma_0=\eta_0 1\upsilon_0\sigma_0$ where $\eta_0=\mathfrak{V}[\![\mathfrak{x}[\![\mathfrak{g}[\![\text{block }\Gamma]\!]\rho_0]\!]1]\!]\zeta_0 1$. For the sake of brevity we let $\nu_0=\#\mathfrak{J}[\![\Gamma]\!]$, $\nu_1=\#\mathfrak{K}[\![\Gamma]\!]$, $\nu_2=\nu_0+\nu_1$, $\nu_3=3+2\times\nu_0+\nu_1$ and $\nu_4=3+5\times\nu_0+\nu_1$.

By forming $\mathfrak{g}[\![\text{block }\Gamma]\!]\rho_0$ in the manner suggested in appendix 6 we are able to calculate as in 5.5.2 that

$\eta_0 1=\lambda\upsilon\sigma.\eta_0 2(\langle size(lift\rho_0)1(arid)\upsilon\sigma\rangle\S\upsilon)\sigma$

and that

$\eta_0 2=\lambda\upsilon\sigma.\eta_0 3(aid\nu_2(grow(\mathfrak{H}[\![\Gamma]\!]\S\mathfrak{K}[\![\Gamma]\!])(arid)(lift\rho_0)0)\upsilon)\sigma$

so if $\upsilon_1=\langle size(lift\rho_0)(1+\nu_2)(grow(\mathfrak{H}[\![\Gamma]\!]\S\mathfrak{K}[\![\Gamma]\!])(arid)(lift\rho_0)0)\upsilon_0\sigma_0\rangle\S\upsilon_0$ then

$\eta 1\upsilon_0\sigma_0=\eta 3\upsilon_1\sigma_0$.

We now let $\rho_1=grow(\mathfrak{J}[\![\Gamma]\!]\S\mathfrak{K}[\![\Gamma]\!])\rho_0(lift\rho_0)0$ and $\zeta_1=\eta_0(1+\nu_4+\#\mathfrak{c}[\![\Gamma]\!]\rho_1)$. Since $C[\![\Gamma]\!]=true$ $\mathfrak{c}[\![\Gamma]\!]\rho_1$ is coherent; moreover $\mathfrak{c}[\![\Gamma]\!]\rho_1$ is embedded in $\mathfrak{g}[\![\text{block }\Gamma]\!]\rho_0$ after ν_4. Hence, according to 5.4.5, when ν is any integer for which $1+\#\mathfrak{c}[\![\Gamma]\!]\rho_1\geq\nu\geq1$,

$\eta_0(\nu_4+\nu)=\eta_1\nu$

where $\eta_1=\mathfrak{V}[\![\mathfrak{x}[\![\mathfrak{c}[\![\Gamma]\!]\rho_1]\!]1]\!]\zeta_1$. In particular, the knowledge that $P[\![\Gamma]\!]=true$ ensures that $1+\#\mathfrak{c}[\![\Gamma]\!]\rho_1\geq\mathfrak{p}[\![\Gamma]\!]\downarrow\nu\geq1$ whenever $\nu_0\geq\nu\geq1$, so

$\eta_0(\nu_4+\mathfrak{p}[\![\Gamma]\!]\downarrow\nu)=\eta_1(\mathfrak{p}[\![\Gamma]\!]\downarrow\nu)$

whenever $\nu_0\geq\nu\geq1$; however, as $P[\![\Gamma]\!]=true$,

$\lambda\upsilon.\langle\eta_1(\mathfrak{p}[\![\Gamma]\!]\downarrow\nu),-1+\#\upsilon\rangle=\lambda\upsilon.\mathfrak{P}[\![\Gamma]\!]\rho_1\zeta(-1+\#\upsilon)\downarrow\nu$

whenever $\nu_0\geq\nu\geq1$, and in fact

$\lambda\upsilon.\langle\eta_0(\nu_4+\mathfrak{p}[\![\Gamma]\!]\downarrow\nu),-1+\#\upsilon\rangle=\lambda\upsilon.\mathfrak{P}[\![\Gamma]\!]\rho_1\zeta_1(-1+\#\upsilon)\downarrow\nu$

whenever $\nu_0 \geq \nu \geq 1$. The fact that $Q[\![\Gamma]\!]=true$ allows us to deduce in a similar fashion that

$\lambda\upsilon.\langle \eta_0(\nu_4+\mathfrak{q}[\![\Gamma]\!]\downarrow\nu),\nu+\nu_0+\#\upsilon\rangle=\lambda\upsilon.\mathfrak{Q}[\![\Gamma]\!]\rho_1\zeta_1(\nu+\nu_0+\#\upsilon)\rangle\downarrow\nu$

whenever $\nu_1 \geq \nu \geq 1$.

If ν is any integer such that $\nu_1 \geq \nu \geq 1$ then

$$\begin{aligned}
\eta_0(\nu_1-\nu+3)&=\mathscr{A}[\![\mathfrak{a}[\![\mathfrak{g}[\![\mathtt{block}\ \Gamma]\!]\rho_0\downarrow(\nu_1-\nu+3)]\!](\nu_1-\nu+4)]\!]\eta_0(\nu_1-\nu+4)\\
&=\mathscr{A}[\![\mathfrak{a}[\![\mathtt{load}\ \langle -1+\nu+5\times\nu_0+\mathfrak{q}[\![\Gamma]\!]\downarrow\nu,\nu+\nu_0\rangle]\!](\nu_1-\nu+4)]\!]\eta_0(\nu_1-\nu+4)\\
&=\mathscr{A}[\![\mathtt{load}\ \langle \nu_4+\mathfrak{q}[\![\Gamma]\!]\downarrow\nu,\nu+\nu_0\rangle]\!]\eta_0(\nu_1-\nu+4)\\
&=\lambda\upsilon\sigma.\eta_0(\nu_1-\nu+4)(\langle\langle \eta_0(\nu_4+\mathfrak{q}[\![\Gamma]\!]\downarrow\nu),\nu+\nu_0+\#\upsilon\rangle\rangle\,\S\,\upsilon)\sigma\\
&=\lambda\upsilon\sigma.\eta_0(\nu_1-(\nu-1)+3)(\langle\mathfrak{Q}[\![\Gamma]\!]\rho_1\zeta_1(\nu+\nu_0+\#\upsilon)\downarrow\nu\rangle\,\S\,\upsilon)\sigma.
\end{aligned}$$

Hence by induction on $\nu_1-\nu$ we see that when $\nu_1 \geq \nu \geq 0$

$\eta_0 3=\lambda\upsilon\sigma.\eta_0(\nu_1-\nu+3)((\mathfrak{Q}[\![\Gamma]\!]\rho_1\zeta_1(\nu_0+\nu_1+\#\upsilon)\dagger\nu)\,\S\,\upsilon)\sigma;$

in particular, when $\upsilon_2=\mathfrak{Q}[\![\Gamma]\!]\rho_1\zeta_1(\nu_0+\nu_1+\#\upsilon_1)\,\S\,\upsilon_1$,

$\eta_0 3\upsilon_1\sigma_0=\eta_0(\nu_1+3)\upsilon_2\sigma_0.$

If ν is any integer such that $\nu_0 \geq \nu \geq 1$ then

$$\begin{aligned}
\eta_0(1+\nu_1+2\times\nu)&=\mathscr{A}[\![\mathfrak{a}[\![\mathfrak{g}[\![\mathtt{block}\ \Gamma]\!]\rho_0\downarrow(1+\nu_1+2\times\nu)]\!](2+\nu_1+2\times\nu)]\!]\eta_0(2+\nu_1+2\times\nu)\\
&=\mathscr{A}[\![\mathfrak{a}[\![\mathtt{find}]\!](2+\nu_1+2\times\nu)]\!]\eta_0(2+\nu_1+2\times\nu)\\
&=\mathscr{A}[\![\mathtt{find}]\!]\eta_0(2+\nu_1+2\times\nu)\\
&=\lambda\upsilon\sigma.\eta_0(2+\nu_1+2\times\nu)(\langle \mathit{false}\rangle\,\S\,\upsilon)\sigma,
\end{aligned}$$

whilst

$$\begin{aligned}
\eta_0(2+\nu_1+2\times\nu)&=\mathscr{A}[\![\mathfrak{a}[\![\mathfrak{g}[\![\mathtt{block}\ \Gamma]\!]\rho_0\downarrow(2+\nu_1+2\times\nu)]\!](2+\nu_1+2\times\nu+1)]\!]\eta_0(2+\nu_1+2\times\nu+1)\\
&=\mathscr{A}[\![\mathfrak{a}[\![\mathtt{nv}]\!](2+\nu_1+2\times\nu+1)]\!]\eta_0(2+\nu_1+2\times\nu+1)\\
&=\mathscr{A}[\![\mathtt{nv}]\!]\eta_0(2+\nu_1+2\times\nu+1)\\
&=\lambda\upsilon\sigma.\mathit{nv}(\eta_0(3+\nu_1+2\times\nu+1))\upsilon\sigma.
\end{aligned}$$

Consequently when $\nu_0 \geq \nu \geq 1$

$\eta_0(1+\nu_1+2\times\nu)=\lambda\upsilon\sigma.\mathit{nv}(\eta_0(1+\nu_1+2\times(\nu+1)))(\langle \mathit{false}\rangle\,\S\,\upsilon)\sigma,$

so the definition of *tie* given in 3.3.4 indicates that by induction on ν we can demonstrate that if $\nu_0 \geq \nu \geq 0$

$\eta_0(\nu_1+3)=\lambda\upsilon\sigma.\mathit{tie}(\lambda\alpha^*.\eta_0(3+\nu_1+2\times\nu)(\alpha^*\S\upsilon))\nu\sigma;$

in particular,

$\eta_0(\nu_1+3)\upsilon_2\sigma_0=\mathit{tie}(\lambda\alpha^*.\eta_0\nu_3(\alpha^*\S\upsilon_2))\nu_0\sigma_0$

and

$\eta_0 1 \upsilon_0 \sigma_0 = tie(\lambda\alpha^*.\eta_0 \nu_3(\alpha^* \S \upsilon_2))\nu_0 \sigma_0$.

Unless $news\nu_0\sigma_0 \in L^*$ the definition of *tie* makes it plain that

$\mathfrak{G}[\![\texttt{block } \Gamma]\!]\rho_0\zeta_0\upsilon_0\sigma_0 = tie(\lambda\alpha^*.\eta_0\nu_3(\alpha^*\S\upsilon_2))\nu_0\sigma_0$

and therefore that

$\eta_0 1\upsilon_0\sigma_0 = \mathfrak{G}[\![\texttt{block } \Gamma]\!]\rho_0\zeta_0\upsilon_0\sigma_0$.

Accordingly we shall concentrate henceforth on what happens if $news\nu_0\sigma_0 \in L^*$, and we shall let $\alpha^* = news\nu_0\sigma_0|L^*$, $\upsilon_3 = \alpha^*\S\upsilon_2$ and $\sigma_1 = updates\alpha^*(use\nu_0)\sigma_0$, so that

$\eta_0 1\upsilon_0\sigma_0 = \eta_0\nu_3\upsilon_3\sigma_1$.

If ν is any integer such that $\nu_0 \geq \nu \geq 1$ then

$$\begin{aligned}\eta_0(\nu_4-3\times\nu) &= \mathcal{A}[\![\mathfrak{a}[\![\mathfrak{g}[\![\texttt{block } \Gamma]\!]\rho_0{\downarrow}(\nu_4-3\times\nu)]\!](\nu_4-3\times\nu+1)]\!]\eta_0(\nu_4-3\times\nu+1)\\ &= \mathcal{A}[\![\mathfrak{a}[\![\texttt{view } \langle lift\rho_0, 1-\nu+\nu_2\rangle]\!](\nu_4-3\times\nu+1)]\!]\eta_0(\nu_4-3\times\nu+1)\\ &= \mathcal{A}[\![\texttt{view } \langle lift\rho_0, 1-\nu+\nu_2\rangle]\!]\eta_0(\nu_4-3\times\nu+1)\\ &= \lambda\upsilon\sigma.\eta_0(\nu_4-3\times\nu+2)(\langle\upsilon{\downarrow}(\#\upsilon-display\upsilon{\downarrow}(lift\rho_0)-(1-\nu+\nu_2)+1)\rangle\S\upsilon)\sigma\end{aligned}$$

and

$$\begin{aligned}\eta_0(\nu_4-3\times\nu+1) &= \mathcal{A}[\![\mathfrak{a}[\![\mathfrak{g}[\![\texttt{block } \Gamma]\!]\rho_0{\downarrow}(\nu_4-3\times\nu+1)]\!](\nu_4-3\times\nu+2)]\!]\eta_0(\nu_4-3\times\nu+2)\\ &= \mathcal{A}[\![\mathfrak{a}[\![\texttt{load } \langle -2+3\times\nu+\mathfrak{p}[\![\Gamma]\!]{\downarrow}\nu, -1\rangle]\!](\nu_4-3\times\nu+2)]\!]\eta_0(\nu_4-3\times\nu+2)\\ &= \mathcal{A}[\![\texttt{load } \langle \nu_4+\mathfrak{p}[\![\Gamma]\!]{\downarrow}\nu, -1\rangle]\!]\eta_0(\nu_3-3\times\nu+2)\\ &= \lambda\upsilon\sigma.\eta_0(\nu_4-3\times\nu+2)(\langle\langle\eta_0(\nu_4+\mathfrak{p}[\![\Gamma]\!]{\downarrow}\nu, -1+\#\upsilon\rangle\rangle\S\upsilon)\sigma\\ &= \lambda\upsilon\sigma.\eta_0(\nu_4-3\times\nu+2)(\langle\mathcal{P}[\![\Gamma]\!]\rho_1\zeta_1(-1+\#\upsilon){\downarrow}\nu\rangle\S\upsilon)\sigma\end{aligned}$$

whereas

$$\begin{aligned}\eta_0(\nu_4-3\times\nu+2) &= \mathcal{A}[\![\mathfrak{a}[\![\mathfrak{g}[\![\texttt{block } \Gamma]\!]\rho_0{\downarrow}(\nu_4-3\times\nu+2)]\!](\nu_4-3\times\nu+3)]\!]\eta_0(\nu_4-3\times\nu+3)\\ &= \mathcal{A}[\![\mathfrak{a}[\![\texttt{insert}]\!](\nu_4-3\times\nu+3)]\!]\eta_0(\nu_4-3\times\nu+3)\\ &= \mathcal{A}[\![\texttt{insert}]\!]\eta_0(\nu_4-3\times\nu+3)\\ &= \lambda\upsilon\sigma.assign(\eta_0(\nu_4-3\times\nu+3)(\upsilon{\dagger}2))(\upsilon{\downarrow}2)(\upsilon{\downarrow}1)\sigma;\end{aligned}$$

hence

$\eta_0(\nu_4-3\times\nu)\upsilon_3=\eta_0(\nu_4-3\times\nu+1)(\langle\alpha^*\downarrow\nu\rangle\S\upsilon_3)$

$=\eta_0(\nu_4-3\times\nu+2)(\langle\mathfrak{P}[\![\Gamma]\!]\rho_1\zeta_1(\#\upsilon_3)\downarrow\nu\rangle\S\langle\alpha^*\downarrow\nu\rangle\S\upsilon_3)$

$=assign(\eta_0(\nu_4-3\times\nu+3)\upsilon_3)(\alpha^*\downarrow\nu)(\mathfrak{P}[\![\Gamma]\!]\rho_1\zeta_1(\#\upsilon_3)\downarrow\nu)$

$=\lambda\sigma.\eta_0(\nu_4-3\times(\nu-1))(update(\alpha^*\downarrow\nu)(\mathfrak{P}[\![\Gamma]\!]\rho_1\zeta_1(\#\upsilon_3)\downarrow\nu)\sigma)$.

An induction on ν now reveals that when $\nu_0\geq\nu\geq 0$

$\eta_0(\nu_4-3\times\nu)\upsilon_3=\lambda\sigma.\eta_0\nu_4\upsilon_3(updates(\alpha^*\dagger\nu)(\mathfrak{P}[\![\Gamma]\!]\rho_1\zeta_1(\#\upsilon_3)\dagger\nu)\sigma)$

so in fact, as $\nu_3=\nu_4-3\times\nu_0$, writing $\sigma_2=updates\,\alpha^*(\mathfrak{P}[\![\Gamma]\!]\rho_1\zeta_1(\nu_2+\#\upsilon_2))\sigma_1$ allows us to assert that

$\eta_0\nu_3\upsilon_3\sigma_1=\eta_0\nu_4\upsilon_3\sigma_2$.

By updating the proof of 5.5.2 we observe that

$\eta_0\nu_4=\lambda\upsilon\sigma.\eta_0(\nu_4+1)(\langle size(lift\,\rho_0+1)1(arid)\upsilon\sigma\rangle\S\upsilon)\sigma$,

while, because $1+\#\mathfrak{e}[\![\Gamma]\!]\rho_1\geq\nu\geq 1$ when $\nu=1$,

$\eta_0(\nu_4+1)=\eta_1 1$;

however, $C[\![\Gamma]\!]=true$ so, according to the definitions in 5.4.6,

$\eta_1 1=\mathfrak{C}[\![\Gamma]\!]\rho_1\zeta_1$

and we may assert that if $\upsilon_4=\langle size(lift\,\rho_0+1)1(arid)\upsilon_3\sigma_2\rangle\S\upsilon_3$ then

$\eta_0\nu_4\upsilon_3\sigma_2=\mathfrak{C}[\![\Gamma]\!]\rho_1(\eta_0(1+\nu_4+\#\mathfrak{e}[\![\Gamma]\!]\rho_1))\upsilon_4\sigma_2$

as $\zeta_1=\eta_0(1+\nu_4+\#\mathfrak{e}[\![\Gamma]\!]\rho_1)$. We can calculate that

$\eta_0(1+\nu_4+\#\mathfrak{e}[\![\Gamma]\!]\rho_1)=\lambda\upsilon\sigma.lose(2+\nu_2)(\eta_0(2+\nu_4+\#\mathfrak{e}[\![\Gamma]\!]\rho_1))\upsilon\sigma$

and that

$\eta_0(2+\nu_4+\#\mathfrak{e}[\![\Gamma]\!]\rho_1)=\lambda\upsilon\sigma.\eta_0(3+\nu_4+\#\mathfrak{e}[\![\Gamma]\!]\rho_1)(\upsilon\dagger 1)\sigma$.

Since $\zeta_0=\eta_0(3+\nu_4+\#\mathfrak{e}[\![\Gamma]\!]\rho_1)$,

$\eta_0\nu_4\upsilon_3\sigma_2=\mathfrak{C}[\![\Gamma]\!]\rho_1(lose(2+\nu_2)(\lambda\upsilon\sigma.\zeta_0(\upsilon\dagger 1)\sigma))\upsilon_4\sigma_2$.

In addition a rudimentary calculation demonstrates that

$\mathfrak{G}[\![\mathtt{block}\ \Gamma]\!]\rho_0\zeta_0\upsilon_0\sigma_0=\mathfrak{C}[\![\Gamma]\!]\rho_1(lose(2+\nu_2)(\lambda\upsilon\sigma.\zeta(\upsilon\dagger 1)\sigma))\upsilon_4\sigma_2$;

so, because

$\eta_0 1\upsilon_0\sigma_0=\eta_0\nu_4\upsilon_3\sigma_2$,

we actually know that

$\eta_0 1\upsilon_0\sigma_0=\mathfrak{G}[\![\mathtt{block}\ \Gamma]\!]\rho_0\zeta_0\upsilon_0\sigma_0$.

As $\mathfrak{G}[\![\mathtt{block}\ \Gamma]\!]\rho_0\zeta_0\upsilon_0\sigma_0=\mathfrak{V}[\![\mathfrak{X}[\![\mathfrak{g}[\![\mathtt{block}\ \Gamma]\!]\rho_0]\!]1]\!]\zeta_0 1\upsilon_0\sigma_0$ for any ρ_0, ζ_0, υ_0 and σ_0 (and as $\mathfrak{g}[\![\mathtt{block}\ \Gamma]\!]\rho_0$ is coherent for any ρ_0), $G[\![\mathtt{block}\ \Gamma]\!]=true$.▷

5.5.5. Lemma.

If Γ_0 and Γ_1 are Sal commands such that $C[\![\Gamma_0]\!] \wedge C[\![\Gamma_1]\!] = \mathit{true}$ then $C[\![\Gamma_0;\Gamma_1]\!] = \mathit{true}$.

$\lhd$For any ρ and ζ we let $\eta = \mathfrak{V}[\![\mathfrak{z}[\![\mathfrak{c}[\![\Gamma_0;\Gamma_1]\!]\rho]\!]1]\!]\zeta$ and we attempt to show that $\mathfrak{C}[\![\Gamma_0;\Gamma_1]\!]\rho\zeta = \eta 1$ provided that $C[\![\Gamma_0]\!] = \mathit{true}$ and $C[\![\Gamma_1]\!] = \mathit{true}$.

The proviso above ensures that $\mathfrak{c}[\![\Gamma_0]\!]\rho$ and $\mathfrak{c}[\![\Gamma_1]\!]\rho$ are coherent; moreover as $\mathfrak{c}[\![\Gamma_0;\Gamma_1]\!]\rho$ is $\mathfrak{c}[\![\Gamma_0]\!]\rho \S \mathfrak{c}[\![\Gamma_1]\!]\rho$ $\mathfrak{c}[\![\Gamma_0]\!]\rho$ and $\mathfrak{c}[\![\Gamma_1]\!]\rho$ are embedded in $\mathfrak{c}[\![\Gamma_0;\Gamma_1]\!]\rho$ after 0 and $\#\mathfrak{c}[\![\Gamma_0]\!]\rho$ respectively. Consequently by applying 5.4.5 twice we may deduce that

$\eta 1 = \mathfrak{V}[\![\mathfrak{z}[\![\mathfrak{c}[\![\Gamma_0]\!]\rho]\!]1]\!](\eta(1+\#\mathfrak{c}[\![\Gamma_0]\!]\rho))1$

and that

$\eta(1+\#\mathfrak{c}[\![\Gamma_0]\!]\rho) = \mathfrak{V}[\![\mathfrak{z}[\![\mathfrak{c}[\![\Gamma_1]\!]\rho]\!]1]\!](\eta(1+\#\mathfrak{c}[\![\Gamma_0]\!]\rho+\#\mathfrak{c}[\![\Gamma_1]\!]\rho))1.$

In addition, as $C[\![\Gamma_0]\!] = \mathit{true}$ and $C[\![\Gamma_1]\!] = \mathit{true}$ we may presume that

$\mathfrak{C}[\![\Gamma_0]\!]\rho(\eta(1+\#\mathfrak{c}[\![\Gamma_0]\!]\rho)) = \mathfrak{V}[\![\mathfrak{z}[\![\mathfrak{c}[\![\Gamma_0]\!]\rho]\!]1]\!](\eta(1+\#\mathfrak{c}[\![\Gamma_0]\!]\rho))$

and that

$\mathfrak{C}[\![\Gamma_1]\!]\rho(\eta(1+\#\mathfrak{c}[\![\Gamma_0]\!]\rho+\#\mathfrak{c}[\![\Gamma_1]\!]\rho)) = \mathfrak{V}[\![\mathfrak{z}[\![\mathfrak{c}[\![\Gamma_1]\!]\rho]\!]1]\!](\eta(1+\#\mathfrak{c}[\![\Gamma_0]\!]\rho+\#\mathfrak{c}[\![\Gamma_1]\!]\rho))1.$

Since $1+\#\mathfrak{c}[\![\Gamma_0]\!]\rho+\#\mathfrak{c}[\![\Gamma_1]\!]\rho = 1+\#\mathfrak{c}[\![\Gamma_0;\Gamma_1]\!]\rho$ we also know that

$\eta(1+\#\mathfrak{c}[\![\Gamma_0]\!]\rho+\#\mathfrak{c}[\![\Gamma_1]\!]\rho) = \zeta.$

Because $\mathfrak{C}[\![\Gamma_0;\Gamma_1]\!]\rho\zeta = \mathfrak{C}[\![\Gamma_0]\!]\rho(\mathfrak{C}[\![\Gamma_1]\!]\rho\zeta)$ and because $\mathfrak{c}[\![\Gamma_0]\!]\rho$ and $\mathfrak{c}[\![\Gamma_1]\!]\rho$ are coherent we may conclude that $\mathfrak{C}[\![\Gamma_0;\Gamma_1]\!]\rho\zeta = \mathfrak{V}[\![\mathfrak{z}[\![\mathfrak{c}[\![\Gamma_0;\Gamma_1]\!]\rho]\!]1]\!]\zeta 1$ and that $\mathfrak{c}[\![\Gamma_0;\Gamma_1]\!]\rho$ is coherent. Hence $C[\![\Gamma_0;\Gamma_1]\!] = \mathit{true}$.$\rhd$

When $P[\![\Gamma_0]\!] = \mathit{true}$ and $P[\![\Gamma_1]\!] = \mathit{true}$ as well we can establish that $P[\![\Gamma_0;\Gamma_1]\!] = \mathit{true}$, for owing to 5.4.5, when $1+\#\mathfrak{c}[\![\Gamma_0]\!]\rho \geq \nu \geq 1$,

$\mathfrak{V}[\![\mathfrak{z}[\![\mathfrak{c}[\![\Gamma_0;\Gamma_1]\!]\rho]\!]1]\!]\zeta\nu = \mathfrak{V}[\![\mathfrak{z}[\![\mathfrak{c}[\![\Gamma_0]\!]\rho]\!]1]\!](\mathfrak{C}[\![\Gamma_1]\!]\rho\zeta)\nu;$

and that, when $1+\#\mathfrak{c}[\![\Gamma_1]\!]\rho \geq \nu \geq 1$,

$\mathfrak{V}[\![\mathfrak{z}[\![\mathfrak{c}[\![\Gamma_0;\Gamma_1]\!]\rho]\!]1]\!]\zeta(\nu+\#\mathfrak{c}[\![\Gamma_0]\!]\rho) = \mathfrak{V}[\![\mathfrak{z}[\![\mathfrak{c}[\![\Gamma_1]\!]\rho]\!]1]\!]\zeta\nu.$

Thus, because $1+\#\mathfrak{c}[\![\Gamma_0]\!]\rho \geq \mathfrak{p}[\![\Gamma_0]\!]\downarrow\nu \geq 1$ whenever $\#\mathfrak{p}[\![\Gamma_0]\!] \geq \nu \geq 1$,

$\mathfrak{P}[\![\Gamma_0]\!]\rho(\mathfrak{C}[\![\Gamma_1]\!]\rho\zeta) = \lambda\nu.\mathit{map}(\lambda\nu'.\langle\mathfrak{V}[\![\mathfrak{z}[\![\mathfrak{c}[\![\Gamma_0;\Gamma_1]\!]\rho]\!]1]\!]\zeta\nu',\nu\rangle)(\mathfrak{p}[\![\Gamma_0]\!])$

and, because $1+\#\mathfrak{c}[\![\Gamma_1]\!]\rho \geq \mathfrak{p}[\![\Gamma_1]\!]\downarrow\nu \geq 1$ whenever $\#\mathfrak{p}[\![\Gamma_1]\!] \geq \nu \geq 1$,

$\mathfrak{P}[\![\Gamma_1]\!]\rho\zeta = \lambda\nu.\mathit{map}(\lambda\nu'.\langle\mathfrak{V}[\![\mathfrak{z}[\![\mathfrak{c}[\![\Gamma_0;\Gamma_1]\!]\rho]\!]1]\!]\zeta\nu',\nu\rangle)(\mathit{map}(\lambda\nu''.\nu''+\#\mathfrak{c}[\![\Gamma_0]\!]\rho)(\mathfrak{p}[\![\Gamma_1]\!])).$

Hence the semantic equations reveal that

$\mathbf{P}[\![\Gamma_0;\Gamma_1]\!]\rho\zeta=\lambda\nu.map(\lambda\nu'.\langle\mathbf{V}[\![\mathbf{z}[\![\mathbf{t}[\![\Gamma_0;\Gamma_1]\!]\rho]\!]1]\!]\zeta\nu',\nu\rangle)(\mathbf{p}[\![\Gamma_0;\Gamma_1]\!])$;

likewise if $Q[\![\Gamma_0]\!]=true$ and $Q[\![\Gamma_1]\!]=true$ they show that

$\mathbf{Q}[\![\Gamma_0;\Gamma_1]\!]\rho\zeta=\lambda\nu.map(\lambda\nu'.\langle\mathbf{V}[\![\mathbf{z}[\![\mathbf{t}[\![\Gamma_0;\Gamma_1]\!]\rho]\!]1]\!]\zeta\nu',\nu\rangle)(\mathbf{q}[\![\Gamma_0;\Gamma_1]\!])$.

5.5.6. Lemma.

If E is a Sal expression and Γ is a Sal command such that $\mathcal{R}[\![E]\!]\wedge\mathcal{C}[\![\Gamma]\!]=true$ then $\mathcal{C}[\![\mathtt{while}\ E\ \mathtt{do}\ \Gamma]\!]=true$.

◁After fixing our attention on an environment, ρ, and a continuation, ζ, we set $\eta_0=\mathfrak{V}[\![\mathfrak{z}[\![\mathfrak{c}[\![\mathtt{while}\ E\ \mathtt{do}\ \Gamma]\!]\rho]\!]1]\!]\zeta$, $\nu_0=\#\mathfrak{r}[\![E]\!]\rho$ and $\nu_1=\#\mathfrak{c}[\![\Gamma]\!]\rho$ for some E and Γ having $\mathcal{R}[\![E]\!]=true$ and $\mathcal{C}[\![\Gamma]\!]=true$. In appendix 6 $\mathfrak{c}[\![\mathtt{while}\ E\ \mathtt{do}\ \Gamma]\!]\rho$ is $\mathfrak{r}[\![E]\!]\rho\S\langle\mathtt{pick}\ 1+\#\mathfrak{c}[\![\Gamma]\!]\rho\rangle\S\mathfrak{c}[\![\Gamma]\!]\rho\S\langle\mathtt{move}\ -(2+\#\mathfrak{r}[\![E]\!]\rho+\#\mathfrak{c}[\![\Gamma]\!]\rho)\rangle$; from appendix 3, however, we know that we wish to prove that $\eta_0 1=fix\xi$, where

$\xi=\lambda\zeta'.\mathfrak{R}[\![E]\!]\rho(\lambda\upsilon\sigma.test\langle\mathfrak{C}[\![\Gamma]\!]\rho\zeta'(\upsilon\dagger1),\zeta(\upsilon\dagger1)\rangle(\upsilon\downarrow1)\sigma)$.

Since $\mathfrak{r}[\![E]\!]\rho$ and $\mathfrak{c}[\![\Gamma]\!]\rho$ are coherent programs embedded in $\mathfrak{c}[\![\mathtt{while}\ E\ \mathtt{do}\ \Gamma]\!]\rho$ after 0 and $1+\nu_0$ respectively we may use 5.4.5 to show that

$\eta_0 1=\mathfrak{V}[\![\mathfrak{z}[\![\mathfrak{r}[\![E]\!]\rho]\!]1]\!](\eta_0(1+\nu_0))1$

and that

$\eta_0(2+\nu_0)=\mathfrak{V}[\![\mathfrak{z}[\![\mathfrak{c}[\![\Gamma]\!]\rho]\!]1]\!](\eta_0(2+\nu_0+\nu_1))1$

However, we are also assuming that

$\mathfrak{R}[\![E]\!]\rho(\eta_0(1+\nu_0))=\mathfrak{V}[\![\mathfrak{z}[\![\mathfrak{r}[\![E]\!]\rho]\!]1]\!](\eta_0(1+\nu_0))1$

and that

$\mathfrak{C}[\![\Gamma]\!]\rho(\eta_0(2+\nu_0+\nu_1))=\mathfrak{V}[\![\mathfrak{z}[\![\mathfrak{c}[\![\Gamma]\!]\rho]\!]1]\!](\eta_0(2+\nu_0+\nu_1))1$.

Moreover the remarks in 5.4.3 ensure that

$$\begin{aligned}\eta_0(1+\nu_0)&=\mathfrak{A}[\![\mathfrak{a}[\![\mathfrak{c}[\![\mathtt{while}\ E\ \mathtt{do}\ \Gamma]\!]\rho\downarrow(1+\nu_0)]\!](2+\nu_0)]\!]\eta_0(2+\nu_0)\\&=\mathfrak{A}[\![\mathfrak{a}[\![\mathtt{pick}\ 1+\#\mathfrak{c}[\![\Gamma]\!]\rho]\!](2+\nu_0)]\!]\eta_0(2+\nu_0)\\&=\mathfrak{A}[\![\mathtt{pick}\ 3+\#\mathfrak{r}[\![E]\!]\rho+\#\mathfrak{c}[\![\Gamma]\!]\rho]\!]\eta_0(2+\#\nu_0)\\&=\lambda\upsilon\sigma.test\langle\eta_0(2+\nu_0)(\upsilon\dagger1),\eta_0(3+\nu_0+\nu_1)(\upsilon\dagger1)\rangle(\upsilon\downarrow1)\sigma\end{aligned}$$

whereas

$$\begin{aligned}\eta_0(2+\nu_0+\nu_1)&=\mathfrak{A}[\![\mathfrak{a}[\![\mathfrak{c}[\![\mathtt{while}\ E\ \mathtt{do}\ \Gamma]\!]\rho\downarrow(2+\nu_0+\nu_1)]\!](3+\nu_0+\nu_1)]\!]\eta_0(3+\nu_0+\nu_1)\\&=\mathfrak{A}[\![\mathfrak{a}[\![\mathtt{move}\ -(2+\#\mathfrak{r}[\![E]\!]\rho+\#\mathfrak{c}[\![\Gamma]\!]\rho)]\!](3+\nu_0+\nu_1)]\!]\eta_0(3+\nu_0+\nu_1)\\&=\mathfrak{A}[\![\mathtt{move}\ 1]\!]\eta_0(3+\nu_0+\nu_1)\\&=\eta_0 1.\end{aligned}$$

As $3+\#\mathcal{r}\llbracket E\rrbracket\rho+\#\mathcal{c}\llbracket\Gamma\rrbracket\rho=1+\#\mathcal{c}\llbracket\texttt{while}\ E\ \texttt{do}\ \Gamma\rrbracket\rho$ it is also the case that

$\eta_0(3+\nu_0+\nu_1)=\zeta$;

hence combining these equations shows that

$$\begin{aligned}\eta_0 1&=\mathcal{R}\llbracket E\rrbracket\rho(\eta_0(1+\#\nu_0))\\&=\mathcal{R}\llbracket E\rrbracket\rho(\lambda\upsilon\sigma.\mathit{test}\langle\eta_0(2+\nu_0)(\upsilon\dagger 1),\eta_0(3+\nu_0+\nu_1)(\upsilon\dagger 1)\rangle(\upsilon\downarrow 1)\sigma)\\&=\mathcal{R}\llbracket E\rrbracket\rho(\lambda\upsilon\sigma.\mathit{test}\langle\eta_0(2+\nu_0)(\upsilon\dagger 1),\zeta(\upsilon\dagger 1)\rangle(\upsilon\downarrow 1)\sigma)\\&=\mathcal{R}\llbracket E\rrbracket\rho(\lambda\upsilon\sigma.\mathit{test}\langle\mathcal{C}\llbracket\Gamma\rrbracket\rho(\eta_0(2+\nu_0+\nu_1))(\upsilon\dagger 1),\zeta(\upsilon\dagger 1)\rangle(\upsilon\downarrow 1)\sigma)\\&=\mathcal{R}\llbracket E\rrbracket\rho(\lambda\upsilon\sigma.\mathit{test}\langle\mathcal{C}\llbracket\Gamma\rrbracket\rho(\eta_0 1)(\upsilon\dagger 1),\zeta(\upsilon\dagger 1)\rangle(\upsilon\downarrow 1)\sigma)\\&=\xi(\eta_0 1)\end{aligned}$$

and that $\eta_0 1\sqsupseteq \mathit{fix}\xi$ (since $\mathit{fix}\xi$ is the least fixed point of ξ).

In order to show that $\mathit{fix}\xi\sqsupseteq\eta_0 1$ we introduce a consecution, η_1, by writing

$$\begin{aligned}\eta_1=\lambda\nu.(1+\nu_0\geq\nu\geq 1)&\to\mathcal{V}\llbracket\mathcal{z}\llbracket\mathcal{r}\llbracket E\rrbracket\rho\rrbracket 1\rrbracket(\lambda\upsilon\sigma.\mathit{test}\langle\mathcal{C}\llbracket\Gamma\rrbracket\rho(\mathit{fix}\xi)(\upsilon\dagger 1),\zeta(\upsilon\dagger 1)\rangle(\upsilon\downarrow 1)\sigma)\nu,\\(2+\nu_0+\nu_1\geq\nu\geq 2+\nu_0)&\to\mathcal{V}\llbracket\mathcal{z}\llbracket\mathcal{c}\llbracket\Gamma\rrbracket\rho\rrbracket 1\rrbracket(\mathit{fix}\xi)(\nu-1-\nu_0),\\&\zeta.\end{aligned}$$

Next we show that $\eta_1=\mathcal{ll}\llbracket\mathcal{z}\llbracket\mathcal{c}\llbracket\texttt{while}\ E\ \texttt{do}\ \Gamma\rrbracket\rho\rrbracket 1\rrbracket\zeta\eta_1$ in the following manner. Because $\mathcal{V}\llbracket\mathcal{z}\llbracket\mathcal{r}\llbracket E\rrbracket\rho\rrbracket 1\rrbracket(\eta_1(1+\nu_0))\nu=\eta_1\nu$ whenever $1+\nu_0\geq\nu\geq 1$ and because $\mathcal{r}\llbracket E\rrbracket\rho$ is a coherent program embedded in $\mathcal{c}\llbracket\texttt{while}\ E\ \texttt{do}\ \Gamma\rrbracket\rho$ after 0 we may apply 5.4.4, thereby deducing that if ν is any integer for which $\nu_0\geq\nu\geq 1$ then

$$\begin{aligned}\eta_1\nu&=\mathcal{V}\llbracket\mathcal{z}\llbracket\mathcal{r}\llbracket E\rrbracket\rho\rrbracket 1\rrbracket(\eta_1(1+\nu_0))\nu\\&=\mathcal{ll}\llbracket\mathcal{z}\llbracket\mathcal{r}\llbracket E\rrbracket\rho\rrbracket 1\rrbracket(\eta_1(1+\nu_0))(\mathcal{V}\llbracket\mathcal{z}\llbracket\mathcal{r}\llbracket E\rrbracket\rho\rrbracket 1\rrbracket(\eta_1(1+\nu_0))\nu\\&=\mathcal{ll}\llbracket\mathcal{z}\llbracket\mathcal{c}\llbracket\texttt{while}\ E\ \texttt{do}\ \Gamma\rrbracket\rho\rrbracket 1\rrbracket\zeta\eta_1\nu.\end{aligned}$$

As $\mathcal{V}\llbracket\mathcal{z}\llbracket\mathcal{c}\llbracket\Gamma\rrbracket\rho\rrbracket 1\rrbracket(\eta_1(2+\nu_0+\nu_1))(\nu-1-\nu_0)=\eta_1\nu$ whenever $2+\nu_0+\nu_1\geq\nu\geq 2+\nu_0$ and as $\mathcal{c}\llbracket\Gamma\rrbracket\rho$ is a coherent program embedded in $\mathcal{c}\llbracket\texttt{while}\ E\ \texttt{do}\ \Gamma\rrbracket\rho$ after $1+\nu_0$, when we apply 5.4.4 again we may infer that if ν is any integer such that $1+\nu_0+\nu_1\geq 2+\nu_0$ then

$$\begin{aligned}\eta_1\nu&=\mathcal{V}\llbracket\mathcal{z}\llbracket\mathcal{c}\llbracket\Gamma\rrbracket\rho\rrbracket 1\rrbracket(\eta_1(2+\nu_0+\nu_1))(\nu-1-\nu_0)\\&=\mathcal{ll}\llbracket\mathcal{z}\llbracket\mathcal{c}\llbracket\Gamma\rrbracket\rho\rrbracket 1\rrbracket(\eta_1(2+\nu_0+\nu_1))(\mathcal{V}\llbracket\mathcal{z}\llbracket\mathcal{c}\llbracket\Gamma\rrbracket\rho\rrbracket 1\rrbracket(\eta_1(2+\nu_0+\nu_1)))(\nu-1-\nu_0)\\&=\mathcal{ll}\llbracket\mathcal{z}\llbracket\mathcal{c}\llbracket\texttt{while}\ E\ \texttt{do}\ \Gamma\rrbracket\rho\rrbracket 1\rrbracket\zeta\eta_1\nu.\end{aligned}$$

In addition when $1>\nu$ or $\nu>2+\nu_0+\nu_1$

$\eta_1\nu=\zeta$,

so actually

$$\eta_1(1+\nu_0)=\lambda\upsilon\sigma.\,test\langle \mathcal{C}[\![\Gamma]\!]\rho(fix\xi)(\upsilon\dagger 1),\zeta(\upsilon\dagger 1)\rangle(\upsilon\downarrow 1)\sigma$$
$$=\lambda\upsilon\sigma.\,test\langle \mathcal{C}[\![\Gamma]\!]\rho(fix\xi)(\upsilon\dagger 1),\eta_1(3+\nu_0+\nu_1)(\upsilon\dagger 1)\rangle(\upsilon\downarrow 1)\sigma$$
$$=\lambda\upsilon\sigma.\,test\langle \mathcal{V}[\![\mathfrak{z}[\![\mathfrak{c}[\![\Gamma]\!]\rho]\!]1]\!](fix\xi)1(\upsilon\dagger 1),\eta_1(3+\nu_0+\nu_1)(\upsilon\dagger 1)\rangle(\upsilon\downarrow 1)\sigma$$
$$=\lambda\upsilon\sigma.\,test\langle \eta_1(2+\nu_0),\eta_1(3+\nu_0+\nu_1)(\upsilon\dagger 1)\rangle(\upsilon\downarrow 1)\sigma$$
$$=\mathcal{A}[\![\mathtt{pick}\ 3+\#\mathfrak{r}[\![E]\!]\rho+\#\mathfrak{c}[\![\Gamma]\!]]\!]\eta_1(2+\nu_0)$$
$$=\mathcal{A}[\![\mathfrak{a}[\![\mathtt{pick}\ 1+\#\mathfrak{c}[\![\Gamma]\!]\rho]\!](2+\nu_0)]\!]\eta_1(2+\nu_0)$$
$$=\mathcal{A}[\![\mathfrak{a}[\![\mathfrak{c}[\![\mathtt{while}\ E\ \mathtt{do}\ \Gamma]\!]\rho\downarrow(1+\nu_0)]\!](2+\nu_0)]\!]\eta_1(2+\nu_0)$$
$$=\mathcal{U}[\![\mathfrak{z}[\![\mathfrak{c}[\![\mathtt{while}\ E\ \mathtt{do}\ \Gamma]\!]\rho]\!]1]\!]\zeta\eta_1(1+\nu_0)$$

whilst

$$\eta_1(2+\nu_0+\nu_1)=fix\xi$$
$$=\xi(fix\xi)$$
$$=\mathcal{R}[\![E]\!]\rho(\lambda\upsilon\sigma.\,test\langle \mathcal{C}[\![\Gamma]\!]\rho(fix\xi)(\upsilon\dagger 1),\zeta(\upsilon\dagger 1)\rangle(\upsilon\downarrow 1)\sigma)$$
$$=\mathcal{V}[\![\mathfrak{z}[\![\mathfrak{r}[\![E]\!]\rho]\!]1]\!](\lambda\upsilon\sigma.\,test\langle \mathcal{C}[\![\Gamma]\!]\rho(fix\xi)(\upsilon\dagger 1),\zeta(\upsilon\dagger 1)\rangle(\upsilon\downarrow 1)\sigma)1$$
$$=\eta_1 1$$
$$=\mathcal{A}[\![\mathtt{move}\ 1]\!]\eta_1(3+\nu_0+\nu_1)$$
$$=\mathcal{A}[\![\mathfrak{a}[\![\mathtt{move}\ -(2+\#\mathfrak{r}[\![E]\!]\rho+\#\mathfrak{c}[\![\Gamma]\!]\rho)]\!](3+\nu_0+\nu_1)]\!]\eta_1(3+\nu_0+\nu_1)$$
$$=\mathcal{A}[\![\mathfrak{a}[\![\mathfrak{c}[\![\mathtt{while}\ E\ \mathtt{do}\ \Gamma]\!]\rho\downarrow(2+\nu_0+\nu_1)]\!](3+\nu_0+\nu_1)]\!]\eta_1(3+\nu_0+\nu_1)$$
$$=\mathcal{U}[\![\mathfrak{z}[\![\mathfrak{c}[\![\mathtt{while}\ E\ \mathtt{do}\ \Gamma]\!]\rho]\!]1]\!]\zeta\eta_1(2+\nu_0+\nu_1)$$

Hence $\eta_1=\mathcal{U}[\![\mathfrak{z}[\![\mathfrak{c}[\![\mathtt{while}\ E\ \mathtt{do}\ \Gamma]\!]\rho]\!]1]\!]\eta_1$ and, since η_0 is the least fixed point of $\mathcal{U}[\![\mathfrak{z}[\![\mathfrak{c}[\![\mathtt{while}\ E\ \mathtt{do}\ \Gamma]\!]\rho]\!]1]\!]\zeta$, $\eta_1\sqsupseteq\eta_0$; in particular, because $fix\xi=\eta_1 1$, $fix\xi\sqsupseteq\eta_0 1$.

We now know that $\mathcal{C}[\![\mathtt{while}\ E\ \mathtt{do}\ \Gamma]\!]\rho\zeta=\mathcal{V}[\![\mathfrak{z}[\![\mathfrak{c}[\![\mathtt{while}\ E\ \mathtt{do}\ \Gamma]\!]\rho]\!]1]\!]\zeta 1$, so as $\mathfrak{c}[\![\mathtt{while}\ E\ \mathtt{do}\ \Gamma]\!]\rho$ is coherent $C[\![\mathtt{while}\ E\ \mathtt{do}\ \Gamma]\!]=true$.▸

When we assume also that $P[\![\Gamma]\!]=true$ we can show that $P[\![\mathtt{while}\ E\ \mathtt{do}\ \Gamma]\!]=true$, since $1+\#\mathfrak{c}[\![\Gamma]\!]\rho\geq\mathfrak{p}[\![\Gamma]\!]\downarrow\nu\geq 1$ whenever $\#\mathfrak{p}[\![\Gamma]\!]\geq\nu\geq 1$. In terms of the notation adopted above,

$$
\begin{aligned}
\mathcal{P}[\![\Gamma]\!]\rho(fix\xi) &= \lambda\nu.map(\lambda\nu'.\langle\mathcal{V}[\![\mathcal{z}[\![\mathcal{c}[\![\Gamma]\!]\rho]\!]1]\!](fix\xi)\nu',\nu\rangle)(\wp[\![\Gamma]\!]) \\
&= \lambda\nu.map(\lambda\nu'.\langle\eta_1(\nu'+1+\#\mathcal{r}[\![E]\!]\rho),\nu\rangle)(\wp[\![\Gamma]\!]) \\
&= \lambda\nu.map(\lambda\nu'.\langle\eta_0(\nu'+1+\#\mathcal{r}[\![E]\!]\rho),\nu\rangle)(\wp[\![\Gamma]\!]) \\
&= \lambda\nu.map(\lambda\nu'.\langle\eta_0\nu',\nu\rangle)(map(\lambda\nu''.\nu''+1+\#\mathcal{r}[\![E]\!]\rho)(\wp[\![\Gamma]\!])) \\
&= \lambda\nu.map(\lambda\nu'.\langle\eta_0\nu',\nu\rangle)(\wp[\![\texttt{while E do }\Gamma]\!]) \\
&= \lambda\nu.map(\lambda\nu'.\langle\mathcal{V}[\![\mathcal{z}[\![\mathcal{c}[\![\texttt{while E do }\Gamma]\!]\rho]\!]1]\!]\zeta\nu',\nu\rangle)(\wp[\![\texttt{while E do }\Gamma]\!])
\end{aligned}
$$

where, according to appendix 3, $\mathcal{P}[\![\texttt{while E do }\Gamma]\!]\rho\zeta=\mathcal{P}[\![\Gamma]\!]\rho(fix\xi)$.

Consequently $\mathcal{P}[\![\texttt{while E do }\Gamma]\!]\rho\zeta$ coincides with

$\lambda\nu.map(\lambda\nu'.\langle\mathcal{V}[\![\mathcal{z}[\![\mathcal{c}[\![\texttt{while E do }\Gamma]\!]\rho]\!]1]\!]\zeta\nu',\nu\rangle)(\wp[\![\texttt{while E do }\Gamma]\!])$;

similarly when $Q[\![\Gamma]\!]=true$ $\mathcal{Q}[\![\texttt{while E do }\Gamma]\!]\rho\zeta$ coincides with

$\lambda\nu.map(\lambda\nu'.\langle\mathcal{V}[\![\mathcal{z}[\![\mathcal{c}[\![\texttt{while E do }\Gamma]\!]\rho]\!]1]\!]\zeta\nu',\nu\rangle)(\mathcal{q}[\![\texttt{while E do }\Gamma]\!])$.

5.5.7. Theorem.

Suppose that if Ξ is any secret instruction then $\mathcal{A}[\![\Xi]\!]=\lambda\eta\nu.\psi(map\eta\nu^{*})(\eta\nu)$ for some $\nu^{*}\in\mathsf{N}^{*}$ which may depend on the parameters of Ξ and for some $\psi\in\mathsf{Z}^{*}\to\mathsf{O}$ which may not depend on the parameters of Ξ. Assume also that for every B, Ω and O the programs $\mathfrak{b}[\![B]\!]$, $\mathfrak{o}[\![O]\!]$ and $\mathfrak{w}[\![\Omega]\!]$ are coherent and satisfy $\mathcal{B}[\![B]\!]=\lambda\zeta.\mathcal{V}[\![\mathfrak{z}[\![\mathfrak{b}[\![B]\!]]\!]1]\!]\zeta 1$, $\mathcal{O}[\![O]\!]=\lambda\zeta.\mathcal{V}[\![\mathfrak{z}[\![\mathfrak{o}[\![O]\!]]\!]1]\!]\zeta 1$ and $\mathcal{W}[\![\Omega]\!]=\lambda\zeta.\mathcal{V}[\![\mathfrak{z}[\![\mathfrak{w}[\![\Omega]\!]]\!]1]\!]\zeta 1$. All E, Φ, Σ, Δ, Θ and Γ are such that, in terms of the predicates of 5.4.6, $E[\![E]\!]\wedge L[\![E]\!]\wedge R[\![E]\!]=true$, $F[\![\Phi]\!]=true$, $S[\![\Sigma]\!]=true$, $D[\![\Delta]\!]\wedge T[\![\Delta]\!]=true$, $G[\![\Theta]\!]=true$ and $C[\![\Gamma]\!]\wedge P[\![\Gamma]\!]\wedge Q[\![\Gamma]\!]=true$; thus any Sal program has a meaning according to stack semantics which is identical with the meaning ascribed to the Sam program obtained by compiling and loading it.

◁This theorem, which simply summarizes the results preceding it, goes some way towards vindicating our claim that underlying the stack semantics of Sal is a particular kind of implementation. Our task is not yet at an end, however, as should become clear in 5.6.1.▷

5.6. The conformity between consecution semantics and pointer semantics.

5.6.1. Pointers.

Coming as it does in the wake of 5.3.9, the proof of 5.5.7 has an elegant simplicity which is rather beguiling, for we have yet to introduce a semantics which indubitably models the workings of a machine. We want to feel sure that certain Sal programs are properly compiled by the functions defined in appendix 6, in the sense that the effect of executing the code obtained can be gauged by standard semantics. Consequently we cannot be content until we have related the valuations defined in appendix 3 to a semantics for Sam which depends on only those entities that can actually be manipulated during the execution of a Sam program. The equations of appendix 12 do not provide such a semantics, for they imply that members of function spaces such as Z can be kept on the stack or in the store, whereas in reality computers merely handle bit patterns. In this section we shall therefore consider the equations of appendix 13, which give a semantics that obviously imitates what happens in a computer. Only after we have shown this semantics to be congruent with that described in 5.4.2 will we be able to appeal to 5.5.7 in order to establish that our compiling functions do indeed allow many Sal programs to be executed in accordance with the intentions of their authors.

In 5.4.2 we remarked that for every Sam instruction Ξ there is some $\nu^*\epsilon N^*$ and some $\psi\epsilon Z^*\to O$ such that $\mathcal{A}[\![\Xi]\!]=\lambda\eta\nu.\psi(map\eta\nu^*)(\eta\nu)$; furthermore usually ψ has a simple form which does not depend on the detailed structure of W. This fact suggests that we try to construct a valuation which ignores the consecution supplied as an argument to our present version of $\mathcal{A}$. This new valuation ought to describe how executing any particular instruction would modify the code pointer, the stack and the store but it must not entail applying a consecution, so we might expect it to belong to $Ins \to N \to Y \to S \to (N \times Y \times S)$. There are some instructions on which such a valuation can be defined; among them are drop and turn, which must yield the values $\lambda\nu\upsilon\sigma.\langle \nu, \upsilon\dagger 1, \sigma\rangle$ and $\lambda\nu\upsilon\sigma.\langle \nu, \langle \upsilon\downarrow 2\rangle \S \langle \upsilon\downarrow 1\rangle \S \upsilon\dagger 2, \sigma\rangle$ respectively. Instructions such as read, however, oblige us to introduce a treatment of errors. This could be done by allowing $\mathcal{A}$ to produce the result *error*, so that $\mathcal{A}$ would be in $Ins \to N \to Y \to S \to (\{error\} + (N \times Y \times S))$, but to gain consistency with the equations of appendix 12 we adopt $wrong \in S \to A$ and take $\mathcal{A}$ to be a member of $Ins \to N \to Y \to S \to (A + (N \times Y \times S))$. This new domain called A is intended to contain whatever answers a Sam program may produce (even if they are only error messages) in much the same way as the domain A provided in 4.4.2 contains the answers yielded by Sap programs.

Because a consecution can no longer be an argument of $\mathcal{A}$, the value placed on the stack by executing link $\langle \nu', \nu''\rangle$, for instance, has not a continuation among its components; instead

$\mathcal{A}[\![$link $\langle \nu', \nu''\rangle]\!] = \lambda\nu\upsilon\sigma.\langle \nu, \langle\langle \nu', \nu'' + \#\upsilon\rangle\rangle \S \upsilon, \sigma\rangle$.

By the same token, jump serves not to apply a continuation but to set up a new code pointer. Thus whereas in 5.4.2 W was assumed to be $L+B+E^*+J+F+J+Z+((L \to T) \times N \times N \times U)$, now it is $L+B+E^*+J+F+N+((L \to T) \times N \times N \times U)$ where J is $N \times N$ and F is $N \times N \times U$. The other domains can still be constructed from W by applying the functors of 5.2.5 so we can continue to use the basic functions described in 3.3.2.

In appendix 13, which provides the version of $\mathcal{A}$ discussed here, the absence of consecutions forces us to analyse the meanings of Sam programs without the use of $\mathcal{U}$ and $\mathcal{V}$. We know that a program Π is executed from the instruction resulting from the execution of $\Pi\downarrow\nu$ and then executing Π from the position resulting from the execution of $\Pi\downarrow\nu$ (unless an error occurs in the meantime). When there are no more instructions to be executed parts of the final stack and store are viewed as the answer yielded by Π. This answer is obtained by applying

$success \in Y \rightarrow S \rightarrow A$, a function which we shall leave unspecified. We shall, however, define $succeed \in (Pro \rightarrow N \rightarrow Y \rightarrow S \rightarrow A) \rightarrow (Pro \rightarrow N \rightarrow Y \rightarrow S \rightarrow A)$, the function which models each successive stage of execution, by setting

$$succeed = \lambda \psi \Pi \nu \upsilon \sigma . (\nu > \# \Pi) \vee (1 > \nu) \rightarrow success\, \upsilon \sigma ,$$
$$\mathcal{A}[\![\Pi \downarrow \nu]\!] (\nu + 1) \upsilon \sigma \mathsf{E} A \rightarrow \mathcal{A}[\![\Pi \downarrow \nu]\!] (\nu + 1) \upsilon \sigma | A ,$$
$$(\lambda \langle \nu', \upsilon', \sigma' \rangle . \psi [\![\Pi]\!] \nu' \upsilon' \sigma')(\mathcal{A}[\![\Pi \downarrow \nu]\!] (\nu + 1) \upsilon \sigma | (N \times Y \times S));$$

the valuation which describes the whole course of execution, $\mathcal{Z}$, can now be set up by writing $\mathcal{Z} = fix(succeed)$. Whereas the control supplied as an argument to the valuation $\mathcal{Z}$ in 4.4.2 differs as execution proceeds, here the program provided as an argument to our new version of $\mathcal{Z}$ remains constant throughout execution (as befits an implementation in which pointers to code are manipulated instead of code itself); consequently there is actually some $\phi \in Pro \rightarrow (N \rightarrow Y \rightarrow S \rightarrow A) \rightarrow (N \rightarrow Y \rightarrow S \rightarrow A)$ such that $\mathcal{Z} = \lambda \Pi . fix(\phi [\![\Pi]\!])$.

This sort of semantics, which we shall refer to as 'pointer semantics', has an intuitive appeal which is lacked by the 'consecution semantics' given in appendix 12. The explanation for this is to be found in the clarity with which $\mathcal{A}$ displays the steps in the execution of a program and in the fact that W is structured without the aid of spaces such as Z. Though the function spaces $(Ide \rightarrow (N \times N)^*) \times N^*$ and $L \rightarrow T$ are still needed by W they could be eliminated by using slightly different models for the environment and the store. More unfortunate is the presence in W of a summand E*, which necessitates defining W recursively; yet even this unrealistic aspect of W could be removed by replacing this summand by a domain M containing pointers to structures and by giving S another factor, such as $M \rightarrow E^*$. Were this done we could discard the redundant members of W, so that instead of being a domain containing $\perp$ and $\top$ it would simply be a set of incomparable elements.

Pointer semantics illuminates one defect of our compiling function which consecution semantics hides. According to the comments in 5.4.1, every monadic operator O gives rise to a Sam program $\mathfrak{z}[\![\mathfrak{o}[\![O]\!]]\!]$ which must be coherent and satisfy $\mathcal{O}[\![O]\!]=\lambda\zeta.\mathcal{V}[\![\mathfrak{z}[\![\mathfrak{o}[\![O]\!]]\!]1]\!]\zeta 1$ if the statement of 5.5.7 is to hold. However when O is the operator £ discussed in 3.4.1, a difficulty emerges: we imagine that $\lambda\zeta.\mathcal{V}[\![\mathfrak{z}[\![\mathfrak{o}[\![£]\!]]\!]1]\!]\zeta 1$ is $\lambda\zeta.rv(\lambda\upsilon\sigma.\upsilon{\downarrow}1{\in}\mathsf{F}\rightarrow\zeta(\langle\langle tv(nv(\upsilon{\downarrow}1{\downarrow}1)),\upsilon{\downarrow}1{\downarrow}2,\upsilon{\downarrow}1{\downarrow}3\rangle\rangle\S\upsilon{\dagger}1)\sigma,\mathit{wrong}\sigma)$, but there is no obvious choice for the value of $\mathcal{Z}[\![\mathfrak{z}[\![\mathfrak{o}[\![£]\!]]\!]1]\!]$, since in pointer semantics the first component of a procedure value is not a continuation but a code pointer. The same problem is caused by every other Sal operator which takes a label or procedure value as an argument. In store semantics this problem can be solved by treating such an operator as a procedure, but in stack semantics this approach entails passing the results of applying an operator out of their scopes. The other solutions of the problem are ugly and will not be considered, because no conventional programming language provides operators that act on label and procedure values. Even for the purposes of appendix 7 we wish to apply £ only to abstractions, so when E is Φ we could take $\mathfrak{e}[\![£\mathrm{E}]\!]$ to be $\lambda\rho.\mathfrak{r}[\![\mathrm{E}]\!]\rho\S\langle\mathbf{give}\ 1\rangle\S\langle\mathbf{move}\ 3\rangle\S\langle\mathbf{tv}\rangle\S\langle\mathbf{nv}\rangle\S\langle\mathbf{move}\ {-}(3+\#\mathfrak{r}[\![\mathrm{E}]\!]\rho)\rangle$, where in consecution semantics $\mathcal{A}[\![\mathbf{give}\ \nu']\!]$ would have the value $\lambda\eta\nu\upsilon\sigma.(\upsilon{\downarrow}1{\in}\mathsf{F}\rightarrow\eta\nu(\langle\langle\nu',\upsilon{\downarrow}1{\downarrow}2,\upsilon{\downarrow}1{\downarrow}3\rangle\rangle\S\upsilon{\dagger}1)\sigma,\mathit{wrong}\sigma)$ and $\mathfrak{a}[\![\mathbf{give}\ \nu']\!]$ would have the value $\lambda\nu.\mathbf{give}\ \nu+\nu'$. Were we to modify appendix 6 in accordance with this suggestion, then $\mathfrak{z}[\![\mathfrak{e}[\![£\mathrm{E}]\!]\rho]\!]1$ would be coherent when $\mathfrak{z}[\![\mathfrak{r}[\![\mathrm{E}]\!]\rho]\!]1$ was coherent and $\mathcal{E}[\![£\Phi]\!]$ would be $\lambda\rho\zeta.\mathcal{V}[\![\mathfrak{z}[\![\mathfrak{e}[\![£\Phi]\!]\rho]\!]1]\!]\zeta 1$ for every abstraction Φ; moreover $\lambda\rho.\mathcal{V}[\![\mathfrak{z}[\![\mathfrak{e}[\![£\mathrm{E}]\!]\rho]\!]1]\!]$ could be given the "right" meaning. To avoid complicating the compiling algorithm in this uninteresting way henceforth we shall ignore £ entirely.

We could obtain equations for Sal by combining appendix 13 with appendix 14 and appendix 6 in the way that in 5.4.6 we combined appendix 12 with appendix 14 and appendix 6. The resulting equations would resemble those in appendix 4 (which we obtained in 4.4.3 by a similar process), but would have little intuitive significance.

5.6.2. The explicit connection between functions and bit patterns.

In 4.6.1 we indicated how to convert members of the domain W appropriate to appendix 11 into members of the domain W for appendix 10 by using *furl*. The parallel between our sorts of semantics for Sap and our sorts of semantics for Sam suggests that there should be a function *hurl* intended to change witnessed values taken from the domain W provided by appendix 13 into witnessed values in the domain W for appendix 12. Because we can turn a control, H, into a continuation simply by forming $\mathcal{Y}[\![H]\!]\zeta$ for any ζ, in 4.6.1 $furl\zeta$ could be allowed to map one version of W into the other. However, to make a code pointer, ν, into a continuation we need not another continuation but a consecution, η, from which the continuation $\eta\nu$ may be obtained; hence here $hurl\eta$ must be the mapping between the two versions of W. If, therefore, $\tilde{\omega}$ is any witnessed value suitable for the pointer semantics of Sam, $hurl\eta\tilde{\omega}$ should belong to the domain W required by the consecution semantics of Sam.

As was mentioned in 5.6.1, even in the pointer semantics of Sam the domains have a recursive structure (albeit one that would not seriously hamper the construction of an implementation). Consequently we are obliged to make *hurl* satisfy a recursive equation formed with the aid of a continuous function, *hurling*, having *hurl* as its least fixed point. When η is a consecution, ψ is a function taking H (the domain of consecutions) into a continuous mapping between the two versions of W and $\tilde{\omega}$ is a witnessed value suited to pointer semantics we let $hurling\psi\eta\tilde{\omega}$ (a witnessed value suited to consecution semantics) be defined implicitly by the equation

$hurling = \lambda\psi\eta\grave{\omega}.\grave{\omega}EL \to \acute{\omega},$

$\grave{\omega}EB \to \acute{\omega},$

$\grave{\omega}EE^* \to (E(\psi\eta))^*(\grave{\omega}|E^*),$

$\grave{\omega}EJ \to \langle \eta((\grave{\omega}|J)\downarrow 1),(\grave{\omega}|J)\downarrow 2\rangle,$

$\grave{\omega}EF \to \langle \eta((\grave{\omega}|F)\downarrow 1),(\grave{\omega}|F)\downarrow 2,(\grave{\omega}|F)\downarrow 3\rangle,$

$\grave{\omega}EJ \to \langle \eta((\grave{\omega}|J)\downarrow 1),(\grave{\omega}|J)\downarrow 2\rangle,$

$\grave{\omega}EN \to \eta(\grave{\omega}|N),$

$\grave{\omega}.$

Though $\psi\eta$ is not a retraction we may still refer to $E(\psi\eta)$ so long as we presume that E is defined on all the continuous functions taking the underlying universal domain into itself. Naturally, we set up E and its counterparts just as in 5.2.5, so we let:

$V = \lambda X.push\langle 4,-1\rangle \circ X \circ push\langle 3,1\rangle;$

$E = \lambda X.X \circ mask4.$

In addition when handling the domains given in appendix 13 and appendix 12 (or appendix 3) we have:

$S = \lambda X.(L \to (VX \times T)) \times (VX)^* \times (VX)^*;$

$Y = \lambda X.X^*.$

We shall manipulate $S(\psi\eta)$ and $Y(\psi\eta)$ as freely as we manipulate $E(\psi\eta)$; in particular, when $\grave{\sigma}$ is a store and $\grave{\upsilon}$ is a stack provided by appendix 13 we shall be interested in $S(fix(hurling)\eta)\grave{\sigma}$ and $Y(fix(hurling)\eta)\grave{\upsilon}$ which are a stack and a store that could be used in appendix 12.

We can now construct *hurl*, the function that is really of interest to us, by setting

$hurl = fix(hurling)$

so that when $\acute{\omega}EE^*$ $hurl\eta\grave{\omega}$ is $map(hurl\eta \circ mask4)(\grave{\omega}|E^*)$.

The analogy between our present situation and that of 4.6.1 extends to assuming that the version of A appropriate to appendix 13 and the version of A for appendix 12 have a common overall structure (in terms of W); we also suppose that these domains can be obtained from their respective versions of W by combining $\times$, $+$, $*$ and $\rightarrow$ without "placing W to the left of $\rightarrow$". By stipulating this much about the answer domains we are able to guarantee that when ϑ belongs to the domain A provided in 5.6.1 and when η is any consecution $A(\mathit{hurl}\,\eta)\vartheta$ belongs to the version of A needed in 5.1.2.

To assure ourselves that pointer semantics is congruent with consecution semantics we have to show that for any program Π the outcome of executing Π can be modelled as well by $\mathcal{Z}$ as it can by $\mathcal{V}$. Thus for any integer ν, any stack υ and any store ϑ it is natural to try to relate $\mathcal{V}[\![\Pi]\!]\zeta\nu(Y(\mathit{hurl}\,\eta_0)\upsilon)(S(\mathit{hurl}\,\eta_1)\vartheta)$ to $A(\mathit{hurl}\,\eta_2)(\mathcal{Z}[\![\Pi]\!]\nu\upsilon\vartheta)$ when η_0, η_1 and η_2 are certain consecutions. When $\hat{\omega}$, say, is a label value contained in υ or ϑ $(\hat{\omega}|J)\downarrow 1$ is interpreted as a pointer into Π, so the counterpart of $\hat{\omega}$ in consecution semantics is $\langle\mathcal{V}[\![\Pi]\!]\zeta((\hat{\omega}|J)\downarrow 1),(\hat{\omega}|J)\downarrow 2\rangle$ (which is $\mathit{hurl}(\mathcal{V}[\![\Pi]\!]\zeta)\hat{\omega}$); similar remarks apply when $\hat{\omega}$ is any other kind of witnessed value and when $\hat{\omega}$ is present in $\mathcal{Z}[\![\Pi]\!]\nu\upsilon\vartheta$, which is the answer produced by Π. Hence we take η_0, η_1 and η_2 to be $\mathcal{V}[\![\Pi]\!]\zeta$. Because $\Pi\downarrow\nu$ might be move $1+\#\Pi$, whatever relation exists between $\mathcal{V}[\![\Pi]\!]\zeta\nu(Y(\mathit{hurl}\,\eta_0)\upsilon)(S(\mathit{hurl}\,\eta_1)\vartheta)$ and $A(\mathit{hurl}\,\eta_2)(\mathcal{Z}[\![\Pi]\!]\nu\upsilon\vartheta)$ must also exist between $\zeta(Y(\mathit{hurl}\,\eta_0)\upsilon)(S(\mathit{hurl}\,\eta_1)\vartheta)$ and $A(\mathit{hurl}\,\eta_2)(\mathit{success}\,\upsilon\vartheta)$. Accordingly we accept that our goal must be to demonstrate that if $\zeta(Y(\mathit{hurl}(\mathcal{V}[\![\Pi]\!]\zeta))\upsilon)(S(\mathit{hurl}(\mathcal{V}[\![\Pi]\!]\zeta))\vartheta)=A(\mathit{hurl}(\mathcal{V}[\![\Pi]\!]\sigma))(\mathit{success}\,\upsilon\vartheta)$ for all suitable υ and ϑ then

$$\mathcal{V}[\![\Pi]\!]\zeta\nu(Y(\mathit{hurl}(\mathcal{V}[\![\Pi]\!]\zeta))\upsilon)(S(\mathit{hurl}(\mathcal{V}[\![\Pi]\!]\zeta))\vartheta)=A(\mathit{hurl}(\mathcal{V}[\![\Pi]\!]\zeta))(\mathcal{Z}[\![\Pi]\!]\nu\upsilon\vartheta)$$

for all suitable ν, υ and ϑ.

The congruence that we wish to establish between the two sorts of semantics for Sam is thus very similar to that between the two sorts of semantics for Sap, which we discussed in 4.6.1. The arguments of 4.6.2 and 4.6.5 therefore suggest that we split our problem in two by trying to show first that

$$\mathcal{V}[\![\Pi]\!]\zeta\nu(Y(\mathit{hurl}(\mathcal{V}[\![\Pi]\!]\zeta))\upsilon)(S(\mathit{hurl}(\mathcal{V}[\![\Pi]\!]\zeta))\vartheta)\sqsupseteq A(\mathit{hurl}(\mathcal{V}[\![\Pi]\!]\zeta))(\mathcal{Z}[\![\Pi]\!]\nu\upsilon\vartheta)$$

and then that

$$\mathcal{V}[\![\Pi]\!]\zeta\nu(Y(hurl(\mathcal{V}[\![\Pi]\!]\zeta))\grave{\upsilon})(S(hurl(\mathcal{V}[\![\Pi]\!]\zeta))\grave{\partial})\sqsubseteq A(hurl(\grave{\mathcal{V}}[\![\Pi]\!]\zeta))(\mathcal{Z}[\![\Pi]\!]\nu\grave{\upsilon}\grave{\partial})$$

for all reasonable Π, ν, $\grave{\upsilon}$, $\grave{\partial}$ and ζ. This is in fact what we shall do, but our proofs for Sam will look somewhat simpler than their counterparts for Sap, because in 5.6.3 and 5.6.6 we shall be able to establish results about individual instructions without placing them in the context of a program. When analysing Sap we could not adopt an analogous approach (by mentioning orders instead of controls in 4.6.3 and 4.6.6), as the treatment of amend I, t $\langle\nu,\Delta\rangle$ and q $\langle\nu,\Gamma\rangle$ in appendix 10 did not tally with the semantics provided by appendix 11 unless the controls containing these orders are constrained to be adhesive. No such constraint need be imposed on Sal programs, and similarly when in 5.6.8 we come to verify that

$$\acute{\mathcal{V}}[\![\Pi]\!]\zeta\nu(Y(hurl(\acute{\mathcal{V}}[\![\Pi]\!]\zeta))\grave{\upsilon})(S(hurl(\grave{\mathcal{V}}[\![\Pi]\!]\zeta))\grave{\partial})=A(hurl(\grave{\mathcal{V}}[\![\Pi]\!]\zeta))(\mathcal{Z}[\![\Pi]\!]\nu\grave{\upsilon}\grave{\partial}).$$

we shall require no restrictions on ν, $\grave{\upsilon}$ or $\grave{\partial}$.

Yet again a succinct notation is provided for us by the diacritical convention of 2.5.4. However, whereas in 4.6.2 acute accents signified the use of the operational semantic equations and grave accents signified the use of the denotational semantic equations, here the pairing is reversed: a typical witnessed value is represented as $\acute{\omega}$ when it is manipulated by the denotational semantic equations (those in appendix 12) and as $\grave{\omega}$ when it is manipulated by the operational semantic equations (those in appendix 13). The reason for this reversal is, paradoxically, a desire for consistency: throughout all of this book acute accents distinguish members of the domains needed by appendix 3 (or by appendix 1) while grave accents distinguish members of the domains needed by appendix 2 (and by appendix 10), so acute accents mark out entities in the domains appropriate to appendix 10, which are the same as the domains for appendix 2.

As is usual when proving congruences we have to make certain plausible assumptions about those aspects of the semantics of Sam which we have deliberately left vague. In particular we insist that $\lambda\eta.A(hurl\,\eta)=\lambda\eta.\bot$, $\lambda\eta.A(hurl\,\eta)\top=\lambda\eta.\top$, $\lambda\eta.wrong\circ S(hurl\,\eta)=\lambda\eta.A(hurl\,\eta)\circ wrong$ and $\lambda\eta.new\circ S(hurl\,\eta)=\lambda\eta.new$ when the versions of *wrong* and *new* found in appendix 12 appear on the left hand sides of these equations and the versions found in appendix 13 appear on the right hand sides. If Ξ is any secret instruction, ν is any integer, $\grave{\upsilon}$ is any stack, $\grave{\sigma}$ is any store and η is any consecution we shall assume that setting $\acute{\upsilon}=Y(hurl\,\eta)\grave{\upsilon}$ and $\acute{\sigma}=S(hurl\,\eta)\grave{\sigma}$ provides a stack $\acute{\upsilon}$ and a store $\acute{\sigma}$ such that, when $\mathcal{A}[\![\Xi]\!]\nu\grave{\upsilon}\grave{\sigma}$ is not in $N\times Y\times S$, $\mathcal{A}[\![\Xi]\!]\eta\nu\acute{\upsilon}\acute{\sigma}=A(hurl\,\eta)(\mathcal{A}[\![\Xi]\!]\nu\grave{\upsilon}\grave{\sigma}|A)$ and, when $\mathcal{A}[\![\Xi]\!]\nu\grave{\upsilon}\grave{\sigma}$ is in $N\times Y\times S$, $\mathcal{A}[\![\Xi]\!]\eta\nu\acute{\upsilon}\acute{\sigma}=(\lambda\langle\nu',\grave{\upsilon}',\grave{\sigma}'\rangle.\,\eta\nu'(Y(hurl\,\eta)\grave{\upsilon}')(S(hurl\,\eta)\grave{\sigma}'))(\mathcal{A}[\![\Xi]\!]\nu\grave{\upsilon}\grave{\sigma}|(N\times Y\times S))$; that this is a reasonable assumption will become obvious when we consider the instructions which are not secret (as we shall do in 5.6.3).

5.6.3. Lemma.

Let Ξ be a Sam order, let ν be an integer, let υ be a stack and let σ be a store; take η to be any consecution and set $\acute{\upsilon}=Y(hurl\eta)\upsilon$ and $\acute{\sigma}=S(hurl\eta)\sigma$. Unless $\mathcal{A}[\![\Xi]\!]\nu\upsilon\sigma\in N\times Y\times S$, $\mathcal{A}[\![\Xi]\!]\eta\nu\acute{\upsilon}\acute{\sigma}=A(hurl\eta)(\mathcal{A}[\![\Xi]\!]\nu\upsilon\sigma|A)$. If $\mathcal{A}[\![\Xi]\!]\nu\upsilon\sigma\in N\times Y\times S$,

$$\mathcal{A}[\![\Xi]\!]\eta\nu\acute{\upsilon}\acute{\sigma}=(\lambda\langle\nu',\upsilon',\sigma'\rangle.\eta\nu'(Y(hurl\eta)\upsilon')(S(hurl\eta)\sigma'))(\mathcal{A}[\![\Xi]\!]\nu\upsilon\sigma|(N\times Y\times S)).$$

◁The version of $\mathcal{A}$ formulated in appendix 12 is required on the right hand sides of the equations above, whereas the version of $\mathcal{A}$ described in appendix 13 is required on the left hand sides. In order to establish these equations we have merely to inspect the meanings ascribed to each Sam instruction in the appendices and to remember the assumptions about *wrong* and *new* (and about secret instructions) made in 5.6.2. We shall consider only one order, apply, and we shall take υ and σ to be such that $\acute{\upsilon}=Y(hurl\eta)\upsilon$ and $\acute{\sigma}=S(hurl\eta)\sigma$ for some η.

When ν is any integer, appendix 12 indicates that $\mathcal{A}[\![\text{apply}]\!]\eta\nu\acute{\upsilon}\acute{\sigma}$ is $\bot$, $\top$, $wrong\acute{\sigma}$ or $\eta\nu(\langle\acute{\upsilon}\downarrow1\rangle\S\langle\acute{\upsilon}\downarrow2\downarrow1\rangle\S\langle\acute{\omega}\rangle\S\langle\eta(\nu+1)\rangle\S\acute{\upsilon}\dagger2)\acute{\sigma}$ (where $\acute{\omega}=bulk(\acute{\upsilon}\downarrow2\downarrow2)0(\acute{\upsilon}\downarrow2\downarrow3)\acute{\upsilon}\acute{\sigma}$), depending on whether $\acute{\upsilon}\downarrow2$ is $\bot$, $\top$, a member of a summand of W other than F or a member of F, whilst appendix 13 shows that $\mathcal{A}[\![\text{apply}]\!]\nu\upsilon\sigma$ is $\bot$, $\top$, $wrong\sigma$ or $\langle\nu,\langle\upsilon\downarrow1\rangle\S\langle\upsilon\downarrow2\downarrow1\rangle\S\langle\grave{\omega}\rangle\S\langle\nu+1\rangle\S\upsilon\dagger2,\sigma\rangle$ (where $\grave{\omega}=bulk(\upsilon\downarrow2\downarrow2)0(\upsilon\downarrow2\downarrow3)\upsilon\sigma$), depending on whether $\upsilon\downarrow2$ is $\bot$, $\top$, a member of a summand of W other than F or a member of F. Since $\acute{\upsilon}\downarrow2=hurl\eta(\upsilon\downarrow2)$ and $wrong\acute{\sigma}=A(hurl\eta)(wrong\sigma)$ it is evident that, unless $\mathcal{A}[\![\text{apply}]\!]\nu\upsilon\sigma\in N\times Y\times S$, $\mathcal{A}[\![\text{apply}]\!]\eta\nu\acute{\upsilon}\acute{\sigma}=A(hurl\eta)(\mathcal{A}[\![\text{apply}]\!]\nu\upsilon\sigma|A)$. Moreover, if $\mathcal{A}[\![\text{apply}]\!]\nu\upsilon\sigma\in N\times Y\times S$, we know that $\acute{\upsilon}\downarrow2\downarrow1=\eta(\upsilon\downarrow2\downarrow1)$ and $\acute{\omega}=\grave{\omega}$ (owing to the way in which in 5.6.1 we transferred the basic functions of 5.1.5 to new domains), so

$$\langle\acute{\upsilon}\downarrow1\rangle\S\langle\acute{\upsilon}\downarrow2\downarrow1\rangle\S\langle\acute{\omega}\rangle\S\langle\eta(\nu+1)\rangle\S\acute{\upsilon}\dagger2=Y(hurl\eta)(\langle\upsilon\downarrow1\rangle\S\langle\upsilon\downarrow2\downarrow1\rangle\S\langle\grave{\omega}\rangle\S\langle\nu+1\rangle\S\upsilon\dagger2)$$

and

$$\mathcal{A}[\![\text{apply}]\!]\eta\nu\acute{\upsilon}\acute{\sigma}=(\lambda\langle\nu',\upsilon',\sigma'\rangle.\eta\nu'(Y(hurl\eta)\upsilon')(S(hurl\eta)\sigma'))(\mathcal{A}[\![\text{apply}]\!]\nu\upsilon\sigma|(N\times Y\times S))$$

as required. The other instructions are as easy to analyse as apply.▷

5.6.4. Proposition.

If Π is a Sam program, η is a consecution and ζ is a continuation such that $\eta=\mathcal{V}[\![\Pi]\!]\zeta$ and

$\lambda\upsilon\partial.\zeta(Y(\mathit{hurl}\eta)\upsilon)(S(\mathit{hurl}\eta)\partial)=\lambda\upsilon\partial.A(\mathit{hurl}\eta)(\mathit{success}\upsilon\partial)$ then

$\lambda\nu\upsilon\partial.\mathcal{V}[\![\Pi]\!]\zeta\nu(Y(\mathit{hurl}\eta)\upsilon)(S(\mathit{hurl}\eta)\partial)\sqsupseteq\lambda\nu\upsilon\partial.A(\mathit{hurl}\eta)(\mathcal{Z}[\![\Pi]\!]\nu\upsilon\partial)$.

◁The parallel with 4.6.4 leads us to try to prove this result by exploiting the knowledge that $\mathcal{Z}=\mathit{fix}(\mathit{succeed})$ and by appealing to the induction principle of 2.3.2. Accordingly we select any program and any continuation ζ such that

$\lambda\upsilon\partial.\zeta(Y(\mathit{hurl}\eta)\upsilon)(S(\mathit{hurl}\eta)\partial)=\lambda\upsilon\partial.A(\mathit{hurl}\eta)(\mathit{success}\upsilon\partial)$,

where for brevity we have let $\eta=\mathcal{V}[\![\Pi]\!]\zeta$.

We suppose that $\psi\in\mathrm{Pro}\to\mathrm{N}\to\mathrm{Y}\to\mathrm{S}\to\mathrm{A}$ is such that

$\lambda\nu\upsilon\partial.\mathcal{V}[\![\Pi]\!]\zeta\nu(Y(\mathit{hurl}\eta)\upsilon)(S(\mathit{hurl}\eta)\partial)\sqsupseteq\lambda\nu\upsilon\partial.A(\mathit{hurl}\eta)(\psi[\![\Pi]\!]\nu\upsilon\partial)$.

In order to show that

$\lambda\nu\upsilon\partial.\mathcal{V}[\![\Pi]\!]\zeta\nu(Y(\mathit{hurl}\eta)\upsilon)(S(\mathit{hurl}\eta)\partial)\sqsupseteq\lambda\nu\upsilon\partial.A(\mathit{hurl}\eta)(\mathit{succeed}\psi[\![\Pi]\!]\nu\upsilon\partial)$

we choose arbitrarily an integer ν, a stack υ and a store ∂. When $\nu>\#\Pi$ or $1>\nu$,

$$\begin{aligned}\mathcal{V}[\![\Pi]\!]\zeta\nu(Y(\mathit{hurl}\eta)\upsilon)(S(\mathit{hurl}\eta)\partial)&=\zeta(Y(\mathit{hurl}\eta)\upsilon)(S(\mathit{hurl}\eta)\partial)\\&=A(\mathit{hurl}\eta)(\mathit{success}\upsilon\partial)\\&=A(\mathit{hurl}\eta)(\mathit{succeed}\psi[\![\Pi]\!]\nu\upsilon\partial)\end{aligned}$$

owing to our assumptions about ζ. When $\#\Pi\geq\nu\geq1$ but $\mathcal{A}[\![\Pi\downarrow\nu]\!](\nu+1)\upsilon\partial$ is not a member of $\mathrm{N}\times\mathrm{Y}\times\mathrm{S}$,

$$\begin{aligned}\mathcal{V}[\![\Pi]\!]\zeta\nu(Y(\mathit{hurl}\eta)\upsilon)(S(\mathit{hurl}\eta)\partial)&=\mathcal{A}[\![\Pi\downarrow\nu]\!]\eta(\nu+1)(Y(\mathit{hurl}\eta)\upsilon)(S(\mathit{hurl}\eta)\partial)\\&=A(\mathit{hurl}\eta)(\mathcal{A}[\![\Pi\downarrow\nu]\!](\nu+1)\upsilon\partial\,|\,A)\\&=A(\mathit{hurl}\eta)(\mathit{succeed}\psi[\![\Pi]\!]\nu\upsilon\partial)\end{aligned}$$

because Ξ can be taken as $\Pi\downarrow\nu$ in 5.6.3. When $\#\Pi\geq\nu\geq1$ and $\mathcal{A}[\![\Pi\downarrow\nu]\!](\nu+1)\upsilon\partial$ is a member of $\mathrm{N}\times\mathrm{Y}\times\mathrm{S}$, by applying 5.6.3 and by recalling the inductive hypothesis we demonstrate that if $\langle\nu',\upsilon',\partial'\rangle=\mathcal{A}[\![\Pi\downarrow\nu]\!](\nu+1)\upsilon\partial\,|\,(\mathrm{N}\times\mathrm{Y}\times\mathrm{S})$ then

$$\mathcal{V}[\![\Pi]\!]\zeta\nu(Y(hurl\eta)\mho)(S(hurl\eta)\eth)=\mathcal{A}[\![\Pi\downarrow\nu]\!]\eta(\nu+1)(Y(hurl\eta)\mho)(S(hurl\eta)\eth)$$
$$=\eta\nu'(Y(hurl\eta)\mho')(S(hurl\eta)\eth')$$
$$=\mathcal{V}[\![\Pi]\!]\zeta\nu'(Y(hurl\eta)\mho')(S(hurl\eta)\eth')$$
$$\sqsupseteq A(hurl\eta)(\psi[\![\Pi]\!]\nu'\mho'\eth')$$
$$=A(hurl\eta)(succeed\psi[\![\Pi]\!]\nu\mho\eth).$$

The cases examined in the three preceding sentences exhaust all the possibilities other than the trivial ones (when $\nu=\bot$ or $\nu=\top$), so as $\mho$ and $\eth$ can be chosen quite freely we may safely claim that

$$\lambda\nu\mho\eth.\mathcal{V}[\![\Pi]\!]\sigma\nu(Y(hurl\eta)\mho)(S(hurl\eta)\eth)\sqsupseteq\lambda\nu\mho\eth.A(hurl\eta)(succeed\psi[\![\Pi]\!]\nu\mho\eth)$$

provided that $\eta=\mathcal{V}[\![\Pi]\!]\zeta$.

Obviously $\mathcal{V}[\![\Pi]\!]\zeta\nu\acute{\mho}\acute{\eth}\sqsupseteq A(hurl(\mathcal{V}[\![\Pi]\!]\zeta))(\bot[\![\Pi]\!]\nu\hat{\mho}\hat{\eth})$ for all ν, $\hat{\mho}$ and $\hat{\eth}$; in particular, the inequality

$$\lambda\nu\mho\eth.\mathcal{V}[\![\Pi]\!]\zeta\nu(Y(hurl(\mathcal{V}[\![\Pi]\!]\zeta))\mho)(S(hurl(\mathcal{V}[\![\Pi]\!]\zeta))\eth)\sqsupseteq\lambda\nu\mho\eth.A(hurl(\mathcal{V}[\![\Pi]\!]\zeta))(\bot[\![\Pi]\!]\nu\mho\eth)$$

must hold. Because $\mathcal{Z}=fix(succeed)$ and the inequality relation corresponds with an inclusive predicate, the argument of the previous paragraph allows us to infer that

$$\lambda\nu\mho\eth.\mathcal{V}[\![\Pi]\!]\zeta\nu(Y(hurl\eta)\mho)(S(hurl\eta)\eth)\sqsupseteq\lambda\nu\mho\eth.A(hurl\eta)(\mathcal{Z}[\![\Pi]\!]\nu\mho\eth)$$

no matter what form is taken by the Sam program Π so long as $\eta=\mathcal{V}[\![\Pi]\!]\zeta$ and $\lambda\mho\eth.\zeta(Y(hurl\eta)\mho)(S(hurl\eta)\eth)=\lambda\mho\eth.A(hurl\eta)(success\mho\eth)$. $\blacktriangleright$

5.6.5. The implicit connection between functions and bit patterns.

When Π is a program and ζ is a continuation for which $\lambda\grave{\upsilon}\grave{\sigma}.\zeta(Y(\mathit{hurl}(\mathcal{V}[\![\Pi]\!]\zeta))\grave{\upsilon})(S(\mathit{hurl}(\mathcal{V}[\![\Pi]\!]\zeta))\grave{\sigma})=\lambda\grave{\upsilon}\grave{\sigma}.A(\mathit{hurl}(\mathcal{V}[\![\Pi]\!]\zeta))(\mathit{success}\grave{\upsilon}\grave{\sigma})$, we can make use of methods like those put forward in 4.6.2 in order to demonstrate that for all ν, $\grave{\upsilon}$ and $\grave{\sigma}$ $\mathcal{V}[\![\Pi]\!]\zeta\nu(Y(\mathit{hurl}(\mathcal{V}[\![\Pi]\!]\zeta))\grave{\upsilon})(S(\mathit{hurl}(\mathcal{V}[\![\Pi]\!]\zeta))\grave{\sigma})\sqsupseteq A(\mathit{hurl}(\mathcal{V}[\![\Pi]\!]\zeta))(\mathcal{Z}[\![\Pi]\!]\nu\grave{\upsilon}\grave{\sigma})$. We therefore naturally expect to be able to apply the techniques discussed in 4.6.5 when verifying that $\mathcal{V}[\![\Pi]\!]\zeta\nu(Y(\mathit{hurl}(\mathcal{V}[\![\Pi]\!]\zeta))\grave{\upsilon})(S(\mathit{hurl}(\mathcal{V}[\![\Pi]\!]\zeta))\grave{\sigma})\sqsubseteq A(\mathit{hurl}(\mathcal{V}[\![\Pi]\!]\zeta))(\mathcal{Z}[\![\Pi]\!]\nu\grave{\upsilon}\grave{\sigma})$. Thus we wish to arrange that when $\acute{\upsilon}$ corresponds with $\grave{\upsilon}$ and $\acute{\sigma}$ corresponds with $\grave{\sigma}$ (in some suitable sense) then $\mathcal{V}[\![\Pi]\!]\zeta\nu\acute{\upsilon}\acute{\sigma}$ corresponds with $\mathcal{Z}[\![\Pi]\!]\nu\grave{\upsilon}\grave{\sigma}$ for every integer ν.

In order to set up these correspondences we observe that from any inclusive predicate x mapping pairs of witnessed values into elements of T′ we can form vx and ex, which are defined on V×V and E×E respectively, by converting members of V×V and E×E into members of W×W. By referring to the function definitions in 2.4.4 we see that:

$\mathrm{v}=\lambda x.x\circ(\mathit{push}\langle 3,1\rangle\times\mathit{push}\langle 3,1\rangle)\circ(\lambda\hat{\beta}.\hat{\beta})$;

$\mathrm{e}=\lambda x.x\circ(\mathit{mask}4\times\mathit{mask}4)\circ(\lambda\hat{\varepsilon}.\hat{\varepsilon})$.

These mappings allow us to define inclusive predicates sx and yx on S×S and Y×Y in terms of the notation of 2.5.5 by taking *check* to be *false* and by setting:

$\mathrm{s}=\lambda x.((l\rightarrow(\mathrm{v}x\times t))\times(\mathrm{v}x)^{*}\times(\mathrm{v}x)^{*})\circ(\lambda\hat{\sigma}.\hat{\sigma})$;

$\mathrm{y}=\lambda x.x^{*}\circ(\lambda\hat{\upsilon}.\hat{\upsilon})$.

As in 4.2.3, the tests for equality between members of T and between members of L are given by the equations $t=\lambda\hat{\varepsilon}.(\acute{\varepsilon}\equiv\grave{\varepsilon})$ and $l=\lambda\hat{\alpha}.(\acute{\alpha}\equiv\grave{\alpha})$.

We might hope to define a predicate w on W×W such that $w\hat{\omega}=\mathit{true}$ if and only if the witnessed values $\acute{\omega}$ and $\grave{\omega}$ correspond, but for the following reason this cannot be done. When $\acute{\omega}$ and $\grave{\omega}$ are drawn from their respective versions of J, $w\hat{\omega}$ should be *true* if and only if

$z\langle(\acute{\omega}|J)\downarrow 1,(\grave{\omega}|J)\downarrow 1\rangle = true$ and $(\acute{\omega}|J)\downarrow 2=(\grave{\omega}|J)\downarrow 2$, where z is a predicate which maps any pair comprising a continuation ζ and an integer ν into a truth value; however, we would like $z\langle\zeta,\nu\rangle$ to be *true* if and only if when $yw\mathrm{\mho}=true$ and $sw\sigma=true$ $\zeta\acute{\upsilon}\acute{\sigma}$ corresponds with the answer $\mathcal{Z}[\![\Pi]\!]\nu\grave{\upsilon}\grave{\sigma}$ for some Π. Only by making the program Π into a parameter of z (and therefore into a parameter of w) can we set up our predicates properly. This contrasts with the situation in 4.6.5, where z took as its argument a pair consisting of a control and a continuation, neither of which needed to be viewed in the context of a whole program ; the difference between our two versions of z is related to the fact that in appendix 13 $\mathcal{Z}$ is of the form $\lambda\Pi.fix(\phi[\![\Pi]\!])$ for some $\phi\in\mathrm{Pro}\to(\mathrm{N}\to\mathrm{Y}\to\mathrm{S}\to\mathrm{A})\to(\mathrm{N}\to\mathrm{Y}\to\mathrm{S}\to\mathrm{A})$ whilst in appendix 11 $\mathcal{Z}$ is not of the form $\lambda\mathrm{H}.fix(\phi[\![\mathrm{H}]\!])$ for any $\phi\in\mathrm{Con}\to(\mathrm{U}\to\mathrm{Y}\to\mathrm{S}\to\mathrm{A})\to(\mathrm{U}\to\mathrm{Y}\to\mathrm{S}\to\mathrm{A})$.

For convenience we shall let z be a certain function such that when Π is a Sam program and x is an inclusive predicate which maps pairs of witnessed values into elements of T′ then $\mathrm{z}[\![\Pi]\!]x$ is an inclusive predicate which acts on continuations and code pointers. In the symbolism of 2.5.5,

$\mathrm{z}=\lambda\Pi x.(yx\to sx\to ax)\circ(\lambda\langle\zeta,\nu\rangle.\langle\zeta,\mathcal{Z}[\![\Pi]\!]\nu\rangle)$.

Obviously we shall suppose that $\mathrm{a}=\lambda x.ax\circ(\lambda\hat{\sigma}.\grave{\sigma})$ when $\acute{\sigma}$ is a typical answer suited to appendix 12 and when $\grave{\sigma}$ is an answer supplied by appendix 13; we shall also presume that $\mathrm{a}x\langle\bot,\bot\rangle=true$, $\mathrm{a}x\langle\top,\top\rangle=true$ and $\mathrm{a}x\langle\bot,\grave{\sigma}\rangle=true$ for every $\grave{\sigma}$ and for every x.

Along with z we need a function w such that if Π is a program and x is an inclusive predicate then $\mathrm{w}[\![\Pi]\!]x$ is an inclusive predicate which coincides with $\mathrm{w}[\![\Pi]\!]x\circ(\lambda\hat{\omega}.\hat{\omega})$. The versions of W defined in appendix 13 and appendix 12 are $\mathrm{L+B+E^*+(N\times N)+(N\times N\times U)+(N\times N)+N+((L\to T)\times N\times N\times U)}$ and $\mathrm{L+B+E^*+(Z\times N)+(Z\times N\times U)+(Z\times N)+Z+((L\to T)\times N\times N\times U)}$ respectively, which suggests that we take $\mathrm{w}[\![\Pi]\!]x$ to be

$(l+b+(\mathrm{e}x)^*+(\mathrm{z}[\![\Pi]\!]x\times n)+(\mathrm{z}[\![\Pi]\!]x\times n\times u)+(\mathrm{z}[\![\Pi]\!]x\times n)+\mathrm{z}[\![\Pi]\!]x+((l\to t)\times n\times n\times u))\circ(\lambda\hat{\omega}.\hat{\omega})$;

here we are adopting the notation of 2.5.5 by letting the tests for equality between members of N, between members of B and between members of U be given by the equations $n=\lambda\hat{\nu}.(\acute{\nu}\equiv\grave{\nu})$, $b=\lambda\hat{\beta}.(\acute{\beta}\equiv\grave{\beta})$ and $u=\lambda\hat{\rho}.(\acute{\rho}\equiv\grave{\rho})$. In 5.6.8, however, the recursive nature of *hurl* will require us to assume that $w[\![\Pi]\!]w\langle\bot,\grave{\omega}\rangle=true$ for every $\grave{\omega}$ and for a certain inclusive predicate w; thus we actually follow the practice of 4.6.5 by writing

$w=\lambda\Pi x\hat{\omega}.(\acute{\omega}\equiv\bot)\rightarrow true,$

$$(l+b+(ex)^*+(z[\![\Pi]\!]x\times n)+(z[\![\Pi]\!]x\times n\times u)+(z[\![\Pi]\!]x\times n)+z[\![\Pi]\!]x+((l\rightarrow t)\times n\times n\times u))\hat{\omega}.$$

Our choice of equation for w leads inevitably to introducing two particular functors called W which are used in connection with our two domains named W. The version of W used to form the domain W for pointer semantics satisfies the equation

$W=\lambda X.L+B+(\mathrm{E}X)^*+(N\times N)+(N\times N\times U)+(N\times N)+N+((L\rightarrow T)\times N\times N\times U),$

in which the retractions T, N, L and B are familiar to us from 3.3.5 and in which $U=(Ide\rightarrow(N\times N)^*)\times N^*$. Similarly the version of W needed by consecution semantics is given by

$W=\lambda X.L+B+(\mathrm{E}X)^*+(\mathrm{Z}X\times N)+(\mathrm{Z}X\times N\times U)+(\mathrm{Z}X\times N)+\mathrm{Z}X+((L\rightarrow T)\times N\times N\times U);$

here Z is such that

$\mathrm{Z}=\lambda X.\mathrm{Y}X\rightarrow\mathrm{S}X\rightarrow\mathrm{A}X.$

We shall keep quiet about the two functors called A (that for pointer semantics and that for consecution semantics) though we shall continue to accept that they are built up in the manner described in 5.6.1.

For both sorts of semantics we define other functors by using the equations of 5.2.5 thus:

$\mathrm{V}=\lambda X.push\langle 4,-1\rangle\circ X\circ push\langle 3,1\rangle;$

$\mathrm{E}=\lambda X.X\circ mask4.$

In addition we suppose as usual that:

$\mathrm{S}=\lambda X.(L\rightarrow(\mathrm{V}X\times T))\times(\mathrm{V}X)^*\times(\mathrm{V}X)^*;$

$\mathrm{Y}=\lambda X.X^*.$

These are the only other functors needed in the present case.

For a short while we require a set of retractions, y, such that X is in y if and only if $X=acute(X)\times grave(X)$, $X\circ(\lambda\hat{\omega}.\hat{\omega})=(\lambda\hat{\omega}.\hat{\omega})\circ X$ and

$X\circ(mask4\times mask4)=(mask4\times mask4)\circ X$. It is plain from 2.5.6 that y is a predictor for Y⊛Y based on $\langle(\lambda\chi.true),(\lambda\chi.\bot)\times(\lambda\chi.\bot)\rangle$ and bounded by y and that s is a predictor for S⊛S based on $\langle(\lambda\chi.true),(\lambda\chi.\bot)\times(\lambda\chi.\bot)\rangle$ and bounded by y. We therefore make the reasonable assumption that a is a predictor for A⊛A based on $\langle(\lambda\chi.true),(\lambda\chi.\bot)\times(\lambda\chi.\bot)\rangle$ and bounded by y. In this situation, for every Π z⟦Π⟧ is a predictor for $Z\circledast(\lambda X.N)$ based on $\langle(\lambda\chi.true),(\lambda\chi.\bot)\times(\lambda\chi.\bot)\rangle$ and bounded by y, so according to 2.5.6 w⟦Π⟧ is a predictor for W⊛W based on $\langle(\lambda\chi.true),(\lambda\chi.\bot)\times(\lambda\chi.\bot)\rangle$ and bounded by y. Moreover

$\langle w(\lambda\chi.true),(W\circledast W)((\lambda\chi.\bot)\times(\lambda\chi.\bot))\rangle\geq\langle\lambda\chi.true,(\lambda\chi.\bot)\times(\lambda\chi.\bot)\rangle$ and

$\lambda\acute{\omega}.\acute{\omega}=fix(W)$, while naturally we postulate that $\lambda\grave{\omega}.\grave{\omega}=fix(W)$. Consequently $\lambda\hat{\omega}.\hat{\omega}=\bigsqcup\{(W\circledast W)^n((\lambda\chi.\bot)\times(\lambda\chi.\bot))\mid n\geq 0\}$ and 2.5.3 allows us to infer the existence of a mapping w such that for every Π w⟦Π⟧ is the sole inclusive predicate for which w⟦Π⟧=w⟦Π⟧(w⟦Π⟧) and w⟦Π⟧$\langle\bot,\bot\rangle=true$. We now let $z=\lambda\Pi.$z⟦Π⟧(w⟦Π⟧) for this particular w, so that

$z=\lambda\Pi.(y(w[\![\Pi]\!])\rightarrow s(w[\![\Pi]\!])\rightarrow a(w[\![\Pi]\!]))\circ(\lambda\langle\zeta,\nu\rangle.\langle\zeta,\mathcal{Z}[\![\Pi]\!]\nu\rangle)$,

and, in addition,

$w=\lambda\Pi\hat{\omega}.(\hat{\omega}\equiv\bot)\rightarrow true,$

$$(l+b+(e(w[\![\Pi]\!]))^*+(z[\![\Pi]\!]\times n)+(z[\![\Pi]\!]\times n\times u)+(z[\![\Pi]\!]\times n)+z[\![\Pi]\!]+((l\rightarrow t)\times n\times n\times u))\hat{\omega}.$$

Shortly we shall set about proving that if $z[\![\Pi]\!]\langle\zeta,1+\#\Pi\rangle=true$ then $z[\![\Pi]\!]\langle\mathcal{V}[\![\Pi]\!]\zeta\nu,\nu\rangle=true$ when Π is any program and ν is any integer. We might try to do this by a simple induction in which we would endeavour to show $z[\![\Pi_0]\!]\langle\mathcal{V}[\![\Pi_0]\!]\zeta\nu,\nu\rangle=true$ for every ν provided that whenever Π_1 is a program having $\#\Pi_0-1\geq\#\Pi_1\geq 0$ $z[\![\Pi_1]\!]\langle\mathcal{V}[\![\Pi_1]\!]\zeta\nu,\nu\rangle=true$ for every ν; however we woud fail to achieve our object, for $\mathcal{V}$ is defined not by recursion on the lengths of Sam programs but by the construction of a fixed point involving $\mathcal{U}$. Thus the proper induction to perform is one in which the inductive step entails showing that if $z[\![\Pi]\!]\langle\zeta,1+\#\Pi\rangle=true$ and $z[\![\Pi]\!]\langle\eta\nu,\nu\rangle=true$ for every ν then $z[\![\Pi]\!]\langle\mathcal{U}[\![\Pi]\!]\zeta\eta\nu,\nu\rangle=true$ for every ν; once this step has been justified, it will follow from the fact that $z[\![\Pi]\!]\langle\bot,\nu\rangle=true$ for every ν (and from the inclusive nature of $z[\![\Pi]\!]$) that if $z[\![\Pi]\!]\langle\zeta,1+\#\Pi\rangle=\mathit{true}$ then $z[\![\Pi]\!]\langle\mathcal{V}[\![\Pi]\!]\zeta\nu,\nu\rangle=\mathit{true}$ for every ν. The details of this induction will be given in 5.6.6 and 5.6.7.

Once again we have to impose conditions on *wrong* and *new* in order to justify our claims about the semantic equations; in particular, for every program Π we assume that if $\hat{\eth}$ is any pair of stores such that $s(w[\![\Pi]\!])\hat{\eth}=\mathit{true}$ and if $\eth$ is any answer then $a(w[\![\Pi]\!])\langle\bot,\eth\rangle=\mathit{true}$, $a(w[\![\Pi]\!])\langle\top,\top\rangle=\mathit{true}$, $a(w[\![\Pi]\!])\langle \mathit{wrong}\acute{\eth},\mathit{wrong}\grave{\eth}\rangle=\mathit{true}$ and $\mathit{new}\acute{\eth}\sqsubseteq\mathit{new}\grave{\eth}$; the versions of *wrong* and *new* appropriate to consecution semantics appear on the left hand sides of these equations, whereas the versions appropriate to pointer semantics are used on the right hand sides. If Ξ is a secret instruction, Π is a program and η is a consecution such that $\lambda\nu.z[\![\Pi]\!]\langle\eta\nu,\nu\rangle=\lambda\nu.\mathit{true}$ we shall suppose that (for any ν, $\hat{\mho}$ and $\hat{\eth}$ having $y(w[\![\Pi]\!])\hat{\mho}=\mathit{true}$ and $s(w[\![\Pi]\!])\hat{\eth}=\mathit{true}$), when $\mathcal{A}[\![\Xi]\!]\nu\grave{\mho}\grave{\eth}$ is not in $N\times Y\times S$, $a(w[\![\Pi]\!])\langle\mathcal{A}[\![\Xi]\!]\eta\nu\acute{\mho}\acute{\eth},\mathcal{A}[\![\Xi]\!]\nu\grave{\mho}\grave{\eth}|A\rangle=\mathit{true}$ and, when $\mathcal{A}[\![\Xi]\!]\nu\grave{\mho}\grave{\eth}$ is in $N\times Y\times S$, $a(w[\![\Pi]\!])\langle\mathcal{A}[\![\Xi]\!]\eta\nu\acute{\mho}\acute{\eth},(\lambda\langle\nu',\grave{\mho}',\grave{\eth}'\rangle.\mathcal{Z}[\![\Pi]\!]\nu'\grave{\mho}'\grave{\eth}')(\mathcal{A}[\![\Xi]\!]\nu\grave{\mho}\grave{\eth}|(N\times Y\times S))\rangle=\mathit{true}$; because in 5.6.6 we shall indicate that this supposition is correct if Ξ is not secret, we may contend plausibly that it ought to hold if Ξ is secret.

5.6.6. Lemma.

Let Ξ be any Sam instruction, let Π be any Sam program and let η be any consecution having $\lambda\nu.z[\![\Pi]\!]\langle\eta\nu,\nu\rangle=\lambda\nu.true$; take ν, $\hat{\upsilon}$ and $\hat{\sigma}$ to be such that $y(w[\![\Pi]\!])\hat{\upsilon}=true$ and $s(w[\![\Pi]\!])\hat{\sigma}=true$. Unless $\mathcal{A}[\![\Xi]\!]\nu\grave{\upsilon}\grave{\sigma}\in N\times Y\times S$, $a(w[\![\Pi]\!])\langle\mathcal{A}[\![\Xi]\!]\eta\nu\acute{\upsilon}\acute{\sigma},\mathcal{A}[\![\Xi]\!]\nu\grave{\upsilon}\grave{\sigma}|A\rangle=true$. If $\mathcal{A}[\![\Xi]\!]\nu\grave{\upsilon}\grave{\sigma}\in N\times Y\times S$, $a(w[\![\Pi]\!])\langle\mathcal{A}[\![\Xi]\!]\eta\nu\acute{\upsilon}\acute{\sigma},(\lambda\langle\nu',\grave{\upsilon}',\grave{\sigma}'\rangle.\mathcal{Z}[\![\Pi]\!]\nu'\grave{\upsilon}'\grave{\sigma}')(\mathcal{A}[\![\Xi]\!]\nu\grave{\upsilon}\grave{\sigma}|(N\times Y\times S))\rangle=true$.

$\triangleleft$The version of $\mathcal{A}$ needed by pointer semantics is that appearing in the term $\mathcal{A}[\![\Xi]\!]\eta\nu\acute{\upsilon}\acute{\sigma}$, whilst the version of $\mathcal{A}$ needed by consecution semantics is that appearing in $\mathcal{A}[\![\Xi]\!]\nu\grave{\upsilon}\grave{\sigma}$. The result itself can be obtained by examining the definitions of the valuations and by recalling the suppositions about *wrong* and *new* (and about the secret instructions) made in 5.6.5. Thus we shall content ourselves with checking only what happens when Ξ is apply and when $y(w[\![\Pi]\!])\hat{\upsilon}=true$ and $s(w[\![\Pi]\!])\hat{\sigma}=true$.

According to appendix 12, $\mathcal{A}[\![\text{apply}]\!]\eta\nu\acute{\upsilon}\acute{\sigma}$ is $\bot$, $\top$, *wrong*$\acute{\sigma}$ or $\eta\nu(\langle\acute{\upsilon}\downarrow1\rangle\S\langle\acute{\upsilon}\downarrow2\downarrow1\rangle\S\langle\acute{\omega}\rangle\S\langle\eta(\nu+1)\rangle\S\acute{\upsilon}\dagger2)\acute{\sigma}$ (where $\acute{\omega}=bulk(\acute{\upsilon}\downarrow2\downarrow2)0(\acute{\upsilon}\downarrow2\downarrow3)\acute{\upsilon}\acute{\sigma}$); similarly from appendix 13 it follows that $\mathcal{A}[\![\text{apply}]\!]\nu\grave{\upsilon}\grave{\sigma}$ is $\bot$, $\top$, *wrong*$\grave{\sigma}$ or $\langle\nu,\langle\grave{\upsilon}\downarrow1\rangle\S\langle\grave{\upsilon}\downarrow2\downarrow1\rangle\S\langle\grave{\omega}\rangle\S\langle\nu+1\rangle\S\grave{\upsilon}\dagger2,\grave{\sigma}\rangle$ (where $\grave{\omega}=bulk(\grave{\upsilon}\downarrow2\downarrow2)0(\grave{\upsilon}\downarrow2\downarrow3)\grave{\upsilon}\grave{\sigma}$). Furthermore, unless $\grave{\upsilon}\downarrow2$ is $\bot$ (in which case $\mathcal{A}[\![\text{apply}]\!]\nu\grave{\upsilon}\grave{\sigma}$ is $\bot$, so that $a(w[\![\Pi]\!])\langle\mathcal{A}[\![\text{apply}]\!]\eta\nu\acute{\upsilon}\acute{\sigma},\mathcal{A}[\![\text{apply}]\!]\nu\grave{\upsilon}\grave{\sigma}|A\rangle=true$ automatically), $\mathcal{A}[\![\text{apply}]\!]\eta\nu\acute{\upsilon}\acute{\sigma}$ takes whichever of its four possible values corresponds with the value actually taken by $\mathcal{A}[\![\text{apply}]\!]\nu\grave{\upsilon}\grave{\sigma}$, since $w[\![\Pi]\!]\langle\acute{\upsilon}\downarrow2,\grave{\upsilon}\downarrow2\rangle=true$. As $a(w[\![\Pi]\!])\langle\bot,\bot\rangle=true$, $a(w[\![\Pi]\!])\langle\top,\top\rangle=true$ and $(s(w[\![\Pi]\!])\rightarrow a(w[\![\Pi]\!]))\langle wrong,wrong\rangle=true$, we may therefore certainly assert that, unless $\mathcal{A}[\![\text{apply}]\!]\nu\grave{\upsilon}\grave{\sigma}\in N\times Y\times S$, $a(w[\![\Pi]\!])\langle\mathcal{A}[\![\text{apply}]\!]\eta\nu\acute{\upsilon}\acute{\sigma},\mathcal{A}[\![\text{apply}]\!]\nu\grave{\upsilon}\grave{\sigma}|A\rangle=true$. If $\mathcal{A}[\![\text{apply}]\!]\nu\grave{\upsilon}\grave{\sigma}\in N\times Y\times S$, however, $\acute{\upsilon}\downarrow2$ and $\grave{\upsilon}\downarrow2$ are drawn from their respective domains called F so (since $z[\![\Pi]\!]\langle\eta\nu,\nu\rangle=true$, $z[\![\Pi]\!]\langle\eta(\nu+1),\nu+1\rangle=true$, $y(w[\![\Pi]\!])\hat{\upsilon}=true$ and $s(w[\![\Pi]\!])\hat{\sigma}=true$) we may infer from the equations governing z in 5.6.5 that $w[\![\Pi]\!]\langle\acute{\upsilon}\downarrow2\downarrow1,\grave{\upsilon}\downarrow2\downarrow1\rangle=true$ and $w[\![\Pi]\!]\hat{\omega}=true$, that

$a(w[\![\Pi]\!])\langle\langle\acute{\upsilon}\downarrow1\rangle\S\langle\acute{\upsilon}\downarrow2\downarrow1\rangle\S\langle\acute{\omega}\rangle\S\langle\eta(\nu+1)\rangle\S\acute{\upsilon}\dagger2,\langle\grave{\upsilon}\downarrow1\rangle\S\langle\grave{\upsilon}\downarrow2\downarrow1\rangle\S\langle\grave{\omega}\rangle\S\grave{\upsilon}\dagger2\rangle=true$

and that

$a(\omega[\![\Pi]\!])\langle \mathcal{A}[\![\text{apply}]\!]\eta\nu\acute{\vartheta}\acute{\sigma},(\lambda\langle\nu',\vartheta',\eth'\rangle.\mathcal{Z}[\![\Pi]\!]\nu'\vartheta'\eth')(\mathcal{A}[\![\text{apply}]\!]\nu\vartheta\eth\,|\,(N\times Y\times S))\rangle = \mathit{true}.$

Calculations very similar to these are required by other instructions, such as jump and adjust.▷

5.6.7. Proposition.

If Π is a Sam program and ζ is a continuation such that $z[\![\Pi]\!]\langle\zeta,1+\#\Pi\rangle=true$ then $\lambda\nu.z[\![\Pi]\!]\langle\mathcal{V}[\![\Pi]\!]\zeta\nu,\nu\rangle=\lambda\nu.true$.

⊲We are now in a position to carry out the induction mentioned in 5.6.5; in this we take Π to be any program and ζ to be any continuation such that $z[\![\Pi]\!]\langle\zeta,1+\#\Pi\rangle=true$, and we note that $\mathcal{V}[\![\Pi]\!]\zeta=fix(\mathcal{U}[\![\Pi]\!]\zeta)$.

For our inductive hypothesis we adopt the assumption that η is a certain consecution for which $\lambda\nu.z[\![\Pi]\!]\langle\eta\nu,\nu\rangle=\lambda\nu.true$; doing this entails trying to prove that $\lambda\nu.z[\![\Pi]\!]\langle\mathcal{U}[\![\Pi]\!]\zeta\eta\nu,\nu\rangle=true$. We therefore select any ν, $\grave{\upsilon}$ and $\grave{\sigma}$ for which $y(w[\![\Pi]\!])\grave{\upsilon}=true$ and $s(w[\![\Pi]\!])\grave{\sigma}=true$, and we check what can happen as ν varies by examining the equations given for $\mathcal{U}$ and $\mathcal{Z}$ in appendix 12 and appendix 13. When $\nu>\#\Pi$ or $1>\nu$,

$$\begin{aligned}a(w[\![\Pi]\!])\langle\mathcal{U}[\![\Pi]\!]\zeta\eta\nu\acute{\upsilon}\acute{\sigma},\mathcal{Z}[\![\Pi]\!]\nu\grave{\upsilon}\grave{\sigma}\rangle &= a(w[\![\Pi]\!])\langle\zeta\acute{\upsilon}\acute{\sigma},\mathcal{Z}[\![\Pi]\!]\nu\grave{\upsilon}\grave{\sigma}\rangle\\ &= a(w[\![\Pi]\!])\langle\zeta\acute{\upsilon}\acute{\sigma},success\,\grave{\upsilon}\grave{\sigma}\rangle\\ &= a(w[\![\Pi]\!])\langle\zeta\acute{\upsilon}\acute{\sigma},\mathcal{Z}[\![\Pi]\!](1+\#z[\![\Pi]\!])\grave{\upsilon}\grave{\sigma})\\ &= true\end{aligned}$$

since $z[\![\Pi]\!]\langle\zeta,1+\#\Pi\rangle=true$. When $\#\Pi\geq\nu\geq1$ but $\mathcal{A}[\![\Pi\dagger\nu]\!](\nu+1)\grave{\upsilon}\grave{\sigma}$ is not a member of $N\times Y\times S$,

$$\begin{aligned}a(w[\![\Pi]\!])\langle\mathcal{U}[\![\Pi]\!]\zeta\eta\nu\acute{\upsilon}\acute{\sigma},\mathcal{Z}[\![\Pi]\!]\nu\grave{\upsilon}\grave{\sigma}\rangle &= a(w[\![\Pi]\!])\langle\mathcal{A}[\![\Pi\dagger\nu]\!]\eta(\nu+1)\acute{\upsilon}\acute{\sigma},\mathcal{Z}[\![\Pi]\!]\nu\grave{\upsilon}\grave{\sigma}\rangle\\ &= a(w[\![\Pi]\!])\langle\mathcal{A}[\![\Pi\dagger\nu]\!]\eta(\nu+1)\acute{\upsilon}\acute{\sigma},\mathcal{A}[\![\Pi\dagger\nu]\!](\nu+1)\grave{\upsilon}\grave{\sigma}\,|\,A\rangle\\ &= true\end{aligned}$$

in accordance with 5.6.6 (so long as Ξ is taken to be $\Pi\dagger\nu$). When $\#\Pi\geq\nu\geq1$ and $\mathcal{A}[\![\Pi\dagger\nu]\!](\nu+1)\grave{\upsilon}\grave{\sigma}$ is a member of $N\times Y\times S$, the inductive hypothesis allows us to apply 5.6.6 again, thereby demonstrating that if $\langle\nu',\grave{\upsilon}',\grave{\sigma}'\rangle=\mathcal{A}[\![\Pi\dagger\nu]\!](\nu+1)\grave{\upsilon}\grave{\sigma}\,|\,(N\times Y\times S)$ then

$$\begin{aligned}a(w[\![\Pi]\!])\langle\mathcal{U}[\![\Pi]\!]\zeta\eta\nu\acute{\upsilon}\acute{\sigma},\mathcal{Z}[\![\Pi]\!]\nu\grave{\upsilon}\grave{\sigma}\rangle &= a(w[\![\Pi]\!])\langle\mathcal{A}[\![\Pi\dagger\nu]\!]\eta(\nu+1)\acute{\upsilon}\acute{\sigma},\mathcal{Z}[\![\Pi]\!]\nu\grave{\upsilon}\grave{\sigma}\rangle\\ &= a(w[\![\Pi]\!])\langle\mathcal{A}[\![\Pi\dagger\nu]\!]\eta(\nu+1)\acute{\upsilon}\acute{\sigma},\mathcal{Z}[\![\Pi]\!]\nu'\grave{\upsilon}'\grave{\sigma}'\rangle\\ &= true.\end{aligned}$$

Since $a(w[\![\Pi]\!])\langle\bot,\bot\rangle=true$ and $a(w[\![\Pi]\!])\langle\top,\top\rangle=true$ we also know that $a(w[\![\Pi]\!])\langle\mathcal{U}[\![\Pi]\!]\zeta\eta\nu\acute{\upsilon}\acute{\sigma},\mathcal{Z}[\![\Pi]\!]\nu\grave{\upsilon}\grave{\sigma}\rangle=true$ when $\nu=\bot$ or $\nu=\top$; in addition $\grave{\upsilon}$ and $\grave{\sigma}$

may be any pairs for which $y(w\llbracket\Pi\rrbracket)\hat{\upsilon}=\mathit{true}$ and $s(w\llbracket\Pi\rrbracket)\hat{\sigma}=\mathit{true}$. Hence $(y(w\llbracket\Pi\rrbracket)\to s(w\llbracket\Pi\rrbracket)\to a(w\llbracket\Pi\rrbracket))\langle\mathfrak{U}\llbracket\Pi\rrbracket\zeta\eta\nu,\mathfrak{Z}\llbracket\Pi\rrbracket\nu\rangle=\mathit{true}$ for every ν, or, in other words, $\lambda\nu.z\llbracket\Pi\rrbracket\langle\mathfrak{U}\llbracket\Pi\rrbracket\zeta\eta\nu,\nu\rangle=\lambda\nu.\mathit{true}$.

In 5.6.5 we stipulated that $a(w\llbracket\Pi\rrbracket)\langle\bot,\eth\rangle=\mathit{true}$ for every $\eth$, so certainly $a(w\llbracket\Pi\rrbracket)\langle(\lambda\nu\acute{\upsilon}\acute{\sigma}.\bot)\nu\acute{\upsilon}\acute{\sigma},\mathfrak{Z}\llbracket\Pi\rrbracket\nu\hat{\upsilon}\eth\rangle=\mathit{true}$ whenever ν, $\hat{\upsilon}$ and $\hat{\sigma}$ are such that $y(w\llbracket\Pi\rrbracket)\hat{\upsilon}=\mathit{true}$ and $s(w\llbracket\Pi\rrbracket)\hat{\sigma}=\mathit{true}$. Consequently $\lambda\nu.z\llbracket\Pi\rrbracket\langle(\lambda\nu.\bot)\nu,\nu\rangle=\lambda\nu.\mathit{true}$; however as we have just proved that if $\lambda\nu.z\llbracket\Pi\rrbracket\langle\eta\nu,\nu\rangle=\lambda\nu.\mathit{true}$ then $\lambda\nu.z\llbracket\Pi\rrbracket\langle\mathfrak{U}\llbracket\Pi\rrbracket\zeta\eta\nu,\nu\rangle=\lambda\nu.\mathit{true}$ (and as $\lambda\eta.z\llbracket\Pi\rrbracket\langle\eta\nu,\nu\rangle$ is inclusive for any ν), we may conclude that $\lambda\nu.z\llbracket\Pi\rrbracket\langle \mathit{fix}(\mathfrak{U}\llbracket\Pi\rrbracket\zeta)\nu,\nu\rangle=\lambda\nu.\mathit{true}$. This means that $\lambda\nu.z\llbracket\Pi\rrbracket\langle\mathfrak{V}\llbracket\Pi\rrbracket\zeta\nu,\nu\rangle=\lambda\nu.\mathit{true}$ provided only that Π and ζ are constrained by the equation $z\llbracket\Pi\rrbracket\langle\zeta,1+\#\Pi\rangle=\mathit{true}$.▷

<u>5.6.8. Theorem.</u>

Suppose that $\lambda\eta.A(hurl\eta)\bot=\bot$, $\lambda\eta.A(hurl\eta)\top=\top$, $a(w[\![\Pi]\!])\langle\bot,\grave{\sigma}\rangle=true$ and $a(w[\![\Pi]\!])\langle\top,\top\rangle=true$ for every $\grave{\sigma}$ and for every Π. Assume that $wrong\acute{\sigma}=A(hurl\eta)(wrong\grave{\sigma})$ and $new\acute{\sigma}=new\grave{\sigma}$ for all $\hat{\sigma}$ and η having $\acute{\sigma}=S(hurl\eta)\grave{\sigma}$ and that $a(w[\![\Pi]\!])\langle wrong\acute{\sigma},wrong\grave{\sigma}\rangle=true$ and $new\acute{\sigma}\sqsubseteq new\grave{\sigma}$ for all $\hat{\sigma}$ and Π having $s(w[\![\Pi]\!])\hat{\sigma}=true$. Take the secret orders to be restricted in the ways mentioned in 5.6.2 and 5.6.5. Let ζ be any continuation such that

$\lambda\grave{\upsilon}\grave{\sigma}.\zeta(Y(hurl(\mathcal{V}[\![\Pi]\!]\zeta))\grave{\upsilon})(S(hurl(\mathcal{V}[\![\Pi]\!]\zeta))\grave{\sigma})=\lambda\grave{\upsilon}\grave{\sigma}.A(hurl(\mathcal{V}[\![\Pi]\!]\zeta))(success\grave{\upsilon}\grave{\sigma})$

for each Π and such that $z[\![\Pi]\!]\langle\zeta,1+\#\Pi\rangle=true$ for each Π. If Π is any Sam program and if $\eta=\mathcal{V}[\![\Pi]\!]\zeta$ then

$\lambda\nu\grave{\upsilon}\grave{\sigma}.\mathcal{V}[\![\Pi]\!]\sigma\nu(Y(hurl\eta)\grave{\upsilon})(S(hurl\eta)\grave{\sigma})=\lambda\nu\grave{\upsilon}\grave{\sigma}.A(hurl\eta)(\mathcal{Z}[\![\Pi]\!]\nu\grave{\upsilon}\grave{\sigma})$ provided that $\acute{\sigma}\sqsubseteq A(hurl(\mathcal{V}[\![\Pi]\!]\zeta))\grave{\sigma}$ whenever $a(w[\![\Pi]\!])\hat{\sigma}=true$.

⊲We start off with a Sam program Π and a continuation ζ for which

$\lambda\grave{\upsilon}\grave{\sigma}.\zeta(Y(hurl(\mathcal{V}[\![\Pi]\!]\zeta))\grave{\upsilon})(S(hurl(\mathcal{V}[\![\Pi]\!]\zeta))\grave{\sigma})=\lambda\grave{\upsilon}\grave{\sigma}.A(hurl(\mathcal{V}[\![\Pi]\!]\zeta))(success\grave{\upsilon}\grave{\sigma})$

and $z[\![\Pi]\!]\langle\zeta,1+\#\Pi\rangle=true$, and for convenience we set $\eta=\mathcal{V}[\![\Pi]\!]\zeta$. According to 5.6.7, $\lambda\nu.z[\![\Pi]\!]\langle\eta\nu,\nu\rangle=\lambda\nu.true$; indeed, as we shall see in the following two paragraphs, $\lambda\hat{\omega}.w[\![\Pi]\!]\langle hurl\eta\hat{\omega},\hat{\omega}\rangle=\lambda\hat{\omega}.true$.

Naturally we suppose that ψ is a mapping for which $\psi\eta$ is a continuous function taking the version of W needed by pointer semantics into the version of W needed by consecution semantics in such a way that $\lambda\hat{\omega}.w[\![\Pi]\!]\langle\psi\eta\hat{\omega},\hat{\omega}\rangle=\lambda\hat{\omega}.true$. This equation guarantees that $\lambda\hat{\varepsilon}^*.(e(w[\![\Pi]\!]))^*\langle(E(hurling\psi\eta))^*\hat{\varepsilon}^*,\hat{\varepsilon}^*\rangle=\lambda\hat{\varepsilon}^*.true$, so when $\hat{\omega}$ is any witnessed value appropriate to appendix 13 by inspecting the summands in which $\hat{\omega}$ may lie we can confirm that $w[\![\Pi]\!]\langle hurling\psi\eta\hat{\omega},\hat{\omega}\rangle=true$; if $\hat{\omega}\in J$, for example, $\langle\eta(\hat{\omega}|J)\downarrow1,(\hat{\omega}|J)\downarrow2\rangle$ is $hurling\psi\eta\hat{\omega}|J$, so as $z[\![\Pi]\!]\langle\eta(\hat{\omega}|J)\downarrow1,(\hat{\omega}|J)\downarrow1\rangle=true$ and $n\langle(\hat{\omega}|J)\downarrow2,(\hat{\omega}|J)\downarrow2\rangle=true$ we know that $w[\![\Pi]\!]\langle hurling\psi\eta\hat{\omega},\hat{\omega}\rangle=true$.

Thus it is possible to claim fairly that if ψ is such that $\lambda\hat{\omega}.w[\![\Pi]\!]\langle\psi\eta\hat{\omega},\hat{\omega}\rangle=\lambda\hat{\omega}.true$ then $hurling\psi$ is such that

$\lambda\hat{\omega}.w[\![\Pi]\!]\langle \mathit{hurling}\psi\eta\hat{\omega},\hat{\omega}\rangle = \lambda\hat{\omega}.\mathit{true}$. However, the equations $w[\![\Pi]\!]=\mathrm{w}[\![\Pi]\!](w[\![\Pi]\!])$ and $\lambda x\hat{\omega}.\mathrm{w}[\![\Pi]\!]x\langle \bot,\hat{\omega}\rangle = \lambda x\hat{\omega}.\mathit{true}$ which were provided in 5.6.5 ensure that $\lambda\hat{\omega}.w[\![\Pi]\!]\langle(\lambda\eta\hat{\omega}.\bot)\eta\hat{\omega},\hat{\omega}\rangle = \lambda\hat{\omega}.\mathit{true}$. Since $\lambda\psi.w[\![\Pi]\!]\langle\psi\eta\hat{\omega},\hat{\omega}\rangle$ is an inclusive predicate for each $\hat{\omega}$, by applying the induction rule of 2.3.2 we can deduce that $w[\![\Pi]\!]\langle \mathit{fix}(\mathit{hurling})\eta\hat{\omega},\hat{\omega}\rangle = \mathit{true}$ for each $\hat{\omega}$, or, in other words, $\lambda\hat{\omega}.w[\![\Pi]\!]\langle \mathit{hurl}\eta\hat{\omega},\hat{\omega}\rangle = \lambda\hat{\omega}.\mathit{true}$.

As $w[\![\Pi]\!]\langle \mathit{hurl}\eta\hat{\omega},\hat{\omega}\rangle = \mathit{true}$ for every $\hat{\omega}$, a trivial calculation using the equations in 5.6.5 demonstrates that $\mathrm{y}(w[\![\Pi]\!])\langle \mathrm{Y}(\mathit{hurl}\eta)\grave{\upsilon},\grave{\upsilon}\rangle = \mathit{true}$ for every $\grave{\upsilon}$ and that $\mathrm{s}(w[\![\Pi]\!])\langle \mathrm{S}(\mathit{hurl}\eta)\grave{\sigma},\grave{\sigma}\rangle = \mathit{true}$ for every $\grave{\sigma}$. We already know from 5.6.7 that $z[\![\Pi]\!]\langle\mathcal{V}[\![\Pi]\!]\zeta\nu,\nu\rangle = \mathit{true}$ for every ν, so actually $\mathrm{a}(w[\![\Pi]\!])\langle\mathcal{V}[\![\Pi]\!]\zeta\nu(\mathrm{Y}(\mathit{hurl}\eta)\grave{\upsilon})(\mathrm{S}(\mathit{hurl}\eta)\grave{\sigma}),\mathcal{Z}[\![\Pi]\!]\nu\grave{\upsilon}\grave{\sigma}\rangle = \mathit{true}$ for all ν, $\grave{\upsilon}$ and $\grave{\sigma}$. If we assume that $\hat{\sigma}\sqsubseteq \mathrm{A}(\mathit{hurl}\eta)\grave{\sigma}$ whenever $\hat{\sigma}$ is such that $\mathrm{a}(w[\![\Pi]\!])\hat{\sigma}=\mathit{true}$ the equation $\eta=\mathcal{V}[\![\Pi]\!]\zeta$ indicates that

$$\lambda\nu\grave{\upsilon}\grave{\sigma}.\mathcal{V}[\![\Pi]\!]\zeta\nu(\mathrm{Y}(\mathit{hurl}\eta)\grave{\upsilon})(\mathrm{S}(\mathit{hurl}\eta)\grave{\sigma})\sqsubseteq\lambda\nu\grave{\upsilon}\grave{\sigma}.\mathrm{A}(\mathit{hurl}\eta)(\mathcal{Z}[\![\Pi]\!]\nu\grave{\upsilon}\grave{\sigma});$$

moreover, from 5.6.4 it follows that

$$\lambda\nu\grave{\upsilon}\grave{\sigma}.\mathcal{V}[\![\Pi]\!]\zeta\nu(\mathrm{Y}(\mathit{hurl}\eta)\grave{\upsilon})(\mathrm{S}(\mathit{hurl}\eta)\grave{\sigma})\sqsupseteq\lambda\nu\grave{\upsilon}\grave{\sigma}.\mathrm{A}(\mathit{hurl}\eta)(\mathcal{Z}[\![\Pi]\!]\nu\grave{\upsilon}\grave{\sigma}),$$

so in fact we may conclude that

$$\lambda\nu\grave{\upsilon}\grave{\sigma}.\mathcal{V}[\![\Pi]\!]\zeta\nu(\mathrm{Y}(\mathit{hurl}\eta)\grave{\upsilon})(\mathrm{S}(\mathit{hurl}\eta)\grave{\sigma})=\lambda\nu\grave{\upsilon}\grave{\sigma}.\mathrm{A}(\mathit{hurl}\eta)(\mathcal{Z}[\![\Pi]\!]\nu\grave{\upsilon}\grave{\sigma}).\triangleright$$

5.6.9. The correctness of implementations.

All the assumptions made in the statement of 5.6.8 have counterparts in the statement of 4.6.8, so justifying them simply entails repeating the bulk of 4.6.9. This we shall not do; we shall, however, introduce a retraction, W_0, which sets up members of the version of W needed by appendix 3. When $Z_0=\lambda\chi.Z(\lambda\acute{\omega}.\acute{\omega})\bot$,
$W_0=L+B+(EW_0)^*+(Z_0\times N)+(Z_0\times N\times U)+(Z_0\times N)+Z_0+((L\to T)\times N\times N\times U)$.
By performing an induction (which involves the obvious continuous function having W_0 as its least fixed point) we can verify that $W_0\circ hurl\bot=W_0\circ hurl\eta$, $W_0\acute{\omega}\sqsubseteq hurl\bot\grave{\omega}$ and $w[\![\Pi]\!]\langle W_0\acute{\omega},\grave{\omega}\rangle=true$ for any Π, for any η and for any $\hat{\omega}$ such that $w[\![\Pi]\!]\hat{\omega}=true$. The suppositions about *new* made in 5.6.2 and 5.6.5 can therefore be vindicated by an argument analogous to that in 4.6.9 provided that the *new* function for stack semantics satisfies the equation $new=new\circ SW_0\circ S(\lambda\acute{\omega}.\acute{\omega})$.

Henceforth we shall confine our attention to one continuation, $\acute{\zeta}$, such that for each Sam program, Π say,
$\lambda\breve{\upsilon}\breve{\sigma}.\acute{\zeta}(Y(hurl(\mathcal{V}[\![\Pi]\!]\acute{\zeta}))\breve{\upsilon})(S(hurl(\mathcal{V}[\![\Pi]\!]\acute{\zeta}))\breve{\sigma})=\lambda\breve{\upsilon}\breve{\sigma}.A(hurl(\mathcal{V}[\![\Pi]\!]\acute{\zeta}))(success\breve{\upsilon}\breve{\sigma})$
and $z[\![\Pi]\!]\langle\acute{\zeta},1+\#\Pi\rangle=true$; remarks like those in 4.6.9 demonstrate that such a continuation exists when A is constructed sensibly. Indeed, we could even follow the pattern set in 4.6.9 by providing a transitive ordering, $\leq$, such that $\acute{\sigma}\leq A(hurl(\mathcal{V}[\![\Pi]\!]\acute{\zeta}))\grave{\sigma}$ for any Π and for any $\hat{\sigma}$ having $a(w[\![\Pi]\!])\hat{\sigma}=true$. Instead, however, we shall arrange that $\acute{\sigma}\sqsubseteq A(hurl(\mathcal{V}[\![\Pi]\!]\acute{\zeta}))\grave{\sigma}$ for any Π and for any $\hat{\sigma}$ having $a(w[\![\Pi]\!])\hat{\sigma}=true$ by insisting that a coincide with $\lambda x\hat{\sigma}.ax\hat{\sigma}\wedge(\acute{\sigma}\equiv AW_0\acute{\sigma})$ (and that, in addition, $\acute{\zeta}=\lambda\acute{\upsilon}\acute{\sigma}.AW_0(\acute{\zeta}\acute{\upsilon}\acute{\sigma})$ and $A=\lambda X.AW_0\circ AX$); in this situation we are able to infer from 5.6.8 that for every Π if $\eta=\mathcal{V}[\![\Pi]\!]\acute{\zeta}$ then
$\lambda\nu\breve{\upsilon}\breve{\sigma}.\mathcal{V}[\![\Pi]\!]\acute{\zeta}\nu(Y(hurl\eta)\breve{\upsilon})(S(hurl\eta)\breve{\sigma})=\lambda\nu\breve{\upsilon}\breve{\sigma}.A(hurl\eta)(\mathcal{Z}[\![\Pi]\!]\nu\breve{\upsilon}\breve{\sigma})$
whilst $\lambda\nu\breve{\upsilon}\breve{\sigma}.A(hurl\eta)(\mathcal{Z}[\![\Pi]\!]\nu\breve{\upsilon}\breve{\sigma})=\lambda\nu\breve{\upsilon}\breve{\sigma}.AW_0(A(hurl\bot)(\mathcal{Z}[\![\Pi]\!]\nu\breve{\upsilon}\breve{\sigma}))$.

To model the execution of entire Sam programs we introduce suitable forms of $\langle\rangle$ (the empty stack) and *empty* (the initial store, which was defined in 3.3.2); evidently for every η we can write $Y(hurl\,\eta)\langle\rangle$ as $\langle\rangle$ and $S(hurl\,\eta)(empty)$ as *empty*. Since the execution of a program begins at the first instruction in the presence of the empty stack and the initial store, we specialize the equations given above by noting that

$\mathcal{V}[\![\Pi]\!]\acute{\zeta}1\langle\rangle(empty)=AW_0(A(hurl\,\bot)(\mathcal{Z}[\![\Pi]\!]1\langle\rangle(empty)))$

(and indeed that $AW_0\circ A(hurl\,\bot)=AW_0$).

If we were to insist on defining languages in terms of machine operations in the manner mentioned in 3.1.4 we would take the meaning of a Sal expression E to be just $\lambda\Pi\rho.\mathcal{Z}[\![\mathfrak{z}[\![\mathfrak{e}[\![E]\!]\rho]\!]1\S\Pi]\!]1$. For our purposes, however, it is enough to note that the effect of compiling, loading and executing E is captured by $\mathcal{Z}[\![\mathfrak{z}[\![\mathfrak{e}[\![E]\!](arid)]\!]1]\!]1\langle\rangle(empty)$; we could, of course, complicate this in a trivial way by using a "library" environment instead of *arid* or by using a store with basic values in its input component. According to 5.5.7, $E[\![E]\!]=true$ when E is the predicate defined in 5.4.6, so

$\mathfrak{E}[\![E]\!](arid)\acute{\zeta}\langle\rangle(empty)=\mathcal{V}[\![\mathfrak{z}[\![\mathfrak{e}[\![E]\!](arid)]\!]1]\!]\acute{\zeta}1\langle\rangle(empty)$,

where $\mathfrak{E}$ is the valuation constructed in appendix 3.

We now suppose that $E[\![E]\!]=true$ when E is defined as in 5.2.6; this supposition is certainly valid when E contains no recursive declarations by incidence (provided that the bases and operators behave properly), but, as was mentioned in 5.3.9, it is actually true for any "sensible" expression. Plainly

$p\langle\langle arid,\langle\rangle,empty\rangle,\langle arid,\langle\rangle,empty\rangle\rangle=true$ for suitable versions of *arid*, $\langle\rangle$ and empty, so if ν and $\grave{\zeta}$ can be chosen in such a way that $e[\![E]\!](arid)\nu=true$ and $j\hat{\zeta}\nu\langle\langle arid,\langle\rangle,empty\rangle,\langle arid,\langle\rangle,empty\rangle\rangle=true$ then

$a\langle\mathfrak{E}[\![E]\!](arid)\acute{\zeta}\langle\rangle(empty),\mathcal{E}[\![E]\!]\grave{\zeta}(arid)\langle\rangle(empty)\rangle=true$,

where we require the form of $\mathcal{E}$ given in appendix 2 as well as that given in appendix 3 and where we insist that E have no free variables.

In addition we may introduce the valuation $\mathcal{E}$ appropriate to appendix 1 by noting that, under the terms of 4.3.7, $E\llbracket \mathrm{E}\rrbracket = true$ when E is taken to be the predicate of that name set up in 4.2.5. Consequently if we can find a continuation κ for standard semantics such that $k\langle\kappa,\langle\grave{\zeta},arid,\langle\rangle\rangle\rangle = true$ then we may assert that

$a\langle\mathfrak{E}\llbracket \mathrm{E}\rrbracket(arid)\kappa(empty),\mathfrak{E}\llbracket \mathrm{E}\rrbracket\grave{\zeta}(arid)\langle\rangle(empty)\rangle = true$;

naturally the version of a used here differs from that used in the preceding paragraph.

For clarity we now restrict our attention to the output components of stores, so that all four domains named A become V*; however, we could equally well consider other interpretations of A, which might, for instance, provide error flags. The versions of a which interest us are $(\lambda\hat{\beta}.(\acute{\beta}\equiv \mathrm{V}W_0\grave{\beta}))^*$ and $(\lambda\hat{\beta}.(\acute{\beta}\equiv \mathrm{V}X_0\grave{\beta}))^*$ (rather than $(\lambda\hat{\beta}.w_0\hat{\beta}\langle\langle arid,\langle\rangle,empty\rangle,\langle arid,\langle\rangle,empty\rangle\rangle)^*$ and v^*); here the retraction called W_0 is that mentioned above whereas the retraction called X_0 is that introduced in 4.2.6, while the two occurrences of $\acute{\beta}$ refer to members of different domains called V. As these versions of a can be set up by predictors subject to the constraints imposed in 5.2.5 and 4.2.3 we know that setting $\acute{\zeta}=\lambda\acute{\upsilon}\acute{\sigma}.(\mathrm{V}W_0)^*(\acute{\sigma}\downarrow 3)$ and $\grave{\zeta}=\lambda\hat{\rho}\hat{\upsilon}\hat{\sigma}.(\mathrm{V}W_0)^*(\hat{\sigma}\downarrow 3)$ gives

$\mathfrak{E}\llbracket \mathrm{E}\rrbracket(arid)\acute{\zeta}\langle\rangle(empty) = (\mathrm{V}W_0)^*(\mathfrak{E}\llbracket \mathrm{E}\rrbracket\grave{\zeta}(arid)\langle\rangle(empty))$

and, by the same token, setting $\kappa=\lambda\acute{\epsilon}\acute{\sigma}.(\mathrm{V}X_0)^*(\acute{\sigma}\downarrow 3)$ gives

$\mathfrak{E}\llbracket \mathrm{E}\rrbracket(arid)\kappa(empty) = (\mathrm{V}X_0)^*(\mathfrak{E}\llbracket \mathrm{E}\rrbracket\grave{\zeta}(arid)\langle\rangle(empty))$

since $\mathrm{V}X_0\circ \mathrm{V}W_0 = \mathrm{V}X_0$. We may combine these results with our earlier ones, thereby obtaining the equation

$\mathfrak{E}\llbracket \mathrm{E}\rrbracket(arid)(\lambda\acute{\epsilon}\acute{\sigma}.(\mathrm{V}X_0)^*(\acute{\sigma}\downarrow 3))(empty) = (\mathrm{V}X_0)^*(\mathfrak{Z}\llbracket \mathfrak{z}\llbracket \mathfrak{e}\llbracket \mathrm{E}\rrbracket(arid)\rrbracket 1\rrbracket 1\langle\rangle(empty))$.

If we knew in addition that there was no possibility whatsoever of transmitting structured values, label values and procedure values as output, we would consider the third components of stores to be members of B*; under these circumstances, which are very realistic, we would be able to establish that

$\mathfrak{E}\llbracket \mathrm{E}\rrbracket(arid)(\lambda\acute{\epsilon}\acute{\sigma}.\acute{\sigma}\downarrow 3)(empty) = \mathfrak{Z}\llbracket \mathfrak{z}\llbracket \mathfrak{e}\llbracket \mathrm{E}\rrbracket(arid)\rrbracket 1\rrbracket 1\langle\rangle(empty)$.

Were we to include occurrences of *restore* in the equations of appendix 1 and appendix 2 in positions analogous to those occupied by *lose* in the equations of appendix 3 we could even prove that

$$\mathcal{E}[\![E]\!](arid)(\lambda\varepsilon\sigma.SX_0\sigma)(empty)=SX_0(\mathcal{X}[\![\chi[\![\mathcal{e}[\![E]\!](arid)]\!]1]\!]1\langle\rangle(empty))$$

when the domains called A are identified with those called S. For this proof we would amend the definition of p_0 given in 5.2.4 and take the versions of a implicit in 5.3.9 and 4.3.7 to be $\lambda\hat{\sigma}.(\acute{\sigma}\equiv SW_0\grave{\sigma})$ and $\lambda\hat{\sigma}.(\acute{\sigma}\equiv SX_0\grave{\sigma})$ respectively (instead of $\lambda\hat{\sigma}.p\langle\langle arid,\langle\rangle,\acute{\sigma}\rangle,\langle arid,\langle\rangle,\grave{\sigma}\rangle\rangle$ and s, which are also obvious choices); naturally the restrictions which we have continually imposed on *wrong* and *new* would still need to be valid.

Remarks analogous to those above are valid for every construct available in Sal, so we can fairly claim to have proved that by using standard semantics we can predict what will happen when we compile, load and execute any Sal program to which 5.3.9 applies. Putting this more briefly, we have established that the compiling function adopted is correct relative to the semantics given for Sal and for Sam.

It should be noted that the pointer semantics of Sam that we have given departs from realism in three respects. The first of these, the presence of function spaces and of E* in the domains, was discussed fully in 5.6.1; the second, the assumption that each member of W occupies one machine word, is no more important and can be rectified by equally trivial means. The third respect concerns the fact that the semantic equations of appendix 13 contain checks on the summands of W to which entities belong, whereas many real machines make no provision for type-checking. This departure might seem to vitiate our method of proving the correctness of compiling functions, for *hurl* and functions such as w evidently depend on the ability to test the types of values. However, we could set up semantic equations for Sam which would differ from those of appendix 13; in them W would reduce to a domain of integers, Y would still be W* and S would become W*×W*×W*. A member of L (or of L→T) could be represented by a member of W, a member of E* could be represented by a list of members of W (the first element of the list being intended to indicate the length of the list) and a member of J could be represented by two adjacent members of W in one of the domains of the form W*; by altering U somewhat we could even regard members of U as lists of members of W, but there is little point in doing this, since the fourth factor of $(L\to T)\times N\times N\times U$ and the third factor of $Z\times N\times U$ could be eliminated from appendix 3 in the manner outlined in 5.1.5. We could therefore set up a simple relation between members of the domain W appropriate to appendix 13 and members of this new version of W*; moreover we could prove without difficulty that if the equations of appendix 13 were supplied with a stack and a store which were properly related to the stack and store supplied to semantic equations using the domain W which did not permit type-checking, the equations of appendix 13 would produce an answer in A related to the answer obtained by applying these new equations (provided that *success* and its counterpart in the new equations matched properly). Indeed we could connect these new equations to those set up in appendix 1 by extending the arguments given above.

Even though a language may ostensibly be a high-level one, if it permits any bit pattern to be treated by the programmer as an integer, a location or a procedure value it can only be given a semantics like that outlined in the preceding paragraph; thus we have to arbitrarily select a compiler for it which produces programs written in the code for a machine such that W is a domain of integers. The only meaning that can be ascribed to an expression E in BCPL [72], for instance, takes the form $\lambda\Pi\rho.\mathcal{Z}[\![\mathfrak{z}[\![\mathcal{e}[\![\mathrm{E}]\!]\rho]\!]1\S\Pi]\!]1$, where the version of $\mathcal{Z}$ is akin to that discussed in 5.6.1. Programs involving iteration and recursion cannot readily be proved correct when this is the sole sort of semantics available; furthermore only those implementations in which the machine used has a structure similar to that of the machine chosen for the definition can be validated easily.

In our opinion the method we have developed for proving the correctness of implementations is sufficiently general to cater for any programming language or machine, despite the fact that it requires nothing more than induction and the use of predicates constructed in accordance with 2.5.3. To proceed from the standard semantics of a language to a form of pointer semantics for a stack machine we have to perform several steps, which we shall now summarize.

Firstly, those portions of the machine state which are hidden in standard semantics must be brought out into the open, as was done in the transition from standard semantics to store semantics; in particular, label and procedure values must be split into their components, and the stack must appear in the semantic equations (as must the entire set of available denoted values, though this may, of course be incorporated in the stack). By this means we ensure that the continuations can be formed simply from "pure code" without the introduction of any quantities which are known when programs are executed but not when programs are compiled.

Secondly, the continuation which in standard semantics is supplied as a separate argument to a procedure application must be kept on the stack, as happens in many conventional implementations; this entails taking the first factor of the domain of procedure values to be Z, not C. In this book this feature of implementations first made its appearance in association with stack semantics, but it could equally well have been present in store semantics. Were the original semantics for the language to differ from standard semantics by not using continuations (as it could do if the language did not contain labels of any kind) it would of course need to be shown to be congruent with a semantics in which continuations were present, since otherwise there would be no continuations to preserve on the stack.

These two initial steps could be combined and the resulting semantic equations could be shown to be congruent with those for standard semantics by the simple methods adopted in the proof of 4.3.7. However, the third step, the removal of *fix* from the equations governing recursive declarations and label settings, is best carried out independently. The reason for this is that, because equations from which *fix* has been removed rely on pointing into the machine state to explicate recursive declarations and label settings, a proof of the congruence of two semantic equations, only one of which uses *fix*, generally appears to involve a comparison of two machine states in which no details are covert. Standard semantics does not, of course, provide such states except for very small languages. This point has already been discussed in 5.2.1 and is illuminated by the fact that the proof of 4.3.5 depends on the inclusive nature of the predicates required whereas the proof of 5.3.8 does not.

Semantic equations that manipulate the entire state without substantial aid from *fix* can be shown to correspond exactly with ones obtained by transforming programs into a machine code which is given meaning by consecution semantics. Verifying this, as we did in 5.5.7, provides the fourth step in the proof that an implementation is correct. The technique underlying 5.5.7 is satisfactory for all languages, since any compiler should produce programs which will inevitably be "coherent" (in the sense appropriate to the machine code chosen) and each coherent program will satisfy an analogue of 5.4.5. Were we to include a linkage editor (in addition to a relocating loader) in the implementation, programs would naturally not be tested for coherence until they had been subjected to the function corresponding with the editor.

For many purposes the correctness proof might end with the introduction of consecution semantics, but there could in fact be two further steps. One of these would establish the connection between consecution semantics and a version of pointer semantics in which type-checking was permitted; this step was completed in the present instance by 5.6.8. The other would relate the form of pointer semantics which gave rise to type-checking to a form without type-checking; although have discussed how to do this we have not provided a full proof in this essay because it raises no new principles whatever.

It might be hoped that the fourth and fifth steps could be combined so that consecution semantics would become redundant. However, there seems to be no prospect of there being a direct connection between the stack semantics of Sal and the pointer semantics of Sam because no result akin to 5.4.5 holds for pointer semantics. Thus, in contrast with $\lambda E\rho\zeta.\mathcal{V}[\![\mathfrak{z}[\![\mathfrak{e}[\![E]\!]\rho]\!]1]\!]\zeta 1$, $\lambda E\Pi\rho.\mathcal{Z}[\![\mathfrak{z}[\![\mathfrak{e}[\![E]\!]\rho]\!]1\S\Pi]\!]1$ does not provide a homomorphism of Exp, regarded as a word algebra [57], into an algebra of meanings, so even if $\mathcal{R}[\![E_0]\!]$ depended on E_0 only through $\lambda\Pi\rho.\mathcal{Z}[\![\mathfrak{z}[\![\mathfrak{r}[\![E_0]\!]\rho]\!]1\S\Pi]\!]1$ and $\mathfrak{E}[\![E_1]\!]$ depended on E_1 only through $\lambda\Pi\rho.\mathcal{Z}[\![\mathfrak{z}[\![\mathfrak{e}[\![E_1]\!]\rho]\!]1\S\Pi]\!]1$ there would be no guarantee that, for instance, $\mathfrak{E}[\![E_0E_1]\!]$ would depend on E_0E_1 only through $\lambda\Pi\rho.\mathcal{Z}[\![\mathfrak{z}[\![\mathfrak{e}[\![E_0E_1]\!]\rho]\!]1\S\Pi]\!]1$.

By the same token straightforward structural induction does not allow us to demonstrate directly the connection between the standard semantics of Sal and the pointer semantics of Sam; we are obliged instead to prove intermediate results involving machine states. In these states can be kept values belonging to domains such as J and F and having components that are effectively state transformations. This situation arises in any language which provides expressed label or procedure values, even when there is no facility for stored label and procedure values (and even when there is no store at all). Hence although setting up the standard semantics of a language may not entail solving recursive domain equations, proving the correctness of an implementation of the language may well do so, in which case the recursive predicate equations provided by 2.5.3 may also be required.